NTC's
Compact
Dutch
and
English
Dictionary

NTC Publishing Group

Library of Congress Cataloging-in-Publication Data

NTC's compact Dutch and English dictionary.
    p.   cm.
    ISBN 0-8442-8351-7
    1. English language—Dictionaries—Dutch.   2. Dutch language—
Dictionaries—English.   I. National Textbook Company.
PF640.N73   1998
439.31'321—dc21   97-48917
                                   CIP

This edition published 1998 by NTC Publishing Group
A division of NTC/Contemporary Publishing Group, Inc.
4255 West Touhy Avenue, Lincolnwood (Chicago), Illinois 60646-1975 U.S.A.
Copyright © 1996 by Het Spectrum B.V., Utrecht
Printed in the United States of America
International Standard Book Number: 0-8442-8351-7

18   17   16   15   14   13   12   11   10   9   8   7   6   5   4   3   2   1

Contents

List of Abbreviations

aanw vnw	demonstrative pronoun
AE	American English
anat.	anatomy
archit.	architecture
betr vnw	relative pronoun
bez vnw	possessive pronoun
bijv.	for example
bijw	adverb
bio.	biology
bnw	adjective
chem.	chemistry
comp.	computer science
econ.	economics
ev	singular
fig.	figurative
form.	formal
foto.	photography
geb. wijs	imperative
geo.	geography
gesch.	history
hand.	commerce
hww	auxiliary verb
inf.	informal
iron.	ironic
jur.	legal
kind.	children's language
kww	copula; linking verb
lit.	literature
luchtv.	aviation
lw	article
m.b.t.	pertaining to
med.	medical
mil.	military
muz.	music
mv	plural
neol.	neologism
on ww	intransitive verb
onb vnw	indefinite pronoun
onp ww	impersonal verb
onv ww	non-conjugable verb
overtr. trap	superlative
ov ww	transitive verb
p.	person
pej.	pejorative
pers vnw	noun
plantk.	botany
pol.	politics
rel.	religion
scherts	mocking
sl.	slang
s.o.	someone
s.th.	something
taalk.	linguistics
techn.	technology
telecom.	telecommunication
telw	numeral
tw	interjection
typ.	typography
uitr vnw	exclamation
vergr. trap	comparative degree
verl tijd	past tense
vero.	antiquated
volt. deelw.	past participle
voorv.	prefix
vr. vrn	interrogative pronoun
vulg.	vulgar
vw	conjunction
vz	preposition
wisk.	mathematics
wkd vnw	reflexive pronoun
wkg vnw	reciprocal pronoun
ww	verb

Special Symbols

Entry words are printed in bold-faced type.

•	The translations of an entry word are organized according to meaning. Each of the meanings is indicated with a dot. Prepositions in the foreign language that lead to a difference in meaning when combined with an entry word also appear following a dot (and in parentheses).
<. . . .>	Each specification of a translation, descriptions of specialty fields, and descriptions of style are enclosed in pointed brackets.
[. . .]	Grammatical categories are in square brackets.
/. . ./	Grammatical information appears between slashes.
★	Example sentences are preceded by an asterisk.
I,II etc.	Descriptions of grammatical categories (nouns, adjectives, types of verbs, etc.) are preceded by Roman numerals.
~	A tilde replaces the entry word.
/	A slash separates words that are mutually interchangeable.
↑	This sign indicates that the translation is more formal than the translated word or example.
↓	This sign indicates that the translation is less formal than the translated word or example.
≈	This sign indicates that the translation is an approximation of the translated word or example; an exact translation cannot be given in this case.

a [lw] *een*
abandon [ov ww] *opgeven, verlaten*
abandoned [bnw] • *losbandig*
  • *verlaten*
abase [ov ww] *verlagen, vernederen*
abate [ov ww] *verlagen <v. prijs>, doen afnemen*
abbess [znw] *abdis*
abbey [znw] *abdij*
abbot [znw] *abt*
abbreviate [ov ww] *af-/be-/verkorten*
abbreviation [znw] *afkorting*
abdicate [ov ww] *aftreden, afstand doen van troon*
abdomen [znw] *(onder)buik*
abdominal [bnw] *in/van de onderbuik*
abduct [ov ww] *ontvoeren, afvoeren*
aberrant [bnw] *abnormaal, afwijkend, afdwalend*
aberration [znw] • *afwijking* • *misstap*
abet [ov ww] *ophitsen, aanstoken*
abhor [ov ww] *verfoeien*
abhorrence [znw] *afschuw*
abide I [ov ww] • *verdragen*
  • *af-/verwachten* II [on ww]
  • *overblijven, vertoeven* • *verblijven, wonen* • *(~ by) trouw blijven aan, z. schikken naar, z. houden aan*
ability [znw] *bekwaamheid, bevoegdheid*
abject [bnw] • *rampzalig* • *verachtelijk*
abjure [ov ww] *afzweren*
ablaze [bijw] *in vlammen, gloeiend*
able [bnw] *in staat, bekwaam, bevoegd*
ably [bijw] *in staat, bekwaam, bevoegd*
abnormal [bnw] • *onregelmatig*
  • *abnormaal, afwijkend*
abnormality [znw]
  • *onregelmatigheid* • *afwijking*
aboard [bijw + vz] • *aan boord (v.)*
  • *langszij*

abode I [ww] *verl.tijd + volt.deelw.*
  → abide II [znw] *verblijf, woonplaats*
abolish [ov ww] *afschaffen*
abominable [bnw] *verfoeilijk*
abominate [ov ww] *verfoeien*
abomination [znw] *gruwel*
abort [ov ww] • *ontijdig bevallen*
  • *(vroegtijdig) afbreken*
  • *verschrompelen* • *doen mislukken*
abortion [znw] • *miskraam* • *abortus provocatus*
abortive [bnw] • *ontijdig* • *mislukt*
abound [on ww] • *overvloedig zijn*
  • *wemelen* • *(~ in/with) rijk zijn aan, wemelen van*
about [bijw + vz] • *om(trent), over* • *in de buurt (v.)* • *in het rond* • *ongeveer*
above I [znw] *bovengenoemde/-staande* II [bnw] *bovengenoemd*
  III [vz] *boven, over*
abrasion [znw] • *schaafwond*
  • *afschuring*
abrasive [bnw] • *schurend, krassend*
  • *ruw, scherp*
abreast [bijw] *naast elkaar*
abridge [ov ww] *be-/verkorten*
abrogate [ov ww] *afschaffen, intrekken*
absence [znw] *afwezigheid*
absent I [wkd ww] *afwezig zijn*
  II [bnw] *afwezig*
absentee [znw] *afwezige*
absolute [bnw] *onvoorwaardelijk, absoluut*
absolution [znw] *absolutie, vergiffenis*
absolve [ov ww] *vergeven*
  • *(~ from/of) vrijspreken van*
absorb [ov ww] • *absorberen* • *geheel in beslag nemen* • *in z. opnemen*
absorbent [bnw] *absorberend*
abstain [on ww] • *(~ from) z. onthouden v.*
abstemious [bnw] *matig*
abstention, abstinence [znw] *onthouding*
abstract I [znw] *overzicht, uittreksel*
  II [bnw] • *abstract* • *theoretisch*

abstracted [bnw] *verstrooid, in gedachten verzonken*
abstraction [znw] • *abstractie* • *afleiding* • *ontvreemding*
abundance [znw] *overvloed*
abundant [bnw] *overvloedig*
abuse I [ov ww] • *misbruiken* • *uitschelden* II [znw] • *misbruik* • *scheldwoorden*
abyss [znw] • *afgrond* • *hel, bodemloze put*
academic I [znw] *academicus* II [bnw] • *academisch* • *theoretisch* • *nuchter*
academy [znw] • *academie, onderwijsinrichting* • *instituut voor speciaal vak* • *genootschap*
accelerate [ov + on ww] *versnellen*
accelerator [znw] *gaspedaal*
accent I [ov ww] *nadruk leggen op* II [znw] • *klemtoon* • *stembuiging, uitspraak*
accentuate [ov ww] • *accentueren* • *verergeren*
accept [ov + on ww] *aannemen/-vaarden*
acceptable [bnw] • *acceptabel* • *welkom*
acceptance [znw] • *gunstige ontvangst* • *accept*
access I [ov ww] z. *toegang verschaffen tot* II [znw] *vlaag*
accessible [bnw] *toegankelijk*
accession [znw] • *troonsbestijging* • *toegang* • *toename*
accident [znw] • *toeval* • *ongeluk*
accidental [bnw] *toevallig*
acclimatize [ov + on ww] *acclimatiseren, wennen aan*
accommodating [bnw] *inschikkelijk, coulant*
accommodation [znw] *accomodatie*
accompaniment [znw] *begeleiding*
accompany [ov ww] *vergezellen, begeleiden* • (~ **with**) *vergezeld doen gaan v.*
accomplice [znw] *medeplichtige*
accomplish [ov ww] *volbrengen*

accomplished [bnw] • *volleerd* • *voldongen* • *volkomen* • *begaafd, (veelzijdig) getalenteerd*
accomplishment [znw] • *prestatie* • *talent* • *vaardigheid*
accord [ov ww] • *overeenstemmen* • *verlenen*
accordingly [bijw] *dienovereenkomstig, derhalve*
account I [ov ww] • *rekenen* • *beschouwen als* • (~ **for**) *verantwoorden, verklaren* II [znw] • *rekenschap* • *rekening* • *belang* • *verslag* • *kostenraming* • *(vaste) klant, opdrachtgever*
accountable [bnw] • *verantwoordelijk* • *verklaarbaar* • *aansprakelijk*
accredit [ov ww] *officieel erkennen* • (~ **to**) *geloof hechten aan, toeschrijven aan*
accrue I [ov ww] *doen aangroeien, kweken* II [on ww] *aangroeien*
accumulate [ov + on ww] (z.) *ophopen, verzamelen*
accumulation [znw] • *verzameling* • *op(een)hoping*
accumulative [bnw] (z.) *opstapelend*
accuracy [znw] *nauwkeurigheid*
accurate [bnw] *nauwkeurig*
accusal, accusation [znw] • *beschuldiging* • *aanklacht*
accuse [ov ww] *beschuldigen, aanklagen*
accustom [ov ww] *wennen* • (~ **to**) *wennen aan*
ace [znw] • *aas* <v. kaarten> • *uitblinker* <in competitie> • *ace* <tennis>
acerbity [znw] *wrangheid, bitterheid*
ache I [on ww] • *pijn lijden, pijn doen* • *hunkeren* II [znw] *(voortdurende) pijn*
achieve [ov ww] *volbrengen, bereiken*
achievement [znw] *succes, prestatie*
acid I [znw] • *zuur* • <sl.> *LSD* II [bnw] • *scherp* • *zuur*
acknowledge [ov + on ww] • *erkennen, bevestigen* • *beantwoorden* <v. groet>

acme [znw] *toppunt*
acorn [znw] *eikel*
acoustic(al) [bnw] *gehoor/geluid betreffend, akoestisch*
acquaintance [znw] • *kennis* <persoon> • *bekendheid* • *kennismaking*
acquiesce [on ww] *berusten* • (~ in) *instemmen met*
acquire [ov ww] • *verwerven* • *aanleren*
acquisitive [bnw] *hebzuchtig*
acquit [ov ww] *vrijspreken*
acquittal [znw] • *vrijspraak* • *vervulling*
acre [znw] *4000 m²*
acreage [znw] *oppervlakte*
acrid [bnw] • *bijtend* • *bitter*
acrimonious [bnw] *bits, boos*
acrimony [znw] • *bitsheid* • *boosheid*
acrobat [znw] *acrobaat*
acrobatics [mv] *acrobatiek*
across [bijw] • *kruiselings* • *aan/naar de overzijde* • *dwars (over)*
act I [on ww] • *optreden* • *handelen* • *werken* • *acteren* • (~ (up)on) *handelen volgens* • (~ up) <inf.> z. *aanstellen, slecht functioneren* • (~ up to) *handelen volgens* II [znw] • *handeling, daad* • *wet* • *bedrijf* <toneel> • *nummer* <variété>
acting I [znw] *het acteren* II [bnw] *waarnemend*
action [znw] • *handeling, werking* • *mechaniek* • *gevecht* • <jur.> *proces*
activate [ov ww] *aanzetten, activeren*
active [bnw] • *actief* • *werkzaam* • *werkend* • *levendig*
activity [znw] *werk(zaamheid), bedrijvigheid*
actor [znw] *acteur*
actress [znw] *actrice*
actual [bnw] *(daad)werkelijk, feitelijk*
actuality [znw] *werkelijkheid*
actually [bijw] • *zowaar* • *eigenlijk*
acute [bnw] • *acuut* • *scherpzinnig* • *dringend* • *scherp* <hoek>

adage [znw] *gezegde*
adamant, adamantine [bnw] *onvermurwbaar*
adapt [ov + on ww] • (~ from...to) *bewerken van(uit)...naar* • (~ to) *aanpassen aan*
adaptable [bnw] *aanpasbaar*
addict [znw] *verslaafde*
addiction [znw] *verslaving*
addictive [bnw] *verslavend*
addition [znw] • *vermeerdering* • *toevoeging*
additional [bnw] *aanvullend*
additive I [znw] *toevoeging* II [bnw] *toevoegend*
address I [ov ww] • *toespreken, aanspreken* • *adresseren* II [znw] • *adres* • *toespraak* • *behendigheid*
addressee [znw] *geadresseerde*
adept I [znw] *deskundige* II [bnw] *ingewijd*
adequacy [znw] *geschiktheid*
adequate [bnw] • *voldoende* • *geschikt*
adhere [on ww] (aan)kleven • (~ to) *trouw blijven aan, vastplakken aan*
adherent I [znw] *aanhanger* II [bnw] *aanklevend*
adhesive [znw] *kleefmiddel*
adjective [znw] *bijvoeglijk naamwoord*
adjoin I [ov ww] *bijvoegen* II [on ww] *grenzen aan*
adjourn I [ov ww] *verdagen* II [on ww] *op reces gaan*
adjournment [znw] • *verdaging* • *onderbreking*
adjunct I [znw] • *toevoegsel* • *onderdeel* • <taalk.> *bepaling* II [bnw] *toegevoegd*
adjust [ov + on ww] *schikken, regelen, afstellen* <v. apparatuur> • (~ to) *aanpassen aan*
adjustable [bnw] *verstelbaar*
adjustment [znw] *regeling, instelling, aanpassing*
administer [ov ww] • *beheren* • *toedienen* <v. medicijnen> • *uitvoeren* <v. wet>

administration [znw] • *administratie*
• *regering* • *ministerie* • *uitvoering*
administrative [bnw] • *administratief*
• *ministerieel*
administrator [znw] • *administrateur*
• *executeur, curator*
admirable [bnw] *bewonderenswaardig*
admiral [znw] *admiraal*
admire [ov ww] *bewonderen*
admirer [znw] *bewonderaar, aanbidder*
admissible [bnw] *geoorloofd*
admission [znw] • *erkenning*
• *toegang, toelating*
admit [ov ww] • *binnenlaten* • *toestaan*
• *erkennen* • (~ **to**) *toelaten*
admittance [znw] *toegang*
admittedly [bijw] *toegegeven*
admonish [ov ww] *aanmanen,*
vermanen
ado [znw] *drukte*
adolescence [znw] *puberteit*
adolescent I [znw] *puber* II [bnw]
opgroeiend
adopt [ov ww] *aan-/op-/overnemen*
adorable [bnw] *aanbiddelijk, schattig*
adoration [znw] *aanbidding*
adore [ov ww] *aanbidden*
adorn [ov ww] *versieren*
adroit [bnw] *handig*
adult I [znw] *volwassene* II [bnw]
volwassen
adulterate [ov ww] *vervalsen*
adulterer [znw] *overspelige man*
adulteress [znw] *overspelige vrouw*
adultery [znw] *overspel*
advance [ov + on ww] • *vooruitbrengen*
• *vervroegen* • *voorschieten* • *verhogen*
• *vorderen* • *naderen* • *opdrukken*
• *stijgen*
advanced [bnw] *geavanceerd, gevorderd*
advancement [znw] • *bevordering*
• *vervroeging* • *vooruitgang* • *voorschot*
advantage [znw] *voordeel*
advantageous [bnw] *voordelig*
adventure [znw] • *avontuur* • *risico*
• *speculatie*

adventurer [znw] • *avonturier*
• *speculant*
adversary [znw] *tegenstander*
adverse [bnw] • *ongunstig* • *vijandig*
adversity [znw] *tegenspoed*
advert [znw] *advertentie*
advertise I [ov ww] • *adverteren*
• *aankondigen* II [on ww] *reclame*
maken
advertisement [znw] • *advertentie*
• *aankondiging*
advertiser [znw] • *advertentieblad*
• *adverteerder*
advertising [znw] *reclame*
advice [znw] • *raad* • *bericht*
advisable [bnw] *raadzaam*
advise [ov + on ww] *raad geven*
adviser [znw] *adviseur, raadgever*
advisory [bnw] *adviserend*
advocacy [znw] *voorspraak, verdediging*
advocate I [ov ww] *voorstaan,*
aanbevelen II [znw] • *verdediger*
• *voorstander*
aerial I [znw] *antenne* II [bnw] *lucht-,*
luchtig
aerobatics [znw] *stuntvliegen,*
luchtacrobatiek
aeroplane [znw] *vliegtuig*
afar [bijw] *in de verte*
affable [bnw] *minzaam*
affair [znw] • *zaak, kwestie* • *ding*
• *buitenechtelijke verhouding*
affect [ov ww] • *voorwenden*
• *aantasten* • *beïnvloeden* • *(ont)roeren*
affectation [znw] *aanstellerij*
affected [bnw] • *aanstellerig*
• *betrokken* • *getroffen*
affecting [bnw] *aandoenlijk*
affection [znw] • *genegenheid,*
tederheid • *aandoening* <ziekte>
affectionate [bnw] • *aanhankelijk*
• *hartelijk*
affinity [znw] *verwantschap*
affirmative I [znw] *bevestiging*
II [bnw] *bevestigend*
affix I [ov ww] • (~ **on/to**) *aanhechten,*

toevoegen II [znw]
achter-/in-/voorvoegsel
afflict [ov ww] teisteren, kwellen
affluence [znw] rijkdom
affluent I [znw] zijrivier II [bnw]
overvloedig
afford [ov ww] • verschaffen • z.
veroorloven
affront I [ov ww] • beledigen • tarten
II [znw] belediging
afloat [bijw] • drijvend • in volle gang
afraid [bnw] bang
afresh [bijw] • opnieuw • v. voren af aan
African I [znw] Afrikaan(se) II [bnw]
Afrikaans
after I [bijw] • nadat • daarna, later
II [vz] • na, achter, achterna • naar
<volgens>
afternoon [znw] namiddag
afterwards [bijw] naderhand, daarna
again [bijw] • weer • daarentegen
against [vz] tegen(over)
agape [bijw] met open mond <v.
verbazing>
age I [on ww] ouder worden, verouderen
II [znw] • ouderdom • tijdperk • eeuw
aged [bnw] bejaard
agency [znw] • bureau, agentschap
• bemiddeling
agenda [znw] • agenda <v.
vergadering> • werkprogram
agent [znw] vertegenwoordiger,
tussenpersoon
aggravate [ov ww] (ver)ergeren
aggregate I [ov ww] • z. verenigen
• bedragen II [znw] • aggregaat
• totaal • verzameling III [bnw]
gezamenlijk
aggression [znw] • aanval • agressie
• strijdlust
aggressive [bnw] • strijdlustig
• ondernemend, actief, dynamisch
aghast [bnw + bijw] onthutst,
ontzet
agile [bnw] vlug en lenig
agitate [ov ww] • beroeren, opwinden

• opruien
agitator [znw] opruier
ago I [znw] verleden II [bijw] geleden
agonize [on ww] • kwellen • gekweld
worden • (~ over) z. suf piekeren over
agonized [bnw] doodsbenauwd
agonizing [bnw] kwellend,
hartverscheurend
agony [znw] • foltering • (doods)angst
agrarian I [znw] agrariër II [bnw]
m.b.t. grondbezit/landbouw, agrarisch
agree [on ww] afspreken • (~ on) het
eens zijn over • (~ to) toestemmen in,
goedkeuren • (~ with)
overeenstemmen met
agreeable [bnw] aangenaam
agreement [znw] • overeenstemming
• contract, afspraak
agricultural [bnw] v. landbouw
agriculture [znw] landbouw
ahead [bijw] • in het vooruitzicht
• vooruit • vóór
aid I [ov ww] helpen II [znw] hulp,
helper
ailment [znw] kwaal
ain't <vulg.> [samentr.]
/am/are/has/have/is not/ —> be,
have
air I [ov ww] uitlaten, luchten II [znw]
• lucht • melodie • houding
airing [znw] • uiting, bekendmaking
• het luchten, het drogen • wandeling,
ritje
airmail [znw] luchtpost
airy [bnw] • vluchtig • luchtig
aisle [znw] • zijbeuk • gangpad
ajar [bijw] • op een kier • knorrig
alacrity [znw] • levendigheid
• bereidwilligheid
alarm I [ov ww] • alarmeren
• verontrusten II [znw] • alarm
• schrik, ontsteltenis • wekker
alarming [bnw] verontrustend,
alarmerend
Albanian I [znw] het Albanees II [bnw]
Albanees

albeit [bijw] zij het, al is het dan,
ofschoon
album [znw] • album • langspeelplaat,
cd
alchemy [znw] alchemie
alcoholic I [znw] alcoholist II [bnw]
alcoholhoudend, alcoholisch
alcoholism [znw] alcoholisme,
drankzucht
ale [znw] bier
alert I [znw] luchtalarm II [bnw]
waakzaam, kwiek
Algerian I [znw] Algerijn II [bnw]
Algerijns
alien I [znw] • niet genaturaliseerde
vreemdeling • buitenaards wezen
II [bnw] • buitenlands
• weerzinwekkend
alienate [ov ww] vervreemden
alight I [on ww] • afstijgen
• uitstappen • landen II [bijw]
• verlicht • brandend
align [on ww] (z.) richten, verbinden
alignment [znw] • richting • opstelling
alike [bijw] • hetzelfde • gelijk,
gelijkend op
alimentary [bnw] voedings-
alimony [znw] alimentatie, onderhoud
alive [bijw] in leven
all I [bnw] • al(le) • geheel II [onb vnw]
• alle(n) • alles • het enige III [bijw]
helemaal
allay [ov ww] • verminderen • tot
bedaren brengen
allegation [znw] bewering, aantijging
allege [ov ww] beweren
allegiance [znw] (eed v.) trouw
allergic [bnw] • allergisch • afkerig
allergy [znw] • allergie • afkeer
alleviate [ov ww] verzachten, verlichten
alley [znw] • steeg • kegelbaan • pad
alliance [znw] • verbond • huwelijk
• verwantschap
allied [bnw] • geallieerd • verbonden
allocate [ov ww] toewijzen
allocation [znw] toewijzing

allotment [znw] • aandeel
• volkstuintje
allow [ov ww] • erkennen • toelaten,
toestaan • (~ for) rekening houden met
allowance [znw] • compensatie,
toegeving • toelage • vergoeding,
tegemoetkoming <kosten>
alloy [ov ww] legéren
allure [ov ww] aanlokken
alluring [bnw] aanlokkelijk
allusion [znw] toespeling
ally [ov ww] • verbinden • bondgenoot
almanac [znw] almanak
almighty [bnw] almachtig
almond [znw] amandel
almost [bijw] bijna
alms [mv] aalmoes, aalmoezen
aloft [bijw] (om)hoog
along [vz] langs
alongside [vz] langszij
aloof [bnw + bijw] op een afstand,
gereserveerd
aloud [bijw] hardop
alphabet [znw] alfabet
alpine [bnw] alpen-, berg-
already [bijw] reeds, al(weer)
Alsatian [znw] • Elzasser • Duitse
herder
also [bijw] ook, bovendien
altar [znw] altaar
alteration [znw] wijziging,
verandering
altercation [znw] woordenwisseling
alternate I [on ww] afwisselen II [bnw]
afwisselend, verwisselend
alternative [znw] alternatief
although [bijw] ofschoon
altitude [znw] hoogte
alto [znw] alt(viool), altstem
altogether [bijw] helemaal, in alle
opzichten
always [bijw] altijd
am [ww] → be
amalgamate [ov ww] • samenstellen
• verenigen
amass [ov ww] vergaren

amaze [ov ww] *verbazen*
amazement [znw] *verbazing*
amazing [bnw] *verbazingwekkend*
ambassador [znw] *ambassadeur,*
afgezant
amber I [znw] *barnsteen* II [bnw]
• *vaalgeel* • *oranje <verkeerslicht>*
ambiguous [bnw] *dubbelzinnig*
ambition [znw] • *eerzucht* • *streven,*
ideaal
ambitious [bnw] • *eerzuchtig* • *groots,*
grootscheeps
ambush I [ov ww] *in hinderlaag laten*
lopen/vallen II [on ww] *in hinderlaag*
liggen III [znw] *hinderlaag*
amenable [bnw] *handelbaar*
amend [ov ww] • *wijzigen* • z.
(*ver*)*beteren*
amendment [znw] *amendement*
American I [znw] *Amerikaan* II [bnw]
Amerikaans
amiable [bnw] *beminnelijk*
amicable [bnw] *vriendschappelijk*
amiss [bnw + bijw] *verkeerd, te onpas*
ammunition, ammo [znw]
(*am*)*munitie*
amnesia [znw] *geheugenverlies*
amnesty [znw] *amnestie*
amorous [bnw] • *verliefdheid* • *liefdes-*
amount I [on ww] • (*~ to*) *bedragen,*
gelijk staan met II [znw] • *bedrag*
• *grootte, hoeveelheid, mate* • *omvang*
amphibian I [znw] • *amfibie,*
tweeslachtig dier
• *amfibievliegtuig/-voertuig* II [bnw]
tweeslachtig, amfibieachtig
amphibious [bnw] *tweeslachtig,*
amfibisch
ample [bnw] • *ruim* • *uitvoerig*
• *overvloedig*
ampler [znw] *merklap*
amplifier [znw] *versterker*
amplify [ov + on ww] *versterken*
amputate [ov + on ww] *amputeren,*
afzetten
amuse [ov ww] *vermaken, aangenaam*

bezighouden
amusement [znw] *plezier*
amusing [bnw] *amusant, vermakelijk*
an [lw] • *een* • *één*
anaemia [znw] • *bloedarmoede*
• *lusteloosheid*
anaemic [bnw] • *bloedarm* • *lusteloos*
anaesthesia [znw] *narcose, verdoving*
anaesthetic I [znw] *verdovingsmiddel*
II [bnw] *verdovend*
anal [bnw] *aars-, anaal*
analyse [ov ww] *ontbinden, ontleden*
analysis [znw] • *analyse*
• (*psycho*)*analyse*
analyst [znw] • *analist*
• (*psycho*)*analyticus*
anarchy [znw] *anarchie*
anathema [znw] *banvloek*
anatomical [bnw] *anatomisch*
anatomy [znw] • *anatomie* • *ontleding*
ancestral [bnw] • *voorouderlijk*
• *prototypisch*
ancestry [znw] • *voorouders* • *afkomst*
anchor I [ov + on ww] (*ver*)*ankeren*
II [znw] • *anker* • *steun*
anchorage [znw] • *ligplaats*
• *verankering* • *steun <fig.>*
anchoret, anchorite [znw] *kluizenaar*
anchovy [znw] *ansjovis*
ancient I [znw] *grijsaard* II [bnw] (*zeer*)
oud
ancillary I [znw] *assistent* II [bnw]
• *ondergeschikt* • *hulp-*
and [vw] *en*
anemone [znw] *anemoon*
anew [bijw] *opnieuw*
angel [znw] • *engel* • *schat*
anger I [ov + on ww] *boos maken*
II [znw] *toorn*
angle I [ov ww] *hengelen* • (*~ for*) *iets*
proberen te bereiken II [znw] • *hoek*
• *gezichtspunt*
angler [znw] *hengelaar*
angry [bnw] • *boos* • *dreigend* • *pijnlijk*
ontstoken
anguish [znw] • *zielensmart* • *angst*

• *pijn*
anguished [bnw] *gekweld, vol angst, vol smart*
angular [bnw] • *hoekig* • *nukkig*
animal I [znw] *dier* II [bnw] *dierlijk*
animate I [ov ww] *bezielen* II [bnw] *levend*
animation [znw] *levendigheid*
animosity [znw] *vijandigheid*
aniseed [znw] *anijszaad(je)*
ankle [znw] *enkel*
annals [mv] *annalen*
annex I [ov ww] *aanhechten, annexeren* II [znw] *annexe* • *aanhangsel* • *bijgebouw*
annihilate [ov ww] *vernietigen*
anniversary [znw] *verjaardag, (jaarlijkse) gedenkdag*
annotate [ov + on ww] *aantekeningen maken van*
announce [ov ww] *aankondigen, omroepen*
announcement [znw] *aankondiging*
announcer [znw] *aankondiger, omroeper*
annoy [ov + on ww] • *ergeren* • *lastig vallen*
annoyance [znw] *ergernis*
annoying [bnw] *hinderlijk, vervelend*
annual I [znw] • *eenjarige plant* • *jaargetijde* • *jaarboekje* II [bnw] *jaarlijks*
annul [ov ww] *tenietdoen*
anoint [ov ww] *zalven, inwrijven*
anonymity [znw] *anonimiteit, naamloosheid*
anonymous [bnw] *anoniem, naamloos*
another [onb vnw] • *een ander* • *een tweede* • *nog een*
answer I [ov + on ww] • *(be)antwoorden (aan)* • z. *verantwoorden voor* • *(~ back) een brutaal antwoord geven* • *(~ for) instaan voor, boeten voor* • *(~ to) antwoorden op* II [znw] *antwoord*
ant [znw] *mier*

antecedent [bnw] *voorafgaand*
antelope [znw] *antilope(leer)*
antenna [znw] • *antenne* • *voelspriet*
anthem [znw] *beurtzang*
anthology [znw] *bloemlezing*
anthropology [znw] *antropologie, leer v.d. mens*
anticipate [ov ww] • *vóór zijn, vooruitlopen op* • *verwachten* • *voorzien*
antipathetic [bnw] *antipathiek*
antipathy [znw] *antipathie, afkeer*
antiquarian I [znw] • *oudheidkundige* • *antiquaar* II [bnw] *oudheidkundig*
antiquated [bnw] *verouderd*
antique [znw] *antiek voorwerp*
antiquity [znw] • *de oudheid* • *antiquiteit*
antithesis [znw] *tegenstelling*
antler [znw] *tak van gewei*
anvil [znw] *aambeeld*
anxiety [znw] • *bezorgdheid* • *verlangen* • *angst*
anxious [bnw] • *bezorgd* • *verontrust* • *verlangend*
any [onb vnw] • *enig* • *ieder* • *soms ook*
anyhow [bijw] *hoe dan ook, in ieder geval*
anyone [onb vnw] • *iemand* • *wie dan ook, iedereen*
anything [onb vnw] • *iets* • *wat dan ook, alles*
anyway [bijw] *in ieder geval, toch*
apart [bnw + bijw] • *apart* • *uit elkaar* • *terzijde*
apartment [znw] • *vertrek* • <AE> *appartement*
apathetic [bnw] *lusteloos*
apathy [znw] *apathie, lusteloosheid*
ape I [ov ww] *na-apen* II [znw] *staartloze aap*
apiece [bijw] *per stuk*
aplomb [znw] *zelfverzekerheid*
apologetic [bnw] *verontschuldigend*
apologize [on ww] z. *verontschuldigen*
apology [znw] *verontschuldiging*
apoplexy [znw] *beroerte*

apostle [znw] apostel
apostolic [bnw] apostolisch
apostrophe [znw] <taalk.> apostrof
appal, appall [ov ww] ontzetten
apparatus [znw] • hulpmiddelen
• apparaat
apparent [bnw] • ogenschijnlijk
• duidelijk • blijkbaar
apparition [znw] spook(verschijning)
appeal I [on ww] • in beroep gaan
• spreken tot <fig.> • (~ to) beroep doen
op, z. beroepen op, aantrekkingskracht
uitoefenen II [znw]
• aantrekkingskracht • beroep
appealing [bnw] • smekend
• aantrekkelijk
appease [ov ww] • verzoenen • sussen
append [ov ww] bijvoegen
appendage [znw] bijvoegsel
appendicitis [znw]
blindedarmontsteking
appendix [znw] • aanhangsel • <med.>
appendix
appetite [znw] eetlust
appetizer [znw] • aperitief
• voorgerecht
appetizing [bnw] • smakelijk • de
eetlust opwekkend
applaud I [ov ww] toejuichen
II [on ww] applaudisseren
applause [znw] applaus
apple [znw] appel
applicable [bnw] • toepasselijk
• doelmatig
applicant [znw] sollicitant
application [znw] • toepassing
• sollicitatie • aanvraag • toewijding
applied [bnw] toegepast
apply [on ww] doen/leggen op • (~ for)
solliciteren naar, aanvragen • (~ to)
van toepassing zijn op, toepassen op, z.
wenden tot
appoint [ov ww] • vaststellen
• aanstellen
apposite [bnw] • passend • adrem
appraise [ov ww] • schatten

• waarderen
appreciable [bnw] • schatbaar
• merkbaar
appreciate [ov ww] • waarderen
• inzien • beoordelen • verhogen in
koers/prijs
appreciation [znw] • waardering
• beoordeling
appreciative [bnw] • goedkeurend
• erkentelijk
apprehend [ov ww] aanhouden
apprehensive [bnw] • ongerust
• intelligent
apprentice I [ov ww] in de leer
doen/nemen • (~ to) in de leer doen bij
II [znw] leerjongen
apprenticeship [znw] • leerlingschap
• leerjaren
approach I [ov ww] • aanpakken
• (be)naderen II [znw] • (be)nadering
• aanpak • opzet
approbation [znw] goedkeuring
appropriate I [ov ww] z. toe-eigenen
II [bnw] • geschikt • passend
approval [znw] goedkeuring
approve [on ww] akkoord gaan • (~ of)
goedkeuren
approximate I [ov ww] (be)naderen
II [bnw] bij benadering (aangegeven)
apricot [znw] abrikoos(kleurig)
apt [bnw] • geneigd • gevat • bekwaam
aquatic [bnw] water-
Arab I [znw] Arabier II [bnw] Arabisch
Arabic [bnw] Arabisch
arable [bnw] bebouwbaar
arbiter [znw] scheidsrechter
arbitrate I [ov ww] beslissen II [on ww]
als scheidsrechter optreden
arbitration [znw] arbitrage
arbitrator [znw] scheidsrechter
arbour [znw] beschutte tuin
arc [znw] (cirkel)boog
arcade [znw] • galerij
• speelautomatenhal
arch I [on ww] (zich) welven II [znw]
• boog • gewelf III [bnw] schalks

archaeology [znw] archeologie, oudheidkunde
archer [znw] boogschutter
archery [znw] • boogschieten • pijl en boog
archipelago [znw] archipel
architectural [bnw] bouwkundig
architecture [znw] architectuur, bouwkunde
ardent [bnw] • vurig • ijverig
ardour [znw] • gloed • vuur
arduous [bnw] • steil • inspannend
are [ww] → be
area [znw] • oppervlakte • gebied • souterrain
argue [on ww] • betogen • debatteren • ruzie maken • bewijzen
argument [znw] • betoog • woordentwist • argument
arid [bnw] dor, droog
arise [on ww] • z. voordoen • opstaan, verrijzen • (~ from) voortkomen uit, ontstaan uit
aristocracy [znw] aristocratie, adel
arithmetic [znw] rekenkunde
arm I [ov ww] bewapenen II [on ww] z. wapenen III [znw] • tak • arm
armadillo [znw] gordeldier
armed [bnw] • gewapend • uit-/toegerust
armistice [znw] wapenstilstand
armour I [ov ww] • pantseren • wapenen II [znw] • bepantsering • tanks • wapenrusting • harnas • duikerpak
armourer [znw] • wapensmid • wapenmeester
armoury [znw] wapenzaal
army [znw] • leger • menigte
aromatic [bnw] geurig
arose [ww] verl. tijd → arise
around I [bijw] • rondom • in de buurt II [vz] • rond(om) • om...heen
arouse [ov ww] (op)wekken
arrangement [znw] • regeling • afspraak • <muz.> arrangement

array I [ov ww] • opstellen • uitdossen II [znw] • kledertooi • mars-/slagorde • stoet, rij
arrest I [ov ww] • arresteren • tegenhouden, stuiten II [znw] • stilstand • arrest(atie)
arrival [znw] • aankomst • aangekomene
arrive [on ww] aankomen, arriveren
arrogance [znw] arrogantie, aanmatiging
arrow [znw] pijl
arse <vulg.> [znw] • achterste, gat • klootzak
arsenal [znw] kruithuis
arsenic [znw] arsenicum
arson [znw] brandstichting
art I [ww] → be II [znw] • kunst • list • vaardigheid
artefact [znw] kunstproduct
arterial [bnw] v.d. slagader
artery [znw] • slagader • verkeersader
artful [bnw] • listig • gekunsteld • kundig
arthritis [znw] artritis, jicht, gewrichtsontsteking
artichoke [znw] artisjok
article I [ov ww] • in de leer doen • aanklacht indienen • (~ to) in de leer doen bij II [znw] • artikel • statuut • <taalk.> lidwoord
artifact [znw] → artefact
artifice [znw] list, kunstgreep
artificial [bnw] • kunstmatig • gekunsteld
artillery [znw] artillerie, geschut
artisan [znw] handwerksman
artist [znw] • artiest • kunstenaar
artistic [bnw] artistiek
artistry [znw] kunstenaarschap, kunstenaarstalent, kunstzinnigheid
artless [bnw] • ongekunsteld • naïef • onhandig
arty [bnw] • te mooi • pseudo-/quasi-artistiek
as I [bijw] zo II [vw] • (zo)als

• *aangezien* • *naarmate* • *terwijl*
asbestos [znw] *asbest*
ascend [ov ww] • *(be)stijgen*
• *teruggaan* ‹in de geschiedenis›
ascendancy, ascendency [znw]
overwicht
ascendant, ascendent I [znw]
• *overwicht, ascendant* • *voorouder*
II [bnw] • *stijgend* • *dominant*
ascent [znw] • *be-/opstijging* • *helling*
• *opkomst*
ascertain [ov ww] • *vaststellen* • *te*
weten komen
ash [znw] • *as* • *es* ‹boom›
ashamed [bnw] *beschaamd*
ashen [bnw] • *asgrauw* • *doodsbleek*
ashore [bijw] *aan land*
Asian, Asiatic I [znw] *Aziaat* II [bnw]
Aziatisch
aside I [znw] • *terzijde* ‹toneel›
• *terloops gemaakte opmerking*
II [bijw] *terzijde*
ask [ov + on ww] *vragen* • *(~ after)*
vragen naar • *(~ for) vragen om,*
uitlokken • *(~ out) uitnodigen*
askance [bijw] • *achterdochtig* • *van*
terzijde
askew [bijw] *scheef*
asleep [bnw + bijw] *in slaap*
aspect [znw] • *gezichtspunt* • *aanblik*
• *ligging*
aspen [znw] • *esp* • *ratelpopulier*
asperity ‹form.› [znw] • *ongeduldige*
strengheid • *ruwheid* • *guurheid*
• *scherpheid*
aspirant I [znw] *kandidaat* II [bnw]
strevend, eerzuchtig
aspiration [znw] *streven*
aspire [on ww] • *streven* • *(ver)rijzen*
aspirin [znw] *aspirine*
ass [znw] • *ezel* • ‹AE vulg.› —> **arse**
assail [ov ww] *bestormen, aanvallen*
assailant [znw] *aanvaller*
assassin [znw] *sluipmoordenaar*
assassinate [ov ww] *vermoorden*
assault I [ov ww] • *aanvallen*

• *bestormen* II [znw] • *aanval*
• *bestorming* • *aanranding*
assemble I [ov ww] • *monteren*
• *verzamelen* II [on ww] *bijeenkomen,*
z. *verzamelen*
assembly [znw] • *montage*
• *vergadering* • *verzameling*
assent I [on ww] *instemmen* • *(~ to)*
instemmen met II [znw] *instemming*
assert [ov ww] • *beweren* • *laten gelden*
assertive [bnw] • *aanmatigend*
• *zelfbewust* • *bevestigend*
assess [ov ww] • *vaststellen* • *belasten*
• *waarderen, beoordelen* • *schatten*
assessment [znw] • *schatting*
• *beoordeling* ‹v. (school)werk›,
waardering • *aanslag*
assessor [znw] *taxateur*
asset [znw] • *aanwinst* • *voordeel,*
pluspunt • *geschiktheid* • ‹econ.›
creditpost
assiduous [bnw] *vlijtig*
assign [ov ww] • *overdragen*
• *toewijzen* • *opgeven*
assignation [znw] • *afspraak*
• *toewijzing*
assignment [znw] • *opdracht* • *opgave*
• ‹AE› *benoeming*
assimilate I [ov ww] • *gelijk maken*
• *opnemen* II [on ww] • *opgenomen*
worden • *gelijk worden*
assist [ov ww] • *bijstaan* • *hulp*
verlenen • *(~ at) (iets) bijwonen*
assistance [znw] *hulp, steun*
assistant I [znw] • *assistent* • *bediende*
II [in samenst.] *adjunct-*
associate I [on ww] (z.) *verenigen*
• *(~ with) omgaan met* II [znw]
• *compagnon, deelgenoot* • *metgezel,*
collega III [bnw] • *verbonden*
• *begeleidend* • *mede-*
association [znw] • *vereniging*
• *samenwerking*
assorted [bnw] • *bij elkaar passend*
• *gemengd*
assortment [znw] • *assortiment*

• *sortering*
assume [ov ww] • *aannemen*
• *veronderstellen* • *op zich nemen* • z.
aanmatigen
assumption [znw] • *veronderstelling*
• *vermoeden* • *aanneming* <v. ambt>
• *overname* <v. macht>
assurance [znw] • *zekerheid*
• *verzekering* • *zelfvertrouwen*
astonish [ov ww] *verbazen*
astonishing [bnw] *verbazingwekkend*
astonishment [znw] (*stomme*)
verbazing
astound [ov ww] • *zeer verbazen*
• *ontstellen*
astray [bnw] *op een dwaalspoor, op het*
slechte/verkeerde pad
astride [bijw] *schrijlings*
astrologer [znw] *astroloog,*
sterrenwichelaar
astrology [znw] *astrologie,*
sterrenwichelarij
astronomer [znw] *astronoom,*
sterrenkundige
astronomy [znw] *astronomie,*
sterrenkunde
asylum [znw] *asiel* <ook politiek>,
gesticht
at [vz] • *met* • *aan* • *bij* • *om* • *in* • *tegen*
ate [ww] verl. tijd → **eat**
atheism [znw] *atheïsme*
athlete [znw] *atleet*
athletic [bnw] *atletisch*
atmosphere [znw] • *atmosfeer* • *sfeer*
atom [znw] • *atoom* • *greintje*
atomic [bnw] *atoom-*
atonement [znw] *verzoening*
atrocious [bnw] • *gruwelijk* • *slecht*
atrocity [znw] *wreedheid*
attach [on ww] • *verbinden, aansluiten*
• (*aan zich*) *hechten* • (~ **to**)
vastmaken aan
attaché [znw] *diplomatenkoffertje*
attachment [znw] • *verbinding*
• *aanhangsel* • *gehechtheid*
attack I [ov ww] *aanvallen* II [znw]

aanval
attain [ov + on ww] • *bereiken*
• *verwerven*
attainable [bnw] • *verkrijgbaar*
• *bereikbaar*
attainment [znw] • *verworvenheid*
• *prestatie* • *talent*
attempt I [ov ww] *pogen* II [znw]
poging
attend [ov ww] • *bijwonen* • *begeleiden*
• *aanwezig zijn* • (~ **to**) *zorgen voor,*
verzorgen, opletten
attendant I [znw] • *begeleider*
• *bediende* II [bnw] • *aanwezig*
• *begeleidend* • *bedienend*
attention [znw] *aandacht, attentie*
attentive [bnw] *aandachtig*
attenuate [ov ww] • *verzachten*
• *afzwakken* • *verdunnen*
attest [ov ww] • *instaan voor* • *beëdigen*
• *getuigen*
attic [znw] *zolder*(kamer)
attitude [znw] *houding*
attorney [znw] *gevolmachtigde,*
procureur
attract [ov ww] *aantrekken, boeien*
attraction [znw] • *aantrekkingskracht*
• *attractie*
attractive [bnw] *aantrekkelijk*
attributable [bnw] *toe te schrijven*
attribute I [ov ww] • (~ **to**)
toeschrijven aan II [znw] *kenmerk*
auburn [bnw] *kastanjebruin* <vnl.
haar>
auction I [ov ww] *veilen, openbaar bij*
opbod verkopen • (~ **off**) *bij opbod*
uit-/verkopen II [znw] *veiling*
auctioneer I [ov ww] *veilen* II [znw]
veilingmeester
audacious [bnw] • *dapper*
• *onbeschaamd*
audacity [znw] • *dapperheid*
• *onbeschaamdheid*
audible [bnw] *hoorbaar*
audience [znw] • *toehoorders* • *publiek*
• *audiëntie*

audition [znw] • gehoor • auditie
auditor [znw] • toehoorder • accountant
auditorium [znw] gehoorzaal, aula
augment I [ov ww] doen toenemen
II [on ww] toenemen
August [znw] augustus
aunt [znw] tante
aura [znw] • (atmo)sfeer • uitstraling
aural [bnw] van/via het gehoor, oor-
auspicious [bnw] gunstig
austere [znw] • sober • grimmig, streng
austerity [znw] • soberheid • strengheid
Australian I [znw] Australiër II [bnw]
Australisch
Austrian I [znw] Oostenrijker II [bnw]
Oostenrijks
authentic [znw] • origineel • oprecht
<gevoelens> • rechtsgeldig
• betrouwbaar • echt
authenticity [znw] • echtheid
• betrouwbaarheid
author [znw] • schrijver • schepper
• <jur.> dader
authoritarian [bnw] autoritair,
eigenmachtig
authoritative [bnw] gezaghebbend
authority [znw] • gezag, autoriteit
• expert
authorization [znw] • machtiging,
volmacht • goedkeuring
authorize [ov ww] machtigen
autocrat [znw] alleenheerser
automatic I [znw] • automatisch
wapen • automaat <auto/apparaat>
II [bnw] • automatisch • werktuiglijk,
zonder nadenken • noodzakelijk
• on-/onderbewust
automaton [znw] automaat, robot
autonomous [bnw] autonoom, met
zelfbestuur
autonomy [znw] zelfbestuur,
autonomie
autopsy [znw] lijkschouwing
autumn [znw] herfst
autumnal [bnw] herfstachtig
auxiliary I [znw] • hulpstuk • helper

• <taalk.> hulpwerkwoord II [bnw]
• hulp- • aanvullend
avail I [on ww] baten II [znw] baat, nut
available [bnw] • beschikbaar • geldig
avalanche [znw] lawine
avarice [znw] • hebzucht • gierigheid
avenge [ov ww] wreken
avenue [znw] • laan • toegang • weg
• <AE> brede straat
average I [ov ww] • gemiddeld halen
• schatten • (~ out) gemiddeld op
hetzelfde neerkomen II [znw]
gemiddelde III [bnw] gemiddeld
averse [bnw] afkerig
aversion [znw] afkeer
avert [ov ww] afwenden
aviary [znw] volière
aviation [znw] • vliegsport • vliegkunst
avid [bnw] • begerig • vurig • fervent
avoid [ov ww] vermijden
avoidable [bnw] vermijdbaar
avoidance [znw] • vermijding
• ontwijking
avow [ov ww] • bekennen • erkennen
avowal [znw] (openlijke) bekentenis
await [ov ww] (af)wachten
awake [bnw] wakker
awakening [znw] het ontwaken
award I [ov ww] • toekennen • belonen
• (~ to) toekennen aan II [znw]
• bekroning, prijs • toelage • <jur.>
vonnis, uitspraak
aware [bnw] • bewust • gewaar
away I [bnw] II [bijw] weg
awe I [ov ww] ontzag inboezemen
II [znw] ontzag
awful [bnw] • afschuwelijk
• indrukwekkend
awkward [bnw] • pijnlijk • onhandig
• lastig
awoke [ww] verl. tijd + volt. deelw.
→ awake
awry [bnw + bijw] • scheef • verkeerd
axis [znw] as, middellijn
azure [bnw] hemelsblauw

B

babble I [on ww] • leuteren, babbelen
• kabbelen • verklappen II [znw]
geleuter

babe [znw] • baby • ‹sl.› meisje, liefje

baboon [znw] baviaan

baby I [ov ww] als (een) kind
behandelen II [znw] • baby, kind
• schat • de jongste

babyish [bnw] kinderachtig, kinderlijk

bachelor [znw] • vrijgezel
• ≈ kandidaat ‹universitair›

back I [ov ww] • steunen • wedden op
• (~ up) steunen II [on ww]
achteruitrijden • (~ away)
terugdeinzen • (~ down) zich
terugtrekken, toegeven, terugkrabbelen
• (~ off) terugtrekken, terugdeinzen
• (~ out) terugkrabbelen III [znw]
• rug, achterkant • ‹sport› achterspeler
IV [bijw] • achter • terug

backing [znw] steun

backward [bnw] achterlijk

backwards [bnw + bijw] achteruit

bacon [znw] spek

bacterial [bnw] bacterie-

bacteriology [znw] bacteriologie

bacterium [znw] bacterie

bad [bnw] • slecht, ondeugdelijk
• kwaad • bedorven

bade [ww] verl. tijd → bid

badge [znw] onderscheidingsteken,
insigne, embleem

badger I [ov ww] • tergen • lastig
vallen, zeuren om iets II [znw] das
‹dier›

badly [bnw + bijw]

baffle I [ov ww] • verijdelen
• verbijsteren II [znw] schot, scherm

bag I [ov ww] vangen, schieten,
bemachtigen II [on ww] (op)zwellen
III [znw] • zak, tas • vangst • wal

‹onder oog›

baggy [bnw] uitgezakt

bail I [ov ww] hozen • (~ out) uit de
puree helpen, door borgtocht vrij
krijgen II [znw] • (muur v.) voorhof
• borgtocht

bait I [ov ww] • van aas of voer voorzien
• sarren II [znw] (lok)aas

bake [ov + on ww] bakken

baker [znw] bakker

bakery [znw] bakkerij

balance I [ov ww] • wegen • wikken • in
evenwicht houden/brengen II [znw]
• weegschaal, balans • evenwicht
• saldo, rest

balcony [znw] balkon

bald [bnw] • kaal • nuchter

bale I [ov ww] hozen II [on ww]
• (~ out) met parachute uit vliegtuig
springen, uitstappen

baleful [bnw] • kwaadaardig
• verderfelijk

balk I [ov ww] • voorbijgaan, overslaan
• z. onttrekken aan • verijdelen
• weigeren II [znw] • balk • struikelblok

ball I [ov + on ww] (zich) ballen II [znw]
bal, bol, kogel

ballad [znw] ballade

ballast I [ov ww] bezwaren II [znw]
ballast

ballistic [bnw] ballistisch

balloon I [on ww] • bol staan
• opzwellen II [znw] bol, ballon

ballot I [on ww] • stemmen • balloteren
• loten II [znw] • stembriefje
• stemming • loting

balm [znw] balsem

balmy [bnw] • mild, • stapelgek

bamboo [znw] bamboe

banal [bnw] banaal

banana [znw] banaan

band I [ov ww] strepen II [znw] • bende
• orkest ‹v. blaasinstrumenten›
• band, lint, strook • drijfriem

bandage I [ov ww] verbinden • (~ up)
verbinden II [znw] verband

bandit [znw] (struik)rover
bandy [ov ww] uitwisselen • (~ about)
heen en weer werpen of slaan
bandy-legged [bnw] met o-benen
bane [znw] • vloek, pest • vergif
bang I [ov + on ww] • hard slaan
• smakken, dichtslaan • knallen
• (~ about) ruw behandelen
• (~ away) blijven bonzen of hameren
II [ov ww] recht afknippen <v. pony>
III [znw] • klap, smak, knal • pony
<haar> IV [tw] pats!, bom!
banger [znw] • worstje • vuurwerk
• wrak <auto>
bangle [znw] armring, armband
banish [ov ww] verbannen
bank I [ov + on ww] • indammen
• hellend rijden of vliegen <bij bank>
II [znw] • oever • zandbank • berm
• bank
banker [znw] bankier
banking [znw] bankwezen
bankrupt [bnw] failliet
bankruptcy [znw] faillissement
banner [znw] • banier • spandoek
banquet I [on ww] feesten, smullen
II [znw] feestmaal
baptism [znw] doop
baptize [ov ww] dopen
bar I [ov ww] • versperren, beletten
• grendelen II [znw] • balk • staaf,
tralie, stang • slagboom • reep
<chocolade>, stuk <zeep> • zandbank
<voor haven- of riviermonding>
• buffet, bar • belemmering, bezwaar
• maat(streep)
barb [znw] • baarddraad <v. vis>
• weerhaak
barbarian I [znw] barbaar II [bnw]
barbaars
barbaric, barbarous [bnw] barbaars
barbarity [znw] barbaarsheid,
wreedheid
barbecue I [ov ww] barbecueën
II [znw] • feest, barbecue • groot
braadrooster

barbed [bnw] * ~ wire prikkeldraad
barber [znw] • barbier • kapper
bare I [ov ww] blootleggen, ontbloten
II [bnw] naakt, kaal
bargain I [on ww] • overeenkomen
• marchanderen II [znw] • afspraak
• koop(je)
barge I [on ww] • (~ into) ergens
tegenaanlopen II [znw] • woonschip
• aak, praam • officierssloep,
staatsiesloep
bark I [ov ww] • afschillen • schaven <v.
huid> II [on ww] blaffen III [znw]
• geblaf • schors, bast • bark
barley [znw] gerst
barn [znw] schuur
barnacle [znw] eendenmossel
baroness [znw] barones
baroque [bnw] barok
barrack(s) I [ov ww] • kazerneren
• uitjouwen <cricket> II [znw] kazerne
barrage [znw] • versperring • spervuur
• stuwdam
barrel [znw] • vat • cilinder • loop <v.
geweer>
barren [znw] onvruchtbaar, dor
barricade I [ov ww] barricaderen
II [znw] barricade
barrier [znw] • hinderpaal, slagboom
• dranghek
barring [vz] behoudens
barrister [znw] advocaat, pleiter
barrow [znw] • kruiwagen • berrie
• handkar • grafheuvel
barter I [ov + on ww] ruilhandel drijven
II [znw] ruilhandel
base I [ov ww] baseren II [znw]
• grondgetal • voetstuk, basis • <sport>
honk • <chem.> base III [bnw] laag,
gemeen
baseless [bnw] ongegrond
basement [znw] souterrain
bash I [ov ww] • (in elkaar) rammen
• inslaan, kapot slaan • (~ up) in
elkaar slaan II [znw] slag
bashful [bnw] verlegen, bedeesd

basin [znw] • bekken • bassin • kom
• dok • stroomgebied
basis [znw] basis, grondslag
bask [on ww] z. koesteren
basket [znw] mand, korf
bass I [znw] • (zee)baars • soort bier
II [bnw] • lage frequenties, lage tonen
• bas
bassoon [znw] fagot
bastard I [znw] • schoft • bastaard
II [bnw] onecht
bat I [ov + on ww] batten II [znw]
• vleermuis • slaghout, bat
batch [znw] • partij, groep, stel • baksel
bath I [ov ww] een bad geven II [znw]
• bad • badkuip
bathe [ov + on ww] • baden • natmaken
bather [znw] bader, zwemmer
bathroom [znw] • badkamer • <AE> wc
baton [znw] • dirigeerstok • gummistok
• staf
battalion [znw] bataljon
batten [znw] (vloer)plank
batter I [ov + on ww] • beuken
• rammen • deuken, havenen II [znw]
• beslag • slagman
battery [znw] • (leg)batterij • accu
• aanranding
battle I [ov + on ww] strijden II [znw]
strijd, veldslag
bauble [znw] snuisterij, prul
baulk [ov ww] → balk
bawdy [bnw] liederlijk
bawl [ov + on ww] brullen, schreeuwen
• (~ out) <inf.> de mantel uitvegen
be I [on ww] • (~ for) zijn voor,
voorstander zijn van • (~ in)
aanwezig/binnen, aan slag zijn, aan
het bewind zijn, erbij, in de mode,
opgenomen zijn • (~ off) afgesloten
zijn <elektra/gas/water>, niet in orde
zijn, verwijderd zijn, niet doorgaan,
afgelast zijn, weg zijn, starten,
ervandoor gaan/zijn • (~ on) tipsy
zijn, aan/op zijn <v. kledingstuk>,
doorgaan, bezig zijn, aan de

gang/beurt zijn, meedoen • (~ out)
gepubliceerd zijn, (er)buiten/eruit zijn,
om/weg zijn, in staking zijn, werkloos
zijn, onmogelijk zijn • (~ over)
over/uit/voorbij zijn, op bezoek zijn,
overschieten • (~ through) het niet
meer zien zitten, klaar zijn, erdoorheen
zijn • (~ up) hoger/gestegen zijn,
op/wakker zijn, op/over/voorbij zijn,
aan de gang/hand zijn, ter discussie
staan II [kww] • zijn • bestaan
• worden • liggen, staan
beach [znw] strand
beacon [znw] (vuur)baken, vuurtoren
bead I [ov ww] van kralen voorzien,
rijgen II [znw] • vizierkorrel • kraal
• parel <v. zweet>
beady [bnw] • kraalvormig • parelend
beagle [znw] speurder
beak [znw] • scherpe snavel • <sl.> neus
beaker [znw] beker(glas)
beam I [ov + on ww] • stralen
• uitzenden <op tv> • glunderen
II [znw] • balk • drijfstang • straal
• stralenbundel • radiosignaal
bean [znw] boon
bear I [ov ww] • (ver)dragen • dulden
• uitstaan • opbrengen • baren
• (~ (up)on) betrekking hebben op
• (~ down (up)on) afkomen op
• (~ out) bevestigen • (~ up against)
het hoofd bieden aan • (~ with)
geduld hebben met II [znw] beer
bearable [bnw] te (ver)dragen
beard I [ov ww] tarten II [znw] baard
bearded [bnw] met een baard
bearer [znw] • toonder • brenger • stut
• drager • houder
bearing [znw] • gedrag, houding
• verband • invloed
beast [znw] • viervoeter • beest
beaten [bnw] • verslagen • gedreven <v.
goud>
beater [znw] drijver <bij jacht>
beating [znw] pak slaag
beautician [znw] schoonheidsspecialist

beautiful [bnw] *mooi*
beautify [ov ww] *verfraaien*
beauty [znw] *schoonheid*
beaver [znw] • *hoed v. bevervilt • bever*
became [ww] verl. tijd → **become**
beck [znw] • *wenk, knik • beek*
beckon [ov ww] *wenken*
become I [ov ww] *goed staan* II [kww] *worden*
becoming [bnw] • *betamelijk • flatterend*
bed I [ov ww] • (~ **down**) *een slaapplaats geven, naar bed brengen* II [on ww] • (~ **down**) *naar bed gaan, gaan slapen* III [znw] • *bed • leger* ‹v. dier› • *bedding • (onder)laag*
bedding [znw] • *beddengoed • onderlaag*
bedeck [ov ww] *(op)tooien, versieren*
bedevil [ov ww] • *bederven • in de war brengen*
bedlam [znw] *gekkenhuis*
bedroom [znw] *slaapkamer*
bee [znw] *bij*
beech [znw] *beuk*
beef I [ov ww] • (~ **up**) ‹sl.› *versterken, opvoeren, opkalefateren* II [on ww] *klagen* III [znw] • *rundvlees • spierkracht*
beefy [bnw] *stevig, gespierd*
beer [znw] *bier*
beet [znw] *biet, kroot*
beetle I [on ww] • (~ **off**) ‹sl.› *zich uit de voeten maken* II [znw] • *tor • stamper • heiblok*
befit [ov ww] *betamen*
befitting [bnw] *passend*
before [vz] • *voor • tevoren • voordat*
beforehand [bijw] *van tevoren*
befriend [ov ww] *een vriend zijn voor*
beg [ov + on ww] *bedelen, smeken* • (~ **for**) *verzoeken om* • (~ **off**) (z.) *verontschuldigen voor het niet nakomen van plicht of afspraak*
beget [ov ww] • *verwekken, voortbrengen • veroorzaken*

beggar [znw] • *bedelaar • schooier(tje)*
beggarly [bnw] *armoedig, armzalig*
begin [ov + on ww] *beginnen*
beginner [znw] *beginneling*
beginning [znw] *oorsprong, begin*
begot [ww] verl. tijd → **beget**
begrudge [ov ww] *misgunnen*
beguile [ov ww] • *bekoren • bedriegen*
begun [ww] volt. deelw. → **begin**
behalf [znw] * on your ~ *namens u*
behaviour [znw] • *werking • gedrag*
behead [ov ww] *onthoofden*
beheld [ww] verl. tijd + volt. deelw. → **behold**
behind I [znw] *achterste* II [vz] • *achter • na*
behindhand [bnw + bijw] • *te traag, te laat • achter(op)*
behold [ov ww] *waarnemen, zien*
being I [ww] tegenw. deelw. → **be** II [znw] *bestaan, wezen*
belabour [ov ww] • *ervan langs geven • te uitvoerig behandelen*
belated [bnw] *te laat, erg laat*
belfry [znw] *klokkentoren*
Belgian I [znw] *Belg* II [bnw] *Belgisch*
belie [ov ww] *verloochenen*
belief [znw] *geloof*
believable [bnw] *geloofwaardig*
believe [ov + on ww] *geloven*
belittle [ov ww] • *verkleinen • kleineren*
bell I [ov ww] *de bel aanbinden* II [znw] • *bel • klok*
bellicose [bnw] • *agressief • oorlogszuchtig*
belligerent I [znw] *oorlogvoerende partij* II [bnw] • *oorlogvoerend • agressief*
bellow I [ov + on ww] *loeien, brullen* II [znw] *gebrul*
belly [znw] • *schoot • buik*
belong [on ww] *horen bij iets* • (~ **to**) *behoren aan/tot*
belongings [mv] • *eigendom • bagage*
beloved I [znw] *geliefde* II [bnw] *geliefd*
below [vz] *onder, (naar) beneden*

belt I [ov ww] • aangorden • afranselen
II [on ww] racen • (~ up) zijn
veiligheidsriem omdoen III [znw]
• gordel, riem • zone • opdonder
bench [znw] • bank • rechtbank
• werkbank
bend I [ov + on ww] (zich) buigen
II [znw] bocht, buiging
beneath [vz] onder, beneden
benediction [znw] • zegen • lof ‹r.-k.›
benefactor [znw] weldoener
benefactress [znw] weldoenster
beneficent [bnw] liefdadig
beneficial [bnw] heilzaam
beneficiary I [znw] • vazal • predikant
• begunstigde II [bnw] leenroerig
benefit I [ov + on ww] baten • (~ by)
voordeel trekken uit II [znw] • voordeel,
baat • toelage • uitkering
benevolence [znw] • gift
• welwillendheid • vriendelijkheid
• weldadigheid
benevolent [bnw] • welwillend
• weldadig
benign [bnw] • vriendelijk • heilzaam
• goedaardig ‹v. ziekte›
bent I [ww] verl.tijd + volt.deelw.
→ bend II [znw] • neiging • voorliefde
bequeath [ov ww] nalaten, vermaken
bequest [znw] legaat
bereavement [znw] • verlies
• sterfgeval
beret [znw] alpinomuts
berry [znw] bes
berserk [bnw] gek van woede
berth I [ov ww] meren II [znw] • kooi
• couchette • ankerplaats • betrekking
beseech [ov ww] (af)smeken
beset [ov ww] • omringen • blokkeren
‹v. weg› • aanvallen
beside [vz] naast
besides [vz] benevens, bovendien
besiege [ov ww] • belegeren
• overstelpen
best I [ov ww] overtreffen
II [bnw + bijw] best(e)

bestial [bnw] beestachtig
bestow [ov ww] • (~ upon) schenken
aan
bet I [ov + on ww] (ver)wedden II [znw]
• inzet • weddenschap
betray [ov ww] • verraden • bedriegen
betrayal [znw] verraad
betrothal [znw] verloving
better I [ov ww] verbeteren II [bnw]
beter
between [vz] tussen
beverage [znw] drank
bevy [znw] • troep • vlucht ‹v. vogels›
beware [ov + on ww]
bewilder [ov ww] verbijsteren
bewildering [bnw] verbijsterend
bewilderment [znw] verbijstering
bewitch [ov ww] betoveren, beheksen
beyond I [znw] hiernamaals II [vz]
• verder dan • aan de andere kant (van)
• boven • behalve
bias I [ov ww] richting of neiging geven
aan II [znw] • neiging • vooroordeel
bibliography [znw] bibliografie
bicker [on ww] • kibbelen • kletteren ‹v.
regen› • kabbelen • flikkeren
bicycle [znw] rijwiel
bid I [ov + on ww] • bieden • pogen
• bevelen • verzoeken • wensen II [znw]
• bod • poging • ‹AE› uitnodiging
bidder [znw] bieder
biennial [bnw] tweejarig
bier [znw] lijkbaar
big [bnw + bijw] • groot • belangrijk
bigamy [znw] bigamie
bigot [znw] • dweper • kwezel
bigotry [znw] • dweepzucht • kwezelarij
bike I [on ww] fietsen II [znw] fiets
bilge [znw] • buik v. schip of vat • onzin
bilious [bnw] • galachtig • gemelijk
bill I [ov ww] • volplakken met biljetten
• aankondigen II [znw] • rekening
• wetsontwerp • document • lijst
• snavel • aanplakbiljet • ‹AE›
bankbiljet
billet I [ov ww] • (~ on) inkwartieren

bij II [znw] • kwartier • bestemming
• ‹inf.› baantje
billion [znw] • biljoen • ‹AE› miljard
billow I [on ww] golven II [znw] golf
bin [znw] • bak, kist • mand • wijnrek
bind [ov ww] • binden ‹ook v. saus,
beslag›, inbinden, vastbinden,
verbinden • verplichten • bekrachtigen
binder [znw] • (boek)binder • omslag,
band • bindmiddel • bint
• verbindingssteen
binding [znw] • (boek)band • boordsel
binge [znw] braspartij, drinkgelag, fuif
biography [znw] levensbeschrijving
biological [bnw] biologisch
biology [znw] biologie
birch [znw] • roede • berk
bird [znw] • vogel • meisje • vent
birth [znw] • geboorte • ontstaan
• afkomst
birthday [znw] verjaardag
biscuit I [znw] • beschuit, biscuit,
koekje • ongeglazuurd porselein
II [bnw] lichtbruin
bisect [ov ww] in tweeën delen
bisexual [bnw] biseksueel
bishop [znw] • bisschop • bisschopwijn
• loper ‹v. schaakspel›
bishopric [znw] • bisdom • ambt v.
bisschop
bit I [ww] verl. tijd → bite II [znw]
• kleinigheid, beetje, stukje • bit ‹v.
hoofdstel› • ‹comp.› bit
bitch I [ov + on ww] • zaniken
• afkraken • kankeren II [znw] • teef
• wijf, griet, del
bitchy [bnw] hatelijk, boosaardig,
kattig
bite I [ov + on ww] • bedriegen
• (uit)bijten • happen • steken
• (~ back) inslikken ‹v. woorden,
opmerking› II [znw] • hap, beet
• greep • scherpte
biting [bnw] bijtend, scherp
bitten [ww] volt. deelw. → bite
bitter I [znw] • bitter bier • maagbitter

II [bnw] bitter, scherp
bivouac I [on ww] bivakkeren II [znw]
bivak
bizarre [bnw] bizar, grillig
blab I [ov ww] eruit flappen, verklappen
II [znw] flapuit
blacken [ov + on ww] zwartmaken,
zwart worden
bladder [znw] • blaas • blaaskaak
blade [znw] • halm • spriet • lemmet
• scheermesje • platte scherpe kant v.
allerlei werktuigen
blame I [ov ww] berispen • (~ for) de
schuld geven van II [znw] schuld
blameless [bnw] onberispelijk
blameworthy [bnw] afkeurenswaardig
blanch [ov + on ww] bleken, (doen)
verbleken
bland [bnw] • flauw • saai • minzaam
• poeslief
blank I [znw] • streepje ‹i.p.v. lelijk
woord› • niet ‹in loterij› • open ruimte
‹op formulier› • leegte II [bnw] • leeg,
blanco • bot • vruchteloos • wezenloos,
verbijsterd, stom ‹v. verbazing›
blanket I [ov ww] • met een deken
bedekken • sussen • jonassen
• monopoliseren II [znw] wollen deken
III [bnw] allesomvattend, insluitend
blare I [ov + on ww] schallen, brullen
II [znw] gebrul
blarney [znw] vleierij
blaspheme [ov + on ww] godslasterlijk
spreken (over), spotten (met)
blasphemous [bnw] (gods)lasterlijk
blasphemy [znw] godslastering
blast I [ov ww] • bezoedelen
• vernietigen • laten springen
• verdorren II [on ww] • (~ off)
lanceren ‹v. ruimteschip› III [znw]
• sterke luchtstroom, windstoot
• (luchtdruk bij) explosie
• springlading • stoot ‹op
koperinstrument› • plaag • vloek
• meeldauw
blasted [bnw] vervloekt

blatant [bnw] • schaamteloos
• opvallend

blaze I [ov ww] rondbazuinen
• (~ away) afvuren II [on ww]
• vlammen • schitteren • uitbarsten
• (~ away) losbarsten, oplaaien <v.
vuur> • (~ up) opvliegen III [znw]
• merk <op boom> • vlam • gloed
• uitbarsting • bles

blazing [bnw] • (fel) brandend,
verblindend • <inf.> overduidelijk

blazon I [ov ww] • blazoeneren
• verkondigen II [znw] blazoen

bleach I [ov + on ww] bleken II [znw]
bleekmiddel

bleak [bnw] • kaal • guur • somber,
troosteloos

bleat I [ov + on ww] blaten II [znw]
geblaat

bleed [ov + on ww] aderlaten, (laten)
bloeden

bleeding <sl.> [bnw] verdomd

bleep I [on ww] oproepen II [znw]
• (elektronische) fluittoon
• oproepsignaal • (tijd)sein

bleeper [znw] pieper <om iem. op te
roepen>

blemish I [ov ww] bevlekken,
bekladden II [znw] smet, klad

blench [on ww] • verbleken
• terugdeinzen

blend I [ov + on ww] (zich) vermengen
II [znw] melange, mengsel

blender [znw] mixer, mengbeker

blessed [bnw] • zalig, gezegend
• vervloekt

blessing [znw] zegen

blew [ww] verl. tijd → blow

blight I [ov ww] • doen verdorren
• vernietigen II [znw] • meeldauw
• brand • bladluis • verderfelijke
invloed

blighter [znw] • ellendeling • kerel

blind I [ov ww] • verblinden, blind
maken • blinderen II [znw] • rolgordijn
• oogklep • camouflage • blinde

granaat III [bnw] • blind • doodlopend
• onzichtbaar

blindfold I [ov ww] blinddoeken
II [bnw + bijw] geblinddoekt

blink I [ov + on ww] knipperen <v. ogen
of licht> II [znw] glimp

blissful [bnw] zalig

blister I [ov + on ww] • blaren (doen)
krijgen • bladderen <v. verf> II [znw]
• blaar • trekpleister

blithe [bnw] blij, vrolijk

blithering <pej.> [bnw] stom, aarts-,
ongelooflijk

blitz [znw] • Blitz(krieg), bliksemoorlog
• (overrompelende) actie

blizzard [znw] hevige sneeuwstorm

bloated [bnw] opgeblazen, pafferig

bloater [znw] bokking

blob [znw] klodder, druppel

bloc [znw] blok, coalitie

block I [ov ww] versperren, blokkeren,
afsluiten • (~ in) insluiten <v.
geparkeerde auto>, invullen
• (~ in/out) in ruwe trekken
schetsen/opzetten • (~ out)
buitensluiten, in de doofpot stoppen
II [znw] • blok • huizenblok
• obstructie • onaandoenlijk mens

blockade I [ov ww] • blokkeren
• afzetten II [znw] blokkade

blockage [znw] • verstopping
• stagnatie

bloke <inf.> [znw] kerel, vent

blood [znw] • bloed • sap
• temperament

bloodless [bnw] • bloedeloos • bleek
• saai • harteloos

bloody [bnw] • bloederig • bloeddorstig
• verdomd

bloom I [on ww] • prijken • bloeien
II [znw] • bloei • blos • waas • bloem

blooming [bnw] vervloekt

blossom I [on ww] tot bloei komen
II [znw] bloesem, bloei

blot I [ov + on ww] • bevlekken • vloeien
• (~ out) vernietigen, overstemmen,

uitwissen • (~ **up**) absorberen II [znw]
vlek, smet
blotchy [bnw] met vlekken
blotter [znw] vloeiblok
blow I [ov + on ww] • waaien • blazen
• doorslaan • doorbranden • verklikken
• verkwisten • (~ **in**) binnen komen
waaien • (~ **over**) voorbijgaan
• (~ **up**) vergroten <v. foto>, tekeergaan
II [znw] klap, slag
blower [znw] • blazer • orgeltrapper
• ventilatieklep • (gas)uitlaat • <sl.>
telefoon
blubber [ov + on ww] grienen
bludgeon I [ov ww] ranselen II [znw]
knuppel
blue I [ov ww] • blauw maken • erdoor
jagen <v. geld> II [znw] • blauw • lucht
• zee III [bnw] • blauw • neerslachtig,
somber • schunnig
bluff I [ov + on ww] (over)bluffen
II [znw] • steile oever, rots of kaap
• bluf III [bnw] • steil • stomp
• openhartig • joviaal
blunder I [on ww] een flater begaan
• (~ **into**) onbeholpen ergens tegenaan
lopen • (~ **upon**) toevallig ontdekken
II [znw] stommiteit
blunt I [ov ww] bot maken II [bnw]
• bot • dom
blur I [ov ww] • uitwissen • bekladden
II [on ww] vervagen III [znw] • veeg
• waas
blush I [on ww] blozen II [znw] • blik
• blos • schaamrood, rode kleur, rose
gloed
bluster I [on ww] • tekeergaan, razen
• snoeven II [znw] • geraas • snoeverij
boar [znw] • wild zwijn • beer <varken>
board I [ov ww] • met planken
betimmeren • aan boord gaan
• aanklampen • stappen in • (~ **out**)
uitbesteden • (~ **with**) in de kost doen
bij II [on ww] laveren • (~ **out**)
buitenshuis eten • (~ **with**) in de kost
zijn bij III [znw] • plank • bord

• karton • kost • bestuur, commissie
• boord
boarder [znw] • leerling v. kostschool
• kostganger
boarding [znw] • betimmering,
schutting • het inschepen, het aan
boord gaan
boast I [ov ww] (kunnen) bogen op
II [on ww] pochen • (~ **about/of**)
opscheppen over III [znw]
• grootspraak, bluf • trots
boastful [bnw] pocherig
boat [znw] • boot • sauskom
boatswain [znw] bootsman
bob I [ov ww] • couperen <staart> • kort
knippen II [on ww] • dobberen • korte
buiging maken III [znw] • op en neer
gaande beweging • shilling
• gecoupeerde staart • korte buiging
bobbin [znw] klos, spoel
bode [znw] voorspellen
bodice [znw] • keurslijf • onderlijfje
bodily [bijw] • lichamelijk • in zijn
geheel
body I [ov ww] II [znw] • lichaam • lijk
• persoon • romp • carrosserie
• voornaamste deel • groep • corporatie
• volume • volheid <v. wijn>
bog I [ww] II [znw] moeras, veen
bogey [znw] • boeman • duivel
boggle I [ov ww] verprutsen II [on ww]
• aarzelen • morrelen III [znw] warboel
boggy [bnw] moerasachtig
bogus [bnw] • gefingeerd • pseudo
• vals
boil I [ov ww] aan de kook brengen
• (~ **down**) inkoken II [znw]
• kook(punt) • steenpuist
bold [bnw] • (stout)moedig, vrij
• onbeschaamd • fors
Bolivian [bnw] Boliviaans
bollard [znw] • meerpaal
• verkeerszuiltje
bolster I [ov ww] • (~ **up**) steunen, in
stand houden II [znw] kussen

bolt I [ov ww] • *onderzoeken*
• *schrokken* • *grendelen* II [on ww]
ervandoor gaan III [znw] • *bout* • *pin*
• *grendel* • *bliksemschicht* • *rol* ‹stof›
bomb I [ov ww] *bombarderen*
II [on ww] *totaal mislukken* III [znw]
bom
bombard [ov ww] *bombarderen*
bombardment [znw] *bombardement*
bombastic [bnw] *bombastisch,*
hoogdravend
bomber [znw] *bommenwerper*
bonanza I [znw] • *voorspoed* • *grote*
productie ‹v. mijn› II [bnw]
voorspoedig
bond [znw] • *band* • *contract*
• *obligatie* • *entrepot*
bondage [znw] *slavernij*
bone I [ww] *uitbenen* II [znw] *been, bot,*
kluif III [bnw] *van been*
bonkers [bnw] ∗ *raving/stark* ~
stapelgek
bonnet [znw] • *Schotse baret*
• *dameshoed* • *motorkap*
bonus [znw] • *bonus* • *premie, extra*
dividend • *tantième* • *bijslag*
bony [bnw] *mager, benig*
boo I [ov ww] *uitjouwen* II [znw]
boegeroep
boob [znw] • *tiet* • ‹sl.› *domoor, ezel*
book I [ov ww] • *boeken* • *bespreken*
• *noteren* • *een kaartje geven* II [znw]
boek
bookable [bnw] *bespreekbaar, te*
reserveren
bookie [znw] *bookmaker*
booking [znw] *bespreking, reservering*
bookish [bnw] • *geleerd* • *pedant*
booklet [znw] *boekje*
boom I [on ww] • *dreunen* • *grote*
vlucht nemen • *plotseling stijgen* ‹v.*
prijzen› II [znw] • *hausse* • *(ge)dreun*
• *versperring*
boon [znw] • *zegen* • *geschenk* • *verzoek*
boor [znw] *boerenkinkel*
boorish [bnw] *lomp*

boost I [ov ww] • *duwen* • *verhogen*
• *opjagen* II [znw] • *duw* • *verhoging*
booster [znw] • *opduwraket* • *aanjager*
• *stroomversterker*
boot I [ov ww] *trappen* II [znw] • *laars*
• *hoge schoen* • *laadbak, bagageruimte*
‹v. auto›
booth [znw] • *tent, kraam* • *telefooncel,*
hokje
booty [znw] *buit*
booze ‹inf.› I [on ww] *zuipen* II [znw]
• *drank* • *zuippartij*
border I [ov + on ww] • *grenzen*
• *omzomen* • (~ **on**) *grenzen aan*
II [znw] • *grens(streek)* • *rand, zoom*
bore I [ww] *verl. tijd* → **bear**
II [ov ww] • *boren* • *vervelen* III [znw]
• *boorgat* • *vervelende persoon/zaak*
• *vloedgolf*
boredom [znw] *verveling*
boring [bnw] *vervelend*
born I [ww] *volt. deelw.* → **bear**
II [bnw] *geboren*
borne [ww] *volt. deelw.* → **bear**
borough [znw] • *stad* • *gemeente*
• *kiesdistrict*
borrow [ov + on ww] • *lenen* • *ontlenen*
bosh [znw] *onzin*
bosom [znw] • *boezem, borst* • *schoot*
boss I [ov ww] • *de baas spelen* • *leiden*
• *commanderen* II [znw] • *baas*
• *kopstuk* • *uitsteeksel* • *knop*
bossy [bnw] • *bazig* • *eigenzinnig*
botany [znw] *plantkunde*
botch ‹inf.› I [ov + on ww] • *verknoeien*
• *slordig verstellen* • (~ **up**) ‹inf.›
verknallen II [znw] *slordige reparatie*
both [bnw + bijw] *beide*
bother I [ov ww] *lastig vallen, kwellen*
II [on ww] • (~ **about**) *z. druk maken*
over III [znw] • *drukte* • *gezeur, last*
bothersome [bnw] *ergerlijk, vervelend*
bottle I [ov ww] *bottelen* • (~ **up**)
oppotten, insluiten II [on ww]
• (~ **out**) *ergens op het laatste moment*
van afzien III [znw] *fles*

bottom I [ov ww] • *v. bodem voorzien*
• *peilen* • *doorgronden* II [on ww]
• (~ **out**) *het laagste punt bereiken*
III [znw] • *bodem* • *zitvlak*
• *benedeneinde* • *laagste score, nul*
IV [bnw] • *onderste* • *laatste*
• *fundamenteel*
bough [znw] *grote dikke tak*
bought [ww] verl. tijd + volt. deelw.
→ **buy**
boulder [znw] • *grote steen* • *kei*
bounce I [ov + on ww] • *snoeven*
• *opveren* • *naar binnen/buiten stuiven*
• (~ **along**) z. *levendig gedragen*
• (~ **back**) z. *herstellen* • (~ **off**)
terugkaatsen II [znw] • *sprong*
• *opvering* • *snoeverij*
bouncer [znw] *uitsmijter* ‹in bar of
disco›
bouncing [bnw] • *flink, stevig*
• *luidruchtig*
bound I [ww] verl.tijd + volt.deelw.
→ **bind** II [ov ww] *beperken,
begrenzen* III [on ww] • *springen*
• *stuiteren* IV [znw] • *grens*
• *veerkrachtige sprong* • *stuitering*
boundary [znw] *grens*
boundless [bnw] *onbegrensd*
bounty [znw] • *geschenk* • *premie*
• *gulheid*
bouquet [znw] • *ruiker, boeket* • *geur*
‹v. wijn›
bourgeois [bnw] *burgerlijk*
bout [znw] • *beurt* • *tijdje* • *aanval*
bow I [ov + on ww] *buigen* II [znw]
• *strijkstok* • *strik* • *beugel, hengsel*
• *buiging* • *boeg* • *boog*
bowels [mv] • *ingewanden* • *medelijden*
bowl I [ov + on ww] • *voortrollen*
• *werpen* ‹bij cricket› • (~ **out**)
uitgooien II [znw] • *kom, schaal* • *bal*
‹bij bowling›
bowler [znw] *werper* ‹bij cricket›
boxer [znw] *bokser*
boxing [znw] *het boksen*
boy [znw] • *jongen* • *bediende*

boycott I [ov ww] *boycotten* II [znw]
boycot
bra [znw] *beha*
brace I [ov ww] • *steunen, versterken*
• *opwekken* II [znw] • *muuranker*
• *beugel* • *paar, koppel*
bracelet [znw] • *armband* • *handboei*
bracing [bnw] *verkwikkend*
bracken [znw] *(adelaars)varen(s)*
bracket I [ov ww] • *tussen haakjes
zetten* • *in één naam noemen*
• *samenkoppelen* II [znw] • *plank aan
de muur* • *console* • *klamp* • *haakje*
• *groep, klasse, categorie* • ‹archit.›
karbeel
brackish [bnw] *brak*
brag I [ov + on ww] *snoeven* II [znw]
soort kaartspel
braggart I [znw] *snoever* II [bnw]
snoeverig
braid I [ov ww] • *vlechten* • *omboorden*
II [znw] • *vlecht* • *tres*
brain I [ov ww] *de hersens inslaan*
II [znw] *hersenen, verstand, brein*
brainy ‹inf.› [bnw] *knap*
braise [ov ww] *smoren* ‹v. vlees›
brake I [ov + on ww] *remmen* II [znw]
• *rem* • *kreupelhout* • *egge* • *varen*
bramble [znw] *braamstruik*
bran [znw] *zemelen*
branch I [on ww] z. *vertakken* • (~ **off**)
afslaan • (~ **out**) z. *uitbreiden* ‹v.
zaken› II [znw] • *(zij)tak* • *branche*
• *filiaal*
brand I [ov ww] *brandmerken* II [znw]
• *brandmerk* • *soort, merk* • *fakkel*
brandish [ov ww] *zwaaien met*
brandy [znw] • *cognac* • *brandewijn*
brash I [znw] • *steenslag* • *oprisping
van (maag)zuur* II [bnw]
onverschrokken, brutaal
brass I [znw] • *geelkoper, brons* • *centen*
• *brutaliteit* • *bronzen grafplaat*
• ‹muz.› *koperen instrumenten*
II [bnw] *koperen, bronzen*
brassy [bnw] • *koperachtig* • *brutaal*

brat [znw] blaag, jochie
bravado [znw] vertoon van moed/lef
brave I [ov ww] tarten, trotseren
II [znw] indianenkrijger III [bnw]
dapper, flink
brawl I [on ww] ruziën II [znw] ruzie
brawny [bnw] gespierd
bray I [on ww] balken II [znw] gebalk
brazen I [ov ww] II [bnw] • koperen
• schel • brutaal
breach I [ov ww] bres maken II [on ww]
springen <v. walvis> III [znw] • bres
• breuk • stortzee • sprong <v. walvis>
bread [znw] • brood • voedsel • <sl.>
poen
breadth [znw] • breedte, breedheid
• baan
break I [ov + on ww] • (ver)breken
• aanbreken, afbreken, losbreken
• (laten) springen <v. bank> • temmen
• overtreden • veranderen • (~ away)
zich losrukken, onafhankelijk worden,
wegrennen <v. land> • (~ down)
tekortschieten, in tranen uitbarsten,
afbreken, bezwijken, vast komen te
zitten • (~ in) interrumperen
• (~ into) aanbreken, aanspreken <v.
geld>, inbreken in • (~ off) pauzeren,
onderbreken, beëindigen
• (~ through) doordringen, ontdekt
worden • (~ with) (band) verbreken
met II [znw] • kans • breuk
• verandering • pauze • <hand.>
plotselinge prijsdaling
breakable [bnw] breekbaar
breakage [znw] • breuk • gebroken
waar
breakdown [znw] • instorting • defect,
storing • specificatie
breaker [znw] • vaatje • hoge golf
breakfast I [on ww] ontbijten II [znw]
ontbijt
breast I [ov ww] • worstelen tegen
• trotseren • doorklieven II [znw]
• borst, boezem • voorkant
breath [znw] adem, zuchtje

breathe [ov + on ww] • ademen • ruisen
• blazen • fluisteren
breather [znw] korte rust
breathing [znw] ademhaling
breathless [bnw] • ademloos, buiten
adem • bladstil
bred [ww] verl. tijd + volt. deelw.
→ breed
breed I [ov + on ww] • voortbrengen
• kweken, fokken • opvoeden II [znw]
soort, ras
breeder [znw] fokker
breeding [znw] opvoeding, manieren
breezy [bnw] • joviaal • winderig, fris
brethren [mv] → brother
brevity [znw] kortheid, bondigheid
brew I [ov + on ww] • brouwen • broeien
• uitbroeden II [znw] brouwsel
brewer [znw] brouwer
briar [znw] → brier
bribe I [ov ww] omkopen II [znw]
steekpenning
bribery [znw] omkoperij
brick I [ov ww] • (~ in/up)
dichtmetselen • (~ off) ommuren
II [znw] • blok <v. bouwdoos>
• baksteen III [bnw] van bakstenen
bridal I [znw] bruiloft II [bnw] bruids-
bride [znw] bruid
bridge I [ov ww] overbruggen II [znw]
• brug • rug <v. neus> • kam <v. viool>
• bridge
bridle I [ov ww] beteugelen II [on ww]
het hoofd in de nek werpen III [znw]
hoofdstel en bit
brief I [ov ww] instrueren II [znw]
• dossier • instructie III [bnw] kort,
bondig
briefing [znw] • voorlichting
• instructie(s)
brier [znw] • wilde roos • heidesoort
• doornstruik
bright [bnw] • helder, schitterend
• pienter • levendig
brilliance [znw] schittering, glans
brilliant I [znw] briljant II [bnw]

briljant, schitterend
brim I [on ww] • (~ **over**) overlopen
II [znw] • boord • rand
brimful(l) [bnw] boordevol
brine I [ov ww] pekelen II [znw] • het
zilte nat • pekel
bring [ov ww] • (mee)brengen,
aanvoeren • indienen • (~ **about**)
veroorzaken • (~ **along**) meebrengen,
aanmoedigen • (~ **back**) (in de
herinnering) terugbrengen • (~ **down**)
neerhalen, verslaan, doen vallen
• (~ **forth**) opleveren, baren,
veroorzaken • (~ **forward**) vervroegen,
naar voren brengen • (~ **in**)
binnenhalen <v. oogst>, inbrengen
• (~ **on**) veroorzaken • (~ **out**) doen
uitkomen, in de handel brengen
• (~ **over**) laten overkomen
• (~ **round**) overtuigen, bijbrengen <v.
bewusteloos iem.> • (~ **through**)
erbovenop helpen • (~ **to**) bijbrengen
• (~ **together**) samenbrengen
• (~ **under**) bedwingen, onderdrukken
• (~ **up**) naar voren brengen, opvoeden
brink [znw] rand
brisk [bnw] • levendig, kwiek
• opwekkend
bristle I [ov + on ww] • overeind gaan
staan • nijdig worden • (~ **with**) vol
zitten met, wemelen van II [znw]
• borstel(haar) • stoppel
bristly [bnw] borstelig, stekelig
Britannic, British [bnw] Brits
brittle [bnw] bros, broos
broach I [ov ww] • aanbreken
• aansnijden <v. onderwerp> II [znw]
• braadspit • torenspits
broad I [znw] <AE> meisje, vrouw
II [bnw] • breed, wijd • plat <v.
taalgebruik> • algemeen • uitgestrekt
broadcast I [ov + on ww] omroepen,
uitzenden II [znw] uitzending
III [bnw] uitgezonden
brocade [znw] brokaat
brogue [znw] • zware schoen

• (Iers/Schots) accent
broil I [ov + on ww] • heet zijn <v. weer>
• <AE> op rooster braden II [znw]
• trammelant • <AE> geroosterd vlees
broiler [znw] • herrieschopper
• braadrooster • braadkip
broke I [ww] verl. tijd → **break**
II [znw] III [bnw] geruïneerd, op zwart
zaad
broken I [ww] volt. deelw. → **break**
II [bnw] gebroken
broker [znw] • uitdrager • makelaar
bronze I [ov + on ww] bruin worden
II [znw] • kunstwerk in brons
• bronskleur III [bnw] • bronzen
• bronskleurig
brooch [znw] broche
brood I [on ww] broeden • (~ **on/over**)
tobben over II [znw] broedsel, gebroed
broody [bnw] broeds
brook I [ov ww] dulden II [znw] beek
broom [znw] • bezem • brem
broth [znw] bouillon
brothel [znw] bordeel
brother [znw] • broer • collega
brotherly [bnw + bijw] broederlijk
brought [ww] verl. tijd + volt. deelw.
→ **bring**
brow [znw] • voorhoofd • wenkbrauw
• top <v. heuvel> • uitstekende rand
brown [bnw] bruin
brownie [znw] • camera • goedaardige
kabouter • kabouter
<padvinder> • gebak met noten
browse I [ov + on ww] • rondneuzen
• grazen • knabbelen • grasduinen
II [znw] twijgen, scheuten <als veevoer>
bruise I [ov ww] • fijnstampen
• kneuzen • kwetsen II [znw] blauwe
plek
brunt [znw] • geweld • schok
brush I [ov + on ww] • vegen • borstelen
• (~ **aside**) opzijschuiven, negeren
• (~ **by**) langssnellen • (~ **down**)
afborstelen • (~ **off**) schoonvegen,
afwijzen • (~ **up**) <inf.> opfrissen <v.

kennis> II [ov ww] • (~ off)
afborstelen, afschepen III [znw]
• borstel • kwast, penseel
brusque [bnw] bruusk, kortaf
brutal [bnw] • wreed, beestachtig • grof
brutality [znw] • wreedheid
• beestachtigheid
brutalize [ov ww] onmenselijk
behandelen
brute I [znw] • bruut • beest II [bnw]
• redeloos • wreed
brutish [bnw] dierlijk
bubble I [on ww] borrelen • (~ over
with) overlopen van II [znw] (lucht)bel
buck I [ov + on ww] bokken • (~ up)
<inf.> moed houden/inspreken II [znw]
• (ree)bok • fat • <AE> dollar
bucket [znw] emmer
buckle I [ov + on ww] • vastgespen
• kromtrekken, verbuigen • in elkaar
zakken • (~ down to) <inf.> z. ertoe
zetten II [znw] gesp
bud I [ov + on ww] • uitbotten
• ontluiken • z. ontwikkelen • enten
II [znw] • knop • kiem
Buddhism [znw] boeddhisme
buddy <AE inf.> [znw] broer, maat,
vriend
budget I [ov + on ww] II [znw] budget,
begroting
budgetary [bnw] budgettair
buff I [ov ww] polijsten II [znw]
• bruingeel leer • enthousiasteling, fan
• dreun, stoot III [bnw] bruingeel
buffalo [znw] • bizon, buffel
• amfibietank
buffet I [ov ww] • worstelen • slaan,
stompen II [znw] • buffet <v. station>
• restauratie(wagon) • koude maaltijd
• klap <met de hand> • buffet(kast)
buffoon <vero.> I [on ww] de pias
spelen II [znw] clown, pias
bug I [ov ww] • afluisteren • hinderen,
dwars zitten II [znw] • wandluis
• insect • ziektekiem, bacil, virus
• verborgen microfoon • storing

bugger <pej.> I [ov ww]
• (~ about/around) pesten, sollen
met • (~ up) verknallen II [on ww]
• (~ about) donderjagen, rondklooien
III [znw] • sodomiet • viezerik
bugle I [ov + on ww] signaal blazen
II [znw] signaalhoorn
build I [ov ww] bouwen II [on ww]
• (~ on) vertrouwen op
builder [znw] • bouwer • aannemer
built [ww] verl. tijd + volt. deelw.
→ build
bulb I [on ww] bolvormig opzwellen
II [znw] • (bloem)bol, knol • gloeilamp
bulbous [bnw] • bolvormig
• uitpuilend <v. ogen>
Bulgarian I [znw] Bulgaar II [bnw]
Bulgaars
bulge I [ov + on ww] (doen) uitpuilen
II [znw] bobbel, uitzetting
bulk [znw] • partij • het grootste deel
• lading • massa, omvang
bulky [bnw] omvangrijk
bull I [ov + on ww] à la hausse
speculeren II [znw] • stier • <AE> smeris
bullet [znw] • geweerkogel
• loodkogeltje
bullock [znw] os
bully I [ov ww] • kwellen • tiranniseren
• pesten II [znw] • laffe kwelgeest • het
kruisen v.d. sticks <bij hockey> • tiran
III [bnw] reuze
bulwark [znw] • verschansing • bolwerk
bum <sl.> I [ov ww] bedelen, bietsen
II [on ww] rondzwerven • (~ around)
nutteloos rondhangen III [znw]
• achterste • <AE> landloper IV [bnw]
van slechte kwaliteit
bumf, bumph <inf.> [znw] • saai
(verplicht) reclame-/studiemateriaal
• <vero.> closetpapier • <pej.> paperassen
bump I [ov + on ww] • botsen • stoten
• (~ into) <inf.> bij toeval ontmoeten,
botsen tegen • (~ off) <inf.>
vermoorden • (~ up) <inf.> verhogen <v.
prijs> II [ov ww] • (~ up) opkrikken,

opvijzelen III [znw] • botsing • bult
bumper [znw] • bumper • buffer ‹v.
spoorwagen› • vol glas
bumpy [bnw] bultig, hobbelig
bun [znw] • broodje • haarwrong
bunch I [ov + on ww] een bos vormen
II [znw] • troep • bos • tros
bundle I [ov + on ww] • oprollen
• inpakken • (~ off) wegwerken ‹v.
persoon› • (~ up) samenvoegen, z.
warm kleden II [znw] bundel, bos, pak
bung I [ov ww] dichtstoppen • (~ up)
‹inf.› verstoppen II [znw] stop
bungle I [ov + on ww] (ver)prutsen
II [znw] prutswerk
bungler [znw] prutser
bunion [znw] eeltknobbel onder grote
teen
bunk [znw] • kooi, couchette • onzin
bunker [znw] • kolenruim • betonnen
schuilplaats
bunny [znw] konijntje
buoy I [ov ww] • (~ up) aanmoedigen,
drijvende houden, kracht geven
II [znw] ton, boei
buoyancy [znw] • opgewektheid
• levendigheid • drijfvermogen
• veerkracht
buoyant [bnw] • drijvend • opgewekt
burden I [ov ww] • belasten • drukken
II [znw] • vracht • last • tonnage
• refrein • hoofdthema
bureau [znw] • schrijfbureau • kantoor
bureaucracy [znw] bureaucratie
burgeon [on ww] snel groeien,
uitbotten
burglar [znw] inbreker
burglary [znw] inbraak
burgle [ov + on ww] inbreken bij/in
burial [znw] begrafenis
burly [bnw] zwaar, stevig
burn [ov + on ww] • (~ out)
uitbranden, opbranden
burner [znw] pit ‹v. fornuis›, brander
burning [bnw] • gloeiend • vurig
burnish [ov ww] • glanzen • polijsten

• bruineren
burnt [ww] verl. tijd + volt. deelw.
→ burn
burp ‹inf.› [ov + on ww] een boer(tje)
laten
burrow I [ov + on ww] • een hol maken
• wroeten II [znw] hol
bursary [znw] • kantoor v.d.
penningmeester • studiebeurs
burst I [ov + on ww] • (open)barsten
• (open)breken • (~ with) overlopen
van II [znw] • barst, scheur • vlaag
• opwelling
bury [ov ww] • begraven • verbergen
• (~ away) naar een afgelegen oord
verplaatsen
bus I [on ww] met de bus gaan II [znw]
bus
bush [znw] • oerwoud • haarbos
• struik • rimboe
bushel [znw] schepel
bushy [bnw] • ruig • begroeid
business [znw] • taak • zaken • zaak
• beroep • bedrijf • kwestie • agenda
businesslike [bnw] zakelijk
bust I [ov ww] kapot maken • (~ up) in
de war sturen, verknallen II [on ww]
kapot gaan • (~ out) ‹inf.› met geweld
ontsnappen • (~ up) trammelant
hebben, uit elkaar gaan III [znw] buste
bustle I [ov ww] opjagen II [on ww]
• (~ about) druk in de weer zijn
III [znw] • queue • drukte
busy I [znw] detective II [bnw] • druk
bezig • rusteloos • bemoeiziek
but [vw] • behalve • slechts • maar
butane [znw] butaan, butagas
butcher I [ov ww] • slachten
• vermoorden II [znw] • moordenaar
• slager
butt I [ov + on ww] stoten • (~ in) in de
rede vallen, z. ergens mee bemoeien
• (~ up against) botsen tegen II [znw]
• vat • achtereind • peukje • stronk
• doel, mikpunt
butter I [ov ww] smeren • (~ up) vleien

II [znw] • *boter* • *vleierij*
butterfly [znw] *vlinder*
buttery I [znw] *provisiekamer* II [bnw]
als boter
button I [ov + on ww] • (~ **up**)
dichtknopen, afronden II [znw] • *knoop*
• *knop*
buttress I [ov ww] II [znw] *steunbeer,*
stut
buxom [bnw] • *knap* • *mollig*
buy I [ov ww] • *(in)kopen* • *omkopen*
• *slikken, geloven, pikken* • (~ **in**)
inkopen • (~ **into**) z. *inkopen* • (~ **off**)
<inf.> *afkopen, uitkopen* • (~ **out**)
uitkopen • (~ **over**) *omkopen* • (~ **up**)
opkopen II [znw] *aankoop*
buyer [znw] • *(in)koper* • *klant*
buzz I [ov + on ww] *gonzen*
• (~ **about**) *rondfluisteren,*
ronddraven II [znw] • *telefoontje*
• *soort kever* • *gezoem*
buzzard [znw] *buizerd*
buzzer [znw] • *zoemer* • *stoomfluit*
• *insect*
by [vz] • *door* • *bij* • *volgens* • *langs*
• *van* • *per* • *via* • *ten opzichte van*
• *ten* <v. kompas>
bye [tw] *tot ziens*
bygone [bnw] *vroeger*

C

cab [znw] • *taxi* • *cabine* • *kap*
cabbage [znw] *kool*
cabin [znw] *hut*
cabinet [znw] *kabinet, ministerraad*
cable I [ov + on ww] *telegraferen*
II [znw] • *kabel, (anker)ketting*
• *kabellengte* <185,31 meter>
• *(kabel)telegram*
cache I [ov ww] *verbergen* II [znw]
verborgen (voedsel)voorraad
cackle I [ov + on ww] • *snoeven*
• *zwammen* II [znw] *gekakel, gesnater*
cadaver [znw] *lijk*
cadaverous [bnw] *lijkkleurig,*
lijkachtig
caddie I [on ww] *als caddie optreden*
II [znw] *caddie*
cadence [znw] *cadans, ritme*
cadre [znw] *kader(lid)*
cafeteria [znw] *cafetaria*
cage I [ov ww] *in een kooi opsluiten*
II [znw] • *kooi* • *gevangenis*
cairn [znw] • *steenhoop* <als grens- of
grafteken> • *cairnterriër*
cajole [ov ww] *door vleien ompraten*
cake I [ov + on ww] *samenkoeken*
II [znw] • *veekoek* • *gebak(je)*
• <Schots> *haverbrood*
calamitous [bnw] *rampzalig*
calamity [znw] *ramp(spoed), ellende*
calculate [ov ww] *berekenen, uitrekenen*
calculating [bnw] *weloverwogen,*
berekend
calculation [znw] *berekening*
calculator [znw] • *(be)rekenaar*
• *rekenmachine* • *berekeningstafel*
calendar I [ov ww] *registreren* II [znw]
• *kalender* • *register* • <jur.> *rol*
calf [znw] • *kalf* • *jong* • *kalfsleer* • *kuit*
<v. been>
calibrate [ov ww] • *het kaliber bepalen*

van • *van schaalverdeling voorzien, kalibreren*

call I [ov + on ww] • (~ **back**) *terugbellen* II [ov ww] *(aan-/af-/op-/toe)roepen, noemen, opbellen* • (~ **down on**) *uitkafferen, afsmeken* • (~ **forth**) *te voorschijn roepen* • (~ **in**) *binnenroepen, inroepen, opvragen* • (~ **off**) *wegroepen, afgelasten, uitmaken* ‹v. verloving› • (~ **over**) *afroepen, appel houden* • (~ **up**) *doen denken aan, in (zijn) herinnering roepen, opbellen, oproepen, wekken* III [on ww] *(aan)komen* • (~ **(up)on**) *beroep doen op, bezoeken, aanmanen* • (~ **for**) *vereisen, roepen, vragen om* IV [znw] • *kreet* • *premie te leveren* • *(op)roep, (oproep tot) telefoongesprek* • *bod* ‹kaartspel› • *aanmaning* • *aanleiding, noodzaak* • *vraag* • *kort bezoek*

caller [znw] • *bezoeker* • *beller*

calligraphy [znw] • *schoonschrift* • *kalligrafie*

calling [znw] • *roeping* • *beroep*

callous [bnw] *ongevoelig*

callow [bnw] • *kaal* • *groen* ‹fig.›, *onervaren*

callus [znw] *eelt(plek)*

calm I [ov ww] *kalmeren, bedaren* II [on ww] • (~ **down**) *kalmeren* III [znw] *windstilte, kalmte* IV [bnw] *kalm*

calumny [znw] *laster*

calve [ov + on ww] *(af)kalven*

calves [mv] → **calf**

cambric I [znw] *batist* II [bnw] *batisten*

came [ww] verl. tijd → **come**

camel [znw] *kameel*

cameo [znw] • *camee* • ‹lit.› *karakterschets*

camp I [on ww] • (z.) *legeren* • *kamperen* II [znw] • *kamp* • ‹inf.› *nichterig gedrag* III [bnw] • *homoseksueel*

campaign I [on ww] *een*

campagne/veldtocht voeren II [znw] • *campagne* • ‹mil.› *veldtocht*

camper [znw] • *kampeerder* • *kampeerwagen*

campus [znw] • *universiteitsterrein* • *de academische wereld*

can I [ov ww] *inblikken* II [hww] *kunnen* III [znw] • *kan* • *inmaakblik* • ‹AE inf.› *bajes* • ‹AE inf.› *wc*

Canadian I [znw] *Canadees* II [bnw] *Canadees*

canal [znw] • *kanaal* • *vaart, gracht*

canalize [ov ww] *kanaliseren*

canary I [znw] *kanarie* II [bnw] *kanariegeel*

cancel I [ov ww] • *afgelasten, annuleren* • *schrappen, doorhalen* • *afstempelen* • *opheffen, intrekken* II [on ww] • (~ **out**) *tegen elkaar wegvallen* ‹v. factoren› III [znw] • *annulering* • *doorhaling, het doorgehaalde, vervanging*

cancer [znw] *kanker*

cancerous [bnw] *kankerachtig*

candidacy, candidature [znw] *kandidatuur*

candidate [znw] *kandidaat*

candle [znw] *kaars*

candour [znw] *oprechtheid, openheid*

candy I [ov ww] *confijten, glaceren* II [znw] • *chocola* • *kandij* • ‹AE› *snoepgoed*

cane I [ov ww] *ranselen* II [znw] • *riet, suikerriet* • *wandelstok* • *stengel* • *scheut*

canine [bnw] *honds-*

canister [znw] *trommeltje*

canker I [ov ww] *aantasten met kanker, wegvreten* II [znw] • *bladrups* • *slechte invloed* • *mondkanker* • *voetzeer*

cannery [znw] *inleggerij, conservenfabriek*

cannibal [znw] *kannibaal*

cannibalism [znw] *kannibalisme*

cannon I [ov + on ww] *caramboleren* • (~ **into**) *opbotsen tegen* II [on ww]

kanon(nen) afschieten III [znw]
• kanon(nen) • carambole
cannonade [znw] beschieting
cannot [samentr.] /can not/ → can
canny [bnw] • slim, handig, verstandig
• zuinig
canoe I [on ww] kanoën II [znw] kano
canon [znw] • canon • kanunnik
canonize [ov ww] heilig verklaren
canopy [znw] • baldakijn, (troon)hemel
• bedekking
cant I [ov ww] op zijn kant zetten,
kantelen II [on ww] • kwezelen
• huichelachtige of boeventaal spreken
III [znw] • schuine kant, helling • stoot
• kanteling • jargon, boeventaal
• sentimenteel of huichelachtig gepraat
can't [samentr.] /can not/ → can
canteen [znw] • kantine • eetketeltje
• veldfles • cassette <v. bestek> • set
kookgerei
canter I [ov ww] in handgalop laten
gaan II [on ww] in handgalop gaan
III [znw] • kwezelaar, huichelaar
• handgalop
canvas [znw] • zeildoek, tentdoek
• linnen <schildersdoek> • schilderij
canvass I [ov + on ww] • colporteren,
werven, bewerken • onderzoeken,
uitpluizen • bespreken II [znw]
• opinieonderzoek • werving
canyon, cañon [znw] diep ravijn
cap I [ov ww] • een muts opzetten
• promotiegraad verlenen • beslaan
• (be)dekken • voorzien v.e. dop
• overtreffen II [znw] • muts, pet • hoed
<v. paddestoel> • kap(je), dop(je)
• wieldop • klappertje • speler in 1e
elftal • <inf.> pessarium
capability [znw] bekwaamheid
capable [bnw] • bekwaam • begaafd
• vatbaar
capacious [bnw] ruim
capacity [znw] • inhoud, vermogen
• (berg)ruimte • capaciteit • volume
• hoedanigheid • bevoegdheid

cape [znw] • kaap • pelerine, cape, kap
caper I [on ww] bokkensprongen maken
II [znw] • bokkensprong, gril
• (kwajongens)streek
capital I [znw] • hoofdletter • kapiteel
• kapitaal • hoofdstad II [bnw]
• voornaamste, hoofd-, zeer belangrijk
• prachtig, magnifiek III [tw] prima!
capitalism [znw] kapitalisme
capitalize [ov + on ww] • kapitaliseren
• munt slaan uit
caprice [znw] gril(ligheid)
capricious [bnw] grillig
capsize I [ov ww] omwerpen II [on ww]
omslaan III [znw] het omslaan, het
omwerpen
captain [znw] • aanvoerder, leider
• eerste piloot • ploegbaas • <scheepv.>
kapitein • <luchtv.> gezagvoerder
caption [znw] • inleiding <v.
document> • opschrift, onderschrift
captive I [znw] gevangene II [bnw]
gevangen
captivity [znw] gevangenschap
capture I [ov ww] • innemen, veroveren
• gevangennemen II [znw] buit, prijs
car [znw] • auto • wagen, kar(retje)
• schuitje, gondel • <AE> liftkooi • <AE>
spoorwagen, tram
carafe [znw] karaf
caramel I [znw] karamel II [bnw]
karamelkleurig
carat [znw] karaat
carbon [znw] • carbonpapier • koolspits
• <chem.> kool(stof)
carbuncle [znw] • karbonkel
• (steen)puist
carburettor [znw] carburator
carcase, carcass [znw] • lijk
• geraamte • geslacht dier
card [znw] • kaart(je) • <inf.> vent,
snoeshaan
cardiac [bnw] hart-
cardigan [znw] wollen vest
cardinal I [znw] • kardinaal
• kardinaalvogel • (schouder)manteltje

II [bnw] • voornaamst, essentieel, belangrijk(st) • donkerrood
care I [on ww] • geven om • (wel) willen, (graag) willen • (~ about) z. bekommeren om • (~ about/for) houden van, geven om • (~ for) zorgen voor II [znw] zorg, bezorgdheid
careful [bnw] • voorzichtig • zorgvuldig • nauwkeurig
careless [bnw] • onvoorzichtig • nonchalant, zorgeloos • onnauwkeurig
caress I [ov ww] liefkozen, strelen II [znw] liefkozing
cargo [znw] • vracht • scheepslading
caricature I [ov ww] tot een karikatuur maken II [znw] karikatuur
caries [znw] cariës, tandbederf
carnage [znw] slachting, bloedbad
carnal [bnw] vleselijk, zinnelijk
carnation I [znw] anjer II [bnw] felrose
carnival [znw] • carnaval • kermis • zwelgpartij
carnivore [znw] vleeseter
carnivorous [bnw] vleesetend
carouse [on ww] zwelgen, brassen
carousel <AE> [znw] • draaimolen • <luchtv.> draaiende bagageband
carp I [on ww] • zeuren • vitten II [znw] karper
carpenter [znw] timmerman
carpet I [ov ww] • met tapijt bedekken • een uitbrander geven II [znw] tapijt, loper
carriage [znw] • rijtuig • vervoer, vracht(prijs) • houding • wagon, wagen • <techn.> slede
carrier [znw] • vliegdekschip • postduif • vrachtrijder, expediteur, bode • vrachtvaarder • drager v.e. ziekte • patroonhouder • bagagedrager
carrion I [znw] kadaver II [bnw] rottend, weerzinwekkend
carrot [znw] wortel(tje)
carroty [bnw] met rood haar
carry I [ov ww] • (ver)voeren,

mee-/wegvoeren, (mee-/over)brengen, bij z. hebben/dragen, dragen • verdragen, houden • (be)halen, erdoor halen doorzetten, uitoefenen, (actie) voeren • (~ about) ronddragen, met z. meedragen • (~ along) meedragen, meeslepen • (~ away) wegvoeren, wegdragen, meeslepen, verliezen, verspelen • (~ back) terugvoeren • (~ off) wegdragen, af-/wegvoeren, (prijs) behalen, het eraf brengen • (~ out) uitvoeren, volbrengen, vervullen • (~ over) overhalen, transporteren, laten liggen • (~ through) volhouden, volvoeren, tot een goed einde brengen II [on ww] • dragen, reiken • (~ on) z. aanstellen, doorgaan III [znw] draagwijdte
cart I [ov ww] per kar vervoeren II [znw] • kar • winkelwagentje
cartel [znw] <hand.> kartel
carton [znw] karton(nen doos)
cartoon [znw] • modelblad • spotprent • tekenfilm
cartoonist [znw] spotprenttekenaar
cartridge [znw] • patroon • cassette
carve I [ov + on ww] (voor)snijden • (~ up) verdelen II [ov ww] • kerven, splijten • beeldhouwen, beeldsnijden • graveren
carving [znw] beeldhouwwerk, snijwerk
cascade I [on ww] bruisend/golvend neerstorten II [znw] (kleine) waterval
case I [ov ww] • in een huis of andere verpakking doen • overtrekken II [znw] • overtrek, tas(je), etui, kist, koffer, kast, bus, koker • geval • staat, toestand • zaak • (rechts)zaak, proces, geding • naamval • patiënt
cash I [ov ww] incasseren • (~ in) verzilveren, te gelde maken, wisselen • (~ up) opdokken II [on ww] • (~ in) sterven • (~ in on) munt slaan uit III [znw] • kassa, kas • (gereed) geld • contant(en)
cashew [znw] cashewnoot

cashier [znw] *caissière, kassier*
cashmere [znw] • *cachemir • sjaal*
cask [znw] *vat, fust*
casket [znw] *kistje, cassette*
cassock [znw] *soutane*
cast I [ov + on ww] *rekenen, optellen*
• (~ off) *losgooien* • (~ on) *opzetten*
<v. breiwerk> II [ov ww] • (~ aside)
aan de kant zetten, afdanken,
wegwerpen • (~ away) *verwerpen,*
verkwisten • (~ down) *neerslaan* <v.
ogen>, *terneerdrukken* • (~ off)
verstoten, (van z.) afwerpen • (~ out)
verjagen, verdrijven • (~ up) *(iem.)*
opnemen, aan land werpen, optellen,
berekenen III [on ww] • *indelen,*
toewijzen <v. rollen> • *werpen*
• *af-/neer-/wegwerpen* • *verwerpen,*
afwijzen, wegsturen • *veroordelen*
• *opwerpen* <v. twijfels> • <techn.>
gieten • (~ about) *wenden* • (~ about*
for) *omzien naar* • (~ back)
teruggaan IV [znw] • *worp*
• *rolbezetting* • *afgietsel, vorm* • *aard,*
type, soort • *tint(je), zweem(pje)*
• *berekening, optelling*
caste [znw] *kaste*
castellated [bnw] • *kasteelachtig*
• *gekanteeld*
caster [znw] • *werper* • *gieter* • *rekenaar*
• *rolverdeler*
castigate [ov ww] • *kastijden*
• *corrigeren*
castle [znw] *kasteel*
castrate [ov ww] *castreren*
cat [znw] • *kat* • *karwats* • <inf.> *knul,*
jongen, vent
cataclysm [znw] • *overstroming*
• *aardbeving* • *geweldige beroering,*
omwenteling
catalogue I [ov ww] *catalogiseren*
II [znw] • *catalogus* • *lijst* • *reeks*
catalyst [znw] *katalysator*
catapult I [ov ww] *met een katapult*
af-/beschieten II [on ww] *afgeschoten*
worden III [znw] *katapult*

cataract [znw] • *waterval* • <med.>
grauwe staar
catarrh [znw] *ontsteking v.h. slijmvlies,*
neusloop
catastrophe [znw] • *ramp*
• *ontknoping* <v. tragedie>
catastrophic [bnw] *rampzalig*
catch I [ov + on ww] • (~ up)
op-/overnemen, in de rede vallen, gelijk
komen met, inhalen II [ov ww]
• (op)*vangen* • (aan-/vast)*grijpen*
• *treffen* <v. gelijkenis> • *aansteken*
<ziekte> • 'doorhebben', *begrijpen*
• *boeien, treffen* • *halen* <trein>
• *vatten, betrappen* • *aantreffen*
• (weg)*grissen* III [on ww] • *haken* <aan
een spijker> • *pakken, sluiten* <v.
grendel> • *om z. heen grijpen*
• *aanstekelijk zijn* • *populair worden*
• (~ at) *grijpen naar, aangrijpen,*
betrappen op • (~ on) *aanslaan,*
snappen IV [znw] • *vangst* • *vangbal*
• *strikvraag, valstrik* • *haak*
• *aanwinst* • *goede partij* • *lokmiddel*
• *het stokken* <v.d stem>
catching [bnw] • *besmettelijk*
• *pakkend, aanlokkelijk*
catchy [bnw] • *pakkend, aantrekkelijk*
• *goed in het gehoor liggend*
• *misleidend, bedrieglijk*
• *onregelmatig bewegend*
catechism [znw] *catechismus*
categorize [ov ww] *categoriseren*
category [znw] *categorie*
cater [on ww] *provianderen, voedsel*
verschaffen/leveren • (~ for) *zorgen*
voor, leveren aan
caterer [znw] • *leverancier* <v.
maaltijden> • *cuisinier*
• *proviandmeester*
caterpillar [znw] • *rups* • *rupsband*
caterwaul I [on ww] *krollen* II [znw]
kattengejank
cathedral [znw] *kathedraal*
cathode [znw] *kathode*
Catholicism [znw] *katholicisme*

cattle [znw] *(rund)vee*
caucus [znw] • *kiescomité* • *kliek*
caught [ww] *verl. tijd + volt. deelw.*
  → catch
cauldron [znw] • *grote ketel*
  • *heksenketel*
cauliflower [znw] *bloemkool*
causal [bnw] *causaal, oorzakelijk*
causality [znw] *causaliteit*
cause I [ov ww] • *veroorzaken,*
  teweegbrengen • *zorgen dat* II [znw]
  • *motief* • *reden* • *oorzaak*
caustic I [znw] *bijtmiddel* II [bnw]
  • *brandend* • *bijtend* • *sarcastisch*
caution I [ov ww] *waarschuwen*
  II [znw] • *omzichtigheid,*
  voorzichtigheid
  • *waarschuwing(scommando)*
  • *berisping*
cautionary [bnw] *waarschuwend*
cautious [bnw] *voorzichtig, omzichtig*
cavalier I [znw] • *(galante) ridder*
  • *royalist* <in de 17e eeuw> II [bnw]
  • *nonchalant* • *aanmatigend, uit de*
  hoogte • *koningsgezind* • *zwierig*
cavalry [znw] *cavalerie*
cave I [on ww] • *(~ in) instorten,*
  bezwijken II [znw] • *hol, grot* • *deuk*
cavern [znw] *hol, spelonk*
cavernous [bnw] *vol holen,*
  spelonkachtig
cavil [on ww] *vitten*
cavity [znw] *holte*
caw [on ww] *krassen* <v. raaf, kraai>
cease I [ov + on ww] *ophouden*
  • *(~ from) ophouden met* II [znw] *het*
  ophouden
ceaseless [bnw] *onafgebroken,*
  aanhoudend
cede [ov ww] *afstaan*
ceiling [znw] • *plafond* • *maximale*
  hoogte • *prijslimiet, loonlimiet*
celebrate [ov + on ww] • *vieren*
  • *verheerlijken* • *loven* • *de mis*
  opdragen
celebrated [bnw] *gevierd, beroemd*

celebration [znw] • *viering* • *feestelijke*
  herdenking • *huldiging* • *het opdragen*
  v.d. mis
celebrity [znw] *roem, beroemdheid*
  <persoon>
celery [znw] *selderie*
celestial [bnw] *hemels*
cell [znw] • *kluis* • *cel*
cellar [znw] *kelder*
cellular [bnw] *celvormig, met cellen*
Celt [znw] *Kelt*
Celtic [bnw] *Keltisch*
cement I [ov ww] • *bevestigen* • *één*
  worden • *met cement verbinden*
  II [znw] • *cement* • *bindmiddel* • *iets*
  dat verbindt <fig.>
censor I [ov ww] *censuur uitoefenen*
  over, censureren II [znw] *censor*
censorious [bnw] • *bedillerig* • *vol*
  kritiek
censure I [ov ww] • *berispen* • *afkeuren*
  • *kritiseren* II [znw] • *berisping*
  • *afkeuring*
census [znw] *volkstelling*
centenarian I [znw] *100-jarige*
  II [bnw] *100-jarig*
centenary, centennial I [znw]
  eeuw(feest) II [bnw] *100-jarig*
centigrade [bnw] *met/op schaal v. 100*
  graden Celsius
centimetre [znw] *centimeter*
centipede [znw] *duizendpoot*
central I [znw] • *centraal geheugen* <v.
  computer> • <AE> *centrale* II [bnw]
  • *centraal, midden-* • *voornaamste,*
  hoofd-
centralize [ov + on ww] *centraliseren*
centre I [ov ww] • *in het midden*
  plaatsen • *het midden zoeken/bepalen*
  van • <sport> *voorzetten, naar het*
  midden spelen II [on ww] *z.*
  concentreren III [znw] • *voorzet*
  • *plaats v. samenkomst* • *basis*
  • *hoofdkwartier* • *centrum* • *kern, bron*
centrifugal [bnw] *middelpuntvliedend*
century [znw] • *eeuw* • *100 runs* <bij

cricket> • *Romeinse legereenheid v. 100
man* • *100 pond*
ceramic [bnw] *pottenbakkers-*
cereal I [znw] *graan* II [bnw] *graan-*
cerebral [bnw] *hersen-*
ceremonial I [znw] *ceremonieel, ritueel*
II [bnw] *plechtig, ceremonieel*
ceremonious [bnw] • *plechtstatig*
• *vormelijk*
ceremony [znw] • *ceremonie,
plechtigheid* • *vormelijkheid*
• *formaliteit(en)*
certifiable [bnw] • *certificeerbaar*
• *krankzinnig*
certificate [znw] • *verklaring, attest,
akte, bewijs* • *diploma*
certify [ov ww] • *verzekeren, verklaren*
• *getuigen* • *waarmerken, attesteren*
• *krankzinnig verklaren*
certitude [znw] *zekerheid*
cessation [znw] • *het ophouden*
• *stilstand*
cesspit, cesspool [znw] *beerput*
chafe I [ov + on ww] • *sarren* • *z. dood
ergeren* • *koken* <v. woede>
• *(warm)wrijven* • *schuren*
• *(stuk)schaven* II [znw] • *schaafwond*
• *ergernis*
chaff I [ov + on ww] • *voor de gek
houden, plagen* • *gekheid maken*
II [znw] • *kaf* • *haksel* • *waardeloos
spul* • *scherts* • *plagerij*
chagrin I [ov ww] • *verdriet doen*
• *ergeren* • *kwellen* II [znw]
• *teleurstelling* • *verdriet*
chain I [ov ww] • *(aaneen)ketenen, aan
de ketting leggen* • *schakelen* II [znw]
• *ketting* • *reeks, keten*
chair I [ov ww] • *in triomf ronddragen*
• *voorzitten, presideren* II [znw] • *zetel,
stoel* • *voorzittersstoel, voorzitterschap*
• *leerstoel* • *professoraat*
• *burgemeesterschap* • <AE> *de
elektrische stoel*
chalice [znw] *kelk*
chalk I [ov ww] • *met krijt inwrijven*

• *tekenen, merken* • *(be)schrijven*
• *(~ out) schetsen, aangeven* • *(~ up)
opschrijven* II [znw] *krijt*
chalky [bnw] • *krijtachtig* • *krijtwit*
• *vol krijt*
challenge I [ov ww] • *eisen, vragen*
• *uitdagen* • *betwisten* • *ontkennen*
II [znw] • *uitdaging* • *opwekking*
• *aanroeping* • <jur.> *wraking*
challenging [bnw] *een uitdaging
vormend*
chamber [znw] • *kamer* • <pol.> *kamer*
chamois [znw] • *gemzenleer, zeemleer*
• *gems*
champ I [ov + on ww] • *(hoorbaar)
kauwen* • *knagen* • *bijten* II [znw]
• *gekauw* • <inf.> *kampioen*
champion I [ov ww] *verdedigen,
krachtig opkomen voor* II [znw]
• *kampioen* • *voorvechter*
championship [znw]
• *kampioenschap* • *verdediging,
krachtige steun*
chance I [ov ww] *wagen, riskeren*
II [on ww] *gebeuren*
• *(~ across/upon) toevallig
tegenkomen* III [znw] • *toeval* • *geluk*
• *gelegenheid, kans, mogelijkheid*
IV [bnw] *toevallig*
chancel [znw] *(priester)koor*
chancellor [znw] • *kanselier* • *titulair
hoofd v.e. universiteit*
chancy [bnw] *gewaagd, riskant*
chandelier [znw] *kroonluchter*
change I [ov + on ww] • *veranderen*
• *(ver)wisselen, (om)ruilen*
• *omschakelen* • *overstappen* • *z.
verkleden* • *(~ down) terugschakelen*
• *(~ into) overgaan in, z. verkleden*
• *(~ over) omschakelen, omzwaaien*
• *(~ up) naar hogere versnelling
schakelen* II [znw] • *verandering*
• *verwisseling, (ver)ruiling* • *variatie*
• *overgang* • *overstap* • *kleingeld*
changeable, changeful [bnw]
veranderlijk

channel I [ov ww] • *groef maken,
uithollen* • *kanaliseren* II [znw]
• *kanaal* • *waterloop* • *stroombed*
• *vaargeul*
chant I [ov + on ww] *reciteren, zingen*
II [znw] • *lied, melodie* • *koraal, psalm*
• *zangerige toon*
chaotic [bnw] *chaotisch*
chap I [ov + on ww] *splijten, scheuren*
II [znw] • *kloof, spleet* • *kaak, kinnebak*
• *kerel, vent*
chapel [znw] • *kapel* • *kerk* • *kerkdienst*
chaplain [znw] • *veldprediker,
aalmoezenier* • *huiskapelaan*
chapter [znw] • *hoofdstuk* • *kapittel*
char I [ov + on ww] *(doen) verkolen,
branden, schroeien* II [znw] • *bergforel*
• *werkster* • *klusje*
character [znw] • *reputatie, goede
naam* • *getuigschrift* • *hoedanigheid,
rol* • *karakter* • *kenmerk* • *merkteken*
• *aard* • *type* • *persoon* • *teken, letter*
• *(hand)schrift*
characteristic I [znw] • *kenmerk*
• ‹wisk.› *index v.* logaritme II [bnw]
kenmerkend
characterless [bnw] *karakterloos*
charade [znw] • *woordspelletje*
• *schertsvertoning*
charcoal [znw] *houtskool*
charge I [ov + on ww] • *in rekening
brengen* • *gelasten, opdragen*
• *losstormen op, aanvallen* • *laden*
• *vullen* • *verzadigen* • *(~ with)
bezwaren met, beschuldigen, ten laste
leggen* II [znw] • *uitgave(n), (on)kosten*
• *prijs* • *belasting* • *taak, plicht, hoede,
zorg* • *pleegkind, pupil* • *instructie*
• *parochie* • *vermaning* • *last, lading*
• *aanval* • ‹jur.› *beschuldiging*
chargeable [bnw] • *schuldig* • *in
rekening te brengen*
chariot [znw] *zegekar*
charitable [bnw] • *liefdadig*
• *welwillend* • *mild*
charity [znw] • *liefdadigheid* • *aalmoes*

• *(naasten)liefde*
• *liefdadigheidsinstelling* • *mildheid*
charlatan [znw] • *kwakzalver*
• *beunhaas*
charm I [ov ww] *betoveren, bekoren*
• *(~ away) wegtoveren* II [znw]
• *betovering, bekoring, charme*
• *tovermiddel, toverspreuk* • *amulet*
charmer [znw] • *tovenaar* • *charmeur*
• *verlokker*
charming [bnw] *betoverend,
charmant, allerliefst*
chart I [ov ww] • *in kaart brengen*
• *grafisch voorstellen/nagaan* II [znw]
• *zeekaart* • *grafiek* • *tabel*
charter I [ov ww]
• *octrooi/privilege/recht verlenen aan*
• *charteren, huren* II [znw] • *contract*
• *octrooi* • *voorrecht* • *oorkonde,
handvest*
charwoman [znw] *werkster*
chase I [ov ww] • *jagen* • *achtervolgen,
vervolgen* II [znw] • *jacht* • *jachtterrein*
• *vervolging, achtervolging*
chaste [bnw] *kuis*
chasten [ov ww] *kuisen*
chastise [ov ww] *kastijden, tuchtigen*
chastity [znw] *kuisheid*
chat I [ov + on ww] *babbelen* II [znw]
• *gekeuvel, geklets* • *roddel*
chatter [on ww] • *kakelen, snateren*
• *klapperen* • *rammelen* II [znw]
• *geklets* • *geklapper*
chatty [bnw] *babbelziek*
cheap [bnw + bijw] • *goedkoop*
• *waardeloos*
cheapen [ov + on ww] • *in prijs
verminderen* • *kleineren* • *afdingen,
pingelen*
cheat I [ov + on ww] • *afzetten* • *vals
spelen* • *spieken* • *bedriegen* • *(~ (out)
of) beroven van, door de neus boren*
II [znw] • *bedrog, zwendel* • *bedrieger*
• *valsspeler*
check I [ov + on ww] • *intomen*
• *belemmeren* • *stopzetten* • *inhouden,*

tegenhouden, ophouden • *het spoor
bijster raken en blijven staan* • *schaak
zetten* • *controleren* • <AE>
afgeven/ophalen tegen reçu • *(~ **in**)
aankomen, z. melden* • *(~ **out**)
vertrekken* • *(~ **up**) controleren*
II [znw] • *beteugeling, belemmering*
• *fiche* • *cheque* • *(plotselinge) stilstand*
• *remmende factor* • *terechtwijzing*
• *controle(merk)* • *reçu* • <AE> *rekening*
checked [bnw] *geruit*
checker [znw] *controleur*
cheek [znw] • *wang* • *brutaliteit*
cheeky [bnw] *brutaal*
cheer I [ov + on ww] • *opvrolijken*
• *aanmoedigen* • *(toe)juichen* • *(~ **up**)
moed scheppen* II [znw] • *hoera(atje)*
• *stemming* • *vrolijkheid* • *onthaal*
• *aanmoediging, bijval*
cheerful [bnw] *vrolijk, opgeruimd*
cheerio(h) [tw] • *dag, tot ziens!*
• *succes!* • *prosit!*
cheerless [bnw] *triest, somber*
cheery [bnw] *vrolijk, opgewekt*
cheese I [ov ww] II [znw] *kaas*
chef [znw] *chef-kok*
chemical I [znw] *scheikundige stof*
II [bnw] *scheikundig*
chemistry [znw] *scheikunde*
cherish [ov ww] • *koesteren* • *liefhebben*
cherry I [znw] • *kersenboom,
kersenhout* • *kers* II [bnw] *kerskleurig*
cherub [znw] • *cherub(ijn)* • *engel*
chess [znw] *schaakspel*
chest [znw] • *koffer, kist* • *kas* • *borstkas*
chestnut I [znw] • *kastanje* • *vos*
<paard> II [bnw] *kastanjebruin*
chic I [znw] *stijl, elegance* II [bnw] *chic*
chick [znw] • *kuiken(tje), jong vogeltje*
• <inf.> *grietje*
chicken I [on ww] II [znw] • *kuiken*
• *kip* • <inf.> *lafaard*
chicory [znw] • *cichorei* • *Brussels lof*
chide [ov + on ww] • *berispen*
• *tekeergaan*
chief I [znw] *leider, hoofd, chef* II [bnw]

voornaamste, leidend(e)
chiefly [bijw] *voornamelijk*
chieftain [znw] *aanvoerder, opperhoofd*
child [znw] *kind*
childish [bnw] *kinderachtig*
children [mv] → **child**
chilly [bnw] • *kil* • *huiverig*
chime I [ov + on ww] • *luiden*
• *samenklinken, harmoniëren* • *(~ **in**
with) overeenstemmen met* II [znw]
• *klokkenspel* • *samenklank, harmonie*
chimney [znw] • *schoorsteen*
• *lampenglas*
chimp, chimpansee [znw]
chimpansee
chin [znw] *kin*
china [znw] • *Chinese thee* • *porselein*
Chinese [bnw] *Chinees*
chink I [ov + on ww] *rinkelen* II [znw]
• *spleet* • *gerinkel*
chip I [ov ww] • *inkerven* • *(af)bikken,
(af)hakken* • *stukjes breken uit*
II [on ww] *schilferen* • *(~ **in**) in de rede
vallen, meebetalen* III [znw]
• *spaan(der), schilfer, splintertje*
• *plakje, schijfje* • *fiche* • <comp.> *chip*
chiropodist [znw] *pedicure*
chirp I [ov + on ww] • *tjilpen, kwelen*
• *opgewekt praten* II [znw] *getjilp*
chirrup I [on ww] • *tjilpen*
• *aanmoedigen door met de tong te
klakken* II [znw] *getjilp*
chisel I [ov ww] • *beitelen, beeldhouwen*
• *bedriegen, beetnemen* II [znw] *beitel*
chit [znw] • *hummel* • *getuigschrift,
briefje, bonnetje* • *kattebelletje*
chivalric, chivalrous [bnw] *ridderlijk,
hoofs*
chivalry [znw] • *ridderschap*
• *ridderlijkheid*
chlorine [znw] *chloor*
chocolate I [znw] • *bonbon*
• *chocolaatje, chocolade* II [bnw]
chocoladebruin
choice I [znw] • *keuze* • *voorkeur* • *het
puikje, het beste* II [bnw] • *uitgelezen*

• *kieskeurig*
choir [znw] *koor*
choke I [ov ww] • *smoren, verstikken*
• *verstoppen, afsluiten* • *onderdrukken*
• *vernauwen* • (~ **down**)
onderdrukken, inslikken, met moeite
verwerken • (~ **off**) (*iem.*) *dwingen iets*
op te geven, (*iem.*) *de mond snoeren*
• (~ **up**) *verstoppen* II [on ww]
• *verstopt raken* • *zich verslikken*
III [znw] • *verstikking(sgevoel)* • *snik*
• *verstopping* • *vernauwing*
choker [znw] • *wurger* • *dooddoener*
• *hoge stijve boord* • (*strop*)*das*
choleric [bnw] *opvliegend*
choose [ov + on ww] *kiezen,*
uitverkiezen
chop I [ov + on ww] (*fijn*)*hakken,*
kappen • (~ **up**) *fijnhakken* II [znw]
• *slag, houw* • *kotelet*
chopper [znw] • *hakmes* • *helikopter*
• *hakker*
choppy [bnw] *vol kloven of barsten*
choral [bnw] * ~ *society*
zangvereniging
chord [znw] • *snaar* • *streng* • <muz.>
akkoord
chore [znw] *karweitje*
choreography [znw] *choreografie*
chorister [znw] *koorzanger, koorknaap*
chortle [on ww] • *schateren* • *grinniken*
chorus [znw] • *koor, rei* • *refrein*
chose [ww] *verl. tijd* → **choose**
chosen [ww] *volt. deelw.* → **choose**
chow [znw] • *chow-chow* • <sl.> *eten*
chowder [znw] *stoofpot met vis*
christen [ov ww] *dopen*
Christendom [znw] *de christenheid*
christening [znw] *doop, het dopen*
Christianity [znw] • *christelijkheid*
• *het christendom*
Christmas [znw] *Kerstmis*
chrome [znw] *chroom*
chromium [znw] *chroom*
chronic [bnw] • *chronisch* • <sl.>
verschrikkelijk

chronicle I [ov ww] *te boek stellen*
II [znw] *kroniek, geschiedenis*
chronologic(al) [bnw] *chronologisch*
chronology [znw] *chronologie*
chubby [bnw] *mollig*
chuck I [ov ww] • *onder de kin*
strijken/aaien • *gooien, smijten* • *de*
bons geven • *klikken* <met tong>
• (~ **away**) *weggooien* • (~ **out**) *eruit*
smijten • (~ **up**) *er de brui aan geven*
II [znw] • *aai, streek* <onder kin>
• *gooi, het van z. afsmijten, worp*
• *geklik* <met tong>
chuckle I [on ww] • *gniffelen,*
grinniken • *z. verkneuteren* II [znw]
lachje
chug I [on ww] *ronken* II [znw] *geronk*
chum I [on ww] • *bij elkaar op kamer(s)*
wonen • *dikke vrienden zijn* II [znw]
goede vriend, gabber
chummy [bnw] *intiem*
chump [znw] • *blok hout* • *dik einde* <v.
lendestuk> • *kop* • *stomkop*
chunk [znw] *homp, blok, stuk*
chunky [bnw] • *bonkig* • *gezet*
church [znw] *kerk*
churlish [bnw] *lomp*
churn I [ov ww] • *omwoelen* • *doen*
schuimen II [znw] • *karn* • *melkbus*
• *het schuimen*
chute [znw] • *stroomversnelling*
• *glijbaan* • *helling* • *parachute*
cigar [znw] *sigaar*
cigarette [znw] *sigaret*
cinch I [ov ww] • *singelen* <v. paard>
• *te pakken krijgen* II [znw] • *iets dat*
zeker is • *makkie*
cinema [znw] *bioscoop*
cinnamon I [znw] *kaneel(boom)*
II [bnw] *geelbruin*
cipher I [ov + on ww] • *cijferen*
• *coderen* II [znw] • *nul* • *cijfer*
• *monogram* • *geheimschrift, code*
circle I [ov ww] *omcirkelen* II [on ww]
rondgaan, ronddraaien, rondzwaaien
III [znw] • *cirkel, (k)ring*

• (omme)zwaai
circuit [znw] • omtrek, omsloten gebied
• tournee, rondgang, rondreis
• kringloop • omweg • ronde baan
• schakeling • ‹techn.› stroombaan
circuitous [bnw] omslachtig
circular I [znw] • circulaire • rondweg
II [bnw] cirkelvormig, rond(gaand)
circulation [znw] • (bloeds)omloop
• circulatie • oplage • omzet
• betaalmiddel
circumcise [ov ww] besnijden
circumference [znw] omtrek v. cirkel
circumlocution [znw] omhaal v.
woorden
circumscribe [ov ww] • omschrijven
• begrenzen
circumspect [bnw] omzichtig
circumspection [znw] omzichtigheid
circumstance [znw] • praal, drukte
• omstandigheid • bijzonderheid
circumstantial [bnw] uitvoerig
circumvent [ov ww] • omsingelen
• ontwijken
cissy [znw] melkmuil, mietje
cistern [znw] • waterreservoir • stortbak
citadel [znw] fort, bolwerk
citation [znw] • dagvaarding • eervolle
vermelding
cite [ov ww] • dagvaarden • aanhalen
citizen [znw] • burger • stedeling
citizenship [znw] burgerschap
city [znw] (grote) stad
civic [bnw] stads-, burger-
civics [znw] burgerlijk recht, staatsbestel
civil [bnw] • privaatrechtelijk • beleefd,
beschaafd • burgerlijk, burger-
civilian I [znw] burger II [bnw] burger-
civility [bnw] beleefdheid
civilization [znw] • beschaving
• beschaafde wereld
civilize [ov ww] beschaven
clack [on ww] ratelen, kletteren
clad [ww] volt. deelw. → clothe
claim I [ov ww] • vorderen • beweren
• aanspraak maken op, (op)eisen

II [znw] • aanspraak, recht, eis,
vordering • claim • concessie ‹in
mijnbouw›
claimant [znw] • eiser • pretendent
clairvoyance [znw] helderziendheid
clam [znw] ≈ mossel
clamorous [bnw] luidruchtig,
schreeuwerig
clamour I [on ww] • schreeuwen
• protesteren • eisen II [znw]
• geschreeuw, misbaar • luid protest
• eis
clamp I [ov ww] • vastzetten, krammen
• ophopen • inkuilen II [on ww]
onderdrukken, de kop indrukken
III [znw] • (muur)anker • klem, kram
clan [znw] • stam ‹in Schotse
Hooglanden› • familie • kliek
clandestine [bnw] clandestien
clang I [ov + on ww] • (laten) klinken
• bellen, rinkelen II [znw] • metalige
klank • klokgelui, belgerinkel
clank I [ov + on ww] rammelen,
kletteren II [znw] metaalgerinkel
clap I [ww] • klappen, klapperen ‹met
vleugels› • applaudisseren, toejuichen
II [znw] • donderslag • klap, slag
• applaus • ‹vulg.› druiper
clapper [znw] • klepel • ratel
claret I [znw] • rode bordeaux(wijn)
• bloed II [bnw] wijnrood
clarify I [ov ww] • ophelderen,
verhelderen • helder/zuiver maken
II [on ww] helder/zuiver worden
clarity [znw] zuiverheid, klaarheid
clash I [ov + on ww] botsen, kletteren
• (~ with) in botsing komen met
II [znw] • botsing, conflict
• tegenstrijdigheid
clasp I [ov + on ww] • sluiten
• (aan)haken, pakken • omhelzen
II [znw] • gesp, broche • slot • beugel
• omhelzing • handdruk
class I [znw] • klas(se) • stand • stijl
• klassestelsel • les(uur), cursus II [bnw]
superieur

classic I [znw] • klassiek werk, klassieke schrijver • classicus II [bnw] klassiek
classical [bnw] klassiek
classification [znw] classificatie
classified [bnw] • geclassificeerd • ‹AE› geheim
classify [ov ww] rangschikken, classificeren
classy [bnw] superieur
clatter I [ov + on ww] kletteren, ratelen II [znw] gekletter, geratel
claustrophobia [znw] claustrofobie
claw I [ov + on ww] • krabben • grissen, grijpen II [znw] • klauw, poot • (klem)haak
clay I [znw] klei, leem II [bnw] van klei
clean I [ov + on ww] schoonmaken, reinigen • (~ out) schoonmaken, leegmaken, opmaken • (~ up) schoonmaken, opruimen, winst maken II [bnw] • schoon, zuiver, rein • zindelijk • welgevormd • handig • glad • van de drugs/drank af III [bijw] totaal
cleaner [znw] • schoonmaker • stofzuiger • wasserij
cleanly [bnw] zindelijk
cleanse [ov ww] zuiveren, reinigen
clear I [ov + on ww] • ledigen • verdwijnen • nemen ‹v. hindernis› • ophelderen, verhelderen, opklaren, verduidelijken • wegnemen • vrijspreken, zuiveren • opruimen, afruimen ‹v. tafel› • (~ away) opruimen, afruimen, optrekken ‹v. mist› • (~ off) afdoen, wegtrekken, verdwijnen • (~ out) ertussenuit knijpen, wegdoen, opruimen, uitmesten • (~ up) opklaren, ophelderen, opruimen II [bnw + bijw] • klaar, helder, duidelijk • zuiver, onbezwaard • vrij • veilig • netto • totaal, helemaal III [bijw] totaal, helemaal
clearing [znw] • open plek in bos • ontginning
cleavage [znw] kloof, kloving

cleave I [ov + on ww] kloven, splijten II [on ww] trouw blijven, (aan)kleven
cleaver [znw] hakmes
clef [znw] sleutel
cleft I [ww] verl.tijd + volt.deelw. → cleave II [znw] spleet, barst III [bnw] gekloven
clench [ov ww] • opeenklemmen ‹v. tanden› • ballen ‹v. vuist› • vastpakken
clergy [znw] geestelijkheid, geestelijken
clerical [bnw] • administratief • geestelijk • van dominee
clerk I [on ww] als klerk/secretaris optreden II [znw] • kantoorbediende • secretaris, griffier • koster en voorlezer • ‹AE› winkelbediende
clever [bnw] • knap, goed bij • handig
click I [ov + on ww] • verliefd worden • het samen goed kunnen vinden • klikken, klakken II [znw] klik, tik
client [znw] cliënt
cliff [znw] steile rots(wand) aan zee, klif
climate [znw] klimaat
climatic [bnw] klimaat-
climax I [ov ww] • klaarkomen • een hoogtepunt bereiken II [znw] • toppunt • orgasme
climb I [ov + on ww] stijgen, (be)klimmen • (~ down) een toontje lager zingen II [znw] • klim • helling • stijgvermogen
climber [znw] • klimplant • streber • (bergbe)klimmer
clinch I [ov ww] • klinken • beklinken II [on ww] elkaar vastgrijpen III [znw] • het vastgrijpen • klinknagel
cling [on ww] • (aan)kleven • nauw aansluiten • (blijven) aanhangen • (~ to) z. vastklampen aan
clinic [znw] verpleeginrichting, kliniek
clinical [bnw] • geneeskundig, klinisch • aan het ziekbed
clink I [ov ww] doen klinken II [on ww] klinken III [znw] • het klinken • gevangenis, nor

clip I [ov ww] • *afknippen, kortknippen,
uitknippen, knippen* • *half uitspreken*
<v. woorden> • *klemmen* II [znw]
• *hoeveelheid geschoren wol* • *klem*
• *knip* • *patroonhouder*
clipper [znw] • *knipper* • *schaar*
clipping [znw] *(kranten)knipsel*
clique [znw] *kliek*
cloak I [ov ww] *omhullen* II [znw]
mantel
clock [znw] *klok*
clod [znw] • *kluit, klont*
• *boerenpummel*
clog I [ov + on ww] • *verstoppen,
verstopt raken* • *klonteren, vastkoeken*
II [ov ww] • *aan het blok leggen*
• *belemmeren* III [znw] • *klompschoen,
klomp* • *blok* <aan been>
cloister [znw] *klooster(gang)*
close I [ov + on ww] • *(~ down)
sluiten, eindigen* II [ov ww] • *besluiten,
(af)sluiten* • *langszij komen* • *(~ up)
verstoppen, afsluiten* III [on ww] *het
slot vormen van* • *(~ (up)on)
omsluiten, sluiten achter, het eens
worden* • *(~ in) insluiten, naderen*
• *(~ up) dichtgaan* • *(~ with)
naderen, handgemeen worden, akkoord
gaan met* IV [znw] • *binnenplaats*
• *speelveld* • *erf* • *terrein* • *hofje*
• *besluit, einde* V [bnw] • *dichtbij*
• *bondig* • *benauwd* • *geheim,
verborgen* • *gierig* • *samenhangend*
• *nauwkeurig* • *innig, intiem*
• *gesloten, dicht* • *nauw* • *nauwsluitend*
closet [znw] • *(privé)kamertje, kabinet*
• *kast*
closure [znw] • *slot* • *sluiting*
clot I [ov + on ww] *klonteren* II [znw]
klont
cloth [znw] • *laken, stof* • *tafellaken*
• *doek, dweil*
clothe [ov ww] *(be)kleden*
clothes [mv] • *kleding* • *(was)goed*
clothing [znw] *kleding*
cloud I [ov + on ww] *bewolken,*

verduisteren, een schaduw werpen over
• *(~ over) somber worden, betrekken*
II [znw] *wolk*
cloudless [bnw] *onbewolkt*
clout I [ov ww] *een klap geven, slaan*
II [znw] • *lap, doek* • *kleren* • *invloed*
• *slag, mep*
clove I [ww] verl. tijd → **cleave**
II [znw] • *kruidnagel* • *anjer*
cloven [ww] volt. deelw. → **cleave**
clover [znw] *klaver*
clown I [on ww] *de clown spelen*
II [znw] *clown*
club I [ov ww] • *met knuppel slaan*
• *zijn steentje bijdragen* II [on ww] (z.)
verenigen III [znw] • *klaverkaart*
• *knuppel* • *golfstick* • *club, sociëteit*
clue I [ov ww] *een tip geven* II [znw]
• *(lei)draad* • *aanwijzing* • *sleutel tot
oplossing*
clump I [ov ww] *bij elkaar
doen/planten* II [on ww] *klossen*
III [znw] *groep* <v. bomen>
clumsy [bnw] *lomp, onhandig*
clung [ww] verl. tijd + volt. deelw.
→ **cling**
cluster I [ov ww] *groeperen* II [on ww]
• *z. groeperen* • *in trossen/bosjes
groeien* III [znw] • *groep* • *bos, tros*
• *zwerm, troep*
clutch I [ov ww] *pakken, grijpen*
II [on ww] • *(~ at) grijpen naar*
III [znw] • *broedsel* • *greep* • *koppeling*
clutter I [ov ww] • *(~ up) rommelig
maken* II [znw] • *bende, rommel*
• *verwarring*
coach I [ov ww] *coachen* II [znw]
• *repetitor* • *koets, rijtuig* • *autobus*
• *coach*
coal [znw] *(steen)kool, kolen*
coalesce [on ww] *samensmelten,
samenvallen*
coalition [znw] *verbond, coalitie*
coarse [bnw] *grof, ruw*
coarsen I [ov ww] *ruw maken*
II [on ww] *ruw worden*

coast I [on ww] • *langs de kust varen*
• *glijden* • *freewheelen* II [znw] • *kust*
• *het freewheelen* • ‹AE› *bobsleebaan*
• ‹AE› *het glijden*
coastal [bnw] *kust-*
coaster [znw] • *kustvaartuig* • *bierviltje*
coat I [ov ww] • *(be)dekken* • *bekleden*
• *vernissen* • *van een laag(je) voorzien*
II [znw] • *jas, mantel* • *bedekking,*
huid, pels • *laag(je)*
coating [znw] • *bekleding, overtrek*
• *laag(je)*
coax [ov + on ww] *vleien* • (~ (in)to)
vleiend overhalen om/tot
cobalt [znw] *kobalt(blauw)*
cobweb I [znw] *spinnenweb, rag*
II [bnw] *ragfijn*
cocaine [znw] *cocaïne*
cock I [ov ww] • *scheefzetten/-houden*
• *(op)steken* • *(op)zetten* II [znw]
• *mannetje* • *leider* • *belhamel*
• *opwaartse buiging* • *haan* • ‹vulg.›
pik
cockatoo [znw] *kaketoe*
cockerel [znw] *jonge haan*
cockney I [znw] • *geboren Londenaar*
• *Londens dialect* II [bnw] *cockney*
cocky [bnw] *verwaand, eigenwijs*
coco [znw] *kokospalm*
cocoa [znw] *cacao*
coconut [znw] *kokosnoot*
cocoon I [ov ww] *inspinnen* II [on ww]
z. inspinnen III [znw] *cocon*
cod I [ov + on ww] *bedotten* II [znw]
kabeljauw
code I [ov ww] • *coderen* • *als wet of*
regel stellen II [znw] • *wet(boek)*
• *reglement, gedragslijn* • *code*
codify [ov ww] *codificeren*
coefficient [znw] *coëfficiënt*
coerce [ov ww] *(af)dwingen*
coercion [znw] *dwang*
coexist [on ww] *naast elkaar bestaan*
coexistence [znw] *coëxistentie*
coffee [znw] *koffie*
coffer [znw] *(geld)kist*

coffin [znw] *doodskist*
cog [znw] *tand* ‹v. wiel›
cogency [znw] *overtuigingskracht*
cogent [bnw] *overtuigend*
cogitate [ov + on ww] *overdenken*
cognate [znw] *(bloed)verwant*
cognizance [znw] • *kennis*
• *competentie* • *onderscheidingsteken*
cohabit [on ww] *samenwonen*
cohere [on ww] *samenhangen*
coherent, cohesive [bnw]
samenhangend
coil I [ov ww] *oprollen* II [on ww] (z.)
kronkelen III [znw] • *spiraal(veer)*
• *tros* • *kronkel* • *rol*
coin I [ov ww] • *munten* • *verzinnen*
II [znw] • *munt* • *geld*
coinage [znw] • *munt(stelsel)* • *het*
munten
coincide [on ww] • *samenvallen*
• *overeenstemmen*
coincidence [znw] *toeval*
coke [znw] • *cokes* • *cola* • ‹inf.› *cocaïne*
cold I [znw] • *kou(de)* • *verkoudheid*
II [bnw] *koud, koel*
colic [znw] *(darm)koliek*
collaborate [on ww] • *collaboreren*
• *samenwerken*
collaborator [znw] • *collaborateur*
• *medewerker*
collapse I [on ww] • *invallen,*
in(elkaar)zakken • *mislukken* II [znw]
• *ineenstorting* • *mislukking*
collapsible [bnw] *opvouwbaar*
collar I [ov ww] • *een halsband*
aandoen • *bij de kraag pakken* • *tot*
rollade maken • *inpikken* II [znw]
• *kraag, boord* • *(hals)keten, (hals)band*
• *zwaar werk* • *rollade*
collateral I [znw] *bloedverwant in*
zijlinie II [bnw] • *zij aan zij* • *zijdelings*
colleague [znw] *collega*
collect I [ov ww] • *verzamelen* • *innen,*
ophalen • *inpikken* II [on ww] z.
verzamelen
collection [znw] • *zelfbeheersing*

• buslichting • *verzameling*
collective [bnw] • *samengesteld*
• *verzamelend* • *gemeenschappelijk*
collectivize [ov ww] *tot collectief bezit maken*
college [znw] • *college* • *zelfstandig universiteitsinstituut* • *grote kostschool*
collide [on ww] *botsen*
colliery [znw] *kolenmijn*
collision [znw] *botsing*
colloquial [bnw] *tot de spreektaal behorend*
colloquialism [znw] *alledaagse uitdrukking*
collusion [znw] *geheime verstandhouding*
collywobbles [mv] *buikpijn* <v. zenuwen/angst>
colon [znw] • *dikke darm* • *dubbele punt*
colonel [znw] • *kolonel* • *overste*
colonial [bnw] *koloniaal*
colonize [ov + on ww] *koloniseren*
colonnade [znw] *zuilengalerij*
colony [znw] *kolonie*
colossal [bnw] *kolossaal*
colour I [ov ww] • *verkeerd voorstellen* • *kleuren, verven* II [znw] • *kleur* • *verf* • *blos*
colourful [bnw] *kleurrijk*
colouring [znw] • *kleur(sel)* • *schijn*
colourless [bnw] • *kleurloos* • *oninteressant*
column [znw] • *kolom, zuil* • *colonne* • *column*
comatose [bnw] • *diep bewusteloos* • *slaperig*
comb I [ov ww] *kammen* • (~ **out**) *uitkammen, zuiveren* II [znw] • *kam* • *honingraat*
combat [znw] *gevecht*
combatant [znw] *strijder*
combination [znw] *combinatie*
combine I [ov ww] • *verenigen* • *combineren* II [on ww] • *z. verenigen* • *samenwerken, samenspelen* III [znw]

syndicaat
combustible I [znw] *brandbare stof* II [bnw] *brandbaar*
combustion [znw] *verbranding*
come [on ww] • *(aan-/neer-/op)komen, erbij komen, terechtkomen* • *naderen* • *worden* • *meegaan* • *afleggen* <v. afstand> • <vulg.> *klaarkomen*
• (~ **about**) *gebeuren, tot stand komen, overstag gaan, richting veranderen* • (~ **across**) *tegenkomen, aantreffen* • (~ **after**) *komen na, achterna komen* • (~ **along**) *voortmaken, eraan komen* • (~ **apart**) *losgaan, uit elkaar vallen*
• (~ **around**) <AE> *langs komen, bijkomen* <na flauwte>, *bijtrekken* <na ruzie> • (~ **at**) *aanvallen, verkrijgen*
• (~ **away**) *losgaan* • (~ **back**) *weer voor de geest komen, terugkomen, iets terugzeggen* • (~ **between**) *tussenbeide komen* • (~ **by**) *voorbijkomen, (ver)krijgen, komen aan* • (~ **down**) *naar beneden komen, kalmeren, rustig worden* • (~ **down on**) *neerkomen op, straffen, uitvaren tegen* • (~ **down to**) *z. uitstrekken tot* • (~ **down with**) *krijgen* <v. ziekte>, *dokken* • (~ **for**) *komen om, afhalen, (dreigend) afkomen op* • (~ **forth**) *te voorschijn komen* • (~ **forward**) *z. aanmelden, naar voren komen* • (~ **from**) *komen van/uit, het resultaat zijn van* • (~ **home to**) *duidelijk worden* • (~ **in**) *thuiskomen, erin komen, aankomen* <v. post>, *beginnen, eraan te pas komen, aan de macht komen, binnenkomen* • (~ **in for**) (als aandeel) *krijgen* • (~ **off**) *eraf gaan/komen, afgeven, uitkomen, uit de strijd komen, lukken* • (~ **on**) *opkomen, naderen, vorderen, op gang komen* • (~ **out**) (er) *uitkomen, te voorschijn komen, blijken, in staking gaan, debuteren* • (~ **over**) *komen over, overkómen, óverkomen, oversteken*

• (~ **round**) *aankomen, vóórkomen,*
bijkomen, weer goed worden
• (~ **through**) *doorkomen, overleven,*
over de brug komen • (~ **to**) *bijkomen,*
bijdraaien • (~ **under**) *vallen onder*
• (~ **up**) *opkomen, bovenkomen, ter*
sprake komen • (~ **up to**) *eropaf*
komen, de hoogte bereiken van, voldoen
aan • (~ **up with**) *inhalen, gelijk*
komen met • (~ **upon**) *overvallen,*
tegen 't lijf lopen, te binnen schieten,
ten laste komen van, opkomen bij
comedian [znw] • *blijspelspeler*
• *blijspelschrijver*
comedy [znw] *blijspel*
comely [bnw] *knap, keurig*
comer [znw] • *aangekomene, bezoeker*
• ‹AE inf.› *veelbelovend iem.*
comet [znw] *komeet*
comfort I [ov ww] *troosten* II [znw]
• *troost, bemoediging* • *gemak, gerief,*
comfort • *welstand*
comfortable [bnw] *geriefelijk,*
gemakkelijk
comforter [znw] • *trooster* • *fopspeen*
• *wollen sjaal*
comic I [znw] *komiek* II [bnw] *komisch*
coming I [znw] *komst* II [bnw]
• *veelbelovend* • *komend, aanstaand*
command I [ov ww] • *bevelen,*
commanderen • *het commando voeren*
over • *beheersen* • *beschikken over*
II [znw] • *beheersing* • *beschikking*
• *bevel, order* • *commando*
commandeer [ov ww] *vorderen*
commander [znw] • *commandant*
• *gezagvoerder*
commanding [bnw] • *indrukwekkend*
• *met goed uitzicht*
commandment [znw] *gebod*
commemorate [ov ww] *herdenken*
commence [ov ww] • *beginnen*
• *promoveren*
commend [ov ww] *prijzen, aanbevelen*
commendable [bnw]
prijzenswaardig, aanbevelenswaardig

commensurate [bnw] • *evenredig*
• *samenvallend*
comment I [on ww] • *van commentaar*
voorzien • *aan- of opmerkingen maken*
II [znw] *commentaar, kritiek*
commentary [znw] • *uiteenzetting,*
commentaar • *reportage*
commentator [znw] • *commentator*
• *verslaggever* ‹v. radio/tv›
commerce [znw] *handel, verkeer*
commercial I [znw] *reclameboodschap*
‹op radio›, *reclamefilm/-spot* ‹op tv›
II [bnw] *handels-, commercieel*
commission I [ov ww] • *opdragen*
• *machtigen* • *bestellen* • *aanstellen*
II [znw] • *opdracht, taak, ambt*
• *commissie* • *provisie*
commit [ov ww] • *toevertrouwen*
• *plegen, bedrijven* • (z.)
compromitteren • *verwijzen* ‹naar
commissie› • *binden* • (~ **to**)
prijsgeven aan
committal [znw] *gevangenzetting*
committee [znw] • *commissie, comité*
• *bestuur*
commodious [bnw] *ruim en geriefelijk*
commodity [znw] *handelsartikel*
common I [znw] • *onbebouwd (stuk)*
land • *gemeenschappelijke wei* II [bnw]
• *gemeenschappelijk* • *algemeen*
• *openbaar* • *gewoon* • *vulgair, ordinair*
commoner [znw] • *(gewoon) burger*
• *lid v. House of Commons*
• *niet-beursstudent*
commotion [znw] *opschudding*
communal [bnw] *gemeente-,*
gemeenschaps-
commune I [on ww] ‹AE› *de communie*
ontvangen • (~ **with**) z. *onderhouden*
met II [znw] • *gemeente* • *kommune*
communicate I [ov ww] • (~ **to**)
mededelen aan II [on ww]
• *communiceren* • *het Avondmaal*
ontvangen • (~ **with**) *een goede relatie*
aanknopen/hebben met, in verbinding
staan met

communication [znw] • mededeling,
het mededelen • verbinding(sweg)
communicative [bnw] mededeelzaam
communion [znw] • gemeenschap
• verbinding • omgang
• kerkgenootschap
communism [znw] communisme
communist I [znw] communist
II [bnw] communistisch
community [znw] genootschap,
gemeenschap
commute I [ov ww] • afkopen en
omzetten <v. schuld of verplichting>
• verzachten <v. straf> II [on ww]
forenzen
commuter [znw] pendelaar, forens
companion [znw] • makker, metgezel,
deelgenoot • gezelschapsdame
• bijbehorende deel
companionable [bnw] gezellig
company I [on ww] II [znw]
• gezelschap • vennootschap,
maatschappij • bedrijf • genootschap
• compagnie
comparable [bnw] vergelijkbaar
comparative I [znw] <taalk.>
vergrotende trap II [bnw] vergelijkend
compare I [ov ww] vergelijken
II [on ww] vergeleken worden
comparison [znw] vergelijking
compartment [znw] • afdeling • coupé
compartmentalize [ov ww] in vakken
verdelen, onderverdelen
compass I [ov ww] • beramen
• omvatten, insluiten • begrijpen
• volvoeren • gaan om II [znw]
• kompas • gebied, terrein • omvang,
draagwijdte <v. stem> • omweg
• omtrek
compassion [znw] medelijden
compassionate [bnw] meelevend,
medelijdend
compatriot [znw] landgenoot
compel [ov ww] (af)dwingen,
verplichten
compelling [bnw] onweerstaanbaar,

boeiend, fascinerend
compensate [ov ww] goedmaken,
vergoeden
compete [on ww] • concurreren
• mededingen
competence [znw] • bevoegdheid
• competentie
competent [bnw] • geoorloofd
• bekwaam, bevoegd
competition [znw] • concurrentie
• competitie
competitive [bnw] • m.b.t. competitie
• prestatiegericht
competitor [znw] concurrent,
mededinger
compilation [znw] samenstelling,
verzameling
compile [ov ww] compileren,
bijeenbrengen
complacent [bnw] (zelf)voldaan, kalm
complain [on ww] klagen
complaint [znw] kwaal, (aan)klacht
complaisant [bnw] minzaam,
inschikkelijk
complement I [ov ww] aanvullen
II [znw] aanvulling, complement,
vereist aantal
complementary [bnw] aanvullend
complete I [ov ww] maken, afmaken,
invullen II [bnw] compleet, volkomen,
voltallig
completion [znw] voltooiing
complex I [znw] complex, samenstel,
geheel II [bnw] samengesteld,
ingewikkeld
complexion [znw] • gelaatskleur
• voorkomen
complexity [znw] complexiteit
compliance [znw] toestemming,
nakoming, inwilliging
compliant [bnw] meegaand, soepel
complicate [ov ww] ingewikkeld
maken
complicated [bnw] ingewikkeld
complication [znw] complicatie
complicity [znw] medeplichtigheid

compliment I [ov ww]
complimenteren II [znw] compliment
complimentary [bnw] gratis
comply [on ww] • (~ with) handelen
overeenkomstig, inwilligen, toestaan
component I [znw] bestanddeel
II [bnw] samenstellend
compose [ov + on ww] • samenstellen
• zetten <drukwerk> • schikken
• kalmeren • componeren
composed [bnw] beheerst, bedaard
composer [znw] componist
composite [bnw] gezamenlijk,
samengesteld
composition [znw] • samenstelling
• compositie • mengsel • opstel • aard
compositor [znw] (letter)zetter
compound I [ov ww] • afkopen
• samenstellen, (ver)mengen II [on ww]
schikken, tot een akkoord komen
III [znw] • kamp • samenstelling,
mengsel IV [bnw] samengesteld,
gecompliceerd
comprehend [ov ww] • insluiten
• begrijpen
comprehension [znw] • omvang
• begrip
comprehensive I [znw] middenschool,
scholengemeenschap II [bnw]
veelomvattend
compress I [ov ww] samendrukken
II [znw] compres
compressor [znw] • drukverband
• compressor
comprise [ov ww]
be-/om-/samenvatten
compromise I [ov ww]
compromitteren II [on ww] tot een
akkoord komen III [znw] compromis,
overeenkomst, middenweg
compulsion [znw] • dwangneurose
• dwang
compulsive [bnw] dwingend
compulsory [bnw] verplicht
compunction [znw] wroeging, spijt
computation [znw] berekening

compute [ov + on ww] (be)rekenen,
calculeren
computer [znw] computer,
elektronisch brein
computerize I [ov + on ww] op de
computer overgaan, computeriseren
II [ov ww] met computer verwerken, in
computer opslaan
comrade [znw] kameraad
con [znw] • zwendel • oplichter
concave I [znw] (hemel)gewelf II [bnw]
hol
conceal [ov ww] verbergen, geheim
houden
concealment [znw] het verborgen
houden
concede I [ov ww] toegeven, toestaan
II [on ww] z. gewonnen geven
conceit [znw] eigendunk, verwaandheid
conceited [bnw] verwaand
conceivable [bnw] denkbaar
conceive I [ov + on ww] z. indenken
II [on ww] zwanger worden
concentrate I [on ww] • samenkomen
• (z.) concentreren II [znw]
geconcentreerde stof
concentration [znw] concentratie
concept [znw] begrip
conception [znw] • bevruchting
• voorstelling <mentaal>
conceptual [bnw] conceptueel, begrips-
concern I [ov ww] aangaan, betrekking
hebben op II [znw] • zaak, firma
• bezorgdheid • deelneming
• betrekking • (aan)deel
concerning [bijw] betreffende
concert [znw] • concert
• overeenstemming
concerto [znw] concert
concession [znw] concessie,
toestemming, inwilliging
conch [znw] schelp(dier)
conciliatory [bnw] verzoeningsgezind
concise [bnw] beknopt
conclave [znw] conclaaf
conclude I [ov ww] concluderen,

beëindigen, (be)sluiten • (~ from)
opmaken uit II [on ww] ten einde
komen, aflopen
conclusion [znw] besluit, conclusie
conclusive [bnw] beslissend,
overtuigend
concoct [ov ww] • verzinnen • bereiden,
brouwen
concord [znw] • verdrag • eendracht,
overeenstemming
concrete I [znw] • beton • concreet
ding/woord II [bnw] • concreet • vast
• v. beton • hard
concubine [znw] bijzit
concur [on ww] • samenvallen
• mee-/samenwerken • 't eens zijn
concurrent [bnw] samenwerkend, in
samenwerking
concussion [znw] • botsing • schol
• hersenschudding
condemn [ov ww] • afkeuren
• veroordelen • onbruikbaar verklaren,
onbewoonbaar verklaren
condemnation [znw]
• veroordelingsgrond • veroordeling
condense [ov + on ww] condenseren,
concentreren, bekorten
condescend [on ww] afdalen, z.
verwaardigen
condescension [znw]
neerbuigendheid, minzaamheid
condiment [znw] kruiderij, bijspijs
condition I [ov ww] • in goede staat
brengen • als voorwaarde stellen,
vereist zijn voor • bepalen II [znw]
• staat, toestand • bepaling
• voorwaarde • conditie • rang, stand
conditional [bnw] voorwaardelijk
condone [ov ww] • goedmaken
• vergeven • gedogen, door de vingers
zien
conducive [bnw] bevorderlijk
conduct I [ov + on ww] geleiden <v.
elektriciteit> II [ov ww] • (aan)voeren,
leiden • dirigeren III [wkd ww] z.
gedragen IV [znw] • optreden, gedrag

• leiding • behandeling
conduction [znw] geleiding
conductor [znw] • dirigent
• conducteur • gids, leider
• bliksemafleider • geleider
conductress [znw] conductrice
conduit [znw] • leiding • kanaal
confection I [ov ww] bereiden II [znw]
• jurk • suikergoed, snoepgoed
• bereiding • mantel • (dames)confectie
confectioner [znw] suikerbakker,
snoepgoedfabrikant
confectionery [znw] suikergoed,
snoepgoed, banket, suikerbakkerij
confederacy [znw] • complot
• (ver)bond, statenbond, federatie
confederate I [on ww] (z.) verbinden,
samenspannen II [znw] • bondgenoot
• medeplichtige III [bnw] in een
federatie verenigd
confederation [znw] (con)federatie
confer I [ov ww] verlenen II [on ww]
beraadslagen
conference [znw] conferentie
confess I [ov + on ww] • bekennen
• erkennen • (~ to) bekennen
II [on ww] biechten
confession [znw] • (geloofs)belijdenis
• biecht, bekentenis
confessional I [znw] biechtstoel
II [bnw] confessioneel, biecht-
confessor [znw] biechtvader
confidant [znw] • vertrouweling
• deelgenoot <v.e. geheim>
confide [ov ww] vertrouwen • (~ in)
vertrouwen op • (~ to) toevertrouwen
aan
confidence [znw] • (zelf)vertrouwen,
vrijmoedigheid • vertrouwelijke
mededeling
confident [bnw] vol zelfvertrouwen,
vertrouwend, vrijmoedig
confidential [bnw] vertrouwelijk
confiding [bnw] vertrouwend, vol
vertrouwen
confine I [ov ww] • opsluiten

• begrenzen, beperken II [znw] grens
confined [bnw] nauw ∗ be ~ bevallen
confinement [znw] • opsluiting
• beperking • kraambed, bevalling
confirm [ov ww] bevestigen,
bekrachtigen
confirmation [znw] bevestiging
confirmed [bnw] overtuigd
confiscate [ov ww] • afnemen • in
beslag nemen, verbeurd verklaren
conflagration [znw] grote brand
conflict I [on ww] botsen • (~ with) in
tegenspraak zijn met II [znw] ruzie,
strijd, conflict
confluence [znw] • toeloop
• samenvloeiing
conform I [ov ww] aanpassen • (~ to)
in overeenstemming brengen met
II [on ww] inschikkelijk zijn • (~ to) z.
voegen naar, z. richten naar
conformity [znw] • overeenstemming
• gelijkvormigheid
confound [ov ww] • verwarren
• beschamen • verijdelen
confront [ov ww] • het hoofd bieden
• confronteren • tegenover elkaar
staan/stellen
confrontation [znw] confrontatie
confuse [ov ww] verwarren
confused [bnw] • verward, beduusd
• rommelig
congenial [bnw] • gezellig
• sympathiek, geschikt
congestion [znw] • verstopping <v.
wegen> • ophoping
• verkeersopstopping
conglomerate I [ov + on ww]
conglomereren II [znw] conglomeraat
III [bnw] opeengepakt
conglomeration [znw] conglomeraat
congratulate [ov ww] feliciteren
• (~ on) gelukwensen met
congratulatory [bnw] feliciterend
congregate [ov + on ww] (z.)
verzamelen
congress [znw] congres

congressional [bnw] v.h. congres
congruent [bnw] congruent, passend,
overeenstemmend
conifer [znw] conifeer
conjecture I [on ww] gissen,
vermoeden II [znw] gissing, vermoeden
conjugal [bnw] echtelijk
conjunction [znw] • samenloop
• <taalk.> voegwoord
conjure [ov + on ww] • aanroepen <v.
geest> • toveren, goochelen • (~ up)
voor de geest roepen
conjurer, conjuror [znw] goochelaar
conk I [ov ww] een opdonder geven
II [znw] • kokkerd, harses • stomp,
dreun
connect I [ov ww] in verband brengen,
aansluiten II [on ww] in verband
staan, (z.) verbinden
connection, connexion [znw]
• verbinding, aansluiting
• koppeling • omgang
• (familie)relatie, familielid • klandizie
connivance [znw] samenspanning
connive [on ww] samenspannen
connoisseur [znw] kenner, fijnproever
connotation [znw] bijbetekenis
connote [ov ww] • insluiten • (ook nog)
betekenen
conquer [ov + on ww] • veroveren
• overwinnen
conqueror [znw] veroveraar,
overwinnaar
conquest [znw] verovering
conscious [bnw] • bij kennis • (z.)
bewust
conscript I [ov ww] aanwijzen voor
militaire dienst
II [znw] dienstplichtige III [bnw]
dienstplichtig
conscription [znw] dienstplicht
consecrate [ov ww] heiligen, wijden
consecutive [bnw] (opeen)volgend
consent I [on ww] • (~ to) toestemmen
in II [znw] toestemming
consequence [znw] (logisch) gevolg

consequent I [znw] *gevolg* II [bnw]
• *consequent* • *daaruit*
volgend/voortvloeiend
consequential [bnw] *consequent*
conservation [znw] *natuurbehoud,*
milieubescherming
conservatism [znw] *conservatisme*
conservative I [znw] *lid v.e.*
conservatieve partij, conservatief
II [bnw] *conservatief*
conservatory I [znw] • *broeikas*
• *conservatorium* II [bnw] *conserverend*
conserve [ov ww] *in stand houden,*
bewaren, behouden, goed houden <v.
voedsel>
consider I [ov ww] • *overwegen*
• *bedenken* • *in aanmerking nemen* • *v.*
mening zijn • *beschouwen (als)*
II [on ww] *nadenken*
considerable [bnw] • *belangrijk*
• *aanzienlijk*
considerate [bnw] *attent*
consideration [znw] • *inachtneming*
• *overweging* • *consideratie* • *beloning,*
compensatie • *welwillendheid* • *achting*
considering [bijw] *in aanmerking*
genomen/nemend
consign [ov ww] • *overleveren,*
overdragen • *consigneren* • *zenden*
• *deponeren, storten <v. geld>* • *(~ to)*
toevertrouwen aan
consist [on ww] • **(of)** *bestaan uit*
consistence, consistency [znw]
• *consequentie* • *vaste lijn* • *dichtheid,*
vastheid
consistent [bnw] • *consequent*
• *samengaand*
console I [ov ww] *troosten* II [znw]
• *speeltafel van orgel* • *console,*
bedieningspaneel
consolidate I [ov ww] • *bevestigen,*
consolideren • *hecht maken* II [on ww]
hechter worden
consonant [znw] *medeklinker*
consort I [on ww] • **(~ with)** *optrekken*
met, overeenstemmen II [znw] *gemalin,*

gemaal
consortium [znw] *consortium,*
syndicaat
conspicuous [bnw] *in het oog*
springend, opvallend
conspiracy [znw] *samenzwering*
conspirator [znw] *samenzweerder*
conspire [on ww] • *samenwerken*
• *samenzweren, beramen*
constancy [znw] *standvastigheid*
constant [bnw] • *voortdurend*
• *standvastig, trouw*
constellation [znw] • *sterrenbeeld*
• *constellatie*
consternation [znw] *consternatie,*
ontsteltenis
constituency [znw] • *de clientèle*
• *<pol.> kiesdistrict, de kiezers*
constituent I [znw] • *lastgever*
• *bestanddeel* • *<pol.> kiezer* II [bnw]
• *constituerend* • *afvaardigend*
• *samenstellend*
constitute [ov ww] • *stichten*
• *samenstellen, vormen, uitmaken*
• *instellen* • *aanstellen (tot)*
constitution [znw] • *gestel*
• *staatsbestel, grondwet, reglement*
constitutional [bnw] *m.b.t. de*
grondwet
constrain [ov ww] • *gevangen zetten*
• *af-/bedwingen* • *noodzaken*
constraint [znw] • *(zelf)beheersing*
• *dwang* • *verlegenheid* • *beperking*
constrict [ov ww] *samentrekken*
constriction [znw] *samentrekking*
construct [ov ww] *construeren,*
(op)bouwen, aanleggen
construction [znw] *constructie,*
opbouw, aanleg
constructive [bnw] • *opbouwend <vnl.*
v. kritiek> • af te leiden, niet
rechtstreeks
construe [ov ww] • *construeren*
• *af-/uitleiden*
consular [bnw] *consulair*
consulate [znw] *consulaat*

consult I [ov ww] • raadplegen
• rekening houden met II [on ww]
beraadslagen, overleggen
consultant [znw] • consulterend
geneesheer • raadpleger, adviseur
consultation [znw] • consult <bij arts>
• beraadslaging
consume I [ov ww] verbruiken,
nuttigen II [on ww] ver-/wegteren
consumer [znw] verbruiker, consument
consummate I [ov ww] voltooien
II [bnw] volkomen, volmaakt
consumption [znw] • verbruik,
consumptie • tuberculose, tering
contact I [ov ww] • z. in verbinding
stellen met, in contact komen met
• aanklampen II [znw] • contact,
aanraking, raakpunt • bacillendrager
contagion [znw] • verderf • besmetting
contagious [bnw] besmettelijk <m.b.t.
ziekte>
contain [ov ww] • bevatten • z.
beheersen, bedwingen • vasthouden
• binden <vijand>
container [znw] • doos • reservoir • vat
• (diepvries)kast • voorwerp dat iets
be-/omvat • laadkist • bus • (plastic)
fles
contaminate [ov ww] bevuilen,
besmetten
contemplate I [ov ww] beschouwen,
overpeinzen, overwegen II [on ww]
bespiegelen, peinzen
contemplative [bnw] beschouwend,
bespiegelend
contemporaneous [bnw] gelijktijdig
contemptible [bnw] verachtelijk
contemptuous [bnw] minachtend
contend I [ov ww] beweren II [on ww]
strijden, twisten, wedijveren
contender [znw] mededinger
content I [ov ww] tevredenstellen
II [znw] • inhoud • tevredenheid
III [bnw] tevreden
contented [bnw] tevreden
contention [znw] geschil

contentious [bnw] • betwistbaar
• twistziek
contentment [znw] tevredenheid
contest I [ov ww] • dingen naar
• betwisten, debatteren • (~ for)
wedijveren om, strijden om II [znw]
• wedstrijd • (woorden)twist, geschil
contestant [znw] deelnemer <aan
wedstrijd>
contiguous [bnw] naburig,
aangrenzend
continence [znw] • (seksuele)
onthouding • continentie
• zelfbeheersing
continent I [znw] • werelddeel
• Europese vasteland II [bnw] • kuis
• z. beheersend
continental I [znw] bewoner v.h. Eur.
vasteland II [bnw] continentaal
contingency [znw] • samenloop
• onvoorziene uitgave • toevallige
omstandigheid
contingent I [znw] • bijkomendheid
• eventualiteit • aandeel, bijdrage
II [bnw] • bijkomend • onzeker,
toevallig
continual [bnw] • herhaaldelijk
• voortdurend
continuance [znw] verblijf
continuation [znw] vervolg,
voortzetting
continue I [ov ww] door (laten) gaan
met, voortzetten II [on ww] blijven
(bestaan)
continuity [znw] continuïteit,
doorlopend verband
continuous [bnw] onafgebroken
contort [ov ww] (ver)draaien
contortion [znw] (ver)draaiing
contortionist [znw] slangenmens
contra [znw] tegendeel
contraband I [znw]
smokkelhandel/-waar II [bnw]
smokkel-
contraception [znw] anticonceptie
contraceptive I [znw]

voorbehoedmiddel II [bnw]
anticonceptioneel
contract I [ov ww] • *contracteren,*
aannemen • *oplopen* ‹v. ziekte›
• (~ **for**) z. *verbinden tot, aannemen,*
overeenkomen II [on ww] *inkrimpen, z.*
samentrekken III [znw] • *contract,*
verdrag, overeenkomst • *verloving*
contraction [znw] *samentrekking*
contractor [znw] • ‹hand.› *leverancier*
• ‹archit.› *aannemer* • ‹anat.› *sluitspier*
contractual [bnw] *contractueel, m.b.t.*
contract
contradict [ov ww] *ontkennen,*
tegenspreken
contradiction [znw]
• *tegenstrijdigheid* • *tegenspraak*
contradictory [bnw] *tegenstrijdig*
contralto [znw] *alt*
contrary I [znw] *tegengestelde* II [bnw]
• *ongunstig* • *tegen(gesteld)*
• *tegendraads*
contribute [ov + on ww] *bijdragen*
• (~ **to**) *bevorderen*
contribution [znw] *bijdrage*
contributor [znw] *medewerker*
contributory I [znw] *medewerker*
II [bnw] *secundair*
contrivance [znw] • *overleg* • *middel,*
toestel • *vindingrijkheid, vernuft, list*
contrive [ov ww] *het klaarspelen,*
uitdenken
contrived [bnw] *onnatuurlijk,*
gekunsteld
control I [ov ww] • *controleren*
• *beheersen* • *beheren, leiden, besturen*
II [znw] • *toezicht, beheer* • *bediening*
‹v. apparaat›, *besturing* ‹v. voertuig›
• *bedwang* • *macht* • *controle*
• *regelorgaan, stuurorgaan*
controller [znw] *controleur, regulateur*
controversial [bnw] *controversieel*
controversy [znw] • *polemiek*
• *dispuut* • *geschil, twistpunt*
conundrum [znw] *woordraadsel*
conurbation [znw] *agglomeratie*

convalesce [on ww] *herstellende zijn*
convalescence [znw] *herstel(periode)*
convalescent I [znw] *herstellende zieke*
II [bnw] *herstellend* ‹v. ziekte›
convene [ov ww] *oproepen,*
bijeenroepen
convenience I [ov ww] *gerieven*
II [znw] *gerief*
convent [znw] *klooster*
convention [znw] • *afspraak*
• *akkoord* • *conventie, gebruik*
• *bijeenroeping, vergadering*
conventional [bnw] • *vormelijk*
• *(stilzwijgend) overeengekomen,*
gebruikelijk
converge I [ov ww] *in één punt laten*
samenkomen II [on ww] *in één punt*
samenkomen
conversant [bnw] *bedreven*
conversation [znw] *het praten, gesprek*
conversational [bnw] *gespreks-*
converse I [on ww] *converseren* II [znw]
het omgekeerde III [bnw] *omgekeerd*
conversion [znw] • *conversie* • *bekering*
convert I [ov ww] • *bekeren* • *omzetten,*
converteren II [on ww] *veranderen*
III [znw] *bekeerling*
convertible I [znw] *cabriolet* II [bnw]
omkeerbaar, in-/verwisselbaar
convex [bnw] *bol*
convey [ov ww] • *mededelen,*
uitdrukken • *vervoeren*
convict I [ov ww] • *overtuigen* ‹v.
dwaling› • *schuldig bevinden,*
veroordelen II [znw] • *dwangarbeider*
• *gevangene* III [bnw] *straf-*
convince [ov ww] *overtuigen*
convocation [znw] *senaat, synode*
convoy I [ov ww] *begeleiden* II [znw]
konvooi
convulsion [znw] *stuiptrekking*
coo [on ww] *kirren*
cook I [ov + on ww] *koken, bereiden*
• (~ **up**) *verwarmen* II [znw] *kok,*
keukenmeid
cooker [znw]

• kookfornuis/-pan/-toestel • *stoofpeer*
cookery [znw] *kookkunst*
cooking [znw] *het koken, kookkunst*
cool I [ov + on ww] *bekoelen*
• (~ **down/off**) *afkoelen* II [znw]
koelte III [bnw] • *koel, kalm • brutaal*
• *ongeïnteresseerd*
cooler [znw] *koeler*
coop I [ov ww] *opsluiten* • (~ **in/up**)
opsluiten II [znw] • *fuik*
• *kippenhok/-mand*
cop I [ov ww] *pakken, inrekenen*
II [znw] *smeris*
cope I [ov ww] *bedekken* II [on ww] *'t*
aankunnen • (~ **with**) *het hoofd*
bieden aan
co-pilot [znw] *tweede piloot*
copious [bnw] *overvloedig,*
(woorden)rijk
copper I [znw] • *koperen ketel • smeris*
• *(rood)koper* II [bnw] *koperen*
coppice, copse [znw] *kreupelbosje*
copulate [on ww] • *paren • z. koppelen*
copy I [ov ww] • *nabootsen*
• *overschrijven, kopiëren* • (~ **out**)
letterlijk overschrijven II [znw]
• *exemplaar • kopie, afschrift*
• *reclame-inhoud, kopij • model*
coral I [znw] *koraal* II [bnw]
• *koraalrood • koralen*
cord [znw] *streng, koord*
cordial I [znw] • *likeur*
• *hartversterkend middel* II [bnw]
hartelijk, hartversterkend
cordon I [ov ww] • (~ **off**) *met een*
kordon afzetten II [znw] • *kordon*
• *ordelint, sierkoord*
core [znw] • *klokhuis • binnenste, kern*
cork I [ov ww] *kurken* • (~ **up**)
(dicht)kurken II [znw] *kurk(eik)*
III [bnw] *kurken-*
cormorant [znw] • *veelvraat*
• *aalscholver*
corn I [ov ww] *zouten* II [znw] • *korrel*
• *likdoorn • koren, graan* • ‹AE› *maïs*
• ‹AE› *whisky*

cornea [znw] *hoornvlies*
corner I [ov ww] • *in de hoek*
drijven/zetten • opkopen om prijzen op
te drijven • *v. hoek voorzien* II [on ww]
de hoek nemen/omslaan III [znw]
• *hoek • hoekschop*
cornice [znw] *(kroon)lijst, lijstwerk*
Cornish I [znw] *taal v. Cornwall*
II [bnw] *m.b.t. Cornwall*
corny [bnw] • *sentimenteel • flauw* ‹fig.›
coronary I [znw] ‹inf.› *hartinfarct*
II [bnw] *kroonvormig*
coronation [znw] *kroning*
coroner [znw] • ≈ *rechter v. instructie*
• *lijkschouwer*
corporal I [znw] *korporaal, corporale*
II [bnw] *lichamelijk*
corporate [bnw] *gemeenschappelijk,*
gezamenlijk
corporation [znw] • *rechtspersoon(lijk*
lichaam) • onderneming, maatschappij
• ‹AE› *bedrijf*
corporeal [bnw] *lichamelijk, stoffelijk*
corpse [znw] *lijk*
corpulent [bnw] *zwaarlijvig*
corral [znw] • *wagenkamp • omheining*
• *kraal*
correct I [ov ww] • *verbeteren*
• *terechtwijzen, afstraffen • verhelpen,*
reguleren II [bnw] • *goed, juist*
• *correct, netjes*
correction [znw] *verbetering*
corrective I [znw] *verbeterend middel*
II [bnw] *verbeterend*
correlate I [ov + on ww] *in onderling*
verband brengen/staan II [znw]
wisselbegrip
correspond [on ww] *corresponderen*
• (~ **to**) *beantwoorden aan*
correspondent I [znw]
• *correspondent • zakenrelatie* II [bnw]
overeenkomend
corresponding [bnw]
corresponderend, overeenkomstig
corridor [znw] *gang*
corroborate [ov ww] *bekrachtigen,*

bevestigen
corroborative [bnw] *bevestigend*
corrode I [ov ww] *aan-/wegvreten*
II [on ww] *wegteren, (ver)roesten,*
oxyderen
corrosion [znw] *roest*
corrupt I [ov ww] • *omkopen*
• *be-/verderven* II [on ww] *ontaarden*
III [bnw] • *omkoopbaar, corrupt,*
be-/verdorven • *verknoeid, vervalst*
corruption [znw] *corruptie, omkoping*
cosine [znw] *cosinus*
cosmetic I [znw] *schoonheidsmiddel*
II [bnw] *schoonheids-*
cosmic(al) [bnw] *kosmisch*
cosmonaut [znw] *ruimtevaarder*
cosmopolitan I [znw] *wereldburger*
II [bnw] *cosmopolitisch*
cosmos [znw] *heelal*
cosset [ov ww] *verwennen*
cost I [ov ww] *kosten* II [znw] *prijs,*
kosten
co-star [znw] *tegenspeler/-speelster* ‹in
film/toneelstuk›
costly [bnw] *duur, kostbaar*
costume I [ov ww] *kleden* II [znw]
kostuum, klederdracht
cosy I [ov ww] *sussen* • (~ **up to**) z.
nestelen bij II [znw] *theemuts* III [bnw]
gezellig, knus
cot [znw] *ledikant(je), krib*
cottage [znw] *huisje, villaatje, hut*
cotton I [on ww] • (~ **on**) *het snappen*
• (~ **up to**) z. *bemind maken bij*
II [znw] *katoen, garen* III [bnw]
katoenen
couch I [ov ww] • *verwoorden,*
formuleren • *neerleggen* II [on ww]
gaan liggen, klaar liggen voor de
sprong III [znw] • *sofa* • *(rust)bed,*
divan
could [ww] *verl. tijd* → **can**
council [znw] • *(raad)svergadering*
• *concilie*
counsel I [ov + on ww] *adviseren*
II [znw] • *advocaten, advocaat*

• *adviseur* • *plan* • *beraadslaging,*
overleg, raad(geving)
counsellor [znw] • *raadgever*
• *welzijnswerker*
count I [ov ww] *(mee-/op)tellen,*
rekenen • (~ **down**) *aftellen* • (~ **in**)
meerekenen • (~ **out**) *uittellen, aftellen*
II [on ww] *meetellen, gelden* • (~ **for**)
meetellen als • (~ **on**) *rekenen op*
III [znw] • *graaf* • *tel(ling), aantal*
countenance I [ov ww] • *goedvinden*
• *steunen, aanmoedigen* II [znw]
• *gelaat(suitdrukking)* • *steun,*
aanmoediging
counterfeit I [ov ww] *vervalsen*
II [on ww] *huichelen* III [znw] *namaak*
IV [bnw] *nagemaakt, vals*
countermand I [ov ww] • *afbestellen,*
annuleren • *een tegenbevel geven*
II [znw] *tegenbevel*
countess [znw] *gravin*
countless [bnw] *talloos*
country [znw] • *land* • *streek*
• *platteland, de provincie*
county [znw] • *graafschap* • ‹AE›
provincie
coup [znw] • *coup* • *goede slag/zet*
coupé [znw] • *tweedeursauto* • *coupé*
• *tweepersoonsrijtuig*
couple I [ov ww] *koppelen* • (~ **with**)
paren aan II [on ww] • *paren* • *paren*
vormen III [znw] *paar(tje), tweetal*
couplet [znw] *twee rijmende versregels*
courage [znw] *moed*
courageous [bnw] *moedig*
courier [znw] *koerier*
course I [ov ww] *jagen op, najagen*
II [on ww] *snellen, stromen* III [znw]
• *loop, (be-/ver)loop* • *kuur* • *reeks*
• *cursus* • *gang* ‹v. maaltijd› • *weg,*
(ren)baan • *gedragslijn, koers*
court I [ov ww] • *streven naar*
• *uitlokken* • *het hof maken* II [on ww]
verkering hebben, vrijen III [znw] • *hof*
• *rechtzitting, rechtbank, gerechtshof*
• *hofhouding* • *vergadering, college*

courtesy [znw] *hoffelijkheid*
courtier [znw] *hoveling*
courtly [bnw] *hoofs, vleierig*
cousin [znw] *neef* ‹zoon v. oom en tante›, *nicht* ‹dochter v. oom en tante›
cove [znw] *inham*
covenant I [ov + on ww] *overeenkomen* II [znw] *verbond, verdrag*
cover I [ov ww] • *beschermen* • *insluiten* • *verbergen* • *v. toepassing zijn op* • *overstelpen met* • *z. uitstrekken over* • *be-/overdekken* • (z.) *dekken* • (~ **over**) *geheel bedekken* • (~ **up**) *verbergen, toedekken, in de doofpot stoppen* II [on ww] • (~ **for**) *invallen voor* III [znw] • *bedekking, deksel* • *buitenband* • *couvert* • *dekmantel* • *boekomslag* • *bescherming, schuilplaats*
coverage [znw] *(pers)verslag*
covering [znw] *dekking*
covert I [znw] *schuilplaats, struikgewas* II [bnw] • *impliciet* • *heimelijk*
covet [ov ww] *begeren*
covetous [bnw] *begerig, hebzuchtig*
cow [znw] • *koe* • *wijfje* ‹bij zoogdieren›
coward [znw] *lafaard*
cowardice [znw] *lafheid*
cowardly [bnw + bijw] *lafhartig*
cower [on ww] *(neer)hurken, ineenkrimpen*
coy [bnw] • *afgezonderd* • *bedeesd, zedig*
crab I [on ww] *mopperen* II [znw] • *krab* • *laagste worp* ‹bij dobbelspel› • *lier* • *platluis*
crabbed [bnw] • *kriebelig* ‹handschrift› • *kribbig, nors*
crack I [ov ww] • *doen barsten* • *laten knallen* • *kraken* ‹v. codes›, *ontcijferen* II [on ww] • *knallen* • *breken/overslaan* ‹v. stem› • *geestelijk instorten* ‹onder druk› • *snoeven* • *scheuren, barsten, kraken* III [znw] • *inbraak* • *gekraak, (ge)knal, klap* • *kier, spleet, barst* • *eersteklas paard/schutter/speler, enz.* • *inbreker*

IV [bnw] *prima, eersteklas*
cracked [bnw] *getikt*
cracker [znw] • *spetter* ‹persoon› • *giller* • *cracker, dun biscuitje* • *voetzoeker, knaller* • *leugen*
cracking ‹sl.› [bnw] • *uitstekend, geweldig* • *snel*
crackle I [on ww] *knetteren, knappen* II [znw] • *geknetter* • *craquelé* III [bnw] *craquelé*
crackling [znw] • *gebraden zwoerd* • *geknetter*
cradle [znw] *wieg*
crafty [bnw] *listig*
crag [znw] • *steile rots* • *schelpzand*
craggy [bnw] • *rotsig* • *woest* • *verweerd* ‹fig.›
cram I [ov ww] *volproppen, inpompen* ‹kennis› II [on ww] (z.) *volstoppen* III [znw] *gedrang*
cramp I [ov ww] • *verankeren* • *belemmeren, vastklemmen* • *kramp veroorzaken (in)* • (~ **up**) *in nauwe ruimte opsluiten* II [znw] • *kramp* • *muuranker, klemhaak*
cramped [bnw] • *bekrompen* • *met kramp* • *kriebelig, gewrongen*
cranberry [znw] *veenbes*
cranium [znw] *schedel*
crank I [znw] • *zonderling* • *slinger* • *kruk(stang)* II [bnw] *zwak, wankel* • (~ **up**) *aanslingeren* ‹v. auto›
cranky [bnw] • *excentriek* • *humeurig* • *wankel* • *kronkelend*
cranny [znw] *scheur, spleet*
crap ‹vulg.› [znw] • *gelul* • *rotzooi, troep*
crash I [ov ww] *verbrijzelen* II [on ww] • *te pletter vallen* • *failliet gaan* • *daveren* • *galmen* • (~ **against/into**) *aanbotsen tegen* III [znw] • *botsing* • *klap* • ‹econ.› *krach*
crashing ‹inf.› [bnw] *verpletterend, ongelooflijk*
crass [bnw] *grof, lomp*
crate [znw] • *krat* • *tenen mand*

crater [znw] • krater • bomtrechter
crave I [ov ww] smeken, verzoeken
II [on ww] hunkeren • (~ **for**) vurig
verlangen naar
craving [znw] verzoek, smeekbede
crawl I [on ww] • crawlen • (de) hielen
likken • kruipen • langzaam
bewegen/voortgaan • (~ **with**)
krioelen van II [znw] crawl
crayon [znw] • koolspits • kleurpotlood,
tekenkrijt • pastel(tekening)
craze I [ov ww] • krankzinnig maken
• craqueleren II [on ww] gecraqueleerd
zijn III [znw] manie, rage
crazy [bnw] • gek, krankzinnig
• bouwvallig • grillig, met
onregelmatig patroon
creak I [on ww] piepen, knarsen II [znw]
geknars
creaky [bnw] knarsend
cream I [ov ww] • tot room maken
• afromen • room doen bij II [on ww]
room/schuim vormen III [znw] • room
• crème • crème de la crème, het puikje
creamy [bnw] • smeuïg • zacht, vol
crease I [ov + on ww] vouwen, kreukelen
II [znw] • streep <bij cricket> • vouw,
kreukel
create [ov ww] • scheppen,
teweegbrengen • verheffen tot
• benoemen
creator [znw] schepper
creature [znw] • voortbrengsel
• schepsel, dier
credence [znw] • geloof • credens(tafel)
credentials [mv] geloofsbrieven
credible [bnw] geloofwaardig
credit I [ov ww] • geloven • crediteren
II [znw] • verdienste, eer, merite
• invloed • goede naam • krediet
• credit(zijde) • vertrouwen, geloof
creditable [bnw] eervol,
achtenswaardig
creditor [znw] schuldeiser, crediteur
credulity [znw] lichtgelovigheid
creed [znw] geloof(sbelijdenis)

creek [znw] • kreek • inham • <AE>
riviertje
creep I [on ww] sluipen, kruipen
II [znw] griezel
creeper [znw] • kruiper
• kruipdier/-plant
creepy [bnw] griezelig
cremate [ov ww] cremeren
crept [ww] verl. tijd + volt. deelw.
→ **creep**
crescent I [znw] • maansikkel, halve
maan • rij huizen in halve cirkel
• halve cirkel II [bnw] • wassend <v.
maan> • halvemaanvormig
cress [znw] tuinkers, waterkers
crest [znw] • hoogtepunt, top
• (schuim)kop op golf • pluim • kuif,
kam
cretin [znw] • idioot • gedrochtje
crevice [znw] spleet, scheur
crew [znw] • bemanning, personeel
• zootje, troep
crib I [ov ww] • gappen • opsluiten
II [on ww] • spieken • plagiaat plegen
III [znw] • hut • krib • plagiaat,
gespiekte vertaling, spiekbriefje
crick [znw] kramp
cricket [znw] • krekel • cricket(spel)
cricketer [znw] cricketspeler
crier [znw] • huiler • omroeper,
schreeuwer
crikey [tw] allemachtig!
crime [znw] misdaad
crimp [ov ww] krullen <v. haar>, plooien
crimson I [ov ww] rood kleuren
II [on ww] rood worden III [znw]
karm(oz)ijnrood IV [bnw]
karm(oz)ijnrood
cringe I [on ww] ineenkrimpen • (~ **to**)
kruipen voor II [znw] slaafse buiging
crinkle I [ov + on ww] rimpelen,
(ver)frommelen II [znw] kreuk, rimpel
crinkly [bnw] verkreukt, rimpelig
cripple I [ov ww] • verminken
• verlammen, belemmeren II [znw]
kreupele

crisp I [znw] *chip* II [bnw] • *netjes en
verzorgd* • *levendig* • *kroes-, gekruld*
• *kort en bondig* • *pittig, krachtig* • *fris*
• *bros, krokant*
criterion [znw] *criterium, maatstaf*
critic [znw] • *vitter* • *criticus,
beoordelaar*
critical [bnw] • *hachelijk, kritiek*
• *vitterig* • *kritisch*
criticism [znw] • *kritiek* • *kritische
bespreking*
criticize [ov ww] • *bespreken*
• *beoordelen* • *aanmerkingen maken op*
croak I [ov ww] ‹sl.› *mollen* II [on ww]
• *krassen, kwaken* • *ongeluk
voorspellen* • ‹vulg.› *kreperen*
crochet I [ov + on ww] *haken* ‹met wol
of garen› II [znw] *haakwerk*
crock [znw] *pot(scherf)*
crockery [znw] *aardewerk, serviesgoed*
crocodile [znw] *krokodil*
croft [znw] *perceeltje bouwland, kleine
pachtboerderij*
crofter [znw] *keuterboer, pachtboertje*
crone [znw] *oud wijf*
crony [znw] *boezemvriend(in)*
crook I [on ww] *buigen, z. krommen*
II [znw] • *kromstaf* • *oplichter, boef*
• *kromte, bocht, haak* III [bnw]
→ **crooked**
crooked [bnw] • *oneerlijk, onoprecht*
• *met krom handvat* • *krom, gebogen*
croon I [ov + on ww] • *croonen*
• *neuriën* II [znw] • *liedje* • *zacht
stemgeluid*
crop I [ov ww] • *bebouwen, oogsten,*
• *afknippen, afsnijden* • *bijsnijden*
II [on ww] *opbrengen* • (~ **out/up**)
vóórkomen, (plotseling) opduiken
III [znw] • *gewas, oogst, krop*
• *rijzweepje* • *zeer kort geknipt haar*
cross I [ov + on ww] *oversteken, dwars
gaan door* II [ov ww] • *strepen* ‹v.
cheque› • *dwarsbomen* • *dwars over
elkaar leggen* • (~ **out**) *doorhalen*
III [on ww] *(elkaar) kruisen* IV [znw]

• *kruis(ing), kruisteken* • *bedrog,
zwendel* V [bnw] • *oneerlijk* • *gekruist*
• *tegengesteld, dwars* • *uit zijn humeur*
crotch [znw] • *kruis* ‹v. menselijk
lichaam› • *vertakking*
crotchet [znw] • *haakje* • *gril* • ‹muz.›
kwartnoot
crotchety [bnw] *grillig, nukkig*
crouch [on ww] • *neerhurken, z.
bukken* • *kruipen*
crow I [on ww] *kraaien* • (~ **over**)
victorie kraaien II [znw] • *koevoet*
• *kraai, gekraai*
crowd I [ov ww] *samenpakken in,
volproppen* • (~ **into/out**) *naar
binnen/buiten dringen* II [on ww] (z.
ver)dringen III [znw] *menigte,
gedrang, troep, gezelschap, hoop*
crowded [bnw] *druk, gedrongen, vol*
crown I [ov ww] *kroon zetten op,
(be)kronen, alles overtreffen* II [znw]
• *kroon* • *kruin, hoogste punt* • *bol* ‹v.
hoed›
crucial [bnw] *cruciaal, beslissend,
kritiek*
crucible [znw] • *vuurproef* ‹fig.›
• *smeltkroes*
crucifix [znw] *kruisbeeld*
crucify [ov ww] • *kruisigen* • *kastijden*
crude [bnw] *onrijp, ruw, onafgewerkt,
grof, rauw*
cruel [bnw] *wreed*
cruelty [znw] *wreedheid*
cruet [znw] • *ampul* • *azijn-/olieflesje*
cruise I [ov ww] *bevaren* II [on ww]
• *kruisen* • *varen* • *patrouilleren*
III [znw] • *cruise* • *tocht*
crumpet [znw] • *bol* • *kop* • *plaatkoek*
crumple I [ov ww] *kreuk(el)en,
(op)frommelen* II [on ww] *in elkaar
schrompelen, zakken*
crunch I [ov ww] • *doen knerpen*
• *kapotkauwen* II [on ww] *knarsen,
knerpen* III [znw] *geknars*
crusade I [on ww] *een kruistocht voeren*
II [znw] *kruistocht*

crusader [znw] *kruisvaarder*
crush I [ov + on ww] *dringen,
verfomfaaien* • (~ **into**) (z.) *dringen in*
II [ov ww] *verpletteren, in elkaar
persen, de kop indrukken* • (~ **out**)
uitroeien III [znw] *drukte*
crust I [ov ww] *met een korst bedekken*
II [on ww] *aankoeken, een koek vormen*
III [znw] *korst*
crustacean I [znw] *schaaldier* II [bnw]
m.b.t. schaaldieren
crutch I [ov ww] *steunen* II [znw] *kruk,
steun*
crux [znw] *moeilijkheid, probleem*
cry I [ov + on ww] • *schreeuwen,
(uit)roepen* • *huilen* • *omroepen*
• (~ **for**) *schreeuwen om/van* • (~ **off**)
ervan afzien • (~ **out**) *het
uitschreeuwen, luid protesteren*
II [znw] • *kreet, roep* • *huilbui*
• *(ge)schreeuw, gehuil, geblaf, geluid*
<v. dier> • *gerucht* • *publieke opinie*
crying [bnw] *dringend, ten hemel
schreiend*
crypt [znw] *crypte*
crystal I [znw] *kristal* II [bnw] *kristal-*
crystalline [bnw] *kristallijn*
cub I [on ww] *jongen werpen* II [znw]
welp, jong <v. beer, vos, grote kat>
Cuban I [znw] *Cubaan* II [bnw]
Cubaans
cube [znw] • *blok(je)* • *dobbelsteen*
• *kubus*
cubic(al) [bnw] • *kubiek* • *kubusvormig*
cubicle [znw] *hokje, stemhokje,
slaaphokje*
cubism [znw] *kubisme*
cucumber [znw] *komkommer*
cuddle I [ov ww] *knuffelen* II [on ww]
z. *nestelen, knus tegen elkaar gaan
liggen* III [znw] *knuffel*
cuddly [bnw] *van knuffelen houdend,
aanhalig*
cue [znw] • *biljart-/pool-/snookerkeu*
• *stemming* • *aanwijzing, wenk*
cuff I [ov ww] *klap/stomp geven*

II [znw] • *manchet* • *stomp, klap*
culinary [znw] *keuken-, kook-*
cull I [ov ww] *plukken, selecteren*
II [znw] *sukkel*
culminate [on ww] *op 't toppunt zijn,
culmineren*
culpable [bnw] *schuldig*
cult [znw] • *rage* • *eredienst* • *cultus*
cultivate [ov ww] • *beoefenen*
• *verzorgen, koesteren* • *veredelen,
beschaven* • *kweken, bebouwen*
cultivated [bnw] *beschaafd, ontwikkeld*
cultural [bnw] *cultureel*
culture I [ov ww] → **cultivate**
II [znw] • *kweek* • *cultuur*
cultured [bnw] *ontwikkeld, beschaafd*
cumbersome, cumbrous [bnw]
moeilijk hanteerbaar, omslachtig
cumulative [bnw] *aangroeiend*
cumulus [znw] *stapel(wolk)*
cunning I [znw] *listigheid* II [bnw]
listig, sluw
cup I [ov ww] *tot een kom vormen*
II [znw] • *kelk* • *kom* • *beker, kop(je)*
• *holte*
curable [bnw] *geneeslijk, te genezen*
curate [znw] *hulppredikant, kapelaan*
curator [znw] • *directeur* • *curator,
conservator*
curd I [ov + on ww] → **curdle** II [znw]
curdle I [ov ww] *doen stremmen*
II [on ww] *stollen, stremmen* III [znw]
gestremde melk
cure I [ov + on ww] *genezen, verhelpen*
II [znw] • *genezing* • *kuur*
• *vulcanisatie* • *geneesmiddel*
curfew [znw] *avondklok*
curio [znw] *rariteit*
curiosity [znw] • *rariteit*
• *nieuwsgierigheid*
curious [bnw] • *nauwgezet*
• *merkwaardig, eigenaardig*
• *weetgierig, nieuwsgierig*
curlew [znw] *wulp*
currant [znw] • *krent* • *aalbes*
currency [znw] • *(om)loop(tijd),*

circulatie • valuta, koers, deviezen
• algemene geldigheid
current I [znw] • strekking • stroom,
richting, loop II [bnw] • actueel, lopend
• (algemeen) gangbaar • geldig,
geldend
curriculum [znw] leerplan, cursus
curry I [ov ww] • roskammen • met
kerrie kruiden II [znw] kerrie(schotel)
curse I [ov + on ww] (uit)vloeken
• (~ **with**) bezoeken met II [znw]
(ver)vloek(ing)
cursed [bnw] vervloekt
cursory [bnw] vluchtig
curt [bnw] kort(af), beknopt
curtail [ov ww] korten, beperken
• (~ **of**) beroven van
curtain [znw] gordijn
curvaceous [bnw] met goed gevormde
rondingen <v. (vrouwelijk) lichaam>
curvature [znw] kromming
curve I [on ww] (z.) buigen II [znw]
curve, gebogen lijn
cushion I [ov ww] van kussen voorzien,
met kussen steunen II [znw] • kussen
• (biljart)band
cushy [bnw] • fijn, lekker • <sl.>
gemakkelijk
custodian [znw] bewaarder, voogd
custody [znw] • bewaring, hechtenis
• hoede
custom [znw] gewoonte(recht), gebruik
customary [bnw] gewoonlijk
customer [znw] klant
cut I [ov + on ww] • (~ **back**) snoeien,
inkrimpen II [ov ww] • (~ **down**)
omhakken, beperken, bezuinigen
• (~ **off**) afsnijden, stopzetten,
uitsluiten van, afsluiten van • (~ **out**)
ophouden (met), uitsnijden,
uitknippen, verwijderen, uitschakelen,
verdringen • (~ **up**) kapotsnijden,
uitroeien, afkraken, erg aangrijpen,
opsnijden, vernielen III [on ww]
• kapothakken • verdelen • modelleren
• (bij)slijpen • bijknippen • monteren

<film> • verlagen • negeren • snijden
• versnijden • (af)knippen • (~ **across**)
dwars doorsteken, ingaan tegen,
doorbreken • (~ **at**) uithalen naar,
inhakken op • (~ **into**) aansnijden,
onderbreken, een aanslag doen op
• (~ **out**) weigeren IV [znw] • geul
• snit, coupe, stijl • snede • knip • het
snijden • het (haar) knippen • slag,
houw, jaap • houtsnede • verlaging,
vermindering
cute [bnw] • bijdehand • schattig • <AE>
leuk
cutlet [znw] kotelet
cutter [znw] • sloep, kotter
• montagetechnicus <film> • soort
baksteen • snijder, snijmachine
cutting I [znw] • stek <v. plant>
• af-/uitgeknipt stuk II [bnw]
afgesneden, uitgesneden
cybernetics [mv] cybernetica
cycle I [on ww] fietsen II [znw] • hertz
• periode • (motor)fiets • kringloop
• cyclus
cyclist [znw] fietser
cyclone [znw] cycloon
cylinder [znw] cilinder, rol
cymbal [znw] bekken
cynic I [znw] cynicus II [bnw] cynisch
cynical [bnw] cynisch
cypher [znw] → **cipher**
cypress [znw] cipres
Cypriot I [znw] Cyprioot II [bnw]
Cyprisch
cyst [znw] • cyste • vruchtvlies • blaas
• abces
czar [znw] tsaar
czarina [znw] keizerin <v. Rusland>
Czech I [znw] Tsjech II [bnw] Tsjechisch
Czechoslovak I [znw]
Tsjecho-Slowaak II [bnw]
Tsjecho-Slowaaks

D

dab I [ov + on ww] *betten* II [znw]
• *veeg(je), likje* ‹verf› • *schar*
dabbler [znw] • *dilettant* • *beunhaas*
dachshund [znw] *taks(hond)*
dado [znw] • *voetstuk* • *lambrisering*
daffodil [znw] *gele narcis*
daft ‹vulg.› [bnw] *dwaas, dol*
dagger [znw] • *dolk* • *(het teken)* +
dago [znw] • *Spanjool* • *Portugees*
• *Italiaan*
daily [bnw + bijw] *dagelijks*
dainty I [znw] *lekkernij* II [bnw] • *fijn,*
tenger • *kieskeurig*
dairy [znw] • *zuivelfabriek* • *melkwinkel*
dais [znw] *podium*
daisy [znw] *madeliefje*
dally [on ww] • *dartelen* • *talmen*
• *(~ with) flirten/spelen met*
dam I [ov ww] • *(~ up) afdammen,*
indijken II [znw] • *opgestuwd water*
• *moer* ‹v. dier› • *dam, dijk*
damage I [ov ww] *beschadigen* II [znw]
schade
damask I [ov ww] *damasceren* II [znw]
damast III [bnw] *damasten*
dame [znw] • *moedertje* • *vrouwe* • ‹AE›
griet
damn I [ov ww] • *verdoemen*
• *vervloeken* II [bnw + bijw] *vervloekt*
damnable [bnw] *vervloekt*
damnation [znw] • *vervloeking*
• *verdoemenis*
damned [bnw] • *uiterst, totaal*
• *verdomd*
damp I [ov ww] *bevochtigen* II [bnw]
vochtig, klam
damper [znw] • *domper* ‹fig.›
• *bevochtiger* • *demper* • *regelklep* ‹v.
kachel›, *sleutel* ‹v. kachel›
dance I [on ww] • *dansen* • *wiegen*
II [znw] *bal*

dancer [znw] *danser*
dandelion [znw] *paardenbloem*
dandruff [znw] *hoofdroos*
dandy I [znw] *fat* II [bnw] • *fatterig*
• *chic*
Dane [znw] • *Deen* • *Noorman*
• *Deense dog*
danger [znw] *gevaar*
Danish [bnw] *Deens*
dank [bnw] *vochtig*
dapper [bnw] *parmantig, kwiek*
dare [ov + on ww] *durven*
daring I [znw] *vermetelheid* II [bnw]
• *vermetel* • *gewaagd*
dark I [znw] *het donker* II [bnw] *donker*
darken [ov ww] *donker maken,*
verduisteren
darling I [znw] *lieveling* II [bnw]
geliefd
darn I [on ww] *stoppen* ‹v. sokken›
II [znw] *stop*
dart I [ov ww] *(af)schieten, werpen*
• *(~ out) razendsnel uitsteken*
II [on ww] • *(~ away) wegstuiven*
III [znw] • *schijf* ‹bij darts› • *pijl(tje),*
werpspies • *angel* • *plotselinge sprong*
vooruit • *worp*
dash I [ov + on ww] *slaan, smijten,*
smakken, kletsen • *(~ against)*
(ergens) tegenaan smijten II [ov ww]
• *(~ in) inslaan/smijten,*
binnenstuiven • *(~ off) wegsnellen*
III [znw] • *gedachtestreepje* • *streep*
• *pennenstreek* • *zwier* • *scheutje, tintje,*
tikje
dashboard [znw] • *spatscherm*
• *dashboard*
dashing [bnw] • *onstuimig* • *kranig,*
kloek • *chic, zwierig*
data [mv] • *informatie* • *gegevens, data*
date I [ov ww] • *dateren* • *ouderdom*
vaststellen van • *afspraakjes hebben*
met • *dagtekenen* II [znw]
• *dadel(palm)* • *datum, jaartal* • ‹AE›
afspraak(je)
dated [bnw] *gedateerd, ouderwets*

daub I [ov ww] • bepleisteren
• bekladden II [znw] pleisterkalk
daughter [znw] dochter
daunt [ov ww] ontmoedigen, bang
maken
dauntless [bnw] onvervaard
dawdle [on ww] • beuzelen, lummelen
• talmen
dawn I [on ww] • dagen, licht worden
• aanbreken • ontluiken <fig.> II [znw]
dageraad
day [znw] dag
daze I [ov ww] • verbijsteren, doen
duizelen • verblinden II [znw]
verbijstering
dazzle I [ov ww] • verbijsteren
• verblinden II [znw] schittering, pracht
deacon [znw] • diaken • ouderling
dead I [znw] II [bnw] • dood
• uitgedoofd • totaal, volstrekt
III [bijw] • dodelijk • uiterst • volkomen
deaden I [ov ww] • geestelijk doden
• krachteloos maken II [on ww] • glans
verliezen • krachteloos worden
deaf [bnw] doof
deafen [ov ww] doof maken
deal I [ov ww] • handelen • uitdelen
• (~ with) behandelen, handelen over,
klant zijn bij II [znw] • (vuil) zaakje
• transactie
dealer [znw] • dealer • handelaar
dean [znw] • deken • decaan
dear I [znw] liefste II [bnw] • duur,
kostbaar • lief, dierbaar
dearie, deary [znw] lieveling
dearly [bijw] • duur • zeer, dolgraag
deathly [bnw] • dodelijk • doods
debar [ov ww] • uitsluiten • verhinderen
debase [ov ww] • vernederen • vervalsen
debatable [bnw] betwistbaar
debate I [ov ww] • betwisten
• overpeinzen II [on ww] debatteren
III [znw] debat
debauch [ov ww] op 't slechte pad
brengen
debauchery [znw] losbandigheid

debilitate [ov ww] verzwakken
debility [znw] zwakte, zwakheid
debit I [ov ww] • (~ against) debiteren
• (~ with) debiteren voor II [znw]
debetpost, debetzijde
debonair [bnw] vriendelijk, goedig
debrief [ov ww] verslag laten
uitbrengen
debris [znw] • puin • resten
debtor [znw] schuldenaar, debiteur
debug [ov ww] • fouten opsporen en
verwijderen <in
computerprogramma>
• afluisterapparatuur weghalen
debunk [ov ww] ontmaskeren, van zijn
voetstuk stoten
decad(e) [znw] • 10-tal • decennium
decadence [znw] decadentie
decadent I [znw] decadent II [bnw]
• decadent • in verval
decamp [on ww] opbreken, ervandoor
gaan
decant [ov ww] voorzichtig uitschenken
<v. wijn>
decanter [znw] wijnkaraf
decapitate [ov ww] onthoofden
decay I [on ww] vervallen, bederven,
rotten II [znw] • bederf • verval
deceased [bnw] overleden, pas
gestorven
deceit [znw] • misleiding
• bedrieglijkheid
deceitful [bnw] bedrieglijk
deceive [ov ww] bedriegen
decelerate [on ww] vaart minderen
decency [znw] fatsoen
decentralize [ov + on ww]
decentraliseren
deception [znw] bedrog, misleiding
deceptive [bnw] bedrieglijk
decide [ov + on ww] beslissen
decided [bnw] • beslist • uitgesproken
deciduous [bnw] loof <v. boom>
decimal I [znw] • decimaal • <wisk.>
tiendelige breuk II [bnw] • tientallig
• decimaal • <wisk.> tiendelig <v.

breuk>
decimalize [ov ww] *tiendelig maken*
decimate [ov ww] *decimeren*
decipher [ov ww] *ontcijferen*
decision [znw] • *vastberadenheid*
• *beslissing*
decisive [bnw] • *beslissend* • *beslist*
deck I [ov ww] • *(~ out) versieren*
II [znw] • *dek* • *spel kaarten*
declaim [ov + on ww] *declameren*
declaration [znw] *verklaring*
declare [ov ww] • *verklaren*
• *vaststellen* • *aangeven* <bij douane>
decode [ov ww] *decoderen*
decompose [on ww] *rotten*
decomposition [znw] *ontbinding*
decontaminate [ov ww] *ontsmetten*
decorate [ov ww] • *versieren* • *decoreren*
• *schilderen, behangen*
decoration [znw] *decoratie*
decorative [bnw] *decoratief*
decorator [znw] *huisschilder, behanger*
decorous [bnw] *waardig, fatsoenlijk*
decorum [znw] *waardigheid, fatsoen*
decoy I [ov ww] *(in de val) lokken*
II [znw] *lokeend, lokvogel, lokmiddel*
decrease I [ov ww] *verminderen*
II [on ww] *afnemen, dalen* III [znw]
afname
decrepit [bnw] *vervallen, afgeleefd*
dedicate [ov ww] • *(~ to) opdragen
aan, toewijden aan*
dedication [znw] *toewijding*
deduce [ov ww] *nagaan* • *(~ from)
afleiden uit*
deduct [ov ww] *aftrekken*
deduction [znw] • *aftrek, korting*
• *deductie*
deductive [bnw] *deductief*
deed [znw] • *daad* • *akte*
deem I [ov ww] *achten* II [on ww]
oordelen
deep I [znw] *diepte, zee* II [bnw]
• *diepzinnig, verdiept* • *diep, hoog*
<sneeuw>, *diepliggend*
deepen I [ov ww] *dieper maken*

II [on ww] *dieper worden*
deer [znw] *hert(en)*
deface [ov ww] *schenden, ontsieren*
defamation [znw] *smaad*
defamatory [bnw] *lasterlijk*
defame [ov ww] *belasteren*
default I [on ww] *in gebreke blijven,
nalatig zijn* II [znw] • *gebrek*
• *nalatigheid* • *verzuim* • *wanbetaling*
• *wanprestatie*
defeat I [ov ww] • *verslaan* • *verijdelen*
• *nietig verklaren* • *verwerpen* II [znw]
nederlaag
defeatism [znw] *defaitisme*
defence, defense [znw] • *verdediging*
• *afweermiddel* • *verweer*
defend [ov ww] *verdedigen, beschermen*
defendant [znw] *gedaagde*
defender [znw] *verdediger*
defensible [bnw] *verdedigbaar,
houdbaar* <fig.>
defensive [bnw] *verdedigend, defensief*
defer I [ov ww] *uitstellen* II [on ww]
• *(~ to) z. onderwerpen aan*
deference [znw] • *eerbied* • *eerbiediging*
deferential [bnw] *eerbiedig,
onderdanig*
defiance [znw] • *verzet* • *trotsering,
uitdaging*
defiant [bnw] • *uitdagend, tartend*
• *trotserend*
deficiency [znw] *tekort*
deficient [bnw] • *onvoldoende,
gebrekkig* • *zwakzinnig*
deficit [znw] • *tekort* • *achterstand*
defile I [on ww] • *bevuilen* • *ontwijden,
onteren* II [znw] *(berg)pas*
definable [bnw] *definieerbaar*
define I [ov ww] • *afbakenen, bepalen*
• *beschrijven, omschrijven* II [on ww]
definiëren
definite [bnw] • *bepaald* • *precies*
definition [znw] • *(beeld)scherpte*
• *definitie*
definitive [bnw] *beslissend, definitief*
deflate [ov ww] *laten ontsnappen* <v.

gas>, leeg laten lopen
deflect I [ov ww] *doen afwijken, opzij*
buigen • (~ **from**) *afketsen/-schampen*
van II [on ww] *afwijken*
deflection [znw] *afbuiging*
deflower [ov ww] *ontmaagden*
defoliant [znw] *ontbladeringsmiddel*
defoliate [ov + on ww] *ontbladeren*
deforest [ov ww] *ontbossen*
deform [ov ww] • *ontsieren*
• *misvormen*
deformation [znw] • *verbastering*
• *misvorming*
deformity [znw] • *mismaaktheid*
• *perversiteit* • *wangedrocht*
defray [ov ww] *bekostigen*
deft [bnw] • *handig, behendig* • *vlug*
defunct [bnw] *niet meer bestaand*
defuse [ov ww] *demonteren* <v.
explosieven>
defy [ov ww] *trotseren, uitdagen (tot)*
degenerate I [on ww] *degenereren*
II [znw] *gedegenereerde, ontaarde*
III [bnw] *gedegenereerd, ontaard*
degradation [znw] • *degradatie*
• *ontaarding*
degrade [ov ww] • *z. verlagen,*
ontaarden • *degraderen*
degree [znw] • *mate* • *graad* <ook
academisch>
dehumanize [ov ww] *ontmenselijken*
dehydrate [ov ww] *(uit)drogen*
deify [ov ww] *vergoddelijken*
deign [ov + on ww] *z. verwaardigen*
deity [znw] *godheid*
dejected [bnw] ↓ *down, ontmoedigd,*
neerslachtig
dejection [znw] *neerslachtigheid*
delay I [ov ww] *uitstellen* II [znw]
vertraging
delectable [bnw] *verrukkelijk*
delectation [znw] *genot*
delegate I [ov ww] *overdragen* II [znw]
• *afgevaardigde* • *gemachtigde*
delegation [znw] • *delegatie*
• *machtiging*

delete [ov ww] *wissen, schrappen*
deliberate I [on ww] *overwegen,*
overleggen II [bnw] • *opzettelijk*
• *weloverwogen* • *bedachtzaam*
deliberation [znw] • *behoedzaamheid*
• *bedachtzaamheid* • *overleg,*
afweging, overweging
deliberative [bnw] *beraadslagend*
delicacy [znw] • *fijngevoeligheid*
• *delicatesse* • *teerheid*
delicate [bnw] • *kies, fijn(gevoelig)*
• *zwak, teer* • *netelig, moeilijk* • *lekker*
delicatessen [mv] • *delicatessezaak*
• *delicatessen, comestibles*
delicious [bnw] *lekker, heerlijk*
delight I [on ww] *verheugen* II [znw]
genot, vreugde, genoegen
delightful [bnw] *verrukkelijk*
delineate [ov ww] • *omlijnen*
• *schetsen, tekenen*
delinquency [znw] • *vergrijp*
• *misdadig gedrag*
delinquent I [znw] *delinquent*
II [bnw] • *misdadig* • *schuldig* <aan
vergrijp>
delirious [bnw] • *ijlend* • *uitzinnig*
deliver I [ov ww] • *overhandigen,*
(af)leveren • *verlossen* II [on ww]
bevallen
deliverance [znw] *bevrijding*
delivery [znw] • *bestelling* • *het*
afleveren • *verlossing* • *(het houden*
v.e.) toespraak
delude [ov ww] *misleiden*
deluge I [ov ww] *overstelpen,*
overstromen II [znw]
• *(woorden)stroom* • *wolkbreuk*
delusion [znw] • *bedrog*
• *zinsbegoocheling*
delusive [bnw] *misleidend, bedrieglijk*
delve [on ww] *grondig doorvorsen*
demagogue [znw] *volksmenner*
demand I [ov ww] *eisen, verlangen*
II [znw] • *eis* • <econ.> *vraag*
demarcate [ov ww] • *demarqueren*
• *afbakenen*

demented [bnw] • krankzinnig
• dement
demerit [znw] • gebrek • minpunt
demilitarize [ov ww] demilitariseren
demise [znw] • het vermaken,
overdraging • overlijden
demist [ov ww] ontwasemen
demobilize, demob [ov + on ww]
<mil.> afzwaaien, demobiliseren
democracy [znw] democratie
democrat [znw] democraat
democratize [ov + on ww]
democratiseren
demolish [ov ww] slopen
demolition [znw] • vernietiging • het
slopen
demonstrable [bnw] aantoonbaar
demonstrate I [ov ww]
• demonstreren, bewijzen • aan de dag
leggen II [on ww] demonstreren,
betoging houden
demonstration [znw] • demonstratie
• actie • protestmars • vertoon
• betoging
demonstrative I [znw] aanwijzend
voornaamwoord II [bnw]
• aanwijzend, bewijzend • z. uitend
• demonstratief
demonstrator [znw] • demonstrator
• betoger
demoralize [ov ww] demoraliseren
demur I [on ww] bezwaar maken
II [znw] • bedenking • aarzeling
den [znw] • hol • hok • (werk)kamer
denationalize [ov ww] privatiseren
denial [znw] • ontkenning
• zelfverloochening
denigrate [ov ww] • denigreren
• belasteren
denomination [znw] • coupure,
(munt)eenheid • benaming • gezindte,
kerkgenootschap
denominator [znw] <wisk.> noemer
<in breuk>
denote [ov ww] • aanduiden • wijzen op
denounce [ov ww] aanklagen

dense [bnw] • dicht • dom
dent I [ov ww] deuken II [znw] deuk
dental I [znw] <taalk.> dentaal II [bnw]
tand-
dentist [znw] tandarts
dentistry [znw] tandheelkunde
denude [ov ww] blootleggen
denunciation [znw] → denounce
deny [ov ww] • ontkennen
• (ver)loochenen • ontzeggen, weigeren
depart [on ww] • vertrekken
• heengaan, doodgaan
department [znw] • sectie, vakgroep
• afdeling • departement
departmental [bnw] • afdelings-
• <AE> ministerieel
departure [znw] vertrek
depend [on ww] eropaan kunnen,
vertrouwen • (~ (up)on) afhangen van
dependence [znw] afhankelijkheid
depict [ov ww] • uitbeelden, afbeelden
• afschilderen
depilatory I [znw] ontharingsmiddel
II [bnw] ontharend
deplorable [bnw] betreurenswaardig
deplore [on ww] betreuren
depopulate [ov ww] ontvolken
deport [ov ww] • verbannen
• deporteren
deportment [znw] • houding • gedrag
depose [ov ww] afzetten
deposit I [ov ww] • deponeren, in
bewaring geven • als waarborg storten
• (neer)leggen • afzetten II [znw]
• deposito • waarborgsom • storting
• afzetting, aanslibbing, geologische
laag
deposition [znw] • het deponeren
• afzetting • (aflegging v.) verklaring
deprave [ov ww] slecht maken, bederven
depravity [znw] verdorvenheid
deprecate [ov ww] afkeuren
depreciate [ov + on ww] in waarde
(doen) verminderen
depress [ov ww] • neerslachtig maken
• (neer)drukken • verlagen

depression [znw] • *het neerdrukken*
• *slapte, malaise, depressie*
• *neerslachtigheid* • *gebied van lage luchtdruk*
deprivation [znw] • *ontbering* • *verlies*
deprive [ov ww] *beroven*
depth [znw] *diepte*
deputation [znw] *afvaardiging*
depute [ov ww] • *machtigen*
• *afvaardigen*
deputize I [ov ww] *aanstellen als waarnemer* II [on ww] *waarnemen*
deputy I [znw] • *plaatsvervanger* • ‹AE› *hulpsheriff* II [bnw] • *waarnemend, plaatsvervangend* • *gevolmachtigd*
• *afgevaardigd*
derail [ov ww] *doen ontsporen*
derelict [bnw] • *verlaten* • *vervallen*
dereliction [znw] *het onbeheerd laten*
deride [ov ww] *uitlachen*
derision [znw] *spot*
derisive [bnw] *spottend*
derivation [znw] • *afleiding* • *afkomst*
derivative I [znw] • *derivaat* • *afgeleid woord* II [bnw] *afgeleid, niet oorspronkelijk*
derive I [ov ww] • (~ **from**) *afleiden van, ontlenen aan* II [on ww]
• (~ **from**) *voortkomen uit, afstammen van*
derogatory [bnw] *geringschattend*
derrick [znw] • *kraan, bok* • *boortoren*
descale [ov ww] *ontkalken*
descendant [znw] *afstammeling*
descent [znw] • *afdaling* • *afkomst, geslacht*
describe [ov ww] *beschrijven*
description [znw] *beschrijving*
descriptive [bnw] *beschrijvend*
desecrate [ov ww] *ontwijden, profaneren*
desert I [ov ww] *in de steek laten, verlaten* II [on ww] ‹mil.› *deserteren* III [znw] *woestijn*
deserter [znw] *deserteur*
deserve [ov ww] *verdienen*

deserving [bnw] *waardig*
design I [ov + on ww] *ontwerpen* II [znw] • *schets, ontwerp(tekening)*
• *vormgeving* • *aanzien* • *plan, opzet*
designate [ov ww] • *(be)noemen, aanduiden* • *bestemmen*
designation [znw] • *benoeming*
• *bestemming*
designer [znw] • *intrigant* • *ontwerper*
designing [bnw] *intrigerend, sluw*
desire I [ov ww] • *wensen* • *begeren* II [znw] • *verlangen, wens* • *begeerte*
desist [on ww] *stoppen* • (~ **from**) *afzien van, ophouden met*
desk [znw] • *schrijftafel, lessenaar*
• *afdeling* • *balie* • ‹AE› *preekstoel*
desolate I [ov ww] • *verwoesten*
• *ontvolken* II [bnw] • *eenzaam*
• *verwaarloosd* • *troosteloos*
desolation [znw] • *eenzaamheid, verlatenheid* • *verwoesting*
despair I [on ww] *wanhopen* II [znw] *wanhoop*
despairing [bnw] *wanhopig*
desperate [bnw] • *wanhopig* • *hopeloos*
desperation [znw] *wanhoop, vertwijfeling*
despicable [bnw] *verachtelijk*
despise [ov ww] *verachten*
despite [vz] *ondanks, in weerwil van*
despondent [bnw] • *wanhopig, vertwijfeld* • *zwaarmoedig*
despot [znw] *despoot*
despotic [bnw] *despotisch*
despotism [znw] *despotisme, tirannie*
destination [znw] *bestemming*
destitute I [znw] *noodlijdende* II [bnw] *noodlijdend, behoeftig*
destitution [znw] *gebrek, armoede*
destroy [ov ww] • *afmaken* ‹v. dier›
• *vernietigen, vernielen*
destroyer [znw] • *vernietiger*
• *torpedojager*
destruction [znw] *vernietiging*
destructive [bnw] *destructief*
desultory [bnw] • *zonder vaste lijn*

• onsamenhangend • vluchtig
detach [ov ww] • detacheren • eraf
halen, losmaken • los raken
detachable [bnw] afneembaar
detached [bnw] • objectief • los
• emotieloos, afstandelijk • vrijstaand
<v. huis>
detachment [znw] • detachement
• gereserveerdheid
detail [znw] • bijzonderheid, detail
• bijzaak • <mil.> kleine afdeling
detain [ov ww] • vasthouden
• ophouden
detect [ov ww] • betrappen • bespeuren
detection [znw] • waarneming
• speurwerk
detective I [znw] • detective
• rechercheur II [bnw] recherche-
detention [znw] • nablijven <op
school> • het vasthouden
deter [ov ww] afschrikken
detergent [znw] (af)wasmiddel
deteriorate [on ww] slechter worden
determinant [znw] beslissende factor
determination [znw] • bepaling,
besluit • vastberadenheid • richting
determine I [ov ww] vaststellen,
bepalen II [on ww] besluiten
determined [bnw] vastberaden
deterrent I [znw] afschrikwekkend
middel II [bnw] afschrikwekkend
detest [ov ww] verafschuwen, haten
detestable [bnw] afschuwelijk
detonate I [ov ww] doen ontploffen
II [on ww] ontploffen
detour [znw] • omweg • omleiding
detract [on ww] • (~ from) afbreuk
doen aan
detriment [znw] nadeel
detrimental [bnw] schadelijk
deuce [znw] • twee <op dobbelstenen,
speelkaarten> • 40 gelijk <tennis>
• du(i)vel, de donder
devalue [ov + on ww] in waarde (doen)
dalen
devastate [ov ww] verwoesten

devastating [bnw] • ontzettend
• verwoestend
develop I [ov ww] • ontginnen
• ontwikkelen II [on ww] • z.
ontwikkelen • aan de dag leggen
developer [znw] • uitwerker • <foto.>
ontwikkelaar
development [znw] ontwikkeling
deviant [bnw] afwijkend, abnormaal
deviate [on ww] • afwijken • afdwalen
deviation [znw] afwijking
device [znw] • middel • opzet, plan
• list • apparaat, uitvinding, toestel
• ontwerp • devies, motto
devil [znw] duivel
devious [bnw] • slinks • kronkelend
devise [ov ww] bedenken, beramen
devoid [bnw] verstoken
devolution [znw] • delegatie
• decentralisatie v. bestuur, overdracht
van bestuur(sbevoegdheden)
devolve I [ov ww] overdragen,
afwentelen II [on ww] te beurt vallen
devote [ov ww] besteden <v. tijd,
aandacht>, (toe)wijden, geheel geven
devoted [bnw] toegewijd
devotee [znw] • dweper • enthousiast
liefhebber
devotion [znw] • toewijding
• godsvrucht
devotional [bnw] • godsdienstig
• devoot
devour [ov ww] verslinden
devout [bnw] • vroom • toegewijd
dew [znw] dauw
dewy [bnw] • vochtig • dauwachtig
dexterity [znw] • handigheid
• rechtshandigheid
dext(e)rous [bnw] handig
dextrose [znw] druivensuiker
diabetes [znw] suikerziekte, diabetes
diabetic I [znw] iem. die aan
suikerziekte lijdt, diabeticus/-ca
II [bnw] m.b.t. suikerziekte
diadem [znw] diadeem
diagnose [ov ww] • constateren • de

diagnose opmaken van
diagnosis [znw] *diagnose*
diagonal I [znw] *diagonaal* II [bnw]
diagonaal
diagram [znw] • *diagram* • *figuur*
• *grafiek*
diagrammatic [bnw] *schematisch*
dialogue [znw] *dialoog*
diameter [znw] *middellijn*
diamond I [znw] • *diamant* • *ruit*
II [bnw] *diamanten*
diaper [znw] *luier*
diaphanous [bnw] *doorschijnend*
diaphragm [znw] • *pessarium*
• *middenrif* • ‹foto.› *diafragma*
diarist [znw] *dagboekschrijver*
diarrh(o)ea [znw] *diarree*
diary [znw] • *dagboek* • *agenda*
diatribe [znw] *felle aanval* ‹met
woorden›
dice I [on ww] • *dobbelen* • *in blokjes
snijden* II [znw] [mv] *dobbelspel,
dobbelstenen*
dicey ‹inf.› [bnw] • *riskant* • *link*
dictate [ov + on ww] • *dicteren*
• *voorschrijven*
dictation [znw] • *het dicteren* • *dictee,
dictaat* • *voorschrift, wet*
dictator [znw] • *dictator* • *dicteelezer*
dictatorial [bnw] *dictatoriaal*
dictatorship [znw] *dictatuur*
diction [znw] • *zegging, voordracht*
• *manier v. uitdrukken*
dictionary [znw] *woordenboek*
dictum [znw] • *gezegde* • *uitspraak*
did [ww] *verl. tijd* → **do**
didactic [bnw] *didactisch*
diddle ‹inf.› [ov ww] • *inpikken*
• *bedotten*
die I [on ww] • *sterven, omkomen*
• *kwijnen* • ‹vulg.› *z. doodlachen*
• (~ **away/down**) *bedaren,
wegsterven* • (~ **for**) *hevig verlangen
naar* • (~ **off/out**) *uitsterven,
wegsterven* • (~ **to**) *ongevoelig worden
voor* II [znw] *dobbelsteen*

diet I [on ww] *op dieet leven* II [znw]
• *voedsel, kost* • *menu* • *dieet*
dietary [bnw] *dieet-*
dietician [znw] • *diëtist(e)*
• *voedingsexpert*
differ [on ww] *verschillen*
difference [znw] *punt v. verschil*
different [bnw] *ander(e)*
differential I [znw] • *differentiaal*
• *loonklasseverschil* II [bnw]
• *kenmerkend* • *differentieel*
difficult [bnw] *moeilijk*
diffidence [znw] *gebrek aan
zelfvertrouwen*
diffident [bnw] *bedeesd*
diffuse I [ov ww] *verspreiden, uitstralen*
II [on ww] *z. verspreiden* III [bnw]
• *diffuus* • *verspreid, verstrooid*
• *omslachtig*
dig I [ov + on ww] *graven* II [ov ww]
• *uitgraven, opgraven* • *duwen, porren*
• ‹AE sl.› *iets snappen, iets/iem. zien
zitten* III [on ww] *ploeteren, blokken*
• (~ **in**) *zich ingraven, aanvallen*
‹opeten› IV [znw] • *por, stoot* • *steek
onder water*
digest I [ov ww] • *verteren, slikken,
verwerken* • *in z. opnemen* II [on ww]
• *voedsel opnemen* • *verteren* III [znw]
• *overzicht* • *compendium*
digestible [bnw] • *verteerbaar*
• *aanvaardbaar*
digestion [znw] • *spijsvertering*
→ **digest**
digestive I [znw] *spijsvertering
bevorderend middel* II [bnw] *de
spijsvertering bevorderend*
digger [znw] ↑ *excavateur*
digit [znw] • *vinger* • *teen* • *cijfer,
geheel getal onder de tien*
• *vingerbreedte*
digital [bnw] *digitaal*
dignify [ov ww] • *waardigheid
toekennen* • *opluisteren*
dignitary [znw] *kerkelijk
waardigheidsbekleder*

digress [on ww] *afdwalen*
dike I [ov ww] *indijken, omwallen*
II [znw] • *dijk* • <vulg.> *lesbienne*
dilate I [ov ww] *wijder maken*
II [on ww] • *wijder worden* • (z.)
uitzetten
dill [znw] *dille*
dilute I [ov ww] *met water verdunnen*
II [bnw] *waterig*
dim I [ov ww] • *donker/mat/schemerig*
maken • *ontluisteren, doen beslaan*
II [on ww] *beslaan* III [bnw] • *mat*
• *donker, schemerig* • *flauw, vaag*
dimension [znw] • *dimensie*
• *afmeting* • *omvang*
diminish [ov + on ww] *verminderen*
diminutive I [znw] *verkleinwoord*
II [bnw] • *verkleinend* • *miniatuur*
dimmer [znw] *dimschakelaar, dimmer*
dimple [znw] *kuiltje*
din [znw] • *lawaai* • *gekletter*
dine [on ww] *dineren* • (~ *in*) *thuis*
dineren • (~ *off/on*) *zijn*
(*middag*)*maal doen met* • (~ *out*)
buitenshuis dineren
diner [znw] • *restauratiewagen* • *eter*
• <AE> *klein* (*weg*)*restaurant*
dingy [bnw] *vuil, smerig*
dinner [znw] *diner, middagmaal*
dinosaur [znw] *dinosaurus*
dip I [ov ww] • (*onder*)*dompelen*
• *dimmen* <v. koplampen> II [on ww]
(*even*) *duiken* III [znw] • *het*
(*onder*)*dompelen* • *bad* • (*dip*)*saus*
diphtheria [znw] *difterie*
diplomacy [znw] *diplomatie*
diplomat, diplomatist [znw]
diplomaat
diplomatic [bnw] *diplomatisch*
dipper [znw] *pollepel*
dire [bnw] *gruwelijk*
direct I [ov ww] • *regisseren* • *richten,*
adresseren <v. post> • *aanwijzingen*
geven II [bnw] • *rechtstreeks* • *zonder*
omwegen • *oprecht*
direction [znw] • *richting* • *bestuur*

• *regie*
directional [bnw] *richtings-*
directive I [znw] *richtlijn* II [bnw]
leidend
directly [bijw] • *rechtstreeks* • *meteen,*
dadelijk
director [znw] • *regisseur*
• *commissaris* <v. NV> • *bestuurder*
• *adviseur* • *directeur, hoofd* <v.
afdeling>
directorate [znw] *raad v.*
commissarissen
directorship [znw] *directeurschap*
directory I [znw] *gids, adresboek*
II [bnw] *adviserend*
dirge [znw] *klaagzang*
dirt [znw] • *vuil* • *drek* • *modder, drab*
• *grond, aarde*
dirty I [ov ww] *bevuilen* II [bnw] *vuil*
disable [ov ww] • *onbekwaam maken*
• *buiten gevecht stellen*
disadvantage I [ov ww] *benadelen*
II [znw] *nadeel*
disadvantageous [bnw] *nadelig*
disaffection [znw] • *afvalligheid*
• *ontrouw*
disagree [on ww] • *het oneens zijn*
• *niet passen bij*
disagreeable [bnw] *onaangenaam*
disagreement [znw] • *meningsverschil*
• *verschil*
disappoint [ov ww] *teleurstellen*
disappointing [bnw] *teleurstellend,*
tegenvallend
disappointment [znw] *teleurstelling*
disapprove [ov + on ww] • (~ *of*)
afkeuren
disarm I [ov + on ww] *ontwapenen*
II [ov ww] *ontmantelen*
disarrange [ov ww] *in de war brengen*
disarray [znw] *wanorde*
disaster [znw] • *narigheid* • *ramp*
disavow [ov ww] • *ontkennen,*
loochenen • *verwerpen*
disband I [ov ww] *ontbinden*
II [on ww] • z. *ontbinden* • *ontbonden*

worden
disbelief [znw] *ongeloof*
disc [znw] • *grammofoonplaat*
• *parkeerschijf* • *rond bord* • *discus*
• *schijf* • *schotelantenne*
discard [ov ww] • *verwerpen* • *afdanken*
discern [ov ww] • *bespeuren,*
waarnemen • *onderscheiden*
discernible [bnw] *waarneembaar*
discerning [bnw] *scherpzinnig*
discernment [znw] • *vermogen om te*
onderscheiden • *inzicht*
discharge I [ov ww] • *afschieten*
• *ontlasten* • *lossen* • *betalen*
• *ontheffen, ontslaan* • *lozen* II [znw]
• *schot* • *ontslag*
disciple [znw] *leerling, volgeling*
disciplinarian [znw] *tuchtmeester*
disciplinary [bnw] *disciplinair*
disclaim [ov ww] *niet erkennen,*
afwijzen
disclaimer [znw] *ontkenning,*
afwijzing
disclose [ov ww] *onthullen*
discolour I [ov ww] *doen verkleuren*
II [on ww] *verkleuren, verschieten*
discomfit [ov ww] *in verlegenheid*
brengen
discomfiture [znw] *verwarring*
discomfort [znw] • *onbehaaglijkheid*
• *ongemak*
disconcert [ov ww] • *verwarren*
• *ontstellen*
disconnect [ov ww] • *verbinding*
verbreken • *verband verbreken*
• *uitschakelen*
disconsolate [bnw] • *troosteloos*
• *ontroostbaar*
discontent [znw] *ontevredenheid*
discontinue I [ov ww] • *opzeggen*
• *opheffen* II [on ww] • *niet voortzetten*
• *ophouden*
discontinuity [znw] • *onderbreking*
• *discontinuïteit*
discontinuous [bnw] *onderbroken,*
niet doorgaand

discord, discordance [znw]
• *tweedracht* • *wanklank*
discordant [bnw] • *strijdig*
• *wanklanken producerend*
discount I [ov ww] • *korten* • *buiten*
beschouwing laten • *weinig*
geloof/belang hechten aan II [znw]
korting
discourage [ov ww] • *ontmoedigen*
• *afschrikken*
discouragement [znw] *moedeloosheid*
discourse I [on ww] *converseren*
II [znw] • *verhandeling* • *rede* • *preek*
discover [ov ww] *ontdekken*
discoverer [znw] *ontdekker, uitvinder*
discovery [znw] *ontdekking*
discredit I [ov ww] • *niet geloven* • *in*
diskrediet brengen II [znw] • *schande,*
diskrediet • *opspraak*
discreditable [bnw] *schandelijk*
discreet [bnw] • *discreet* • *stemmig*
discrepancy [znw] *discrepantie*
discrete [bnw] • *afzonderlijk* • *zonder*
samenhang
discretion [znw] • *discretie*
• *geheimhouding* • *wijsheid, beleid,*
tact, voorzichtigheid
discriminate I [ov ww] *onderscheiden,*
herkennen II [on ww] *onderscheid in*
acht nemen • (~ **against**) *onderscheid*
maken (ten nadele van)
discriminating [bnw] *scherpzinnig*
discrimination [znw] • *discriminatie*
• *onderscheidingsvermogen* • *inzicht,*
doorzicht
discursive [bnw] • *logisch* • *uitweidend*
discuss [ov ww] *bespreken*
discussion [znw] *discussie*
disdain I [ov ww] *verachten* II [znw]
minachting
disdainful [bnw] *minachtend,*
hooghartig
disease [znw] • *ziekte* • *kwaal*
disembark [ov + on ww] (z.) *ontschepen*
disembowel [ov ww] • *ontweien*
• *openrijten*

disengage [ov + on ww] (z.) *vrijmaken*
disentangle [ov + on ww] (z.)
ontwarren
disgorge I [ov ww] *uitbraken,*
uitstorten II [on ww] z. *uitstorten*
disgrace I [ov ww] • *in ongenade doen*
vallen • *degraderen* • *te schande maken*
• *ontsieren* II [znw] • *ongenade*
• *schande*
disguise I [ov ww] *vermommen,*
onherkenbaar maken II [znw]
vermomming
disgust I [ov ww] *doen walgen* II [znw]
afschuw
dish I [ov ww] *opdienen* II [znw]
• *schotel, schaal* • *schotelantenne*
• *gerecht*
dishonest [bnw] *oneerlijk*
dishonesty [znw] *oneerlijkheid*
dishonourable [bnw] *schandelijk*
disillusion I [ov ww] *ontgoochelen*
II [znw] *ontgoocheling*
disinclination [znw] *tegenzin*
disinfect [ov ww] *ontsmetten*
disinfectant I [znw] *ontsmettend*
middel II [bnw] *ontsmettend*
disingenuous [bnw] *onoprecht*
disinherit [ov ww] *onterven*
disinterested [bnw] • *belangeloos*
• *onbevooroordeeld* • *ongeïnteresseerd*
disjointed [bnw] *onsamenhangend*
dislike I [ov ww] *een hekel hebben aan,*
niet mogen II [znw] *afkeer*
dislocate [ov ww] • *ontwrichten*
• *verplaatsen*
dislocation [znw] • *dislokatie*
• *ontwrichting*
dislodge I [ov ww] *loswrikken*
II [on ww] z. *losmaken*
disloyal [bnw] *trouweloos*
disloyalty [znw] *trouweloosheid*
dismal [mv] [bnw] *akelig, naar, triest*
dismay I [ov ww] *totaal ontmoedigen,*
ontstellen II [znw] *ontzetting,*
verslagenheid
dismember [ov ww] *aan stukken*
hakken
dismiss [ov ww] • *wegzenden*
• *ontslaan* • *van z. afzetten*
dismissal [znw] • *wegzending*
• *verwerping* • *ontslag*
dismount [on ww] *afstijgen, afstappen*
disobedience [znw]
ongehoorzaamheid
disobedient [bnw] *ongehoorzaam*
disobey [ov + on ww] *ongehoorzaam*
zijn
disorder [znw] • *oproer* • *wanorde*
• *ongesteldheid, kwaal* • *ontregeling*
disorderly [bnw] • *wanordelijk*
• *oproerig*
disorganize [ov ww] • *ontwrichten*
• *ontredderen*
disown [ov ww] • *(ver)loochenen*
• *verwerpen* • *ontkennen*
disparage [ov ww] • *kleineren*
• *afgeven op*
disparaging [bnw] *geringschattend,*
kleinerend
disparate [bnw] *wezenlijk verschillend*
disparity [znw] *(essentieel) verschil*
dispassionate [bnw] • *onpartijdig*
• *bedaard, koel*
dispatch I [ov ww] • *uit de weg ruimen*
• *goed en snel afdoen* • *vlug opeten*
• *(met spoed) verzenden* II [znw]
• *depêche* • *nota* • *spoed* • *sterfgeval*
dispel [ov ww] *verdrijven*
dispensable [bnw] *niet noodzakelijk*
dispensary [znw]
(fonds-/huis)apotheek
dispensation [znw] *dispensatie*
dispense [on ww] • *uitdelen*
• *toedienen* • *(~ from) vrijstellen van*
• *(~ with) het (kunnen) stellen zonder*
dispenser [znw] • *apotheker*
• *automaat* • *doseerbuisje, houder*
disperse I [ov ww] • *verspreiden*
• *verjagen* II [on ww] • z. *verspreiden*
• *uiteen gaan*
displace [ov ww] • *verplaatsen*
• *verdringen*

displacement [znw] verplaatsing
display I [ov ww] • (ver)tonen
• ontplooien • aan de dag leggen
II [znw] • beeldscherm • uitstalling
• visueel hulpmiddel
displease [ov ww] mishagen
disposable I [znw] wegwerpartikel
II [bnw] • beschikbaar • wegwerp-
disposal [znw] regeling, stemming
dispose [on ww] • (~ of) verkopen,
beschikken over, afdoen (met),
tenietdoen
disposition [znw] neiging, aard,
gezindheid
dispossess [ov ww] • onterven
• onteigenen
disproportion [znw] onevenredigheid
disproportionate [bnw] onevenredig
disprove [ov ww] weerleggen
disputation [znw] dispuut, discussie
dispute I [ov ww] betwisten II [on ww]
redetwisten III [znw] geschil
disqualification [znw] diskwalificatie
disqualify [ov ww] diskwalificeren
disquiet I [ov ww] onrustig maken
II [znw] • ongerustheid • onrust
III [bnw] onrustig
disregard I [ov ww] negéren, z. niets
aantrekken van II [znw]
veronachtzaming
disrepair [znw] vervallen staat
disreputable [bnw] • berucht,
schandelijk • onfatsoenlijk
disrepute [znw] diskrediet
disrespect [znw] gebrek aan eerbied
disrespectful [bnw] oneerbiedig,
onbeschaamd
disrupt [ov ww] ontwrichten
disruption [znw] ontwrichting
disruptive [bnw] ontwrichtend
dissatisfaction [znw] ontevredenheid
dissect [ov ww] ontleden
dissemble I [ov ww] • verhullen
• veinzen • verbergen II [on ww]
huichelen
disseminate [ov ww] verspreiden

dissension [znw] onenigheid
dissent I [on ww] verschillen v. mening
II [znw] verschil v. inzicht
dissenter [znw] andersdenkende
dissertation [znw] verhandeling
disservice [znw] slechte dienst
dissident I [znw] andersdenkende
II [bnw] andersdenkend
dissimilar [bnw] ongelijk
dissimilarity, dissimilitude [znw]
• verschil • ongelijkheid
dissimulate [ov + on ww] • huichelen
• verbergen
dissipate I [ov ww] • verdrijven • doen
verdwijnen • verspillen, verkwisten
II [on ww] verdwijnen
dissipated [bnw] liederlijk
dissipation [znw] losbandigheid
dissociate [ov ww] • (~ from) los
maken/zien van
dissolute [bnw] losbandig
dissolution [znw] • ontbinding • dood
dissolve I [ov ww] • oplossen
• ontbinden, opheffen II [on ww] • z.
oplossen • z. ontbinden
dissonance [znw] • wanklank
• onenigheid
dissuade [ov ww] afraden
distance [znw] • verte • afstand
distant [bnw] • ver (weg) • hautain
distaste [znw] • afkeer • tegenzin
distasteful [bnw] • onaangenaam
• onsmakelijk
distemper [znw] • dierenziekte
• tempera • muurverf
distend [ov + on ww] (doen) opzwellen
distension [znw] zwelling
distil [ov ww] • distilleren • zuiveren
distillery [znw] distilleerderij, stokerij
distinct [bnw] • duidelijk • apart
• onderscheiden
distinction [znw] • onderscheid(ing)
• voornaamheid, aanzien • apartheid
distinctive [bnw] • onderscheidend
• kenmerkend
distinguish I [ov ww] onderscheiden

II [on ww] • (~ **among/between**) *onderscheid maken tussen*

distinguishable [bnw] • *(goed) te onderscheiden* • *duidelijk waarneembaar*

distortion [znw] *vervorming*

distract [ov ww] • *afleiden* • *verwarren, verbijsteren*

distraction [znw] • *afleiding* • *ontspanning* • *waanzin* • *verwarring*

distress I [ov ww] • *benauwen* • *smart veroorzaken aan* II [znw] • *pijn* • *angst* • *nood, ellende* • *uitputting*

distressing [bnw] • *pijn/angst veroorzakend* • *verontrustend*

distribution [znw] *distributie, verspreiding*

distributor [znw] • *groothandelaar* • *verdeler*

district [znw] • *district, streek, gebied* • *wijk*

distrust I [ov ww] *wantrouwen* II [znw] *wantrouwen*

distrustful [bnw] *wantrouwig*

disturb [ov ww] • *(ver)storen* • *in beroering brengen*

disturbance [znw] *verstoring*

disuse [znw] *onbruik*

ditch I [ov ww] *achterlaten, in de steek laten* II [znw] *sloot, greppel*

dither I [on ww] *treuzelen* II [znw] *opgewonden toestand*

ditto [znw] *dezelfde, hetzelfde*

ditty [znw] *deuntje, wijsje*

diurnal [bnw] • *overdag* • *gedurende de dag*

divan [znw] *divan*

dive I [on ww] *duiken* II [znw] *duik*

divergent [bnw] • *divergent* • *afwijkend*

diverse [bnw] *verschillend*

diversify [ov ww] • *variëren, afwisselen* • *wijzigen*

diversion [znw] • *afleidingsmanoeuvre* • *omlegging* • *verstrooiing*

diversity [znw] • *variatie*

• *verscheidenheid*

divert [ov ww] • *een andere richting of wending geven* • *afleiden* • *vermaken*

divide I [ov ww] • *verdelen, (in)delen* • *scheiden* II [on ww] z. *verdelen*

divination [znw] • *voorspelling* • *waarzeggerij*

divinity [znw] • *goddelijkheid* • *god(heid)* • *godgeleerdheid*

division [znw] • *stemming* <voor of tegen> • *afdeling* • *branche* • *groep* • *divisie* • *district, wijk*

divorce I [ov ww] *scheiden van* II [znw] *echtscheiding*

divulge [ov ww] *openbaar (bekend) maken*

dizzy I [ov ww] *duizelig maken* II [bnw] *duizelig*

do I [ov ww] • *doen* • *maken* • *(gaar) koken, bereiden* • *spelen (voor)* • *uitputten, moe maken* • *ertussen nemen* • (~ **for**) <sl.> *ruïneren/doden* • (~ **in**) <inf.> *van kant maken* • (~ **up**) *opknappen, vastmaken* II [on ww] • *doen* • *deugen, genoeg zijn, (ermee door) gaan* • (~ **away with**) *afschaffen, van kant maken* • (~ **by/to**) *behandelen* • (~ **for**) *dienen als* • (~ **without**) *ontberen, niet nodig hebben* III [znw] • *fuif* • <muz.> *do*

doc <sl.> [znw] → **doctor**

docile [bnw] • *gedwee* • *volgzaam*

dock I [ov ww] • *korten* • *dokken, binnengaan* II [on ww] *meren, dokken* III [znw] • *dok* • *haven* • *beklaagdenbank* • *zuring* • *staartwortel*

docker [znw] *dokwerker, havenarbeider*

docket I [ov ww] *labelen* II [znw] *korte inhoudsaanduiding* <op document>

doctor I [ov ww] • *de graad van doctor verlenen* • *behandelen* • *dokteren (aan)* II [znw] • *dokter* • *doctor, geleerde*

doctrinal [bnw] *leerstellig*

document I [ov ww] *documenteren*

II [znw] *document, bewijsstuk*
documentary [znw] *documentaire*
documentation [znw] *documentatie*
dodder I [on ww] • *beven*
• *(voort)sukkelen* II [znw] *warkruid*
dodge I [ov ww] • *ontwijken* • *handig ontduiken* II [on ww] *uitwijken*
III [znw] • *ontwijkende beweging*
• *smoesje* • *truc, foefje*
dodger [znw] • *slimme vos* • <AE> *strooibiljet*
dodgy [bnw] *gehaaid, slinks*
does [ww] → **do**
dog I [ov ww] *achtervolgen* II [znw]
• *hond* • *mannetjeswolf, mannetjesvos*
• *kerel*
dogged [bnw] • *hardnekkig, koppig*
• *nors*
doggerel [znw] *kreupel vers, rijmelarij*
dogmatic [bnw] • *dogmatisch*
• *autoritair*
dogmatism [znw] *dogmatisme, dogmatiek*
do-gooder <iron.> [znw] *wereldverbeteraar*
do-it-yourself [bnw] *doe-het-zelf*
dole I [ov ww] • *(~ out) (karig) uitdelen* II [znw] • *steun* • *aalmoes*
doleful [bnw] • *somber, akelig*
• *smartelijk*
doll I [wkd ww] • *(~ up) z. opdirken*
II [znw] *pop*
dollop [znw] • *kwak* • *scheut*
dolphin [znw] • *dolfijn* • *dukdalf*
dolt [znw] *dommerd, stommeling*
domain [znw] *gebied, domein*
dome [znw] • *koepel* • *gewelf*
domed [bnw] *koepelvormig*
domesticity [znw] *het huiselijke leven*
domicile [znw] *woonplaats, domicilie*
dominance [znw] *dominantie*
dominant [bnw] *dominant*
dominate I [ov ww] *overheersen*
II [on ww] • *heersen, domineren* • *de overhand hebben*
domineering [bnw] *bazig*

dominion [znw] • *heerschappij*
• *eigendomsrecht*
domino [znw] *domino(steen)*
don I [ov ww] *aantrekken* <v. kleren>
II [znw] *docent aan een universiteit*
donate [ov ww] • *begiftigen* • *schenken*
donation [znw] *schenking, gift*
done [ww] *volt. deelw.* → **do**
donkey [znw] *ezel*
donor [znw] • *donor* • *donateur, schenker*
don't [samentr.] /do not/ → **do**
doodle I [on ww] *poppetjes tekenen*
II [znw] *krabbel*
doom I [ov ww] *doemen, veroordelen*
II [znw] *ondergang*
door [znw] *deur*
dope I [ov ww] *toedienen* • *(~ out) ontdekken* • *(~ up) behandelen met dope* II [znw] • *sufferd* • *tip, inlichting*
• *doping* • <sl.> *dope, heroïne*
dopey [bnw] • *(ver)suf(t)* • *dom*
dormant [bnw] • *latent* • *slapend, ongebruikt*
dormitory [znw] • *slaapzaal*
• *woonwijk*
dormouse [znw] *relmuis*
dorsal [bnw] *van/aan de rug, rug-*
dosage [znw] • *dosering* • *dosis*
dose I [ov ww] • *doseren* • *een dosis geven* II [znw] *dosis*
dot I [ov ww] • *punten plaatsen op*
• *stippelen* II [znw] *stip, punt*
double I [ov ww] • *verdubbelen*
• *dubbelslaan, dubbelvouwen*
• *doubleren* • *een dubbelrol spelen*
II [on ww] • *(~ back) omdraaien en terugkomen* • *(~ up) ineenkrimpen* <v. pijn>, *een kamer delen* III [znw] • *'t dubbele* • *dubbelganger, duplicaat, doublure* • *dubbelspel* • *looppas*
IV [bnw + bijw] • *dubbel* • *niet oprecht*
doubly [bijw] *dubbel, extra*
doubt I [ov + on ww] *twijfelen* II [znw]
• *twijfel* • *onzekerheid*
doubtful [bnw] • *weifelend*

• *bedenkelijk, precair*
doubtless [bijw] *ongetwijfeld*
dough [znw] • *deeg* • *poen*
dour [bnw] *streng, hard, koel,*
ongenaakbaar
douse [ov ww] → **dowse**
dove [znw] *duif(je)*
dovetail I [ov + on ww] • *met*
zwaluwstaarten verbinden • *in elkaar*
sluiten II [znw] *zwaluwstaart <in*
timmervak>
dowager [znw] *douairière*
dowdy [bnw] *smakeloos gekleed*
dowel [znw] *deuvel*
down I [znw] • *dons* • *tegenslag*
• *hooggelegen land* II [bnw]
benedenwaarts III [bijw] • *neer, onder,*
(naar) beneden, af • *stroomafwaarts*
IV [vz] *langs, (naar beneden) in, van ...*
af
downy [bnw] *donzig*
dowry [znw] • *bruidsschat* • *talent, gave*
dowse I [ov ww] • *uitdoen <v. licht>*
• *natgooien* II [on ww] *met de*
wichelroede lopen
doyen [znw] *nestor, oudste*
doze I [on ww] *dutten, soezen* • *(~ off)*
indutten II [znw] *sluimering*
dozen [znw] *dozijn*
dozy <inf.> [bnw] *soezerig, loom,*
slaperig
drab [bnw] • *vaalbruin* • *saai, eentonig*
draft I [ov ww] • *ontwerpen, opstellen,*
schetsen • *detacheren* • *inlijven* II [znw]
• *trekking <v. wissel>* • *detachement*
• *schets, ontwerp, concept, klad* • *het*
trekken <v. wissel> • *wissel, cheque*
• *tocht <luchtstroom>* • *<AE>*
dienstplicht
drag I [ov ww] • *trekken* • *dreggen*
• *(~ down) omlaaghalen <ook fig.>,*
deprimeren • *(~ out) rekken, eruit*
trekken, ophalen met dreg II [on ww]
• *niet opschieten* • *slepen* • *dreggen*
• *(~ on) (z.) voortslepen* III [znw]
• *dreg* • *sleepnet*

dragon [znw] *draak*
dragoon [znw] *dragonder, huzaar*
drain I [ov ww] • *afwateren,*
droogleggen, draineren, rioleren
• *leegmaken, opmaken* • *uitputten*
• *aftappen, afgieten* II [on ww]
• *leeglopen* • *wegtrekken* • *afwateren*
III [znw] *afvoerbuis, afvoerpijp, riool*
drainage [znw] *afgevoerd water,*
rioolwater
drake [znw] *woerd*
drama [znw] • *toneel* • *toneelstuk*
• *drama*
dramatist [znw] *toneelschrijver*
dramatize I [ov ww] • *dramatiseren*
• *voor toneel bewerken* II [on ww] *z.*
aanstellen
drank [ww] *verl. tijd* → **drink**
drape [ov ww] • *bekleden* • *draperen*
• *omfloersen*
draper [znw] *manufacturier*
drapery [znw] *manufacturen(zaak)*
drastic [bnw] • *drastisch, doortastend*
• *ingrijpend*
draught [znw] • *teug, slok* • *tocht,*
zucht
draughtsman [znw] • *tekenaar*
• *damschijf*
draughty [bnw] *tochtig*
draw I [ov + on ww] • *tekenen, schetsen*
• *trekken* • *(op)halen, binnenhalen,*
uithalen • *lot trekken, winnen*
• *(~ (up)on) gebruik maken van*
• *(~ out) (uit)rekken* • *(~ up)*
vóórrijden, optrekken, opstellen, tot
staan brengen/komen II [ov ww]
• *klanten trekken* • *aftappen* • *uithoren*
• *(~ forth) te voorschijn halen*
III [on ww] *pistool/zwaard trekken*
• *(~ apart) uiteendrijven* • *(~ away)*
terugwijken • *(~ back) terugdeinzen,*
terugwijken • *(~ near) naderen*
IV [znw] • *gelijkspel* • *opmerking om*
iem. uit te horen • *het trekken* • *vangst*
• *successtuk, succesnummer,*
succesartikel • *loterijtrekking*

drawer [znw] lade
drawing [znw] tekening
drawl I [on ww] lijzig spreken II [znw] lijzige manier van praten
drawn I [ww] volt. deelw. → **draw** II [bnw] * ~ face lang gezicht
dreadful [bnw] vreselijk
dream I [ov + on ww] dromen II [znw] droom
dreamer [znw] dromer
drear(y) [bnw] akelig, somber
dredge I [ov + on ww] • dreggen • baggeren II [znw] • sleepnet • dreg • baggermachine
dredger [znw] baggermachine
dregs [mv] bezinksel
drench [ov ww] doorweken
dress I [ov ww] • kleden • kostumeren • optuigen • aanmaken <v. etenswaren> • bereiden • verbinden <v. wond> • (~ down) een aframmeling/schrobbering geven • (~ up) opsmukken II [on ww] • toilet maken • z. (aan)kleden • <mil.> z. richten • (~ down) z. zeer eenvoudig kleden • (~ out) z. uitdossen • (~ up) z. verkleden, z. opdirken III [znw] • kleding • avondkleding, rok • japon, jurk
dresser [znw] • soort kast • <AE> toilettafel
dressing [znw] • (sla)saus • verband(stoffen)
dressy [bnw] • chic • pronkziek
drew [ww] verl. tijd → **draw**
dribble I [ov + on ww] • druppelen • <sport> dribbelen (met) II [on ww] kwijlen III [znw] • stroompje • dribbel <bij voetbal>
drier I [znw] droger II [bnw] vergr. trap → **dry**
drift I [on ww] • afdrijven • afwijken • z. laten meeslepen • (z.) ophopen • doelloos rondzwalken • (~ apart) van elkaar vervreemden II [znw] • stroom, koers • strekking • neiging, hang

• afwijking • opeenhoping, drijvende massa
drifter [znw] iem. die doelloos rondzwalkt
drill I [ov ww] • drillen, africhten • doorboren • (~ in(to)) erin stampen II [on ww] • boren • stampen <v. leerstof> • oefenen III [znw] • drilboor • exercitie, het africhten • oefening • dril <stof> • drilaap
drink I [ov ww] (op)drinken • (~ in) gretig in z. opnemen • (~ up) opdrinken II [on ww] drinken • (~ to) drinken op • (~ up) leegdrinken III [znw] • dronk • borrel • drank
drinker [znw] • drinker • alcoholist
drip I [ov ww] laten druppelen II [on ww] druppelen • (~ with) druipen van III [znw] • druppel • infusie
dripping [znw] braadvet
drive I [ov ww] • slaan <v. bal, paal> • drijven, aandrijven, voortdrijven, (aan)jagen • (be)sturen, mennen • (~ in(to)) aanzetten tot/om te II [on ww] rijden • (~ at) bedoelen • (~ up) vóórrijden, oprijden III [znw] • rit, tocht • drijfjacht • slag • energie • rijweg, oprijlaan
drivel [on ww] • kwijlen • kletspraat verkopen
driven [ww] volt. deelw. → **drive**
driver [znw] • koetsier, voerman, chauffeur, bestuurder • machinist
dromedary [znw] dromedaris
drool <AE> [on ww] kwijlen
droop [on ww] • (neer)hangen, kwijnen • de moed verliezen
drop I [ov ww] • laten vallen • droppen • vergieten • niet doorzetten, laten verlopen • verliezen • afzetten • afgeven II [on ww] vallen • (~ away) afvallen, een voor een weggaan • (~ behind) achter(op) raken • (~ by) even langskomen, binnenwippen • (~ in) eens komen aanlopen • (~ off)

in slaap komen, insluimeren • (~ **out**)
uitvallen, wegraken III [znw] • *druppel*
• *zuurtje* • *borreltje, slokje* • *helling
naar beneden, daling, achteruitgang,
(ver)val* • *scherm* <v. toneel>
droppings [mv] *uitwerpselen*
dross [znw] • *metaalslak(ken)*
• *verontreiniging(en)*
drought [znw] *droogte*
drove I [ww] *verl. tijd* → **drive**
II [znw] *samengedreven kudde, menigte*
drown I [ov ww] • *verdrinken*
• *overstromen* • *overstemmen* • (~ **out**)
*overstemmen, met water
verdrijven/uitdrijven, overschreeuwen*
II [on ww] • *verdrinken* • *overstromen*
drowse [on ww] *dutten, soezen*
drowsy [bnw] • *slaperig*
• *slaapverwekkend*
drudge I [on ww] *zwoegen* II [znw]
werkezel, zwoeger
drudgery [znw] • *'t zwoegen* • *saai
werk*
drug I [ov ww] • *bedwelmende
middelen toedienen* • *een drug mengen
in* II [znw] • *medicijn, drankje*
• *bedwelmend middel, drug*
drum I [ov + on ww] *trommelen*
II [znw] • *trom* • *tamboer* • *cilinder*
• *grote bus* • *draadklos* • *(metalen) vat*
• *olievat*
drummer [znw] *tromslager, tamboer*
drunk I [ww] *volt. deelw.* → **drink**
II [znw] *dronkenman* III [bnw] *dronken*
drunkard [znw] *dronkaard*
drunken [bnw] *dronken*
dry I [ov ww] • (~ **out**) *door en door
droog laten worden, laten afkicken,
uitdrogen* II [on ww] *door en door
droog worden, afkicken* • (~ **up**)
verdrinken, verdorren, vastzitten <v.
toneelspeler> III [bnw] • *droog* • *sec,
niet zoet* • *nuchter* • *saai*
dryer [znw] *droger, (haar)droogkap*
dubious [bnw] *twijfelachtig*
duchess [znw] *hertogin*

duchy [znw] *hertogdom*
duck I [ov ww] *onderdompelen*
II [on ww] • *onderduiken* • *z. bukken*
• (~ **out**) *er onderuit komen, ontkomen
(aan)* III [znw] • *eend(en)* • *schat* • *duik*
duckling [znw] *jonge eend*
duct [znw] *(afvoer)kanaal, afvoerbuis*
dud <sl.> [znw] • *blindganger*
• *vogelverschrikker* • *prul, fiasco* • *valse
cheque, vals bankbiljet*
dudgeon [znw] • *kwaadheid* • *wrok*
due I [znw] *wat iem. toekomt* II [bnw]
• *(ver)schuldig(d)* • *behoorlijk, gepast*
duel I [on ww] *duelleren* II [znw] *duel*
duet [znw] • *duet* • *paar*
duffer [znw] *sufferd, stomkop*
dug I [ww] *verl.tijd + volt.deelw.*
→ **dig** II [znw] *uier* <v. zoogdier>
duke [znw] • *hertog* • <sl.> *vuist*
dukedom [znw] *hertogdom*
dull I [ov ww] *somber maken* II [on ww]
somber worden III [bnw] • *saai* • *dom*
• *stompzinnig, idioot* • *bot, stomp*
• *lusteloos* • *somber* • *dof*
duly [bijw] → **due**
dumb [bnw] • *dom* • *stom, sprakeloos*
• *zwijgzaam*
dummy I [znw] • *lege verpakking*
• *fopspeen* • *pop* <op schietbaan> • *pop,
modepop, kostuumpop* • *blinde* <bij
kaartspel> • *figurant, stroman*
• *stommerd* • *exercitiepatroon* II [bnw]
namaak-
dump I [ov ww] • *neergooien* • *storten*
<v. vuil> II [znw] • *opslagplaats*
• *vuilnisbelt* • <sl.> *huis, kamer*
dumpling [znw] • *(appel)bol*
• *dikkerdje*
dumpy [bnw] • *kort, gezet* • *dwars*
• *verdrietig*
dun [bnw] *grijsbruin, vaal*
dunce [znw] *domkop, uilskuiken,
stommeling*
dune [znw] *duin*
dung I [ov ww] *bemesten* II [znw] *mest*
dunk [ov ww] *dopen, soppen*

duo [znw] • duo, paar • duet
duodenum [znw] twaalfvingerige
darm
dupe I [ov ww] beetnemen II [znw]
• dupe, gedupeerde • onnozele hals
duplex [bnw] tweevoudig, dubbel
duplicate I [ov ww] kopiëren,
dupliceren II [znw] duplicaat, kopie
III [bnw] dubbel
duplicator [znw] kopieermachine
duplicity [znw] onbetrouwbaarheid
durable [bnw] duurzaam
duress(e) [znw] • vrijheidsberoving
• dwang
during [vz] gedurende
dusk [znw] schemering
dusky [bnw] duister, donker <v. kleur>,
schemerig
dust I [ov ww] • afstoffen, afkloppen
• bestuiven, stoffig maken
• (~ down/off) afkloppen, afstoffen
• (~ off) afstoffen, afranselen II [znw]
• stof • stuifmeel • pegels, geld
duster [znw] • stofjas • stofdoek
dusty [bnw] • stoffig • dor
Dutch [bnw] Nederlands
duty [znw] • plicht • functie, dienst
dwarf I [ov ww] nietig doen lijken
II [znw] dwerg
dwell [on ww] • wonen • verblijven
dwelling [znw] woning
dwindle [on ww] afnemen, kwijnen,
achteruitgaan
dying [bnw] stervend, sterf-
dyke [znw] → dike
dynamic I [znw] stuwkracht II [bnw]
dynamisch, energiek
dynamism [znw] • dynamisme
• dynamiek
dynamite I [ov ww] met dynamiet
vernielen II [znw] dynamiet
dynasty [znw] dynastie
dysentery [znw] dysenterie

E

each [onb vnw] elk
ear [znw] • oor • gehoor • aar
earl [znw] graaf
early [bnw + bijw] vroeg
earn [ov ww] • verdienen • behalen
earnest I [znw] ernst II [bnw] ijverig,
ernstig
earth I [ov ww] <techn.> aarden
II [znw] • aarde, grond • hol <v. dieren>
earthen [bnw] van aarde(werk)
earthly [bnw] aards
earthy [bnw] laag-bij-de-gronds,
platvloers
ease I [ov ww] • op zijn gemak stellen,
vergemakkelijken • verlichten • losser
maken • vieren II [on ww] • (~ off)
gemakkelijker worden, afnemen <in
ernst> III [znw] gemak
easily [bijw] → easy
east I [znw] het oosten II [bnw] oost
easterly [bnw + bijw] oostelijk
easy [bnw + bijw] • gemakkelijk
• meegaand • ongedwongen
eat I [ov + on ww] • (op)eten • verteren
• (~ up) helemaal opeten, verslinden
<ook fig.> II [on ww] • (~ away)
wegteren, verteren • (~ into)
wegvreten, invreten, uitbijten • (~ out)
buitenshuis eten
eatable [bnw] eetbaar
eater [znw] • eter • handappel/-peer
eaves [mv] onderste dakrand
ebb I [on ww] teruglopen, afnemen
II [znw] • eb • verval, het afnemen
ebullient [bnw] kokend, (op)bruisend
eccentric I [znw] zonderling,
excentriekeling II [bnw] • excentrisch
• onregelmatig • zonderling
eccentricity [znw] excentriciteit
ecclesiastic [znw] geestelijke
ecclesiastical [bnw] kerkelijk

eclipse I [ov ww] • *verduisteren*
• *overschaduwen* II [znw]
• *verduistering* • *verdwijning*
ecological [bnw] *ecologisch*
ecology [znw] *ecologie*
economics [mv] *economie*
economist [znw] *econoom*
economize [ov ww] • *spaarzaam
beheren* • *bezuinigen (op)*
economy [znw] • *economie,
huishoudkunde* • *spaarzaamheid*
• *besparing*
ecstasy [znw] *extase, geestvervoering*
ecstatic [bnw] *in vervoering*
ecumenical [bnw] *oecumenisch*
eczema [znw] *eczeem, huiduitslag*
eddy I [ov + on ww] *dwarrelen* II [znw]
• *draaikolk* • *dwarreling*
edge I [ov ww] *begrenzen* II [on ww]
• *zich in (schuine) richting bewegen*
• *langzaam vorderen* • *(~ away)*
<scheepv.> *afhouden* • *(~ on)
langzaam vooruitkomen, aanzetten*
III [znw] • *scherpe kant* • *rand* • *sne(d)e*
edging [znw] *rand, franje*
edgy [bnw] • *scherp* • *met scherpe
contouren* • *zenuwachtig* • *ongedurig*
edible I [znw] II [bnw] *eetbaar*
edict [znw] *edict, bevelschrift*
edifice [znw] *gebouw*
edify [ov ww] *geestelijk verheffen*
edit [ov ww] • *bewerken en doen
uitgeven* • *redactie voeren* • *monteren*
<v. film of geluidsband> • *verfraaien,
aanpassen* • *(~ out) schrappen*
edition [znw] *editie*
editor [znw] • *bewerker* • *redacteur*
editorial I [znw] *hoofdartikel* II [bnw]
redactioneel
educate [ov ww] • *onderwijzen*
• *opvoeden*
education [znw] *opleiding*
educational [bnw] • *m.b.t. de
opleiding* • *leerzaam*
educator [znw] *opvoeder*
eel [znw] *paling, aal(tje)*

efface [ov ww] • *uitwissen* • *in de
schaduw stellen*
effect I [ov ww] • *teweeg brengen* • *tot
stand brengen* II [znw] *effect*
effective I [znw] <AE> *soldaat in
werkelijke dienst* II [bnw] *doeltreffend,
werkzaam*
effectual [bnw] • *doeltreffend* • *bindend*
effeminate [bnw] *verwijfd*
effervescent [bnw] • *borrelend*
• *bruisend*
effete [bnw] *uitgeput, versleten*
efficacious [bnw] • *werkzaam*
• *probaat*
efficacy [znw] • *uitwerking*
• *doeltreffendheid*
efficiency [znw] *efficiëntie*
efficient [bnw] • *bekwaam*
• *voortvarend* • *doeltreffend, doelmatig*
• *krachtig* • *economisch*
effigy [znw] *(af)beeld(ing), beeldenaar*
effort [znw] • *poging*
• *(krachts)inspanning*
effortless [bnw] *moeiteloos,
ongedwongen*
effrontery [znw] *onbeschaamdheid*
effusion [znw] *uitstorting,
ontboezeming*
egg I [ov ww] • *(~ on) aanzetten,
ophitsen* II [znw] *ei*
egoism [znw] *zelfzucht*
egoist [znw] *egoïst*
egotism [znw] • *egocentrisme* • *egoïsme*
egotist [znw] • *egoïst* • *egocentrisch
persoon*
Egyptian I [znw] *Egyptenaar* II [bnw]
Egyptisch
eh [tw] *hè*
eight [telw] *acht*
eighteen [telw] *achttien*
eighth [telw] *achtste*
eightieth [telw] *tachtigste*
eighty [telw] *tachtig*
either [bnw + bijw] • *elk (v. beide)*
• *(een van) beide(n)*
ejaculate [ov ww] • *uitroepen*

• uitstorten
eject [ov ww] • verdrijven • uitwerpen
elaborate I [on ww] uitweiden II [bnw]
• nauwgezet • met zorg uitgewerkt,
uitgebreid
elastic I [znw] elastiek II [bnw]
• rekbaar • ruim • veerkrachtig
elasticity [znw] elasticiteit
elation [znw] opgetogenheid
elbow I [on ww] (met de elleboog)
dringen II [znw] elleboog
elder I [znw] • oudere, oudste
• ‹plantk.› vlier II [bnw] ouder, oudste
elderly [bnw] op leeftijd
eldest [bnw] oudste
elect [ov ww] (ver)kiezen
election [znw] verkiezing
elective [bnw] • gekozen • kies- • met
kiesrecht
elector [znw] kiezer, kiesman
electoral [bnw] m.b.t. verkiezing
electorate [znw] alle kiezers
electric [bnw] elektrisch
electrical [bnw] → electric
electrician [znw] elektricien
electricity [znw] elektriciteit
electrify [ov ww] • elektrificeren • onder
stroom zetten • schokken ‹fig.›
electrocute [ov ww] elektrocuteren,
terechtstellen op elektrische stoel
electrode [znw] elektrode
electrolysis [znw] elektrolyse
elegant [bnw] • sierlijk, smaakvol
• elegant
elegy [znw] treurdicht/-zang
elemental [bnw] • m.b.t. de elementen
• natuur- • enorm • essentieel
elementary [bnw] eenvoudig,
elementair
elephant [znw] olifant
elephantine [bnw] • als een olifant
• plomp
elevate [ov ww] • (op-/ver)heffen
• veredelen
elevation [znw] • verhoging • hoogte
elevator [znw] • silo • ‹AE› lift

eleven I [znw] elftal II [telw] elf
elevenses [znw] elfuurtje
eleventh [telw] elfde
elicit [ov ww] ontlokken
eligible [bnw] • verkiesbaar, verkieslijk
• wenselijk
eliminate [ov ww] • verwijderen
• elimineren
elk [znw] • eland • ‹AE› wapiti(hert)
ellipse [znw] ovaal, ellips
ellipsis [znw] ‹taalk.› weglating
elm [znw] iep
elocution [znw] voordracht
elongate [ov + on ww] • (uit)rekken
• (z.) verlengen
elope [on ww] (van huis) weglopen om
te trouwen
eloquence [znw] welsprekendheid
eloquent [bnw] welsprekend,
welbespraakt
else [bnw] anders
elucidate [ov ww] ophelderen,
toelichten
elude [ov ww] ontwijken, ontgaan
elusive, elusory [bnw] • onvindbaar
• ontwijkend
emancipate [ov ww] vrij maken,
emanciperen
embalm [ov ww] • balsemen • geurig
maken
embankment [znw] • opgehoogde
weg • kade • spoordijk
embargo I [ov ww] beslag leggen op
II [znw] • embargo • verbod v. in- of
uitvoer
embark I [ov ww] aan boord nemen
II [on ww] aan boord gaan
• (~ in/upon) z. begeven/wagen in
embarrass [ov ww] in verlegenheid
brengen
embarrassing [bnw] lastig, pijnlijk
embarrassment [znw] verlegenheid
embassy [znw] ambassade
embattled [bnw] • omringd door
vijand(en) • belaagd, in moeilijkheden
embed [ov ww] (vast)leggen, insluiten

embezzle [ov ww] *verduisteren <v. geld>*
embitter [ov ww] *verbitteren*
emblem [znw] • *symbool* • *embleem*
emblematic [bnw] *symbolisch*
embodiment [znw] *belichaming*
embody [ov ww] • *belichamen* • *vorm geven* • *uitdrukken* • *omvatten*
embolden [ov ww] *aanmoedigen*
embrace I [ov ww] • *omvatten* • *(elkaar) omhelzen* II [znw] *omhelzing*
embroider [ov ww] *borduren*
embroidery [znw] *borduurwerk*
embroil [ov ww] *verwikkelen*
embryonic [bnw] *nog niet ontwikkeld*
emend [ov ww] *verbeteren*
emerald I [znw] *smaragd* II [bnw] • *smaragden* • *smaragdgroen*
emerge [on ww] • *(naar) boven komen* • *naar buiten komen*
emergence [znw] • *uitwas* • *het verschijnen*
emergency [znw] *nood(toestand)*
emery [znw] *amaril*
eminence [znw] • *hoge positie* • *eminentie*
eminent [bnw] *eminent, verheven, uitstekend*
emirate [znw] *emiraat*
emission [znw] • *uitstraling, uitzending* • *uitlaatgas <v. auto>*
emit [ov ww] • *uiten* • *uitgeven/-zenden*
emolument [znw] *emolumenten, (bij)verdienste*
emotion [znw] *emotie, ontroering*
emotional [bnw] • *gevoels-* • *ontvankelijk, licht geroerd*
emotive [bnw] *roerend*
emperor [znw] *keizer*
emphasis [znw] • *nadruk* • *overwicht*
emphasize [ov ww] *nadruk leggen op*
emphatic [bnw] *nadrukkelijk*
empire [znw] • *(keizer-/wereld)rijk* • *heerschappij*
employ I [ov ww] • *gebruiken* • *in dienst hebben* II [znw] • *bezigheid*

• *dienst(betrekking)*
employee [znw] *werknemer*
empower [ov ww] • *machtigen* • *in staat stellen*
empress [znw] *keizerin*
emptiness [znw] *leegheid, leegte*
empty I [ov ww] *leeg maken/raken* II [on ww] *leeg worden* III [bnw] • *leeg* • *nietszeggend*
emu [znw] *emoe*
emulate [ov ww] • *wedijveren met* • *navolgen*
emulsify [ov ww] *emulgeren*
emulsion [znw] *emulsie*
enable [ov ww] • *in staat stellen* • *machtigen*
enact [ov ww] *spelen <v. rol op toneel>*
enactment [znw] *verordening*
enamel I [ov ww] *emailleren* II [znw] • *vernis* • *email* • *lak*
encamp [on ww] • *(zich) legeren* • *kamperen*
encampment [znw] *kamp(ement)*
encase [ov ww] *omhullen, omsluiten*
enchant [ov ww] • *betoveren* • *verrukken*
enchanting [bnw] *aantrekkelijk, verrukkelijk, charmant, betoverend*
enchantment [znw] *betovering*
enchantress [znw] • *toverkol* • *verleidster*
encircle [ov ww] *omringen, insluiten, omsingelen*
enclose [ov ww] • *omgeven, omheinen* • *insluiten <bij brief>*
enclosure [znw] • *eigen terrein, omheind gebied* • *bijlage*
encompass [ov ww] • *omgeven* • *omvatten*
encore I [znw] *toegift* II [tw] *bis*
encourage [ov ww] • *aanmoedigen* • *bevorderen*
encouragement [znw] *aanmoediging*
encouraging [bnw] *bemoedigend*
encroach [on ww] • *(~ (up)on) inbreuk maken op*

encroachment [znw] • aantasting
• overschrijding
encumber [ov ww] • belemmeren
• belasten
encumbrance [znw] last <ook fig.>
endanger [ov ww] in gevaar brengen
endear [ov ww] zich bemind maken
endearing [bnw] sympathiek,
vertederend
endearment [znw] liefkozing
endeavour [on ww] • (~ after) streven
naar
endemic I [znw] inheemse ziekte
II [bnw] inheems
ending [znw] • einde • <taalk.> uitgang
<v. woord>
endive [znw] andijvie
endless [bnw] eindeloos
endorse [ov ww] • endosseren
• onderschrijven
endorsement [znw] onderschrijving
endow [ov ww] • subsidiëren
• begiftigen
endowment [znw] talent, gave
endurance [znw] • lijdzaamheid,
geduld • uithoudingsvermogen
• duur(zaamheid)
endure I [ov ww] verdragen, uithouden
II [on ww] in stand blijven,
(voort)duren
enema [znw] lavement, darmspoeling
enemy I [znw] vijand II [bnw]
vijandelijk
energetic [bnw] • krachtig • energiek
enfold [ov ww] in-/omwikkelen, hullen
in
enforce [ov ww] • kracht bijzetten
• streng handhaven • (af)dwingen (tot)
enforceable [bnw] af te dwingen
engage I [ov ww] • bespreken <v.
plaatsen> • in dienst nemen • op z.
nemen • voor zich innemen II [on ww]
• (zich) verbinden • zich verloven
• slaags raken met • (~ in) z. begeven
in • (~ upon) beginnen met
• (~ with) in dienst gaan bij

engagement [znw] • afspraak
• verloving
engaging [bnw] charmant,
aantrekkelijk
engender [ov ww] teweegbrengen,
verwekken
engine [znw] machine, motor,
locomotief
engineer I [ov ww] • construeren • op
touw zetten, bewerken II [znw]
• aanstichter • ingenieur • technicus
• <scheepv.> machinist • <AE>
(trein)machinist
engineering [znw]
(machine)bouwkunde
English I [znw] Engelsen II [bnw]
Engels
engrave [ov ww] • graveren • inprenten
engraver [znw] graveur
engraving [znw] gravure
engulf [ov ww] verzwelgen
enhance [ov ww] • verhogen
• versterken
enjoy [ov ww] genieten (van)
enjoyable [bnw] prettig
enjoyment [znw] plezier
enlarge [ov ww] vergroten, verruimen
• (~ (up)on) uitweiden over
enlargement [znw] vergroting
enlighten [ov ww] toe-/verlichten
• (~ about/on) inlichten over
enlightened [bnw] verlicht
enlist I [ov ww] • inlijven • te hulp
roepen II [on ww] (z. laten) inschrijven
enliven [ov ww] verlevendigen
enmity [znw] vijandschap
ennoble [ov ww] • adelen • veredelen
enormity [znw] • enormiteit
• gruweldaad
enormous [bnw] enorm, kolossaal
enough [bnw + bijw] genoeg
enquire [ov + on ww] → inquire
enrich [ov ww] rijk(er) maken, verrijken
enroll, enrol [ov ww] • inschrijven
• registreren • (~ in) opnemen in
enrol(l)ment [znw] register, lijst

enshrine [ov ww] • (als heiligdom)
bewaren • in-/omsluiten • bevatten
ensign [znw] • vaandel • vaandrig
enslave [ov ww] tot slaaf maken
ensnare [ov ww] verstrikken
ensue [on ww] • volgen • intreden
ensure [ov ww] • verzekeren (van)
• waarborgen
entail [ov ww] als gevolg/nasleep
hebben
entangle [ov ww] verwikkelen
entanglement [znw] intrige
enter I [ov + on ww]
binnengaan/-komen • (~ for) gaan
deelnemen aan II [ov ww] boeken
• (~ (up)on) aannemen, ter hand
nemen III [on ww] • opkomen <op
toneel> • (zich laten) inschrijven
enterprise [znw]
• onderneming(sgeest), initiatief
• waagstuk
enterprising [bnw] ondernemend
entertain [ov ww] • onderhouden
• vermaken • gastvrij ontvangen
entertainer [znw] conferencier,
kleinkunstenaar
entertaining [bnw] amusant
entertainment [znw] amusement
enthuse I [ov ww] enthousiast maken
II [on ww] enthousiast zijn, dwepen
enthusiasm [znw] enthousiasme,
geestdrift
enthusiast [znw] enthousiasteling,
geestdriftig bewonderaar
enthusiastic [bnw] enthousiast
entice [ov ww] (aan-/ver)lokken
entire [bnw] • (ge)heel • compleet
• ongecastreerd
entirely [bijw] helemaal, totaal
entirety [znw] geheel
entitle [ov ww] betitelen • (~ to) het
recht geven te/op
entity [znw] • iets bestaands • wezen
entourage [znw] gevolg, begeleiding
entrails [mv] ingewanden, binnenste
entrance I [ov ww] in verrukking of

trance brengen II [znw] • intocht
• toegang, ingang • entree
• aanvaarding • binnenkomst
entreat [ov ww] dringend verzoeken
entreaty [znw] smeekbede
entrée [znw] entree
entrench [on ww] verschansen
entrepreneur [znw] ondernemer
entrust [ov ww] toevertrouwen
entry [znw] • (binnen)komst • ingang
• inschrijving, boeking • notitie <in
dagboek>
enumerate [ov ww] opnoemen,
opsommen
enunciate [ov ww] • uitspreken
• verkondigen • stellen
envelop [ov ww] (in-/om)hullen,
omgeven
enviable [bnw] benijdenswaardig
envious [bnw] afgunstig
environment [znw] milieu
environmental [bnw] milieu-
environs [mv] omstreken
envisage [ov ww] beschouwen
envoy [znw] (af)gezant
envy I [ov ww] benijden II [znw]
(voorwerp van) afgunst
enzyme [znw] enzym
ephemeral [bnw] van één dag,
kortstondig
epic I [znw] episch gedicht II [bnw]
episch
epicentre [znw] epicentrum
epidemic I [znw] epidemie II [bnw]
epidemisch
epigram [znw] puntdicht
epileptic I [znw] epilepsiepatiënt
II [bnw] epileptisch
epilogue [znw] slotwoord, naschrift
Epiphany [znw] Driekoningen
episcopal [bnw] m.b.t. bisschoppelijke
hiërarchie
epitaph [znw] grafschrift
epithet [znw] scheldwoord
epitome [znw] • toonbeeld • korte
samenvatting

epoch [znw] • *tijdvak* • *tijdstip*
equable [bnw] • *gelijkvormig*
• *evenwichtig*
equal I [ov ww] • *gelijk zijn aan*
• *evenaren* II [znw] *gelijke* III [bnw]
gelijk
equalize [ov ww] *gelijk maken/stellen*
equally [bijw] *even*
equator [znw] *evenaar*
equatorial [bnw] *equatoriaal*
equine [bnw] *paarden-*
equip [ov ww] *uit-/toerusten*
equipment [znw] *uitrusting*
equitable [bnw] *billijk*
equity [znw] *billijkheid*
equivalent I [znw] *equivalent* II [bnw]
gelijkwaardig
equivocal [bnw] *twijfelachtig,*
dubbelzinnig
era [znw] • *jaartelling* • *tijdperk*
eradicate [ov ww] *uitroeien*
erase [ov ww] *doorhalen*
eraser [znw] • *vlakgum* • *bordenwisser*
erasure [znw] *uitwissing*
erect I [ov ww] • *oprichten* • *stichten*
II [bnw] *omhoog-/opgericht, overeind*
erection [znw] • *erectie* • *gebouw* • *het*
oprichten
ermine [znw] *hermelijn*
erode [ov ww] • *uitbijten* ‹door zuur›
• *uitschuren* • *wegvreten*
erosion [znw] *erosie*
eroticism [znw] *erotiek*
errand [znw] *boodschap*
errant I [znw] II [bnw] *dolend*
erratic [bnw] • *dwalend*
• *onevenwichtig* • *grillig*
erroneous [bnw] *onjuist*
error [znw] • *fout, vergissing* • *dwaling*
erudite [bnw] *geleerd*
erudition [znw] *uitgebreide kennis*
erupt [on ww] • *uitbarsten* • *oplaaien*
escalate [on ww] • *toenemen* • *escaleren*
escalator [znw] *roltrap*
escape I [on ww] *ontsnappen,*
ontkomen II [znw] • *brandladder*

• *ontsnapping*
escapee [znw] *ontsnapte gevangene*
escarpment [znw] *glooiing, talud*
escort I [ov ww] *begeleiden* II [znw]
escorte, geleide
esoteric [bnw] *geheim, voor ingewijden*
especial [bnw] *bijzonder*
espionage [znw] *spionage*
essay [znw] • *essay, korte studie* • *poging*
essayist [znw] *essayschrijver*
essence [znw] • *wezen, kern* • *extract*
• *parfum*
essential I [znw] • *het wezenlijke* • *het*
onontbeerlijke II [bnw] • *wezenlijk*
• *onontbeerlijk*
establish [ov ww] • *oprichten*
• *vestigen* • *instellen, vaststellen*
• *bewijzen*
establishment [znw] • *instelling,*
organisatie • *personeel* • *handelshuis,*
grote zaak
estate [znw] • *onroerend goed* • *boedel,*
nalatenschap • *landgoed* • *plantage*
esteem I [ov ww] • *achten*
• *beschouwen* II [znw] *achting*
estimation [znw] • *oordeel* • *mening*
• *achting*
etch [ov + on ww] *etsen*
etching [znw] *ets*
eternal [bnw] *eeuwig*
ethereal [bnw] • *etherisch* • *vluchtig*
• *hemels*
ethic(al) [bnw] *ethisch*
ethnic [bnw] • *etnisch, heidens*
• *volkenkundig*
ethnology [znw] *volkenkunde*
Eucharist [znw] • *eucharistie*
• *Avondmaal*
eugenics [mv] *eugenetiek*
eulogize [ov ww] *prijzen*
eulogy [znw] *lof(rede)*
euphemism [znw] *eufemisme*
euphemistic [bnw] *eufemistisch*
euphoria [znw] *euforie, gelukzalig*
gevoel
Eurasian I [znw] *Eurazïer* II [bnw]

Europees-Aziatisch
European I [znw] *Europeaan* II [bnw]
Europees
euthanasia [znw] *euthanasie*
evacuate [ov ww] • *evacueren*
• *ontruimen*
evacuee [znw] *evacué*
evade [ov ww] *ontduiken/-wijken*
evaluate [ov ww] *de waarde bepalen*
van
evaluation [znw] • *waardebepaling*
• *nabeschouwing*
evangelize [ov ww] • *het evangelie*
prediken • *kerstenen*
evaporate [ov + on ww] *(doen)*
verdampen
evasion [znw] *ontwijking*
evasive [bnw] *ontwijkend*
eve [znw] • *vooravond* • *dag vóór*
even I [ov + on ww] • *(~ out)*
gelijkmatig verdelen/-spreiden
II [bnw] • *effen* • *even* • *vlak*
• *gelijk-/regelmatig* III [bijw] *zelfs*
evening [znw] *avond*
event [znw] • *gebeurtenis* • *geval*
• *evenement*
eventful [bnw] *veelbewogen*
eventual [bnw] *uiteindelijk*
eventuality [znw] *mogelijke*
gebeurtenis
eventually [bijw] *tenslotte*
ever [bijw] *ooit*
evergreen [znw] • *altijdgroene plant*
• *liedje dat populair blijft*
everlasting [bnw] *eeuwig(durend)*
every [telw] *ieder*
everybody [onb vnw] *iedereen*
everyday [bnw] • *alledaags* • *dagelijks*
everything [onb vnw] *alles*
everywhere [bnw + bijw] *overal*
evict [ov ww] *uitwijzen/-zetten*
eviction [znw] *uitzetting, ontruiming*
evidence I [ov ww] *getuigen (van)*
II [znw] • *bewijs,*
bewijsstuk/-materiaal • *getuige(nis)*
evident [bnw] *duidelijk*

evince [ov ww] *bewijzen, (aan)tonen*
evocation [znw] • *evocatie* • *oproeping*
evocative [bnw] *beeldend* <*v.*
taalgebruik>
evoke [ov ww] • *aanhalen* • *oproepen*
evolution [znw] *evolutie*
evolutionary [bnw] *evolutie-*
evolve I [ov ww] *ontwikkelen*
II [on ww] • *zich ontplooien*
• *geleidelijk ontstaan*
ewe [znw] *ooi*
ewer [znw] • *kruik* • *lampetkan*
exact I [ov ww] *eisen* II [bnw] • *precies,*
nauwkeurig • *juist*
exacting [bnw] *veeleisend*
exactitude [znw] *nauwkeurigheid*
exaggerate [ov ww] *overdrijven*
exalt [ov ww] *verheffen*
exaltation [znw] • *verheerlijking*
• *verrukking*
examine [ov + on ww] *ondervragen,*
onderzoeken
examiner [znw] *examinator*
example [znw] *voorbeeld*
exasperate [ov ww] • *ergeren* • *kwaad*
maken
excavate [ov ww] *op-/uitgraven*
excavator [znw] *excavateur,*
graafmachine
exceed [ov ww] *overschrijden/-treffen*
exceeding(ly) [bnw] *buitengewoon*
excel I [ov ww] *overtreffen* II [on ww]
uitmunten
excellence [znw] *uitmuntende*
eigenschap
excellent [bnw] *uitstekend*
except [vz] *uitgezonderd, behalve*
exception [znw] *uitzondering*
exceptional [bnw] *uitzonderlijk*
excerpt [znw] *uittreksel*
excess [znw] • *overmaat* • *exces*
• *uitspatting*
excessive [bnw] *buitensporig*
exchange I [ov ww]
• *(ver-/uit-/om)wisselen* • *ruilen*
II [znw] • *wisselkoers* • *beurs*

• *telefooncentrale*
excise I [ov ww] *uitsnijden* II [znw]
accijns
excitable [bnw] *prikkelbaar*
excite [ov ww] • *(op)wekken* • *prikkelen*
• *opwinden*
excited [bnw] *opgewonden*
excitement [znw] • *opwinding* • *roes*
exciting [bnw] *opwindend, spannend*
exclaim [ov ww] *uitroepen*
exclamation [znw] *uitroep*
exclude [ov ww] *uitsluiten, onmogelijk*
maken
exclusion [znw] *uitsluiting*
excommunicate [ov ww] *in de*
kerkelijke ban doen
excrete [ov ww] *afscheiden*
excruciating [bnw] *folterend,*
ondraaglijk
excursion [znw] • *excursie* • *uitstapje*
excuse I [ov ww] • *excuseren,*
verontschuldigen • *vrijstellen* II [znw]
• *verontschuldiging* • *uitvlucht*
execrable [bnw] *afschuwelijk*
execute [ov ww] • *uitvoeren, ten uitvoer*
brengen • *vervullen* • *ter dood brengen*
executioner [znw] *beul*
executive I [znw] • *directeur*
• *topambtenaar* • *uitvoerende macht*
• *bewindsman* II [bnw] *uitvoerend,*
verantwoordelijk
executor [znw] *executeur-testamentair*
exemplary [bnw] • *voorbeeldig*
• *kenschetsend*
exemplify [ov ww] • *als voorbeeld*
dienen • *met voorbeeld toelichten*
exempt I [ov ww] *vrijstellen* II [bnw]
vrijgesteld
exercise I [ov ww] • *(be-/uit)oefenen*
• *in acht nemen* • *beweging laten*
nemen • *<mil.> (laten) exerceren*
II [on ww] • *oefeningen doen/maken*
• *sporten* III [znw] • *oefening*
• *(lichaams)beweging*
exert [ov ww] *inspannen, uitoefenen*
exertion [znw] • *inspanning*

• *krachtige poging*
exhale [ov ww] • *uitademen*
• *uitwasemen*
exhaust I [ov ww] • *uitputten*
• *verbruiken* II [znw] • *uitlaatgassen*
• *uitlaat <v. motor>*
exhaustion [znw] *uitputting*
exhaustive [bnw] *volledig, grondig*
exhibit I [ov ww] • *(ver)tonen*
• *tentoonstellen* II [znw] • *bewijsstuk*
• *inzending <op tentoonstelling>*
• *vertoon, vertoning*
exhibition [znw] *tentoonstelling*
exhibitionism [znw] *exhibitionisme*
exhort [ov ww] *aansporen, vermanen*
exhume [ov ww] *opgraven*
exile I [ov ww] *verbannen* II [znw]
• *ballingschap* • *balling* • *verbanning*
exist [on ww] *bestaan* • *(~ on) bestaan*
van
existence [znw] *het bestaan*
existent [bnw] *bestaand*
exit I [on ww] *(v.h. toneel) verdwijnen*
II [znw] • *uitgang* • *dood* • *vertrek*
exodus [znw] *uittocht*
exorbitant [bnw] *buitensporig*
exorcism [znw] *duivelbezwering*
exotic I [znw] *uitheemse plant* II [bnw]
uitheems
expand I [ov ww]
• *uitbreiden/-spreiden* • *uitwerken <v.*
aantekeningen> II [on ww]
• *toenemen* • *uitzetten*
expanse, expansion [znw]
• *uitgestrektheid* • *uitbreiding*
expansive [bnw] • *uitzettings-* • *wijd*
• *open <v. karakter>*
expatriate [ov ww] *verbannen*
expect [ov ww] *verwachten*
expectancy [znw] *verwachting,*
afwachting, kans
expectation [znw] *vooruitzicht*
expedient I [znw] *(red)middel* II [bnw]
• *doelmatig, raadzaam*
• *opportunistisch*
expedite [ov ww] *bespoedigen,*

voorthelpen

expedition [znw] • *expeditie* • *vlotheid*

expeditious [bnw] *vlot*

expel [ov ww] *verdrijven, verjagen,*
verwijderen

expend [ov ww] *besteden, uitgeven*

expendable [bnw] *te verwaarlozen*

expenditure [znw] *uitgaven*

expense [znw] *uitgave(n), (on)kosten*

expensive [bnw] *duur*

experience I [ov ww] *ervaren* II [znw]
• *mystieke ervaring* • *ondervinding*
• *ervaring*

experiment I [on ww] *proeven nemen*
II [znw] *proef*

expert I [znw] *deskundige* II [bnw]
deskundig, bedreven

expiration [znw] *uitademing, expiratie*

expire I [ov + on ww] *uitademen*
II [on ww] • *sterven* • *aflopen, vervallen*

explain [ov ww] *uitleggen, verklaren*

expletive [znw] • *verwensing*
• *krachtterm*

explicable [bnw] *verklaarbaar*

explicit [bnw] • *expliciet* • *nauwkeurig*
omschreven • *uitdrukkelijk* • *stellig*
• *duidelijk*

explode [ov + on ww] *(doen) ontploffen*

exploit I [ov ww] • *exploiteren*
• *uitbuiten* II [znw] • *heldendaad*
• *prestatie*

exploratory [bnw] *verkennend,*
onderzoekend

explore [ov ww] • *onderzoeken*
• *verkennen*

explorer [znw] *ontdekkingsreiziger,*
verkenner

explosion [znw] *explosie*

explosive I [znw] *springstof* II [bnw]
• *ontplofbaar* • *ontploffend*
• *opvliegend*

exponent [znw] • *exponent* <bij
algebra> • *vertolker, vertegenwoordiger*
• *vertolking*

export I [ov ww] *exporteren* II [znw]
export

exporter [znw] *exporteur*

expose [ov ww] • *ontmaskeren*
• *uiteenzetten* • *tentoonstellen* • (~ **to**)
blootstellen aan

exposition [znw] *uiteenzetting*

expound [ov ww] *uiteenzetten,*
verklaren

express I [ov ww] *uitdrukken* II [znw]
• *expresse* • *sneltrein* III [bnw + bijw]
• *expresse* <post> • *uitdrukkelijk, stellig*
• *met opzet*

expression [znw] *uitdrukking*

expressionism [znw] *expressionisme*

expressive [bnw] • *expressief*
• *veelzeggend*

expropriate [ov ww] • *onteigenen*
• *afnemen*

exquisite [bnw] *voortreffelijk,*
(ver)fijn(d)

extemporize [ov ww] *improviseren*

extend I [ov ww] • *uitsteken* • *rekken,*
verlengen II [on ww] *zich uitstrekken*

extension [znw] • *uitgebreidheid*
• *bijkantoor*

extensive [bnw] • *groots opgezet*
• *veelomvattend*

extenuate [ov ww] *verzachten*

exterior I [znw] *buitenkant* II [bnw]
• *uiterlijk* • *uitwendig* • *buiten-*

external [bnw] • *uitwendig* • *van*
buiten af • *uiterlijk*

extinct [bnw] *uitgestorven*

extinction [znw] *het uitsterven*

extinguish [ov ww] *blussen, (uit)doven*

extinguisher [znw] *blusapparaat*

extort [ov ww] *afdwingen/-persen*

extra I [znw] • *extraatje* • *figurant* <in
film> II [bnw] *extra* III [voorv] *buiten-*

extract I [ov ww] • *(uit)trekken*
• *afdwingen* • *uitpersen* II [znw]
• *passage* <uit boek> • *extract*

extraction [znw] *afkomst*

extramarital [bnw] *buitenechtelijk*

extraneous [bnw] *buiten de zaak*
staand

extraordinary [bnw] *buitengewoon*

extravagance [znw] *extravagantie*
extravagant [bnw] • *buitensporig,*
overdreven • *verkwistend* • *ongerijmd*
extreme I [znw] • *(uit)einde* • *hoogste*
graad II [bnw] • *uiterst, laatst, hoogst*
• *buitengewoon*
extremism [znw] *extremisme*
extremist I [znw] *extremist* II [bnw]
extremistisch
extremity [znw] • *uiterste nood*
• *uiterste maatregel* • *uiterste*
• *uitsteeksel*
extricate [ov ww] • *uit de knoop halen*
• *bevrijden*
exuberant [bnw] • *overvloedig*
• *uitbundig*
exude [ov ww] *uitzweten*
exult [on ww] *juichen* • *(~ over)*
triomferen over
exultant [bnw] • *juichend*
• *opgewonden* • *dol van blijdschap*
eye I [ov ww] *na-/aankijken* II [znw] *oog*

F

fable [znw] • *fabel* • *leugen, praatje*
fabled [bnw] *legendarisch*
fabric [znw] *geweven stof, weefsel*
fabricate [ov ww] • *verzinnen*
• *namaken*
fabrication [znw] • *verzinsel* • *namaak*
fabulous [bnw] *wonderbaarlijk,*
fabelachtig
face I [ov ww] • *uitzicht geven op*
• *onder ogen (durven) zien*
• *liggen/staan tegenover* • *(~ up to)*
flink aanpakken, onder ogen zien
II [znw] • *gelaat, gezicht* • *voorkomen*
• *beeldzijde, voorkant* • *oppervlakte*
• *wijzerplaat*
facet [znw] *facet*
facetious [bnw] *schertsend*
facial I [znw] *gezichtsmassage* II [bnw]
gelaats-
facilitate [ov ww] *vergemakkelijken*
facility [znw] • *gemak* • *voorziening,*
faciliteit
facing I [znw] • *revers* • *(aanbrenging*
van) buitenlaag <op muur > II [vz]
(staande) tegenover
fact [znw] • *feit, gebeurtenis*
• *werkelijkheid*
faction [znw] • *politieke partij*
• *partijgeest*
factitious [bnw] *nagebootst,*
kunstmatig, onecht
factor [znw] *factor*
factory [znw] *fabriek*
factotum [znw] *manusje-van-alles*
factual [bnw] *feitelijk, feiten-*
faculty [znw] • *vermogen* • *faculteit*
fad [znw] *rage, gril*
fade [on ww] • *wegzakken <v.*
radio-ontvangst> • *verwelken*
• *geleidelijk verdwijnen*
• *(~ away/out) (doen) verbleken,*

wegkwijnen • (~ **in/up**) *volume
regelen, inregelen* <v. beeld> • (~ **into**)
overgaan in • (~ **out**) *uitregelen* <v.
beeld/film>
faeces [znw] *uitwerpselen*
fag [znw] • *vermoeiend en
onaangenaam werk* • <inf.> *sigaret*
• <pej.> *homo*
fail I [ov ww] • *in gebreke blijven* • *laten
zakken* <bij examen> II [on ww]
• *mislukken* • *zakken* <bij examen>
• *falen* • *opraken* • *wegsterven*
failing I [znw] *gebrek, zwak(te)* II [vz]
bij gebrek aan
faint I [on ww] *flauwvallen* II [znw]
flauwte III [bnw] • *zwak* • *vaag*
fair I [znw] • *beurs* • *kermis* • *jaarmarkt*
II [bnw] • *mooi* • *blond* • *zuiver*
• *eerlijk, geoorloofd* • *tamelijk* • *gunstig*
fairly [bijw] • *eerlijk* • *tamelijk*
fairy I [znw] *fee* II [bnw] *feeachtig,
tover-*
faith [znw] • *geloof, vertrouwen*
• *leer(stelling)*
faithful [bnw] • *gelovig* • *trouw*
• *nauwgezet*
fake I [ov ww] *vervalsen, fingeren*
II [znw] • *namaak* • *bedrog,
voorwendsel* III [bnw] *vals, nep*
falcon [znw] *valk*
falconer [znw] *valkenier*
falconry [znw] *valkenjacht*
fall I [on ww] • *vallen* • *worden*
• *afdalen* • *betrekken* <v. gezicht>
• (~ **away**) *weg-/uit-/afvallen,
verminderen, hellen, verdwijnen*
• (~ **back**) *achteropraken, terugvallen*
• (~ **behind**) *achteropraken* • (~ **for**)
verliefd worden op • (~ **in**) *instorten, z.
aansluiten* • (~ **in with**) *het eens zijn
met* • (~ **into**) *vervallen tot* • (~ **on**)
zich storten op • (~ **out**) *uitvallen,
ruzie krijgen, gebeuren, blijken (te zijn)*
• (~ **through**) *in duigen vallen,
mislukken* • (~ **to**) *z. toeleggen op,
beginnen met* • (~ **upon**) *vallen op,*

aanvallen • (~ **within**) *binnen het
kader vallen* II [znw] • *val* • *daling*
• *helling* • *verval, ondergang*
• *waterval* • <AE> *herfst*
fallacious [bnw] *bedrieglijk*
fallacy [znw] • *bedrog* • *drogrede(n)*
fallen [ww] *volt. deelw.* → **fall**
fallible [bnw] *feilbaar*
fallow [bnw] *braak(liggend)*
false [bnw] • *vals, onjuist* • *ontrouw*
• *onecht*
falsehood [znw] *leugen(s)*
falsify [ov ww] *vervalsen, verkeerd
voorstellen*
falsity [znw] • *valsheid* <in geschrifte>
• *oneerlijkheid* • *bedrog* • *onjuistheid*
famed [bnw] *beroemd*
familiar [bnw] • *familiaar* • *vertrouwd,
bekend*
familiarity [znw] • *vertrouwdheid*
• *familiariteit*
familiarize [ov ww] *bekend/vertrouwd
maken met*
family [znw] • *familie, gezin* • *geslacht*
famine [znw] *schaarste, hongersnood*
famous [bnw] *vermaard, beroemd*
fan I [ov ww] • *aanwakkeren* • *koelte
toewaaien* II [znw] • *waaier*
• *ventilator* • *enthousiast(eling), fan*
fanatic I [znw] *fanatiekeling* II [bnw]
fanatiek
fanaticism [znw] *fanatisme,
dweepzucht*
fanciful [bnw] • *ingebeeld, fantastisch*
• *kieskeurig*
fancy I [ov ww] *z. inbeelden, verbeelden*
II [znw] • *in-/verbeelding(skracht)*
• *gril, zin, voorliefde* III [bnw] • *luxe*
• *chic*
fang [znw] *slagtand, giftand*
fanny [znw] • <sl.> *kut* • <AE sl.> *kont*
fantastic [bnw] • *grillig, vreemd*
• *fantastisch*
fantasy [znw] *fantasie*
far [bnw + bijw] *ver, afgelegen*
farcical [bnw] *bespottelijk*

fare [znw] • *vrachttarief* • *vrachtje* <taxi> • *kost* <eten>

farewell [znw] *vaarwel*

farm I [on ww] *boerenbedrijf uitoefenen* II [znw] • *landerij, boerderij* • *kwekerij, fokkerij*

farmer [znw] *boer, pachter*

farming I [znw] *landbouw* II [bnw] *landbouw-*

fart I [on ww] *een scheet laten* II [znw] *scheet*

farther [bnw + bijw] vergr. trap → far

farthest [bnw] overtr. trap → far

fascinate [ov ww] • *betoveren* • *fascineren*

fashion I [ov ww] *vormen, pasklaar maken* II [znw] • *fatsoen* • *mode* • *aard, wijze*

fast I [on ww] *vasten* II [znw] *vastentijd* III [bnw + bijw] • *snel* • *wasecht* • *onbeweeglijk, vast* • *los* <v. zeden> • *vóór* <v. klok>

fasten [ov ww] *bevestigen, sluiten, vastmaken* • (~ **on**) *vasthouden aan, uitkiezen* <voor kritiek e.d.> • (~ **up**) *vastmaken* <japon>

fastener [znw] *sluiting*

fastness [znw] • *bolwerk* • → fast

fat I [ww] → fatten II [znw] *het vet(te)* III [bnw] *vet, dik*

fatal [bnw] • *noodlottig, rampspoedig* • *fataal, dodelijk* • *onvermijdelijk*

fatalism [znw] *fatalisme*

fatality [znw] • *noodlot, voorbeschikking* • *ramp, ongeluk met dodelijke afloop*

fate [znw] *dood, (nood)lot*

fateful [bnw] *noodlottig*

father I [ov ww] • *voortbrengen* • *een vader zijn voor* II [znw] • *vader* • *voorvader* • *nestor* • *pater, biechtvader* • *kerkvader* • *God* • *leider*

fatherly [bnw] *vaderlijk*

fathom I [ov ww] *peilen, doorgronden* II [znw] *vadem, 3 voet (ca. 1.80 m)*

fathomless [bnw] *peilloos, ondoorgrondelijk*

fatigue I [ov ww] *vermoeien* II [znw] *vermoeidheid*

fatten I [ov ww] *mesten* II [on ww] *dik/vet worden*

fatty I [znw] <inf.> *dikke(rd)* II [bnw] *vet(tig)*

fatuous [bnw] *sullig, idioot*

fault I [ov ww] *aanmerking maken* II [znw] • *fout* • *schuld* • *overtreding* • *gebrek*

faultless [bnw] *onberispelijk*

faulty [bnw] • *gebrekkig* • *onjuist*

favour I [ov ww] • *(willen) begunstigen, bevoordelen* • *goedkeuren, steunen* • *verkiezen* • *lijken op* • <inf.> *ontzien* II [znw] • *begunstiging, gunst* • *achting* • *genade, vriendelijkheid*

favourable [bnw] *gunstig*

favourite I [znw] *gunsteling, lieveling* II [bnw] *lievelings-*

favouritism [znw] *(oneerlijke) bevoorrechting*

fawn I [on ww] • *kwispelstaarten* <v. hond> • *vleien, kruipen voor* II [znw] • *jong hert* • *geelbruin*

fear I [ov ww] *bang zijn voor, vrezen, duchten* • (~ **for**) *bang/bezorgd zijn voor* II [znw] *vrees, angst*

fearful [bnw] • *vreselijk* • *bang*

fearless [bnw] *onbevreesd*

fearsome [bnw] *vreselijk*

feasible [bnw] • *uitvoerbaar* • *waarschijnlijk*

feast I [on ww] *feest vieren* • (~ **on**) z. te goed doen aan II [znw] • *kerkelijk feest* • *feest(maal)*

feat [znw] *heldendaad, prestatie*

feather I [ov ww] *met veren bedekken* II [znw] *veer*

February [znw] *februari*

fecund [bnw] *overvloedig, vruchtbaar*

fed [ww] verl. tijd + volt. deelw. → feed

federal [bnw] *federaal, bonds-*

federation [znw] statenbond
fee [znw] • schoolgeld • loon,
honorarium
feeble [bnw] futloos, zwak
feed I [ov ww] voeden, voederen,
instoppen <computer> II [on ww] eten,
z. voeden III [znw] veevoer
feeder [znw] • eter • zijlijn/-tak
• aanvoerapparaat
feel I [ov ww] voelen, gewaarworden
II [on ww] gevoelens hebben, voelen,
gevoel/tastzin hebben • (~ for) zoeken
naar, voelen voor • (~ out) aan de tand
voelen • (~ with) meevoelen met
III [znw] gevoel
feeler [znw] voelhoorn/-spriet
feeling [znw] gevoel(en)
feet [mv] → foot
feint I [on ww] doen alsof II [znw]
• schijnbeweging • voorwendsel
felicitous [bnw] goed (gevonden) en
toepasselijk
felicity [znw] • groot geluk, zegen(ing)
• gelukkige vondst • toepasselijkheid
feline I [znw] katachtige II [bnw]
katachtig
fell I [ov ww] vellen II [on ww] verl. tijd
→ fall III [znw] • vel, huid • berg
• heidevlakte <N.-Engeland>
fellow I [znw] • makker • kerel, vrijer,
vent II [bnw] • -genoot, mede- • gelijke
fellowship [znw]
• kameraadschappelijke omgang,
collegialiteit • broederschap,
genootschap • studiebeurs, betrekking
van wetenschapper
felt I [on ww] verl.tijd + volt.deelw.
→ feel II [znw] vilt III [bnw] vilten
female I [znw] wijfje, vrouw(spersoon)
II [bnw] vrouwelijk, wijfjes-
feminism [znw] feminisme
feminist [znw] feminist(e)
fen [znw] moeras, ondergelopen land
fence I [ov ww] beschutten, omheinen
• (~ off) afschermen II [on ww] <sport>
schermen III [znw] • hek, omheining

• schutting • <inf.> heler(shuis)
fencing [znw] • omheining
• schermkunst/-sport
fend [ww] • (~ for) zorgen voor
• (~ off) afweren
fender [znw] • bescherming,
haardhekje • bumper • <AE> spatbord
<v. auto>
fennel [znw] venkel
ferment I [on ww] fermenteren, gisten
II [znw] gist, gisting
fern [znw] varen(s)
ferry I [ov ww] overzetten II [znw]
veer(boot)
fertile [bnw] vruchtbaar, rijk (in/aan)
fertilize [ov ww] • vruchtbaar maken
• met kunstmest behandelen
• bevruchten
fertilizer [znw] (kunst)mest
fervent [bnw] heet, vurig
fervour [znw] hitte, drift
fester [on ww] zweren
festive [bnw] feest-, feestelijk
festivity [znw] feestelijkheid,
feestvreugde
festoon I [ov ww] versieren met slingers
II [znw] guirlande
fetch [ov ww] • toebrengen <slag>
• halen • opbrengen <prijs>
fetching [bnw] • innemend
• aantrekkelijk • pakkend
fetid [bnw] stinkend
fetish [znw] fetisj
fetter I [ov ww] boeien, belemmeren
II [znw] • voetboei • belemmering
fettle [znw] conditie
fetus [znw] foetus, vrucht, ongeboren
kind
feud [znw] vete
feudal [bnw] leen-
feudalism [znw] leenstelsel
fever [znw] • koorts • (koortsachtige)
opwinding
feverish [bnw] koorts(acht)ig
few [onb vnw] weinige(n)
fib I [on ww] jokken II [znw] leugentje

fibber, fibster [znw] jokkebrok
fibre [znw] • karakter • *vezelachtige
stof* • <AE> *vezel(s)*
fibroid, fibrous [bnw] *vezelachtig*
fiddle I [ov ww] <sl.> bedriegen, knoeien
<vooral met de boekhouding>
II [on ww] vioolspelen III [znw] • *vedel,
viool* • *knoeierij, bedrog, geklungel*
fiddler [znw] • *vedelaar* • *bedrieger*
fiddling [bnw] • onbetekenend
• *prullerig*
fidelity [znw] (ge)trouw(heid)
fidget I [on ww] (z.) zenuwachtig
bewegen • (~ **about**) niet stil kunnen
zitten II [znw] druk en nerveus persoon
fidgety [bnw] druk, gejaagd
field I [ov ww] • bal vangen • in 't veld
brengen <v. team> II [znw] • veld
• slagveld • akker • gebied, terrein
fielder [znw] balvanger
fiend [znw] • duivel • maniak
fiendish, fiendlike [bnw] duivels
fierce [bnw] • woest, onstuimig, hevig
• erg
fiery [bnw] • vurig, opvliegend
• gloeiend
fifteen [telw] vijftien
fifth [telw] vijfde
fiftieth [telw] vijftigste
fifty [telw] vijftig
fig [znw] vijg(enboom)
fight I [ov ww] • vechten tegen • laten
vechten II [on ww] vechten III [znw]
• gevecht, strijd • vechtlust
figment [znw] verzinsel
figurative [bnw] • figuurlijk,
zinnebeeldig • beeld-
figure I [ov ww] <AE> geloven • (~ **on**)
rekenen op, vertrouwen op • (~ **out**)
uitrekenen, bedenken II [on ww]
verschijnen, voorkomen III [znw]
• figuur, vorm, gestalte • patroon
• bedrag • cijfer
filament [znw] • gloeidraad • vezel
• <plantk.> helmdraad
filch [ov ww] gappen

file I [ov ww] • vijlen • in archief
opbergen • indienen <v.
eis/klacht/verzoek> II [on ww]
• (~ **in/out**) achterelkaar naar
binnen/buiten lopen III [znw] • vijl
• briefordener • dossier • gelid
filial [bnw] v. dochter/zoon
fill I [ov ww] • vullen • plomberen
• stoppen <pijp> • verzadigen
• bekleden <ambt> • (~ **in**) invullen,
dempen, inlichten • (~ **out**) opvullen,
inschenken, invullen <formulier>
• (~ **up**) volproppen, tanken, dempen
II [on ww] z. vullen III [znw] • vulling
• bekomst
filler [znw] (op)vulsel
filling [znw] vulling
fillip [znw] aansporing, prikkel, knip
<met duim en vinger>, tikje
filmy [bnw] • fijn • wazig
filter I [ov ww] filtreren, zuiveren
II [on ww] • (~ **through**)
door-/uitlekken III [znw] filter
filth [znw] • vuile taal • vuiligheid
filthy [bnw] vuil
fin [znw] • vin • <luchtv.> kielvlak
final I [znw] • eindwedstrijd • <inf.>
laatste editie v. krant op de dag
II [bnw] • definitief, afdoend • eind-,
slot-, laatste
finalist [znw] • eindexamenkandidaat
• speler in eindwedstrijd
finalize [ov ww] besluiten, afmaken
finance I [ov ww] financieren II [znw]
financieel beheer, financiën,
financiewezen
financial [bnw] financieel
finch [znw] vink
find I [ov + on ww] oordelen, uitspreken
II [ov ww] • (be)vinden • zien,
ontdekken • (gaan) halen • verschaffen,
bekostigen III [znw] vondst
finder [znw] • zoeker <op fototoestel>
• vinder
fine I [ov ww] beboeten II [znw]
geldboete III [bnw] • fijn, mooi

• *verfijnd, subtiel, zuiver* • *hard*
<potlood> • *scherp* <pen> • *uitstekend*
<conditie> • *goed, gelukkig, schoon,*
waardig • *helder of droog* <weer>
IV [bijw] *prima*
finery [znw] • *opschik* • <techn.>
frishaard
finesse [znw] *handigheid,*
spitsvondigheid
finger [znw] *vinger*
finicky [bnw] *overdreven precies,*
pietepeuterig
finish I [ov + on ww] • *voltooien,*
(be)eindigen • *opeten/-drinken/-roken,*
enz. • *garneren* • *uitlezen* • *afwerken,*
lakken • *v. kant maken* II [znw]
• *laatste laag, afwerkingslaag,*
glanslaag • *vernis* • *finish, einde,*
afwerking
finite [bnw] *begrensd, eindig*
fink [znw] *verrader, aanbrenger*
Finn [znw] Fin
Finnish [bnw] Fins
fiord [znw] *fjord*
fir [znw] *den(nenboom), dennenhout,*
spar
fire I [ov ww] • *aanvuren* • *bakken*
<stenen> • *afvuren* • *ontslaan*
• (~ **away**) *er op los schieten, v. leer*
trekken, beginnen • (~ **off**) *afvuren*
II [znw] *vuur, brand, gloed, hitte*
firm I [znw] *firma* II [bnw] • *vast, hard*
• *vastberaden, standvastig*
first I [znw] *eerste* II [bnw] *eerst,*
belangrijkst III [bijw] • *voor 't eerst*
• *ten eerste* • *liever*
firstly [bijw] *ten eerste*
fiscal [bnw] *fiscaal, belasting-*
fish I [ov + on ww] *vissen* II [znw] *vis*
fisherman [znw] *visser*
fishery [znw] *visgrond/-plaats*
fishing [znw] *het vissen*
fishy [bnw] • *naar vis smakend*
• *visachtig* • <inf.> *niet helemaal pluis,*
verdacht
fission [znw] *splijting, celdeling,*

splitsing v. atoom
fissure [znw] *kloof, spleet*
fist [znw] *vuist*
fit I [ov + on ww] • *passen (bij), geschikt*
maken • *monteren* • (~ **in**) *inlassen*
• (~ **in with**) *kloppen met* • (~ **on**)
(aan)passen • (~ **out**) *uitrusten* <bijv.
schip> • (~ **up**) *monteren, uitrusten*
• (~ **with**) *voorzien van* II [znw] • *bui*
• *aanval, stuip* • *beroerte* • *'t*
passen/zitten III [bnw] • *geschikt,*
gepast • *gezond, in goede conditie*
fitful [bnw] *afwisselend, bij vlagen*
fitment [znw] *wandmeubel*
fitter [znw] • *monteur* • *bankwerker*
• *fitter*
fitting I [znw] • *pasbeurt* • *armatuur*
II [bnw] *passend*
five [telw] *vijf*
fiver <inf.> [znw] *bankbiljet v. vijf pond*
fix I [ov ww] • *vastleggen/-maken,*
bevestigen, vaststellen <v. datum>
• *monteren, installeren, fixeren*
• *repareren* • *opmaken* <v. haar>
• *aanleggen* <vuur> • *klaarspelen*
• (~ **up**) *regelen, organiseren* II [znw]
• *moeilijkheid, dilemma*
• *doorgestoken kaart* • <sl.> *shot* <drugs>
fixation [znw] *obsessie*
fixed [bnw] *vast*
fixture [znw] • *wat vast is* • *datum v.*
wedstrijd
fizz I [on ww] *sissen* II [znw]
• *champagne* • *gesis*
fizzle [on ww] *sissen, sputteren*
• (~ **out**) *met een sisser aflopen*
flabby, flaccid [bnw] • *slap, zwak*
• *willoos*
flag I [ov ww] • (~ **down**) *teken geven*
om te stoppen <aan auto> II [on ww]
kwijnen, verflauwen III [znw] *vlag*
flagellate [ov ww] *kastijden, geselen*
flagon [znw] • *schenkkan* • *fles*
flagrant [bnw] • *flagrant* • *opvallend*
• *schandelijk* <belediging>
flair [znw] • *flair* • *bijzondere*

handigheid
flake I [ov ww] *doen afschilferen*
II [on ww] • *als vlokken vallen*
• *afschilferen* • *(~ out) 't bewustzijn*
verliezen III [znw] • *vlok* • *schilfer*
• *plakje*
flaky [bnw] • *vlokkig* • *schilferachtig*
flame I [on ww] • *ontvlammen*
• *vuurrood worden* II [znw] *vlam, vuur*
flaming [bnw] • *zeer heet* • *felgekleurd*
flammable [bnw] *brandbaar*
flan [znw] *vlaai, jamgebak*
flange [znw] *flens*
flank I [ov ww] *flankeren* II [znw] *zijde,*
flank
flannel I [znw] • *flanel* • *flanellen*
wrijflap, dweil, washandje II [bnw]
flanellen
flap I [ov + on ww] • *klapperen,*
fladderen • *klapwieken* • *(~ away/off)*
wegvliegen II [znw] • *klep*
• *neerhangend deel* <v. tafelblad> • *slip*
<jas> • *kieuwdeksel* • *omslag* <v. boek>
flare I [on ww] • *flikkeren, gloeien* • *z.*
buitenwaarts bollen, uitstaan <v. rok>
• *(~ up) oplaaien* II [znw] • *helle vlam*
• *lichtkogel* <met parachute>,
signaalvlam
flash I [ov ww] • *seinen* • *doen flitsen,*
laten schijnen, schieten <vuur v. ogen>
II [on ww] *schijnen, opvlammen,*
flitsen III [znw] • *vlam* • *oogwenk*
• *vertoon* • *vlaag* • *kiekje* • *nieuwsflits*
flasher [znw] • *exhibitionist,*
potloodventer • *knipperlicht* <auto>
flashy [bnw] *opzichtig, fatterig, poenig*
flatten I [ov ww] • *plat maken* • *pletten*
• *klein krijgen* • *met de grond gelijk*
maken II [on ww] *plat/vlak worden*
• *(~ out) plat worden*
flatter [ov ww] *vleien, strelen* <v.
ego/ijdelheid>
flatterer [znw] *vleier*
flattery [bnw] *vleierij*
flatulence [znw] • *winderigheid*
• *aanmatiging*

flaunt [ov ww] *pronken met*
flautist [znw] *fluitist*
flavouring [znw] *'t kruiden, kruiderij*
flavourless [bnw] *smakeloos*
flaw [znw] • *regen-/windvlaag* • *barst,*
scheur • *onvolkomenheid, fout*
flawless [bnw] *perfect, onberispelijk,*
smetteloos
flay [ov ww] • *bekritiseren* • *villen*
flea [znw] *vlo*
fleck [znw] *vlek, spat, spikkel*
flee I [ov ww] *vluchten* II [on ww]
ontvluchten
fleece I [ov ww] • *scheren* <schapen>
• *geld afhandig maken* II [znw]
schapenvacht
fleecy [bnw] *wollig, vlokkig*
fleet [znw] • *vloot* • *wagenpark* <auto's>
fleeting [bnw] *snel, vergankelijk,*
vluchtig
Flemish [bnw] *Vlaams*
flesh I [ov ww] • *(~ out) nader*
preciseren, uitwerken II [znw] *vlees*
flew [ww] verl. tijd → **fly**
flex I [ov ww] *buigen* II [znw]
(elektrisch) snoer
flexible [bnw] *buigzaam, handelbaar*
flick [ov ww] *tikken, rukken, knippen*
flicker I [on ww] *flikkeren* II [znw]
opflikkering
flight [znw] • *vlucht* • *zwerm*
• *formatie* <vliegtuigen>
flighty [bnw] • *grillig* • *wispelturig*
flimsy [bnw] *ondeugdelijk, zwak, nietig*
flinch [on ww] • *wijken* • *ineenkrimpen*
<v.d. pijn> • *(~ from) terugdeinzen*
voor
fling I [ov ww] • *smijten* • *gooien*
II [znw] • *worp* • *onstuimige*
hooglandse dans • *kortstondige,*
stormachtige liefdesaffaire, uitspatting
flint [znw] *keisteen, vuursteen*
flip I [ov + on ww] • *(~ over)*
omdraaien II [ov ww] • *(weg)knippen,*
tikken • *(om) laten kantelen* • *(snel)*
omdraaien • *(~ through)*

doorbladeren III [on ww] • *flippen*
<door drugs>, *ongunstig reageren op,
door het dolle heen raken,
wildenthousiast worden* • *een salto
maken* IV [znw] • *knip, tik* • *salto*
flippancy [znw] • *spot* • *oneerbiedige
opmerking*
flippant [bnw] *ongepast luchthartig,
zonder de nodige ernst, spottend*
flirt I [on ww] *flirten* • (~ **with**) *spelen*
<met de gedachte> II [znw] *flirt*
flirtatious [bnw] *koket(terend)*
float I [ov ww] *laten drijven, doen
zweven* II [on ww] • *vlot komen*
• *drijven, zweven* • *doelloos
rondtrekken* III [znw] • *vlotter* <v.
stoomketel> • *dobber* • *vlot* • *lage
wagen* <in optocht>
floating [bnw] *drijvend, vlottend*
<kapitaal>
flock I [on ww] *samenstromen* II [znw]
schare, kudde, troep
floe [znw] *drijvende ijsschots(en)*
flog [ov ww] • *slaan* • *verpatsen*
flood I [ov ww] • *(doen) overstromen*
• *overvoeren* <v.d. markt> II [on ww]
overstromen III [znw] • *vloed* • *stroom,
overstroming*
floor I [ov ww] • *vloeren, neerslaan*
• *overdonderen, te machtig zijn*
II [znw] • *vloer, bodem* • *verdieping*
• *loonminimum*
flop I [on ww] • *klossen*
• *neerploffen/-smijten* • *mislukking
worden* II [znw] • *plof, plons* • <inf.>
flop, fiasco III [bijw] *ineens*
floppy [bnw] *flodderig, zwak*
floral [bnw] *m.b.t. bloemen*
florid [bnw] • *opzichtig* • *blozend*
florist [znw] *bloemist, bloemenkweker*
flotilla [znw] *flotille*
flotsam [znw] • *aanspoelende
wrakgoederen, rommel* • *zwervers*
flounce I [on ww] *woedend (weg)lopen*
II [znw] • *ruk* • *strook*
flounder I [on ww] • *ploeteren* <door

modder> • *fouten maken* • *in de war
raken* II [znw] *bot* <vis>
flour I [ov ww] *bestrooien met meel*
II [znw] *bloem, meel*
flourish I [ov ww] *wuiven met, gebaren*
II [on ww] *gedijen, in de bloeitijd
leven/zijn* III [znw] • *krul* <als
versiering> • *zwierig gebaar*
floury [bnw] *melig, bedekt met meel*
flout [ov ww] *in de wind slaan*
flow I [on ww] • *stromen, golven*
• *opkomen* <v. getij> • (~ **from**)
(voort)vloeien uit II [znw] • *vloed*
• *stroming, golving*
flower I [on ww] *(op)bloeien* II [znw]
• *bloem* • *bloei* • *keur*
flowered [bnw] *gebloemd, versierd met
bloemen*
flowery [bnw] *bloemrijk, gebloemd,
bloemen-*
flown [ww] *volt. deelw.* → **fly**
flu <inf.> [znw] *griep*
fluctuate [on ww] *golven, op en neer
gaan*
flue [znw] *rookkanaal, vlampijp*
fluency [znw] • *spreekvaardigheid*
• *welbespraaktheid*
fluent [bnw] • *vaardig* <vnl.
spreekvaardigheid>, *welbespraakt*
• *vloeiend, sierlijk*
fluff I [ov ww] *donzig maken,
opschudden* <v. bed> • (~ **out/up**)
laten uitstaan <haar> II [znw] • *pluis,
donzig spul* • *onhandige slag* • <sl.>
blunder, verspreking
fluffy [bnw] *donzig* <v. kussen>, *pluizig*
fluid I [znw] *vloeistof* II [bnw]
vloeibaar, beweeglijk
fluke [znw] *(gelukkig) toeval*
flummox [ov ww] *versteld doen staan*
flung [ww] *verl. tijd + volt. deelw.*
→ **fling**
flunk <inf.> [ov ww] *laten zakken* <bij
examen> • (~ **out**) *weggestuurd
worden* <v. school/universiteit>
fluorescent [bnw] *fluorescerend*

flurry I [ov ww] *zenuwachtig maken*
II [znw] *(wind)vlaag*
flush I [ov ww] • *doorspoelen* • *opjagen*
<v. vogels> II [on ww] *blozen* III [znw]
• *gesloten serie* <poker> • *doorspoeling*
• *plotselinge stroom* • *opwinding* • *blos*
IV [bnw] • *in één vlak liggend* • *goed
bij kas zijnde*
fluster [ov ww] *gejaagd maken*
flute [znw] *fluit*
flutist [znw] *fluitist*
flutter I [on ww] *fladderen, trillen, vlug
heen en weer bewegen* II [znw] *trilling,
gefladder*
fly I [on ww] *vliegen, zweven* II [znw]
• *vlieg* • *gulp*
flying [bnw] *vliegend*
foal [znw] *veulen*
foam I [on ww] *schuimen* II [znw]
schuim
foamy [bnw] *schuimend*
fob I [ov ww] • (~ **off**) *(met smoesjes)
afschepen* II [znw] *horlogeketting*
focal [bnw] *brandpunt(s)-*
focus I [ov + on ww] • *concentreren* <v.
gedachten> • *instellen* <v. camera>
II [znw] • *brandpunt* • *scherpstelling*
fodder [znw] *stalvoer*
foe [znw] *vijand* <dichterlijk>
fog I [ov ww] *vertroebelen, benevelen*
II [znw] *mist*
foggy [bnw] • *mistig* • *vaag*
foible [znw] *zwakke zijde*
foil I [ov ww] *verijdelen, in de war
brengen* II [znw] • *folie* • *zilverpapier*
foist [ov ww] • (~ **on/upon**) *opdringen*
fold I [ov ww] *vouwen* • (~ **up**) <inf.>
failliet gaan II [znw] • *vouw, kronkel*
• *schaapskooi*
folder [znw] *folder, vouwblad, map*
<voor documenten>
foliage [znw] *gebladerte, loof*
folk, folks [znw] <inf.> *volk, luitjes,
ouders, familieleden*
folksy [bnw] *gezellig, plattelands-,
eenvoudig*

follow I [ov ww] • *uitoefenen* <v.
ambacht> • *volgen* • *najagen*
• *begrijpen* II [on ww] *volgen (op/uit)*
• (~ **up**) *nagaan, werk maken van*
follower [znw] *volgeling*
following I [znw] • *aanhang*
• *volgelingen* • *het volgende* II [bnw]
volgend
folly [znw] *dwaasheid*
foment [ov ww] *aanstoken/-vuren*
fond [bnw] • *dwaas* • *innig, teder*
fondle [ov ww] *liefkozen*
font [znw] • *doopvont* • *wijwaterbakje*
• *oliereservoir* <v. lamp> • <AE> *lettertype*
food [znw] *voedsel, eten, voedingsartikel*
fool I [ov ww] *bedriegen* • (~ **into**)
wijsmaken • (~ **out of**) *(iets)
aftroggelen* II [on ww]
• (~ **about/around**) *rondhangen*
III [znw] • *dwaas, gek, nar*
• *(kruisbessen)vla* IV [bnw] <AE inf.>
dwaas
foolhardy [bnw] *roekeloos*
foolish [bnw] • *belachelijk* • *dwaas*
foolscap [znw] • *narrenkap, papieren
muts* • *schrijfpapier* <17 x 13,5 in.>
foot [znw] • *voet* • *pas, tred* • *versvoet*
• *voet* < 30,5 cm>
football [znw] • *voetbal* • *rugby*
footballer [znw] • *(prof)voetballer*
• *rugbyspeler*
footing [znw] • *voet* • *'t plaatsen van
de voeten* • *vaste betrekking, vaste voet*
• *verhouding*
foppish [bnw] *fatterig*
for I [vz] • *om, wegens* • *wat aangaat*
• *naar* • *gedurende* II [vw] *want,
aangezien*
forage I [ov ww] *plunderen* II [on ww]
• *fourageren* • *snuffelen in* III [znw]
• *voer* • *'t fourageren*
foray I [ov ww] *plunderen* II [znw]
rooftocht
forbear [on ww] z. *onthouden van*
forbearance [znw] *verdraagzaamheid*
forbid [ov ww] *verbieden*

forbidden I [ww] volt. deelw.
→ **forbid** II [bnw] *verboden*
forbidding [bnw] *onaanlokkelijk*
force I [ov ww] • *tot 't uiterste
inspannen* • *forceren, doorbreken*
• *noodzaken, dwingen tot* • *geweld
aandoen, overweldigen* • *(voort)drijven,
iem. iets opdringen* • *met geweld
nemen* • *(~ from) afdwingen,
ontwringen* II [znw] • *kracht, macht*
• *invloed* • *strijdkracht*
• *overtuigingskracht* • *noodzaak*
• *ploeg werklui*
forceful [bnw] *krachtig*
forcemeat [znw] *gehakt*
forceps [znw] *tang* ‹v. chirurg›
forcible [bnw] *krachtig, gedwongen*
fore I [bnw] *voor-* II [bijw] *voor(aan)*
forearm [znw] *voorarm*
foreboding [znw] *(slecht) voorgevoel*
forecast I [ov ww] *voorspellen* II [znw]
• *(weers)voorspelling* • *prognose*
forecourt [znw] *voorhof/-terrein*
forefinger [znw] *wijsvinger*
forefoot [znw] *voorpoot*
forefront [znw] *voorste deel, voorste
geledeen*
forego [ov ww] *voorafgaan (aan)*
foregoing [bnw] • *bovenvermeld*
• *voorafgaand*
foreground [znw] *voorgrond*
forehead [znw] *voorhoofd*
foreign [bnw] • *vreemd* • *buitenlands*
foreigner [znw] *buitenlander*
foreknowledge [znw] *voorkennis*
foreleg [znw] *voorpoot/-been*
forelock [znw] *lok haar op voorhoofd*
foreman [znw] • *voorzitter v. jury*
• *meesterknecht, ploegbaas*
foremost [bnw] *voorste, eerste,
voornaamste*
forename [znw] *voornaam*
foreshorten [ov ww] *in perspectief
afbeelden, verkort weergeven*
foreskin [znw] *voorhuid*
forest I [ov ww] *bebossen* II [znw]
woud, bos
forestry [znw] • *boscultuur* • *bosgrond*
foretaste [znw] *voorproefje*
foretell [ov ww] *voorspellen*
forethought [znw] *overleg*
forever [bijw] • *voor eeuwig/altijd,
voortaan* • *de hele tijd, steeds maar
(door)*
forewarn [ov ww] *van tevoren
waarschuwen*
foreword [znw] *voorwoord*
forfeit I [ov ww] *verspelen* II [znw]
• *boete* • *'t verbeurde, pand* III [bnw]
verbeurd verklaard
forgave [ww] verl. tijd → **forgive**
forge I [ov + on ww] • *smeden*
• *verzinnen, vervalsen* II [znw]
• *smidse, smidsvuur* • *smeltoven,
smelterij* • *vervalsing*
forgery [znw] *valsheid in geschrifte*
forget [ov + on ww] *vergeten*
forgetful [bnw] *vergeetachtig*
forgive [ov ww] *vergeven, kwijtschelden*
forgiveness [znw] *vergeving,
vergevingsgezindheid*
forgiving [bnw] *vergevingsgezind*
forgo [ov ww] • *z. onthouden van*
• *opgeven, afstand doen van*
fork I [ov ww] • *(~ out) dokken, over de
brug komen* II [on ww] *z. vertakken*
III [znw] • *vork, gaffel* • *vertakking*
• *splitsing* ‹in weg›
forlorn [bnw] • *wanhopig, hopeloos*
• *verlaten, troosteloos* • *ellendig
uitziend*
form I [ov ww] *vormen* II [on ww] *zich
vormen* • *(~ after) (z.) vormen naar*
• *(~ up) (z.) opstellen* III [znw] • *vorm,
gedaante* • *schoolklas* • *formulier*
• *gedrag* • ‹sport› *conditie*
formal [bnw] *formeel, nadrukkelijk*
formalism [znw] *formalisme,
vormelijkheid*
formality [znw] *formaliteit*
format I [ov ww] *formatteren* II [znw]
• *formaat* • *het formatteren*

formation [znw] *vorming, formatie*
formative [bnw] • *vormend*
• *buigings-, afleidings-*
former [bnw] • *vroeger, voormalig*
• *eerstgenoemde*
formidable [bnw] *ontzagwekkend, geducht*
formula [znw] • *recept* • *formule* • <AE> *babyvoeding*
formulate [ov ww] *formuleren*
fornicate [on ww] *ontucht plegen*
forsake [ov ww] *in de steek laten, verlaten*
forswear [ov ww] *afzweren*
forte [znw] • *sterke kant* • <muz.> *forto*
forth [bijw] *voort, uit, weg, buiten*
forthcoming [bnw] • *aanstaande, komend* • *tegemoetkomend* <v. personen>
forthright [bnw] • *open, eerlijk, oprecht* • *direct, onmiddellijk*
forthwith [bijw] *onmiddellijk*
fortieth [telw] *veertigste*
fortify [ov ww] *(ver)sterken*
fortitude [znw] *vastberadenheid*
fortnight [znw] *twee weken*
fortnightly [bijw] *iedere twee weken*
fortress [znw] *vesting*
fortuitous [bnw] • *toevallig* • *fortuinlijk*
fortunate [bnw] *gelukkig*
fortune [znw] *geluk, lot, fortuin* <geld>
forty [telw] *veertig*
forward I [ov ww] • *bevorderen, vooruithelpen* • *(door)sturen, (ver)zenden* II [znw] <sport> *voorspeler* III [bnw] • *vooruitstrevend* • *voorwaarts, naar voren* • *vroegrijp, vroegtijdig* • *vrijpostig* IV [bijw] *voorwaarts, vooruit*
fossil I [znw] *fossiel* II [bnw] • *versteend* • *opgedolven*
foster I [ov ww] *koesteren* II [bnw] *pleeg-*
fought [ww] *verl. tijd + volt. deelw.* → fight

foul I [ov ww] *bezoedelen* • (~ up) *verprutsen, verknoeien* II [on ww] *vuil worden* III [znw] <sport> *overtreding* IV [bnw] • *walgelijk, stinkend* • *oneerlijk* • *smerig* <weer> • *vuil, bedorven* <lucht>
found I [ww] *verl.tijd + volt.deelw.* → find II [ov ww] *stichten*
foundation [znw] • *basis, fundering* • *oprichting* • *stichting*
founder I [on ww] • *mislukken* • *vergaan* <schip> II [znw] • *oprichter* • *gieter* <v. metaal>
foundling [znw] *vondeling*
foundry [znw] *metaalgieterij*
fount [znw] *bron* <dichterlijk>
fountain [znw] • *waterstraal, fontein* • *bron*
four I [znw] *boot met 4 riemen* II [telw] *vier*
fourteen [telw] *veertien*
fourth [telw] *vierde*
fourthly [bijw] *ten vierde*
fowl [znw] • *gevogelte* <ook 't vlees> • *kip, haan*
fox I [ov ww] *onbegrijpelijk zijn voor* II [znw] • *sluwaard* • *vos*
foxy [bnw] • *sluw* • *aantrekkelijk*
fracas [znw] *herrie, vechtpartij*
fraction [znw] • *breuk* • *onderdeel*
fractional [bnw] • *gebroken, gedeeltelijk* • *onbeduidend*
fracture I [ov ww] *breken* II [znw] • *barst* • *botbreuk*
fragile [bnw] *broos, bros, zwak, teer, breekbaar*
fragment I [ov + on ww] • *verdelen in (brok)stukken* • *versplinteren* II [znw] • *fragment* • *scherf, (brok)stuk*
fragmental, fragmentary [bnw] *fragmentarisch*
fragrant [bnw] *geurig*
frail [bnw] *broos, zwak*
franchise [znw] • *burgerrecht* • *stemrecht* • *vrijstelling* • *vergunning*
frank [bnw] *openhartig*

frankincense [znw] *wierook*
frantic [bnw] *razend, krankzinnig*
fraternal [bnw] *broederlijk*
fraternity [znw] • *broederschap* • <AE>
studentenclub/-corps
fraternize [on ww] *z. verbroederen*
fraud [znw] • *fraude, bedrog* • *bedrieger*
fraudulent [bnw] *frauduleus*
fraught [bnw] *beladen, vol van*
fray I [ov + on ww] *rafelen* II [znw]
gekrakeel, strijd
freak I [on ww] • (- out) *hallucinaties*
krijgen <bij drugs> II [znw] • *gril*
• *gedrocht, rariteit* • *zonderling, hippie*
• *fanaat*
freckle [znw] *sproet*
free I [ov ww] • *bevrijden,*
los-/vrijmaken • *ontslaan* <v. belofte>
II [bnw] • *vrij, onbelemmerd*
• *onafhankelijk* • *gratis*
freedom [znw] *vrijheid*
freeze I [ov ww] • (doen) *bevriezen* <ook
fig.> • *laten stilstaan* <beeldband of
film> • *stabiliseren* <prijzen of lonen>
• (doen) *stollen* • (- out) *uitsluiten,*
boycotten II [on ww] • *bevriezen*
<plotseling onbeweeglijk worden>
• *vriezen* • (- over) *dichtvriezen*
III [znw] • *vorst* • *bevriezing* <v. loon>
freezer [znw] *diepvries*
freight I [ov ww] • *verzenden* • *laden,*
bevrachten II [znw] *vracht(prijs),*
lading
freighter [znw] • *bevrachter*
• *vrachtboot/-vliegtuig*
French I [znw] *de Fransen* II [bnw]
Frans
frenetic [bnw] *dwaas, waanzinnig*
frequent I [ov ww] *regelmatig/vaak*
bezoeken II [bnw] *veelvuldig*
fresh [bnw] • *nieuw, anders, fris, vers*
• *onervaren* • *zoet* <water> • *brutaal*
freshen [ov ww] • *ontzouten*
• *opfrissen, aanzetten* • (- up) (z.)
opfrissen
fret I [ov ww] • *versieren met snijwerk*

• *knagen, in-/wegvreten* • (z.) *ergeren*
• *verdrietig zijn, kniezen* II [znw]
• *ergernis* • *vingerzetting* <v.
snaarinstrument>
fretful [bnw] • *verdrietig, gemelijk*
• *vingerzetting* <v. snaarinstrument>
• *stormachtig* <weer>
friction [znw] *wrijving*
Friday [znw] *vrijdag*
fridge [znw] *koelkast*
friend [znw] • *vriend(in), kennis*
• *relatie*
friendless [bnw] *zonder vrienden*
friendly I [znw] *vriendschappelijke*
wedstrijd II [bnw] • *welwillend*
• *vriendschappelijk, bevriend* <naties>
friendship [znw] *vriendschap*
frieze [znw] *fries* <rand v. versiering>
frigate [znw] *fregat*
fright [znw] *schrik, vrees*
frighten [ov ww] *doen schrikken*
• (- away) *verjagen*
frightful [bnw] • *afschuwelijk* • <inf.>
ontzaglijk
frigid [bnw] • *frigide* • *koud, ijzig, kil*
frill [znw] *geplooide strook*
frilly [bnw] *met*
kantjes/strookjes/prullaria
fringe [znw] • *franje, zoom,*
buitenkant, zelfkant • *ponyhaar*
frippery [znw] *opschik, snuisterijen*
frisk I [ov ww] • *fouilleren* • <AE>
zakkenrollen II [on ww] • *springen*
• *dartelen*
fritter I [ov ww] • (- away)
verklungelen II [znw] *(appel)beignet*
frivolity [znw] *lichtzinnigheid*
frivolous [bnw] • *dwaas* • *lichtzinnig,*
wuft
frizz [ov + on ww] *krullen* <haar>
frock [znw] *japon, jurkje*
frog [znw] • *kikker, kikvors* • <pej.>
Fransoos
frolic I [on ww] *rondspringen, pret*
maken II [znw] *grap, fuif*
from [vz] • *naar, volgens* • *als gevolg v.,*

wegens, door • van, weg van, van ... af,
uit

front I [ov ww] staan tegenover II [znw]
• front • gezicht • voorgevel
• voorhoofd <dichterlijk> • brutaliteit
• strandboulevard • camouflage
III [bnw] voorste, voor-

frontage [znw] • vóór gelegen terrein
• front

frontal [bnw] front(en)-, voorhoofds-

frontier [znw] grens

frontispiece [znw] • voorgevel • plaat
tegenover titelblad <in boek>

frost I [ov ww] • doen bevriezen
<planten> • glaceren <gebak> • berijpen
• mat maken <glas> II [znw] vorst

frosting [znw] glazuur <voor gebak>

frosty [bnw] • vriezend, ijzig • berijpt

froth [znw] schuim

frown I [on ww] 't voorhoofd fronsen,
dreigend kijken II [znw] frons,
afkeurende blik

froze [ww] verl. tijd → freeze

frozen I [ww] volt. deelw. → freeze
II [bnw] bevroren, ijzig

frugal [bnw] matig, sober

fruit [znw] fruit, vrucht(en)

fruitful [bnw] vruchtbaar, resultaat
gevend

fruition [znw] • verwezenlijking
• vervulling

fruitless [bnw] • onvruchtbaar
• vruchteloos

fruity [bnw] • vrucht- • geurig, pikant
• klankrijk, vol <v. stem>

frump [znw] slons

fry I [ov ww] braden, bakken II [znw]
jonge vissen

fuck <vulg.> [ov + on ww] neuken
• (~ about/around) rotzooien,
aanklooien

fudge I [ov ww] eromheen draaien
II [znw] • onzin, bedotterij • zachte
karamel

fuel I [ov ww] voorzien v. brandstof
II [znw] brandstof

fug [znw] bedompte atmosfeer <in
kamer>

fugitive I [znw] • voortvluchtige
• vluchteling II [bnw] • kortstondig
• voortvluchtig

fulcrum [znw] • steunpunt, draaipunt
<v. hefboom> • <plantk.> aanhangsel

fulfil [ov ww] • vervullen,
beantwoorden aan <doel> • uitvoeren

fulfilment [znw] bevrediging

fully [bijw] • volledig • v. ganser harte

fulminate [ov ww] uitvaren tegen

fulsome [bnw] kruiperig vleiend

fumble [on ww] op onhandige manier
doen

fumigate [ov ww] • ontsmetten
• doorgeuren

fun [znw] pret

function I [on ww] functioneren
II [znw] • functie, beroep
• plechtigheid, feest

functional [bnw] doelmatig,
functioneel

functionary I [znw] • ambtenaar,
beambte • functionaris II [bnw]
→ functional

fund I [ov ww] bekostigen II [znw]
fonds, voorraad

fundamental I [znw] basis,
grondbeginsel, grondtoon II [bnw]
grond-, fundamenteel

funeral I [znw] • begrafenis(stoet) • <AE>
rouwdienst II [bnw] begrafenis-, lijk-

funereal [bnw] • begrafenis- • somber,
treur- • diepzwart

fungus [znw] • paddestoel • zwam

funk I [ov ww] ontwijken <uit angst>
II [znw] • bangerd • <muz.> funk

funnel I [ov ww] afvoeren door trechter
II [znw] • trechter • lichtkoker,
luchtkoker • schoorsteen

funny [bnw] • grappig, raar
• bedrieglijk

fur I [znw] • bont(werk) • aanzetsel <v.
wijn>, beslag <op de tong>, ketelsteen
II [bnw] bont(en)-

furbish [ov ww] • (~ **up**) *oppoetsen,*
opknappen, vernieuwen
furious [bnw] • *woedend* • *wild*
furl [ov ww] *reven <zeil>, opvouwen*
furlong [znw] *1/8 Eng. mijl <201 m.>*
furnace [znw] *oven, vuurhaard*
furnish [ov ww] • *leveren* • *meubileren*
• (~ **with**) *voorzien v.*
furore [znw] *furore, opwinding*
furrier [znw] *bontwerker,*
bonthandelaar
furrow I [ov ww] *rimpelen* II [znw]
voor, groef, rimpel
furry [bnw] • *met bont bekleed* • *zacht*
further I [ov ww] *bevorderen*
II [bnw + bijw] • *verder* • *meer*
furthest [bnw] *verst(e)*
fury [znw] • *woeste vrouw, feeks, furie*
• *woede*
fuse I [ov ww] • *v. lont voorzien*
• *(samen)smelten* II [on ww] *doorslaan*
<v. zekeringen> III [znw] • *zekering <v.*
elektr.> • *lont*
fuselage [znw] *romp v. vliegtuig*
fusion [znw] *smelting, fusie*
fuss I [on ww] • *druk maken*
• *zenuwachtig maken* • (~ **over**) *z.*
druk maken over II [znw] *drukte, ophef*
fussy [bnw] • *gejaagd, druk* • *pietluttig*
fusty [bnw] *muf*
futile [bnw] *doelloos, nutteloos,*
waardeloos
futility [znw] • *futiliteit* • *nutteloosheid*
future I [znw] *toekomst, toekomende*
tijd II [bnw] *toekomstig, aanstaand*
futuristic [bnw] *futuristisch*
fuzz [znw] • *dons* • <sl.> *politie*
fuzzy [bnw] • *beneveld, wazig* • *donzig*

G

gab [on ww] *praten, kletsen*
gabble I [ov + on ww] *haastig praten*
II [znw] *haastig gepraat*
gable [znw] *gevelspits*
gadget [znw] • *machineonderdeel(tje),*
instrument(je) • *truc, foefje*
gadgetry [znw] *allerlei spullen*
Gaelic I [znw] *de Keltische taal* II [bnw]
Keltisch
gaffe [znw] *blunder, ongepaste*
daad/opmerking
gag I [ov ww] *knevelen, de mond snoeren*
II [on ww] *kokhalzen* III [znw] • *knevel*
• *grap*
gaga [bnw] *kinds, dement*
gaggle I [on ww] *snateren* II [znw]
• *vlucht ganzen* • *het snateren*
gaiety [znw] • *vrolijkheid* • *opschik*
gaily [bijw] • *vrolijk* • *fleurig*
gain I [ov ww] • *winnen, behalen,*
krijgen, verwerven • *bereiken*
• *toenemen <v. lichaamsgewicht>*
• (~ (**up**)**on**) *inhalen* II [znw] *winst,*
voordeel
gainful [bnw] *winstgevend*
gainsay [ov ww] *tegenspreken,*
ontkennen
gait [znw] *manier v. lopen, pas*
gaiter [znw] • *slobkous* • <AE> *bottine*
gal <inf.> [znw] *meisje*
galaxy [znw] • *de melkweg*
• *schitterende groep/schare/stoet*
gale [znw] • *storm* • <plantk.> *gagel*
gall I [ov ww] *verbitteren, kwetsen*
II [znw] • *gal* • *bitterheid* • *(oorzaak v.)*
verdriet • <AE> *arrogantie*
gallant I [znw] *galante ridder <fig.>*
II [bnw] • *fier, statig* • *dapper* • *galant*
gallantry [znw] • *dapperheid*
• *hoffelijkheid*
gallery [znw] • *galerij*

- *(schilderijen)museum* • *toonzaal*
- *schellinkje* • ‹AE› *veranda*
galley [znw] • *galei* • *sloep*
- *scheepskeuken*
Gallic [bnw] • *Gallisch* • *Frans*
gallivant [on ww] • *flaneren* • *flirten*
gallop I [ov + on ww] *(laten)*
galopperen II [znw] *galop*
gallows [mv] *galg*
galvanize [ov ww] • *galvaniseren*
- *opzwepen*
gambit [znw] • *gambiet* • *listige zet*
gamble I [ov + on ww] *dobbelen,*
gokken, speculeren II [znw] *gok*
gambler [znw] *gokker*
gambol [on ww] *dartelen*
game I [znw] • *spel(letje)* • *wild*
II [bnw] *moedig*
gammon [znw] *gerookte ham*
gamut [znw] • *het hele register*
- *toonladder, toonschaal*
- *(toon)omvang*
gander [znw] • *gent* • ‹inf.› *stomme*
idioot
gang I [on ww] • *(~ up) samenklitten,*
een bende vormen • *(~ up*
against/on) z. collectief keren tegen,
samenspannen tegen II [znw] *troep,*
bende
gangling [bnw] *slungelig*
gangrene [znw] *gangreen, koudvuur*
gangrenous [bnw] *gangreneus*
gangster [znw] *gangster, bendelid*
gantry [znw] *stellage, seinbrug, rijbrug*
‹onder kraan›
gaol [znw] → **jail**
garb [znw] • *kledij* • *klederdracht*
garbage [znw] *afval, vuilnis*
garden I [on ww] *tuinieren* II [znw]
tuin
gardener [znw] *tuinman, tuinier*
gargantuan [bnw] *reusachtig*
gargle I [ov + on ww] *gorgelen* II [znw]
gorgeldrank
gargoyle [znw] *waterspuwer*
garish [bnw] *opzichtig, bont*

garland I [ov ww] *bekransen* II [znw]
bloemslinger, bloemkrans
garlic [znw] *knoflook*
garment [znw] *kledingstuk, gewaad*
garnet I [znw] *granaat(steen)* II [bnw]
granaatrood
garnish I [ov ww] *versieren, opmaken*
II [znw] *versiering, garnering*
garret [znw] *zolderkamer(tje)*
garrison I [ov ww] *bezetten* II [znw]
garnizoen
garrulous [bnw] *praatziek*
garter [znw] *kousenband*
gas I [ov ww] *vergassen* II [on ww]
zwammen III [znw] • *gas* • *gezwam*
- ‹AE› *benzine*
gash I [ov ww] *een jaap toebrengen*
II [znw] *diepe snede, jaap*
gasolene, gasoline [znw] • *gasoline*
- *benzine*
gasometer [znw] *gashouder*
gasp I [on ww] • *hijgen* • II [znw] *het*
stokken van de adem
gastric [bnw] *v.d. maag, maag-*
gastronomic [bnw] *gastronomisch*
gastronomy [znw] *gastronomie*
gate [znw] • *poort* • *hek* • *deur* ‹ook v.
sluis›
gather [ov + on ww] • *(z.) verzamelen*
- *oogsten, plukken, oprapen* • *rimpelen,*
plooien • *afleiden* • *(~ from) besluiten,*
v. iets afleiden
gathering [znw] • *vergadering*
- *bijeenkomst*
gauche [bnw] *onhandig, lomp*
gaudy [bnw] *opzichtig*
gauge I [ov ww] • *meten, peilen*
- *normaliseren, ijken* II [znw]
- *standaard (inhouds)maat* • *omvang,*
inhoud • *spoorwijdte* • *regenmeter,*
oliedrukmeter
gaunt [bnw] *mager, ingevallen*
gauntlet [znw] *dikke handschoen*
gave [ww] *verl. tijd* → **give**
gavel [znw] *(voorzitters)hamer*
gawky [bnw] *onhandig, klungelig*

gay [bnw] • vrolijk • fleurig
• homo(seksueel), lesbisch
gaze I [on ww] staren II [znw] starende
blik
gear I [ov ww] (op)tuigen • (~ to)
aanpassen aan, afstemmen op II [znw]
• gereedschappen, spullen • raderwerk,
tandwieloverbrenging,
versnelling(smechanisme) • vlotte
kledij, snelle kleren • tuig
geese [mv] → goose
gel I [on ww] (meer) vaste vorm krijgen
II [znw] gel
gelding [znw] ruin
gem [znw] edelsteen, kleinood, juweel
gen I [ov ww] • (~ up) grondig van
informatie voorzien II [on ww]
• (~ up) zich volledig laten inlichten
gender [znw] geslacht
gene [znw] gen
genealogic(al) [bnw] genealogisch
genealogy [znw] • stamboom
• genealogie
genera [mv] → genus
general I [znw] • generaal • strateeg
II [bnw] algemeen, gewoon(lijk)
generality [znw] algemeenheid
generalization [znw] generalisatie
generate [ov ww] • genereren
• voortbrengen
generation [znw] • wording
• generatie, geslacht
generator [znw] • dynamo, stoomketel
• generator
generic [bnw] • algemeen • generisch,
kenmerkend voor de soort
generosity [znw] vrijgevigheid
generous [bnw] • overvloedig • gul
• mild
genesis [znw] ontstaan, oorsprong
genial [bnw] • mild • gezellig, joviaal
genie [znw] geest
genital [bnw] m.b.t. de geslachtsdelen,
voortplantings-
gent ‹inf.› [znw] meneer
genteel ‹iron.› [bnw] chic, deftig

gentility [znw] deftigheid
gentle [bnw] • zacht, rustig, matig
• vriendelijk
gentleman [znw] heer
gentry [znw] • lagere adel • ridders en
baronets
genuflect [on ww] de knie buigen
genuine [bnw] • onvervalst, echt
• oprecht
genus [znw] geslacht, soort, klasse
geography [znw] aardrijkskunde
geology [znw] geologie
geometry [znw] meetkunde
geophysics [znw] geofysica
Georgian I [znw] • Georgiër • inwoner
van Georgia II [bnw] • Georgisch
• 18e-eeuws
geriatric [bnw] geriatrisch
germ [ov ww] doen ontkiemen
Germanic [bnw] Germaans
germinate [ov + on ww] (doen)
ontkiemen
gestation [znw] • groeiperiode • dracht
gesticulate [on ww] gebaren maken
gesture I [on ww] gebaren maken
II [znw] • gebaar • geste
get I [ov ww] • krijgen • (te) pakken
(krijgen) • (be)halen • verdienen • ertoe
brengen • snappen • laten • (~ across)
begrijpelijk maken • (~ back)
terugkrijgen • (~ down) deprimeren,
doorslikken, noteren • (~ in)
erin/ertussen komen, instappen
• (~ on) aantrekken • (~ out of)
krijgen/halen uit • (~ over) te boven
komen • (~ through) erdoor krijgen
• (~ to~her) bijeenbrengen • (~ up)
op touw zetten II [on ww]
• terechtkomen • (ge)raken • bereiken
• worden • (~ about) z. verspreiden,
rondlopen • (~ across) begrepen
worden • (~ ahead) vooruitkomen
• (~ along) vorderen • (~ around)
rondreizen • (~ around to) ertoe
komen, tijd vinden om te • (~ at)
bereiken, er komen • (~ away)

wegkomen • (~ **back**) *terugkomen*
• (~ **down**) *naar beneden komen*
• (~ **in**) *binnenhalen* • (~ **into**)
komen/belanden in • (~ **off**) *afstijgen,
er afkomen, uitstappen* • (~ **on**)
opschieten, 't stellen • (~ **out**) *eruit
komen, uitlekken* • (~ **over**) *begrepen
worden, overkomen* • (~ **through**)
erdoor komen • (~ **to**) *komen/krijgen
te, bereiken* • (~ **to**~**her**) *bijeenkomen*
• (~ **up**) *opstaan*
geyser [znw] • *natuurlijke hete bron,
geiser* • *geiser, heetwatertoestel*
ghastly [bnw] • *gruwelijk, afgrijselijk*
• *doodsbleek*
gherkin [znw] *augurk*
ghetto [znw] *getto*
ghost [znw] *geest, spook*
ghostly [bnw] *spookachtig*
ghoul [znw] • *(lugubere) geest, monster*
• *lijkeneter, grafschender*
giant I [znw] *reus* II [bnw] *reusachtig*
gibber [on ww] *brabbelen*
gibberish [znw] *brabbeltaal*
gibe I [ov + on ww] *(be)spotten, honen*
II [znw] *schimpscheut, spottende
opmerking*
giddy [bnw] • *duizelig*
• *duizelingwekkend* • *wispelturig,
onbezonnen, dwaas*
gig [znw] • *optreden* • *sjees*
gigantic [bnw] *reusachtig*
giggle I [on ww] *giechelen* II [znw]
gegiechel
gild I [ov ww] *vergulden* II [znw]
→ **guild**
gill [znw] *kieuw*
gilt I [ww] *verl.tijd + volt.deelw.*
→ **gild** II [bnw] *verguld*
gimlet [znw] *handboor(tje)*
gimmick [znw] *truc, foefje, vondst*
gin [znw] *jenever*
ginger I [znw] *gember* II [bnw] *rood* <v.
haar>
gingerly [bijw] *behoedzaam*
giraffe [znw] *giraf*

gird [ov ww] • *een gordel omdoen,
(aan)gorden* • *insluiten*
girder [znw] *dwarsbalk*
girdle [znw] *gordel*
girl [znw] *meisje*
girlie [bnw] *met veel vrouwelijk naakt*
girlish [bnw] *meisjesachtig*
girth [znw] • *omvang* • *buikriem, gordel*
gist [znw] • *kern, hoofdzaak* • *strekking*
give I [ov ww] • *geven* • *opleveren*
• (~ **away**) *verklappen, weggeven,
verraden* • (~ **back**) *teruggeven*
• (~ **forth**) *afgeven, verspreiden*
• (~ **in**) *inleveren, erbij geven* • (~ **off**)
afgeven • (~ **out**) *aankondigen,
bekend maken, afgeven* • (~ **over**)
opgeven, laten varen • (~ **up**)
ophouden met II [on ww] • *geven*
• *toegeven, meegeven, 't begeven*
• (~ **in**) *toegeven, zwichten*
• (~ **on(to)**) *uitkomen op* • (~ **out**)
opraken • (~ **up**) *'t opgeven* III [znw] *'t
meegeven, elasticiteit*
given I [ww] *volt. deelw.* → **give**
II [znw] *gegeven* III [bnw] *bepaald*
glacial [bnw] • *m.b.t. ijs, m.b.t. gletsjers*
• *gekristalliseerd*
glacier [znw] *gletsjer*
glad [bnw] *blij*
gladiator [znw] *zwaardvechter,
gladiator*
glamorize [ov ww] *verheerlijken,
vergulden* <fig.>
glance I [on ww] *(vluchtig) kijken*
• (~ **aside/off**) *afschampen* • (~ **at**)
een blik werpen op, even aanroeren
• (~ **over/through**) *dóórkijken*
II [znw] *(vluchtige) blik*
glandular [bnw] *m.b.t. klier,
klierachtig*
glare I [on ww] • *wild/woest kijken*
• *zinderen, fel schijnen of stralen*
II [znw] • *schittering, fel licht* • *woeste
blik*
glass I [znw] • *glas(werk)* • *spiegel*
• *monocle* • *barometer* II [bnw] *glazen*

glassy [bnw] • glazen • spiegelglad
glaucoma [znw] groene staar
glaze I [ov ww] • van glas voorzien
• verglazen, glazuren, glaceren <v.
gebak>, vernissen • glazig maken
II [on ww] glazig worden III [znw]
• glans, vernis, glacé, glazuur • waas
gleam I [on ww] glimmen, glanzen,
schijnen II [znw] glans, schijnsel
glean [ov ww] lezen, bijeengaren
glee [znw] • vrolijkheid • meerstemmig
lied
gleeful [bnw] vrolijk
glen [znw] nauw dal
glib [bnw] rad v. tong, welbespraakt
glide I [on ww] glijden, sluipen II [znw]
glijvlucht
glider [znw] zweefvliegtuig
gliding [znw] het zweefvliegen,
zweefvliegsport
glimmer I [on ww] flikkeren, (zwak)
schijnen II [znw] zwak licht
glimpse I [ov + on ww] even vluchtig
zien/kijken II [znw] glimp, vluchtige
blik, kijkje
glint I [on ww] glinsteren, blinken
II [znw] schijnsel
glisten [on ww] glinsteren
glitter I [on ww] schitteren, flonkeren,
blinken II [znw] glans
gloat [on ww] • (~ on/over) met
leedvermaak bekijken
global [bnw] globaal, wereldomvattend
globe [znw] • aarde • globe • (aard)bol
• hemellichaam • rijksappel • viskom
globular [bnw] bolvormig
globule [znw] • bolletje
• bloedlichaampje
gloom [znw] • duisternis • somberheid
glorify [ov ww] verheerlijken
gloss I [ov ww] • glanzend maken
• commentariëren • (~ over) met de
mantel der liefde bedekken, verbloemen
II [znw] • glans • valse schijn
• kanttekening, glosse, tekstuitleg
glossary [znw] verklarende woordenlijst

glossy [bnw] glanzend
glove [znw] handschoen
glow I [on ww] gloeien, stralen II [znw]
gloed
glower [on ww] • (~ at) woedend kijken
naar
glowing [bnw] • gloeiend, vlammend
• geestdriftig, levendig
glue I [ov ww] lijmen II [znw] lijm
glum [bnw] somber, triest
glut [ov ww] verzadigen
glutinous [bnw] lijmachtig, kleverig
glutton [znw] gulzigaard, veelvraat
gluttonous [bnw] vraatzuchtig,
gulzig
gnash [ov + on ww] knarsen <v. tanden>
gnat [znw] mug
gnaw [ov + on ww] • knabbelen (aan),
knagen (aan) • (uit)bijten
gnome [znw] kabouter, aardmannetje
gnu [znw] gnoe, wildebeest
go I [on ww] • gaan • vertrekken • lopen
• eropuit gaan, reizen • in elkaar
zakken, eraan gaan • gelden
• (~ about) rondgaan, aanpakken
• (~ against) indruisen tegen
• (~ along) gaan, heengaan • (~ at)
aanvliegen, aanpakken • (~ back
from) terugkomen op, niet houden
• (~ beyond) overschrijden, verder
gaan dan, te boven gaan • (~ by)
voorbijgaan, afgaan op • (~ for) te lijf
gaan, kiezen • (~ in for) gaan doen
aan, z. ten doel stellen, doen in
• (~ into) ingaan (op) • (~ off)
bederven • (~ on) doorgaan (met),
volhouden, z. aanstellen • (~ on at)
tekeergaan tegen • (~ over) dóórlopen
<v. thema/huis>, nakijken
• (~ round) voldoende zijn (voor
allen) • (~ through) nagaan,
doorzoeken, doorstaan, beleven
• (~ through with) doorgaan (met),
volhouden • (~ to) gaan naar/tot
• (~ together) (bij elkaar) passen,
samengaan, met elkaar gaan

• (~ **under**) ten onder gaan, te gronde
gaan • (~ **up**) opgaan, stijgen
• (~ **upon**) afgaan op • (~ **with**)
passen bij, overeenkomen met,
samengaan, het eens zijn met
• (~ **without**) het stellen zonder
II [kww] worden III [znw] • gang
• energie • poging • beurt • ‹sl.› zaak
goad I [ov ww] prikkelen II [znw]
prikkel
goal [znw] • doel • doelpunt
• bestemming
goat [znw] geit, bok
gobble I [ov ww] naar binnen
schrokken II [on ww] • schrokken
• klokken ‹v. kalkoen›
goblet [znw] • glas met hoge voet
• drinkbeker
goblin [znw] kabouter, plaaggeest
goggle [on ww] uitpuilen ‹v. ogen›
going I [znw] • het vooruitkomen • het
gaan II [bnw] voorhanden
gold I [znw] goud II [bnw] gouden
golliwog [znw] pop met uiterlijk van
neger
golly [tw] gossie!
gondola [znw] gondel
gone I [ww] volt. deelw. → go
II [bnw] • weg, dood • bedorven
• verloren, op
goo [znw] • slijmerig spul • slijm
good I [znw] • goed, welzijn • voordeel,
nut • bestwil II [bnw] • goed • braaf,
zoet • flink, best • vriendelijk, aardig
goodly [bnw] • knap, mooi • flink
goody [znw] bonbon
goody-goody [znw] sul
gooey [bnw] • klef, kleverig • mierzoet
• sentimenteel
goof [znw] sufferd, halve gare
goofy [bnw] niet goed wijs
goon [znw] • sul, sukkel • boeman
goose [znw] • gans • uilskuiken
gooseberry [znw] kruisbes
gore I [ov ww] doorboren, priemen
II [znw] (geronnen) bloed

gorge I [ov + on ww] (z.) volproppen,
gulzig (op)eten II [znw] bergengte
gorgeous [bnw] prachtig, schitterend
gormless [bnw] onnozel, stom
gorse [znw] gaspeldoorn
gory [bnw] bloedig
gosh [tw] gossiemijne!, tjemig!
gosling [znw] jonge gans
gospel [znw] • evangelie • ‹AE›
gospelmuziek
gossamer I [znw] • ragfijn weefsel
• herfstdraad/-draden II [bnw]
vluchtig, ragfijn, teder
gossip I [on ww] roddelen II [znw]
• kletskous, roddelaarster • geklets,
geroddel
gossipy [bnw] roddelachtig, praatziek
got [ww] verl. tijd + volt. deelw. → **get**
Gothic I [znw] gotiek II [bnw] gotisch
gouge I [ov ww] gutsen, uithollen
II [znw] • groef • guts
gourd [znw] kalebas, pompoen
gout [znw] • jicht • kleine hoeveelheid,
bloeddruppel/-spat
govern [ov ww] • leiden • bepalen
• regeren • beheersen
governess [znw] gouvernante
government [znw] • overheid,
regering • ministerie
governor [znw] • gouverneur • patroon
• ‹inf.› ouwe heer
gown [znw] • japon • toga
grab I [ov ww] • grissen • inpikken
II [znw] greep
grace I [ov ww] (ver)sieren, opluisteren
• (~ **with**) vereren met II [znw]
• genade • gratie, elegantie
• gepastheid, fatsoen • gunst
graceful [bnw] elegant, sierlijk, gracieus
graceless [bnw] • onbeschaamd • lomp
gracious [bnw] • genadig
• goedgunstig • minzaam, hoffelijk
gradation [znw] • onmerkbare
overgang, gradatie • nuance, trap,
stadium
grade I [ov ww] beoordelen met cijfer

II [znw] • graad • klasse • klas • cijfer
<op school> • centigraad • helling
• loonschaal
gradient [znw] • helling • gradiënt
gradual [bnw] geleidelijk
graduate I [ov ww] graad verlenen,
diplomeren II [on ww] • graad behalen
• geleidelijk opklimmen III [znw]
afgestudeerde
graduation [znw] • schaalverdeling
• promotie • progressie • buluitreiking,
het afstuderen
graft I [ov ww] enten II [znw]
• entspleet • transplantatie • entloot
• enting
grain [znw] • korrel • graan • greintje
• korrelstructuur, ruwe kant v. leer
• nerf, draad <v. hout> • aard, natuur
grammar [znw] grammatica
grammatical [bnw] grammaticaal
gramophone [znw] grammofoon
grand [bnw] • voornaam • groot(s),
weids, imposant • prachtig, prima
grandeur [znw] pracht
grandiloquent [bnw] bombastisch,
hoogdravend
grandiose [bnw] grandioos, groots
granite [znw] graniet
granny [znw] (groot)moedertje
grant I [ov ww] • vergunnen, toestaan,
verlenen • toegeven • schenken II [znw]
subsidie, concessie, uitkering, toelage,
(studie)beurs
granular [bnw] korrelig
granule [znw] korreltje
grape [znw] druif
graph [znw] grafiek
graphic [bnw] grafisch
graphite [znw] grafiet
grapnel [znw] • klein anker
• enterhaak • dreg
grapple I [ov ww] aanpakken,
beetpakken II [znw] • klein anker
• worsteling
grasp I [ov ww] • aangrijpen,
vasthouden • begrijpen, inzien II [znw]

• vat, houvast • bereik, volledig begrip
• bevattingsvermogen
grasping [bnw] hebberig, inhalig
grass I [on ww] <sl.> verklikken II [znw]
• gras • <sl.> marihuana, hasjiesj
grassy [bnw] grasachtig
grate I [ov ww] • raspen • knarsen
II [on ww] knarsen III [znw] • rooster
• open haard
grateful [bnw] • dankbaar • weldadig
grater [znw] rasp
grating [znw] tralies, traliewerk
gratitude [znw] dankbaarheid
gratuitous [bnw] • ongegrond
• nodeloos
gratuity [znw] • fooi • gratificatie
grave I [znw] graf II [bnw] ernstig,
somber
gravel [znw] grind, kiezel
gravitate [on ww] • (over)hellen, neigen
• (be)zinken • aangetrokken worden
gravitation [znw] zwaartekracht
gravitational [bnw] gravitatie-
gravity [znw] • gewicht(igheid)
• zwaartekracht
gravy [znw] jus
gray [znw] → **grey**
graze I [ov + on ww] • grazen • weiden
• schaven, schampen II [znw]
schaafwond, schram, schampschot
grease I [ov ww] insmeren, invetten
II [znw] vet
greasy [bnw] vettig
great [bnw] • groot • gewichtig,
voornaam • prachtig
greatly [bijw] zeer, grotelijks
Grecian [bnw] Grieks
greed [znw] begerigheid, hebzucht
greedy [bnw] hebzuchtig
Greek I [znw] Griek II [bnw] Grieks
green I [znw] grasveld II [bnw] • groen
• onrijp • onervaren
greenery [znw] planten
greenish [bnw] groen
greet [ov ww] (be)groeten
greeting [znw] groet

gregarious [bnw] • *in kudden levend* • *(op) gezellig(heid gesteld)*
grenade [znw] *handgranaat*
grew [ww] verl. tijd → **grow**
grey I [ov + on ww] *grijs maken/worden* II [znw] *grijze schimmel* III [bnw] • *grijs* • *somber* • *vergrijsd, met ervaring*
grid [znw] • *rooster* • *net(werk)* • *accuplaat*
griddle [znw] *bakplaat*
grief [znw] *verdriet*
grievance [znw] *grief*
grieve [on ww] *bedroeven* • (~ **at/for**) *treuren om/over*
grievous [bnw] • *pijnlijk, smartelijk* • *ernstig, afschuwelijk*
grill I [ov + on ww] *grillen, roosteren* II [ov ww] *stevig aan de tand voelen* III [znw] • *rooster* • *grill* • *geroosterd vlees* • *traliewerk*
grim [bnw] • *grimmig, akelig* • *streng, meedogenloos, onverbiddelijk*
grime [znw] *(vettig) vuil, goorheid*
grimy [bnw] *goor, vies*
grin I [on ww] *grijnzen* II [znw] *brede glimlach*
grip I [ov + on ww] *grijpen, pakken* II [ov ww] *vat hebben op, boeien* III [znw] • *greep* • *handvat* • *macht* • *beheersing*
gripe [on ww] *klagen, jammeren*
grisly [bnw] *griezelig*
grist [znw] • *koren* • *mout*
gristle [znw] *kraakbeen*
grit I [ov + on ww] *knarsen* II [ov ww] *met zand bestrooien* III [znw] • *zand(korreltje)* • *(steen)gruis* • *pit, durf*
grizzle [ov + on ww] • *grienen* • *(klagend) zeuren*
grizzled [bnw] • *grijs* • 'peper en zout', *grijzend*
grizzly [znw] *grijze beer*
groan I [on ww] *kreunen* • (~ **under**) *zuchten onder* II [znw] *gekreun*

grocer [znw] *kruidenier*
grocery [znw] *het kruideniersvak*
groggy [bnw] • *beneveld, dronken* • *niet vast op de benen*
groin [znw] • *lies* • ‹archit.› *graatrib*
groom I [ov ww] *verzorgen* II [znw] • *stalknecht* • *kamerheer* • *bruidegom*
groove I [ov ww] *een sleuf maken in* II [znw] *sleuf, sponning*
groovy ‹sl.› [bnw] *gaaf, in (de mode), tof, blits*
grope [ov + on ww] • (~ **after/for**) *(rond)tasten naar*
gross I [ov ww] *verdienen* II [znw] *gros* III [bnw] • *grof, lomp, walgelijk, monsterlijk* • *vet* • *bruto*
grotesque I [znw] *groteske* II [bnw] *potsierlijk*
grotto [znw] *grot*
grotty [bnw] • *akelig, beroerd* • *rot, gammel*
grouch I [on ww] *mopperen* II [znw] *mopperaar*
grouchy [bnw] *humeurig, met de bokkenpruik op*
ground I [ov ww] • *gronden, baseren* • *(grondig) onderleggen* • *aan/op de grond zetten* • *aarden* ‹v. elektriciteit› II [on ww] *aan de grond lopen* III [znw] • *terrein, park* • *grondkleur-/toon/-verf* • *ondergrond* • *reden* • *grond*
grounding [znw] *basis, vooropleiding, grondbeginselen*
group I [ov + on ww] *(z.) groeperen* II [znw] *groep*
grouping [znw] *groepering*
grouse I [on ww] *kankeren, mopperen* II [znw] • *korhoen(deren)* • *gemopper, gekanker*
grove [znw] *bosje*
grovel [on ww] z. *vernederen, kruipen* ‹fig.›
grow I [ov ww] *verbouwen, kweken* II [on ww] • *groeien* • *worden*
grown [ww] volt. deelw. → **grow**
growth [znw] • *groei* • *gewas* • *gezwel*

grub I [ov ww] *uitgraven, opgraven*
II [on ww] *graven, wroeten* III [znw]
• *larve, made* • *eten*

grubby [bnw] *slonzig, smoezelig,
smerig*

grudge I [ov ww] *misgunnen* II [znw]
wrok

grudging [bnw] *onwillig,
schoorvoetend, met tegenzin*

gruel [znw] *watergruwel*

gruelling [bnw] *hard, meedogenloos*

gruesome [bnw] *ijzingwekkend, akelig*

gruff [bnw] *bars, nurks, nors*

grumble [on ww] *mopperen, grommen*
• (~ **about/at/over**) *zich beklagen
over*

grumpy [bnw] *knorrig, gemelijk*

grunt [on ww] • *knorren* • *grommen*

guarantee I [ov ww] *garanderen*
II [znw] *waarborg, garantie*

guard I [ov ww] *beschermen, bewaken,
hoeden* • (~ **against/from**) *behoeden
voor, beschermen tegen* II [on ww] z.
hoeden • (~ **against/from**) z. *hoeden
voor* III [znw] • *bescherming, wacht*
• *hoede, waakzaamheid* • *garde,
beschermer, bewaker*

guarded [bnw] *voorzichtig*

guardian [znw] • *beschermer* • *voogd*
• *curator*

guess I [ov + on ww] *raden* • (~ **at**)
raden naar II [znw] *gissing*

guest [znw] • *gast* • *introducé*

guffaw I [on ww] *schaterlachen*
II [znw] *schaterlach*

guidance [znw] • *(bege)leiding*
• *voorlichting*

guide I [ov ww] • *(bege)leiden*
• *besturen* II [znw] • *gids* • *(reis)leider*
• *leidraad*

guild [znw] *gilde*

guile [znw] *bedrog, list*

guileless [bnw] *argeloos*

guillotine I [ov ww] *onthoofden*
II [znw] *guillotine*

guilt [znw] *schuld*

guise [znw] *uiterlijk, gedaante*

guitar [znw] *gitaar*

gulch [znw] *ravijn*

gulf [znw] • *golf* • *afgrond, kloof*

gull [znw] *zeemeeuw*

gullet [znw] *slokdarm*

gull(e)y [znw] • *ravijn* • *geul, goot,
afwatering*

gullible [bnw] *goedgelovig, onnozel*

gulp I [ov + on ww] *(in)slikken,
(op)slokken* • (~ **down**) *in één keer
achteroverslaan/opslokken* II [on ww]
bijna stikken III [znw] *slok*

gum I [ov ww] *met gom plakken*
II [znw] • *gom(boom)* • *kauwgom*
• *tandvlees*

gummy [bnw] • *gomachtig* • *kleverig*

gun I [ov ww] *schieten* • (~ **down**)
neerschieten II [znw] • *geweer*
• *revolver* • *kanon*

gunner [znw] • *artillerist*
• *boordschutter*

gurgle I [on ww] • *kirren* • *klokken*
• *rochelen* • *murmelen* II [znw] • *gekir*
• *geklok* • *gemurmel*

guru [znw] *goeroe*

gush I [on ww] • *gutsen, stromen*
• *dwepen, sentimenteel doen* II [znw]
• *stroom* • *opwelling* • *sentimentaliteit*

gust [znw] *(wind)vlaag*

gusto [znw] *smaak, genot, animo*

gut I [ov ww] • *uithalen, kaken* <v. vis>
• *leeghalen, uitbranden* <v. huis>
II [znw] • *darm* • <pej.> *pens*

gutless [bnw] *laf, zonder ruggengraat*
<fig.>

gutter I [on ww] *druipen* <v. kaars>
II [znw] *goot*

guttural [bnw] *keel-*

guy [znw] • *stormlijn* <v. tent> • <AE>
vent, kerel

gym [znw] • *gymzaal* • *gymnastiekles*

gymkhana [znw] *gymkana,
ruiterwedstrijd/-show*

gymnasium [znw] *gymnastiekzaal*

gynaecology [znw] *gynaecologie*

gypsy [znw] *zigeuner*
gyrate [on ww] *(rond)draaien, wentelen*
gyroscope [znw] *gyroscoop*

H

haberdasher [znw]
• *fourniturenhandelaar* • ‹AE› *verkoper van herenmode(artikelen)*
haberdashery [znw]
• *fournituren(zaak/-afdeling)* • ‹AE› *herenmodezaak/-afdeling*
habit [znw] • *gewoonte* • *pij, habijt*
habitable [bnw] *bewoonbaar*
habitat [znw] *verspreidingsgebied* ‹v. dier/plant›, *woongebied*
habitation [znw] • *woning* • *bewoning*
habitual [bnw] *gewoon(lijk)*
hack I [ov + on ww] *(af-/fijn)hakken*
II [on ww] • *computerkraken*
• *(paard)rijden* III [znw] • *huurpaard, rijpaard* • *knol* • *broodschrijver* • ‹AE› *huurrijtuig, taxi*
had [ww] verl. tijd + volt. deelw.
→ have
haddock [znw] *schelvis*
hadn't [samentr.] /had not/ → have
haemoglobin [znw] *hemoglobine*
haemophilia [znw] *hemofilie, bloederziekte*
haemophiliac [znw] *hemofiliepatiënt*
haemorrhoids [znw] *aambeien*
hag [znw] *heks*
haggard [bnw] *verwilderd uitziend, wild*
haggle [on ww] *(af)pingelen*
hail I [on ww] *hagelen* II [znw] • *hagel*
• *welkom, groet* III [tw] *heil!, hoezee!*
hair [znw] *haar, haren*
hairy [bnw] • *harig* • *hachelijk*
hale I [ov ww] *trekken, sleuren, slepen*
II [bnw] *gezond, kras*
half I [znw] • *de helft* • *een halve*
II [bnw] *half* III [bijw] *half*
halibut [znw] *heilbot*
hall [znw] • *zaal, eetzaal* • *hal, vestibule, gang* • *groot huis, gildehuis,*

stadhuis, kasteel
hallucinogenic [bnw] *hallucinogeen*
halo [znw] *stralenkrans, nimbus*
halt I [ov ww] *halt (laten/doen) houden* II [znw] • *halt(e)* • *rust*
halter [znw] • *halster* • *bovenstukje* ‹v. bikini›, *topje*
halve [ov ww] *halveren*
ham [znw] • *dij, bil* • *ham* • *prulacteur* • *zendamateur*
hamlet [znw] *gehucht*
hammer I [ov ww] *hameren* • (~ **out**) *(met moeite) bereiken/tot stand doen komen* II [on ww] • *hameren* • *klop geven* • (~ (**away**) **at**) *erop los kloppen, zwoegen op* III [znw] *hamer*
hammock [znw] *hangmat*
hamper I [ov ww] *belemmeren, verwarren* II [znw] *pakmand, sluitmand*
hand I [ov ww] *aanreiken* II [znw] • *hand* • *knecht*
handicap I [ov ww] • *nadelige invloed hebben op* • *belemmeren, hinderen* II [znw] *handicap*
handicraft [znw] *handarbeid, handwerk*
handiwork [znw] *schepping, werk, handwerk*
handkerchief [znw] *zakdoek*
handle I [ov ww] • *hanteren* • *onder handen nemen* • *bedienen* • *aanraken* II [znw] • *stuur* • *handgreep, handvat* • *kruk* • *knop* • *oor, heft*
handler [znw] • *africhter, trainer* ‹v. honden› • *afhandelaar* ‹v. bagage›
handsome [bnw] • *knap* • *royaal, overvloedig*
handy [bnw] • *handig* • *bij de hand*
hang I [ov ww] *hangen, ophangen, behangen* II [on ww] • *hangen* • *niet opschieten* • (~ **about**) *(doelloos) rondhangen* • (~ **back**) *dralen, niet mee willen komen* • (~ **behind**) *achterblijven* • (~ **on**) *met aandacht luisteren naar, volhouden*

• (~ **on/onto**) z. *vastklampen aan*
• (~ **together**) *samenhangen* • (~ **up**) *(telefoon) ophangen* • (~ **upon**) *afhangen van*
hank [znw] *streng* ‹garen›
hanker [on ww] *hunkeren*
hankering [znw] *hunkering, hang*
hanky-panky ‹inf.› [znw] *gescharrel*
haphazard [bnw] *willekeurig, op goed geluk*
happen [on ww] *gebeuren, voorvallen* • (~ (**up**)**on**) *toevallig aantreffen*
happening [znw] • *gebeurtenis* • *manifestatie*
happy [bnw] • *gelukkig* • *tevreden* • *blij*
harangue I [on ww] *een heftige toespraak houden* II [znw] *(heftige) rede, filippica*
harass [ov ww] *lastig vallen, teisteren, bestoken*
harbinger [znw] *voorbode*
harbour I [ov ww] • *herbergen* • *koesteren* II [znw] • *haven* • *(veilige) schuilplaats*
hard [bnw + bijw] • *hard* • *moeilijk* • *moeizaam* • *streng* • *onbuigzaam*
harden [on ww] *hard of vast worden, stollen*
hardly [bijw] • *met moeite* • *nauwelijks, zelden*
hardship [znw] *last, ongemak, ontbering*
hardy [bnw] • *stoutmoedig* • *sterk, gehard*
hare [znw] *haas*
hark [on ww] *luisteren* • (~ **back**) *(doen) herinneren*
harm I [ov ww] *kwaad doen, benadelen, letsel toebrengen* II [znw] *kwaad, letsel*
harmful [bnw] *schadelijk, nadelig*
harmless [bnw] *onschadelijk*
harmonic I [znw] *flageolettoon* II [bnw] *harmonisch*
harmonica [znw] *(mond)harmonica*
harmonize I [ov ww] *harmoniseren* II [on ww] *harmoniëren*

harmony [znw] • *harmonie*
• *eensgezindheid*
harness I [ov ww] • *inspannen*
• *benutten* II [znw] • *paardentuig*
• *babytuigje*
harp I [on ww] *op harp spelen* • (~ **on**
(**about**)) *over iets doorzeuren* II [znw]
harp
harpoon I [ov ww] *harpoeneren*
II [znw] *harpoen*
harpsichord [znw] *klavecimbel*
harrow [znw] *eg*
harrowing [bnw] *aangrijpend,
schokkend*
harry [ov ww] • *lastig vallen* • *zeuren
om*
harsh [bnw] • *hard(vochtig)* • *ruw*
harvest I [ov ww] *oogsten* II [znw] *oogst*
harvester [znw] • *oogster*
• *oogstmachine*
has [ww] → **have**
hash [znw] • *hachee* • *hasj(iesj)*
hashish [znw] *hasj(iesj)*
hasp [znw] *knip, klamp, beugel* ‹v.
hangslot›
haste I [on ww] *z. haasten* II [znw]
haast
hasten I [ov ww] *verhaasten* II [on ww]
z. haasten
hasty [bnw] • *haastig* • *overhaast*
hat [znw] *hoed*
hatch I [ov ww] (*uit*)*broeden* II [on ww]
uitkomen III [znw] • *onderdeur*
• *luikgat* • *broedsel*
hatchery [znw] *kwekerij* ‹vnl. vis›
hatchet [znw] *bijl(tje)*
hate I [ov ww] • *een hekel hebben aan*
• *haten* II [znw] *haat*
hateful [bnw] • *erg vervelend, akelig*
• *hatelijk* • *haatdragend*
hatred [znw] *haat*
hatter [znw] *hoedenmaker/-maakster*
haughty [bnw] *uit de hoogte,
hooghartig*
haul I [ov ww] • (*op*)*halen, slepen*
• *vervoeren* • (~ **up**) *dagvaarden*

II [znw] • *haal, trek* • *illegale vangst,
buitenkansje*
haunch [znw] *lende(stuk), schoft, bil*
haunt I [ov ww] • (*veelvuldig*) *bezoeken*
• *rondspoken in/om* • *z. ophouden in*
II [on ww] *rondwaren* III [znw] • *veel
bezochte plaats* • *verblijf(plaats)* • *hol*
have I [ov ww] • *hebben* • *houden*
• *krijgen* • *beetnemen* • (~ **on**)
beetnemen II [hww] *hebben*
haven [znw] *haven, toevluchtsoord*
haven't [samentr.] /*have not*/ → **have**
havoc [znw] *plundering, verwoesting*
haw I [znw] *hagendoorn* II [tw] *ahum*
hawk I [ov ww] *leuren met, venten*
II [on ww] *met valken jagen* III [znw]
havik, valk
hawker [znw] • *valkenier* • *venter*
hawser [znw] *kabel*
hawthorn [znw] *hagendoorn*
hay I [on ww] *hooien* II [znw] *hooi*
hazard I [ov ww] • *riskeren, in de
waagschaal stellen* • *wagen* II [znw]
• *gevaar* • *risico*
hazardous [bnw] • *onzeker* • *gewaagd*
haze I [ov ww] • *benevelen, in nevel
hullen* • ‹AE› *treiteren* II [znw] • *nevel,
waas* • *zweem*
hazel I [znw] • *hazelaar* • (*stok v.*)
hazelnotenhout II [bnw] *lichtbruin*
hazy [bnw] • *vaag* • *aangeschoten*
• *heiig*
he [pers vnw] *hij*
head I [ov ww] • *de leiding
geven/nemen/hebben*
• *voor-/bovenaan staan* • ‹sport›
koppen • (~ **off**) *de pas afsnijden,
verhinderen* II [on ww] *gaan* • (~ **for**)
aangaan op, onderweg zijn naar
III [znw] • *hoofd, kop* • *top* • *chef,
directeur* • *rector* • *bovenstuk,
bovenkant* • *voorste stuk, voorkant*
• *voorgebergte* • *schuimkraag*
• *categorie, rubriek, post* • *stuk* ‹vee›
header [znw] • *duik met hoofd voorover*
• *kopbal*

heading [znw] opschrift, titel, kop, rubriek
heady [bnw] • onstuimig • koppig
heal [ov + on ww] genezen
healer [znw] genezer
health [znw] gezondheid
healthy, healthful [bnw] gezond
heap I [ov ww] • ophopen • laden, beladen, overladen II [znw] hoop
hear I [ov + on ww] horen II [ov ww] • horen, vernemen • luisteren naar • (~ of) horen over • (~ out) aanhoren tot het einde
hearer [znw] toehoorder
hearing [znw] • hoorzitting • publiek • gehoor
hearsay [znw] praatjes
hearse [znw] lijkkoets, lijkauto
heart [znw] • hart • gemoed • moed • kern
hearten [ov ww] bemoedigen
hearth [znw] haard
heartily [bijw] • hartgrondig • van harte • flink
hearty [bnw] • hartelijk • grondig • stevig • gezond
heat I [ov + on ww] heet/warm maken/worden, warmlopen II [ov ww] • (~ up) verwarmen III [znw] • bronst • onderdeel v. wedstrijdtoernooi, loop, manche • hitte, warmte • drift
heated [bnw] verhit, razend, woest
heater [znw] • verwarmer • kacheltje
heath [znw] heide
heathen I [znw] heiden II [bnw] heidens
heather [znw] heide(struik)
heating [znw] verwarming(sinstallatie)
heave I [ov ww] • (op)heffen, optillen • gooien • ophijsen • slaken II [on ww] op (en neer) gaan, deinen • (~ to) <scheepv.> stil gaan liggen, bijdraaien III [znw] hijs, ruk
heaven [znw] hemel
heavenly [bnw] hemels
heavy [bnw + bijw] • zwaar • moeilijk • somber, zwaarmoedig

Hebrew I [znw] • Hebreeër • Hebreeuws <taal> II [bnw] Hebreeuws
heck [tw] verdomme!
heckle [ov ww] • hekelen • (luidruchtig) interrumperen
heckler [znw] querulant
hectic [bnw] • tering- • hectisch, koortsachtig, opgewonden
hector I [ov ww] • overdonderen, intimideren • afblaffen II [znw] • bullebak • schreeuwer
he'd [samentr.] /he had/ /he would/ → have, will
hedge I [ov ww] omheinen II [on ww] • z. gedekt houden • z. dekken III [znw] heg, haag
heed I [ov ww] aandacht schenken aan II [znw] aandacht
heedless [bnw] achteloos
heel [znw] • hiel, hak • <AE> schlemiel
hefty [bnw] • stoer • log • <AE> zwaar
hegemony [znw] hegemonie
heifer [znw] vaars
height [znw] hoogte(punt)
heighten [ov ww] verhogen
heirloom [znw] erfstuk
held [ww] verl. tijd + volt. deelw. → hold
helicopter [znw] helikopter
heliport [znw] helihaven
he'll [samentr.] /he will/ → will
hellish [bnw] hels
hello [tw] hallo
helm [znw] roer
helmet [znw] helm
help I [ov + on ww] • helpen, bijstaan • (be)dienen II [znw] hulp
helpful [bnw] • behulpzaam • handig, nuttig
helping [znw] portie
helpless [bnw] hulpeloos
helter-skelter [bijw] holderdebolder
hem I [ov ww] omzomen • (~ in) insluiten, omsingelen II [znw] zoom
hemisphere [znw] halve bol
hemlock [znw] dolle kervel

hen [znw] *kip*
hence [bijw] • *van hier, vandaar* • *weg*
henchman [znw] *volgeling, trawant*
henna I [ov ww] *met henna verven*
II [znw] *henna*
hepatitis [znw] *hepatitis, geelzucht*
her [pers vnw] *haar*
heraldry [znw] *heraldiek*
herb [znw] *kruid*
herbaceous [bnw] *kruidachtig, met*
kruiden
herbal I [znw] *kruidenboek* II [bnw]
kruiden-
herbalist [znw] • *kruidenkenner*
• *kruidendokter*
herbivorous [bnw] *plantenetend*
herd I [ov ww] *hoeden, bijeendrijven* ‹v.
kudde› II [znw] • *kudde* • *hoeder,*
herder
here [bijw] *hier(heen)*
hereditary, hereditable [bnw] *erfelijk*
heredity [znw] *erfelijkheid, overerving*
heresy [znw] *ketterij*
heretic [znw] *ketter*
heritage [znw] *erfenis, erfgoed, erfdeel*
hermaphrodite [znw] *hermafrodiet*
hermetic [bnw] *hermetisch*
hermit [znw] *kluizenaar*
hernia [znw] *(ingewands)breuk*
hero [znw] • *held* • *halfgod*
heroic [bnw] *heldhaftig*
heroin [znw] *heroïne*
heroine [znw] • *halfgodin* • *heldin*
heroism [znw] *heldenmoed*
heron [znw] *reiger*
herring [znw] *haring*
hers [bez vnw] • *van haar* • *het/de hare*
herself [wkd vnw] *haar(zelf), zich(zelf)*
he's [samentr.] /he is/ /he has/ → be,
have
hesitancy [znw] *aarzeling*
hesitant [bnw] *aarzelend*
hesitate [on ww] • *aarzelen* • *weifelen*
hesitation [znw] *aarzeling*
heterosexual [bnw] *heteroseksueel*
hew [ov + on ww] • *kappen, houwen*

• *hakken*
hexagon [znw] *zeshoek*
heyday [znw] *bloei, fleur*
hi [tw] • *hé, hela* • *hallo*
hiatus [znw] *leemte, hiaat*
hibernate [on ww] *winterslaap doen*
hide I [ov ww] • (~ from) *verbergen*
voor II [on ww] (z.) *verbergen* III [znw]
• *huid* • *hachje* • *schuilplaats*
hideous [bnw] *afschuwelijk*
hiding [znw] *pak rammel*
hierarchy [znw] *hiërarchie*
hieroglyph [znw] *hiëroglief*
higgledy-piggledy [bnw + bijw]
schots en scheef, overhoop
high I [znw] *record, hoogtepunt*
II [bnw + bijw] • *hoog* • *verheven*
• *opgewekt* • *dronken* • *bedwelmd*
highly [bijw] • *zeer, hoogst* • *met lof*
hijack I [ov ww] *kapen* II [znw] *kaping*
hike I [on ww] *rondtrekken* II [znw]
trektocht
hiker [znw] *wandelaar, trekker*
hilarious [bnw] *vrolijk*
hilarity [znw] *hilariteit*
hill [znw] *heuvel*
hillock [znw] *heuveltje*
hilly [bnw] *heuvelachtig*
hilt [znw] *gevest*
him [pers vnw] *hem*
himself [wkd vnw] • *zich(zelf)* • *zelf*
hind I [znw] *hinde* II [bnw] *achter(ste)*
hinder I [ov ww] *(ver)hinderen, beletten*
II [bnw] *achter(ste)*
hindrance [znw] *obstakel,*
belemmering
hindsight [znw] • *vizier* • *beschouwing*
achteraf
Hindu I [znw] *hindoe* II [bnw]
• *hindoes* • *van het hindoeïsme*
Hinduism [znw] *hindoeïsme*
hinge I [on ww] • *rusten op* • *draaien*
II [znw] • *scharnier* • *spil* ‹fig.›
hint I [on ww] • (~ at) *zinspelen op*
II [znw] • *wenk, aanwijzing*
• *zinspeling*

hinterland [znw] achterland
hip I [znw] • heup • rozenbottel II [bnw]
hip
hippo [znw] nijlpaard
hippopotamus [znw] nijlpaard
hire I [ov ww] huren • (~ out) verhuren
II [znw] • huur • loon
hireling [znw] huurling
his [bez vnw] 't zijne, zijn, van hem
hiss I [ov + on ww] sissen II [ov ww]
(uit)fluiten III [znw] sissend geluid
historian [znw] • geschiedschrijver
• geschiedkundige
hit I [ov + on ww] • raken • slaan
• (~ (up)on) toevallig
aantreffen/stoten op II [ov ww] treffen
• (~ off) precies treffen III [on ww] <AE>
(aan)komen (bij/op) IV [znw]
succes(nummer/-stuk)
hitch I [ov ww] vastmaken, vastraken
• (~ up) optrekken <met een rukje>
II [on ww] liften III [znw] hapering,
kink in de kabel
hither [bijw] hierheen
hoard I [ov + on ww] hamsteren
II [ov ww] vergaren III [znw]
• voorraad • spaargeld • schat
hoarding [znw] aanplakbord
hoarse [bnw] schor, hees
hoary [bnw] • grijs • eerbiedwaardig
hoax I [ov ww] een poets bakken
II [znw] grap
hob [znw] haardplaat
hobble I [ov ww] kluisteren II [on ww]
III [znw] • strompelgang • kluister
hobby [znw] liefhebberij
hock [znw] • hielgewricht <v. paard>
• rijnwijn
hod [znw] kalkbak
hoe I [ov + on ww] schoffelen II [znw]
schoffel
hog I [ov ww] voor zich opeisen II [znw]
• (slacht)varken • zwijn <fig.>
hoist I [ov ww] (op)hijsen II [znw]
hijstoestel
hoity-toity [bnw] nuffig

hold I [ov ww] • (be)houden
• in-/tegen-/vasthouden • eropna
houden • (kunnen) bevatten • v.
mening zijn • <AE> gevangenhouden
• (~ against) kwalijk nemen,
verwijten • (~ back) aarzelen, z.
onthouden • (~ in) (z.) inhouden
• (~ off) uitstellen, op een afstand
houden • (~ on) niet loslaten • (~ up)
ophouden, omhooghouden,
aanhouden, overvallen II [on ww] • het
(uit)houden • v. kracht zijn
• aanhouden • (~ aloof) z. afzijdig
houden • (~ back) tegenhouden,
geheim houden • (~ by) blijven bij, z.
houden aan • (~ forth) betogen,
oreren • (~ off) wegblijven • (~ on) z.
vasthouden, doorgaan, aanblijven
• (~ on to) vasthouden aan • (~ out)
het uithouden, toereikend zijn
• (~ with) het houden bij/met,
goedkeuren III [znw] • houvast, vat,
greep • <scheepv.> ruim
holder [znw] • huurder, pachter
• houder
holiness [znw] heiligheid
holler [ov + on ww] schreeuwen
hollow I [ov ww] (uit)hollen, hol
maken II [znw] • holte • dal, laagte
III [bnw + bijw] • hol • voos, geveinsd,
leeg
holly [znw] hulst
holy [bnw] heilig
homage [znw] hulde
home I [znw] • t(e)huis • huis
• geboortegrond, vaderland • verblijf
• honk II [bnw] • huis(houd)elijk
• eigen • binnenlands • raak III [bijw]
• naar huis, thuis • naar/op z'n plaats,
raak
homeward(s) [bijw] huiswaarts
homicidal [bnw] moord-, moorddadig
homicide [znw] • doodslag • pleger v.
doodslag
homing [znw] het naar huis gaan
homoeopath [znw] homeopaat

homogeneity [znw] homogeniteit
homosexual [znw] homoseksueel
hone [ov ww] aanzetten, slijpen
honest [bnw] • rechtschapen • eerlijk
• deugdelijk
honesty [znw] • eerlijkheid,
oprechtheid • <plantk.> judaspenning
honey [znw] • honing • schat, liefje
honeyed [bnw] (honing)zoet
honeymoon I [on ww] de
huwelijksreis/wittebroodsweken
doorbrengen II [znw] huwelijksreis,
wittebroodsweken
honorary [bnw] ere-
honour I [ov ww] • eren • honoreren
II [znw] eer, eergevoel
honourable [bnw] • eervol
• rechtschapen • ≈ edelachtbaar
hood [znw] • kap, capuchon • huif
• <AE> motorkap
hoodlum [znw] vandaal, relschopper
hoodwink [ov ww] misleiden, zand in
de ogen strooien
hoof [znw] hoef
hook I [ov ww] • (z.) vasthaken,
aanhaken • aan de haak slaan • (~ up)
aansluiten II [on ww] blijven haken
III [znw] • haak, vishaak • sikkel,
snoeimes, kram
hooked [bnw] • haakvormig • met
haak • verslaafd
hoop [znw] • hoepel • basket <bij
basketbal>, poortje <bij croquet>
hoot I [ov ww] uitjouwen II [on ww]
• krassen <v. uil> • toeteren,
claxonneren • jouwen • (hard) lachen
III [znw] • gekras • getoeter
hooter [znw] • stoomfluit • sirene
hooves [mv] → hoof
hop I [on ww] springen (op), hinken,
huppelen • (~ off) ophoepelen,
afspringen (van), afstijgen II [znw]
• sprong(etje) • etappe • <plantk.> hop
hope I [ov + on ww] hopen II [znw] hoop
hopeful [bnw] hoopvol
hopefully [bijw] hopelijk

hopper [znw] (graan)schudder
hormone [znw] hormoon
horn [znw] • hoorn • voelhoorn
• trompet, kornet • claxon
horned [bnw] met hoorns
hornet [znw] horzel
horny [bnw] • hoornachtig, vereelt
• <sl.> heet, geil
horoscope [znw] horoscoop
horrible, horrid [bnw] afschuwelijk
horror [znw] afgrijzen, gruwel
horse I [ov ww] van paard(en) voorzien
II [on ww] • (~ around) ravotten
III [znw] • paard • <inf.> heroïne
hose I [ov ww] (schoon)spuiten
• (~ down) schoonspuiten • (~ out)
uitspuiten II [znw] slang, tuinslang,
brandslang
hosiery [znw] kousen en gebreide
artikelen
hospitable [bnw] gastvrij
hospital [znw] • ziekenhuis • hospitaal
hospitality [znw] gastvrijheid
hospitalize [ov ww] in ziekenhuis
opnemen
host I [ov ww] gastheer/-vrouw zijn
II [znw] • gastheer <ook biologisch>
• waard • hostie • menigte
hostage [znw] • gijzelaar • onderpand
hostel [znw] tehuis, jeugdherberg
hostess [znw] • gastvrouw • waardin
• stewardess
hostile [bnw] vijandig, vijandelijk
hot [bnw] • heet, warm • driftig, heftig
• pikant • kersvers, gloednieuw
hotelier [znw] hotelhouder
hound I [ov ww] vervolgen • (~ out)
verjagen II [znw] (jacht)hond
hour [znw] uur
hourly [bnw + bijw] • per uur • van uur
tot uur, voortdurend
house I [ov ww] • huisvesten
• herbergen • stallen II [znw] • huis
• schouwburg(zaal) • firma
household I [znw] gezin, huishouden
II [bnw] huis-

householder [znw] • hoofd v.h. gezin • hoofdbewoner • bewoner v.e. eigen huis

housing [znw] • behuizing • bijgebouwen • huisvesting • ‹techn.› (metalen) kast/ombouw

hove [ww] verl. tijd + volt. deelw. → heave

hovel [znw] hut, krot

hover [on ww] • rondhangen, zwerven, zweven • bidden ‹v. roofvogel›

how [bijw] • hoe • wat

however [bijw] • echter • hoe ... ook

howl I [on ww] brullen, huilen, janken II [znw] gehuil

howler [znw] • brulaap • enorme blunder

howling I [znw] gebrul II [bnw] enorm

hub [znw] • naaf • middelpunt

hubbub [znw] kabaal, herrie

huckster [znw] venter

huddle I [on ww] in elkaar duiken • (~ up) zich zo klein mogelijk maken II [znw] dicht opeengepakte groep

hue [znw] tint, kleur

huff I [on ww] z. nijdig maken II [znw] nijdige bui, lichtgeraaktheid

huffy [bnw] lichtgeraakt

hug I [ov ww] omhelzen II [znw] omhelzing

huge [bnw] reusachtig

hulk [znw] • bonk (van een vent) • (romp v.) afgetuigd schip • log schip/gevaarte

hulking [bnw] log, lomp

hull I [ov ww] pellen II [znw] (scheeps)romp

hum I [ov + on ww] neuriën II [on ww] zoemen, brommen III [znw] gezoem, gebrom

human [bnw] menselijk

humane [bnw] humaan, menslievend

humanitarian I [znw] filantroop II [bnw] • filantropisch • humanitair

humanity [znw] • menselijkheid • mensdom • het mens zijn

• menslievendheid

humanize [ov ww] • beschaven • vermenselijken

humble I [ov ww] vernederen II [bnw] • nederig, onderdanig • bescheiden

humbug [znw] • branieschopper • zwendel • kouwe drukte • nonsens

humdinger [znw] • kei ‹fig.›, geweldenaar • meesterstukje • knaller

humdrum [bnw] alledaags, saai

humid [bnw] vochtig

humidity [znw] vochtigheid

humiliate [ov ww] vernederen

humility [bnw] nederigheid

humour I [ov ww] • zijn zin geven • toegeven (aan) II [znw] • humor • stemming • humeur

hump I [on ww] • krommen • (met moeite) dragen II [znw] bult

hunch I [ov ww] optrekken II [on ww] buigen, krommen III [znw] • bult • voorgevoel

hundred [telw] honderd, honderdtal

hundredth [telw] honderdste

hung [ww] verl. tijd + volt. deelw. → hang

Hungarian I [znw] • Hongaar(se) • het Hongaars II [bnw] Hongaars

hunger I [on ww] hongeren II [znw] • honger • verlangen

hungry [bnw] hongerig

hunk [znw] brok, homp

hunt I [ov ww] • jagen op • afzoeken • (~ down) in 't nauw drijven, achterna zitten • (~ out) opsporen, achterhalen II [on ww] • jagen ‹met honden/paard› • zoeken III [znw] • jacht • zoektocht

hunter [znw] jager

hunting [znw] • jacht • zoektocht

huntsman [znw] jager

hurdle [znw] horde ‹om over te springen›

hurl [ov ww] werpen, smijten

hurly-burly [znw] rumoer

hurricane [znw] orkaan

hurried [bnw] *gehaast*
hurry I [ov ww] • *overhaasten* • *tot*
haast aanzetten • (~ **along/on**)
voortjagen, opjagen • (~ **away**) *in*
haast wegbrengen II [on ww] • *z.*
haasten • *haast maken met*
• (~ **along/on**) *voortijlen* • (~ **away**)
wegsnellen • (~ **up**) *haast maken,*
voortmaken III [znw] *haast*
hurt I [ov + on ww] *pijn doen* II [znw]
pijn
hurtful [bnw] *nadelig*
hurtle [on ww] *kletteren, snorren*
husband I [ov ww] *zuinig beheren*
II [znw] *man, echtgenoot*
husbandry [znw] *landbouw en veeteelt*
hush I [ov ww] • *sussen* • *tot zwijgen*
brengen • (~ **up**) *in de doofpot stoppen*
II [on ww] *zwijgen* III [znw] *stilte*
IV [tw] *sst!*
husk I [ov ww] *v. schil enz. ontdoen,*
pellen II [znw] *peul, dop, schil, kaf*
husky [bnw] • *schor* • *potig*
hussy [znw] *brutale meid, feeks*
hustings [mv] *verkiezingsactiviteiten*
hustle I [ov ww] *door elkaar schudden*
II [on ww] • *dringen* • *jachten* III [znw]
gedrang
hustler [znw] *oplichter*
hut [znw] • *hut* • *barak*
hutch [znw] *(konijnen)hok*
hyacinth [znw] *hyacint*
hyaena [znw] *hyena*
hybrid I [znw] *bastaard(vorm)* II [bnw]
bastaard-, hybridisch
hydrant [znw] *brandslang, standpijp*
hydraulic [bnw] *hydraulisch*
hydrogen [znw] *waterstof*
hygiene [znw] *hygiëne*
hygienic [bnw] *hygiënisch*
hymen [znw] *maagdenvlies*
hymn [znw] *lofzang, hymne*
hymnal [znw] *hymneboek,*
gezangenboek
hyphen [znw] *verbindingsstreepje*
hypnosis [znw] *hypnose*

hypnotic [bnw] *hypnotiserend*
hypnotism [znw] *hypnotisme*
hypochondria [znw]
zwaarmoedigheid
hypocrisy [znw] *huichelarij*
hypocrite [znw] *huichelaar*
hypocritical [bnw] *huichelachtig*
hypodermic [bnw] *onderhuids*
hypotenuse [znw] *hypotenusa,*
schuine zijde
hypothesis [znw] *hypothese,*
veronderstelling
hysteria [znw] *hysterie*
hysterical [bnw] *hysterisch*
hysterics [mv] *hysterische aanval*

I

I [pers vnw] ik
ice I [ov ww] glaceren <v. gebak>
II [on ww] • (~ over/up) vastvriezen,
met ijs bedekt worden III [znw] (portie)
ijs
Icelander [znw] IJslander
Icelandic I [znw] IJslands II [bnw]
IJslands
icing [znw] suikerglazuur
icon [znw] ikoon
iconoclast [znw] beeldenstormer
icy [bnw] • ijsachtig, ijs- • met ijs
bedekt, vriezend, bevroren • kil,
afstandelijk
I'd [samentr.] /I had, I should, I
would/ → have, will, shall
idea [znw] • idee, plan • bedoeling
ideal I [znw] ideaal II [bnw] • ideaal
• ideëel
idealism [znw] idealisme
idealistic [bnw] idealistisch
idealize [ov ww] idealiseren
identic(al) [bnw] gelijkwaardig,
identiek
identification [znw] identificatie
identify I [ov ww] identificeren,
gelijkstellen II [on ww] • (~ with) zich
identificeren met
identity [znw] identiteit,
persoonlijkheid
ideological [bnw] ideologisch
ideology [znw] ideologie
idiocy [znw] zwakzinnigheid, idioterie
idiom [znw] idioom
idiomatic(al) [bnw] idiomatisch
idiot [znw] idioot
idiotic(al) [bnw] idioot
idle I [on ww] luieren II [bnw]
• nutteloos • ongegrond • braak <v.
land> • lui • niet aan 't werk zijnde
idler [znw] leegloper

idol [znw] • afgod(sbeeld) • idool
idolatrous [bnw] m.b.t. afgoderij
idolatry, idolization [znw] afgoderij
idolize [ov ww] verafgoden
idyl(l)ic [bnw] idyllisch
if [vw] • indien, als, ingeval • of
igloo [znw] iglo
ignite I [ov ww] in brand steken
II [on ww] ontbranden
ignition [znw] • ontsteking <v. motor>
• ontbranding
ignoble [bnw] • v. lage komaf • gemeen
ignominious [bnw] • schandelijk
• oneervol
ignominy [znw] schande, smaad
ignoramus [znw] domkop
ignorance [znw] • onervarenheid
• domheid
ignorant [bnw] • onkundig • onwetend
ignore [ov ww] negeren
ilk [bnw] soort, slag
ill I [znw] • kwaad • kwaal II [bnw]
• ziek, misselijk • slecht III [bijw]
slecht, kwalijk
I'll [samentr.] /I shall/ /I will/
→ shall, will
illegal [bnw] onwettig
illegible [bnw] onleesbaar
illegitimacy [znw] onwettigheid,
illegitimiteit
illegitimate [bnw] onwettig, onecht
illiberal [bnw] weinig vrijheid
toestaand
illicit [bnw] onwettig, ongeoorloofd
illiteracy [znw] ongeletterdheid
illiterate I [znw] analfabeet II [bnw]
niet kunnende lezen
illness [znw] ziekte
illogical [bnw] onlogisch
illuminate, illumine [ov ww]
• verlichten, licht werpen op
• verluchten <v. manuscript>
illusion [znw] • illusie • visioen
illustrate [ov ww] • illustreren
• verduidelijken
illustrator [znw] illustrator, tekenaar

illustrious [bnw] • doorluchtig
• beroemd
I'm [samentr.] /I am/ → be
image [znw] • gelijkenis, beeld,
voorstelling, beeltenis • idee • reputatie
imagery [znw] • beelden • beeldspraak
imaginable [bnw] denkbaar
imaginary [bnw] denkbeeldig
imagination [znw] verbeelding
imaginative [znw] • fantasierijk
• fantastisch
imagine [ov ww] z. voorstellen
imbalance [znw] onevenwichtigheid
imbecile [bnw] imbeciel
imitate [ov ww] nabootsen, navolgen
imitation [znw] imitatie, namaak
imitative [bnw] nabootsend
immaterial [bnw] • onstoffelijk
• onbelangrijk
immature [bnw] onrijp, niet volwassen
immeasurable [bnw] oneindig,
onmeetbaar
immediacy [znw] • nabijheid
• dringendheid
immediate [bnw] onmiddellijk
immediately I [bijw] • onmiddellijk
• rechtstreeks II [vw] meteen als/toen,
zodra
immense [bnw] onmetelijk
immerse [ov ww] onderdompelen,
indopen
immersion [znw] onderdompeling
immigrant I [znw] immigrant
II [bnw] immigrerend
immigration [znw] immigratie
imminent [bnw] dreigend, op handen
zijnde
immobile [bnw] onbeweeglijk
immobilize [ov ww] onbeweeglijk
maken
immoderate [bnw] buitensporig,
onmatig
immodest [bnw] • onbetamelijk
• onbescheiden
immoral [bnw] • immoreel • onzedelijk
immortal I [znw] onsterfelijke II [bnw]

• onsterfelijk • ‹inf.› onverslijtbaar
immortalize [ov ww] onsterfelijk
maken, vereeuwigen
immovable [bnw] onbeweeglijk
immune [bnw] immuun
immunize [ov ww] immuun maken
immutable [bnw] onveranderlijk
imp [znw] • kabouter • stout kind
• duiveltje
impact I [ov ww] indrijven II [znw]
• botsing • invloed • uitwerking • effekt
• slag • stoot
impair [ov ww] • verzwakken
• beschadigen
impale [ov ww] spietsen
impart [ov ww] mededelen
impartial [bnw] onpartijdig
impassable [bnw] • onbegaanbaar
• onoverkomelijk
impassioned [bnw] hartstochtelijk
impassive [bnw] • ongevoelig
• onverstoorbaar
impatience [znw] • ongeduld
• gretigheid • onverdraagzaamheid
impatient [bnw] verlangend,
ongeduldig, vurig
impeach [ov ww] in staat v.
beschuldiging stellen
impeachment [znw] aanklacht en
vervolging
impeccable [bnw] smetteloos, zonder
zonden
impecunious [bnw] • (altijd) arm
• zonder geld
impede [ov ww] verhinderen
impediment [znw] beletsel
impel [ov ww] • aanzetten • dringen
impenetrable [bnw]
ondoordringbaar, ondoorgrondelijk,
onbegrijpelijk
imperative I [znw] II [bnw]
• gebiedend • noodzakelijk
imperceptible [bnw] onmerkbaar
imperfect I [znw] onvoltooid verleden
tijd II [bnw] onvolkomen, onvolmaakt
imperfection [znw] • onvolmaaktheid

• zonde
imperial [bnw] • keizerlijk, keizer(s)-
• rijks-
imperialism [znw] imperialisme
imperil [ov ww] in gevaar brengen
imperishable [bnw] onvergankelijk
impermeable [bnw] ondoordringbaar
impersonate [ov ww]
• verpersoonlijken • vertolken • nadoen,
imiteren
impertinence [znw] onbeschaamdheid
imperturbable [bnw] onverstoorbaar
impervious [bnw] ondoordringbaar
impetuous [bnw] onstuimig, heftig
impetus [znw] • bewegingsstuwkracht
• stoot
impiety [znw] • oneerbiedigheid
• goddeloosheid
impious [bnw] • goddeloos • profaan
impish [bnw] • ondeugend
• duivelachtig
implacable [bnw] onverzoenlijk
implant [ov ww] • planten • inprenten
implausible [bnw] onwaarschijnlijk
implement I [ov ww] nakomen
<contract> II [znw] werktuig
implicate [ov ww] insluiten, omvatten
• (~ in) betrekken bij
implication [znw] gevolgtrekking
implicit [bnw] • onvoorwaardelijk
• erin begrepen
implore [ov ww] (af)smeken
imply [ov ww] suggereren
impolite [bnw] onbeleefd
impolitic [bnw] onoordeelkundig
imponderable [bnw] • onweegbaar
• niet te schatten
import I [ov ww] • invoeren
• betekenen • v. belang zijn II [znw]
• betekenis • belang(rijkheid) • invoer
importance [znw] • belang
• gewicht(igheid)
important [bnw] • belangrijk
• gewichtig
importer [znw] importeur
importunate [bnw] lastig, (z.

op)dringend
importune [ov ww] lastig vallen
importunity [znw] opdringerigheid
impose [ov ww] • (~ on) imponeren, z.
opdringen, opleggen <v. plicht,
belasting>, misbruik maken van
imposing [bnw] • indrukwekkend
• veeleisend
impossible [bnw] onmogelijk
imposture [znw] bedrog
impotence [znw] • onmacht,
onvermogen • impotentie
impotent [bnw] • machteloos
• impotent
impound [ov ww] • insluiten • in
beslag nemen
impoverish [ov ww] verarmen
impracticable [bnw] • onbegaanbaar
• onuitvoerbaar
impractical [bnw] onpraktisch
impregnable [bnw] onneembaar
impress [ov ww] stempelen, inprenten,
indruk maken op
impression [znw] • oplage • indruk
impressionable [bnw] ontvankelijk
impressionist [znw] • impressionist
• imitator
impressionistic [bnw]
impressionistisch
impressive [bnw] indrukwekkend
imprint I [ov ww] • stempelen
• inprenten II [znw] stempel
imprison [ov ww] in de gevangenis
zetten
imprisonment [znw] gevangenschap
improbable [bnw] onwaarschijnlijk
improper [bnw] • onjuist • ongepast
impropriety [znw] ongepastheid
improve [ov + on ww] verhogen,
verbeteren
improvement [znw] • beterschap,
vooruitgang • hoger bod
• (bodem)verbetering
improvidence [znw] zorgeloosheid
improvise [ov ww] improviseren
imprudent [bnw] onvoorzichtig

impudent [bnw] *onbeschaamd, schaamteloos*
impugn [ov ww] *betwisten*
impulse [znw] • *stoot* • *prikkel* • *opwelling*
impulsive [bnw] • *aandrijvend, stuw-* • *impulsief*
impunity [znw] *straffeloosheid*
impure [bnw] • *onrein* • *onkuis* • *vervalst*
impurity [znw] *onreinheid*
impute [ov ww] • *ten laste leggen* • *toeschrijven, wijten (aan)*
inability [znw] *onbekwaamheid*
inaccessible [bnw] *ongenaakbaar, ontoegankelijk*
inaccuracy [znw] *onnauwkeurigheid, fout(je)*
inaccurate [bnw] *onnauwkeurig*
inaction [znw] • *traagheid* • *werkeloosheid*
inactive [bnw] • *werkeloos* • *traag*
inadequacy [znw] *onvolledigheid*
inadmissible [bnw] *ontoelaatbaar*
inadvertent [bnw] • *onoplettend* • *onbewust*
inalienable [bnw] *onvervreemdbaar*
inane [bnw] • *leeg* • *idioot* • *zinloos*
inapplicable [bnw] *niet toepasselijk*
inappropriate [bnw] • *ongepast* • *ongeschikt*
inapt [bnw] • *ongeschikt* • *ongepast*
inarticulate [bnw] *niet uit te spreken*
inattention [znw] *onachtzaamheid*
inattentive [bnw] *onoplettend*
inaudible [bnw] *onhoorbaar*
inaugural [bnw] *inaugureel*
inaugurate [ov ww] • *openen* • *installeren* • *inwijden*
inauspicious [bnw] *onheilspellend, ongunstig*
inborn, inbred [bnw] *aangeboren*
inbreeding [znw] *inteelt*
incalculable [bnw] *onberekenbaar*
incandescent [bnw] *gloeiend*
incantation [znw] *toverformule*

incapable [bnw] *onbekwaam*
incapacitate [ov ww] *ongeschikt maken*
incapacity [znw] *onbekwaamheid*
incarcerate [ov ww] *gevangenzetten*
incarnate I [ov ww] *belichamen* II [bnw] *vleselijk*
incarnation [znw] *verpersoonlijking*
incautious [bnw] *onvoorzichtig*
incendiary I [znw] *brandbom* II [bnw] *brandstichtend*
incense I [ov ww] • *woedend maken* • *bewieroken* II [znw] *wierook*
incentive [znw] • *prikkeling* • *motief* • *aansporing*
inception [znw] *aanvang*
incessant [bnw] *onophoudelijk*
inch I [on ww] z. *zeer langzaam voortbewegen* II [znw] *Engelse duim* ‹2,54 cm›
incidence [znw] *aantal gevallen*
incident [znw] *incident, voorval, episode*
incidental [bnw] *bijkomstig*
incinerate [ov ww] *verassen, verbranden*
incipient [bnw] *aanvangs-*
incise [ov ww] • *insnijden* • *graveren*
incisive [bnw] • *scherp* • *snij-*
incisor [znw] *snijtand*
incite [ov ww] • *aansporen* • *opruien*
inclement [bnw] *streng* ‹v. weer›, *guur*
inclination [znw] • *neiging* • *aanleg*
incline I [ov ww] • *geneigd maken* • *doen (over)hellen* II [on ww] • *(over)hellen* • *geneigd zijn* III [znw] • *hellend vlak* • *helling*
include [ov ww] *insluiten, omvatten*
inclusion [znw] • *insluitsel* • *insluiting*
inclusive [bnw] *insluitend, omvattend*
incoherent [bnw] • *verward* • *onsamenhangend*
income [znw] *inkomsten, inkomen*
incoming [bnw] • *binnenkomend* • *opkomend* ‹v. getij›
incommunicado [bnw] *(v.d. buitenwereld) afgeschermd, geïsoleerd*

incompatible [bnw] • onverenigbaar
• tegenstrijdig
incomplete [bnw] • onvolledig
• gebrekkig
incomprehensible [bnw]
onbegrijpelijk
inconceivable [bnw] onbegrijpelijk
inconclusive [bnw] niet beslissend,
niet overtuigend
incongruity [znw]
• ongelijksoortigheid • inconsequentie
incongruous [bnw] • ongelijksoortig
• inconsequent
inconsiderable [bnw] onbelangrijk
inconsiderate [bnw] onbedachtzaam,
onattent
inconsistent [bnw] • tegenstrijdig
• inconsequent
inconsolable [bnw] ontroostbaar
inconspicuous [bnw] onopvallend
incontrovertible [bnw] onbetwistbaar
inconvenience I [ov ww] in
ongelegenheid brengen II [znw]
ongemak, ongerief
inconvenient [bnw] • ongeriefelijk
• lastig
incorporate [ov ww] verenigen
• (~ in(to)/with) inlijven bij
incorrect [bnw] onjuist
incorrigible [bnw] onverbeterlijk
incorruptible [bnw] • onkreukbaar
• onvergankelijk
incredible [bnw] ongelofelijk
incredulity [znw] ongeloof
increment [znw] • loonsverhoging
• toename
incriminate [ov ww] • beschuldigen
<v. misdaad> • betrekken in aanklacht
incubate [ov + on ww] (uit)broeden
incubator [znw] • broedmachine
• couveuse
inculcate [ov ww] inprenten
incumbent [bnw] verplicht
incur [ov ww] • oplopen • maken <v.
schulden>
incurable [bnw] ongeneeslijk

incursion [znw] vijandelijke inval,
onverwachte aanval
indebted [bnw] • (ver)schuldig(d)
• verplicht
indecency [znw] onfatsoenlijkheid
indecent [bnw] onzedelijk,
onfatsoenlijk
indecision [znw] besluiteloosheid
indecisive [bnw] besluiteloos
indeed [bijw] trouwens, dan ook, zelfs,
werkelijk, weliswaar, inderdaad
indefatigable [bnw] onvermoeid,
onvermoeibaar
indefensible [bnw] onverdedigbaar
indefinable [bnw] ondefinieerbaar,
niet te bepalen
indefinite [bnw] • onbepaald • vaag
indelible [bnw] onuitwisbaar
indemnity [znw] • schadeloosstelling
• vrijwaring • amnestie, kwijtschelding
indent [ov + on ww] • inspringen <v.
regel> • vorderen <v. goederen>
indentation [znw] inkeping, het
inspringen
independence [znw]
onafhankelijkheid
independent I [znw] iem. die niet
politiek gebonden is II [bnw]
onafhankelijk
indestructible [bnw] onverwoestbaar
Indian I [znw] • Indiër • indiaan
II [bnw] • indiaans • Indisch
indicate [ov ww] • aangeven <v.
richting> • tonen • aanwijzen • wijzen
op
indication [znw] aanwijzing
indicative I [znw] aantonende wijs
II [bnw] aantonend
indicator [znw] • spanningmeter
• richtingaanwijzer
indict [ov ww] beschuldigen, aanklagen
indictable [bnw] vervolgbaar
indifference [znw] onverschilligheid
indigenous [bnw] • inheems
• aangeboren
indigent [bnw] arm, behoeftig

indigestible [bnw] *onverteerbaar*
indigestion [znw] *indigestie*
indignant [bnw] *verontwaardigd*
indignation [znw] *verontwaardiging*
indignity [znw] *belediging*
indirect [bnw] • *bedrieglijk* • *indirect, zijdelings*
indiscernible [bnw] *niet te onderscheiden*
indiscreet [bnw] *onbezonnen*
indiscretion [znw] *onbezonnen daad/gedrag*
indiscriminate [bnw] • *geen verschil makend* • *in het wilde weg, zo maar*
indispensable [bnw] *onmisbaar*
indisposition [znw] *ongesteldheid*
indisputable [bnw] *onbetwistbaar*
indistinct [bnw] *onduidelijk*
individual I [znw] *individu, persoon* II [bnw] • *individueel, persoonlijk* • *eigenaardig*
individualism [znw] *individualisme*
individualist I [znw] *individualist* II [bnw] *individualistisch*
individuality [znw] *individualiteit*
individualize [ov ww] *individualiseren*
indoctrinate [ov ww] *indoctrineren*
indolent [bnw] *lui*
indomitable [bnw] *ontembaar, onoverwinnelijk*
Indonesian I [znw] *Indonesiër, Indonesische* II [bnw] *Indonesisch*
indoor [bnw] *binnenshuis, huis-*
indubitable [bnw] *zonder twijfel*
induce [ov ww] • *bewegen, ertoe krijgen* • *afleiden*
inducement [znw] • *beweegreden* • *lokmiddel*
induct [ov ww] *installeren, bevestigen* <v. predikant>
induction [znw] • *installatie* • *gevolgtrekking* • *inductie* • *kunstmatig ingeleide bevalling*
inductive [bnw] *aanleiding gevend, inductief*
indulge I [ov ww] • *verwennen*

• *toegeven (aan)* II [on ww] • (~ in) z. *overgeven aan*
indulgence [znw] *overdreven toegeeflijkheid*
indulgent [bnw] *(al te) toegeeflijk*
industrial [bnw] *industrieel, bedrijfs-, nijverheids-*
industrialist [znw] • *industrieel* • *fabriekseigenaar*
industrious [bnw] *hardwerkend, arbeidzaam*
industry [znw] • *industrie, bedrijf* • *ijver*
inebriate I [znw] *dronkaard* II [bnw] *(altijd) dronken*
inedible [bnw] *oneetbaar*
ineffable [bnw] *onuitsprekelijk*
ineffective [bnw] *ondoeltreffend*
ineffectual [bnw] • *vruchteloos* • *ontoereikend*
inefficient [bnw] • *onbekwaam* • *ondoelmatig*
inelegant [bnw] *onelegant, niet fraai*
ineligible [bnw] *niet te verkiezen*
inept [bnw] *onbekwaam*
ineptitude [znw] *onbekwaamheid*
inequality [znw] • *verschil* • *ongelijkheid*
inequitable [bnw] *onrechtvaardig, onbillijk*
inert [bnw] *traag, log*
inertia [znw] *traagheid*
inescapable [bnw] *onontkoombaar*
inessential [bnw] *niet essentieel, bijkomstig*
inestimable [bnw] *onschatbaar*
inevitable [bnw] *onvermijdelijk*
inexact [bnw] *onjuist*
inexcusable [bnw] *onvergeeflijk*
inexhaustible [bnw] *onuitputtelijk*
inexorable [bnw] *onverbiddelijk*
inexpensive [bnw] *goedkoop*
inexperience [znw] *onervarenheid*
inexperienced [bnw] *onervaren*
inexpert [bnw] *onbedreven, ondeskundig*

inexplicable [bnw] *onverklaarbaar*
inextricable [bnw] *onontwarbaar*
infallible [bnw] *onfeilbaar*
infamous [bnw] *berucht*
infamy [znw] • *beruchtheid* • *schande*
infancy [znw] • *kindsheid*
• *minderjarigheid*
infant I [znw] • *zuigeling* • *kind
beneden 7 jaar* • *minderjarige* II [bnw]
kinderlijk, kinder-
infanticide [znw] *kindermoord*
infantile [bnw] *kinder-, kinderlijk,
kinderachtig*
infantry [znw] *infanterie*
infatuation [znw] *dwaze verliefdheid*
infection [znw] *besmetting*
infectious [bnw] *besmettelijk,
aanstekelijk*
infer [ov ww] *gevolg trekken*
inference [znw] *gevolgtrekking*
inferior I [znw] *ondergeschikte* II [bnw]
• *minder(waardig)* • *onder-* • *lager*
infernal [bnw] *hels, duivels*
inferno [znw] *hel, onderwereld*
infertile [bnw] *onvruchtbaar*
infest [ov ww] *teisteren*
infidel I [znw] *ongelovige* II [bnw]
ongelovig
infidelity [znw] • *ontrouw* • *ongeloof*
infiltrate [ov + on ww] • *dóórdringen*
• *infiltreren*
infinitesimal [bnw] *zeer klein*
infinitive [znw] *onbepaalde wijs*
infinity [znw] *oneindigheid*
infirm [bnw] *onvast, zwak*
infirmary [znw] *ziekenhuis, ziekenzaal*
inflame [ov ww] *opgewonden maken*
inflammable [bnw] *ontvlambaar*
inflammation [znw] *ontsteking*
inflammatory [bnw] • *ontstekings-*
• *opwindend*
inflatable [bnw] *opblaasbaar*
inflate [ov ww] *oppompen, opblazen*
inflation [znw] *inflatie*
inflect [ov ww] ‹taalk.› *verbuigen*
inflection, inflexion [znw]

• *verbuiging* • *stembuiging*
inflexible [bnw] • *standvastig*
• *onbuigzaam*
inflict [ov ww] *toedienen/opleggen* ‹v.
straf›
inflow [znw] *binnenstromende
hoeveelheid*
influence I [ov ww] *beïnvloeden*
II [znw] *invloed*
influential [bnw] *invloedrijk*
influenza [znw] *griep*
influx [znw] • *instroming* • *toevloed*
inform [ov ww] *mededelen*
informal [bnw] *informeel, niet officieel*
information [znw] • *mededeling*
• *inlichtingen*
informative [bnw] *informatief*
informer [znw] • *aanklager*
• *verklikker*
infrastructure [znw] *infrastructuur*
infrequent [bnw] *niet vaak*
infringe [ov + on ww] *overtreden*
infuriate [ov ww] *woedend maken*
infuse I [ov ww] • *laten trekken* ‹v.
thee› • *ingieten* II [on ww] *trekken* ‹v.
thee›
infusion [znw] • *infusie* • *aftreksel*
ingenious [bnw] *vernuftig*
ingenuity [znw] *vernuft*
ingenuous [bnw] *onschuldig*
ingrained [bnw] *diepgeworteld*
ingratiate [ov ww] • *(~ with) in de
gunst komen bij*
ingratitude [znw] *ondankbaarheid*
ingredient [znw] *bestanddeel*
inhabit [ov ww] *wonen in*
inhabitant [znw] *bewoner, inwoner*
inhale [ov ww] *inademen, inhaleren*
inherit [ov ww] *erven*
inheritance [znw] *erfenis, overerving*
inhibit [ov ww] *remmen, beletten*
inhibited [bnw] *verlegen, geremd*
inhibition [znw] *geremdheid*
inhospitable [bnw] • *ongastvrij*
• *onherbergzaam*
inhuman [bnw] • *onmenselijk*

• *monsterlijk*
inhumane [bnw] *wreed*
inhumanity [znw] *wreedheid*
inimical [bnw] • *vijandig* • *schadelijk*
inimitable [bnw] *onnavolgbaar,*
weergaloos
iniquitous [bnw] • *zondig*
• *onrechtvaardig*
iniquity [znw] • *onrechtvaardigheid*
• *zonde*
initial I [ov ww] *paraferen* II [znw]
voorletter III [bnw] *eerste, begin-, voor-*
initiate I [ov ww] • *beginnen*
• *inwijden, inleiden* II [znw] *ingewijde*
III [bnw] *ingewijd*
initiative I [znw] *initiatief* II [bnw]
aanvangs-
inject [ov ww] *inspuiten*
injection [znw] *injectie*
injudicious [bnw] *onverstandig*
injunction [znw] • *dringend verzoek*
• *verbod, bevel*
injure [ov ww] • *verwonden* • *krenken*
injurious [bnw] • *beledigend*
• *schadelijk*
injury [znw] • *belediging* • *letsel, schade*
injustice [znw] *onrecht(vaardigheid)*
ink I [ov ww] *met inkt insmeren* II [znw]
inkt
inkling [znw] *flauw vermoeden*
inky [bnw] *inktachtig*
inlaid [bnw] *ingelegd*
inland I [znw] *binnenland*
II [bnw + bijw] • *binnenlands* • *in of*
naar 't binnenland
inlay I [ov ww] *inleggen* II [znw]
• *mozaïek* • *vulling* <v. kies>
inlet [znw] *inham*
inn [znw] • *herberg, taveerne*
• *(dorps)hotel*
innate [bnw] *aangeboren, natuurlijk*
inner [bnw] *inwendig, innerlijk,*
binnen-
innocence [znw] *onschuld*
innocent I [znw] *onschuldig iem.*
<vooral klein kind> II [bnw]

• *onschuldig* • *onschadelijk*
innocuous [bnw] *onschadelijk,*
ongevaarlijk
innovator [znw] *vernieuwer*
innuendo [znw] • *beledigende*
insinuatie • *verdachtmaking*
innumerable [bnw] *ontelbaar*
inoculate [ov ww] *inenten*
inoculation [znw] *inenting*
inoffensive [bnw] • *geen aanstoot*
gevend • *onschadelijk*
inoperable [bnw] *niet te opereren*
inoperative [bnw] • *niet werkend*
• *ongeldig* <v. wet>
inopportune [bnw] • *ontijdig*
• *ongelegen*
inordinate [bnw] *buitensporig*
inorganic [bnw] *anorganisch*
input [znw] • *invoer van gegevens*
• *toevoer*
inquest [znw] *gerechtelijk onderzoek*
inquire [ov + on ww] *navragen*
• (~ **about/after**) *informeren naar*
• (~ **into**) *onderzoeken*
inquisition [znw] • *onderzoek*
• *inquisitie*
insalubrious [bnw] *ongezond* <v.
omgeving>
insane [bnw] *krankzinnig*
insanity [znw] *krankzinnigheid,*
dwaasheid
insatiable [bnw] *onverzadigbaar*
inscribe [ov ww] • *graveren* • *opdragen*
<v. boek>
inscription [znw] *inscriptie*
inscrutable [bnw] *ondoorgrondelijk*
insect [znw] *insect*
insecure [bnw] *onveilig,*
onbetrouwbaar
insensible [bnw] • *bewusteloos*
• *ongevoelig*
insensitive [bnw] • *ongevoelig*
• *onattent*
inseparable [bnw] *onafscheidelijk, niet*
te scheiden
insert I [ov ww] • *invoegen* • *insteken*

II [znw] *inlas*
inshore [bnw] *naar of dichtbij de kust*
inside I [znw] *binnenkant* II [bnw]
binnen-, binnenste III [bijw] *van/naar
binnen* IV [vz] *binnen, in*
insider [znw] • *lid v. vereniging*
• *ingewijde*
insidious [bnw] *verraderlijk*
insight [znw] *inzicht*
insignificant [bnw] *onbeduidend*
insincere [bnw] *bedrieglijk, oneerlijk*
insinuate [ov ww] *insinueren*
insipid [bnw] • *saai, oninteressant*
• *smakeloos*
insist [ov + on ww] *volhouden, met
klem beweren*
insistence [znw] *aandrang*
insistent [bnw] • *aanhoudend* • *urgent*
insole [znw] *binnenzool*
insolent [bnw] *onbeschaamd*
insoluble [bnw] *onoplosbaar*
insolvency [znw] *insolventie*
insolvent [bnw] • *insolvent* • <scherts>
blut
insomnia [znw] *slapeloosheid*
inspect [ov ww] *onderzoeken,
inspecteren, bezichtigen*
inspector [znw] • *onderzoeker*
• *inspecteur* • *opzichter*
inspiration [znw] *inspiratie, ingeving*
inspire [ov ww] *inspireren, bezielen*
instability [znw] *onstandvastigheid*
installation [znw] • *installatie*
• *plaatsing*
instalment [znw] • *termijn* <v.
betaling> • *aflevering* • *installatie*
instead [bijw] *in plaats
hiervan/daarvan*
instigate [ov ww] *aansporen,
aanzetten tot*
instil(l) [ov ww] • *doordringen van
gevoelens/ideeën* • *indruppelen*
instinct [znw] • *instinct* • *intuïtie*
instinctive [bnw] *instinctmatig*
institute I [ov ww] *stichten* II [znw]
instelling, instituut

institution [znw] • *instituut,
instelling* • *gesticht* • *wet* • <inf.>
bekend of vast voorwerp of persoon
instruct [ov ww] • *onderrichten*
• *bevelen*
instruction [znw] • *aanwijzing,
instructie* • *bevel*
instructive [bnw] *leerzaam*
instructor [znw] • *instructeur* • *docent*
<aan universiteit>
instrument [znw] *instrument,
werktuig*
instrumental [bnw] *instrumentaal*
instrumentalist [znw] *bespeler v.
instrument*
instrumentation [znw]
instrumentatie
insubordinate [bnw] *ongehoorzaam*
insubstantial [bnw] *onbelangrijk*
insufferable [bnw] *on(ver)draaglijk*
insufficient [bnw] *onvoldoende*
insular [bnw] *bekrompen* <v. geest>
insulate [ov ww] • *isoleren* • *afscheiden*
insulation [znw] *isolatie(materiaal)*
insulator [znw] *isolatie(middel)*
insulin [znw] *insuline*
insult I [ov ww] *beledigen* II [znw]
belediging
insuperable [bnw] *onoverkomelijk*
insupportable [bnw] *ondraaglijk*
insurance [znw] *verzekering*
insure [ov ww] *verzekeren*
insurer [znw] *verzekeraar, assuradeur*
insurgent I [znw] *rebel* II [bnw]
oproerig
insurmountable [bnw]
onoverkomelijk
insurrection [znw] *opstand*
intact [bnw] *intact, heel, ongeschonden*
intake [znw] • *nieuwe instroom* <v.
personen> • *opname* • *opgenomen
hoeveelheid* <v. energie, vermogen>
intangible [bnw] • *ongrijpbaar*
• *onstoffelijk*
integer [znw] *geheel getal*
integral [bnw] *essentieel deel*

uitmakend
integrate [ov + on ww] *integreren*
integrity [znw] • *eerlijkheid*
• *onkreukbaarheid*
intelligence [znw] *verstand, begrip*
intelligentsia [znw] *intellectuelen*
intelligible [bnw] *begrijpelijk*
intemperate [bnw] *overdreven, hevig*
intend [ov ww] • *v. plan zijn*
• *bestemmen*
intended I [znw] *verloofde* II [bnw]
• *aanstaande* • *met opzet*
intense [bnw] *intens, krachtig, vurig,*
diep gevoeld
intent I [znw] *bedoeling* II [bnw]
• *(in)gespannen* • *doelbewust*
• *(~ (up)on) vastbesloten*
intention [znw] • *voornemen* • *doel,*
bedoeling
intentional [bnw] *opzettelijk*
inter I [ov ww] *begraven* II [bnw]
tussen, onder
interact [on ww] *op elkaar inwerken*
intercession [znw] *tussenkomst*
interchange I [ov ww] *ruilen,*
(uit)wisselen II [znw] • *verandering*
• *ruil, uitwisseling* • ‹AE› *oprit naar*
viaduct
interchangeable [bnw] *verwisselbaar*
intercontinental [bnw]
intercontinentaal
intercourse [znw] *(geslachts)verkeer,*
omgang
interdependent [bnw] *onderling*
afhankelijk
interest I [ov ww] • *(~ in)*
belangstelling wekken voor II [znw]
• *belangstelling, (eigen)belang* • *rente*
interested [bnw] *geïnteresseerd*
interesting [bnw] *interessant,*
belangwekkend
interfere [on ww] ‹techn.› *interfereren*
• *(~ with) z. bemoeien met, verstoren*
interference [znw] • *bemoeiing,*
tussenkomst • *hinder* • *interferentie,*
storing • ‹sport› *blokkeren*

interior I [znw] • *'t inwendige,*
interieur • *binnenland* • *binnenste*
II [bnw] • *binnenlands* • *inwendig*
• *innerlijk*
interject [ov ww] *tussenwerpen*
interjection [znw] • *tussenwerpsel*
• *uitroep*
interlock [on ww] *in elkaar sluiten of*
grijpen
interlocutor [znw] *gesprekspartner*
interloper [znw] *indringer*
interlude [znw] • *pauze* • *tussenspel,*
intermezzo
intermarriage [znw] *gemengd*
huwelijk
intermarry [on ww] *huwen tussen*
verschillende stammen of volkeren
intermediary [znw] *bemiddelaar*
intermediate [bnw] *tussenkomend*
interment [znw] *begrafenis*
interminable [bnw] *eindeloos*
intermingle [ov + on ww] *(ver)mengen*
intermission [znw] • *pauze*
• *onderbreking*
internal I [znw] II [bnw] • *inwendig,*
innerlijk • *binnenlands* • *inwonend*
international I [znw] ‹sport›
(deelnemer aan) internationale
wedstrijd II [bnw] *internationaal*
internationalism [znw]
internationalisme
internecine [bnw] *bitter* ‹in gevecht›
internee [znw] *geïnterneerde*
internment [znw] *internering*
interplay [znw] *wisselwerking*
interpolate [ov ww] *tussenvoegen,*
inlassen
interpose I [ov ww] *plaatsen tussen*
II [on ww] • *tussen beide komen* • *in de*
rede vallen
interpret I [ov ww] • *verklaren,*
uitleggen • *vertolken* II [on ww] *als*
tolk fungeren
interpretation [znw] • *vertolking*
• *uitleg, verklaring*
interpreter [znw] *tolk*

interrelate [ov ww] *onderling verbinden*
interrogate [ov ww] *ondervragen*
interrupt [ov ww] *onderbreken, afbreken*
interruption [znw] *interruptie, onderbreking*
intersect I [ov ww] • *doorsnijden* • *verdelen* II [on ww] *elkaar snijden*
intersection [znw] *snijpunt, kruispunt*
intersperse [ov ww] *hier en daar ertussen zetten*
intertwine [ov ww] *in elkaar vlechten*
interval [znw] • *tussenruimte* • *pauze*
intervention [znw] *interventie*
interview I [ov ww] • *interviewen* • *ondervragen* II [znw] • *onderhoud* • *sollicitatiegesprek* • *vraaggesprek*
interviewer [znw] • *interviewer* • *ondervrager*
interweave I [ov ww] *vervlechten* II [on ww] *zich dooreen weven*
intimacy [znw] *intimiteit*
intimate I [ov ww] *min of meer laten blijken* II [bnw] *intiem, vertrouwelijk*
intimation [znw] • *wenk* • *teken*
intimidate [ov ww] *intimideren*
into [vz] *in, tot*
intolerable [bnw] *on(ver)draaglijk*
intolerant [bnw] *onverdraagzaam*
intonation [znw] *intonatie*
intone [ov ww] *aanheffen*
intoxicant I [znw] *bedwelmend middel, sterkedrank* II [bnw] *bedwelmend*
intractable [znw] *weerspanning*
intransigent [bnw] *onverzoenlijk*
intransitive [bnw] *onovergankelijk*
intravenous [bnw] • *intraveneus* • *in de ader(en)*
intricacy [znw] *ingewikkeldheid*
intricate [bnw] • *ingewikkeld* • *gedetailleerd*
intrigue I [ov + on ww] • *bevreemden* • *intrigeren* II [znw] *intrige*
intrinsic [bnw] • *innerlijk* • *inherent*

introduce [ov ww] • *voorstellen* <v. persoon> • *ter sprake brengen* • *invoeren, inleiden*
introduction [znw] *inleiding, voorwoord*
introductory [bnw] *inleidend*
introspection [znw] *zelfonderzoek*
introspective [bnw] *zelfbespiegelend*
intrude [ov + on ww] • *storen* • *binnen dringen*
intruder [znw] *indringer*
intrusion [znw] *inbreuk*
intrusive [bnw] *indringerig*
intuitive [bnw] *intuïtief*
inundate [ov ww] *onder water zetten, overstromen*
inure [ov ww] • (~ *to*) *gewennen aan*
invade [ov ww] *binnenvallen* <v. vijand>
invalid I [znw] • *zieke* • *invalide* II [bnw] • *ziek* • *invalide* • *ongeldig*
invalidate [ov ww] *ongeldig maken*
invaluable [bnw] *onschatbaar*
invasion [znw] *inval*
invective [znw] *scheldwoorden*
inveigh [on ww] • (~ *against*) (*heftig*) *uitvaren tegen, schelden op*
inveigle [ov ww] (*ver*)*lokken*
invent [ov ww] • *uitvinden* • *verzinnen*
invention [znw] *uitvinding*
inventive [bnw] *vindingrijk*
inventor [znw] *uitvinder*
inventory [znw] *inventaris*
inverse I [znw] *'t omgekeerde* II [bnw] *omgekeerd*
inversion [znw] • *omkering* • <taalk.> *inversie*
invert [ov ww] *omkeren*
invertebrate I [znw] *ongewerveld dier* II [bnw] *ongewerveld*
invest I [ov ww] • *beleggen* <v. geld> • *bekleden* • *installeren* II [on ww] *investeren*
investigate [ov ww] *onderzoeken*
investigator [znw] *onderzoeker*
investment [znw] *geldbelegging, investering*

investor [znw] *investeerder, belegger*
inveterate [bnw] *verstokt, ingeworteld*
invidious [bnw] • *aanstootgevend*
• *gehaat, hatelijk* • *jaloers*
invincible [bnw] *onoverwinnelijk*
inviolable [bnw] *onschendbaar*
invisible [bnw] *onzichtbaar*
invite I [ov ww] • *aanlokken*
• *uitnodigen* II [znw] ‹inf.› *uitnodiging*
invocation [znw] • *inroeping* ‹v. hulp›
• *aanroeping* ‹v. God› • *oproeping* ‹v.
geest›
invoice I [ov ww] *factureren* II [znw]
factuur
invoke [ov ww] *inroepen*
involuntary [bnw] *onwillekeurig*
involvement [znw] • *verwikkeling*
• *(financiële) betrokkenheid* • *(seksuele)
verhouding*
inward I [bnw] *inwendig, innerlijk*
II [bijw] *naar binnen*
iota [znw] • *jota* • *schijntje*
IOU [afk] • *(I owe you) schuldbekentenis*
Iranian I [znw] *Iraniër* II [bnw] *Iraans*
Iraqi [bnw] *Irakees*
irascible [bnw] *opvliegend* ‹v. aard›
irate [bnw] *woedend*
iridescent [bnw] • *met de kleuren van
de regenboog, regenboogkleurig*
• *weerschijnend*
iris [znw] • *iris* • ‹foto.› *diafragma*
Irish I [znw] *het Iers* II [bnw] *Iers*
irk [ov ww] • *vervelen* • *vermoeien*
irksome [bnw] *vervelend*
iron I [ov ww] *strijken* • (~ **out**)
gladstrijken, oplossing vinden voor
II [znw] • *ijzer* • *beenbeugel*
• *strijkijzer* III [bnw] • *ijzeren* • *niet
wijkend* • *stevig* • *meedogenloos*
ironing [znw] • *het strijken* • *strijkgoed*
irony [znw] *ironie, spot*
irrational [bnw] *irrationeel*
irredeemable [bnw] • *onherstelbaar*
• *onaflosbaar* • *niet inwisselbaar* ‹v.
geld›
irreducible [bnw] • *onherleidbaar*

• *wat niet meer vereenvoudigd kan
worden*
irrefutable [bnw] *onweerlegbaar*
irregular [bnw] • *ongeregeld*
• *onregelmatig*
irrelevant [bnw] *irrelevant, niet ter
zake doend*
irremediable [bnw] *onherstelbaar*
irreparable [bnw] *onherstelbaar*
irreplaceable [bnw] *onvervangbaar*
irrepressible [bnw] *niet te
onderdrukken*
irreproachable [bnw] *onberispelijk,
keurig*
irresistible [bnw] *onweerstaanbaar*
irrespective [bnw]
irresponsible [bnw] • *ongeacht*
• *onverantwoordelijk*
irretrievable [bnw] *reddeloos (verloren)*
irreverent [bnw] *oneerbiedig*
irrevocable [bnw] *onherroepelijk*
irrigate [ov ww] *bevloeien, irrigeren*
irritable [bnw] *prikkelbaar*
irritant I [znw] *prikkelend middel*
II [bnw] *prikkelend*
irritate [ov ww] • *irriteren* • *prikkelen*
• *ergeren*
irritation [znw] • *geprikkeldheid*
• *branderigheid*
is [ww] → *be*
Islamic [bnw] *islamitisch*
island [znw] *eiland*
isle [znw] *eiland*
islet [znw] *eilandje*
isolate [ov ww] *isoleren, afzonderen*
isolation [znw] *afzondering, isolement*
issue I [ov ww] • *in circulatie brengen,
uitgeven* • *verstrekken* • *uitvaardigen*
• (~ **with**) *voorzien van* II [on ww]
• *uitgaan, uitkomen* • *afstammen*
• (~ **forth**) *verschijnen* • (~ **from**) *'t
gevolg zijn van* III [znw] • *uitgang*
• *nakomelingen* • *geschilpunt,
probleem* • *kwestie* • *uitgave* • *oplage*
• *uitstroming*
isthmus [znw] *istmus, landengte*

it [pers vnw] • *het, hèt* • *het einde*
Italian I [znw] *Italiaan* II [bnw]
Italiaans
itch I [on ww] • *jeuken* • *hunkeren*
II [znw] *jeuk*
item [znw] • *agendapunt,*
programmaonderdeel • *artikel* • *post*
<op rekening> • *nieuwsbericht*
itemize [ov ww] • *artikelsgewijze*
noteren • *specificeren*
itinerant [bnw] *rondreizend*
itinerary I [znw] • *route*
• *reisbeschrijving* • *gids* II [bnw] *reis-*
it'll [samentr.] /it will/ / it shall/
→ will, shall
it's [samentr.] /it is/ /it has/ → be,
have
itself [wkd vnw] z.(*zelf*)
I've [samentr.] /I have/ → have
ivory I [znw] *ivoor* II [bnw] *ivoren*
ivy [znw] *klimop*

J

jab I [ov ww] *porren, steken* II [znw]
steek
jabber I [on ww] *snateren, wauwelen*
II [znw] *het snateren, het wauwelen*
jack I [ov + on ww] • (~ in) *eraan geven,*
opgeven II [ov ww] • (~ off) <vulg.> z.
aftrekken • (~ up) *opvijzelen,*
opkrikken III [znw] • *stekker* • *boer* <in
kaartspel> • *dommekracht, krik*
jackal [znw] *jakhals*
jacket I [ov ww] *voorzien v.e.*
mantel/omslag II [znw] • *buis*
• *colbert, jasje* • *omslag* <v. boek> • *hoes*
<v. plaat> • *schil* <v. aardappel>
jagged [bnw] • *hoekig, getand*
• *gekarteld*
jail I [ov ww] *gevangen zetten* II [znw]
gevangenis, gevangenisstraf
jam I [ov ww] • *samendrukken,*
vastzetten, versperren • <telecom.>
storen II [on ww] • *knellen* • *vastlopen*
<v. machine> • <muz.> *improviseren*
III [znw] • *jam* • *klemming, gedrang,*
(verkeers)opstopping
jamb [znw] *deur-/raamstijl*
jangle I [ov ww] *doen rinkelen*
II [on ww] *ratelen, rinkelen* III [znw]
gerinkel
janitor [znw] • *portier* • <AE> *conciërge*
January [znw] *januari*
jar I [ww] • *onaangenaam aandoen* • *in*
strijd zijn met • *knarsen, krassen*
II [znw] • *geknars* • *schok* • *wanklank*
• *onenigheid* • *pot, kruik, fles*
jargon [znw] • *bargoens* • *jargon*
jaundice [znw] *geelzucht*
jaunt I [on ww] *'n uitstapje maken*
II [znw] *uitstapje*
jaunty [bnw] *luchtig, vrolijk*
javelin [znw] *speer*
jaw [znw] • *kaak* • <inf.> *geklets*

jay [znw] *Vlaamse gaai*
jazz I [on ww] • (~ **up**) <sl.> *levendiger
maken, opvrolijken* II [znw] *jazz*
jazzy [bnw] *lawaaierig, bont, druk,
grillig*
jealous [bnw] *jaloers, afgunstig*
jealousy [znw] *jaloezie, naijver, afgunst*
jeans [mv] *spijkerbroek*
jeer I [ww] *honen* II [znw] *hoon, spot*
jell [on ww] • *stollen* • <inf.> *vaste vorm
aannemen*
jelly [znw] *gelei, pudding*
jemmy [znw] *breekijzer*
jeopard(ize) [ov ww] *in gevaar brengen*
jeopardy [znw] *gevaar*
jerk I [ov + on ww] *rukken, trekken,
schokken* • (~ **off**) <sl.> *aftrekken*
II [znw] • *ruk, trek, schok, spiertrekking*
• <sl.> *stomme meid/vent*
jerkin [znw] *wambuis*
jerky [bnw] *met rukken, met horten en
stoten*
jersey [znw] *gebreide wollen trui*
jest I [on ww] *schertsen* II [znw] *scherts*
jester [znw] *grappenmaker, nar*
Jesuit [znw] *jezuïet*
jet I [on ww] *per straalvliegtuig reizen*
II [znw] • *(water)straal* • *git*
• *straalvliegtuig* III [bnw] *gitzwart*
jettison [ov ww] *overboord gooien v.
lading, afwerpen v. lading*
jewel [znw] *(edel)steen, juweel*
jeweller [znw] *juwelier*
jewellery, jewelry [znw] *juwelen*
Jewess [znw] *jodin*
Jewish [bnw] *joods*
jib [on ww] • *koppig zijn* • *onverwachts
stilstaan* <v. paard> • *bezwaar maken*
jibe [znw] → **gibe**
jiff(y) [znw] *ogenblikje*
jig I [ov + on ww] *bepaalde Schotse dans
uitvoeren, huppelen, met korte rukjes
bewegen, hossen* II [znw] *soort Schotse
dans*
jiggle [ov ww] *schudden, wiegelen, even
rukken aan*

jilt [ov ww] *de bons geven*
jingle I [ov + on ww] *(doen) klingelen,
(laten) rinkelen* II [znw] • *geklingel*
• *deuntje* • *jingle*
jingoism [znw] *chauvinisme*
jinx I [ov ww] *beheksen* II [znw] *doem,
vloek*
job [znw] • *werk, karwei* • *klus*
• *baan(tje), betrekking, arbeidsplaats,
functie, vak*
jodhpurs [mv] *rijbroek*
jog I [ov ww] • *(iem.) aanstoten*
• *opfrissen* <v. geheugen> II [on ww]
• *joggen, trimmen* • *op een sukkeldrafje
lopen* • (~ **along**) *voortsukkelen*
III [znw] • *duwtje* • *sukkeldraf*
jogger [znw] • *afstandsloper* • *trimmer*
joggle [ww] *schudden*
join I [ov + on ww] *dienst nemen* <in
het leger>, *bij elkaar brengen,
ontmoeten, (z.) aansluiten bij, meedoen
aan/met, lid worden v.* • (~ **in**)
meedoen • (~ **up**) *verbinden, in mil.
dienst gaan* • (~ **with**) *z. aansluiten
bij* II [znw]
• *verbindingslijn/-punt/-las, enz.*
• *naad*
joiner [znw] *meubelmaker*
joinery [znw] *vak/werk v. meubelmaker*
joint I [ov ww] • *verbinden* • *voegen*
<muur> II [znw] • *verbinding(sstuk),
voeg, naad, gewricht, stengelknoop,
geleding* • *stuk vlees* • *tent, speelhol,
dansgelegenheid* • <sl.> *stickie* III [bnw]
gezamenlijk
joist [znw] *bint*
joke I [ov + on ww] *grappen maken*
II [znw] *grap*
joker [znw] • *grappenmaker* • *joker* <in
kaartspel>
jolliness, jollity [znw] • *festiviteit*
• *jool*
jolly I [bnw] *vrolijk* II [bijw] <inf.> *heel,
zeer*
jostle I [ov + on ww] *duwen,
(ver)dringen* II [znw] *drukte, gewoel*

jot I [ov ww] • (~ **down**) *vlug
opschrijven* II [znw] • *jota* <fig.>
• *kleine hoeveelheid*
jotter [znw] *aantekenboekje*
journal [znw] • *dagboek* • *tijdschrift,
dagblad*
journalism [znw] *journalistiek*
journey I [on ww] *reizen* II [znw] *reis*
joust [on ww] *steekspel houden*
jovial [bnw] *gezelschaps-, opgewekt,
joviaal*
jowl [znw] *kaak, wang*
joy [znw] • *succes* • *vreugde, genot*
joyful, joyous [bnw] *blij*
joyless [bnw] *treurig*
jubilant [bnw] *juichend*
jubilation [znw] *gejubel*
jubilee [znw] *jubileum*
judder [on ww] *hevig schudden*
judge I [ov ww] • *be-/veroordelen*
• *beslissen* II [on ww] • *rechtspreken*
• *als scheidsrechter optreden* III [znw]
• *rechter* • *iem. die beoordeelt, kenner*
• *jurylid*
jug [znw] *kan, kruik*
juggernaut [znw] • *moloch* • *grote
vrachtwagen*
juggle [ov + on ww] *jongleren (met)*
juggler [znw] *jongleur*
jugular I [znw] II [bnw] *keel-, hals-*
juice [znw] • *benzine* <in motor> • *sap,
vocht, afscheiding* • *fut* • <sl.>
elektriciteit
July [znw] *juli*
jumble I [on ww] *door elkaar
gooien/rollen, verwarren* II [znw]
rommel, warboel
jumbo [znw] • *jumbojet* • *olifant*
jump I [ov ww] • *springen over*
• *toespringen op* • *overslaan* II [on ww]
• *omhoogschieten* • *springen* III [znw]
• *sprong* • *plotselinge beweging* • *slag*
<bij damspel> • <sport> *hindernis*
jumper [znw] • *gebreide (dames)trui*
• *springer, springpaard* • <AE> *slipover*
jumpy [bnw] *zenuwachtig, opgewonden*

junction [znw] *knooppunt, kruispunt*
juncture [znw] *samenloop v.
omstandigheden*
June [znw] *juni*
jungle [znw] • *rimboe* • *warwinkel*
junior [znw] • *junior* • *jongere, mindere*
• *zoon*
juniper [znw] *jeneverbes(struik)*
junk [znw] • *jonk* • *afval, rommel, oud
roest*
junket [znw] *snoepreisje*
jurisdiction [znw] • *jurisdictie*
• *rechtspraak*
jurisprudence [znw] *jurisprudentie*
juror [znw] • *jurylid* • *gezworene*
jury [znw] *jury, gezworenen*
just I [bnw] • *gegrond* • *terecht* II [bijw]
• *precies, net* • *gewoon(weg), alleen
maar*
justice [znw] *rechtvaardigheid, recht*
justifiable [bnw] *gerechtvaardigd*
justification [znw] *rechtvaardiging,
verantwoording*
justify [ov ww] • *rechtvaardigen*
• *verdedigen* • *uitvullen* <v. tekst>
jut [ov ww] • (~ **out**) *uitsteken*
juxtaposition [znw] *het naast elkaar
geplaatst zijn*

K

kale [znw] (boeren)kool
kaleidoscope [znw] kaleidoscoop
kangaroo [znw] kangoeroe
kayak [znw] kajak
keel I [on ww] • (~ over) omslaan,
kapseizen II [znw] kiel <v. schip>
keen [bnw] scherp(zinnig),
doordringend, intens, levendig, vurig
keep I [ov ww] • in orde houden
• bijhouden <v. boeken> • hebben <v.
winkel/bedrijf> • erop na houden
• iem. onderhouden • in voorraad
hebben • vasthouden, gevangen
houden • (z.) houden (aan) • bewaren
• (~ away) uit de buurt houden
• (~ back) terug-/achterhouden
• (~ down) (onder)drukken
• (~ from) verzwijgen voor,
verhinderen te, weerhouden van
• (~ in) inhouden, binnen houden,
school laten blijven • (~ off) op afstand
houden, afblijven van, afweren
• (~ on) ophouden, blijven houden,
aanhouden <bijv. v. huis> • (~ out)
buiten houden • (~ under)
onderhouden, onderdrukken,
bedwingen • (~ up) de moed erin
houden, in stand houden, aanhouden
<vuur>, wakker houden, ophouden,
onderhouden <contact> II [on ww]
• goed houden, goed blijven <v.
voedsel> • blijven doen, doorgaan met
• (~ at) blijven werken aan • (~ away)
wegblijven • (~ from) z. onthouden
van • (~ in with) <inf.> contact
houden met • (~ on) doorgaan, blijven
praten • (~ on at) blijven praten tegen,
vragen aan, vitten, treiteren • (~ up)
bijhouden III [znw] • toren,
versterking, fort • hoede, bewaring
• onderhoud, kost

keeper [znw] • bewaker, bewaarder,
houder • doelverdediger • hoeder,
opzichter
keeping [znw] • overeenstemming
• hoede
keg [znw] vaatje
kennel [znw] • kennel • hondenhok
• meute
kept I [ww] verl.tijd + volt.deelw.
→ keep II [bnw] (goed) onderhouden
kerb [znw] trottoirband
kernel [znw] kern, pit
kerosene [znw] kerosine
key I [ov + on ww] spannen, stemmen
• (~ down) 'n toontje lager (doen)
zingen, afzwakken • (~ in) intoetsen
• (~ up) verhogen, opdrijven II [znw]
• sleutel • toets • grondtoon, toonaard
• rif III [bnw] voornaamste, sleutel-
khaki [znw] kaki
kick I [ov + on ww] schoppen,
achteruitslaan, trappen • (~ about)
ruw behandelen • (~ off) uitgooien <v.
schoenen> • (~ out) eruit trappen
II [znw] • energie, fut • trap • kick
kidnap [ov ww] ontvoeren
kidney [znw] • nier • gesteldheid, aard
kill I [ov ww] • doden • slachten
• overstelpen met • vernietigend oordeel
uitspreken <over wetsontwerp>
• stoppen <v. bal> • afzetten <v. motor>
• (~ off) afmaken <doden> II [znw]
(door jager) gedood dier
killer [znw] • slachter • moordenaar
killing I [znw] prooi II [bnw] dodelijk
kiln [znw] kalkoven, stookoven
kilt [znw] kilt, Schotse rok
kin [znw] familie, bloedverwantschap
kind I [znw] soort, aard II [bnw]
vriendelijk, aardig
kindergarten [znw] kleuterschool
kindle [ov + on ww] ontsteken,
aansteken, aanvuren, vlam vatten,
gloeien
kindling [znw] aanmaakhout
kindly I [bnw] gemoedelijk, vriendelijk

II [bijw] wilt u zo vriendelijk zijn om,
alstublieft
kindness [znw] • vriendelijkheid • iets
aardigs
kindred I [znw] verwanten II [bnw]
verwant
kinetic [bnw] bewegings-
king [znw] • koning, vorst • heer
• magnaat
kingdom [znw] • (konink)rijk • terrein
• gebied
kink [znw] slag, knik, hersenkronkel
kinky [bnw] • kroezend • vreemd,
ongewoon • pervers • kronkelig
kinship [znw] verwantschap
kiosk [znw] • stalletje • kiosk
• telefooncel
kip <inf.> I [on ww] maffen • (~ down)
gaan maffen II [znw] bed, slaap
kipper [znw] gerookte haring
kiss I [ov ww] kussen II [znw] kus
kitchen [znw] keuken
kitchenette [znw] keukentje
kite [znw] • vlieger • wouw
kittenish [bnw] speels
kitty [znw] • poesje • pot <bij kaartspel>
• (huishoud)potje • kas
klaxon [znw] claxon
kleptomania [znw] kleptomanie
kleptomaniac [znw] kleptomaan
knack [znw] handigheid, slag
knapsack [znw] ransel, rugzak
knave [znw] boer <in kaartspel>
knead [ov ww] • kneden • masseren
knee I [ov ww] een knietje geven
II [znw] knie(stuk)
kneel [on ww] knielen • (~ to) knielen
voor
knell [znw] • (geluid v.) doodsklok
• aankondiging v. dood of onheil
knew [ww] verl. tijd → **know**
knickers [mv] onderbroek
knife I [ov ww] steken <met mes>
II [znw] mes
knight I [ov ww] tot ridder slaan,
ridderen II [znw] • ridder • paard <in

schaakspel>
knighthood [znw] • ridderschap • titel
v. ridder
knightly [bnw] ridderlijk
knit [ov + on ww] • knopen, breien • (z.)
verenigen • fronsen <v. wenkbrauwen>
• (~ up) stoppen <v. kousen>,
verbinden, eindigen
knitting [znw] • 't breien • breiwerk
knives [mv] → **knife**
knob [znw] • knop, knobbel • kluitje,
klont(je)
knobbly [bnw] • bultig • knobbelig
knock I [ov ww] • kloppen • slaan
• (~ about/around) toetakelen,
afranselen • (~ back) achteroverslaan
<borrel> • (~ down) neerslaan,
afbreken, verslaan • (~ off) afslaan,
korting geven, naar de andere wereld
helpen, stelen, aftrekken <v. kosten>,
naaien <fig.> • (~ out) verslaan,
uitkloppen <pijp>, k.o. slaan • (~ over)
omslaan <een glas> • (~ together)
haastig in elkaar zetten • (~ up)
omhoog slaan, vlug in elkaar zetten
<huis/plan>, afmatten, zwanger
maken II [on ww] kloppen <ook v.
motor> • (~ about/around)
rondslenteren, ronddolen • (~ off)
ophouden • (~ under) z. onderwerpen
• (~ up) <sport> vooraf inslaan
III [znw] klop, duw, slag
knocker [znw] • deurklopper • <sl.>
borst
knoll [znw] heuveltje
knot I [ov ww] vast-/dichtknopen
II [on ww] in de knoop raken III [znw]
• knoest in hout • strik, knoop <in
touw> • groep(je) • <scheepv.> knoop
knotty [bnw] vol knopen, ingewikkeld
know I [ov ww] (her)kennen, weten,
merken, bekend zijn met II [on ww]
weten
knowing [bnw] schrander, handig,
geslepen
knowledge [znw] kennis, wetenschap

knowledgeable [bnw] *goed ingelicht*
known I [ww] *volt. deelw.* → know
II [bnw] *erkend, berucht, gereputeerd*
knuckle I [on ww] • (~ down) *hard
aan 't werk gaan* • (~ down/under)
z. *gewonnen geven* II [znw] *knokkel*
Korean I [znw] • *Koreaan* • *het
Koreaans* II [bnw] *Koreaans*

L

label I [ov ww] • *van etiket voorzien*
• *bestempelen (als), beschrijven (als)*
II [znw] *etiket*
laboratory [znw] *laboratorium*
laborious [bnw] • *hardwerkend*
• *moeizaam* • *geforceerd* <v. stijl>
labour [znw] • *arbeid, taak, werk,
inspanning* • *arbeidskrachten*
• *barensweeën*
labourer [znw] *arbeider*
laburnum [znw] *goudenregen*
labyrinth [znw] *labyrint, doolhof*
lace I [ov ww] • *scheutje sterkedrank
toevoegen* • *rijgen* • (~ in) *inrijgen*
• (~ up) *vastrijgen* II [znw] • *veter*
• *kant, vitrage* III [bnw] *kanten*
lacerate [ov ww] *(ver)scheuren*
laceration [znw] *scheur, rijtwond*
lachrymose [bnw] • *huilend* • *huilerig*
lackadaisical [bnw] *lusteloos, dromerig*
lackey [znw] *lakei*
laconic [bnw] *kortaf, laconiek*
lacquer I [ov ww] *vernissen, lakken*
II [znw] • *vernis* • *lakwerk*
lacy [bnw] • *kanten* • *kantachtig*
lad [znw] *knaap, jongeman, jongen*
laden [bnw] • *beladen* • *bezwaard*
• *bezwangerd*
ladle I [ov ww] • (~ out) *opscheppen,
uitscheppen* II [znw] • *soeplepel*
• *gietlepel*
lady [znw] • *dame* • *vrouwe*
lag I [ov ww] • *van bekleding voorzien*
<v. stoomketel> • *isoleren*
• *achterblijven* II [on ww] III [znw]
• *achterstand* • *vertraging* • <sl.>
recidivist
lager [znw] *soort bier*
lagging [znw] *isolatiemateriaal*
lagoon [znw] *lagune*
laid [ww] *verl.tijd + volt.deelw.* → lay

lain [ww] volt. deelw. → lie
lair [znw] • leger <v. dier>, hol • <inf.> kamer
laity [znw] • de leken • lekenpubliek
lake [znw] meer
lamb [znw] • lam(svlees) • lammetje <fig.>
lame I [ov ww] kreupel maken II [bnw] • kreupel • stotend <v. metrum> • slapjes, niet overtuigend <v. excuus>
lament I [ww] (be)treuren, lamenteren II [znw] klaaglied
lamentable [bnw] • jammerlijk • betreurenswaardig
lamentation [znw] weeklacht, klaaglied
lamp [znw] lamp, lantaarn
lampoon I [ov ww] aanvallen in een satire II [znw] satire
lance I [ov ww] • met lancet doorprikken • slingeren II [znw] lans, speer
land I [ov ww] • doen landen <v. vliegtuig> • toedienen <v. klap of slag> • ophalen <v. vis> • in de wacht slepen <v. prijs> • doen belanden • (~ with) opschepen met II [on ww] • aankomen, bereiken, terechtkomen • landen III [znw] land(streek), grond, landerij(en)
landau [znw] landauer
landed [bnw] • grond bezittend • ontscheept • in moeilijkheden • grond-, land-
landing [znw] • landingsplaats, losplaats • overloop <tussen twee trappen> • vangst • aanvoer • landing
lane [znw] • landweg, weggetje • rijstrook • steeg • route <v. schepen, vliegtuigen> • (kegel)baan
language [znw] taal, spraak
languid [bnw] traag, lusteloos
languish [on ww] • (weg)kwijnen, verzwakken • smachtend kijken
languor [znw] loomheid
languorous [bnw] • loom • zwoel

lank [bnw] • mager en lang • sluik <v. haar>
lanky [bnw] slungelachtig
lantern [znw] lantaarn
lanyard [znw] • koord om fluit/mes, enz. aan te bevestigen • draagriem <v. kijker>
lap I [ov + on ww] • likken • kabbelen • (~ up) gretig luisteren of aannemen II [znw] • schoot • ronde <bij wedstrijd>
lapel [znw] revers <v. jas>
lapse I [on ww] • (ver)vallen • glijden • verlopen II [znw] • verloop <v. tijd> • vergissing, misstap • afvalligheid • het vervallen <v. recht>
lapwing [znw] kievit
larch [znw] • lariks • larikshout
lard I [ov ww] • larderen • doorspekken II [znw] varkensvet
larder [znw] provisiekast, provisiekamer
large [bnw] groot, veelomvattend, omvangrijk, fors
lark I [on ww] • (~ about) keet trappen, tekeergaan II [znw] • leeuwerik • dolle grap, lolletje • vermakelijk voorval
larva [znw] larve
larynx [znw] strottenhoofd
lascivious [bnw] wellustig, wulps
lash I [ov + on ww] • slaan • zwiepen II [ov ww] • geselen • vastsjorren III [on ww] om z. heen slaan • (~ out) uitvaren tegen IV [znw] • (zweep)slag • zweepkoord • wimper
lashing [znw] • pak slaag • bindtouw • grote hoeveelheid
lassitude [znw] moeheid, traagheid
lasso I [ov ww] met een lasso vangen II [znw] lasso
last I [ov + on ww] • duren • 't uithouden • goed blijven <v. voedsel> • voldoende zijn II [znw] • leest • (de) laatste III [bnw] • laatste • verleden • vorig IV [bijw] het laatst
lasting [bnw] • voortdurend, blijvend • duurzaam

lastly [bijw] *laatst, ten slotte,*
uiteindelijk
latch I [ov ww] *op de klink doen*
II [on ww] • (~ **on**) *'t begrijpen*
• (~ **on to**) *begrijpen, zich realiseren,*
niet loslaten, zich vastklampen aan
III [znw] • *klink* • *slot* ‹in deur›
late [bnw + bijw] • *van de laatste tijd*
• *laat* • *te laat* • *wijlen, overleden,*
vorig, vroeger
lately [bijw] • *onlangs, kort tevoren* • *de*
laatste tijd
lateral [bnw] • *zijdelings* • *zij-*
lath [znw] *lat*
lathe [znw] *draaibank*
lather I [ov ww] • *inzepen* • *afranselen*
II [on ww] • *schuimen* • *schuimend*
zweet afscheiden ‹v. paard› III [znw]
• *zeepsop* • *schuimend zweet* ‹bij paard›
Latin I [znw] • *Latijn* • *Romaan*
II [bnw] *Latijns*
latitude [znw] • *ruime opvatting*
• *omvang* • *vrijheid* • ‹geo.› *breedte*
latter [bnw] *laatstgenoemde* ‹v.d. twee›
laud [ov ww] *loven*
laudable [bnw] *prijzenswaardig,*
lofwaardig
laugh I [ov + on ww] *lachen* • (~ **at**)
lachen om/tegen, uitlachen • (~ **off**) *z.*
lachend ergens v. afmaken, door een
lach verdrijven II [znw] *(ge)lach*
laughter [znw] *gelach*
launch I [ov ww] • *werpen, slingeren*
• *afschieten, lanceren* • *uitbrengen, op*
de markt brengen • *te water laten*
• *uitzetten* ‹v. boten› • *loslaten, laten*
gaan • *op touw zetten* • *ontketenen*
• (~ **against/at**) *naar het hoofd*
slingeren II [on ww] • (~ **forth**)
beginnen • (~ **into**) *zich storten in,*
zich begeven in • (~ **out**) *met*
enthousiasme beginnen aan III [znw]
• *tewaterlating, lancering* • *sloep*
• *boot* • *begin*
launder [ov ww] *wassen (en strijken)*
launderette [znw] *wasserette*

laundry [znw] • *wasserij* • *was(goed)*
laurel [znw] • *laurier* • *lauwerkrans*
lavatory [znw] • *wasvertrek* • *wc*
lavender I [znw] *lavendel* II [bnw]
zacht lila
lavish I [ov ww] *kwistig geven* II [bnw]
verkwistend
law [znw] • *wet* • *recht* • *justitie, politie*
lawful [bnw] *wettig, rechtmatig*
lawless [bnw] • *wetteloos* • *losbandig*
lawn [znw] • *gazon* • *grasperk*
• *grasveld* ‹om op te sporten› • *batist*
lawyer [znw] • *advocaat* • *jurist*
• *rechtsgeleerde*
lax [bnw] • *laks* • *slordig* • *vaag, slap*
laxative I [znw] *laxerend middel*
II [bnw] *laxerend*
lay I [ww] *verl. tijd → lie* II [ov ww]
• *dekken* ‹de tafel› • *aanleggen* ‹vuur›
• *leggen, zetten, plaatsen* • *beleggen,*
bekleden, bedekken • *bezweren* ‹geest›
• ‹sl.› *pak slaag geven* • (~ **aside/by**)
opzij leggen, sparen • (~ **down**)
neerleggen, voorschrijven • (~ **in**)
voorraad inslaan • (~ **low**) *verslaan,*
neerslaan • (~ **off**) *afleggen, z. niet*
inlaten met, ontslaan • (~ **on**)
opleggen, toedienen ‹klappen›,
aanleggen • (~ **out**)
klaarleggen/-zetten, afleggen ‹v. lijk›,
aanleggen, ontwerpen, buiten gevecht
stellen • (~ **out on**) *geld besteden aan*
• (~ **to**) *wijten aan* • (~ **up**) *sparen,*
bewaren, uit de vaart nemen, 't bed
doen houden III [on ww] *leggen*
• (~ **about**) *wild slaan* • (~ **over**) *een*
reis onderbreken • (~ **to**) ‹scheepv.›
stilleggen IV [znw] • *lied* • *leg* ‹v. kip›
• *laag* ‹v. metselwerk› • ‹geo.› *ligging*
V [bnw] *leken-, wereldlijk*
layer I [ov ww] ‹plantk.› *afleggen*
II [znw] • *laag* • *legger* • *legkip*
• ‹plantk.› *aflegger*
laze [on ww] • *luilakken* • *uitrusten*
lazy [bnw] • *lui* • *traag* • *loom*
lead I [ov + on ww] • *leiden, aanvoeren*

• *de eerste viool spelen, de toon
aangeven* • *voorspelen* ‹kaartspel›
• (~ **off**) *beginnen, openen* • (~ **off
with**) *uitkomen met* • (~ **out**) *ten
dans leiden, beginnen* • (~ **out of**) *in
directe verbinding staan met* • (~ **up
to**) *aansturen op* II [ov ww] • *leiden,
overreden* • *in lood vatten, verloden,
verzwaren met lood* • (~ **astray**)
misleiden, verleiden • (~ **away**)
wegleiden • (~ **on**) *verder leiden,
aanmoedigen, uithoren* • (~ **on to**)
brengen op, aansturen op III [znw]
• *leiding, voorbeeld* • *'t uitkomen*
‹kaartspel› • *hondenriem*
• *hoofdrol(vertolker)* • *hoofdartikel* ‹v.
krant› • *toevoerleiding* • *lood, peillood*
IV [bnw] *loden*
leaden [bnw] • *loden* • *drukkend*
• *loodkleurig*
leader [znw] • *(ge)leider* • *gids*
• *concertmeester* • *hoofdartikel*
• *voorste paard in een span* • ‹AE›
dirigent • ‹plantk.› *hoofdscheut*
leadership [znw] • *leiding* • *leiderschap*
leaf I [ov ww] *doorbladeren* II [znw]
• *blad, gebladerte* • *deurvleugel*
• *vizierklep*
leaflet [znw] *blaadje, circulaire*
leafy [bnw] • *bladachtig* • *bladerrijk*
league I [ov ww] *verbinden* II [znw]
• *(ver)bond* • *4800 m* ‹op land› • *5500
m* ‹op zee› • *(voetbal)competitie*
leak I [ov ww] • *lekken* • *laten uitlekken*
II [on ww] *lek zijn, lekken, uitlekken*
• (~ **out**) *uitlekken* III [znw] *lek(kage)*
leakage [znw] *lek(kage)*
leaky [bnw] *lek*
lean I [ov ww] *laten steunen* II [on ww]
• *leunen* • *schuin staan* • (~ **over**)
overhellen • (~ **towards**) *begunstigen,
meegaan met* • (~ **upon**) *steunen op*
III [znw] *schuine stand* IV [bnw]
• *schraal* • *mager*
leaning [znw] *neiging*
leap I [on ww] *springen* II [znw] *sprong*

leapfrog I [on ww] • *haasje-over spelen*
• *zich aan een ander ophalen* II [znw]
haasje-over
learn [ov + on ww] • *leren* • *vernemen,
horen, erachter komen*
learned I [ww] verl.tijd + volt.deelw.
→ **learn** II [bnw] *geleerd*
learner [znw] *leerling, volontair*
learning [znw] *geleerdheid, wetenschap*
lease I [ov ww] *(ver)huren, (ver)pachten*
II [znw] *(ver)huur(contract),
(ver)pacht(ing)*
leash I [ov ww] *koppelen* II [znw] *riem,
band*
least [bnw] *kleinst, geringst, minst*
leather I [znw] • *leer* • *leder, leertje*
• *zeemlap* • *riem v. stijgbeugel* II [bnw]
leren
leathery [bnw] *leerachtig, taai* ‹v.
vlees›
leave I [ov ww] • *vertrekken* • *verlaten,
nalaten, laten, overlaten, achterlaten*
• *in de steek laten* • (~ **behind**)
achterlaten, achter zich laten • (~ **off**)
ophouden (met) • (~ **on**) *laten liggen
(op), aan laten (staan)* • (~ **out**)
overslaan II [znw] *verlof, vakantie*
leaven I [ov ww] *zuren* ‹v. deeg›
II [znw] *zuurdeeg, zuurdesem*
leavings [mv] *afval, kliekjes, wat
overblijft*
Lebanese I [znw] *Libanees* II [bnw]
Libanees
lecher [znw] *geilaard*
lecherous [bnw] *wellustig, geil*
lechery [znw] *ontucht, wellust*
lectern [znw] *lezenaar, lessenaar*
lecture I [ov ww] *de les lezen* II [on ww]
college geven • (~ **about/on**) *een
lezing houden over* III [znw] • *lezing*
• *college* • *berisping*
lecturer [znw] • *lector* • *spreker,
conferencier*
led [ww] verl. tijd + volt. deelw.
→ **lead**
ledge [znw] *overstekende rand, lijst,*

richel
ledger [znw] • *grootboek* • ‹AE› *register*
lee [znw] *lijzijde, luwte*
leech [znw] *bloedzuiger*
leek [znw] *look, prei*
leer I [on ww] • (~ **at**) *lonken naar*
II [znw] *wellustige, sluwe blik*
leeway [znw] *koersafwijking*
left [ww] *verl.tijd + volt.deelw.*
→ **leave** II [znw] *linkerhand,*
linkerkant III [bnw] *links, linker*
IV [bijw] *links*
leftist ‹pol.› I [znw] *links iem.* II [bnw]
links
leg [znw] • *been, poot, schenkel*
• *broekspijp* • *etappe*
legacy [znw] • *erfenis, nalatenschap*
• *legaat*
legal [bnw] • *wets-* • *wettelijk, wettig*
• *rechtsgeldig* • *rechterlijk*
• *rechtskundig*
legality [znw] *wettigheid*
legalize [ov ww] • *legaliseren* • *wettigen*
legation [znw] *legatie, gezantschap*
legend [znw] • *legende* • *inscriptie*
• *legenda*
legendary [bnw] *legendarisch*
leggy [bnw] *met lange of mooie benen*
legible [bnw] *leesbaar*
legion [znw] • *legioen* • *enorm aantal,*
legio
legislate [on ww] *wetten maken*
legislation [znw] *wetgeving*
legislative [bnw] *wetgevend*
legislature [znw] *wetgevende macht*
legitimacy [znw] • *wettigheid*
• *geldigheid*
legitimate I [ov ww] • *wettigen* • *als*
echt erkennen II [bnw] *wettig,*
rechtmatig, gerechtvaardigd
leisure [znw] *vrije tijd*
leisurely [bnw + bijw] • *op zijn gemak*
• *bedaard, rustig*
lemonade [znw] *(citroen)limonade*
lend I [ov ww] *(uit)lenen, verlenen*
II [znw]

lenient [bnw] *toegevend, mild*
lent [ww] *verl. tijd + volt. deelw.*
→ **lend**
lentil [znw] *linze*
leopard [znw] *luipaard*
leotard [znw] *nauwsluitend tricot,*
gympak
leper [znw] *melaatse, lepralijder*
leprosy [znw] *melaatsheid, lepra*
lesbian I [znw] *lesbienne* II [bnw]
lesbisch
lesion [znw] ‹med.› *laesie*
less I [bnw + bijw] *kleiner, minder*
II [vz] *min*
lessen I [ov ww] *doen afnemen*
II [on ww] *kleiner worden,*
verminderen, afnemen
lesser [bnw] *kleiner, minder*
lesson [znw] • *les* • *schriftlezing*
let I [ov ww] • *laten, toestaan* • *verhuren*
• (~ **down**) *neerlaten, in de steek laten,*
teleurstellen, uitleggen ‹v. zoom›,
verraden • (~ **in**) *binnenlaten* • (~ **off**)
afvuren, laten ontsnappen, vrijlaten,
ontslaan van • (~ **out**) *uitlaten,*
verklappen, verhuren, uitleggen
‹kledingstuk› II [on ww] • (~ **on**)
‹inf.› *iets verklappen* • (~ **up**) *minder*
streng worden, ophouden III [znw]
verhindering
lethal [bnw] *dodelijk*
lethargic [bnw] *loom, slaperig*
lethargy [znw] • *loomheid* • *apathische*
toestand
letter [znw] • *letter* • *brief*
lettered [bnw] • *geleerd* • *voorzien v.*
letters
lettuce [znw] *(krop) sla*
level I [ov + on ww] • *waterpassen*
• *aanleggen* ‹geweer›
• (~ **at/against**) *richten tegen* ‹v.
kanon/beschuldiging› • (~ **off/out**)
vlakmaken, vlak worden, horizontaal
(gaan) vliegen II [ov ww]
• *gelijkmaken, op gelijke hoogte*
plaatsen • *nivelleren, met de grond*

gelijkmaken III [on ww] • (~ **with**)
<sl.> *open/eerlijk spreken* IV [znw]
• *peil, stand, niveau* • *waterpas*
• *vlak(te)* V [bnw + bijw] • *horizontaal*
• *gelijk(elijk)* • *naast elkaar* • *uniform*
• *evenwichtig*
lever I [ov ww] • *met een hefboom*
opheffen • *opvijzelen* II [znw]
• *hefboom* • *versnellingspook*
leverage [znw] • *hefboomwerking,*
hefboomkracht • *invloed, macht*
leveret [znw] *jonge haas*
leviathan I [znw] *krachtpatser,*
zeemonster, gevaarte II [bnw] *reuzen-*
levitate I [ov ww] *doen opstijgen*
II [on ww] *opstijgen*
levity [znw] • *onstandvastigheid,*
lichtzinnigheid • *ongepaste vrolijkheid*
levy I [ov ww] *heffen* II [znw] *heffing* <v.
gelden>
lewd [bnw] • *wulps* • *obsceen*
lexicography [znw] *lexicografie*
lexicon [znw] • *woordenboek* • *lexicon*
liability [znw] • *betalingsverplichting*
• *blok aan het been* • *aansprakelijkheid*
liable [bnw] *aansprakelijk*
liar [znw] *leugenaar*
libel I [ov ww] • *valselijk beschuldigen*
• *belasteren* II [znw] *smaadschrift*
libellous [bnw] *lasterlijk*
liberal I [znw] *liberaal* II [bnw] • *mild,*
overvloedig • *van brede opvatting*
• <pol.> *liberaal*
liberalism [znw] *liberalisme*
liberalize [ov + on ww] *verruimen*
liberate [ov ww] *bevrijden, vrijmaken*
liberator [znw] *bevrijder*
libertine I [znw] • *vrijdenker* • *losbol*
II [bnw] • *vrijdenkend* • *losbandig*
liberty [znw] *vrijheid*
librarian [znw] *bibliothecaris*
library [znw] *bibliotheek*
lice [mv] → **louse**
licence [znw] • *verlof, vergunning* <vnl.
om drank te verkopen> • *vrijheid,*
losbandigheid • *licentie* • *diploma*

• *bewijs* v. *voorwaardelijke*
invrijheidstelling
licentious [bnw] *ongebreideld,*
losbandig
lichen [znw] *korstmos*
lick I [ov ww] • *likken* • *lekken* <v.
vlammen> • *zacht overspoelen* <v.
golven> • <sl.> *overwinnen* • <sl.>
afranselen II [znw] • *lik* • *veeg*
• *snelheid, vaart* • *zoutlik*
licking <sl.> [znw] *pak slaag, nederlaag*
lid [znw] • *deksel* • *ooglid*
lido [znw] • *badstrand, lido*
• *openluchtbad*
lie I [on ww] • *liegen* • *liggen*
• *gaan/blijven liggen* • *rusten*
• (~ **about**) *rondslingeren, lui zijn,*
niets uitvoeren • (~ **back**) *achterover*
(gaan) liggen • (~ **by**) z. *rustig houden,*
ongebruikt liggen • (~ **down**) z. *iets*
laten welgevallen, liggen te rusten,
gaan liggen • (~ **in**) *lang uitslapen*
• (~ **up**) *het bed houden* • (~ **with**)
liggen bij, slapen met, zijn aan,
berusten bij II [znw] • *leugen* • *ligging,*
richting
lieu [znw] *plaats*
lieutenant [znw] • *luitenant ter zee*
• *plaatsvervanger* • <AE> *inspecteur* <v.
politie>
life [znw] • *leven* • *energie,*
levendigheid, bezieling • <AE sl.>
levenslang <gevangenisstraf>
lifeless [bnw] • *levenloos* • *saai,*
vervelend
lift I [ov ww] • *verheffen* • *stelen*
• *opheffen, hijsen* • *opslaan* <v. ogen>
II [on ww] • *omhoog getild worden*
• *zich verheffen* • *wegtrekken,*
optrekken <v. mist> • (~ **off**) *opstijgen*
<v. vliegtuig> III [znw] • *hulp, steun*
• *lift* • *opwaartse druk, stijgkracht* <v.
vliegtuigvleugel>
ligament [znw] *gewrichtsband*
light I [ov ww] • *lichten, verlichten,*
belichten • *aansteken, opsteken*

• (~ **up**) *aansteken* II [on ww] • *vlam*
vatten • *schitteren* • (~ **(up)on**)
toevallig aantreffen • (~ **up**) *aangaan,*
vlam vatten, opvrolijken ‹v.
gezicht› III [znw] • *(dag)licht* • *vuurtje*
• *verlichting, lamp* IV [bnw + bijw]
• *licht, verlicht, helder* • *licht* ‹v.
gewicht› • *v. lichte kleur* • *luchtig*
• *lichtzinnig*
lighten I [ov ww] • *(ver)lichten*
• *verhelderen* II [on ww] • *lichter*
worden • *opklaren*
lighter [znw] *aansteker*
lighting [znw] *verlichting*
lightning [znw] *bliksem*
like I [ov ww] • *houden van* • *(graag)*
willen II [znw] • *voorliefde* • *gelijke,*
weerga III [bnw] • *gelijk(end)*
• *dergelijk* • *geneigd* IV [vz] *(zo)als*
V [vw] *zoals*
likelihood [znw] *waarschijnlijkheid*
likely [bnw + bijw] • *waarschijnlijk,*
vermoedelijk • *veelbelovend* • *geschikt*
(lijkend) • *aannemelijk*
liken [ov ww] *vergelijken*
likeness [znw] • *gelijkenis* • *portret*
• *getrouwe kopie*
likewise [bijw] *eveneens, bovendien, ook*
liking [znw] *voorkeur, zin, smaak*
lilac I [znw] *sering* II [bnw] *lila*
lilt I [ov + on ww] *(melodieus en*
ritmisch) zingen II [znw] *wijsje*
lily I [znw] *lelie* II [bnw] *wit, lelieblank,*
bleek
limb [znw] • *lid(maat)* • *tak* • *arm* ‹v.
kruis›
limber I [ov + on ww] • (~ **up**) ‹sport›
opwarmen II [bnw] *lenig, buigzaam*
limbo [znw] • *limbo* ‹dans›
• *gevangenis* ‹fig.› • *toestand v.*
vergetelheid
lime [znw] • *kalk* • *limoen*
limit I [ov ww] *begrenzen* II [znw]
grens, limiet
limitation [znw] *begrenzing, grens*
limited [bnw] *begrensd, beperkt*

limitless [bnw] *grenzeloos, onbeperkt*
limousine, limo [znw] *limousine,*
grote auto, slee
limp I [on ww] *kreupel/mank lopen,*
hinken II [znw] *kreupele gang*
III [bnw] • *buigzaam* • *lusteloos*
limpet [znw] *soort zeeslak*
limpid [bnw] *helder, doorschijnend*
linden [znw] *linde(boom)*
line I [ov ww] • *strepen* • *opgesteld*
staan langs, opstellen • *(v. binnen)*
bekleden, voeren, als voering dienen
• *vullen* ‹maag›, *spekken* ‹v. beurs›
• *liniëren* II [on ww] • (~ **up**) z.
opstellen, aantreden III [znw] • *(stuk)*
touw, lijn, koord, snoer • *linie*
• *grens(lijn)* • *rimpel* ‹in gezicht›
• *streep* • *omtrek, contour* • *regel,*
versregel • *briefje* • *lijndienst*
• *afkomst, familie* • *gedragslijn*
• *gedachtegang* • *vak, branche* • *rij*
lineage [znw] • *geslacht* • *voorouders*
lineal [bnw] *afstammend in rechte lijn*
lineament [znw] *(gelaats)trek*
linear [bnw] • *lineair* • *lang, smal en v.*
gelijke breedte • *lengte-, lijn-*
linen [znw] • *linnen* • *linnengoed*
liner [znw] *lijnboot/-vliegtuig*
linger [on ww] • *talmen, dralen, blijven*
zitten • *blijven hangen*
linguist [znw] • *talenkenner*
• *taalkundige*
linguistic [bnw] *taal-, taalkundig*
liniment [znw] *smeersel*
lining [znw] • *voering* • *omlijning*
link I [ov ww] • *schakelen, verbinden*
• *ineenslaan* ‹v. handen› • *steken door*
‹v. armen› II [on ww] *zich verbinden,*
zich aansluiten III [znw] • *schakel,*
verbinding, verband • *manchetknoop*
lint [znw] *pluis, pluksel*
lion [znw] • *leeuw* • *beroemdheid*
lioness [znw] • *leeuwin* • *vrouwelijke*
beroemdheid
lip I [znw] • *lip* • *rand* • ‹sl.› *brutale*
praat, onbeschaamdheid II [bnw]

lip(pen)-
liquefy [ov + on ww] *smelten, vloeibaar maken* ‹v. gas›
liquid I [znw] *vloeistof* II [bnw]
• *waterig, vloeibaar* • *harmonieus of vloeiend* ‹v. klanken› • *onvast, vlottend* ‹v. kapitaal›
liquidate [ov ww] • *liquideren* • *vereffenen* ‹v. schuld› • *uit de weg ruimen*
liquidity [znw] • *onvastheid* • *vloeibaarheid* • ‹econ.› *liquiditeit*
liquidizer [znw] *mengbeker*
liquor [znw] *(sterke)drank*
lisp I [on ww] *lispelen* II [znw] *gelispel*
list I [ov ww] • *lijst opmaken van, catalogiseren* • *noteren* II [on ww] • *overhellen* • *slagzij maken* III [znw] • *lijst, catalogus* • *het overhellen* ‹bijv. v. muur› • *slagzij*
listen [on ww] *luisteren* • (~ **in** (**to**)) *afluisteren, luisteren naar radiostation*
listener [znw] *luisteraar*
listless [bnw] *lusteloos*
lit I [ww] *verl.tijd + volt.deelw.* → **light** II [bnw] *verlicht*
litany [znw] *litanie*
literacy [znw] *geletterdheid*
literal [bnw] • *prozaïsch, nuchter* • *letterlijk* • *letter-*
literary [bnw] • *letterkundig* • *geletterd*
literate [bnw] • *kunnende lezen en schrijven* • *geletterd*
literature [znw] • *literatuur, letterkunde* • *de publicaties over een bep. onderwerp* • ‹inf.› *propaganda-/voorlichtingsmateriaal*
lithe(some) [bnw] *lenig, buigzaam*
lithography [znw] *lithografie, steendrukkunst*
Lithuanian I [znw] *Litouwer* II [bnw] *Litouws*
litigant [znw] *partij voor de rechtbank*
litigation [znw] *proces(voering)*
litigious [bnw] • *pleitziek, twistziek* • *betwistbaar* • *proces-*

litre [znw] *liter*
litter I [ov ww] *jongen werpen* • (~ **about/around/over**) *bezaaien, door elkaar gooien* II [znw] • *draagstoel, draagbaar* • *strobedekking* • *rommelboeltje* • *afval* • *worp* ‹v. dieren›
little [bnw + bijw] • *klein* • *weinig* • *beetje* • *kleinzielig* • *onbelangrijk*
liturgy [znw] *liturgie*
live I [ov ww] • *leven* • *doorléven* • *in praktijk brengen* • (~ **down**) *te boven komen* • (~ **out**) *zijn leven slijten* II [on ww] • *leven, bestaan* • *leven van, aan de kost komen* • *blijven leven* • *wonen* • (~ **by**) *leven van* • (~ **in**) *inwonend zijn* • (~ **off**) *leven (op kosten) van* • (~ **on**) *blijven leven* • (~ **out**) *uitwonend zijn* • (~ **through**) *doormaken* • (~ **up to**) *naleven, nakomen, waarmaken* III [bnw] • *levend, in leven* • *gloeiend* ‹v. kolen›, *onder stroom* ‹v. elektriciteitsdraad› • ‹scherts› *echt* • ‹telecom.› *rechtstreeks uitgezonden*
livelihood [znw] *levensonderhoud*
lively [bnw] • *levendig, krachtig* • *vrolijk, opgewekt* • *bedrijvig* • *helder, fris* ‹v. kleur›
liver [znw] • *lever* • *leverkleur* • *iem. die leeft, levende* • *bewoner*
liverish [bnw] *misselijk*
livery [znw] *livrei*
lives [mv] → **life**
livid [bnw] • *loodkleurig, donkerpaars* • ‹inf.› *razend, boos*
living I [znw] • *levensonderhoud* • *leven* II [bnw] *levend*
lizard [znw] *hagedis*
llama [znw] *lama(wol)*
load I [ov ww] • *inladen, beladen, verzwaren, belasten, laden* • *vervalsen door zwaarder/sterker te maken* ‹vnl. v. dobbelstenen› • (~ **up**) *(be)laden* II [znw] • *last, vracht, lading* • *hoeveelheid* • *druk* • *belasting*

loaded [bnw] • *ingeladen* • *beladen*
• *rijk*
loaf I [ov + on ww] *rondslenteren,*
lummelen II [znw] *brood*
loafer [znw] • *leegloper* • *(comfortabele)*
schoen
loam [znw] • *leem* • *potgrond*
• *bloemistenaarde*
loathe [ov ww] *verafschuwen, walgen*
van
loathing [znw] *afschuw, walging*
loathsome [bnw] *walgelijk*
loaves [mv] → **loaf**
lobby I [ov + on ww] • *lobbyen* • *druk*
uitoefenen op (politieke)
besluitvorming II [znw] • *foyer*
• *portaal, vestibule* • *pressiegroep*
• *(wandel)gang* • <AE> *conversatiezaal*
<in hotel>
lobe [znw] • *(oor)lel* • *lob* • *kwab*
lobster [znw] *zeekreeft*
local I [znw] • *plaatselijke bewoner*
• <inf.> *(dorps)café* II [bnw] *plaatselijk,*
gewestelijk, plaats-
locale [znw] *plaats van handeling,*
toneel
locality [znw] • *ligging* • *plaats, streek*
localize [ov ww] • *lokaliseren* • *een*
plaatselijk karakter geven
• *decentraliseren* • *(~ upon)*
(aandacht) concentreren op
locate [ov ww] • *in 'n plaats vestigen*
• *de plaats bepalen van*
location [znw] • *plaats(bepaling)*
• *ligging*
loch <Schots> [znw] *meer*
lock I [ov + on ww] *insluiten, omsluiten,*
sluiten II [ov ww] • *op slot doen*
• *vastzetten* <v. kapitaal> • *(~ away)*
wegsluiten • *(~ in) insluiten, opsluiten,*
omsluiten • *(~ out) buitensluiten,*
uitsluiten • *(~ up) wegsluiten,*
opsluiten <v. patiënt>, *op (nacht)slot*
doen, vastzetten <v. geld>, *sluiten*
III [on ww] • *vastlopen* <v. wiel>
• *klemmen* • *op slot kunnen* • *(~ on)*

doel zoeken en automatisch volgen <v.
raket, radar> IV [znw] • *slot*
• *(haar)lok* • *dol* <v. roeiboot> • *sluis*
locker [znw] • *bagagekluis* • *doosje of*
kastje met slot
locket [znw] *medaillon*
locomotion [znw] *(voort)beweging,*
verkeer, vervoer
locomotive I [znw] *locomotief* II [bnw]
z. *(voort)bewegend, bewegings-,*
beweeg-
locust [znw] *sprinkhaan*
locution [znw] *spreekwijze, manier v.*
(z.) uitdrukken
lodger [znw] *kamerbewoner*
lodging [znw] *logies, verblijf*
loft I [ov ww] *hoog slaan* <v. bal bij
golf> II [znw] • *vliering, zolder*
• *tribune, galerij* • *duiventil*
lofty [bnw] • *hoog, verheven*
• *hooghartig*
log I [ov ww] *optekenen in 't logboek*
II [znw] • *logaritme* • *blok hout*
• *logboek*
logarithm [znw] *logaritme*
logical [bnw] *logisch*
loin [znw] *lende(stuk)*
loiter [ov + on ww] *dralen, talmen,*
rondhangen • *(~ about/away)*
rondslenteren
lollipop(s) [znw] *(ijs)lolly*
lollop <inf.> [on ww] • *lui*
liggen/hangen • *slenteren* • *zwalken*
lolly [znw] *lolly*
lone [bnw] *eenzaam, verlaten*
long I [on ww] • *(~ for) verlangen naar*
II [bnw] • *lang(gerekt)* • *ver reikend*
longevity [znw] *lang leven*
longing [znw] *verlangen*
longitude [znw] *geografische lengte*
longitudinal [bnw] *lengte-*
loo [znw] <inf.> *wc*
look I [ov ww] • *(~ over) doorkijken,*
onderzoeken • *(~ up) opzoeken* <v.
woord/persoon> II [on ww] *kijken,*
zien • *(~ about) rondkijken*

• (~ **after**) *zorgen voor, waarnemen* <*v.*
dokterspraktijk> • (~ **ahead**)
vooruitzien • (~ **at**) *kijken naar,
bezien, beoordelen, bekijken, overwegen*
• (~ **back**) *achterom kijken, z.
herinneren* • (~ **down**) *de ogen
neerslaan* • (~ **for**) *zoeken naar,
verwachten, vragen om*
<moeilijkheden> • (~ **forward to**)
(verlangend) uitzien naar • (~ **in**)
aanlopen • (~ **on**) *toekijken* • (~ **out**)
uitkijken • (~ **out** (**up**)**on**) *uitzicht
geven op/over* • (~ **out for**) *uitzien
naar, verwachten* • (~ **over**) *uitzien
op/over* • (~ **round**) *omkijken, om z.
heen zien* • (~ **round for**) *uitkijken
naar* • (~ **through**) *kijken door,
doorkijken, doorzien* • (~ **to**) *zorgen
voor, denken om, vertrouwen*
• (~ **towards**) *uitzien op, overhellen
naar* • (~ **up**) *opkijken* • (~ **upon as**)
beschouwen als **III** [kww] *lijken,
uitzien, eruitzien* • (~ **like**) *eruitzien
als, lijken op* **IV** [znw] • *blik, gezicht*
• *uiterlijk* • *uitzicht*
loom I [on ww] *opdoemen* II [znw]
weefgetouw
loop I [ov ww] *een lus maken in* II [znw]
• *lus, strop* • *bocht*
loose I [ov ww] *losmaken, loslaten*
II [bnw] • *los* • *losbandig* • *slap*
loosen I [ov ww] • *los(ser) maken* • *doen
verslappen* II [on ww] • *los(ser) worden*
• *losraken* • *verslappen* • (~ **up**) *vrijuit
praten, opdokken, opwarmen* <voor het
sporten>
loot I [ov ww] *plunderen, (be)roven*
II [znw] • *buit, plundering* • <sl.>
luitenant, luit
lop [ww] • (~ **away/off**) *snoeien*
• (~ **off**) *afhakken*
lope I [on ww] • *z. met grote sprongen
voortbewegen* <v. dier> • *draven*
II [znw] *sprong, dravende gang*
loquacious [bnw] *babbelziek*
lordly [bnw] • *hooghartig* • *groots*

• *vorstelijk* • *als v.e. heer*
lore [znw] *traditionele kennis* <v. bep.
onderwerp>
lorry [znw] • *lorrie* <op spoorweg>
• *vrachtwagen*
lose [ov + on ww] • *verknoeien* <v. tijd>
• *missen* <v. kans, trein> • *(doen)
verliezen, verspelen, verlies lijden*
• (~ **out** (**with**)) *het afleggen (tegen)*
loser [znw] *verliezer*
loss [znw] • *verlies* • *schade*
lost [ww] *verl.tijd + volt.deelw.* → **lose**
lot [znw] • *heel wat, een boel* • *aandeel*
• *partij* • *stuk grond, perceel* • *lot*
lottery [znw] *loterij*
lotus [znw] • *lotusplant* • *bep.
waterlelie*
loud [bnw] • *lawaaierig, luid*
• *opvallend, schreeuwend* <v. kleuren>,
opzichtig
lounge I [on ww] • *slenteren* • *lui
(gaan) liggen, luieren* II [znw]
• *zitkamer* • *sofa* • *grote hal* <in
huis/hotel>
louse I [ov ww] *ontluizen* • (~ **up**)
verknoeien, in de soep laten lopen
II [znw] • *luis* • *ploert*
lousy [bnw] • *beroerd, laag, gemeen*
• *armzalig*
lout [znw] *lummel, boerenpummel*
lovable [bnw] *lief, beminnelijk*
love I [ov ww] • *houden van, beminnen*
• *dol zijn op, dolgraag doen* • *liefkozen*
II [znw] • *liefde* • *geliefde* • *lief(je),
schat(je)* • *nul* <bij tennis> • *groet(en)*
lover [znw] • *minnaar* • *bewonderaar*
loving [bnw] *liefhebbend, teder*
low I [ov + on ww] • *loeien* <v. koe>
II [znw] • *geloei* • *lagedrukgebied*
• *laag peil* III [bnw + bijw] • *laag*
• *diep* <v. buiging> • *eenvoudig*
• *(laag)uitgesneden* <v. japon>
• *gemeen, ruw, plat* • *minnetjes* • *bijna
leeg* <v. batterij> • *neerslachtig* • *zacht*
<v. stem>
lower I [ov ww] • *strijken* <v. vlag, zeil>

• *verlagen* ‹v. prijs› • *vernederen*
• *neerlaten* II [on ww] • *afhellen,*
afdalen • *dreigend eruit zien* ‹v.
hemel› III [bnw] *onder-, onderste-,*
beneden-
lowly [bnw] • *nederig, bescheiden* • *laag*
loyal [bnw] *(ge)trouw, loyaal*
loyalist [znw] *regeringsgetrouwe*
loyalty [znw] *loyaliteit, trouw*
lozenge [znw] • *ruitvormig facet* ‹bijv.
v. diamant› • *(hoest)tablet*
lubricant [znw] • *smeermiddel*
• ‹med.› *glijmiddel*
lucid [bnw] *helder, klaar, stralend*
luck [znw] *geluk, toeval, succes*
luckily [bijw] • *toevallig* • *gelukkig*
luckless [bnw] *onfortuinlijk*
lucky [bnw] • *gelukkig, fortuinlijk*
• *geluk brengend*
lucrative [bnw] *winstgevend*
ludicrous [bnw] *koddig, belachelijk*
lug I [ov ww] *sleuren, slepen*
• *(~ along) meeslepen* • *(~ in) met de*
haren erbij slepen II [on ww] • *(~ at)*
rukken aan
luggage [znw] *bagage*
lugubrious [bnw] *luguber,*
naargeestig, somber, treurig
lukewarm [bnw] • *lauw* • *onverschillig*
lull I [ov ww] *in slaap wiegen/sussen*
II [on ww] • *gaan liggen* ‹v. wind›
• *kalm worden* III [znw] • *tijdelijke*
stilte • *slapte in bedrijf*
lumbago [znw] *lendepijn, spit*
lumber I [ov ww] • *volstoppen met*
rommel • *opzadelen met* II [on ww]
met logge tred gaan, botsen III [znw]
• *rommel* • *ruw timmerhout*
luminary [znw] *uitblinker*
luminous [bnw] *lichtgevend, stralend*
lump I [ov ww] *bij elkaar op een hoop*
gooien II [znw] *brok, klontje*
lumpy [bnw] • *klonterig* • *met bulten*
lunar [bnw] *v.d. maan, maanvormig,*
sikkelvormig
lunatic I [znw] *krankzinnige* II [bnw]

• *krankzinnig* • *dwaas*
lunch I [on ww] *lunchen, koffiedrinken*
II [znw] • *lunch* • *lichte maaltijd*
lung [znw] *long*
lunge I [ov ww] *longeren* ‹v. paard›
II [on ww] *vooruitschieten* • *(~ at)*
slaan of stoten naar • *(~ for) grijpen*
naar • *(~ into) binnenvallen* III [znw]
• *longe* ‹paardensport› • *plotselinge*
voorwaartse beweging • *stoot* • *uitval*
lurch I [on ww] *slingeren, wankelen*
II [znw] *plotselinge slingerbeweging,*
plotselinge zijwaartse beweging, ruk
lure I [ov ww] *(ver)lokken* II [znw]
lokaas, lokstem
lurid [bnw] • *fel gekleurd* • *shockerend*
lurk [on ww] • *z. schuil houden*
• *verscholen zijn*
luscious [bnw] • *heerlijk* • *zinnelijk*
lush [bnw] • *weelderig* • *mals* ‹v. gras›
lust I [on ww] • *(~ after/for) haken*
naar, begeren, hevig verlangen naar
II [znw] *(wel)lust*
lustre [znw] *schittering, glans*
lustrous [bnw] *glanzend, schitterend*
lusty [bnw] *krachtig, flink, vitaal*
lute [znw] *luit*
luxuriance [znw] • *luxe* • *rijkdom*
luxuriant [bnw] *weelderig, welig*
luxuriate [on ww] • *zijn gemak er van*
nemen • *welig tieren* • *(~ in) genieten*
van, zwelgen in
luxurious [bnw] • *weelderig* • *v. alle*
gemakken voorzien
luxury I [znw] • *luxe, weelde*
• *luxeartikel* • *genot(middel)* II [bnw]
luxe-
lying I [ww] *tegenw. deelw.* → **lie**
II [bnw] *leugenachtig, vals*
lyre [znw] *lier*
lyric I [znw] *lyrisch gedicht* II [bnw]
lyrisch
lyrical [bnw] *lyrisch*

M

macaroon [znw] bitterkoekje
mace [znw] • foelie • scepter
machine I [ov ww] machinaal
vervaardigen II [znw] • machine,
toestel • automaat
machinery [znw] • machinerie
• mechanisme
machinist [znw] • monteur
• machineconstructeur
• machinebediener
mackerel [znw] makreel
mackintosh [znw] regenjas
macrocosm [znw] macrokosmos, heelal
mad I [on ww] II [bnw] gek, dwaas,
krankzinnig • (~ about/at) woest over
• (~ on) dol op, verliefd op • (~ with)
nijdig op
madam [znw] mevrouw, juffrouw
madden [ov ww] dol/gek maken
maddening [bnw] gek makend
made [ww] verl.tijd + volt.deelw.
→ make
maelstrom [znw] maalstroom
mag [znw] → magazine
magazine [znw] • actualiteitenrubriek
op radio/tv • kruitmagazijn
• tijdschrift
maggot [znw] made
Magi [mv] de drie wijzen uit het oosten
magic I [znw] toverkunst II [bnw]
toverachtig, betoverend, tover-
magician [znw] • tovenaar • goochelaar
magisterial [bnw] • gezaghebbend,
autoritair • magistraats-
magnanimity [znw] grootmoedigheid
magnanimous [bnw] grootmoedig
magnate [znw] magnaat
magnetic [bnw] magnetisch,
onweerstaanbaar
magnetism [znw] magnetisme
magnetize [ov ww] • magnetiseren

• biologeren
magnification [znw] vergroting
magnificence [znw] • grootsheid
• pracht, praal
magnify [ov ww] • vergroten
• overdrijven
magnitude [znw] • grootte
• belangrijkheid
magnum [znw] wijnfles van tweemaal
de normale grootte
magpie [znw] ekster
mahogany [znw] • mahoniehout
• mahonieboom
maid [znw] • meid • ongetrouwd meisje
maiden I [znw] • meisje • maagd
II [bnw] • nieuw • eerst(e) • ongetrouwd
mail I [ov ww] per post verzenden, op de
post doen II [znw] (brieven)post
maim [ov ww] verminken
main I [znw] hoofdleiding II [bnw]
hoofd-, voornaamste
maintain [ov ww] • volhouden,
beweren, handhaven • steunen,
onderhouden, voeren
maintenance [znw] onderhoud,
alimentatie, handhaving
maize [znw] maïs
major I [on ww] • (~ in) <AE> als
(hoofd)vak kiezen, als hoofdvak(ken)
hebben II [znw] • majoor
• sergeant-majoor • meerderjarige
• hoofdvak • <muz.> majeur III [bnw]
• groter, grootste, hoofd- • meerderjarig
• de oudere <v. twee> • <muz.> majeur
majority [znw] • meerderheid
• meerderjarigheid
make I [ov ww] • benoemen tot
• dwingen, laten, zorgen dat • maken,
fabriceren, bereiden, zetten <v. thee,
koffie>, aanleggen <v. vuur>, houden
<v. toespraak> • opmaken <v. bed>
• aankomen te, bereiken, halen <v.
trein, bus> • verdienen, vorderen
• schatten op • (~ out) opmaken,
uitschrijven, begrijpen, beweren
• (~ over) overdragen, vermaken

• (~ **up**) *vergoeden, opmaken, bereiden, verzinnen, z. grimeren, bijleggen* **II** [on ww] • (~ **away/off**) *ervandoor gaan* • (~ **for**) *bijdragen tot, gaan naar, aansturen op* • (~ **out**) *'t redden, 't klaar spelen* **III** [znw] • *gesteldheid, aard, soort* • *(lichaams)bouw* • *maaksel, merk, fabricaat*

maker [znw] *maker, fabrikant, schepper*

making [znw] *fabricage, het maken*

maladjusted [bnw] • *onaangepast* • *onevenwichtig*

maladroit [bnw] *onhandig*

Malay **I** [znw] • *Maleis* • *Maleier* **II** [bnw] *Maleis*

Malaysian **I** [znw] *Maleier, Maleisiër* **II** [bnw] *Maleis*

malcontent **I** [znw] *ontevredene* **II** [bnw] *ontevreden*

male **I** [znw] • *mannelijk persoon* • *mannetje* **II** [bnw] *mannen-, mannelijk*

malformation [znw] *misvorming*

malice [znw] *kwaadwilligheid*

malign **I** [ov ww] *belasteren* **II** [bnw] *kwaadwillig*

malignancy [znw] *kwaadaardigheid* <ook v. ziekte>, *kwaadwilligheid*

malignant [bnw] *kwaadaardig* <ook v. ziekte>

malinger [on ww] *ziekte voorwenden, simuleren*

malingerer [znw] *simulant*

malleable [bnw] • *pletbaar, smeedbaar* • *gedwee*

mallet [znw] *houten hamer*

malnutrition [znw] *ondervoeding*

malodorous [bnw] *stinkend*

malpractice [znw] *kwade praktijk*

malt **I** [ov + on ww] *mouten* **II** [znw] *mout*

Maltese **I** [znw] *Maltees, Maltezer* **II** [bnw] *Maltees*

maltreat [ov ww] *slecht behandelen, mishandelen*

mammal [znw] *zoogdier*

mammary [bnw] *m.b.t./van de borst, borst-*

mammoth [znw] *mammoet*

man **I** [ov ww] *v. bemanning voorzien, bemannen* **II** [znw] • *man* • *mens, persoon* • *iem., men* • *bediende, knecht, werkman*

manacle **I** [ov ww] *boeien* **II** [znw] *(hand)boei*

manage [ov + on ww] • *het redden* • *leiden, beheren* • *onder controle houden*

manageable [bnw] *te hanteren, handelbaar*

management [znw] • *(bedrijfs)leiding, beheer* • *bestuur, directie*

manager [znw] • *directeur, bedrijfsleider, bestuurder* • *impresario*

manageress [znw] *bestuurster, cheffin*

managerial [bnw] *directeurs-, bestuur-*

mandarin [znw] • *mandarijntje* <vrucht> • *mandarijn* • *Mandarijns* • *bureaucraat*

mandate [znw] *mandaat, bevel, opdracht*

mandatory [bnw] • *verplicht* • *bevel-*

mandible [znw] *(onder)kaak*

mane [znw] *manen*

manganese [znw] *mangaan*

manger [znw] *kribbe, voerbak*

mangy [bnw] • *schurftig* • *sjofel*

manhood [znw] • *mannelijkheid* • *mannelijke leeftijd* • *mannelijke bevolking*

mania [znw] • *manie, rage* • <med.> *waanzin*

maniac **I** [znw] • *maniak* • *waanzinnige* **II** [bnw] *maniakaal*

maniacal [bnw] *dollemans-, waanzinnig*

manicurist [znw] *manicure, manicuurster*

manifest **I** [ov ww] • *openbaar maken* • *aan de dag leggen* **II** [bnw] *in 't oog vallend, klaarblijkelijk, zichtbaar, duidelijk*

manifestation [znw] *manifestatie*
manifesto [znw] *manifest*
manifold [bnw] *menigvuldig*
manipulate [ov ww] • *hanteren*
• *behandelen, manipuleren* • *knoeien*
met <cijfers, tekst>
manly [bnw] • *mannelijk, manhaftig*
• *manachtig <v. vrouw>*
mannequin [znw] • *mannequin*
• *etalagepop*
manner [znw] *manier, wijze*
mannered I [bnw] *geaffecteerd*
II [in samenst.] *met...manieren*
mannerism [znw] *hebbelijkheid,
aanwensel*
mannish [bnw] *manachtig <v. vrouw>*
manoeuvre I [ov ww] • *manoeuvreren*
• *klaarspelen* II [on ww] *manoeuvreren*
III [znw] • *kunstgreep* • *manoeuvre*
manor [znw] • ≈ *riddergoed* • *<sl.>
politiedistrict*
manpower [znw] • *mankracht*
• *arbeidskracht(en), personeel*
mansion [znw] *groot herenhuis*
manual I [znw] *handboek, handleiding*
II [bnw] *hand-, handmatig*
manufacture I [ov ww] *fabriceren*
II [znw] • *fabricage* • *fabrikaat*
manufacturer [znw] *fabrikant*
manure [znw] *mest*
Manx I [znw] • *bewoners v.h. eiland
Man* • *taal v.h. eiland Man* II [bnw]
Manx-
many I [onb vnw] *vele(n)* II [telw] *veel,
menige*
map I [ov ww] *in kaart brengen*
• *(~ out) voorbereiden, arrangeren,
indelen* II [znw] *(land)kaart*
maple [znw] *esdoorn*
mar [ov ww] *ontsieren, bederven*
marble I [znw] • *marmer* • *knikker*
II [bnw] *marmeren, als marmer*
march I [ov ww] • *(~ away) wegvoeren*
• *(~ off) laten afmarcheren* • *(~ up)
laten aanrukken* II [on ww] *marcheren*
• *(~ off) afmarcheren* • *(~ on)*

voortmarcheren • *(~ past) defileren*
• *(~ up) aanrukken* III [znw] • *mars*
• *loop, vooruitgang*
March [znw] *Maart*
marchioness [znw] *markiezin*
mare [znw] *merrie*
margin [znw] • *rand, kant, marge,
grens* • *overschot, saldo, winst* • *speling*
marginal [bnw] • *rand-, kant-* • *in
grensgebied gelegen, aangrenzend*
• *bijkomstig, ondergeschikt* • *weinig
productief*
marigold [znw] *goudsbloem*
marina [znw] *jachthaven*
mariner [znw] *matroos, zeeman*
marionette [znw] *marionet*
marital [bnw] • *v.d. echtgeno(o)t(e)*
• *huwelijks-*
maritime [bnw] *zee(vaart)-, kust-,
maritiem*
marjoram [znw] *marjolein*
mark I [ov ww] • *onderscheiden,
(ken)merken* • *noteren, nakijken,
cijfer/punt toekennen* • *bestemmen*
• *opmerken, letten op* • *(~ down)
opschrijven, afprijzen, bestemmen*
• *(~ off) onderscheiden, afscheiden*
• *(~ out) bestemmen, afbakenen,
onderscheiden* • *(~ up) de prijs hoger
maken* II [on ww] *markeren <bij jacht>*
III [znw] • *onderscheiding* • *mark
<munt>* • *aanwijzing, teken, blijk*
• *zegel* • *stempel, merk, litteken, vlek*
• *cijfer, punt* • *kruisje <i.p.v.
handtekening>*
marked [bnw] • *opvallend* • *getekend
<dier>, gemerkt*
marker [znw] • *iem. die optekent*
• *merkstift* • *boekenlegger*
market I [ov ww] *verkopen,
verhandelen* II [znw] • *markt*
• *marktprijs, handel*
marketable [bnw] • *verkoopbaar*
• *markt-*
marketing [znw] *marketing,
commercieel beleid*

marmalade [znw] *marmelade*
maroon I [ov ww] • *aan zijn lot overlaten, op onbewoonde kust aan land zetten en achterlaten* • *isoleren* II [bnw] *paarsrood*
marquee [znw] *grote tent*
marriage [znw] *huwelijk*
married [bnw] • *huwelijks-* • *gehuwd*
marrow [znw] • *merg* • *kern* • *(eetbare) pompoen, (soort) courgette*
marry I [ov ww] • *huwen (met), trouwen* • *uithuwelijken* • *nauw verbinden* • *(~ up) samenbrengen* II [on ww] • *trouwen* • *z. nauw verbinden*
marsh [znw] *moeras*
marshal I [ov ww] • *rangschikken, opstellen* • *aanvoeren, leiden* II [znw] • *maarschalk* • *ceremoniemeester* • *≈ griffier* • *‹AE› hoofd v.d. politie*
marshy [bnw] *moerassig*
marsupial I [znw] *buideldier* II [bnw] *buidelvormig, buideldragend*
mart [znw] • *verkooplokaal* • *handelscentrum* • *‹form.› markt*
marten [znw] *marter*
martial [bnw] *krijgs-, krijgshaftig, krijgslustig*
Martian I [znw] *Marsbewoner* II [bnw] *v. Mars, Mars-*
martyr I [ov ww] • *de marteldood doen sterven* • *martelen* II [znw] *martelaar*
martyrdom [znw] • *martelaarschap* • *marteldood* • *marteling*
marvel I [on ww] *z. afvragen* • *(~ at) z. verwonderen over* II [znw] *wonder*
marvellous [bnw] *fantastisch*
Marxist I [znw] *marxist* II [bnw] *marxistisch*
marzipan [znw] *marsepein*
mascot [znw] *mascotte, talisman*
masculine [bnw] • *mannelijk ‹ook v. rijm›* • *manachtig ‹v. vrouw›* • *krachtig*
mash I [ov ww] *fijnstampen* II [znw] • *warm voer* • *aardappelpuree*

mask I [ov ww] *maskeren, verbergen* II [znw] *masker*
masochism [znw] *masochisme*
masonry [znw] *metselwerk*
masquerade I [on ww] *z. vermommen* • *(~ as) vermomd zijn als* II [znw] • *maskerade* • *valse schijn*
massacre I [ov ww] *een slachting aanrichten onder* II [znw] *bloedbad, slachting*
massage I [ov ww] *masseren* II [znw] *massage*
massive [bnw] • *massief* • *zwaar, stevig* • *indrukwekkend, gigantisch*
master I [ov ww] *beheersen, overmeesteren, de baas worden, te boven komen, besturen* II [znw] • *patroon* • *leermeester* • *directeur, hoofd ‹v. college›* • *gezagvoerder* • *baas, werkgever* • *heer des huizes* • *jongeheer* • *mijnheer* • *moederblad, origineel* III [bnw] *voornaamste, hoofd-*
masterful [bnw] • *meesterlijk* • *bazig*
masterly [bnw + bijw] *meesterlijk*
mastery [znw] *meesterschap*
masticate [ov + on ww] *kauwen*
masturbate [on ww] *masturberen*
mat I [znw] *mat, kleedje* II [bnw] *dof, mat*
match I [ov ww] • *opgewassen zijn tegen, een partij zijn voor, de gelijke zijn van* • *in overeenstemming brengen met, iets bijpassends vinden* II [on ww] *bij elkaar passen* • *(~ up to) opgewassen zijn tegen* III [znw] • *gelijke, tegenhanger, evenknie* • *paar* • *wedstrijd* • *lucifer*
matchless [bnw] *weergaloos, niet te evenaren, onvergelijkelijk*
mate I [ov ww] • *doen paren* • *mat zetten* II [on ww] *paren* III [znw] • *levensgezel(lin)* • *mannetje, wijfje* • *stuurman* • *schaakmat* • *kameraad*
material I [znw] • *stof* • *materiaal, bestanddeel* II [bnw] • *stoffelijk, materieel, lichamelijk* • *wezenlijk,*

essentieel, belangrijk
materialism [znw] *materialisme*
materialize [on ww] *verstoffelijken,*
verschijnen, materialiseren
maternal [bnw] *moederlijk, moeder-, v.*
moederszijde
maternity [znw] *moederschap*
mathematical [bnw] *wiskundig,*
wiskunde-
mathematics, maths [mv] *wiskunde*
matrices [mv] → **matrix**
matriculate [on ww] *als student*
toegelaten worden, z. als student
inschrijven
matrix [znw] • *voedingsbodem*
• *gietvorm, matrijs* • *matrix*
matron [znw] • *matrone, getrouwde*
dame • *directrice, hoofd, moeder* ‹v.
instituut›
matronly [bnw] *aan de dikke kant* ‹v.
vrouw›
matt [bnw] *dof, mat*
matter I [on ww] *v. belang zijn,*
betekenen II [znw] • *materie, stof*
• *zaak, aangelegenheid, kwestie* • *kopij*
matting [znw] *matwerk*
mattock [znw] *houweel*
mattress [znw] *matras*
mature I [ov ww] *rijpen* II [on ww]
• *volwassen worden, tot ontwikkeling*
komen, rijpen • *vervallen* ‹v. wissel›
III [bnw] • *volwassen, volledig*
ontwikkeld, rijp • *weloverwogen*
• *vervallen* ‹v. wissel›
maturity [znw] • *rijpheid* • *vervaltijd*
‹v. wissel›
maudlin [bnw] *overdreven sentimenteel*
maul [ov ww] • *afkraken* ‹door
recensent› • *bont en blauw slaan,*
toetakelen
mauve [bnw] *mauve, zachtpaars*
maverick [znw] *politiek dissident,*
non-conformist
maw [znw] *bek, muil*
mawkish [bnw] *overdreven*
sentimenteel

maxim [znw] *stelregel, spreuk, principe*
maximize [ov ww] *maximaliseren, tot*
het uiterste vergroten
may [hww] • *mogen* • *kunnen*
‹mogelijkheid›
May [znw] *mei*
maybe [bijw] *misschien*
mayhem [znw] *chaos, wanorde*
mayonnaise [znw] *mayonaise*
mayor [znw] *burgemeester*
mayoress [znw] *vrouw v.d.*
burgemeester
me [pers vnw] • *mij* • ‹inf.› *ik*
meadow [znw] *weide, hooiland,*
grasland
meagre [bnw] *mager, schraal*
meal [znw] • *meel* • *maal(tijd)*
mealy [bnw] *melig, meelachtig*
mean I [ov ww] • *betekenen* • *bedoelen,*
(serieus) menen • *willen* • *v. plan zijn*
• *(~ for) bestemmen voor* II [on ww]
bedoelen III [znw] *middelste term*
IV [bnw] • *gemiddeld, middelmatig*
• *middelste, middel-, tussen-* • *gemeen,*
laag • *gering* • *bekrompen, gierig*
• *slechtgehumeurd* • ‹AE› *onbehaaglijk*
• ‹inf.› *beschaamd*
meander I [on ww] • *z. slingeren*
• *dolen* II [znw] *bocht* ‹in rivier›
meaning [znw] • *bedoeling* • *betekenis*
meaningful [bnw] *veelbetekenend,*
belangrijk
meaningless [bnw] • *nietszeggend*
• *zinloos*
meant [ww] *verl. tijd + volt. deelw.*
→ **mean**
meantime [znw] *tussentijd*
measles [mv] *mazelen*
measly [bnw] ‹inf.› *armzalig, min,*
waardeloos
measurable [bnw] • *meetbaar*
• *gematigd*
measure I [ov ww] • *meten, de maat*
nemen, bep. lengte hebben • *beoordelen*
• *(~ out) uitdelen* II [on ww] *meten*
• *(~ up to) voldoen aan* III [znw]

• *grootte, afmeting* • *bedrag, hoeveelheid* • *maatstaf* • *maatregel* • ‹muz.› *maat*
measured [bnw] • *gelijkmatig* • *weloverwogen*
measurement [znw] *(af)meting*
meat [znw] *vlees*
meaty [bnw] *vlezig, vleesachtig, vlees-*
mechanic [znw] • *werktuigkundige, mecanicien* • *monteur*
mechanical [bnw] • *machinaal, werktuiglijk* • *werktuigkundig*
mechanism [znw] • *mechaniek* • *mechanisme*
mechanize [ov ww] *mechaniseren*
medal [znw] *medaille*
medallist [znw] *medaillewinnaar*
meddler [znw] *bemoeial*
meddlesome, meddling [bnw] *bemoeiziek*
media I [znw] → **medium** II [mv] • *media, kranten, radio en tv*
mediaeval [bnw] → **medieval**
mediate [ov + on ww] *als bemiddelaar optreden*
medical I [znw] *medisch onderzoek* II [bnw] *geneeskundig*
medicament [znw] *geneesmiddel*
medication [znw] • *geneeskundige behandeling* • *geneesmiddel*
medicinal [bnw] *genezend, geneeskrachtig*
medicine [znw] • *geneeskunde* • *geneesmiddelen*
medieval [bnw] *m.b.t. de Middeleeuwen*
mediocre [bnw] *middelmatig*
mediocrity [znw] *middelmatigheid*
meditative [bnw] *nadenkend, bespiegelend*
Mediterranean I [znw] *Middellandse Zee, Middellandse-Zeegebied* II [bnw] *mediterraan*
medium I [znw] • *tussenpersoon* • *medium* • *voertaal* • *oplosmiddel* II [bnw] *gemiddeld*

medley [znw] *mengelmoes, potpourri*
meek [bnw] • *zachtmoedig* • *gedwee* • *deemoedig*
meet I [ov ww] • *ontmoeten, (aan)treffen, kennis maken met* • *afhalen* • *voldoen aan, voorzien in* • *bestrijden* ‹v. onkosten› II [on ww] • *elkaar ontmoeten* • *samenkomen* • *(~ up with) ontmoeten* • *(~ with) ervaren, ondervinden, tegenkomen*
meeting [znw] • *wedstrijd, ontmoeting* • *bijeenkomst, vergadering*
megalomania [znw] *megalomanie*
megalomaniac [znw] *megalomaan*
megaphone [znw] *megafoon*
melancholic I [znw] *melancholicus* II [bnw] *melancholiek, melancholisch*
melancholy I [znw] *melancholie, zwaarmoedigheid, droefgeestigheid* II [bnw] *zwaarmoedig, droefgeestig*
mellifluous [bnw] *honingzoet, zoetvloeiend*
mellow I [ov + on ww] • *rijpen, zacht maken/worden* • *benevelen* II [bnw] • *zacht, sappig, rijp* • *vol, zuiver* ‹v. klank, kleur› • *vriendelijk, hartelijk, joviaal* • *lichtelijk aangeschoten*
melodic [bnw] *melodisch, melodieus*
melodious [bnw] *melodieus, welluidend*
melodramatic [bnw] *melodramatisch*
melody [znw] *melodie*
melon [znw] *meloen*
melt I [ov ww] *doen smelten* • *(~ down) versmelten* II [on ww] *smelten, z. oplossen* • *(~ away) wegsmelten, verdwijnen* • *(~ into) langzaam overgaan in*
member [znw] • *lid* • *lichaamsdeel, (mannelijk) lid* • *afgevaardigde*
membership [znw] • *lidmaatschap* • *ledental*
memento [znw] *herinnering, aandenken*
memo [znw] ‹inf.› *korte notitie, briefje*
memoir [znw] *gedenkschrift,*

(auto)biografie
memorable [bnw] gedenkwaardig
memorandum [znw] • memorandum
• diplomatieke nota
memorial I [znw] gedenkteken,
aandenken II [bnw] gedenk-,
herinnerings-
memorize [ov ww] v. buiten leren
memory [znw] • geheugen
• herinnering • gedachtenis
men [mv] → man
menace I [ov + on ww] (be)dreigen
II [znw] • bedreiging • vervelend iem.,
lastig iets
mend I [ov ww] • verbeteren
• herstellen, repareren, stoppen <v.
kousen> II [on ww] • z. (ver)beteren
• herstellen
mendacious [bnw] leugenachtig
mendacity [znw] leugen(achtigheid)
mending [znw] verstelwerk
menial I [znw] <pej.> bediende, knecht
II [bnw] • dienstbaar, dienst- • slaafs,
ondergeschikt, laag
meningitis [znw]
hersenvliesontsteking
menopause [znw] menopauze
menstrual [bnw] menstruatie-
mental [bnw] • geestelijk, geest(es)-,
verstandelijk • <inf.> zwakzinnig
mentality [znw] mentaliteit, denkwijze
mention I [ov ww] (ver)melden,
zeggen, noemen II [znw] (ver)melding
mercantile [bnw] handels-, koopmans-
mercenary I [znw] huurling II [bnw]
geldbelust
merchant I [znw] groothandelaar,
koopman II [bnw] koopmans-,
koopvaardij, handels-
merciless [bnw] genadeloos,
meedogenloos
mercurial [bnw] • levendig
• veranderlijk
mercury [znw] kwikzilver
mercy [znw] • zegen(ing) • genade,
barmhartigheid

mere [bnw] louter, alleen maar, niets
anders dan, (nog) maar
meretricious [bnw] bedrieglijk
meridian [znw] meridiaan
merit I [ov ww] verdienen II [znw]
verdienste
meritocracy [znw] meritocratie,
prestatiemaatschappij
mermaid [znw] (zee)meermin
merriment [znw] vreugde, vrolijkheid
merry [bnw] • vrolijk • aangeschoten
mesh I [on ww] in elkaar grijpen
II [znw] • maas • net(werk)
mesmerize [ov ww] magnetiseren,
hypnotiseren, biologeren
mess I [ov ww] • (~ up) in de war
sturen, verknoeien, vuil maken
II [on ww] • (~ about)
(rond)scharrelen • (~ with) z.
bemoeien met III [znw] • kantine,
gemeenschappelijke tafel • knoeiboel
• (vuile) rommel
message [znw] bericht, boodschap
messenger [znw] bode, boodschapper
messy [bnw] vuil, rommelig, verward
met [ww] verl. tijd + volt. deelw.
→ meet
metabolic [bnw] stofwisselings-
metabolism [znw] metabolisme,
stofwisseling
metal [znw] metaal
metallic [bnw] metaal-, metalen,
metaalachtig
metallurgy [znw] metallurgie,
metaalkunde
metamorphosis [znw] metamorfose
metaphor [znw] beeldspraak
metaphoric(al) [bnw] figuurlijk
metaphysical [bnw] metafysisch,
bovennatuurlijk
metaphysics [znw] metafysica
meteor [znw] meteoor
meteoric [bnw] • meteoor- • als een
komeet, bliksemsnel
meteorite [znw] meteoorsteen,
meteoriet

meteorology [znw] *meteorologie,*
weerkunde
meter I [ov ww] *meten* II [znw]
meetinstrument
methane [znw] *methaan(gas)*
method [znw] • *methode*
• *regelmaat*
meticulous [bnw] • *angstvallig*
nauwkeurig, pietluttig • *nauwgezet*
metre [znw] • *metrum* • *meter*
metronome [znw] *metronoom*
metropolis [znw] *wereldstad,*
hoofdstad
metropolitan I [znw] *bewoner v.*
hoofd-/wereldstad II [bnw] • *tot het*
moederland behorend • *tot*
hoofd-/wereldstad behorend
mettle [znw] • *aard* • *vuur, moed*
mew [on ww] *miauwen*
Mexican I [znw] *Mexicaan(se)* II [bnw]
Mexicaans
miaow I [on ww] *miauwen* II [znw]
miauw
microwave [znw] *magnetron*
midday [znw] *12 uur 's middags*
middle I [znw] • *midden* • *middel*
II [bnw] *midden(-), middel-, middelst*
middling I [bnw] *middelmatig, vrij*
goed II [bijw] *tamelijk*
midge [znw] *mug*
midget I [znw] • *klein voorwerp*
• *dwerg* II [bnw] *miniatuur*
midriff [znw] *middenrif*
midst ‹form.› [znw] *midden*
midwife [znw] *vroedvrouw*
might I [hww] verl. tijd → may
II [znw] *kracht, macht*
mightily [bijw] *erg, geweldig, zeer*
mighty I [bnw] *machtig, geweldig*
II [bijw] ‹inf.› *zeer, verbazend*
migrant I [znw] • *trekvogel* • *migrant,*
zwerver II [bnw] *migrerend, zwervend,*
trek-
migrate [on ww] • *migreren, verhuizen*
• *trekken* ‹v. vogels›
migratory [bnw] *migrerend, trekkend,*

zwervend, trek-
mike [znw] *microfoon*
mild [bnw] • *mild, zacht* • *kalm en*
warm ‹v. weer› • *licht* ‹v. bier, tabak›
• *gematigd* • *onschuldig* ‹v. ziekte›
mildew [znw] *meeldauw, schimmel*
mile [znw] *mijl* ‹1609 m.›
militant I [znw] *militant persoon*
II [bnw] *strijdend, strijdlustig,*
strijdbaar
militarism [znw] *militarisme*
military I [znw] *soldaten, leger* II [bnw]
militair
militate [on ww] *strijden*
• (~ **against**) *bestrijden*
militia [znw] • *militie, burgerwacht*
• *landweer*
milk I [ov ww] *(uit)melken* II [znw]
melk
milky [bnw] • *melkachtig* • *vol melk*
mill I [ov ww] *malen* II [on ww]
• (~ **about/around**) *krioelen,*
(ordeloos) rondlopen III [znw] • *molen*
• *fabriek* • *(maal)machine*
miller [znw] *molenaar*
millet [znw] *gierst*
milliner [znw] *modiste*
millinery [znw] *dameshoeden*
million [znw] *miljoen*
millipede [znw] *duizendpoot*
mime I [ov ww] • *door gebaren*
voorstellen • *nabootsen* II [znw]
• *gebarenspel* • *mimespeler*
mimic I [ov ww] *nabootsen, naäpen*
II [znw] • *mimespeler* • *nabootser,*
naäper
mimicry [znw] • *mimiek* • *nabootsing,*
naäperij
mince I [ov ww] *fijnhakken* II [on ww]
gemaakt lopen/spreken III [znw]
gehakt ‹vlees›
mincer [znw] *vleesmolen*
mind I [ov ww] • *denken om, in acht*
nemen • *zorgen voor, bedienen*
‹machine› II [on ww] *bezwaren*
hebben • (~ **out (for)**) *oppassen (voor)*

III [znw] • *geest, verstand* • *zin*
minded I [bnw] *geneigd, van zins*
II [in samenst.] *aangelegd, -bewust,*
-gezind, georiënteerd
mindful [bnw] • *indachtig*
• *voorzichtig*
mine I [ov + on ww] • *graven* ‹v.
onderaardse gang› • *mijnen leggen*
• *in mijn werken* **II** [ov ww]
ondermijnen, winnen, ontginnen
III [znw] • *mijn* • *bron* ‹fig.›
IV [bez vnw] • *de/het mijne, van mij*
• *de mijnen*
mineral I [znw] *mineraal, delfstof*
II [bnw] *mineraal*
mineralogy [znw] *mineralogie*
mingle [ov + on ww] (z.) *(ver)mengen*
• *(~ with)* z. *begeven onder, meedoen*
met
mini I [znw] • *minirok* • *mini* ‹auto›
II [in samenst.] *kort, miniatuur-, klein*
miniature I [znw] *miniatuurportret*
II [bnw] *klein, op kleine schaal*
minim [znw] *halve noot*
minimal [bnw] *minimaal*
minimize [ov ww] • *onderwaarderen*
' • *verkleinen*
mining [znw] *mijnbouw*
minion [znw] *onbelangrijke*
medewerker
minister I [on ww] • *(~ to) hulp*
verlenen, bedienen **II** [znw] • *minister*
• *gezant* ‹beneden rang v.
ambassadeur› • *predikant*
ministerial [bnw] *ministerieel*
ministry [znw] • *geestelijkheid*
• *ministerschap* • *ministerie, kabinet*
mink [znw] • *nerts* • *nerts-/bontmantel*
minnow [znw] *witvis, voorn*
minstrel [znw] *minstreel*
mint I [ov ww] • *munten* • *uitvinden,*
fabriceren **II** [znw] • *munt*
‹gebouw/instelling› • ‹plantk.› *munt*
minus I [znw] *minteken* **II** [bnw]
• *min(us), negatief* • ‹scherts› *zonder*
minuscule [bnw] *piepklein*

minute I [ov ww] *notuleren* **II** [znw]
• *minuut* • *ogenblik* **III** [bnw] • *zeer*
nauwkeurig, minutieus • *zeer klein,*
nietig
miracle [znw] *wonder*
miraculous [bnw] *miraculeus,*
wonderbaarlijk
mire [znw] • *modder, slijk*
• *moeilijkheden*
mirror I [ov ww] *afspiegelen,*
weerkaatsen **II** [znw] • *spiegel*
• *afspiegeling*
mirth [znw] *vrolijkheid*
mirthless [bnw] *vreugdeloos, triest,*
somber
misadventure [znw] *tegenspoed,*
ongeluk
misanthrope [znw] *misantroop,*
mensenhater
misanthropic [bnw] *misantropisch*
misapply [ov ww] *verkeerd gebruiken*
misapprehend [ov ww] *verkeerd*
begrijpen
misapprehension [znw] *misverstand*
misappropriate [ov ww] z.
wederrechtelijk toe-eigenen,
verduisteren
misbehaviour [znw] *wangedrag*
miscarriage [znw] • *miskraam*
• *mislukking*
miscarry [on ww] • *mislukken, niet*
slagen • *een miskraam krijgen*
miscast [ov ww] *een niet-passende rol*
geven ‹bij film/theater›
miscellaneous [bnw] • *gemengd*
• *veelzijdig*
miscellany [znw] *mengeling*
mischance [znw] *ongeluk*
mischief [znw] • *streken* • *plaaggeest,*
rakker, onheilstoker • *ondeugendheid*
• *onheil, kwaad*
misconception [znw] *verkeerd begrip,*
dwaling
misconduct [znw] *wangedrag*
misconstruction [znw] *verkeerde*
interpretatie

misdeed [znw] *wandaad, misdaad*
misdemeanour [znw] • *misdrijf*
• *wangedrag*
misdirect [ov ww] • *verkeerd leiden/richten* • *verkeerde inlichtingen geven*
miser [znw] *gierigaard, vrek*
miserable [bnw] *ellendig, miserabel, armzalig*
miserly [bnw + bijw] *gierig, vrekkig*
misery [znw] • *ellende* • *zeurpiet*
misfire [on ww] *mislukken* <v. plan>
misfit [znw] *buitenbeentje, mislukkeling in de maatschappij*
misfortune [znw] *ongeluk, tegenslag*
misgiving [znw] *twijfel, angstig voorgevoel, wantrouwen*
misguided [bnw] • *misplaatst* • *misleid*
mishap [znw] *ongeluk(je)*
misinform [ov ww] *verkeerd inlichten*
misinterpret [ov ww] *verkeerd interpreteren, verkeerd uitleggen*
misjudge [ov + on ww] • *verkeerd (be)oordelen* • *z. vergissen (in)*
mislay [ov ww] *op verkeerde plaats leggen, zoek maken*
mislead [ov ww] *misleiden*
misleading [bnw] • *misleidend* • *bedrieglijk*
mismanage [ov ww] *verkeerd besturen, verkeerd beheren, verkeerd aanpakken*
mismanagement [znw] *wanbestuur, wanbeheer*
misnomer [znw] *verkeerde benaming*
misogynist [znw] *vrouwenhater*
misprint [znw] *drukfout*
mispronounce [ov ww] *verkeerd uitspreken*
misquote [ov + on ww] *onjuist aanhalen*
misread [ov ww] • *verkeerd lezen* • *verkeerd interpreteren*
misrepresent [ov ww] *een verkeerde voorstelling geven van*
miss I [ov ww] *missen* • (~ **out**)

overslaan II [on ww] • (~ **out** (on))
mislopen III [znw] • *misstoot, misslag* • *(me)juffrouw*
misshapen [bnw] *mismaakt, misvormd*
missile I [znw] • *raket* • *projectiel* II [bnw] *werp-*
missing [bnw] *ontbrekend*
mission [znw] • *missie* • *gezantschap* • *roeping*
missionary I [znw] *missionaris, zendeling* II [bnw] *zend(el)ings-*
mist I [ov ww] *benevelen* II [on ww] • *beneveld worden* • *misten* III [znw] • *mist, nevel* • *waas*
mistake I [ov ww] *verkeerd begrijpen, z. vergissen* II [znw] *fout, vergissing, dwaling*
mistaken [bnw] • *verkeerd, onjuist* • *misplaatst*
mister [znw] *mijnheer*
mistime [ov ww] *op het verkeerde ogenblik doen/zeggen*
mistletoe [znw] *maretak, vogellijm*
mistress [znw] • *meesteres* • *mevrouw* • *vrouw des huizes* • *baas, hoofd* • *geliefde, maîtresse* • *lerares, onderwijzeres*
mistrust I [ov ww] *wantrouwen* II [znw] *wantrouwen*
mistrustful [bnw] *wantrouwend*
misty [bnw] • *vol tranen* • *vaag* • *beslagen, wazig* • *mistig*
misunderstand [ov ww] *verkeerd begrijpen*
misuse I [ov ww] • *misbruiken* • *verkeerd gebruiken* II [znw] • *misbruik* • *verkeerd gebruik*
mite [znw] • *beetje, zier* • *dreumes* • *mijt*
miter, mitre [znw] *mijter*
mitigate [ov ww] • *verlichten, verzachten* • *matigen* <v. straf>
mitt(en) [znw] • *want* • *vuisthandschoen* <als bij honkbal>
mix I [ov ww] • *(ver)mengen* • *kruisen* <v. dieren> • (~ **in**) (goed) *vermengen* • (~ **up**) *verwarren, door elkaar gooien*

II [on ww] z. (ver)mengen • (~ **with**) z.
aansluiten bij, omgaan met III [znw]
mengeling, mengsel
mixed [bnw] gemengd, vermengd
mixture [znw] mengsel, mengeling
mnemonic [znw] geheugensteuntje,
ezelsbruggetje
moan I [ov ww] betreuren II [on ww]
kreunen, jammeren III [znw] gekreun
moat [znw] slotgracht
mob I [ov ww] in een grote groep
omringen II [znw] • (wanordelijke)
menigte • <inf.> kring, kliek
mobile I [znw] mobile II [bnw]
• beweeglijk, mobiel • vlottend <v.
kapitaal>
mobilize [ov ww] mobiel maken,
mobiliseren
mobster <AE> [znw] bendelid, gangster
mock I [ov ww] de spot drijven met
II [on ww] • (~ **at**) spotten met
III [bnw] zogenaamd, schijn-, onecht,
vals
mockery [znw] • bespotting
• schijnvertoning
modal [bnw] modaal
mode [znw] • manier • gebruik
model I [ov ww] modelleren, vormen,
boetseren • (~ **after/upon**) vormen
naar II [on ww] als mannequin
fungeren III [znw] • type • maquette,
model • mannequin IV [bnw] • model-
• voorbeeldig
moderate I [ov ww] matigen
II [on ww] • bedaren, z. matigen
• bemiddelen III [znw] gematigde
IV [bnw] gematigd, matig
modernism [znw] • modernisme
• neologisme
modernist [znw] nieuwlichter
modernize I [ov ww] moderniseren
II [on ww] z. aan de moderne tijd
aanpassen
modest [bnw] • bescheiden • ingetogen,
zedig
modicum [znw] een beetje, een weinig

modification [znw] • wijziging
• aanpassing
modify [ov ww] • matigen • wijzigen
modish [bnw] modieus
modulate [ov ww] regelen, moduleren
• (~ **to**) in overeenstemming brengen
met
module [znw] • maatstaf,
standaardmaat • onderdeel v.
ruimtevaartuig • modulus
Mohammedan I [znw]
mohammedaan II [bnw]
mohammedaans
moist [bnw] vochtig, klam
moisten [ov ww] bevochtigen
molasses [znw] melasse, stroop
mole [znw] • moedervlek • haven(dam),
pier • mol • <inf.> spion
molecular [bnw] moleculair
molest [ov ww] • lastig vallen
• aanranden
mollify [ov ww] vertederen, bedaren,
matigen
molten I [ww] volt. deelw. → **melt**
II [bnw] gesmolten
moment [znw] • ogenblik • belang
momentary [bnw] • gedurende een
ogenblik • vluchtig
momentous [bnw] belangrijk,
gedenkwaardig, gewichtig
momentum [znw] • stuwkracht
• <techn.> moment
monarchy [znw] monarchie
monastic [bnw] klooster-
Monday [znw] maandag
monetary [bnw] monetair, financieel-,
munt-
money [znw] geld
moneyed [bnw] vermogend
mongrel [znw] bastaard(hond)
monitor I [ov ww] controleren II [znw]
• iem. die radiouitzendingen afluistert
• monitor
monk [znw] monnik
monkey I [on ww] • (~ **about**)
donderjagen, klooien

• (~ **about/around**) *streken uithalen*
II [znw] • *aap* • *deugniet*
monochrome [bnw] *zwart-wit,*
monochroom
monogamous [bnw] *monogaam*
monogamy [znw] *monogamie*
monograph [znw] *monografie*
monolith [znw] *monoliet*
monolithic [bnw] *monolitisch*
monopolize [ov ww] • *monopoliseren*
• *totaal in beslag nemen*
monopoly [znw] *monopolie*
monotone I [znw] *eentonige stem of*
geluid II [bnw] *monotoon, eentonig*
monotonous [bnw] *eentonig*
monotony [znw] *eentonigheid*
monsoon [znw] *moesson*
monstrosity [znw]
monster(achtigheid)
monstrous [bnw] *kolossaal,*
monsterlijk
month [znw] *maand*
monthly I [znw] *maandelijks*
tijdschrift II [bnw + bijw] *maandelijks*
monumental [bnw] • *gedenk-,*
monumentaal • *kolossaal, enorm*
moo I [on ww] *loeien* II [znw] *geloei*
mooch I [ov ww] *klaplopen, schooien*
II [on ww] *slenteren* • (~ **about**)
rondhangen, lummelen
mood [znw] • *stemming* • <taalk.> *wijs*
moody [bnw] *humeurig, somber*
gestemd, zwaarmoedig
moon I [on ww] *rondhangen*
• (~ **about**) *rondhangen,*
rondslenteren • (~ **over**) *dagdromen*
over, nalopen II [znw] *maan*
moor I [ov + on ww] *aan-/afmeren*
II [znw] • *heide* • *veen, veengrond*
moose [znw] *Amerikaanse eland*
mop I [ov ww] *zwabberen, dweilen,*
betten • (~ **up**) *opvegen* II [znw]
• *zwabber* • *vaatkwast*
mope [on ww] *kniezen*
moped [znw] *bromfiets*
moral I [znw] *moraal* II [bnw]

zedelijkheids-, moreel, zedelijk
morale [znw] *moreel*
morality [znw] • *zedenleer* • *zedelijk*
gedrag, moraliteit
moralize [on ww] *moraliseren*
morass [znw] *moeras*
moratorium [znw] • *moratorium,*
algemeen uitstel van betaling
• *(tijdelijk) verbod/uitstel*
mordant [bnw] *scherp, bijtend*
more I [onb vnw] *meer* II [bijw] *meer,*
verder
moreover [bijw] *bovendien*
morgue [znw] *lijkenhuis*
moribund [bnw] *stervend, zieltogend*
morning [znw] *morgen, voormiddag*
moron [znw] • *zwakzinnige* • <pej.>
imbeciel, rund
morose [bnw] • *gemelijk, knorrig*
• *somber*
morsel [znw] *hapje, stukje*
mortal I [znw] *sterveling* II [bnw]
• *sterfelijk* • *dodelijk* • <inf.>
verschrikkelijk, vreselijk vervelend
mortality [znw] • *sterfelijkheid*
• *sterfte(cijfer)*
mortar [znw] • *vijzel* • *mortier*
• *metselkalk*
mortgage I [ov ww] • *verhypothekeren*
• *verpanden* <fig.> II [znw] *hypotheek*
mortician <AE> [znw]
begrafenisondernemer
mortify [ov ww] *in hevige verlegenheid*
brengen
mortise, mortice [znw] *tapgat*
mortuary [znw] *lijkenhuisje*
mosaic [znw] *mozaïek*
Moslem I [znw] *mohammedaan,*
moslim II [bnw] *mohammedaans*
mosque [znw] *moskee*
moss [znw] *mos*
mossy [bnw] • *met mos bedekt*
• *mosachtig*
most I [onb vnw] *meest, grootst,*
meeste(n) II [bijw] *meest, hoogst, zeer*
mostly [bijw] *meestal, voornamelijk*

moth [znw] • *mot* • *nachtvlinder*
mother I [ov ww] *als een moeder*
zorgen voor II [znw] *moeder*
motherlike, motherly [bnw]
moederlijk
motif [znw] *motief, thema*
motion I [ov + on ww] • *wenken* • *door*
gebaar te kennen geven II [znw]
• *beweging* • *gebaar* • *voorstel, motie*
motivate [ov ww] *motiveren, ingeven,*
aanzetten
motive I [znw] *motief, beweegreden*
II [bnw] *beweging veroorzakend*
motley I [znw] *bonte mengeling*
II [bnw] *bont*
motor I [ov + on ww] *in auto*
rijden/vervoeren II [znw] *motor*
III [bnw] *beweging-, motorisch*
motoring [znw] *(rond)toeren met de*
auto, het autorijden
motorist [znw] *automobilist*
mottled [bnw] *gevlekt, gespikkeld*
motto [znw] *devies, spreuk*
mould I [ov ww] *gieten, kneden*
• (~ **on**) *vormen naar* II [on ww]
beschimmelen III [znw] • *losse*
teelaarde • *(giet)vorm, mal, bekisting*
• *gesteldheid, aard* • *schimmel*
moulder [on ww] • *rotten, vermolmen*
• *vervallen*
moulding [znw] • *(kroon)lijst, fries*
• *afdruk*
mouldy [bnw] *beschimmeld*
moult I [on ww] *verharen, vervellen,*
ruien II [znw] *het ruien*
mound [znw] • *aardverhoging,*
(graf)heuveltje, terp • *wal* • *werpheuvel*
<honkbal>
mount I [ov ww] • *opstellen, plaatsen*
• *zetten* <v. juwelen> • *bestijgen*
• *monteren* <v. toneelstuk>
• *opplakken* II [on ww] *stijgen,*
opstijgen • (~ **up**) *oplopen* III [znw]
• *berg* • *rijpaard*
mountain [znw] *berg*
mountaineer [znw] *bergbeklimmer*

mountaineering [znw] *bergsport*
mountainous [bnw] *bergachtig*
mourn I [ov ww] *betreuren* II [on ww]
rouw dragen, rouwen
mourner [znw] *treurende, rouwdrager*
mournful [bnw] *treurig, droevig*
mourning [znw] • *het treuren*
• *weeklacht* • *rouw(kleding)*
mouse [znw] *muis*
mouth I [ov ww] • *in de mond nemen*
• *iets zeggen waarin men zelf niet*
gelooft II [znw] • *monding* • *mond,*
bek, muil • *opening*
mouthful [bnw] • *mond(je)vol* • <inf.>
hele mond vol, moeilijk uit te spreken
woord
move I [ov ww] • *bewegen* • *verhuizen,*
verzetten, vervoeren • *opwekken* <v.
gevoelens>, *ontroeren, aanzetten tot*
• (~ **down**) *in rang terugzetten, naar*
een lagere klas terugzetten II [on ww]
• *in beweging komen, z. bewegen*
• *optreden, stappen nemen* • *opschieten*
• *verhuizen* • (~ **about**) *heen en weer*
trekken • (~ **down**) *naar een lagere*
klas teruggezet worden, in rang
teruggezet worden • (~ **out**) *verhuizen,*
vertrekken III [znw] • *zet, beurt*
• *beweging* • *maatregel* • *verhuizing*
movement [znw] • *mechaniek*
• *beweging*
mover [znw] • *iem. die iets voorstelt*
• *drijfveer* • *verhuizer*
movie [znw] *film*
moving [bnw] • *bewegend, beweeg-*
• *ontroerend, aandoenlijk*
mow [ov ww] *maaien* • (~ **down**)
neerschieten, neermaaien
mower [znw] *maaier*
Mr [afk] • (Mister) *dhr., meneer*
Mrs [afk] • (Mistress) *mevrouw*
Ms [afk] • (Miss/Mrs)
mejuffrouw/mevrouw
much I [onb vnw] *zeer, ten zeerste, veel*
II [bijw] *veel, zeer*
muck I [ov ww] • (~ **out**) *uitmesten*

• (~ **up**) *bederven, verknoeien*
II [on ww] • (~ **about/around**)
rondhangen • (~ **in**) ‹inf.› *meehelpen*
• (~ **in** (**with**)) *een handje helpen*
III [znw] • *mest* • *vuile boel* • *iets v.*
slechte kwaliteit
mucky [bnw] *vuil, smerig*
mucus [znw] *slijm*
mud [znw] • *leem* • *modder*
muddle I [ov ww] • *benevelen* • *door*
elkaar gooien II [on ww] • (~ **along**)
aanmodderen • (~ **through**) *z.*
erdoorheen scharrelen III [znw]
warboel, wanorde
muddy I [ov ww] • *troebel maken*
• *bemodderen* II [bnw] • *modderig*
• *wazig, troebel*
muff I [ov ww] *verknoeien* II [znw] *mof*
muffin [znw] *soort gebakje, met boter*
gegeten
muffle [ov ww] • *omfloersen, dempen*
‹v. geluid› • *inpakken* ‹in kleren›
muffler [znw] • *das* • *(geluid)demper*
mug I [ov ww] *gewelddadig beroven*
• (~ **up**) *blokken* II [znw] • *kroes*
• *smoel* • *sul*
mugger [znw] *straatrover*
muggy [bnw] *benauwd, drukkend* ‹v.
weer›
mulberry [znw] *moerbei*
mule [znw] • *muildier* • *muiltje*
mulish [bnw] • *weerspannig* • *(als) v.e.*
muildier
mull I [ov ww] • (~ **over**) *overdenken*
II [on ww] *piekeren*
multifarious [bnw] *veelsoortig,*
verscheiden
multiple I [znw] *veelvoud* II [bnw]
• *veelvoudig* • *veelsoortig*
multiplication [znw]
vermenigvuldiging
multiplicity [znw] • *veelheid, menigte*
• *verscheidenheid*
multiply I [ov ww] *vergroten* • (~ **by**)
vermenigvuldigen met II [on ww] *z.*
voortplanten, z. vermenigvuldigen

multitude [znw] • *menigte* • *groot*
aantal
mum I [znw] • *stilte, stilzwijgen* • ‹inf.›
mamma, mammie II [bnw] *stil*
mumble I [ov + on ww] *mompelen,*
prevelen, mummelen II [znw]
gemompel
mummify [ov ww] *mummificeren*
mummy [znw] • *mummie* • *mammie,*
moedertje
mumps [mv] *de bof* ‹ziekte›
munch [ov + on ww] *(hoorbaar)*
kauwen (op), knabbelen (aan)
mundane [bnw] *alledaags*
municipal [bnw] *gemeentelijk,*
gemeente-, stads-
municipality [znw] • *gemeentebestuur*
• *gemeente*
munificent [bnw] *gul, mild(dadig)*
mural I [znw] *muurschildering* II [bnw]
muur-, wand-
murder I [ov ww] *(ver)moorden*
II [znw] • *moord* • *hels karwei, een hel,*
gruwel
murderer [znw] *moordenaar*
murderess [znw] *moordenares*
murderous [bnw] *moorddadig*
muscle I [on ww] • (~ **in**) *z. indringen*
II [znw] • *spier* • *(spier)kracht*
muscular [bnw] • *spier-* • *gespierd*
muse I [on ww] *peinzen* • (~ (**up**)**on**)
peinzen over, peinzend kijken naar
II [znw] *muze*
mush [znw] • *pulp* • *sentimentaliteit*
• ‹AE› *maïsmeelpap*
mushroom I [on ww] *z. snel*
verspreiden, als paddestoelen verrijzen
II [znw] • *champignon, (eetbare)*
paddestoel • *atoomwolk*
mushy [bnw] • *papperig* • *slap,*
sentimenteel
music [znw] • *muziek* • *bladmuziek*
musical I [znw] *musical* II [bnw]
• *muzikaal* • *muziek-* • *melodieus*
musician [znw] *musicus, muzikant*
musk [znw] *muskus*

musky [bnw] *muskusachtig*
Muslim I [znw] *mohammedaan,*
  moslim II [bnw] *mohammedaans*
muslin [znw] • *mousseline* • ‹AE› *katoen*
mussel [znw] *mossel*
must I [hww] *moet(en)* II [znw] ‹inf.›
  noodzaak, must
mustard I [znw] • *mosterd*
  • *mosterdplant* II [bnw] *mosterdgeel*
muster I [ov ww] *bijeenbrengen* ‹voor
  inspectie› II [on ww] *aantreden* ‹voor
  inspectie›, z. *verzamelen* III [znw]
  inspectie
musty [bnw] • *schimmelig* • *muf*
mutation [znw] • *mutatie*
  • *verandering*
mute I [ov ww] • *tot zwijgen brengen*
  • ‹muz.› *dempen* II [znw]
  • *(doof)stomme* • ‹muz.› *demper*
  III [bnw] • *zwijgend, stom* • *sprakeloos*
mutilate [ov ww] *verminken*
mutineer [znw] *muiter*
mutinous [bnw] *muitend, oproerig,*
  opstandig
mutiny I [on ww] *muiten, in opstand*
  komen II [znw] *muiterij, opstand*
mutt [znw] • *dwaas, sukkel* • *mormel*
mutter I [ov + on ww] *mompelen*
  II [znw] • *gemompel* • *gemopper*
mutual [bnw] *wederzijds, wederkerig*
muzzle I [ov ww] *muilkorven* II [znw]
  • *bek, snuit* • *mond* ‹v. vuurwapen›
  • *muilkorf*
muzzy [bnw] • *beneveld* ‹door drank›
  • *wazig*
my [bez vnw] *mijn*
myopic [bnw] *bijziend*
myriad I [znw] • *tienduizend(tal)*
  • *groot aantal* II [bnw] *ontelbaar*
myself [wkg vnw] • *mijzelf* • *(ik)zelf*
mysterious [bnw] *mysterieus,*
  geheimzinnig
mystery [znw] • *geheim*
  • *geheimzinnigheid* • *detectiveroman*
mystic I [znw] *mysticus* II [bnw]
  → **mystical**

mystical [bnw] *verborgen, mystiek*
mysticism [znw] • *mystiek*
  • *mysticisme*
mystify [ov ww] • *voor een raadsel*
  stellen • *bedotten*
mystique [znw] *wereldbeschouwing,*
  mystiek
myth [znw] *mythe*
mythology [znw] *mythologie*

N

nab [ov ww] ‹sl.› *betrappen*
nadir [znw] • *laagste punt* • *voetpunt, dieptepunt*
nag I [ov + on ww] *klagen (tegen)* • (~ **at**) *vitten op* II [znw] • *gevit* • ‹inf.› *paard*
nail I [ov ww] • *(vast)spijkeren* • *grijpen, betrappen* • (~ **down**) *vastspijkeren, dichtspijkeren, vastleggen, houden aan* ‹belofte› • (~ **up**) *vastspijkeren, dichtspijkeren* II [znw] • *nagel* • *spijker*
naked [bnw] • *naakt, bloot* • *weerloos* • *kaal, onopgesmukt* • *niet geïsoleerd* ‹v. stroomdraad›
name I [ov ww] *(be)noemen* II [znw] *naam, benaming*
namely [bijw] *namelijk, dat wil zeggen*
nanny [znw] *kinderjuffrouw*
nap I [on ww] *dutten, soezen* II [znw] *dutje*
nape [znw] *(achterkant v.d.) nek*
napkin [znw] *servet*
nappy [znw] *luier*
narcissus [znw] *narcis*
narcotic I [znw] *verdovend middel* II [bnw] *verdovend*
narrate [ov + on ww] *vertellen*
narrative [znw] *verhaal*
narrator [znw] *verteller*
narrow I [ov + on ww] • *vernauwen* • *minderen* ‹bij breien› II [ov ww] *z. vernauwen* III [bnw] • *nauw, smal* • *bekrompen*
nasal [bnw] *nasaal, neus-*
nascent [bnw] *wordend, ontluikend*
nasturtium [znw] *Oost-Indische kers*
nasty [bnw] • *beroerd* ‹v. o.a. weer› • *hatelijk* • *lastig* • *onsmakelijk* • *lelijk, gemeen* • *ernstig*
nation [znw] *natie, volk*

national [bnw] *nationaal, volks-, staats-*
nationalism [znw] • *streven naar nationale onafhankelijkheid* • *vaderlandsliefde*
nationalist I [znw] *nationalist* II [bnw] *nationalistisch*
nationality [znw] • *nationaliteit* • *ethnische groep*
nationalize [ov ww] *onteigenen* ‹door de staat›
native I [znw] • *iem. uit het land of de plaats zelf* • *inboorling, inlander* • *inheems(e) dier of plant* II [bnw] • *inheems* • *geboorte-* • *natuurlijk, aangeboren*
natty [bnw] • *keurig* • *handig*
natural I [znw] *getalenteerd iem.* II [bnw] • *aangeboren, natuurlijk* • *gewoon, normaal* • *eenvoudig, ongekunsteld* • *onwettig* ‹v. kind› • *natuur-*
naturalism [znw] *naturalisme*
naturalist [znw] • *naturalist* • *bioloog*
naturalistic [bnw] *naturalistisch, realistisch*
naturalize [ov ww] *naturaliseren*
naturally [bijw] • *van nature* • *op natuurlijke wijze* • *vanzelfsprekend*
nature [znw] • *(de) natuur* • *aard, soort*
naturism [znw] *naturisme, nudisme*
naught [znw] • *nul* • *niets*
naughty [bnw] *ondeugend, stout*
nausea [znw] • *(gevoel v.) misselijkheid* • *walging*
nauseate [ov ww] *misselijk maken*
nauseous [bnw] *walgelijk*
naval [bnw] • *zee-* • *scheeps-* • *vloot-* • *marine-*
nave [znw] • *naaf* ‹v. wiel› • *schip* ‹v. kerk›
navel [znw] *navel*
navigable [bnw] *bevaarbaar* ‹v. rivier›
navigate I [ov ww] • *bevaren* • *besturen* II [on ww] • *navigeren* • *sturen* ‹v. schip, vliegtuig›

navigation [znw] *navigatie*
navigator [znw] • *zeevaarder*
• *navigator ‹v. vliegtuig›*
navvy [znw] *polderjongen, grondwerker*
navy I [znw] • *vloot, zeemacht* • *marine*
II [bnw] *marineblauw*
nay I [znw] *neen, weigering* II [bijw] *ja zelfs*
near I [bnw] • *nauw (verwant)* • *intiem*
• *dichtbijzijnd* • *krenterig* • *‹AE› grenzend aan* II [bijw] • *dichtbij*
• *nabij* • *bijna*
nearly [bijw] *bijna, haast*
neat [bnw] • *handig, knap* • *keurig*
• *onvermengd ‹v. drank›*
nebulous [bnw] *nevelachtig, vaag*
necessarily [bijw] *noodzakelijk(erwijs), onvermijdelijk*
necessary [bnw] *noodzakelijk*
necessitate [ov ww] *noodzaken*
necessity [znw] *noodzaak, noodzakelijkheid*
neck [znw] *nek, hals*
necklace [znw] *halssnoer*
née [bnw] ⋆ *Mrs Smith, née Jones mevr. Smith, geboren Jones*
need I [ov ww] • *nodig hebben, vereisen*
• *moeten* II [hww] *hoeven* III [znw]
• *nood(zaak)* • *armoede, tekort*
needle I [ov ww] *ergeren, prikkelen, lastig maken* II [znw] *naald ‹ook v. naaldboom of magneet›*
needless [bnw] *nodeloos*
needy [bnw] *behoeftig, armoedig*
negate [ov ww] • *tenietdoen*
• *ontkennen*
negation [znw] • *ontkenning*
• *weigering*
negative I [znw] • *ontkenning*
• *negatieve grootheid ‹in algebra›*
• *vetorecht* • *‹techn.› negatieve pool*
• *‹foto.› negatief* II [bnw] • *ontkennend*
• *verbods-* • *weigerend* • *negatief*
neglect I [ov ww] • *veronachtzamen, verwaarlozen* • *over 't hoofd zien*
II [znw] • *verzuim* • *verwaarlozing*

neglectful [bnw] • *nalatig*
• *verwaarloosd*
negligence [znw] • *nalatigheid*
• *ongedwongenheid, achteloosheid*
negligent [bnw] *nalatig, achteloos*
negotiable [bnw] • *verhandelbaar ‹v. effecten›* • *oplosbaar* • *bespreekbaar*
• *begaanbaar*
negotiate I [ov ww] • *nemen ‹v. hindernis›* • *onderhandelen over*
II [on ww] *onderhandelen*
negotiation [znw] *onderhandeling*
negotiator [znw] *onderhandelaar*
neigh I [on ww] *hinniken* II [znw] *gehinnik*
neighbour, neighbor I [ov ww] *grenzen aan* II [on ww] *grenzen, benaderen* • *(~ on) grenzen aan*
III [znw] • *buurman, buurvrouw*
• *‹rel.› naaste* IV [bnw] *naburig*
neighbourhood, neighborhood [znw] • *buurt* • *omtrek*
neighbouring, neighboring [bnw] *naburig*
neighbourly, neighborly [bnw]
• *een goede buur betamend, als buren*
• *gezellig* • *vriendelijk*
neither [bnw + bijw] • *noch, en ... ook niet* • *evenmin* • *geen v. beide* • *‹rel.› zelfs niet*
neolithic [bnw] *neolithisch*
nephew [znw] *neef ‹zoon v. broer of zuster›, oom-/tantezegger*
nepotism [znw] *nepotisme*
nerve I [ov ww] *kracht of moed geven*
II [znw] • *zenuw* • *moed, zelfbeheersing*
• *‹inf.› brutaliteit*
nerveless [bnw] • *krachteloos, lusteloos, zwak* • *zonder zenuwen*
nervous [bnw] • *zenuwachtig* • *zenuw-*
• *bang*
nervy [bnw] *zenuwachtig*
nest I [on ww] *nesten* II [znw] *nest*
nestle I [ov ww] *vlijen* II [on ww] • *z. (neer)vlijen* • *half verborgen liggen*
nestling [znw] *nestvogel*

net I [ov ww] • (als) met een net
bedekken/omgeven/vangen/afvissen,
voorzien v. netwerk • in de wacht slepen
II [znw] • net • valstrik • spinnenweb
• vitrage, netwerk • netto bedrag/prijs
III [bnw] netto
nettle I [ov ww] ergeren, prikkelen
II [znw] brandnetel
network [znw] • netwerk
• radio-/tv-station
neural [bnw] zenuw-, ruggenmergs-
neuralgia [znw] zenuwpijn
neurology [znw] neurologie
neurosis [znw] neurose
neurotic I [znw] zenuwlijder II [bnw]
neurotisch, zenuwziek
neuter [bnw] onzijdig
neutral [bnw] • neutraal • onbepaald,
vaag • v.e. grijze kleur
neutralize [ov ww] opheffen,
neutraliseren
never [bijw] • nooit • helemaal niet,
toch niet
nevertheless [bijw] • niettegenstaande
dit/dat • toch
new [bnw] • nieuw, onbekend • vers <v.
brood>
news [znw] • nieuws • opzienbarend
iets/iem.
newspaper [znw] • krant
• krantenpapier
newsy [bnw] <inf.> vol nieuws
newt [znw] watersalamander
next I [bnw] • naast • (eerst)volgende,
aanstaande II [bijw] • naast • daarna,
de volgende keer, vervolgens III [vz]
naast
nexus [znw] band, schakel, verbinding
nib [znw] • punt <v. ganzenpen,
gereedschap> • pen
nibble I [on ww] knabbelen II [znw]
geknabbel
nice [bnw] • genuanceerd, subtiel
• nauwgezet, nauwkeurig, aandachtig
• kies • aardig, prettig, leuk • lekker
• fatsoenlijk

nicety [znw] • nauwgezetheid,
nauwkeurigheid • finesse
niche [znw] • leuke baan • nis • passend
plaatsje
nick I [ov ww] • inkepen, kerven • <sl.>
arresteren, snappen • <sl.> gappen
II [znw] • inkeping, kerf • <sl.> bajes,
nor
nickel I [znw] • nikkel • Amerikaans
vijfcentstuk II [bnw] nikkelen
niece [znw] nicht <oom-/tantezegger>
Nigerian I [znw] Nigeriaan II [bnw]
Nigeriaans
niggardly [bnw + bijw] gierig, karig
niggle [on ww] beuzelen, vitten
night [znw] avond, nacht
nightingale [znw] nachtegaal
nightly I [bnw] nachtelijk, avond-
II [bijw] • iedere nacht/avond • 's
avonds/nachts
nihilism [znw] nihilisme
nil [znw] niets, nul
nimble [bnw] vlug, handig
nimbus [znw] stralenkrans
nincompoop [znw] lomperd, domoor,
stommeling
nine [telw] negen
nineteen [telw] negentien
ninetieth [bnw] negentigste
ninety [telw] negentig
ninny [znw] onnozele hals, sukkel
ninth [bnw] negende
nip I [ov ww] • bijten • knijpen
II [on ww] <inf.> snellen, rennen
• (~ in) binnenwippen • (~ out) vlug
ervandoor gaan III [znw] • kneep • beet
• borreltje, hartversterking
nipper [znw] • (klein) ventje
• straatjongen
nipple [znw] • tepel • speen • <techn.>
nippel
nippy [bnw] frisjes <v. weer>
nit [znw] • neet, luizenei • stommeling,
leeghoofd
nitrate [znw] • nitraat,
salpeterzuurzout • nitraatmeststof

nitty-gritty [znw] *detail, bijzonderheid*
nitwit [znw] *leeghoofd*
no [bijw] • *geen* • *niet* • *neen*
nobility [znw] *adel, adelstand*
noble I [znw] *edelman* II [bnw]
• *adellijk* • *edel, grootmoedig* • *statig,*
indrukwekkend
nobody [onb vnw] *niemand*
nocturnal [bnw] *nacht-, nachtelijk*
nod I [on ww] *knikken, knikkebollen,*
slaperig zijn • (~ **off**) *in slaap vallen*
II [znw] *knik*
node [znw] • *knooppunt* • *knoest,*
knobbel
nodule [znw] • *knoestje* • *knobbeltje,*
klein gezwel • *knolletje*
noise [znw] *lawaai, ruis*
noiseless [bnw] • *zonder lawaai*
• *geruisloos*
noisy [bnw] • *schreeuwend* <v. kleuren>
• *luidruchtig, druk*
nomad [znw] *nomade*
nomadic [bnw] *nomadisch, nomaden-,*
zwervend
nomenclature [znw] *terminologie*
nominal [bnw] • *naamwoordelijk*
• *nominaal, in naam*
nomination [znw] • *benoeming*
• *voordracht, kandidaatstelling*
nominee [znw] • *benoemde*
• *kandidaat*
nondescript [bnw] • *onbepaald* • *saai,*
oninteressant
none [bnw + bijw] *niemand, niet een,*
totaal niet, niets
nonentity [znw] • *niet-bestaan(d iets)*
• *onbeduidend iem. of iets*
nonsense [znw] *onzin*
nonsensical [bnw] *onzinnig*
noodle [znw] *soort mie, soort vermicelli*
nook, nookery [znw] *(gezellig) hoekje*
noon [znw] *12 uur's middags*
noose [znw] *lus, schuifknoop, strop*
nope <AE inf.> [bijw] *nee*
nor [bijw] • *noch, (en) ook niet*
• *evenmin*

Nordic I [znw] *Noord-Europeaan*
II [bnw] *Noord-Europees*
norm [znw] *standaard, norm, patroon*
normal [bnw] *normaal*
normalize [ov ww] *normaliseren*
Norman I [znw] *Normandiër* II [bnw]
Normandisch
north I [znw] *noorden* II [bnw + bijw]
noordwaarts, noordelijk, noord(en)-,
noorder-
Norwegian I [znw] *Noor* II [bnw]
Noors
nose I [ov ww] • *ruiken (aan),*
(be)snuffelen • *met de neus wrijven*
tegen • (~ **out**) <inf.> *ontdekken,*
erachter komen II [on ww] *zijn weg*
zoeken <v. voertuig> • (~ **about**)
rondneuzen, rondsnuffelen III [znw]
• *reuk, geur* • *neus, neusstuk* <v.
instrument>
nosh <sl.> I [ov + on ww] *eten* II [znw]
eten, voedsel, hapje
nostalgia [znw] *nostalgie, heimwee*
nostalgic [bnw] • *heimwee-*
• *nostalgisch, vol verlangen*
not [bijw] *niet*
notable I [znw] *vooraanstaand*
persoon, notabele II [bnw]
• *merkwaardig, opvallend* • *merkbaar*
<v. o.a. hoeveelheid>
notation [znw] *schrijfwijze*
note I [ov ww] • *notitie nemen van,*
opmerken • *aantekenen* • *annoteren*
II [znw] • *aantekening* • *(order)briefje*
• *nota* • *bankbiljet* • *aandacht*
• *reputatie, aanzien* • *toon* • *toets* <v.
piano> • *noot* • *geluid, gezang* <v.
vogels> • *teken, kenmerk*
noted [bnw] *beroemd*
nothing [bnw + bijw] *niets, nul, niet*
bestaan(d iets)
nothingness [znw] • *'t niets (zijn)*
• *nietigheid*
notice I [ov ww] *opmerken* II [znw]
• *recensie* <v. boek> • *aankondiging,*
waarschuwing • *aandacht*

- *bekendmaking, mededeling*
- *opzegging <v. contract>* • *convocatie*
noticeable [bnw] • *merkbaar*
- *opmerkelijk*
notifiable [bnw] *die/dat aangegeven moet worden, met aangifteplicht <v. ziekten>*
notification [znw] • *bekendmaking*
- *aankondiging*
notify [ov ww] *aankondigen, verwittigen, aangeven <v. ziekte>, bekendmaken*
notion [znw] • *notie* • *idee, begrip*
- *neiging*
notional [bnw] *denkbeeldig, begrips-*
notoriety [znw] • *bekendheid*
- *beruchtheid* • *bekende persoonlijkheid*
notorious [bnw] • *berucht* • *bekend*
notwithstanding I [bijw] *ondanks dat* II [vz] *niettegenstaande*
nougat [znw] *noga*
nought [znw] *niets, nul*
noun [znw] *zelfstandig naamwoord*
nourish [ov ww] • *koesteren <v. o.a. hoop>* • *voeden*
nourishment [znw] *onderhoud, voedsel, voeding*
novel I [znw] *roman* II [bnw] *nieuw, ongebruikelijk*
novelette [znw] *novelle*
novelist [znw] *romanschrijver*
novice [znw] • *novice* • *nieuweling*
now I [znw] *heden* II [bijw] *op 't ogenblik, nu*
nowaday(s) I [znw] *'t heden* II [bnw + bijw] *tegenwoordig*
nowhere [bijw] *nergens*
noxious [bnw] • *schadelijk* • *ongezond*
nozzle [znw] • *pijp, tuit* • *<techn.> mondstuk*
nuance [znw] *nuance, schakering*
nub [znw] • *knobbel* • *kernpunt*
nubile [bnw] *huwbaar*
nuclear [bnw] *nucleair, atoom-, kern-*
nucleus [znw] *kern*
nude I [znw] *naakt(model)* II [bnw]

naakt, bloot
nudge I [ov ww] *even aanstoten met elleboog* II [znw] *duwtje*
nudism [znw] *nudisme*
nudity [znw] *naaktheid*
nugget [znw] • *juweel(tje) <fig.>*
- *goudklomp*
nuisance [znw] *overlast, onaangenaam iets, lastpost*
null [bnw] *niet bindend, ongeldig, nietig*
nullify [ov ww] *opheffen, annuleren, nietig verklaren*
numb I [ov ww] • *verdoven, verzachten <v. pijn>* • *doen verstijven* • *verlammen <fig.>* • *verstommen* II [bnw] *verkleumd, verdoofd, verstijfd*
number I [ov ww] • *tellen, nummeren*
- *bedragen* • *(~ among) rekenen onder* II [znw] • *nummer* • *aantal*
numeral I [znw] • *getalteken*
- *nummer* II [bnw] *getal-*
numerate [bnw] • *bekend met wis- en natuurkundige grondbegrippen*
- *kunnende tellen en rekenen*
numerous [bnw] *talrijk*
nun [znw] *non*
nunnery [znw] *nonnenklooster*
nuptial I [znw] II [bnw] *bruilofts-, huwelijks-*
nurse I [ov ww] • *de borst geven*
- *koesteren* • *voorzichtig vasthouden*
- *verplegen* II [on ww] *de borst krijgen* III [znw] *verpleegster*
nursery [znw] • *pootvijver*
- *kinderkamer* • *(kinder)bewaarplaats, crèche* • *kwekerij* • *verpleging* • *periode v. borstvoeding*
nurture I [ov ww] • *verzorgen, koesteren* • *grootbrengen* II [znw] *'t grootbrengen, verzorging*
nut [znw] • *(hazel)noot* • *gek, ezel*
- *moer <v. schroef>* • *<sl.> hoofd, kop*
nutrient [znw] *voedingsstof/-middel*
nutriment [znw] *voedsel*

nutrition [znw] *voedsel,*
voeding(swaarde)
nutty [bnw] • *nootachtig* • *vol noten*
• *‹sl.› niet goed bij 't hoofd*
nuzzle [on ww] *met de neus wrijven*
tegen, besnuffelen
nymph [znw] • *nimf* • *onvolwassen*
vorm v. lager insect

oaf [znw] *pummel*
oak I [znw] *eik(enhout)* II [bnw]
eikenhouten
oar [znw] *roeiriem*
oasis [znw] *oase*
oath [znw] • *eed* • *vloek*
obduracy [znw] • *onverbeterlijkheid*
• *onverzettelijkheid*
obdurate [bnw] *verstokt, verhard*
obedience [znw] *gehoorzaamheid*
obedient [bnw] *gehoorzaam*
obeisance [znw] • *diepe buiging*
• *eerbetoon*
obese [bnw] *corpulent*
obey [ov + on ww] *gehoorzamen (aan)*
object I [on ww] *bezwaar maken*
II [znw] • *object* • *doel* • *voorwerp*
objection [znw] *bezwaar*
objectionable [bnw] • *laakbaar*
• *onaangenaam*
objective I [znw] *doel* II [bnw]
• *objectief* • *voorwerps-*
obligation [znw] • *contract*
• *verbintenis* • *(zware) verplichting*
obligatory [bnw] • *bindend* • *verplicht*
oblige I [ov + on ww] *iem. een plezier*
doen II [ov ww] *(ver)binden, (aan zich)*
verplichten
obliging [bnw] *voorkomend, gedienstig*
oblique I [znw] *schuine streep* II [bnw]
schuin, scheef, indirect
obliterate [ov ww] • *vernietigen*
• *uitwissen*
oblivion [znw] *vergetelheid,*
veronachtzaming
oblong I [znw] *rechthoek* II [bnw]
langwerpig
obnoxious [bnw] • *gehaat,*
onaangenaam • *aanstotelijk*
oboe [znw] *hobo*
oboist [znw] *hoboïst*

obscene [bnw] *vuil, onzedelijk*
obscenity [znw] *iets obsceens*
obscure I [ov ww] *verduisteren, verdoezelen, verbergen, in de schaduw stellen* II [bnw] • *donker, duister* • *obscuur, onbekend, onduidelijk*
obscurity [znw] • *onbekendheid* • *vaagheid* • *duisternis*
observable [bnw] *waarneembaar*
observance [znw] • *inachtneming* • *viering*
observant [bnw] *opmerkzaam*
observation [znw] • *aandacht, waarneming* • *opmerking*
observer [znw] *waarnemer*
obsess [ov ww] *vervolgen ‹v. idee›, kwellen, obsederen*
obsession [znw] • *obsessie* • *nachtmerrie ‹fig.›*
obsessive [bnw] • *obsederend* • *bezeten*
obsolescent [bnw] *in onbruik gerakend*
obsolete [bnw] *verouderd, overbodig, in onbruik geraakt*
obstacle [znw] *hindernis, beletsel*
obstinacy [znw] *koppigheid*
obstinate [bnw] *koppig, hardnekkig*
obstreperous [bnw] *lawaaierig, weerspannig*
obstruct [ov ww] *belemmeren, versperren*
obstruction [znw] • *beletsel* • *obstructie*
obstructive [bnw] • *hinderlijk* • *obstructievoerend*
obtain I [ov ww] *verkrijgen, verwerven* II [on ww] *heersen, algemeen in gebruik zijn*
obtainable [bnw] *verkrijgbaar*
obtrusive [bnw] • *opdringerig* • *opvallend*
obtuse [bnw] • *stomp, bot* • *traag v. begrip*
obviate [ov ww] *verhelpen, uit de weg ruimen*
obvious [bnw] *klaarblijkelijk, vanzelfsprekend, duidelijk, opvallend*

occasion I [ov ww] *aanleiding geven tot, veroorzaken* II [znw] • *plechtige gelegenheid* • *gelegenheid* • *grond, aanleiding, reden*
occasional [bnw] • *toevallig* • *af en toe plaatsvindend*
occult I [znw] *het occulte* II [bnw] • *occult* • *geheim, verborgen*
occupancy [znw] • *bezit* • *bewoning* • *bezitneming*
occupant [znw] *bewoner, inzittende*
occupation [znw] • *beroep, bezigheid* • *bezetting ‹ook mil.›* • *bewoning*
occupational [bnw] *beroeps-*
occupier [znw] *bewoner*
occupy [ov ww] • *bezetten* • *bewonen* • *innemen, in beslag nemen ‹v. tijd›, bezighouden*
occur [on ww] *gebeuren* • *(~ to) in gedachte komen bij, opkomen bij*
ocean [znw] *oceaan*
oceanic [bnw] • *oceaan-* • *onmetelijk*
oceanography [znw] *oceanografie*
o'clock [bijw] ★ *five ~ vijf uur*
octagon [znw] *achthoek*
octane [znw] *octaan*
octave [znw] *octaaf, achttal*
October [znw] *oktober*
octogenarian [znw] *tachtigjarige*
oculist [znw] *oogarts*
odd [bnw] • *oneven ‹getal›* • *ongeregeld* • *vreemd, eigenaardig*
oddity [znw] *eigenaardig iem./iets*
odour [znw] • *geur* • *stank*
of [vz] *van*
off I [bnw] *ver(der), verst* II [bijw] • *weg, (er)af* • *af, uit* III [vz] • *van(af)* • *naast, op de hoogte van*
offal [znw] *slachtafval*
offence, offense [znw] • *belediging* • *‹jur.› overtreding, vergrijp*
offend [ov + on ww] • *beledigen* • *overtreden ‹v. wet›*
offender [znw] *dader, schuldige*
offensive I [znw] *offensief* II [bnw] • *aanvals-, aanvallend* • *beledigend*

• weerzinwekkend, kwalijk riekend
offer I [ov ww] (aan)bieden II [znw]
• aanbod, offerte • bod
offering [znw] • offerande, aanbieding
• gift
office [znw] • ambt, taak • dienst
• kerkdienst, mis, officie • kantoor
• ministerie • <AE> spreekkamer
officer [znw] • ambtenaar, beambte
• politieagent • deurwaarder • officier
official I [znw] ambtenaar, beambte
II [bnw] • ambtelijk, officieel • officieel
erkend
officialdom [znw] • de ambtenarij • 't
ambtenarenkorps
officiate [on ww] een ceremonie leiden
officious [bnw] • overgedienstig
• opdringerig • officieus <in
diplomatie>
offing [znw] ★ in the ~ in het verschiet
offset [ov ww] opwegen tegen,
neutraliseren, compenseren
often [bijw] vaak, dikwijls
oh [tw] o!, och!, ach!
oil I [ov ww] smeren, oliën II [znw]
• olieverf • olie • petroleum
oily [bnw] • olieachtig, olie- • vleiend,
glad v. tong
ointment [znw] smeersel, zalf
old [bnw] • oud, versleten, ouderwets
• vroeger
oligarchy [znw] oligarchie
olive I [znw] • olijf • olijfgroen, olijftak
II [bnw] olijfkleurig
Olympic [bnw] olympisch
omen [znw] voorteken
ominous [bnw] onheilspellend,
dreigend
omission [znw] weglating, 't weglaten,
verzuim
omit [ov ww] • weglaten • verzuimen
omniscient [bnw] alwetend
omnivorous [bnw] • verslindend <vnl.
v. boeken> • <bio.> allesetend
on I [bijw] • (er)op • aan II [vz] • over,
aangaande • op • aan

once I [bijw] eens, een keer II [vw] zodra
one I [znw] een II [onb vnw] • iem.
• men III [telw] • één, enige • een,
dezelfde
oneself [wkd vnw] (zich)zelf
onion [znw] ui
onlooker [znw] toeschouwer
only I [bnw] enig II [bijw] • (alleen)
maar • pas, eerst III [vw] maar, alleen
onrush [znw] toeloop, toestroom,
stormloop
onset [znw] • aanval • begin, eerste
symptomen
onshore I [bnw] aanlandig II [bijw]
• land(in)waarts • aan land
onslaught [znw] woeste aanval
onus [znw] • (bewijs)last, plicht • schuld
onward [bnw] voorwaarts
oodles [mv] massa's
ooze I [ov + on ww] • sijpelen • druipen
van <ook fig.> II [znw] slib, slijk
opacity [znw] duisternis
opal [znw] opaal
opaque [bnw] • mat • ondoorschijnend,
duister • onduidelijk
open I [ov + on ww] openen II [bnw]
open
opening I [znw] • opening, begin
• kans • vacante betrekking II [bnw]
openend, inleidend
openly [bijw] • openlijk • openbaar
• openhartig
operate I [ov ww] • bewerken,
teweegbrengen • <AE> exploiteren, leiden
II [on ww] • opereren • werken,
uitwerking hebben
operation [znw] • operatie • financiële
transactie • exploitatie • werking,
handeling
operative I [znw] • werkman,
fabrieksarbeider • <AE> spion II [bnw]
• in werking • van kracht • praktisch,
doeltreffend
operator [znw] • (be)werker • operateur
• iem. die machine bedient
• telegrafist(e), telefonist(e) • eigenaar

v. bedrijf
operetta [znw] *operette*
ophthalmic [bnw] *oogheelkundig*
opiate [znw] *geneesmiddel dat opium bevat*
opinionated [bnw] • *dogmatisch* • *eigenzinnig*
opponent I [znw] *tegenpartij/-stander* II [bnw] *tegengesteld, strijdig*
opportune [bnw] *gelegen, geschikt*
opportunism [znw] *opportunisme*
opportunity [znw] *(gunstige) gelegenheid, kans*
oppose [ov ww] *z. verzetten (tegen)* • *(~ to) stellen tegenover*
opposed [bnw] *tegengesteld*
opposite I [znw] *tegen(over)gestelde, tegenpool* II [bnw] *tegenovergelegen, overstaand* <v. blad of hoek>, *ander(e), tegen-, over-* III [vz] • *tegenover* • *aan de overkant*
opposition [znw] • *verzet, oppositie* <ook politiek> • *tegenstelling, plaatsing tegenover*
oppress [ov ww] • *onderdrukken, verdrukken* • *bezwaren, drukken op*
oppression [znw] *verdrukking, onderdrukking*
oppressive [bnw] *verdrukkend, onderdrukkend*
oppressor [znw] *onderdrukker, tiran*
opt [on ww] *opteren, keuze doen* • *(~ out) niet meer (willen) meedoen, z. terugtrekken*
optic [bnw] *gezichts-*
optical [bnw] *gezichts-, optisch*
optician [znw] *opticien*
optimism [znw] *optimisme*
optimum [znw] *optimum, beste, meest begunstigde*
option [znw] • *keus* • *optie*
optional [bnw] *naar keuze, facultatief*
opulent [bnw] *rijk, weelderig, overvloedig*
oracle [znw] *orakel*
oracular [bnw] • *als een orakel*

• *dubbelzinnig*
oral I [znw] <inf.> *mondeling examen* II [bnw] *mondeling, mond-*
orange I [znw] *sinaasappel* II [bnw] *oranje*
oration [znw] *redevoering*
orator [znw] *redenaar*
oratoric(al) [bnw] *oratorisch*
oratory [znw] • *(huis)kapel* <r.-k. kerk> • *welsprekendheid*
orb [znw] • *bol* • *hemellichaam* • *rijksappel* • <form.> *oog(bal)*
orbit I [ov + on ww] *draaien in een baan om* II [znw] • *(gebogen) baan v. hemellichaam* • *invloedssfeer*
orbital [znw] *verkeersweg om voorsteden heen*
orchard [znw] • *boomgaard* • *fruittuin*
orchestra [znw] • *orkest* • <AE> *stalles*
orchid, orchis [znw] *orchidee*
ordain [on ww] • *(tot priester) wijden* • *beschikken, voorschrijven*
ordeal [znw] • *godsgericht* • *beproeving*
order I [ov ww] • *bestellen* • *ordenen, regelen* • *verordenen, bevelen* • *(~ out) wegsturen, laten uitrukken* II [znw] • *rang* • *klasse, stand* • *volgorde* • *order, bevel* • *soort* • *bestelling*
orderly I [znw] *ziekenoppasser* II [bnw] *ordelijk, geregeld*
ordinance [znw] *verordening*
ordinary [bnw] *alledaags, normaal, gewoon*
ordination [znw] *wijding* <tot geestelijke>
ordnance [znw] *tak v. openbare dienst voor mil. voorraden en materieel*
ordure [znw] • *mest, gier* • *uitwerpselen, drek*
ore [znw] *erts*
organ [znw] • *orgaan* • *orgel*
organic [bnw] • *organisch* • *structureel*
organism [znw] *organisme*
organization [znw] *organisatie*
organize [ov ww] *organiseren*
organizer [znw] *organisator*

orgasm [znw] *orgasme*
orgy [znw] *orgie, drinkgelag,*
uitspatting
oriental I [znw] *oosterling* II [bnw]
oosters
orientate [ov ww] • z. *oriënteren* • z.
naar een bepaald punt richten • z. *naar*
de omstandigheden richten
orientation [znw] • *richtingsgevoel*
• *oriëntering*
orifice [znw] *opening, mond(ing)*
origin [znw] *afkomst, oorsprong, begin*
original I [znw] *origineel* II [bnw]
aanvankelijk, oorspronkelijk, origineel,
eerste
originate [ov + on ww] • *voortbrengen*
• *ontstaan (in)* • (~ **from**) *voortkomen*
uit • (~ **with**) *opkomen bij*
ornament I [ov ww] *versieren, tooien*
II [znw] *ornament, sieraad, versiersel*
ornamental [bnw] *decoratief,*
ornamenteel, sier-
ornate [bnw] • *sierlijk, bloemrijk* <v.
taal> • *ornaat*
orphan [znw] *wees*
orphanage [znw] *weeshuis*
orthodox [bnw] • *orthodox* • *algemeen*
geaccepteerd, conventioneel
• *ouderwets, v.d. oude stempel*
orthodoxy [znw] *orthodoxie*
orthography [znw] *spellingsleer,*
orthografie
orthopaedic [bnw] *orthopedisch*
oscillate [on ww] • *schommelen,*
slingeren • *oscilleren* <v. radio>
• *aarzelen*
osier [znw] • *soort wilg* • *rijs*
ossify I [ov ww] *(doen) verstenen*
II [on ww] • *in been veranderen*
• *verharden* <fig.>
ostensible [bnw] *ogenschijnlijk,*
zogenaamd
ostentation [znw] *uiterlijk vertoon*
ostentatious [bnw] *opzichtig, in 't oog*
lopend
osteopath [znw] *(onbevoegd)*

orthopedist, osteopaat
ostrich [znw] *struisvogel*
other I [znw] *de/het andere* II [bnw]
anders, verschillend
otherwise [bijw] • *anders* • *(of) anders*
• *verder*
ouch [tw] *au!*
ounce [znw] • *283 gram* • *greintje*
our [bez vnw] *ons, onze*
ours [bez vnw] *het onze, de onze(n)*
ourselves [wkd vnw] *ons(zelf),*
wij(zelf), zelf
out I [bnw] • *in staking* • *in bloei* • *uit*
(op) • *over* • *fout* II [bijw] • *weg, (er)uit,*
(er)buiten • *uit de mode* • *voorbij,*
afgelopen, om • *verschenen, publiek*
• *zonder betrekking, af* <in spel> III [vz]
langs, uit
out- [voorv] *meer, groter, beter, harder*
out-and-out [bnw] *volledig,*
voortreffelijk
outback [znw] *binnenland* <v.
Australië>
outbreak [znw] • *het uitbreken* • *oproer*
outbuilding [znw] *bijgebouw*
outburst [znw] *uitbarsting*
outcast [znw] *verschoppeling*
outclass [on ww] *de meerdere zijn van*
outcry [znw] • *verontwaardiging*
• *geschreeuw*
outdo [ov ww] *overtreffen*
outdoor [bnw] *openlucht-,*
buiten(shuis)
outer [bnw] *buiten-, uitwendig*
outfit [znw] • *kleding* • *uitrusting*
• <inf.> *gezelschap, troep, stel*
<mensen>, *ploeg* <werklui>, *bataljon*
outgoing [bnw] • *extrovert*
• *vertrekkend, aftredend*
outing [znw] *uitstapje*
outlandish [bnw] *vreemd, afgelegen*
outlast [ov ww] *langer duren dan*
outlaw I [ov ww] *vogelvrij verklaren*
II [znw] *vogelvrij verklaarde*
outlay I [ov ww] *besteden, uitgeven*
II [znw] *uitgave(n)*

outlet [znw] • *uitgang/-weg*
• *afvoerbuis* • *afzetgebied* • *afnemer*
• *verkooppunt* • ‹AE› *stopcontact*
outline I [ov ww] *schetsen, in grote
lijnen aangeven* • (~ **against**)
aftekenen tegen II [znw] *(om)trek,
schets*
outlook [znw] *uitkijk/-zicht, kijk*
outnumber [ov ww] *overtreffen in
aantal*
output [znw] • *output* ‹v. computer›
• *productie, prestatie, vermogen* ‹v.
elektriciteit› • *opbrengst, uitkomst*
• *uitvoer*
outrage I [ov ww] • *geweld aandoen,
verkrachten* • *grof beledigen* II [znw]
• *grove belediging* • *verontwaardiging*
• *gewelddaad*
outrageous [bnw] • *beledigend,
ergerlijk* • *schandelijk, verschrikkelijk*
• *extravagant, buitensporig*
outré [bnw] *onbehoorlijk, buitenissig*
outright I [bnw] *totaal* II [bijw]
• *ineens* • *helemaal* • *ronduit*
outside I [znw] • *buiten(kant), uiterlijk*
• *uiterste prijs* ∗ *at the ~ op z'n hoogst*
II [bnw] *buitenste* III [bijw] *naar/van
buiten* IV [vz] • *buiten* • ‹AE› *behalve*
outsider [znw] • *buitenstaander*
• *niet-lid* • ‹sport› *mededinger met
weinig kans om te winnen* ‹vnl. paard›
outspoken [bnw] *openhartig, ronduit*
outstanding [bnw] • *uitstekend,
voortreffelijk* • *onbeslist* • *overduidelijk*
outward(s) [bnw] *buitenwaarts,
uiterlijk, uitwendig*
oval [bnw] *ovaal*
ovary [znw] • *eierstok* • *vruchtbeginsel*
ovation [znw] *ovatie*
oven [znw] *oven, fornuis*
over I [bnw] • *al te groot/veel, enz.*
• *klaar, beëindigd* • *over, opper-*
II [bijw] • *voorbij* • *om, over* • ‹AE›
z.o.z. III [vz] • *over, boven* • *bij,
aangaande* • *over... heen*
over- [voorv] *over-, te*

overall I [znw] • *overall*
• *huishoudschort* II [bnw] *geheel,
totaal, globaal*
overboard [bijw] *overboord*
overcharge [ov ww] • *te sterk laden* ‹v.
batterij› • *overdrijven* • *overvragen, te
veel in rekening brengen*
overcoat [znw] *overjas*
overcome [ov ww] *te boven komen*
overdo [ov ww] • *overdrijven* • *te gaar
koken/worden* • *uitputten*
overflow I [on ww] *overstromen*
II [znw] • *overloop(pijp)*
• *overstroming* • *overvloed*
overhead I [bnw] *boven 't hoofd,
bovengronds* ‹geleiding› II [bijw]
boven 't hoofd
overheads [mv] *vaste bedrijfsuitgaven*
overhear [ov ww] • *toevallig horen*
• *afluisteren*
overjoyed [bnw] *opgetogen, dolblij*
overlap I [ov ww] *gedeeltelijk bedekken,
overlappen* II [on ww] *gedeeltelijk
samenvallen (met)* III [znw] *overlap*
overlook [ov ww] • *uitzien op* • *over
het hoofd zien* • *door de vingers zien*
overly [bijw] *al te, te zeer*
overnight I [bnw] *v.d. avond/nacht*
II [bijw] • *gedurende de nacht* • *in 'n
wip* • *zo maar, ineens*
overpower [ov ww]
overmannen/-weldigen
override [ov ww] • *belangrijker zijn
dan* • *tenietdoen*
overrule [ov ww] • *verwerpen*
• *overstemmen* • *overreden*
overrun [ov ww] • *overstromen* • *geheel
begroeien*
overseas [bnw + bijw] *overzee(s)*
overshoot [ov ww]
voorbijschieten/-streven
oversight [znw] *onoplettendheid,
vergissing*
overt [bnw] *publiek, open(lijk)*
overtake [ov ww] • *inhalen* ‹i.h.
verkeer› • *overvallen*

overtime [znw] *overuren/-werk*
overtone [znw] • *bijbetekenis,
ondertoon* ‹fig.› • ‹muz.› *boventoon*
overture [znw] • *(eerste) voorstel*
• *inleiding* • ‹muz.› *ouverture*
overweight [bnw] *te zwaar* ‹in
lichaamsgewicht›
overwhelm [ov ww] *overstelpen*
overwhelming [bnw] *overweldigend,
verpletterend*
overwrought [bnw] *op v.d. zenuwen*
ovum [znw] *ei(cel)*
owe [ov ww] • *schuldig/verschuldigd
zijn* • *te danken hebben*
owl [znw] *uil*
owlish [bnw] *uilachtig*
own I [ov ww] • *bezitten, (in eigendom)
hebben* • *toegeven, erkennen* • *(~ up)*
‹inf.› *opbiechten* II [bnw] *eigen*
owner [znw] *eigenaar*
ownership [znw] *eigendom(srecht)*
ox [znw] *os*
oxide [znw] *oxide*
oxidize [ov + on ww] *oxideren*
oxygen [znw] *zuurstof*
oyster [znw] *oester*
ozone [znw] • *ozon* • ‹inf.› *frisse lucht*

P

pace I [ov + on ww] • *stappen* • *ijsberen*
• *in telgang lopen* • *(~ out) afpassen,
afmeten* II [znw] • *stap, pas* • *gang,
tempo* • *telgang*
pacifier [znw] • *vredestichter* • ‹AE›
fopspeen
pacifism [znw] *pacifisme*
pacify [ov ww] *tot bedaren/rust/vrede
brengen*
pack I [ov ww] • *inpakken, verpakken*
• *omwikkelen* • *beladen* • *partijdig
samenstellen* ‹vnl. v. jury› • ‹AE›
dragen • *(~ up) (in)pakken* II [on ww]
zijn biezen pakken • *(~ up)* ‹sl.› *tot
stilstand komen* ‹v. machine›,
(moeten) stoppen, ophouden III [znw]
• *bende* • *veld drijfijs* • *bepakking*
• *stel, partij* • *pak(je)* • *last* • *zekere
hoeveelheid* ‹v. goederen› • *meute* ‹v.
jachthonden›
package I [ov ww] *'n pak maken van*
II [znw] • *emballage* • *verpakking* • *pak*
packer [znw] *emballeur*
packet [znw] • *pakje* ‹vnl. v.
sigaretten› • *pakketboot* • ‹sl.› *grote
som geld*
packing [znw] *(ver)pakking*
pad I [ov ww] • *bekleden* • *opvullen*
II [on ww] *lopen* ‹vnl. v. dier› III [znw]
• *(stoot)kussen* • *vulsel* • *kladblok,
blocnote* • *poot* ‹v. vos of haas›
paddock [znw] *omheind veld* ‹bij
paardenstoeterij of renbaan›
paddy [znw] *rijstveld*
padlock I [ov ww] *v. hangslot voorzien*
II [znw] *hangslot*
padre ‹sl.› [znw] *aalmoezenier*
pagan I [znw] *heiden* II [bnw] *heidens*
page I [ov ww] • *pagineren* • *oproepen*
II [znw] • *page* • *piccolo,
bruidsjonkertje* • *bladzijde*

pageant [znw] • *(historische)*
optocht/vertoning • *opzienbarend*
schouwspel
pageantry [znw] *praal*
pagination [znw] *paginering*
pagoda [znw] *pagode*
paid [ww] *verl.tijd* + *volt.deelw.*
→ **pay**
pail [znw] • *emmer* • ‹AE› *eetketeltje*
pain I [ov + on ww] *pijnigen* II [znw]
• *pijn, lijden* • *lastpost*
painful [bnw] • *pijnlijk* • *moeizaam*
painless [bnw] *pijnloos*
painstaking [bnw] *nauwkeurig,*
zorgvuldig
paint I [ov ww] *(be)schilderen, (z.)*
verven • *(~ over) overschilderen*
II [znw] *verf*
painter [znw] • *vanglijn* • *schilder*
painting [znw] • *schildering, schilderij*
• *schilderkunst*
pair I [ov + on ww] • *(~ off) in paren*
heengaan, koppelen • *(~ off (with))*
‹inf.› *trouwen (met)* II [znw] • *paar*
• *tweede van paar*
Pakistani I [znw] *Pakistaan, Pakistani*
II [bnw] *Pakistaans*
pal ‹sl.› I [on ww] • *(~ up (to/with))*
vrienden zijn/worden (met) II [znw]
(goeie) vriend
palatable [bnw] • *smakelijk*
• *aangenaam*
palate [znw] • *verhemelte* • *smaak*
palatial [bnw] *paleisachtig*
palaver [znw] *over-en-weergepraat*
pale I [on ww] *verbleken (naast)*
II [znw] *omsloten ruimte* III [bnw]
bleek, mat, dof, licht
palette [znw] *palet*
pall I [on ww] *vervelend worden*
II [znw] • *pallium* • *sluier* • *lijkkleed*
pallet [znw] • *strozak, stromatras*
• *pallet*
pallid [bnw] *bleek*
pally ‹inf.› [bnw] *bevriend*
palm I [ov ww] *verbergen* ‹in de hand›

II [znw] • *palm(tak)* • *handpalm*
palmistry [znw] *handlijnkunde*
palpable [bnw] *tastbaar*
palpitation [znw] *hartklopping*
palsy [znw] *verlamming*
paltry [bnw] *verachtelijk, armetierig,*
armzalig, nietig
pamper [ov ww] *te veel geven,*
verwennen
pamphlet [znw] *vlugschrift, brochure*
pan I [ov ww] ‹AE› *afkammen, vitten op*
II [on ww] • *panoramisch filmen*
• *(goud)erts wassen* III [znw]
• *duinpan, koekenpan, kruitpan*
• *ketel, schaal, toiletpot* • ‹AE› *gezicht*
panacea [znw] *panacee, wondermiddel*
pancake [znw] *pannenkoek*
pancreas [znw] *alvleesklier*
pane [znw] *(glas)ruit*
panel I [ov ww] *lambrisering*
aanbrengen II [znw] • *paneel*
• *tussenzetsel* ‹in jurk› • *schakelbord*
• *panel*
panelling [znw] *paneelwerk,*
lambrisering
pang [znw] *pijnscheut*
panic I [on ww] *in paniek raken*
II [znw] *paniek* III [bnw] *panisch*
pannier [znw] *(draag)mand*
panoply [znw] • *volle wapenrusting*
• *praal*
pant [on ww] *hijgen* • *(~ after/for)*
snakken naar
pantheism [znw] *pantheïsme*
panther [znw] *panter*
pantry [znw] *provisiekamer,*
provisiekast
pants [mv] *(onder)broek*
papacy [znw] • *pausschap* • *pausdom*
papal [bnw] *pauselijk*
paper I [ov ww] *behangen* II [znw]
• *papiergeld* • *wissels* • *examenopgave*
• *krant, blad* • *document* • *opstel*
• *scriptie* • *voordracht* • *papillot*
• *papier* III [bnw] • *op papier* • *van*
papier

papery [bnw] *papierachtig*
papyrus [znw] • *papyrus* • *papyrus(rol)*
• *papyrus(plant)*
par [znw] • *gelijkheid* • *pari*
• *gemiddelde*
parabola [znw] *parabool*
parabolic [bnw] *van/zoals een parabool*
parachute I [ov ww] *met parachute
neerlaten* II [on ww] *met parachute
afdalen* III [znw] *valscherm, parachute*
parade I [ov + on ww] • *paraderen*
• *doortrekken, laten marcheren*
• *optocht houden* • *pronken (met)*
II [znw] • *parade* • *promenade,
boulevard* • *vertoon* • *optocht*
paradigm [znw] *paradigma*
paradise [znw] *paradijs*
paradoxical [bnw] *paradoxaal,
tegenstrijdig*
paraffin [znw] *kerosine*
paragon [znw] *toonbeeld* <v.
volmaaktheid>
paragraph [znw] *alinea*
parakeet [znw] *parkiet*
parallel I [ov ww] • *evenaren*
• *evenwijdig zijn met* II [znw] *gelijke*
III [bnw] • *evenwijdig* • *analoog, gelijk*
parallelogram [znw] *parallellogram*
paralysis [znw] *verlamming*
paramilitary [bnw] *paramilitair*
paramount [bnw] *opper-, hoogst,
overwegend, opperst*
paranoia [znw] *paranoia,
vervolgingswaanzin*
parapet [znw] • *borstwering* • *muurtje,
stenen leuning*
paraphernalia [mv] *spullen,
uitrusting, rompslomp*
paraphrase I [ov ww] *in andere
woorden weergeven* II [znw] *parafrase*
parapsychology [znw]
parapsychologie
parasite [znw] • *parasiet* • *klaploper*
paratrooper [znw] *para(chutist),
paratroeper*
paratroops [mv] *valschermtroepen*

parboil [ov ww] *blancheren, even aan
de kook brengen*
parcel I [ov ww] • (~ **out**) *verdelen,
uitdelen, kavelen* • (~ **up**) *inpakken*
II [znw] • *partij* <v. goederen> • *pak(je)*
• *perceel, kaveling*
parch [ov + on ww] *opdrogen, verdorren*
parchment [znw] *perkament*
pardon I [ov ww] *vergiffenis schenken,
vergeven* II [znw] *vergiffenis,
vergeving, gratie, pardon*
pardonable [bnw] *vergeeflijk*
pare [ov ww] • *besnoeien, beknibbelen*
• *schillen* • *afknippen, afsnijden*
• (~ **away/off**) *afsnijden*
parent [znw] • *ouder* • *vader, moeder*
• *bron*
parentage [znw] *afkomst*
parental [bnw] *ouderlijk*
parenthesis [znw] • *inlassing* • *haakje*
parenthood [znw] *ouderschap*
pariah [znw] *paria, uitgestotene*
parish [znw] *parochie, kerspel,
kerkelijke gemeente*
parishioner [znw] • *parochiaan*
• *gemeentelid*
parity [znw] • *gelijkheid, overeenkomst*
• *pariteit*
park I [ov + on ww] *parkeren* II [ov ww]
deponeren III [znw] • *(artillerie)park*
• *parkeerterrein*
parking [znw] *het parkeren,
parkeergelegenheid*
parky [bnw] *kil*
parlance [znw] *wijze v. zeggen, taal*
parley I [on ww] *onderhandelen*
II [znw] *onderhandeling*
parliament [znw] *parlement*
parliamentarian [znw] *parlementariër*
parliamentary [bnw] • *parlements-*
• *parlementair*
parlour [znw] • *zitkamer* • <AE> *salon*
parody I [ov ww] *parodiëren* II [znw]
parodie
parole I [ov ww] *op erewoord vrijlaten*
II [znw] • *parool, erewoord* • <AE>

voorwaardelijke invrijheidstelling
paroxysm [znw] *hevige aanval*
parquet [znw] *parketvloer*
parricide [znw] *vadermoord(enaar)*
parrot I [ov ww] *nadoen, napraten*
II [znw] *papegaai*
parry I [ov ww] • *pareren, afweren* ‹v.
slag› • *ontwijken* ‹v. vraag› II [znw]
afweringsmanoeuvre
parse [ov ww] *taal-/redekundig
ontleden*
parsimonious [bnw] • *spaarzaam*
• *gierig*
parsimony [znw] *spaarzaamheid,
gierigheid*
parsley [znw] *peterselie*
parsnip [znw] *pastinaak*
parson [znw] *dominee*
parsonage [znw] *pastorie*
part I [ov ww] *van elkaar scheiden,
scheiding maken* ‹in haar› II [on ww]
• *z. verdelen* • *uit elkaar gaan* • ‹sl.›
betalen • (~ **from/with**) *afscheid
nemen van, scheiden van* • (~ **with**)
opgeven, v.d. hand doen, afgeven ‹vnl.
v. hitte› III [znw] • *gedeelte, deel*
• *toneelrol* • *zijde* • *partij* • (*aan*)*deel*
• ‹muz.› *stem*
partake [on ww] *deel hebben aan*
partial [bnw] • *partijdig* • *gedeeltelijk*
participant I [znw] *deelgenoot,
deelnemer* II [bnw] *deelhebbend,
deelnemend*
participate [on ww] *delen* (*in*),
deelnemen aan, deel hebben in
participle [znw] *deelwoord*
particle [znw] • *partikel* • *deeltje*
particular I [znw] *bijzonderheid*
II [bnw] • *veeleisend* • *afzonderlijk,
speciaal* • *nauwkeurig, precies*
particularize [ov ww] • *specificeren*
• *in details treden*
parting [znw] • *afscheid* • *scheiding* ‹v.
haar›
partisan, partizan [znw]
• *aanhanger, voorstander* • *guerrilla*

partition I [ov ww] (*ver*)*delen* • (~ **off**)
afscheiden II [znw] • (*ver*)*deling*
• *tussenschot*
partly [bijw] *gedeeltelijk*
partner I [ov ww] *partner zijn van*
II [znw] • *deelgenoot,* (*levens*)*gezel(lin)*
• *partner* • *vennoot, compagnon*
partnership [znw] *vennootschap,
deelgenootschap*
party [znw] • *partij* • *fuif, feestje*
• *gezelschap*
pass I [ov ww] • *gaan* (*door*) • *inhalen,
voorbij gaan* • *aangeven, doorgeven*
II [on ww] • *gaan* • *verstrijken*
• (~ **away**) *sterven* • (~ **out**)
flauwvallen III [znw] *pas*
passable [bnw] • *tamelijk, vrij
behoorlijk* • *toelaatbaar*
• *doorwaadbaar, begaanbaar*
passage [znw] • *gang, passage,
overgang, doorgang* • *recht v.
doorgang* • *overtocht* • *stoelgang* • '*t
aannemen* ‹v.e. wet› • *passage* ‹in
boek›
passenger [znw] *passagier*
passer-by [znw] *voorbijganger*
passing I [znw] • '*t voorbijgaan*
• *overlijden* II [bnw] *voorbijgaand*
passion [znw] *hartstocht, passie*
passionate [bnw] *hartstochtelijk*
Passover [znw] *joods paasfeest*
passport [znw] • *paspoort* • *toegang*
‹fig.›
past I [znw] *verleden* (*tijd*) II [bnw]
• *voorbij*(*gegaan*) • *verleden* • *vroeger*
• *gewezen* III [bijw] *voorbij* IV [vz]
• *langs, voorbij* • *over, na*
paste I [ov ww] (*be*)*plakken* II [znw]
• *deeg* ‹v. gebak› • (*amandel*)*spijs*
• (*stijfsel*)*pap, plaksel* • *simili,
namaakdiamanten*
pastel [znw] • *pastel*(*tekening*)
• *pastelkleur*
pasteurize [ov ww] *pasteuriseren*
pastime [znw] *tijdverdrijf*
pasting ‹inf.› [znw] *flink pak slaag*

pastor [znw] • *geestelijke leider*
• *zielenherder* • ‹AE› *pastoor*
pastoral I [znw] *pastorale* II [bnw]
• *herderlijk, herders-* • *landelijk*
pastry [znw] *gebak(jes), (korst)deeg*
pasture I [on ww] *(af)grazen* II [znw]
• *gras* • *weide*
pasty I [znw] *vleespastei* II [bnw]
deegachtig
pat I [ov ww] • *zachtjes slaan/kloppen*
op • *aaien* • *strelen* II [znw] • *tikje*
• *klompje, kluitje* ‹vnl. v. boter›
III [bnw + bijw] • *klaar* • *precies v. pas,*
toepasselijk
patch I [ov ww] *(op)lappen* • *(~ up)*
oplappen, bijleggen ‹v. geschil›
II [znw] • *plek* • *stukje grond* • *lap,*
pleister
patchy [bnw] • *onregelmatig* • *met*
vlekken
patent I [ov ww] • *patenteren* • *patent*
nemen op II [znw] • *patent* • *octrooi*
III [bnw] • *gepatenteerd*
• *voortreffelijk, patent* • *open, zichtbaar*
paternal [bnw] • *vaderlijk, vader-*
• *van vaderszijde*
paternalism [znw] *overdreven*
vaderlijke zorg
paternity [znw] • *vaderschap* • *bron*
‹fig.›
path [znw] *pad, weg, baan*
pathetic [bnw] • *aandoenlijk* • *zielig*
• *bedroevend*
pathological [bnw] *pathologisch,*
ziekelijk
pathologist [znw] *patholoog*
pathology [znw] *pathologie*
pathos [znw] • *pathos*
• *aandoenlijkheid*
patience [znw] • *patience* ‹kaartspel›
• *geduld, lijdzaamheid, volharding*
patient I [znw] *patiënt, zieke* II [bnw]
geduldig, lijdzaam, volhardend
patina [znw] • *schijn, waas* • *glans* ‹op
meubels› • *kopergroen*
patio [znw] *patio, binnenhof*

patriarch [znw] • *nestor* • *patriarch,*
aartsvader
patrician I [znw] *patriciër* II [bnw]
patricisch
patricide [znw] → **parricide**
patrimony [znw] *vaderlijk erfdeel,*
erfgoed
patriot I [znw] *patriot* II [bnw]
patriottisch
patriotic [bnw] *vaderlandslievend*
patriotism [znw] *patriottisme,*
vaderlandsliefde
patrol I [ov + on ww] *patrouilleren, de*
ronde doen II [znw] *patrouille, ronde*
patron [znw] • *beschermheilige*
• *beschermheer* • *klant, begunstiger*
patronage [znw] • *beschermheerschap*
• *recht v. voordracht tot ambt*
• *klandizie, steun* • *neerbuigendheid*
patronize [ov ww] • *beschermen,*
begunstigen • *neerbuigend behandelen*
patronizing [bnw] *neerbuigend*
patter I [on ww] • *trippelen, ritselen*
• *babbelen, praten* • *kletteren* II [znw]
• *(verkoop)praatje* • *getrippel, geritsel*
• *gekletter*
pattern I [ov ww] *schakeren*
• *(~ after/upon)* *vormen naar*
II [znw] *tekening, patroon* III [bnw]
model-
patty [znw] *pasteitje*
paunch [znw] • *buik* • *pens*
pauper [znw] *armlastige, minder*
bedeelde
pause I [on ww] • *even ophouden,*
pauzeren • *nadenken* II [znw] *pauze,*
onderbreking, rust
pavement [znw] *stoep, trottoir*
pavilion [znw] • *tent* • *paviljoen*
• *clubhuis*
paving [znw] *bestrating, plaveisel,*
bevloering
paw I [ov + on ww] • *aanraken* ‹met
poot› • *krabben* ‹met hoef› II [ov ww]
‹inf.› *betasten* III [znw] • *poot* ‹met
klauw› • ‹inf.› '*poot', hand*

pawn I [ov ww] *belenen, verpanden*
II [znw] • *onderpand* • *pion* ‹fig.›,
gemanipuleerd persoon • *pion* ‹in
schaakspel›
pay I [ov ww] • *(uit)betalen* • *vergelden*
• *vergoeden* • *schenken* ‹v. aandacht›
• *(~ away) uitgeven* ‹v. geld›
• *(~ away/out)* ‹scheepv.› *vieren* ‹v.
kabel› • *(~ back) betaald zetten,
terugbetalen* • *(~ into) storten* ‹v.
geld› • *(~ off) (af)betalen, afrekenen*
• *(~ out) (uit)betalen* • *(~ towards)
bijdragen voor* • *(~ up) betalen,
volstorten* ‹v. aandelen› II [on ww]
• *betalen, boeten* • *renderen* ‹v. zaak›
III [znw] *betaling, loon, soldij*
payable [bnw] • *te betalen* • *betaalbaar*
payer [znw] *betaler*
payment [znw] • *betaling* • *beloning*
pea [znw] *erwt*
peace [znw] • *vrede* • *rust*
peaceable [bnw] • *vreedzaam* • *vredig*
peaceful [bnw] *vredig*
peach [znw] • *perzik* • ‹inf.› *schat* ‹v.e.
meisje›, *snoes*
peak I [on ww] *hoogtepunt bereiken*
II [znw] • *piek, spits* • *hoogtepunt*
• *klep* ‹v. pet› III [bnw] *hoogste*
peaked [bnw] *puntig, scherp*
peaky ‹inf.› [bnw] *mager* ‹v. gezicht›,
pips
peal I [on ww] *klinken, weergalmen*
II [znw] • *gelui* ‹v. klokken›
• *(donder)slag* • *geschater*
peanut [znw] *pinda*
pear [znw] *peer*
pearl [znw] • *parel* • *juweel* ‹fig.›
pearly [bnw] • *parelachtig* • *vol parels*
peat [znw] • *veen* • *turf*
peaty [bnw] *turfachtig, veenachtig*
peccadillo [znw] *pekelzonde, kleine
zonde*
peck I [ov + on ww] • *hakken*
• *knabbelen* • *pikken* • *(~ at) pikken
naar/in, in kleine hapjes verorberen,
vitten op* II [ov ww] *oppervlakkig een*

kus geven • *(~ up) oppikken* III [znw]
• *pik* ‹met snavel› • *vluchtige kus*
pecker [znw] • ‹inf.› *moed* • ‹sl.› *penis*
peculiar [bnw] *eigenaardig*
peculiarity [znw] *eigenaardigheid*
pedagogy [znw] *pedagogie*
pedal I [ov + on ww] *fietsen* II [znw]
pedaal
pedant [znw] *muggenzifter*
pedantic [bnw] *pedant*
peddle [ov + on ww] • *venten, verkopen*
‹vnl. drugs› • *opdringen* ‹v.
denkbeelden›
pedestrian I [znw] *voetganger* II [bnw]
• *voet-* • *wandel-* • *prozaïsch, laag bij
de grond*
pedigree [znw] • *stamboom* • *afkomst*
pedlar [znw] *marskramer*
pee ‹sl.› I [on ww] *plassen* II [znw] *plasje*
peek [on ww] *gluren, kijken*
peel I [ov ww] • *(af)schillen* • *villen,
(af)stropen* II [on ww] • *vervellen* • ‹sl.›
bladderen ‹v. verf›, z. *uitkleden*
III [znw] *schil*
peeler [znw] *schilmesje*
peep I [ov ww] • z. *vertonen* • *heimelijk
'n blik werpen op* • *(~ at) gluren naar*
II [znw] • *gepiep* • *kijkje*
peer I [on ww] • *(~ at/in(to)) turen
naar* II [znw] • *weerga, gelijke*
• *edelman*
peerage [znw] • *adel(stand)* • *boek v.
edelen en hun stamboom*
peeress [znw] • *vrouw v.e. edelman*
• *vrouw met adellijke titel*
peevish [bnw] *knorrig, gemelijk*
peg I [ov ww] *met pennen/knijpers
vastmaken/steunen* • *(~ down (to))
binden (aan)* • *(~ out) afpalen,
afbakenen, wasgoed ophangen*
II [on ww] • *(~ away) ploeteren op*
• *(~ out) het hoekje omgaan,
doodgaan* III [znw] • *kapstok* • *knijper*
• *schroef* ‹v. snaarinstrument›
• *houten nagel, pen* • *haring* ‹v. tent›
• ‹inf.› *houten been*

pejorative [bnw] • *ongunstig*
• *kleinerend*
pelican [znw] *pelikaan*
pellet [znw] • *hagelkorrel* • *balletje,*
propje • *kogeltje*
pellucid [bnw] *helder, doorschijnend*
pelt I [ov ww] *beschieten* II [on ww]
• *kletteren* • *rennen* III [znw] • *vacht,*
huid • *slag(regen)*
pelvis [znw] *bekken*
pen I [ov ww] • *opsluiten*
• *(op)schrijven, neerpennen* II [znw]
• *schaapskooi, hok* • *pen*
penal [bnw] *straf(baar), straf-*
penalize [ov ww] • *strafbaar stellen*
• *benadelen*
penalty [znw] *straf, boete*
penance [znw] *boetedoening*
pence [mv] → **penny**
penchant [znw] *neiging*
pencil I [ov ww] *met potlood*
merken/(op)schrijven II [znw]
• *potlood* • *stiftje*
pendant I [znw] *(oor)hanger, pendant*
II [bnw] *(over)hangend, hangende,*
onbeslist
pending I [bnw] *hangende, onbeslist*
II [vz] • *hangende, gedurende* • *in*
afwachting v., tot
pendulous [bnw] • *hangend*
• *schommelend*
pendulum [znw] *slinger*
penetrate [ov + on ww] • *doordringen*
• *doorgronden*
penetrating [bnw] • *doordringend*
• *scherpzinnig*
penguin [znw] *pinguïn*
penicillin [znw] *penicilline*
peninsula [znw] *schiereiland*
penitence [znw] *berouw*
penitent I [znw] • *boetvaardige*
zondaar • *biechteling* • *boeteling*
II [bnw] *boetvaardig*
penitential [bnw] *boete-, boetvaardig*
penitentiary I [znw]
• *verbeteringsgesticht* • *penitentiaire*

II [bnw] *straf-, boete-*
pennant [znw] *wimpel*
penniless [bnw] *arm, zonder geld*
penny I [znw] *stuiver* II [bnw]
goedkoop, prul-
pension I [ov ww] • *(~ off) met*
pensioen laten gaan II [znw] • *pensioen*
• *jaargeld* • *pension*
pensionable [bnw]
• *pensioengerechtigd* • *recht gevend op*
pensioen
pensioner [znw] *pensioentrekker*
pensive [bnw] • *peinzend*
• *zwaarmoedig*
pentathlon [znw] *vijfkamp*
Pentecost [znw] • *joods Pinksteren*
• *pinksterzondag*
penthouse [znw] <AE> *hoogste*
verdieping van wolkenkrabber
penultimate [bnw] *voorlaatste*
penurious [bnw] *behoeftig*
penury [znw] *armoede*
peony [znw] *pioen(roos)*
people I [ov ww] *bevolken* II [znw]
• *mensen* • *men* • *volk*
pepper I [ov ww] *beschieten,*
bombarderen II [znw] *peper*
peppery [bnw] • *peperachtig, gepeperd*
• *driftig*
perambulator [znw] *kinderwagen*
perceive [ov ww] *(be)merken,*
waarnemen
perception [znw] *gewaarwording*
perceptive [bnw] *opmerkzaam*
perch I [ov ww] *gaan zitten of plaatsen*
op iets hoogs II [on ww] *neerstrijken*
III [znw] • *roest* <v. vogel> • *hoge plaats*
• *baars*
percolate [ov + on ww] • *filtreren*
• *sijpelen, dóórdringen, doordringen*
percolator [znw] *koffiezetapparaat*
percussion [znw] <muz.> *slagwerk*
perdition [znw] *verderf, verdoemenis*
peremptory [bnw] *gebiedend,*
dictatoriaal
perennial I [znw] *overblijvende plant*

II [bnw] • eeuwigdurend • <plantk.> overblijvend

perfect I [ov ww] verbeteren, perfectioneren II [znw] voltooid tegenwoordige tijd III [bnw] • volmaakt, volledig, perfect • volslagen • voortreffelijk

perfection [znw] perfectie, toppunt

perfidious [bnw] trouweloos, verraderlijk

perforate [ov ww] doorboren, perforeren

perforation [znw] • doorboring, perforatie • gaatje

performance [znw] • (toneel)voorstelling, optreden • prestatie

performer [znw] zanger, iem. die iets doet of presteert, toneelspeler

perfume I [ov ww] parfumeren II [znw] geur, parfum

perfunctory [bnw] oppervlakkig, nonchalant

perhaps [bijw] misschien

peril [znw] gevaar

perilous [bnw] hachelijk, gevaarlijk

perimeter [znw] omtrek

period I [znw] • punt <na zin> • menstruatie • periode • duur • lesuur II [bnw] behorend tot 'n bepaalde tijd/stijl

periodic [bnw] periodiek

periodical I [znw] periodiek, tijdschrift II [bnw] periodiek

peripatetic I [znw] iem. die rondtrekt II [bnw] rondtrekkend

peripheral [bnw] • perifeer • de buitenkant rakend

periphery [znw] • omtrek • oppervlak, buitenkant

periscope [znw] periscoop

perish [on ww] omkomen of vergaan

perishable [bnw] • vergankelijk • aan bederf onderhevig

perishing [bnw + bijw] <sl.> beestachtig <vnl. v. kou>

perjury [znw] meineed

perk [on ww] • (~ up) z. oprichten, opfleuren

perky [bnw] • verwaand, zelfbewust, brutaal • zwierig

perm [znw] permanent <in haar>

permanent [bnw] blijvend, duurzaam, permanent

permeable [bnw] doordringbaar

permeate [ov + on ww] doordringen

permissible [bnw] toelaatbaar, geoorloofd

permission [znw] verlof, vergunning

permissive [bnw] (al te) toegeeflijk

permit I [ov + on ww] toestaan II [znw] vergunning, verlof

pernicious [bnw] • verderfelijk • kwaadaardig

peroration [znw] • slotwoord • oratie

peroxide [znw] peroxide

perpendicular I [znw] loodlijn II [bnw] loodrecht, steil, recht(op)

perpetrate [ov ww] • bedrijven, begaan • <inf.> z. bezondigen aan

perpetrator [znw] dader

perpetual [bnw] • eeuwig • <inf.> geregeld, herhaaldelijk

perpetuate [ov ww] • bestendigen • vereeuwigen

perpetuity [znw] eeuwigheid

perplex [ov ww] verwarren, verlegen maken

perplexity [znw] verwarring

perquisite [znw] fooi, neveninkomst(en)

persecute [ov ww] • vervolgen • lastigvallen

persecution [znw] vervolging

persevere [on ww] volharden, volhouden

Persian I [znw] • 't Perzisch • Pers II [bnw] Perzisch

persist [on ww] • blijven volhouden • voortduren • (~ in) doorgaan met

persistent [bnw] • hardnekkig • blijvend

person [znw] • persoon • iemand

personable [bnw] • knap ‹v. uiterlijk›
• innemend
personage [znw] • personage • persoon
personal I [znw] II [bnw] persoonlijk
personality [znw] persoonlijkheid
personalize [ov ww] verpersoonlijken
personally [bijw] wat mij betreft,
persoonlijk
personify [ov ww] verpersoonlijken
personnel [znw] • personeel
• manschappen
perspective [znw] • perspectief
• vooruitzicht
perspiration [znw] zweet, transpiratie
persuade [ov ww] overreden, overtuigen
persuasion [znw] • overreding(skracht)
• geloof • overtuiging • ‹scherts› ras,
soort, geslacht
persuasive [bnw] overredend,
overredings-
pert [bnw] vrijpostig, brutaal
pertinacious [bnw] hardnekkig,
volhardend
pertinent [bnw] ter zake, adrem,
toepasselijk
perusal [znw] 't doorlezen
peruse [ov ww] onderzoeken,
aandachtig bekijken, even doorlezen
Peruvian I [znw] Peruviaan II [bnw]
Peruviaans
pervade [ov ww] doordringen
perverse [bnw] • pervers, verdorven,
verkeerd • onhandelbaar
perversion [znw] • verdraaiing ‹vnl. v.
woorden› • perversie
pervert I [ov ww] • verdraaien ‹vnl. v.
woorden› • pervers maken II [znw]
pervers iem.
pessary [znw] pessarium
pessimism [znw] pessimisme
pest [znw] • plaag • lastig mens
• schadelijk dier • pest
pester [ov ww] plagen • (~ for) lastig
vallen om
pesticide [znw] pesticide,
verdelgingsmiddel

pestilence [znw] dodelijke epidemie
pet I [ov ww] liefkozen, vertroetelen
II [znw] • lieveling(sdier) • boze bui
III [bnw] lievelings-
petal [znw] bloemblad
petite [bnw] klein en tenger
petition I [ov + on ww] een verzoek
richten tot • (~ for) smeken om
II [znw] smeekschrift, adres,
verzoek(schrift)
petitioner [znw] verzoeker, adressant,
eiser
petrify I [ov ww] • doen verstenen
• versteend doen staan II [on ww]
verstenen
petrochemical I [znw] petrochemische
stof II [bnw] petrochemisch
petrol [znw] benzine
petticoat [znw] (onder)rok
pettifogging [bnw] kleinzielig
pettish [bnw] • humeurig • lichtgeraakt
petty [bnw] • onbeduidend, nietig
• kleinzielig • klein
pew [znw] • kerkbank • ‹inf.› zitplaats
pewter [znw] tinlegering
phalanx [znw] • slagorde • dicht
aaneengesloten menigte
• teen-/vingerkootje
phallic [bnw] fallisch
phallus [znw] fallus, penis
phantasmagoria [znw] schimmenspel
phantom I [znw] spook,
geestverschijning II [bnw] • schijnbaar
• onbekend • geheim • spook-
pharmaceutical [bnw] farmaceutisch
pharmacist [znw] farmaceut,
apotheker
pharmacology [znw] farmacologie
pharmacy [znw] apotheek, farmacie
phase I [ov ww] • (~ in) gelijdelijk
invoeren II [znw] • schijngestalte ‹v.d.
maan› • stadium, fase
pheasant [znw] fazant
phenomenal [bnw] enorm,
buitengewoon
phenomenon [znw] • verschijnsel

• *fenomeen* • *wonderbaarlijk iem./iets*
phew [tw] *foei!, hè!*
philanderer [znw] *flirter*
philatelist [znw] *filatelist*
philately [znw] *filatelie*
philology [znw] *filologie*
philosopher [znw] *wijsgeer*
philosophize [on ww] *filosoferen*
philosophy [znw] • *wijsbegeerte*
• *levensbeschouwing*
phobia [znw] *fobie*
phoenix [znw] *feniks*
phone [znw] ‹inf.› *telefoon*
phonograph [znw] • *fonograaf* • ‹AE›
grammofoon
phonology [znw] *klankleer*
phosphate [znw] *fosfaat*
phosphorescent [bnw] *fosforescerend*
phosphorus [znw] *fosforus*
photo [znw] *foto*
photogenic [bnw] *fotogeniek*
photograph I [ov + on ww]
fotograferen II [znw] *foto, portret*
photographer [znw] *fotograaf*
photographic [bnw] • *fotografisch*
• *fotografie-*
phrase I [ov ww] *onder woorden*
brengen II [znw] • *uitdrukking,*
gezegde • *bewoording, woorden* • *frase*
phrasing [znw] • *bewoording,*
uitdrukking • ‹muz.› *frasering*
phut [bijw] * *go phut kapotgaan; niet*
meer functioneren
physical I [znw] ‹AE› *lichamelijk*
onderzoek II [bnw] • *natuurkundig*
• *materieel, natuur-* • *lichamelijk*
physician [znw] *geneesheer, dokter*
physicist [znw] *natuurkundige*
physiognomy [znw] • *gelaat,*
voorkomen • *aanblik v. iets*
physique [znw] *lichaamsbouw, gestel*
piano I [znw] *piano* II [bnw + bijw]
‹muz.› *piano*
picaresque [bnw] *schurken-,*
schurkachtig
pick I [ov + on ww] • *plukken*

• (op)pikken • (uit)kiezen • *bekritiseren*
• (~ at/on) ‹AE› *vitten/afgeven op*
• (~ on) *uitkiezen* • (~ out) *uitkiezen*
• (~ up) *ontvangen/krijgen* ‹v.
inlichtingen›, *oprapen, opnemen,*
(aan)leren, *opknappen, beter worden,*
terugvinden ‹v. spoor›, *aanwakkeren*
‹v. wind›, *aanslaan* ‹v. motor›
II [ov ww] • *uiteenrafelen, pluizen*
• *peuteren* • (~ off) *afplukken,*
uitpikken, de een na de ander
neerschieten III [znw] • *houweel*
• *keuze* • *'t beste* • *pluk*
picker [znw] *plukker*
picket I [ov ww] *posten* ‹v. stakers›
II [znw] • *paal, staak* • *post* ‹v. stakers›
pickle I [ov ww] • *pekelen* • *inmaken*
II [znw] • *pekel* • *azijn*
picnic I [on ww] *picknicken* II [znw]
picknick
picnicker [znw] *picknicker*
pictorial [bnw] • *beeld-* • *geïllustreerd*
picture I [ov ww] *afbeelden, schilderen*
II [znw] *portret, beeld, voorstelling,*
plaat, toonbeeld, schilderij
picturesque [bnw] • *schilderachtig*
• *beeldend, levendig*
piddle I [on ww] ‹inf.› *een plasje doen*
II [znw] ‹inf.› *plasje*
piddling ‹inf.› [bnw] *onbenullig*
pidgin I [znw] *pidgin(taal)* II [bnw]
pidgin-
pie [znw] • *pastei(tje)* • *taart, gebak*
piebald [bnw] *bont, zwart-wit gevlekt*
‹v. paard›
piece I [ov ww] • (~ together)
uitvogelen, in elkaar zetten (van
stukjes) II [znw] • *stuk(je)*
• *schaakstuk, damschijf* • *muziekstuk*
pier [znw] • *steiger* • *havenhoofd, pier*
pierce [ov + on ww] *doordringen,*
doorboren
piercing [bnw] *doordringend*
piety [znw] *piëteit, vroomheid*
piffle ‹inf.› [znw] *onzin*
pig I [wkd ww] *schrokken, veel eten*

II [znw] • *varken(s*vlees) • (wild) zwijn
• *lammeling* • *schrokop* • *smeerlap*
pigeon [znw] *duif*
piglet [znw] *big*
pigment [znw] *kleurstof, verfstof*
pike [znw] • *piek, spies* • *snoek*
pilchard [znw] *soort kleine haring*
pile **I** [ov ww] *opstapelen* • (~ **up**)
opstapelen, doen toenemen **II** [on ww]
• (~ **up**) *zich opstapelen, toenemen*
III [znw] • *hoop, stapel* • *pool, nop* ‹op
stof› • *aambei* • *(hei)paal* • ‹inf.›
fortuin, geld
pilfer [ov ww] *gappen*
pill [znw] *pil*
pillage **I** [ov ww] *plunderen, roven*
II [znw] *plundering*
pillar [znw] *(steun)pilaar, zuil*
pillow **I** [ov ww] *op een kussen (laten)
rusten* **II** [znw] *hoofdkussen*
pilot **I** [ov ww] *besturen, loodsen*
II [znw] • *leidsman, gids* • *piloot*
• *controlelampje* • *loods* **III** [bnw] *test-*
pimp [znw] *souteneur*
pimple [znw] *puistje*
pimpled, pimply [bnw] *puistig*
pin **I** [ov ww] • *(op)prikken*
• *vastspelden* • (~ **up**) *opprikken* ‹v.
insecten›, *opspelden* **II** [znw] • *speld*
• *pen*
pinch **I** [ov ww] • *knijpen* • *bekrimpen*
• ‹sl.› *jatten* **II** [on ww] • *gierig zijn*
• *(te) strak zitten* **III** [znw] • *kneep*
• *kritieke toestand* • *heel klein beetje,
snuifje*
pine **I** [on ww] • (~ **after/for**)
smachten naar • (~ **away**) *wegkwijnen*
II [znw] *grenenhout, vurenhout*
pineapple [znw] *ananas*
pinion [ov ww] *vastbinden* ‹v.d.
armen›
pink **I** [on ww] • *roze worden* • *kloppen*
‹v. motor› **II** [znw] • *anjelier*
• *perfectie, puikje* **III** [bnw] • *roze*
• ‹pol.› *met 'rood' sympathiserend*
pinkish [bnw] *rozeachtig*

pinnacle [znw] • *torentje* • *top*
• *hoogtepunt*
pint [znw] • *pint* ‹6 dl› • *glas bier*
pioneer **I** [ov ww] • *de weg bereiden*
• *leiden* **II** [znw] *pionier, baanbreker*
pip **I** [ov ww] *verslaan* **II** [znw] • *pit*
• *pip*
pipe **I** [ov ww] *door buizen laten lopen*
II [on ww] *met lage stem spreken*
• (~ **down**) ‹sl.› *rustig worden*
III [znw] • *pijp* • *buis*
piper [znw] *doedelzakspeler, fluitspeler*
pipette [znw] *pipet*
piping **I** [znw] • *pijpen, buizen*
• *biesversiering* **II** [bnw + bijw]
• *sissend, kokend* • *fluitend*
piquant [bnw] *pikant, prikkelend*
pique **I** [ov ww] *kwetsen* **II** [znw] *wrok*
piracy [znw] • *zeeroverij* • *plagiaat*
pirate **I** [ov ww] *ongeoorloofd boeken
e.d. nadrukken* **II** [znw] • *zeerover*
• *plagiaris*
piss ‹sl.› **I** [ov + on ww] *pissen* • (~ **off**)
wegwezen **II** [znw] *pis*
pissed [bnw] *dronken*
pistol [znw] *pistool*
piston [znw] *zuiger*
pit **I** [ov ww] • (~ **against**) *stellen
tegenover, opzetten tegen* **II** [znw]
• *kuil, groeve, schacht* • *putje, kuiltje*
• *diepte* • *pit* ‹tijdens autorace›
• *parterre* ‹in schouwburg›
pitch **I** [ov ww] • *gooien, werpen*
• *opslaan* ‹v. tent› **II** [on ww]
• *voorovervallen, z. storten* • *stampen*
‹v. schip› • (~ **in**) ‹inf.› *een handje
helpen* • (~ **into**) ‹inf.› *te lijf gaan*
III [znw] • *toonhoogte* • *pek* • *worp*
• *standplaats* • ‹sport› *veld*
pitcher [znw] • *kan, kruik* • *werper* ‹bij
honkbal›
pitfall [znw] • *valkuil* • *valstrik* ‹fig.›
pith [znw] *essentie, kern*
pithy [bnw] *pittig, krachtig*
pitiable [bnw] *meelijwekkend*
pitiful [bnw] • *medelijdend* • *armzalig*

• *verachtelijk*
pitiless [bnw] *meedogenloos*
pity I [ov ww] *medelijden hebben met,*
beklagen II [znw] *medelijden*
pitying [bnw] *vol medelijden,*
medelijdend
pivot I [on ww] *draaien om spil* II [znw]
spil <ook fig.>
pivotal [bnw] *hoofd-, centraal*
pixie [znw] *fee*
placard [znw] ≈ *spandoek*
placate [ov ww] *tevredenstellen,*
verzoenen
place I [ov ww] • *plaatsen* • *herinneren,*
thuisbrengen <fig.> II [znw] • *plaats,*
woonplaats • *zitplaats* • *huis, gebouw,*
buitengoed • *pleintje, hofje* • *plek*
• *ruimte* • *betrekking, positie*
placid [bnw] *vredig, rustig, kalm*
plagiarism [znw] *plagiaat*
plagiarist [znw] *plagiaris*
plagiarize [ov ww] *plagiaat plegen*
plague I [ov ww] • *bezoeken* <fig.>
• <inf.> *pesten, treiteren* II [znw] • *pest*
• *plaag* • *vervelend/lastig iem./iets*
plaice [znw] *schol*
plaid [znw] • *(geruite) reisdeken*
• *Schotse omslagdoek* • *(geruite) wollen*
stof • *plaid*
plain I [znw] *vlakte* II [bnw] • *duidelijk*
• *eenvoudig* • *onversierd* • *openhartig*
• *alledaags, gewoon* • *lelijk* <v. meisje>
• *vlak, glad* <v. ring> III [bijw] *gewoon*
plainly [bijw] *ronduit, zonder meer*
plaintive [bnw] *klagend*
plait I [ov ww] *vlechten* II [znw] *vlecht*
plan I [ov ww] • *een plan maken*
• *regelen* II [on ww] • (~ **on**) *rekenen*
op III [znw] • *plan* • *schema, ontwerp*
• *schets, tekening* • *plattegrond*
plane I [ov ww] *schaven* II [znw]
• *plataan* • *schaaf* • *vlak* • *niveau, peil,*
plan • <inf.> *vliegtuig*
planet [znw] *planeet*
plank [znw] • *programmapunt* • *plank*
planking [znw] • *bevloering* • *planken*

planner [znw] *ontwerper*
planning [znw] *planning, regeling,*
opzet, 't ontwerpen
plant I [ov ww] • *planten* • *plaatsen,*
posteren • *toebrengen* <v. slag> • <sl.>
verbergen • (~ **out**) *vanuit pot in de*
open grond zetten, uitpoten II [znw]
• *plant* • *installatie, materieel* • <AE>
fabriek
plantain [znw] *weegbree*
plantation [znw] *plantage*
planter [znw] • *planter*
• *plantage-eigenaar*
plaque [znw] • *(gedenk)plaat*
• *tandplak*
plastic I [znw] *plastic* II [bnw] • *van*
plastic • *kneedbaar*
plate I [ov ww] *pantseren* II [znw]
• *naamplaat, pantserplaat,*
fotografische plaat • *nummerbord*
• *gravure* • *bord* • *tafelzilver, metalen*
vaatwerk • *collecteschaal*
plateau [znw] • *plateau* • *stilstand* <in
groei>
plateful [znw] *bordvol*
platform [znw] • *podium,*
spreekgestoelte • *verhoging* • *perron*
• *balkon* <v. tram> • <AE> *program v.*
politieke partij
plating [znw] • *verguldsel* • *pantsering*
platinum [znw] *platina*
platitude [znw] *gemeenplaats*
platoon [znw] *peloton*
platter [znw] • *plat bord of schaal*
• *plateau*
plausible [bnw] *aannemelijk,*
geloofwaardig
play I [ov ww] • *spelen, bespelen*
• *uithalen* <v. grap> • *spelen, uitspelen*
<v. kaart> • (~ **back**) *terugspelen van*
geluidsband • (~ **down**)
bagatelliseren, kleineren • (~ **out**)
uitspelen II [on ww] *spelen*
• (~ **(up)on**) *bespelen, beïnvloeden,*
misbruik maken van • (~ **up**) *beginnen*
te haperen, last bezorgen • (~ **up to**)

vleien, helpen, steunen III [znw] • *spel*
• *toneelstuk* • *speling,*
bewegingsvrijheid
player [znw] *(beroeps)speler*
playful [bnw] *schertsend, speels*
plaza [znw] *plein*
plea [znw] • *pleidooi, betoog*
• *verontschuldiging*
plead I [ov ww] • *bepleiten, verdedigen*
• *als verontschuldiging aanvoeren*
II [on ww] *pleiten, z. verdedigen*
pleading [bnw] *smekend*
pleasant [bnw] *aangenaam, prettig*
please I [ov + on ww] • *bevallen,*
behagen • *believen* II [bijw] *alstublieft*
pleat I [ov ww] *plooien* II [znw] *plooi*
plebeian I [znw] *plebejer* II [bnw]
plebejisch
pledge I [ov ww] *plechtig beloven*
II [znw] *belofte, gelofte*
plenary [bnw] • *geheel* • *volledig,*
voltallig
plenty I [znw] *overvloed* II [bnw] ‹AE›
overvloedig III [bijw] ‹inf.› *ruimschoots*
pleurisy [znw] *pleuris*
pliable [bnw] *plooibaar, volgzaam*
pliers [mv] *buigtang*
plight [znw] • *conditie, (hopeloze)*
toestand • *(onaangename) situatie*
plinth [znw] *plint*
plod I [on ww] *sjokken* • (~ **along/on**)
voortsukkelen II [znw] *gezwoeg*
plodder [znw] *zwoeger, ploeteraar*
plonk I [ov ww] *met 'n smak neergooien*
II [znw] • *plof, smak* • *goedkope wijn*
plop I [ov + on ww] *neerploffen* II [znw]
plons, plof
plot I [ov ww] • *intrigeren, plannen*
smeden/beramen • *in kaart brengen*
II [znw] • *stukje grond* • *plot, intrige*
• *samenzwering*
plotter [znw] *samenzweerder*
plough I [ov ww] *(door)ploegen*
• (~ **in**) *onderploegen* • (~ **up**)
omwoelen II [znw] *ploeg*
plover [znw] *pluvier*

plow → **plough**
ploy ‹inf.› [znw] *tactische zet*
pluck I [ov ww] *plukken* ‹ook v.
gevogelte›, *trekken (aan)* II [znw]
moed, durf
plucky [bnw] *moedig*
plug I [ov ww] • *dichtstoppen, vullen* ‹v.
tand› • *ophemelen* • ‹sl.› *neerschieten*
• (~ **in**) *contact maken, de stekker*
insteken II [on ww] • (~ **away**)
doorploeteren, doorzwoegen III [znw]
• *stop, plug, stekker, vulling* • *propje* ‹v.
tabak› • *bougie*
plum I [znw] *pruim* II [bnw] *paars,*
dieprood
plumage [znw] *gevederte*
plumb I [ov ww] *peilen* II [bnw]
• *volkomen, volslagen* • *precies*
plumber [znw] *loodgieter*
plumbing [znw] *loodgieterswerk,*
sanitair
plume [znw] *pluim, vederbos*
plummy [bnw] • *bekakt* • *dieprood*
plump I [ov ww] *opschudden* • (~ **for**)
als één man stemmen op, z. verklaren
voor II [on ww] *neerploffen*
• (~ **down**) *neerploffen* III [znw] *plof*
IV [bnw] *mollig, vol, vlezig, dik*
plunder I [ov ww] *plunderen, (be)roven*
II [znw] • *plundering* • *buit, roof*
plunge I [ov ww] • *onderdompelen*
• *storten* II [on ww] • *kelderen* ‹v.
prijzen› • (z.) *storten* III [znw] • *duik*
• *kritiek ogenblik*
plunger [znw] *ontstopper*
plunk I [ov + on ww] *neerploffen*
II [znw] *dof geluid*
plural [bnw] *meervoudig, meervoud(s)-*
pluralism [znw] *pluralisme*
plurality [znw] • *meervoudigheid*
• *meerderheid v. stemmen*
plus I [znw] • *plusteken* • *voordeel*
II [bnw] • *extra* • ‹wisk.› *positief*
III [vz] *plus*
plush I [znw] *pluche* II [bnw] *piekfijn*
plushy [bnw] ‹inf.› *chic, luxueus*

plutocracy [znw] *plutocratie*
ply I [ov + on ww] • *(krachtig) hanteren*
‹v. wapen› • *lastig vallen met,*
overstelpen met II [on ww] *pendelen* ‹v.
boot› III [znw] • *laag* • *multiplex*
pneumatic [bnw] • *pneumatisch,*
lucht(druk)- • *geestelijk*
poach [ov ww] • *pocheren* • *stropen* • *op*
oneerlijke manier verkrijgen
poacher [znw] *stroper*
pock [znw] *pok*
pocket I [ov ww] • *in de zak steken*
• *potten* ‹bij poolbiljart› II [znw] • *zak*
• *pocketboek* • ‹mil.› *geïsoleerd gebied*
III [bnw] *in zakformaat, miniatuur*
pocketful [znw] *heel veel*
pod [znw] *dop, peul*
podgy [bnw] *dik, rond*
poem [znw] *gedicht*
poetry [znw] *dichtkunst, poëzie*
poignancy [znw] • *scherpheid*
• *pijnlijkheid*
poignant [bnw] *scherp, pijnlijk,*
schrijnend
point I [ov ww] *richten* • (~ **at**) *richten*
op • (~ **out**) *wijzen op* • (~ **up**)
benadrukken II [on ww] *gericht zijn*
• (~ **at**) *wijzen op* • (~ **to**) *wijzen op,*
aangeven III [znw] • *het voornaamste,*
kern • *zin, nut* • *punt, decimaalteken,*
stip • *(kompas)streek* • *spits, naald*
• *(doel)punt*
pointed [bnw] • *puntig* • *nadrukkelijk*
pointer [znw] • *wijzer* • *aanwijsstok*
• *staande hond* • ‹inf.› *aanwijzing,*
wenk
pointless [bnw] • *doelloos* • *zinloos,*
nodeloos
poise [znw] • *zelfbeheersing* • *houding*
• *evenwicht*
poison I [ov ww] • *vergiftigen*
• *verpesten, bederven* II [znw] *vergif*
poisonous [bnw] • *vergiftig*
• *verderfelijk*
poke I [ov ww] • *oppoken* • *stoten,*
duwen II [znw] *stoot, duw, por*

poker [znw] • *pook* • *poker*
poky [bnw] *klein en lelijk* ‹v.
onderkomen›
polar [bnw] *polair, pool-*
polarity [znw] *polariteit*
polarize [ov + on ww] *polariseren*
pole [znw] • *paal, stok, staak, mast*
• *pool*
polemic [znw] *polemiek*
police I [ov ww] • *onder politietoezicht*
stellen • *toezicht houden op* II [znw]
politie
policy [znw] • *(staats)beleid* • *polis*
polish I [ov ww] *polijsten, poetsen*
• (~ **off**) ‹inf.› *afmaken, verorberen*
• (~ **up**) *verfraaien, oppoetsen* II [znw]
• *glans, politoer, poets* • *elegantie*
polite [bnw] • *beleefd* • *beschaafd*
politic [bnw] *politiek, handig*
political [bnw] *staatkundig, politiek*
politician [znw] *politicus*
polity [znw] • *staatsinrichting* • *staat*
poll I [ov ww] • *stemmen behalen*
• *ondervragen* II [znw] *opiniepeiling*
pollen [znw] *stuifmeel*
pollinate [ov ww] *bestuiven*
polls [mv] *verkiezingen*
pollute [ov ww] *verontreinigen* ‹vnl. v.
milieu›
pollution [znw] *verontreiniging,*
vervuiling
polygamy [znw] *polygamie*
polyglot [znw] *polyglot, iem. die veel*
talen beheerst
polytechnic [znw] ≈ *hoger*
beroepsonderwijs
polythene [znw] *polytheen,*
polyethyleen
pom, pommy ‹pej.› [znw] *Engelsman*
pomegranate [znw] *granaatappel-*
(boom)
pomp [znw] *pracht, luister*
pomposity [znw] *gewichtigheid*
pompous [bnw] • *hoogdravend*
• *gewichtig*
ponce [znw] • *pooier* • ‹sl.› *verwijfd type*

pond [znw] *vijver*
ponder I [ov ww] *overpeinzen*
II [on ww] • *(~ on) peinzen over*
ponderous [bnw] • *zwaar, log* • *saai, vervelend* <v. stijl> • *zwaarwichtig*
pong I [on ww] *stinken* II [znw] *stank*
pontifical [bnw] *pontificaal, pauselijk*
pontificate I [on ww] *gewichtig doen, orakelen* II [znw] *pontificaat*
pontoon I [ov ww] *in pontons oversteken* II [znw] • *ponton* • *caisson* • *eenentwintigen*
poodle [znw] *poedel*
pooh [tw] *bah!*
pool I [ov ww] • *samenbundelen* <fig.> • *verenigen* • *poolen* II [znw] • *poel, plas* • *zwembad* • *reservoir* • *pot* <bij spel> • *gemeenschappelijk fonds*
poop [znw] • *achtersteven* • *achterdek*
poor I [znw] *de armen* II [bnw] *belabberd, arm, schraal, armetierig*
pop I [ov ww] • *laten knallen* • *laten verschijnen* • *even neerzetten/-leggen* • <AE> *poffen* <v. maïs> • *(~ on) haastig aantrekken, aanschieten* <v. kleren> II [on ww] • *knallen* • *snel of plotseling gaan of komen* • *glippen* • *wippen* • *(~ down) even naar beneden gaan* • *(~ in (on)) even binnenlopen (bij)* • *(~ off) wegglippen, de pijp uit gaan* • *(~ over/round) even aanwippen, even binnenlopen* • *(~ up) weer boven water komen, opduiken* III [znw] • *knal, plof, klap* • *gemberbier* • *popmuziek* • <AE inf.> *papa*
popish [bnw] *paaps*
poplar [znw] *populier*
poppet <inf.> [znw] *popje, lieverd*
poppy [znw] *papaver, klaproos*
populace [znw] *gewone volk*
popular [bnw] *populair, volks-*
popularize [ov ww] *populariseren*
population [znw] *bevolking*
populous [bnw] *dichtbevolkt, volkrijk*
porcelain I [znw] *porselein* II [bnw] *porseleinen*

porch [znw] • *portiek* • <AE> *veranda*
porcupine [znw] *stekelvarken*
pore I [on ww] • *(~ over) z. verdiepen in* <vnl. boek> II [znw] *porie*
pork [znw] *varkensvlees*
porn(o) [znw] *porno*
pornography [znw] *pornografie*
porous [bnw] *poreus*
porridge [znw] *pap*
port [znw] • *bakboord* • *port* • *haven(plaats)*
portable [bnw] *draagbaar*
portal [znw] *ingang, poort*
portend [ov ww] *voorspellen*
portent [znw] *voorteken*
portentous [bnw] • *onheilspellend* • *plechtig* • *veelbetekenend*
porter [znw] • *portier* • *kruier, drager, besteller*
portico [znw] *zuilengang, portiek*
portion I [ov ww] • *(~ out) uitdelen, verdelen* II [znw] • *lot* • *(aan)deel, portie*
portly [bnw] *gezet* <v. persoon>
portrait [znw] • *portret* • *beeld* • *levendige beschrijving*
portray [ov ww] *portretteren*
pose I [ov ww] • *plaatsen, opstellen* • *stellen* <v. vraag of stelling> II [on ww] • *z. aanstellen, 'n houding aannemen* • *z. uitgeven voor* • *poseren* III [znw] *pose, houding, aanstellerij*
poser [znw] • *moeilijke vraag, moeilijk probleem* • *poseur*
posh <sl.> [bnw] *chic*
position I [ov ww] *plaatsen* II [znw] • *stelling, bewering* • *houding, plaats(ing)* • *stand, rang* • *toestand* • *post, betrekking*
positive [bnw] • *positief* • <inf.> *echt, volslagen*
posse [znw] • *groep gewapende mannen* • *troep*
possess [ov ww] *hebben, beheersen, bezitten*
possession [znw] *bezit, bezitting*

possessive I [znw] • tweede naamval • bezittelijk voornaamwoord II [bnw] • bezit-, bezittelijk • aanmatigend
possessor [znw] bezitter
possibility [znw] mogelijkheid
possible I [znw] mogelijkheid II [bnw] mogelijk
possibly [bijw] mogelijkerwijs
post I [ov ww] • (aan)plakken, bekend maken • op de post doen • posten II [znw] • post(kantoor) • post, (stand)plaats • betrekking, post • post, staak, paal III [voorv] na, post-
postage [znw] porto
postal [bnw] post-
poster [znw] affiche, aanplakbiljet
posterior I [znw] zitvlak II [bnw] • later • volgend op
posterity [znw] nakomelingschap, nageslacht
posthumous [bnw] na de dood, postuum
postpone [ov ww] uitstellen
posture I [on ww] poseren II [znw] houding
pot I [ov ww] • potten <v. plant> • stoppen <bij biljart> • neerschieten II [on ww] • (~ at) schieten op III [znw] • kan, beker, pot • <sl.> cannabis, hasj, marihuana
potassium [znw] kalium
potato [znw] aardappel
potence, potency [znw] • macht, invloed • potentie • kracht
potent [bnw] • potent • machtig • sterk <v. medicijn>
potentate [znw] vorst
potential I [znw] • potentieel • mogelijkheid II [bnw] eventueel, latent, potentieel, mogelijk
potentiality [znw] mogelijkheid
potion [znw] drankje <v. medicijn of vergif>
potted [bnw] • ingemaakt • verkort
potter I [on ww] • (~ about) rondscharrelen II [znw] pottenbakker

pottery [znw] • aardewerk • pottenbakkerij
potty I [znw] po II [bnw] gek
pouch [znw] • zak • wangzak • krop, buikje • buidel <v. buideldier> • wal <onder ogen>
poultry [znw] pluimvee
pounce I [on ww] • (~ on) zich werpen op II [znw] plotselinge beweging/sprong
pound I [ov ww] fijnstampen, beuken II [on ww] bonzen <v. hart> • (~ away) at/on) losbeuken op • (~ along) voortsjokken III [znw] • bons, slag, klap • pond < 454 gram of 373 gram> • pond sterling • omsloten ruimte <om vee, goederen te bewaren>
pour [ov + on ww] • gieten, schenken, storten • stortregenen • (~ forth/out) uitstromen, uitstorten <v. hart> • (~ in) binnenstromen
pout I [ov + on ww] pruilen II [znw] gepruil
poverty [znw] • schraalheid • armoede
powder I [ov ww] • poederen • besprenkelen • tot poeder maken II [znw] poeder
power I [ov ww] drijfkracht verschaffen <aan motor> II [znw] • macht • kracht • volmacht • gezag • invloed • mogendheid • vermogen • energie • stroom • net(spanning)
powerful [bnw] • krachtig, machtig, invloedrijk • indrukwekkend
pox [znw] • pokken • <vulg.> syfilis
practicable [bnw] • uitvoerbaar, doenlijk • begaanbaar • doorwaadbaar • geschikt (voor)
practical [bnw] praktisch, werkelijk
practicality [znw] praktische zaak
practice [znw] • praktijk • gewoonte • toepassing • (uit)oefening
practise I [ov ww] • studeren <op muziekinstrument> • uitoefenen <v. beroep> • (~ in) zich oefenen op II [on ww] • (~ (up)on) misbruik

maken
pragmatic [bnw] *pragmatisch,
feitelijk, zakelijk*
pragmatism [znw] *zakelijkheid,
praktische zin*
praise I [ov ww] *prijzen, loven* II [znw]
lof(spraak)
praiseworthy [bnw] *lofwaardig*
pram [znw] *kinderwagen*
prance [on ww] • *steigeren* • *trots
stappen* • z. *arrogant gedragen*
prank [znw] *(dolle) streek, poets*
prattle I [ov + on ww] *babbelen*
II [znw] *gebabbel*
prawn [znw] *steurgarnaal*
pray [ov + on ww] • (~ **for**) *bidden om,
smeken om*
prayer [znw] • *gebed* • *verzoek*
preach [ov + on ww] *preken* • (~ **at**) *een
preek houden tegen*
preacher [znw] *prediker, predikant*
preamble [znw] *inleiding*
precarious [bnw] *precair, wisselvallig,
onzeker*
precaution [znw] *voorzorgsmaatregel*
precautionary [bnw] *voorzorgs-*
precede [ov ww] *(laten) voorafgaan,
voorgaan*
precedence [znw] *prioriteit, (recht v.)
voorrang*
precedent I [znw] • *precedent* • *traditie*
II [bnw] *voorafgaand*
precept [znw] • *voorschrift, bevel*
• *lering*
precinct [znw] • *ingesloten ruimte
<vooral om kerk>* • *gebied* • *autovrij
gebied* • <AE> *politiedistrict, kiesdistrict*
precious I [bnw] • *kostbaar* • *edel <v.
steen of metaal>* • *dierbaar*
• *gekunsteld* • <inf.> *geweldig* • <iron.>
mooi • <inf.> *totaal* II [bijw]
• *verduiveld* • <inf.> *buitengewoon*
precipice [znw] • *steile rotswand*
• *afgrond <fig.>*
precipitate I [ov ww] • *aanzetten,
(ver)haasten* • <chem.> *neerslaan*

II [znw] <chem.> *neerslag* III [bnw]
• *onbezonnen* • *overhaast*
precipitation [znw] • *onbezonnenheid*
• *neerslag*
precipitous [bnw] *steil*
précis [znw] *beknopte samenvatting*
precise [bijw] • *juist <v. tijdstip>,
nauwkeurig* • *(al te) precies*
precision [znw] *nauwkeurigheid*
preclude [ov ww] • *uitsluiten*
• *beletten, voorkómen, verhinderen*
precocious [bnw] *vroegrijp, voorlijk*
preconceived [bnw] *vooraf gevormd*
preconception [znw] *vooroordeel,
vooropgezette mening*
precursor [znw] *voorloper*
predator [znw] • *roofdier* • *plunderaar*
predecessor [znw] • *voorganger*
• *voorvader*
predestination [znw] • *bestemming*
• *voorbeschikking*
predicament [znw] *netelige of
moeilijke positie of kwestie*
predicate I [ov ww] *beweren* II [znw]
<taalk.> *gezegde*
predict [ov ww] *voorspellen*
predictable [bnw] *voorspelbaar*
prediction [znw] *voorspelling*
predilection [znw] *voorliefde, voorkeur*
predispose [ov ww] • *aanleg hebben
<vnl. voor ziekte>* • *neigen tot*
predisposed [bnw] *vatbaar (voor)*
predisposition [znw] *aanleg, neiging*
predominance [znw] *heerschappij,
overheersing, overhand*
predominant [bnw] *overheersend*
predominate [ov ww] *overheersen, de
overhand hebben*
pre-eminent [bnw] *uitblinkend,
uitstekend boven*
pre-empt [ov ww] • *zich toe-eigenen*
• *overbodig maken*
pre-emptive [bnw] *voorkomend,
preventief*
preen [ov ww] *gladstrijken <v. veren>*
prefab [znw] *montagewoning*

preface I [ov ww] *v.e. inleiding
voorzien, inleiden* II [znw] *inleiding*
prefer [ov ww] *prefereren* • (~ to)
verkiezen boven
preferable [bnw] *te verkiezen*
preference [znw] *voorkeur*
prefix [znw] *voorvoegsel*
pregnancy [znw] *zwangerschap*
pregnant [bnw] • *zwanger* • *geladen
‹fig.›*
prehistoric [bnw] *voorhistorisch*
prejudice I [ov ww] *schaden, nadeel
berokkenen* • (~ against) *innemen
tegen* II [znw] • *vooroordeel* • *nadeel,
schade*
prejudicial [bnw] *schadelijk*
prelate [znw] *prelaat*
preliminary I [znw] *inleiding* II [bnw]
• *inleidend* • *voorlopig*
premature [bnw] • *vroegtijdig*
• *ontijdig* • *voorbarig*
premeditation [znw] *opzet*
premier I [znw] • *premier* • *eerste
minister* II [bnw] ‹sl.› *voornaamste,
eerste*
premise I [ov ww] *vooropstellen, vooraf
laten gaan* II [znw] *premisse*
premium I [znw] *premie* II [bnw]
super-
premonition [znw] • *waarschuwing*
• *voorgevoel*
preoccupation [znw] *iets waar
voortdurend aan gedacht wordt*
preoccupy [ov ww] *geheel in beslag
nemen*
preparation [znw] • *huiswerk*
• *preparaat* • *voorbereiding*
preparatory [bnw] *voorbereidend*
prepare [ov + on ww] • *bereiden ‹v.
voedsel›* • *prepareren*
• *voorbereidingen treffen* • *instuderen*
• (~ for) (z.) *voorbereiden op/voor*
preponderant [bnw] *overwegend*
preposterous [bnw] *dwaas, belachelijk*
prerequisite I [znw] *eerste vereiste*
II [bnw] *allereerst vereist*

prerogative [znw] *(voor)recht*
presage [ov ww] *voorspellen*
presbytery [znw] *pastorie ‹v. r.-k.
pastoor›*
prescience [znw] *vooruitziende blik*
prescribe [ov + on ww] *voorschrijven*
prescription [znw] *recept ‹v. dokter›*
presence [znw] *aanwezigheid*
present I [ov + on ww] *presenteren*
II [znw] • *cadeau* • *het heden* III [bnw]
• *aanwezig* • *huidig*
presentable [bnw] *geschikt om
voorgedragen of voorgesteld te worden,
geschikt als geschenk*
presentation [znw] • *'t voorstellen*
• *aanbieding* • *presentatie*
• *voorstelling*
presentiment [znw] *(angstig)
voorgevoel*
presently [bijw] • *dadelijk, aanstonds*
• *weldra, kort daarop* • *nu,
tegenwoordig*
preservative I [znw] *conserverend
middel* II [bnw] *conserverend*
preserve I [ov ww] • *beschermen,
redden, bewaren* • *goed houden,
conserveren, inmaken* • (~ from)
behoeden voor II [znw] • *wildpark,
eigen viswater* • *eigen gebied*
preside [on ww] *voorzitten, de leiding
hebben*
president [znw] • *hoofd v. bep. colleges*
• *president* • ‹AE› *directeur ‹v. bank of
bedrijf›*
presidential [bnw] *presidents-,
voorzitters-*
press I [ov + on ww] • *uitpersen,
oppersen* • *pressen, aandringen (op)*
• *bestoken ‹v. vijand›* • *dringen* • z.
verdringen • *drukken, de hand drukken*
II [znw] *pers*
pressing [bnw] *(aan)dringend*
pressure I [ov ww] *onder druk zetten*
II [znw] • *druk* • *dwang, pressie*
prestigious [bnw] *gezaghebbend*
presume I [ov ww] • *aannemen,*

vermoeden, geloven • 't wagen
II [on ww] • (~ (up)on) misbruik
maken van, z. laten voorstaan op
presumption [znw] • aanmatiging
• vermoeden • veronderstelling
presumptive [bnw] vermoedelijk
presumptuous [bnw] aanmatigend
presuppose [ov ww] vooronderstellen,
insluiten
presupposition [znw]
vooronderstelling
pretend [ov + on ww] • voorwenden,
doen alsof • (valselijk) beweren
pretender [znw] pretendent
pretension [znw] aanmatiging
pretentious [bnw] aanmatigend
pretext [znw] • voorwendsel • excuus
pretty I [bnw] aardig, mooi II [bijw]
nogal, tamelijk
pretzel [znw] zoute krakeling
prevail [on ww] • de overhand krijgen
of hebben • (over)heersen • zegevieren
• overreden, overhalen
prevailing [bnw] heersend, gangbaar
prevaricate [on ww] liegen, eromheen
draaien
prevent [ov ww] (ver)hinderen
preventative, preventive [bnw]
preventief
prevention [znw] 't voorkómen
preview [znw] beoordeling vooraf <v.
film of boek>
previous [bnw] voorafgaand
prey I [on ww] • (~ upon) azen op,
aantasten II [znw] prooi
price I [ov ww] • prijzen <v. goederen>
• schatten II [znw] • prijs • koers
priceless [bnw] • onschatbaar • <sl.>
vermakelijk, kostelijk
prick I [ov ww] (door)prikken II [znw]
• prik • stekel • <vulg.> pik, lul
prickle I [ov + on ww] prikk(el)en
II [znw] • doorntje • stekel
prickly [bnw] • stekelig • kriebelig
pride I [wkd ww] • (~ on) trots zijn op
II [znw] • trots, hoogmoed • troep <v.

leeuwen>
priest [znw] • geestelijke • priester
priestess [znw] priesteres
priestlike, priestly [bnw] als 'n
priester
prig [znw] pedant iem.
priggish [bnw] pedant
prim [bnw] vormelijk, stijf
primacy [znw] • primaatschap
• voorrang
primal [bnw] • oorspronkelijk
• voornaamst
primarily [bijw] allereerst
primary I [znw] <AE> voorverkiezing
voor presidentschap II [bnw] • eerst
• voornaamste • oorspronkelijk
primate [znw] • primaat
• aartsbisschop • mens(aap)
prime I [ov ww] • voorbereiden,
inlichten • in de grondverf zetten
• laden <v. vuurwapen> II [znw]
• hoogste volmaaktheid • 't beste
• bloeitijd • priemgetal III [bnw]
• hoofd- • prima • grond-
primer [znw] • boek voor beginners,
inleiding • grondverf
primitive [bnw] • primitief, grond-
• oer- • vroeg, eerste, primair
• eenvoudig, ruw
primordial [bnw] oer-, oorspronkelijk
primrose [znw] sleutelbloem
prince [znw] prins
princely [bnw] prinselijk
princess [znw] prinses
principal I [znw] • kapitaal • rector
II [bnw] voornaamste, hoofd-
principle [znw] principe, grondbeginsel
print I [ov ww] • in druk uitgeven
• bedrukken • (laten) drukken • (~ out)
afdrukken II [znw] • afdruk, stempel,
teken, merk • bedrukte stof • drukwerk,
gedrukt werk, druk • reproductie,
gravure, plaat, prent
printing I [ww] tegenw. deelw.
→ print II [znw] (boek)drukkunst
prior I [znw] prior II [bnw + bijw]

vroeger
priority [znw] *voorrang*
priory [znw] *priorij*
prise [ov ww] *openbreken*
prism [znw] • *prisma* • *spectrum*
prison [znw] *gevangenis*
prisoner [znw] *gevangene*
pristine [bnw] *ongerept, zuiver*
privacy [znw] *afzondering*
private I [znw] *gewoon soldaat* II [bnw]
• *geheim* • *privé, persoonlijk,*
vertrouwelijk • *afgelegen, afgezonderd*
• *particulier*
privation [znw] *ontbering, gebrek*
privet [znw] *liguster*
privy I [znw] *privaat, toilet* II [bnw] *op*
de hoogte van
prize I [ov ww] *waarderen* II [znw]
• *prijs, beloning* • *buit* III [bnw]
bekroond ‹op tentoonstelling›
pro I [znw] ‹inf.› → **professional**
II [bnw] *pro, vóór*
probability [znw] *waarschijnlijkheid*
probable I [znw] *vermoedelijke*
winnaar of kandidaat II [bnw]
waarschijnlijk
probation [znw] • *proef(tijd),*
onderzoek • *voorwaardelijke*
veroordeling • *reclassering*
probationary [bnw] *proef-*
probationer [znw]
• *leerling-verpleegster* • *voorwaardelijk*
veroordeelde
probe I [ov ww] • *sonderen*
• *doordringen in, onderzoeken* II [znw]
• *sonde* • *onderzoek*
probity [znw] *oprechtheid, eerlijkheid*
problem [znw] *probleem, vraagstuk*
proboscis [znw] • *slurf* • *zuigmond* ‹v.
insect›
procedural [bnw] *betreffende een*
procedure
procedure [znw] *methode, procedure*
proceed [on ww] *verder (voort)gaan,*
vorderen, vervolgen ‹v. rede›
• (~ **against**) *gerechtelijk vervolgen*

• (~ **from**) *uitgegeven worden door,*
komen uit • (~ **to**) *behalen* ‹v. graad›
• (~ **upon**) *tewerkgaan volgens*
• (~ **with**) *verder gaan*
process I [ov ww] • *behandelen* ‹vnl. v.
stof› • *conserveren* ‹v. voedsel›
• *verwerken* II [znw] • *proces* • *(ver)loop*
• *verrichting, methode, werkwijze*
procession [znw] • *processie, defilé,*
stoet • *opeenvolging, reeks*
proclaim [ov + on ww] *verkondigen*
proclamation [znw] • *proclamatie*
• *verkondiging*
proclivity [znw] *neiging*
procreate [ov ww] *voortplanten*
procure [ov ww] *verkrijgen, bezorgen*
procuress [znw] *bordeelhoudster,*
koppelaarster
prod I [ov + on ww] • *prikken, porren*
• *(aan)sporen* II [znw] • *por* • *(vlees)pen*
prodigal I [znw] *verkwister* II [bnw]
verkwistend
prodigious [bnw] *wonderbaarlijk,*
enorm, abnormaal
prodigy [znw] *wonder(kind)*
produce I [ov ww] • *opleveren* • *te*
voorschijn halen • *opbrengen*
• *aanvoeren* ‹v. bewijs› • *opvoeren* ‹v.
toneelstuk› • *produceren* • *ontwerpen*
‹v. kleding› • *veroorzaken* II [znw]
• *opbrengst* • *producten* ‹v.d. bodem›
• *resultaat*
producer [znw] • *producent*
• *productieleider* ‹v. film, toneel›
• *ontwerper* • *regisseur*
product [znw] • *product* • *resultaat*
production [znw] • *productie* • *product*
productive [bnw] • *producerend*
• *productief*
productivity [znw] *productiviteit*
profess [ov ww] • *betuigen* ‹v.
gevoelens› • *openlijk verklaren*
• *beweren* • *belijden* ‹v. rel.›
professed [bnw] *zogenaamd*
profession [znw] • *beroep* • *verklaring,*
betuiging

professional I [znw] • beroepsspeler
• vakman II [bnw] • beroeps-, vak-
• tot de gestudeerde stand behorend
professionalism [znw]
professionalisme, vakbekwaamheid
professor [znw] • professor • belijder
• ‹AE› docent
professorial [bnw] professoraal
professorship [znw] professoraat
proffer [ov ww] aanbieden
proficient [bnw] bekwaam
profile [znw] • profiel • korte
levensbeschrijving, karakterschets ‹in
de journalistiek›
profit I [on ww] profiteren II [znw]
• voordeel, nut • winst
profitable [bnw] • winstgevend
• nuttig
profiteer [znw] ‹pej.› iem. die
woekerwinst maakt
profligacy [znw] losbandigheid
profligate I [znw] losbol II [bnw]
losbandig
profound [bnw] diep(gaand), grondig
profundity [znw] diepte
profuse [bnw] overvloedig
profusion [znw] overvloed
progenitor [znw] • voorvader
• geestelijke vader, voorganger
progeny [znw] nageslacht
prognosis [znw] prognose
program(me) I [ov ww]
programmeren II [znw] • program(ma)
• ‹AE› agenda
progress I [on ww] vooruitgaan,
vorderen II [znw] voortgang,
vordering(en)
progression [znw] • vooruitgang,
vordering • progressie • reeks
progressive I [znw] voorstander v.
progressieve politiek II [bnw]
• vooruitgaand • vooruitstrevend
• progressief
prohibitive [bnw] • belemmerend
• enorm hoog ‹vnl. v. prijs›
project I [ov ww] • projecteren

• slingeren II [on ww] vooruitsteken
III [znw] • project, plan, schema
• (school)taak
projectile [znw] projectiel
projection [znw] • uitsteeksel
• projectie ‹in meetkunde› • 't
projecteren
projectionist [znw] filmoperateur
projector [znw] projectietoestel
proletarian I [znw] proletariër II [bnw]
proletarisch
proliferate [on ww] zich snel
vermenigvuldigen, z. verspreiden
prolific [bnw] overvloedig
prolix [bnw] • uitvoerig • langdradig
prologue [znw] proloog, inleiding
prolong [ov ww] aanhouden ‹v. noot›,
verlengen
promenade I [on ww] wandelen
II [znw] • wandeling • wandelpad
prominence [znw] • uitsteeksel,
verhevenheid • onderscheiding
prominent [bnw] • vooraanstaand
• vooruitstekend • opvallend
promiscuity [znw] vrije liefde
promiscuous [bnw] • veel relaties
hebbend • gemengd, zonder onderscheid
promise I [ov + on ww] beloven,
toezeggen II [znw] belofte
promising [bnw] veelbelovend
promontory [znw] • voorgebergte
• kaap
promote [ov ww] • bevorderen,
vooruithelpen • aanmoedigen
promoter [znw] • bevorderaar,
begunstiger • oprichter van
maatschappij
promotion [znw] • bevordering
• reclameactie
prompt I [ov ww] • aanzetten,
aanmoedigen • souffleren, voorzeggen
II [znw] ‹comp.› prompt III [bnw]
onmiddellijk, vlug, vlot, prompt
IV [bijw] precies
prompter [znw] • iem. die aanmoedigt
• souffleur

promulgate [ov ww] *bekend maken*
prone [bnw] • *vatbaar (voor)*
• *voorover(liggend), plat*
prong [znw] *tand <v. vork>*
pronoun [znw] *voornaamwoord*
pronounce [ww] • *uitspreken, uiten*
• *uitspraak doen*
pronouncement [znw] *verklaring*
pronunciation [znw] *uitspraak*
proof I [znw] • *bewijs* • *drukproef*
II [bnw] *bestand*
prop I [ov ww] • *steunen* • *schragen*
• *(~ against) zetten tegen* • *(~ up)
ondersteunen, overeind houden* II [znw]
• *decorstuk* • *stut, steunpilaar*
propagate I [ov ww] • *propageren*
• *voortplanten* • *verbreiden,
verspreiden* II [on ww] • z. *verspreiden*
• z. *voortplanten*
propel [ov ww] *(voort)drijven*
propeller [znw] *propeller, schroef*
propensity [znw] *geneigdheid, neiging*
proper [bnw] • *eigen(lijk)* • *juist, goed*
• *gepast, netjes, fatsoenlijk*
• *onvervalst, echt*
propertied [bnw] *(land) bezittend*
property [znw] • *bezit(ting),
land(goed)* • *eigendom(srecht)*
• *eigenschap*
prophecy [znw] *profetie, voorspelling*
prophesy [ov + on ww] *profeteren,
voorspellen*
prophet [znw] • *profeet* • *voorstander*
prophetess [znw] *profetes*
propitiate [ov ww] *gunstig stemmen*
propitious [bnw] *genadig, gunstig*
proportion [znw] • *evenredigheid*
• *deel* • *verhouding*
proportional [bnw] *evenredig*
proportionate [bnw] *evenredig*
proposal [znw] • *voorstel*
• *huwelijksaanzoek*
propose I [ov ww] *voorstellen, van plan
zijn* II [on ww] *huwelijksaanzoek doen*
proposition [znw] • *bewering*
• *stelling* • *voorstel*

propound [ov ww] *voorstellen*
proprietary [bnw] • *eigendoms-,
particulier* • *bezittend <v. klasse>*
• *gepatenteerd*
proprietor [znw] *eigenaar*
proprietress [znw] *eigenares*
propriety [znw] • *juistheid* • *fatsoen,
welvoeglijkheid*
propulsion [znw] • *voortstuwing*
• *stuwkracht*
prosaic [bnw] *prozaïsch*
proscribe [ov ww] • *vogelvrij
verklaren, verbannen* • *verwerpen <v.
bep. praktijk>*
proscription [znw] • *verbod*
• *verbanning*
prose [znw] *proza*
prosecute [ov ww] • *vervolgen* • *klacht
indienen tegen*
prosecution [znw] • *vervolging* • *eiser*
prosecutor [znw] *aanklager*
prosper [on ww] *voorspoed genieten,
gedijen*
prosperity [znw] *voorspoed, bloei*
prostitute I [ov ww] • *prostitueren*
• *vergooien, verlagen, misbruiken*
II [znw] *prostituee*
prostitution [znw] • *prostitutie*
• *misbruik*
prostrate I [ov ww] • *ter aarde werpen*
• *(lichamelijk) uitputten* II [bnw]
• *voorooverliggend, uitgestrekt*
• *verslagen, gebroken <v. smart>*
• *(lichamelijk) uitgeput*
prosy [bnw] *vervelend, saai, langdradig*
protagonist [znw] • *hoofdpersoon*
• *kampioen, voorvechter*
protect [ov ww] *beveiligen*
• *(~ against) beschermen tegen*
• *(~ from) beschutten tegen,
beschermen tegen*
protection [znw] *bescherming*
protective [bnw] *beschermend*
protector [znw] *beschermer*
protectorate [znw] *protectoraat*
protein [znw] *proteïne, eiwit*

protest I [on ww] • *protesteren*
• *betuigen* II [znw] • *protest* • *betuiging*
protestation [znw] • *protest*
• *betuiging*
protester [znw] *iem. die protesteert of*
betuigt
protrude [on ww] • *(voor)uitsteken*
• *uitpuilen*
protrusion [znw] *uitsteeksel*
proud [bnw] • *fier* • *trots*
prove I [ov ww] *bewijzen* II [on ww]
blijken (te zijn)
provenance [znw] *(plaats v.) herkomst*
proverb [znw] • *spreekwoord* • *gezegde*
proverbial [bnw] *spreekwoordelijk*
provide [ov ww] • *(~ for) zorgen voor*
• *(~ with) voorzien van*
providence [znw] *voorzienigheid*
providential [bnw] • *v.d.*
voorzienigheid • *geschikt, te juister*
tijd, gelukkig
provider [znw] • *kostwinner*
• *leverancier*
provincialism [znw] *provincialisme*
provision I [ov ww] *provianderen*
II [znw] • *voorziening*
• *(mond)voorraad* • *wetsbepaling*
provisional [bnw] *voorlopig*
proviso [znw] • *bepaling* • *voorbehoud*
Provo [znw] *lid van extremistische*
vleugel v.d. IRA
provocation [znw] *provocatie*
provocative [bnw] • *provocerend*
• *prikkelend*
provoke [ov ww] • *(op)wekken*
• *uitlokken, tarten, verlokken*
• *veroorzaken*
provost [znw] • *hoofd v. sommige*
colleges • ‹Schots› *burgemeester*
prow [znw] *boeg, voorsteven*
prowl [ov + on ww] *rondzwerven,*
rondsluipen
prowler [znw] *sluiper*
proxy [znw] *(ge)volmacht(igde),*
procuratie(houder)
prude [znw] *preuts iem.*

prudence [znw] *voorzichtigheid,*
omzichtigheid
prudery, prudishness [znw]
preutsheid
prudish [bnw] *preuts*
prune I [ov ww] *snoeien* II [znw]
pruimedant
pry I [ov ww] *openbreken* II [on ww]
gluren • *(~ into) zijn neus steken in*
psyche [znw] • *ziel* • *geest*
psychiatric [bnw] *psychiatrisch*
psychiatrist [znw] *psychiater*
psychiatry [znw] *psychiatrie*
psychological [bnw] *psychologisch*
psychopath [znw] *psychopaat*
psychotherapy [znw] *psychotherapie*
psychotic [bnw] *psychotisch*
pub ‹inf.› [znw] *café, kroeg*
puberty [znw] *puberteit*
pubic [bnw] *schaam-*
public I [znw] *publiek* II [bnw] *publiek,*
openbaar, algemeen staats-
publican [znw] *kroegbaas*
publication [znw] • *afkondiging*
• *publicatie, uitgave*
publicist [znw] • *journalist* • *publicist*
publicity [znw] • *openbaarheid,*
bekendheid • *reclame*
publish [ov ww] • *publiceren, uitgeven*
• *bekend maken*
publisher [znw] *uitgever*
pucker [ov + on ww] • *rimpelen, (z.)*
plooien • *samentrekken*
puddle [znw] *poel, plas*
puerile [bnw] *kinderachtig*
puff I [on ww] • *puffen, snuiven, blazen,*
hijgen • *opbollen, opzwellen* II [znw]
• *rookwolkje* • *poederdonsje* • *luchtig*
gebak • *windstoot, ademstoot* • *trekje,*
pufje
puffy [bnw] *dik, opgeblazen, pafferig*
pug [znw] *mopshond*
pugnacious [bnw] *strijdlustig,*
twistziek
puke ‹inf.› I [ov + on ww] *(uit)braken*
II [znw] *braaksel*

pull I [ov ww] • trekken (aan), rukken
• verrekken • (~ back) (doen)
terugtrekken • (~ down) neerhalen,
afbreken, klein krijgen • (~ in)
inrekenen • (~ off) uittrekken,
klaarspelen • (~ on) aantrekken
• (~ out) uithalen, uittrekken • (~ up)
optrekken, inhouden, tot
nadenken/staan brengen, onder
handen nemen II [on ww] trekken,
rukken • (~ at) trekken aan, een flinke
teug nemen • (~ back) terugkrabbelen,
(zich) terugtrekken • (~ in)
binnenlopen <v. trein> • (~ out)
vertrekken <v. trein>, wegrijden, z. uit
iets terugtrekken • (~ over) (naar de
kant rijden en) stoppen, opzij gaan
• (~ round/through) 't halen,
erdoorheen komen • (~ together) één
lijn trekken, samenwerken • (~ up)
stilhouden III [znw] • teug
• aantrekkingskracht • trekkracht
• trek, ruk

pullet [znw] jonge kip

pulley [znw] katrol

pulmonary [bnw] long-

pulp I [ov ww] tot pulp maken II [znw]
• vruchtvlees • merg • houtpap, pulp

pulpit [znw] kansel, preekstoel

pulsate [on ww] kloppen, slaan, trillen

pulse I [on ww] kloppen, slaan, trillen,
tikken II [znw] • pols(slag), slag
• peulvrucht

pulverize [ov ww] • fijnwrijven, doen
verstuiven, tot poeder/stof maken
• volkomen vernietigen

puma [znw] poema

pummel [ov ww] afrossen, toetakelen

pump I [ov + on ww] pompen
II [ov ww] • uithoren • krachtig
schudden <v. hand> • (~ out) in grote
hoeveelheden produceren III [znw]
• pump • pomp

pumpkin [znw] pompoen

pun I [on ww] woordspelingen maken
II [znw] woordspeling

punch I [ov ww] • stompen • ponsen <v.
kaartjes> • (~ in/out) intoetsen
II [znw] • punch • pons • slag, stomp
• <sl.> fut, flink optreden

punctual [bnw] punctueel, precies op
tijd

punctuate [ov ww] • interpungeren
• onderbreken <v. redevoering>

punctuation [znw] interpunctie

puncture I [ov ww] (door)prikken
II [znw] gaatje, lek <in fietsband>

pundit [znw] <scherts> geleerde

pungent [bnw] • scherp • bijtend
• prikkelend

punish [ov ww] straffen

punishable [bnw] strafbaar

punishing [bnw] verpletterend

punishment [znw] straf, bestraffing

punitive [bnw] • straffend • straf-

punk I [znw] punker II [bnw] punk-

punnet [znw] spanen mandje

punt I [ov + on ww] bomen II [znw]
boot met platte bodem

punter [znw] • bomer • beroepswedder

puny [bnw] klein, zwak, nietig

pup [znw] jonge hond

pupil [znw] • leerling, scholier • pupil

puppet [znw] marionet

puppy [znw] jonge hond

purchase I [ov ww] (aan)kopen
II [znw] inkoop, aankoop

purchaser [znw] koper

pure [bnw] • zuiver • louter

purely [bijw] uitsluitend

purgative [znw] purgeermiddel

purgatory [znw] • vagevuur • hel <fig.>

purge I [ov ww] • zuiveren • purgeren
II [znw] zuivering

purify [ov ww] • reinigen, zuiveren,
louteren • klaren <v. vloeistof>

purist [znw] taalzuiveraar

purl I [ov ww] averechts breien II [znw]
averechtse steek

purple [bnw] paars

purplish [bnw] paarsachtig

purport I [ov ww] beweren,

voorwenden II [znw] *strekking,
betekenis*
purpose I [ov ww] *van plan zijn*
II [znw] • *doel, plan, opzet*
• *vastberadenheid*
purposeful [bnw] *doelbewust*
purposeless [bnw] *doelloos*
purposely [bijw] *met opzet*
purr I [on ww] *spinnen* ‹v. kat› II [znw]
gespin
purse I [ov ww] *samentrekken* ‹v.
lippen› II [znw] • *geldprijs* • *fondsen,
gelden* • *zak(je), portemonnee, beurs*
• ‹AE› *damestas*
purser [znw] *administrateur* ‹vooral
op schip›
pursuance [znw] *uitvoering*
pursue [ov ww] • *najagen* ‹v. genot›
• *vervolgen, achtervolgen* • *voortzetten*
‹vnl. v. gedragslijn› • *volgen* ‹v. plan›
• *uitoefenen, beoefenen*
pursuit [znw] *vervolging*
purvey [ov + on ww] • *leveren* ‹v.
voedsel› • *verschaffen*
purveyor [znw] • *verschaffer*
• *leverancier* ‹v. levensmiddelen›
push I [ov + on ww] • *handelen in
heroïne* • *duwen, stoten* • *schuiven*
• *aanzetten* • z. *inspannen, doorzetten*
• *pousseren* ‹v. handelsartikel›
• (~ **on**) ‹inf.› *verder gaan, zijn weg
vervolgen* • (~ **through**) *doorzetten,
zich een weg banen* II [on ww] • (~ **in**)
voordringen III [znw] • *duw* • *stoot,
zetje* • *energie*
pushy [bnw] *opdringerig*
pussy [znw] • *poes* • ‹vulg.› *kut*
put I [ov ww] • *brengen, doen, plaatsen,
leggen, zetten* • *stellen* • *zeggen, onder
woorden brengen* • (~ **about**)
rondstrooien ‹praatjes› • (~ **across**)
iets duidelijk maken • (~ **aside**) *opzij
leggen/zetten, uitschakelen* • (~ **at**) *de
prijs stellen op, schatten op* • (~ **away**)
*wegleggen, opzijleggen, sparen,
verorberen, gevangen zetten* • (~ **back**)

vertragen, achteruitzetten • (~ **by**)
opzijleggen • (~ **down**) *neerzetten,
neerleggen, onderdrukken* ‹v. opstand›,
op zijn plaats zetten ‹fig.› • (~ **forth**)
verkondigen • (~ **forward**) *naar voren
brengen, komen met, verkondigen*
• (~ **in**) *installeren* • (~ **into**) *erin
zetten* • (~ **off**) *uitstellen, afzeggen,
misselijk maken, v.d. wijs brengen*
• (~ **on**) *voorwenden, aannemen* ‹een
houding›, *opvoeren* ‹v. toneelstuk›,
aantrekken, opzetten, opleggen
• (~ **out**) *ontwrichten, irriteren,
uitblazen, uitdoen, inspannen,
uitvaardigen, uitzetten, uitsteken* ‹v.
hand›, *blussen* • (~ **over**) *bedriegen*
• (~ **through**) *doorverbinden*
• (~ **together**) *samenstellen,
samenvoegen, in elkaar zetten, punten
maken* ‹cricket› • (~ **up**) *aanplakken,
aanbieden, opzenden, opjagen* ‹v.
wild›, *opvoeren* ‹v. toneelstuk›, *als
jockey laten rijden, opstellen, opslaan,
ophangen, verhogen* ‹v. prijs›,
beschikbaar stellen, voordragen ‹als
lid›, *te koop aanbieden, samenstellen,
bouwen, opsteken, logies verlenen,
stallen* ‹v. paard›, *in de schede doen,
opbergen* II [on ww] • (~ **about**)
draaien, de steven wenden • (~ **forth**)
uitbotten, uitschieten • (~ **in**)
binnenlopen ‹v. schip› • (~ **off**) *de zee
kiezen* • (~ **out**) *vertrekken* • (~ **up**)
logeren • (~ **up with**) *tolereren,
verdragen* III [znw] → **putt**
putative [bnw] *vermeend*
putrefaction [znw] *(ver)rotting, bederf*
putrefy [on ww] *rotten*
putrid [bnw] • *vuil, (ver)rot* • ‹sl.›
waardeloos
putsch [znw] *staatsgreep*
putt I [on ww] *(zachtjes) met golfstok
tegen bal slaan* II [znw] *zachte slag
met golfstok*
putter I [on ww] *liefhebberen* II [znw]
golfstick

puzzle I [ov ww] *verbijsteren, in de war brengen* II [on ww] *piekeren* III [znw]
• *moeilijkheid, probleem* • *raadsel, puzzle*
puzzlement [znw] *verwarring, verlegenheid*
pygmy I [znw] *pygmee, dwerg* II [bnw] *dwergachtig*
pyramid [znw] *piramide*
pyre [znw] *brandstapel*

Q

quack I [ww] *kwaken* II [znw] *kwakzalver*
quad [znw] → quadrangle
quadrangle [znw] • *vierhoek*
• *(vierkant) binnenplein*
quadrilateral I [znw] *vierhoek*
II [bnw] *vierzijdig*
quadruped [znw] *viervoetig dier*
quadruple I [ov + on ww] (z.) *verviervoudigen* II [znw] *viervoud*
III [bnw] *viervoudig*
quail I [on ww] • *de moed verliezen*
• *wijken* II [znw] *kwartel*
quaint [bnw] • *vreemd, eigenaardig, typisch* • *ouderwets*
quake I [on ww] *beven* II [znw] *(aard)beving, trilling*
qualification [znw] • *matiging*
• *geschiktheid* • *voorwaarde, vereiste*
• *kwalificatie*
qualified [bnw] • *bevoegd, bekwaam*
• *getemperd* ‹v. optimisme›
qualifier [znw] • *beperking* • *bepalend woord*
qualify I [ov ww] • *bevoegd maken*
• *verzachten* • *kwalificeren, kenschetsen, bepalen* II [on ww] *zich kwalificeren*
qualitative [bnw] *kwalitatief*
quality [znw] • *eigenschap, kwaliteit*
• *deugd* • *bekwaamheid*
qualm [znw] • *gevoel v. misselijkheid*
• *angstig voorgevoel* • *wroeging*
quantum [znw] • *kwantum, hoeveelheid* • *klein beetje*
quarantine I [ov ww] *afzonderen in quarantaine* II [znw] *quarantaine*
quarrel I [on ww] • *kritiek hebben*
• *ruzie hebben, ruzie maken* II [znw]
• *ruzie, twist* • *pijl voor kruisboog*
quarrelsome [bnw] *twistziek*

quarry I [ov ww] (uit)graven II [znw]
• prooi, slachtoffer • achtervolgd wild
• (steen)groeve
quart [znw] 1/4 gallon (ruim 1 l)
quarter I [ov ww] • in vieren delen
• inkwartieren II [znw] • kwart, vierde
deel • kwartier <v. maan> • 1/4 cwt < 12
1/2 kg> • 1/4 dollar • kwartaal
• (wind)streek • wijk <v. stad>
quartz [znw] kwarts
quash [ov ww] • een einde maken aan,
verijdelen, onderdrukken • <jur.>
vernietigen
quatrain [znw] vierregelig vers
quaver I [on ww] trillen, beven <v.
stem> II [znw] • trilling <v. stem> • 1/8
noot
quay [znw] kade
queasy [bnw] misselijk
queen [znw] • koningin • vrouw <in
kaartspel> • <sl.> homo, flikker
queenlike, queenly [bnw] als een
koningin
queer I [znw] homoseksueel II [bnw]
• vreemd, eigenaardig • homoseksueel
quell [ov ww] • onderdrukken • met
kracht een einde maken aan
quench [ov ww] • lessen <v. dorst>
• blussen
querulous [bnw] klagend
query I [ww] • een vraag stellen
• betwijfelen II [znw] • vraag
• vraagteken • twijfel • bezwaar
quest I [ov + on ww] • speuren (naar)
• zoeken II [znw] het zoeken, speurtocht
questionable [bnw] twijfelachtig
questioning [bnw] vragend
questionnaire [znw] vragenlijst
queue I [on ww] een rij vormen II [znw]
rij, queue
quibble I [on ww] chicaneren II [znw]
onbetekenende ruzie
quick I [znw] levend vlees II [bnw]
• vluchtig • levendig • vlug III [bijw]
vlug, snel
quicken [ov + on ww] versnellen

quickie [znw] • iets dat zeer snel of in
korte tijd gebeurt • vluggertje
quid [znw] <sl.> pond sterling
quiet I [ov + on ww] • tot rust brengen,
kalmeren • rustig worden II [znw]
• rust • vrede III [bnw] • rustig, kalm
• stil • stemmig <v. kleding>
quieten I [ov ww] kalmeren, tot
bedaren brengen II [on ww] rustig
worden, bedaren
quill [znw] • slagpen • ganzenpen
• stekel <v. stekelvarken>
quilt I [ov ww] watteren, doorstikken
II [znw] • gewatteerde deken • sprei
quince [znw] kwee(peer)
quinine [znw] kinine
quintessence [znw] • het zuiverste
• het wezenlijke • het voornaamste
quip I [on ww] geestige of spitsvondige
opmerking maken II [znw] geestigheid,
spitsvondigheid
quirk [znw] • eigenaardigheid • toeval
quit [ov ww] • ontslag nemen
• ophouden • opgeven • weggaan
quite [bijw] • geheel, volkomen • zeer
• absoluut
quitter [znw] iem. die bij
moeilijkheden ervandoor gaat
quiver I [on ww] trillen, beven II [znw]
• trilling • pijlkoker
quizzical [bnw] • vragend • spottend
quotation [znw] • aanhaling <v.
passage> • notering <v. prijs>,
prijsopgave
quote I [ov ww] • citeren • noteren <v.
prijs> II [znw] citaat
quotient [znw] quotiënt

R

rabbit I [on ww] • (~ **on**) *wauwelen*
II [znw] *konijn*
rabble [znw] • *gepeupel* • *tuig, gespuis*
rabid [bnw] • *verbeten* • *hondsdol*
rabies [znw] *hondsdolheid*
raccoon [znw] *wasbeer*
race I [ov ww] • *laten snellen* • *om 't*
hardst laten rijden/lopen enz.
II [on ww] • *snellen, jagen* • *om 't*
hardst rijden/lopen enz. III [znw]
• *wedloop* • *ras*
racer [znw] *snelle fiets/auto*
racial [bnw] *ras(sen)-*
racing [znw] • *het wedrennen* • *de*
rensport
racism [znw] *racisme, rassenhaat*
rack I [ov ww] *folteren, pijnigen,*
afbeulen II [znw] • *rek* • *(bagage)net*
• *pijnbank*
racket I [on ww] *lawaai maken* II [znw]
• *(tennis)racket* • *herrie, lawaai, drukte*
• *zwendel*
racketeer [znw] *zwarthandelaar,*
bandiet, geldafperser
racketeering [znw]
gangsterpraktijken <afpersing,
chantage, omkoperij>
racquet [znw] *(tennis)racket*
racy [bnw] *pittig, pikant*
radial [bnw] • *straal-* • *stervormig*
• *spaakbeen-* • *radium-*
radiance [znw] *straling, schittering*
radiant [bnw] *stralend*
radiate I [ov ww] • *uitstralen*
• *draadloos uitzenden* II [on ww]
• *stralen* • *straalsgewijs uitlopen*
radiation [znw] *straling*
radiator [znw] • *koeler* • *radiator*
radical I [znw] *radicaal* II [bnw]
• *fundamenteel, grond-, grondig,*
wezenlijk • *wortel-* • *radicaal*

radicalism [znw] *radicalisme*
radii [mv] → **radius**
radio I [ov + on ww] *uitzenden* II [znw]
• *radio* • *radiotelegrafie*
radioactive [bnw] *radioactief*
radish [znw] *radijs*
radius [znw] • *straal* • *spaak(been)*
raft [znw] • *(hout)vlot* • *luchtbed*
rafter [znw] • *dakspar, balk* • *vlotter*
rag I [ov ww] *plagen, treiteren,*
ontgroenen II [znw] • *vod, lomp(en)*
• *doek, lap* • <pej.> *krant*
rage I [on ww] *woeden, razen* • (~ **at**)
tekeergaan tegen II [znw] • *woede*
• *rage, manie*
ragged [bnw] • *haveloos, gerafeld,*
onverzorgd • *ruig, ruw* • *ongelijk*
raid I [ov ww] *teisteren, afstropen*
II [on ww] *een inval doen* III [znw]
• *inval, overval* • *razzia* • *rooftocht*
• *(lucht)aanval*
raider [znw] *stroper, kaper*
rail I [ov ww] *omheinen* II [on ww]
schelden • (~ **at**) *tekeergaan tegen*
III [znw] • *dwarsbalk, stang, staaf, lat*
• *hek(werk), leuning, reling* • *rail*
railing [znw] *hek, leuning, reling*
railroad [znw] <AE> *spoorweg*
railway [znw] *spoorweg*
rain I [ov + on ww] *regenen, (doen)*
neerstromen • (~ **down**) *(doen)*
neerkomen/-dalen II [onp ww] *regenen*
III [znw] *regen*
rainbow [znw] *regenboog*
rainy [bnw] *regenachtig*
raise I [ov ww] • *rechtop zetten* • *doen*
opstaan/rijzen • *verhogen,*
aan-/op-/verheffen • *doen ontstaan*
• *oprichten, stichten* • *lichten*
• *grootbrengen* • *fokken, planten,*
kweken • *wekken* II [znw] *verhoging,*
opslag
raisin [znw] *rozijn*
rake I [ov ww] • *aanharken,*
bijeenharken • *(door)snuffelen,*
doorzoeken • (~ **in**) *(met hopen)*

binnenhalen • (~ **up**) oprakelen,
optrommelen, opscharrelen II [znw]
• hark • losbol, boemelaar • helling
rakish [bnw] • liederlijk, lichtzinnig
• chic
rally I [ov + on ww] • (zich) groeperen
• (zich) verzamelen • zich herstellen
II [znw] • bijeenkomst • (signaal tot)
verzamelen • slagenwisseling <bij
tennis> • sterrit, rally
ram I [ov ww] • rammen, heien
• aan-/vaststampen • stoten II [znw]
• ram • stormram
ramble I [on ww] • zwerven,
rondtrekken, ronddolen • tieren, welig
groeien • (~ **on**) raaskallen II [znw]
zwerftochtje
rambler [znw] zwerver
rambling [bnw] • onregelmatig
gebouwd • systeemloos,
onsamenhangend
ramification [znw] vertakking
ramp [znw] • glooiing, talud
• oneffenheid, drempel • oprit
• loopplank • vliegtuigtrap
rampage [on ww] razen, rondrennen
rampant [bnw] • alom heersend
• onbeheerst, wild, dolzinnig
ramrod [znw] laadstok
ramshackle [bnw] bouwvallig, gammel
ran [ww] verl. tijd → **run**
rancorous [bnw] haatdragend,
rancuneus
rancour [znw] wrok, rancune
random I [znw] II [bnw] willekeurig
randy [bnw] geil
rang [ww] verl. tijd → **ring**
range I [ov ww] • opstellen,
rangschikken, plaatsen • laten gaan
langs/over • (~ **among/with**) indelen
bij II [on ww] • zich opstellen • zich
uitstrekken, reiken, bestrijken
• (~ **among/with**) behoren tot
• (~ **between**) z. bewegen tussen,
gevonden worden III [znw] • bereik,
gebied, draagwijdte, omvang • sfeer

• (schoots)afstand, schootsveld
• schietbaan • rij, serie • assortiment,
reeks • (berg)keten
• verspreiding(sgebied), sector
• weide-/jachtgebied • (kook)fornuis
ranger [znw] boswachter
rank I [ov ww] • opstellen, in gelid
plaatsen • een plaats geven
• (~ **among**) rekenen tot II [on ww]
• een plaats hebben • voorkeurspositie
innemen • (~ **among**) behoren tot
III [znw] • rang • stand • gelid • rij
• taxistandplaats IV [bnw] • grof
• overwoekerd • ranzig, sterk
rankle [on ww] knagen, (blijven) pijn
doen
rant [on ww] • fulmineren
• bombastische taal uitslaan
• (~ **against**) uitvaren tegen
rap I [ov + on ww] kloppen • (~ **out**)
blaffen <fig.> II [znw] • tik, klop(teken)
• strenge terechtwijzing
rapacious [bnw] roofzuchtig
rapacity [znw] roofzucht
rape I [ov ww] onteren, verkrachten
II [znw] • verkrachting • koolzaad
rapid I [znw] stroomversnelling
II [bnw] snel
rapidity [znw] snelheid
rapist [znw] verkrachter
rapport [znw] • relatie
• verstandhouding
rapt [bnw] • verzonken • in vervoering,
in hoger sferen
rapture [znw] vervoering, extase
rare [bnw] • zeldzaam • dun, ijl
• voortreffelijk • niet gaar
rascal [znw] • schelm • kwajongen
rascally [bnw] schelmachtig
rash I [znw] huiduitslag II [bnw]
• overhaast • onbezonnen
rasher [znw] plakje spek of ham
rasp I [ov ww] raspen II [on ww]
krassen, schrapen, raspen III [znw] rasp
raspberry [znw] framboos
rat I [on ww] • (~ **on**) verraden, in de

steek laten II [znw] • *rat*
• *onderkruiper, overloper*
rate I [ov ww] • *achten, schatten,*
aanslaan • *rekenen tot, waarderen, een*
waarde toekennen • (~ **among/with**)
rekenen tot II [on ww] *gerekend worden*
• (~ **among/with**) *behoren tot*
III [znw] • *tarief, prijs* • *snelheid*
rather [bijw] • *liever* • *nogal*
ratify [ov ww] *bekrachtigen,*
ratificeren
rating [znw] • *taxering* • *klasse,*
classificatie • *aanslag* • *matroos*
ratio [znw] • *verhouding* • *rede*
ration I [ov ww] *rantsoeneren* II [znw]
rantsoen
rational [bnw] • *redelijk, verstandelijk*
• *rationeel* • *rationalistisch*
rationale [znw] • *basis, grond(reden)*
• *redenering* • *argument*
rationalism [znw] *rationalisme*
rationalize [ov + on ww]
• *verstandelijk verklaren*
• *rationaliseren* • *rationalistisch*
beschouwen
rattle I [ov ww] • *doen rammelen,*
rammelen (met) • *nerveus maken,*
opjagen, op stang jagen • (~ **off**)
afraffelen II [on ww] • *rammelen*
• *kletteren* • (~ **away/on**) *erop los*
kletsen, maar door ratelen III [znw]
• *gerammel* • *ratel*
rattling [bnw + bijw] *denderend*
ratty [bnw] *prikkelbaar, nijdig*
raucous [bnw] *rauw, schor*
raunchy [bnw] *geil*
ravage I [ov ww] • *verwoesten* • *teisteren*
• *plunderen* II [znw] *ravage*
rave I [on ww] • *razen, ijlen, dazen*
• *dwepen met* II [znw] *rage* III [bnw]
hip
raven I [znw] *raaf* II [bnw] *ravenzwart*
ravenous [bnw] *uitgehongerd*
ravine [znw] *ravijn*
raving [bnw] *stapel(gek)*
ravish [ov ww] • *meeslepen* <fig.>

• *verkrachten*
raw [bnw] • *rauw* • *ruw, onbewerkt,*
puur • *onervaren, ongeoefend* • *pijnlijk,*
gevoelig
ray [znw] • *straal* • *rog* <vis>
rayon [znw] *rayon, kunstzijde*
raze [ov ww] *met de grond gelijk maken*
razor [znw] *scheermes*
re I [znw] <muz.> *re* II [vz] *betreffende*
reach I [ov ww] • *aanreiken* • *pakken*
• *bereiken, komen bij* II [on ww] *reiken*
• (~ **for**) *grijpen naar* • (~ **forward**)
voorover reiken/leunen • (~ **out**) *de*
hand uitstrekken III [znw] • *bereik*
• *rak* <v.e. rivier>
reaction [znw] *reactie*
read I [ov ww] • *lezen, oplezen,*
voorlezen, aflezen • *(kunnen) verstaan,*
horen • *ontvangen* <v. radio> • (~ **into**)
(een betekenis) willen leggen in
• (~ **out**) *voorlezen* • (~ **to**) *voorlezen*
• (~ **up**) *(grondig) bestuderen*
II [on ww] • *geschreven staan* • *lezen*
• *studeren*
readable [bnw] • *lezenswaard*
• *leesbaar*
reader [znw] • *(voor)lezer* • *lector*
• *leesboek*
readership [znw] • *lectoraat* • *de lezers*
readily [bijw] *gaarne*
readiness [znw] *gevatheid*
reading [znw] • *(meter)stand* • *lezing*
• *lectuur*
readjust [ov + on ww] *(z.) weer*
aanpassen
ready [bnw] • *klaar* • *bereid(willig)*
• *handig, vlug*
real [bnw + bijw] • *echt, werkelijk* • *reëel*
• *onroerend*
reality [znw] *werkelijkheid, realiteit*
realizable [bnw] *realiseerbaar, te*
verwezenlijken
realize [ov ww] • *verwezenlijken*
• *beseffen, inzien, z. realiseren* • *(te*
gelde) maken • *opbrengen*
really I [bijw] *werkelijk* II [tw]

inderdaad, heus
ream [znw] • *riem* <papier> • *grote hoeveelheid* <informeel>
reap [ov + on ww] *oogsten, maaien*
reaper [znw] • *oogster* • *oogstmachine*
reappear [on ww] *weer verschijnen*
reappearance [znw] *herverschijning*
reappraisal [znw] *herwaardering*
rear I [ov ww] • *bouwen, oprichten* • *verheffen, opheffen* • *kweken, fokken, grootbrengen* II [on ww] *steigeren* III [znw] • *achterkant, achterste gedeelte* • *achterhoede* IV [bnw] *achter-, achterste*
rearmost [bnw] *achterste*
rearrange [ov ww] *herschikken*
reason I [ov ww] *beredeneren* II [on ww] *redeneren* • (~ **from**) *uitgaan van* III [znw] • *reden* • *verstand, rede* • *redelijkheid, billijkheid*
reasonable [bnw] • *redelijk* • *billijk*
reasonably [bijw] • *redelijkerwijs* • *vrij, tamelijk*
reassurance [znw] *geruststelling*
reassure [ov ww] *geruststellen*
rebel I [on ww] *in opstand komen* II [znw] *opstandeling, oproerling*
rebellion [znw] *opstand, oproer*
rebellious [bnw] *opstandig*
rebirth [znw] *wedergeboorte*
reborn [bnw] *herboren*
rebound [on ww] *terugspringen* • (~ (**up**)**on**) (*weer*) *neerkomen op*
rebuff I [ov ww] *afwijzen* II [znw] *afwijzing*
rebuild [ov ww] *herbouwen*
rebuke I [ov ww] *berispen* II [znw] *berisping*
rebut [ov ww] *weerleggen*
rebuttal [znw] *weerlegging*
recalcitrant [bnw] *recalcitrant, weerspannig*
recall I [ov ww] • *terugroepen* • *weer in 't geheugen roepen, weer voor de geest roepen* • *herinneren aan* • *herroepen,*

intrekken, terugnemen II [znw] • *herinnering* • <AE> *dwang om af te treden*
recant [ov ww] (*openlijk*) *herroepen*
recapture I [ov + on ww] *heroveren, terugnemen* II [znw] *terugname, herovering*
recast I [ov ww] • *omwerken* • *rol toewijzen aan andere acteur* II [znw] • *hervorming* • *veranderde rolverdeling*
recede [on ww] *achteruitgaan, (terug)wijken van* • (~ **from**) *terugkomen van, z. terugtrekken uit*
receipt [znw] • *ontvangst* • *kwitantie, reçu*
receive I [ov + on ww] *verwelkomen* II [ov ww] • *ontvangen, krijgen* • *opnemen*
receiver [znw] • *curator* • *ontvangtoestel, telefoonhoorn*
recent [bnw] • *kortgeleden* • *van onlangs* • *nieuw*
reception [znw] • *ontvangst* • *receptie* • *erkenning*
receptive [bnw] *ontvankelijk, vatbaar*
recess [znw] • *nis, alkoof* • *schuilhoek* • *reces, vakantie*
recession [znw] *achteruitgang, recessie*
recipe [znw] *recept*
recipient I [znw] *ontvanger, belanghebbende* II [bnw] *ontvankelijk*
reciprocal [bnw] *wederzijds, wederkerig, als tegenprestatie*
reciprocate [ov ww] • *uitwisselen* • *wederdienst bewijzen, wederkerig van dienst zijn*
reciprocity [znw] • *gelijke behandeling v. weerskanten* • *wisselwerking*
recital [znw] • *concert, recital* • *verhaal* • *voordracht*
recitation [znw] • *voordracht* • *verhaal*
reckless [bnw] *roekeloos*
reckon I [ov ww] *houden voor, beschouwen* • (~ **in**) *meetellen* • (~ **with**) *rekening houden met* II [on ww] *menen*

reckoning [znw] • *berekening*
• *vergelding, verrekening*
reclaim [ov ww] • *terugwinnen* • *weer*
op 't goede pad brengen, beschaven
• *cultiveren* • *droogmaken* ‹v. land›
• *hergebruiken*
recline [on ww] • *leunen* • *liggen*
• *steunen*
recluse [znw] *kluizenaar*
recognition [znw] • *herkenning*
• *erkenning*
recognizable [bnw] *herkenbaar*
recognize [ov ww] • *herkennen*
• *erkennen*
recoil I [on ww] • *terugdeinzen*
• *terugstoten* ‹v. vuurwapen›
• (~ **from**) *terugdeinzen voor* • (~ **on**)
z. wreken op II [znw] • *terugslag*
• *reactie*
recollect [ov + on ww] *zich (weten te)*
herinneren
recollection [znw] *herinnering*
recommend [ov ww] *aanbevelen,*
adviseren
recommendation [znw] *aanbeveling*
recompense I [ov ww] • *vergoeden,*
vergelden • *belonen* II [znw] *vergoeding*
reconcile [ov ww] • *verzoenen,*
overeenbrengen • *bijleggen*
• (~ **to/with**) *verzoenen met*
recondite [bnw] *obscuur, diep(zinnig)*
recondition [ov ww] *opkalefateren,*
opknappen
reconnaissance [znw] • *verkenning*
• *verkenningspatrouille*
reconsider [ov + on ww] *heroverwegen*
reconstruct [ov ww] • *opnieuw*
opbouwen • *reconstrueren*
reconstruction [znw] • *reconstructie*
• *wederopbouw*
record I [ov + on ww] • *aantekenen,*
registreren, te boek stellen, optekenen
• *vastleggen* ‹op geluidsdrager›
• *vermelden* II [znw] • *record*
• *afschrift, document* • *verslag, verhaal*
• *reputatie, antecedenten* • *opname,*

grammofoonplaat
recorder [znw] • *griffier* • *archivaris*
• *(band)recorder* • *blokfluit*
recording [znw] *opname*
recount I [ov ww] *uitvoerig vertellen*
II [znw] *nieuwe telling*
recoup [ov ww] *terugwinnen*
recourse [znw] *toevlucht*
recover I [ov ww] *terugwinnen,*
terugkrijgen, terugvinden II [on ww]
genezen, herstellen, bijkomen, er weer
bovenop komen
recoverable [bnw] • *terug te krijgen*
• ‹jur.› *verhaalbaar*
recovery [znw] *herstel*
recreate [ov ww] • *opnieuw creëren*
• *terugroepen*
recreation [znw] • *speelkwartier*
• *ontspanning, recreatie* • *vermaak*
recreational [bnw] *recreatie-, recreatief*
recrimination [znw] *tegenverwijt*
recruit I [ov ww] *aanwerven, rekruteren*
II [on ww] • *rekruten (aan)werven*
• ‹vero.› *herstellen, herstel zoeken*
III [znw] *rekruut*
rectangle [znw] *rechthoek*
rectangular [bnw] *rechthoekig*
rectitude [znw] • *rechtschapenheid*
• *correctheid*
rector [znw] • *rector* • *predikant* ‹v.
angl. kerk›
rectory [znw] • *predikantsplaats*
• *pastorie*
recumbent [bnw] *(achterover)liggend*
recuperate I [ov ww] *doen herstellen, er*
weer bovenop brengen II [on ww]
herstellen, er weer bovenop komen
recur [on ww] *terugkeren, terugkomen,*
z. herhalen
recurrence [znw] • *herhaling*
• *toevlucht*
recurrent [bnw] *telkens terugkerend*
recycle [ov ww] *opnieuw in omloop*
brengen, verwerken tot nieuw product
red [bnw] *rood*
redden [ov + on ww] *rood*

maken/worden
reddish [bnw] *roodachtig, rossig*
redeem [ov ww] • *terugkopen, afkopen, vrijkopen, aflossen, inlossen* • *loskopen, verlossen* • *goedmaken*
redeemable [bnw] • *aflosbaar* • *inwisselbaar*
redemption [znw] • *aflossing* • *verlossing*
redouble [ov + on ww] (z.) *verdubbelen*
redoubtable [bnw] *geducht*
redress I [ov ww] *weer goedmaken, herstellen, vergoeden* II [znw] *herstel, vergoeding*
reduce [ov ww] • *verlagen, verminderen, verzwakken* • *(terug)brengen, herleiden*
reduction [znw] *vermindering*
redundancy [znw] *overtolligheid*
redundant [bnw] *overtollig*
reedy [bnw] *schel*
reef [znw] *rif*
reefer [znw] • *korte jas* • <sl.> *stickie*
reek I [on ww] • *stinken, rieken* <ook fig.> • *dampen, roken* II [znw] • *stank* • *damp, rook*
reel I [ov ww] • (~ **off**) *afrollen, afraffelen* II [on ww] • *duizelen* • *wankelen, waggelen* III [znw] • *film(strook)* • *Schotse dans* • *klos(je), haspel, spoel*
re-entry [znw] *herintreding*
refectory [znw] *refter*
refer I [ov ww] *verwijzen* II [on ww] • (~ **to**) *raadplegen, betrekking hebben op, zich wenden tot, zinspelen op*
referee [znw] *scheidsrechter*
referendum [znw] *volksstemming*
refill I [ov ww] *opnieuw vullen* II [znw] *vulling*
refine [ov ww] *verfijnen, raffineren, veredelen, zuiveren*
refined [bnw] *verfijnd, elegant, geraffineerd*
refinement [znw] *raffinement*
refinery [znw] *raffinaderij*

refit [ov ww] *herstellen*
reflect [ov ww] • *weerspiegelen, weergeven, terugkaatsen* • *bedenken, (over)peinzen*
reflection [znw] • *weerschijn, (spiegel)beeld* • *overdenking, 't nadenken, gedachte*
reflective [bnw] *nadenkend, peinzend*
reflex [znw] *reflex(beweging)*
reflexive [bnw] *wederkerend*
reform I [ov ww] *hervormen, verbeteren, bekeren, tot inkeer brengen* II [on ww] *zich bekeren* III [znw] *beterschap, herziening*
reformer [znw] *hervormer*
refract [ov ww] *breken* <v. licht>
refractory [bnw] *onhandelbaar*
refrain I [on ww] *z. onthouden* • (~ **from**) *afzien van* II [znw] *refrein*
refresh [ov + on ww] (z.) *opfrissen, (z.) verfrissen*
refreshing [bnw] • *verfrissend* • *aangenaam, verrassend*
refreshment [znw] • *verversing* • *verfrissing*
refrigerate [ov + on ww] (af)koelen
refuel [ov + on ww] *tanken*
refuge [znw] • *toevlucht(soord)* • *redmiddel*
refugee [znw] *vluchteling*
refusal [znw] *weigering*
refute [ov ww] *weerleggen*
regain [ov ww] *herkrijgen, terugwinnen*
regal [bnw] *koninklijk*
regale [ov ww] *onthalen* • (~ **with**) *vergasten op*
regard I [ov ww] *beschouwen* II [znw] *achting*
regardless I [bnw] *onattent, onachtzaam* II [bijw] *niettemin, desondanks*
regatta [znw] *roeiwedstrijd, zeilwedstrijd*
regency [znw] *regentschap*
regicide [znw] *koningsmoord(enaar)*
regimental [bnw] *regiments-*

region [znw] *streek, gebied*
regional [bnw] *gewestelijk*
register I [ov + on ww] *registreren*
II [ov ww] • *(laten) inschrijven,*
aangeven • *uitdrukken, tonen* • *(laten)*
aantekenen ‹v. brief› III [on ww] • *z.*
(laten) inschrijven • *in zich opnemen*
IV [znw] *register, lijst*
registrar [znw] • *griffier* • *ambtenaar*
v.d. burgerlijke stand • *bewaarder der*
registers
registry [znw] • *registratie* • *archief*
regress [on ww] *achteruitgaan*
regret I [ov ww] *betreuren* II [znw]
spijt, berouw
regretful [bnw] *spijtig, treurig*
regrettable [bnw] *betreurenswaardig*
regroup [ov + on ww] *(z.) hergroeperen*
regular I [znw] *vaste afnemer, vaste*
klant, stamgast II [bnw] • *regelmatig,*
geregeld, vast ‹klant› • *correct, zoals*
het hoort • ‹inf.› *echt, doortrapt* • ‹AE›
gewoon, normaal
regularity [znw] *regelmatigheid*
regularize [ov ww] *regulariseren*
regulate [ov ww] *reguleren,*
reglementeren, regelen
regulation [znw] • *voorschrift*
• *voorgeschreven*
regulator [znw] *regulateur*
regurgitate [ov ww] • *uitbraken*
• *na-apen*
rehabilitate [ov ww] • *rehabiliteren*
• *revalideren* • *renoveren*
rehash I [ov ww] *weer uit de kast halen,*
opnieuw brengen II [znw]
herbewerking, oude kost ‹fig.›
rehearse [ov ww] • *herhalen, weer*
opzeggen • *repeteren* ‹toneel›
rehouse [ov ww] *een nieuw onderdak*
geven
reign I [on ww] *regeren, heersen*
II [znw] *regering*
reimburse [ov ww] *terugbetalen,*
vergoeden
reindeer [znw] *rendier*

reinforce [ov ww] *versterken*
reinforcement [znw] *versterking*
reinstate [ov ww] *herstellen*
reissue [ov ww] *opnieuw uitgeven*
reiterate [ov ww] *herhalen*
reject [ov ww] *verwerpen, afwijzen*
rejoice [on ww] *zich verheugen*
rejoinder [znw] *(bits) antwoord*
rejuvenate [ov + on ww] *weer jong*
maken/worden
relapse I [on ww] *(weer) instorten,*
(weer) terugvallen II [znw] *instorting,*
terugval
relate I [ov ww] • *vertellen* • *(onderling)*
verband leggen • *(~ to/with) in*
verband brengen met II [on ww] *in*
verband staan
relation [znw] • *betrekking,*
verhouding • *(bloed)verwantschap*
• *familielid*
relationship [znw] • *verhouding*
• *verwantschap*
relative I [znw] *familielid* II [bnw]
• *betrekkelijk* • *in betrekking staand*
relativity [znw] • *betrekkelijkheid*
• *relativiteit*
relax [ov + on ww] *(z.) ontspannen*
relaxation [znw] *ontspanning*
relay I [ov ww] • *aflossen* • *relayeren*
II [znw] • *aflossing* ‹v. wacht,*
*paarden› • *relais*
release I [ov ww] • *loslaten, bevrijden,*
vrijlaten • *vrijgeven* • *voor 't eerst*
vertonen ‹film›, *op de markt brengen*
• *(~ from) ontheffen van* II [znw]
• *bevrijding, vrijgeving* • *nieuwe*
film/lp • *perscommuniqué*
relegate [ov ww] *degraderen,*
overplaatsen
relent [on ww] *medelijden tonen, z.*
laten vermurwen
relentless [bnw] *meedogenloos*
relevance [znw] *relevantie*
relevant [bnw] *relevant, toepasselijk*
reliable [bnw] *betrouwbaar*
reliance [znw] *afhankelijkheid*

reliant [bnw] afhankelijk
relic [znw] • reliek, relikwie • overblijfsel
relief [znw] • verlichting, opluchting,
    welkome afwisseling • steun, hulp
    • ontheffing • aflossing • reliëf, plastiek
religion [znw] godsdienst
religious [bnw] religieus
relinquish [ov ww] opgeven, afstand
    doen v.
relish I [ov ww] genoegen scheppen in
    II [znw] kruiderij
relive [ov ww] opnieuw beleven
reluctance [znw] tegenzin
reluctant [bnw] onwillig
remain [on ww] (over)blijven, nog over
    zijn
remand [znw] • voorarrest • preventief
    gedetineerde
remark I [ov ww] opmerken II [on ww]
    opmerkingen maken III [znw]
    opmerking
remarkable [bnw] merkwaardig
remarry [on ww] hertrouwen
remedial [bnw] verbeterend
remedy I [ov ww] verhelpen, genezen
    II [znw] • (genees)middel • herstel
remember I [ov + on ww] (z.)
    herinneren, nog weten, niet vergeten,
    onthouden II [ov ww] • denken aan
    • bedenken <met fooi, legaat>
remembrance [znw] • geheugen
    • aandenken
reminder [znw] • waarschuwing
    • aanmaning
reminisce [on ww] herinneringen
    ophalen, mijmeren
reminiscence [znw] herinnering
reminiscent [bnw] met plezier
    terugdenkend
remiss [bnw] nonchalant, lui
remission [znw] • vermindering
    • vergeving
remit I [ov ww] • overmaken
    • toezenden II [znw] gebied <fig.>
remittance [znw] geldzending, remise
remnant [znw] • rest, restant • coupon

remodel [ov ww] opnieuw modelleren
remonstrate I [ov ww] tegenwerpen
    II [on ww] protesteren
remorse [znw] berouw
remorseful [bnw] berouwvol
remorseless [bnw] meedogenloos
remote [bnw] • ver weg • afgelegen
removal [znw] verplaatsing,
    verwijdering
remove [ov ww] • verwijderen,
    afnemen, wegnemen, eraf doen
    • opruimen, uit de weg ruimen
remover [znw] vlekkenwater,
    afbijtmiddel, remover <v. nagellak>
remunerative [bnw] lonend
rename [ov ww] hernoemen
rend [ov ww] • stukscheuren,
    verscheuren • klieven
render [ov ww] • teruggeven
    • weergeven • betuigen, betonen
    • verlenen
rendering [znw] weergave
rendition [znw] uitvoering, weergave,
    vertaling
renegade [znw] afvallige, overloper
renew [ov ww] • vernieuwen,
    hernieuwen • doen herleven • hervatten
    • vervangen, verversen • prolongeren,
    verlengen
renewable [bnw] • vernieuwbaar
    • verlengbaar
renewal [znw] • vernieuwing
    • verlenging
rennet [znw] stremsel
renounce [ov ww] • afstand doen v.,
    afzien v. • verwerpen, verloochenen
renovate [ov ww] renoveren
renowned [bnw] vermaard
rent I [ww] verl.tijd + volt.deelw.
    → rend II [ov ww] (ver)huren,
    (ver)pachten, in huur of pacht hebben
    III [znw] • kloof, scheur • huur, pacht
rental [znw] huursom, pachtsom
renunciation [znw] het afstand doen
reopen [ov ww] heropenen
reorganize [ov + on ww] reorganiseren

rep [afk] • (representative)
vertegenwoordiger • (repertory)
reprisetheater
repair I [ov ww] • repareren
• vergoeden, weer goedmaken
II [on ww] • (~ to) z. begeven naar
III [znw] onderhoud
reparation [znw] • schadeloosstelling,
herstelbetaling • reparatie
repartee [znw] gevat antwoord
repatriate [ov + on ww] naar 't
vaderland terugkeren/-zenden
repay [ov ww] • terugbetalen
• vergelden, vergoeden
repayable [bnw] aflosbaar
repayment [znw] → repay
repeal I [ov ww] herroepen II [znw]
herroeping
repeat I [ov ww] • herhalen • opzeggen,
navertellen II [on ww] repeteren
III [znw] • herhaling • bis • <muz.>
herhalingsteken, reprise
repeater [znw] repeteergeweer
repel [ov ww] • terugdrijven • afstoten
repellent I [znw] afweermiddel
II [bnw] weerzinwekkend, onprettig
repent [ov + on ww] berouw hebben
repentance [znw] berouw
repentant [bnw] berouwvol
repercussion [znw] • reactie
• weerklank
repetition [znw] herhaling
repetitious, repetitive [bnw] (zich)
herhalend
replace [ov ww] • terugzetten
• vervangen
replaceable [bnw] vervangbaar
replacement [znw] vervanging
replay I [ov + on ww] opnieuw laten
zien/horen, herhalen II [znw]
• overgespeelde wedstrijd • herhaling
<v. beeldscène/geluidsfragment>
replenish [ov ww] bijvullen, aanvullen
replete [bnw] vol, verzadigd
replica [znw] duplicaat
reply I [ov + on ww] antwoorden

• (~ to) beantwoorden II [znw]
antwoord
report I [ov ww] • verslag doen v.,
rapport uitbrengen v. • melden
II [on ww] verslag doen/uitbrengen,
rapporteren • (~ to) zich melden bij
III [znw] • verslag • gerucht • knal,
schot
reportedly [bijw] naar verluidt
reporter [znw] • verslaggever
• rapporteur
repose I [on ww] rusten II [znw] rust
reprehensible [bnw] laakbaar
represent [ov ww] • voorstellen
• vertegenwoordigen
representation [znw] • voorstelling
• vertegenwoordiging, inspraak
representative I [znw]
(volks)vertegenwoordiger II [bnw]
• vertegenwoordigend • representatief
• kenmerkend, typisch
repress [ov ww] onderdrukken,
bedwingen
repression [znw] • verdringing
• onderdrukking
repressive [bnw] onderdrukkend
reprieve I [ov ww] gratie verlenen
II [znw] gratie
reprimand I [ov ww] berispen II [znw]
officiële berisping
reprint I [ov ww] herdrukken II [znw]
herdruk
reprisal [znw] vergelding, represaille
reproach I [ov ww] • verwijten
• berispen II [znw] verwijt
reproachful [bnw] verwijtend
reprobate [znw] verworpene
reproduce I [ov ww] • weergeven,
reproduceren, kopiëren • (opnieuw)
voortbrengen II [on ww] zich
voortplanten
reproduction [znw] reproductie
reproductive [bnw] • reproducerend
• voortplantings-
reproof [znw] • verwijt • berisping
• afkeuring

reptile [znw] *reptiel*
republic [znw] *republiek*
repugnance [znw] *afkeer, weerzin*
repugnant [bnw] *weerzinwekkend*
repulse [ov ww] • *afslaan, terugslaan*
• *afwijzen*
repulsion [znw] • *tegenzin* • *afstoting*
repulsive [bnw] *weerzinwekkend*
reputable [bnw] *fatsoenlijk, goed*
bekend staand
reputation [znw] *reputatie, (goede)*
naam
repute [znw] *vermaardheid, (goede)*
naam, roep
reputed [bnw] • *befaamd* • *vermeend*
request I [ov ww] *verzoeken* II [znw]
verzoek
requiem [znw] *requiem, uitvaartdienst*
require [ov ww] • *eisen* • *nodig hebben,*
vereisen
requirement [znw] *eis, vereiste*
requisite I [znw] *vereiste* II [bnw]
vereist
requisition I [ov ww] *vorderen*
II [znw] *(op)vordering*
requite [ov ww] *beantwoorden*
rescind [ov ww] *opheffen, nietig*
verklaren
rescue I [ov ww] *redden, bevrijden*
II [znw] *redding*
rescuer [znw] *redder*
research [znw] *(wetenschappelijk)*
onderzoek
researcher [znw] *onderzoeker,*
wetenschapper
resemblance [znw] *gelijkenis*
resemble [ov ww] *lijken op*
resent [ov ww] *kwaad zijn over,*
kwalijk nemen
resentful [bnw] • *kwaad, boos*
• *lichtgeraakt*
resentment [znw] *rancune, wrevel*
reservation [znw] • *voorbehoud*
• *(indianen)reservaat* • *reservering*
• *reservatie*
reserve I [ov ww] *reserveren* II [znw]

• *voorbehoud* • *gereserveerdheid*
reserved [bnw] *gesloten, gereserveerd,*
zwijgzaam
reservoir [znw] • *reservoir*
• *reservevoorraad*
reset [ov ww] <comp.> • *zetten* <v. bot>
• <comp.> *opnieuw opstarten*
resettle [ov ww] *opnieuw vestigen*
reshuffle I [ov ww] *herschikken,*
opnieuw schudden <kaartspel> II [znw]
herverdeling
reside [on ww] *wonen, zijn standplaats*
hebben • *(~ in) berusten bij*
residence [znw] • *woning*
• *woonplaats, standplaats* • *residentie*
resident I [znw] *inwoner, vaste*
bewoner II [bnw] *(in)wonend*
residential [bnw] *woon-*
residual [bnw] *resterend*
residue [znw] *rest, overschot*
resign I [ov ww] • *afstand doen v.,*
overgeven • *opgeven* II [on ww] *ontslag*
nemen, aftreden
resignation [znw] • *ontslag* • *berusting*
resigned [bnw] *gelaten*
resilience [znw] *veerkracht*
resilient [bnw] *veerkrachtig*
resin [znw] *hars*
resinous [bnw] *harsig*
resist I [ov ww] • *bestand zijn tegen,*
weren • *z. verzetten tegen* II [on ww]
weerstand bieden, z. verzetten
resistance [znw] • *verzet* • <techn.>
weerstand
resistant [bnw] *weerstand biedend,*
immuun, bestand
resolute [bnw] *vastberaden*
resolution [znw] • *besluit* • *resolutie*
• *ontknoping* • *vastberadenheid*
resolve I [ov ww] • *oplossen*
• *ontbinden, herleiden* II [on ww]
besluiten, beslissen III [znw] *besluit*
resound [ov + on ww] *(doen)*
weerklinken, galmen
resounding [bnw] • *luid klinkend,*
galmend • *eclatant, daverend*

resource [znw] • hulpbron • middel, toevlucht, uitweg • vindingrijkheid
respect I [ov ww] eerbiedigen II [znw] • eerbied, achting, respect • opzicht
respectable [bnw] • fatsoenlijk • behoorlijk
respectful [bnw] eerbiedig
respective [bnw] onderscheidenlijk, respectief
respiration [znw] ademhaling
respirator [znw] • ademhalings-/zuurstofmasker • gasmasker
respiratory [bnw] ademhalings-
resplendent [bnw] schitterend
respond [on ww] antwoorden • (~ to) reageren op
response [znw] • antwoord • reactie, weerklank • tegenzang, responsorium
responsibility [znw] verantwoordelijkheid
responsible [bnw] • verantwoordelijk • aansprakelijk
responsive [bnw] • antwoordend • reagerend • sympathiek
rest I [ov ww] • laten rusten, rust geven • steunen, liggen II [on ww] • uitrusten, berusten • blijven III [znw] • steun, houder, statief • rust
restate [ov ww] herformuleren
restful [bnw] • rustig • kalmerend
restitution [znw] schadeloosstelling
restive [bnw] koppig, prikkelbaar, onhandelbaar
restless [bnw] • ongedurig • rusteloos
restoration [znw] restauratie
restorative I [znw] herstellend middel II [bnw] herstellend
restore [ov ww] • herstellen, restaureren • teruggeven • weer op zijn plaats zetten
restorer [znw] restaurateur <v. kunstwerken>
restrain [ov ww] • weerhouden, bedwingen • beperken
restrained [bnw] beheerst, rustig, kalm

restraint [znw] • beperking • terughoudendheid
restrict [ov ww] beperken
restriction [znw] beperking
restrictive [bnw] beperkend
result I [on ww] • (~ from) volgen uit • (~ in) uitlopen op II [znw] • gevolg, resultaat • afloop, uitkomst
resume [ov + on ww] hervatten
résumé [znw] resumé, samenvatting
resumption [znw] hervatting
resurgent [bnw] terugkerend, herlevend
resurrect [ov ww] doen herleven
resuscitate I [ov ww] weer opwekken, bijbrengen, reanimeren II [on ww] weer opleven, bijkomen
retail I [ov ww] • verkopen • uitvoerig vertellen II [znw] kleinhandel
retailer [znw] kleinhandelaar
retain [ov ww] • nemen <v. advocaat> • behouden, onthouden • tegenhouden, vasthouden
retainer [znw] • vooruitbetaald honorarium • vazal
retake [ov ww] opnieuw nemen
retaliate [on ww] wraak nemen
retaliative, retaliatory [bnw] vergeldings-
retard [ov ww] vertragen
retch [on ww] kokhalzen
retentive [bnw] vasthoudend
rethink [ov + on ww] heroverwegen, nog eens bekijken
reticence [znw] • zwijgzaamheid • terughoudendheid
reticent [bnw] zwijgzaam, gesloten
retinue [znw] gevolg
retire I [ov ww] • terugtrekken, intrekken • ontslaan II [on ww] • met pensioen gaan, ontslag nemen • zich terugtrekken, naar bed gaan
retired [bnw] • eenzaam • gepensioneerd
retirement [znw] • pensionering • eenzaamheid
retiring [bnw] • pensioen- • bescheiden

retouch [ov ww] bijwerken, retoucheren
retrace [ov ww] volgen, (weer) nagaan
retract I [ov ww] intrekken,
terugtrekken II [on ww] ingetrokken
(kunnen) worden
retractable [bnw] intrekbaar
retraction [znw] intrekking, herroeping
retread [znw] gecoverde autoband
retreat I [on ww] terugwijken, (zich)
terugtrekken II [znw] • wijkplaats
• terugtocht • afzondering
• retraite(huis)
retribution [znw] vergelding,
genoegdoening
retributive [bnw] vergeldend
retrieval [znw] het terughalen
retrieve [ov ww] • terugkrijgen,
terugvinden • apporteren
retroactive [bnw] met terugwerkende
kracht
retrograde [bnw] • achteruitgaand
• omgekeerd
retrogressive [bnw] achteruitgaand
retrospect, retrospection [znw]
terugblik
return I [ov ww] • teruggeven,
terugzetten • beantwoorden II [on ww]
terugkomen, teruggaan, terugkeren
III [znw] • omzet, opbrengst
• terugkomst • retour(biljet) • opgave
returnable [bnw] retour-
reunion [znw] • hereniging • reünie
reunite [ov ww] herenigen
rev [ov + on ww] • (~ up) plankgas
geven, sneller draaien <v. motor>
revalue [ov ww] revalueren,
herwaarderen
reveal [ov ww] openbaren,
bekendmaken
revealing [bnw] onthullend,
veelzeggend
revel I [on ww] fuiven, boemelen,
feesten • (~ in) genieten van II [znw]
pret, feest
revelation [znw] onthulling,
openbaring

reveller [znw] pretmaker
revelry [znw] pretmakerij
revenue [znw] (staats)inkomen,
inkomsten, baten
reverberate [ov + on ww]
terugkaatsen, weerkaatsen
revere [ov ww] (ver)eren, met eerbied
opzien tegen
reverence [znw] eerbied, verering
reverend I [znw] geestelijke II [bnw]
eerwaard(ig)
reverent, reverential [bnw] eerbiedig
reverie [znw] mijmering
reversal [znw] het wisselen, ommekeer
reverse I [ov ww] • omkeren,
omschakelen • achteruitrijden
• herroepen, intrekken II [on ww]
achteruitrijden III [znw]
• tegenovergestelde, omgekeerde
• tegenslag • achteruit <v. auto>
IV [bnw] tegenovergesteld, omgekeerd
reversion [znw] terugkeer
revert [on ww] • terugkeren,
terugkomen • terugvallen <v.e. erfgoed
aan oorspr. schenker of diens
erfgenamen>
review I [ov ww] • nog eens onder de
loep nemen, opnieuw bekijken
• inspecteren • recenseren • herzien
II [znw] • recensie • inspectie, parade
• tijdschrift • overzicht • herziening
reviewer [znw] recensent
revile [ov ww] uitschelden, tekeergaan
tegen
revise I [ov + on ww] blokken II [ov ww]
nazien, herzien, reviseren
revision [znw] • herziening • herziene
uitgave
revival [znw] • opleving • reprise
<toneel>
revive [ov + on ww] (doen) herleven,
(doen) bijkomen
revocation [znw] herroeping
revoke [ov ww] herroepen
revolt I [ov ww] doen walgen
II [on ww] • in opstand komen

• *walgen* III [znw] *opstand*
revolting [bnw] • *opstandig*
• *weerzinwekkend*
revolutionary I [znw] *revolutionair*
II [bnw] *revolutionair*
revolutionize [ov ww] *'n ommekeer*
teweegbrengen in
revolve [ov ww] *omwentelen,*
(om)draaien
revulsion [znw] *walging*
reward I [ov ww] *belonen* II [znw]
beloning
rewarding [bnw] *lonend, de moeite*
waard
rewind [ov ww] *opnieuw opwinden,*
terugspoelen
rewrite [ov ww] *omwerken*
rhapsody [znw] *rapsodie*
rhetoric [znw] • *retorica* • *retoriek*
rhetorical [bnw] *retorisch*
rheumatic I [znw] *reumalijder*
II [bnw] *reumatisch*
rhino [znw] *neushoorn*
rhubarb [znw] *rabarber*
rhyme I [on ww] *rijmen* II [znw]
rijm(pje), poëzie
rhythm [znw] *ritme*
rib I [ov ww] ‹inf.› *plagen* II [znw] • *rib*
• *nerf* • *richel* • *balein*
ribald [bnw] *onbehoorlijk, schunnig*
ribbon [znw] *lint, strook*
rice [znw] *rijst*
rich [bnw] • *kostbaar* • *machtig* ‹v.
spijzen› • *vol, warm* ‹v. kleur, klank›
• *rijk* • *vruchtbaar*
richly [bijw] *rijkelijk*
rick I [ov ww] *verrekken* II [znw] *hoop*
hooi, hooimijt
rickets [znw] *Engelse ziekte*
rickety [bnw] *wankel, gammel*
ricochet I [on ww] *afketsen* ‹v. kogel›
II [znw] *verdwaalde kogel*
rid [ov ww] *bevrijden* • (~ **of**) *ontdoen*
van
ridden [ww] volt. deelw. → **ride**
riddle I [ov ww] *doorzeven* II [znw]

raadsel
ride I [ov + on ww] • *rijden* • *drijven,*
varen II [znw] *rit, reis, tocht*
rider [znw] • *ruiter, (be)rijder*
• *toegevoegde clausule, toevoeging*
ridge [znw] • *heuvelrug, bergkam*
• *richel* • *nok*
ridicule I [ov ww] *belachelijk maken*
II [znw] *spot*
ridiculous [bnw] *belachelijk*
rife [bnw] *algemeen heersend*
rifle I [ov ww] • *plunderen*
• (~ **through**) *doorzoeken* II [znw]
geweer
rift [znw] *spleet, scheur*
rig I [ov ww] • *slinks bewerken,*
manipuleren • *uitrusten* • (~ **out**)
uitdossen • (~ **up**) *in elkaar flansen*
II [znw] • *boortoren, booreiland*
• *aankleding, kledij*
rigging [znw] *tuigage*
right I [ov ww] *(iets) rechtzetten*
II [znw] • *recht* • *rechts* III [bnw]
• *recht* • *juist* • *goed* • *passend*
IV [bijw] • *rechts* • *meteen*
rightful [bnw] • *rechtmatig*
• *rechtvaardig*
rightist I [znw] *rechtse* II [bnw] *rechts*
(georiënteerd)
rigid [bnw] • *stijf* • *onbuigzaam, streng*
rigmarole [znw] *rompslomp*
rigorous [bnw] *streng, hard*
rigour [znw] *strengheid, hardheid*
rile [ov ww] *kwaad maken*
rim [znw] • *rand* • *(bril)montuur*
rimless [bnw] *zonder rand*
rind [znw] • *(kaas)korst, schil*
• *(spek)zwoerd*
ring I [ov ww] • *bellen, laten klinken,*
luiden • *opbellen* • *ringen, ring*
aandoen • *omringen* • (~ **in**) *inluiden*
• (~ **out**) *uitluiden* • (~ **up**) *opbellen*
II [on ww] • *klinken* • *bellen* • *gaan* ‹v.
bel›, *overgaan* ‹v. telefoon› • (~ **for**)
bellen (om) • (~ **off**) *neerleggen* ‹v.
telefoon› • (~ **with**) *weerklinken van*

III [znw] • *ring* • *kring* • *kliek,*
combinatie • *circus, (ren)baan* • *klank*
• *gelui, gebel*
ringer [znw] *klokkenluider*
ringlet [znw] *haarkrulletje*
rink [znw] • *ijs(hockey)baan*
• *rolschaatsbaan*
rinse I [ov ww] *(om)spoelen* II [znw]
spoeling
riot I [on ww] *oproer maken* II [znw]
• *oproer, rel* • *vrolijke bende*
riotous [bnw] *oproerig*
rip I [ov + on ww] *scheuren* • (~ **off**)
bedriegen, stelen • (~ **up**) *verscheuren*
II [znw] *scheur, torn*
ripe [bnw] *rijp, belegen*
ripple I [ov + on ww] *rimpelen, golven*
II [znw] *rimpeling, golfje(s)*
rise I [on ww] • *groter/hoger worden,*
opkomen, (ver)rijzen, stijgen • *(zich)*
verheffen • *uiteengaan* <v.
vergadering> • *opstaan* • *opgaan,*
omhooggaan • (~ **from**) *ontspringen*
uit, voortkomen uit • (~ **up**) *in*
opstand komen II [znw] • *helling,*
verhoging • *opslag*
riser [znw] * *early* ~ *vroege vogel*
rising I [znw] *opstand* II [bnw]
opkomend
risk I [ov ww] *wagen, riskeren* II [znw]
risico, gevaar
risky [bnw] *gewaagd*
ritual I [znw] *ritueel* II [bnw] *ritueel*
rival I [ov ww] *wedijveren met, trachten*
te evenaren II [znw] *mededinger,*
medeminnaar III [bnw] *mededingend,*
concurrerend
rivalry [znw] *rivaliteit, wedijver*
river [znw] *rivier*
rivet I [ov ww] • *(vast)klinken* • *boeien*
<ook fig.>, *vestigen* <de ogen>,
concentreren <de aandacht> II [znw]
klinknagel
rivulet [znw] *riviertje, beekje*
roach [znw] *voorn*
road [znw] *(straat)weg*

roam I [ov + on ww] *zwerven (door)*
II [znw] *zwerftocht* <te voet>
roar I [ov + on ww] *brullen, bulderen*
II [znw] *gebulder*
roaring [bnw] • *denderend* • *bulderend*
roast I [ov + on ww] • *braden, roosteren*
• *branden* II [ov ww] *in de maling*
nemen III [znw] *gebraad* IV [bnw]
geroosterd
rob [ov + on ww] *(be)stelen, (be)roven*
robber [znw] *dief, rover*
robbery [znw] *roof, diefstal*
robe I [ov ww] *zich kleden* II [znw]
• *kamerjas* • *toga, ambtsgewaad*
• *robe, gewaad*
robin [znw] *roodborstje*
robust [bnw] • *robuust* • *inspannend*
rock I [ov + on ww] • *schommelen,*
wieg(el)en • *(doen) wankelen* II [znw]
• *rots(blok), steen* • *kandij, suikerstok*
• *rock(muziek)*
rocker [znw] • *schommelstoel* • *nozem*
• *gebogen hout onder wieg*
rocket I [on ww] *omhoog schieten*
II [znw] • *raket* • *uitbrander* • *vuurpijl*
rocky [bnw] • *rotsachtig* • *gammel,*
wankel
rod [znw] • *staf, staaf, stang* • *hengel*
rode [ww] *verl. tijd* → **ride**
rodent [znw] *knaagdier*
roe [znw] *ree*
roguish [bnw] *schurkachtig*
role [znw] *rol*
roll I [ov ww] *(op)rollen* • (~ **up**)
oprollen II [on ww] • *rollen, rijden*
• *woelen* III [znw] • *rol* • *broodje*
roller [znw] • *roller* • *wals*
rolling [bnw] *golvend, deinend*
roly-poly [bnw] *mollig*
Roman I [znw] • *rooms-katholiek*
• *Romein* II [bnw] • *Romeins*
• *rooms(-katholiek)*
romantic I [znw] *romanticus* II [bnw]
romantisch
romanticism [znw] *romantiek*
romanticize [ov ww] *romantisch*

maken
romp I [on ww] *stoeien, ravotten*
II [znw] *stoeipartij*
roof I [ov ww] *onder dak brengen,*
overdekken II [znw] *dak*
roofing [znw] • *dakbedekking*
• *dekmateriaal*
rook I [ov ww] *afzetten* II [znw] • *roek*
• *toren* ‹schaakspel›
rookie [znw] *rekruut*
room I [on ww] ‹AE› *op (een) kamer(s)*
wonen II [znw] • *kamer, zaal* • *ruimte,*
plaats • *gelegenheid, aanleiding*
roomy [bnw] *ruim, breed*
roost I [on ww] *op stok gaan* II [znw]
roest, (kippen)stok, nachthok
rooster [znw] *haan*
root I [ov ww] *omwroeten* • (~ **out**) *te*
voorschijn brengen, opscharrelen,
opsnorren • (~ **up**) *uittrekken* ‹v.*
plant› II [on ww] *inwortelen,*
wortelschieten • (~ **for**) *zich inzetten*
voor III [znw] • *wortel* • *kern, bron,*
grondslag
rope I [ov ww] • *vastbinden* • *vangen*
‹m. lasso› II [znw] *touw*
rosary [znw] *rozenkrans*
rose I [znw] *roos* II [bnw] *rozerood,*
bruinroze
rosemary [znw] *rozemarijn*
rosette [znw] *rozet*
roster [znw] *dienstrooster*
rostrum [znw] *spreekgestoelte,*
podium, publieke tribune
rosy [bnw] • *roze* • *rooskleurig*
rot I [ov ww] *doen rotten, bederven*
II [on ww] *rotten, verrotten, bederven*
III [znw] • *rotheid, rotte plek* • *onzin*
rota [znw] *(dienst)rooster*
rotary [bnw] *roterend*
rotate [ov + on ww] • *draaien, wentelen*
• *rouleren*
rotation [znw] • *rotatie, roulering*
• *vruchtwisseling*
rote [znw] *domme routine*
rotor [znw] *(draai)wiek v.e. helikopter*

rotten [bnw] • *(ver)rot* • *corrupt*
• *waardeloos, beroerd, slecht*
rotter [znw] *mispunt, vent/vrouw van*
niks
rotund [bnw] *mollig, gezet*
rough I [znw] *ruwe klant* II [bnw]
• *ruw, ruig* • *guur, stormachtig*
• *onbeschaafd* • *hard, drastisch*
• *globaal*
roughage [znw] • *ruwvoer* • *vezelrijk*
voedsel
roughen [ov + on ww] *ruw*
maken/worden
round I [ov ww] • (~ **off**) *afronden*
II [znw] • *ronde, reeks* • *sport* ‹v.*
ladder› • *canon* • *toer* ‹breien›
III [bnw] • *rond* • *afgerond* IV [bijw]
• *rond, om* • *in 't rond, rondom* V [vz]
rondom
roundabout I [znw] • *draaimolen*
• *verkeersrotonde* II [bnw] *omslachtig,*
wijdlopig
roundly [bijw] *botweg, rondweg,*
ronduit
rouse I [ov ww] • *prikkelen* • *wakker*
maken, (op)wekken, opschrikken
II [on ww] *wakker worden*
rove [ov + on ww] *rondzwerven (door),*
ronddolen (door), dwalen (door)
row I [ov + on ww] *roeien (tegen)*
II [znw] • *rij* • *huizenrij, straat* • *herrie,*
drukte • *ruzie*
rowdy I [znw] *herrieschopper* II [bnw]
lawaaierig
rower [znw] *roeier*
royal I [znw] *lid v. koninklijk huis*
II [bnw] • *konings-, koninklijk*
• *schitterend, heerlijk*
royalty [znw] • *koningschap,*
koninklijke waardigheid • *vorstelijke*
personen • *royalty*
rub I [ov ww] • *poetsen, boenen*
• *inwrijven, afwrijven* • (~ **down**)
afwrijven, stevig afdrogen • (~ **in**)
inwrijven, erin stampen ‹v. les›
• (~ **off**) *eraf wrijven* • (~ **out**)

uitgummen • (~ **together**) *tegen elkaar wrijven* II [znw] • *moeilijkheid, hindernis* • *poetsbeurt* • *robber*
rubber I [znw] • *wrijfkussen* • *rubber, gummi, elastiek* • *robber* II [bnw] *rubberen*
rubbish [znw] • *rommel* • *onzin*
rubble [znw] *puin*
rubicund [bnw] *blozend*
rubric [znw] *rubriek*
ruby I [znw] *robijn* II [bnw] *robijnrood*
ruck I [on ww] *verkreukelen* II [znw] • *kreukel* • *(de) massa*
rucksack [znw] *rugzak, ransel*
rudder [znw] *roer*
ruddy [bnw] • *verdomd(e)* • *rood, blozend* • *rossig*
rude [bnw] • *ruw* • *lomp* • *primitief, onbeschaafd*
rudimentary [bnw] • *rudimentair* • *in een beginstadium*
rue [ov ww] *berouw hebben over/van, treuren om*
rueful [bnw] *verdrietig, treurig*
ruff [znw] • *Spaanse plooikraag* • *verenkraag*
ruffian [znw] *bullebak, schurk, woesteling*
ruffle [ov ww] • *verfrommelen* • *rimpelen* • *uit zijn humeur brengen*
rug [znw] • *(haard)kleedje* • *(reis)deken*
rugged [bnw] • *ruw, hobbelig* • *hoekig* • *hard, nors* • *krachtig*
ruin I [ov ww] *te gronde richten, vernielen, ruïneren* II [znw] • *ondergang* • *wrak* ‹fig.›
rule I [ov ww] *heersen* • (~ **out**) *uitsluiten* II [on ww] *heersen, regeren* III [znw] • *regel* • *liniaal* • *heerschappij, bestuur*
ruler [znw] • *regeerder, heerser* • *liniaal*
rum I [znw] *rum* II [bnw] *vreemd, raar*
rumble I [ov ww] *doorhebben* II [on ww] *rommelen* III [znw] • *storend signaal, brom* ‹elektronica› • *geroezemoes*

ruminate I [ov ww] *(nog eens) overdenken* II [on ww] *herkauwen*
ruminative [bnw] *peinzend*
rummage I [ov ww] • *doorsnuffelen* • *overhoop halen, rommel maken* • (~ **out**) *opscharrelen* II [on ww] *rommelen, snuffelen*
rumour [znw] *gerucht*
rump [znw] *staart(stuk), achterste*
rumple [ov ww] *in de war maken*
rumpus [znw] *tumult, herrie, hooglopende ruzie*
run I [ov ww] • *lopen over* • *laten lopen, laten gaan, rijden, laten stromen* • *aan 't hoofd staan van, leiden, sturen* • *brengen* ‹v. artikel, toneelstuk› • *rijgen* • *(binnen)smokkelen* • (~ **down**) *overrijden, afgeven op* • (~ **in**) *inrekenen* • (~ **into**) *laten vervallen tot, steken in* • (~ **off**) *laten weglopen* • (~ **out**) *afrollen* • (~ **over**) *overrijden, laten gaan over* • (~ **through**) *doorsteken, doorhalen, erdoor brengen* II [on ww] • *hardlopen* • *z. haasten* • *doorlopen, uitlopen, z. snel verspreiden* • *een run maken* ‹bij cricket› • (~ **about**) *heen en weer lopen, rondsjouwen* • (~ **across**) *(toevallig) tegenkomen* • (~ **after**) *achternalopen* • (~ **away**) *weglopen, ervandoor gaan* • (~ **down**) *opraken, uitgeput raken, vervallen* • (~ **for**) *kandidaat zijn voor* • (~ **in**) *binnenlopen* • (~ **into**) *in botsing komen met* • (~ **off**) *de benen nemen, weglopen* • (~ **on**) *doordraven, doorlopen, doorgaan* • (~ **out**) *opraken, verlopen, ongeldig worden* • (~ **over**) *overlopen* • (~ **through**) *doorlopen, lopen door, doornemen* • (~ **to**) *(op)lopen tot, gaan tot* • (~ **together**) *in elkaar lopen* • (~ **up**) *oplopen* III [znw] • *(kippen)ren* • *vrij gebruik, vrije toegang* • *run* ‹bij cricket› • *(ver)loop* • *toeloop, gang* • *ritje* • *uitstapje*

rung I [ww] volt. deelw. → ring
II [znw] • sport <v. ladder> • spijl
runner [znw] • hardloper • wisselloper,
ordonnans • uitloper, scheut <v. plant>
running [bnw] • doorlopend,
achterelkaar • strekkend
runt [znw] • dwerg, kriel • uilskuiken
rupture I [ov ww] • een breuk
veroorzaken • doorbreken, verbreken
II [on ww] een breuk hebben III [znw]
breuk, scheuring
rural [bnw] landelijk, plattelands-
rusk [znw] (scheeps)beschuit
russet [bnw] roodbruin
Russian I [znw] • Rus(sin) • het
Russisch II [bnw] Russisch
rust I [on ww] roesten, verroesten
II [znw] roest
rustic [bnw] • landelijk • boers
rustle I [ov ww] doen ritselen
II [on ww] ruisen, ritselen III [znw]
geritsel, geruis
rusty [bnw] • roestig • roestrood
rut [znw] • karrenspoor • groef • (oude)
sleur • bronst
ruthless [bnw] meedogenloos
rye [znw] rogge

S

sabbatical [znw] sabbatsjaar
sable [znw] sabelbont
sabotage I [ov + on ww] saboteren
II [znw] sabotage
sabre [znw] cavaleriesabel
sachet [znw] parfumkussentje
sack I [ov ww] • de bons geven
• plunderen II [znw] zak
sacking [znw] • paklinnen • ontslag
sacred [bnw] • heilig • gewijd
• onschendbaar
sacrifice I [ov ww] (op)offeren
II [on ww] offeren III [znw]
• (op)offering • offerande
sacrificial [bnw] offer-
sacrilege [znw] heiligschennis
sacrilegious [bnw] heiligschennend
sacristy [znw] sacristie
sacrosanct [bnw] • onschendbaar
• heilig
sad [bnw] droevig, treurig
saddle I [ov ww] • opzadelen • belasten,
in de schoenen schuiven II [znw] • zadel
• lendestuk
saddler [znw] zadelmaker
sadistic [bnw] sadistisch
safe I [znw] brandkast II [bnw] • veilig
• betrouwbaar
safety [znw] veiligheid
saffron I [znw] saffraan II [bnw]
saffraangeel
sag I [on ww] • doorbuigen/-zakken
• (scheef)hangen II [znw] • verzakking
• doorhanging
saga [znw] • (lang) verhaal • sage
• familiekroniek
sagacious [bnw] • schrander • wijs
sage I [znw] • wijze • salie II [bnw] wijs
sago [znw] sago(palm)
said I [ww] volt. deelw. → say II [bnw]
voornoemd(e)

sail I [ov ww] (be)zeilen II [on ww]
• (uit)varen • stevenen • zeilen III [znw]
• zeil • zeiltochtje • molenwiek
sailing [znw] • het zeilen • bootreis
• afvaart
sailor [znw] zeeman, matroos
saint [znw] heilige, sint
sainthood [znw] heiligheid
saintlike, saintly [bnw] • vroom
• volmaakt
sake [znw] ★ for God's sake in
godsnaam ★ for the sake of terwille van
salable [bnw] → saleable
salacious [bnw] wellustig, wulps
salad [znw] salade, sla
salaried [bnw] bezoldigd
salary [znw] salaris
sale [znw] • verkoop • uitverkoop
• verkoping, veiling
saleable [bnw] verkoopbaar
salient I [znw] saillant II [bnw]
• (voor)uitspringend • in 't oog vallend
saline [bnw] zout(houdend)
saliva [znw] speeksel
salivary [znw] speeksel-
salivate [on ww] kwijlen
salmon [znw] zalm
saloon ‹AE› [znw] • bar • sedan
salt I [ov ww] zouten, pekelen
• (~ away) wegzetten als appeltje voor
de dorst • (~ down) inpekelen,
wegzetten als appeltje voor de dorst
II [znw] zout III [bnw] zout-
salty [bnw] zout(ig)
salubrious [bnw] gezond
salutation [znw] • (be)groet(ing)
• aanhef ‹in brief›
salute I [ov ww] begroeten, huldigen
II [on ww] salueren, groeten III [znw]
• groet • saluut(schot)
salvage I [ov ww] bergen, redden
II [znw] geborgen of geredde goederen
salvation [znw] behoudenis, redding
salve I [ov ww] sussen II [znw] • zalf
• pleister ‹fig.›
salver [znw] presenteerblad

same [vnw] • zelfde • dezelfde, hetzelfde
sameness [znw] • gelijkheid
• eentonigheid
sample I [ov ww] • proeven ‹v. voedsel›
• een monster geven/nemen v. iets
• keuren • ondervinding opdoen v.
II [znw] monster, staal(tje)
sanctimonious [bnw] schijnheilig
sanction I [ov ww] • bekrachtigen
• sanctie geven aan II [znw] sanctie
sanctity [znw] • heiligheid
• onschendbaarheid
sanctuary [znw] • kerk, heiligdom
• (vogel)reservaat
sand I [ov ww] • (~ down) polijsten,
schuren II [znw] zand
sandal [znw] sandaal
sandwich I [ov ww] inklemmen
(tussen) II [znw] dubbele boterham
sandy [bnw] • zanderig • rossig
sane [bnw] • gezond • verstandig
sang [ww] verl. tijd → sing
sanguinary [bnw] bloedig
sanitary [bnw] gezondheids-,
hygiënisch
sanitation [znw] • sanering
• volksgezondheid
sanity [znw] geestelijke gezondheid
sank [ww] verl. tijd → sink
sap I [ov ww] uitputten II [znw]
(levens)sap
sapling [znw] jonge boom
sapphire I [znw] saffier II [bnw]
saffierblauw
sarcasm [znw] sarcasme
sarcophagus [znw] sarcofaag
sardine [znw] sardientje
sardonic [bnw] cynisch, bitter,
sardonisch
sartorial [bnw] kleermakers-,
(maat)kledings-
sash [znw] • sjerp • schuifraam
sat [ww] verl. tijd + volt. deelw. → sit
satchel [znw] • pukkel ‹schooltas›
• geldtas
satellite [znw] satelliet

satiate I [ov ww] (over)verzadigen
II [bnw] verzadigd, zat
satin I [znw] satijn II [bnw] satijnen
satirist [znw] • satiricus • hekeldichter
satirize [ov ww] hekelen
satisfaction [znw] • tevredenheid
• voldoening • voldaanheid • genoegen
• genoegdoening
satisfactory [bnw] • bevredigend
• voldoende
satisfy I [ov ww] • overtuigen • tevreden
stellen • bevredigen • stillen <v.
honger> II [on ww] • voldoen(de zijn)
• genoegdoening geven
saturate [ov ww] • verzadigen
• doordrenken
saturated [bnw] • verzadigd • doornat
saturation [znw] (over)verzadiging
Saturday [znw] zaterdag
satyr [znw] sater
sauce [znw] saus
saucy [bnw] brutaal
saunter I [on ww] slenteren, kuieren
II [znw] wandelingetje
sausage [znw] worst(je)
sauté [ov ww] licht (en snel) bakken,
sauteren
savage I [ov ww] • aanvallen,
mishandelen • fel bekritiseren II [znw]
• wilde • woesteling, barbaar III [bnw]
• wild, primitief • wreed, fel • woest
save I [ov ww] • redden • (be-/uit)sparen
II [on ww] sparen III [vz] behalve
saving [znw] besparing
savour I [ov ww] • proeven • genieten
(van) II [on ww] • (~ of) smaken naar,
rieken naar III [znw] • smaak • aroma
savoury I [znw] (pikant) tussengerecht
II [bnw] • smakelijk • hartig, pikant
saw I [ww] verl. tijd → see II [ov ww]
(door)zagen III [on ww] zagen
IV [znw] • zaag • gezegde, spreuk
sax, saxophone [znw] saxofoon
Saxon I [znw] Angelsakser II [bnw]
Angelsaksisch
say I [ov ww] opzeggen II [on ww]

zeggen III [znw] • zegje • zeggenschap
saying [znw] gezegde
scab [znw] • korstje • iem. die werkt
tijdens staking
scabbard [znw] schede
scabby [bnw] met korsten bedekt
scabies [znw] schurft
scaffold [znw] • stellage, steiger
• schavot
scaffolding [znw] stellage, steigers
scald I [ov ww] • branden <aan hete
vloeistof of stoom> • met heet water
uitwassen • tegen de kook aan brengen
II [znw] brandwond
scalding [bnw] kokend (heet)
scale I [ov ww] beklimmen
• (~ down/up) evenredig
verlagen/-hogen II [znw] • schaal
• schub, schilfer • ketelsteen • tandsteen
• toonladder
scallop [znw] • sint-jakobsschelp,
kamschelp • ribbel
scallywag [znw] apenkop
scalp I [ov ww] • scalperen • afmaken
<met kritiek> II [znw] • scalp
• hoofdhuid
scalpel [znw] scalpel, ontleedmes
scaly [bnw] geschubd
scamp [znw] deugniet, rakker
scamper I [on ww] hollen II [znw]
drafje
scampi [znw] • garnalengerecht • grote
garnalen
scandal [znw] schandaal
scandalize [ov ww] ergernis wekken bij,
shockeren
scandalous [bnw] • ergerlijk,
schandelijk • schandalig
Scandinavian I [znw] • Scandinaviër
• Scandinavisch II [bnw] Scandinavisch
scanner [znw] • aftaster • radarantenne
scant [bnw] gering, karig
scanty [bnw] • krap • schaars
scapegoat [znw] zondebok
scar I [ov ww] • een litteken bezorgen
<ook emotioneel> • met littekens

bedekken II [znw] *litteken*
scarce I [bnw] • *schaars* • *zeldzaam*
II [bijw] *nauwelijks*
scare I [ov ww] *bang maken,*
verschrikken • (~ **away/off**) *wegjagen*
II [on ww] *bang worden* III [znw]
• *schrik, vrees, angst* • *bangmakerij*
scarf [znw] • *sjaal* • *das*
scarlet [bnw] *scharlaken, (vuur)rood*
scary [bnw] *schrikaanjagend, eng*
scatter [on ww] (z.) *verspreiden*
scattered [bnw] • *sporadisch* • *her en*
der verspreid
scavenge [ov + on ww] • *doorzoeken* ‹v.
afval› • *aas eten*
scavenger [znw] • *afvaleter* • *aaseter*
scene [znw] • *decor* • *landschap*
• *toneel, tafereel* • *scène*
scenery [znw] • *natuurschoon,*
landschap • *decor(s)*
scenic [bnw] • *schilderachtig*
• *verhalend, dramatisch*
scent I [ov ww] • *vermoeden* • *ruiken*
• *parfumeren* II [znw] • *geur, lucht*
• *parfum* • *reuk* • *spoor*
sceptic I [znw] *scepticus* II [bnw]
sceptisch
scepticism [znw] *scepticisme*
sceptre [znw] *scepter*
schedule I [ov ww] *plannen* II [znw]
• *bijlage* • *dienstregeling, rooster*
schematic [bnw] *schematisch*
scheme I [ov ww] • *beramen*
• *intrigeren (tegen)* II [on ww] *konkelen*
III [znw] • *plan* • *schema* • *stelsel*
• *(gemeen) spelletje, intrige*
schemer [znw] *intrigant*
schizophrenia [znw] *schizofrenie*
schizophrenic I [znw] *schizofreen*
persoon II [bnw] • *schizofreen*
• *gespleten*
scholar [znw] • *leerling* • *geleerde*
• *beursstudent*
scholarship [znw] • *geleerdheid*
• *studiebeurs*
scholastic [bnw] • *schools* • *school-,*

academisch • *schoolmeesterachtig*
• *scholastisch*
school I [ov ww] • *scholen* • *trainen*
• *africhten* II [znw] • *faculteit* • *school,*
universiteit
schooling [znw] • *onderwijs* • *scholing*
• *dressuur*
schooner [znw] *schoener*
sciatica [znw] *ischias*
science [znw] • *wetenschap*
• *natuurwetenschap(pen)*
scientific [bnw] *wetenschappelijk*
scientist [znw] *wetenschapper*
scion [znw] • *ent* • *spruit, telg*
sclerosis [znw] *sclerose*
scoff [ov ww] • *bespotten* • *gulzig opeten*
scold I [ov ww] *'n uitbrander geven*
II [on ww] *schelden*
scone [znw] *klein afgeplat broodbolletje*
scoop I [ov ww] *(uit)scheppen* • (~ **out**)
uithollen • (~ **up**) *opscheppen* II [znw]
• *scheplepel* • *schoep* • *'t scheppen* ‹in
één beweging› • *primeur*
scoot [on ww] • *rennen* • *'m smeren*
scooter [znw] • *step* • *scooter*
scope [znw] • *(draag)wijdte, bereik,*
strekking, omvang • *gelegenheid* ‹tot
ontplooiing›
scorch I [ov ww] *(ver)schroeien*
II [on ww] • *(ver)schroeien* • *woest*
rijden, scheuren III [znw] *schroeiplek*
scorcher [znw] *snikhete dag*
scorching [bnw] • *snikheet, bloedheet*
• *gloeiend (heet)*
score I [ov + on ww] • *scoren*
• *schrammen, krassen* II [znw] • *score*
• *partituur*
scorer [znw] *(doel)puntenmaker, scorer*
scornful [bnw] *minachtend*
scorpion [znw] *schorpioen*
scoundrel [znw] *schurk*
scour [ov ww] • *(op)wrijven,*
(uit)schuren • *reinigen* • *doorzoeken*
scourer [znw] • *pannenspons*
• *vagebond*
scourge I [ov ww] *teisteren* II [znw]

gesel

scout I [ov ww] *verkennen* II [on ww] *op verkenning zijn* • (~ **(around) for**) *speuren naar* III [znw] • *verkenner* • *padvinder*

scowl I [on ww] *dreigend kijken* II [znw] *dreigende blik*

scrabble I [on ww] • *krabbelen* • *graaien* II [znw] *het scrabblespel*

scraggy [bnw] *mager, schriel*

scram [on ww] *opkrassen*

scramble I [ov ww] • *door elkaar gooien* • *te grabbel gooien* II [on ww] • *klauteren* • *scharrelen, grabbelen* III [znw] • *gedrang, wedloop* • *motorcross* • *klimpartij*

scrap I [ov ww] *afdanken* II [znw] • *ruzie, herrie* • *stukje* • *zweem, zier*

scrape I [ov ww] • *schuren (langs)* • *(af)krabben, schrap(p)en* • *krassen* • (~ **away/off**) *(er) afkrabben, wegkrabben* • (~ **down**) *afschrap(p)en* • (~ **out**) *uithollen/-krabben* • (~ **together/up**) *bijeenschrapen* II [on ww] *krassen* • (~ **through**) *het nèt halen* III [znw] • *schaafwond* • *moeilijke situatie*

scrappy [bnw] *onsamenhangend*

scratch I [ov ww] • *(z.) krabben* • *krassen* • *schrammen* • *schrappen* • *afgelasten* • (~ **out**) *doorhalen, wegschrappen* II [on ww] *krassen* III [znw] • *schram* • *kras*

scrawl I [ov + on ww] *(be)krabbelen* II [znw] *krabbel(tje)*

scream I [on ww] • *gillen* • *krijsen* • *gieren* II [znw] • *dolkomisch iets of iem.* • *(ge)krijs, (ge)gil*

scree [znw] *(berghelling met) steenslag*

screech I [on ww] • *krijsen* • *knarsend piepen* II [znw] • *krijs* • *gil*

screen I [ov ww] • *af-/beschermen* • *doorlichten* • *vertonen <v. film>* II [znw] • *beeldscherm* • 't *witte doek* • *bescherming, scherm* • *schot*

screening [znw] *doorlichting*

screw I [ov + on ww] • *vastdraaien/-schroeven, aandraaien, opschroeven* • *onder pressie zetten* • <vulg.> *neuken* • (~ **up**) *verfrommelen, verkreukelen, het verknallen* II [znw] *schroef, bout*

screwy [bnw] *getikt*

scribble I [ov ww] • *pennen* • *(be)krabbelen* II [on ww] • *een beetje aan schrijven doen* • *krabbelen* III [znw] • *gekrabbel* • *kattebelletje*

scribe [znw] • *(af)schrijver* • *klerk, secretaris* • *schriftgeleerde*

scrimmage [znw] • *scrimmage <bij rugby>* • *vechtpartij*

scrimp [on ww] *bezuinigen, karig zijn*

scriptural [bnw] *m.b.t. de bijbel*

scroll [znw] • *(boek)rol* • *krul*

scrotum [znw] *scrotum, balzak*

scrounge [ov ww] *bietsen*

scrounger [znw] *bedelaar*

scrub I [ov ww] • *wassen* • *schrobben* II [znw] *(terrein met) struikgewas*

scrubby [bnw] *bedekt met struikgewas*

scruff [znw] * ~ *of the neck nekvel*

scrumptious [znw] *verrukkelijk <vnl. eten>*

scruple [znw] *gewetensbezwaar*

scrupulous [bnw] *gewetensvol, nauwgezet*

scrutinize [ov ww] *nauwkeurig onderzoeken*

scud [on ww] *(voort)jagen, snellen*

scuff [ov + on ww] *sloffen, schuifelen*

scuffle I [on ww] *vechten, elkaar afrossen* II [znw] *handgemeen*

scull I [ov + on ww] • *roeien* • *wrikken* II [znw] • *roeiriem* • *wrikriem*

scullery [znw] *bijkeuken*

sculpt [ov + on ww] → **sculpture**

sculptor [znw] *beeldhouwer*

sculptural [bnw] • *(als) gebeeldhouwd* • *beeldhouwers-*

sculpture I [ov + on ww] *beeldhouwen* II [znw] • *beeldhouwwerk* • *beeldhouwkunst*

scum [znw] • *schuim* • *uitschot*

scupper I [ov ww] *overrompelen en afmaken* II [znw] *spuigat*

scurrility [znw] *schunnigheid, gemeenheid*

scurrilous [bnw] • *gemeen, schunnig* • *grof*

scurry I [on ww] • *vlug trippelen* • *snellen* II [znw] • *het getrippel* • *draf* • *holletje*

scurvy [znw] *scheurbuik*

scuttle I [on ww] • *gejaagd (weg)lopen* • *z. ijlings uit de voeten maken* II [znw] *kolenbak*

scythe I [ov + on ww] *maaien* II [znw] *zeis*

sea [znw] *zee*

seal I [ov ww] • *be-/verzegelen* • *(dicht)plakken* • *stempelen* • *(~ up) sluiten, dichten, dichtsolderen* II [znw] • *(lak)zegel* • *bezegeling* • *stempel* • *afsluiter, sluiting* • *zeehond, rob*

seam [znw] • *naad* • ‹geo.› *dunne tussenlaag*

seaman [znw] • *zeeman* • *matroos*

seamless [bnw] *naadloos*

seamstress [znw] *naaister*

seamy [bnw] * *the ~ side of life de zelfkant*

sear [on ww] • *schroeien* • *verzengen*

search I [ov ww] • *doorzoeken* • *nasporen* • *doordringen in* • *doorgronden* • *(~ out) grondig nasporen* II [znw] • *zoekactie* • *huiszoeking* • *visitatie*

searching [bnw] *onderzoekend*

season I [ov ww] *kruiden* II [znw] • *jaargetijde* • *seizoen* • *moesson* • *(geschikte) tijd*

seasonable [bnw] • *gelegen* • *op de juiste tijd (komend)* • *overeenkomstig de tijd v.h. jaar*

seasonal [bnw] *seizoen-*

seasoning [znw] • *het kruiden* • *kruiderij*

seat I [ov ww] *doen zitten, plaatsen, een plaats geven* II [znw] • *zetel* • *zitting* • *zitvlak* • *houding* ‹te paard› • *(zit)plaats, stoel, bank*

seating [znw] *zitplaats(en)*

secateurs [znw] *snoeischaar*

secede [on ww] z. *terugtrekken, z. afscheiden*

secluded [bnw] *afgezonderd*

seclusion [znw] *afzondering*

second I [ov ww] *(onder)steunen, helpen* II [znw] • *de tweede* • *seconde* • *begeleiding* • *secondant* III [bnw] • *ander* • *op tweede plaats komend* • *op een na* IV [bijw] *ten tweede* V [telw] *tweede*

secondary [bnw] • *bij-* • *bijkomend* • *secundair* • *voortgezet* ‹v. onderwijs›

secrecy [znw] *geheimhouding*

secret I [znw] *geheim* II [bnw] *geheim*

secretarial [bnw] *van 'n secretaris/secretaresse*

secretariat [znw] *secretariaat*

secretary [znw] • *secretaresse* • *secretaris* • *minister*

secretive [bnw] *terughoudend, gesloten*

sect I [znw] *sekte* II [afk] • *(section) sectie*

sectarianism [znw] • *hokjesgeest* • *sektegeest*

section [znw] • *partje* ‹v. citrusvrucht› • *snede* • *sectie* • *paragraaf* • *afdeling* • *(ge)deel(te)*

sectional [bnw] *begrensd*

secular [bnw] • *seculier* • *wereldlijk* • *seculair*

secure I [ov ww] • *beveiligen* • *vastleggen/-zetten* • *bemachtigen* II [bnw] • *veilig* • *zeker* • *vast*

security [znw] • *zekerheid* • *waarborg* • *veiligheid* • *onderpand*

sedan [znw] • *draagstoel* • *sedan*

sedate I [ov ww] *kalmeren* ‹d.m.v. kalmeringsmiddel› II [bnw] *bedaard, rustig, stil*

sedation [znw] *verdoving*

sedative I [znw] *kalmeringsmiddel*

II [bnw] *kalmerend* ‹medicijn›
sedentary [bnw] *zittend*
sedge [znw] *moerasgras, zegge*
sedimentary [bnw] *sedimentair*
sedition [znw] *opruiing*
seditious [bnw] *oproerig*
seduce [ov ww] *verleiden*
seduction [znw] *verleiding*
seductive [bnw] *verlokkend, verleidelijk*
see I [ov + on ww] • *zien* • *inzien,*
snappen II [ov ww] • *brengen*
• *bezoeken, spreken, naar... gaan*
• *toelaten, ontvangen* • (~ **off**)
wegbrengen • (~ **out**) *uitlaten*
• (~ **through**) *doorzien* III [on ww]
('ns) kijken • (~ **about**) *zorgen voor*
• (~ **to**) *zorgen voor*
seed I [ov ww] *inzaaien* II [on ww] *zaad*
vormen III [znw] *zaad*
seedy [bnw] • *vol zaad* • *sjofel, verlopen*
seek I [ov ww] *trachten te*
bereiken/verkrijgen • (~ **out**)
(op)zoeken II [on ww] • (~ **after/for**)
(af)zoeken naar
seem [on ww] *schijnen*
seeming [bnw] *schijnbaar*
seemly [bnw + bijw] *betamelijk*
seen [ww] *volt. deelw.* → **see**
seep [on ww] *sijpelen*
seer [znw] • *ziener* • *profeet*
segment I [ov ww] *verdelen* II [znw]
segment, deel, stukje
segmentation [znw] *segmentatie*
segragated [bnw] *gescheiden*
segregate [ov ww] • *scheiden*
• *afzonderen*
segregation [znw] • *(af)scheiding*
• *segregatie*
seismic [bnw] *aardbevings-*
seize [ov ww] *(aan)grijpen*
seizure [znw] • *inbeslagname*
• *(machts)greep* • *attaque, vlaag*
seldom [bijw] *zelden*
select I [ov ww] *uitkiezen* II [bnw]
• *gedistingeerd* • *chic* • *select, uitgelezen*
selection [znw] • *keur, keuze*

• *bloemlezing*
selective [bnw] • *(uit)kiezend* • *op*
keuze gebaseerd • *selectief*
selector [znw] • *selecteur, lid van*
keuzecommissie • *keuzeschakelaar*
• *versnellingshendel/-pook*
self I [znw] • *(eigen) ik* • *persoon*
II [voorv] • *zelf-* • *eigen-* • *van/voor*
zichzelf
selfish [bnw] *egoïstisch*
selfless [bnw] *onbaatzuchtig*
sell I [ov ww] *verkopen* • (~ **off**)
uitverkopen II [on ww] *verkocht*
worden • (~ **out**) *iem. verraden*
seller [znw] *verkoper, handelaar*
selves [mv] → **self**
semaphore I [ov + on ww] *met vlaggen*
seinen II [znw] • *seinsysteem met*
vlaggen • *seinpaal*
semblance [znw] • *gedaante* • *schijn*
semen [znw] *sperma*
seminal [bnw] • *primitief* • *kiem-,*
zaad-
seminar [znw] *cursus, studiegroep*
seminary [znw] *seminarie*
Semitic [bnw] *Semitisch*
semolina [znw] *griesmeel*
senator [znw] • *senator* • *lid v.d. Am.*
Senaat
senatorial [bnw] *senaats-*
send I [ov + on ww] *uitzenden*
II [ov ww] *verzenden, op-/versturen*
• (~ **down**) *wegzenden* ‹wegens
wangedrag› • (~ **for**) *laten komen*
• (~ **forth**) *uitgeven/-zenden, afgeven*
• (~ **in**) *inzenden* • (~ **off**)
af-/wegzenden • (~ **on**) *doorsturen*
• (~ **out**) *uitzenden, verspreiden*
sender [znw] *afzender*
senile [bnw] *seniel, ouderdoms-*
seniority [znw] • *hogere leeftijd*
• *anciënniteit*
sensation [znw] • *gewaarwording*
• *sensatie*
sensational [bnw] *sensationeel*
sensationalism [znw] *sensatiezucht*

sense I [ov ww] *(aan)voelen, bespeuren*
II [znw] • *verstand* • *zintuig*
• *betekenis* • *zin* • *besef* • *gevoel(en)*
senseless [bnw] • *bewusteloos* • *zinloos*
sensibility [znw] • *gevoeligheid <v.*
kunstenaar>, ontvankelijkheid
• *lichtgeraaktheid*
sensible [bnw] *verstandig*
sensorial, sensory [bnw] *zintuiglijk*
sensual [bnw] *zinnelijk*
sensuous [bnw] *de zinnen strelend*
sent [ww] verl. tijd + volt. deelw.
→ **send**
sentence I [ov ww] ‹jur.› *veroordelen,*
vonnissen II [znw] • *zin* • ‹jur.› *vonnis,*
oordeel
sententious [bnw] *moraliserend,*
prekerig
sentient [bnw] *met*
waarnemingsvermogen/gevoel
sentiment [znw] • *gevoel(en)*
• *sentimentaliteit*
sentimental [bnw] • *gevoelvol, wat tot*
't hart spreekt • *weekhartig*
• *sentimenteel*
separate I [ov ww] • *(af)scheiden*
• *afzonderen* II [on ww] • *uiteengaan*
• *zich afscheiden* III [bnw] *gescheiden,*
afzonderlijk, apart
separation [znw] • *het uit elkaar*
gaan/zijn van twee partners zonder
officiële scheiding • *het uiteengaan*
separatism [znw] *separatisme*
septic [bnw] *geïnfecteerd*
sepulchral [bnw] • *graf-* • *begrafenis-*
sepulchre [znw] *graf*
sequel [znw] • *vervolg* • *gevolg,*
resultaat
sequence [znw] • *volgorde*
• *opeenvolging* • *reeks*
sequential [bnw] • *(erop)volgend* • *als*
gevolg, als complicatie
sequester [ov ww] • *afzonderen* • ‹jur.›
beslag leggen op
sequin [znw] *lovertje, paillet*
serenade I [ov + on ww] *een serenade*

brengen II [znw] • *serenade* • *pastorale*
cantate
serene [bnw] *rustig, bedaard, helder*
serenity [znw] • *sereniteit*
• *doorluchtigheid*
serf [znw] *lijfeigene*
serfdom [znw] *lijfeigenschap*
sergeant [znw] • *sergeant,*
wachtmeester • *brigadier <v. politie>*
serial I [znw] *tv-serie, feuilleton*
II [bnw] • *serie-* • *opeenvolgend*
serialize [ov ww] *in afleveringen*
publiceren/uitzenden
series [znw] • *serie(s)* • *reeks(en)*
serious [bnw] *ernstig*
sermon [znw] *preek*
sermonize [ov + on ww] *preken*
serpent [znw] *slang*
serpentine [bnw] • *slangachtig*
• *kronkelend*
servant [znw] • *bediende, knecht,*
dienstbode • *diena(a)r(es)*
serve I [ov + on ww] • *bedienen*
• *opdienen* • ‹sport› *serveren* II [ov ww]
• *voldoende zijn (voor)* • *in dienst zijn*
(bij) • *baten* • *(~ out) uitdelen,*
verstrekken • *(~ up) opdienen* III [znw]
‹sport› *serve, service*
service I [ov ww] *onderhoudsbeurt*
geven II [znw] • *dienst* • *service* • *servies*
serviceable [bnw] *bruikbaar*
serviette [znw] *servet*
servile [bnw] • *slaafs* • *kruiperig*
• *slaven-*
servitude [znw] • *slavernij*
• *dienstbaarheid*
sesame [znw] *sesamzaad*
session [znw] *zitting*
set I [ov ww] • *aanzetten, scherpen*
• *bezetten, versieren* • *zetten, stellen,*
plaatsen • *instellen* • *opeenklemmen*
‹v. tanden› • *vaststellen, opstellen*
• *(~ against) stellen tegenover,*
opzetten tegen • *(~ apart) reserveren,*
scheiden, opzij leggen/zetten
• *(~ aside) aan de kant zetten,*

afschaffen • (~ **at**) *ophitsen tegen*
• (~ **back**) *achteruitzetten, hinderen,*
terugzetten • (~ **before**) *voorleggen*
• (~ **by**) *terzijde leggen, reserveren*
• (~ **down**) *neerzetten, opschrijven*
• (~ **forth**) *uiteenzetten*
• (~ **forward**) *vooruithelpen,*
vooruitzetten, verkondigen • (~ **off**)
doen uitkomen, contrasteren, doen
afgaan, aan 't ... brengen, afpassen,
compenseren • (~ **on**) *ophitsen tegen*
• (~ **out**) *uitstallen, klaarzetten,*
uiteenzetten • (~ **over**) *(aan)stellen*
over • (~ **up**) *rechtop zetten, instellen,*
aanheffen, (eropna) gaan houden,
installeren • (~ **upon**) *aanvallen*
II [on ww] • *(blijven) staan ‹v. hond›*
• *ondergaan ‹v. zon, maan›* • *vrucht*
zetten, vast worden, stollen
• (~ **about**) *aanpakken, beginnen*
• (~ **forth**) *op weg gaan* • (~ **in**)
inzetten • (~ **off**) *vertrekken* • (~ **on**)
oprukken • (~ **out**) *vertrekken,*
beginnen, z. ten doel stellen • (~ **to**)
beginnen, aanvallen • (~ **up**)
erbovenop komen III [znw] • *stand*
• *toestel, installatie, apparatuur*
• *servies* • *ligging* • *rij, stel, serie*
• *filmlokatie* IV [bnw] • *bestendig*
• *gestold* • *vast(gesteld), formeel*
• *opgesteld* • *strak, opeengeklemd*
setter [znw] • *setter ‹(jacht)hond›*
• → **set**
setting [znw] • *achtergrond*
• *arrangement* • *montuur* • *omlijsting,*
omgeving • *tegenwoordig deelwoord*
→ **set**
settle I [ov + on ww] • *vaststellen*
• *afspreken* • *(doen) bedaren*
• (~ **down**) *tot bedaren/rust komen*
• (~ **up**) *vereffenen, afrekenen*
II [ov ww] • *regelen* • *vestigen*
• *koloniseren* • *vereffenen* III [on ww]
• *vaste voet krijgen* • *gaan zitten*
• *rustig worden* • *geregeld gaan leven*
• *z. installeren/vestigen, vaste*

woonplaats kiezen • *bezinken*
• (~ **down**) *geregeld gaan leven,*
wennen, vast worden • (~ **in**) *zich*
installeren/vestigen • (~ **out**)
neerslaan ‹in vloeistof›
settlement [znw] • *verrekening*
• *officiële overeenkomst* • *nederzetting,*
kolonie
settler [znw] *kolonist*
seven [telw] *zeven*
seventeen [telw] *zeventien*
seventh [telw] *zevende*
seventieth [telw] *zeventigste*
seventy [telw] *zeventig*
sever [ov ww] • *verbreken* • *(af)scheiden*
• *afhouwen*
several [bnw] • *verscheiden(e)*
• *afzonderlijk*
severance [znw] • *verbreking*
• *scheiding*
severe [bnw] • *streng* • *sober* • *hevig*
• *meedogenloos, hard*
sew [ov + on ww] *naaien*
sewage [znw] *rioolvuil/-water*
sewer [znw] *riool*
sex [znw] • *seks* • *geslacht* • *het seksuele*
sexist [znw] *seksist*
sexton [znw] • *koster* • *doodgraver*
sexual [bnw] *geslachtelijk, seksueel*
sexuality [znw] *seksualiteit*
shabby [bnw] • *haveloos* • *onverzorgd*
• *gemeen*
shackle I [ov ww] • *boeien* • *kluisteren*
• *belemmeren* II [znw] • *belemmering*
• *boei* • *kluister*
shade I [ov ww] • *beschaduwen,*
(over)schaduwen • *afschermen* • *arceren*
II [on ww] • (~ **into**) *overgaan in*
III [znw] • *schakering, tint* • *nuance*
• *lampenkap* • *scherm* • *zweem(pje),*
schijntje • *schaduw*
shading [znw] • *schaduw(partij)* • *het*
schaduwen ‹in tekeningen› • *nuance,*
nuancering
shadow I [ov ww] *schaduwen* II [znw]
• *schim* • *schijn(tje), zweem* • *schaduw*

• *detective*
shadowy [bnw] *onduidelijk,
schaduwrijk*
shady [bnw] • *schaduwrijk* • *duister*
• *onbetrouwbaar* • *twijfelachtig*
shaft [znw] • *schacht* • *stang* • *steel*
• *pijl, schicht* • *zuil* • *disselboom*
shag [znw] • *(bosje) ruig haar* • *shag*
‹tabak› • *aalscholver*
shaggy [bnw] *ruig(harig)*
shake I [ov + on ww] • *(doen) schudden*
• *schokken* • *trillen, beven* • *wankelen*
• *vibreren* • *(~ down) een uiltje
knappen* • *(~ off) (van z.) afschudden*
• *(~ up) door elkaar schudden, van
streek maken* II [znw] • *milkshake*
• *schok, ruk* • *(t)rilling*
shaky [bnw] • *gammel*
• *onbetrouwbaar* • *zwak*
shale [znw] *zachte leisteen*
shall [hww] *zal, zullen, zult*
shallot [znw] *sjalot*
shallow I [on ww] *ondiep/oppervlakkig
worden* II [znw] *ondiepte* III [bnw]
• *oppervlakkig* • *ondiep*
sham I [on ww] *simuleren, voorwenden*
II [znw] • *namaak, schijn* • *verlakkerij*
• *komediant* III [bnw] • *vals*
• *voorgewend*
shamble I [on ww] *sloffen, schuifelen*
II [znw] *schuifelende gang*
shame I [ov ww] • *beschamen* • *schande
aandoen* II [znw] • *schaamte* • *schande*
shamefaced [bnw] *bedeesd, schuchter*
shampoo I [ov ww] *'t haar wassen*
II [znw] • *shampoo* • *haarwassing,
wasbeurt*
shank [znw] • *schacht* • *steel* • ‹anat.›
(scheen)been
shan't [samentr.] /shall not/ → **shall**
shanty [znw] • *hut, keet* • *matrozenlied*
shape I [ov ww] • *modelleren* • *vormen*
• *(~ to) aanpassen* II [znw] • *vorm,
gedaante* • *(lichamelijke) conditie*
shapely [bnw] *goedgevormd, mooi,
knap*

shard [znw] *scherf*
share I [ov + on ww] *(ver)delen* II [znw]
(aan)deel, portie
shark [znw] • *haai* • *afzetter*
sharp I [znw] ‹muz.› *kruis*
II [bnw + bijw] • *scherp* • *puntig* • *goed
bij, pienter* • *bits, vinnig* • *hevig*
• *gehaaid* • ‹muz.› *te hoog*
sharpen [ov ww] *scherp maken, slijpen*
sharpener [znw]
(punten-/messen)slijper
shatter [ov ww] • *verbrijzelen*
• *vernietigen* ‹ook fig.› • *(in stukken)
breken* • *schokken* ‹v. zenuwen› • *de
bodem inslaan*
shave I [ov + on ww] • *(z.) scheren*
• *schaven* • *(~ off) afscheren* II [znw]
scheerbeurt
shaver [znw] *scheerapparaat*
shawl [znw] • *sjaal* • *omslagdoek*
she I [pers vnw] *zij* II [in samenst.]
• *vrouwelijk* • *wijfjes-*
sheaf [znw] *schoof, bundel*
shear [ov ww] *scheren* ‹v. wol›
sheath [znw] • *schede* • *condoom*
sheaves [mv] → **sheaf**
shed I [ov ww] • *vergieten* • *afwerpen*
• *verliezen* ‹v. haar› • *wisselen* ‹v.
tanden› • *ruien* • *z. ontdoen v.* II [znw]
• *schuur, keet* • *afdak*
she'd [samentr.] /she would/ /she
had/ → **will, have**
sheen [znw] *glans, pracht*
sheep [znw] *schaap, schapen*
sheer I [on ww] *plotseling uitwijken*
II [bnw + bijw] • *louter, puur* • *steil,
loodrecht* • *ijl, doorschijnend*
sheet I [ov ww] *met een laken, enz.
bedekken* II [znw] • *blad* • *vlak(te)* • *vel
(papier)* • *laken*
shelf [znw] • *plank, schap* • *vak*
• *(rots)rand* • *klip, zandbank*
shell I [ov ww] • *schillen, pellen, uit
dop/schaal halen* • ‹mil.› *beschieten,
onder artillerievuur nemen* II [on ww]
• *(~ out) opdokken* III [znw] • *schelp,*

schaal • dop, peul • (om)huls(el)
• granaat • geraamte, romp • <AE>
patroon
she'll [samentr.] /she will/ → **will**
shelter I [ov ww] beschutten II [on ww]
(z. ver)schuilen III [znw] • beschutting,
bescherming, onderdak • schuilplaats
• tram-/wachthuisje
shelve I [ov ww] op de lange baan
schuiven II [on ww] glooien
shelving [znw] • (kast)planken,
schappen • materiaal voor planken
shepherd I [ov ww] hoeden, (ge)leiden
II [znw] herder
sherbet [znw] • sherbet, bruispoeder
<voor maken v. frisdrank> • <AE> sorbet
she's [samentr.] /she has/ /she is/
→ **have, be**
shield I [ov ww] • beschermen • de hand
boven 't hoofd houden II [znw]
• wapenschild • bescherming,
beschermer • schild
shift I [ov + on ww] • z. (zien te) redden
• draaien • veranderen (van), wisselen
(van) • verschuiven, verleggen, (z.)
verplaatsen • (~ **away**) wegwerken,
ertussenuit knijpen II [znw]
• hulp-/redmiddel • truc, list • ploeg <v.
arbeiders> • verband <v. metselwerk>
shiftless [bnw] • zonder initiatief
• onbeholpen
shifty [bnw] louche, onbetrouwbaar
shilly-shally [on ww] aarzelen,
weifelen
shimmer I [on ww] glinsteren II [znw]
glinstering
shin I [on ww] klauteren II [znw] scheen
shine I [ov ww] • (~ **up**) (op)poetsen
II [on ww] • schijnen • (uit)blinken
• schitteren III [znw] zonneschijn
shiner [znw] blauw oog
shingle [znw] • dekspaan, plank <v.
dak> • kiezelste(e)n(en) • <AE> naambord
shining [bnw] blinkend, schitterend
shiny [bnw] glimmend
ship I [ov ww] per schip vervoeren

II [znw] schip
shipment [znw] • (ver)zending • lading
shipping I [znw] • scheepvaart • de
schepen II [bnw] • scheeps- • expeditie-
shire [znw] graafschap
shirk [ov ww] • z. onttrekken aan
• lijntrekken
shirt [znw] • (over)hemd
• overhemdbloes
shit <vulg.> I [on ww] schijten II [znw]
• stront • rotzooi • onzin III [tw] verrek!
shitty [bnw] <vulg.> klotig, klote-
shiver I [on ww] rillen, trillen II [znw]
rilling
shivery [bnw] rillerig
shoal [znw] school <v. vissen>
shock I [ov ww] • aanstoot geven
• hevig ontstellen II [znw] • bos <haar>
• schok • ontzetting • shock(toestand)
shocker [znw] gruwelroman/-film
shocking [bnw] • schokkend
• gruwelijk • zeer onbehoorlijk
shod [ww] volt. deelw. → **shoe**
shoddy [bnw] prullerig
shoe I [ov ww] • schoeien • beslaan
II [znw] • schoen • hoefijzer
shone [ww] verl. tijd → **shine**
shoo I [ov ww] • (~ **away**) verjagen,
wegjagen II [tw] kssj!
shook [ww] verl. tijd → **shake**
shoot I [ov ww] • (af-/uit-/ver)schieten
• doodschieten • jagen, afjagen
• spuiten <v. heroïne> • <foto.> filmen,
kieken II [on ww] vuren, schieten
• (~ **ahead of**) voorbijschieten
III [znw] • jacht • scheut, loot
shooting I [znw] jachtrecht,
jacht(gebied) II [in samenst.] • schiet-
• jacht-
shop I [ov ww] verlinkenII [on ww]
winkelen, boodschappen doen III [znw]
• werkplaats • winkel
shopper [znw] koper, klant
shopping [znw] boodschappen,
inkopen
shore I [ww] verl. tijd → **shear**

II [ov ww] *stutten* III [znw] • *schoor,*
stut • *oever* • *strand* • *kust*
shorn [ww] volt. deelw. → **shear**
short I [znw] • *korte voorfilm* • *borrel*
• *kortsluiting* II [bnw] • *te kort,*
bekrompen, karig • *kort, klein* • *kortaf*
III [bijw] • *niet genoeg* • *plotseling,*
opeens
shortage [znw] *tekort*
shorten [ov ww] *(ver)minderen*
shortening [znw] • *verkorting,*
verkorte vorm • *bakvet*
shortly [bijw] • *binnenkort* • *kort*
daarna • *in 't kort* • *kortaf*
shot I [ww] verl.tijd + volt.deelw.
→ **shoot** II [znw] • *stoot* • *slag*
• *hagel* • *kogel(s)* • *schutter* • *borrel*
• *injectie* • *spuitje* <v. heroïne> • *schot*
• <foto.> *(korte) opname, beeldje*
III [bnw] *changeant (geweven)*
should [ww] verl.tijd → **shall**
shoulder I [ov + on ww] *duwen* <met
de schouder>, *dringen* II [ov ww] *op de*
schouder(s) nemen III [znw] *schouder*
shout I [ov + on ww] *schreeuwen*
• *(~ at) schreeuwen tegen* • *(~ down)*
overschreeuwen II [znw] *schreeuw*
shove I [ov + on ww] • *duwen*
• *schuiven* • *(z.) dringen* • *(~ off)*
opduvelen II [znw] *zet, duw*
shovel I [ov ww] *scheppen* II [znw]
schop
show I [ov ww] • *blijk geven van*
• *tentoonstellen, laten zien, vertonen,*
(aan)tonen, uitstallen • *wijzen,*
bewijzen • *(~ down) de kaarten op*
tafel leggen • *(~ in) binnenlaten*
• *(~ off) pronken met* • *(~ out)*
uitlaten • *(~ round) rondleiden*
• *(~ up) in verlegenheid brengen*
II [on ww] *te zien zijn, vertoond*
worden, z. laten zien • *(~ off) z.*
aanstellen, branie schoppen • *(~ up) z.*
vertonen, verschijnen III [znw]
• *(uiterlijk) vertoon, schijn*
• *tentoonstelling* • *schouwspel* • *revue,*

variété • <inf.> *organisatie, zaak(je),*
spul
shower I [ov ww] • *doen neerstorten,*
doen dalen • z. *uitstorten* II [on ww]
douchen III [znw] • *bui* • *(stort)regen*
• *douche*
showery [bnw] *buiig*
showing [znw] • *voorstelling* • *opgave*
shown [ww] volt. deelw. → **show**
showy [bnw] *opzichtig*
shrank [ww] verl. tijd → **shrink**
shrapnel [znw] *granaatsplinters*
shred I [ov ww] • *aan flarden/repen*
scheuren/snijden • *rafelen* II [znw]
reep, flard
shrewd [bnw] • *schrander* • *gewiekst*
shriek I [ov + on ww] • *gieren* • *krijsen,*
gillen II [znw] • *krijs* • *gil*
shrill I [on ww] *schel/schril klinken*
II [bnw] *schril, schel*
shrimp [znw] • *klein kereltje* • *garnaal*
shrine [znw] • *heiligdom* • *graf v.e.*
heilige • *reliekschrijn*
shrink I [ov ww] *doen krimpen*
II [on ww] • *(in elkaar) krimpen*
• *verschrompelen* • *verminderen*
III [znw] <AE> *zielenknijper*
shrinkage [znw] *be-/inkrimping*
shrivel I [ov ww] *doen*
ineenschrompelen II [on ww]
ineenkrimpen
shroud I [ov ww] • *in doodskleed*
wikkelen • *hullen* • *(~ from) verbergen*
voor II [znw] • *doodskleed* • *waas, sluier*
shrub [znw] *heester*
shrubbery [znw] *heesters*
shrug [ov + on ww] *de schouders*
ophalen • *(~ off) naast zich*
neerleggen, negeren
shrunk(en) [ww] volt. deelw.
→ **shrink**
shudder I [on ww] *huiveren, rillen*
II [znw] *huivering*
shuffle I [ov ww] • *schuiven* • *schudden*
<v. kaarten> II [on ww] *schuifelen,*
sloffen III [znw] *schuifelende loop,*

geschuifel
shun [ov ww] • (ver)mijden, ontlopen
• links laten liggen
shunt I [ov ww] verplaatsen II [on ww]
(op zijspoor) rangeren of gerangeerd
worden
shush [ov ww] sussen
shut I [ov ww] • (z.) sluiten • dicht doen
• (~ **down**) stopzetten • (~ **in**)
in-/opsluiten • (~ **off**) af-/uitsluiten
• (~ **up**) op-/in-/afsluiten, de mond
snoeren II [on ww] dicht gaan
• (~ **down**) stilliggen • (~ **up**)
ophouden met praten III [bnw] dicht
shutter [znw] • blind <voor raam>
• <foto.> sluiter
shuttle [znw] • schietspoel • schuitje <v.
naaimachine>
shy I [ov ww] gooien II [on ww] opzij
springen • (~ **away from**)
(terug)schrikken voor III [bnw]
• verlegen • schuw
Siamese I [znw] Siamees II [bnw]
Siamees
sibling [znw] • broer • zuster
sick I [on ww] braken • (~ **up**)
uitbraken II [znw] braaksel III [bnw]
• misselijk • naar • zeeziek • ziek
sicken I [ov ww] • ziek maken • doen
walgen II [on ww] • ziek worden
• walgen
sickening [bnw] misselijkmakend
sickle [znw] sikkel
sickly [bnw] • ziekelijk • ongezond
• wee, weeïg • bleek
sickness [znw] • ziekte • misselijkheid
side I [on ww] • (~ **with**) partij kiezen
voor II [znw] • kant, zijde • zijkant
• aspect • partij • elftal, team
sideways [bnw + bijw] naar opzij
siding [znw] rangeerspoor
sidle [on ww] • zijdelings lopen • met
eerbied/schuchter naderen
siege [znw] • belegering • beleg
sieve I [ov ww] zeven II [znw] zeef
sift [ov ww] • zeven, ziften • strooien <v.

o.a. suiker> • nauwkeurig uitpluizen,
uithoren
sigh I [on ww] zuchten • (~ **for**)
smachten naar II [znw] zucht
sight I [ov ww] in 't oog krijgen II [znw]
• (ge)zicht • schouwspel
• bezienswaardigheid • vizier • <inf.>
heleboel
sighting [znw] waarneming
sign I [ov + on ww] ondertekenen
II [on ww] in gebarentaal spreken
• (~ **away**) schriftelijk afstand doen
van • (~ **on**) stempelen bij de sociale
dienst • (~ **on/up (for/to)**)
aanmonsteren (bij), tekenen <als o.a.
lid> III [znw] • teken • uithangbord
• bordje • reclameplaat
signal I [ov ww] • seinen • door
signalen/tekens te kennen geven
II [znw] • verkeerslicht • sein, signaal
III [bnw] opmerkelijk
signatory [znw] ondertekenaar
signature [znw] • handtekening
• signatuur
significance [znw] • betekenis
• gewichtigheid
significant [bnw] veelbetekenend
silence I [ov ww] tot zwijgen brengen
II [znw] • stilte • het zwijgen
silencer [znw] • geluiddemper • knalpot
silent [bnw] • stil • zwijgend
• zwijgzaam
silhouette [znw] silhouet
silica [znw] kiezelzuur
silicon [znw] silicium
silk I [znw] • zijde • II [bnw] zijden
silken, silky [bnw] zijdeachtig,
zijdezacht
sill [znw] vensterbank
silly [bnw] • dwaas, idioot • flauw,
kinderachtig
silo [znw] • (graan)silo • kuil voor
groenvoer
silt I [ov + on ww] • (~ **up**) dichtslibben
II [znw] slib
silver I [znw] • zilver • tafelzilver

II [bnw] • zilveren • zilverachtig
silvery [bnw] • *met zilveren klank*
• *zilverachtig*
similar [bnw] *gelijksoortig*
similarity [znw] • *gelijkvormigheid*
• *overeenkomst*
simile [znw] *vergelijking* <stijlfiguur>
simmer I [ov ww] *laten sudderen*
II [on ww] *sudderen* **III** [znw] *gesudder*
simper I [on ww] *gemaakt/onnozel*
lachen **II** [znw] *onnozele glimlach*
simple [bnw] • *eenvoudig, enkelvoudig*
• *ongekunsteld* • *gewoon* • *onnozel*
simpleton [znw] • *imbeciel* • *sul*
simplicity [znw] • *eenvoud*
• *ongekunsteldheid*
simplify [ov ww] *vereenvoudigen*
simply [bijw] *simpel(weg),*
eenvoudig(weg), domweg
simulate [ov ww] • *veinzen* • *nabootsen*
simulator [znw] • *simulant* • *simulator*
simultaneous [bnw] *gelijktijdig*
sin I [on ww] *zondigen* **II** [znw] *zonde*
sincere [bnw] *oprecht*
sinew [znw] *pees*
sinewy [bnw] • *pezig* • *gespierd, sterk*
sinful [bnw] *zondig*
sing I [ov + on ww] *zingen* **II** [ov ww]
bezingen **III** [on ww] *zoemen, suizen*
• (~ **of**) *bezingen* • (~ **out**) *uitzingen,*
brullen
singe [ov ww] *afschroeien, (ver)schroeien*
singer [znw] *zanger(es)*
singing [znw] • *het zingen* • *gezang*
• *zang(kunst)*
single I [ov ww] • (~ **out**) *uitkiezen,*
eruit pikken **II** [znw] • *single*
<grammofoonplaat of cd> • *enkelspel*
• *enkele reis* • *enkele bloem* • <taalk.>
enkelvoud **III** [bnw] • *enkel,*
afzonderlijk • *ongetrouwd*
singlet [znw] • *interlockje* • *borstrok*
singular I [znw] <taalk.> *enkelvoud(ig*
woord) **II** [bnw] • *vreemd, zonderling*
• *uniek* • *enkelvoudig*
sinister [bnw] • *sinister*

• *onheilspellend* • *onguur*
sink I [ov ww] • *doen zinken* • *laten*
zakken • *in de grond boren* • *torpederen*
II [on ww] • *zinken, dalen, zakken*
• *boren, graven* • *achteruitgaan,*
bezwijken • *gaan liggen* <wind>
• (~ **in**) *tot iem. doordringen, bezinken,*
inzinken **III** [znw] *gootsteen*
sinuous [bnw] *bochtig, kronkelend*
sinus [znw] • *holte* • *schedelholte*
sip I [ov + on ww] *nippen, met kleine*
teugjes drinken **II** [znw] *teugje, slokje*
siphon [znw] *sifon*
sir [znw] *mijnheer*
sire I [ov ww] *de vader zijn van* <bij
dieren> **II** [znw] • *stamvader,*
(voor)vader • *Sire*
siren [znw] • *sirene* • *zeekoe*
sirloin [znw] *lendestuk v. rund*
sissy [znw] *mietje, fatje*
sister [znw] *zuster*
sisterhood [znw] • *zusterschap*
• *congregatie*
sit [on ww] • *zitten* • *zich bevinden*
• *poseren* • (~ **around**) *nietsdoen*
• (~ **down**) *gaan zitten*
site I [ov ww] *plaatsen* **II** [znw]
• *terrein, perceel, kavel* • *plaats, ligging*
sit-in [znw] *bezetting*
sitter [znw] • *model* • *oppas*
sitting [znw] *zittingsperiode*
situate [ov ww] *plaatsen*
situation [znw] • *ligging, stand*
• *toestand, situatie* • *betrekking*
six [telw] *zes*
sixteen [telw] *zestien*
sixth [telw] *zesde*
sixtieth [bnw] *zestigste*
sixty [telw] *zestig*
size I [ov ww] • (~ **up**) *taxeren, schatten*
II [znw] • *grootte* • *maat*
sizzle [on ww] *sissen*
skate I [on ww] *schaatsen* **II** [znw]
• *schaats* • *vleet* <vis>
skater [znw] *schaatser*
skein [znw] • *knot, streng* • *vlucht wilde*

ganzen
skeleton [znw] • *skelet, geraamte*
• *schema, kern*
sketch I [ov + on ww] *schetsen* II [znw]
schets
sketchy [bnw] *oppervlakkig, niet*
afgewerkt
skew I [on ww] *v.* koers afwijken
II [bnw] *schuin*
skewer I [ov ww] *doorsteken* II [znw]
• *vleespen* • *spit*
ski I [on ww] *skiën* II [znw] *ski*
skid I [on ww] • *slippen* • *remmen*
II [znw] *'t slippen, slip*
skier [znw] *skiër*
skilled [bnw] *geschoold, vakkundig*
skillet [znw] *koekenpan*
skim I [ov + on ww] *vluchtig*
doornemen II [ov ww] • *afromen*
• *afschuimen* III [on ww] *scheren* ‹over
(water)oppervlak›
skimp [on ww] *zuinig zijn, bekrimpen*
skimpy [bnw] *krap, karig, krenterig*
skin I [ov ww] • *villen* • *ontvellen*
II [znw] • *huid* • *vlies* • *schil* • *leren*
wijnzak
skinny [bnw] • *vel over been*
• *broodmager*
skint ‹sl.› [bnw] *blut, platzak*
skip I [ov ww] *overslaan* II [on ww]
• *huppelen* • (*touwtje*)*springen*
• (~ *over*) *overslaan* III [znw]
• *sprong(etje)* • *afvalcontainer*
skipper [znw] • *schipper,*
(*scheeps*)*kapitein* • ‹sport› *aanvoerder*
skirmish I [on ww] *schermutselen*
II [znw] *schermutseling*
skirt I [ov ww] • *bewegen langs de rand*
v. • *grenzen aan* • *vermijden* II [znw]
• *rok* • *slip, pand* • ‹sl.› *meid, griet*
skit [znw] *kort satirisch toneelstuk*
skittish [bnw] • *dartel, frivool*
• *schichtig*
skittle [znw] *kegel*
skive [on ww] *zich drukken, niet komen*
werken

skulk [on ww] • *sluipen* • *z.* verschuilen
skull [znw] • *schedel* • *doodskop*
skunk [znw] • *stinkdier* • ‹sl.› *vuns,*
schoft
sky [znw] *lucht, hemel*
slab [znw] • *platte steen* • *plak*
slack I [ov + on ww] • *treuzelen,*
lijntrekken • *lessen* • (~ **away/off**)
vieren • (~ **off**) *verslappen, kalmpjes*
aan (*gaan*) *doen* • (~ **up**) *vaart*
minderen, het rustiger aandoen
II [znw] • *slap hangend deel v.* touw of
zeil • *dood tij* • *slapte* III [bnw] • *slap*
• *los* • *lui, traag, laks, loom*
slacken I [ov ww] • *laten vieren* • *slap*
doen worden II [on ww] • *vieren* • *vaart*
minderen • *afnemen* • *slap worden*
slag [znw] • *slons* • *slak(ken)* • *sintel(s)*
slain [ww] *volt. deelw.* → **slay**
slake [ov ww] • *lessen* • *koelen* • *blussen*
‹v. kalk›
slam I [ov + on ww] *hard dichtslaan*
II [znw] *harde klap* III [bijw] • *met een*
harde klap • *pardoes*
slander I [on ww] (*be*)*lasteren* II [znw]
laster
slanderous [bnw] *lasterlijk*
slang [znw] • *spreektaal* • *jargon*
• *schuttingtaal*
slant I [ov ww] *schuin houden/zetten*
II [on ww] *schuin lopen/staan*
III [znw] • *helling* • *schuine streep*
• ‹AE› *kijk* ‹op de zaak›
slap I [ov ww] • *slaan* • *klappen, kletsen*
II [znw] • *klap* ‹met de vlakke hand›
• *slag* III [bijw] • *pardoes* • *met een klap*
slash I [ov ww] • *houwen* • *een jaap*
geven • *snijden* • *striemen* II [znw]
• *houw, jaap* • *striem*
slat [znw] *dun latje*
slate I [ov ww] • *met leien dekken*
• *scherp kritiseren, met kritiek afmaken*
• *bestemmen* (*als*) II [znw] *lei(steen)*
III [bnw] *leien*
slattern [znw] • *slons* • *slet*
slatternly [bnw] *slordig*

slaughter I [ov ww] (af)slachten
II [znw] • slachting • 't slachten
• bloedbad
slave I [on ww] z. afbeulen II [znw]
• slavin • slaaf
slaver I [ov ww] kwijlen II [znw] kwijl
slavery [znw] slavernij
slavish [bnw] slaafs
slay <vero.> [ov ww] doden
sleazy [bnw] louche en verlopen
sled I [on ww] sleeën II [znw] slee
sledge I [on ww] sleeën II [znw] • slee
• moker
sleek [bnw] • glad • glanzend
sleep I [ov ww] (kunnen) bergen
II [on ww] slapen • (~ in) lang door
blijven slapen, z. verslapen • (~ out)
buitenshuis overnachten III [znw] slaap
sleeper [znw] • dwarsligger • slaper
• slaapwagen
sleepless [bnw] slapeloos
sleepy [bnw] • slaperig • dromerig
sleet I [onp ww] sneeuwen, hagelen
II [znw] hagel met regen, natte sneeuw
sleeve [znw] • mouw • hoes
sleeveless [bnw] zonder mouwen,
mouwloos
sleigh [znw] slee
slender [bnw] • slank • dun • karig
slept [ww] verl. tijd + volt. deelw.
→ sleep
slew I [ww] verl. tijd → slay
II [ov + on ww] slippen
slice [znw] plakje
slick I [ov ww] • (~ down)
gladkammen <v. haar>, plakken
II [znw] olievlek III [bnw] • vlot
• handig • glad
slide I [on ww] • schuiven • (uit)glijden
II [znw] • glijbaan/-plank • glijbank
• dia(positief) • objectglaasje <v.
microscoop> • schuifje • schuifraampje
• aardverschuiving • <foto.> chassis
slight I [ov ww] met geringschatting
behandelen, kleineren II [znw]
• geringschatting • kleinering III [bnw]

• gering • tenger • klein • vluchtig
• zwak • licht
slim I [ov ww] aan de lijn doen II [bnw]
slank
slime [znw] • slijk • slijm
slimy [bnw] • kruiperig • glibberig
sling I [ov ww] • slingeren • gooien
II [znw] • (werp)slinger • mitella,
draagverband
slink [on ww] sluipen
slip I [ov ww] • in de hand stoppen
• vieren • laten glijden II [on ww]
• los-/wegschieten, van zijn plaats
schieten • (uit)glijden • 'n fout maken
• zich vergissen • (~ away/out)
ertussenuit knijpen • (~ by) ongemerkt
voorbijgaan • (~ up) zich vergissen
III [znw] • vergissing • stukje <v.
papier>, strook, reep(je) • onderjurk
• broekje
slipper [znw] pantoffel
slippery [bnw] • glad • glibberig
• onbetrouwbaar • gewetenloos
slippy [bnw] glad
slit I [ov ww] af-/opensnijden II [znw]
spleet
slither [on ww] glibberen, glijden
sliver [znw] • splinter • stuk(je)
slob [znw] luiwammes, vetzak
slobber I [ov ww] bekwijlen II [on ww]
kwijlen
sloe [znw] • sleedoorn • sleepruim
slog I [ov ww] hard slaan • (~ away at)
hard werken aan II [on ww] moeizaam
vooruitkomen III [znw] • moeizame
voetreis • taaie klus
slogan [znw] • strijdkreet • leuze
• slagzin
sloop [znw] sloep
slop I [ov ww] bemorsen II [on ww]
morsen
slope I [ov ww] • doen hellen • schuin
zetten II [on ww] • hellen • schuin
liggen/staan • (~ off) ervandoor gaan
III [znw] • helling • talud
sloppy [bnw] • sentimenteel • slordig

slosh [ov + on ww] • (~ **on**) er dik
opkwakken/-smeren
slot I [ov ww] gleuf maken in II [znw]
gleuf
sloth [znw] • luiheid • luiaard <dier>
slouch I [on ww] (slap) naar beneden
hangen • (~ **about**) rondlummelen
II [znw] slungelige gang/houding
slough I [ov ww] • (~ **off**) de huid
afwerpen <v. slang, reptiel>, laten
vallen, opgeven II [on ww] vervellen
III [znw] moeras
slovenly [bnw] slordig
slow I [on ww] • (~ **down**/ **up**)
vertragen, langzamer gaan, rijden of
laten werken, kalm(er) aan (gaan) doen
II [bnw + bijw] • saai • langzaam
• traag <v. begrip>
sludge [znw] • slik • drab
slug I [ov ww] een klap geven II [znw]
• (naakt)slak • kogel • slok
sluggish [bnw] • lui • traag(werkend)
sluice I [ov ww] afspoelen II [znw] sluis
slum [znw] slop, achterbuurt
slumber I [on ww] • slapen • sluimeren
II [znw] • slaap • sluimering
slump I [on ww] • plotseling sterk
dalen • kelderen II [znw] • plotselinge
(sterke) prijsdaling • malaise
• achteruitgang in populariteit
slung [ww] verl. tijd + volt. deelw.
→ **sling**
slunk [ww] verl. tijd + volt. deelw.
→ **slink**
slur I [ov + on ww] onduidelijk
schrijven/uitspreken II [on ww] <muz.>
legato spelen/zingen, slepen III [znw]
<muz.> verbindingsboogje, legatoteken
slush [znw] • sneeuwdrab/-modder
• vals sentiment
slushy [bnw] • vals sentimenteel
• modderig
slut <pej.> [znw] • slons • slet
sly [bnw] geslepen, sluw
smack I [on ww] • klappen • smakken
• kletsen • (~ **of**) rieken/smaken naar,

doen denken aan II [znw] • smaak(je)
• geur(tje) • tikje, tikkeltje • smak
• klap • 't smakken <v. o.a. tong>
• klapzoen • smak <schip> III [bijw]
met een klap
small [bnw] • klein • kleingeestig,
flauw • onbenullig • zwak <v. stem>
smarmy [bnw] flemerig
smart I [on ww] • pijn doen • z.
gekwetst voelen • lijden II [znw] • pijn
• smart III [bnw] • behoorlijk • pijnlijk
• vinnig • handig • vlug • bijdehand
• gevat • keurig • chic <kleding>
smarten [ov + on ww] opknappen
smash I [ov ww] • vernielen • slaan
• verpletteren • keihard slaan <bij
tennis> • (~ **up**) kapotslaan II [on ww]
• kapotvallen • te pletter slaan • botsen
III [znw] • smak • hevige klap of slag
• verpletterende nederlaag • botsing
• smash <bij tennis> IV [bijw] met een
klap
smasher [znw] • prachtexemplaar
• kanjer
smashing [bnw] denderend, mieters
smattering [znw] heel klein beetje
smear I [ov ww] • besmeren, (in)smeren
(met) • vuil maken II [znw] • veeg
• uitstrijkje
smell I [ov + on ww] ruiken
• (~ **about**) rondsnuffelen • (~ **at**)
ruiken aan • (~ **of**) ruiken naar
• (~ **out**) opsporen, uitvissen II [znw]
• reuk • lucht • geur, stank
smelly [bnw] vies ruikend
smelt I [ww] verl.tijd + volt.deelw.
→ **smell** II [ov ww] smelten III [znw]
spiering
smile I [on ww] glimlachen • (~ **at**)
lachen om, toelachen II [znw] glimlach
smithereens [mv] gruzelementen
smithy [znw] smederij
smock I [ov ww] smokken II [znw]
• kiel • mouwschort
smoke I [ov + on ww] • roken • walmen
• be-/uitroken • (~ **out**) uitroken

II [znw] • rook • walm • sigaar, sigaret
smoker [znw] • roker • rookcoupé
smoky [bnw] rokerig
smooth I [ov ww] glad maken
• (~ **away/out**) glad-/wegstrijken, uit
de weg ruimen • (~ **over**) vergoelijken,
goed praten II [bnw + bijw] • vloeiend
• kalm <v. zee of water> • glad, effen
• vlak
smother [ov ww] • smoren, doven
• verstikken, doen stikken
• onderdrukken • (~ **with**) overladen
met
smoulder [on ww] smeulen
smudge I [ov ww] • bevlekken • vuil
maken II [znw] • veeg, vlek • vuile vlek
smug [bnw] zelfingenomen
smuggle [ov ww] smokkelen
smut [znw] • roetdeeltje • (zwarte) vlek
• vuil(igheid) • pornografie
smutty [bnw] vuil
snack [znw] • snelle hap • hapje
snag I [ov ww] met kleding ergens aan
blijven haken II [znw] moeilijkheid
snail [znw] slak
snake I [on ww] kronkelen II [znw]
slang
snap I [ov + on ww] • happen, bijten
• snauwen • (doen) afknappen, breken
• klikken • knippen (met) • kieken
• (~ **at**) happen naar, snauwen tegen
• (~ **off**) afbijten/-knappen • (~ **up**)
mee-/wegpikken, gretig aannemen
II [znw] • klik, tik • kiekje
• kaartspelletje III [bnw] haastig
IV [bijw] • knap • krak • klik • pang
snappy [bnw] • pittig • snauwend
snare I [ov ww] • strikken • vangen
II [znw] strik
snarl I [ov ww] • (~ **up**) vastlopen, in de
knoop raken II [on ww] • grommen
• grauwen, snauwen III [znw] grauw
snatch I [ov ww] • pakken • grissen
• pikken • (~ **away**) wegrukken
• (~ **up**) bemachtigen, oppikken
II [znw] • greep • (brok)stuk • <vulg.>

kut
sneak I [on ww] • sluipen • klikken
II [znw] • gluiperd • klikspaan
sneaker [znw] schoen met zachte zool
sneaking [bnw] • stiekem • gluiperig
sneeze I [on ww] niezen II [znw]
nies(geluid)
snicker [on ww] zacht grinniken
snide [bnw] • gemeen • spottend,
sarcastisch
sniff I [ov ww] opsnuiven II [on ww]
• snuiven • de neus ophalen • (~ **at**)
ruiken aan, de neus optrekken voor
III [znw] snuif(je)
sniffle I [on ww] snotteren II [znw]
gesnotter
sniffy [bnw] • hautain • smalend
snigger I [on ww] (gemeen) grinniken
II [znw] gegrinnik
snip I [ov ww] (af-/door)knippen
II [znw] • knip • snippertje • koopje
snipe I [ov + on ww] uit hinderlaag
(dood)schieten II [znw] snip(pen)
sniper [znw] sluipschutter
snippet [znw] • snipper(tje), stuk(je)
• fragment
snitch [on ww] klikken
snivel [on ww] grienen, jengelen,
snotteren
snobbery [znw] snobisme
snobbish [bnw] snobachtig, snobistisch
snoop <AE> [on ww] rondneuzen
snooper [znw] bemoeial
snooty <inf.> [bnw] verwaand
snooze I [on ww] dutten II [znw] dutje
snore I [on ww] snurken II [znw]
(ge)snurk
snorkel I [on ww] met de snorkel
zwemmen/duiken II [znw] snorkel
snort I [ov + on ww] snuiven II [on ww]
• briesen • ronken III [znw] (ge)snuif
snot <vulg.> [znw] snot
snotty [bnw] • snotterig • verwaand
snout [znw] • snuit • kokkerd
snow I [ov ww] <inf.> vleien II [onp ww]
sneeuwen III [znw] • sneeuw • <sl.>

cocaïne

snub I [ov ww] *bits/hooghartig afwijzen* II [znw] *hatelijke opmerking* III [bnw] *stomp*

snuff I [ov ww] *snuiten* ‹v. kaars›
• (~ **out**) *een eind maken aan, uitdoven* II [znw] • *snufje* • *snuif*

snuffle [on ww] *snuffelen*

snug I [on ww] z. *behaaglijk nestelen, lekker (knus) gaan liggen* II [znw] *gezellig plekje* III [bnw] • *knus, gezellig, behaaglijk* • *goed gedekt*

so [bijw] • *zo, aldus* • *dus* • *het, dat*

soak I [ov ww] • *(door)weken* • *doordringen* • (~ **up**) *opzuigen, absorberen* II [on ww] • (~ **in**) *doordringen in* • (~ **through**) *doorsijpelen* III [znw] • *plensbui* • *regen* • *zatlap*

soap I [ov ww] *inzepen* II [znw] *zeep*

soapy [bnw] • *zeep-, vol zeep* • *zeepachtig*

soar [on ww] • *zich verheffen* • *zweven*

sob I [on ww] *snikken* II [znw] *snik*

sober I [on ww] • (~ **up**) *nuchter worden* II [bnw] • *nuchter* • *sober* • *stemmig*

soccer [znw] *voetbal*

sociable [bnw] • *gezellig* • *vriendelijk* • *prettig in de omgang*

social I [znw] *gezellig avondje* II [bnw] • *sociaal, maatschappelijk* • *gezellig*

socialism [znw] *socialisme*

socialize I [ov + on ww] *socialiseren* II [ov ww] *socialistisch inrichten* III [on ww] *veel mensen ontmoeten, gezelligheid zoeken*

society I [znw] • *(de) maatschappij* • *vereniging* • *genootschap* • *de grote wereld* II [bnw] • *van de grote wereld* • *mondain*

sociologist [znw] *socioloog*

sociology [znw] *sociologie*

sock I [ov ww] *slaan* II [znw] *sok*

socket [znw] • *stopcontact* • *(oog)kas* • *holte*

sod I [on ww] • (~ **off**) *oprotten* II [znw] • *rotzak* • *stakker* • *zode*

soda [znw] • *soda* • *spuitwater* • ‹AE› *frisdrank*

sodden [bnw] • *klef* • *doordrenkt*

sodium [znw] *natrium*

sofa [znw] *sofa, canapé*

soft [bnw + bijw] • *zacht, week* • *zachtaardig, verwijfd, sentimenteel*

soften I [ov ww] • *zacht(er) maken* • *vermurwen* • (~ **up**) *murw maken* II [on ww] *zacht(er) worden*

softener [znw] *wasverzachter*

softy [znw] • *sukkel* • *doetje*

soggy [bnw] • *drassig, nat* • *klef* ‹brood of cake›

soil I [ov ww] *vuil maken* II [znw] • *grond* • *bodem*

solace I [ov ww] *troosten* II [znw] *(ver)troost(ing)*

solar [bnw] *zons-, m.b.t. de zon, zonne-*

sold [ww] *verl. tijd + volt. deelw.*
→ **sell**

solder I [ov ww] *solderen* II [znw] *soldeer*

soldier I [on ww] • (~ **on**) *moedig volhouden, volharden* II [znw] *soldaat*

sole I [ov ww] *(ver)zolen* II [znw] • *zool* • *tong* ‹vis› III [bnw] *enig, enkel*

solemn [bnw] • *plechtig* • *plechtstatig* • *ernstig*

solicitor [znw] • ≈ *notaris* • ≈ *advocaat-procureur* • *juridisch adviseur*

solicitous [bnw] • *bezorgd* • *gretig*

solicitude [znw] • *zorg* • *aandacht*

solid I [znw] • *vast lichaam* • *stereometrische figuur* II [bnw] • *stevig* • *degelijk* • *vast* • *massief*

solidarity [znw] *solidariteit*

solidify I [ov ww] *in vaste toestand brengen* II [on ww] *in vaste toestand komen*

soliloquy [znw] • *alleenspraak* • *'t in zichzelf praten*

solitary [bnw] • *eenzaam* • *enkel*

• *alleenlevend*
solitude [znw] *eenzaamheid*
solo I [znw] *solo* II [bnw] *alleen-*
soloist [znw] *solist(e)*
soluble [bnw] *oplosbaar*
solution [znw] • *oplossing* • *solutie*
solvable [bnw] *oplosbaar*
solve [ov ww] *oplossen*
solvent I [znw] *oplosmiddel* II [bnw]
‹hand.› *solvabel*
sombre [bnw] *somber*
some I [bnw] • *sommige* • *ongeveer, een*
• *nogal wat, heel wat* • *een of ander(e),*
een zeker(e) • *wat, een paar, enige*
II [vnw] • *enige(n), sommige(n), een*
stuk of wat • *een beetje, wat* III [bijw]
een beetje, een tikje
somehow [bijw] • *op een of andere*
manier • *om de een of andere reden*
someone [vnw] *een of andere persoon,*
iemand
someplace [bijw] *ergens*
somersault I [on ww] *duikelen*
II [znw] • *duikeling* • *salto mortale*
something [vnw] *iets, wat*
sometime [bijw] • *te zijner tijd, wel 'ns*
een keer ‹in de toekomst› • *te eniger*
tijd • *vroeger, voorheen*
sometimes [bijw] *soms*
somnambulist [znw] *slaapwandelaar*
somnolent [bnw] • *slaperig*
• *slaapwekkend*
son [znw] *zoon*
sonata [znw] *sonate*
song [znw] • *lied(je)* • *gezang*
sonic [bnw] *m.b.t. geluid*
sonority [znw] *sonoriteit*
sonorous [bnw] • *klankvol, sonoor*
• *melodieus* • *mooi klinkend*
soon [bijw] *spoedig, weldra, gauw*
soot [znw] *roet*
soothe [ov ww] *sussen, kalmeren*
sooty [bnw] • *roetig* • *roetkleurig*
sop I [ov ww] • *(~ up)*
opnemen/-zuigen II [znw] • *aanbod*
‹om iem. mee om te kopen› • *concessie*

sophisticated [bnw]
• *intellectualistisch* • *ontwikkeld*
• *geavanceerd, geraffineerd, subtiel*
soporific [bnw] *slaapverwekkend*
‹middel›
sopping I [ww] *tegenw. deelw.*
→ **sop** II [bnw] *doorweekt*
soppy [bnw] *sentimenteel*
soprano [znw] *sopraan*
sorcerer [znw] *tovenaar*
sorceress [znw] *tovenares, heks*
sorcery [znw] *toverij, hekserij*
sordid [bnw] • *onverkwikkelijk*
‹kwestie› • *vuil* • *laag* • *gemeen*
sore I [znw] • *zeer* • *pijnlijke plek*
• *zweer* II [bnw] • *pijnlijk* • *gevoelig*
• *gekrenkt* • *ernstig, dringend*
sorrel I [znw] • *vos* ‹paard› • *zuring*
II [bnw] *roodbruin, rossig*
sorrow I [on ww] *bedroefd zijn, treuren*
II [znw] • *verdriet, droefheid* • *lijden*
sorrowful [bnw] • *treurig* • *bedroefd*
sorry I [bnw] • *zielig* • *pathetisch*
• *spijtig* II [tw] • *sorry* • *pardon*
sort I [ov ww] • *sorteren* • *indelen*
• *(~ out)* *uitzoeken, sorteren* II [znw]
soort
sortie [znw] • *uitje* • ‹mil.› *uitval*
sought [ww] *verl. tijd + volt. deelw.*
→ **seek**
soul [znw] • *ziel* • *geest*
soulful [bnw] • *zielvol* • *met vuur*
• *gevoelvol*
soulless [bnw] *zielloos, dood(s)*
sound I [ov + on ww] • *laten horen*
• *polsen* • *onderzoeken* • *luiden* • *(doen)*
klinken • *blazen op* • *peilen* • *(~ off)*
‹AE› *zijn mening zeggen, z. laten horen*
II [znw] • *geluid, klank* • *peiling*
• *zee-engte* III [bnw] • *gezond*
• *degelijk, flink* • *solide* • *betrouwbaar*
soundless [bnw] *geluidloos*
soup I [ov ww] • *(~ up) opvoeren*
II [znw] *soep*
sour I [ov + on ww] *verzuren* II [bnw]
zuur

source [znw] *bron*
south I [znw] *zuiden* II [bnw] • *zuid-*
• *zuiden-* • *op 't zuiden*
southerly [bnw + bijw] *zuidelijk,*
zuiden-
southern [bnw] • *zuidelijk* • *zuider-*
southerner [znw] *zuiderling*
sovereignty [znw] • *soevereiniteit*
• *oppergezag*
sow I [ov ww] *zaaien* II [znw] *zeug*
sozzled [bnw] *dronken*
spa [znw] • *badplaats, kuuroord*
• *geneeskrachtige bron*
space [znw] • *ruimte* • *tijdsruimte, poos*
• <typ.> *spatie*
spacing [znw] *spatiëring, tussenruimte,*
spatie
spacious [bnw] *ruim, uitgestrekt*
spade [znw] • *spade, schop*
• *schoppenkaart* • <pej.> *nikker*
span I [ov ww] *(om-/over)spannen,*
overbruggen II [znw]
• *reik-/spanwijdte* • *vleugelbreedte*
spangle I [ov ww] *bespikkelen* II [znw]
• *pailletje, lovertje* • *glinsterend*
spikkeltje
Spaniard [znw] *Spanjaard, Spaanse*
Spanish [bnw] *m.b.t. Spanje, Spaans*
spank I [ov ww] *slaan* <met platte
hand>, *op achterwerk slaan* II [znw]
klap
spanking I [znw] *billenkoek, pak voor*
de broek II [bnw] • *prima* • *flink*
spanner [znw] *moersleutel*
spar I [on ww] *boksen* II [znw] *paal,*
mast
spare I [ov ww] *(be)sparen* II [znw]
reserveonderdeel/-wiel III [bnw]
• *mager, schraal* • *reserve-* • *extra*
sparing [bnw] • *matig* • *karig, zuinig*
spark I [on ww] *vonken (uitslaan)*
II [znw] • *vonk* • *sprankje*
sparkle I [on ww] • *sprankelen*
• *schitteren* II [znw] *schittering*
sparkler [znw] *sterretje* <vuurwerk>
sparrow [znw] *mus*

sparse [bnw] • *dun gezaaid* <fig.>
• *schaars*
spasm [znw] • *kramp* • *scheut*
spasmodic [bnw] • *met vlagen,*
onregelmatig • *krampachtig*
spastic [bnw] • *kramp-* • *spastisch*
spat I [ww] *verl.tijd + volt.deelw.*
→ spit II [znw] *slobkous*
spate [znw] *stroom, (toe)vloed* <fig.>
spatial [bnw] • *ruimtelijk* • *m.b.t.*
ruimte
spatter I [ov ww] *besprenkelen,*
bespatten II [znw] *spat(je)*
spatula [znw] *spatel*
spawn I [ov ww] *voortbrengen*
II [on ww] *kuit schieten* III [znw] • *kuit*
• *kikkerdril*
speak [ov + on ww] • *spreken* • *zeggen*
• *tegen elkaar spreken* • (~ for) *spreken*
namens/voor • (~ of) *spreken over*
• (~ out) *vrijuit spreken* • (~ up)
harder spreken
speaker [znw] • *luidspreker* • *spreker*
speaking [bnw] *spreek-*
spear I [ov ww] • *doorboren* • *spietsen*
• *aan de speer rijgen* II [znw] • *speer*
• *piek*
speciality [znw] • *specialiteit*
• *bijzondere eigenschap* • *speciaal*
onderwerp/vak
specialize [on ww] *specialiseren*
• (~ in) z. *speciaal gaan toeleggen op*
specially [bijw] *speciaal, (in het)*
bijzonder
species [znw] *soort(en)* <levensvormen>
specific [bnw] • *specifiek* • *soortelijk,*
soort- • *bepaald*
specifically [bijw] • *specifiek* • *wat je*
noemt
specification [znw] • *bestek*
• *specificatie*
specify [ov + on ww] • *specificeren*
• *nader bepalen*
specimen [znw] • *staaltje, (voor)proef*
• *voorbeeld, exemplaar*
specious [bnw] *vals, misleidend*

speck [znw] • *vlekje, stip* • *greintje*
speckle I [ov ww] *(be)spikkelen* II [znw]
spikkeltje
spectacle [znw] *tafereel, schouwspel*
spectacular I [znw] • *schouwspel*
• *show* II [bnw] • *opzienbarend,
spectaculair* • *opvallend* • *sensationeel*
spectator [znw] *toeschouwer*
spectral [bnw] • *spookachtig* • *spook-*
• *spectraal*
speculate [on ww] • *peinzen, mediteren*
• *speculeren*
speculative [bnw] *speculatief*
speculator [znw] *speculant*
sped [ww] verl. tijd + volt. deelw.
→ speed
speech [znw] • *toespraak, rede* • *spraak*
• *taal*
speechless [bnw] *sprakeloos*
speed I [on ww] • *z. haasten, spoeden*
• *(te) snel rijden* • *(~ up) het tempo
opvoeren* II [znw] • *snelheid* • *spoed*
• *versnelling* • *amfetamine*
speedometer [znw] *snelheidsmeter*
speedy [bnw] • *snel* • *met spoed*
• *spoedig*
spell I [ov + on ww] • *spellen*
• *betekenen* • *(~ out) (voluit) spellen*
II [znw] • *toverspreuk* • *betovering*
• *(korte) periode*
spend [ov ww] • *verspelen* • *uitgeven*
• *besteden* • *doorbrengen* • *verbruiken*
spender [znw] • *uitgever* <v. geld>
• *opmaker*
spent I [ww] verl.tijd + volt.deelw.
→ spend II [bnw] *uitgeput, op,
versleten, leeg* <huls>
sperm [znw] *sperma*
spew [ov + on ww] *spuwen, (uit)braken*
sphere [znw] • *bol* • *sfeer* • *terrein*
spheric(al) [bnw] • *bolvormig* • *bol-*
sphinx [znw] *sfinx*
spicy [bnw] • *kruidig, geurig* • *pikant,
pittig*
spider [znw] *spin*
spidery [bnw] • *spinachtig* • *spichtig*

spiel [znw] *(verkoop)praatje*
spike I [ov ww] • *spietsen* • *alcohol
toevoegen aan* II [znw] • *(ijzeren) punt*
• *schoennagel* • *lange bout/spijker*
• *piek*
spiky [bnw] • *met scherpe punten*
• *stekelig* <ook v. personen>
spill I [ov ww] • *morsen* • *gemorst
worden* • *overlopen* II [znw] • *gemorste
hoeveelheid vloeistof* • *val* <v. paard of
(motor)fiets>
spilt [ww] volt. deelw. → spill
spin I [ov + on ww] • *spinnen* • *snel
ronddraaien, rondtollen* • *(~ out)
uitrekken/-spinnen* II [znw] • *spinsel*
• *draaiing* • *tochtje, ritje, dans*
spinach [znw] *spinazie*
spinal [bnw] *m.b.t. de ruggengraat*
spindle [znw] • *spoel, klos* • *spil, as,
stang*
spindly [bnw] *spichtig*
spine [znw] • *stekel, doorn*
• *ruggengraat* • *rug* <v.e. boek>
spineless [bnw] *zonder ruggengraat*
<vooral fig.>, *futloos*
spinner, spinster [znw] *spinner* <bij
cricket>
spinney [znw] *bosje*
spinster [znw] *oude vrijster*
spiny [bnw] *stekelig*
spiral I [on ww] *spiraalvormig lopen*
II [znw] *spiraal* III [bnw]
spiraalvormig, spiraal-
spire [znw] *(toren)spits*
spirit I [ov ww] • *(~ away/off)
heimelijk doen verdwijnen, wegtoveren*
II [znw] • *geest* • *spook* • *fut,
(levens)moed, energie, pit* • *alcohol,
spiritus*
spirited [bnw] *levendig, vurig*
spiritualism [znw] • *spiritualisme*
• *spiritisme*
spit I [ov + on ww] *blazen* <v. kat>,
sputteren, spuwen II [ov ww]
doorboren, aan spit steken III [on ww]
• *(~ upon) verachten, spugen op*

IV [znw] • (braad)spit • landtong
• speeksel • spuug
spite I [ov ww] • dwars zitten • kwellen,
pesten, plagen II [znw] • wrevel,
rancune, wrok • boosaardigheid
spiteful [bnw] • rancuneus • hatelijk
• uit haat
spittoon [znw] kwispedoor
splash I [ov + on ww] • (be)spatten
• rondspatten • plenzen II [znw]
• kwak • plons
splay [ov + on ww] • (~ out) uitspreiden
spleen [znw] • milt • woede, gal
splendid [bnw] • prachtig • groots
• prima • schitterend
splendour [znw] • pracht • luister
splice [ov ww] • splitsen ‹touw› • in
elkaar vlechten • ‹inf.› trouwen
splint [znw] spalk
splinter I [ov ww] versplinteren
II [znw] splinter
split I [ov + on ww] • splijten • (z.)
splitsen • uiteengaan • (z. ver)delen
• klikken II [znw] • scheur • split
• scheuring, breuk
splitting [bnw] barstend ‹v. hoofdpijn›
splodge, splotch [znw] • veeg, vlek
• spat
splurge [on ww] • met geld smijten • z.
te buiten gaan (aan)
splutter [on ww] • vochtig praten
• sputteren
spoil I [ov ww] • schaden • in de war
sturen • verwennen • bederven II [znw]
• roof • buit
spoke I [ww] verl. tijd → **speak**
II [znw] spaak
spoken I [ww] volt. deelw. → **speak**
II [bnw] spreek-
spokesman [znw] woordvoerder
sponge I [ov ww] afsponsen
• (~ **down**) afsponsen II [on ww]
parasiteren • (~ **off/on**) op (iem.s) zak
teren III [znw] • spons • sponsdeeg
sponger [znw] klaploper
spongy [bnw] sponsachtig

sponsor I [ov ww] financieel steunen
II [znw] sponsor
sponsorship [znw] financiële steun v.
sponsor(s)
spontaneous [bnw] • spontaan
• vanzelf, uit zichzelf
spoof [znw] parodie, satire
spook I [ov ww] bang maken II [znw]
spook
spooky [bnw] spookachtig
spool [znw] spoel
spoon I [ov ww] lepelen, scheppen
II [znw] lepel
spoonful [znw] lepel ‹hoeveelheid›
sporadic [bnw] sporadisch
spore [znw] • spore ‹v. plant of zwam›
• kiem
sport I [ov ww] dragen, pronken met
II [znw] • sport • spel • vermaak
• fideel/sportief persoon • speelbal ‹fig.›
sporting [bnw] • sport-, jacht-
• sportief
spot I [ov ww] • in de gaten krijgen
• ontdekken II [znw] • plek, plaats
• spikkeltje • puistje • beetje, tikje
• reclamespotje • vlek
spotless [bnw] smetteloos
spotted [bnw] gevlekt, bont
spotty [bnw] met puistjes
spouse [znw] • echtgenoot, echtgenote
• bruid(egom) • gade
spout I [ov ww] spuiten, gutsen,
stromen II [znw] • tuit • spuit(gat)
• straal
sprat [znw] sprot
sprawl I [on ww] languit (gaan) liggen
II [znw] • luie houding • spreiding
spray I [ov ww] • besproeien
• verstuiven II [znw] • stuifwolk • wolk
‹parfum› • spray • sproeier • verstuiver
• vaporisator • twijgje ‹met bloemen›
• aigrette
sprayer [znw] sproeier
spread I [ov ww] • verspreiden
• verbreiden • (uit)spreiden
• uitstrekken • smeren • (~ **out**)

uitspreiden II [on ww] • z. verspreiden,
z. verbreiden • z. uitspreiden III [znw]
• breedte • smeerbeleg • omvang, wijdte
spree [znw] vrolijk uitje
sprig [znw] twijgje, takje
sprightly [bnw] • vrolijk • dartel
spring I [ov ww] • helpen ontsnappen
• plotseling aankomen met II [on ww]
• springen • ontspringen • ontstaan,
voortkomen • barsten • (~ up)
plotseling ontstaan III [znw] • lente
• bron, oorsprong • veer, veerkracht
springy [bnw] veerkrachtig
sprinkle [ov ww] (be)sprenkelen,
(be)strooien
sprinkler [znw] strooier, sproeiwagen
sprinkling [znw] → sprinkle
sprint I [ov + on ww] sprinten II [znw]
sprint
sprung I [ww] volt. deelw. → spring
II [bnw] • gebarsten • met veren <v.
matras>
spry [bnw] vlug, kwiek, kittig
spud [znw] pieper <aardappel>
spun [ww] verl.tijd + volt.deelw.
→ spin
spunk [znw] pit, moed, lef
spunky [bnw] vurig, moedig
spur I [ov ww] de sporen geven • (~ on)
aansporen, aanvuren II [znw] • spoor
• prikkel • uitloper <v. berg>
spurious [bnw] vals, niet echt
spurn [ov ww] versmaden
spurt I [ov + on ww] • spuiten • spatten
<v. pen> II [on ww] spurten III [znw]
• straal • spurt
sputter I [on ww] sputteren, spetteren,
knetteren II [znw] gesputter
spy I [ov + on ww] • (be)spioneren
• (be)loeren • in 't oog krijgen
• (~ (up)on) bespioneren • (~ out)
proberen achter... te komen II [znw]
spion
squabble I [on ww] kibbelen, ruzie
maken II [znw] kibbelpartij
squad [znw] • groep, ploeg

• (politie)patrouille
squalid [bnw] vunzig, smerig
squall I [ov + on ww] • gillen • brallen
II [znw] • windstoot • vlaag
squalor [znw] • vunzigheid, smerigheid
• ellende
squander [ov ww] verkwisten,
vergooien
square I [ov ww] • in kwadraat brengen
• vierkant maken, recht/haaks maken
• in orde maken, afrekenen
• (~ to/with) in overeenstemming
brengen met, aanpassen aan • (~ up)
vereffenen, afrekenen, betalen
II [on ww] • (~ with) kloppen met
III [znw] • ouderwets iem. • vierkant
• kwadraat • plein, exercitieterrein
• huizenblok • carré IV [bnw]
• ouderwets • vierkant • stoer, stevig
• eerlijk, oprecht, betrouwbaar
• ondubbelzinnig • gelijk, quitte V
[bijw] • vierkant • oprecht • vlak,
ronduit
squash I [ov ww] • plat drukken • tot
moes maken/slaan II [znw] • gedrang
• pulp, moes • limonade, kwast
• vruchtvlees v.e. kalebas <als groente>
squashy [bnw] zacht
squat I [ov ww] kraken <v. huis, stuk
land> II [on ww] hurken III [znw]
gekraakt pand IV [bnw] kort,
gedrongen
squatter [znw] kraker
squaw [znw] (indiaanse) vrouw
squawk I [on ww] krijsen II [znw]
schreeuw
squeak I [on ww] piepen II [znw] gepiep
squeal I [on ww] • gillen • gieren • <sl.>
verraden II [znw] gil
squeamish [bnw] • overgevoelig
• (gauw) misselijk
squeeze I [ov ww] • knijpen, uitknijpen
• uitpersen, afpersen • (tegen z.
aan)drukken • eruit dwingen <bridge>
II [on ww] (z.) dringen • (~ through)
't met moeite halen III [znw]

- moeilijke situatie • kneep(je)
- gedrang • (hand)druk • hartelijke omhelzing

squelch I [on ww] zuigend geluid maken <als bij lopen door modder>
II [znw] zuigend geluid

squid [znw] pijlinktvis

squiggle [znw] golvend lijntje, slangetje

squire [znw] • landjonker • <gesch.> schildknaap

squirm [on ww] • wriemelen, kronkelen • krimpen <v. schaamte>

squirrel [znw] eekhoorn

squirt I [ov + on ww] • spuiten • sprietsen II [znw] • straal • spuitje • branieschopper

stab I [ov + on ww] steken <vnl. met dolk, of v. wond> II [znw] • dolkstoot, doodsteek • (pijn)scheut

stability, stableness [znw] bestendigheid, evenwichtigheid

stabilize [ov + on ww] stabiliseren

stack I [ov ww] stapelen • (~ up) opstapelen, optassen II [znw] • stapel, hoop • groep schoorstenen <op dak> • (schoorsteen)pijp • (hooi)mijt

stadium [znw] • stadion • stadium

staff I [ov ww] van personeel e.d. voorzien II [znw] • (leidinggevend) personeel • staf

stag [znw] (mannetjes)hert

stage I [ov ww] • opvoeren • ensceneren • op touw zetten II [znw] • stage, leertijd • fase, stadium • toneel • podium • etappe, traject

stagger I [ov ww] • ontstellen • (doen) duizelen • zigzagsgewijs of om en om plaatsen II [on ww] • wankelen • waggelen

stagnant [bnw] • stilstaand • traag, dood <fig.>

stagnate [on ww] • stilstaan • op 'n dood punt staan of komen

stagy [bnw] theatraal

staid [bnw] • bedaard, bezadigd

- degelijk

stain I [ov ww] • vlek(ken) maken op • kleuren, verven • beitsen • onteren, bezoedelen II [on ww] • vlekken geven • afgeven <v. stoffen> III [znw] • smet, vlek • blaam • kleurstof, verfstof, beits

stair [znw] • trede • trap

stake I [ov ww] aan paal/staak (op)binden • (~ out) afbakenen
II [znw] • inzet • aandeel, belang(en) • paal, staak

stale [bnw] • niet fris meer, muf • verschaald • oud(bakken)

stalemate [znw] • pat(stelling) • schaakmat

stalk I [ov ww] (be)sluipen <v. prooi> II [znw] stengel

stall I [ov + on ww] • vertragen • treuzelen • afslaan <v. motor> II [znw] • afdeling in stal • box • koorbank • koorstoel • stalletje, kiosk, kraam

stallion [znw] hengst

stalwart I [znw] getrouwe, trawant II [bnw] • robuust, stoer, struis • trouw

stamina [znw] uithoudingsvermogen

stammer I [ov + on ww] • stotteren • stamelen II [znw] het stotteren

stamp I [ov + on ww] stampen
II [ov ww] • (be)stempelen • frankeren, zegelen • karakteriseren, kenmerken • (~ out) uittrappen, vernietigen, uitroeien III [znw] • stempel, merk • postzegel • (ge)stamp • soort, karakter

stampede I [ov ww] paniek/vlucht veroorzaken II [on ww] massaal op hol slaan III [znw] • massale plotselinge vlucht v. paarden/vee • toeloop, stormloop

stand I [ov ww] • plaatsen, zetten • uithouden, verdragen, uitstaan • bestand zijn tegen • trakteren (op)
II [on ww] • blijven staan, er (nog) staan • standhouden, geldig zijn, steekhouden, gehandhaafd blijven • (gaan) staan • (~ back) z. afzijdig

houden • (~ **by**) lijdelijk toezien, klaar
(gaan) staan om te helpen, een handje
helpen • (~ **down**) z. terugtrekken
• (~ **for**) steunen, voorstaan,
betekenen, symboliseren, kandidaat
zijn voor • (~ **in**) iem. vervangen
• (~ **out**) in 't oog vallen, niet
toegeven, standvastig zijn, volhouden
• (~ **up**) opstaan, rechtop blijven/gaan
staan, het opnemen (voor) III [znw]
• tribune • standaard, rek, tafeltje,
statief • standplaats • standpunt
• kraam, kiosk
standard I [znw] • standaard • vaandel
• standaardmaat • maatstaf, norm
• stander II [bnw] • standaard,
normaal • algemeen
erkend/gewaardeerd
standardize [ov ww] normaliseren
standing I [znw] • duur, ouderdom
• reputatie, aanzien II [bnw] • staand
• blijvend, voortdurend, permanent
stank [ww] verl. tijd → **stink**
staple I [ov ww] (vast)nieten, krammen
II [znw] • hoofdmiddel van bestaan
• hoofdexportartikel, hoofdproduct
• kern, hoofdschotel ‹fig.› • kram
• hechtnietje III [bnw] • hoofd- • kern-
stapler [znw] nietmachine
star I [ov ww] • met sterren
tooien/versieren • sterretjes zetten bij
• als ster laten optreden II [on ww] • de
hoofdrol spelen • als ster optreden
III [znw] • ster(retje) • gesternte
IV [bnw] • ster- • hoofd- • eerste
starch I [ov ww] stijven II [znw]
• zetmeel • stijfsel
starchy [bnw] • zetmeelrijk • gesteven
• vormelijk
stardom [znw] de status van ster
stare I [ov + on ww] • grote ogen
opzetten • staren • (~ **at**) aangapen
II [znw] • (hol) starende blik • blik
stark I [bnw] • absoluut, volkomen
• spiernaakt • grimmig II [bijw]
volkomen

starkers [bnw] spiernaakt
starlet [znw] sterretje
starling [znw] spreeuw
starry [bnw] met sterren bezaaid
start I [ov + on ww] • beginnen (met)
• starten II [ov ww] • startsein geven
• aan de gang krijgen • op gang/weg
helpen • aanzetten • (~ **up**) starten,
aanzetten III [on ww] • vertrekken
• (op)springen • (op)schrikken
• aanslaan ‹v. motor› • (~ **at**)
schrikken van • (~ **for**) vertrekken naar
• (~ **from/with**) uitgaan van
• (~ **off/out**) op weg gaan • (~ **up**)
opspringen, opschrikken IV [znw]
• vertrekpunt, beginpunt, start
• voorsprong
starter [znw] • starter • deelnemer ‹aan
wedstrijd› • begin • voorgerecht
startle [ov ww] opschrikken
starvation [znw] hongerdood
starve I [ov ww] uithongeren II [on ww]
• honger lijden, honger/trek hebben
• verhongeren
state I [ov ww] • verklaren, beweren
• uiteenzetten • formuleren II [znw]
• staat • toestand • stand • staatsie,
praal III [bnw] • staats- • staatsie-
stately [bnw] • statig • imposant
statement [znw] verklaring
statesman [znw] staatsman
statesmanship [znw] (goed)
staatsmanschap, staatkunde
static [bnw] statisch
station I [ov ww] • opstellen
• stationeren • postvatten II [znw]
• station • (stand)plaats • positie • post
• politiebureau • schapenranch ‹in
Australië›
stationary I [znw] II [bnw] • stationair
• stilstaand • vast • onveranderd
stationery [znw] • kantoorboekhandel
• postpapier
statistic(al) [bnw] statistisch
statue [znw] standbeeld
statuesque [bnw] statig

statuette [znw] beeldje
stature [znw] gestalte, postuur
statute [znw] • wet • statuut
• verordening • reglement
statutory [bnw] • statutair • volgens de
wet
staunch I [ov ww] stelpen II [bnw]
trouw (aan)
stave I [ov ww] • (~ off) opschorten
II [znw] • notenbalk • staf
stay I [on ww] • blijven • logeren
II [znw] verblijf
stead [znw] plaats
steadfast [bnw] • standvastig,
onwrikbaar • strak <v. blik>
steady I [ov ww] • in evenwicht brengen
• tot bedaren brengen II [on ww]
rustig/kalm worden III [znw] <sl.> vaste
vrijer IV [bnw] • stevig, vast • gestadig
• bedaard, rustig
steak [znw] • runderlap • moot vis
steal I [ov + on ww] stelen II [on ww]
• sluipen, glijden • onmerkbaar gaan of
komen • (~ away) ongemerkt
voorbijgaan • (~ out) er stilletjes
vandoor gaan
stealth [znw] heimelijkheid
stealthy [bnw] • heimelijk • steels
steam I [ov + on ww] • stomen • (~ up)
beslaan II [znw] • stoom • damp
steamer [znw] • stoomboot
• stoomkoker
steamy [bnw] • warm en vochtig • <inf.>
erotisch
steed [znw] • paard • strijdros
steel I [wkd ww] zich vermannen
II [znw] • staal • wetstaal III [bnw]
stalen
steely [bnw] • van staal • staalachtig
steep I [ov + on ww] weken II [ov ww]
(in)dompelen III [bnw] • steil
• abnormaal (hoog) • overdreven
steeple [znw] torenspits
steer I [ov ww] (be)sturen II [znw]
gecastreerde stier
stellar [bnw] sterren-

stem I [ov ww] • stremmen
• tegenhouden, stuiten II [on ww]
• (~ from) teruggaan op III [znw]
• stengel • stam <ook v. woord> • steel
<v. pijp>
stench [znw] stank, (onaangename)
lucht
stencil I [ov ww] stencillen II [znw]
• stencil • sjabloon
stenographer [znw] stenograaf
step I [ov ww] stappen • (~ up)
opvoeren II [on ww] stappen, treden,
opstappen • (~ aside) opzij gaan
staan, afdwalen, een misstap doen
• (~ aside/down) af-/terugtreden
• (~ back) teruggaan <fig.>, z.
terugtrekken • (~ between)
tusenbeide komen • (~ in) erin stappen,
er even tussenkomen III [znw]
• (voet)stap, pas • tred • tree, sport
stereophonic [bnw] stereofonisch
stereotype I [ov ww] stereotyperen
II [znw] stereotype
sterile [bnw] • onvruchtbaar
• onproductief • steriel
sterilize [ov ww] • onvruchtbaar
maken • steriliseren
sterling [bnw] • van standaardgehalte
• onvervalst, echt • degelijk
stern I [znw] • achtersteven • achterste
<v. dier> II [bnw] • streng • hard
sternum [znw] borstbeen
stevedore [ov ww] stuwadoor
stew I [ov + on ww] stoven II [znw]
stamppot <met vlees of vis>
steward [znw] • kelner <aan boord>
• administrateur • rentmeester
• beheerder
stewardess [znw] stewardess
stick I [ov ww] • steken, zetten
• vastplakken • uithouden, uitstaan
• (~ on) plakken op, opplakken
• (~ out) naar buiten/voren steken
• (~ up) overeind zetten II [on ww]
• blijven hangen/steken/zitten, vast
blijven zitten • klitten, kleven, plakken

- (~ **around**) *in de buurt blijven*
- (~ **at**) *volhouden, doorgaan met*
- (~ **by**) *trouw blijven, z. houden aan*
- (~ **out**) *naar buiten/voren steken*
- (~ **to**) *trouw blijven aan, blijven bij, volhouden* • (~ **up**) *overeind staan* III [znw] • *tak* • *stok, staaf, steel* • *rare snijboon*

stickleback [znw] *stekelbaarsje*

stickler [znw] * a ~ *for discipline iem. die discipline eist*

sticky [bnw] • *lastig, penibel* • *kleverig* • *kleef-*

stiff [bnw] • *stijf* • *onbuigzaam* • *vormelijk* • *moeilijk* • *stroef* • *stevig*

stiffen I [ov ww] *stijf maken* II [on ww] *verstijven*

stifle I [ov ww] • *doen stikken* • *smoren* • *de kop indrukken* • *onderdrukken* • *inhouden* II [on ww] *(ver)stikken*

stigma [znw] • *schandvlek* • *stigma, wondteken v. Christus* • *stempel* <v. bloem>

stigmatize [ov ww] • *brandmerken* • *stigmatiseren*

stile [znw] • *overstap* • *deurstijl*

stiletto [znw] • *stiletto* • *schoen met naaldhak*

still I [ov ww] • *stillen* • *kalmeren* II [bnw] • *stil, rustig* • *niet mousserend* <v. wijn> III [bijw] • *nog* • *nog altijd* • *toch, toch nog*

stilt [znw] *stelt*

stilted [bnw] *onhandig, harkerig*

stimulant [znw] • *prikkel* • *opwekkend middel*

stimulate [ov ww] • *prikkelen* • *(op)wekken* • *stimuleren* • *aansporen*

stimulus [znw] *stimulans*

sting I [ov + on ww] • *steken* • *prikken* II [ov ww] *afzetten, 't vel over de neus halen* III [on ww] *pijn doen* IV [znw] • *steek, beet* • *angel* • <plantk.> *brandhaar*

stingy [bnw] *gierig, vrekkig*

stink I [on ww] *stinken* • (~ **of**) *stinken*

naar II [znw] *stank*

stinking [bnw] *rot, gemeen*

stipend [znw] • *salaris* • *bezoldiging*

stir I [ov ww] • *verroeren* • *poken* • *roeren* • *in beweging brengen* • *(op)wekken* • *op de verbeelding werken* • (~ **up**) *doen opwarrelen, opruien (tot), doen oplaaien* II [on ww] *z. verroeren* III [znw] *sensatie, herrie*

stirring [bnw] *ontroerend, prikkelend*

stirrup [znw] *stijgbeugel*

stoat [znw] • *hermelijn* • *wezel*

stock I [ov ww] • *inslaan* • *bevoorraden, voorzien van, uitrusten (met)* • *in voorraad hebben* II [on ww] *z. bevoorraden, voorraad inslaan* III [znw] • *bouillon* • *stam, (wortel)stronk* • *afkomst, geslacht* • *'t geheel* • *voorraad, inventaris, materieel* • *grondstof, materiaal* • *obligatie, fonds, aandelenkapitaal* IV [bnw] *gewoon, stereotiep, afgezaagd*

stocking [znw] *kous*

stockist [znw] *leverancier*

stocky [bnw] *kort en breed*

stodge [znw] *machtige of zware kost*

stodgy [bnw] • *zwaar, machtig* <v. eten> • *saai, plechtig*

stoic I [znw] *stoïcijn* II [bnw] *stoïcijns*

stoke [ov ww] • *stoken* • *brandstof/kolen bijgooien*

stole I [ww] *verl. tijd* → **steal** II [znw] *stola*

stolen [ww] *volt. deelw.* → **steal**

stolid [bnw] • *bot* • *flegmatisch* • *onaandoenlijk*

stomach I [ov ww] • *verteren* • *verdragen* • *(voor lief) nemen* II [znw] • *buik* • *maag*

stomp I [ov ww] <AE> *stampen* II [on ww] *klossen*

stone I [ov ww] • *stenigen* • *ontpitten* II [znw] • *steen* • *kei* • *natuursteen* • *pit* • *Eng. gewichtseenheid* III [bnw] *stenen*

stony [bnw] *(steen)hard, hardvochtig*

stood [ww] *verl. tijd + volt. deelw.*

→ **stand**
stooge [znw] • knechtje, slaafje
• mikpunt, aangever <v. conferencier>
stool [znw] kruk
stoop I [on ww] • z. vernederen/
verwaardigen • voorover
lopen/staan/zitten • (z.) bukken
II [znw] • kromme rug • <AE> stoep
stop I [ov ww] • ophouden met,
neerleggen <werk> • afzetten,
stilleggen, beletten, weerhouden, doen
ophouden, stil doen staan • afsluiten,
verstoppen, dichtstoppen • versperren,
stelpen, tegenhouden, dempen • (~ up)
doen verstoppen, dichtstoppen
II [on ww] • stoppen, ophouden, niet
meer werken/gaan • stil (blijven) staan
• logeren, blijven • (~ at) logeren bij/te
• (~ in) binnenblijven • (~ out)
uitblijven • (~ up) opblijven III [znw]
• punt <leesteken> • stilstand
• stopplaats, halte • register <v. orgel>,
klep, demper • <taalk.> ploffer
stoppage [znw] inhouding, blokkering
stopper [znw] stop <op fles>
storage [znw] opslag, 't opslaan
store I [ov ww] opslaan • (~ up)
opslaan, bewaren II [znw] • voorraad
• hoeveelheid • opslagplaats • <AE>
winkel
storey [znw] verdieping, etage
stork [znw] ooievaar
storm I [ov ww] bestormen II [on ww]
• woeden, razen • <AE> stormen • (~ at)
tekeergaan tegen III [znw] • (hevige)
bui • noodweer • storm
stormy [bnw] • stormachtig • storm-
• heftig
story [znw] • verhaal • geschiedenis
• gerucht • leugentje • <AE> verdieping,
etage
stout I [znw] donker bier II [bnw]
• krachtig • stevig • dik, gezet
stove [znw] • kachel • fornuis
stow I [ov ww] • (vakkundig) laden
• opbergen, wegbergen • (~ away)

opbergen, wegstoppen II [on ww]
• (~ away) als verstekeling meereizen
straddle I [ov ww] • over iets heen
staan • over een heel gebied verspreid
zijn II [on ww] wijdbeens (gaan)
lopen/staan/zitten III [znw]
spreidstand
straggle [on ww] • achterblijven
• verspreid of verward
groeien/hangen/liggen • zwerven,
afdwalen • (~ behind) achterblijven,
niet meekomen
straight I [znw] hetero II [bnw]
• eerlijk, oprecht • betrouwbaar • in
orde, op orde • puur, onvermengd
• recht • rechtstreeks • recht op de man
af III [bijw] • recht(streeks) • rechtop
• direct • ronduit
straighten I [ov ww]
• rechtmaken/-zetten/-leggen
• strekken • in orde brengen • (~ up) in
orde brengen II [on ww] • recht worden
• rechttrekken • (~ up) rechtop gaan
staan
strain I [ov + on ww] • zeven • filteren
• (~ off/out) uitzeven, filtreren
II [ov ww] • verrekken • inspannen
• zwoegen • overspannen • (te) veel
vergen van • forceren III [on ww] z.
inspannen IV [znw] • spanning
• belasting • soort, variëteit • melodie
strainer [znw] zeef
strait [znw] zee-engte
strand I [ov ww] aan de grond doen
lopen II [on ww] vastlopen, stranden
III [znw] • strand • streng • lok, wrong
strange [bnw] • vreemd • raar
• eigenaardig
stranger [znw] vreemde(ling)
strangle [ov ww] • wurgen
• onderdrukken
strangler [znw] wurger
strangulation [znw] • wurging
• economische druk
strap I [ov ww] gespen II [znw]
• riem(pje) • band(je) • lus <in tram>

strategist [znw] *strateeg*
strategy [znw] *strategie*
stratification [znw] *gelaagdheid*
stratum [znw] *(geologische) laag*
straw I [znw] • *strootje* • *strohoed*
• *stro(halm)* • *rietje* II [bnw] *strooien*
strawberry [znw] *aardbei*
streak I [ov ww] *strepen* II [on ww]
• *snellen, ijlen* • <inf.> *naakt over plein
e.d. rennen* III [znw] • *streep* • *flits*
streaker [znw] *iem. die naakt over plein
e.d. rent*
streaky [bnw] • *gestreept* • *doorregen*
stream I [ov ww] *doen stromen*
II [on ww] • *stromen* • *wapperen*
III [znw] • *beek(je)* • *groep met zelfde
leerprogram* • *stroom*
streamline [znw] *stroomlijn*
streamlined [bnw] *gestroomlijnd*
street [znw] *straat*
strength [znw] • *kracht(en)* • *sterkte*
strengthen I [ov ww] *versterken*
II [on ww] *sterker worden*
strenuous [bnw] *inspannend*
stress I [ov ww] *de nadruk leggen op*
II [znw] • *nadruk* • *gewicht* • *accent*
• *spanning* • *druk*
stretch I [ov ww] • *(uit)strekken*
• *uitrekken, (op)rekken* • *spannen*
• (~ **forth**) *uitsteken* II [on ww] • *zich
(uit)strekken* • *(zich) uitrekken* • *reiken
(tot)* • *lopen tot* • (~ **down to**) z.
uitstrekken tot, lopen tot III [znw]
• *uitgestrektheid* • *stuk* • *periode, duur*
• *traject* • *afstand*
stretcher [znw] *brancard*
strew [ov ww] • *bezaaien* • *verspreid
liggen op* • *(be)strooien*
stricken [bnw] • *getroffen* • *geteisterd*
strict [bnw] • *strikt* • *stipt* • *nauwgezet*
• *streng*
stricture [znw] *kritiek*
stride I [on ww] • *grote stappen nemen*
• *schrijden* II [znw] *(grote) stap*
strident [bnw] *hard en schel*
strife [znw] • *strijd* • *conflict*

strike I [ov ww] • *slaan (met), raken*
• *aanslaan* • *aanstrijken, aangaan*
• *opvallen* • *opkomen bij* • (~ **down**)
neerslaan, vellen • (~ **off**) *royeren*
• (~ **out**) *doorhalen* • (~ **up**)
aanheffen II [on ww] • *toeslaan, treffen*
• *staken* • *luiden* • (~ **at**) *slaan naar*
• (~ **out**) *een andere richting inslaan*
• (~ **up**) *inzetten, beginnen te
spelen/zingen* III [znw] • *staking* • *slag*
<honkbal> • <AE> *succes, bof*
striker [znw] • *staker* • <sport>
spitsspeler
string I [ov ww] • *met touw vastbinden*
• *besnaren* II [on ww] • (~ **along**)
meeboemelen III [znw] • *touw(tje)*
• *serie* • *snaar*
stringent [bnw] • *bindend* • *streng*
• *strikt*
stringy [bnw] • *draderig* • *pezig*
strip I [ov + on ww] • *strippen* • *ontdoen
van* II [znw] • *strip* • *(smalle) rand*
• *landingsbaan* • *sportkleding*
stripe [znw] • *streep* • *chevron* • *striem*
striped [bnw] *gestreept*
stripper [znw] *stripteasedanser(es)*
strive [on ww] z. *inspannen*
• (~ **after/for**) *streven naar*
strode [ww] verl. tijd → **stride**
stroke I [ov ww] *strijken, aaien, strelen*
II [znw] • *aai* • *klap* • *slag* • *beroerte*
stroll I [on ww] • *slenteren* • *wandelen*
II [znw] *wandeling(etje)*
stroller [znw] *wandelwagentje*
strong [bnw] • *sterk* • *krachtig* • *zwaar*
<v. tabak, bier> • *vast* <v. geldkoers,
prijzen> • *overdreven*
stroppy [bnw] • *tegendraads* • *dwars,
koppig*
strove [ww] verl. tijd → **strive**
struck [ww] verl. tijd + volt. deelw.
→ **strike**
structural [bnw] *structureel*
structure [znw] • *(op)bouw*
• *bouwwerk* • *structuur*
struggle I [on ww] • *worstelen*

• *vechten* • *tegenspartelen* • (~ **to**)
moeite hebben om II [znw] *strijd,*
gevecht
strum I [ov + on ww] *trommelen,*
tjingelen II [znw] *getrommel, getjingel*
strung [ww] *verl. tijd + volt. deelw.*
→ **string**
strut I [ov + on ww] *trots stappen*
II [znw] *stut*
stub I [ov ww] *stoten* II [znw] • *stompje*
• *peukje*
stubble [znw] *stoppels*
stubborn [bnw] • *koppig* • *hardnekkig*
stuck [ww] *verl. tijd + volt. deelw.*
→ **stick**
stud [znw] • *fokstal* • *dekhengst*
• *metalen sierknopje* • *boordenknoopje,*
manchetknoopje
student [znw] • *student* • *leerling*
studio [znw] • *atelier* • *studio*
studious [bnw] • *vlijtig, ijverig*
• *studerend*
study I [ov ww] • *(be)studeren*
• *observeren* II [on ww] *studeren*
III [znw] • *studie* • *etude*
• *studeerkamer*
stuff I [ov ww] • *(vol)stoppen* • *opvullen*
• *farceren* • *volproppen* • *opzetten* <v.
dier> II [znw] • *stof, materiaal* • *spul,*
goedje • *waardeloze rommel* • *onzin*
stuffing [znw] *vulling*
stuffy [bnw] • *benauwd, bedompt*
• *ouderwets*
stultify [ov ww] • *belachelijk maken*
• *tenietdoen*
stumble I [on ww] • *struikelen*
• *stuntelen* • *hakkelen*
• (~ **across/(up)on**) *toevallig*
aantreffen, tegen 't lijf lopen
• (~ **along**) *voortstrompelen* II [znw]
misstap, struikeling
stump I [ov + on ww] • (~ **up**) <sl.>
betalen, dokken II [ov ww]
• *af-/uitgooien* <bij cricket>
• *sprakeloos doen staan* III [on ww]
• *klossen* • *onbehouwen lopen* IV [znw]

• *stomp(je)* • *(boom)stronk*
• *wicketpaaltje* <bij cricket>
stumpy [bnw] *dik en kort, gezet*
stun [ov ww] • *verdoven* • *verbijsteren*
stung [ww] *verl. tijd + volt. deelw.*
→ **sting**
stunk [ww] *verl. tijd + volt. deelw.*
→ **stink**
stunning [bnw] • *verbijsterend*
• *fantastisch*
stunt I [ov ww] *de groei belemmeren*
II [znw] *stunt*
stupefaction [znw] • *versuffing*
• *verbijstering*
stupefy [ov ww] • *afstompen*
• *versuffen* • *stomverbaasd doen staan*
stupendous [bnw] • *verbluffend*
• *enorm* • *kolossaal*
stupid [bnw] • *dom* • *stom*
stupidity [znw] *domheid*
stupor [znw] • *verdoving* • *coma*
• *apathie*
sturdy [bnw] • *struis* • *fors* • *flink* • *stoer*
stutter I [ov + on ww] *stotteren* II [znw]
gestotter
sty [znw] • *strontje* <op oog> • *stal, kot*
style I [ov ww] • *noemen* • *betitelen*
II [znw] • *stijl* • *distinctie* • *trant*
stylish [bnw] • *gedistingeerd* • *chic*
stylist [znw] *stilist*
stylistic [bnw] *stilistisch*
stylus [znw] *naald* <v. platenspeler>
stymie [ov ww] *dwarsbomen*
suave [bnw] • *hoffelijk* • *minzaam*
subdue [ov ww] • *temperen*
• *onderwerpen* • *bedwingen*
subject I [ov ww] *onderwerpen* • (~ **to**)
blootstellen aan II [znw] • *onderdaan*
• *onderwerp* • *vak* III [bnw]
onderworpen
subjective [bnw] • *subjectief*
• *onderwerps-*
subjugate [ov ww] *onderwerpen*
subjunctive [znw] *aanvoegende wijs*
sublimate [ov ww] *sublimeren*
sublime [bnw] • *verheven* • *subliem*

submarine I [ov ww] *torpederen vanuit onderzeeër* II [znw] *onderzeeër* III [bnw] *onderzees*
submerge I [ov ww] • *onder water zetten* • *(onder)dompelen* II [on ww] • *onder water gaan* • *onderduiken*
submission [znw] • *onderdanigheid* • *nederigheid*
submissive [bnw] *onderdanig*
submit I [ov + on ww] *(z.) onderwerpen* II [ov ww] • *voorleggen* • *in het midden brengen*
subnormal [bnw] *beneden de norm, achterlijk*
subordinate I [ov ww] • *(~ to) ondergeschikt maken aan* II [znw] *ondergeschikte* III [bnw] *ondergeschikt*
subscribe [ov ww] *bijeenbrengen* ‹v. geld› • *(~ to) z. abonneren op, onderschrijven*
subscriber [znw] • *abonnee* • *donateur*
subscription [znw] • *donatie* • *abonnement*
subsection [znw] *onderafdeling*
subsequent [bnw] • *(daarop)volgend* • *later*
subservient [bnw] • *onderdanig* • *kruiperig*
subside [on ww] • *(ver)zakken, inzakken* • *bedaren*
subsidize [ov ww] *subsidiëren, geldelijk steunen*
subsidy [znw] *subsidie*
subsist [on ww] • *bestaan* • *(voort)leven*
subsistence [znw] *bestaansminimum*
substance [znw] • *essentie* • *stof* • *substantie* • *hoofdzaak, kern*
substandard [bnw] *beneden de norm*
substantial [bnw] • *stevig* • *aanzienlijk*
substantiate [ov ww] *bewijzen*
substantive [bnw] *iets om het lijf hebbend, wezenlijk*
substitute I [ov ww] *vervangen* II [znw] • *vervanger* • *surrogaat*
substructure [znw] *onderbouw,*

grondslag, fundament
subsume [ov ww] *onder één noemer brengen, opnemen*
subterfuge [znw] *uitvlucht*
subterranean [bnw] • *ondergronds* • *heimelijk*
subtle [bnw] • *subtiel* • *spitsvondig* • *geraffineerd*
subtlety [znw] *subtiliteit*
subtract [ov + on ww] *aftrekken*
subtraction [znw] *aftrekking*
suburb [znw] *voorstad*
suburbia [znw] *de (mensen in/v.d.) buitenwijken*
subversion [znw] *omverwerping*
subversive [bnw] *subversief*
subway [znw] • *tunnel* • ‹AE› *metro, ondergrondse*
succeed I [ov + on ww] *opvolgen* • *(~ to) volgen op* II [on ww] • *slagen* • *succes hebben*
success [znw] *succes*
successful [bnw] • *geslaagd* • *succesrijk*
succession [znw] • *op(een)volging* • *successie*
successive [bnw] • *achtereenvolgend* • *successievelijk*
successor [znw] *opvolger*
succinct [bnw] *beknopt, bondig*
succour I [ov ww] *helpen, te hulp komen* II [znw] *helper*
succulent [bnw] *sappig*
succumb [on ww] *bezwijken* • *(~ to) sterven aan*
such [bnw] • *zulk (een)* • *zo'n* • *zo* • *zodanig, zo groot* • *degenen* • *zulks*
suck I [ov + on ww] *zuigen (op)* • *(~ from) halen uit* • *(~ in) inzuigen, in zich opnemen* • *(~ out of) halen uit* • *(~ up) hielen likken* II [znw] *slokje*
sucker [znw] • *sukkel* • *zuignap* • *spruit*
suckle [ov ww] *zogen*
sudden [bnw] • *plotseling* • *overijld*
suds [mv] *zeepsop*
sue [ov ww] *een proces aandoen*
suet [znw] *niervet*

suffer I [ov ww] • *ondergaan*
• *(toe)laten* • *verdragen* • *uitstaan*
II [on ww] • *beschadigd worden*
• *lijden* • *(~ from) lijden aan*
sufferance [znw] • *stilzwijgende*
toestemming, instemming • *toelating*
sufferer [znw] • *lijder* • *slachtoffer*
suffering [znw] *beproeving, ellende*
suffice [ov + on ww] • *voldoende zijn*
(voor) • *tevreden stellen*
sufficiency [znw] *voldoende*
hoeveelheid
sufficient [bnw] *genoeg, voldoende*
suffocate I [ov ww] • *doen stikken*
• *verstikken* II [on ww] *stikken*
suffrage [znw] *stemrecht*
suffuse [ov ww] *overgieten* ‹vnl. met
licht›
sugar I [ov ww] *(be)suikeren* II [znw]
• *suiker* • *lieveling*
sugary [bnw] • *suikerachtig* • *suikerzoet*
suggest [ov ww] • *suggereren* • *opperen*
• *doen denken aan* • *voorstellen*
suggestible [bnw] *gemakkelijk te*
beïnvloeden
suggestion [znw] • *suggestie* • *zweem,*
spoor
suggestive [bnw] *suggestief*
suicidal [bnw] *zelfmoord-*
suicide [znw] *zelfmoord(enaar)*
suit I [ov + on ww] • *schikken* • *gelegen*
komen • *passen (bij/voor)* • *staan*
II [znw] • *proces* • *pak* • *mantelpak*
• *kleur* ‹in kaartspel›
suitable [bnw] • *geschikt, gepast*
• *passend*
suitcase [znw] *(platte) koffer*
suite [znw] • *suite* ‹kamer›
• *ameublement* • ‹muz.› *suite*
suitor [znw] *aanbidder*
sulk I [on ww] *mokken* II [znw] *boze bui*
sulky I [znw] *sulky* II [bnw] *mokkend*
sullen [bnw] • *nors, knorrig* • *somber*
sully [ov ww] • *bevlekken* • *vuil maken*
sulphur [znw] *zwavel*
sultry [bnw] *drukkend, zwoel*

sum I [ov ww] • *(~ up) opsommen,*
optellen, samenvatten II [znw] • *som*
• *totaal*
summarize [ov + on ww] *samenvatten*
summary I [znw] *samenvatting*
II [bnw] • *beknopt* • *summier* • *kort*
summation [znw] *optelling, totaal*
summer [znw] *zomer*
summery [bnw] *zomerachtig*
summit [znw] *top(punt)*
summon [ov ww] • *(op)roepen*
• *bijeenroepen* • *verzamelen*
• *dagvaarden* • *(~ up) vergaren,*
bijeenrapen, optrommelen
summons [znw] *meervoud*
• *oproep(ing)* • *dagvaarding*
sump [znw] *oliereservoir*
sumptuous [bnw] • *kostbaar*
• *weelderig*
sun I [ov + on ww] *zonnen* II [znw] *zon*
Sunday [znw] *zondag*
sundry [bnw] • *allerlei* • *diverse,*
verscheiden(e)
sung [ww] volt. deelw. → **sing**
sunk [ww] volt. deelw. → **sink**
sunken [bnw] • *ingevallen*
• *diepliggend* • *hol*
sunny [bnw] *zonnig*
super [bnw] • *super-* • ‹sl.› *grandioos,*
prima
superabundant [bnw] • *meer dan*
overvloedig • *in rijke mate*
superannuation [znw] *pensionering*
superb [bnw] • *voortreffelijk* • *zeer*
indrukwekkend • *groots* • *meesterlijk*
supercilious [bnw] *verwaand*
superficial [bnw] *oppervlakkig*
superficiality [znw] *oppervlakkigheid*
superfluity [znw] *overtolligheid*
superfluous [bnw] *overbodig,*
overtollig
superimpose [ov ww] • *(er) bovenop*
plaatsen • *(~ (up)on) plaatsen op,*
bouwen op
superintend [ov + on ww] • *toezicht*
houden op • *met controle belast zijn op*

superintendent [znw] • *inspecteur*
• *opzichter* • *directeur*
• *hoofdinspecteur* ‹v. politie›
superior I [znw] • *meerdere* • *overste*
II [bnw] • *uitmuntend* • *bijzonder goed*
• *superieur* • *hooghartig, neerbuigend*
superlative I [znw] *overtreffende trap*
II [bnw] *uitstekend*
supermarket [znw] *supermarkt*
supernatural I [znw] *het*
bovennatuurlijke II [bnw]
bovennatuurlijk
supersede [ov ww] *vervangen*
supersonic [bnw] *supersonisch*
superstition [znw] *bijgeloof*
superstructure [znw] *bovenbouw*
supervise [ov + on ww] *toezicht*
houden op
supervision [znw] *supervisie*
supervisor [znw] • *inspecteur*
• *(afdelings)chef* • *controleur*
• *surveillant*
supervisory [bnw] • *toezichthoudend*
• *toeziend*
supine [bnw] *achteroverliggend*
supper [znw] *souper, avondmaal(tijd)*
supplant [ov ww] • *(listig) verdringen*
• *vervangen*
supplement I [ov ww] • *aanvullen*
• *toevoegen* II [znw] *supplement*
supplementary [bnw] *aanvullend*
supplication [znw] *smeekbede*
supplier [znw] *leverancier*
supply I [ov ww] *bevoorraden* II [znw]
voorraad
support I [ov ww] *(onder)steunen*
II [znw] *steun*
supporter [znw] • *aanhanger*
• *supporter*
suppose [ov ww] • *veronderstellen*
• *menen* • *denken*
supposition [znw] *veronderstelling*
suppress [ov ww] • *de kop indrukken*
• *verbieden* ‹v. krant, boek›
• *achterhouden*
suppression [znw] *onderdrukking*

suppurate [on ww] *etteren*
supremacy [znw] • *suprematie*
• *hoogste gezag of macht*
supreme [bnw] • *hoogste, opperste*
• *laatst, uiterst*
surcharge [znw] *toeslag*
sure I [bnw] *zeker* II [bijw] ‹AE› *(ja)zeker*
surely [bijw] • *gerust* • *zeker*
surety [znw] *borg*
surf I [on ww] *surfen* II [znw] *branding*
surface [znw] • *oppervlakte*
• *buitenkant*
surfeit I [ov ww] *oververzadigen*
II [znw] *overlading, oververzadiging*
surge I [on ww] • *(hoog) golven*
• *deinen* • *opwellen, opbruisen* II [znw]
• *stijging* • *opwelling* • *golfslag*
surgeon [znw] *chirurg*
surgery [znw] • *spreekuur* • *chirurgie*
• *operatieve ingreep* • *spreekkamer*
surgical [bnw] *chirurgisch*
surly [bnw] *nors*
surmise I [ov + on ww] • *gissen*
• *vermoeden* II [znw] • *gissing*
• *vermoeden*
surmount [ov ww] • *overtrekken* ‹v.
berg› • *te boven komen* • *staan op*
surmountable [bnw] *overwinbaar*
surname [znw] *achternaam*
surpass [ov ww] *overtreffen*
surplus I [znw] *teveel, overschot*
II [bnw] *overtollig*
surprise I [ov ww] • *verwonderen*
• *verrassen* • *overrompelen* II [znw]
verrassing III [bnw] *verrassings-*
surprising [bnw] • *verwonderlijk*
• *wonderbaarlijk*
surrender I [ov ww] • *overgeven*
• *opgeven* • *afstand doen v.* II [on ww]
• *capituleren* • *z. overgeven* III [znw]
overgave
surreptitious [bnw] *heimelijk*
(verkregen), clandestien
surrogate [znw] *surrogaat*
surround I [ov ww] • *omringen*
• *omsingelen* • *omgeven* II [znw]

vloerbedekking tussen los kleed en wanden

surrounding [bnw] *naburig*

surtax [znw] *extra belasting*

surveillance [znw] *toezicht*

survey I [ov ww] • *inspecteren*
• *opmeten • taxeren • in ogenschouw nemen, bekijken* II [znw] • *overzicht*
• *rapport • onderzoek*

survive [ov + on ww] • *overleven • nog (voort) leven of bestaan*

survivor [znw] • *langstlevende*
• *overlevende*

susceptibility [znw] *ontvankelijkheid*

susceptible [bnw] • *ontvankelijk*
• *gemakkelijk te beïnvloeden*
• *lichtgeraakt*

suspect I [ov ww] • *verdenken*
• *wantrouwen* II [on ww] • *vermoeden*
• *geloven* III [znw] *verdachte* IV [bnw] *verdacht*

suspend [ov ww] • *opschorten*
• *verdagen • uitstellen • schorsen*
• *tijdelijk intrekken • (~ from) ophangen aan, ontheffen van*

suspender [znw] • *sokophouder*
• *jarretelle*

suspense [znw] • *spanning*
• *onzekerheid*

suspension [znw] • *schorsing*
• *uitstelling • suspensie • vering*

suspicion [znw] • *argwaan*
• *wantrouwen • verdenking • (flauw) vermoeden • tikkeltje*

suspicious [bnw] • *verdacht*
• *achterdochtig*

sustain [ov ww] • *steunen • verdragen*
• *doorstaan • in stand houden*
• *aanhouden* <v. noot>

sustenance [znw] *voeding, voedsel*

svelte [bnw] • *soepel, slank*
• *welgevormd*

swab I [ov ww] *zwabberen* II [znw]
<med.> *dotje watten*

swaddle [ov ww] • *inbakeren*
• *inpakken* <v. baby>

swagger I [on ww] *branieachtig lopen*
II [znw] *branie*

swallow I [ov ww] • *(in)slikken*
• *verslinden • (~ down) inslikken*
• *(~ up) verzwelgen* II [on ww] *slikken*
III [znw] • *slok • slikbeweging*
• *zwaluw*

swam [ww] *verl. tijd* → **swim**

swamp I [ov ww] *vol of onder water doen lopen* II [znw] *moeras*

swampy [bnw] *moerassig, drassig*

swan [znw] *zwaan*

swank I [on ww] *opscheppen* II [znw] *opschepperij*

swap → **swop**

swarm I [on ww] *zwermen • (~ with) wemelen van* II [znw] • *zwerm • troep*

swarthy [bnw] • *donker(bruin)*
• *gebruind*

swashbuckling [bnw] *branieachtig, blufferig*

swastika [znw] *swastika, hakenkruis*

swat [ov ww] *(dood)slaan* <v. vlieg>

swathe [ov ww] • *zwachtelen*
• *omhullen*

sway I [ov + on ww] • *zwiepen*
• *slingeren • zwaaien* II [ov ww]
beïnvloeden III [znw] • *zwaai • invloed*
• *overwicht • heerschappij*

swear I [ov + on ww] • *onder ede verklaren • zweren • (~ by) zweren bij*
• *(~ in) beëdigen* II [on ww] *vloeken*

sweat I [ov + on ww] *zweten* II [znw]
• *zweet • lastig werk*

sweater [znw] *wollen trui*

Swedish [bnw] *Zweeds*

sweep I [ov ww] • *vegen • snellen door, slaan over, woeden over, teisteren*
• *bestrijken • afzoeken, afdreggen*
• *(~ away) wegvagen • (~ up) opvegen, aanvegen* II [on ww] • *vegen*
• *statig schrijden • z. uitstrekken, met een wijde bocht lopen • gaan, snellen, woeden • strijken over • (~ over) razen over, slaan over • (~ through) gaan/snellen door* III [znw] • *veeg*

• *schoorsteenveger* • *bocht* • *draai,*
zwaai, slag • *streek* • *omvang, bereik,*
sector
sweeper [znw] • *veger* • *straatveger,*
schoorsteenveger • *veegmachine*
sweeping [bnw] • *overweldigend*
• *radicaal* • *(te) veelomvattend* • *(te)*
algemeen • *z. uitstrekkend over een*
(grote) oppervlakte
sweet I [znw] • *bonbon, snoepje*
• *dessert* • *het aangename*
II [bnw + bijw] • *lief* • *leuk* • *zoet*
sweeten [ov ww] • *zoet maken* • *lijmen*
‹fig.›
swell I [ov ww] • *doen zwellen*
• *opblazen* II [on ww] • *uitdijen* • *bol*
gaan staan • *zwellen* • *aanzwellen,*
opzetten, uitzetten III [znw] • *crescendo*
• *deining* IV [bnw] *prima, eersteklas*
swelling [znw] *zwelling*
swelter [on ww] *stikken v.d. hitte*
swept [ww] *verl. tijd + volt. deelw.*
→ **sweep**
swerve I [ov + on ww] *zwenken* II [znw]
zwenking
swig I [ov + on ww] ‹sl.› *drinken, zuipen*
II [znw] *teug*
swill I [ov ww] • *(~ out) uitspoelen*
II [on ww] *zuipen*
swim I [ov + on ww] • *zwemmen*
• *overzwemmen* II [znw] *zwempartij*
swimmer [znw] *zwemmer*
swimming [bnw] *zwem-*
swimmingly [bnw] ‹inf.› *van een leien*
dakje
swindle I [ov ww] • *bezwendelen*
• *oplichten* II [znw] • *zwendel*
• *oplichterij*
swindler [znw] *oplichter*
swine [znw] *zwijn(en)*
swing I [ov + on ww] • *zwaaien*
• *slingeren* • *schommelen* • *swingen*
• *(~ from) hangen aan, bengelen aan*
• *(~ round) (zich) omdraaien* II [znw]
• *ommekeer* • *schommel* • *vaart, gang*
• *slag* • ‹muz.› *swing*

swingeing [bnw] *vernietigend*
swinging [bnw] • *actief, kwiek*
• *bruisend* ‹fig.›
swipe I [ov + on ww] • *hard slaan* • ‹sl.›
gappen, wegpikken II [znw] *harde slag,*
mep
swirl I [ov + on ww] *warrelen, wervelen*
II [znw] *werveling*
swish I [ov + on ww] *zwiepen*
II [on ww] *ruisen* III [znw] *gesuis*
Swiss I [znw] *Zwitser(s)* II [bnw]
Zwitsers
switch I [ov + on ww] • *aan de knop*
draaien, (over)schakelen • *slaan,*
zwiepen (met) • *(~ off) uit-/afdraaien,*
uitschakelen • *(~ on) aandraaien,*
inschakelen II [znw] • *schakelaar*
• *knop* • *twijg*
swivel [ov + on ww] *(om zijn as) draaien*
swollen [ww] *volt. deelw.* → **swell**
swoop I [on ww] • *(~ down (upon))*
neerschieten op ‹als 'n roofvogel›,
aanvallen • *(~ up) (weg)grissen,*
(plotseling) klimmen II [znw]
plotseling duikvlucht
swop I [ov + on ww] • *verwisselen,*
(uit)wisselen • *verruilen, (om)ruilen*
II [znw] *ruil*
sword [znw] *zwaard*
swore [ww] *verl. tijd* → **swear**
sworn I [ww] *volt. deelw.* → **swear**
II [bnw] • *gezworen* • *beëdigd*
swot I [on ww] • *blokken* • *zwoegen*
II [znw] *serieuze student, blokker*
sycamore [znw] • *esdoorn* • ‹AE›
plataan
sycophant [znw] *vleier*
symbol [znw] • *symbool* • *letter, cijfer*
symbolism [znw] *symboliek*
symbolize [ov ww] *symboliseren*
symmetry [znw] *symmetrie*
sympathetic [bnw] • *hartelijk*
• *sympathisch*
sympathize [on ww] • *meevoelen*
• *sympathiseren*
sympathizer [znw] • *aanhanger*

• *sympathisant*
sympathy [znw] • *medegevoel*
• *medeleven* • *eensgezindheid*
• *solidariteit(sgevoel)* • *sympathie*
symposium [znw] • *reeks artikelen*
van verschillende schrijvers over zelfde
onderwerp • *kring, bijeenkomst v.*
wetenschappers
symptom [znw] • *symptoom* • *teken*
symptomatic [bnw] *symptomatisch*
synagogue [znw] *synagoge*
synchronize [ov + on ww]
• *samenvallen* • *synchroniseren* • *gelijk*
zetten
syncopate [ov ww] *syncoperen*
syndicate I [ov ww] • *tot syndicaat e.d.*
verenigen • *gelijktijdig in verschillende*
kranten publiceren II [znw]
• *consortium* • *perssyndicaat*
• *syndicaat*
synod [znw] • *synode* • *kerkvergadering*
synonym [znw] • *synoniem*
synonymous [bnw] *synoniem*
synopsis [znw] *overzicht, korte*
samenvatting
syntax [znw] *syntaxis*
synthesis [znw] *synthese*
synthesize [ov ww] *synthetisch*
bereiden
synthetic [bnw] • *kunst-* • *synthetisch*
• *onoprecht*
syphilis [znw] *syfilis*
Syrian I [znw] • *Syriër* • *Syrisch* II [bnw]
Syrisch
syringe [znw] • *injectiespuit* • *spuit(je)*
syrup [znw] • *stroop* • *siroop*
system [znw] • *systeem* • *stelsel* • *gestel*
• *maatschappij* • *formatie* ‹in geologie›
systematic [bnw] *systematisch*
systematize [ov ww] *systematiseren*

T

ta [tw] *dank u, dank je*
tab [znw] • *labeltje* • *metalen lipje*
tabby I [znw] *cyperse kat* II [bnw]
gestreept
tabernacle [znw] • *tabernakel*
• *bedehuis* ‹o.a. bij methodisten›
table I [ov ww] • *indienen* ‹v. voorstel,
motie, enz.› • ‹AE› *voorlopig opzij*
zetten II [znw] • *tafel* ‹ook v.
vermenigvuldiging› • *plateau* • *tabel*
tableau [znw] • *tableau* • *tableau*
vivant
tablet [znw] • *tablet* • *gedenkplaat*
tabloid [znw] *blad met sensationeel*
nieuws en societyroddels
taboo I [znw] *taboe* II [bnw] *verboden,*
taboe
tabular [bnw] *in tabelvorm*
tabulate [ov ww] *rangschikken in*
tabellen
taciturn [bnw] *zwijgend, stil*
tack I [ov ww] • *vastspijkeren* • *rijgen*
• (~ **on**) *(iets overbodigs) toevoegen*
II [on ww] *laveren, overstag gaan*
III [znw] • *gedragslijn* • *kopspijker*
tackle I [ov + on ww] • *aanvallen*
• *aanpakken* ‹v. probleem› • ‹sport›
tackelen II [znw] • *tuig, uitrusting*
• *takel*
tacky [bnw] • *kleverig* • *slecht gemaakt,*
lelijk • ‹AE› *haveloos*
tact [znw] *tact*
tactful [bnw] *tactvol*
tactical [bnw] *tactisch*
tactician [znw] *tacticus*
tactile [bnw] • *tactiel* • *tastbaar*
tactless [bnw] *tactloos, ontactisch*
tag I [ov ww] • *van labels voorzien*
• *etiketteren* • ‹AE› *bestempelen als*
II [on ww] • (~ **along** (**with**)) *op de*
voet volgen III [znw] • *tikkertje* ‹spel›

• *label*
tail I [ov ww] *schaduwen* II [on ww]
• (~ **off**) *geleidelijk afnemen* III [znw]
• *staart* • *(uit)einde* • *pand* <v. jas>
tailor I [ov ww] *aanpassen* II [znw]
kleermaker
taint I [ov ww] • *bevlekken, bezoedelen*
• *aantasten* II [znw] • *smet* • *bederf*
take I [ov ww] • *nemen, gebruiken* <v.
eten, drinken> • *aannemen* • *afnemen*
• *innemen* • *opnemen* • *meenemen*
• *oplopen, vatten* <kou> • *begrijpen,*
beschouwen, opvatten, opnemen
• *aanvaarden* • (~ **apart**) *uit elkaar*
halen, demonteren, kritisch analyseren
• (~ **away**) *wegnemen, meenemen,*
afnemen • (~ **back**) *terugnemen,*
terugbrengen • (~ **down**) *'n toontje*
lager doen zingen, afnemen, neerhalen,
opschrijven • (~ **for**) *houden voor*
• (~ **from**) *aftrekken, afnemen van,*
slikken van • (~ **in**) *onderdak verlenen,*
inademen, in z. opnemen, beetnemen,
innemen, binnenkrijgen • (~ **off**)
uittrekken, van 't repertoire nemen,
afnemen, afzetten, opheffen,
wegbrengen, karikaturiseren • (~ **on**)
aannemen, op z. nemen, overnemen
• (~ **out**) *uitnemen, verwijderen,*
aanvragen • (~ **over**) *overnemen*
• (~ **up**) *ingaan op, innemen, in beslag*
nemen, beginnen, opnemen II [on ww]
• *werkzaam zijn* • *aanslaan* <v. plant>
• (~ **after**) *aarden naar* • (~ **off**)
afnemen, opstijgen • (~ **on**) *opgang*
maken, tekeergaan • (~ **over**)
overnemen • (~ **to**) *graag mogen,*
gewoonte maken van III [znw] *opname*
taken [ww] volt. deelw. → **take**
tale [znw] • *verhaal* • *sprookje* • *smoesje*
talent [znw] • *talent* • *iem. met talent*
talented [bnw] *begaafd*
talk I [ov ww] *spreken over* • (~ **down**)
tot zwijgen brengen • (~ **into**)
overreden • (~ **round**) *iem. bepraten*
II [on ww] *praten, spreken*

• (~ **about/of**) *praten over* • (~ **back**)
brutaal antwoord geven • (~ **down**)
neerbuigend praten III [znw] • *gepraat*
• *gesprek* • *bespreking* • *praatjes,*
gerucht
talkative [bnw] *praatziek*
talker [znw] *prater*
tall [bnw] • *hoog* • *lang*
tallow [znw] • *talk* • *kaarsvet*
tally I [on ww] *kloppen, stroken met*
II [znw] • *aantal* • *score*
talon [znw] *klauw* <v. roofvogel>
tambourine [znw] *tamboerijn*
tame I [ov ww] *temmen* II [bnw] *tam*
tan I [ov ww] • *looien* • <sl.> *afranselen*
II [on ww] *bruin worden* <v. huid>
III [znw] *bruinere huidskleur als gevolg*
v. zonlicht IV [bnw] *geelbruin*
tang [znw] *sterke smaak of geur*
tangent [znw] • *raaklijn* • <wisk.>
tangens
tangential [bnw] • *tangentiaal*
• *oppervlakkig*
tangle I [ov ww] *verwikkelen* II [on ww]
in de war maken/raken/zijn • (~ **with**)
in conflict raken met III [znw]
• *verwarring* • *verwarde toestand*
• *wirwar*
tank [znw] • *reservoir* • *tank*
tankard [znw] *(bier)pul*
tanker [znw] *tankschip*
tanner [znw] *looier*
tannery [znw] *looierij*
tantalize [ov ww] *doen watertanden*
tantamount [bnw] *gelijkwaardig*
tantrum [znw] *woedeaanval*
tap I [ov ww] • *aftappen* • *afluisteren* <v.
telefoon> • *aanbreken* <v. fles>
• *uithoren* II [on ww] *zacht tikken,*
zacht kloppen III [znw] • *tikje, klopje*
• *kraan*
tape I [ov ww] • *opnemen* <op geluids-
of beeldband> • *met lint verbinden*
II [znw] • *geluidsband* • *plakband*
• *lint*
taper I [ov ww] *taps/spits doen toelopen*

• (~ **off**) uitlopen in punt, scherp toelopen II [on ww] taps/spits toelopen III [znw] kaars

tapestry [znw] wandtapijt

tar I [ov + on ww] teren II [znw] teer

tarantula [znw] tarantel, vogelspin, wolfsspin

tardy [bnw] • te laat • langzaam, traag

target [znw] • schietschijf • mikpunt • doel • productiecijfer

tariff [znw] (tol)tarief

tarmac [znw] asfalt(weg)

tarn [znw] bergmeertje

tarnish I [ov ww] • mat/dof maken • bezoedelen II [on ww] mat/dof worden

tarpaulin [znw] • zeildoek • dekkleed

tarragon [znw] dragon

tarry I [on ww] dralen II [bnw] • teer- • teerachtig • geteerd

tart I [ov ww] • (~ **up**) opdirken II [znw] • taart(je) • <sl.> slet III [bnw] wrang, zuur, scherp

tartan [znw] Schotse ruit

task I [ov ww] veel vergen v. II [znw] taak

tassel [znw] kwastje

taste I [ov ww] proeven II [on ww] smaken <ook fig.> III [znw] • smaak(je) • slokje • <inf.> 'n weinig

tasteful [bnw] smaakvol, v. goede smaak getuigend

tasteless [bnw] • v. slechte smaak getuigend, smakeloos • smaakloos

tasty [bnw] • smakelijk • aantrekkelijk

tat [znw] goedkope rommel

tattered [bnw] haveloos

tattoo I [ov ww] tatoeëren II [on ww] trommelen III [znw] • taptoe • militair schouwspel • tatoeage

tatty [bnw] smerig, sjofel, slordig

taught [ww] verl. tijd + volt. deelw. → teach

taunt I [ov ww] beschimpen II [znw] beschimping

taut [bnw] strak, gespannen

tautology [znw] tautologie

tavern [znw] taveerne, café, herberg

tawdry [bnw] • opzichtig • opgedirkt • smakeloos

tawny [bnw] taankleurig

tax I [ov ww] • belasten • veel vergen v. • op de proef stellen • (~ **with**) beschuldigen v. II [znw] belasting

taxable [bnw] belastbaar

taxation [znw] belasting

taxi I [on ww] taxiën <v. vliegtuig> II [znw] taxi

taxidermist [znw] iem. die dieren opzet

tea [znw] • thee • theemaaltijd • hoofdmaaltijd

teach [ov + on ww] onderwijzen, leren

teacher [znw] leraar, onderwijzer

teaching I [znw] • het onderwijs • leer II [bnw] onderwijzend

teak [znw] • teakboom • teakhout

team I [on ww] • (~ **up**) <inf.> samen een team vormen • (~ **up with**) <inf.> samenwerken met II [znw] • ploeg, span <paarden> • elftal

tear I [ov ww] • (ver)scheuren • trekken (aan) • uitrukken <v. haren> • openrijten • (~ **apart**) verscheuren, kapotscheuren • (~ **at**) rukken aan • (~ **down**) afbreken <v. gebouw> • (~ **up**) verscheuren, uitroeien II [on ww] scheuren • (~ **about**) wild rondvliegen III [znw] • traan • druppel • scheur

tearful [bnw] • vol tranen • betraand

tease I [ov ww] • plagen • kwellen • <vulg.> opgeilen • (~ **out**) ontwarren II [znw] • plaaggeest • vrouw die beurtelings met een man flirt en hem afwijst

teasel [znw] kaarde

teaser [znw] • plager • <inf.> moeilijke vraag

teat [znw] tepel <v. dier>, uier, speen

tech <inf.> [znw] technische school, ≈ hogere technische school

technical [bnw] • technisch

• *vaktechnisch*
technicality [znw] *technisch detail*
technician [znw] *technicus*
technique [znw] • *techniek, werkwijze*
• *manier v. optreden, handelen*
technocracy [znw] *technocratie*
technocrat [znw] *technocraat*
technologist [znw] *technoloog*
technology [znw] *technologie*
tedious [bnw] *saai, vervelend*
teem [on ww] • (~ **with**) *wemelen v.*
teeter [on ww] *wankelen*
teeth [mv] → **tooth**
teethe [on ww] *tanden krijgen*
teetotal [bnw] *geheelonthouders-,
alcoholvrij*
teetotaller [znw] *geheelonthouder*
telegraphese [znw] *telegramstijl*
telegraphic [bnw] • *telegrafisch*
• *telegram-*
telepathy [znw] *telepathie*
telephone I [ov + on ww] *telefoneren*
II [znw] *telefoon*
telephonist [znw] *telefonist(e)*
teleprinter [znw] *telex*
telescope I [ov + on ww] • *in elkaar
schuiven* • *inschuifbaar zijn* II [znw]
verrekijker
telescopic [bnw] *telescopisch*
television [znw] *televisie*
telex I [ov + on ww] *telexen* II [znw]
telex
tell I [ov ww] • (op)tellen <v. stemmen
in parlement> • *uit elkaar houden*
• *zeggen* • *vertellen* • (~ **off**) *berispen*
II [on ww] • *vertellen* • *zeggen*
• *klikken* • *effect hebben, indruk maken*
• (~ **against**) *pleiten tegen* • (~ **of**)
getuigen v.
teller [znw] • *kassier* • *stemopnemer*
<lid v.h. parlement>
telling [bnw] • *indrukwekkend*
• *tekenend*
telly [znw] *tv*
temerity [znw] • *onbezonnenheid*
• *roekeloosheid*

temp I [on ww] *werken als
uitzendkracht* II [znw] *uitzendkracht*
temper I [ov ww] • *harden* <v. staal>
• *matigen, verzachten* II [znw] • *aard,
aanleg, natuur* • *stemming, humeur*
• *boze bui*
temperamental [bnw] • *aangeboren*
• *onbeheerst*
temperance [znw] • *matigheid*
• *(geheel)onthouding*
temperate [bnw] *matig, gematigd*
tempest [znw] *storm*
tempestuous [bnw] *stormachtig,
onstuimig*
temple [znw] • *slaap* <v.h. hoofd>
• *tempel, kerk*
temporary [bnw] *tijdelijk*
temporize [on ww] *trachten tijd te
winnen*
tempt [ov ww] *verleiden, bekoren*
temptation [znw] *verleiding, bekoring*
tempting [bnw] *verleidelijk*
ten [telw] *tien*
tenable [bnw] *te verdedigen, houdbaar*
tenacious [bnw] *vasthoudend*
tenacity [znw] *vasthoudendheid*
tenancy [znw] *huur, pacht*
tenant [znw] *huurder, pachter*
tend I [ov ww] • *hoeden* <dieren>
• *oppassen* <op zieke> • *zorgen voor*
II [on ww] • *in de richting gaan v.*
• *geneigd zijn* • (~ **to**) *leiden tot,
neigen tot*
tendency [znw] • *neiging, aanleg*
• *tendens*
tendentious [bnw] *tendentieus*
tender I [ov ww] *aanbieden* II [znw]
• *oppasser* • *tender* <v. locomotief>
• *aanbod, offerte* III [bnw]
• *liefhebbend* • *mals* • *teder, zacht*
• *gevoelig* • *pijnlijk*
tenderize [ov ww] *mals maken* <v.
vlees>
tendon [znw] *pees*
tendril [znw] *scheut, rank, dunne twijg*
tenement [znw] *huurflat*

tenet [znw] *dogma, leerstelling*
tenner <inf.> [znw] *bankbiljet van tien pond*
tenon [znw] *(houten) pen*
tenor [znw] • *gang* <v. zaken> • *geest, strekking, bedoeling* • *tenor* • *altviool*
tense I [ov ww] *spannen* II [znw] <taalk.> *grammaticale tijd* III [bnw] *(in)gespannen, strak*
tensile [bnw] *rekbaar, elastisch*
tension [znw] • *(in)spanning* • *spankracht*
tentacle [znw] • *voelhoorn* • *vangarm*
tentative [bnw] • *voorzichtig* • *weifelend*
tenth [telw] *tiende*
tenuous [bnw] • *(te) subtiel, vaag* • *onbeduidend*
tenure [znw] • *(periode v.) bezit* • *(ambts)periode* • *eigendomsrecht*
tepee, tipi [znw] *wigwam*
term I [ov ww] *(be)noemen* II [znw] • *beperkte periode* • *trimester* • *term*
terminal I [znw] • *(pool)klem* <elektriciteit> • *einde* • <comp.> *eindstation, terminal* II [bnw] • *slot-, eind-* • *dodelijk* <v. ziekte>
terminate [ov + on ww] • *beëindigen* • *opzeggen of aflopen* <v. contract>
terminus [znw] • *eindstation* • *eind(punt)*
termite [znw] *termiet*
tern [znw] *stern*
terrace [znw] • *bordes* • *terras* • *rij v. rijtjeshuizen*
terrestrial [bnw] • *aards, ondermaans* • *land-*
terrible [bnw] *verschrikkelijk, ontzettend*
terribly [bijw] • *vreselijk, verschrikkelijk, erg* • *geweldig*
terrier [znw] *terriër*
terrific [bnw] *ontzettend (goed), schrikbarend*
terrify [ov ww] • *(doods)bang maken* • *doen schrikken*

territorial I [znw] *soldaat v.d. vrijwillige landweer* II [bnw] • *territoriaal* • *land-*
terror [znw] • *angst* • *verschrikking* • *terreur*
terrorism [znw] *terrorisme*
terrorize [ov ww] *terroriseren*
terse [bnw] *kort, beknopt*
tertiary [bnw] *tertiair*
test I [ov ww] • *beproeven, op de proef stellen* • *overhoren* II [znw] • *proef* • *beproeving* • *proefwerk*
testicle [znw] *testikel, zaadbal*
testify I [ov ww] • *verklaren* • *getuigen v.* • *(~ to) getuigen v., getuigenis afleggen v.* II [on ww] *getuigen*
testimonial [znw] *getuigschrift*
testimony [znw] *bewijs, verklaring onder ede*
testy [bnw] *prikkelbaar*
tetchy [bnw] *gemelijk, prikkelbaar*
text [znw] *tekst*
textile [znw] *textiel*
textual [bnw] • *letterlijk* • *m.b.t. de tekst*
texture [znw] *structuur*
Thai I [znw] • *Thai* • *Thailander* II [bnw] *Thais, Thailands*
than [vw] *dan*
thank [ov ww] *(be)danken*
thankful [bnw] *dankbaar*
thankless [bnw] *ondankbaar*
that I [aanw vnw] *dat, die* II [betr vnw] *die, dat, welke, wat* III [vw] • *opdat* • *dat*
thatch I [ov ww] *met riet dekken* II [znw] • *(dak)stro* • *rieten dak* • <inf.> *dik hoofdhaar*
thaw I [ov + on ww] *(doen) (ont)dooien* II [znw] *dooi*
the [lw] *de, het*
theatre, theater [znw] • *theater* • *operatiezaal* • *toneel*
theatrical [bnw] *theatraal, toneel-*
theft [znw] *diefstal*
their [bez vnw] *hun, haar*

theirs [bez vnw] *de/het hunne, hare*
them [pers vnw] *hen, hun, haar, ze, zich*
theme [znw] • *onderwerp* • *thema*
themselves [wkd vnw] *zich(zelf)* <mv>
thence [bijw] *vandaar, om die reden*
theocracy [znw] *theocratie*
theologian [znw] *godgeleerde*
theologic(al) [bnw] *theologisch*
theology [znw] *godgeleerdheid*
theoretician [znw] *theoreticus*
theorize [on ww] *theoretiseren*
theory [znw] *theorie*
therapy [znw] *therapie, behandeling*
there [bijw] • *daar, er* • *daarheen*
therefore [bijw] • *daarom* • *bijgevolg, dus*
therm [znw] *bepaalde warmte-eenheid*
thermal I [znw] *thermiek* II [bnw] *warmte-*
thermostat [znw] *thermostaat*
these [aanw vnw] *deze*
thesis [znw] • *dissertatie* • *te verdedigen stelling*
they [pers vnw] *zij* <mv>, *men*
thick [bnw + bijw] • *dik, breed* • *intiem* • *dicht begroeid* • *onduidelijk klinkend door slechte articulatie* • *dom* • *sterk* <fig.>, *kras*
thicken I [ov ww] • *verdikken* • *binden* <v. saus, jus, soep> II [on ww] *talrijker worden, dikker*
thicket [znw] *struikgewas*
thickness [znw] • *dikte* • *laag*
thief [znw] *dief*
thieving [znw] *diefstal*
thigh [znw] *dij*
thimble [znw] *vingerhoed*
thimbleful [znw] *vingerhoedje, heel klein beetje*
thin I [ov + on ww] *dunner worden, verdunnen* II [bnw] • *dun* • *ijl* <lucht> • *mager* • *doorzichtig*
think I [ov ww] *vinden, achten* • (~ **out**) *uitdenken, ontwerpen* <plan>, *overwegen* • (~ **over**) *overdenken* • (~ **up**) <AE> *bedenken, verzinnen*

II [on ww] • *denken* • *bedenken* • *(erover) nadenken* • *z. voorstellen* • (~ **about**) *denken over* • (~ **of**) *denken aan/over/van*
thinker [znw] *denker*
third [telw] *derde*
thirst I [on ww] • (~ **after/for**) *dorsten naar* II [znw] *dorst*
thirsty [bnw] *dorstig*
thirteen [telw] *dertien*
thirtieth [telw] *dertigste*
thirty [telw] *dertig*
this [aanw vnw] *dit, deze* <enkelvoud>
thistle [znw] *distel*
thither [bijw] *derwaarts*
thorax [znw] • *borstkas* • *borststuk* <v. insect>
thorn [znw] *stekel, doorn*
thorny [bnw] • *doornachtig, stekelachtig* • *netelig*
thorough [bnw] • *volkomen* • *grondig* • *degelijk*
those [aanw vnw] • *degenen* • *die* <mv>, *zij* <mv>
thou <vero.> [pers vnw] *gij* <enkelvoud>
though I [bijw] *maar toch, evenwel* II [vw] *ofschoon, niettegenstaande*
thoughtless [bnw] *gedachteloos, onnadenkend*
thousand [telw] *duizend*
thread I [ov ww] *aanrijgen* <kralen>, *een draad doen door* II [znw] *draad, garen*
threat [znw] *bedreiging*
threaten [ov ww] • *(be)dreigen* • *dreigen met*
three I [znw] *drietal* II [telw] *drie*
thresh [ov ww] *dorsen*
threshold [znw] • *drempel* • *grens(gebied)*
threw [ww] *verl. tijd* → **throw**
thrift [znw] *zuinigheid, spaarzaamheid*
thrifty [bnw] *zuinig*
thrill I [ov ww] *aangrijpen* II [on ww] • (~ **to**) *aangegrepen/ontroerd worden, verrukt/zeer enthousiast zijn* III [znw]

• *spanning* • *sensatie*
thrilling [bnw] • *sensationeel*
• *spannend*
thrive [on ww] *gedijen, voorspoed hebben*
throat [znw] *keel*
throaty [bnw] *schor*
throb I [on ww] • *pulseren, kloppen, bonzen* • *ronken* <v. machine> II [znw] • *(ge)bons* • *(ge)klop*
thrombosis [znw] *trombose*
throne [znw] • *troon* • *soevereine macht*
throng I [on ww] • z. *verdringen* • *opdringen, toestromen* II [znw] • *menigte* • *gedrang*
throttle I [ov ww] *wurgen* II [on ww] • *(~ back/down) gas minderen* III [znw] • *smoorklep* • *gaspedaal*
through [vz] *door*
throughout [vz] *door, langs*
throve [ww] verl. tijd → **thrive**
throw I [ov ww] • *(uit)werpen, (weg)gooien* • *verslaan* • *maken* <scène> • *(~ about) heen en weer gooien, smijten* <met geld> • *(~ away) voorbij laten gaan, weggooien* • *(~ in) ingooien, ertussen gooien* <opmerking> • *(~ off) uitgooien* <kleren>, z. *bevrijden v.* • *(~ on) aanschieten* <kleren> • *(~ out) eruit gooien, afgeven* <hitte>, *verwerpen* • *(~ over) in de steek laten* • *(~ up) opgooien, voortbrengen, kappen* <met baan> II [on ww] *gooien* • *(~ back) oude koeien uit de sloot halen* • *(~ up) braken* III [znw] *worp, gooi*
thru <AE> → **through**
thrum I [ov + on ww] *ronken* II [znw] *geronk*
thrush [znw] • *lijster* • *spruw*
thrust I [ov + on ww] • *duwen* • *werpen* • *steken* • *stuwen* II [znw] • *stoot* • *steek* • *aanval* • *stuwkracht*
thud I [on ww] *ploffen, dreunen* II [znw] *doffe slag, plof*
thug [znw] *gangster*

thumb I [ov ww] • *liften* • *snel doorbladeren* <v. boek> II [znw] *duim*
thump I [ov + on ww] *beuken, stompen, erop slaan* II [znw] • *zware slag* • *stomp*
thumping [bnw] *geweldig*
thunder I [on ww] *donderen* II [znw] *donder*
thundering [bnw] *kolossaal*
thunderous [bnw] *donderend*
thundery [bnw] *met kans op onweer*
Thursday [znw] *donderdag*
thus [bijw] • *op deze/die manier, zo, aldus* • *als gevolg van*
thwack I [ov ww] *een dreun geven* II [znw] *(harde) klap, dreun*
thwart [ov ww] • *dwarsbomen* • *verijdelen*
thy <vero.> [bez vnw] *uw*
thyme [znw] *tijm*
thyroid [znw] *schildklier*
tiara [znw] *tiara, diadeem*
tick I [ov ww] *tekentje zetten* • *(~ off) aanstrepen* <op lijst>, *een standje geven* II [on ww] *tikken* • *(~ over) stationair lopen* <v. motor> III [znw] • *(ge)tik* • *tekentje* <om aan te strepen> • *krediet* • *teek* • *ogenblik*
ticking [znw] *beddentijk*
tickle I [ov ww] • *kietelen* • *amuseren* II [znw] • *gekietel* • *kriebel*
ticklish [bnw] • *kittelig* • *netelig, teer, lastig*
tidbit [znw] → **titbit**
tiddler [znw] *(klein) visje*
tiddly [bnw] • *aangeschoten* • *nietig, klein*
tide I [ov ww] • *(~ over) te boven komen* <v. tegenslag> II [znw] • *getij* • *stroom*
tidings [mv] *nieuws, bericht(en)*
tidy I [ov ww] • *opruimen* • *in orde brengen* • *(~ up) (z.) opknappen* II [znw] • *sponsbakje en zeepbakje* • *iets om allerlei spullen in op te bergen, werkmandje* III [bnw] • *netjes,*

proper • *flink* ‹v. bedrag›
tie I [ov ww] • *(vast)binden* • *verbinden*
• *(~ up) vastmaken, vastmeren,*
verbinden, afbinden II [znw]
• *onbesliste wedstrijd, gelijke stand*
• *knoop* • *das* • *verbinding, iets dat*
bindt
tight [bnw] • *strak* • *precair* • *dronken*
• *gierig*
tights [mv] [ov ww] *panty*
tilt I [ov + on ww] *schuinhouden, schuin*
zijn II [znw] *schuine hoek*
timber I [znw] • *hout* • *bomen* • *balk*
• *spant* ‹v. schip› II [bnw] *houten*
time I [ov ww] *klokken* II [znw] • *tijd*
• *periode* • *keer* • *gelegenheid* • *maat*
timeless [bnw] • *oneindig* • *tijdloos*
timely [bnw] *te juister tijd*
timid, timorous [bnw] *bedeesd,*
verlegen
timing [znw] *de keuze v.h. juiste*
tijdstip
tin I [znw] • *tin* • *blik(je)* • *trommel*
• *bakvorm* II [bnw] *tinnen*
tincture [znw] *tinctuur*
tinder [znw] *tondel*
ting I [ov + on ww] *tingelen* II [znw]
getingel
tinge I [ov ww] *een tintje geven* II [znw]
• *tint, kleur* • *zweem*
tingle [on ww] *tintelen*
tinkle [ov + on ww] *tingelen, rinkelen*
tinny [bnw] • *blikkerig, schel*
• *derderangs*
tinsel I [znw] *kerstslingers* II [bnw]
schijn-, vals
tint I [ov ww] *een tint geven* II [znw]
tint
tiny [bnw] *(zeer) klein*
tip I [ov ww] • *fooi geven* • *doen hellen,*
kantelen • *doen doorslaan* ‹v.*
weegschaal› • *wippen* ‹met stoel›
• *wenk geven* • *(~ off) voor iets*
waarschuwen • *(~ up) schuin zetten*
II [on ww] *hellen* III [znw] • *eind(je)*
• *punt* • *topje* ‹v. vingers› • *mondstuk*

‹v. sigaret› • *fooi* • *tip* • *vuilnisbelt*
tipple I [ov + on ww] *pimpelen* II [znw]
sterkedrank
tipster [znw] *iem. die tips geeft*
tipsy [bnw] *aangeschoten, dronken*
tire I [ov ww] • *vermoeien* • *vervelen*
• *tooien* • *(~ out) afmatten* II [on ww]
• *(~ with) iets/iem. beu worden,*
vermoeid worden v. III [znw] • *band*
‹om wiel› • ‹vero.› *(hoofd)tooi* • ‹AE›
schort
tired [bnw] • *vermoeid* • *versleten*
• *vervelend*
tireless [bnw] *onvermoeibaar*
tiresome [bnw] *vervelend*
tiro [znw] *beginneling*
tissue [znw] *weefsel* ‹v. stof of
organisme›
tit [znw] • *mees* • ‹vulg.› *tiet, tepel*
titbit [znw] • *lekker hapje*
• *interessants, juweeltje* ‹fig.›, *iets*
moois
tithe [znw] *tiende deel, tiend*
title [znw] • *(eigendoms)recht* • *titel*
titled [bnw] *met titel*
titular [bnw] • *in naam* • *zogenaamd*
tizzy [znw] *opwinding*
to I [bijw] II [vz] • *naar, tot, aan, tot aan*
• *bij* • *tegen* • *in* • *op* • *van* • *om te*
toad [znw] • *pad* ‹dier› • *walgelijk*
persoon, vuilak
toady [znw] *vleier, kruiper*
toast I [ov ww] • *roosteren* • *verwarmen*
• *dronk instellen op* II [znw] • *populair*
iem. • *heildronk* • *geroosterd brood*
toaster [znw] *broodrooster*
tobacco [znw] *tabak*
tobacconist [znw] • *sigarenwinkelier*
• *sigarenfabrikant*
toboggan I [on ww] *met slede helling*
afgaan, rodelen II [znw] *platte slee*
today [bijw] • *vandaag* • *tegenwoordig*
toddle [on ww] *waggelen*
toddler [znw] *peuter, dreumes*
toe [znw] • *teen* • *neus* ‹v. schoen›
together [bijw] • *samen, tegelijk*

- *aaneen*
togetherness [znw] *saamhorigheid, solidariteit*
toggle [znw] *dwarshoutje, knevel(tje)*
toil I [on ww] *hard werken* II [znw] *zware arbeid, inspanning*
toilet [znw] *toilet* • wc
token I [znw] • *bewijs* • *aandenken* • *(boeken-/cadeau-/platen)bon* II [bnw] *symbolisch*
told [ww] verl.tijd + volt.deelw. → **tell**
tolerable [bnw] • *draaglijk* • *tamelijk*
tolerance [znw] • *verdraagzaamheid* • *'t dulden*
tolerant [bnw] *verdraagzaam*
toll I [ov + on ww] *luiden* ‹v. klok› II [znw] • *tol(geld)* • *slag* ‹v. klok›
tomato [znw] *tomaat*
tomboy [znw] *robbedoes, wildebras*
tome [znw] *boekdeel*
tomorrow [bijw] *morgen*
ton [znw] • *2240 Eng. pond ‹1016 kg›* • *‹AE› 2000 Eng. pond ‹907 kg›*
tonal [bnw] *de toon betreffend*
tonality [znw] • *toonaard* • *toonzetting*
tone I [ov ww] • *(~ down) temperen* • *(~ up) sterker maken ‹v. spieren›* II [on ww] • *(~ down) verflauwen* • *(~ in) (qua kleur) passen bij* III [znw] • *tonus* • *toon* • *klank* • *stemming, geest* • *tint* • *cachet*
toneless [bnw] *toonloos*
tongs [mv] *tang*
tongue [znw] • *tong* • *spraak* • *taal*
tonic [znw] • *tonic ‹frisdrank›* • *tonicum, versterkend middel* • *‹muz.› grondtoon*
tonight [bijw] • *vanavond* • *vannacht, komende nacht*
tonnage [znw] • *laadruimte in schip* • *gewicht in tonnen*
tonsil [znw] *amandel ‹klier›*
tonsure [znw] *tonsuur*
too [bijw] • *(al) te* • *ook, nog wel*
took [ww] verl. tijd → **take**
tool [znw] *gereedschap, instrument,*

hulpmiddel, werktuig
toot [on ww] *toeteren*
tooth [znw] *tand, kies*
tootle [on ww] • *kuieren* • *toeteren ‹op instrument›*
top I [ov ww] *overtreffen* • *(~ up) bijvullen* II [znw] • *top, hoogtepunt* • *bovenkant* • *deksel, dop* • *topje*
topaz [znw] *topaas*
topic [znw] *onderwerp v. gesprek*
topical [bnw] *actueel*
topography [znw] *topografie*
topping I [znw] *toplaag* II [bnw] *tiptop*
topple I [ov ww] • *(~ down/over) omvergooien* II [on ww] • *(~ down/over) omvallen*
torch [znw] *fakkel, toorts*
tore [ww] verl. tijd → **tear**
torment I [ov ww] *martelen, kwellen* II [znw] *marteling ‹emotioneel, psychologisch›, kwelling, plaag*
tormentor [znw] *beul, kwelgeest*
torn [ww] volt. deelw. → **tear**
torpedo I [ov ww] *torpederen* II [znw] *torpedo*
torpid [bnw] *traag*
torque [znw] • *halssnoer van gevlochten metaal* • *‹techn.› torsie*
torrent [znw] *stroom, stortvloed*
torrential [bnw] *als een stortvloed*
torso [znw] *torso, tors*
tortoise [znw] *landschildpad*
tortuous [bnw] • *verwrongen, gedraaid* • *slinks*
torture I [ov ww] *martelen, folteren, kwellen* II [znw] *foltering, marteling, kwelling*
torturer [znw] *folteraar*
Tory [znw] • *conservatief* • *lid v.d. Engelse Conservatieve Partij* • *‹AE› Britsgezinde*
toss I [ov ww] • *gooien* • *mengen ‹v. salade›* II [znw] *worp*
tot I [ov ww] • *(~ up) optellen* II [znw] • *klein kind, hummeltje* • *borreltje, glaasje*

total I [on ww] *bedragen* II [znw] *totaal* III [bnw] *totaal, volslagen*

totalitarianism [znw] *totalitarisme, eenpartijstelsel*

totality [znw] *totaliteit*

totter [on ww] *waggelen, wankelen*

touch I [ov ww] • *(aan)raken, (aan)roeren* • *betreffen* • *(~ off) veroorzaken* • *(~ up) retoucheren, afmaken, bijwerken* II [on ww] *raken* • *(~ down) neerkomen, landen* • *(~ on) even aanroeren* ‹v. onderwerp› III [znw] • *aanraking, betasting* • *tastzin* • *vaardigheid*

touched [bnw] • *ontroerd* • *getikt*

touchy [bnw] • *(over)gevoelig* • *lichtgeraakt* • *teer*

tough I [znw] ‹AE› *misdadiger* II [bnw] • *taai* • *hardnekkig* • *moeilijk* ‹v. werk, opdracht› • ‹AE› *gemeen, misdadig*

toughen [ov + on ww] *hard (doen) worden*

tour I [ov + on ww] *een (rond)reis maken (door)* II [znw] • *(rond)reis* • *uitstapje* • *tournee*

tourism [znw] *toerisme*

tourist [znw] *toerist*

tournament [znw] *toernooi*

tout I [on ww] *klandizie trachten te krijgen* II [znw] *klantenlokker*

tow I [ov ww] *slepen, trekken* II [znw] *sleepboot*

towards [vz] *naar ... toe*

towel I [ov + on ww] *(z.) afdrogen* II [znw] *handdoek*

tower I [on ww] *hoog uitsteken boven, z. hoog verheffen* II [znw] • *verdediger* • *toren*

towering [bnw] • *verheven* • *torenhoog*

town [znw] *stad*

township [znw] *gemeente*

toxic [bnw] *giftig, vergiftigings-*

toxicology [znw] *toxicologie*

toxin [znw] *toxine*

toy I [on ww] • *(~ with) spelen met* II [znw] • *(stuk) speelgoed* • *speelbal*

trace I [ov ww] • *nasporen* • *overtrekken* • *(~ back) terugvoeren* • *(~ out) duidelijk en netjes schrijven* II [znw] • *(voet)spoor* • *kleine hoeveelheid*

tracing [znw] *overgetrokken tekening*

track I [ov ww] • *(~ down) volgen, opsporen* II [znw] • *spoor* • *weg, pad, baan* • *spoorbaan*

tract [znw] • *gebied, uitgestrektheid* • *verhandeling* • ‹anat.› *ademhalings-/spijsverteringsstelsel*

tractable [bnw] *gemakkelijk te behandelen, volgzaam, gedwee*

traction [znw] *tractie, 't (voort)getrokken worden*

tractor [znw] *tractor, trekker*

trade I [ov ww] *ruilen, verhandelen* • *(~ in) ‹AE› inruilen* • *(~ off) ‹AE› verhandelen* II [on ww] *handel drijven* • *(~ on) misbruik maken van* ‹iem.'s goedheid› III [znw] • *(ruil)handel* • *ambacht* • *vak, beroep*

trader [znw] *koopman*

tradition [znw] *traditie, overlevering*

traditional [bnw] *traditioneel, volgens overlevering, aloud*

traffic I [ov + on ww] • *helen* • *drugs verkopen* II [znw] *(koop)handel*

trafficker [znw] *dealer*

tragedy [znw] *treurspel, tragedie*

trail I [ov + on ww] *slepen* II [ov ww] *de sporen volgen van* III [znw] • *spoor* • *pad* • *spoorweg*

train I [ov ww] • *leiden* ‹v. plant in bep. richting› • *vormen, trainen* II [on ww] *trainen* III [znw] • *sleep* • *nasleep* • *reeks* • *trein*

trainee [znw] *iem. die getraind wordt, leerling*

trainer [znw] *trainer, oefenmeester, africhter*

training [znw] *opleiding*

traipse [on ww] *doelloos rondslenteren, zwerven, (rond)zwalken*

trait [znw] *(karakter)trek*

traitor [znw] *verrader*

trajectory [znw] *baan* ‹v. projectiel›
trammel I [ov ww] *belemmeren*
II [znw] *belemmering*
tramp I [on ww] *sjokken* II [znw]
• *zware stap* • *voetreis* • *landloper* • *slet*
trample [ov ww] *vertrappen, met*
voeten treden
tranquil [bnw] *kalm, rustig*
tranquillize [ov ww] *kalmeren,*
verzachten
tranquillizer [znw] *kalmerend middel*
transact [ov ww] • *verrichten* • *zaken*
doen
transaction [znw] *transactie*
transatlantic [bnw] *transatlantisch*
transcend [ov ww] *te boven gaan,*
overtreffen
transcendence [znw] *transcendentie*
transcendent [bnw] *overtreffend*
transcendental [bnw] *bovenzinnelijk*
transcript [znw] *afschrift*
transfer I [ov ww] • *overdrukken*
• *vervoeren* • *overdragen, overbrengen*
• *overmaken, overschrijven* ‹op
rekening› • *overplaatsen* II [on ww]
overgeplaatst worden III [znw]
• *plakplaatje* • *overdracht,*
overbrenging
transferable [bnw] *over te dragen*
transference [znw] *overdracht*
transfix [ov ww] *doorboren*
transgress [ov ww] • *overtreden,*
schenden • *zondigen*
transience [znw] *vergankelijkheid*
transient I [znw] *passant* II [bnw]
vergankelijk, v. korte duur
transistor [znw] • *transistor*
• *transistor(radio)*
transit [znw] • *doortocht, doorvoer*
• *vervoer*
transition [znw] *overgang(speriode)*
transitive [bnw] *overgankelijk*
transitory [bnw] *vergankelijk, tijdelijk*
translate [ov ww] • *vertalen* • *omzetten*
• *uitleggen, verklaren*
translation [znw] *vertaling*

translator [znw] *vertaler*
translucent [bnw] • *doorschijnend*
• *doorzichtig*
transmission [znw] • *uitzending,*
overbrenging • *transmissie*
transmit [ov ww] • *overbrengen,*
overzenden • *overleveren* • ‹techn.›
geleiden
transmitter [znw] *radiozender*
transmute [ov ww] • *veranderen*
• *verwisselen*
transparency [znw] • *doorzichtigheid,*
doorschijnendheid • *dia*
transparent [bnw] *doorzichtig*
transpire [on ww] ‹inf.› *gebeuren*
transplant I [ov ww] • *verplanten,*
overplanten • *overbrengen,*
transplanteren II [znw] *transplantatie*
transport I [ov ww] • *vervoeren,*
transporteren • *verrukken* II [znw]
• *transport* • *vervoer*
transportation [znw] • *transport*
• *openbaar vervoer* • ‹AE› *middelen v.*
vervoer
transporter [znw] *vervoerder*
transpose [ov ww] • *verplaatsen*
• *omzetten*
transverse [bnw] *dwars*
transvestite [znw] *travestiet*
trap I [ov ww] • *in de val laten lopen*
• *met vallen vangen* II [znw]
• *val(strik)* • *licht rijtuig* • ‹sl.› *mond*
trapper [znw] *pelsjager*
trash [znw] *rommel*
trashy [bnw] *prullerig*
traumatic [bnw] *traumatisch*
travel I [ov + on ww] • *reizen* • *afleggen*
‹v. afstand› • z. *voortplanten* ‹v.
(geluids)golven› II [znw] *'t reizen*
traveller [znw] *reiziger*
traverse [ov ww] • *doortrekken*
• *oversteken*
travesty I [ov ww] *parodiëren* II [znw]
parodie, karikatuur
trawl I [on ww] *treilen* II [znw] *sleepnet*
trawler [znw] *treiler*

tray [znw] *presenteerblad*
treacherous [bnw] *verraderlijk*
treachery [znw] *verraad*
treacle [znw] *stroop*
tread I [ov + on ww] • *stappen*
• *(be)treden* • *vertrappen* II [znw]
• *stap, tred* • *trede* • *profiel* ‹v. band›
treason [znw] *verraad*
treasonable [bnw] *verraderlijk*
treasure I [ov ww] • *waarderen*
• *bewaren als een schat* II [znw]
• *schat(ten)* • *schat* ‹fig.›
treasurer [znw] *penningmeester*
treasury [znw] *schatkist, schatkamer*
treat I [ov ww] *behandelen* • (~ to)
trakteren op II [znw] *traktatie*
treatise [znw] *verhandeling*
treatment [znw] *behandeling*
treaty [znw] *verdrag, overeenkomst*
treble I [ov ww] *verdrievoudigen*
II [on ww] z. *verdrievoudigen* III [znw]
• *het drievoudige* • *sopraan* IV [bnw]
• *drievoudig* • *sopraan-* • *hoge tonen*
‹v. audioapparatuur›
tree [znw] *boom*
trek I [on ww] *trekken* II [znw] *lange*
tocht
trellis [znw] *traliewerk*
tremble I [on ww] *trillen, rillen, beven*
II [znw] *trilling*
tremendous [bnw] • *verschrikkelijk*
• *reusachtig*
tremor [znw] • *beving* • *(t)rilling*
• *huivering*
tremulous [bnw] • *bevend* • *bedeesd*
trench [znw] • *greppel* • *loopgraaf*
trenchant [bnw] • *scherp, snijdend*
• *krachtig*
trend [znw] • *neiging* • *trend*
trendy [bnw] • *modern, van deze tijd*
• *modieus*
trepidation [znw] *opwinding,*
bezorgheid
trespass I [on ww] *overtreding begaan,*
overtreden • (~ upon) *misbruik*
maken v. II [znw] *zonde*

trespasser [znw] *overtreder*
trestle [znw] *schraag, bok*
trial [znw] • *proef* • *beproeving* • ‹jur.›
proces
triangle [znw] • *driepotige takel*
• *triangel* • *driehoek*
triangular [bnw] • *driehoekig*
• *drievoudig*
tribal [bnw] *stam-*
tribe [znw] • *stam* • ‹pej.› *troep*
tribulation [znw] *tegenspoed,*
beproeving
tribunal [znw] *rechterstoel, rechtbank*
tributary I [znw] *zijrivier* II [bnw] *bij-,*
zij-
tribute [znw] • *bijdrage, schatting*
• *huldeblijk*
trice [znw] *ogenblik*
trick I [ov ww] *bedotten, bedriegen*
• (~ out) *versieren* II [znw]
• *aanwensel, hebbelijkheid* • *poets,*
grap • *slag* ‹bij kaartspel› • *truc, list*
• *handigheid*
trickery [znw] *bedotterij*
trickle I [on ww] • *druppelen* • *druipen*
• *sijpelen* II [znw] *straaltje*
trickster [znw] *bedrieger*
tricky [bnw] • *bedrieglijk* • ‹inf.› *lastig,*
moeilijk
tricycle [znw] *driewieler*
trifle I [on ww] • (~ with) *lichtvaardig*
behandelen II [znw] • *kleinigheid,*
beetje • *cake in vla*
trifling [bnw] *onbeduidend*
trigger I [ov ww] • (~off)
teweegbrengen II [znw] *trekker* ‹v.*
geweer›
trigonometry [znw] *driehoeksmeting*
trike ‹inf.› [znw] *driewieler*
trill I [ov + on ww] • *zingen* ‹v. vogel›
• *met hoge stem praten* II [znw] ‹muz.›
triller
trilogy [znw] *trilogie*
trim I [ov ww] • *opknappen, versieren*
• *garneren* • *bijknippen* ‹v. haar›
• *snoeien* II [znw] *orde* III [bnw]

• netjes, goed onderhouden • goed
passend
trimmings [mv] garnering
trinket [znw] • goedkoop sieraad
• kleinood
trio [znw] trio, drietal
trip I [ov ww] • (~ **up**) doen struikelen
II [on ww] • trippelen • struikelen
III [znw] • reis(je) • trip <v.
drugsverslaafde>
tripe [znw] • (rol)pens <als voedsel>
• onzin
triple I [ov ww] verdrievoudigen
II [on ww] z. verdrievoudigen III [bnw]
drievoudig, driedelig
triplets [mv] drieling
triptych [znw] triptiek, drieluik
trite [bnw] afgezaagd
triumph I [on ww] triomferen II [znw]
triomf
triumphal [bnw] triomferend, triomf-
triumphant [bnw] triomfantelijk,
triomferend
trivia [mv] onbelangrijke dingen/zaken
trivial [bnw] onbeduidend
triviality [znw] trivialiteit
trod [ww] verl. tijd + volt. deelw.
→ **tread**
trodden [ww] volt. deelw. → **tread**
Trojan I [znw] Trojaan II [bnw]
Trojaans
trolley [znw] wagentje, karretje,
serveerwagen, winkelwagentje
trollop [znw] • slons • slet
troop I [on ww] in grote groep lopen
II [znw] • troep, menigte • afdeling v.
cavalerie
trooper [znw] • cavalerist • <AE>
staatspolitieagent
trophy [znw] trofee
trot I [on ww] draven II [znw] draf
trotter [znw] schapenpoot
trouble I [ov ww] • kwellen • lastig
vallen • storen II [on ww] z.
bekommeren, z. moeite geven III [znw]
• pech • probleem • onrust • kwaal,

ongemak • onlusten
trough [znw] • trog • laagte tussen
twee golven • dieptepunt
trounce [ov ww] volledig verslaan
troupe [znw] troep <v. toneelspelers,
acrobaten>
trout [znw] forel(len)
trowel [znw] • troffel • plantenschepje
truancy [znw] 't spijbelen
truant [znw] spijbelaar
truce [znw] wapenstilstand
truck I [ov ww] vervoeren per
vrachtwagen II [znw] omgang
trucker [znw] vrachtwagenchauffeur
trudge I [on ww] sjokken II [znw]
gesjok
true [bnw + bijw] • waar • juist • zuiver
• recht • echt
truffle [znw] truffel
truism [znw] cliché
truly [bijw] • waarlijk • goed • juist
trumpet I [ov ww] uitbazuinen
II [on ww] trompetteren III [znw]
trompet, bazuin
trumpeter [znw] trompetter
truncate [ov ww] besnoeien, afknotten
truncheon [znw] gummiknuppel
trundle I [ov ww] doen rollen of rijden
II [on ww] • rollen, rijden • kuieren
trunk [znw] • boomstam • romp • slurf
<v. olifant> • koffer • <AE> kofferruimte
<v. auto>
truss I [ov ww] • (vast)binden, armen
langs lichaam binden • opmaken <v.
gevogelte, voor het bereiden> II [znw]
<med.> breukband
trust I [ov ww] • toevertrouwen
• vertrouwen (op) • (v. harte) hopen
II [on ww] • (~ **in**) vertrouwen op
III [znw] • stichting • trust
• vertrouwen • voor ander beheerde
goederen
trustee [znw] beheerder, curator,
executeur, regent <v. instelling>
trustful [bnw] vertrouwend
trustworthy [bnw] te vertrouwen,

betrouwbaar
truth [znw] waarheid
truthful [bnw] waarheidlievend
try I [ov + on ww] proberen II [ov ww]
• beproeven, op de proef stellen
• gerechtelijk onderzoeken • verhoren
• (~ on) passen ‹v. kleren› • (~ out)
(uit)proberen III [znw] poging
trying [bnw] • lastig ‹v. gedrag›
• vermoeiend
tub [znw] • tobbe • badkuip • schuit
tubby [bnw] rond, corpulent
tube [znw] • tube • buis • ‹inf.› tv,
metro
tuber [znw] knol ‹v. plant›
tuberculosis [znw] tbc
tubular [bnw] buisvormig
tuck I [ov + on ww] • (~ in) verorberen
II [ov ww] • instoppen • stoppen,
wegzetten, opbergen • (~ away)
verstoppen • (~ in/up) instoppen,
verorberen III [znw] • plooi • lekkers,
snoep
Tuesday [znw] dinsdag
tuft [znw] bosje
tug I [ov + on ww] rukken (aan), trekken
II [znw] • ruk • sleepboot
tuition [znw] • lesgeld • onderricht
tumble I [ov ww] ondersteboven gooien
II [on ww] • tuimelen • duikelen
• (~ down) instorten • (~ over)
omvallen • (~ to) ‹sl.› iets snappen
III [znw] val
tumbler [znw] • bekerglas • acrobaat
tummy ‹kind.› [znw] buikje
tumour [znw] gezwel
tumultuous [bnw] • lawaaierig
• woelig
tun [znw] ton, kuip
tundra [znw] toendra
tune I [ov ww] • afstemmen, stemmen
• afstellen • (~ to) afstemmen op,
aanpassen aan II [on ww] • (~ in)
afstemmen ‹bij radio› III [znw] melodie
tuneful [bnw] • welluidend • muzikaal
tuneless [bnw] onwelluidend

tuner [znw] • stemmer
• radio-ontvanger
tunic [znw] tuniek
tunnel I [ov ww] tunnel maken II [znw]
tunnel
tuppence [znw] twee pence
tuppenny [bnw] van twee pence
turban [znw] tulband
turbid [bnw] troebel, dik
turbulent [bnw] onstuimig
turd [znw] • drol • rotkerel, rotmeid
tureen [znw] soepterrine
turf I [ov ww] graszoden leggen
• (~ out) ‹sl.› (iem.) eruit gooien
II [znw] • gras(tapijt) • graszode
turgid [bnw] gezwollen, hoogdravend
‹v. taal›
Turkish [bnw] Turks
turmoil [znw] verwarring, herrie,
opwinding
turn I [ov ww] • richten • afwenden
• vormen, doen draaien, doen keren,
omslaan, omdraaien
• doen worden, veranderen • (~ back)
omslaan • (~ down) weigeren, lager
zetten • (~ in) inleveren, arresteren
• (~ into) veranderen in • (~ off)
uitdraaien, uitzetten • (~ on)
aanzetten, (seksueel)
opwinden/prikkelen, opendraaien
• (~ out) beurt geven ‹v. kamer›,
produceren, uitdraaien, eruit gooien,
binnenstebuiten keren • (~ over)
kantelen • (~ up) omslaan II [on ww]
• z. keren • z. richten • zuur worden
• (~ about) ronddraaien
• (~ aside/away/from) z. afwenden
van • (~ back) terugkeren • (~ down)
inslaan • (~ in) naar bed gaan
• (~ into) veranderen in, inslaan
• (~ off) z. afkeren, afslaan • (~ on) z.
keren tegen, afhangen v. • (~ out) te
voorschijn komen, blijken te zijn
• (~ over) z. omkeren • (~ round) z.
omdraaien • (~ to) z. wenden tot,
raadplegen, z. toeleggen op • (~ up) te

voorschijn komen III [znw] • *draai,*
wending, richting, bocht • *keerpunt,*
verandering • *wandelingetje* • *schok*
• *beurt* • *afslag*
turning [znw] • *(zij)straat* • *afslag*
turnip [znw] *raap, knol*
turnover [znw] • *verloop* ‹v. personeel›
• *omzet* • *appelflap*
turpentine [znw] *terpentijn*
turret [znw] • *torentje* • *geschuttoren*
turtle [znw] *zeeschildpad*
tusk [znw] *(slag)tand*
tussle I [on ww] *vechten* II [znw]
worsteling, strijd
tutelage [znw] *voogdij(schap)*
tutorial [znw] *werkcollege*
twaddle [znw] *kletspraat*
twang I [ov + on ww] *tjingelen,*
tokkelen ‹op instrument› II [on ww]
snorren ‹v. pijl› III [znw] *getokkel*
tweak I [ov ww] • *(draaien en) trekken*
aan • *knijpen* II [znw] *ruk*
tweet I [on ww] *sjilpen* II [znw] *gesjilp*
twelfth I [znw] *twaalfde deel* II [telw]
twaalfde
twelve [telw] *twaalf*
twentieth [telw] *twintigste*
twenty [telw] *twintig*
twerp [znw] *sul*
twice [bijw] *twee keer*
twiddle I [ov + on ww] *spelen met*
‹klein voorwerp› II [znw] *draai*
twig I [ov ww] ‹inf.› *begrijpen, snappen*
II [znw] • *twijg* • *wichelroede*
twilight [znw] *schemering*
twin I [ov ww] *verbinden met* ‹v. stad›
II [znw] *tweelingbroer/-zus* III [bnw]
• *tweeling-* • *gepaard* • *dubbel*
twine I [ov + on ww] *(z.) draaien om*
II [znw] *dun touw*
twinge [znw] *steek, pijnscheut*
twinkle I [on ww] • *flikkeren*
• *schitteren* ‹v. pret› II [znw]
schittering ‹v. pret›
twirl I [ov + on ww] *(rond)draaien*
II [znw] *(snelle) draai*

twist I [ov ww] • *(in elkaar) draaien*
• *verdraaien* • *verrekken* II [on ww]
• *draaien* • *kronkelen* • *vertrekken* ‹v.
gezicht› III [znw] • *draaiing*
• *gedraaid iets* • *(onverwachte)*
verandering • *twist* ‹dans›
twister [znw] • *bedrieger* • *lastig*
probleem • ‹AE› *cycloon*
twit [znw] *dom iem.*
twitch I [ov ww] *rukken of trekken* ‹aan
mouw, om aandacht te trekken›
II [on ww] *trekken* ‹v. spier› III [znw]
• *ruk* • *zenuwtrek*
twitter [on ww] • *sjilpen* • *met*
piepstem spreken
two [telw] *twee*
tycoon ‹AE› [znw] *groot zakenman,*
magnaat
type I [ov + on ww] *typen* II [znw]
• *voorbeeld, type, model* • *(zinne)beeld*
• *lettervorm*
typhoid [znw] *tyfus*
typhoon [znw] *wervelstorm*
typical [bnw] *typisch, kenmerkend*
typify [ov ww] *typeren*
typist [znw] *typiste*
typography [znw] *typografie*
tyrannize [ov + on ww] *tiranniseren*
tyranny [znw] *tirannie*
tyrant [znw] *tiran*
tyre [znw] *band* ‹v. wiel›
tyro [znw] → *tiro*
tzar [znw] *tsaar*

U

ubiquitous [bnw] *alomtegenwoordig*
ubiquity [znw] *alomtegenwoordigheid*
udder [znw] *uier*
ugly [bnw] *lelijk*
ulcer [znw] *(maag)zweer*
ulterior [bnw] *heimelijk*
ultimate I [znw] *het beste* II [bnw]
• *ultieme* • *uiteindelijke*
ultimately [bijw] *ten slotte*
umber I [znw] *omber* ‹kleur v. aarde›
II [bnw] *omberkleurig*
umbrage [znw] *aanstoot*
umbrella [znw] • *tuinparasol*
• *overkoepeling(sorgaan)* • *paraplu*
umpire I [ov + on ww] *optreden als
scheidsrechter* II [znw] *scheidsrechter*
umpteen ‹inf.› [telw] • *heel wat*
• *zoveel*
umpteenth [bnw] *zoveelste*
unabashed [bnw] • *niet verlegen*
• *onbeschaamd*
unabated [bnw] *onverminderd,
onverzwakt*
unacceptable [bnw] *onaanvaardbaar*
unaccompanied [bnw] *zonder
begeleiding*
unaccountable [bnw]
• *onverklaarbaar* • *niet
verantwoordelijk* • *ontoerekenbaar*
unaccustomed [bnw] • *ongewoon*
• *niet gewend*
unacquainted [bnw] *onbekend (met)*
unaffected [bnw] • *niet beïnvloed*
• *eerlijk, open, natuurlijk,
ongedwongen*
unafraid [bnw] *niet bang, onversaagd*
unaided [bnw] *zonder hulp*
unalloyed [bnw] *onvermengd, zuiver*
unalterable [bnw] *onveranderlijk*
unaltered [bnw] *ongewijzigd*
unambiguous [bnw] *ondubbelzinnig,*

helder
unanimity [znw] *eenstemmigheid*
unanimous [bnw] *eenstemmig*
unanswered [bnw] *onbeantwoord*
unapproachable [bnw]
ontoegankelijk
unarmed [bnw] *ongewapend*
unashamed [bnw] • *schaamteloos*
• *onbeschroomd*
unasked [bnw] *ongevraagd*
unassuming [bnw] *niet aanmatigend,
bescheiden*
unattached [bnw] • *alleenstaand,
ongebonden* • *extern*
unattended [bnw] • *niet vergezeld,
zonder gevolg* • *onbeheerd*
• *verwaarloosd*
unattractive [bnw] *onaantrekkelijk*
unauthorized [bnw] *niet gemachtigd*
unavailable [bnw] *niet beschikbaar*
unavailing [bnw] *vergeefs*
unavoidable [bnw] *onvermijdelijk*
unaware [bnw] *z. niet bewust v.*
unawares [bijw] • *onbewust*
• *onverhoeds*
unbalance [ov ww] *uit 't evenwicht
brengen*
unbalanced [bnw] *onevenwichtig*
unbearable [bnw] *ondraaglijk,
onduldbaar*
unbecoming [bnw] • *ongepast*
‹gedrag› • *niet goed staand*
unbelievable [bnw] *ongelooflijk*
unbeliever [znw] *ongelovige*
unbelieving [bnw] *ongelovig*
unbend [ov + on ww] *z. losser gedragen*
unbending [bnw] *onbuigzaam*
unbidden [bnw] *ongenood*
unborn [bnw] *ongeboren*
unbounded [bnw] *onbegrensd*
unburden [ov ww] • *ontlasten* • *z.
bevrijden van*
uncanny [bnw] • *geheimzinnig*
• *griezelig*
unceasing [bnw] *onophoudelijk*
unceremonious [bnw] *zonder*

plichtplegingen
uncertain [bnw] *onzeker, twijfelachtig, onbetrouwbaar*
unchallenged [bnw] *onbetwist*
unchanged [bnw] *onveranderd*
uncharitable [bnw] *liefdeloos, onbarmhartig*
uncharted [bnw] *niet in kaart gebracht*
unchecked [bnw] • *niet gecontroleerd* • *onbelemmerd*
uncivil [bnw] *onbeleefd*
uncivilized [bnw] *onbeschaafd*
unclaimed [bnw] • *onopgevraagd* • *niet opgehaald*
unclassified [bnw] • *niet geclassificeerd, niet geregistreerd* • *niet (meer) geheim*
uncle [znw] *oom*
unclean [bnw] *onrein, smerig*
unclear [bnw] *onduidelijk*
uncoloured [bnw] *ongekleurd*
uncomfortable [bnw] • *ongemakkelijk* • *niet op zijn gemak*
uncommitted [bnw] *niet gebonden, neutraal*
uncommon [bnw] *ongewoon*
uncompromising [bnw] *onverzoenlijk*
unconcealed [bnw] *openlijk, onverholen*
unconcern [znw] *onverschilligheid*
unconcerned [bnw] *onverschillig, onbezorgd*
unconditional [bnw] *onvoorwaardelijk*
unconscionable [bnw] *onredelijk, schandalig*
unconscious I [znw] *het onderbewustzijn* II [bnw] • *onbewust* • *bewusteloos*
unconsidered [bnw] • *onbezonnen* • *ondoordacht*
uncontrollable [bnw] • *niet te beïnvloeden* • *niet te beheersen*
uncontrolled [bnw] • *onbeheerst* • *onbeperkt*

unconvincing [bnw] *niet overtuigend*
uncork [ov ww] *ontkurken, opentrekken* ‹v. fles›
uncouth [bnw] *lomp*
uncover [ov ww] *ontbloten, bloot leggen*
uncritical [bnw] • *onkritisch* • *klakkeloos*
unctuous [bnw] • *vettig* • *zalvend* ‹fig.›
uncultivated [bnw] *onbebouwd*
uncut [bnw] • *ongesnoeid* • *ongeslepen* ‹diamant› • *onverkort*
undaunted [bnw] *onverschrokken, onversaagd*
undecided [bnw] *onbeslist*
undemonstrative [bnw] *terughoudend, gesloten*
undeniable [bnw] *ontegenzeglijk*
under I [bnw] *onder, beneden* II [bijw] *hieronder, (daar)onder* III [vz] • *onder, lager/minder dan, beneden* • *krachtens* • *onder beschutting van*
underground I [znw] • *ondergrondse spoorweg* • *ondergrondse verzetsbeweging* II [bnw + bijw] • *ondergronds* • *geheim*
underneath I [znw] *onderkant* II [bnw] *onder-* III [bijw] *hieronder, daaronder, beneden* IV [vz] *onder, beneden*
understand [ov ww] • *begrijpen* • *verstaan* • *(ergens uit) opmaken*
understandable [bnw] *begrijpelijk*
understanding I [znw] • *begrip* • *verstandhouding* • ‹inf.› *schikking* II [bnw] *begripvol tegemoetkomend*
understate [ov ww] *te zwak uitdrukken*
understatement [znw] *te zwakke uitdrukking*
understudy I [ov ww] *doublure zijn voor, instuderen v.e. rol ter eventuele vervanging v.e. toneelspeler* II [znw] *doublure*
undertake [ov ww] • *op z. nemen* • *ondernemen* • ‹AE› *wagen*

undeserved [bnw] onverdiend
undesirable I [znw] ongewenste persoon II [bnw] ongewenst
undeveloped [bnw] onontwikkeld
undignified [bnw] onwaardig, onbetamelijk, ongepast
undisputed [bnw] onbetwist
undistinguished [bnw] onbetekenend, middelmatig
undisturbed [bnw] ongestoord, onverstoord
undivided [bnw] ongedeeld, onverdeeld
undo [ov ww] • tenietdoen, ongedaan maken • losmaken, openmaken • ruïneren
undone [bnw + bijw] • on(af)gedaan • losgemaakt • geruïneerd
undoubted [bnw] ongetwijfeld
undress [ov + on ww] (z.) uitkleden
undue [bnw] overdreven
undulate [ov + on ww] • (doen) golven • (doen) trillen
unearth [ov ww] • opgraven, rooien • aan 't licht brengen, opdiepen
unearthly [bnw] • bovenaards • griezelig, spookachtig, akelig
uneasy [bnw] • ongerust • onrustig • ongemakkelijk, onbehaaglijk
uneducated [bnw] ongeschoold, onontwikkeld
unemployable [bnw] ongeschikt voor werk
unemployed [bnw] werkloos
unemployment [znw] werkloosheid
unenviable [bnw] niet benijdenswaardig, onaangenaam
unequal [bnw] • niet opgewassen tegen • ongelijk
unequalled [bnw] ongeëvenaard
unequivocal [bnw] ondubbelzinnig, duidelijk
unerring [bnw] onfeilbaar
uneven [bnw] ongelijk(matig)
unexpected [bnw] onverwacht
unexplained [bnw] onverklaard
unfailing [bnw] zeker, onfeilbaar

unfair [bnw] • oneerlijk • onsportief
unfaithful [bnw] trouweloos
unfamiliar [bnw] • onbekend • ongewoon
unfashionable [bnw] niet modieus
unfasten [ov ww] losmaken, openmaken
unfathomable [bnw] ondoorgrondelijk
unfavourable [bnw] ongunstig
unfinished [bnw] onafgedaan, onafgewerkt, onaf
unfit [bnw] • ongeschikt • niet in goede conditie
unflagging [bnw] onvermoeibaar, onverflauwd
unflappable [bnw] onverstoorbaar
unfold [ov + on ww] • (z.) ontvouwen, (z.) uitspreiden • opengaan
unforeseen [bnw] onvoorzien
unforgettable [bnw] onvergetelijk
unforgivable [bnw] onvergeeflijk
unfortunate I [znw] ongelukkige II [bnw] onfortuinlijk, ongelukkig
unfounded [bnw] ongegrond
unfriendly [bnw] onsympathiek, nors
unfulfilled [bnw] onvervuld, niet in vervulling gegaan
unfurl [ov + on ww] • (z.) ontrollen, (z.) ontplooien • uitspreiden
unfurnished [bnw] ongemeubileerd
ungainly [bnw] • onbeholpen • lelijk
ungenerous [bnw] • kleinzielig, hard • krenterig, gierig
ungodly [bnw] • goddeloos, zondig • ergerlijk, onmenselijk
ungovernable [bnw] niet bestuurbaar, onhandelbaar
ungracious [bnw] onvriendelijk
ungrateful [bnw] • ondankbaar • onaangenaam
unguarded [bnw] • niet beschermd • onvoorzichtig • onbewaakt
unhappy [bnw] ongelukkig, ongepast
unhealthy [bnw] ongezond
unheard [bnw] niet gehoord

unhelpful [bnw] niet hulpvaardig
unhesitating [bnw] prompt, zonder
aarzelen
unhinge [ov ww] ontwrichten, iem. uit
z'n evenwicht slaan
unholy [bnw] • goddeloos, zondig
• <inf.> verschrikkelijk
unhook [ov ww] losmaken, loshaken
unicorn [znw] eenhoorn
unidentified [bnw] niet geïdentificeerd
unification [znw] eenmaking
uniform I [znw] uniform II [bnw]
• uniform, gelijk • onveranderlijk,
eenparig
uniformed [bnw] in uniform
uniformity [znw] uniformiteit
unify [ov ww] • verenigen
• gelijkschakelen
unilateral [bnw] eenzijdig
unimaginable [bnw] ondenkbaar
unimaginative [bnw] zonder enige
fantasie
unimpaired [bnw] ongeschonden
unimpeachable [bnw] onberispelijk
unimportant [bnw] onbelangrijk
uninformed [bnw] niet op de hoogte
(gebracht), niet ingelicht
uninspiring [bnw] oninteressant, niet
inspirerend, saai
uninterested [bnw] ongeïnteresseerd
uninteresting [bnw] niet interessant
uninterrupted [bnw] onafgebroken,
ongestoord
uninvited [bnw] ongenood, niet
uitgenodigd
union [znw] • eendracht • vakbond
• vereniging • verbinding, verbond
• <form.> huwelijk
unionism [znw] • vakbeweging
• beginselen v. unionistische partij
unionist I [znw] • lid v.d. vakbond
• voorstander v. politieke unie II [bnw]
• verenigings- • unionistisch
unique [bnw] • buitengewoon,
ongeëvenaard • uniek, enig <in soort>
• <inf.> opmerkelijk

unison [znw] harmonie,
overeenstemming
unit [znw] • eenheid • <techn.>
onderdeel • <mil.> afdeling
unite I [ov ww] verenigen • (~ in)
(doen) verenigen in II [on ww] z.
verenigen • (~ with) iem./iets met z.
verenigen
united [bnw] • verenigd • eendrachtig
unity [znw] • eenheid
• overeenstemming
universal I [znw] algemeen
begrip/eigenschap/principe II [bnw]
algemeen
unjust [bnw] onrechtvaardig
unjustifiable [bnw] niet te
rechtvaardigen
unjustified [bnw] ongerechtvaardigd
unkempt [bnw] slordig, onverzorgd
unkind [bnw] onvriendelijk, onaardig
unknown I [znw] onbekende II [bnw]
• ongekend • onbekend
unlawful [bnw] onwettig, ongeoorloofd
unleash [ov ww] loslaten
unless I [vz] behalve II [vw] tenzij
unlike [vz] • ongelijk • anders dan • in
tegenstelling met
unlimited [bnw] • vrij • onbeperkt,
niet begrensd
unload [ov ww] • ontladen • lossen
unlock [ov ww] ontsluiten
unlooked-for [bnw] onverwacht
unlucky [bnw] • onzalig • ongelukkig
unmade [bnw] • niet opgemaakt <v.
bed> • niet gemaakt
unmanageable [bnw]
• onhandelbaar, lastig • niet te besturen
unmanned [bnw] onbemand,
onbeheerd
unmarked [bnw] niet v.e. merk
voorzien
unmarried [bnw] ongetrouwd
unmatched [bnw] • ongeëvenaard,
weergaloos • niet bij elkaar passend
unmoved [bnw] onbewogen
unnamed [bnw] niet met name

genoemd, naamloos, onbekend
unnatural [bnw] *onnatuurlijk,
geforceerd, tegennatuurlijk*
unnecessary [bnw] • *onnodig*
• *overbodig*
unnerve [ov ww] *v. kracht beroven,
verslappen, ontzenuwen*
unnoticed [bnw] *onopgemerkt*
unobtainable [bnw] *onverkrijgbaar*
unobtrusive [bnw] *niet
in-/opdringerig*
unoccupied [bnw] *onbewoond*
unofficial [bnw] *officieus, niet
geautoriseerd*
unorthodox [bnw] • *ketters*
• *onconventioneel, ongewoon,
ongebruikelijk*
unpack [ov + on ww] *uitpakken*
unpaid [bnw] *niet betaald, onbezoldigd*
unparalleled [bnw] *zonder weerga*
unparliamentary [bnw]
onparlementair
unpleasant [bnw] *onplezierig,
onaangenaam*
unpleasantness [znw] *onprettige
toestand, wrijving*
unpopular [bnw] *impopulair*
unprecedented [bnw] • *zonder
precedent* • *weergaloos*
unpredictable [bnw] *onvoorspelbaar*
unpretentious [bnw] *niet
aanmatigend, bescheiden*
unprincipled [bnw] *gewetenloos*
unproductive [bnw] *onproductief,
weinig opleverend*
unprofitable [bnw] *geen voordeel
opleverend*
unprotected [bnw] *onbeschermd*
unprovoked [bnw] *onuitgelokt*
unqualified [bnw] • *onbevoegd*
• *onvoorwaardelijk* • *totaal, absoluut*
unquestionable [bnw] *onbetwistbaar*
unquestioned [bnw] *onbetwist*
unquestioning [bnw]
onvoorwaardelijk
unquote [tw] *einde citaat*

unreadable [bnw] • *onleesbaar* • *niet
te lezen*
unreal [bnw] *onwerkelijk, irreëel*
unreasonable [bnw] • *onredelijk*
• *ongegrond*
unreasoning [bnw] *onnadenkend*
unrecognized [bnw] • *niet erkend*
• *niet herkend*
unrelated [bnw] • *niet verwant* • *geen
verband met elkaar houdend*
unrelenting [bnw] *meedogenloos,
onverbiddelijk*
unreliable [bnw] *onbetrouwbaar*
unrelieved [bnw] *niet verzacht*
unremitting [bnw] *aanhoudend,
onverdroten*
unrequited [bnw] • *onvergolden*
• *onbeantwoord ‹liefde›*
unreserved [bnw] *openhartig,
vrijmoedig*
unrest [znw] *onrust*
unrestrained [bnw] *onbeperkt,
onbeteugeld*
unrestricted [bnw] *onbeperkt,
onbegrensd*
unrewarding [bnw] *niet lonend,
teleurstellend*
unripe [bnw] *onrijp*
unrivalled, unrivaled [bnw]
ongeëvenaard
unroll [ov + on ww] *ontplooien, (z.)
ontrollen*
unruffled [bnw] • *ongerimpeld, glad*
• *bedaard*
unsafe [bnw] *onveilig, gevaarlijk,
onbetrouwbaar*
unsaid [bnw] *onuitgesproken,
verzwegen*
unsatisfactory [bnw] *onbevredigend*
unscathed [bnw] *ongedeerd,
onbeschadigd*
unscientific [bnw] *onwetenschappelijk*
unscrew [ov ww] *losschroeven*
unscrupulous [bnw] *gewetenloos*
unseat [ov ww] • *uit het zadel gooien*
• *v. functie beroven* • *wegwerken*

unseeing [bnw] zonder (iets) te zien, blind

unseemly [bnw] • ongelegen • ongepast

unseen I [znw] het onzichtbare II [bnw] ongezien

unselfish [bnw] onbaatzuchtig

unsettle [ov ww] • (beginnen te/doen) wankelen • van streek brengen

unsettled [bnw] • onzeker • zonder vaste woonplaats • niet opgelost • niet gekoloniseerd

unsightly [bnw] afzichtelijk, lelijk

unskilled [bnw] ongeschoold

unsociable [bnw] ongezellig

unsophisticated [bnw] • eenvoudig • geestelijk ongezond

unsound [bnw] • onbetrouwbaar, ondeugdelijk • vals

unspeakable [bnw] • onbeschrijfelijk • afschuwelijk

unspecified [bnw] niet gespecificeerd

unspoken [bnw] niet geuit

unstable [bnw] • onvast • wankelbaar

unsteady [bnw] onvast

unstoppable [bnw] onstuitbaar, niet te stoppen

unstuck [bnw] los

unsuitable [bnw] • ongeschikt • ongepast

unsuited [bnw] ongeschikt

unsung [bnw] • niet gezongen • niet bezongen

unsure [bnw] onzeker

unsuspected [bnw] • onverdacht • niet vermoed

unsuspecting [bnw] geen kwaad vermoedend, argeloos

unswerving [bnw] niet afwijkend, onwankelbaar

unsympathetic [bnw] • geen belangstelling tonend • antipathiek

untangle [ov ww] ontwarren

untapped [bnw] onaangesproken <fig.>, (nog) niet aangeboord

unthinkable [bnw] ondenkbaar

unthinking [bnw] onbezonnen

untidy [bnw] slordig

untie [ov ww] • bevrijden • losmaken

until I [vz] tot (aan) II [vw] tot(dat)

untimely [bnw] • ongelegen, niet op de juiste tijd • voortijdig

untiring [bnw] onvermoeid, onverdroten

unto <vero.> [vz] tot, tot aan

untold <form.> [bnw] onnoemelijk

untouchable I [znw] paria II [bnw] • onaanraakbaar <hindoeïsme> • onaantastbaar

untouched [bnw] onaangeraakt

untoward [bnw] onfortuinlijk

untrained [bnw] ongeoefend

untried [bnw] • niet geprobeerd • onervaren • <jur.> (nog) niet berecht/verhoord

untrue [bnw] • onwaar • ontrouw

untruth [znw] onwaarheid

untruthful [bnw] leugenachtig

untutored [bnw] niet onderwezen

unused [bnw] • niet gewend • ongebruikt

unusual [bnw] niet gebruikelijk, ongewoon

unutterable [bnw] vreselijk, onuitsprekelijk

unveil [ov ww] ontsluieren, onthullen

unwanted [bnw] • niet verlangd • niet nodig

unwarranted [bnw] onverantwoord

unwelcome [bnw] niet welkom

unwell [bnw] onwel

unwieldy [bnw] • log • lastig te hanteren

unwilling [bnw] • met tegenzin • onwillig

unwind I [ov ww] afwinden II [on ww] • zich ontrollen • <inf.> kalmeren

unwise [bnw] onverstandig

unwitting [bnw] onwetend

unworkable [bnw] onuitvoerbaar

unworthy [bnw] onwaardig, niet passend

unwrap [ov ww] loswikkelen

unwritten [bnw] *ongeschreven*
unzip [ov ww] *openritsen, losmaken* ‹v. ritssluiting›
up I [bnw] • *op, omhoog* • *verstreken, afgelopen* • *aan de gang* II [bijw] *op, omhoog, naar boven* III [vz] *op*
upbraid [ov ww] *berispen, verwijten*
upbringing [znw] *opvoeding*
update [ov ww] *moderniseren*
upgrade [ov ww] *verbeteren* ‹positie›
upheaval [znw] • *omwenteling* • *ontreddering*
uphill I [bnw] *moeilijk* II [bijw] • *moeizaam* • *bergopwaarts*
uphold [ov ww] *steunen, verdedigen*
upholstery [znw] *stoffering, bekleding*
upkeep [znw] *onderhoud(skosten)*
upland [bnw] *in/uit/van het hoogland*
uplift I [ov ww] • *helpen, steunen* • *verheffen* ‹i.h.b. geestelijk› II [znw] • *verheffing* • *steun*
upon [vz] • *op* • *meteen na(dat)*
upper I [znw] *bovengedeelte v. schoen* II [bnw] *hoger, boven(ste)*
uppish [bnw] *verwaand*
upright I [znw] *verticale post/stut* II [bnw] • *recht, verticaal* • *eerlijk, eerbaar, oprecht* III [bijw] *rechtop*
uprising [znw] *opstand*
uproarious [bnw] • *bijzonder grappig* • *luid lachend*
upset I [ov ww] • *omverwerpen, omgooien* • *in de war sturen* • *v. streek brengen* II [bnw] *v. streek*
upshot [znw] *resultaat, eind van 't liedje*
upstage [ov ww] *in de schaduw stellen, naar de achtergrond dringen*
upstairs I [bnw] *boven-* II [bijw] *de trap op, naar boven*
upstanding [bnw] *oprecht, hoogstaand*
upstart I [znw] *parvenu* II [bnw] *opschepperig*
upstream [bnw] *tegen de stroom op, stroomopwaarts*
upsurge [znw] *opwelling, plotselinge toename*

uptake [znw] • *verbruikte hoeveelheid* • *begrip*
uptight [bnw] *erg gespannen, zeer nerveus*
up-to-date [bnw] *bij de tijd, modern*
upturn [znw] ‹hand.› *opleving*
urban [bnw] *stedelijk, stads-*
urbane [bnw] *hoffelijk, wellevend*
urbanize [ov ww] *verstedelijken*
urchin [znw] *schelm, kwajongen*
urge I [ov ww] • *aansporen, aanzetten, aandrijven* • *aandringen op* • (~ **on**) *aanzetten, voortdrijven* II [znw] *aandrang, verlangen*
urgency [znw] • *dringende noodzaak* • *urgentie*
urinal [znw] *urinoir*
urn [znw] • *urn* • *koffie-/theeketel*
us [pers vnw] *ons*
usage [znw] *gebruik, gewoonte*
use I [ov ww] *gebruiken, benutten* • (~ **up**) *opmaken, verbruiken, uitputten* II [hww] * I used to smoke *vroeger was ik een roker* III [znw] • *gebruik* • *nut* • *gewoonte*
used [bnw] • *tweedehands, gebruikt* • *gewoon, gewend*
useless [bnw] *nutteloos*
user [znw] *gebruiker, verbruiker*
usher I [ov ww] • *binnenleiden* • *aankondigen* • *als ceremoniemeester/ zaalwachter optreden voor* • (~ **in**) *inleiden* II [znw] • *zaalwachter* • *ceremoniemeester*
usual I [znw] *'t gewoonlijke* II [bnw] *gewoon, gebruikelijk*
usurer [znw] *woekeraar*
usurp [ov ww] *z. aanmatigen, z. wederrechtelijk toe-eigenen*
utensil [znw] *gebruiksvoorwerp*
utility [znw] • *(openbare) voorziening* • *nut* • *bruikbaarheid*
utilize, utilise [ov ww] *gebruik maken van, benutten*
utmost I [znw] *'t uiterste* II [bnw]

hoogste, uiterste, verste
utter I [ov ww] *uiten, uiting geven aan*
II [bnw] *volkomen, totaal, volslagen*
utterance [znw] • *uitspraak* • *uiting*
utterly [bijw] *totaal, volkomen*

vacancy [znw] • *lege (hotel)kamer*
• *vacature*
vacant [bnw] • *onbezet, leeg(staand)*
• *wezenloos* • *leeghoofdig, dom* • *vacant*
vacate [ov ww] • *neerleggen ‹v. ambt›*
• *ontruimen ‹v. huis›*
vacation [znw] *vakantie*
vaccinate [ov ww] *inenten*
vacuity [znw] • *ledigheid*
• *wezenloosheid*
vacuous [bnw] *leeghoofdig, wezenloos, dom*
vacuum I [ov + on ww] ‹inf.› *stofzuigen*
II [znw] • *leegte* • *het luchtledige*
vagabond [znw] *landloper, vagebond,
zwerver*
vagary [znw] *gril, kuur*
vagrancy [znw] *landloperij*
vagrant I [znw] *zwerver, vagebond*
II [bnw] *zwervend*
vague [bnw] *vaag, onbestemd,
onbepaald*
vain [bnw] • *ijdel, prat (op)* • *nutteloos,
vergeefs*
vale [znw] ‹form.› *dal*
valediction [znw] *afscheid*
valedictory [bnw] *afscheids-*
valet [znw] *bediende*
valiant [bnw] *dapper, moedig*
valid [bnw] • *geldig* • *gefundeerd,
deugdelijk*
validate [ov ww] • *geldig verklaren*
• *bekrachtigen, bevestigen*
valise [znw] *valies*
valley [znw] *dal*
valour [znw] *moed, dapperheid*
valuable [bnw] *erg waardevol, kostbaar*
valuation [znw] *schatting, taxatie*
value I [ov ww] • *waarderen, achten*
• *schatten, taxeren* II [znw] *waarde*
valve [znw] *klep, ventiel*
vamp I [ov ww] • *(~ up) spannender*

maken, oplappen, inpalmen II [on ww]
‹inf.› *verstrikken, flirten* III [znw] ‹inf.›
verleidster
vampire [znw] • *vampier* • *uitzuiger*
van [znw] *(bestel-/meubel-/post)wagen*
vanguard [znw] *voorhoede*
vanilla [znw] *vanille*
vanish [on ww] *verdwijnen*
vanity [znw] *ijdelheid, verwaandheid*
vanquish [ov ww] *overwinnen,*
bedwingen
vapid [bnw] *saai, lusteloos*
vaporize I [ov ww] • *doen verdampen*
• *besproeien* II [on ww] *verdampen*
vaporous [bnw] *dampig, damp-*
vapour [znw] *damp*
variable I [znw] *veranderlijke grootheid*
II [bnw] *veranderlijk, ongedurig*
variance [znw] • *onenigheid*
• *tegenspraak*
variant I [znw] *variant* II [bnw]
afwijkend
variation [znw] • *variëteit* • ‹muz.›
variatie
varied [bnw] • *gevarieerd* • *bont* ‹v.
kleur›
variegated [bnw] • *bont* ‹v. kleur›
• *afwisselend*
variety [znw] • *variatie*
• *verscheidenheid* • *soort* • *variété*
various [bnw] *verschillend, verscheiden*
varnish I [ov ww] *vernissen* • *(~ over)*
verbloemen II [znw] • *vernis* • *glazuur*
vary [ov + on ww] • *variëren, veranderen*
• *verschillen*
vascular [bnw] *vaat-*
vase [znw] *vaas*
vassal [znw] • *vazal* • *slaaf*
vast [bnw] • *veelomvattend*
• *onmetelijk, reusachtig*
vault I [ov ww] *springen* ‹steunend op
handen of stok› II [znw] • *wijnkelder,
grafkelder* • *kluis* ‹bank›
veal [znw] *kalfsvlees*
veer [on ww] • *van koers veranderen*
• *omlopen* ‹v. wind› • *draaien*

vegetable I [znw] • *groente* • *plant*
II [bnw] *plantaardig, planten-*
vegetate [on ww] *vegeteren*
vegetation [znw] • *plantengroei*
• *plantenwereld*
vehemence [znw] *heftigheid*
vehement [bnw] *heftig*
vehicle [znw] • *voertuig* • *drager* ‹fig.›
veil I [ov ww] • *sluieren* • *bedekken*
‹fig.›, *vermommen* II [znw] • *sluier,
voile* • *dekmantel*
vein [znw] • *ader* • *nerf, geest* ‹fig.›
velocity [znw] *snelheid*
velvet [znw] *fluweel*
venal [bnw] *omkoopbaar*
vend [ov ww] *verkopen, venten*
vendetta [znw] *bloedwraak*
vendor [znw] *verkoper*
veneer [znw] • *fineer(bladen),
fineerhout* • *vernisje* ‹fig.›
venerable [bnw] • *eerbiedwaardig*
• *hoogeerwaarde* ‹in angl. kerk, als
titel v. aartsdiaken›
venerate [ov ww] *vereren*
vengeance [znw] *wraak*
vengeful [bnw] *wraakgierig*
venial [bnw] *vergeeflijk*
venison [znw] *reebout, wildbraad*
venom [znw] • *vergif* • *venijn*
venomous [bnw] • *(ver)giftig*
• *venijnig*
vent I [ov ww] *lucht geven aan, uiten*
II [znw] • *schoorsteenkanaal* • *uitweg,
opening* • *luchtgat*
ventilate [ov ww] • *luchten* ‹v.
grieven› • *ventileren, luchten* • *in 't
openbaar bespreken*
ventricle [znw] • *holte* ‹in hersenen›
• *hartkamer*
ventriloquism [znw] *het buikspreken*
ventriloquist [znw] *buikspreker*
venture I [ov + on ww] *riskeren, wagen,
op 't spel zetten* • *(~ out)* z. *buiten
wagen* II [znw] • *(riskante)
onderneming* • *avontuurlijke reis*
venturesome [bnw] *stoutmoedig,*

gewaagd
venue [znw] *plaats v. samenkomst*
veracious [bnw] *waarheidlievend*
veracity [znw] *waarheid(sliefde)*
verb [znw] *werkwoord*
verbiage [znw] *woordenstroom*
verbose [bnw] *woordenrijk, breedsprakig*
verdant [bnw] *met weelderige plantengroei overdekt*
verdict [znw] • *uitspraak <v. rechter>* • *oordeel, beslissing*
verge I [on ww] *neigen* • *(~ on) grenzen aan* II [znw] *berm, rand*
verger [znw] *koster*
verifiable [bnw] *verifieerbaar*
verify [ov ww] • *verifiëren* • *bewijzen, bevestigen*
verisimilitude [znw] *waarschijnlijkheid*
veritable [bnw] *echt, waar*
vermin [znw] • *ongedierte* • *schoelje*
verminous [bnw] *vol ongedierte*
vernacular I [znw] *landstaal* II [bnw] *inheems, vaderlands*
versatile [bnw] *veelzijdig*
verse [znw] • *vers(regel)* • *couplet* • *poëzie*
versed [bnw] *ervaren, bedreven*
version [znw] • *lezing, versie* • *bewerking*
vertebra [znw] *wervel*
vertebrate I [znw] <bio.> *gewerveld dier* II [bnw] *gewerveld*
vertical I [znw] *loodlijn* II [bnw] *verticaal*
vertiginous [bnw] *duizelingwekkend*
vertigo [znw] *duizeling <vooral door hoogtevrees veroorzaakt>*
verve [znw] *geestdrift, vuur*
very I [bnw] • *juist, precies* • *zelfde* II [bijw] • *aller-* • *zeer, heel*
vessel [znw] • *vat* • *vaartuig, schip*
vest [znw] • *(onder)hemd* • *<AE> vest*
vestige [znw] *spoortje*
vestry [znw] • *sacristie*

• *consistoriekamer*
vet I [ov ww] *grondig onderzoeken, behandelen* II [znw] • —> **veterinarian** • —> **veteran**
veteran [znw] • *veteraan* • *oud-militair*
veterinarian [znw] *dierenarts*
veterinary [bnw] *dierenarts-*
veto I [ov ww] *verbieden* II [znw] *veto, verbod*
vex [ov ww] *plagen, ergeren, hinderen*
vexation [znw] • *plagerij, kwelling* • *ergernis*
viable [bnw] • *levensvatbaar* • *uitvoerbaar*
vial [znw] *medicijnflesje*
vibrate I [ov ww] *doen vibreren, doen trillen* II [on ww] *vibreren, trillen*
vicar [znw] *dominee <angl. kerk>, predikant*
vicarage [znw] • *predikantsplaats* • *pastorie*
vicarious [bnw] *indirect belevend of beleefd*
vice [znw] • *verdorvenheid, fout, gebrek, ondeugd* • *kuur <v. paard>* • *bankschroef*
vicinity [znw] *buurt, nabijheid*
vicious [bnw] *venijnig*
victim [znw] *(slacht)offer*
victimize [ov ww] *tot slachtoffer maken*
victor [znw] *overwinnaar*
Victorian [bnw] • *Victoriaans, uit de tijd v. koningin Victoria* • *v.d. kolonie Victoria*
victorious [bnw] *zegevierend*
victory [znw] *overwinning*
video [znw] *videorecorder, videotape*
vie [on ww] *wedijveren*
view I [ov ww] *bekijken, beschouwen* II [znw] • *(ver)gezicht, uitzicht* • *standpunt* • *idee, denkbeeld* • *bedoeling*
viewer [znw] • *kijker* • *bezichtiger* • *viewer*
vigil [znw] *(nacht)wake*
vignette [znw] • *vignet* • *karakterschets*

vigorous [bnw] *krachtig, vitaal, energiek*
vigour [znw] *kracht, vitaliteit, activiteit*
vile [bnw] • *walgelijk, verdorven, gemeen* • *afschuwelijk, vies*
vilify [ov ww] *belasteren, beschimpen*
village [znw] *dorp*
villager [znw] *dorpsbewoner*
villain [znw] *schurk*
villainous [bnw] *schurkachtig, gemeen*
villainy [znw] *schurkerij*
vindicate [ov ww] • *staven* • *het gelijk bewijzen van*
vindictive [bnw] *rancuneus, wraakzuchtig*
vine [znw] • *wijnstok* • *klimplant*
vinegar [znw] *azijn*
vintage I [znw] *wijn uit een goed jaar* II [bnw] *v. goede kwaliteit*
vintner [znw] *wijnhandelaar*
viola [znw] • <muz.> *altviool* • <plantk.> *viooltje*
violate [ov ww] • *overtreden* • *breken* <v. gelofte> • *onteren, ontwijden, schenden*
violence [znw] *geweld(dadigheid), gewelddaad*
violent [bnw] • *hevig, heftig* • *gewelddadig*
violet I [znw] *viooltje* II [bnw] *violet*
violin [znw] *viool*
violinist [znw] *violist*
viper [znw] *adder*
virgin I [znw] *maagd* II [bnw] • *maagdelijk* • *onbevlekt, ongerept* • *onbetreden* <gebied>
virginal [bnw] *maagdelijk*
virtual [bnw] *feitelijk, eigenlijk*
virtue [znw] • *deugd(zaamheid)* • *(goede) eigenschap*
virtuoso [znw] *virtuoos*
virtuous [bnw] *deugdzaam*
virulent [bnw] *vergiftig, kwaadaardig*
visa [znw] *visum*
vis-à-vis [vz] *vis-à-vis, (recht) tegenover*
viscosity [znw] *kleverigheid*
viscount [znw] *burggraaf*

viscountess [znw] *burggravin*
viscous [bnw] *kleverig*
visible [bnw] • *zichtbaar* • *duidelijk, merkbaar*
vision [znw] • *gezicht(svermogen)* • *visioen, verschijning*
visionary I [znw] • *ziener* • *fantast* II [bnw] • *fantastisch* • *ingebeeld*
visit I [ov ww] *bezoeken* • (~ (up)on) *teisteren* • (~ with) <AE> *bezoeken* II [znw] *bezoek*
visitation [znw] • *visitatie* • *huisbezoek* <v. geestelijke>
visitor [znw] *gast, bezoeker*
visor [znw] • *vizier* <v. helm> • *klep* <v. pet> • *zonneklep* <in auto>
vista [znw] • *vergezicht* • *perspectief*
visual [bnw] • *gezichts-, oog-* • *zichtbaar*
visualize [ov ww] *zich een beeld vormen van*
vital [bnw] • *levens-* • *vitaal*
vitality [znw] *vitaliteit, levenskracht*
vitamin [znw] *vitamine*
vitiate [ov ww] • *verzwakken* • *aantasten* • *ongeldig maken*
vitreous [bnw] *glazen, glasachtig, glas-*
vitriol [znw] • *vitriool* • *venijn*
vitriolic [bnw] • *vitriool-* • *venijnig, bijtend*
vituperative [bnw] *schimpend*
vivacious [bnw] *opgewekt, levendig*
vivacity [znw] *opgewektheid*
vivisection [znw] *vivisectie*
vivisectionist [znw] *vivisector*
vixen [znw] • *wijfjesvos* • *feeks, helleveeg*
vocabulary [znw] • *woordenlijst* • *woordenschat*
vocal [bnw] • *mondeling* • *mondig* • *stem-*
vocalist [znw] *zanger(es)*
vocation [znw] • *roeping* • *beroep*
vogue [znw] *mode, populariteit*
voice I [ov ww] *uitdrukking geven aan* <gevoelens> II [znw] • *stem* • *geluid* • *inspraak*

void I [znw] • leegte • (ledige) ruimte
II [bnw] • nietig <v. contract>
• onbezet, ledig
volatile [bnw] • vluchtig <vloeistoffen>
• wispelturig
volcanic [bnw] vulkanisch
volcano [znw] vulkaan
volition [znw] het willen, wilskracht
voltage [znw] elektrische spanning
voluble [bnw] veel en enthousiast
pratend
volume [znw] • boekdeel • omvang,
volume <v. zaken> • geluidssterkte
voluminous [bnw] • (te) groot <v.
kleren> • omvangrijk, lijvig
voluntary I [znw] <muz.> solo op orgel
II [bnw] • opzettelijk • door de wil
geregeld <v. spierbeweging> • vrijwillig
volunteer I [ov ww] ongevraagd iets
geven of doen II [on ww] • aanbieden
iets te doen • in dienst gaan III [znw]
vrijwilliger
voluptuous [bnw] • weelderig <v.
vormen> • wellustig • heerlijk
vomit I [ov + on ww] braken II [znw]
• braaksel • braakmiddel
voracious [bnw] gulzig, vraatzuchtig
vortex [znw] draaikolk, maalstroom
vote I [ov + on ww] stemmen (op)
II [znw] stem
voter [znw] • kiezer • stemgerechtigde
vouch [on ww] • (~ for) instaan voor,
borg staan voor
voucher [znw] • (waarde)coupon • bon
• reçu
vouchsafe [ov ww] • in bewaring geven
• verzekeren
vow [znw] eed, gelofte
vowel [znw] klinker(teken)
voyage [znw] (zee)reis
voyager [znw] zeevaarder, (zee)reiziger
voyeur [znw] gluurder, voyeur
vulgar [bnw] vulgair, ordinair, grof,
laag
vulnerable [bnw] kwetsbaar
vulture [znw] gier

W

wacky [bnw] idioot, vreselijk excentriek
wad [znw] • prop • pakje bankbiljetten
waddle [on ww] waggelen
wader [znw] • waadvogel • waterlaars
wafer [znw] • wafel • hostie
waffle I [on ww] kletsen II [znw] • wafel
• geklets
waft I [ov ww] voeren II [on ww] zweven
III [znw] vleugje
wag I [ov ww] • heen en weer bewegen,
schudden • kwispelen II [on ww]
kwispelen III [znw] grappenmaker
wage I [ov ww] voeren <vnl. v. oorlog>
II [znw] loon
wager I [ov + on ww] (ver)wedden
II [znw] weddenschap
waggle [ww] → wag
waif [znw] • zwerver, dakloze
• verwaarloosd kind
wail I [on ww] • jammeren, weeklagen
• huilen, loeien <v. wind> II [znw]
jammerende uitroep
waist [znw] taille, middel
wait I [on ww] • wachten • bedienen
<aan tafel> • (~ (up)on) bedienen, van
dienst zijn • (~ for) wachten op
II [znw] • wachttijd • pauze
waiter [znw] kelner
waitress [znw] serveerster
waive [ov ww] afstand doen van, afzien
van
wake I [ov ww] wekken • (~ up) wakker
maken/schudden II [on ww] wakker
zijn, waken • (~ up) wakker worden
III [znw] (kiel)zog
wakeful [bnw] • slapeloos • waakzaam,
wakker
waken I [ov ww] wakker maken
II [on ww] wakker worden
walk I [ov ww] • lopen/wandelen in/op
• stapvoets doen gaan, laten stappen,

uitlaten II [on ww] *lopen, wandelen,
stapvoets gaan* • (~ **into**) *onverwachts
betrokken raken bij, makkelijk krijgen*
‹v. baan› III [znw] • *wandeling*
• *manier v.* lopen • *wandelpad*
walker [znw] *voetganger, wandelaar*
wall I [ov ww] • (~ **in**) *ommuren*
• (~ **up**) *afsluiten met een muur,
dichtmetselen* II [znw] • *wand, muur*
• *stadswal*
wallaby [znw] *kleine kangoeroe*
wallet [znw] *portefeuille*
wallop I [ov ww] *afranselen* II [znw]
mep, opdonder
walloping [znw] *aframmeling*
wallow I [on ww] *rollen* • (~ **in**) (z.)
wentelen in II [znw] *poel* ‹voor dieren›
walnut [znw] • *walnoot* • *notenhout*
waltz I [on ww] • *walsen* • *ontspannen
en zelfverzekerd lopen* II [znw] *wals*
wan [bnw] *bleek, flets*
wand [znw] (tover)staf
wander [on ww] • *rondwandelen,
zwerven, dwalen, ronddolen* • *afdwalen*
wanderer [znw] *zwerver*
wane I [on ww] *afnemen, tanen* II [znw]
het afnemen
wangle I [ov ww] *voor elkaar krijgen,
gedaan krijgen* II [znw] *knoeierij*
want I [ov ww] • *missen, ontberen*
• *nodig hebben* • *wensen, willen*
II [znw] • *behoefte* • *gemis, gebrek*
wanting [bnw] *ontbrekend*
wanton [bnw] • *speels* • *lichtzinnig*
• *baldadig*
war I [on ww] *strijden* (tegen), *oorlog
voeren* (tegen) II [znw] *oorlog*
ward I [ov ww] • (~ **off**) *afweren,
behoeden voor, pareren* II [znw] • *zaal,
afdeling* • *curatele, voogdij* • *pupil* ‹v.
voogd› • *stadsdistrict*
warden [znw] • *huismeester* • *bewaker*
• (parkeer)wacht
warder [znw] *cipier*
wardrobe [znw] • *kleerkast* • *garderobe*
warehouse [znw] *pakhuis,*

opslagplaats, magazijn
warm I [ov + on ww] (ver)warmen,
warm maken/worden • (~ **up**) *warmer
maken/worden, opwarmen* II [bnw]
• *warm, heet* • *hartelijk*
warmth [znw] • *warmte* • *hartelijkheid*
warn [ov + on ww] *waarschuwen*
warning [znw] *waarschuwing*
warp I [ov ww] • *doen kromtrekken*
• *vervormen, verkeerd richten,*
(verkeerd) *beïnvloeden* II [on ww]
• *kromtrekken* • *afwijken* III [znw]
• *schering* • *kromming* • (psychische)
afwijking
warrant I [ov ww] *rechtvaardigen,
wettigen* II [znw] • *machtiging*
• *bevel(schrift)*
warrior [znw] *krijger*
wart [znw] *wrat*
wary [bnw] *behoedzaam*
was [ww] verl. tijd → **be**
wash I [ov ww] *wassen, spoelen*
• (~ **down**) *wegspoelen* • (~ **out**)
uitwassen • (~ **up**) *afwassen*
II [on ww] • *wassen* • *spoelen/stromen
langs* • (~ **out**) *door wassen eruit gaan*
• (~ **up**) *de afwas doen* III [znw]
• *wasbeurt* • *was* • *deining, het spoelen*
• *dun laagje*
washable [bnw] (af)wasbaar
washer [znw] • *sluitring, kraanleertje,
pakking* • *wasmachine*
wasp [znw] *wesp*
waspish [bnw] *venijnig, nijdig,
prikkelbaar*
wastage [znw] *verkwisting*
waste I [ov ww] *verkwisten, verknoeien,
verloren laten gaan* II [on ww]
• (~ **away**) *wegkwijnen, wegteren*
III [znw] • *verkwisting* • *afval*
• *braakliggend land* IV [bnw] • *woest,
braak* • *afval-*
wasteful [bnw] *verkwistend*
watch I [ov ww] • *bekijken, nakijken*
• *in de gaten houden* • *bewaken, zorgen
voor* II [on ww] *kijken* • (~ **for**)

uitkijken naar III [znw] • wacht
• nachtwake • horloge
watchful [bnw] waakzaam
water I [ov ww] besproeien, water geven
• (~ **down**) verwateren, verzachten
II [on ww] • wateren <v. mand>
• tranen <v. ogen> III [znw] water
watery [bnw] • waterig • verwaterd
wave I [ov ww] • zwaaien met • met een
gebaar te kennen geven • (~ **aside**)
afwijzen • (~ **away**) beduiden weg te
gaan II [on ww] • golven, wapperen
• zwaaien, wuiven III [znw] • golf
• golving • wuivend gebaar
wavy [bnw] golvend
wax I [ov ww] boenen, met was
inwrijven, poetsen II [on ww]
• toenemen • <vero.> worden III [znw]
• lak • oorsmeer • woedeaanval • was
IV [bnw] was-, wassen
waxen [bnw] wasbleek
waxy [bnw] wasachtig
way [znw] • weg • richting, kant
• eind(je), afstand • wijze, manier (van
doen), methode
we [pers vnw] wij
weaken [ov + on ww] verzwakken,
verslappen
weakness [znw] • zwak punt
• zwakheid
weal [znw] striem
weapon [znw] wapen
wear I [ov ww] • dragen, aanhebben
• afslijten, uitslijten, verslijten
• uitputten, afmatten • (~ **away**)
uitslijten • (~ **down**) afmatten
• (~ **out**) verslijten, afdragen,
uitputten II [on ww] afslijten,
verslijten • (~ **away/off**) slijten, steeds
minder worden • (~ **down**) afslijten
• (~ **on**) langzaam voorbijgaan
• (~ **out**) slijten, uitgeput raken
III [znw] • dracht • slijtage
wearing [bnw] • moeizaam
• vermoeiend
wearisome [bnw] • vervelend

• vermoeiend
weary I [on ww] moe worden II [bnw]
• moe • beu • vermoeiend • vervelend
weasel [znw] wezel
weather I [ov ww] doorstaan
II [on ww] verweren III [znw] weer
weave I [ov ww] • weven • in elkaar
zetten II [znw] weeftrant, patroon,
dessin
weaver [znw] wever
web [znw] • web • zwemvlies
wed [ov + on ww] trouwen
we'd [samentr.] /we should/ /we had/
/we would/ → shall, have, will
wedding [znw]
• huwelijksplechtigheid • bruiloft
wedge I [ov ww] • proppen • een wig
slaan/steken in, vastzetten II [znw]
• wig • stuk kaas, taartpunt • sector
wedlock [znw] • huwelijk • echtelijke
staat
Wednesday [znw] woensdag
weed I [ov ww] wieden II [znw]
• onkruid • <inf.> marihuana • <inf.>
zaadje
weekly I [znw] weekblad
II [bnw + bijw] wekelijks
weep [on ww] • wenen • vocht
afscheiden
weigh I [ov ww] • wegen, z. laten wegen
• overwegen • (~ **down**)
(terneer)drukken, doen (door)buigen
• (~ **out**) afwegen II [on ww] • gewicht
in de schaal leggen, (mee)tellen
• wegen
weight I [ov ww] verzwaren II [znw]
• gewicht • belang • zwaar voorwerp
weighting [znw] toelage, toeslag,
standplaatstoelage
weighty [bnw] • gewichtig, belangrijk
• zwaar
weir [znw] • (stuw)dam • weer
weird [bnw] • akelig, griezelig • vreemd
welcome I [ov ww] verwelkomen in
II [znw] ontvangst, verwelkoming
III [bnw] welkom

weld I [ov ww] • *lassen* • *samenvoegen*
II [znw] *las*
welfare [znw] • *uitkering* • *bestwil*
• *sociale voorzieningen*
well I [on ww] *(omhoog) wellen,*
ontspringen II [znw] • *put* • *bron*
III [bnw] • *goed, beter, gezond*
• *in orde* IV [bijw] • *goed, goed en wel*
• *behoorlijk* • *een heel eind*
V [tw] • *nou* • *nou ja* • *och ja*
• *welnu*
we'll [samentr.] /we shall/ /we will/
→ **shall, will**
welt [znw] *striem*
welter [znw] *chaos, verwarring*
went [ww] verl. tijd → **go**
wept [ww] verl. tijd + volt. deelw.
→ **weep**
were [ww] verl. tijd → **be**
we're [samentr.] /we are/ → **be**
weren't [samentr.] /were not/ → **be**
west I [znw] *westen* II [bnw + bijw]
west(en), westelijk
westerner [znw] *westerling*
westernize [ov ww] *westers maken*
wet I [ov ww] *nat maken,*
bevochtigen II [znw] *nat(tigheid)*
III [bnw] *nat, vochtig*
we've [samentr.] /we have/ → **have**
whack I [ov ww] *(erop) slaan,*
meppen II [znw] • *smak, klap, mep*
• *(aan)deel, portie*
whale [znw] *walvis*
whaler [znw] *walvisvaarder*
whaling [znw] *walvisvangst*
wharf [znw] *kade, laad-/lossteiger*
what I [vr vnw] *wat voor, welk(e), wat*
II [betr vnw] *wat* III [tw] *hè*
whatever, whatsoever [vnw]
• *wat/welke...ook* • *wat/welke...toch*
wheat [znw] *tarwe*
wheedle [on ww] *flemen, vleien,*
bedelen
wheel I [ov ww] *duwen, laten rijden,*
kruien II [on ww] • *rijden, rollen*
• *zwenken* • *(~ round) (om)zwenken,*

z. *omdraaien* III [znw] • *wiel, rad*
• *stuur* • *spinnewiel*
• *pottenbakkersschijf*
wheeze I [on ww] • *piepen* ‹bij 't
ademhalen› • *hijgen* II [znw] *foefje*
whelp I [on ww] *jongen, werpen*
II [znw] *welp*
when I [bijw] *wanneer* II [vw] • *terwijl*
• *toen* • *als*
whenever I [bijw] *wanneer ook maar*
II [vw] *telkens wanneer*
where I [bijw] *waarheen, waar* II [vw]
terwijl
whereas [vw] *terwijl*
wherever I [bijw] *waar toch (heen)*
II [vw] *waar(heen) ook, overal*
waar(heen)
whet [ov ww] *prikkelen, opwekken,*
slijpen
whether [vw] *of*
which I [vr vnw] *wie, wat, welk(e)*
II [betr vnw] *die, dat, welke, wat,*
hetwelk
whichever I [bnw] *welk(e)..ook*
II [onb vnw] *welk(e)*
whiff [znw] *zuchtje, vleugje*
while I [ov ww] • *(~ away) verdrijven v.*
tijd II [znw] *tijd(je), poosje* III [vw]
terwijl, hoewel
whim [znw] *gril, nuk*
whimper I [ov + on ww] *zachtjes*
janken II [znw] *zacht gejank*
whimsical [bnw] • *wispelturig*
• *eigenaardig*
whine I [ov + on ww] • *jengelen,*
dreinen, janken • *gieren* II [znw]
• *gezeur* • *gejammer* • *het gieren*
whinny I [on ww] *hinniken* II [znw]
gehinnik
whip I [ov ww] • *kloppen* • *de zweep*
leggen over, geselen, (af)ranselen, slaan
• *opzwepen* • *(~ off) snel te voorschijn*
halen, eruit flappen • *(~ up) haastig in*
elkaar zetten, opzwepen II [on ww]
• *fladderen* • *wippen, schieten*
• *(~ round) z. snel omdraaien*

III [znw] *zweep*
whirl I [ov + on ww] • *draaien* • *snel rond draaien, rondtollen* **II** [znw] • *werveling, draaikolk* • *roes*
whirr I [on ww] *gonzen, snorren* **II** [znw] *snorrend geluid*
whisk I [ov ww] • *tikken, zwaaien, zwiepen, slaan* • *(op)kloppen* • *(~ away) in een flits wegvoeren/-werken* **II** [on ww] *z. snel bewegen, wegglippen* • *(~ round) z. plotseling omdraaien* **III** [znw] • *garde, eierklopper* • *tik, veeg, snelle beweging*
whisker [znw] *snorhaar <v. kat/hond>*
whisper I [on ww] *fluisteren* **II** [znw] • *gefluister* • *geruis*
whistle I [ov + on ww] *fluiten* **II** [znw] • *fluit(je)* • *gefluit*
whit [znw] *greintje*
white I [znw] *blanke* **II** [bnw] • *wit* • *bleek* • *blank*
whiten I [ov ww] *bleken* **II** [on ww] *wit worden*
whitening [znw] • *krijtpoeder* • *witkalk*
whiting [znw] • *witkalk* • *wijting*
whittle [ov ww] *(af)snijden* • *(~ away) verminderen* • *(~ down) besnoeien, kleiner maken*
who I [vr vnw] *wie* **II** [betr vnw] *die, wie*
whoever [vnw] *wie (dan) ook*
whole I [znw] *geheel* **II** [bnw] • *heel* • *ongeschonden, gezond*
wholesale [bnw] • *massaal, op grote schaal* • *m.b.t. de groothandel*
wholesaler [znw] *grossier*
wholly [bijw] *geheel*
whom [vnw] → *who*
whoop I [ov + on ww] *schreeuwen* **II** [znw] *uitroep*
whopper [znw] • *enorme leugen* • *kanjer, knaap*
whopping [bnw] *enorm, kolossaal*
whore [znw] *hoer*
whorl [znw] *spiraalvorm*
whose [vr vnw] *wier, van wie, v. welke,*

wiens, ervan, waarvan
wicked [bnw] • *slecht, gemeen, vals* • *ondeugend*
wicker [znw] *vlechtwerk, mandwerk*
wicket [znw] *wicket <cricket>*
wide I [bnw] • *wijd, breed* • *uitgestrekt, uitgebreid, groot, ruim* **II** [bijw] • *wijdbeens* • *wijd open*
widen [ov + on ww] *verbreden, wijder maken/worden*
widow [znw] *weduwe*
widower [znw] *weduwnaar*
width [znw] • *wijdte, breedte* • *ruimheid*
wield [ov ww] *gebruiken, zwaaien*
wife [znw] *vrouw, echtgenote*
wig [znw] *pruik*
wiggle I [ov ww] *doen wiebelen, (snel op en neer) bewegen* **II** [znw] *gewiebel*
wild [bnw] • *wild* • *woedend* • *enthousiast*
wildcat I [znw] *wilde kat* **II** [bnw] *financieel onbetrouwbaar*
wilful [bnw] • *opzettelijk* • *koppig, dwars*
will I [ov + on ww] *willen* **II** [ov ww] *nalaten, vermaken* **III** [hww] • *zullen* • *willen* **IV** [znw] • *wil, wilskracht* • *testament*
willing [bnw] *bereid(willig), gewillig*
willow [znw] *wilg*
willowy [bnw] *soepel*
willy-nilly [bijw] *goedschiks of kwaadschiks*
wilt I [ww] → *will* **II** [ov + on ww] *(doen) verwelken, slap doen/gaan hangen*
wily [bnw] *sluw*
wimple [znw] *kap <v. non>*
win I [ov ww] • *winnen* • *behalen, verwerven, bereiken* • *(~ back) terugwinnen* **II** [on ww] *winnen* • *(~ out) 't winnen* • *(~ through) te boven komen, z. erdoorheen slaan* **III** [znw] • *overwinning* • *succes*
winch [znw] *lier, windas*

wind I [ov ww] (op)winden, (omhoog)
draaien • (~ **down**) naar beneden
draaien <v. autoruit>, af laten lopen <v.
veer> • (~ **up**) opdraaien <v.
mechaniek>, omhoogdraaien, op stang
jagen, beëindigen, opwinden
II [on ww] zich slingeren • (~ **down**)
aflopen <v. veer>, zich ontspannen
• (~ **round**) kronkelen • (~ **up**)
terechtkomen III [znw] • adem • lucht
• wind
windlass [znw] windas, lier
window [znw] • raam • loket • etalage
windscreen [znw] voorruit
windward [bnw] naar de wind gericht
windy [bnw] • winderig • breedsprakig
• bang
wine [znw] wijn
wing I [on ww] vliegen II [znw]
• vleugel • wiek • spatbord
winged [bnw] met vleugels
wink I [ov + on ww] • knipperen
• knipogen • flikkeren • (~ **at**)
knipogen naar, oogluikend toelaten
II [znw] • knipoog • wenk
winner [znw] • winnaar • succes
winning [bnw] innemend
winsome [bnw] innemend, sympathiek
winter I [ov + on ww] de winter
doorbrengen II [znw] winter
wipe I [ov ww] (af)vegen, afdrogen
• (~ **away**) wegvegen • (~ **out**)
uitvegen, wegvagen, totaal vernietigen
• (~ **up**) opvegen II [znw] • veeg
wiper [znw] ruitenwisser
wire I [ov ww] • met draad
vastzetten/versterken • telegraferen
• <techn.> aansluiten II [znw]
• telegram • (metaal)draad
wireless I [znw] radio II [bnw]
draadloos
wiry [bnw] • taai • weerbarstig
wisdom [znw] wijsheid
wise I [ov + on ww] • (~ **up**) iets
doorkrijgen II [znw] <vero.> wijze,
manier III [bnw] wijs, verstandig

wish I [ov + on ww] • wensen,
toewensen • verlangen II [znw] wens
wisp [znw] • (rook)sliert • bos(je) • piek
<v. haar>
wispy [bnw] piekerig, spichtig
wistful [bnw] treurig, droefgeestig
wit [znw] • geestigheid • geestig persoon
witch [znw] heks
with [vz] • met • van • bij
withdraw I [ov ww] • terugnemen
• terugtrekken II [on ww] z.
terugtrekken
withdrawal [znw] • het terugtrekken
• het terugnemen
withdrawn [bnw] • teruggetrokken
• verlegen
wither [ov + on ww] (doen) verwelken,
verschrompelen, verdorren, (uit)drogen
withhold I [ov ww] terughouden, niet
geven II [on ww] z. weerhouden, z.
onthouden
within I [bijw] (van) binnen, in huis
II [vz] binnen (in)
without [vz] zonder
withstand [ov ww] weerstaan,
weerstand bieden (aan)
witless [bnw] onnozel, stupide, dom
witness I [ov ww] getuige zijn v.
II [znw] getuige
witticism [znw] geestigheid
witty [bnw] geestig
wives [mv] → **wife**
wizard [znw] tovenaar
wizardry [znw] toverkunst(en)
wobble [on ww] wiebelen, schommelen
woe [znw] wee
woke [ww] verl. tijd + volt. deelw.
→ **wake**
woken [ww] volt. deelw. → **wake**
wolf I [ov ww] • (~ **down**) opschrokken
II [znw] wolf
wolves [mv] → **wolf**
woman [znw] • vrouw • werkster
womanish [bnw] verwijfd,
sentimenteel
womankind [znw] de vrouwen

womanly [bnw] *vrouwelijk*
womb [znw] *baarmoeder, schoot*
women [mv] → **woman**
won [ww] *verl. tijd + volt. deelw.*
→ **win**
wonder I [on ww] • *verbaasd staan*
• *zich afvragen* • *benieuwd zijn* • (~ **at**)
zich verwonderen over II [znw]
• *wonder* • *verwondering*
wonderful [bnw] *prachtig, schitterend*
wonderment [znw] *verwondering*
wondrous [bnw + bijw] *verwonderlijk,*
buitengewoon
wont ‹form.› [bnw] *gewoon, gewend*
won't [samentr.] /will not/ → **will**
woo [ov ww] • *de gunst proberen te*
winnen van • *het hof maken*
wood [znw] • *hout* • *bos*
wooded [bnw] *bebost*
wooden [bnw] *houten, houterig, stijf*
woodwind [znw] *blaasinstrumenten*
woodwork [znw] • *houtwerk* ‹in
gebouw› • *houtbewerking*
woody [bnw] • *bosrijk* • *hout-*
woof I [on ww] *blaffen* II [znw] • *inslag*
• *weefsel* • *blaf*
wool [znw] *wol*
woollen [bnw] *wollen*
woolly I [znw] *wollen trui* II [bnw]
wollig
word I [ov ww] *uitdrukken, verwoorden*
II [znw] • *woord* • *bericht, nieuws*
• *bevel* • *parool, wachtwoord*
wording [znw] *bewoordingen, stijl,*
redactie
wordy [bnw] *woordenrijk, langdradig*
wore [ww] *verl. tijd* → **wear**
work I [ov ww] • *laten werken*
• *bedienen, exploiteren* • *bewerken,*
kneden, smeden • (~ **in**) *erin werken,*
ertussen werken • (~ **into**) *tot ...*
brengen • (~ **off**) *te boven komen,*
afreageren • (~ **out**) *berekenen*
• (~ **over**) *aftuigen* • (~ **up**) *opwerken,*
aanzetten II [on ww] • *werken* • *effect*
hebben, gaan, functioneren • (*nerveus*)

trekken • (~ **on**) *dóórwerken, werken*
op • (~ **out**) *uitkomen, trainen, lukken*
III [znw] • *werk, arbeid* • *naaiwerk,*
breiwerk, borduurwerk • *werkstuk*
workable [bnw] *bruikbaar*
workaday [bnw] *alledaags, saai*
worker [znw] *werker, arbeider*
working I [znw] • *werking* • *mijn*
II [bnw] • *werk-, bedrijfs-* • *werkend,*
praktisch, bruikbaar
world [znw] *wereld*
worldly [bnw] • *aards* • *werelds*
worm I [ov ww] *ontwormen* II [znw]
worm
wormy [bnw] • *wormstekig* • *vol*
wormen
worn I [ww] *volt. deelw.* → **wear**
II [bnw] • *versleten* • *gedragen*
worried [bnw] *bezorgd*
worrisome [bnw] *lastig, vervelend,*
zorgelijk
worry I [ov ww] *lastig vallen, vervelen,*
(*aan 't hoofd*) *zaniken* II [on ww]
piekeren, z. zorgen maken III [znw]
• *zorg* • *tobberij*
worrying [bnw] *zorgwekkend, zorgelijk*
worse [bnw + bijw] *slechter, erger*
worsen [ov + on ww] *verergeren*
worship I [ov ww] *aanbidden* II [znw]
• *verering, aanbidding* • *eredienst*
worshipful [bnw] *eerbiedig*
worshipper [znw] • *vereerder*
• *gelovige, kerkganger*
worsted [znw] *wol, kamgaren*
worth I [znw] *waarde* II [bnw] *waard*
worthless [bnw] *waardeloos*
worthy I [znw] *beroemdheid, held*
II [bnw] • *waardig* • *waard*
• (*achtens*)*waardig, braaf*
would [ww] *verl. tijd* → **will**
wound I [ww] *verl.tijd + volt.deelw.*
→ **wind** II [ov ww] (*ver*)*wonden,*
krenken III [znw] *wond*
wove [ww] *verl. tijd* → **weave**
woven [ww] *volt. deelw.* → **weave**
wrangle I [on ww] *ruzie*

hebben/maken, kiften, vitten II [znw]
ruzie
wrap I [ov ww] *inpakken, wikkelen*
• (~ **up**) *afronden, inwikkelen*
II [on ww] • (~ **up**) *z. inpakken*
III [znw] • *omslagdoek* • *reisdeken*
wrapper [znw] *wikkel*
wrapping [znw] *(in)pakmateriaal*
wrath [znw] *toorn*
wreak [ov ww] *aanrichten*
wreath [znw] *krans, guirlande*
wreathe [ov ww] • (~ **in**) *omkransen,*
hullen in
wreck I [ov ww] • *doen schipbreuk*
lijden, doen verongelukken
• *vernietigen* II [znw] *ruïne,*
wrak(stukken), overblijfsel
wreckage [znw] *wrakstukken*
wrecker [znw] *verwoester*
wren [znw] *winterkoninkje*
wrench I [ov ww] • *ontwrichten,*
verstuiken • *wringen, rukken, draaien*
II [znw] • *ruk, draai* • *moersleutel*
• *pijnlijke scheiding*
wrest [ov ww] *wegrukken*
wrestle [ov + on ww] *worstelen (met)*
wrestler [znw] *worstelaar*
wrestling [znw] *het worstelen*
wretched [bnw] • *slecht, miserabel*
• *ellendig, diep ongelukkig*
wriggle I [ov + on ww] *wriemelen,*
(zich) kronkelen • (~ **out of**) *ontkomen*
aan II [znw] *gekronkel, gewriemel*
wring I [ov ww] *wringen* • (~ **out**)
uitwringen II [znw] *draai*
wringer [znw] *mangel*
wrinkle I [ov + on ww] *rimpelen,*
plooien II [znw] *rimpel, plooi*
wrist [znw] *pols*
write I [ov ww] *schrijven* • (~ **down**)
opschrijven • (~ **off**) *als afgeschreven*
beschouwen • (~ **out**) *uitschrijven,*
voluit schrijven • (~ **up**) *in het net*
schrijven II [on ww] *schrijven*
writer [znw] *schrijver*
write-up [znw] *rapport, recensie*

writhe [ov + on ww] *(z.) kronkelen*
writing I [znw] • *schrift* • *geschrift,*
handschrift II [bnw] *schrijf-*
written I [ww] *volt. deelw.* → **write**
II [bnw] *schriftelijk*
wrong I [ov ww] • *verkeerd beoordelen*
• *onrecht aandoen, onheus behandelen*
II [znw] • *kwaad, onrecht* • *iets*
verkeerds • *ongelijk* III [bnw + bijw]
• *verkeerd, niet in orde* • *slecht*
wrongful [bnw] • *onrechtmatig* • *fout*
wrote [ww] *verl. tijd* → **write**
wrung [ww] *verl. tijd + volt. deelw.*
→ **wring**

X

xenophobia [znw]
   vreemdelingenhaat/-angst
Xmas [znw] *Kerstmis*
X-ray I [ov ww] • *röntgenfoto maken*
   (v.) • *nauwkeurig onderzoeken* II [znw]
   röntgenfoto
xylophone [znw] *xylofoon*

Y

yacht [znw] *jacht*
yachting [znw] *zeilsport*
yank I [ov ww] *plotseling (weg)trekken,*
   rukken, trekken aan II [znw] *ruk, stoot,*
   klap
Yank, Yankee I [znw] *inwoner v.d. VS,*
   Amerikaan II [bnw] *Amerikaans*
yap I [on ww] • *keffen* • *kletsen* II [znw]
   gekef
yard [znw] • *yard (=91 cm)*
   • *binnenplaats, erf, plaats(je)* <bij huis>
   • *emplacement, werf*
yarn [znw] • *garen, draad* • *sterk verhaal*
yaw [on ww] • *uit de koers raken*
   • *slingeren* <v. vliegtuig/schip>
yawn I [on ww] *gapen, geeuwen*
   II [znw] • *geeuw* • *vervelend iets*
ye <vero.> I [pers vnw] *gij, u* II [lw] *de,*
   het
yea [znw] *ja*
year [znw] *jaar*
yearly [bnw + bijw] *jaar-, jaarlijks*
yearn [on ww] *smachten (naar)*
yearning I [znw] *vurig verlangen*
   II [bnw] *smachtend*
yeast [znw] *gist*
yell I [on ww] *schreeuwen* • (~ **out**)
   uitbrullen II [znw] *geschreeuw, gil*
yellow I [ov ww] *geel maken* II [on ww]
   vergelen, geel worden III [bnw] • *geel*
   • *laf*
yelp I [on ww] *janken* II [znw] *gejank*
yes [tw] *ja*
yesterday [bijw] *gisteren*
yet I [bijw] • *nog, tot nog toe* • *toch,*
   nochtans • *al* II [vw] *en toch, maar*
Yiddish I [znw] *de Jiddische taal*
   II [bnw] *Jiddisch*
yield I [ov ww] • *op-/voortbrengen,*
   opleveren • *afstaan* • (~ **up**) *opleveren,*
   afstaan II [on ww] • *toegeven* • *z.*

overgeven • bezwijken III [znw]
• *productie • opbrengst • oogst*
yielding [bnw] *meegaand/-gevend*
yippee [tw] *jippie!*
yodel I [ov + on ww] *jodelen* II [znw]
　gejodel
yoke I [ov ww] • *'t juk opleggen*
• *aanspannen* <v. ossen> • *verbinden*
II [znw] • *juk • heup-/schouderstuk* <v.
kledingstuk>
yokel [znw] *boerenpummel*
yolk [znw] *eidooier*
yonder [bijw] *daar(ginds)*
you [pers vnw] • *jullie, je • gij, u • men*
you'd [samentr.] /*you would*/ /*you
had*/ → **will, have**
you'll [samentr.] /*you will*/ /*you
shall*/ → **shall, will**
young [bnw] *jong*
youngster [znw] *jong mens, kind*
your [bez vnw] *uw, je*
you're [samentr.] /*you are*/ → **be**
yours [bez vnw] *jouwe, de/het uwe*
youth [znw] • *jeugd • jongeling*
youthful [bnw] *jeugdig, jong*
you've [samentr.] /*you have*/ → **have**
yowl I [on ww] *janken, huilen,
miauwen* II [znw] • *gejank • gemiauw*

Z

zany [bnw] *grappig, excentriek*
zap I [ov ww] <inf.> *doden, doodschieten*
II [on ww] *snel ergens heengaan*
• (~ **through**) *snel iets afmaken*
zeal [znw] *ijver, vuur*
zealot [znw] *fanatiekeling*
zealous [bnw] *ijverig*
zero I [on ww] • (~ **in/on**) *richten op*
II [znw] *nul(punt)* III [bnw] *nul-, geen*
zest [znw] • *vuur • animo*
zinc [znw] *zink*
zip I [ov ww] • (~ **up**) *dichtritsen*
II [znw] *ritssluiting*
zipper [znw] *ritssluiting*
zodiac [znw] *dierenriem*
zoo [znw] *dierentuin*
zoology [znw] *dierkunde*
zoom [on ww] • *zoemen • snel in prijs
stijgen* • (~ **in (on)**) *inzoomen (op)*

NTC's
Compact
Dutch
and
English
Dictionary

Contents

lijst van afkortingen

aanw vnw	aanwijzend voornaam-woord
adm.	administratie
AE	Amerikaans Engels
astrol.	astrologie
BE	Brits Engels
bel.	beledigend
betr vnw	betrekkelijk voornaam-woord
bez vnw	bezittelijk voornaam-woord
bijv.	bijvoorbeeld
bijw	bijwoord
bio.	biologie
bnw	bijvoeglijk naamwoord
chem.	scheikunde
comp.	informatica
econ.	economie
ev	enkelvoud
fig.	figuurlijk
form.	formeel
foto.	fotografie
geb. wijs	gebiedende wijs
geo.	geografie
gesch.	geschiedenis
hand.	handel
hww	hulpwerkwoord
inf.	informeel
iron.	ironisch
jur.	juridisch
kind.	kindertaal
kww	koppelwerkwoord
lit.	literatuur
luchtv.	luchtvaart
lw	lidwoord
m.b.t.	met betrekking tot
med.	medisch
mil.	militair
muz.	muziek
mv	meervoud
nat.	natuurkunde

neol.	neologisme
on ww	onovergankelijk werk-woord
onb vnw	onbepaald voornaamwoord
onp ww	onpersoonlijk werkwoord
onv ww	onvervoegbaar werkwoord
ov ww	overgankelijk werkwoord
p.	persoon/person
pej.	pejoratief
pers vnw	persoonlijk voornaam-woord
plantk.	plantkunde
pol.	politiek
rel.	godsdienst
s.o.	someone
s.th.	something
scheepv.	scheepvaart
scherts	schertsend
sl.	slang
taalk.	taalkunde
techn.	techniek
telw	telwoord
tw	tussenwerpsel
uitr vnw	uitroepend voornaam-woord
vero.	verouderd
Vl.	Vlaams
volkst.	volkstaal
voorv	voorvoegsel
vr vnw	vragend voornaam-woord
vulg.	vulgair
vw	voegwoord
vz	voorzetsel
wisk.	wiskunde
wkd vnw	wederkerend voornaam-woord
wkg vnw	wederkerig voornaam-woord
ww	werkwoord

6

Bijzondere tekens

Trefwoorden zijn vetgedrukt. Alle informatie die niet cursief is gezet, heeft betrekking op het Nederlands, alle cursieve informatie heeft betrekking op het Engels.

•   Elke betekenisomschrijving van een trefwoord wordt voorafgegaan door een bolletje en staat tussen ronde haken.

‹....›   Elke specificering van een vertaling staat tussen punthaakjes, evenals vakgebied- en stijlaanduidingen.

[...]   Grammaticale informatie staat tussen rechte haken.

★   Voorbeeldzinnen worden voorafgegaan door een sterretje.

▼   Idiomatische uitdrukkingen worden voorafgegaan door een driehoekje.

I,II enz.   Aanduidingen van grammaticale categorieën (zelfstandig naamwoord, bijvoeglijk naamwoord, soorten werkwoorden enz.) worden voorafgegaan door romeinse cijfers.

~   Een tilde vervangt het trefwoord.

/   Een schuine streep scheidt woorden die onderling verwisselbaar zijn.

↑   Dit teken geeft aan dat de vertaling formeler is dan het vertaalde woord of voorbeeld.

↓   Dit teken geeft aan dat de vertaling informeler is dan het vertaalde woord of voorbeeld.

≈   Dit teken geeft aan dat de vertaling een benadering is van het vertaalde woord of voorbeeld; een exacte vertaling kan in dat geval niet worden gegeven.

A

aaien *stroke,* ‹kat› *pet,* ‹romantisch› *caress*

aak *(Rhine-)barge*

aal *eel*

aalbes *redcurrant*

aalmoes *alms* [mv]

aalmoezenier *chaplain,* ‹inf.› *padre*

aambeeld *anvil*

aan I [bijw] • (in werking) *on* • (aan het lichaam) *on* • (op zekere wijze) ★ *rustig aan! easy does it!* • (begonnen) ★ *het is dik aan tussen hen they're very close* II [vz] • (meewerkend vw.) *to* • (op een plaats) *on/in/at* • (als gevolg van) *from/of* • (wat betreft) *of* • (na/naast elkaar) *by/upon*

aanbellen *ring (the bell)*

aanbesteden *put out to contract/tender, invite tenders for*

aanbesteding *contract, (public) tender*

aanbetaling *down payment*

aanbevelen *recommend*

aanbeveling *recommendation*

aanbidden *adore, worship,* ‹rel.› *worship*

aanbidder • (bewonderaar) *admirer* • (rel.) *worshipper*

aanbieden *present, offer,* ‹telegram› *hand in*

aanbieding • (offerte) *offer* • (het geven) *presentation* • (koopje) *bargain, special offer*

aanblijven *stay on,* ‹v. ambt› *remain in office*

aanblik *sight, scene,* ‹v. persoon› *appearance*

aanbod *offer*

aanbouw • (aangebouwd deel) *annex(e), extension* • (het bouwen) building

aanbouwen *build,* ‹uitbreiden› *build on to*

aanbranden *burn, be burnt*

aanbreken I [ov ww] ‹een brood› *cut into,* ‹een fles› *open* II [on ww] • (beginnen) ‹dag› *dawn,* ‹nacht› *fall*

aanbrengen ‹slot› *fix,* ‹veranderingen› *introduce,* ‹verf› *apply*

aandachtig *attentive*

aandeel • (portie) *portion, share* • (bijdrage) *part* • (waardepapier) *share*

aandeelhouder *shareholder*

aandenken • (het in de herinnering houden) *memory, remembrance* • (souvenir, enz.) *souvenir, keepsake*

aandikken • (overdrijven) *exaggerate,* ‹inf.› *lay it on (thick)* • (dikker worden) *thicken*

aandoen • (aantrekken) *put on* • (berokkenen) *cause* • (beroeren) *move, affect*

aandoening *disorder*

aandoenlijk *moving, touching*

aandrang *urge, pressure*

aandrijven *drive*

aandringen I [ov ww] • (met klem betogen) *press the point* II [on ww] • (naar voren dringen) *advance, press forward*

aanduiden *indicate, point out,* ‹met teken› *mark*

aandurven *dare (to)*

aaneen *on end, at a stretch*

aaneenschakeling *chain, sequence, series* [mv]

aanfluiting *farce, mockery*

aangaan I [ov ww] • (beginnen) *contract, enter into* • (betreffen) *concern* II [on ww] ‹v. brandhout› *catch fire,* ‹v. lampen› *go on*

aangaande *concerning, regarding, as for/to*

aangapen *gape/stare at*

aangeboren *inborn/inbred,* <v. talent> *innate*

aangedaan • (ontroerd) *moved, touched* • (aangetast) *affected*

aangelegenheid *matter, affair, business*

aangenaam *agreeable, pleasant, pleasing*

aangeschoten *tipsy*

aangetrouwd *related by marriage*

aangeven • (doorgeven) *hand, pass* • (melden) <bijzonderheden> *state,* <op meetapparatuur> *register*

aangezicht *face, countenance*

aangezien *as, since, because,* <inf.> *seeing (as)*

aangifte <v. belasting> *return,* <v. goederen> *declaration,* <v. misdaad> *report*

aangrenzend *adjacent, adjoining*

aangrijpen • (vastpakken) *seize* • (ontroeren) *move*

aanhalen • (vasttrekken) *tighten* • (citeren) *quote* • (liefkozen) <v. dier> *pet,* <v. mens> *fondle, caress* • (wisk.) *bring down*

aanhalig *affectionate*

aanhang *followers, supporters, adherents*

aanhangen I [ov ww] • (steunen) *follow, support* • (ophangen) *attach, hang* II [on ww] *hang on to, stick to*

aanhanger • (volgeling) *follower, supporter* • (aanhangwagen) *trailer*

aanhangig *pending*

aanhangsel <v. boek/document> *appendix,* <v. polis> *slip,* <v. testament> *codicil*

aanhangwagen *trailer*

aanhankelijk *attached, devoted, affectionate*

aanhef *opening (words),* <v. brief> *salutation*

aanheffen *start, begin*

aanhoren • (beluisteren) *listen to, hear* • (merken) *hear, tell*

aanhouden I [ov ww] • (in stand houden) *prolong,* <vriendschap> *keep up* • (tegenhouden) *stop* • (arresteren) *arrest* • (uitstellen) *hold/leave over,* <v. rechtszaak> *adjourn* II [on ww] • (volhouden) *keep/go on, persist (in), continue*

aanhoudend • (zonder ophouden) *continuous, constant, incessant* • (steeds weer) *continual, time and again*

aanhouding *arrest*

aanjagen <schrik, vrees> *scare, frighten*

aankijken • (bekijken) *look at, regard* • (afwachten) *wait and see* • (~ op) *blame for*

aanklacht *accusation, charge*

aanklagen *accuse (of), charge (with), bring charges against*

aanklager *accuser,* <jur.> *plaintiff*

aanklampen • (aanspreken) *accost, buttonhole* • (enteren) *board*

aankleden *dress*

aankloppen • (op deur kloppen) *knock at the door* • (~ bij) *appeal to*

aanknopen • (vastknopen aan) *tie/fasten to* • (aangaan) <onderhandelingen> *enter into,* <zaken> *establish (with)*

aanknopingspunt *starting-point*

aankomen I [ov ww] • (aanraken) *touch* • (verkrijgen) ★ *hoe ben je eraan gekomen? how did you get it?* • (~ op) *come to* • (~ met) *come up with* II [on ww] • (arriveren) *arrive* • (zwaarder worden) *put on weight* • (op bezoek komen) *come round, drop in* • (doel treffen) *hit home*

aankomend *next, coming*

aankomst *arrival*

aankondigen *announce*

aankondiging *announcement*

aankoop • (het gekochte) *purchase*
• (het kopen) *buying, acquisition*
aankruisen *mark, tick, check*
aankunnen • (opgewassen zijn tegen)
cope (with), be a match for • (erop
vertrouwen) *depend/count/rely on*
aanleg • (constructie) *contruction,
building*, ‹v. tuin› *laying-out*
• (talent) *talent* • (neiging) *tendency*
aanleggen I [ov ww] • (maken,
bouwen) ‹elektriciteit› *put in*,
‹spoorweg› *build*, ‹tuin› *lay out*,
‹voorraad› *build up*, ‹vuur› *lay, make*,
‹weg› *construct* • (aanbrengen)
‹maatstaf› *apply*, ‹verband› *bandage*
II [on ww] • (aanmeren) *moor*
aanleiding *occasion*
aanlengen *dilute*
aanleunen *lean against*
aanlokkelijk *alluring, enticing,
tempting*
aanlokken *lure, entice*, ‹klanten›
attract
aanloop • (bezoek) *visitors*
• (inleidende loop) ‹sport› *run-up*, ‹v.
vliegtuig› *take-off run* • (inleiding)
introduction, preamble
aanlopen • (naderen) ∗ komen ~ *come
walking* • (~ **tegen**) *walk/bump/run
(into)*, *chance (on)*, ‹fig.› *come (across)*
aanmaak *manufacture, production*
aanmanen *urge, exhort*
aanmaning *reminder*, ‹voor
belasting› *summons*
aanmatigen *presume, assume*, ‹form.›
arrogate to o.s.
aanmatigend *presumptuous,
overbearing, arrogant*
aanmelden I [ov ww] • (aandienen)
announce, report • (opgeven) *enter
(for)* II [wkd ww] *come forward*
aanmerkelijk *considerable*
aanmerken • (kritiek leveren) *criticize*
• (beschouwen als) *consider (as),
regard (as)*

aanmerking • (kritiek) *comment,
(critical) remark* • (beschouwing)
consideration
aanmoedigen *encourage*, ‹sport› *cheer*
aanmonsteren I [ov ww] *engage, sign
on* II [on ww] *sign on*
aannemelijk • (geloofwaardig) *fair*,
‹redelijk› *plausible*, ‹waarschijnlijk›
likely
aannemen • (accepteren) *accept, take*,
‹motie› *carry* • (veronderstellen)
assume, suppose • (in dienst nemen)
engage • (geloven) *believe*
• (adopteren) *adopt*
aannemer *contractor, (master)builder*
aanpak *approach*
aanpakken • (vastpakken) *take hold
of, seize* • (ter hand nemen) *deal with,
tackle* • (hard werken) *work hard* ∗ hij
weet van ~ *he is a go-getter*
aanpappen ∗ ~ met *suck up to; get
matey with*
aanpassen I [ov ww] • (passen) *try on*
• (geschikt maken) *adapt* II [wkd ww]
adapt/adjust o.s. to
aanplakbiljet *poster, placard*
aanplant • (het planten) *planting*
• (het geplante) *new plants, plantings*
aanpoten • (hard werken) *slog away
at, slave away* • (voortmaken) *hurry
(up)*, ‹inf.› *get a move on*
aanpraten ∗ iem. iets ~ *talk s.o. into
s.th.*
aanprijzen *recommend, praise*
aanraden *advise, recommend*, ‹plan›
suggest
aanraken *touch*
aanraking • (beroering) *touch*
• (contact) *contact*
aanranden *assail/assault s.o., assault
indecently*
aanrecht *kitchen sink (unit)*
aanreiken *pass, hand, reach*
aanrekenen ‹gunstig› *give credit for*,
‹ongunstig› *blame (for), hold (against)*

aanrichten *cause, bring about*

aanrijden I [ov ww] *collide (with), run into* II [on ww] *drive up*

aanrijding *collision, crash, accident*

aanroepen *call, hail*

aanroeren • (ter sprake brengen) *refer to s.th., mention s.th. (in passing)* • (aanraken) *touch (upon)*

aanrukken *advance*

aanschaffen *purchase, acquire, buy*

aanschieten • (licht verwonden) *hit* • (snel aantrekken) *slip into* • (aanklampen) *buttonhole, accost*

aanschouwelijk *clear, graphic*

aanschouwen *see, behold*

aanschrijven *summon, order, instruct*

aanslaan I [ov ww] • (de waarde bepalen) *estimate, rate,* <belasting> *assess* • (kort raken) <snaar> *touch,* <toets> *strike* II [on ww] • (blaffen) *start barking* • (starten v. motor) *start* • (succes hebben) *be a success, catch on*

aanslag • (het aanslaan) *touch* • (belastingaanslag) *assessment* • (aanval) *attack, attempt* • (aanzetting) *deposit*

aanslagbiljet *tax demand,* <inkomsten> *income tax return*

aanslibben *silt (up)*

aansluiten I [ov ww] • (verbinden) *connect* • (aaneen doen sluiten) *close, link up* II [on ww] • (aaneensluiten) <v. treinen> *connect* III [wkd ww] • (z. voegen bij) *join*

aansluiting • (het aansluiten bij iem./iets) *joining* • (verbinding) *connection, junction*

aansnijden • (eerste stuk afsnijden) *cut (into)* • (aankaarten) *broach, bring up*

aanspannen • (voor een voertuig spannen) *harness, hitch up* • (strak trekken) *tighten* • (rechtzaak beginnen) *take legal proceedings (against s.o.)*

aanspoelen I [ov ww] *wash ashore* II [on ww] *be washed ashore*

aansporen <prikkelen> *stimulate,* <v. paard> *spur*

aansporing *incentive, stimulation, stimulus*

aanspraak • (recht om te eisen) *title, claim* • (sociaal contact) *company*

aansprakelijk *responsible, liable*

aansprakelijkheid *liability, responsibility*

aanspreken • (het woord richten tot) *address, speak to* • (gebruiken) <kapitaal> *break into*

aanstaan <tv, enz.> *be (switched) on,* <v. motor> *be running*

aanstalten *preparations*

aanstaren *stare/gaze at*

aanstekelijk *infectious, contagious, catching*

aansteken • (doen branden) *light, set fire to* • (besmetten) *infect*

aansteker *lighter*

aanstellen I [ov ww] *appoint* II [wkd ww] *pose, put on airs*

aanstellerig *affected, theatrical*

aanstellerij *affectation, pose*

aanstelling *appointment*

aanstippen • (kort noemen) *mention briefly, touch on* • (aankruisen) *tick off* • (even aanraken) *touch,* <med.> *dab*

aanstonds *at once, directly,* <straks> *presently*

aanstoot *offence, scandal*

aanstrepen <in tekst> *mark,* <op lijst> *tick off*

aansturen • (sturen naar) *make/head for* • (bedoelen) *drive at*

aantal *number*

aantasten • (aanvallen) *attack* • (aanvreten) *affect, attack*

aantekenen *record,* <v. brief> *register*

aantekening • (notitie) *note* • (noot) *annotation, (foot)note* • (vermelding) *registration* aantijging *imputation, accusation, allegation*

aantikken I [ov ww] • (even aanraken) *tap* II [on ww] • (oplopen) *mount/tot up*

aantocht *approach, advance*

aantonen • (bewijzen) *prove, demonstrate* • (laten zien) *demonstrate, reveal, show*

aantreden *fall in, line up*

aantreffen *meet (with), find, come across*

aantrekkelijk *attractive, inviting*

aantrekken I [ov ww] • (naar zich toetrekken) *draw*, <fig.> *attract* • (vasttrekken) *draw tighter, tighten* • (aandoen) <kleren> *put on*, <schoeisel> *pull on* • (werven) *employ* II [wkd ww] *take s.th. at heart/ seriously*

aantrekkingskracht • (aantrekkelijkheid) *attractiveness, appeal* • (nat.) *power of attraction, (gravitational) pull*

aanvaardbaar *acceptable*

aanvaarden • (accepteren) <aanbod> *accept*, <commando> *assume* • (beginnen) *begin*

aanval • (offensief) *assault*, <ook bij sport> *attack* • (aandoening) *attack, fit*

aanvallen *attack*, <plotseling en hevig> *charge*

aanvang *beginning, start*, <form.> *commencement*

aanvangen I [ov ww] *begin, commence* II [on ww] *begin*

aanvankelijk I [bnw] *original, first, initial* II [bijw] *initially, at first*

aanvaring *collision*

aanvechtbaar *questionable, debatable*

aanvechten *question*, <v. bewering> *challenge*

aanverwant • (nauw betrokken bij) *related* • (aangetrouwd) *related by marriage,*

aanvliegen *fly at (s.o.)*

aanvoelen I [ov ww] *feel, appreciate, sense (the atmosphere)* II [on ww] *feel*

aanvoer • (het aanvoeren) *supply, delivery* • (het aangevoerde) *supply, arrival(s)*

aanvoerder *commander, leader*, <sport> *captain*

aanvoeren • (aandragen) <bewijs> *submit*, <bezwaren> *raise*, <redenen> *produce* • (leiden) *lead* • (leveren) *supply, bring*

aanvraag • (verzoek) *application, request* • (bestelling) *order, demand*

aanvragen *apply/ask for*

aanvullen <v. leemte> *fill (up)*, <v. tekort> *supply*, <elkaar> *complement*

aanvulling *supplement, addition*

aanvuren *fire, inspire*, <sport> *cheer (on)*

aanwaaien ★ bij iem. komen ~ *drop in on s.o.*

aanwakkeren I [ov ww] • (aanmoedigen) *stimulate* • (verergeren) *stir up, fan* II [on ww] • (heviger worden) <v. wind> *increase*

aanwas • (toename) *increase, growth* • (aangeslibde grond) *accretion*

aanwenden *use, apply*

aanwerven *canvass*

aanwezig *present*

aanwezigheid • (presentie) *attendance* • (het aanwezig/ beschikbaar zijn) *availability, presence*

aanwijzen • (wijzen naar) *indicate, point out/to, show* • (toewijzen) *assign (to), designate*

aanwijzing • (indicatie) *indication, sign* • (wenk) <bij aanpak> *instructions, pointer, directions*, <bij raadsel> *clue*

aanwinst • (verworven bezit) *gain, acquisition* • (verrijking) *gain, asset*

aanwrijven I [ov ww] *blame s.o. (for)* II [on ww] ★ ~ tegen *rub against*

aanzetten • (in werking zetten)
<motor> start, <tv> switch on
• (aansporen) <tot opstand> incite to
aanzien I [het] • (uiterlijk) aspect, look
• (achting) esteem, prestige II [ov ww]
• (bekijken) look at/(up)on, consider
• (aan het uiterlijk zien) ★ men ziet
hem zijn leeftijd niet aan he does not
look his age • (~ voor) take for
aanzienlijk • (groot) considerable,
substantial • (voornaam)
distinguished, notable, noble
aanzitten sit at table
aanzoek proposal
aap monkey
aard • (gesteldheid) nature, character
• (soort) kind, sort
aardappel potato
aardbei strawberry
aardbeving earthquake
aardbodem earth's surface, earth,
ground
aardbol • (de aarde) earth • (globe)
globe
aarde • (teelaarde) soil, (leaf) mould
• (aardbol) earth • (techn.) earth
aarden I [bnw] earthen II [ov ww]
• (techn.) earth III [on ww]
• (thuisraken) feel at home • (~ naar)
take after
aardewerk pottery, crockery,
earthenware
aardgas natural gas
aardig I [bnw] • (vriendelijk) <v.
manieren> pleasant, <v. personen>
nice II [bijw] • (vriendelijk) nicely
• (behoorlijk) fairly, pretty (good)
aardigheid • (plezier) fun, pleasure
• (grap) joke, jest
aardkorst earth's crust
aardolie petroleum, crude oil
aardrijkskunde geography
aardrijkskundig geographical
aards terrestrial
aardschok earthquake

aardverschuiving landslide
aartsbisschop archbishop
aartsengel archangel
aartshertog archduke
aartslui bone-idle
aartsvijand arch-enemy
aarzelen hesitate, waver
aas • (kaart) ace • (lokaas) bait • (kreng)
carrion
abces abscess, boil
abdij abbey
abdis abbess
abonnement <lidmaatschap>
subscription, <plaatsbewijs>
season-ticket
aborteren abort
abortus abortion
abrikoos apricot
abrupt abrupt, sudden
absent absent
absentie absence
absolutie absolution
absoluut absolute
absorberen absorb
abstract abstract
abstraheren abstract
absurd absurd, ridiculous
abt abbot
abuis mistake, error
abusievelijk wrongly
academicus university graduate
academie • (hogeschool) university,
<kunst> academy
academisch academic, university
accent • (tongval) accent • (leesteken)
accent • (klemtoon) stress • (nadruk)
emphasis
accentueren accent, stress, emphasize,
accentuate
acceptabel acceptable
accepteren accept
accijns excise (duty)
acclamatie ★ bij ~ by acclamation
acclimatiseren acclimatize
accolade • (haakje) brace, bracket

• (omarming) *accolade*
accommodatie *accommodation*
accordeon *accordion*
accountant *accountant*
accrediteren • (krediet verschaffen)
*give s.o. credit facilities at a bank, give
s.o. credit* • (met geloofsbrieven
uitzenden) *accredit (to)*
accuraat *accurate, precise*
accuratesse *accuracy, precision*
acht I [de] • (cijfer) *eight* • (aandacht)
attention, heed II [telw] *eight*
achtbaar *respectable*
achteloos *careless, negligent*
achten • (respecteren) *esteem, respect*
• (vinden) *deem, consider, judge*
achter I [bijw] • (aan de achterkant)
at/in the back/rear • (in achterstand)
behind II [vz] • (na) ∗ ~ elkaar *one
after the other* • (met iets/iem. voor
zich) *at*
achteraan *in the rear, behind, at the
back*
achteraf • (naderhand) *after the event*
• (afgelegen) *in the rear, out of the way*
achterbaks I [bnw] *underhand*
II [bijw] *underhand, secretly*
achterban *rank and file, supporters*
achterblijven • (niet mee kunnen
komen) ‹bij wedstrijden› *fall behind,*
‹in ontwikkeling› *be backward*
• (achtergelaten worden) *be left
(behind)*
achterbuurt *back street, slum*
achterdocht *suspicion*
achterdochtig *suspicious, distrustful*
achtereen *without a pause*
achtereenvolgens *successively, in
succession*
achteren *back, further back/backwards*
achtergrond *background*
achterhalen • (te pakken krijgen)
‹misdadiger› *catch (up with)*
• (terugvinden) *retrieve, recover*
achterhoede *rear(guard),* ‹sport›
defence
achterhoofd *back of the head*
achterhouden *keep back, withhold*
achterin *in/at the back*
achterland *hinterland*
achterlaten *leave (behind)*
achterlijk *backward, retarded*
achterlopen *be behind the times,* ‹v.
klok› *be slow*
achterna *behind, after*
achternaam *family name, surname*
achterneef • (zoon van neef/nicht)
second cousin • (zoon van
oom-/tantezegger) *great nephew*
achterom *round the back*
achterop • (op de achterkant) *at the
back* • (met achterstand) *behind*
achterover *back(wards), on one's back*
achteroverdrukken *pinch, knock off*
achterstallig *back, overdue*
achterstand *arrears*
achterstellen *discriminate against,
subordinate to, place at a disadvantage*
achteruit *backwards, back*
achteruitgaan • (naar achteren gaan)
move/go back • (verslechteren)
decline, deteriorate
achtervoegsel *suffix*
achtervolgen • (steeds lastig vallen)
run after, pursue • (nazetten) *pursue*
achtervolging *pursuit, chase*
achterwaarts I [bnw] *backward*
II [bijw] *back(wards)*
achterwege ∗ ~ blijven (v. zaken) *not
come off; be omitted* ∗ ~ laten *omit;
drop*
achting *regard, esteem, respect*
achtste I [bnw] *eighth* II [telw] *eighth*
achttien *eighteen*
acne *acne*
acrobaat *acrobat*
acrobatisch *acrobatic*
acteren • (toneelspelen) *act, perform*
• (doen alsof) *act, pretend*
acteur *actor*

actie • (handeling) *action*
• (protestactie) ∗ ~ *voeren*
agitate/campaign for/against
actief • (in dienst) *active* • (bezig)
active, energetic
activeren *activate*
activiteit *activity*
actrice *actress*
actualiteit • (het actueel zijn)
topicality • (actueel onderwerp)
topical subjet, ‹gebeurtenis› *current
event*
actueel *current, topical*
acupunctuur *acupuncture*
acuut I [bnw] *acute* II [bijw]
immediately, right away
adder *viper, adder*
adel *nobility*
adelaar *eagle*
adellijk • (edel) *noble* • (bijna
bedorven) *high, gamy*
adelstand *nobility*
adem *breath*
adembenemend *breathtaking*
ademen • (ademhalen) *breathe*
• (lucht doorlaten) *breathe*
ademhaling *breathing, respiration*
ademloos *breathless*
adempauze *breathing-space*
adequaat *adequate*
ader • (bloedvat) *vein* • (bodemlaag)
vein, lode, seam
aderlaten *bleed*
aderlating • (behoorlijk verlies) *drain*
• (gesch.) *bleeding, blood-letting*
aderverkalking *hardening of the
arteries,* ‹med.› *arteriosclerosis*
adhesie • (aanklevingskracht)
adhesion • (instemming) *adhesion,
adherence*
adjudant • (toegevoegd officier)
adjutant, A.D.C., aide-de-camp
• (adjudant-onderofficier) ≈ *warrant
officer* • (vogel) *adjutant bird*
administrateur *administrator,*

‹boekhouder› *accountant, bookkeeper*
administratie • (beheer)
administration, management
• (afdeling) *accounts (department),*
‹mil.› *paymaster's department*
administratief *administrative*
admiraal *admiral*
adopteren • (als kind aannemen)
adopt • (onder zijn hoede nemen)
take up
adoptie *adoption*
adres • (gegevens) *address*
• (verzoekschrift) *petition, address*
adresseren *address,* ‹form.› *direct*
adverteerder *advertiser*
advertentie *advertisement*
adverteren *advertise*
advies *advice, counsel*
adviseren *advise, recommend*
adviseur *adviser, counsellor*
advocaat • (drank) ≈ *eggnog*
• (raadsman) *lawyer*
af I [bnw] • (voltooid) *finished, done*
II [bijw] • (vandaan/weg) *from* • (naar
beneden) *off* • (bij benadering) *to*
• (bevrijd/verlost van) *off*
afbakenen ‹fig.› *define,* ‹v. weg› *mark
out, trace*
afbeelden *represent, portray, depict*
afbeelding • (het afbeelden) *portrayal*
• (beeld) *picture, portrait,* ‹in boek›
illustration
afbellen • (afzeggen) *ring off*
• (iedereen opbellen) *ring round*
afbestellen ‹een order› *cancel,* ‹v.
opdracht› *countermand*
afbetalen • (gedeeltelijk betalen) *pay
on account* • (helemaal aflossen) *pay
(off)*
afbetaling *payment*
afbeulen *work (s.o.) to the bone*
afbijten *bite off,* ‹woorden› *clip*
afbinden • (dichtklemmen) *tie up/off*
• (losmaken) *untie, take off*
afblijven *leave alone, keep one's hands*

off

afbraak *demolition,* <chemisch>
degradation

afbraakprijs *knock-down price*

afbreken • (eraf breken) *break off*
• (slopen) *demolish, pull down,* <tent>
strike • (beëindigen) *break off*
• (afkraken) *cry/run down*

afbrengen ⋆ *het er goed/slecht* ~ *do
well/badly*

afbreuk ⋆ ~ *doen aan damage; be
detrimental to; (do) harm (to)*

afdak *shelter, lean-to*

afdalen *go down, descend*

afdanken • (wegsturen) *dismiss,*
<minnaar> *ditch* • (wegdoen) <kleren>
cast off, <machine, enz.> *scrap*

afdeling *department,* <v. leger> *unit,*
<v. ziekenhuis> *ward*

afdingen I [ov ww] *beat/knock down*
II [on ww] *haggle, bargain*

afdoen • (afhandelen) *finish*
• (afzetten) *take off*

afdoend <bewijs> *conclusive,*
<maatregelen> *effective*

afdragen • (verslijten) *wear out*
• (afgeven) *hand over*

afdrijven I [ov ww] • (aborteren) *abort*
II [on ww] • (uit koers drijven) *drift off*

afdrogen *dry, wipe (off)*

afdruipen • (druipen) *trickle down*
• (weggaan) *slink off*

afdruk *print*

afdrukken *print*

afdwalen *stray (off),* <fig.> *digress*

afdwingen <bekentenis> *extort,*
<bewondering> *compel, command*

affaire *affair*

affiche *poster*

affiniteit *affinity*

afgaan • (in werking komen) *go off*
• (een slecht figuur slaan) *lose one's
face* • (het er slecht/goed vanaf
brengen) *do badly/well* • (~ **op**) *make
for,* <fig.> *rely on*

afgang *defeat, flop,* <inf.> *come-down*

afgelasten *countermand, cancel,*
<sport> *abandon, postpone*

afgelegen *distant, remote, out of the
way*

afgemeten • (afgepast) *measured*
• (stijf) *formal, stiff*

afgevaardigde *delegate (to a meeting)*

afgeven I [ov ww] • (overhandigen)
hand in, deliver II [on ww] • (vlekken)
run • (~ **op**) *run (s.o./s.th.) down*
III [wkd ww] • (~ **met**) *associate o.s.
with*

afgezaagd <grap> *corny,* <uitdrukking>
hackneyed

afgezant *envoy, ambassador*

afgieten • (beelden gieten) *cast*
• (vocht verwijderen) *pour off,* <door
vergiet> *strain*

afgifte <v. brief> *delivery,* <v.
document> *issue*

afgod *idol*

afgraven *dig away,* <egaliseren> *level*

afgrijselijk *horrible, ghastly*

afgrijzen *horror, abhorrence*

afgrond *precipice,* <fig.> *abyss, gulf*

afgunst *jealousy*

afgunstig *jealous (of)*

afhaken I [ov ww] • (loskoppelen)
unhook, <v. wagon> *uncouple* II [on
ww] • (opgeven) *drop out*

afhalen <goederen, personen> *collect,*
<met auto> *pick up,* <thuis> *call for*

afhandelen *settle, deal with*

afhandig ⋆ *iem. iets* ~ *maken trick s.o.
out of s.th.; filch s.th from s.o.*

afhangen ⋆ ~ *van depend (on)*

afhankelijk *dependent (on)*

afhouden • (weghouden) *keep
off/from,* <sport> *obstruct* • (inhouden)
deduct, withhold

afkammen *run down*

afkappen • (afhakken) *chop/cut off*
• (plotseling beëindigen) *cut short*

afkeer *aversion (to), dislike (of/to)*

afkeren *turn away, avert*
afkerig *averse (to/from)*
afketsen I [ov ww] • (terugstuiten) *reject, turn down*
II [on ww] • (terugstuiten) *glance off*
• (niet doorgaan) *fall through, fail*
afkeuren • (niet geschikt verklaren) *reject, declare unfit* • (veroordelen) *condemn, disapprove (of)*
• (verwerpelijk vinden) *frown upon*
afkeuring • (het ongeschikt verklaren) *rejection* • (het veroordelen) *condemnation, disapproval*
afkicken *kick (a habit)*
afkijken • (leren door te kijken) *copy*
• (spieken) *copy, crib*
afkloppen • (schoonmaken) *dust*
• (bezweren) *touch wood*
afknappen • (afbreken) *snap*
• (mentaal instorten) *crack up, break down*
afknapper *letdown*
afkoelen *cool down*
afkomen • (klaar krijgen) *get finished*
• (afstappen) *get off* • (naar beneden komen) *come down(stairs)* • (aan iets ontsnappen) *get away* • (kwijtraken) *get rid of*
afkomst *descent, birth, origin*
afkomstig *coming/originating from*
afkondigen *proclaim, declare*
afkopen <iem.> *buy out,* <iets> *buy off*
afkorten *abbreviate, shorten*
afkraken *slate, run down*
afkunnen *be able to get through, manage, cope with*
aflaten I [ov ww] • (niet opdoen) *leave off* II [on ww] • (ophouden) *desist (from), cease*
afleggen • (afdoen) *take off* • (zich ontdoen van) *set/put aside* • (doen) <eed> *take, swear,* <examen> *sit/take*
afleiden • (bezig houden/storen) *divert, distract* • (wegleiden) *guide/lead away (from),* <fig.> *divert*

• (vormen uit iets anders) *derive (from)* • (~ uit) *conclude, gather (from)*
afleiding • (ontspanning) *diversion*
• (woordvorming) *derivation*
afleren *unlearn*
afleveren *turn out, produce, deliver*
aflevering • (deel van reeks) *issue,* <v. tv-serie> *episode* • (bezorging) *delivery*
aflezen *read*
afloop • (einde) <v. vergadering> *end, close* • (uitkomst) *result,* <v. strijd> *outcome*
aflopen • (eindigen) *(come to an) end,* <v. contract, termijn> *expire* • (afgaan) *go off* • (afhellen) *slope (down/away)*
• (~ op) *make for*
aflossen • (vervangen) *relieve*
• (terugbetalen) *pay off*
aflossing • (afbetaling) *repayment*
• (vervanging) *relief*
afluisteren *eavesdrop (on),* <v. telefoon> *tap*
afmaken I [ov ww] • (beëindigen) *finish, complete* • (doden) *kill, finish off* • (afkraken) *pull/tear to pieces* II [wkd ww] • (~ (er) van) *dismiss s.th., shrug s.th. off*
afmatten *exhaust, tire/wear out*
afmelden • (afzeggen) *cancel*
• (vertrek melden) *clock off/out,* <in fabriek> *sign out*
afmeten • (meten) *measure (off)*
• (beoordelen) *judge*
afmeting *dimension, proportion, size*
afmonsteren I [ov ww] • (ontslaan) *pay off* II [on ww] • (ontslag nemen) *sign off*
afname • (aankoop) *purchase* • (het afgenomen worden) *sale*
• (vermindering) *decline*
afnemen I [ov ww] • (laten afleggen) *hold, administer* • (wegnemen) *take away* • (afruimen) *clear* • (kopen) *buy* II [on ww] *decrease,* <v. kracht, maan> *wane,* <v. wind> *subside*

afnemer *buyer, client, customer*
aforisme *aphorism*
afpakken *take/snatch (away)*
afpassen • (afmeten) *pace (out)*,
measure • (gepast betalen) *give/pay
the exact money*
afpersen *extort, blackmail*
afpoeieren *brush off*
afprijzen *mark down, reduce*
afraden *dissuade (a person from s.th.),
advise against*
afraffelen ‹vnl. huiswerk› *rush
through*
afranselen *thrash*, ‹als straf› *flog*
afrastering *railings* [mv], *fence*
afreageren *work/let off steam*
afreizen I [ov ww] • (bereizen) *travel*
II [on ww] • (vertrekken) *depart, leave
(for)*
afrekenen *pay/settle one's bill*
afrekening • (het afrekenen)
payment, settlement • (nota) *receipt*
afremmen I [ov ww] • (temperen)
temper, curb II [on ww] • (remmen)
slow down
africhten *train*, ‹paard› *break*
afrijden • (naar beneden rijden) *drive
down* • (rijexamen doen) *do one's
driving test*
Afrika *Africa*
afrit *sliproad*, ‹autoweg› *exit*
afroepen *call out/off*
afromen *cream, skim*, ‹fig.› *cream off*
afronden • (beëindigen) *round off,
wind up* • (rondmaken) *round off*
• (wisk.) ★ *naar boven/beneden ~
round up/down*
afruimen *clear the table, clear away*
afrukken • (met ruk aftrekken) *tear
away, rip off* • (masturberen) *jerk/jack
off, wank (off)*
afschaffen *abolish, do away with*
afscheid *parting, departure, leave*
afscheiden • (uitscheiden) *secrete*
• (losmaken) *separate, detach*

afscheiding • (het afsplitsen van)
separation, ‹m.b.t. kerk› *schism*
• (uitscheiding) *secretion*
afschepen *put/fob (s.o.) off*
afschermen *mask, screen, protect from*
afschieten • (afvuren) *fire* • (doden)
shoot
afschilderen • (afbeelden) *paint*
• (uitbeelden) *portray, make out*
afschrift *copy*, ‹v. bankrekening›
statement (of account)
afschrijven • (afboeken) *debit*
• (boekwaarde verlagen) *write off*
afschrijving • (afmelding) *letter of
cancellation* • (verlaging v.
boekwaarde) *depreciation* • (bewijs
van afboeking) *debit note*
afschrikken *discourage, put/scare off,
deter*
afschrikwekkend *deterrent,
frightening*
afschudden *shake off*
afschuiven I [ov ww] • (wegschuiven)
push/move away, shift • (afwentelen)
shift, pass on (to) II [on ww] • (betalen)
fork out, cough up
afschuw *horror, disgust*
afschuwelijk I [bnw] • (afgrijselijk)
horrible, abominable • (heel
slecht/lelijk) *shocking, awful* II [bijw]
frightfully, terribly
afslaan I [ov ww] • (prijs verlagen)
reduce • (afwijzen) ‹aanbod› *decline,*
‹verzoek› *refuse* • (eraf slaan) ‹v.
thermometer› *shake down* II [on ww]
• (v. richting veranderen) *turn (off)*,
‹weg› *branch off* • (uitgaan) ‹v.
motor, enz.› *stall*
afslachten • (slachten) *slaughter, kill
off* • (in groten getale doden)
massacre, slaughter
afslag *turn*, ‹v. autoweg› *exit*
afsluiten • (op slot doen) *lock*
• (door-/toevoer staken) ‹door
gasbedrijf› *cut off*, ‹elektriciteit›

disconnect, <gas> turn off, <weg> close
• (beëindigen) <de boeken> balance,
<rekening> close • (overeenkomen)
<contract> conclude, <verzekering>
effect

afsluiting • (beëindiging) closing,
conclusion • (het afsluiten)
<elektriciteit> disconnection, <gas>
shut-off

afsnauwen snap/snarl at

afsnijden <ook fig.> cut (off)

afsnoepen steal

afspelen I [ov ww] play II [wkd ww]
happen, take place

afspiegelen • (afschilderen) portray
• (weerspiegelen) reflect

afsplitsen split off, <v. weg, leiding>
branch off

afspraak • (overeenkomst) agreement
• (ontmoeting) appointment,
engagement (to meet s.o.)

afspreken I [ov ww] agree (on), arrange
II [on ww] make an appointment

afspringen • (naar beneden springen)
jump/leap down • (~ op) jump at

afstaan give (up), hand over

afstammen be descended (from)

afstand • (het opgeven) <v. bezit,
recht> surrender • (distantie) distance

afstandsbediening remote control

afstappen step down/off, <v. fiets,
paard> get off

afsteken I [ov ww] • (wegsteken) cut
off/away, <met beitel> chisel off
• (aansteken) <vuurwerk> let off II [on
ww] • (~ tegen) contrast with, stand
out against

afstellen set, adjust (to)

afstemmen • (met stemming
afwijzen) vote down, • (doen
overeenstemmen) attune to
• (aanpassen) adjust to

afstempelen stamp

afsterven die (off)

afstevenen make for, <dreigend> bear

down on

afstijgen get off, dismount

afstoffen dust

afstompen I [ov ww] • (stomp maken)
blunt • (ongevoelig maken) dull,
numb II [on ww] • (stomp worden)
become blunt • (ongevoelig worden)
become dull/numb

afstoten I [ov ww] • (tegenstaan) repel
• (wegdoen) <v. personeel> discharge,
lay off, <v. zaken> shed, cast off II [on
ww] repel

afstraffen punish, reprimand

afstropen strip (off), <villen> skin

afstuderen finish one's studies,
graduate

aftakelen • (achteruitgaan) go to seed,
go downhill • (aftuigen v. schip) unrig

aftakking branch, fork, <techn.> shunt

aftands decrepit

aftappen draw (off), <ook telefoon> tap

aftasten • (tastend onderzoeken) feel,
<fig.> sound, explore • (techn.) scan

aftekenen I [ov ww] • (voor gezien
tekenen) sign • (afbakenen) outline,
mark off II [wkd ww] show (up),
become visible

aftellen • (uittellen) count off/out
• (van 10 tot 0 tellen) count down
• (aftelrijmpje opzeggen) dip for it

aftocht retreat

aftrap kick-off

aftrappen I [ov ww] • (wegschoppen)
kick away/off • (verslijten) wear out
II [on ww] • (de aftrap doen) kick off

aftreden I [het] resignation II [on ww]
resign, retire (from office)

aftrek • (korting) deduction, <voor
kinderen> allowance

aftrekken I [ov ww] • (eraf halen)
draw off/down • (in mindering
brengen) deduct, <v. getal> subtract
II [wkd ww] • (masturberen) jerk/jack
off

aftreksel extract

aftroeven • (troefkaart gebruiken)
trump • (te vlug af zijn) be too clever
for s.o.
aftroggelen wheedle/coax out of
aftuigen • (het tuig afhalen) <v.
paard> unharness, <v. schip> unrig
• (afranselen) thrash
afvaardigen delegate, depute
afvaardiging delegation, deputation
afval waste, <vuilnis> refuse
afvallen • (uitvallen) drop out • (naar
beneden vallen) fall off/down
• (lichter worden) lose weight
• (ontrouw worden) desert
afvallig disloyal, <v. geloof> lapsed
afvalproduct waste product,
by-product
afvloeien • (wegvloeien) flow down/off
• (ontslagen worden) be laid off
afvoer • (het afvoeren) <v. goederen>
removal, <v. vocht> discharge
• (afvoerbuis) drain
afvoeren • (wegvoeren) <v. goederen>
remove, <v. water> drain away
afvragen wonder, ask o.s.
afvuren fire (off), discharge, <raket>
launch
afwachten I [ov ww] • (op iets/iem.
wachten) wait (for) II [on ww] • (geen
actie ondernemen) wait (and see)
afwachting expectation
afwas washing-up
afwassen I [ov ww] • (schoonmaken)
wash • (verwijderen) wash away/off
II [on ww] • (de vaat doen) do the
dishes/the washing-up
afweer defence
afwegen • (wegen) weigh
• (overwegen) weigh
afwenden I [ov ww] • (afweren) avert
• (in andere richting keren) turn
away, <blik> avert II [wkd ww] • (zich
wegdraaien) turn away
afwennen break/get out of a habit
afwentelen roll off/away/down

afweren • (weghouden) <fig.>
fend/ward off, fend off, <v. slag> parry,
<vijand, enz.> keep/hold off
afwerken • (afmaken) finish (off),
complete, give the finishing touch to
• (uitvoeren) get through
afwerpen • (laten vallen) <v. bladeren,
bommen> drop • (afgooien) throw off,
<ruimtevaart> jettison
afweten * het laten ~ excuse o.s.; fail to
turn up
afwezig • (absent) absent, not in, not at
home • (verstrooid) absent-minded
afwezigheid • (het absent zijn)
absence • (verstrooidheid)
absent-mindedness
afwijken • (andere richting opgaan)
<v. gebruik, programma> depart, <v.
koers> deviate, <v. lijn> diverge
• (verschillen) deviate
afwijking • (het afwijken van een
richting) deviation • (gebrek)
handicap, defect • (het afwijken van
een regel) aberration
afwijzen • (niet toelaten) refuse
admittance to, turn away • (weigeren)
<v. uitnodiging> decline, <v. verzoek>
refuse
afwikkelen • (loswinden) unwind,
unroll • (regelen) wind up
afwimpelen pass over
afwisselen <v. mensen> relieve, <v.
zaken> vary
afwisseling • (variatie) variety
• (opeenvolging) alternation
afzakken • (naar beneden zakken)
come down, sag • (minder worden) <v.
prestaties> tail off, <v. werk> fall off (in
quality)
afzeggen cancel, call off
afzender sender
afzet • (vraag) market • (verkochte
waren) sale(s) • (sport) take-off
afzetten • (uitzetten) <motor> shut off,
<radio> switch off, <wekker> stop

• (bedriegen) *cheat, swindle* • (afdoen) *take off* • (afleveren) <v. passagier> *drop* • (amputeren) *amputate* • (barricaderen) *block, close off*
afzetter *cheat, swindler*
afzetterij *swindle,* <inf.> *rip-off*
afzetting *cordon*
afzichtelijk *hideous, ghastly*
afzien • (sport) *have a hard/tough time (of it)* • (~ **van**) <plan> *abandon* ★ *afgezien van apart from*
afzijdig *aloof* ★ *zich ~ houden hold/keep aloof*
afzonderen I [ov ww] • (afzonderlijk plaatsen) *separate (from)* • (in afzondering plaatsen) *isolate* II [wkd ww] *cut o.s. off, seclude o.s. from*
afzondering *separation, isolation, seclusion*
afzonderlijk • (alleen, apart) *individual, single* • (zonder anderen) *private*
afzwaaien *be demobbed*
afzweren <v. drank> *swear off,* <v. geloof> *abjure*
agenda • (notitieboekje) *diary* • (te behandelen onderwerpen) *agenda*
agent • (politieagent) *policeman, constable* • (vertegenwoordiger) *agent*
agentschap *agency*
ageren *agitate, campaign*
agglomeratie *agglomeration*
aggregaat *aggregate*
agitatie • (het opruien) *agitation* • (opwinding) *excitement*
agrariër *agrarian*
agrarisch *agrarian*
agressie *aggression*
agressief *aggressive*
air *air, look, appearance*
akelig • (naar) *dreary, nasty, dismal* • (onwel) *ill, sick*
akkefietje • (onaangename taak) *chore* • (karweitje) *(little) job*
akker *field*

akkerbouw *agriculture*
akkoord I [het] • (overeenkomst) *agreement, settlement* • (samenklank) *chord* II [bnw] • (in orde) *agreed, correct, all right* ★ ~ *gaan agree* III [tw] *agreed!, ok!*
akoestiek *acoustics*
akoestisch *acoustic*
akte • (vergunning) *diploma, certificate* • (deel v. toneelstuk) *act* • (stuk) *document,* <v. verkoop> *deed of sale*
aktetas *briefcase*
al I [bijw] • (reeds) *already,* <in vraagzin> *yet* II [telw] *all, every (one of), each* III [vw] *(al)though, even if, even though*
alarm *alarm, alert*
alarmeren • (waarschuwen) *alert* • (ongerust maken) *alarm*
albatros *albatross*
albino *albino*
album *album*
alcohol *alcohol*
alcoholisme *alcoholism*
aldaar *there*
aldoor *all the time, all along*
aldus *thus, in this manner*
alfabet *alphabet*
alfabetisch *alphabetic(al)*
algebra *algebra*
algeheel *total, complete*
algemeen I [het] ★ *in het* ~ *in general; on the whole* II [bnw] ★ ~ *bekend common knowledge* ★ *met algemene stemmen unanimously* ★ *het* ~ *belang the public interest* ★ ~ *kiesrecht universal suffrage*
algemeenheid • (het algemeen zijn) *generality, universality* • (vage uitspraak) *commonplace*
alhier *here*
alhoewel *although*
alias *a.k.a, otherwise known as, also known as, alias*

alibi *alibi*
alimentatie *maintenance allowance,*
   <v. scheiding> alimony
alinea *paragraph*
alkoof *alcove*
allebei *both*
alledaags *everyday, ordinary*
alleen I [bnw] • *(zonder anderen)*
   alone • (eenzaam) lonely II [bijw] *only,*
   merely
alleenheerschappij *absolute power*
alleenstaand • *(afgezonderd) isolated,*
   detached • (zonder partner)
   individual, single
allegaartje *hotchpotch, farrago* [mv:
   farragos]
allegorie *allegory*
allemaal *(one and) all, everybody,*
   everyone, <dingen> everything
allemachtig I [bnw] *amazingly* II [tw]
   well, I never!, Good God, good heavens
allengs *gradually, by degrees*
allergie *allergy*
allergisch *allergic* (to)
Allerheiligen *All Saints' Day*
allerlei I [het] *miscellany* II [bnw] *all*
   sorts of
allerminst I [bnw] *least of all* II [bijw]
   not in the least
alles *all, everything, anything*
allesbehalve *anything but, far from*
alleszins *highly, in every respect/way*
alliantie *alliance*
allicht *most probably/likely, likely*
allooi *alloy, <fig.> quality*
almachtig *omnipotent, all-powerful*
almanak *almanac*
alom *everywhere*
alomtegenwoordig *omnipresent*
alomvattend *all-embracing*
aloud *ancient, time-honoured*
alpinist *alpinist, mountaineer*
als • *(zoals) like, (such) as • (in de*
   hoedanigheid van) as • (indien) if
   • *(wanneer) when*

alsmede *and also, also, as well as*
alsnog *as yet, <nu nog> still*
alsof *as if/though*
alt *alto*
altaar *altar*
alternatief *alternative*
althans *at least, at any rate, anyhow*
altijd *always, ever*
altviool *viola*
aluminium *aluminium, <AE>*
   aluminum
aluminiumfolie *tin foil*
alvast *meanwhile*
alvleesklier *pancreas*
alvorens *before, prior to*
alweer *again, once more*
amandel • *(vrucht) almond • (klier)*
   tonsil
amateur *amateur*
amazone • *(paardrijdster)*
   horsewoman • (mythologisch figuur)
   Amazon
ambacht *(handi)craft, trade*
ambassade *embassy*
ambassadeur *ambassador*
ambiëren *aspire to*
ambitie • *(eerzucht) ambition • (ijver)*
   zeal
ambitieus • *(eerzuchtig) ambitious*
   • *(ijverig) zealous*
ambt *position, office, function*
ambtelijk *official*
ambtenaar *official, civil servant*
ambtenarij *civil service, <iron.>*
   officialdom, <pej.> red tape
ambtsaanvaarding *accession to office*
ambtsgeheim • *(geheim) official*
   secret • (geheimhoudingsplicht)
   official secrecy
ambtshalve *by virtue of one's office, ex*
   officio
ambulance *ambulance*
amendement *amendment*
Amerika *America*
ameublement *furniture*

amfetamine *amphetamine*
amfibie *amphibian*
amfitheater *amphitheatre*
amicaal *amicable, friendly*
ammunitie *ammunition*, ‹inf.› *ammo*
amnestie *amnesty*
amok *amok, amuck*
amoreel *amoral*
ampel *ample*
amper *hardly, scarcely*
ampul *ampoule*, ‹AE› *ampule*
amputatie *amputation*
amputeren *amputate*
amulet *amulet, charm, talisman*
amusant *amusing, entertaining*
amusement *amusement, entertainment*
amuseren *amuse, entertain*
analfabeet *illiterate*
analogie *analogy*
analoog *analogous*
analyse *analysis*
analyseren *analyse*
analytisch *analytic(al)*
ananas *pineapple*
anarchie *anarchy*
anarchisme *anarchism*
anarchist *anarchist*
anatomie *anatomy*
anatomisch *anatomical*
anciënniteit *seniority*
ander I [bnw] • (het tegenovergestelde) *other* • (verschillend) *different* II [onb vnw] ‹v. persoon› *another (person)* [mv: *the others*], ‹v. zaken› *another thing* III [telw] *next*
anderhalf *one and a half*
anders I [bnw] *different, other* II [bijw] • (op andere wijze) *differently, otherwise* • (zo niet) *else, otherwise* • (op andere tijd) *at any other time* • (verder) ∗ ~ nog iets? *anything else?*
andersom *the reverse, the other way round, the opposite*

anderszins *otherwise*
anderzijds *on the other hand*
andijvie *endive*
anekdote *anecdote*
anemoon *anemone*
anesthesie *anaesthesia*
anesthesist *anaesthetist*
angel • (steekorgaan) *sting* • (vishaak) *hook*
Angelsaksisch *Anglo-Saxon*
angina *angina*
angst *fear (of)*, ‹hevig› *terror*, ‹zielsangst› *agony*
angstaanjagend *frightening*
angstig *frightened*, ‹predicatief› *afraid*
angstvallig • (nauwkeurig) *scrupulous, conscientious* • (bang) *timid*, ‹form.› *timorous*
angstwekkend *alarming, terrifying*
anijs I [de] • (plant) *anise* • (zaad) *aniseed* II [bnw] *aniseed*
animeren *encourage, stimulate*
animo *zest (for), spirit, gusto (in)*
animositeit *animosity*
anker • (muuranker) *brace* • (scheepsanker) *anchor* • (palletje in uurwerk) *lever* • (techn.) *armature*
ankeren I [ov ww] *anchor* II [on ww] *(cast) anchor*
annalen *annals*
annex *annex(e)*
annexatie *annexation*
annexeren *annex*
annuleren *cancel*, ‹v. contract› *annul*
anomalie *anomaly*
anoniem *anonymous, faceless*
anonimiteit *anonymity*
ansjovis *anchovy*
antecedent • (voorafgaand feit) *antecedent, precedent* • (taalk.) *antecedent*
antenne • (bio.) *antenna* [mv: *antennae*] • (techn.) *aerial*, ‹AE› *antenna*
antibioticum *antibiotic*

antiek I [het] *antiques* [mv] II [bnw]
   antique, ancient, <pej.> *old-fashioned*
antilope *antelope*
antipathie *antipathy, dislike*
antiquair *antique dealer, antiquary*
antiquariaat *antiquarian bookshop*
antiquarisch *antiquarian,*
   second-hand
antiquiteit <gebruik> *antiquity,*
   <voorwerp> *antique*
anti-semiet *anti-Semite*
antiseptisch *antiseptic*
antistof *antibody*
antraciet *anthracite*
antropologie *anthropology*
antropoloog *anthropologist*
antwoord *answer, reply*
antwoorden *answer, reply,* <scherp>
   retort
anus *anus*
apart • (afzonderlijk) *separate, apart*
   • (bijzonder) *special, exclusive*
apartheid *apartheid, racial segregation*
apathie *apathy*
aperitief *aperitif*
apostel *apostle*
apostolisch *apostolic*
apostrof *apostrophe*
apotheek <vnl. kliniek> *dispensary,*
   <winkel> *chemist's (shop)*
apotheker *(dispensing) chemist,*
   pharmacist
apotheose *apotheosis*
apparaat *machine, appliance*
apparatuur *apparatus, equipment,*
   <comp.> *hardware*
appartement *flat,* <AE> *apartment*
appel *apple*
appelleren • (appel aantekenen)
   appeal, lodge an appeal • (een beroep
   doen op) *appeal (to)*
appetijtelijk *appetizing*
applaudisseren *applaud*
applaus *applause*
april *April*

a priori *a priori*
aquaduct *aqueduct*
aquarel *watercolour*
aquarium *aquarium*
Arabier *Arab*
Arabisch *Arab(ian),* <v. taal en cijfers>
   Arabic
arbeid *labour, work*
arbeiden *labour, work*
arbeider *workman, worker,* <voor
   zware arbeid> *labourer*
arbeidsmarkt *labour market*
arbeidsovereenkomst *employment*
   contract
arbeidzaam *hard-working*
arbiter • (jur.) *arbitrator* • (sport)
   referee
arbitrage *arbitration*
archaïsch *archaic*
archaïsme *archaism*
archeologie *archeology*
archief • (gebouw) *record office*
   • (verzameling stukken) *archives, files*
archipel *archipelago*
architect *architect*
architectuur *architecture*
archivaris *archivist*
arctisch *arctic*
are *are*
arena *arena, ring*
arend *eagle*
argeloos • (onopzettelijk) *harmless,*
   inoffensive • (nietsvermoedend)
   unsuspecting, innocent
arglistig *crafty, cunning,* <form.>
   guileful
argument *argument*
argumenteren *argue*
argwaan *suspicion*
argwanend *suspicious*
aria *aria*
aristocraat *aristocrat*
aristocratie *aristocracy*
aristocratisch *aristocratic*
arm I [de] • (vertakking) *arm*

- (bevestiging v. lamp) *bracket*
- (lichaamsdeel) *arm* II [bnw]
- (behoeftig) *poor* • (meelijwekkend) *poor, wretched* • (~ aan) *poor in*

armband *bracelet*
armelijk *poor, shabby*
armoedig • (haveloos) *poor, shabby*
- (karig) *poor, paltry*

armoedzaaier *poor devil, down-and-out*
armslag *elbow room*
armzalig • (armoedig) *poor*
- (onbeduidend) *paltry*

aroma • (geur) *aroma* • (smaakstof) *flavouring*
arrangeren *arrange*
arrest • (hechtenis) *arrest, detention,* ‹voorarrest› *custody*
arrestant • (gedetineerde) *prisoner*
- (gearresteerde) *an arrested person*

arrestatie *arrest*
arresteren • (in hechtenis nemen) *arrest* • (beslag leggen) *seize*
- (vaststellen v. notulen) *confirm*

arriveren *arrive*
arrogant *arrogant*
arrogantie *arrogance*
arrondissement *district*
arrondissementsrechtbank *district court*
arsenaal • (verzameling) *stock*
- (wapenopslag) *arsenal*

arsenicum *arsenic*
articulatie *articulation*
articuleren *articulate*
artiest (variety) *artist, entertainer*
artikel • (geschreven stuk) *article, paper* • (bepaling) *article,* ‹v. wet› *section*
artillerie *artillery*
artisjok (globe) *artichoke*
artistiek *artistic*
arts *physician, doctor*
as • (spil) ‹v. wiel› *axle* • (middellijn) *axis* • (verbrandingsresten) *ashes*

asbest *asbestos*
asceet *ascetic*
ascetisch *ascetic*
asfalt *asphalt*
asfalteren *asphalt*
asiel • (bescherming) *asylum*
- (dierenverblijf) *home for lost animals*

asociaal *anti-social*
asperge *asparagus,* ‹inf.› *sparrow-grass*
aspirant • (kandidaat) *candidate, applicant* • (sport) *junior*
aspiratie *aspiration*
assembleren *assemble*
assistentie *assistance, help*
assisteren *assist, help*
associatie *association*
assortiment *assortment*
assuradeur *insurer,* ‹scheepv.› *underwriter*
assurantie *insurance*
astma *asthma*
astrologie *astrology*
astroloog *astrologer*
astronaut *astronaut*
astronomie *astronomy*
astronoom *astronomer*
asymmetrisch *asymmetric(al)*
atelier *studio*
atheïsme *atheism*
atheïst *atheist*
Atlantisch *Atlantic*
atlas *atlas*
atleet *athlete*
atletiek *athletics*
atmosfeer *atmosphere*
atoom *atom*
atoombom *atom(ic) bomb*
attaché *attaché*
attenderen *draw attention to*
attent • (opmerkzaam) *attentive*
- (vriendelijk) *considerate*

attentie • (aandacht) *attention* • (blijk van vriendelijkheid) *token of attention, present*
attest *testimonial, certificate*

attractie *attraction*
attractief *attractive*
attribuut *attribute*
aubade *aubade*
audiëntie *audience*
auditorium • (publiek) *audience*
• (zaal) *auditorium*
augurk *gherkin*
augustus *August*
aula *auditorium, great hall*
aureool *aureole, halo*
auspiciën ✶ onder ~ van *under the*
auspices of
auteur *author*
authenticiteit *authenticity*
authentiek *authentic*
auto *car*
autobus *bus, coach*
automaat • (distributieapparaat)
vending machine • (persoon, toestel)
automaton, robot
automatisch *automatic*
automatiseren *automatize*
autonomie *autonomy*
autonoom *autonomous*
autoritair *authoritarian*
autoriteit *authority*
autosnelweg *motorway,* <AE> *freeway*
averechts I [bnw] • (verkeerd) *wrong*
II [bijw] (in) *the wrong way*
averij <v. motor> *breakdown,* <v. schip>
damage
avond *evening, night*
avondeten *supper, dinner*
avondkleding *evening dress*
avondklok *curfew*
avondmaal • (avondeten) *evening*
meal, supper, dinner • (rel.) *the Lord's*
Supper
avontuur *adventure*
avontuurlijk *adventurous*
axioma *axiom*
azen *prey (on),* <v. personen> *have one's*
eye on
azijn *vinegar*

azuren *azure*
azuur *azure*

B

baai • (inham aan de kust) *bay* • (stof) *baize* • (tabak) *Virginia*
baal *bale*
baan • (betrekking) *job* • (traject) ‹v. hemellichaam› *orbit*, ‹v. projectiel› *trajectory*
baanbrekend *pioneering, epoch-making*
baanvak *section*
baanwachter *signalman*
baar I [de] • (draagbaar) *stretcher*, ‹voor lijk› *bier* • (staaf edelmetaal) *bar* II [bnw] ★ *baar geld cash; readies*
baard • (haargroei op kin) *beard* • (deel v. veer) *vane* • (deel v. sleutel) *bit*
baarlijk ★ ~e nonsens *utter nonsense* ★ de ~e duivel *the devil incarnate*
baarmoeder *womb*, ‹med.› *uterus*
baars *perch, bass*
baas • (chef) *boss*, ‹inf.› *governor* • (man, jongen) *bloke, fellow*
baat • (nut, voordeel) *benefit, advantage* • (opbrengst) *profit, benefit*
babbelen • (gezellig praten) *chat* • (veel praten) *chatter, babble*, ‹inf.› *natter*
baby *baby*
bacil *bacillus*
bacterie *bacteria* [mv]
bad • (water) *bath* • (badkuip) *bath*
baden I [ov ww] • (in bad doen) *bath* II [on ww] • (een bad nemen) *bathe*
badgast ‹in badplaats› *holidaymaker*, ‹in kuuroord› *patient*
badkamer *bathroom*
badkuip (bath)tub
badmeester *lifeguard*
badplaats *seaside resort*, ‹kuuroord› *spa*

badstof *towelling, terry(cloth)*
bagage *luggage, baggage*
bagagedepot *left-luggage*
bagagedrager *carrier*
bagagekluis *luggage locker*
bagatel *trifle, bagatelle*
bagatelliseren *play down*
bagger *mud, slush*
baggeren I [ov ww] *dredge* II [on ww] *wade*
bajes *slammer, nick*
bajonet *bayonet*
bak • (vergaarplaats) ‹ondiep› *tray*, ‹voor eten› *dish*, ‹voor water› *tank* • (mop) *joke, lark*
bakbeest *giant*, ‹inf.› *whopper*
bakboord *port*
baken *beacon*
bakermat *cradle, origin*
bakfiets *carrier bike*
bakkebaard *sideboards, (side-)whiskers*
bakkeleien • (vechten) *tussle, scuffle*, ‹inf.› *scrap* • (ruziën) *bicker, quarrel*
bakken ‹in oven› *bake*, ‹in pan› *fry*
bakker *baker*
bakkerij *bakery*
bakkes *mug*
baksteen *brick*
bal I [de] • (teelbal) *testicle* • (bol) *ball* • (snob) *snob, stuck-up person* • (sport) *ball* II [het] *ball, dance*
balanceren *balance, poise*
balans • (evenwicht) *balance* • (weeginstrument) *(pair of) scales* • (lijst van bezittingen en schulden) *balance sheet*
baldadig *unruly, disorderly*
baldadigheid *disorderliness, wantonness*
balie *counter*
balk *beam*
balken *bray*
balkon *balcony*, ‹v. tram en trein› *platform*
ballade *ballad*

ballast *ballast*
ballen I [ov ww] ★ de vuisten ~ *clench one's fist* II [on ww] *play ball*
ballet *ballet*
balling *exile*
ballingschap *banishment, exile*
ballon ● (omhulsel v. lamp) *globe* ● (luchtballon) *balloon*
balorig ● (onwillig) *unruly,* ‹form.› *refractory* ● (slecht gehumeurd) *peevish, cross*
balpen *ball-point pen, biro*
balsem *balm*
balsemen *embalm*
balustrade *balustrade,* ‹v. trap› *banisters*
bamboe *bamboo*
ban ● (excommunicatie) *excommunication* ● (betovering) *spell*
banaal *banal, trite, hackneyed*
banaan *banana*
banaliteit ● (het banaal zijn) *banality* ● (cliché) ‹form.› *platitude*
band ● (strook stof) ‹hoed, arm› *band,* ‹lint› *ribbon,* ‹vechtsport› *belt,* ‹verband› *bandage* ● (magneetband) *tape* ● (radiofrequentie) *(wave)band* ● (ring) ‹om wiel› *tyre* ● (boekomslag) *binding* ● (boekdeel) *volume* ● (transportband) ★ lopende band *conveyor-belt; assembly line*
bandeloos *lawless, disorderly, riotously*
bandiet ‹rover› *bandit,* ‹schurk› *ruffian*
bang ● (angstig) ★ hij was bang *he was afraid* ● (ongerust) *anxious*
bangerd *coward*
bangmakerij *intimidation*
banier *banner*
bank ● (geldinstelling) *bank* ● (zitmeubel) ‹bekleed› *sofa, settee, couch,* ‹onbekleed› *bench*
bankbiljet *banknote*
banket ● (feestmaal) *banquet* ● (gebak) (almond) *pastry*

banketbakker *pastry cook,* ‹snoepgoed› *confectioner*
bankier *banker*
bankrekening *bank account*
bankroet I [het] *bankruptcy* II [bnw] *bankrupt*
bankschroef *(bench-)vice*
bankstel *3-piece suite*
bankwerker *fitter, bench worker/operator*
bankwezen *banking*
banneling *exile*
bannen ‹gedachten, personen› *banish,* ‹personen› *exile*
bar I [de] bar II [bnw] ● (dor) *barren* ● (koud) *severe* III [bijw] *awfully (bad)*
barak *shed,* ‹mil.› *hut, barracks*
barbaar *barbarian*
barbaars *barbarous*
barbecue *barbecue*
***barbecueën** (Wdl: barbecuen) *barbecue*
baren ● (ter wereld brengen) *bear, give birth to* ● (veroorzaken) *cause, give*
baret *beret*
bariton *baritone*
barkeeper *barmaid, barman,* ‹AE› *bartender*
barmhartig *charitable, merciful*
barmhartigheid *charity, mercy*
barnsteen *amber*
barok *baroque*
barometer *barometer*
barrevoets I [bnw] *barefooted* II [bijw] *barefoot*
barricade *barricade*
barricaderen *barricade*
bars *grim, stern,* ‹v. stem› *gruff*
barst *crack,* ‹in huid› *chap*
barsten *burst,* ‹v. huid› *chap,* ‹v. ruit› *crack*
bas *bass*
basalt *basalt*
baseren *base, ground (on), ground in*
basilicum *basil*

basiliek *basilica*
basis • (grondslag) *basis, base*
 • (steunpunt) *base* • (wisk.) *base*
basisonderwijs *primary education*
basisschool *primary school*
bassin *basin*
bassist *bass player*
bast • (schors) *bark* • (peul) *husk, shell*
 • (huid) ‹inf.› *skin*
bastaard *bastard*
bataljon *battalion*
baten I [de] *assets* II [on ww] *avail*
batig * ~ saldo *credit balance; surplus*
batterij • (toestel) *battery*
 • (verzameling) *battery*
bauxiet *bauxite*
baviaan *baboon*
bazelen *waffle, talk rubbish*
bazig *masterful, domineering,* ‹inf.›
 bossy
bazin *mistress*
bazuin *trumpet*
beambte *official, officer*
beamen *agree (to)*
beantwoorden *answer, reply to*
bebloed *blood-stained*
beboeten *fine*
bebossen *afforest, plant a forest*
bebouwen • (gebouwen neerzetten)
 build on • (gewassen kweken)
 cultivate
bebouwing • (akkerbouw) *cultivation*
 • (het bouwen) *building* • (de
 gebouwen) *buildings*
becijferen *calculate, figure out, work
 out*
becommentariëren *comment on*
beconcurreren *compete with*
bed *bed*
bedaagd *elderly, getting on in years*
bedaard *calm, composed*
bedacht • (strevend naar) *intent on,
 alive to* • (voorbereid op) *prepared for*
bedachtzaam *thoughtful, cautious,
 circumspect*

bedanken *thank*
bedaren *calm down*
beddengoed *bedding, bedclothes*
bedding *bed*
bede *entreaty, prayer*
bedeesd *timid, shy*
bedekken *cover (up)*
bedekking *cover(ing)*
bedekt • (afgedekt) *covered* • (niet
 openlijk) *covert*
bedelaar *beggar*
bedelen *beg*
bedelven *bury*
bedenkelijk ‹v. middelen, gezicht›
 doubtful
bedenken I [ov ww] • (iets schenken)
 remember • (overwegen) *consider*
 • (uitdenken) *think up, devise, invent*
 II [wkd ww] *change one's mind*
bedenking • (overweging)
 consideration • (bezwaar) *objection*
bedenktijd *time for reflection, time to
 think*
bederf *decay*
bederfelijk *perishable*
bederven I [ov ww] • (verwennen)
 spoil • (beschadigen) ‹gezondheid›
 ruin, ‹plezier› *mar* II [on ww] ‹v.
 etenswaren› *go bad/go off*
bedevaart *pilgrimage*
bedevaartganger *pilgrim*
bediende *servant,* ‹in winkel›
 assistant, ‹op kantoor› *clerk*
bedienen • (laten functioneren)
 operate • (dienen, helpen) *serve,* ‹aan
 tafel› *wait,* ‹in restaurant, enz.› *wait
 on,* ‹in winkel› *serve*
bediening • (het laten functioneren)
 operation, ‹auto› *controls* • (het
 bedienen) *service*
bedillen *find fault with, carp at*
beding *condition*
bedingen *stipulate, insist on,* ‹prijs›
 bargain (for)
bedisselen *arrange, manage*

bedlegerig *bedridden, confined to (one's) bed*

bedoelen • (duiden op) *have in view/mind, mean* • (beogen) *aim at, drive at, intend*

bedoeling • (betekenis) *meaning* • (oogmerk) *intention, purpose, aim*

bedompt *close, stuffy*

bedonderen *fool, dupe, con*

bedorven • (niet meer eetbaar) ∗ de melk is ~ *the milk's off* • (verwend) ‹v. kinderen› *spoilt*

bedotten *trick, dupe, fool*

bedrag *amount*

bedragen *amount to*

bedreigen *threaten*

bedreiging *threat*

bedremmeld *confused, embarrassed, taken aback*

bedreven *skilled, skilful*

bedriegen *cheat, deceive, swindle*

bedrieger *swindler, impostor, cheat, fraud*

bedrieglijk ‹v. aard› *deceitful*, ‹v. uiterlijk› *deceptive*

bedrijf • (werking) *operation* • (onderneming) *enterprise, business*, ‹gas, spoorwegen› *service* • (deel v. toneelstuk) *act*

bedrijfschap *trade organization*

bedrijfsleven *business, trade and industry*

bedrijfstak *branch of industry*

bedrijven *commit, perpetrate*

bedrijvig *busy*, ‹hard werkend› *industrious*

bedrijvigheid *activity, busyness, industriousness*

bedroefd *sad, dejected*

bedroevend *sad, saddening, distressing*

bedrog *fraud, deceit, deception*

bedruipen I [ov ww] *to splash with...*, ‹culinair› *baste* II [wkd ww] ∗ zich(zelf) ~ *support o.s.*

bedrukt • (met inkt bedekt) *printed*

• (terneergeslagen) *dejected, depressed*

bedtijd *bedtime*

beducht *fearful* (of), *apprehensive* (about), *afraid* (of)

beduiden • (betekenen) *mean, represent* • (aanduiden) *indicate*

beduvelen *sell, swindle, double-cross*

bedwang *restraint, control*

bedwelmen ‹door drank, parfum› *intoxicate*, ‹door narcotica› *drug*

bedwingen *check, control, restrain, contain*

beëdigen • (een eed afnemen) *swear in* • (met een eed bekrachtigen) *swear to (s.th.)*

beëindigen *finish, end*, ‹form.› *conclude*

beek *brook*

beeld • (indruk) *image* • (sculptuur) *statue, sculpture*

beeldbuis ‹techn.› *cathode-ray tube*, ‹televisietoestel› (viewing) *screen*

beeldend *plastic, expressive, evocative*

beeldenstorm *iconoclasm*

beeldhouwer *sculptor*

beeldhouwwerk *sculpture*

beeldscherm *screen*

beeldschoon *gorgeous, stunning, ravishing*

beeldspraak *imagery, metaphor*

beeltenis *image, effigy*, ‹portret› *portrait*

been • (ledemaat) *leg* • (bot) *bone*

beer • (waterkering) *dam, weir* • (muurstut) *buttress* • (schuld) *debt* • (fecaliën) *muck, excrement* • (roofdier) *bear* • (mannetjesvarken) *boar*

beerput *cesspool, cesspit*

beest *animal, beast*

beestachtig • (als een beest) *beastly* • (walgelijk) *bestial* • (wreed) *brutal*

beet • (het bijten) *bite*, ‹wesp, slang, enz.› *sting* • (hap) *bite*

beetje ∗ een ~ *a bit/little*

beetnemen • (beetpakken) *seize, grab, take hold of* • (ertussen nemen) *make a fool of, pull s.o.'s leg*

bef *jabot*

befaamd *famous, famed,* ‹form.› *renowned*

begaafd *gifted, talented*

begaafdheid *gift, talent*

begaan I [bnw] ★ ~ zijn met pity; *feel sorry for* II [ov ww] • (uitvoeren) ‹misdaad› *commit,* ‹vergissing› *make* • (betreden) *walk on*

begaanbaar *passable,* ‹form.› *practicable*

begeerlijk *desirable*

begeerte *desire,* ‹erotisch› *lust*

begeleiden *escort,* ‹ook muzikaal› *accompany*

begeleider • (vergezeller) *escort, companion* • (muz.) *accompanist*

begeleiding *escort, accompanying,* ‹muz.› *accompaniment*

begeren *desire, wish, long for,* ‹form.› *covet*

begerig • (verlangend) *desirous (of), eager (for)* • (inhalig) *greedy*

begeven I [ov ww] • (verlaten) ★ het ~ *give out* II [wkd ww] • (gaan) *make one's way (to), go*

begieten *water*

begiftigen *endow (with), present (with)*

begijn *beguine*

begin *beginning, start*

beginnen I [ov ww] • (een begin maken met) *begin, start* • (gaan doen) *do* II [on ww] • (aanvangen) *begin (to)* ★ begin maar *go ahead!; fire away!* ★ om te ~ *to begin with; for a start* • (zich bezighouden) ★ daar kunnen we niet aan ~ *(that's) out of the question* • (~ over) *bring up, broach*

beginsel • (principe) *principle* • (grondslag) *basics*

begluren *spy on, peep at*

begraafplaats *cemetery, burial ground, graveyard*

begrafenis *funeral*

begrafenisstoet *funeral procession*

begraven *bury*

begrenzen • (de grens vormen) *border* • (beperken) *limit, restrict*

begrijpelijk *comprehensible, understandable, intelligible*

begrijpen *understand, comprehend*

begrip • (denkbeeld) *notion, concept, idea* • (inzicht) *comprehension, understanding*

begroeten *greet, welcome,* ‹form.› *salute*

begroten *estimate (at)*

begroting • (raming) *estimate* • (budget) *budget*

begunstigen *favour*

behaaglijk • (prettig) *comfortable, pleasant* • (gezellig) *cosy, snug*

behaagziek *coquettish, flirtatious*

behaard *hairy*

behagen I [het] *pleasure* II [on ww] *please*

behalen *win, gain, get,* ‹winst› *make*

behalve • (uitgezonderd) *except, but* • (benevens) *besides*

behandelen • (omgaan met) *treat,* ‹een vraag› *handle, deal with* • (uiteenzetten) *discuss*

behandeling *treatment*

behang *wallpaper*

behangen • (met behang bekleden) *wallpaper* • (bedekken) *hang (with)*

behartigen *serve, have at heart, look after*

beheer *management,* ‹toezicht› *control*

beheerder *director,* ‹kantine, enz.› *manager*

beheersen • (kennis hebben van iets) *be fluent in* • (heersen over) *control*

beheksen *bewitch*

behelzen *contain*

behendig *adroit*

behept *afflicted with, -ridden*
beheren *manage*
behoeden *keep (from), guard (from)*
behoedzaam *cautious, wary*
behoefte *want, need*
behoeftig *destitute, needy*
behoeve ⋆ *ten ~ van on behalf of*
behoeven I [ov ww] • *(nodig hebben)
need, want* II [on ww] • *(nodig zijn)*
⋆ *we ~ hem niet te schrijven we
needn't write to him; we don't need to
write him*
behoorlijk *proper, decent*
behoren • *(betamen) should, ought to*
• *(~ aan) be owned by, belong to*
• *(~ bij) go with/together* • *(~ tot)
belong to, be among*
behoud *preservation*
behouden I [bnw] ⋆ *~ reis! safe
journey!* II [ov ww] *preserve, keep*
behoudend *conservative*
behoudens • *(met voorbehoud)
subject to* • *(behalve) except for*
behulp ⋆ *met ~ van with the help of*
behulpzaam *obliging, helpful*
beige *beige*
beïnvloeden *influence*
beitel *chisel*
beits *(wood) stain*
bejaard *aged, elderly, old*
bejegenen *treat, use*
bek • *(muil) muzzle, ‹lange snuit›
snout* • *(snavel) bill, ‹kort› beak*
• *(mond) mouth, trap*
bekaf *done in, ‹inf.› dog-tired,
knackered*
bekend ⋆ *algemeen ~ common
knowledge* ⋆ *ik ben hier niet ~ I am a
stranger here* ⋆ *~ voorkomen look
familiar* ⋆ *~ klinken sound familiar*
bekendheid • *(faam) name,
reputation* • *(het bekend zijn met)
acquaintance (with)*
bekennen • *(uitkomen voor) confess,
own up* • *(jur.) admit, ‹v.*

beschuldigde› *plead guilty*
bekentenis *confession, admission*
beker • *(drinkgerei) cup, mug, beaker*
• *(sport) cup*
bekeren I [ov ww] • *(tot andere
overtuiging brengen) convert, ‹in
gunstige zin› reform* II [wkd ww] *be
converted (to), ‹zich beteren› mend
one's ways*
bekeuren *fine*
bekeuring *fine, ticket*
bekijken • *(kijken naar) look at,
examine* • *(beschouwen) look at,
consider*
bekken • *(kom) basin* • *(bio.) pelvis*
• *(muz.) cymbal*
beklaagde *accused*
bekladden *blotch, blot, ‹v. reputatie›
smear*
beklag *complaint*
beklagen I [ov ww] *pity* II [wkd ww]
• *(~ bij) complain to (s.o.)*
bekleden • *(bedekken) cover, hang on*
• *(vervullen) occupy, ‹ambt› hold*
bekleding • *(het bedekken) clothing,
covering, lining* • *(uitoefening) tenure*
beklemmen *oppress*
beklemtonen *stress*
beklimmen *climb, ‹form.› mount,
‹fig.› ascend*
beklinken I [ov ww] • *(afspreken)
clinch, settle* • *(toasten) drink to* II [on
ww] • *(inklinken) set, settle*
beknibbelen *skimp on, ‹loon› cut
back on*
beknopt *brief, concise*
beknotten *curtail, reduce*
bekocht *cheated, taken in*
bekoelen *cool (down)*
bekogelen *pelt*
bekokstoven *cook up, hatch, contrive*
bekomen I [ov ww] • *(krijgen) receive*
II [on ww] • *(herstellen van) recover,
get over*
bekommeren *worry*

bekonkelen plot, hatch, scheme
bekoorlijk charming
bekoren charm
bekoring charm
bekorten shorten, cut short
bekostigen pay the cost of, pay for
bekrachtigen confirm
bekrachtiging confirmation, ‹form.›
  ratification
bekritiseren criticize
bekrompen • (niet ruim) confined
  • (kortzichtig) narrow-minded,
  bigoted
bekronen crown (with success)
bekruipen • (opkomen v. gevoelens)
  steal over, come over • (besluipen)
  steal/creep up on
bekwaam capable, able, competent
bekwaamheid capability, ability
bekwamen I [ov ww] train II [wkd
  ww] qualify, prepare (for), train (to be)
bel • (deurbel) bell • (luchtbel) bubble
  • (oorbel) earring
belabberd wretched, rotten, ‹inf.› lousy
belachelijk ridiculous, laughable
beladen load, burden
belagen waylay (s.o.), beset, ‹vrijheid,
  veiligheid, enz.› threaten
belanden land/end up,
belang • (interesse) interest
  • (voordeel) interest, concern
  • (waarde) importance
belangrijk important, ‹aanzienlijk›
  considerable
belangstelling interest
belangwekkend interesting
belastbaar taxable
belasten • (opdragen) charge
  • (belasting opleggen) tax • (een
  lading plaatsen op) load, burden
belasteren slander, ‹form.› defame
belasting • (gewicht) load
  • (geestelijke druk) pressure, burden
  • (verplichte bijdrage) ‹plaatselijk›
  rates, ‹v.h. rijk› tax(es)

belastingaangifte (tax) return
belastingaanslag tax assessment
belastingbiljet tax form
belazeren diddle
beledigen insult, offend, affront
belediging insult, offence, affront
beleefd civil, polite, obliging, courteous
beleefdheid politeness, civility,
  courtesy
beleg • (belegering) siege
  • (broodbeleg) (sandwich) filling
belegen mellow, ‹kaas, wijn› matured
belegeren besiege
beleggen • (bedekken) cover
  • (investeren) invest
belegging • (bedekking) covering
  • (bijeenroeping) ‹form.› convocation
  • (geldinvestering) investment
beleid • (tact) tact • (gedragslijn)
  conduct, policy
belemmeren hamper, hinder
belemmering obstruction,
  interference, impediment, handicap
belendend adjacent, neighbouring
belenen pawn
beletsel obstacle, impediment
beletten prevent, obstruct
beleven • (meemaken) go through,
  experience • (lang genoeg leven om)
  live to see the day
belevenis experience, adventure
belezen well-read
België Belgium
belhamel • (deugniet) rascal, scamp
  • (raddraaier) ringleader
belichamen embody
belichaming embodiment
belichten • (licht laten vallen op)
  light up • (verhelderen) illustrate
  • (foto.) expose
believen I [het] pleasure II [ov ww]
  please
belijden • (bekennen) confess, admit
  • (aanhangen) ‹form.› profess
belijdenis • (kerkgenootschap)

denomination • (getuigenis van geloof) confirmation • (bekentenis) confession

bellen • (signaal geven) ring/sound the bell • (telefoneren) ring, call

bellettrie belles-lettres

belofte promise

belonen • (vergelden) reward • (betalen) pay, ‹form.› remunerate

beloning ‹voor daad› reward, ‹voor werk› pay

beloop course, way

belopen • (bedragen) amount to, add up to, run into (a large sum) • (te voet afleggen) ★ 't is niet te ~ it's too far to walk

beloven promise

beluisteren listen to

belust ★ ~ op eager for; keen on

bemachtigen • (buitmaken) capture • (te pakken krijgen) get hold of, ‹form.› secure

bemannen man

bemanning crew

bemerken notice, spot, ↑ perceive

bemesten ‹organisch› manure, ‹vnl. met kunstmest› fertilize

bemiddelaar intermediary, ‹inf.› go-between, ‹bij conflict› mediator

bemiddeld well-to-do, ‹inf.› well off

bemiddelen mediate

bemiddeling mediation

beminnelijk ‹in manieren› amiable, ‹v. aard› lovable

beminnen love

bemoederen mother

bemoedigen encourage, cheer up

bemoeial busybody, nos(e)y parker

bemoeienis • (inmenging) interference • (bemoeiing) exertion

bemoeilijken obstruct, impede, hamper, handicap

bemoeizucht meddling, meddlesomeness

benadelen harm, injure

benaderen come close to, ‹bedrag, ideaal› approximate (to)

benadering approach, ‹bedrag› approximation

benadrukken stress, emphasize, underline

benaming name

benard • (moeilijk) awkward • (hachelijk) perilous

benauwd • (niet ruim) cramped, ‹inf.› poky • (drukkend) close, ‹v. weer› sultry, muggy • (angstig) afraid, anxious

benauwen • (beklemmen) oppress • (beangstigen) frighten

bende • (groep) gang • (janboel) mess

beneden I [bijw] • (lager gelegen) down(stairs), at the bottom II [vz] • (onder) under, below, beneath

benedenverdieping ground-floor

benepen • (bekrompen) petty • (verlegen) bashful • (klein van ruimte) ‹kamer› poky

benevens (together) with, in addition to

bengel little scamp, naughty boy

benieuwd curious (about)

benieuwen ★ het zal mij ~ of I wonder if

benijden envy

benodigd required, necessary, requisite

benodigdheden necessities (of life), requisites

benoemen • (naam geven) name • (aanstellen) appoint

benoeming appointment

benul notion, inkling

benutten make the most of, utilize

benzine petrol, ‹AE› gas(oline)

benzinepomp petrol pump/ station

beoefenaar ‹geneeskunde› practitioner, ‹taal, muz.› student

beoefenen ‹deugd, kunst› practise, ‹wetenschap› study

beogen aim at, have in mind

beoordelen • (oordeel geven) *judge*, <v. examenwerk> *mark* • (inschatten) *estimate, assess*

bepaald I [bnw] • (vastgesteld) *specific, fixed* • (een of ander) *certain* II [bijw] *positively, absolutely*

bepakking *pack*

bepalen • (voorschrijven) *fix, stipulate*, <tijdstip, plaats> *appoint* • (vaststellen) *decide, define*

bepaling • (voorwaarde) *condition* • (voorschrift) *provision*

beperken *limit, restrict*

beperking *limitation, restriction*

beplanten *plant*

bepleiten *plead, advocate, argue*

bepraten • (overhalen) *persuade* • (praten over) *discuss*

beproeven • (proberen) *attempt, endeavour* • (op de proef stellen) *try, test*

beproeving • (proef) *trial, test* • (ellende) *trial, ordeal*

beraad *deliberation*

beraadslagen *deliberate (on)*

beraadslaging *consultation, consideration, deliberation*

beramen • (ontwerpen) *devise, plan* • (begroten) *estimate*

berechten *try*, <form.> *adjudicate*

bereden *mounted*

beredeneren *discuss*, <aantonen> *argue*

bereid *ready, willing, prepared*

bereiden *prepare*

bereik *reach, range*

bereikbaar <doel> *attainable*, <plaats> *accessible*

bereiken • (aankomen bij) *arrive in/at*, <v. leeftijd> *reach* • (komen tot iets) *achieve, attain*

bereisd (widely) *travelled*

berekend • (berekenend) *calculating, scheming* • (geschikt voor) <personen> *equal to*, <zaken> *designed for*

• (uitgerekend) *calculated*

berekenen • (becijferen) *calculate* • (in rekening brengen) *charge*

berekening *calculation*

berg *mountain*

bergen • (in veiligheid brengen) *rescue*, <wrak> *recover, salvage* • (opbergen) *store, put away* • (onderbrengen) *hold, accommodate, put up*

berging • (bergruimte) *storeroom* • (scheepv.) *salvage*

bergpas (mountain) *pass*

bergtop (mountain) *top*

bericht *news, message*, <in de krant> *report*

berichten *report, inform (s.o. of s.th.)*

berijden • (rijden op) *ride* • (rijden over) *drive along, ride on*

berispen *rebuke, reprimand*

berisping *rebuke, reprimand*

berm *verge, shoulder*

beroemd *famous, celebrated, renowned*

beroemdheid • (beroemd persoon) *a celebrity* • (het beroemd zijn) *fame, renown*

beroep • (betrekking) *occupation, job*, <hoger opgeleid> *profession* • (jur.) *appeal* ★ in hoger ~ gaan *appeal (to a higher court)*

beroepen *call (on), appeal to*

beroepskeuze *choice of career*

beroerd *rotten, miserable, wretched*

beroeren *stir (up), disturb*

beroering • (onrust) *trouble, agitation* • (commotie) *turmoil*

beroerte *fit, stroke*

berokkenen ★ iem. verdriet ~ *cause s.o. sorrow* ★ iem. schade ~ *harm s.o.*

berooid *penniless*, <form.> *destitute*

berouw *remorse, compunction*, <rel.> *repentance*

berouwvol *penitent*, <rel.> *repentant*

beroven <fig.> *deprive of*, <ook fig.> *rob*

berucht *notorious, disreputable*

berusten • (~ **bij**) *be deposited with, be in the keeping of* • (~ **in**) *acquiesce in/to, resign to* • (~ **op**) *be based on, rest on*

berusting • (gelatenheid) *resignation* • (bewaring) *custody*

bes • (vrucht) *berry* • (muzieknoot) B *flat*

beschaafd *cultivated, educated, well mannered, civilized*

beschaamd *ashamed*

beschadigen *damage*

beschadiging *damage*

beschamen • (beschaamd maken) (put to) *shame* • (teleurstellen) ‹vertrouwen› *betray*, ‹verwachtingen› *disappoint*

beschaving *civilization*

bescheiden *modest*

bescheidenheid *modesty*

beschermeling *protégé*

beschermen *protect, shield*, ‹tegen zon/wind› *screen*

beschermengel *guardian angel*

beschermheer *patron*

beschermheilige *patron saint*

bescherming • (begunstiging) *patronage* • (beveiliging) *protection*

beschieten *fire on/at*

beschikbaar *available*

beschikken • (beslissen) *arrange* • (~ **over**) *have at one's disposal*

beschikking • (besluit) *decision, decree* • (macht over iets te beschikken) *disposal*

beschilderen *paint*

beschimpen *scoff/jeer/sneer (at)*

beschonken *intoxicated*

beschot • (afscheiding) *partition* • (bekleedsel) *panelling*

beschouwen • (beoordelen) *consider, look at* • (houden voor) *consider, regard as*

beschouwing • (beoordeling, overdenking) *view, consideration,*

contemplation • (uiteenzetting) *view*

beschrijven • (omschrijven) *describe* • (schrijven op) *write on (paper)*

beschrijving *description*

beschroomd *timid*

beschuit *biscuit, rusk*

beschuldigen *accuse (of), charge (with)*

beschuldiging *accusation, charge*

beschutten *shelter (from), screen (from), protect (from/against)*

besef • (bewustzijn) *awareness, consciousness* • (begrip) *notion, idea*

beseffen *realize*

beslaan I [ov ww] • (innemen) ‹ruimte› *cover, take up* II [on ww] *mist over/up, steam up*

beslag • (deeg) *batter* • (het in bezit nemen) ‹v. goederen› *seizure*

beslechten *settle, decide*

beslissen *decide*

beslissing *decision*

beslist I [bnw] *decided, resolute* II [bijw] • (stellig) *absolutely* • (zeker) *definitely, decidedly*

besloten *private, closed*

besluipen *creep/steal up on*, ‹wild› *stalk*

besluit • (maatregel) *order*, ‹v. overheid› *decree* • (beslissing) *resolution, decision* • (einde) *conclusion, close* • (slotsom) *conclusion*

besluiteloos *undecided*, ‹form.› *irresolute*

besluiten • (eindigen) *finish (up), wind up (with), end* • (concluderen) *conclude* • (beslissing nemen) *decide*

besmeren *smear*, ‹met verf› *daub*

besmettelijk *contagious, infectious, catching*

besmetten *contaminate, infect*

besmeuren *smear (on/over), stain*

besnoeien ⋆ ~ **op** *cut (down on)*

besparen *save*

besparing *saving*

bespelen • (manipuleren)

manipulate, <gevoelens> play on
• (muz.) play
bespeuren perceive, sense, catch sight
of, spot
bespieden spy on, watch
bespiegeling contemplation
bespioneren spy on
bespoedigen accelerate, speed up
bespottelijk ridiculous
bespotten ridicule, mock, deride
bespreken • (behandelen) speak/talk
about, discuss • (recenseren) review,
<form.> notice • (reserveren) book
bespreking • (recensie) review
• (reservering) booking
• (behandeling) discussion
besproeien <land> irrigate, <planten>
water
best I [het] best II [bnw] • (goed) very
good, best, <zeer goed> excellent
• (aanspreking) dear • (instemming)
★ 't is mij best it's fine with me
III [bijw] • (zeer goed) best, very well
• (mogelijkheid) ★ 't is best mogelijk
it's highly likely ★ hij kan best thuis
zijn he may well be at home
bestaan I [het] existence II [on ww]
• (er zijn) be, exist • (mogelijk zijn) be
possible • (~ **uit**) consist of • (~ **van**)
live on
bestaansminimum subsistence level,
bare minimum
bestand I [het] • (wapenstilstand)
truce • (verzameling gegevens) file
II [bnw] • (~ **tegen**) <regen>
rainproof, <vuur> fireproof
bestanddeel element, ingredient
besteden • (uitgeven) <geld> spend
• (~ **aan**) ★ aandacht ~ aan pay
attention to ★ tijd ~ aan devote/spend
time on
bestek cutlery
bestelauto delivery van
bestellen • (laten komen) order (from)
• (bezorgen) deliver

besteller postman, <v. zaak> delivery
man
bestelling • (opdracht) order
• (bezorging) delivery
bestemmen mean, intend, mark out
bestemming destination
bestemmingsplan development plan
bestempelen • (stempelen) stamp,
• (aanduiden) call, label
bestendig • (duurzaam) <kleur>
permanent, <materialen> durable
• (niet veranderlijk) stable, <karakter>
steady
besterven ★ je zult het nog ~ it will be
the death of you ★ ik bestierf 't bijna
van de schrik I nearly jumped out of
my skin; I nearly died of fright ★ ik
bestierf 't bijna van 't lachen I nearly
died laughing
bestijgen ascend, climb, <paard, enz.>
mount
bestoken • (aanvallen) harass, <met
granaten> shell • (lastig vallen) pester,
<met vragen> assail, bombard
bestormen storm, attack
bestraffen • (straffen) punish
• (berispen) reprimand, rebuke
bestralen shine on, <med.> give
radiotherapy/-treatment
bestrating pavement
bestrijden • (bevechten) fight
(against) • (aanvechten) dispute (a
point) • (kosten, enz. dekken) cover,
reimburse, <form.> defray
bestrijken spread (over), smear, <verf>
coat (with)
bestrooien <poeder> dust, <suiker>
sprinkle
bestuderen study
besturen • (aan het stuur zitten) drive
• (regeren) govern, rule
bestuur • (regering) government
• (beheer) management
bestuurder • (leidinggevende)
governor, director, ruler

• (automobilist) *driver*
bestuurslid <bedrijf> *member of the board of directors*, <instelling> *member of the governors*, <vereniging> *committee member*
bestwil ★ leugentje om ~ *white lie* ★ voor uw/je eigen ~ *for your own good; in your own best interests*
betaalmiddel *currency*, <form.> *means of payment*
betalen • (vergelden) *repay* • (de kosten voldoen) *pay (for)*, <schuld> *settle, pay off*
betaling *payment*, <schuld> *settlement*
betalingsbalans *balance of payments*
betamelijk *proper, decent*
betamen *become*
betasten *finger, feel, handle*
betekenen *mean, signify*
betekenis • (inhoud, bedoeling) *sense, meaning* • (belang) *importance, significance*
beter *better*
beterschap *improvement*, <gezondheid> *recovery*
beteugelen *check, curb*
beteuterd *perplexed, dazed, stunned*
betijen ★ laat hem ~ *leave him alone; let him be*
betitelen *call, style*
betogen • (demonstreren) *demonstrate* • (beredeneren) *argue*
betoging *demonstration*
beton *concrete*
betonen *show, display*
betonmolen *concrete mixer*
betoog *argument*
betoveren • (beheksen) *cast a spell on, bewitch (a person)* • (bekoren) *fascinate, enchant*
betovering • (beheksing) *bewitchment, spell* • (bekoring) *fascination, enchantment*
betrachten *practise*
betrappen *catch*

betreden *set foot on, step onto*
betreffen • (aangaan) *concern, regard* • (betrekking hebben op) *relate to, concern*
betreffende *concerning*
betrekkelijk *relative, comparative*
betrekken I [ov ww] • (zijn intrek nemen) *move into* • (erbij halen) *involve* II [on ww] • (bewolkt worden) *become overcast, cloud over*
betrekking • (baan) *position, job, post* • (verhouding) *relation*
betreuren *regret*, <een verlies> *mourn*
betrouwbaar *reliable, dependable*
betten *bathe, dab*
betuigen *express*, <onschuld> *protest*
betweter <vero.> *wiseacre*
betwijfelen *doubt*
betwistbaar • (te betwisten) *debatable, disputable* • (twijfelachtig) *questionable*
betwisten *challenge, dispute*
beu ★ het beu zijn *be fed up (with s.th.)*
beugel • (bevestiging) *bracket* • (gebitscorrectie) *brace*
beuk • (boom) *beech* • (dreun) *whack*
beuken *batter, pound, hammer*
beul • (scherprechter) *executioner*, <bij ophanging> *hangman* • (wreedaard) *brute, beast*
beunhaas • (prutser) *cowboy* • (zwartwerker) *moonlighter*
beuren • (geld innen) *receive*
beurs I [de] • (tentoonstelling) *fair* • (portemonnee) *purse* • (studiebeurs) *scholarship* • (econ.) *exchange* II [bnw] • (overrijp) *over-ripe* • (bont en blauw) *bruised*
beursstudent *scholarship student*, <form.> *scholar*
beurt *turn*
beurtelings *in turn*
bevaarbaar *navigable*
bevallen • (aanstaan) *please* • (baren) *have a baby*

bevallig *graceful*
bevalling *birth,* ‹med.› *confinement*
bevangen *overcome, seize*
bevattelijk • (schrander) *intelligent*
• (duidelijk) *intelligible*
bevatten • (inhouden) *contain*
• (begrijpen) *comprehend*
bevattingsvermogen *comprehension*
bevechten *fight (against)*
beveiligen *protect, secure
(against/from)*
bevel • (opdracht) *order, command*
• (bevelschrift) *warrant, writ*
bevelen *order, command*
bevelhebber *commander*
beven ‹ook v. kou› *shake, shiver,* ‹ook
v. woede› *tremble*
bever *beaver*
beverig *trembling, shaking,*
‹handschrift› *shaky*
bevestigen • (bekrachtigen) *confirm*
• (vastmaken) *fix, fasten, attach*
bevinden I [ov ww] • (in
toestand/plaats zijn) *find*
• (vaststellen) *find* II [wkd ww] *find
o.s.*
bevinding *experience,* ‹na onderzoek›
finding
bevlieging *caprice, fancy*
bevloeien *irrigate*
bevochtigen *moisten*
bevoegd • (bekwaam) *qualified*
• (gerechtigd) *authorized*
bevoegdheid • (bekwaamheid)
qualification • (autoriteit) *authority*
bevolken *people*
bevolking *population*
bevolkingsregister • (bureau)
registry-office, registrar • (lijst)
Population Register, ‹in UK› *Register
of Births, Deaths and Marriages*
bevoordelen *benefit, favour*
bevooroordeeld *prejudiced, bias(s)ed*
bevoorrechten *privilege*
bevorderen • (begunstigen) *further,*

‹belangen, enz.› *promote,*
‹gezondheid› *benefit,* ‹groei, eetlust›
stimulate • (promoveren) *promote*
bevorderlijk *conducive (to), good (for)*
bevragen ★ te ~ bij *apply to* ★ te ~
alhier *apply within*
bevredigen *satisfy,* ‹lust› *indulge,
gratify*
bevrediging *satisfaction*
bevreemden *surprise*
bevreemding *surprise*
bevreesd *afraid (of), scared (of),
frightened (of)*
bevriend *friendly*
bevriezen *freeze*
bevrijden *liberate, free (from),*
‹gevangenen› *set free,* ‹uit gevaar›
rescue
bevrijding *liberation*
bevruchten *fertilize,* ‹zwanger
maken› *impregnate*
bevruchting • (het zwanger maken)
impregnation • (bio.) *fertilization*
bewaarder *keeper,* ‹cipier› *warder*
bewaken • (waken over veiligheid)
guard, watch over • (controleren)
monitor
bewaking • (het waken over) *guard,
watch* • (het controleren) *monitoring*
bewapenen *arm*
bewapeningswedloop *arms race*
bewaren • (niet wegdoen) *keep, save*
• (opbergen) *store, keep,* ‹etenswaren›
preserve • (behoeden) *protect, save
(from)*
beweegreden *motive*
bewegen I [ov ww] • (in beweging
brengen) *move* II [wkd ww] *move, stir*
beweging • (beroering) *commotion*
• (het bewegen) *movement, motion*
beweren *claim, assert*
bewering *assertion,* ‹betwistbaar›
claim, ‹uitspraak› *statement*
bewerken • (behandeling doen
ondergaan) ‹land› *farm, cultivate,*

<toneelstuk> *rewrite*, <voor toneel, film> *adapt (for)* • (bewerkstelligen) *accomplish, bring about* • (beïnvloeden) *manipulate*
bewerking • (het bewerken) *cultivation, process* • (beïnvloeding) *manipulation*, <muziekstuk> *arrangement*, <voor toneel, film> *adaptation*
bewerkstelligen *bring about, achieve, accomplish*
bewijs *proof, evidence*
bewijzen *prove*
bewind *government, administration*
bewindvoerder *administrator*, <bij faillissement> *trustee*
bewogen • (ontroerd) *moved, stirred* • (vol gebeurtenissen) *eventful, stirring*
bewolking *clouds*
bewonderaar *admirer*
bewonderen *admire*
bewondering *admiration (of/for)*
bewonen *inhabit*, <huis, enz.> *live in, occupy*
bewoner <huis, kamer> *occupant*, <v. stad, huis> *resident*
bewust • (betreffende) *concerned, aware, conscious* • (opzettelijk) *intentional, deliberate*
bewusteloos *unconscious, senseless*
bewustheid *consciousness*
bewustzijn *consciousness, awareness*
bezaaien • (bestrooien) *sow* • (bedekken met) ★ *bezaaid met dotted; studded with; strewn; littered*
bezadigd *sober-minded*, <persoon> *steady*
bezegelen *seal*
bezem *broom*
bezeren *hurt, injure*
bezet • (ingenomen) <v. hotelkamer> *occupied*, <v. persoon> *busy, occupied*, <v. plaats> *taken* • (bedekt) *set*
bezeten <v.d. duivel> *possessed*, <v.e.

gedachte> *obsessed*
bezetten *occupy*
bezetting *occupation*
bezichtigen *inspect, view*
bezielen • (leven geven aan) *animate, breathe life into* • (inspireren) *inspire, animate*
bezieling *animation, inspiration*
bezien • (bekijken) *regard, look at* • (denken over) ★ *het staat/valt te ~ it remains to be seen*
bezienswaardigheid *sight, place of interest*
bezig *busy, engaged (in), occupied (with)*
bezigheid *work, activity, occupation*
bezighouden *keep busy*
bezinken • (naar bodem zakken) *settle (down)* • (verwerken) *digest, assimilate*
bezinksel *sediment*
bezinnen ★ *zich ~ change one's mind*
bezinning • (het zich bezinnen) *reflection, contemplation* • (besef) *reflection*
bezit *possession*, <eigendom> *property*
bezitten *own, possess*
bezitter *owner*, <hotel, huis> *proprietor*
bezitting *property, possession*
bezoek • (het bezoeken) *visit, call* • (personen) *visitors, callers*
bezoeken • (een bezoek brengen aan) *visit, call on*, <kerk, school, theater> *attend*
bezoldigen *pay*
bezoldiging *pay, salary*
bezonken *mature, well-considered*
bezorgd • (ongerust) *uneasy (about), anxious, worried* • (vol goede zorg) *concerned (for/about)*
bezorgen • (verschaffen) *get, provide* • (afleveren) *deliver* • ((een uitgave) verzorgen) *edit*
bezuinigen *economize (on), cut down on one's expenses*
bezuren *regret*

bezwaar • (bedenking) *objection*
• (nadeel) *drawback*
bezwaard *weighed down, burdened*
bezwaarlijk I [bnw] *inconvenient*
II [bijw] *hardly, not very well*
bezwaarschrift *petition*
bezwaren *load, <vooral fig.> burden*
bezweet *perspiring, sweating*
bezweren • (onder ede verklaren)
swear • (uitdrijven) <v. kwade
krachten> *exorcize* • (oproepen)
conjure up
bezwering • (het onder eed
bevestigen) *swearing* • (het
uitdrijven) *exorcism* • (het oproepen)
conjuring • (het afwenden) *allying*
• (formule) *incantation*
bezwijken • (sterven) *go under,
succumb* • (niet bestand zijn tegen
iets) *collapse, give way* • (toegeven)
succumb, give in, yield to
bibberen *quiver, <ook v. kou> tremble,
shiver*
bibliografie *bibliography*
bibliothecaris *librarian*
biceps *biceps*
bidden *pray, <bij maaltijd> say grace*
biecht *confession*
biechten *confess*
bieden • (aanbieden) *offer, <aanblik>
present* • (een bod doen) *(make a) bid*
biefstuk *steak*
bier *beer*
bies • (sierrand) *border* • (plant)
(bul)rush
biet *(sugar)beet*
big *piglet*
bigamie *bigamy*
bij I [de] *bee* II [bnw] • (slim) ★ *hij is
goed bij he's clever/all there* • (bij
bewustzijn) *conscious* • (zonder
achterstand) *up-to-date* III [vz]
• (toegevoegd aan) *(to go) with*
• (aanwezig) *(present) at* • (in een
bepaald geval) *in case of, at*

• (door/wegens) *by* • (omstreeks) *by*
• (in de buurt van) *near/close to*
• (vergeleken met) ★ *het is daar niets
bij it's nothing in comparison with/to
that* • (maal) *by* • (met) *by* • (aan) *by*
• (door middel van) *by* • (~ met wkd
vnw) with ★ *heb je geld bij je? have
you any money on/with you*
bijbaantje *sideline*
bijbedoeling *hidden motive*
bijbehorend ★ *met ~e broek with
trousers to match; matching trousers*
bijbel *bible*
bijbels *biblical*
bijbetalen *pay extra, make an extra
payment*
bijblijven • (op de hoogte blijven)
keep up to date • (bijhouden) *keep
up/pace with*
bijbrengen • (bij bewustzijn
brengen) *bring round* • (leren) *teach,
<form.> impart (to)*
bijdehand *bright, smart*
bijdraaien *<v. personen> come round*
bijdrage *contribution*
bijdragen *contribute (to)*
bijeen *together, assembled*
bijeenkomen *meet, come together,
gather*
bijeenkomst *meeting, gathering,
<inf.> get-together*
bijeenroepen *call together, <v.
vergadering> convene*
bijenhouder *bee-keeper*
bijgaand *enclosed*
bijgebouw *annex(e)*
bijgedachte • (associatie) *association*
• (bijbedoeling) *ulterior motive*
bijgeloof *superstition*
bijgevolg *consequently, as a
consequence*
bijhouden • (bij iets houden) *hold
out* • (bijblijven) *keep up with, keep
pace with* • (niet achter laten raken)
keep up to date

bijkantoor *branch office*
bijkeuken *scullery, pantry, larder*
bijkomen • (bij bewustzijn komen) *come round/to* • (op adem komen) *gain one's breath, pick o.s. up*
bijkomstig • (toevallig) *incidental, accidental* • (als bijzaak) *of minor importance*
bijl *axe,* ‹klein› *hatchet*
bijlage *appendix,* ‹bij brief› *enclosure*
bijles *extra lesson*
bijna *nearly, almost*
bijnaam *nickname*
bijpassen *pay (extra)*
bijproduct *by-product*
bijscholen *retrain*
bijschrift *caption, note in the margin*
bijstellen *adjust*
bijster ∗ 't spoor ~ zijn *be on the wrong track*
bijten I [ov ww] *bite,* ‹v. slang› *sting* II [on ww] • (happen) *bite* • (stekend gevoel geven) *sting*
bijtijds *early,* ‹op tijd› *in time*
bijvak *subsidiary subject,* ‹inf.› *second subject*
bijval *approval, applause*
bijvallen ∗ iem. ~ *back s.o. up; support s.o.*
bijverdienste *extra income*
bijvoegen *add, enclose*
bijvoeglijk *adjectival*
bijvoegsel ‹v. boek› *appendix,* ‹v. brief› *enclosure*
bijvoorbeeld *for example, for instance*
bijwerken • (aanvullen) *bring up to date,* ‹v. tekst› *revise* • (afwerken) *touch up*
bijwonen • (bezoeken) *attend* • (meemaken) *witness*
bijwoord *adverb*
bijzaak *side issue, matter of secondary importance*
bijzetten • (plaatsen) *place* • (ter aarde bestellen) *bury*

bijzijn ∗ in het ~ van *in front of; in the presence of*
bijzin *subordinate clause*
bijzonder I [bnw] • (speciaal) *particular* • (eigenaardig) *peculiar* • (opmerkelijk) *remarkable* II [bijw] • (vooral) *especially* • (zeer) *very*
bijzonderheid • (detail) *particular detail* • (eigenaardigheid) *peculiarity*
bikini *bikini*
bikken *grub, lay into*
bil *buttock,* ‹v. dier› *rump*
biljart • (spel) *billiards* • (tafel) *billiard table*
biljet • (kaartje) *ticket* • (bankbiljet) (bank)*note* • (aanplakbiljet) *poster* • (strooibiljet) *leaflet, handbill*
biljoen *billion*
billijk *fair, reasonable*
billijken *approve (of)*
binair *binary*
binden • (in-/vastbinden) *bind, tie (up)* • (dikker maken) *thicken*
binding *bond*
bindweefsel *connective tissue*
binnen I [bijw] • (in een ruimte) *inside* • (in herinnering) ∗ 't schiet me wel weer te ~ *it will come back to me* II [vz] • (erin) *inside, within* • (minder dan) *within*
binnenband *tube*
binnendringen *penetrate,* ‹met geweld› *force one's way/break into*
binnengaan *go in, enter*
binnenhaven *inner harbour*
binnenhuisarchitect *interior decorator, interior designer*
binnenin *inside*
binnenkant *inside*
binnenkort *before long, soon*
binnenkrijgen *get down*
binnenland • (het inwendige van een land) *interior* • (het eigen land) ∗ in binnen- en buitenland *at home and abroad*

binnenlands *domestic,* ‹waterwegen› *inland*
binnenlaten *let in, show in*
binnenlopen • (op bezoek gaan) *drop in* (at/on) • (naar binnen gaan) *go in*(to)
binnenplaats (inner) *court*(yard)
binnenshuis *indoors*
binnensmonds *under one's breath*
binnenstad *town/city centre*
binnenvallen ‹onverwachts› *barge into*
binnenwaarts *inward*(s)
binnenwerk • (inwendige delen) *mechanism, innards* • (werk binnenshuis) *indoor work*
binnenzak *inside pocket*
biochemie *biochemistry*
biografie *biography*
biologie *biology*
biologisch *biological*
bioloog *biologist*
bioscoop *cinema*
biscuit *biscuit*
bisdom *diocese, bishopric*
bisschop *bishop*
bisschoppelijk *episcopal*
bits *snappy*
bitter I [het] *bitters* II [bnw] *bitter* III [bijw] *awfully*
bivak *bivouac*
bivakkeren • (in de open lucht slapen) *bivouac* • (tijdelijk wonen) *stay, be put up*
bizar *bizarre*
bizon *bison*
blaam *blame, censure*
blaar *blister*
blaas • (orgaan) *bladder* • (luchtbel) *bubble*
blaasinstrument *wind instrument*
blaaskaak *big head*
blad • (deel van plant) *leaf* • (vel papier) *sheet* • (tijdschrift) *magazine*
bladeren ★ in een boek ~ *leaf through a book*

bladgoud *gold leaf*
bladgroente *greens*
bladluis *greenfly*
bladwijzer *bookmark*
bladzijde *page*
blaffen • (geluid v. hond) *bark* • (tekeergaan) *bark* (at), *snap* (at)
blaken *burn,* ‹zon› *blaze*
blakeren *scorch*
blamage *disgrace*
blameren *discredit*
blanco *open,* ‹cheque› *blank*
blank I [bnw] • (ongekleurd, wit) *white* II [bijw] • (onder water) ★ ~ staan *be flooded*
blaten *bleat*
blauw I [het] *blue* II [bnw] *blue*
blauwbekken ★ staan ~ *stand in the cold*
blauwdruk *blueprint*
blazen *blow*
blazer • (bespeler van blaasinstrument) *brass player* • (jasje) *blazer*
bleek I [de] • (het bleken) *bleach*(ing) • (bleekveld) *bleach*(ing)*-field* II [bnw] *pale,* ‹form.› *wan*
bleken *bleach*
blij • (verheugd) *glad, happy, pleased* • (verheugend) *joyful*
blijdschap *gladness, joy* (at)
blijheid *gladness, joy* (at)
blijk *token, sign*
blijkbaar *apparent, evident, obvious*
blijken *appear* (from)
blijkens *according to*
blijmoedig *cheerful*
blijspel *comedy*
blijven *remain, stay*
blijvend *permanent, lasting, enduring*
blik I [de] *look,* ‹lang› *gaze,* ‹vluchtig› *glance* II [het] • (stofblik) *dustpan* • (plaatstaal) *tin* • (bus, doos) *tin*
blikken I [bnw] *tin* II [on ww] *look,*

glance
blikopener tin opener
blikschade damage to the bodywork
bliksem lightning
bliksemafleider lightning conductor
bliksemen I [on ww] flash II [onp ww]
lighten
bliksemflits flash of lightning
bliksemsnel as quick as lightning
blikvanger eye-catcher
blind I [het] shutter II [bnw] blind
blinddoeken blindfold
blinde blind man/woman
blindedarm appendix
blindelings blindly
blindengeleidehond guide dog, ‹AE›
seeing-eye dog
blindganger unexploded shell, ‹inf.›
dud
blindheid blindness
blinken shine, glitter
blocnote notepad, pad
bloed blood
bloedbad slaughter, massacre
bloeddorstig bloodthirsty
bloedeigen ∗ ~ kinderen own flesh
and blood
bloedeloos • (zonder bloed) bloodless
• (slap) listless
bloeden bleed
bloederig bloody
bloedig bloody
bloeding bleeding, ‹hevig›
haemorrhage
bloedlichaampje blood cell, ‹med.›
corpuscle
bloedneus bloody nose
bloedproef blood test
bloedsomloop (blood) circulation
bloeduitstorting bruise
bloedvat blood vessel
bloedvergiftiging blood poisoning
bloedverwant blood relation, relation,
relative
bloei • (het bloeien) blossom,

flowering, bloom • (ontplooiing)
prosperity, ‹form.› flower (of youth)
bloeien • (bloemen dragen) bloom,
blossom, flower • (floreren) flourish,
bloom
bloem • (plant) flower • (meel) flour
bloembol bulb
bloemist florist
bloemkool cauliflower
bloemlezing anthology
bloemperk flowerbed
bloempot flowerpot
bloemrijk flowery
bloemstuk bouquet, ‹form.› floral
tribute
bloes blouse
blok block
blokfluit recorder
blokkade blockade
blokken cram, swot
blokkendoos box of bricks
blokkeren • (de toegang afsluiten)
blockade • (tegenhouden) lock, jam,
‹cheque› stop
blond blond, fair, ‹v. vrouw› blonde
bloot bare, naked
blootgeven show one's hand, commit
o.s.
blootleggen • (van bedekking
ontdoen) lay bare • (onthullen)
disclose, reveal
blootshoofds bareheaded
blootstaan be subject to, be exposed to
blootstellen expose
blootsvoets barefoot
blos flush
blozen ‹v. gezondheid› bloom (with),
‹v. opwinding› flush (with), ‹v.
verlegenheid› blush (with)
bluf • (het overbluffen) bluff
• (opschepperij) bragging, boast(ing)
bluffen • (opscheppen) brag, boast
(of/about), swank (about)
• (overbluffen) bluff
blunder blunder

blussen *extinguish, put out*
blut *broke,* <na spel> *cleaned out*
bluts *dent*
blutsen *dent*
bobbel • (bult) *lump, bump*
• (lucht-/gasbel) *bubble*
bochel • (hoge rug) *hump*
• (gebochelde) *hunchback* • (bobbel)
lump
bocht I [de] *turn, curve, bend* II [het]
plonk, rubbish
bochtig *winding, tortuous*
bod *bid, offer*
bode *messenger*
bodem • (onderkant) *bottom* • (grond)
soil • (grondgebied) *territory*
bodemloos *bottomless*
boedel • (nalatenschap) *estate* • (bezit)
property
boedelscheiding *division of*
estate/property
boef *rogue, rascal,* <gevangene> *convict*
boeg *bow(s)*
boei *buoy*
boeien • (in de boeien slaan) *fetter,*
shackle, handcuff • (fascineren) *grip,*
arrest, enthral
boek *book*
boekbinder *bookbinder*
boekdeel *volume*
boekdrukkunst *printing*
boeken • (behalen) <succes> *score,*
<vooruitgang> *make* • (reserveren)
book
boekenkast *bookcase*
boekenlegger *bookmark*
boekenlijst *reading list*
boekenplank *bookshelf*
boekenrek *bookshelves*
boeket *bouquet*
boekhandel • (boekwinkel) *bookshop*
• (handel in boeken) *book trade*
boekhouden I [het] *bookkeeping*
II [on ww] *keep the books*
boekhouder *bookkeeper*

boekhouding • (het boekhouden)
bookkeeping, accountancy
• (boekhoudafdeling) *accounts*
department
boekjaar *financial year*
boekstaven *put on record*
boekweit *buckwheat*
boel • (bedoening) * de hele boel *the*
whole lot * een mooie boel *a pretty*
kettle of fish • (veel) * een (hele) boel
(quite) a lot (of)*
boeman *bogeyman*
boemelen • (feesten) *be out on the*
town, paint the town red • (met de
boemel reizen) *take the slow train*
boemerang *boomerang*
boenen • (schrobben) *scrub*
• (oppoetsen) *polish*
boer • (agrariër) *farmer*
• (plattelander) *countryman*
• (lomperik) *yokel, country bumpkin*
• (oprisping) *belch* • (speelkaart) *jack*
boerderij • (boerenbedrijf) *farm*
• (woning) *farmhouse*
boeren • (het boerenbedrijf
uitoefenen) *farm* • (een boer laten)
burp, belch
boerenbedrijf *farming (industry)*
boerenkool *curly kale*
boerin • (vrouwelijke boer) *woman*
farmer • (vrouw van de boer) *farmer's*
wife
boers *boorish*
boete • (geldstraf) *penalty, fine*
• (genoegdoening) * ~ doen *do*
penance
boetedoening *penance*
boeten *pay/suffer (for)*
boetiek *boutique*
boetseren *model*
boezem • (borstpartij) *breast,* <form.>
bosom • (binnenste) *heart* • (gemoed,
hart) *heart* • (hartholte) *auricle*
bof • (ziekte) *mumps* • (gelukje) *piece of*
luck

boffen *be lucky*
bok ‹geit› *billy goat,* ‹hert› *buck,* ‹hert,
eland› *stag*
bokaal *goblet,* ‹als prijs› *cup*
bokkensprong *antics*
bokkig *surly, gruff, morose*
bokking *bloater, smoked herring,*
‹vers› *white/fresh herring*
boksbeugel *knuckle-duster,* ‹AE› *brass
knuckles*
boksen *box*
bokser *boxer,* ‹voor geld› *prize-fighter*
bol I [de] • (bolvormig voorwerp)
sphere, ball, globe • (broodje) *roll*
II [bnw] *round,* ‹wangen› *chubby*
bolleboos *clever/bright person, dab,*
‹pej.› *clever-clogs*
bollen *bulge, swell (up),* ‹v. stof› *billow*
bolster *husk*
bolwerk *bulwark*
bolwerken ∗ het ~ *manage*
bom • (grote hoeveelheid) *load, pile*
• (explosief) *bomb*
bomaanslag *bomb attack,
bomb-outrage*
bombardement *bombardment*
bombarderen • (beschieten) ‹fig.›
bombard, ‹met bommen› *bomb,* ‹met
granaten› *shell* • (~ tot) *be appointed
as*
bombast *pompous language*
bombrief *letter-bomb*
bommenwerper *bomber*
bon • (bekeuring) *ticket* • (waardebon)
voucher • (cadeaubon) *token*
• (betalingsbewijs) *receipt*
bonbon *chocolate, sweet*
bond *alliance, league*
bondgenoot *ally*
bondgenootschap *alliance*
bondig *concise, terse*
bonnefooi ∗ op de ~ *on the off chance*
bons • (klap) *thump* • (hoge ome) *big
boss*
bont I [het] *fur* II [bnw] • (veelkleurig)

multi-coloured, ‹was› *coloured* • (met
gevlekte vacht) *spotted,* ‹paard›
piebald
bontjas *fur coat*
bonus *bonus*
bonzen *thump*
boodschap • (bericht) *message* • (het
inkopen) *the shopping*
boodschapper *messenger (boy)*
boog • (boogconstructie) ‹in gebouw›
arch, ‹v. brug› *span* • (kromme lijn)
arc, curve • (wapen) *bow*
boogschutter • (boogschieter) *archer*
• (sterrenbeeld) *Sagittarius*
boom *tree*
boomgaard *orchard*
boomgrens *tree-line*
boomschors *bark*
boomstam *tree-trunk*
boomstronk *stump*
boon *bean*
boor *drill*
boord I [de] • (rand) *border* • (oever)
bank, shore II [het] • (kraag) *collar*
• (scheepv., luchtv.) *board*
boordevol *brimfull, brimming with*
boordwerktuigkundige *flight
mechanic, flight engineer*
booreiland *oil-rig*
boormachine (power) *drill*
boos • (kwaad) *angry,* ‹woedend›
furious ∗ boos worden *lose one's
temper* • (verdorven) *wicked,* ‹daden,
driften› *evil*
boosaardig *malicious*
boosdoener *wrong-doer*
boot *boat*
bootwerker *docker*
bord • (eetgerei) *plate*
• (mededelingenbord) *notice board*
• (schoolbord) *blackboard*
• (speelbord) *board*
bordeel *brothel*
bordes ≈ (flight of) *steps*
borduren *embroider*

boren drill ∗ ~ naar drill for
borg • (persoon) surety, bail
• (onderpand) security
borgsom deposit
borgtocht • (borgstelling) security
• (waarborgsom) bail
borrel drink, drop, ‹Schots› dram
borrelen • (bubbelen) bubble
• (borrels drinken) have a drink
borst • (borstkas) chest
• (vrouwenborst) breast
borstel • (werktuig) brush • (stekels v.
dier) bristle
borstelen brush
borstelig bristly, bushly
borstkas chest
borstwering parapet
bos I [de] ‹bloemen, sleutels› bunch,
‹hout› bundle II [het] wood, ‹groot›
forest
bosbes bilberry
bosbrand forest fire
bosje • (bundeltje) bunch • (groepje
bomen) grove, thicket
boswachter forester
bot I [de] • (vis) flounder II [het] bone
III [bnw] • (niet scherp) dull, ‹mes›
blunt • (onbeleefd) ‹opmerking›
blunt, ‹weigering› flat
boter butter
boteren I [ov ww] • (met boter
besmeren) butter II [on ww] • (tot
boter worden) make butter
boterham (a slice of) bread (and
butter), ‹met beleg› sandwich
botsen • (stoten) collide (with), crash
(into), bump (into) • (in conflict
komen) clash
botsing smash (up), collision, crash
bottelen bottle
botterik • (lomperd) lout • (dom
persoon) dimwit
botvieren ∗ zijn hartstochten ~
indulge one's passions
botweg bluntly, point-blank

boud bold
bougie • (motoronderdeel) spark(ing)
plug • (kaars) candle
bouillon stock
bouillonblokje stock cube
boulevard boulevard, ‹aan zee›
promenade
bout • (schroef) bolt • (strijkijzer) iron
• (stuk vlees) leg, ‹v. gevogelte›
drumstick
bouw • (het bouwen) building,
construction • (postuur) build
bouwdoos • (blokkendoos) box of
bricks • (bouwpakket) do-it-yourself
kit
bouwen • (maken) build • (~ op) rely
on, depend on
bouwgrond • (bouwterrein) building
site • (landbouwgrond) arable land
bouwkunde architecture
bouwkundig architectural
bouwkunst architecture
bouwpakket do-it-yourself kit
bouwstijl architecture, architectural
style
bouwvak I [de] building industry
holiday II [het] building (trade)
bouwval ruin(s)
bouwvallig ramshackle, dilapidated
bouwwerk building
boven I [bijw] • (hoger gelegen) above,
up(stairs) • (erop) on (the) top of ∗ van
~ naar beneden from top to bottom;
(from the top) downward(s) II [vz]
above, over
bovenaan at the top
bovenal above all
bovenarm upper arm
bovenbouw • (de hogere klassen) last
two or three classes of a secondary
school • (bovendeel v. gebouw)
superstructure
bovenbuur upstairs neighbour
bovendien besides, in addition,
moreover

bovengronds ‹leidingen› *overhead*, ‹trein› *overground*
bovenhuis *upstairs flat/apartment*
bovenin *at the top*
bovenkamer *upstairs room*
bovenkomen • (aan de oppervlakte komen) *surface, rise, float to the surface* • (opwellen) *surface* • (een verdieping hoger komen) *come up(stairs)*
bovenleiding *overhead line/cable*
bovenmatig *excessive, extreme*
bovenmenselijk *superhuman*
bovennatuurlijk *supernatural*
bovenop *on top*
bovenstaand ★ 't ~e *the above*
boventoon *overtone*
bovenuit ★ zijn stem klonk overal ~ *his voice drowned (out) everything*
box • (babybox) *playpen* • (afgescheiden bergruimte) *box* • (luidspreker) *(loud)speaker*
boycot *boycott*
boycotten *boycott*
braadpan *frying pan*
braaf *good*
braak I [de] *burglary* II [bnw] *fallow*
braakmiddel *emetic*
braam • (oneffen rand) *burr* • (braambes) *blackberry* • (braamstruik) *blackberry (bush), bramble*
brabbelen *jabber*
braden ‹in de oven› *roast, bake*, ‹in de pan› *fry*
brak I [de] *beagle* II [bnw] *brackish*
braken *vomit, be sick, throw up*
brancard *stretcher*
brand *fire*
brandbaar *combustible, inflammable*
brandblaar *blister*
branden I [ov ww] *burn*, ‹door hete vloeistof› *scald* II [on ww] *burn* • (~ van) *burn (with)*
brander • (vlambek) *burner*

• (distilleerder) *distiller*
branderig • (als van brand) *burnt* • (ontstoken) *inflamed, burning*
brandewijn *brandy*
brandgang *firebreak*
brandhout *firewood*
branding *surf*, ‹golven› *breakers*
brandkast *safe*
brandmerk • (merkteken) *brand* • (schandvlek) *stigma*
brandmerken *brand*, ‹fig.› *stigmatize*
brandnetel *nettle*
brandpunt • (snijpunt van stralen) *focus* • (middelpunt) *focus, centre*
brandslang *fire-hose*
brandstapel *funeral pyre*
brandstichter *arsonist, fire-raiser*, ‹AE› *firebug*
brandstof *fuel*
brandvrij *flame/fire resistant, fireproof*
brandweer *fire brigade*
brandweerman *fireman*
brandwond *burn*
bravoure *bravado*
breed • (wijd) *broad, wide* • (ruim) ★ zij hebben het niet ~ *they are hard up*
breedsprakig *verbose, long-winded*
breedte *width, breadth*, ‹geo.› *latitude*
breedtegraad *degree of latitude*
breedvoerig *detailed, exhaustive*
breekbaar *breakable, fragile*
breekijzer *crowbar*
breien *knit*
brein • (hersenen) *brain* • (verstand) *intellect*
breiwerk *knitting*
breken *break*, ‹v. bot› *fracture*
brem *broom*
brengen • (vervoeren) ‹naar de spreker toe› *bring*, ‹v.d. spreker af› *take* • (doen geraken) *get, bring, make* • (presenteren) *bring* ★ ten gehore ~ *perform* ★ iets naar voren ~ *suggest s.th.*

bres *breach, gap*
breuk • (het breken) *breaking*
• (beschadiging) ‹in glas› *crack*, ‹v.
bot› *fracture* • (navelbreuk) *hernia*
• (verbreking van relatie) *rupture,
split* • (wisk.) *fraction*
brevet *certificate*, ‹luchtvaart› *licence*
brief *letter*, ‹form.› *epistle*
briefkaart *postcard*
briefwisseling *correspondence*
bries *breeze*
briesen ‹v. leeuw› *roar*, ‹v. paard› *snort*
brievenbus *mailbox*, ‹aan huis›
letterbox, ‹om te verzenden› *pillar box*
brigade *brigade*
brigadier ‹bij de politie› *(police)
sergeant*, ‹in het leger› *brigadier*
brij *porridge*, ‹fig.› *pulp*
bril • (wc-bril) *seat* • (kijkglazen) *(pair
of) glasses, spectacles*
briljant I [de] *diamond* II [bnw]
brilliant
brillantine *brilliantine*
Brits I [het] *British-English* II [bnw]
British
brochure *brochure*
broeden *brood, sit (on eggs)*
broeder • (broer) *brother* • (verpleger)
(male) nurse • (rel.) *friar*
broederlijk *brotherly*
broederschap • (het broeders zijn)
brotherhood • (vereniging) *fraternity*
broeien • (heet worden) *heat, get
heated* • (drukkend warm zijn) *be
muggy/sultry* • (dreigen) ⋆ *er broeit
onweer a (thunder)storm is brewing*
broeierig *close, sultry*
broeikas *hothouse*
broeinest *hotbed*
broek *(pair of) trousers*, ‹AE› *pants*
broekpak *trouser suit*
broer *brother*
brok *chunk, piece*, ‹groot› *lump*
brokkelig *crumbly*
brokstuk *fragment, piece*

brombeer *grumbler*
bromfiets *moped*
brommen • (brommend geluid
maken) ‹dier› *growl (at)*, ‹v. motor,
radio› *whirr, hum* • (straf uitzitten)
do time
bron • (opwellend water) *spring*
• (oorsprong) *source, origin*
bronchitis *bronchitis*
brons *bronze*
bronwater *spring water*
bronzen I [bnw] *bronze* II [ov ww]
bronze, tan
brood • (eetwaar) *bread*
• (levensonderhoud) *living*
broodmager (as) *thin as a rake*
broodtrommel *bread-bin*
broodwinning *living, livelihood*
brouwen I [ov ww] • (bereiden) *brew*
• (beramen) *stir up* II [on ww] *speak
with a burr*
brouwsel *brew, concoction*
brug • (sport) *parallel bars* • (scheepv.)
bridge • (gebitsprothese) *bridge(work)*
• (oeververbinding) *bridge*
bruid *bride*
bruidegom *bridegroom*
bruidsjonker ‹v. bruidegom› *best
man*
bruidsmeisje *bridesmaid*
bruidspaar *bride and (bride)groom*
bruidsschat *dowry*
bruikbaar *useful*
bruikleen ⋆ in ~ (hebben) *(have) on
loan*
bruiloft • (huwelijksfeest) *wedding*
• (gedenkfeest) *wedding anniversary*
bruin I [het] *brown* II [bnw] *brown*,
‹v.d. zon› *tanned*
bruinen *brown*, ‹door de zon› *tan*
bruisen ‹v. beek› *bubble*, ‹v. drank›
fizz, sparkle
brullen *roar*
brunette *brunette*
brutaal *insolent, cheeky*

brutaliteit *brashness, impudence, insolence, cheek*
bruto *gross*
bruusk *abrupt, brusque*
bruut I [de] *brute* II [bnw] *coarse, brutal*
budget *budget*
buffel *buffalo*
buffer *buffer*
buffet • (opbergmeubel) *sideboard* • (stationsrestauratie) *buffet, refreshment bar*
bui • (neerslag) *shower* • (humeur) *mood*
buigen I [ov ww] • (krom staan) *bend* II [on ww] • (afbuigen) *bend* • (buiging maken) *bow*
buiging • (kromming) *curve, bend* • (groet) *bow*
buigzaam *flexible*
buiig *showery*
buik *belly*, ‹form.› *abdomen*
buikdanseres *belly dancer*
buikloop *diarrhoea*
buikpijn *stomach-ache*, ‹inf.› *bellyache*, ‹kind.› *tummy-ache*
buikriem • (riem) *belt* • (zadelriem) *girth*
buikspreken I [het] *ventriloquism* II [ww] *practise ventriloquism*
buil *lump, swelling*
buis • (pijp) *tube* • (televisie) *telly, box*
buit *booty, spoils, loot*
buitelen *tumble*
buiteling *tumble*
buiten I [bijw] • (buitenshuis) *outside* • (niet betrokken bij) *out of* • ((op) het platteland) (in) *the country* II [vz] • (zonder) *without, out of* • (behalve) *except for* • (niet binnen een plaats) *outside*
buitenboordmotor *outboard motor*
buitenechtelijk ‹kind› *illegitimate*, ‹verhouding› *extramarital*
buitengaats *off shore*
buitengewoon *extraordinary,*

exceptional
buitenissig *eccentric, strange*
buitenkant *outside*
buitenland *foreign country*
buitenlander *foreigner*
buitenlands *foreign*
buitenlucht ‹buitenshuis› *open air*, ‹op het platteland› *country air*
buitenom ★ ~ het huis/de stad, enz. gaan *go round the house/town*
buitenshuis *out-of-doors*
buitensluiten *lock out*, ‹fig.› *exclude*
buitenspel ‹sport› *offside*
buitensporig *extravagant*
buitenstaander *outsider*
buitenverblijf *country house*
buitenwijk *suburb*
buitenzijde *outside*
bukken *stoop*, ‹snel› *duck*
bul • (oorkonde) *diploma, degree certificate* • (stier) *bull*
bulderen *roar, bellow*
buldog *bulldog*
bulken ★ ~ van het geld *be rolling in money*
bullebak *bully*
bult *lump, bump*, ‹bochel› *hump*
bundel • (bos(je) van iets) *bundle* • (verzameling, boekje) *collection*
bundelen *bundle*, ‹krachten› *join*, ‹teksten› *collect*
bungalow *bungalow*
bunker *bunker, pillbox*
bunzing *polecat*
burcht *castle, citadel, fortress*
bureau • (openbaar gebouw) *office* • (schrijftafel) *(writing) desk* • (afdeling) *bureau, office*
bureaucratie *red tape, bureaucracy*
burgemeester *mayor*
burger • (inwoner) *citizen* • (niet-militair) *civilian*
burgerij • (burgerbevolking) *citizens* • (burgerstand) *middle classes*
burgerlijk • (van/voor staatsburgers)

civil • (kleinburgerlijk) middle-class, (petit) bourgeois
burgerrecht civil right(s)
bus • (autobus) coach, <stadsbus> bus
• (brievenbus) ★ een brief op de bus doen post a letter • (trommel) box, caddy
buskruit gunpowder
buste • (borstbeeld) bust • (boezem) bust, bosom
bustehouder bra, <form.> brassière
butagas calor gas
buur neighbour
buurt • (omgeving) neighbourhood, vicinity • (wijk) quarter, neighbourhood, district, area

C

cabaret cabaret
cabine • (bestuurderscabine) cabin
• (passagiersruimte) cabin
• (projectieruimte) projection room
• (hokje) booth
cacao • (chocolademelk, cacaopoeder) cocoa • (boom, boon) cacao
cactus cactus
cadans rhythm
cadeau present, gift
caféhouder landlord, pub owner, café owner
cafetaria cafeteria
calorie calorie
calvinisme Calvinism
calvinistisch Calvinistic
camera camera
camoufleren camouflage
campagne campaign
canon canon
canoniek canonical
canvas canvass
capabel capable, competent, able
capaciteit • (vermogen) capacity, <v. motor, enz.> power • (bekwaamheid) ability, capability
capitulatie capitulation
capituleren capitulate
capsule capsule, <v. fles> bottle-cap
caravan caravan, <AE> trailer
cardiogram cardiogram
cardioloog cardiologist
cargadoor ship broker
carnaval carnival
carrosserie coachwork, bodywork
cassatie cassation
cassette cassette tape
cassetterecorder cassette/tape recorder
castratie castration
castreren castrate, <v. dieren> geld

catalogus *catalogue*
catastrofaal *catastrophic, disastrous*
catechisatie *confirmation classes*
catechismus *catechism*
categorie *category*
categorisch *categorical*
causaal *causal*
cavalerie *cavalry*
ceder *cedar*
ceintuur • (riem) *belt* • (gordel van stof) *sash*
cel *cell*
celibaat *celibacy*
cellist (violon)*cellist*
cello *cello*
cellofaan *cellophane*
Celsius *Celsius*
cement *cement*
censuur *censorship*
cent • (munt) *cent* • (kleine waarde) *penny*
centraal *central*
centrale • (elektriciteitscentrale) *power station* • (telefooncentrale) *exchange*, ‹binnen een gebouw› *switchboard*
centrifuge ‹techn.› *centrifuge*, ‹voor de was› *spin-drier*
centrum *centre*
ceremonie *ceremony*
ceremonieel *ceremonial*
certificaat *certificate*
chalet *chalet, Swiss cottage*
champagne *champagne*
chantage *blackmail*
chaos *chaos, disorder, confusion*
chaotisch *chaotic*
charmant *charming, delightful*
charmeren *charm*
charteren *charter*
chassis ‹v. auto› *chassis*
chaufferen *drive (a car)*
chauffeur *driver*, ‹in uniform› *chauffeur*
chef *chief*, ‹inf.› *boss*, ‹directeur›

manager, ‹patroon› *employer*, ‹v. afdeling› *office-manager*
chemicaliën *chemicals*
chemicus (research) *chemist, chemical analyst*
chemie *chemistry*
chemisch *chemical*
cheque *cheque*
chic *stylish, smart*
chimpansee *chimpanzee*, ‹inf.› *chimp*
Chinees I [de] • (persoon) *Chinese* [mv: *Chinese*], ‹bel.› *Chink* • (Chinees restaurant) *Chinese restaurant* II [het] *Chinese* III [bnw] *Chinese*
chip (computer) *chip*
chirurg *surgeon*
chirurgisch *surgical*
chloor *chlorine*
cholera *cholera*
cholesterol *cholesterol*
choreografie *choreography*
christelijk *Christian*
christen *Christian*
christendom *Christianity*
chromosoom *chromosome*
chronisch *chronic*
chroom *chromium*
cijfer • (cijferteken) *figure* • (maatstaf) *mark, grade* • (code) *cipher*
cijferen *calculate*
cilinder *cylinder*
cineast *film director*
circa *about, approximately*, ‹jaartallen› *circa, around*
circulatie *circulation*
circuleren *circulate*
circus *circus*
cirkel *circle*
cirkelen *circle*
citaat *quotation*
citeren *cite*, ‹woordelijk› *quote*
citroen *lemon*
civiel *civil(ian)*
claimen *claim*
clandestien *clandestine, secret*,

<handel> illicit
classicus classicist, classical scholar
classificatie classification
classificeren classify, class
claustrofobie claustrophobia
clausule clause, stipulation, rider
claxon horn
claxonneren honk, hoot, sound one's horn
clementie clemency, leniency
clerus clergy
cliënt client, customer
climax climax
clinch clinch
clitoris clitoris
closet water-closet, w.c.
clown clown
club club
coalitie coalition
cocaïne cocaine
code code
coderen encode
codicil codicil
cognac cognac, French brandy
coïtus coitus
cokes coke
collecte collection
collecteren collect
collectief collective
collega colleague
college • (les) lecture
• (bestuurslichaam) board
collegegeld lecture fee, tuition fees
collegialiteit good-fellowship, fellow-feeling
colporteur canvasser, hawker
coltrui turtleneck sweater, polo-neck sweater
coma coma
combinatie combination
combineren combine
comfort comfort
comfortabel comfortable
commandant commander, <v. kamp> commandant

commanderen command, order
commando • (gezag) command
• (bevel) command, order • (soldaat) commando [mv: commandos]
commentaar comment, <krant, tv, enz.> commentary
commentariëren commentate on, comment upon
commentator commentator
commercieel commercial
commies • (kantoorbediende) clerk
• (ambtenaar) civil servant, <v. douane> customs officer
commissaris <v. politie> Chief Constable, <v.d. koningin> provincial governor
commissie • (groep personen) committee • (opdracht) commission
communicatie communication
communicatiesatelliet communications satellite, comsat
communiceren communicate
communie (Holy) Communion
communisme communism
communist communist
communistisch communist
compact compact
compagnie company
compagnon partner
compensatie compensation
compenseren make good, counterbalance, compensate for
competent competent
competentie competence
competitie • (wedijver) competition
• (sport) league
compleet I [bnw] complete, full
II [bijw] clean
complex I [het] complex II [bnw] complex, complicated
compliment compliment
complot plot, intrigue
componeren compose
componist composer
compositie composition

compost *compost*
compressie *compression*
computer *computer*
concentratiekamp *concentration camp*
concentreren *focus, concentrate, centre (a)round/on*
concentrisch *concentric*
concept • *(ontwerp) (rough) draft, outline* • *(begrip) concept*
concert • *(uitvoering) concert* • *(stuk) concerto*
concerteren *give a concert*
concessie *concession*
conciërge *caretaker, <grote gebouwen> janitor*
concilie *council*
concluderen *conclude, infer (from)*
conclusie *conclusion*
concreet *concrete*
concurrent *competitor, rival*
concurrentie *rivalry, competition*
concurreren *compete (with)*
conditie • *(voorwaarde) condition* • *((lichamelijke) toestand) condition, state*
condoleren *condole*
condoom *condom, <inf.> rubber*
conducteur *conductor, <v. trein> guard*
conferentie *conference*
conflict *conflict, dispute*
conform *in conformity/accordance with*
confrontatie *confrontation*
confronteren *confront/face (with)*
congres *congress*
congruent *corresponding, <wisk.> congruent*
conjunctuur *tendency of the market, economic situation*
connectie *connection*
conrector *deputy headmaster, senior master*
consciëntieus *conscientious, scrupulous*
consequent *consistent, logical*

consequentie *consequence*
conservatief I *[de] conservative* II *[bnw] conservative, <pol.> Conservative*
conservatorium *conservatory, school of music*
conserveren • *(goed houden) preserve, keep* • *(inblikken) tin, can*
consideratie *consideration*
consolideren *consolidate*
constateren *ascertain, establish*
constellatie • *(stand van zaken) state of affairs* • *(stand van sterren) constellation*
constitutie *constitution*
constitutioneel *constitutional*
constructie • *(het construeren) construction* • *(het bouwen) building* • *(het geconstrueerde) structure, construction*
constructief *constructive*
construeren • *(samenstellen) construct* • *(bouwen) build* • *(ontwerpen) design*
consul *consul*
consulaat *consulate*
consulent *adviser, <voor belasting, enz.> consultant*
consult *consultation*
consultatiebureau *health centre*
consulteren *consult*
consument *consumer*
consumentenbond *Consumers' Association, <Engeland> Consumer's Council*
consumeren *consume, eat, drink*
consumptie • *(voedsel) refreshment(s)* • *(verbruik) consumption*
contact • *(aanraking) touch, contact* • *(persoon) connection* • *(elektrische verbinding) contact, <v. auto> ignition*
contactdoos *socket*
contactlens *contact lens*
container *container*
contant *cash*

continent *continent*
continentaal *continental*
contingent *contingent*
continubedrijf *continuous working plant, working on a 24-hour basis,* <bedrijfstak> *continuous industry*
conto *account*
contract *contract, agreement*
contractueel *contractual*
contrast *contrast*
contrasteren *contrast (with)*
contributie *subscription*
controle • (het beheersen) *control* • (toezicht) *check (on), supervision,* <med.> *checkup,* <v. kaartjes> *inspection* • (plaats) *ticket gate/barrier*
controleren *check,* <v. feiten> *verify,* <v. kaartjes> *inspect*
controleur *controller, inspector,* <kaartjes> *ticket-inspector*
conventioneel *conventional*
conversatie *conversation*
convocatie *notification,* <aankondiging> *notice,* <bijeenroeping> *convocation*
coöperatie • (samenwerking) *cooperation* • (vereniging) *cooperative*
coördineren *co-ordinate*
corporatie *corporate body, corporation*
corps *corps, body*
correct *correct*
correctie *correction*
correspondent *correspondent*
correspondentie *correspondence*
corresponderen • (overeenstemmen) *correspond (with/to)* • (schrijven) *correspond (with)*
corrigeren • (verbeteren) *correct* • (nakijken) <proefdruk> *(proof)read,* <schoolwerk> *mark*
corrupt *corrupt*
corsage *corsage*
corvee • (vervelend werk) *chore, drudgery* • (huishoudelijk karwei) *chores,* <mil.> *fatique*

coupé • (ruimte in trein) *compartment* • (auto) *coupé*
couplet *stanza,* <v. twee regels> *couplet*
coupon *coupon*
courant *current, marketable*
couvert • (briefomslag) *envelope* • (bestek voor één persoon) *cover*
credit *credit*
crediteren *credit*
creëren *create*
crematie *cremation*
crematorium *crematorium, crematory*
cremeren *cremate*
creperen *kick the bucket*
crisis *crisis*
criterium *criterion* [mv: *criteria*]
criticus *critic*
cruciaal *crucial*
culinair *culinary*
cultureel *cultural*
cultus *cult*
cultuur *culture*
cultuurgeschiedenis *cultural history*
curatele *guardianship*
curator *curator, custodian*
curieus *curious, strange, odd*
curiositeit *curiosity, oddity,* <klein voorwerp> *curio*
cursief *italicized, in italics*
cursus *course*
cycloon *cyclone*
cyclus *cycle*
cynicus *cynic*
cynisch *cynical*
cynisme *cynicism*

D

daad *action, act*
daadwerkelijk *actual*
daags I [bnw] *daily* II [bijw]
 ★ tweemaal ~ *twice a day*
daar *there*
daardoor • (daardoorheen) *through
 that* • (door middel van) *by doing so,
 by these means*
daarentegen ‹keuze› *on the other
 hand,* ‹tegenstelling› *on the contrary*
daarheen *there,* ‹met beweging› *over
 there, that way*
daarin *in it, in there,* ‹met beweging›
 into it
daarlaten *leave s.th. out of
 consideration, leave aside*
daarna *after that, afterwards*
daarnaast *next to it, beside it*
daarom • (om die reden) *therefore*
 • (desondanks) *in spite of..., although*
daaronder • (onder iets) *under that
 (it)* • (onder meer) *among(st) others,
 including*
daarop • (erbovenop) (up) *on it*
 • (vervolgens) *thereupon*
daarover • (eroverheen) *across it,*
 ‹plaats› *over that* • (daaromtrent)
 about that
daartoe *for that purpose, to that end*
daartussen *between (among) them*
daaruit • (eruit) *out of it/that*
 • (daaruit volgend) *from that*
daarvoor • (voor een tijd) *before that*
 • (ten behoeve van) *for that (purpose)*
 • (voor een plaats) *in front of it*
dadel *date*
dadelijk *immediately, directly, at once,*
 ‹straks› *presently*
dader *offender, culprit,* ‹form.›
 perpetrator

dag I [de] *day* [tw] • (groet bij
 ontmoeting) *hello!* • (groet ter
 afscheid) *bye (bye)!*
dagblad *daily (paper)*
dagboek *diary*
dagelijks I [bnw] • (daags) *daily*
 • (gewoon) *everyday* II [bijw] *every
 day, daily*
dagen I [ov ww] • (dagvaarden)
 summon II [on ww] • (dag worden)
 ★ het begon te ~ *day was
 breaking/dawning*
dageraad *dawn*
daglicht *daylight*
dagloon *daily wages*
dagvaarden *summon,* ‹jur.› *subpoena*
dagvaarding *summons,* ‹jur.›
 subpoena
dak *roof*
dakgoot *gutter*
dakloos • (zonder dak) *roofless*
 • (zonder onderdak) *homeless*
dakpan (roof) *tile*
dal *valley*
dalen *descend,* ‹prijs, temperatuur›
 fall, drop
daling *descent,* ‹prijs, temperatuur›
 fall, drop
dam • (waterkering) *dam* • (dubbele
 damschijf) *king*
damast *damask*
dambord ‹BE› *draughtboard(s),* ‹AE›
 checkerboard
dame *lady*
dammen ‹BE› *play draughts,* ‹AE›
 play checkers
damp *vapour,* ‹schadelijk› *fume,
 smoke,* ‹v. water› *steam*
dampen • (damp afgeven) *steam*
 • (rook afgeven) *smoke, fume*
dampkring *atmosphere*
damschijf ‹BE› *draughtsman,* ‹AE›
 checker
damspel ‹BE› (game of) *draughts,* ‹AE›
 checkers

dan I [bijw] *then* II [vw] ★ *ouder dan older than*

danig I [bnw] <afgang> *severe,* <pak slaag> *sound* II [bijw] *soundly, severely, terribly*

dank *thanks*

dankbaar *thankful, grateful*

dankbaarheid *gratitude*

danken I [ov ww] ● (bedanken) *thank, give thanks* ● (verschuldigd zijn) *owe, be indebted* II [on ww] ● (bidden) *say grace*

dans *dance*

dansen *dance*

dapper *brave*

dapperheid *bravery,* <v. soldaat> *gallantry, valour*

darm *intestine, gut*

dartel *playful,* <v. dier> *frisky*

dartelen *frolic,* <v. dier> *frisk*

das ● (stropdas) *tie* ● (sjaal van stof/wol) *scarf* ● (dier) *badger*

dat I [aanw vnw] *that* [mv: *those*] II [betr vnw] *that, which* III [vw] *that*

data *data*

dateren I [ov ww] *date* II [on ww] *date back (to/from)*

datum *date*

dauw *dew*

daveren *boom, thunder*

de *the*

debat *debate*

debet *debit*

debiel I [de] *mentally defective person,* <scheldwoord> *moron* II [bnw] *backward, mentally defective*

debiteren ● (als debet boeken) ★ *we zullen u voor 't bedrag ~ we shall debit you with the amount* ● (vertellen) ★ *'n grap ~ crack a joke*

debiteur *debtor*

debuteren *make one's début, one's first appearance*

debuut *début, first appearance*

decadentie *decadence*

december *December*

decimaal *decimal*

declameren *declaim*

declaratie ● (aangifte voor belasting) *declaration of income* ● (onkostennota) *expenses claim, statement of expenses* ● (aangifte voor douane) *(customs) declaration*

declareren *declare*

decoderen *decode*

decor *scenery,* <fig.> *background,* <film, toneel> *set*

decoratie *decoration*

decoreren *decorate*

decreet *decree*

deductie *deduction*

deeg *dough,* <v. gebak> *paste*

deel I [de] ● (dorsvloer) *threshing-floor* II [het] ● (gedeelte) *part, portion, share*

deelachtig ★ ~ *zijn participate in; share* ★ ~ *worden obtain; acquire* ★ *iem. iets* ~ *maken impart s.th. to s.o.*

deelbaar *divisible*

deelgenoot *sharer, partner*

deelnemen *take part (in), join (in), attend*

deelnemer *participant,* <examen> *candidate,* <wedstrijd> *competitor*

deelneming ● (het meedoen) *participation,* <aan wedstrijd> *entry* ● (meeleven) *sympathy*

deels *partly*

deelwoord *participle*

deerlijk *pitiful*

defect I [het] *defect* II [bnw] *defective,* <opschrift> *out of order*

defensie *defence*

defensief *defensive*

defilé *procession*

defileren *march past*

definiëren *define*

definitie *definition*

definitief <antwoord> *definite,* <besluit> *final*

deftig <huis> *stately,* <persoon>

distinguished, ‹stijl› dignified
degelijk I [bnw] solid, sound, thorough
II [bijw] solidly, soundly, thoroughly
degen sword
degene ⋆ ~ die... he/she who... ⋆ ~n
die... those who...
degeneratie degeneration
degenereren degenerate
degradatie degradation, ‹mil.›
demotion
degraderen degrade, ‹mil.› reduce to
(the ranks), demote
deinen roll, heave
dek ● (scheepsvloer) deck ● (bedekking)
cover
dekbed duvet, ‹donzen› eiderdown
(quilt)
deken blanket
dekken cover ⋆ de tafel ~ set the table
dekmantel ⋆ onder de ~ van under the
cloak of
deksel cover, lid
dekzeil tarpaulin
delegatie delegation
delegeren delegate
delen ● (splitsen) divide (by)
● (gemeenschappelijk hebben) share
deler divisor
delfstof mineral
delicaat delicate
delicatesse delicacy
delict offence, delict
deling division
delinquent delinquent
delta delta
delven dig
dementeren I [ov ww]
● (logenstraffen) deny II [on ww]
● (dement worden) grow demented
demilitariseren demilitarize
demobiliseren demobilize, ‹inf.›
demob
democraat democrat
demonstratie demonstration
demonstreren demonstrate

demonteren dissassemble
demoraliseren demoralize
dempen ● (dichtgooien) fill up
● (onderdrukken) ‹geluid› muffle,
‹licht› dim
Denemarken Denmark
denkbaar imaginable, conceivable
denkbeeld notion, idea
denken ● (nadenken) think, consider
● (van plan zijn) think of/about,
intend to, plan to ● (herinneren)
⋆ doen ~ aan remind (one) of;
remember ⋆ denk om het afstapje
mind the step
denker thinker, philosopher
dennenboom fir-tree
deodorant deodorant
departement department
dependance annex(e)
deponeren deposit
deportatie deportation
deporteren deport
deposito deposit
depot depot
derde third
deren hurt, harm
dergelijk such(-like), similar
derhalve so, consequently, therefore
dermate to such an extent
dertien thirteen
dertig thirty
derven miss out on, ‹mislopen› lose,
‹ontberen› lack
des ⋆ des te meer daar... the more so
as... ⋆ des te beter all the better
desalniettemin nevertheless
deserteren desert
deserteur deserter
desinfecteren disinfect
desnoods if need be
desondanks in spite of it
dessert dessert
destijds at the time
detail detail
detective detective

determineren determine, ‹bio.›
identify
detineren detain
deugd virtue
deugdelijk sound, reliable
deugen ★ nergens voor ~ be a
good-for-nothing ★ die fiets deugt
niet that bike is no good
deugniet • (rakker) scamp
• (slampamper) good-for-nothing
deuk dent
deuken ‹met opzet› indent, ‹per
ongeluk› dent
deur door
deurknop door handle, doorknob
deurwaarder bailiff
devaluatie devaluation, depreciation
devalueren devalue
devies device, motto
devoot pious, devout
deze this [mv: these]
dezelfde the same
dia transparency, slide
diabetes diabetes
diafragma diaphragm
diagnose diagnosis
diagonaal diagonal
diaken deacon
dialect dialect
dialectiek dialectics
dialoog dialogue
diamant I [de] • (de edelsteen)
diamond II [het] • (het materiaal)
diamond
diameter diameter
diametraal diametral, ‹fig.›
diametrical
diarree diarrhoea
dicht I [bnw] • (gesloten) closed, shut
• (opeen) close, dense II [bijw] close
(to), near
dichtbij close at hand, near by
dichtdoen shut, close
dichten I [ov ww] • (dichtmaken)
close, ‹gat, enz.› stop (up) II [on ww]

• (in dichtvorm schrijven) write
verses/poetry
dichter poet
dichterlijk poetic(al)
dichtheid density
dichtkunst (art of) poetry
dichtmaken close
dichtspijkeren nail up
dictaat • (aantekeningen) (lecture)
notes • (het gedicteerde) dictation
dictafoon dictaphone
dictator dictator
dictatuur dictatorship
dictee dictation
dicteren dictate
didactiek didactics
die I [aanw vnw] that [mv: those]
II [betr vnw] that, who, which
dieet diet, regimen
dief thief
diefstal theft
diegene he/she who
dienaangaande as to that, with
respect/reference/regard to that, on
that score
dienaar servant
dienen I [ov ww] • (in dienst zijn van)
serve • (van dienst zijn) ★ waarmee
kan ik u ~? what can I do for you?
• (helpen) ★ dat dient nergens toe
that is no good; that is of no use II [on
ww] • (gebruikt worden voor iets)
• (~ als/voor/tot) serve as/for
dienovereenkomstig accordingly
dienst • (behulpzame daad) service
• (het dienen) service • (het dienen als
militair) ★ generaal buiten ~ retired
general ★ in ~ gaan go into the army
★ ~ weigeren refuse to serve (in the
army) • (werking, gebruik) ★ in ~
stellen put into service ★ ~ doen als
serve for/as ★ buiten ~ out of order/use
★ ten ~e van for the use of
dienstbode maid-servant, servant girl
dienstdoend on duty, ‹waarnemend›

acting
dienster *waitress*
dienstmeisje *servant-girl*
dienstplicht *conscription, compulsory (military) service*
dienstverlening *(rendering of) service*
dienstweigering *conscientious objection*
dientengevolge *therefore, consequently*
diep I [bnw] *deep*, ‹fig.› *profound* II [bijw] *deeply*, ‹fig.› *profoundly*
diepgaand *profound*
diepgang *profundity, depth*
diepte *depth*
diepzinnig *profound*
dier *animal, beast, creature*
dierbaar *dear, beloved*
dierenarts *vet(erinary surgeon)*
dierenbescherming *protection of animals*
dierenriem *zodiac*
dierenrijk *animal kingdom*
dierentuin *Zoo*, ‹form.› *zoological garden(s)*
dierkunde *zoology*
dierlijk • *(als van een dier) bestial* • *(van dier) animal* ∗ ~e *vetten animal fats*
dieselmotor *diesel engine*
dievegge *thief*
differentiëren *differentiate*
digitaal *digital*
dij *thigh*
dijbeen *thigh-bone*
dijk *dike, dyke*
dijkbreuk *giving way of a dike, bursting of a dike*
dik • *(niet dun) thick* • *(mollig) fat, plump* • *(opgezwollen) swollen*
dikte *thickness*
dikzak *fatty, fatso*
dilemma *dilemma*
dimmen *dim,* ‹koplampen› *dip*
diner *dinner*

dineren *dine*
ding *thing*
dingen • *(afdingen) haggle, bargain* • *(trachten te krijgen) compete (for)*
dinsdag *Tuesday*
diocees *diocese*
diploma *membership card, certificate, diploma*
diplomaat *diplomat(ist)*
diplomatie *diplomacy*
diplomatiek *diplomatic*
diplomeren *certificate*
direct I [bnw] *direct* II [bijw] *directly, right away*
directeur *manager, director,* ‹gevangenis› *governor,* ‹maatschappij› *managing director,* ‹school› *head-master, principal*
directie *management, board of directors*
directoraat *directorate*
dirigeerstok *baton*
dirigent *conductor*
dirigeren • *(orkest leiden, enz.) conduct* • *(sturen) direct*
discipel *disciple*
disciplinair *disciplinary*
discipline *discipline*
disconto *(rate of) discount,* ‹bankdisconto› *bankrate*
discotheek • *(fonotheek) record library* • *(dansgelegenheid) disco(thèque)*
discreet • *(geheimhoudend) discreet* • *(bescheiden) modest* • *(kies) discrete, considerate*
discretie • *(kiesheid) discretion, consideration* • *(bescheidenheid) modesty* • *(geheimhouding) discretion*
discriminatie *discrimination*
discrimineren *discriminate*
discus *disc,* ‹sport› *discus*
discussie *discussion, debate*
discutabel *debatable, dubious, disputable*
diskrediet *discredit*

diskwalificeren *disqualify*
dispensatie *dispensation*
dispuut *dispute*
dissertatie *dissertation, thesis*
dissident *dissident*
dissonant *discord*
distel *thistle*
distilleerderij *distillery*
distilleren *distil*
distribueren *distribute,* ‹voedsel› *ration*
distributie *distribution,* ‹voedsel› *rationing*
district *district*
dit *this* [mv: *these*]
ditmaal *this time*
divan *divan, couch*
dividend *dividend*
divisie *division*
dobbelsteen *die* [mv: *dice*]
dobber *float*
dobberen *bob (up and down)*
docent *master, teacher*
doceren *teach*
doch *but, yet*
dochter *daughter*
doctor *doctor*
doctoraal I [het] *Master's exam,* ≈ *Master's degree* II [bnw] ≈ *Master's,* (*post*)*graduate*
doctorandus ≈ ‹Letteren› *Master of Arts, M.A,* ‹exacte wetenschap› *Master of Science, M.Sc*
doctrine *doctrine, dogma*
document *document*
documenteren *document*
dode *dead man/woman,* ‹jur.› *the deceased*
dodelijk *mortal, deadly*
doden *kill,* ‹lit.› *slay*
doedelzak *bagpipes*
doe-het-zelver *do-it-yourselfer*
doek I [de] *cloth* II [het] • (*stof*) *cloth*
 • (*linnen om op te schilderen*) *canvas*
 • (*schilderij*) *painting*

 • (*projectiescherm*) *screen*
doel • (*reisbestemming*) *destination*
 • (*mikpunt*) *target* • (*oogmerk*) *goal, aim, object*(*ive*)
doelbewust *purposeful*
doeleinde • (*oogmerk*) *aim, purpose*
 • (*bestemming*) *aim, end*
doellijn *goal-line*
doelloos • (*zonder doel*) *aimless, useless* • (*nutteloos*) *pointless*
doelman *goal-keeper,* ‹inf.› *goalie*
doelmatig *efficient, appropriate, suitable*
doelpunt *goal*
doelstelling *objective, aim*
doeltreffend *effective, efficient*
doelwit *target, butt*
doen I [ov ww] • (*verrichten*) *make, take* • (*functioneren*) ⋆ *de remmen doen het niet the brakes don't work* • (*plaatsen*) *put* • (*aandoen*) ⋆ *iem. pijn/verdriet doen hurt s.o.; cause s.o. pain/sorrow* II [on ww] • (*zich gedragen*) ⋆ *vreemd doen behave oddly* ⋆ *doen alsof make believe; pretend* • (~ **over**) ⋆ *hoe lang heb je erover gedaan? how long did it take you?* • (~ **aan**) *go in for*
doenlijk *practicable, feasible*
doetje *softy*
doezelen • (*dommelen*) *doze, drowse* • (*dun uitwrijven v. kleur*) *stump*
doezelig *drowsy*
dof *dull,* ‹blik, haren› *lacklustre*
dog *bulldog, mastiff*
dogma *dogma*
dok *dock*
dokken • (*in dok leggen*) *dock* • (*betalen*) *fork out (money)*
dokter *doctor, physician, medical man*
dokteren • (*als dokter optreden*) *practise* • (*onder doktersbehandeling zijn*) *be under doctor's orders, be under medical treatment* • (~ **aan**) *tinker at/with*

dokwerker *dock-labourer, docker*
dol I [bnw] • (gek) *mad, frantic, wild*
• (versleten) *worn* • (verzot op) *crazy
about* II [bijw] • (hoogst) *madly*
dolblij *as pleased as Punch*
dolen *wander (about), roam*
dolfijn *dolphin*
dolgraag *with great pleasure*
dolk *dagger*
dollen • (stoeien) *horse around* • (voor
de gek houden) *make fun of s.o.*
dom I [de] *cathedral,* <v. kerk> *dome*
II [bnw] *stupid*
domein *domain*
domheid *stupidity, dullness*
domicilie *domicile*
dominee *rector, vicar*
domineren *dominate*
dominicaan *Dominican*
domino I [de] • (mantel met kap)
domino II [het] *dominoes*
dommekracht • (werktuig) *jack*
• (log en dom persoon) *mindless hulk*
dompelen *dip, plunge*
domper *extinguisher*
donateur *donor, supporter*
donatie *donation*
donder *thunder*
donderdag *Thursday*
donderen I [ov ww] • (lazeren) *fling,
chuck, hurl* II [on ww] • (tekeergaan)
thunder (away), bluster III [onp ww]
thunder
donders I [bnw] *damn(ed), bloody*
II [tw] *dash it!, damn it!*
donderslag *thunderclap, peal of
thunder*
donderwolk *thunder-cloud*
donker I [het] *dark, darkness* II [bnw]
dark, obscure
donor *donor*
dons *down, fluff*
donzen *down*
dood I [de] *death* II [bnw] • (niet
levend) *dead* • (niet meer

functionerend) ⋆ dode hoek *dead
angle; blind spot* ⋆ de Dode Zee *the
Dead Sea* • (zeer, hevig) ⋆ zich dood
ergeren *be utterly annoyed* ⋆ zich
dood lachen *die laughing; laugh one's
head off* ⋆ zich dood schrikken *be
frightened out of one's wits* ⋆ zich dood
werken *work o.s. to death*
doodbloeden *bleed to death,* <fig.>
blow over
dooddoener *silencer, clincher*
doodgaan *die*
doodgeboren *still-born*
doodgewoon I [bnw] *common or
garden* II [bijw] *simply*
doodgraver *grave digger*
doodlopen <v. straat> *come to a dead
end,* <v. zaak> *peter out*
doods *deathly*
doodsangst • (vrees voor de dood)
fear of death • (grote angst) *agony,
mortal fear*
doodsbed *death bed*
doodsbleek *deathly pale, white as a
sheet*
doodshoofd *death's head, skull*
doodslaan *kill, beat to death*
doodslag *manslaughter, homicide*
doodsnood *agony, death-struggle*
doodsteek *death-blow*
doodstil *stock-still, deadly quiet*
doodstraf *capital punishment*
doodsvijand *mortal enemy*
doodvallen • (doodblijven) *fall dead*
• (dodelijke val maken) *fall to one's
death*
doodvonnis *death-sentence*
doodziek *critically/dangerously ill,*
<fig.> *sick to death*
doodzonde *mortal sin*
doodzwijgen <een zaak> *hush up,*
<iem.> *ignore*
doof *deaf*
doofheid *deafness*
doofpot *extinguisher*

doofstom *deaf and dumb*
dooi *thaw*
dooien *thaw*
dooier *yolk*
doolhof *labyrinth, maze*
doop *christening, baptism*
doopceel *certificate of baptism*
doopvont *font*
door I [bijw] *through* II [vz] • (middels) *by* • (wegens) *owing to* • (van a naar b) ⋆ door de kamer *through the room* ⋆ onder de brug door *under the bridge*
doorberekenen *pass on* (to)
doorbijten *bite through,* ‹fig.› *hold on*
doorbladeren *leaf through, flick through*
doorboren • (boren door) *drill through* • (gaatjes maken) *perforate*
doorbraak *break-through,* ‹v. dijk› *burst*
doorbrengen ‹tijd, vakantie› *spend*
doordacht *well-considered*
doordat *because*
doordraven *rattle on*
doordrijven *force/push through*
doordrukken *press through*
dooreen *pell-mell, in confusion*
doorgaan • (door ruimte, enz. gaan) *go through* • (toch gebeuren) *come off, take place* • (verder gaan) *go on* • (voortduren) *continue* • (beschouwd worden als) *pass* (for)
doorgaans *generally*
doorgang *passage*
doorgeefluik *service hatch*
doorgeven *pass on* (to) ⋆ kun je het zout ~? *pass the salt, please*
doorgronden *fathom*
doorhalen • (ergens doortrekken) *pull through* • (doorstrepen) *cross out*
doorheen *through*
doorkijk (open) *view*
doorkomen *come/get through*
doorkruisen • (dwarsbomen) *thwart* • (gaan door) *traverse*

doorlezen I [ov ww] *read through, peruse* II [on ww] *go on reading*
doorlichten • (onderzoeken) *investigate* • (met röntgenstralen onderzoeken) *X-ray*
doorlopen I [ov ww] • (inzien) ⋆ de tekst ~ *run through the text* II [on ww] • (verder lopen) *move, walk on*
doorlopend *continuous, non-stop*
doormaken *go through*
doormidden *in two*
doorn *thorn*
doornat *wet through, soaked*
doornemen *go over/through*
doorregen ⋆ ~ spek *streaky bacon*
doorreis *passage*
doorslaan I [ov ww] *break* II [on ww] • (doordraven) *run on* • (overhellen) *turn, dip* • (doldraaien) *race* • (stukgaan) *blow*
doorslag *carbon copy*
doorsmeren *grease, lubricate*
doorsnijden *cut in two, intersect*
doorstaan ‹pijn› *endure,* ‹toets, kou› *stand,* ‹ziekte› *pull through*
doortastend *energetic*
doortocht • (het doortrekken) ‹mil.› *march through* • (doorgang) *passage, right of way*
doorvaart *passage*
doorvoed *well-fed*
doorvoer *transit*
doorvoeren *carry through,* ‹v. wet› *enforce*
doorwerken I [ov ww] *work through, finish* II [on ww] *work on*
doorwrocht *thorough, elaborate*
doorzakken • (doorbuigen) *sag* • (teveel drinken) *drink to excess,* ‹inf.› *booze*
doorzetten I [ov ww] *carry through* II [on ww] *persevere, carry on*
doorzettingsvermogen *perseverance*
doorzichtig *transparent*
doorzoeken ‹huis› *search,* ‹streek›

comb out
doos *case, box*
dop • (rond omhulsel) <v. ei, noot>
shell, <v. erwt, boon> *pod* • (dekseltje)
lid, <v. pen, flacon, fles> *cap*
dopen *baptize, christen*
doperwt *green pea*
doppen <bonen> *shell*, <v. ei> *peel*
dor <bladeren> *withered*, <hout> *dry*,
<land> *barren*
dorp *village*
dorps *countrified, rustic, parochial*
dorsen *thresh*
dorsmachine *threshing-machine*
dorst *thirst* ★ ~ *hebben be thirsty*
dorsten *thirst (for)*
dorstig *thirsty*
doseren *dose*
dosis *dose*
dot • (bundeltje) *knot* • (iets liefs)
dream
douane *custom-house,* (the) *Customs*
doubleren *double*, <een klas> *repeat*
douche *shower*
doven *extinguish, put out*
dozijn *dozen*
draad • (lang en dun geheel) *thread*,
<metaal> *wire* • (vezel) *fibre*
draadloos *wireless*
draagbaar I [de] *stretcher* II [bnw]
portable
draagkracht <v. schip, brug, enz.>
carrying-capacity, <v. stem>
carrying-power, <v. vliegtuig> *lift*, <v.
vuurwapen> *range*
draaglijk • (te dragen) *bearable,*
supportable • (niet slecht) *passable,*
tolerable
draagvermogen <v. brug, schip, enz.>
carrying-capacity, <v. vliegtuig>
carrying capacity, lift
draagvlak *plane*, <fig.> *basis*, <v.
vliegtuig> *airfoil*
draagwijdte • (bereik) *range*, <v.
stem> *carrying power* • (strekking)

impact, <v. voorstel> *scope*, <v.
woorden> *import*
draai *turn*, <v. weg> *bend*
draaibaar *revolving*
draaibank *lathe*
draaiboek *script*
draaideur *revolving door*
draaien I [ov ww] • (afspelen) <een
plaat, cd> *play*, <film> *show* • (kiezen)
dial a (telephone) number • (keren)
turn II [on ww] • (in het rond gaan)
turn, rotate • (van richting
veranderen) *shift* • (uitvlucht zoeken)
prevaricate, hedge III [wkd ww] ★ *zich
eruit ~ wriggle out*
draaierig *giddy*
draaiing <om eigen as> *rotation*, <om
iets anders heen> *revolution*
draaikolk *vortex, eddy*
draaimolen *merry-go-round,*
roundabout
draaiorgel *barrel-organ*
draaitol *top, fidgetter*
draak *dragon*
drab *dregs, lees*
dracht • (last) *load* • (kleding) *dress,*
costume • (reikwijdte) *range of a gun*
• (drachtig zijn van dier) *gestation*
drachtig *with young*
draf I [de] • (gang) *trot* II [het]
• (varkensvoer) *swill, pigswill,*
hogwash
dragen I [ov ww] • (aanhebben) *wear*
• (bij zich hebben) *carry* • (op zich
nemen) *bear/take* II [on ww]
• (reikwijdte hebben) *carry*
drager *carrier*, <in hotel, enz.> *porter,*
<v. bril, enz.> *wearer*
draineren *drain*
dralen *tarry, delay*
drama *drama*
dramatisch *dramatic*
dramatiseren *dramatize*
drang • (aandrang) *urge* • (druk)
pressure

drank *drink, beverage*
draperen *drape*
drassig *marshy, swampy*
drastisch *drastic*
draven *trot*
dreef • (laan) *avenue, lane* • (gang) ★ op
~ zijn *be in great form* ★ op ~ komen
*warm up to (a subject); get into one's
stride*
dreggen *drag*
dreigbrief *threatening letter*
dreigement *threat, menace*
dreigen I [ov ww] *threaten* II [on ww]
★ er dreigt onweer *it looks like thunder*
dreiging *threat, menace*
dreinen *whine*
drek *dung, filth*
drempel *threshold*
drenkeling *drowning person, drowned
person*
drenken *water*
drentelen *lounge, saunter*
dresseren *train*
dressuur *training*
dreumes *nipper, toddler*
dreun • (het dreunen) *boom, rumble*
• (klap) *smack* • (eentonig geluid)
drone
dreunen *rumble, boom*
dribbelen <v. kind> *toddle,* <voetbal>
dribble
drie *three*
driehoek *triangle*
driehoekig *triangular*
Driekoningen *Epiphany,
Twelfth-night*
driekwart *three fourths, three quarters*
driekwartsmaat *three-four time*
drieling *triplets*
drieluik *triptych*
driemanschap *triumvirate*
driesprong *three-forked road*
drietal *three, trio*
drietand *trident*
driewieler *tricycle*

drift • (het (af)drijven) *drift*
• (woedeaanval) *passion, temper*
driftig *hot-/quick-tempered*
drijfjacht *battue, drive,* <fig.> *round-up*
drijfkracht <fig.> *driving force,* <v.
machine, enz.> *driving power,* <v.
schip> *driving power, propelling force*
drijfnat *soaking wet, dripping*
drijfveer • (beweegreden) *motive*
• (veer) *main-spring*
drijfzand *quicksand(s)*
drijven I [ov ww] • (~ tot) *drive to*
II [on ww] • (kletsnat zijn) *be soaked,
be sopping wet* • (aan oppervlakte
blijven) *float*
drillen *drill*
dringen I [ov ww] • (drang
uitoefenen) *push* • (dwingen) *force,
compel* II [on ww] • (een weg banen)
push, press • (duwen) *throng*
dringend *urgent,* <afspraak> *pressing*
drinkbaar *drinkable*
drinken I [het] • (het drinken)
drinking • (de drank) *drink(s),
beverage* II [ov ww] *drink*
droefgeestig I [bnw] *melancholy*
II [bijw] *dolefully, sadly*
droesem *dregs, lees*
droevig *sorrowful, sad*
drogen *dry*
drogist • (drogisterij) *chemist's,* <AE>
drugstore • (winkelier) *chemist,* <AE>
druggist
drol <volkst.> *turd*
drom *crowd, throng*
dromedaris *dromedary*
dromen I [ov ww] *dream* II [on ww]
• (een droom hebben) *dream*
• (mijmeren) *daydream*
dromer *dreamer*
dromerig *dreamy*
drommel ★ arme ~ *poor
bastard/devil/sod*
drommels *good grief!*
dronk ★ een ~ uitbrengen *propose a*

toast
dronken ★ zij is ~ she is drunk ★ in een ~ bui in a drunken fit
dronkenschap drunkenness, intoxication
droog dry
droogleggen • (droogmaken) drain (land, bogs), reclaim • (verkoop van alcohol verbieden) make dry
drooglijn clothes-line
droogte • (het droog zijn) dryness • (periode van droogte) drought
droogtrommel tumble dryer
droom dream
droombeeld vision
drop liquorice, <AE> licorice
druif grape
druilerig • (futloos) moping! • (regenachtig) drizzly
druipen • (~ van) drip with
druipnat dripping/sopping/soaking wet
druipsteen • (hangend) stalactite • (staand) stalagmite, sinter
druivensap grapejuice
druivensuiker grape sugar, glucose
druk I [de] • (aandrang) pressure • (oplage) edition II [bnw] • (levendig) busy, <kleuren> loud • (opgewonden) active, excited, fussy III [bijw] busily
drukfout misprint, printer's error
drukken I [ov ww] • (duwen) press, push, squeeze • (afdrukken) print • (verlagen) ★ de prijzen/kosten ~ hold/keep the prices/costs down II [on ww] press
drukkend <gemoed> heavy, <hitte> oppressive, <weer> sultry
drukker printer
drukkerij printing-office
drukpers • (werktuig) printing-press • (medium) press
drukproef galley(proof), proof(-sheet)
drukte • (bedrijvigheid) bustle, rush • (ophef) fuss

druktemaker loudmouth, fuss pot, busy body, noisy fellow
drukwerk printed matter
druppel drop, drip, <med.> drops
druppelen I [ov ww] • (in druppels laten vallen) drip, trickle (of tears) II [on ww] • (in druppels vallen) drip, trickle
dubbel I [het] duplicate, double II [bnw] double III [bijw] doubly
dubbelganger double
dubbelspel doubles [mv]
dubbelzinnig ambiguous, <vaak schunnig> double-meaning
dubben be in two minds
dubieus doubtful, dubious
duchten dread, fear
duchtig sound, thorough
duel duel, single combat
duelleren (fight a) duel
duet duet
duf • (saai) fusty, stale • (muf) musty, stuffy
duidelijk clear, plain, obvious
duiden ★ ~ op point to; suggest
duif pigeon, dove
duig stave
duikboot submarine
duikelen (take a) tumble, fall head over heels
duiken dive
duiker • (persoon) diver • (watergang) culvert
duikvlucht <luchtv.> (nose-)dive
duim • (vinger) thumb • (lengtemaat) inch
duimstok (folding) rule
duin dune
duister • (geheimzinnig) obscure • (donker) dark
duisternis dark(ness)
Duits German
Duitsland Germany
duivelin she-devil
duivelskunstenaar • (tovenaar)

magician, sorcerer [v: *sorceress*] • (erg handig mens) *wizard*
duivenmelker *pigeon-fancier*
duizelen *grow dizzy*
duizelig *dizzy, giddy*
duizelingwekkend ★ ~e hoogte *dizzy heights*
duizend *a/one thousand*
duizendpoot • (geleedpotig dier) *centipede* • (iem. die alles kan) *Jack-of-all-trades*
duizendste *thousandth*
dulden • (verdragen) *bear, endure* • (toelaten) *tolerate*
dun • (niet dik) *thin* • (tenger) *slender*
dunk *opinion*
dunken ★ mij dunkt *I think; it seems to me*
duo • (twee personen) *duo* • (duet) *duet*
dupe *dupe, victim*
duperen *dupe*
duplicaat *duplicate*
duplo ★ in ~ *in duplicate* ★ in ~ opmaken *draw up in duplicate*
duren • (tijd in beslag nemen) *last* • (voortgaan) *continue, go on*
durf *pluck, daring*
durfal *dare-devil*
durven *dare*
dus I [bijw] • (bijgevolg) *consequently* • (aldus) *thus* II [vw] *therefore*
dusdanig I [aanw vnw] *such* II [bijw] *so, in such a way,* <dermate> *to such an extent*
dutten *doze, snooze*
duur I [de] *duration, length* II [bnw] *dear, expensive, costly*
duurte *costliness, expensiveness*
duurzaam *durable, lasting, permanent*
dwaalspoor *wrong track*
dwaas I [de] *fool* II [bnw] *silly, foolish, absurd*
dwaasheid *folly, absurdity*
dwalen • (dolen) *wander, stray* • (zonder doel rondlopen) *roam*

• (zich vergissen) *err*
dwaling *error, mistake*
dwang *compulsion, coercion*
dwangarbeid *hard labour, penal servitude*
dwangbevel *warrant*
dwangbuis *straitjacket*
dwars • (haaks op) *diagonal, transverse* • (onwillig) *contrary, pig-headed*
dwarsbomen *cross, thwart*
dwarsfluit *transverse flute*
dwarsstraat *side-street*
dweepziek *fanatic(al)*
dweil • (doek) *(floor)cloth,* <aan stok> *mop*
dweilen *mop,* <dek> *swab*
dwepen *be fanatical*
dwerg *dwarf, pigmy*
dwingeland *tyrant*
dwingelandij *tyranny*
dwingen *force, coerce, compel*
dynamiet *dynamite*
dynamisch *dynamic*
dynamo *dynamo, generator*
dynastie *dynasty*
dysenterie *dysentery*

E

eb *ebb* ★ eb en vloed *low tide and high tide*
echec *setback*
echo *echo*
echoën *echo, reverberate*
echt I [de] *marriage, matrimony* II [bnw] *real,* <gevoel> *genuine,* <schilderij> *authentic* III [bijw] *true, really, genuinely*
echter *however*
echtgenoot *husband, spouse*
echtheid *authenticity*
echtpaar *married couple*
echtscheiding *divorce*
ecologie *ecology*
ecologisch *ecological*
economie ● (leer) *economy, economics* ● (zuinigheid) *economy*
economisch ● (m.b.t. staatshuishoudkunde) *economic* ● (zuinig) *economical*
econoom *economist*
eczeem *eczema*
edel *noble*
edelman *nobleman*
edelmoedig *generous*
edelmoedigheid *generosity*
edelsteen *precious stone*
editie *edition*
educatief *educative*
eed *oath*
eekhoorn *squirrel*
eelt *callosity*
een I [telw] *one* II [lw] *a,* <voor klinker> *an*
eend ● (watervogel) *duck* ● (domoor) *fool, silly*
eender *the same*
eendracht *concord*
eendrachtig I [bnw] *united,*

unanimous II [bijw] *in unison*
eenheid ● (samenhangend geheel) *unity* ● (team) *unit*
eenheidsprijs *unit price,* <in winkel> *uniform price*
eenkennig *shy, timid*
eenling *individual,* <inf.> *lone wolf*
eenmaal *once, one day*
eens I [bnw] *agreed* II [bijw] ● (eenmaal) *once* ● (ooit) <toekomst> *one day,* <verleden> *once* ● (als versterking) *just, even*
eensgezind *unanimous*
eensklaps *all of a sudden*
eensluidend *uniform with*
eenstemmig *unanimous,* <muz.> *for one voice*
eentonig *monotonous, drab*
eenvormig *uniform*
eenvoud *simplicity*
eenvoudig I [bnw] *plain, simple* II [bijw] *simply*
eenwording *unification*
eenzaam *lonely*
eenzaamheid *seclusion, solitude, loneliness, desolation*
eenzelvig *shy, retiring*
eenzijdig *one-sided, unilateral*
eer I [de] *honour, credit* II [bijw] *before* III [vw] *before*
eerbaar *honourable, virtuous*
eerbied *respect*
eerbiedig *respectful*
eerbiedigen *respect*
eerbiedwaardig *respectable*
eerder *before, sooner, rather*
eergevoel *sense of honour*
eergisteren *the day before yesterday*
eerherstel *rehabilitation*
eerlijk *sincere,* <v. mensen> *honest*
eerlijkheid *honesty, fairness*
eerst *first*
eersterangs *first-rate*
eervol *honourable*
eerzaam *respectable*

eerzucht *ambition*
eetbaar *edible*
eetgelegenheid *place to eat,
eating-place*
eetkamer *dining-room*
eetlepel *table-spoon*
eetlust *appetite*
eetzaal *dining-hall*
eeuw • (periode van honderd jaar)
century • (tijdperk) *age*
eeuwenoud *centuries old, as old as the
hills*
eeuwig *eternal, perpetual, perennial*
eeuwigheid *eternity*
effect *effect*
effectief • (doeltreffend) *effective*
• (werkelijk) *real*
effen • (vlak) *even, smooth* • (zonder
uitdrukking) *plain*
effenen *level, smooth*
eg *harrow*
egaal *smooth, level*
egaliseren *equalize, level*
egel *hedgehog*
eggen *harrow*
egoïsme *egoism, selfishness*
egoïst *egoist, self-seeker*
egoïstisch *egoistic(al), selfish*
ei *egg,* ‹bio.› *ovum*
eigen • (aan iem./iets behorend) *own*
• (persoonlijk) *personal* • (privé)
private
eigenaar *owner, proprietor*
eigenaardig I [bnw] *singular, peculiar*
II [bijw] *in a peculiar way, strangely,
oddly*
eigendom *property*
eigendunk *self-conceit, self-esteem*
eigenhandig *(made/done)with one's
own hands*
eigenlijk I [bnw] *real, proper* II [bijw]
*properly/strictly speaking, really, in
fact, actually*
eigenmachtig *high-handed, arbitrary*
eigennaam *proper name*

eigenschap ‹v. dingen› *property,* ‹v.
mensen› *quality*
eigentijds *contemporary*
eigenwijs (self-)opinionated, self-willed*
eigenzinnig *obstinate, stubborn*
eik *oak*
eikel *acorn*
eiland *island*
eileider ‹mensen› *Falopian tube,*
‹vogels› *oviduct*
eind • (resultaat, afsluiting)
conclusion, close • (stuk van iets) *piece*
• (uiteinde) *extremity, end* • (afloop)
end
einddiploma *certificate, diploma*
eindelijk I [bnw] *ultimate* II [bijw]
finally, at last
eindeloos • (zonder einde) *endless*
• (prachtig) *wonderful*
eindexamen *final examination(s)*
eindig *finite*
eindigen *end, finish*
eindproduct *final product*
eindpunt *end,* ‹v. trein, bus› *terminus*
eindstation ‹v. trein, bus› *terminal*
eindstreep *finish*
eis *demand,* ‹voor examen›
requirement, ‹voor schade› *claim*
eisen *claim (from), demand (from/off),
require of*
eiwit *eggwhite,* ‹proteïne› *protein*
ekster *magpie*
eksteroog *corn*
eland *elk*
elasticiteit *elasticity*
elastiek *elastic, rubber band*
elastisch *elastic*
elders *elsewhere*
elegant *elegant, smart*
elektricien *electrician*
elektriciteit *electricity*
elektrisch *electric*
elektronisch *electronic*
elektrotechniek *electro-technics,
electrical engineering*

element *element*
elementair *elementary*
elf I [de] *elf* II [telw] *eleven*
elfde *eleventh*
elftal *eleven*
elimineren *eliminate*
elite *élite*
elk *every, each*
elkaar *each other, one another*
elleboog *elbow*
ellende *misery, distress*
ellendeling *villain, nasty piece of work*
ellendig *miserable, wretched*
ellips *ellipse*
elliptisch *elliptic(al)*
elpee *LP, long-play(ing) record*
els • (priem) *awl* • (boom) *alder*
email *enamel*
emailleren *enamel*
emancipatie *emancipation*
emanciperen *emancipate*
emballage *packing*
embargo *embargo*
embleem *emblem*
embryo *embryo*
emeritaat *superannuation*
emeritus *emeritus*
emigrant *emigrant*
emigratie *emigration*
emigreren *emigrate*
eminent *eminent*
emissie *issue*
emmer *pail, bucket*
emotie *emotion*
emotioneel *emotional*
empirisch *empiric(al)*
en *and*
encyclopedie *encyclop(a)edia*
encyclopedisch *encyclopedic*
endeldarm *rectum*
energie *energy*, ‹elektrisch› *power*
energiek *energetic*
eng • (nauw) *narrow* • (akelig) *scary, creepy*
engel *angel*

Engeland *England*
engelbewaarder *guardian angel*
Engels I [het] *English* II [bnw] *English*
engerd ‹inf.› *creep, crawler*
engte *narrow(s), strait(s)*, ‹bergengte› *defile*, ‹landengte› *isthmus*
enig I [bnw] • (enkel) *only, unique* • (leuk) *lovely* II [onb vnw] *some*, ‹in vragen› *any*
enigermate *to some extent*
enigszins *somewhat, slightly, rather*
enkel I [de] *ankle* II [bnw] *single* III [bijw] *simply, only* IV [telw] • (een klein aantal) *a few, one or two* • (slechts één) ★ geen ~e kans *not a chance*
enkeling *individual*
enkelvoud *singular*
enorm *enormous*
enquête *inquiry*
ensceneren *stage*
enten • (een ent aanbrengen) *graft* • (inenten) *inoculate*
enteren *board*
enthousiasme *enthusiasm*
enthousiast I [de] *enthusiast* II [bnw] *enthusiastic*
entree • (ingang) *entrance* • (het binnentreden) *entrance, entry* • (toegangsprijs) ★ ~ betalen *pay for admission* ★ ~ vrij *admission free*
epidemie *epidemic*
epidemisch *epidemic*
epiloog *epilogue*
episode *episode*
epos *epic*
equator *equator*
equatoriaal *equatorial*
er I [pers vnw] ★ hoeveel heb je er *how many do you have?* ★ wat is er? *what's the matter?* ★ is er iets? *is anything the matter?* ★ er werd gedanst *there was a dance (going on)* II [bijw] *there*
erbarmelijk • (meelijwekkend) *pitiful, miserable* • (akelig slecht)

awful, dreadful, abominable
eren honour
erewoord word of honour
erfdeel inheritance, ‹fig.› heritage
erfelijk hereditary
erfelijkheid heredity
erfelijkheidsleer genetics
erfenis inheritance, legacy,
  ‹voornamelijk fig.› heritage
erfgenaam heir
erfstuk (family) heirloom
erfzonde original sin
erg I [het] ∗ ik had er geen erg in I was
  not aware of it ∗ voor je er erg in hebt
  before you know where you are II [bnw]
  bad III [bijw] very
ergens • (op een plaats) somewhere,
  anywhere • (in enig opzicht) somehow
  • (iets) something
ergeren I [ov ww] shock, vex, annoy
  II [wkd ww] be vexed, get annoyed,
  take offence (at)
ergerlijk annoying, aggravating,
  shocking
ergernis • (irritatie) annoyance
  • (aanstoot) offence
erkennen • (inzien) acknowledge,
  recognize • (toegeven) confess, admit
  • (als wettig/echt aanvaarden)
  recognize
erkenning acknowledgement,
  recognition, admission
erkentelijk grateful, thankful
erkentelijkheid gratitude,
  appreciation
erker bay window
ernst earnest(ness), seriousness
ernstig ‹gezicht› earnest, ‹ongeluk,
  situatie› serious
erotiek eroticism
erotisch erotic
erts ore
ervaren I [bnw] experienced, skilled
  II [ov ww] • (ondervinden) experience
  • (vernemen) find out, learn

ervaring experience
erven I [de] heirs II [ov ww] inherit
erwt pea
erwtensoep pea-soup
es ash (tree)
escalatie escalation
esdoorn maple (tree)
eskader squadron
eskimo Eskimo
essentieel essential
estafette relay race
esthetisch aesthetic
etage storey, floor
etalage display window, shop-window
etaleren display
etaleur window dresser
etappe stage
eten I [het] • (voedsel) food • (maaltijd)
  meal, dinner II [ov ww] eat,
  ‹avondeten› have dinner, ‹form.› dine
  III [on ww] eat
etenstijd dinner-time
eter eater
ether • (drager van radiogolven) air
  • (chem.) ether
ethisch ethical
etiket label
etmaal twenty-four hours
etnisch ethnic
ets etching
etsen etch
etter matter, pus
etteren • (pus afscheiden) fester,
  ‹med.› suppurate • (klieren) be a pain
  in the neck
etui case
eucharistie Eucharist
eufemisme euphemism
eufemistisch euphemistic
Europa Europe
euvel • (kwaad) evil • (gebrek) fault
evacuatie evacuation
evacueren evacuate
evaluatie evaluation, assessment
evalueren evaluate, assess

evangelie *gospel*
evangelisch *evangelic(al)*
evangelist *evangelist*
even I [bnw] *even* II [bijw] *just*
evenaar *equator*
evenals *(just) as, (just) like*
evenaren *equal*
evenbeeld *image, (very) picture*
eveneens *as well, likewise, too*
evengoed • (evenzeer) *(just) as well,
equally well* • (toch) *all the same*
evenknie *equal*
evenmin * *ik ga niet en mijn
vrienden* ~ *I'm not going, and neither
are my friends*
evenredig *proportional (to),
proportionate (to)*
evenredigheid *proportion*
eventjes *(only) a moment, just*
eventueel I [bnw] *any (possible)*
II [bijw] *possible*
evenveel *as much, as many*
evenwel *however, nevertheless, yet*
evenwicht *balance, equilibrium*
evenwichtig *balanced, well-balanced,
steady*
evenwijdig *parallel*
evenzeer • (in dezelfde mate) *(just) as
much as, (just) as great as* • (ook)
likewise
evenzo *likewise*
evolueren *evolve*
evolutie *evolution*
exact *precise*
examen *examination,* <inf.> *exam*
examinator *examiner*
examineren *examine*
excellentie *excellency*
excentriek *eccentric*
exclusief I [bnw] *exclusive* II [bijw]
exclusive of, excluding
excursie *excursion, trip*
excuseren *excuse*
excuus • (reden van
verontschuldiging) *excuse*

• (verontschuldiging) *apology*
executeren *execute*
executie *execution*
exemplaar *specimen, sample,* <v. boek>
copy
existentialisme *existentialism*
expansie *expansion*
expediteur *forwarding-agent,
shipping-agent*
expeditie • (tocht) *expedition*
• (verzending) *shipping, forwarding*
experiment *experiment*
experimenteel *experimental*
experimenteren *experiment*
expert *expert,* <verzekeringsexpert>
assessor
exploderen *explode*
exploitant <v. hotel> *owner,* <v.
transportlijn> *operator*
exploitatie *exploitation,* <v. bedrijf>
running, <v. mijn> *working,* <v.
transportlijn> *operation*
exploiteren • (gebruikmaken van) <v.
krant> *own* • (misbruiken) *exploit*
exponent *exponent*
export *export*
exporteren *export*
exporteur *exporter*
exposeren *exhibit, show*
expositie *exhibition, show*
expres I [de] *express* II [bnw] *express*
III [bijw] *on purpose*
expresbrief *express letter*
extra *extra*
extract • (aftreksel) *extract*
• (uittreksel) *excerpt*
ezel • (dier) *donkey, ass* • (voorwerp)
easel
ezelsoor *ass's ear,* <v. boek> *dog's ear*

F

faam *fame, reputation*
fabel *fable*
fabelachtig *fabulous*
fabricage *manufacture*
fabriceren *manufacture, ‹leugens, enz.› fabricate*
fabriek *factory, works*
fabrikaat *product, ‹alleen als meervoud› goods*
fabrikant *manufacturer*
facet • *(geslepen vlak) facet* • *(gezichtspunt) facet, aspect, angle*
faciliteit *facility*
factor *factor*
factureren *invoice, charge to s.o.'s account*
factuur *invoice*
facultatief *optional*
faculteit *faculty*
fagot *bassoon*
failliet I *[de] bankrupt* II *[het] bankruptcy* III *[bnw] bankrupt*
faillissement *bankruptcy*
fakkel *torch*
falen *fail*
fallus *phallus*
familie *relatives, family*
familielid *member of the family, relation, relative*
familieziek *overly attatched to ones' family*
fanaticus *fanatic, ‹rel.› zealot*
fanatiek *fanatic(al)*
fanatisme *fanaticism*
fanfare *fanfare*
fantaseren *imagine, ‹dagdromen› fantasize*
fantasie • *(muziekstuk) fantasia* • *(verbeelding(skracht)) imagination, fancy* • *(verzinsel) fantasy*

fantast *fantast, dreamer*
fantastisch *fantastic*
farizeeër *Pharisee*
farmaceutisch *pharmaceutical*
farmacie *pharmacy*
fascisme *fascism*
fase *stage, phase*
fat *dandy, fop*
fataal *fatal*
fatsoen • *(correctheid) decency, good manners* • *(vorm) shape, form*
fatsoeneren *shape, model, fashion*
fatsoenlijk *decent, respectable*
fatsoenshalve *for decency's sake*
fauna *fauna*
favoriet *favourite*
fazant *pheasant*
februari *February*
fee *fairy*
feeëriek *fairytale-like*
feeks *shrew*
feest • *(partij) party* • *(religieuze feestdag) feast, festival*
feestdag *holiday*
feestelijk *festive, ‹form.› festal*
feestmaal *feast, ‹groots› banquet*
feestvieren *feast, celebrate*
feilloos *faultless, ‹regelmaat› unfailing*
feit *fact*
feitelijk I *[bnw] actual* II *[bijw] actually, practically, virtually*
fel *fierce, sharp, ‹brand/zon› blazing, ‹kleur› vivid*
felicitatie *congratulations*
feliciteren *congratulate (on)*
feminisme *feminism*
ferm • *(zeer groot, hevig) ‹portie› generous, ‹v. persoon› strapping* • *(flink) firm*
festiviteit *festivity*
feuilleton *serial (story)*
fiasco *failure, flop, ‹inf.› washout*
fideel *jovial, jolly*
fiducie *faith, confidence*
fier *proud*

fiets *bicycle,* ‹inf.› *bike*
fietsen *cycle*
fietser *cyclist*
fietspad *cycle-track*
fietstocht *cycling-tour*
figuur I [de] • (personage) *figure, character* II [het] • (gestalte) *figure* • (indruk, houding) ∗ *een slecht ~ slaan make a poor figure*
figuurlijk *figurative*
fijn • (klein) *fine* • (niet grof) *fine, tiny* • (verfijnd) *fine, choice* • (prettig) *nice, lovely* • (subtiel) *subtle*
fijngevoelig *sensitive*
fijnhakken *mince*
fijnmaken *pulverize*
fijnproever *connoisseur*
fijntjes *subtly*
fiks ‹borrel, wandeling› *stiff,* ‹pak slaag› *sound*
filantroop *philanthropist*
file *traffic-jam, tailback*
filet *fillet*
filharmonisch *philharmonic*
filiaal *branch*
film *film, feature (film), motion-picture,* ‹AE› *movie*
filmen *film*
filmopname *shot*
filmster *film-star*
filologie *philology*
filosoferen *philosophize*
filosofie *philosophy*
filosofisch *philosophic(al)*
filosoof *philosopher*
filter *filter,* ‹voor koffie› *percolator*
finale *finale,* ‹sport› *final(s)*
finalist *finalist*
financieel *financial*
financiën • (geldwezen) *finance, financial system* • (geld) *finances*
financier *financier, sponsor*
financieren *finance*
fingeren *feign, simulate, fake,* ‹ensceneren› *stage*

Finland *Finland*
firma *firm, concern*
firmant *partner*
fiscaal *fiscal*
fiscus *exchequer, treasury, revenue*
fixeerbad *fixing-bath*
fixeren *fix*
fjord *fjord*
fladderen • (bewegen) *flap* • (vliegen) *flutter*
flakkeren *flicker,* ‹in de tocht› *waver*
flanel • (stof) *flannel* • (kledingstuk) *singlet*
flaneren *lounge, stroll,* ‹inf.› *mooch (about)*
flank *flank, side*
flankeren *flank*
flat • (flatgebouw) *block of flats,* ‹AE› *apartment building* • (appartement) *flat,* ‹AE› *apartment*
flater *blunder, howler*
flatgebouw *block of flats,* ‹AE› *apartment building*
flatteren *flatter*
flauw • (kinderachtig) *silly* • (niet levendig) *dull* • (zwak gebogen) *gentle/slight* • (met weinig smaak) *tasteless* • (zwak) *feeble, weak* • (niet geestig) *silly,* ‹grap› *feeble*
flauwerd • (flauwerik) *a silly person, spoilsport* • (lafaard) *chicken, sissy*
flauwiteit *silly joke/remark*
flauwte *faint, fainting fit*
flegma *phlegm*
flemen *cajole, coax*
fles *bottle*
flessentrekker *swindler*
flessentrekkerij *con, swindle, swindling*
flets • (ongezond) *wan, pale* • (niet helder) ‹kleur› *dull,* ‹kleuren› *faded,* ‹ogen› *lacklustre*
fleurig *blooming, gay*
flikkeren • (schitteren) *glint,* ‹v. kaars› *flicker,* ‹v. ogen› *glitter,* ‹v.

sterren> *twinkle* • (smijten) *dump*
• (vallen) *tumble*
flikkering *flicker, twinkle*
flikkerlicht *flashlight*
flink I [bnw] • (stevig) *robust, sturdy,
stout,* <klein kind> *strapping*
• (moedig) *brave, plucky* II [bijw]
soundly, firmly, considerably
flirt *flirtation,* <persoon> *flirt*
flirten *flirt*
flits *flash*
flitsen *flash*
flodder • (patroon) *blank, dummy*
floers • (stof) *crape, crêpe* • (waas) *veil,
shroud*
flonkeren *twinkle, sparkle*
floreren *flourish, prosper*
floret *foil*
fluim *phlegm,* <inf.> *gob (of spit)*
fluisteren *whisper*
fluit *flute,* <blokfluit> *recorder,*
<signaalfluit> *whistle*
fluiten <op fluit> *play the flute,* <v.
mond of fluitje> *whistle,* <v. vogel>
warble
fluitist *flautist,* <AE> *flutist*
fluitketel *whistling kettle*
fluor *fluor*
fluweel *velvet*
fluwelen *velvet*
fobie *phobia*
foedraal *case*
foei *shame (on you)!,* <m.b.t. kinderen>
naughty, naughty!
foeilelijk *as ugly as sin*
foeteren *storm, rage (at)*
foetus *foetus, fetus*
fokken *rear, breed*
fokker *breeder*
folklore *folklore*
folteren *torture*
fondant *fondant*
fonds *fund, capital*
fondue *fondue*
fonetiek *phonetics*

fonetisch *phonetic*
fonkelen *sparkle*
fonkelnieuw *brand(-)new*
fontein *fountain*
fooi *tip, gratuity*
foppen *fool, kid*
fopspeen *dummy,* <AE> *comforter*
forceren <de ogen, stem> *strain,* <een
deur> *force*
forel *trout*
forens *commuter, non-resident*
formaat *size, format*
formaliteit *formality*
formatie *formation*
formeel *formal*
formeren *form*
formule *formula*
formuleren *phrase, formulate, put
(into words)*
formulier *form*
fornuis *cooking-range, kitchen-range,
cooker*
fors *robust*
fort • (vesting) *fort(ress)* • (sterke zijde)
strong point
fortuin *fortune, (good) luck*
fortuinlijk *lucky*
fosfor *phosphorus*
fossiel I [het] *fossil* II [bnw] *fossil*
foto *photograph, picture, snap(shot),*
<inf.> *photo*
fotoalbum *photo(graph) album*
fotogeniek *photogenic*
fotograaf *photographer*
fotograferen *photograph*
fotografisch *photographic*
fototoestel *camera*
fout I [de] • (schuld) *fault*
• (vergissing) *mistake* • (gebrek) *defect*
II [bnw] *wrong*
fraai *beautiful, fine*
fractie • (politieke partij) *group, party*
• (deeltje) *fraction*
fractuur *fracture, break*
fragment *fragment*

fragmentarisch *fragmentary, sketchy*
framboos *raspberry*
franciscaan *Franciscan*
franco *post-free*
franje *fringe,* <fig.> *frill(s)*
frank I [de] *franc* II [bnw] *frank*
Frankrijk *France*
Frans I [het] *French* II [bnw] *French*
frapperen *strike, cool,* <v. drank> *chill*
frase *phrase*
frater *(lay) brother, friar*
fraude *fraud*
frauduleus *fraudulent, bent, not on the level,* <inf.> *crooked*
fregat *frigate*
frequentie *frequency*
fresco *fresco*
fret • (boor) (twist)*auger, gimlet* • (dier) *ferret*
frezen *mill*
friemelen *fumble*
Friesland *Friesland*
friet *chips*
frigide *frigid*
frik *pedant,* <inf.> *beak*
fris *fresh*
frisheid *freshness*
frisjes *chilly, cool, nippy*
frivool *frivolous*
frommelen • (kreukelen) *crumple* • (friemelen) *fumble*
frons *frown,* <boos> *scowl*
fronsen *frown,* <boos> *scowl*
front *front*
frontaal *frontal*
fruit *fruit*
fruiten *fry*
frustratie *frustration*
frustreren *frustrate, thwart*
fuif *party*
fuik *bow-net, fish-trap*
fuiven *feast, revel, make whoopee*
functie *function*
functionaris *functionary, official*
functioneel *functional*

functioneren *function*
fungeren * ~ als *act/officiate as*
fusie *fusion, merger, amalgamation*
fusilleren *shoot*
fust *barrel,* <vat> *cask*
fut *go, spirit, grit, spunk*
futiliteit *futility, triviality*
futloos *spiritless*
fysica *physics*
fysicus *physicist*
fysiek I [het] *physique* II [bnw] *physical*
fysiologie *physiology*

G

gaaf • (ongeschonden) *whole, perfect*
• (geweldig) *super, great*
gaan I [on ww] • (zich bewegen) *go*
• (weggaan) *go, leave* • (functioneren)
★ de telefoon gaat *the (tele)phone
rings* • (lukken, kunnen) ★ 't gaat niet
it won't work; it's impossible
• (beginnen met) *go* ★ gaan wandelen
go for a walk • (~ **met**) *go out with*
• (~ **over**) *be (about)* ★ wie gaat
hierover? *who is in charge of this?*
II [onp ww] • (vergaan) ★ hoe gaat
het? *how are you (getting on)?; how is
it going* ★ 't gaat nogal/wel *not too
bad* ★ 't ga je goed *good luck to you*
• (~ **om**) *be (about)* ★ 't gaat erom of
the question/point is whether ★ daar
gaat het niet om *that's beside the
point*
gaande • (in beweging) *going* • (aan
de hand) *going on*
gaandeweg *gradually*
gaar • (niet rauw) *done, cooked* • (duf)
done, tired
gaarkeuken *soup kitchen*
gaarne *willingly, gladly*
gaas • (weefsel) *gauze, net(ting)*
• (vlechtwerk van metaal) *wire netting*
gadeslaan *watch, observe*
gading ★ dat is niet van mijn ~ *it is
not in my line; it is not to my taste* ★ ik
kon niets van mijn ~ vinden *I
couldn't find anything I
fancied/wanted*
gaffel *(two-pronged) fork,* ‹hooivork›
pitchfork
gage *salary, pay*
gal *bile*
gala *gala*
galant *gallant*

galblaas *gall bladder*
galei *galley*
galerij *gallery,* ‹v. flatgebouw›
walkway
galg *gallows*
galgenhumor *grim humour*
galgenmaal *last meal*
galm *resonance,* ‹zwaar› *boom*
galmen • (zwaar en luid klinken)
resound, boom • (weerkaatsen van
klank) *echo, reverberate* • (luid
zingen/schreeuwen) *bawl (out)*
galop *gallop*
galopperen *gallop*
galsteen *gallstone*
galvaniseren *galvanize*
gamma • (Griekse letter) *gamma*
• (reeks) *gamut, spectrum,* ‹v. tonen›
scale
gammel *rickety,* ‹v. huis› *tumbledown*
gang • (doorloop) *corridor* • (onderdeel
van menu) *course* • (steeg) *alley*
• (manier van gaan) *walk, gait*
• (werking, beweging) ★ aan de gang
blijven *keep going* ★ aan de gang gaan
set to work ★ aan de gang zijn *be in
progress; have begun; be at work* ★ op
gang komen *get going* • (vlugge
vaart) ★ goed op gang *well under way*
★ in volle gang *in full swing* • (gedrag,
handelen) ★ zijn eigen gang gaan *go
one's own way* ★ ga uw gang! *go
ahead!; do as you please!*
gangbaar ‹v. betaalmiddel› *current,*
‹v. theorie› *accepted*
gangmaker ‹op een feest, enz.› *(the)
life and soul*
gangster *gangster,* ‹inf.› *mobster*
gans I [de] • (vogel) *goose* [mv: *geese*]
• (dom persoon) *goose* II [bnw] *whole,
entire* III [bijw] *wholly, entirely*
gapen *yawn*
gappen *pinch, pilfer*
garage *garage*
garanderen *guarantee*

garant *guarantor*
garantie *guarantee*
garde • (lijfwacht) *guard(s)*
• (keukengerei) *whisk* • (roede) *rod*
garderobe *wardrobe,* ‹in theater, enz.›
cloakroom
gareel *collar, harness*
garen I [het] *thread, yarn* II [ov ww]
collect, gather
garnaal *shrimp,* ‹steurgarnaal› *prawn*
garneren *garnish*
garnering *garnishing*
garnituur *decoration, trimmings,* ‹v.
juwelen› *set of jewels*
garnizoen *garrison*
gas *gas*
gasbedrijf *gas company*
gasfitter *gas fitter*
gasfles *gas cylinder*
gasfornuis *gas cooker*
gaskachel *gas heater/fire*
gaskamer *gas chamber*
gaskraan *gas tap*
gasleiding ‹in huis› *gas pipes,* ‹in
straat› *gas main*
gasmeter *gas meter*
gaspedaal *accelerator*
gaspit *gas jet*
gast • (bezoek) *guest, visitor* • (persoon)
fellow
gastarbeider *(im)migrant/foreign
worker*
gastheer *host*
gasthuis *hospital*
gastvrij *hospitable*
gastvrijheid *hospitality*
gastvrouw *hostess*
gat • (opening) *gap, hole*
• (achterwerk) *bum, backside,*
↑ *bottom* • (afgelegen plaatsje) *hole*
gauw I [bnw] *quick, swift* II [bijw]
quickly, soon
gauwigheid *rush, hurriedness*
gave • (geschenk) *gift* • (talent) *talent,
gift*

gazon *lawn*
geaardheid *disposition*
geacht *esteemed, respected*
geadresseerde *addressee*
geaffecteerd *affected, mannered*
geanimeerd *animated*
gearmd *arm in arm*
gebaar *gesture*
gebarentaal *sign language*
gebed *prayer*
gebeente *bones*
gebelgd *incensed, enraged*
gebergte *mountain range*
gebeten ⋆ ~ zijn op iem. *bear s.o. a
grudge*
gebeuren I [het] *event,* ‹inf.›
happening II [on ww] • (gedaan
worden) ⋆ 't moet ~ *it has to be done*
⋆ 't is zo gebeurd *it will only take a
minute* • (plaatsvinden) *happen, occur*
• (overkomen) *happen, occur*
gebeurtenis *event, occurrence*
gebied • (grondgebied) *territory*
• (streek) *area* • (tak v. wetenschap)
domain • (jur.) *jurisdiction*
gebieden I [ov ww] • (voorschrijven)
order, command II [on ww] • (heersen)
rule
gebit *teeth*
gebladerte *foliage*
gebloemd *flowered*
geblokt *chequered*
gebod *order, command*
geboorte *birth*
geboortedag *birthday*
geboortejaar *year of (one's) birth*
geboortebeperking *family planning,
birth control*
geboren • (van nature) *born, natural*
• (ter wereld gebracht) *born*
gebouw *building,* ‹form.› *edifice*
gebrand • (geroosterd) *roasted*
• (~ op) *be keen on*
gebrek • (tekort) *want, lack, shortage*
• (mankement) *defect* • (kwaal)

infirmity
gebrekkig *defective, faulty,* <v. lichaam> *crippled*
gebroeders * de ~ A *the A.* brothers
gebruik • (het benutten) *use* • (verbruik) *consumption* • (gewoonte) *custom*
gebruikelijk *usual*
gebruiken • (aanwenden) *use* • (nuttigen) *eat,* <v. maaltijd> *have*
gebruiker *user,* <verbruiker> *consumer*
gebruiksaanwijzing *directions for use*
gebruiksvoorwerp <gereedschap> *implement,* <in keuken> *utensil*
gecompliceerd *complicated*
gedaante *shape, figure*
gedachte *thought, idea*
gedachtegang *train of thought*
gedachtenis * ter ~ van *in memory of*
gedachtewisseling *exchange of views*
gedeelte *part, section*
gedeeltelijk I [bnw] *partial* II [bijw] *partially, partly*
gedegen • (degelijk) *solid* • (grondig) *thorough*
gedelegeerde *delegate*
gedenkboek *memorial volume*
gedenkdag *anniversary*
gedenken *remember, commemorate*
gedetineerde *prisoner*
gedicht *poem*
gedienstig *obliging*
gedierte *animals*
gedijen *prosper, thrive*
geding • (rechtszaak) *lawsuit, case* • (punt van discussie) * in het ~ zijn *be at issue*
gedistilleerd *spirits*
gedistingeerd *refined, distinguished*
gedoe *business, goings on*
gedogen *tolerate, allow*
gedonder • (geluid) *thunder* • (gezeur, geduvel) *bullying, nagging* • (ellende) *trouble*
gedrag *conduct, behaviour*

gedragen I [bnw] • (plechtstatig) *lofty* • (al eerder gebruikt) *worn* II [wkd ww] *behave/conduct o.s.*
gedrang *crowd, crush*
gedrocht *monster*
gedrongen • (opeengepakt) *squashed* • (kort en breed) *stocky, thick-set* • (summier) *terse*
gedrukt • (in zetletters) *printed* • (neerslachtig) *down*
geducht *formidable, enormous*
geduld *patience*
geduldig *patient*
gedurende *during, for*
gedurfd *daring*
gedurig • (telkens weer) *continual* • (onafgebroken) *continuous*
gedwee *meek, docile*
geel I [het] • (eidooier) *yolk* • (kleur) *yellow* II [bnw] *yellow*
geen *none,* <bijvoeglijk gebruikt> *no,* <zelfstandig gebruikt> *not one*
geenszins *by no means, not at all*
geest • (denkwijze, sfeer) *spirit* • (onstoffelijk wezen) *spirit, ghost* • (ziel) *soul*
geestdodend *monotonous*
geestdrift *enthusiasm*
geestdriftig *enthusiastic*
geestelijk • (mentaal) *spiritual, mental* • (kerkelijk) *clerical* • (rel.) *spiritual*
geestelijkheid *clergy*
geestesgesteldheid *mentality*
geestig *witty*
geestigheid *witticism*
geestkracht *energy, strength of mind*
geestverwant I [de] *kindred spirit, sympathizer* II [bnw] *kindred, congenial*
geeuw *yawn*
geeuwen *yawn*
gegadigde *interested party, prospective buyer,* <bij sollicitatie> *applicant*
gegeven *data* [ev/mv], *datum*

gehaast *hurried, hastened*
gehakt *minced meat*, ‹inf.› *mince*
gehalte • (hoeveelheid) *percentage,* ‹v.
alcohol› *degrees proof*
• (hoedanigheid) *quality, standard*
geheel I [het] *whole* II [bnw] *whole,
entire* III [bijw] ★ ~ *de uwe yours
faithfully/sincerely; yours truly*
geheelonthouder *teetotaller*
geheim *secret*
geheimhouding *secrecy*
geheimschrift *cipher*
geheimzinnig *mysterious*
geheimzinnigheid *mysteriousness*
geheugen *memory*
geheugenverlies *loss of memory,
amnesia*
gehoor • (het horen) *hearing* ★ *op het
~ by ear* • (toehoorders) *audience*
gehoorapparaat *hearing aid*
gehoorsafstand ★ *op ~ within earshot*
gehoorzaam *obedient*
gehoorzaamheid *obedience*
gehoorzamen *obey*
gehorig *noisy*
gehouden *obliged to, bound to*
gehucht *hamlet*
gehumeurd ★ *goed/slecht ~
good-/ill-tempered*
geijkt • (gebruikelijk) ★ *~e
uitdrukking set phrase* • (voorzien
van ijkmerk) ★ *~e maten legally
stamped measures*
geil *lascivious*
gein • (lol) *fun, humour* • (grapje) *joke*
geiser • (warme bron) *geyser, hot
spring* • (warmwatertoestel) *geyser,
*(gas) *water heater*
geit *(she)goat*
gejaagd *agitated*
gek I [de] • (onnozele) *fool*
• (krankzinnige) *madman, lunatic*
II [bnw] • (onnozel) *silly, foolish*
• (krankzinnig) *mad, crazy* • (raar)
funny, strange, queer • (~ op) *mad on,*

crazy about
gekant ★ *tegen iets ~ zijn be opposed
to s.th.*
gekheid • (krankzinnig zijn) *madness*
• (dwaasheid) *folly,* (tom)*foolery*
• (grapje) *joke*
gekkenhuis *madhouse*
gekkenwerk *madness, folly*
gekleed • (keurige kleren dragend)
★ *het staat ~ it is dressy* • (met kleren
aan) *dressed*
geknipt ★ *~ voor cut out for*
gekunsteld *artificial,* ‹bij spreken›
affected
gelaat *countenance, face*
gelach *laughter*
gelag *score*
gelagkamer *tap-room, bar*(room)
gelang ★ *naar ~ van according to*
gelasten *order*
gelaten *resigned*
gelatine *gelatin(e)*
geld *money,* ‹inf.› *dough*
geldbelegging *investment*
geldelijk *financial, monetary*
gelden • (beschouwd worden als)
count • (aangaan) *concern* • (van
kracht zijn) *be in force, apply*
geldgebrek *lack of money*
geldig *valid*
geldigheid *validity*
geldingsdrang *assertiveness*
geldmarkt *money market*
geldmiddelen • (financiële situatie)
finances • (inkomsten) (*financial*)
means
geldschieter *moneylender, financier,
sponsor*
geldstuk *coin*
geleden *ago* ★ *heel kort ~ quite
recently* ★ *lang ~ long ago*
geleding • (verbindingsplaats) *joint*
• (deel) *section*
geleed *jointed,* ‹v. kust› *indented* ★ *een
gelede bus an articulated bus*

geleerd *scholarly, learned*
geleerdheid *scholarship, erudition*
gelegen • (liggend) *situated*
• (geschikt) *convenient*
gelegenheid • (gunstige omstandigheid) *opportunity*
• (gebeurtenis) *occasion*
• (eetgelegenheid, plaats) *place, café, restaurant*
gelei *jelly*
geleide • (het vergezellen) *attendance,* ‹mil.› *escort,* ‹scheepv.› *convoy* • (de vergezellende personen) *guard*
geleidehond *guide-dog*
geleidelijk *gradual, progressive*
geleiden • (begeleiden) *lead, escort*
• (overbrengen) *conduct*
geleider • (begeleider) *guide*
• (overbrenger) *conductor*
geleiding *leading, conduction*
gelid • (gewricht) *joint* • (rij) *rank*
geliefd *beloved, dear*
geliefkoosd *favourite, pet*
gelijk I [het] *right* II [bnw]
• (hetzelfde) *same, equal,* ‹alleen pred.› *alike,* ‹gelijkend› *similar,* ‹op gelijk niveau› *equal,* ‹precies gelijk› *identical* ★ alle mensen zijn ~ *all men are equal* ★ een-een ~ *one all* • (effen) *level, smooth* III [bijw] ★ ~ handelen *act alike* IV [vw] *as*
gelijkelijk *equally*
gelijken *resemble, look like* ★ een goed ~d portret *a good likeness*
gelijkenis • (overeenkomst) *resemblance, likeness* • (parabel) *parable*
gelijkheid *equality*
gelijklopen *run parallel (to),* ‹v. klok› *keep time*
gelijkluidend *identical*
gelijkmaken *equalize,* ‹v. grond› *level*
gelijkmaker *equalizer*
gelijkmatig *even,* ‹v. klimaat› *equable*
gelijknamig *of the same name*

gelijkschakelen *coordinate (with), standardize*
gelijksoortig *similar*
gelijkspelen *draw*
gelijkstaan • (evenveel punten hebben) ‹sport› *be level (with)*
• (gelijk zijn) *be equal*
gelijkstellen • (gelijk achten) *put on a par (with)* • (gelijke rechten geven) *give equal rights*
gelijkstroom *direct current*
gelijktijdig *simultaneous*
gelijkvloers *on the ground floor,* ‹AE› *on the first floor*
gelijkwaardig *equal (to), equivalent (to)*
gelijkzetten *set (watch), synchronize*
gelijkzijdig *equilateral*
gelofte *vow*
geloof • (vertrouwen) *belief, faith*
• (godsdienst) *religion*
geloofsbelijdenis *creed*
geloofwaardig *credible*
geloven *believe, think* ★ 't is niet te ~ *it's incredible*
gelovig *religious*
geluid *sound*
geluiddemper *silencer*
geluiddicht *soundproof*
geluidloos *soundless, without sound*
geluidsinstallatie *audio/sound system*
geluimd ★ goed ~ *good-humoured*
★ slecht ~ *bad-tempered*
geluk • (aangename toestand) *happiness, bliss* • (fortuin) *fortune*
• (gunstige omstandigheid) ★ van ~ mogen spreken *count o.s. lucky* ★ ~ hebben *be in luck*
gelukkig I [bnw] • (fortuinlijk) *lucky, fortunate* • (blij) *happy*
• (voorspoedig) ★ een ~ nieuwjaar *a happy New Year* ★ ~ kerstfeest *merry Christmas* II [bijw] ★ ~ (maar)! *thank goodness!*

geluksvogel *lucky dog*
gelukwens *congratulation*
gelukwensen *congratulate (on)*
gelukzalig *blessed*
gemaakt • (gekunsteld) *affected,*
pretentious • (geveinsd) *artificial,*
pretended
gemaal I [de] *consort* II [het]
pumping-engine/station
gemachtigde *deputy,* <v. postwissel,
enz.> *endorsee*
gemak • (kalmte) *ease* • (moeiteloos)
ease • (wat gemak verschaft) *comfort,*
convenience • (toilet) *w.c., (public)*
convenience
gemakkelijk • (niet moeilijk) *easy*
• (onbezorgd) *easy* • (gerieflijk)
comfortable
gemakzucht *indolence, laziness*
gemakzuchtig *indolent, lazy*
gemalin *consort*
gematigd *moderate,* <v. klimaat>
temperate
gember *ginger*
gemeen I [bnw] • (slecht) *vile, bad*
• (laag-bij-de-gronds) *low, mean,* <v.
aard> *wicked* • (gemeenschappelijk)
common II [bijw] *meanly, beastly*
gemeengoed *common property*
gemeenplaats *commonplace, platitude*
gemeenschap • (groep,
maatschappij) *community* • (seks)
(sexual) intercourse
gemeenschappelijk I [bnw] • (van
meer dan 1 persoon) *common*
• (gezamenlijk) *joint* II [bijw] *jointly,*
together
gemeenschapszin *public spirit*
gemeente • (bestuurlijke eenheid)
municipality • (parochie) *parish*
gemeentebestuur *municipality,*
corporation
gemeentehuis *town hall*
gemeenteraad *local council*
gemeentesecretaris ≈ *town clerk*

gemeentewerken *municipal works*
gemeenzaam *familiar*
gemelijk *peevish, sullen*
gemenebest *commonwealth*
gemiddeld I [bnw] *average* II [bijw]
on an average
gemis *lack, want*
gemoed *mind, heart*
gemoedelijk *kind(-hearted), genial,*
<v. sfeer> *cosy*
gemoedsrust *tranquillity, peace of*
mind
gems *chamois*
genaamd *called, named*
genade • (gratie) *mercy,* <gerechtelijk>
pardon, <godsdienst> *grace* • (gave,
gunst) *favour*
genadeslag *finishing stroke, deathblow*
genadig • (vol genade) *merciful*
• (neerbuigend) *condescending,*
gracious
gene *that*
geneesheer *physician, medical*
practitioner
geneeskrachtig *healing*
geneeskunde *medical science, medicine*
geneeskundig *medical*
geneesmiddel *remedy, medicine*
geneeswijze *cure, treatment*
genegen *inclined, willing*
genegenheid • (geneigdheid)
inclination • (goedgezindheid)
affection
geneigd *inclined (to),* <tot kwaad>
prone (to)
geneigdheid *inclination, disposition*
generaal I [de] *general* II [bnw] *general*
generaliseren *generalize*
generatiekloof *generation gap*
generator *generator*
generen ⋆ zich ~ *feel embarrassed*
genezen I [ov ww] *cure s.o. of* II [on
ww] *recover (from),* <v. wond> *heal*
geniaal ⋆ een ~ idee *a brilliant idea*
genie I [de] <mil.> *the Royal Engineers*

II [het] *genius* [mv: *geniuses*]
genieten I [ov ww] • (ontvangen)
   receive • (plezier beleven) *enjoy* II [on
   ww] *enjoy o.s.*
genodigde *guest*
genoeg I [bijw] *enough* II [telw]
   enough, sufficient
genoegdoening *satisfaction*
genoegen • (voldoening) *satisfaction*
   • (plezier) *pleasure, joy*
genoeglijk *pleasant*
genoegzaam *sufficient*
genootschap *society*
genot *pleasure, delight, enjoyment*
genotmiddel *luxury, stimulant*
geografie *geography*
geografisch *geographic(al)*
geologie *geology*
gepaard *by twos, in pairs*
gepast • (fatsoenlijk) *proper, becoming*
   • (afgepast) *exact*
gepeins *meditation, reverie*
gepeupel *mob, populace*
gepikeerd *piqued, sore* (at)
geprononceerd *pronounced*
geraakt • (ontroerd) *moved*
   • (gepikeerd) *offended, nettled*
geraamte *skeleton*
geraas *din, noise*
geraden *advisable*
geraffineerd *refined*
gerant *manager*
gerecht I [het] • (schotel) *dish* • (gang
   v. maaltijd) *course* • (rechtbank) *court
   (of justice), tribunal* II [bnw] *just, due*
gerechtelijk ⋆ ~e dwaling *judicial
   error* ⋆ iem. ~ vervolgen *take legal
   proceedings against s.o.*
gerechtigd *qualified, entitled*
gerechtshof *court (of justice)*
gereed *ready,* ‹af› *finished*
gereedheid *readiness*
gereedschap *tools, instruments*
gereedschapskist *tool-box*
gereformeerd ‹rel.› *Calvinist(ic),*

‹kerk› (Dutch) *Reformed*
geregeld • (regelmatig) *regular*
   • (ordelijk) ⋆ een ~ leven leiden *lead
   an orderly life*
gereserveerd • (terughoudend)
   reserved, reticent • (besproken)
   reserved, booked
geriatrie *geriatrics*
gerief *convenience, comfort*
gering *scanty, slight, small*
Germaan *Teuton*
Germaans I [het] *Germanic* II [bnw]
   Germanic
geronnen *clotted*
geroutineerd *experienced, practised*
gerst *barley*
gerucht • (geluid) *noise* • (praatje)
   rumour, report
geruchtmakend *sensational*
geruis • (geluid) *noise* • (geritsel) *rustle*
geruisloos *noiseless*
geruit *checked, chequered*
gerust *easy, quiet, calm*
geruststellen *reassure, set* (s.o.'s *mind*)
   at ease
geruststelling *reassurance*
geschenk *gift, present*
geschieden • (gebeuren) *happen,
   occur* • (overkomen) *befall*
geschiedenis • (historie) *history*
   • (verhaal) *story*
geschiedkundig *historical*
geschiedschrijver *historian*
geschift *curdled,* ‹fig.› *dotty, crazy*
geschikt • (met de juiste kwaliteiten)
   fit, suitable • (aardig) *decent*
geschil *difference, dispute*
geschilpunt *point at issue, controversy*
geschoold *trained, schooled*
geschreeuw *shouting, cries*
geschrift (*piece of*) *writing, pamphlet*
geschut *artillery, guns*
gesel *whip, scourge*
geselen *flog*
geseling *flogging*

geslacht • (familie) race, family, generation • (sekse) ‹bio.› genus, ‹taalk.› gender

geslachtsrijp sexually mature

geslachtsziekte venereal disease, V.D.

geslepen sly, cunning

gesp buckle, clasp

gespen buckle, ‹met riem› strap

gespierd muscular

gespikkeld speckled

gesprek conversation, talk, ‹over telefoon› call

gespuis rabble, scum, riff-raff

gestalte • (uiterlijke vorm) figure • (gedaante) shape

gesteente stone

gestel constitution

gesteld I [bnw] ★ ik ben erg op hem ~ I'm very fond of him II [bijw] ★ ~ dat hij kwam suppose he came

gesteldheid state, condition, constitution

gestemd disposed

gesternte • (alle sterren) stars • (sterrenbeeld) constellation

gesticht I [het] asylum, institution, mental home II [bnw] ‹rel.› edified

gesticuleren gesticulate

gestreept striped

getal number

getand • (met tanden) toothed, ‹v. wiel› cogged • (met insnijdingen) indented, notched

getapt popular (with)

getikt crazy, balmy, mad

getrouw • (nauwkeurig) true, faithful, exact • (trouw) loyal, faithful, true

getto ghetto

getuige witness, ‹bij huwelijk› best man

getuigen I [ov ww] testify II [on ww] • (getuigenis afleggen) appear as a witness, give evidence • (blijk geven) ★ het getuigt van grote moed it shows great courage

getuigenis evidence, testimony

getuigschrift certificate, ‹v. personeel› testimonial

geul • (watergeul) gully, channel • (gleuf) ditch, gap, furrow

geur scent, odour, smell

geuren • (ruiken) smell • (~ met) sport, show off

geurig fragrant

geus (Sea) Beggar, Protestant

gevaar • (gevaarlijke toestand) peril, danger • (risico) risk

gevaarlijk risky, dangerous

gevaarte monster, colossus

geval case

gevarendriehoek hazard/breakdown triangle

gevat quick-witted, sharp, on the ball

gevecht fight, action

gevel façade, front

geven • (schenken) give • (gesteld zijn op) care for/about • (hinderen) matter • (aanreiken) hand, give, ‹kaartspel› deal • (toekennen) give, grant • (opleveren) give, ‹v. rente› yield, ‹v. warmte› give out • (opgeven) give up • (veroorzaken) ‹aanstoot› give, ‹hoop› raise, ‹moeilijkheden› cause

gever ‹bij kaartspel› dealer

gevlamd flamed, ‹v. hout› grained

gevlekt spotted

gevleugeld winged

gevlij ★ bij iem. in het ~ komen humour s.o.

gevoeglijk decently, properly

gevoel • (lichamelijk gevoel, tast) touch, feeling, sensation • (innerlijk gevoel) feeling, sense • (gevoeligheid) sentiment, feeling • (besef) ★ ~ voor humor sense of humour

gevoelen feeling, opinion

gevoelig • (ontvankelijk) sensitive • (lichtgeraakt) touchy • (pijnlijk) tender, sore

gevoelloos unfeeling, callous,

insensitive, ‹v. lichaamsdeel› numb

gevogelte fowls, poultry

gevolg • (personen) retinue, train • (resultaat, uitwerking) consequence, result

gevolgtrekking conclusion

gevuld • (mollig) full, plump • (met vulling) ‹v. gevogelte, enz.› stuffed, ‹v. portemonnee› well-filled

gewaad robe, garment

gewaarworden • (opmerken, zien) perceive, notice • (merken) become aware of, ‹te weten komen› find out

gewaarwording • (ondervinding) sensation, ‹v. zintuigen› perception • (indruk) feeling, impression

gewag * geen ~ maken van iets keep quiet about s.th.

gewas • (soort plant) plant • (plantengroei) vegetation • (oogst) crops

geweer rifle, gun

geweerschot rifle-shot, gunshot

geweervuur rifle-fire, gunfire

gewei antlers [mv: antlers]

geweld violence, force

gewelddaad act of violence, outrage

gewelddadig violent

geweldenaar • (sterk, bekwaam persoon) superman, ‹kundig› crack • (dwingeland) tyrant, bully

geweldig • (ontzaglijk) enormous, tremendous • (goed) great

geweldpleging violence

gewelf vault, arch

gewennen I [ov ww] accustom (to), habituate (to) II [on ww] get used/accustomed to

gewest province, region

gewestelijk regional, ‹accent› local

geweten conscience

gewetenloos unscrupulous

gewetensbezwaar scruple

gewetenswroeging remorse, compunction

gewezen former, ex-

gewicht weight

gewichtig I [bnw] weighty, important, momentous II [bijw] * ~ doen behave pompously

gewiekst cunning, smart, shrewd, astute

gewijd • (geheiligd) consecrated • (liturgisch) sacred

gewild • (in trek) much sought after, popular, ‹v. product› in demand

gewillig willing, ready

gewoel • (drukte) turmoil, bustle • (het woelen) tossing and turning

gewoon I [bnw] • (gebruikelijk) normal, usual, customary • (alledaags) ordinary, common, plain • (gewend aan) accustomed/used to II [bijw] just, simply

gewoonlijk usually

gewoonte • (gebruik) custom, usage • (persoonlijk gebruik) custom, habit

gewoonterecht common law

gewoonweg downright, simply, just

gewricht joint

gezag • (macht) authority • (overtuigende kracht) authority • (overheid) authorities

gezaghebbend authoritative

gezagvoerder ‹scheepv.› commander, captain, ‹luchtv.› captain

gezamenlijk I [bnw] • (collectief) combined, joint, collective II [bijw] together

gezang • (het zingen) singing • (lied) song, ‹rel.› hymn

gezant envoy, ambassador

gezegde • (spreekwoord) proverb, saying • (taalk.) predicate

gezel • (leerling-vakman) mate • (makker) fellow, mate

gezellig enjoyable, pleasant, ‹v. personen› companionable, sociable, ‹v. vertrek› cosy, snug

gezelligheid * voor de ~ for fun

gezelschap • (samenzijn) *company*
• (groep) *company, society*
gezelschapsspel *party/round game*
gezet • (dik) *stout, corpulent*
• (geregeld) ★ op ~te tijden *at set times*
gezeten • (met vaste woonplaats)
settled, resident • (welgesteld)
substantial
gezicht • (gezichtsvermogen)
(eye)sight, vision • (aangezicht) *face*
• (aanblik) *view, sight*
gezichtsbedrog *optical illusion*
gezichtspunt *point of view, viewpoint,*
angle
gezichtsveld *field of vision*
gezichtsvermogen (eye)sight
gezien *in view of, considering*
gezin *family*
gezind *disposed*
gezindheid • (stemming) *disposition*
• (rel.) *conviction, persuasion*
gezindte *denomination*
gezinshoofd *head of the family*
gezinshulp *home help*
gezinszorg *family-welfare (services),*
home help
gezocht • (gekunsteld) *contrived* • (in
trek) ★ zeer ~ *much sought after; in*
great demand
gezond *healthy,* <v. voedsel> *wholesome*
gezondheid I [de] • (gesteldheid)
health • (heilzaamheid) <v. klimaat>
healthiness, <v. voedsel>
wholesomeness II [tw] *Bless you!*
gezondheidsredenen *considerations*
of health
gezondheidszorg *health care*
gezusters ★ de ~ A. *the A. sisters*
gezwel • (opzwelling) *swelling, lump*
• (tumor) *tumour*
gezwollen *swollen*
gids <boek> *guide(book),* <persoon>
guide
gier • (vogel) *vulture* • (mest) *liquid*
manure

gieren • (brullen) <lachen> *scream,* <v.
wind> *whistle, howl*
gierig *stingy*
gierigaard *miser*
gieten *pour*
gieter *watering-can*
gieterij *foundry*
gift *present, gift*
giftig • (vergiftig) *poisonous, toxic*
• (venijnig) <boos> *touchy,* <v.
mensen> *venomous*
gij *thou*
gijzelaar *hostage*
gijzelen *take hostage,* <voor geld>
kidnap
gil *scream, yell, shriek*
gillen *shriek, scream, yell*
ginds *over there*
gips • (mineraal) *gypsum*
• (gipsverband) *plaster*
gipsverband *plaster cast*
gireren *pay/transfer by giro*
giro *giro, clearing, transfer*
girobetaalkaart *Giro cheque card*
gissen *guess, conjecture*
gist *yeast*
gisten *ferment*
gisting *ferment, fermentation*
gitaar *guitar*
glaceren *glaze,* <v. gebak> *ice*
glad I [bnw] • (glibberig) *slippery*
• (strak) *smooth,* <v. haar> *sleek,* <v.
ring> *plain,* <v. water> *calm* • (sluw)
cunning, clever • (vlot) *smooth*
II [bijw] *smoothly*
gladheid • (effenheid) *smoothness*
• (glibberigheid) *slipperiness*
gladiator *gladiator*
glans • (weerschijn) *gloss, lustre, shine*
• (luister) *splendour*
glansrijk *glorious, splendid*
glanzen *shine, shimmer, gleam,*
<vochtig glanzen> *glisten*
glas • (materiaal) *glass* • (ruit)
(window)pane • (brillenglas) *glass,*

lens • (drinkglas) *glass*
glashelder *crystal-clear*
glazen *glass(y)*
glazenwasser *window-cleaner*
glazig *glassy*, <v. aardappel> *waxy*
glazuren *glaze*, <v. gebak> *ice*
gletsjer *glacier*
gleuf *groove*, <v. automaat> *slot*, <v. brievenbus> *slit*
glibberen *slither*
glibberig *slippery*, *slithery*
glijbaan *slide*
glijden • (voortbewegen) <op ijs> *slide*, <op water> *glide*
 • (weg-/uit-/afglijden) *slip*
glijvlucht <v. vliegtuig> *glide*, <v. vogels> *gliding flight*
glimlach *smile*
glimlachen *smile (at)*
glimmen *glimmer*, *shine*, *gleam*, <v. zweet> *glisten*
glimp *glimpse*
glinsteren *sparkle*, *glitter*, *twinkle*
glinstering *glitter(ing)*, *sparkle*
glippen *slip*
globaal *rough*, *broad*
globe *globe*
gloed *glow*
gloednieuw *brand-new*
gloeien • (stralen van hitte) *glow*
 • (branden zonder vlam) *smoulder*
gloeilamp *light bulb*
glooiing *slope*
gloren *glimmer*, <v.d. dag> *dawn*
glorie *glory*
glucose *glucose*
gluiperig *shifty*, *sneaky*
glunderen *beam*, *radiate*
gluren *peep*, <wellustig> *leer*
glycerine *glycerine*
gnuiven *gloat (over)*, *chuckle (over/at)*
goddank *thank God*
goddelijk *divine*
goddeloos • (atheïstisch) *godless*, *ungodly* • (zondig) *wicked*, *unholy*

godgeklaagd *disgraceful*
godgeleerdheid *theology*
godheid • (goddelijk wezen) *deity*, *divine/celestial being*
 • (goddelijkheid) *divinity*, *godhead*
godsdienst *religion*
godsdienstig • (vroom) *pious*, *devout*
 • (religieus) *religious*
godsdienstoefening *divine service*, (practice of) *worship*
godsdienstvrijheid *freedom of religion/worship*
godvergeten *God-forsaken*
goed I [bnw] • (gezond) *good*, *well*
 • (juist) *right* • (uitstekend) *good*
 • (goedhartig) *kind* II [bijw] • (juist) *well*, *right* • (flink) *thoroughly*
 • (behoorlijk) *properly*
goedaardig *good-natured*, *kind-hearted*, *mild*, <v. ziekten, gezwel> *benign*
goeddeels *largely*, *for the greater part*
goedgeefs *generous*, *liberal*, *open-handed*
goedgelovig *credulous*, *gullible*
goedgezind *well-disposed*
goedig *good-natured*, *kind-hearted*
goedkeuren *approve (of)*
goedkeuring *approval*
goedkoop *inexpensive*, <ook fig.> *cheap*
goedmaken *make good*, *make up for*, *put right*, *make amends for*
goedmoedig *good-natured*
goedpraten *gloze over*, *explain away*
goedschiks *with a good grace*, *willingly*
goedvinden • (goedkeuren) *consent*, *approve of* • (nuttig vinden) *think fit*
gokken • (om geld spelen) *gamble*
 • (speculeren) *take a chance* • (raden) *guess*
golf • (van water) *wave*, <grote golf> *roller* • (wijde baai) *gulf*, *bay*
 • (balspel) *golf*
golfbeweging *undulation*

golflengte *wave-length*
golfslag *wash of the waves, surge*
golven *wave, undulate,* ‹v. haar› *flow,*
‹v. vlakte› *roll*
gom • (lijmstof) *gum* • (vlakgom)
rubber, ‹AE› *eraser*
gondel *gondola*
gong *gong*
gonzen ‹v. insect› *hum, buzz*
goochelaar *conjurer, magician*
goochelen • (toveren) *conjure*
• (handig omspringen met) *juggle*
goochem *knowing, smart*
gooi *throw, cast*
gooien *throw, fling,* ‹hard en gericht›
pitch
goot • (dak-/straatgoot) *gutter*
• (stortgoot) *chute, shoot*
gootsteen (kitchen) *sink*
gordel • (riem) *belt, girdle* • (kring)
circle • (geo.) *zone*
gordelroos *shingles*
gordijn *curtain*
gorgelen *gargle*
gorilla *gorilla*
gort ‹gebroken› *groats,* ‹gepeld› *pearl*
barley
gortig ⋆ *het te ~ maken go too far*
gotiek *Gothic*
gotisch *Gothic*
goud *gold*
gouden *gold*
goudsmid *goldsmith*
goudvis *goldfish*
graad *degree*
graaf *count, earl*
graafschap • (status) *countship,*
earldom • (landstreek) *county, shire*
graag I [bnw] *eager, hungry* II [bijw]
gladly, with pleasure, willingly
graaien *grab*
graan *corn, grain*
graat *fish-bone*
grabbel ⋆ *geld te ~ gooien throw away*
money

grabbelen *grabble* (in), *grope* (about)
gracht • (waterweg) *canal,* ‹om
kasteel› *moat* • (straat langs gracht) ≈
quay
gracieus *graceful, elegant*
gradueel • (trapsgewijs opklimmend)
gradual
graf *grave*
grafiek • (kunst) *graphic art* • (wisk.)
graph, diagram
grafiet *graphite*
grafisch *graphic*
grafkelder (family) *vault*
grafschennis *desecration of tombs*
grafschrift *epitaph*
grafsteen *tombstone, gravestone*
grafstem *sepulchral voice*
gram *gram(me)*
grammatica *grammar*
grammaticaal *grammatical*
grammofoon *gramophone*
grammofoonplaat (gramophone)
record
granaat I [de] *shell, grenade* II [het]
garnet
grandioos *magnificent*
graniet *granite*
granieten *granite*
grap • (mop) *joke,* ‹v. komiek› *gag*
• (grappige streek) *practical joke, hoax*
grapjas *joker, funny-man*
grappig *funny, amusing*
gras *grass*
grasduinen *browse*
grasmat *turf*
grasperk *lawn*
grasveld *lawn,* (grass) *field*
grasvlakte *stretch of grass, grassy plain*
graszode *turf*
gratie • (sierlijkheid) *grace* • (gunst)
favour ⋆ *bij de ~ Gods by the grace of*
God • (kwijtschelding) *pardon*
gratificatie *bonus*
gratis I [bnw] *free, gratis* II [bijw]
gratis, free of charge, for free

grauw I [de] *snarl* II [het] *rabble*
III [bnw] *grey*
graveerkunst *(art of) engraving*
graven *dig*
graveren *engrave*
gravin *countess*
gravure *engraving*
grazen *graze*
greep • *(onopzettelijke keus) pick*
• *(handvat) handle* • *(graai) grip, grasp*
grenadier *grenadier*
grendel *bolt*
grendelen *bolt*
grens • *(scheidingslijn) border*
• *(limiet) limit, boundary*
grensgeval *borderline case*
grenspost *border crossing*
grensrechter *linesman*
grenzeloos *boundless*
grenzen ∗ ~ *aan be bounded by; border on*
greppel *ditch, trench*
gretig *eager*
grief *grievance, offence*
Griekenland *Greece*
Grieks I [het] *Greek* II [bnw] *Greek*
grienen *blubber, whimper*
griep *influenza, (the) flu*
grieven *grieve, hurt*
griezel *creep, horror*
griezelen *shudder, get the creeps,*
<Schots> *get the heebie-jeebies*
griezelig *creepy, eerie*
grif *promptly*
griffie *record-office,* ≈ *registry*
griffier <v. rechtbank> *clerk of the court, clerk,* ≈ *registrar*
grijpen I [ov ww] *seize, grip, catch, grasp* II [on ww] • *(~ naar) reach for, grab/snatch at*
grijper *grab, grip(per)*
grijs • *(kleur) grey* • *(oud) hoary, ancient*
grijsaard *(grey) old man*
grijzen *(turn) grey*

gril *caprice, whim*
grillen I [ov ww] *grill,* <AE> *broil* II [on ww] *shudder*
grillig *capricious, whimsical, fanciful,* <v. weer> *changeable*
grimas *grimace*
grimeren *make up*
grimeur *make-up artist*
grimmig *grim*
grind *gravel*
grissen *snatch*
groef *groove*
groei *growth*
groeien • *(groter worden) grow*
• *(ontwikkelen) grow*
groen I [het] *green(ery)* II [bnw] *green*
groente *(green) vegetables, greens*
groenteboer *greengrocer*
groep *group*
groeperen *group*
groepering • *(het groeperen) grouping* • *(groep)* ∗ *een politieke ~ a (political) faction*
groet *greeting,* <mil.> *salute*
groeten *greet,* <mil.> *salute*
groeve *pit,* <steengroeve> *quarry*
groezelig *dingy, grubby*
grof • *(onbeleefd) rude* • *(niet fijn) coarse, rough*
grofheid • *(grof zijn) coarseness, roughness* • *(botheid) rudeness*
grommen • *(grommend geluid maken) growl* • *(morren) grumble*
grond • *(bouwgrond) site* • *(bodem onder water) bottom* • *(kern) ground, foundation* • *(aarde) ground, earth, soil* • *(motief) ground, reason*
grondbegrip *fundamental/basic idea*
grondbelasting *land-tax, property tax*
gronden • *(baseren op) found,* <v. hoop> *ground (on),* <v. mening> *base/ground (on)*
grondgebied *territory*
grondgedachte *basic/underlying idea*
grondig *profound, thorough*

grondlegger *founder*
grondregel *principle*
grondslag • (fundament) *foundation*
• (basis, beginsel) *basis, foundations*
grondstof • (onbewerkt materiaal)
raw material • (hoofdbestanddeel)
(starting) material, component
grondverf *undercoat, primer*
grondvesten I [de] *foundations* II [ov
ww] *found, base (on)*
grondwater *ground/subsoil water*
grondwet *constitution*
grondwettelijk *constitutional*
groot I [het] * ~ en klein *great and
small* * in 't ~ *on a large scale* II [bnw]
• (volwassen) *grown(-up)*
• (belangrijk) *great* • (van afmeting)
* 3 cm ~ *3 cm in size* • (omvangrijk)
big, great • (uitgestrekt) *large, vast*
• (lang, hoog) *tall* III [bijw] * ~ gelijk
quite right
grootbrengen *bring up, raise*
groothandel • (bedrijf) *wholesale
house, wholesaler* • (handelsvorm)
wholesale trade
groothandelaar *wholesale dealer,
wholesaler*
grootheid • (het groot zijn)
magnitude, <v. geest> *greatness*
• (belangrijk persoon) *man/woman of
consequence, celebrity*, <inf.> *big shot*
• (wisk.) *quantity*, <veranderlijk>
variable
groothertogdom *grand duchy*
grootje *granny*
grootkapitaal *big business, high
finance*
grootmeester *Grandmaster*
grootmoedig *magnanimous*
grootouders *grandparents*
groots • (prachtig) *grand(iose)*
• (indrukwekkend) *spectacular*
grootspraak *boast(ing)*
grootte *size*, <lichaamslengte> *height*
grootvader *grandfather*

gros • (12 dozijn) *gross* • (grootste deel)
majority
grossier *wholesale dealer*
grot *cave*, <groot en diep> *cavern*
grotendeels *mainly, largely*
grotesk *grotesque*
gruis *grit*
gruwel • (iets gruwelijks) *horror*
• (watergruwel) (water)gruel
gruwelijk • (afschuwwekkend)
atrocious, gruesome
gruwen *shudder*
guillotine *guillotine*
guitig *roguish, arch*
gul *generous*
gulden I [de] *guilder, Dutch florin*
II [bnw] *golden*
gulheid *generosity*
gulp *fly*
gulpen *gush*
gulzig *greedy*
gummi (india) *rubber*
gunnen • (toewijzen) *place, award*
• (verlenen) *grant, allow*
• (toewensen) * 't is je (van harte)
gegund *you are (heartily) welcome to it*
gunst • (goede gezindheid) * ten ~e
van *on behalf of; in favour of* * iem.
een ~ vragen *ask a favour of s.o.* * in
de ~ komen bij *find favour with* * uit
de ~ raken *fall out of favour*
• (vriendelijk gebaar) * iem. een ~
bewijzen *do s.o. a favour*
gunstig *favourable*
gutsen I [on ww] *gush*, <v. zweet> *pour
(down)* II [onp ww] *pour (down)*
guur <v. weer> *raw*
gymnasiast ≈ *grammar school pupil*
gymnasium ≈ *grammar school*
gymnastiek *physical education, P.E.,
gymnastics*
gynaecologie *gynaecology*
gynaecoloog *gynaecologist*

H

haag • (heg) *hedge* • (rij mensen/ dingen) *row*

haai • (vis) *shark* • (persoon) *shark* • (vrouw) *shrew*

haak *hook*, ‹leesteken› *bracket*, ‹v. kapstok› *peg*

haaks *square*

haakwerk *crochet(ing)*

haal • (ruk) *pull* • (streep) *stroke*

haan • (dier) *cock*, ‹AE› *rooster* • (pal in vuurwapen) *cock* • (weerhaan) *weathercock*

haar I [de] • (fractie) *hair* • (haarvezel) *hair* II [het] • (haardos) *hair* III [pers vnw] *her* IV [bez vnw] *her, hers*

haarband *headband*, ‹lint› *ribbon*

haard • (open haard) *hearth, fireplace* • (kachel) *stove*

haardos *(head of) hair*

haardvuur *fire (burning in the hearth)*

haarfijn I [bnw] ‹fig.› *minute, subtle* II [bijw] *minutely*

haarspeld *hairpin*

haarstukje *hairpiece*

haas • (dier) *hare* • (vlees) *fillet* • (bangerd) *coward* • (sport) *pacemaker*

haast I [de] • (snelheid) *haste* • (drang tot spoed) *hurry* II [bijw] • (bijna) *almost, nearly* • (gauw) *soon*

haasten *hurry*

haastig I [bnw] *hasty, hurried* II [bijw] *hurriedly, in a hurry, hastily*

haat *hatred*

haatdragend *vindictive, spiteful, resentful*

hachelijk *critical, precarious*

hachje *skin, life*

hagedis *lizard*

hagel • (neerslag) *hail* • (jachthagel) *shot*

hagelbui *hailstorm*

hagelen *hail*

hagelsteen *hailstone*

hagelwit *as white as snow*

hak • (hiel) *heel* • (hielstuk v. schoen) *heel* • (houw) *cut* • (werktuig) *hoe*

hakblok *butcher's block, chopping board*

haken I [ov ww] • (vastmaken) *hook, hitch* II [on ww] • (handwerken) *crochet* • (blijven haken) *catch* • (~ naar) *hanker after*

hakenkruis *swastika*

hakkelen *stammer, stutter*

hakken I [ov ww] • (in stukken hakken) *chip, cut (up)* • (sport) *back kick with the heel* II [on ww] • (houwen) *hack* • (vitten) *pick holes in, find fault with*

hakmes *chopper, chopping knife*

hal • (vestibule) *(entrance) hall*, ‹v. hotel, theater› *foyer, lobby* • (zaal) *hall*

halen • (ophalen) *fetch, get* • (naar zich toe trekken) *pull* • (behalen) *obtain* • (bereiken) ★ *dat haalt (het) er niet bij* it can't compare with it ★ *jij haalt de 90 wel* you'll live to be 90 ★ *hij haalde het net* he scraped through; he barely made it ★ *de trein ~* catch the train

half I [bnw] • (de helft zijnd) *half, semi-* • (een groot deel) ★ *de halve wereld* half the world • (halverwege) ★ *half een* half past twelve; twelve-thirty ★ *half mei* the middle of May II [bijw] *half*

halfbakken *half-baked*

halfbloed I [de] • (mens van gemengd bloed) *halfbreed* • (kruising) *crossbreed* II [bnw] *halfbreed*, ‹v. dieren› *crossbred*

halfbroer *half-brother*

halfdood *half dead*

halfjaarlijks *half-yearly, biannual*

halfrond I [het] *hemisphere* II [bnw]

• (cirkel) *semicircular* • (bol)
hemispherical
halfslachtig *half-hearted*
halfstok *half-mast*
halfweg *halfway*
hallucinatie *hallucination*
halm *stalk,* ‹v. gras› *blade*
hals • (halsopening v.
kleding) *neckline* • (nek) *neck* • (persoon)
★ onnozele hals *sucker*
halsband *collar*
halsdoek *scarf*
halsmisdaad *capital crime*
halsstarrig *obstinate, headstrong,
stubborn*
halster *halter*
halswervel *cervical vertebra*
halter ‹kort› *dumbbell,* ‹lang› *barbell*
halvemaan *half-moon, crescent*
halveren • (in tweeën delen) *divide
into halves* • (met de helft
verminderen) *halve*
halverwege I [bijw] *halfway* II [vz]
half-way, midway
ham *ham*
hamer *hammer*
hameren I [ov ww] *hammer* II [on ww]
• (~ op) ★ ergens op blijven ~ *keep
going on about s.th.*
hamster *hamster*
hamsteren *hoard (up)*
hand *hand*
handbal I [de] • (bal) *handball* II [het]
• (sport) *handball*
handboek *manual, handbook*
handbreed ★ geen ~ wijken *not yield*
handdoek *towel*
handdruk *handshake*
handel • (zaak) *business* • (het
kopen/verkopen) *trade, commerce,
business*
handelaar *merchant,* ‹auto's, drugs›
dealer
handelbaar • (handzaam)
manageable, handy, easy to use

• (meegaand) *tractable, manageable*
handelen • (doen) *act* • (handel
drijven) *trade* • (~ **over**) *deal with,
treat (of)*
handeling *act*
handelsmerk *trademark*
handelsverdrag *commercial treaty*
handenarbeid • (schoolvak)
handicraft • (werk met de handen)
manual labour
handgebaar *gesture, motion*
handgeklap *applause, handclapping*
handgeld • (voorschot) *handsel,
earnest money* • (eerste verdienste)
first money of the day
handgemeen *scuffle*
handgranaat (hand) *grenade*
handgreep • (foefje) *trick, dodge*
• (handvat) *handle, grip* • (handvol)
handful • (handigheid) *knack, trick*
handhaven I [ov ww] *maintain*
II [wkd ww] *maintain o.s.*
handicap *handicap, disability*
handig • (behendig) *skilful, clever*
• (makkelijk te hanteren) *handy*
handigheid • (hanteerbaarheid)
handiness • (foefje) *knack, trick* • (het
handig zijn) *skill, cleverness*
handlanger • (medeplichtige)
accomplice, tool • (ondergeschikte
helper) *assistant*
handleiding *manual, handbook*
handomdraai ★ in een ~ *in a trice; in
less than no time*
handpalm *palm of the hand*
handrem *handbrake*
handschoen *glove*
handschrift • (geschreven tekst)
manuscript • (manier v. schrijven)
handwriting
handtastelijk • (slaags) *violent*
• (vrijpostig) *free*
handtekening *signature*
handvest *charter, covenant*
handvol *handful*

handwerk • (ambacht) *trade, craft*
• (met de hand gemaakt) *handwork, handiwork*
handzaam • (handelbaar) *manageable*
• (praktisch) *handy*
hangbrug • (hangsteiger) *cradle*
• (opgehangen brugdek) *suspension bridge*
hangen I [ov ww] *hang (up)* II [on ww]
• (slap hangen) *hang,* <bloemen> *droop* • (vastzitten) *stick to*
• (rondlummelen) *loll* • (nog niet afgedaan zijn) *hang* • (van iets afhangen) *hang*
hanger • (sieraad dat hangt) *pendant*
• (kleerhaak) *hanger*
hangerig *drooping, listless*
hangkast • (klerenkast) *wardrobe,* <AE> *closet* • (hangende kast) *hanging cupboard*
hangmat *hammock*
hangplant *hanging plant*
hangslot *padlock*
hansworst *buffoon, clown*
hanteerbaar *manageable*
hanteren • (in de hand nemen) *manage* • (omgaan met) *handle*
hap • (afgehapt stuk) *morsel* • (stuk) *bit* • (boel) *lot* • (beet) *bite*
haperen • (blijven steken) *stick,* <v. stem> *falter* • (mankeren) ★ *er hapert iets there's s.th. wrong (with)*
happen • (bijten) *bite* • (tot zich nemen) *take a bite* • (reageren) *take the bait*
happig *eager (for), keen (on)*
hard I [bnw] • (niet zacht) *hard*
• (hevig) <regen> *heavy*
• (meedogenloos) *stern, harsh*
• (vaststaand) *hard* • (luid, schel) *loud*
• (kalkrijk) *hard* II [bijw] • (snel) *fast*
• (niet zacht, hevig) *hard* • (luid) *loud*
• (meedogenloos) *hard* • (hevig) *hard*
harden • (hard maken) *harden,* <staal> *temper,* <v. persoon> *steel*

• (uithouden) *stand, bear*
hardhandig *rough*
hardleers • (moeilijk lerend) *dull, dense, thick-skulled* • (eigenwijs) *obstinate, stubborn*
hardlopen I [het] *running* II [on ww] *run*
hardloper *runner,* <op korte afstand> *sprinter*
hardnekkig *obstinate, dogged, stubborn,* <v. gerucht> *persistent*
hardop (out) *loud, aloud*
hardrijden *race, speed*
hardvochtig *callous, harsh, heartless*
harig *hairy*
haring • (pin v. tent) *peg* • (vis) *herring*
hark • (gereedschap) *rake* • (stijf persoon) ★ *stijve hark dull old stick*
harken *rake*
harkerig *stiff, clumsy*
harmonica • (mondharmonica) *harmonica* • (accordeon) *accordion*
harmonie *harmony*
harmoniëren *harmonize*
harmonisch *harmonious*
harnas *armour*
harp *harp*
harpoen *harpoon*
harpoeneren *harpoon*
harrewarren *squabble, bicker*
hars *resin*
hart *heart*
hartaanval *heart attack*
hartelijk *cordial, hearty*
harteloos *heartless, callous*
harten *hearts*
*hartenlust (Wdl: hartelust) ★ naar ~ to one's heart's content
hartgrondig I [bnw] *heartfelt, cordial* II [bijw] *cordially, wholeheartedly*
hartig • (pittig, gekruid) *hearty, tasty*
• (zout) *salt, savoury*
hartinfarct *coronary*
hartklopping *palpitation (of the heart)*

hartroerend I [bnw] *touching* II [bijw]
pathetically
hartslag *heartbeat*
hartstocht *passion*
hartstochtelijk *passionate*
hartverlamming *heart failure*
hartverscheurend *heartrending*
hartzeer *heartache*
haspel *reel*
haspelen I [ov ww] • (met haspel
winden) *reel* • (verwarren) *mix up,
mess (up)* II [on ww] *bicker*
hatelijk • (boosaardig) *nasty, hateful*
• (krenkend) *spiteful, nasty*
hatelijkheid • (het hatelijk zijn)
malice, nastiness • (hatelijke
opmerking) *nasty remark*
haten *hate*
have *property, stock*
haven • (aanlegplaats) *harbour,* <grote
haven> *port* • (toevluchtsoord) *haven*
havenarbeider *dock worker*
havenmeester *harbour master*
havenstad *port*
haver *oats*
havik • (vogel) *hawk* • (begerig mens)
vulture, vampire • (pol.) *hawk*
haviksneus *hook-nose*
hazelaar *hazel*
hazelnoot *hazelnut, nut*
hazenlip *harelip*
hebbelijkheid *way, mannerism, habit*
hebben I [het] ⋆ hun hele ~ en
houden *all their belongings* II [ov ww]
• (beschikken over) *have* • (in
bepaalde omstandigheden verkeren)
⋆ het goed/slecht ~ *be well/badly off*
• (krijgen) ⋆ daar heb je het nou!
there you are! • (verdragen) ⋆ ik kan
veel ~ *I can take a lot* • (behandelen)
⋆ het over iets ~ *talk about s.th.*
⋆ daar heb ik het niet over *that's not
the point* ⋆ iedereen heeft het erover
it's the talk of the town ⋆ Ad weet
waar hij het over heeft *Ad knows*

what he's talking about • (voelen)
⋆ wat heb je? *what's wrong with you?*
• (~ aan) ⋆ daar heb ik niets aan
that's (of) no use to me ⋆ je weet nooit
wat je aan hem hebt *you never know
what to expect of him* ⋆ wat heb je
daaraan? *what use is it?*
hebberig *greedy, covetous*
Hebreeuws I [het] *Hebrew* II [bnw]
Hebrew
hebzucht *greed*
hebzuchtig *greedy*
hecht *strong, firm*
hechten I [ov ww] • (vastmaken)
attach, fasten, <med.> *stitch, suture*
• (toekennen) *attach* II [on ww]
• (gesteld zijn op) *be attached to, be
devoted to* • (blijven kleven) *adhere,
stick* III [wkd ww] • (~ aan) *attach o.s.
to, become attached to*
hechtenis *custody, detention*
hechting *stitch, suture*
hechtpleister *elastoplast, sticking
plaster, bandage*
hectare *hectare*
heden I [het] *present* II [bijw] *today*
hedendaags *modern, present-day*
heel I [bnw] • (niet kapot) *whole, entire*
• (in z'n geheel) *entire, whole* • (veel,
groot) *quite* II [bijw] • (volstrekt)
quite, completely • (geheel en al) *quite,
wholly, completely, entirely* • (zeer)
very
heelal *universe*
heelhuids *without injury, unhurt*
heen • (naar toe) *away* • (heenweg)
⋆ heen en weer *to and fro; up and
down* ⋆ heen en terug *there and back*
• (weg) ⋆ hij is ver heen *he is far gone*
heengaan • (vertrekken) *go away,
leave* • (sterven) *pass away*
heenkomen ⋆ een goed ~ zoeken *run
to safety*
heenreis *outward journey,* <per schip>
outward voyage

heer • (meester) lord • (figuur in kaartspel) king • (God)
★ Onze-Lieve-Heer our Lord
• (beschaafd man) gentleman

heerlijk • (aangenaam) delightful, wonderful, <v. weer> lovely • (lekker) delicious

heerlijkheid • (iets lekkers) delicacies [mv] • (gelukzaligheid) bliss • (gebied) manor

heerschap master, gent

heerschappij mastery, dominion, lordship

heersen • (regeren) rule, <v. vorst> reign • (aanwezig zijn) prevail

heerser ruler

heerszuchtig imperious, domineering

hees hoarse

heester shrub

heet • (warm) hot • (overdadig gekruid) spicy

heethoofd hothead

hefboom lever

heffen • (tillen) raise, lift • (opleggen) <belasting> impose, <boete> fine

heffing • (het heffen) lifting • (vordering) levying, imposition

heft handle, haft

heftig vehement

heftruck fork-lift truck

hegemonie hegemony

heibel • (ruzie) row • (lawaai) racket

heide • (gebied) heath, moor • (plant) heather

heiden heathen, pagan

heidens • (niet christelijk) pagan, heathen • (ontzettend) atrocious

heien ram, drive

heiig hazy

heil • (voordeel) good • (redding) safety, refuge • (zielenheil) salvation • (welzijn) welfare

heilig holy

heiligdom • (plaats) sanctuary, shrine • (voorwerp) relic

heilige saint

heiligen • (louteren) sanctify • (wijden aan) dedicate to • (wijden) hallow, sanctify • (eerbiedigen) keep holy

heiligschennis sacrilege

heiligverklaring canonization

heilloos • (goddeloos) sinful, wicked • (geen geluk brengend) fatal

heilzaam • (geneeskrachtig) curative, healing • (weldadig) beneficial, salutary

heimelijk secret, furtive

heimwee homesickness, <naar vroeger> nostalgia

heinde ★ van ~ en verre from far and near

heipaal pile

hek • (poort) gate • (omheining) railing(s), fence • (versperring) barrier • (horde) hurdle

hekel dislike

hekeldicht satire

hekelen • (vlas over de hekel halen) hackle • (bekritiseren) criticize

heks • (tovenares) witch • (lelijk wijf) (old) hag

heksen practise witchcraft

hel I [de] hell II [bnw] vivid, <v. kleur> bright, <v. licht> glaring

helaas unfortunately, <form.> alas

held hero

heldendicht heroic poem, epic poem

heldenmoed heroism

helder bright, <water> clear

heldhaftig heroic

helemaal • (geheel en al) quite, all, entirely, altogether • (aanduiding van afstand) ★ ~ van/naar Groningen all the way from/to Groningen

helen I [ov ww] • (gestolen goederen kopen) receive, <inf.> fence • (genezen) heal II [on ww] cure, heal

heler receiver, <inf.> fence

helft • (groot deel) half • (elk v. twee

gelijke delen) *half*
helikopter *helicopter*
helium *helium*
Helleens *Hellenic*
hellen • (schuin aflopen) *slope*
• (overhangen) *slant, slope*
helleveeg *hellcat, shrew*
helling • (het overhellen) *inclination*
• (glooiing, talud) *slope*
helm • (hoofddeksel) *helmet*
• (plantk.) *marram*
helpen *aid, help*
hels • (van de hel) *hellish, infernal*
• (kwaad) *furious*
hem *him,* ‹m.b.t. dier, ding› *it*
hemd • (onderkleding) *vest*
• (overhemd) *shirt*
hemdsmouw *shirtsleeve*
hemel • (luchtruim) *sky, heaven*
• (hiernamaals) *heaven* • (God)
Heaven
hemelhoog *sky-high*
hemellichaam *heavenly body*
hemels • (van de hemel) *heavenly*
• (goddelijk) *sublime, divine*
hemelsbreed I [bnw] • (zeer groot)
enormous • (in rechte lijn) ∗ 5 *mijl* ~ 5
miles as the crow flies II [bijw] ∗ *ze*
verschillen ~ *they are as different as*
chalk and cheese; they are poles apart
hemeltergend *outrageous, appalling*
Hemelvaartsdag *Ascension day*
hen I [de] *hen* II [pers vnw] *them*
hengel *fishing rod*
hengelaar *angler*
hengelen • (vissen) *angle* • (~ **naar**)
fish/angle for
hengsel • (beugel) *handle* • (scharnier)
hinge
hengst • (mannelijk paard) *stallion*
• (dreun) *thump*
hennep *hemp*
hens ∗ *alle hens aan dek all hands on*
deck
herademen *breathe more freely*

herbergen *house, lodge*
herboren *reborn, born again*
herdenken *commemorate*
herdenking *commemoration*
herder • (hoeder) ‹v. koeien› *cowherd,*
‹v. schapen› *shepherd* • (hond)
‹Duitse› *Alsatian*
herdershond *sheepdog*
herdruk *reprint*
herenboer *gentleman farmer*
herenhuis *mansion, large house*
herexamen *re-examination*
herfst *autumn,* ‹AE› *fall*
herhaald *repeated*
herhalen *repeat*
herhaling *repetition,* ‹film› *repeat,*
‹televisie› *replay*
herhalingsoefening *revision exercise,*
‹mil.› *retraining*
herinneren I [ov ww] *remind* II [wkd
ww] *remember, recollect*
herinnering • (geheugen) *memory*
• (het herinneren) *recollection*
• (souvenir) *memento, souvenir* • (wat
doet herinneren) *reminder* • (wat
men herinnert) *recollection, memory*
herkauwen *ruminate, chew the cud,*
‹fig.› *go on about s.th.*
herkenbaar *recognizable*
herkennen • (terugkennen) *recognize*
• (onderscheiden) *identify*
herkenning *recognition, identification*
herkiesbaar *eligible for re-election*
herkiezen *re-elect*
herkomst *origin, source*
herleiden *reduce (to), convert (into)*
herleven *revive*
hermetisch *hermetic, airtight*
hernieuwen *renew*
heroïne *heroin, smack,* ‹inf.› *horse*
heropenen *reopen*
heroveren *reconquer, recapture*
herrie • (lawaai) *noise, din, racket, row*
• (ruzie) *row* • (drukte) ∗ ~ *schoppen*
cause trouble; kick up a row

herrijzen *rise again*
herroepen <v. besluit> *revoke,* <v. bevel> *countermand*
herscholen *retrain*
hersenen • (orgaan) *brain* • (verstand) *brains* [mv] • (hersenpan) *skull*
hersenschim *chimera, fantasy*
hersenschudding *concussion*
hersenspoeling *brainwashing*
hersenvliesontsteking *meningitis*
herstel • (het herstellen) <v. economie, gezondheid> *recovery* • (reparatie) *repair*
herstellen I [ov ww] • (repareren) *repair, mend* • (in de oude toestand brengen) *re-establish,* <orde, vrede> *restore* II [on ww] *recover, convalesce* III [wkd ww] *recover (o.s.)*
herstellingsoord *sanitorium, convalescent home*
hert *deer* [mv: *deer*], <mannetje> *stag*
hertenkamp *deer park/forest*
hertog *duke*
hertogdom *dukedom, duchy*
hervatten *resume*
hervormen *reform*
hervorming • (het hervormen) *reform* • (rel.) *Reformation*
herwaarderen *revalue*
herwinnen *regain, recover,* <techn.> *recycle*
herzien *revise*
herziening *revision*
het I [pers vnw] ★ ben jij het? *is it you?* ★ ik ben het *it is me* II [onb vnw] *it* III [lw] *the*
heten I [ov ww] ★ iem. welkom ~ *wish/bid s.o. welcome* II [on ww] • (de naam dragen, aanduiden) *be called/named* • (beweerd worden) *be reputed*
heterdaad ★ iem. op ~ betrappen *catch s.o. in the act; catch s.o. red-handed*
heterogeen *heterogeneous*

hetgeen I [aanw vnw] *what, that which* II [betr vnw] *which*
hetze *witch hunt,* <gestook> *smear campaign*
hetzelfde *the same*
hetzij *either*
heugen ★ dàt zal u ~ *you will be sorry for this; you won't forget this*
heulen *collaborate*
heup *hip,* <v. dier> *haunch*
heus I [bnw] • (echt) *real* • (beleefd) *courteous, polite* II [bijw] *really, indeed*
heuvel *hill*
hevig I [bnw] • (heftig) *violent, vehement* • (intens) <haat, enz.> *intense,* <pijn> *severe* II [bijw] *violently, intensely*
hiaat *hiatus, gap*
hiel *heel*
hier • (op deze plaats) *here* • (alsjeblieft) *here* • (hierheen) *here*
hiërarchie *hierarchy*
hierbij *herewith*
hierdoor • (hierdoorheen) *through here/this* • (daardoor) *because of this, owing to this*
hierheen *this way, here*
hierin *in this,* <plaats> *in here*
hierna • (tijd) *after this,* <form.> *hereafter* • (plaats) *below*
hiernaast *alongside,* <buren> *next door*
hiernamaals *hereafter*
hierom • (hieromheen) *around this* • (daarom) *for this reason, because of this*
hieromtrent • (hier in de buurt) *hereabout(s), around here* • (hierover) *about this*
hieronder • (verderop) *below* • (erbij zijnd) *among these* • (onder het genoemde) *by this*
hierop • (hierbovenop) *(up)on this* • (hierna) *upon this,* <form.> *hereupon*
hiertoe • (voor dit doel) *for this purpose* • (m.b.t. plaats) *(up to) here*

hieruit • (uit het genoemde) *from this* • (uit deze plaats) *out of here*

hiervoor • (in ruil voor) (*in return*) *for this* • (voor het genoemde) <m.b.t. plaats> *in front of this*, <m.b.t. tijd> *before this* • (tot dit doel) *for this purpose, to this end*

hij I [de] *he* II [pers vnw] *he*

hijgen *pant, gasp for breath*

hijsen I [ov ww] • (omhoog trekken) *hoist* II [on ww] • (zuipen) *booze*

hik *hiccup*

hikken *hiccup*

hinde *hind, doe*

hinder *nuissance, bother, impediment*

hinderen • (belemmeren) *hinder, hamper* • (bezwaarlijk zijn) *matter* • (ergeren) *annoy, bother*

hinderlaag *ambush*

hinderlijk • (storend) *troublesome, disturbing* • (belemmerend) *inconvenient* • (ergerlijk) *annoying, aggravating*

hindernis *obstacle, hindrance*

hinderpaal *obstacle*

hinderwet ≈ *nuisance act*

hinkelen *hop,* <spel> *play hopscotch*

hinken *limp*

hinniken • (geluid v. paarden) *neigh, whinny* • (lachen) *bray (with laughter)*

hippie *hippy, hippie*

historicus *historian, student of history*

historisch • (erg belangrijk) *historic* • (als uit de historie) *historical* • (waar gebeurd) *historical, not legendary*

hit • (succes) *hit* • (pony) *pony, cob* • (dienstmeisje) *servant, maid*

hitte *heat*

hittegolf *heat wave*

hobbelen • (schommelen) *rock,* <in rijtuig> *jolt* • (hobbelig zijn) *be bumpy*

hobbelig *rough, bumpy*

hobbelpaard *rocking-horse*

hobo *oboe*

hoboïst *oboist*

hockey *hockey*

hoe • (op welke wijze) *how* • (in welke mate) *how* • (als voegwoord) *how* • (welk) *what* • (waardoor) *how*

hoed *hat, bonnet*

hoedanigheid • (aard) *quality* • (functie) ★ ik spreek in de ~ van *I speak in the capacity of*

hoede • (bescherming) *care* • (voorzichtigheid) *guard*

hoef *hoof*

hoefijzer *horseshoe*

hoegenaamd ★ ~ niets *absolutely nothing*

hoek • (deel v. vertrek) *corner* • (kant) *side* • (verborgen hoekje) *nook* • (straathoek) *corner* • (stoot bij boksen) *hook* • (vishaak) *hook, fishhook* • (wisk.) *angle*

hoekhuis *corner house, house on the corner*

hoekig • (met hoeken) *angular* • (stuntelig) *awkward*

hoeksteen • (steen op de hoek) *cornerstone* • (fundament) *foundation*

hoektand *eyetooth, canine tooth*

hoen *hen, fowl*

hoenderhok *chicken coop*

hoepel *hoop*

hoepelen *play with a hoop, trundle a hoop*

hoer *whore, prostitute*

hoes *cover,* <boek> *slip cover, book jacket,* <grammofoonplaat> *sleeve*

hoest *cough*

hoestbui *coughing fit*

hoesten *cough*

hoeve *farm, farmstead*

hoeveel *how much/many*

hoeveelheid *quantity, amount*

hoeveelste • (verhouding) *what part* • (rangorde) ★ de ~ is het *what is today's date?*

hoeven I [ov ww] ★ dat had je niet ~ doen *you shouldn't have done that*

II [on ww] *need, be necessary*
hoewel *although, though*
hoezeer I [bijw] *how much* II [vw]
however much, as much as
hof I [de] *garden* II [het] *court* ∗ *'t hof*
maken court
hoffelijk *courteous*
hofhouding *royal household*
hofje ● (binnenplaats) *courtyard*
● (tuin) *garden* ● (huis) *almshouse*
hofleverancier *purveyor to the Royal*
Household
hogeschool *college, academy*
hok ● (bergruimte) *shed* ● (kamer) *den*
hokken ● (samenwonen) *shack up*
(with) ● (op één plek blijven) ∗ *bij*
elkaar ~ *huddle together*
hol I [het] ● (grot) *cave, cavern*
● (schuilplaats) *den, haunt* II [bnw]
● (leeg klinkend) *hollow* ● (niet bol)
‹lens› *concave,* ‹ogen› *gaunt* ● (leeg)
hollow, ‹maag› *empty*
Holland *Holland*
Hollander *Dutchman, Hollander*
Hollands *Dutch*
hollen I [ov ww] *hollow (out)* II [on
ww] *run*
holster *holster*
holte ● (holle ruimte) *cavity,* ‹v.d.
hand› *hollow* ● (diepte) *draught*
hom *milt, soft roe*
homeopaat *homoeopath(ist)*
homeopathie *homoeopathy*
hommel *bumblebee*
homogeen *homogeneous*
homoseksualiteit *homosexuality*
homoseksueel *homosexual, gay*
homp *lump, chunk, hunk*
hond *dog, mutt,* ‹jachthond› *hound,*
‹jong› *pup(py),* ‹straathond› *mongrel,*
cur
hondenhok *doghouse*
hondenweer *beastly weather*
honderd *a/one hundred*
honderdduizend *a/one hundred*

thousand
honderdste *hundredth*
honds *churlish, surly, brutal*
hondsdolheid *rabies*
honen *gibe/jeer at*
Hongarije *Hungary*
honger ● (behoefte aan eten) *hunger*
● (begeerte) *lust*
hongerdood *death from starvation*
hongeren ● (honger lijden) *starve*
● (~ **naar**) *be hungry (for)*
hongerig *hungry*
hongerloon *starvation wages*
hongersnood *famine*
hongerstaking *hunger strike*
honk ● (thuis) *home*
● (honkbalkussen) *base*
honkbal *baseball*
honorarium *fee*
honoreren ● (accepteren) *honour*
● (belonen) *pay, remunerate*
hoofd ● (leider) ‹v. groep, partij› *chief,*
‹v. school› *headmaster* ● (bovenste
gedeelte) *heading* ● (voorste deel)
head, front ● (lichaamsdeel) *head*
● (verstand) ∗ *zich het* ~ *breken over
cudgel one's brains about; racking
one's brains about* ∗ *uit 't* ~ *leren
learn by heart* ∗ *uit 't* ~ *rekenen do
mental arithmetic* ● (persoon)
∗ *bedrag per* ~ *amount per head*
hoofdartikel *leading article, leader,
editorial*
hoofdbestuur ‹v. bedrijf› *board of
directors,* ‹v. instelling›
general/executive committee
hoofdbureau *head office,* ‹v. politie›
police headquarters
hoofddeksel *headgear*
hoofdelijk ∗ ~ *stemmen vote by call*
∗ ~*e stemming roll-call vote* ∗ ~*e
omslag poll tax*
hoofdgerecht *main course*
hoofdinspecteur *chief inspector*
hoofdkantoor *head office*

hoofdkussen *pillow*
hoofdkwartier *headquarters*
hoofdletter *capital (letter)*
hoofdpijn *headache*
hoofdprijs *first prize*
hoofdredacteur *editor-in-chief*
hoofdrekenen *mental arithmetic*
hoofdschotel *main course*
hoofdstad *capital*
hoofdsteun *head rest*
hoofdstuk *chapter*
hoofdvak *main subject, major*
hoofdzaak *main point/issue*
hoofdzakelijk *chiefly, mainly*
hoog • (niet laag) *high(-pitched),* <boom, gebouw> *tall,* <stem> *high* • (hoog in rang, status) *exalted* • (aanzienlijk) *advanced*
hoogachten *esteem highly*
hoogachting *esteem, respect*
hoogbejaard *aged*
hoogconjunctuur *boom*
hoogdravend *high-flown, pompous,* <inf.> *highfalutin*
Hooggeacht ⋆ ~e Heer *(Dear) Sir*
hooggebergte *high mountains*
hooggeplaatst *high(-up), highly placed*
hooghartig *haughty*
hoogheid *highness*
hoogleraar *professor*
hooglopend ⋆ een ~e ruzie *flaming row*
hoogmis *high mass*
hoogmoed *pride*
hoogmoedig *haughty, proud*
hoognodig *highly necessary*
hoogoven *blast furnace*
hoogspanning *high tension*
hoogst I [het] *highest, top* II [bijw] *highly, extremely*
hoogstaand *high-principled*
hoogstens *at best, at most, at the utmost*
hoogte • (verheffing) *height, elevation*

• (afmeting omhoog) *height* • (peil, niveau) *level, height* • (klank) *pitch* • (ligging, plaats) ⋆ ter ~ van Dover *off Dover*
hoogtepunt *height, acme, zenith*
hoogtevrees *fear of heights*
hoogtezon *sun(ray) lamp*
hoogverraad *high treason*
hoogvlakte *uplands, plateau*
hoogvlieger *high-flier*
hoogwaardig *highgrade*
hooi *hay*
hooiberg *haystack*
hooien I [het] *haymaking* II [ov ww] *make hay*
hooikoorts *hay fever*
hooimijt *haystack*
hooivork *pitchfork, hayfork*
hooiwagen • (kar) *hay wagon/cart* • (insect) *daddy longlegs*
hoon *scorn*
hoop • (hoopvolle verwachting) *hope (of)* • (stapel) *heap, pile* • (veel) *lot of, great deal of, great many*
hoopvol *hopeful*
hoorapparaat *hearing aid*
hoorbaar *audible*
hoorn I [de] • (uitsteeksel aan kop) *horn* • (telefoonhoorn) *receiver* • (muz.) *horn, bugle* II [het] *horn*
hoornen *horn*
hoorspel *radio play*
hop I [de] • (plant) *hop* • (vogel) *hoopoe* II [tw] *come on, let's go*
hopeloos *hopeless*
hopen *hope*
hopman *chief, scoutmaster*
hor *wire gauze, screen, mesh*
horde • (troep) *horde* • (vlechtwerk) *hurdle* • (sport) *hurdle*
hordeloop *hurdles(race)*
horen I [ov ww] • (vernemen) *hear* • (met gehoor waarnemen) ⋆ van ~ zeggen *by/from hearsay* ⋆ ~ en zien verging je *the noise was deafening*

• (luisteren) ★ *hoor eens listen; look here* II [on ww] • (behoren) *should, ought to* • (toebehoren) *belong (to)* • (thuishoren) ★ *die stoel hoort hier niet that chair does not belong here*
horloge *watch*
horoscoop *horoscope*
hort I [de] *jerk, jolt* II [tw] ★ *hort! gee-up!; giddy-up!*
horzel *horsefly, gadfly,* <wespachtige> *hornet*
hospes *landlord*
hospitaal *hospital*
hospiteren *do one's teaching practice*
hossen • (dansen) *jig* • (hobbelen) *jolt*
hostie *host*
hotel *hotel*
hotelhouder *innkeeper, hotel manager*
houdbaar • (verdedigbaar) *tenable* • (te bewaren) ★ *tenminste ~ tot... best before...*
houden I [ov ww] • (doen plaatsvinden) <toespraak> *make/deliver,* <vergadering> *hold* • (nakomen) *keep* • (uithouden) *keep, maintain* • (erop na houden) *keep* • (behouden) *keep* • (vast-/tegenhouden) *hold* • (in toestand laten blijven) ★ *rechts ~ keep to the right* II [on ww] • (~ van) *love, like, be fond of* III [wkd ww] • (schijn aannemen) *pretend* • (~ aan) *keep to, adhere to*
houder • (beheerder) *keeper* • (klem) *holder* • (voorwerp om iets in te bewaren) *holder, container*
houding • (lichaamshouding) *carriage, bearing, posture* • (voorgewend gedrag) *pose* • (opstelling) *attitude, manner*
hout • (timmerhout) *timber* • (stuk hout) *piece of wood* • (houtgewas) *wood*
houten *wooden*
houtgravure *wood engraving, wood cut*

houthakker *woodcutter, lumberjack*
houtlijm *joiner's glue, glue for joining wood*
houtskool *charcoal*
houtvester *forester*
houtvesterij *forestry*
houtwol *wood wool*
houtzagerij *sawmill*
houvast *hold,* <fig.> *grip*
houw • (slag met bijl) *gash* • (snee) *cut*
houweel *pickaxe*
houwen • (hakken) *hew, cut, slash* • (bewerken) *hew, carve*
hovaardig *presumptuous*
hozen I [ov ww] *bail, bale, scoop* II [onp ww] *pour (down)*
huichelaar *hypocrite*
huichelachtig *hypocritical*
huichelarij *hypocrisy*
huichelen I [ov ww] *simulate, sham* II [on ww] *dissemble, give a false impression*
huid • (vel) *skin* • (afgestroopt dierenvel) *hide*
huidarts *dermatologist*
huidig *present(-day), at the present time*
huifkar *covered waggon*
huig *uvula*
huilbui *fit of crying/weeping*
huilebalk *crybaby*
huilen • (wenen) *cry* • (janken, loeien) *howl*
huilerig *tearful*
huis • (woning) *house* • (gebouw) *house* • (komaf) *house* • (firma) *house*
huisarrest *house arrest*
huisarts *family doctor, physician*
huisbaas *landlord*
huisbezoek *house call*
huisdier *pet*
huisgenoot • (gezinslid) *member of the family* • (medebewoner) *roommate, housemate, flatmate*

huisgezin *family, household*
huishoudelijk • (het huishouden betreffend) *domestic* • (m.b.t. dagelijkse gang van zaken) *domestic*
huishouden I [het] • (gezin) *family, household* • (huishouding) *housekeeping, management* II [on ww] • (een huishouden besturen) *keep house* • (tekeergaan) *carry on*
huishoudgeld *housekeeping money*
huishouding • (organisatie v.e. huishouden) *housekeeping* • (bewoners van huis) *household*
huishoudschool *School of Domestic Science, School of Home Economics*
huishoudster *housekeeper*
huisjesmelker *slumlord, rackrenter*
huiskamer *living room*
huismoeder *housewife, mother*
huismus • (vogel) *house sparrow* • (persoon) *stay-at-home*
huisraad *furniture, furnishings*
huisschilder *house painter*
huisvesten *house, lodge,* <tijdelijk> *accommodate*
huisvesting *accommodation, lodging*
huisvlijt *home industry*
huisvredebreuk *unlawful entry, trespassing*
huisvrouw *housewife*
huiswaarts *homeward(s)*
huiswerk • (werk in huis) *housework* • (schoolwerk) *homework*
huiszoeking *house search*
huiveren • (rillen) <v. afgrijzen> *shudder,* <v. koude> *shiver* • (terugschrikken) *shrink from*
huiverig • (rillerig) *shivery* • (angstig) ⋆ hij was er ~ voor *he was hesitant to do it*
huivering • (rilling) <v. afgrijzen> *shudder,* <v. koude> *shiver(s)*
huiveringwekkend *horrible*
huizen *live, be housed,* <tijdelijk> *lodge*
hulde *tribute, homage*

huldigen *pay homage to*
hullen *wrap (up) in*
hulp • (bijstand) *help, aid, assistance* • (persoon) ⋆ hulp in de huishouding *household help*
hulpbehoevend *helpless,* <door ouderdom> *infirm*
hulpbron *resource*
hulpmiddel • (bron) *resource* • (gereedschap) *tool* • (uitkomst) *expedient*
hulppost *aid station, first-aid post*
hulpvaardig *helpful*
hulpwerkwoord *auxiliary*
huls • (peul) *pod, cod* • (omhulsel) *case, cover,* <v. kogel> *cartridge case*
hulst *holly*
humaan *humane*
humanisme *humanism*
humeur • (stemming) *temper, humour, mood* • (temperament) *temper*
humeurig *moody*
humor *humour*
humorist *humorist*
humoristisch *humorous*
humus *humus*
hun I [pers vnw] *them* II [bez vnw] *their*
hunebed *megalithic tomb*
hunkeren • (~ naar) *yearn/long for*
huppelen *skip, frisk*
huren *hire, rent*
hut • (huisje) *cottage,* <armoedig> *hut, hovel* • (cabine op schip) *cabin*
hutkoffer *cabin trunk*
huur • (het huren) *lease* • (de huursom) *(house) rent*
huurauto *rented/hire(d) car*
huurcontract *lease*
huurder *renter,* <v. woonruimte> *tenant*
huurhuis *rented house*
huurkoop *hire-purchase*
huwbaar *marriageable*

huwelijk • (echtverbintenis)
marriage, matrimony
• (huwelijksvoltrekking) marriage,
wedding
huwelijksaankondiging
wedding-announcement
huwelijksaanzoek proposal of
marriage
huwelijksreis honeymoon
huwen marry
hyacint hyacinth
hydraulisch hydraulic
hyena hyena
hygiëne hygiene
hygiënisch hygienic
hypnose hypnosis
hypnotiseren hypnotize
hypothese hypothesis
hypothetisch hypothetic(al)
hysterie hysteria

I

ideaal I [het] ideal II [bnw] ideal
idealiseren idealize
idealisme idealism
idealist idealist
idealistisch idealistic
idee idea, notion, opinion
ideeënbus suggestion box
identiek identical
identificatie identification
identificeren identify
identiteit identity
ideologie ideology
idioom idiom
idioot I [de] idiot, imbecile II [bnw]
idiotic
idylle idyl(l)
idyllisch idyllic
ieder everybody, anyone, anybody,
everyone, any, ‹bijvoeglijk gebruikt›
every, ‹zelfstandig gebruikt› each
iedereen everyone, everybody
iel thin
iemand someone, somebody
Ierland Ireland
iets I [onb vnw] something, anything
II [bijw] a little, somewhat
ijdel • (vergeefs) ‹hoop› idle, ‹hoop,
poging› vain • (behaagziek) vain, ‹v.
personen› conceited
ijdelheid vanity
ijdeltuit * een ~ a vain creature
ijken stamp and verify, calibrate
ijl I [de] * in aller ijl posthaste II [bnw]
thin, rare
ijlen • (van koorts) be delirious, rave
• (haasten) hasten, hurry
ijlings in great haste
ijs • (roomijs) icecream • (bevroren
water) ice
ijsbaan skating rink

ijsbeer *polar bear*
ijsberen *pace up and down, walk back
and forth*
ijsberg *iceberg*
ijsbreker *icebreaker*
ijscoman *ice-cream vendor*
ijselijk *horrible*
ijsje *ice cream (cone)*
ijskast *refrigerator, icebox,* ‹inf.› *fridge*
ijskoud *ice cold, icy,* ‹bedaard› *cool,*
‹fig.› *frosty*
IJsland *Iceland*
ijstijd *Ice Age*
ijszee *polar sea*
ijver *diligence, industry*
ijveren • (~ **voor**) *advocate zealously*
• (~ **tegen**) *oppose*
ijverig *diligent, industrious*
ijzel *glazed frost*
ijzelen ⋆ *het ijzelt it is icing up; it is
freezing over*
ijzen *shudder (at)*
ijzer *iron*
ijzerdraad *(iron) wire*
ijzeren *iron*
ijzerhandel *ironmongery,
iron/hardware trade, hardware
business, hardware dealer*
ijzersterk *(as) strong as iron*
ijzerwaren *hardware, ironware*
ijzig *icy*
ik I [het] ⋆ *het ik the self; the ego* II [pers
vnw] *I*
illegaal *illegal*
illegaliteit *illegality, resistance
movement*
illusie *illusion*
illustratie *illustration*
illustreren *illustrate*
imaginair *imaginary*
imbeciel I [de] *imbecile* II [bnw]
imbecile
imitatie *imitation*
imiteren *imitate*
imker *beekeeper, apiculturist*

immens *immense*
immer *ever*
immers ⋆ *je kent hem* ~? *you know
him, don't you?*
immigrant *immigrant*
immigratie *immigration*
immigreren *immigrate*
immoreel *immoral*
immuniteit *immunity*
immuun *immune (from, to)*
impasse *impasse, deadlock*
imperiaal *imperial,* ‹AE› *luggage rack,*
‹op auto› *roof rack*
imperium *empire, imperium*
impliceren *imply*
imponeren *impress*
import *import*
importeur *importer*
impotent *impotent*
impotentie *impotence*
improductief *unproductive*
improvisatie *improvisation*
improviseren *improvise*
impuls *impulse*
impulsief *impulsive*
in • (op een bep. plaats) *in(side),*
‹richting› *into* • (op/binnen een bep.
tijd) (with)*in* • (per) *to, in*
inachtneming *observance*
inademen *inhale, breathe (in)*
inaugureel *inaugural (address)*
inbaar *collectable*
inbeelding *fancy, imagination*
inbegrepen *included*
inbegrip ⋆ *met* ~ *van including*
inbinden *bind*
inblazen *blow into*
inboedel *furniture, furnishings*
inboeten *lose*
inboezemen *inspire*
inboorling *aborigine, native*
inborst *disposition, nature*
inbouwen *build in*
inbraak *burglary, housebreaking*
inbreken *break into a house*

inbreker *burglar,* ‹inf.› *cracksman*
inbreng *portion, contribution*
inbrengen • (naar binnen brengen) *bring/take in* • (~ **tegen**) ★ daar valt niets tegen in te brengen *that argument is unanswerable*
inbreuk *infringement,* ‹op rechten› *encroachment,* ‹op wet› *violation*
inburgeren *naturalize, acclimatize*
incasseren *collect,* ‹een cheque› *cash*
incident *incident*
incidenteel *incidental*
incognito *incognito*
incompetent *incompetent*
inconsequent *inconsistent*
incourant *unsalable*
indachtig *mindful of*
indammen *dam, embank*
indelen *class(ify),* ‹in groepen› *divide*
indeling *division, classification, incorporation*
inderdaad *indeed, in (point of) fact*
inderhaast *in haste*
indertijd *formerly, at the time*
indeuken *dent, indent*
index *index*
indexcijfer *index figure*
indexeren *index*
India *India*
indien *if, in case*
indienen *present,* ‹klacht› *lodge,* ‹motie› *move,* ‹ontslag› *tender*
indijken *dike, embank*
indirect *indirect*
Indisch • (Indiaas) (East) *Indian* • (Indonesisch) *of the former Dutch East Indie*
individu *individual*
individueel *individual*
indoctrinatie *indoctrination*
indoctrineren *indoctrinate*
indommelen *drop/nod off*
Indonesië *Indonesia*
indringen *penetrate (into)*
indruisen *clash/conflict (with), run*

counter (to)
indruk *impression*
indrukken ★ een knop ~ *push in a button; press a button*
indrukwekkend *impressive*
industrialiseren *industrialize*
industrie *industry*
industrieel I [de] *industrialist* II [bnw] *industrial*
indutten *doze off*
ineen *together*
ineenkrimpen ‹bij pijn› *double up,* ‹meestal fig.› *wince*
ineens *suddenly, all at once*
ineenschrompelen *shrivel up*
ineenstorten *collapse*
inenten *vaccinate*
infanterie *infantry*
infarct *infarct*
infecteren *infect*
infectie *infection*
infiltreren *infiltrate*
inflatie *inflation*
influenza *influenza,* ‹inf.› *flu*
influisteren *whisper, suggest*
informant *informant*
informeel *informal*
informeren I [ov ww] *inform* II [on ww] *inquire (after/about)*
infrastructuur *infrastructure*
ingaan • (binnengaan) *go into,* ‹kamer› *enter* • (van kracht worden) ‹maatregel› *come into force, take effect,* ‹vakantie, enz.› *begin* • (~ **tegen**) *go against* • (~ **op**) *go into*
ingang *entrance, entry*
ingebeeld • (verwaand) *(self-)conceited* • (imaginair) *imaginary*
ingenieur *engineer*
ingenomen ★ ~ met *pleased with*
ingetogen *quiet, modest*
ingeven • (toedienen) *administer* • (in gedachten geven) *inspire, suggest, dictate*

ingeving *inspiration, brainwave, prompting*
ingevolge *in accordance with*
ingewijde *adept, <inf.> insider*
ingewikkeld *intricate*
ingezetene *resident, inhabitant*
ingooi *throw in*
ingooien • *(breken) smash, break* • *(sport) throw in(to)*
ingrediënt *ingredient*
ingreep *intervention, <med.> operation, surgery*
ingrijpen *intervene, interfere*
inhaalverbod *<op bord> no overtaking*
inhakken ★ *~ op pitch into*
inhalen • *(passeren) overtake* • *(inlopen) make up for*
inhalig *grasping, greedy, covetous*
inham *inlet, creek, bay*
inheems *<gebruiken> native*
inhoud • *(volume) capacity* • *(datgene waarover iets handelt) contents* • *(strekking) purport*
inhouden I *[ov ww]* • *(bevatten) hold, contain* • *(betekenen) imply, mean* • *(bedwingen) restrain* II *[wkd ww] check o.s., restrain o.s.*
inhouding *stoppage*
inhoudsmaat *cubic measure*
inhuldigen *inaugurate, install*
inhuren *hire*
initiatief *initiative*
injectie *injection*
inkeer • *(zelfbeschouwing) introspection* • *(berouw) repentance*
inkijken *look in, have a look at, dip into, glance through*
inklaren *clear*
inklaring *clearance*
inkleden *word, express*
inkomen I *[het] income* II *[on ww] come in*
inkomstenbelasting *income tax*
inkoop *purchase*
inkopen *buy, purchase*

inkorten *shorten, curtail*
inkrimpen I *[ov ww] cut down/back, reduce* II *[on ww] shrink, contract*
inkt *ink*
inktvis *inkfish, squid, cuttlefish*
inkuilen *<aardappels> clamp, <veevoer> ensilage*
inkwartieren *billet*
inladen • *(zich volstoppen) stuff o.s.* • *(beladen) load*
inlander *native*
inlands *native, homemade*
inlassen *insert*
inlaten I *[ov ww] let in, admit* II *[wkd ww] take up with, concern o.s. with (s.th.), associate with (s.o.)*
inleggen • *(invoegen) inlay* • *(geld inbrengen) put in, deposit, <bij gokken> stake*
inlegvel *supplementary sheet*
inleiden • *(binnenleiden) lead/usher in* • *(introduceren) introduce*
inleiding *introduction*
inleveren *hand in, submit*
inlichten • *(~ over) inform about, enlighten on*
inlijsten *frame*
inlijven *incorporate (in), <gebied> annex*
inlopen *walk into, <een gebouw> enter, <een straat> turn into*
inlossen *repay*
inmaak • *(het inmaken) bottling, conserving, preserving, <in zuur> pickling* • *(ingemaakte groenten) preserved vegetables, pickles*
inmaken • *(wecken) preserve, tin, can, <in azijn> pickle, <in zout> salt* • *(verslaan) slaughter*
inmenging *interference*
inmiddels *meanwhile, in the mean time*
innemen • *(binnenhalen) take in, <kaartjes> collect* • *(gebruiken, slikken) take* • *(bezetten) occupy,*

‹ruimte› *take up*

innemend *winning, captivating,*
prepossessing

innen ‹cheque› *cash,* ‹huur› *collect*

innerlijk *inner*

innig *profound, heartfelt,* ‹vurig›
fervent

inpakken • (opbergen, verpakken) ‹in
koffer› *pack,* ‹in papier, enz.› *wrap up*
• (warm kleden) *wrap (o.s.) up*

inpalmen • (binnenhalen) *rope in*
• (voor zich winnen) *win over, charm,*
get round

inpassen *fit in*

inperken *restrict, curtail*

inpikken • (pakken) *snap up, grab*
• (stelen) *pinch*

inpolderen *reclaim land, impolder*

inpompen • (iem. iets bijbrengen)
drill/drum into • (pompen) *pump into*

inprenten *impress (upon), drum into*

inrekenen • (arresteren) *pull in,* ‹inf.›
run in

inrichten • (regelen) *arrange, organize*
• (toerusten) *furnish*

inrichting • (meubilering, stoffering)
furnishing • (samenstelling) *structure,*
‹huis› *layout* • (instelling) *institution*
• (regeling) *organization, arrangement*

inrijden *drive in(to),* ‹op de fiets› *ride*
in(to)

inrit *entry, entrance, driveway*

inroepen *call in, invoke*

inruilen *exchange (for),* ‹v. auto›
trade-in

inruimen ∗ plaats ~ *make room*

inrukken *break ranks,* ‹militair›
dismiss, ‹v. brandweer, politie›
withdraw

inschakelen ‹stroom› *switch on*
• (doen meewerken) *enlist*

inschenken ‹glas› *fill,* ‹kopje thee›
pour

inschepen *ship*

inschieten ∗ er geld bij ~ *lose money*

over it ∗ er zijn leven bij ~ *lose one's*
life in it

inschikkelijk *accommodating,*
obliging

inschrijven • (opgeven) ‹geboorte,
huwelijk› *register,* ‹voor wedstrijd›
enter • (intekenen op iets) *subscribe*

insect *insect, bug*

insgelijks I [bijw] *likewise* II [tw] *(the)*
same to you!

inslaan • (ingaan) *turn (into)* • (in
voorraad nemen) *stock up, lay in*
• (stukslaan) *smash (in)*
• (inhameren) *drive/hammer in*

inslag • (het inslaan) *impact*
• (karakter(trek)) ∗ humoristische ~
humoristic streak • (weefsel) *weft*

inslapen • (in slaap vallen) *fall asleep,*
drop off • (sterven) *pass away*

inslikken *swallow*

insluimeren *doze off, drop off (to sleep)*

insluipen *steal in(to),* ‹fig.› *creep in*

insluiten • (omgeven) *surround,*
encircle • (inhouden) *imply*
• (bijsluiten) *enclose* • (opsluiten) *lock*
in • (omvatten) *include*

insmeren • (~ **met**) ‹met boter, vet›
grease, ‹met lotion, enz.› *rub with*

insneeuwen *snow in*

inspannen I [ov ww] ‹ogen› *strain*
II [wkd ww] *exert o.s., make an effort*

inspanning *effort, exertion,* ‹te grote›
strain

inspecteren *inspect*

inspecteur *inspector*

inspectie *inspection*

inspelen I [ov ww] • (muz.) *play in*
II [on ww] • (~ **op**) *anticipate* III [wkd
ww] • (sport) *warm-up, play o.s. in*

inspiratie *inspiration*

inspireren *inspire*

inspraak *voice, say*

inspreken *record*

inspringen • (inkomen met een
sprong) *leap in(to)* • (terugwijken) ‹v.

regel> indent • (vervangen) substitute
inspuiten inject
instaan be responsible, guarantee
installateur installer, <v. elektriciteit>
electrician
installatie • (stereo) stereo
• (apparatuur) equipment • (techn.)
installation
installeren • (inrichten) <school, enz.>
equip • (techn.) install
instandhouding maintenance
instantie • (orgaan) authority, body
• (jur.) instance, resort
instappen <auto, trein> get in, <bus>
get on
insteken put in
instellen • (oprichten) establish,
institute • (voor gebruik afstellen)
<camera> focus, <instrument> adjust
instelling institution, <houding>
attitude
instemmen fall in with, agree/concur
(with)
instemming agreement, <bijval>
approval
instinct instinct
instituut institution,
<wetenschappelijk, sociaal> institute
instoppen • (toedekken) tuck in
• (indoen) * stop 't hier maar in put it
in here
instorten fall down, collapse
instructeur instructor
instructie • (onderricht) instruction,
tuition • (aanwijzing) direction, <voor
een vlucht, enz.> briefing
instrueren instruct
instrument instrument
instrumentaal instrumental
instuderen <muz.> practise, <rol>
study, <stuk> rehearse
insturen • (inzenden) send in(to)
• (naar binnen sturen) steer in(to)
integendeel on the contrary
integraal integral

integratie integration
intekenen subscribe (to, for)
intellect intellect
intellectueel intellectual
intelligent intelligent
intelligentie intelligence
intens intense
intensief intensive
intensiteit intensity
intensiveren intensify
intercom intercom
interen eat into one's capital
interesseren I [ov ww] interest II [wkd
ww] be interested
intermezzo intermezzo, interlude
intern internal, <aangelegenheden>
domestic, <inwonend> resident,
<patiënt> in-patient
internaat boarding school
internationaal international
internist internal medical specialist,
<AE> internist
interpellatie interpellation
interpelleren interpellate, <in
Engeland> question
interpunctie punctuation
interrumperen interrupt
interruptie interruption
interval interval
interventie intervention
interview interview
interviewen interview
intiem intimate
intimiteit intimacy
intocht entry
intomen curb, check, restrain
intransitief intransitive
intrappen <deur> kick in/down
intreden enter (upon), <v. vriesweer,
toestand> set in
intrek * zijn ~ bij iem. nemen move
in with s.o. * zijn ~ nemen in een
hotel put up at a hotel
intrekken I [ov ww] • (naar binnen
trekken) draw in • (herroepen) <een

bevel> *revoke*, <verlof, een opdracht>
cancel II [on ww] • (binnentrekken)
march into, move in(to) • (gaan
inwonen) *move in*
intrige *intrigue, scheming*
intrigeren *intrigue, scheme*
introducé *guest*
introduceren *introduce*
introductie *introduction*
intuïtie *intuition*
intussen *meanwhile*
inval • (het invallen) <v. politie> *raid*,
<v. vijand> *invasion* • (idee) *idea, brain
wave*
invalide I [de] *invalid, disabled
person* [mv: *disabled*] II [bnw] *invalid*
invaliditeit *invalidity, disablement*
invallen • (binnenvallen v. land)
invade • (beginnen) <v. dooi, enz.> *set
in*, <v. nacht> *fall* • (instorten) *cave in*,
<v. huis> *fall down, collapse*
• (plaatsvervangen) *deputize*, <sport>
stand in • (muz.) *join in*
invaller *substitute, reserve*
invalshoek • (gezichtspunt) *angle*
• (nat.) *angle of incidence* • (luchtv.)
angle of attack
invasie *invasion*
inventaris • (lijst) *inventory*
• (goederen) *equipment, furniture (and
fittings)*
inventarisatie *stocktaking*
inventariseren *make an inventory of*
investeren *invest*
investering *investment*
invetten *grease, oil*
invitatie *invitation*
inviteren *invite (to)*
invloed *influence*, <uitwerking> *effect*
invloedrijk *influential*
invoegen I [ov ww] *insert, put in* II [on
ww] *merge*
invoegstrook *merging lane*
invoer *import*, <computer> *input*,
<goederen> *imports*

invoeren • (importeren) *import*
• (introduceren) *introduce*
invorderen • (innen) *collect*
• (betaling eisen) *demand payment*
invriezen *freeze*
invrijheidstelling *release*
invullen <formulier> *fill in/up*,
<naam> *fill in*
inwendig *inner, inward, interior*
inwerken I [ov ww] * iem. ~ *teach s.o.
the job* II [on ww] • (~ **op**) *act upon,
affect*
inwijden • (in gebruik nemen)
inaugurate • (op de hoogte brengen)
initiate
inwijding *inauguration*
inwilligen *comply with*
inwinnen * inlichtingen ~ *make
inquiries*
inwisselen *change, exchange for*
inwonen *live-in*
inwoner *resident*, <v. stad> *inhabitant*
inwrijven *rub in*
inzage *perusal, inspection*
inzakken *collapse, sag*
inzamelen *collect*
inzameling *collection*
inzegenen <huwelijk> *celebrate*,
<kerk> *consecrate*
inzenden *send in, contribute*
inzet • (wat op het spel staat) <spel>
stake(s) • (toewijding) *devotion,
dedication* • (deel van kaartje, enz.)
inset (map), insert • (begin) *start*
inzetten • (geld inleggen) *stake*
• (beginnen) *start*
inzicht • (begrip) *insight* • (mening)
opinion
inzien • (vluchtig bekijken) *glance
over* • (beseffen) *see, realize*
inzinking • (het verzakken)
subsidence • (achteruitgang) *slump*
• (instorting) *relapse*
inzitten *be worried, worry about*
iris *iris*

ironie *irony*
ironisch *ironical*
irrigatie *irrigation*
irritatie *irritation*
irriteren *irritate*
ischias *sciatica*
islam *Islam*
islamiet *Islamite*
islamitisch *Islamic*
isolatie • (isolement) *isolation* • (het
  isoleren) *insulation*
isolement *isolation*
isoleren • (afzonderen) *isolate* • (nat.)
  insulate
Italië *Italy*
item *item*
ivoor *ivory*

J

ja I [het] *yes* II [tw] *yes*
jaar *year*
jaarbeurs *industries fair, trade fair*
jaarboek • (kroniek, almanak)
  yearbook • (annalen) *annals, chronicles*
jaargang *volume,* <v. wijn> *vintage*
jaarlijks I [bnw] *yearly, annual*
  II [bijw] *every year, annually*
jaartal *date, year*
jaartelling *era*
jacht I [de] • (het jagen) *hunting*
  • (jachtpartij) *hunt* • (het najagen)
  pursuit II [het] *yacht*
jachten I [ov ww] *hurry, rush, hustle*
  II [on ww] *rush, hustle, hurry*
jachthaven *marina*
jachtig *hurried*
jacquet *morning coat,* <inf.> *tails*
jagen I [ov ww] *hunt,* <klein wild>
  shoot II [on ww] • (streven) *pursue*
  • (snel bewegen) *rush, race*
jager • (iem. die jaagt) *hunter*
  • (jachtvliegtuig) *fighter*
jak I [de] *yak* II [het] • (overjasje) *jacket*
  • (bloes) *smock*
jakhals *jackal*
jakkeren *rush,* <vnl. m. auto> *tear
  along*
jaloers *jealous*
jaloezie • (jaloersheid) *jealousy*
  • (zonwering) *Venetian blind*
jam *jam*
jammer I [het] *misery* II [bijw] *a pity*
jammeren *lament, wail, moan,* <inf.>
  yammer
jammerlijk *woeful, pitiful*
jampot *jam jar*
Jan *John*
janken • (huilen) *cry, whine* • (klagend
  blaffen) *yelp, whimper, whine*

januari *January*
Japan *Japan*
japon *dress*
jarenlang I [bnw] *many years'* II [bijw]
for years
jargon *jargon*
jarig ★ *wanneer ben je ~? when is your*
birthday?
jas ● (mantel) *coat* ● (colbert) *jacket*
jasmijn *jasmine*
jaszak *coat pocket*
jawoord *consent*
je I [pers vnw] *you* II [bez vnw] *your*
III [onb vnw] *you*
jegens *to(wards)*
jekker *reefer, jacket*
jenever *gin*
jengelen *whimper, whine*
jeugd *youth*
jeugdherberg *youth hostel*
jeugdig *youthful*
jeuk *itch*
jeuken *itch*
jicht *gout*
Jiddisch *Yiddish*
jij *you*
jobstijding *bad news/tidings*
jodelen *yodel*
jodendom ● (het joodse volk) *Jewry,*
Jews ● (godsdienst) *Judaism*
jodium *iodine*
joelen *shout, howl, roar*
jokken *fib, tell tales/lies*
jolig *jolly*
jong I [het] ● (zeer jong dier) *young one*
● (jongen) *kid, child* II [bnw] ● (niet
oud) *young* ● (recent) *recent, latest*
jongeheer *young gentleman,* <met
naam> *Master*
jongelui *young people, youngsters*
jongen I [de] *boy, lad* II [on ww] *give*
birth, <v. hond> *have pups,* <v. kat>
have kittens
jongensachtig *boyish*
jongleren *juggle*

jonker *(young) nobleman, esquire*
jood *Jew*
joods *Jewish*
journaal ● (dagboek) *journal, diary,*
log book ● (nieuws) *news*
journalist *journalist, newspaperman*
journalistiek I [de] *journalism*
II [bnw] *journalistic*
jouw *your*
joviaal *jovial, genial*
jubelen *shout with joy, exult (at), be*
jubilant
jubilaris *a person celebrating his/her*
jubilee/anniversary
jubileren *celebrate one's*
jubilee/anniversary
jubileum *anniversary, jubilee*
juffrouw ● (ongehuwde vrouw) *Miss*
● (schooljuffrouw) *teacher* ● (pej.) *lady*
juichen *cheer, be jubilant, shout with*
joy
juist I [bnw] ● (correct) *right, correct*
II [bijw] ● (zojuist) *just* ● (precies) *just,*
exactly
juistheid *rightness, correctness,*
exactness
juk *yoke*
jukbeen *cheekbone*
juli *July*
jullie I [pers vnw] *you, you people*
II [bez vnw] *your*
juni *June*
junior *junior*
junta *junta*
juridisch *legal*
jurist ● (rechtsgeleerde) *jurist, lawyer*
● (student in de rechten) *law student*
jurk *dress*
jury *jury*
jurylid *member of the jury*
justitie ● (rechtswezen) *justice*
● (rechtspraak) *justice, judicature*
● (rechterlijke macht) *judiciary,* <inf.>
the law
justitieel *judicial*

jute *jute*
juweel • (sieraad) *jewel, gem*
  • (prachtexemplaar) *treasure, gem*
juwelier *jeweller*

K

kaak • (kaakbeen) *jaw* • (kieuw) *gill*
kaal • (zonder bedekking) *bare,*
  <velden> *barren* • (zonder haar)
  <hoofd> *bald* • (afgesleten) *worn*
kaap *cape, headland*
kaarsrecht *as straight as an arrow, as*
  straight as a die
kaarsvet *candle wax, tallow*
kaart • (visite-/menukaart, enz.) *card,*
  <verzekering> *green card*
  • (toegangsbewijs) *ticket* • (landkaart)
  map
kaarten *play at cards*
kaartspel • (het kaarten) *playing cards*
  • (een pak kaarten) *pack of cards,* <AE>
  deck of cards
kaas *cheese*
kaatsen • (terugstuiten) *bounce*
  • (sport) *play at fives*
kabaal *din, row*
kabbelen *ripple, babble, lap*
kabel *cable,* <elektriciteit> *wire*
kabelbaan *cable-railway, cable car*
kabeljauw *cod*
kabelnet • (elektriciteitsnet) *electric*
  mains • (kabeltelevisienet) *cable*
  network/grid
kabeltelevisie *cable television*
kabinet • (meubel) *cabinet*
  • (expositiezaal) *gallery* • (regering)
  cabinet
kachel *stove, heater, (electric)fire*
kadaster *land registry,* <kantoor> *land*
  registry office
kadaver <lijk> *corpse,* <rottend dier>
  carrion, <voor dissectie> *cadaver*
kader *framework*
kadetje *roll*
kaf *chaff*
kaffer • (lomperd) *boor, lout*

• (Bantoeneger) Kaffir
kaft (paper) cover
kaften cover
kajak kayak
kajuit cabin
kakelen • (roepen van kip) cackle
• (kwebbelen) blabber, chatter, rattle
kaki khaki
kakkerlak cockroach
kalender calendar
kalf calf
kaliber calibre
kalk lime, <geblust> slaked lime,
<metselkalk> mortar, <ongeblust>
quick lime, <pleisterkalk> plaster
kalken • (bepleisteren) plaster
• (witten) whitewash
kalkoen turkey
kalksteen limestone
kalm calm, quiet
kalmeren I [ov ww] calm, soothe II [on
ww] calm down, compose o.s.
kalmte calm(ness), composure,
tranquillity, quiet
kalverliefde puppy love
kam comb, <v. vogel> crest
kameel camel
kameleon chameleon
kamer • (hartholte) ventricle
• (vertrek) room, chamber
kameraad comrade, pal, mate, <inf.>
chum
kameraadschappelijk I [bnw]
companiable, friendly, <inf.> chummy,
pally II [bijw] friendly
kamerjas dressing gown
kamermeisje chambermaid
kamermuziek chamber music
kamerplant houseplant
kamerscherm room-divider, screen
kamertemperatuur
room-temperature
kamfer camphor
kamgaren worsted
kamille <plantk.> camomile

kammen comb
kamp I [de] fight, struggle II [het] camp
kampeerder camper
kampen contend, fight
kamperen camp (out)
kamperfoelie honeysuckle
kampioen champion
kampioenschap championship
kampvuur camp fire
kan jug, can
kanaal channel, <waterweg> canal
kanaliseren canalize
kandelaar candlestick
kandidaat • (gegadigde) candidate
• (sollicitant) applicant
kandidatuur candidature, nomination
kandij candy
kaneel cinnamon
kangoeroe kangaroo
kanjer whopper
kanker cancer
kankeraar grouser, bellyacher
kankeren grouse, grumble, <inf.> chew
the rag
kankergezwel cancerous
tumour/growth
kannibaal cannibal
kano canoe
kanon gun, cannon
kans • (waarschijnlijkheid) chance
• (gelegenheid) ★ de kans doen keren
turn the tide ★ die kans komt nooit
weer it's the chance of a life-time ★ de
kans schoon zien see one's chance
• (risico, gok) ★ een kans wagen take a
chance ★ de kans lopen om te run the
risk of
kansel pulpit
kanselier chancellor
kanshebber favourite
kansspel game of chance
kant I [de] • (zijde) side • (uiterste
rand, zijkant) border, <oever> edge
• (richting) way, direction • (aspect,
visie, partij) side, aspect

• (verwantschap) ★ van moeders kant *on the mother's side* II [het] • (weefsel) *lace*
kantelen I [ov ww] *tilt, overturn, flip (over)* II [on ww] *topple/turn over,* <v. schip> *capsize*
kanten I [on ww] *square* II [wkd ww] *oppose*
kantine *canteen*
kantje • (bladzijde) *page, side*
kantlijn *margin, marginal line*
kantongerecht <BE> ≈ *magistrates court,* <Schotland> *district-court*
kantoor *office*
kantoorboekhandel *stationer's (shop)*
kanttekening • (aantekening in de marge) *marginal note, annotation* • (commentaar) *short/marginal comment*
kap • (hoofddeksel) <v. monnik> *cowl,* <v. non> *wimple* • (bedekking, bovenstuk) <v. auto> *hood,* <v. lamp> *shade*
kapel • (insect) *butterfly* • (muziekkapel) *band* • ((uitbouw v.) kerk) *chapel*
kapelaan <hulppriester> *curate,* <in tehuis, enz.> *chaplain*
kapen • (overmeesteren van een vliegtuig, enz.) *hijack* • (stelen) *pinch* • (gesch.) *capture*
kaper *hijacker*
kapitaal I [het] *capital* II [bnw] *capital, excellent*
kapitaalkrachtig *substantial*
kapitein *captain*
kapittelen ★ iem. ~ *read s.o. a lecture*
kaplaars *top-boot, jackboot*
kapot • (defect) *broken, gone to pieces,* <v. auto> *broken down,* <v. machine> *out of order* • (versleten, enz.) <v. kous> *in holes,* <v. schoenen> *worn out* • (afgemat, doodmoe) *frayed, on edge* • (onder de indruk) ★ ik ben er niet ~ van *I'm not wild about it*

kappen I [ov ww] • (hakken) <hout> *chop,* <v. bomen> *fell, cut down* • (haar opmaken) *style, dress, model* II [on ww] • (inf.) *quit*
kapper *hairdresser, barber*
kapseizen *capsize, keel over*
kapsel *haircut, hair-style*
kapstok <aan muur> *hat-rack,* <haak> *peg,* <staand> *hatstand*
kar *cart,* <handkar> *barrow*
karaat *carat*
karabijn *carabine*
karaf *decanter*
karakter *character, nature*
karakteriseren *characterize*
karakteristiek I [de] *characterization, description* II [bnw] *characteristic*
karate *karate*
karavaan *caravan*
karbonade *chop, cutlet*
kardinaal I [de] *cardinal* II [bnw] *cardinal*
karig • (sober) *scanty, frugal* • (zuinig) *parsimonious, mean*
karikatuur *caricature*
karkas *carcass, skeleton*
karnemelk *buttermilk*
karnen *churn*
karper *carp*
karpet *carpet*
karren *cart*
karton • (verpakking) *carton* • (gelaagd bordpapier) *cardboard*
kartonnen *cardboard*
karwei *job*
kas • (betaalplaats) *pay-desk* • (geldmiddelen) *cash, funds* • (broeikas) *hothouse,* <voor planten> *greenhouse* • (holte voor oog, enz.) *socket*
kassa <v. supermarkt> *check-out,* <v. theater> *box office*
kassier *cashier*
kast • (ombouw, omhulsel) *case* • (bergmeubel) *cupboard,*

<boekenkast> bookcase, <klerenkast>
wardrobe
kastanje chestnut
kaste caste
kasteel castle
kastekort deficit
kastelein innkeeper, landlord
kastijden <het vlees> mortify
kat • (huisdier) cat • (standje, bitse
opmerking) reprimand
katapult catapult
kater • (mannetjeskat) tomcat
• (gevolg van alcoholgebruik)
hangover • (teleurstelling)
disillusionment
katoen cotton
katrol pulley
kattebelletje scribbled note
kattenbak cat's box, <v. auto> dickey
seat
kattenkwaad mischief
katterig chippy, hung over, ropy
kattig catty, bitchy
kauwen chew
kauwgom chewing gum
kavel parcel, lot
kaviaar caviar
kazerne <mil.> barracks, <brandweer>
station
keel throat
keelgat gullet
keelontsteking inflammation of the
throat, throat infection
keelpijn sore throat
keer • (maal) time • (wending,
kentering) turn, change
keerkring tropic
keerpunt turning point
keet • (schuurtje) shed, shanty
• (chaos) row, racket
keffen yap, yelp
kegel • (wiskundige figuur) cone
• (voorwerp) cone • (figuur in
kegelspel) pin, skittle (pin)
• (kegelspel) ninepin • (slechte adem)

bad breath, breath like a brewery
kegelbaan skittle/bowling alley
kegelen I [ov ww] toss(out) II [on ww]
play at skittles/ninepins
kei • (steen) boulder, <straatkei>
cobble(-stone) • (uitblinker) crack
keihard as hard as nails, rock hard,
hard-boiled
keizer emperor
keizerlijk imperial
keizerrijk empire
kelder cellar
kelderen • (in waarde dalen) slump
• (vergaan) sink, founder
kelen cut the throat of
kelk • (beker) cup, chalice • (plantk.)
calyx
kelner waiter
kemphaan fighting-cock
kenbaar familiar
kenmerk feature, characteristic,
distinguishing mark
kenmerken characterize, mark
kenmerkend distinctive, characteristic
(of)
kennel kennel
kennelijk I [bnw] obvious, apparent
II [bijw] clearly, obviously
kennen know
kenner • (deskundige) authority
• (fijnproever) connoisseur, judge
kennis • (het kennen van iets of iem.)
knowledge, acquaintance • (wat men
weet) knowledge, learning
• (bewustzijn) consciousness
• (bekende) acquaintance
kennisgeving notice, announcement
kennismaking acquaintance
kennisneming inspection, perusal
kenschetsen characterize
kenteken <v. auto> licence number
kentekenbewijs ≈ registration
document(s)/card
kenteren • (veranderen) turn
• (kapseizen) turn over, capsize

kentering *turn, change*
kerel *fellow, chap, bloke*
keren I [ov ww] turn II [on ww]
turn(about) III [wkd ww] • (~ tegen)
turn against
kerf *notch, nick*
kerk *church*
kerkdienst *mass*
kerkelijk *ecclesiastical, church(ly)*
kerkenraad • (bestuur van gemeente)
church council • (vergadering) church
council meeting
kerker *jail, gaol, dungeon*
kerkganger *churchgoer, chapel-goer*
kerkgenootschap *denomination*
kerkhof *churchyard, graveyard,* <niet
bij kerk> *cemetery*
kermen *moan, groan, whine*
kermis *(fun)fair, carnival*
kern • (binnenste) <v. atoom> *nucleus,*
<v. noot> *kernel,* <v. pruim, kers> *stone*
• (essentie) *heart, root, nucleus*
kernachtig *pithy, terse, concise*
kerngezond *perfectly healthy*
kernkop *nuclear warhead*
kerrie *curry*
kers *cherry*
kerstavond <24 dec.> *Christmas Eve,*
<24, 25 dec.> *Christmas evening*
kerstdag <eerste> *Christmas Day,*
<tweede> *Boxing Day*
kerstfeest *Christmas (feast)*
kerstlied *Christmas carol*
kersvers *quite fresh, brand new*
kervel *chervil*
kerven *carve, notch*
ketel • (voor theewater, enz.) *kettle*
• (groot formaat pan) *cauldron*
• (stoomketel) *boiler*
keten *chain*
ketenen *chain*
ketsen I [ov ww] turn down, <voorstel>
defeat II [on ww] glance off, <bij
biljart> miscue
ketterij *heresy*

ketting *chain*
kettingbotsing *chain collision,*
pile-up
kettingkast *chain guard*
kettingreactie *chain reaction*
keu • (biljartstok) *cue* • (varken) *pig*
keuken • (plaats) *kitchen* • (kookstijl)
cuisine
Keulen *Cologne*
keur • (keuze) *choice, pick* • (keurmerk)
hall-mark
keuren *inspect, test,* <med.> *examine,*
<voedsel, drank> *sample*
keurig *neat, dainty, trim*
keuring *test,* <med.> *examination,* <v.
voedsel> *inspection*
keuringsdienst ≈ *Food Inspection*
Department
keurkorps *crack troops,* <regiment>
crack regiment
keus • (voorkeur) *choice*
• (recht/mogelijkheid tot kiezen)
choice, option • (waaruit men kan
kiezen) *choice, selection*
keuvelen *chat, natter*
keuzevak *optional subject*
kever *beetle*
kibbelen *squabble, bicker, barney*
kidnappen *kidnap*
kidnapper *kidnapper*
kiel • (kledingstuk) *blouse* • (scheepv.)
keel
kiem *germ*
kiemen • (ontkiemen) *germinate*
• (beginnen te groeien) *sprout, come
up*
kier *chink*
kies *molar, back tooth*
kieskeurig *choosy, fastidious,
particular,* <inf.> *pernickety*
kiespijn *toothache*
kiesrecht *suffrage, franchise, right to
vote*
kiestoon *dialling tone*
kietelen *tickle*

kieuw *gill*
kiezel *gravel, <op strand> shingle*
kiezen • (keus doen) *single out, select, choose* • (stem uitbrengen) *vote*
kiezer *voter, constituent*
kijk *view* ⋆ *er is geen kijk op verbetering there is no hope of improvement*
kijken I [ov ww] • (~ **naar**) *look at* ⋆ *naar een film ~ watch a film* II [on ww] *look, have a look*
kijker • (persoon) *looker-on, spectator, <televisie> viewer* • (verrekijker) *binoculars, <toneel> opera-glass(es)*
kijven *brawl, quarrel, wrangle*
kik ⋆ *ze gaf geen kik she didn't utter a sound*
kikker *frog*
kil *chilly, cold*
kilometer *kilometre*
kim *horizon*
kin *chin*
kind *child, <inf.> kid*
kinderachtig *childish*
kinderarts *children's doctor, paediatrician*
kinderbescherming *child care and protection*
kinderbijslag *family allowance/credit, child benefit*
kinderboek *children's book*
kinderlijk *childlike, <pej.> childish*
kindermeisje *nanny*
kinderrechter *juvenile court magistrate*
kinderspel • (spel) *children's game* • (makkie) *a piece of cake*
kinderverlamming *<vero.> infantile paralysis, <med.> poliomyelitis, <inf.> polio*
kinderwagen *<form.> perambulator, <inf.> pram, <AE> buggy*
kinds *doting, senile*
kinine *quinine*
kinkhoest *whooping-cough*

kiosk *kiosk, <kranten> newspaper stand*
kip *hen, chicken*
kiplekker *fit as a fiddle, on top of the world, as right as rain*
kippengaas *chicken-wire*
kippenhok *hen/chicken house*
kippensoep *chicken soup*
kippenvel *goose flesh/pimples*
kippig *short-sighted*
kirren *coo*
kist • (verpakking) *packing-case, box, case* • (doodkist) *coffin*
kisten *(lay in a) coffin*
kittig *smart, spirited*
klaaglied *lamentation(s)*
klaar • (helder, duidelijk) *<stijl> limpid, <water> clear* • (afgewerkt) *finished* • (gereed voor gebruik) *ready*
klaarblijkelijk *evident, obvious*
klaarheid *clarity, clearness*
klaarkomen • (gereedkomen) *be finished, finish* • (orgasme krijgen) *come*
klaarmaken *get ready, prepare, <eten> make, <warm eten> cook*
klaarspelen ⋆ *'t ~ manage; pull off*
klaarstaan *stand/be ready*
klaarstomen ⋆ *iem. ~ voor een examen cram s.o. for an exam*
klacht *complaint*
klad *rough draught*
kladden *doodle, <schilderen> daub, <schrijven> scrawl, scribble*
klagen *complain*
klager *complainer, complainant, <jur.> plaintiff*
klakkeloos I [bnw] *gratuitous* II [bijw] ⋆ *iets ~ aannemen accept s.th. without thinking*
klam *clammy, damp, moist*
klandizie • (het klant zijn) *custom* • (klanten) *customers*
klank *sound*
klankbord *sound(ing) board*
klankkast *soundbox*

klant *customer*
klap • (fel geluid) *bang* • (slag) *blow, slap* • (tegenslag) ⋆ *een zware klap krijgen be hard hit*
klapband *blow-out, burst tyre*
klaplopen *sponge (on s.o.),* <AE> *freeload*
klappen • (in/met de handen klappen) *clap* • (barsten, springen) ⋆ *uit elkaar* ~ *burst; explode*
klapper • (register) *index* • (ordner) *folder, file* • (uitschieter) *hit*
klapperen <v. tanden> *chatter,* <v. zeil> *flap*
klappertanden ⋆ *ik stond te* ~ *my teeth were chattering*
klaproos *poppy*
klapstoel • (opvouwbare stoel) *folding-chair* • (stoel die omhoogklapt) *tip-up seat*
klapstuk • (vlees) *rib-piece* • (hoogtepunt) *crowning piece*
klaren ⋆ *hij zal het wel* ~ *he'll manage*
klarinet *clarinet*
***klassestrijd** (Wdl: klassenstrijd) *class-struggle*
klassiek *classic(al)*
klassikaal (in) *class*
klateren *splash*
klatergoud *tinsel*
klauteren *clamber*
klauw • (nagel) *claw,* <v. roofvogel> *talon* • (poot) *paw, claw*
klavecimbel *harpsichord*
klaver *clover*
klaverblad *cloverleaf*
klavier • (toetsenbord) *keyboard* • (piano) *piano*
kleden *dress, clothe*
klederdracht *traditional/national costume/dress*
kleed *carpet, rug*
kleedkamer *changing/dressing room*
kleefpleister *sticking plaster*
kleerhanger *coat hanger*

kleermaker *tailor*
klef • (klam) *sodden, clammy* • (kleverig) *sticky* • (vervelend/hinderlijk aanhalig) *clinging*
klei *clay*
klein • (niet groot) *small, little* • (jong) ⋆ *v.* ~ *af aan from a little boy/girl* ⋆ *de* ~*e the little one* • (nederig, benepen) ⋆ *iem.* ~ *houden keep s.o. down* ⋆ *iem.* ~*krijgen break s.o. in* • (niet geheel) ⋆ *een* ~*e tien gulden a little under ten guilders*
kleinbedrijf *small business*
kleindochter *granddaughter*
kleingeestig *petty, narrow-minded*
kleinhandel *retail trade*
kleinigheid *trifle*
kleinkind *grandchild*
kleinmaken *cut up,* <geld> *change*
kleinood *jewel, gem, valuables* [mv]
kleintje • (jong kind/dier) *little one* • (klein ding) *small one, short one*
kleinzerig • (bang voor pijn) *frightened of pain* • (lichtgeraakt) *touchy, over-sensitive*
kleinzielig *petty, narrow-minded*
kleinzoon *grandson*
klem I [de] • (val) *catch, trap* • (nadruk) *emphasis, stress* • (ziekte) *lockjaw* • (benarde omstandigheid) ⋆ *in de klem zitten be in a hole* ⋆ *in de klem raken get into a hole; get in a scrape/jam* II [bnw] *jammed, stuck*
klemmen I [ov ww] *jam,* <lippen> *tighten* II [on ww] *jam,* <v. deur> *stick*
klemtoon *stress*
klep <v. motor, enz.> *valve,* <v. pet> *peak, visor,* <v. zak, enz.> *flap*
klepel *clapper*
kleppen • (klepperen) *clatter* • (kletsen) *chatter*
klepperen *clapper, rattle*
klerikaal *clerical*
klerk *clerk*

klets • (slag) *smack, slap* • (gezwam) *twaddle, rot*
kletsen • (praten) *chat(ter)* • (zwammen) *gas, talk rot*
kletskous *chatterbox*
kletsnat *soaking (wet)*
kleumen *shiver, freeze, chill(to the bone)*
kleur • (wat het oog ziet) *colour* • (kaartspel) *suit* • (gelaatskleur) *complexion*
kleurboek *colouring/painting-book*
kleurecht *fast-dyed, colour fast*
kleuren • (kleur aannemen) *colour* • (blozen) *blush* • (~ bij) *match*
kleurenblind *colour blind*
kleurenfilm *technicolour film*
kleurentelevisie *colour television*
kleurig *colourful*
kleurkrijt *coloured chalk*
kleurling *coloured person*
kleurloos *colourless*
kleurpotlood *crayon, coloured pencil*
kleurstof *pigment, ‹verf› dye*
kleuter *tot, toddler*
kleuterleidster *nursery (school) teacher*
kleuterschool *infant/nursery school*
kleven *adhere, stick, cling*
kleverig *sticky*
kliek • (groepje) *clique* • (etensrestjes) *scraps*
klier • (orgaan) *gland* • (akelig persoon) *pain in the neck, pain in the ass ‹AE› ‹vulg.›*
klieven *cleave*
klikken • (verklappen) *tell tales* • (goed contact hebben) ★ *het klikt tussen hen they hit it off*
klim *climb*
klimaat *climate*
klimmen *climb, ‹op paard› mount*
klimop *ivy*
klimplant *climbing-plant*
klimrek *climbing frame*

kliniek *clinic, clinical hospital*
klinisch *clinical*
klink *latch*
klinken I [ov ww] *rivet, nail* II [on ww] • (geluid maken) *sound, ring* • (toasten) *clink to*
klinker • (steen) *clinker, brick* • (taalk.) *vowel*
klinkklaar *sheer, rank*
klinknagel *rivet*
klip *rock, reef*
klodder *clot, blob*
klodderen *clot, ‹met verf› daub*
kloek I [de] *mother-hen* II [bnw] • (fors, flink) *sturdy, ‹volume› stout* • (dapper) *bold*
klok • (uurwerk) *clock* • (bel) *bell* • (stolp) *bell-glass, bell-jar*
klokgelui *bell-ringing, chiming*
klokhuis *core*
klokken • (geluid) *cluck, chuck, ‹v. kalkoen› gobble, ‹v. water› gurgle* • (tijd opnemen) ‹bij aankomst› *clock in, ‹bij vertrek› clock out*
klokkenspel *chimes*
klokkentoren *bell tower*
klokslag *stroke of the clock*
klomp • (brok) *lump, slug* • (houten schoen) *wooden shoe, clog*
klont ‹suiker› *lump*
klonteren *clot, curdle*
kloof *cleft, gap, ‹huid› chap*
klooster *cloister, convent, ‹mannen› monastery, ‹vrouwen› nunnery*
kloosterling ‹man› *monk, ‹vrouw› nun*
kloot • (teelbal) *ball* • (aardkloot) *globe*
klop • (doffe tik) *knock, tap* • (hartklop) *beat*
klopgeest *poltergeist, rapping spirit*
klopjacht *battue, ‹korhoen› drive*
kloppen • (een klop geven) *knock, tap, pat* • (klutsen) ‹eieren› *beat (up)* • (verslaan) *beat* • (overeenstemmen) ★ *ja, dat klopt! yes, that's right!* ★ *dat*

klopt met *fits in with*
klos • (stukje hout) *reel, spool*
• (elektriciteitsspoel) *coil*
klossen *stump*
klotsen • (spatten) *dash* • (tikken van biljartballen) *kiss*
kloven *cleave, split*
klucht *farce*
kluchtig *farcical*
kluif *bone*
kluis *safe, strong-room*
kluisteren *fetter*
kluit *clod, lump, pat*
kluiven *pick (a bone), gnaw at*
kluizenaar *hermit*
klungelen *bungle*
klutsen <eieren> *whisk*, <room> *whip*
kluwen *ball, clew*
knaagdier *rodent*
knaap • (jongen) *lad, boy*
• (klerenhanger) *coat-hanger*
• (kanjer) *a whopper*
knabbelen *nibble*
knagen *gnaw*
knak *bend*
knakken *break, crack*
knakworst <AE> *frankfurter*, <BE> *hot dog (in brine)*
knal *crack*, <v. kurk> *pop*
knallen <v. geweer, zweep> *crack*, <v. kanon> *bang*, <v. kurk> *pop*
knalpot *silencer*
knap I [bnw] • (aantrekkelijk) *handsome, personable, good-looking* • (slim) *clever* II [bijw] • (slim) *cleverly* • (nogal) *rather, quite, pretty*
knappen *crack*, <v. touw> *snap*
knapperd *clever fellow*, <inf.> *brain*
knarsen • (piepen) <v. scharnier> *creak* • (knarsend geluid maken) <v. grind> *crunch*, <v. tanden> *grind*
knarsetanden *gnash/grit one's teeth*
knauw *bite*
knauwen *gnaw, munch, maul*
knecht *servant, man*

knechten *enslave*
kneden *knead*
kneep • (het knijpen) *pinch* • (handigheidje) *dodge, trick*
knel ★ in de knel zitten *be in a scrape* ★ knel zitten tussen *be wedged between*
knellen I [ov ww] *squeeze, press* II [on ww] *squeeze, pinch*
knelpunt *bottleneck*
knetteren *crackle*, <v. donder> *crash*
kneuzen *bruise*
kneuzing *bruise*
knevel • (snor) *moustache* • (mondprop) *gag* • (dwarspen) *toggle*
knevelen *gag*
knibbelen *haggle*
knie *knee*
kniebuiging <gymnastiek> *knee bend*, <in kerk> *genuflection*, <v. vrouw> *curts(e)y*
knieholte *hollow of the knee*
kniekous *knee stocking*, <nylons> *popsock*
knielen *kneel*
knieschijf *knee-cap*, <med.> *patella*
kniesoor *grump, grouch*
knieval *genuflection*
kniezen *mope, fret, worry*
knikkebollen *nod (off)*
knikken *nod*
knikker *marble*
knikkeren I [ov ww] ★ iem. eruit ~ *chuck s.o. out* II [on ww] *play (at) marbles*
knip • (sluiting) *catch, clasp*
knipmes *clasp-knife*
knipogen *wink*
knippen I [ov ww] <coupons> *clip*, <haar> *cut*, <heg> *trim*, <nagels> *pare* II [on ww] • (knippend geluid maken) <met de vingers> *snap*
knipperen *flicker, blink*
knipperlicht *flashing light, flasher*
knipsel *cutting, clipping*

knobbel *bump*
knobbelig *knotty, gnarled*
knoei ★ in de ~ zitten *be in a jam*
knoeiboel • (bedrog) *swindle*
• (smeerboel) *mess*
knoeien • (morsen) *make a mess*
• (slecht werken) *bungle*
• (zwendelen) *swindle*
knoeier *bungler, swindler*
knoeiwerk *bungle, blunder*
knoest *knot*
knoet *knout*
knoflook *garlic*
knokken *scrap*
knol • (bol, stengel) ‹aardappel› *tuber,*
‹raap› *turnip* • (paard) *jade*
knoop • (sluiting) *button*
• (snelheidsmaat) *knot*
• (verstrikking) ★ in de ~ raken *knot*
★ een ~ leggen *tie a knot*
knooppunt ‹v. spoorw.› *junction*
knoopsgat *button-hole*
knop • (klink) *knob* • (schakelaar)
button, ‹v. elektr. licht› *switch*
• (bloem-/bladknop) *bud*
knopen • (een knoop leggen) *tie, knot*
• (dichtknopen) *button*
knorren • (brommen) *grunt* • (slapen)
kip
knorrepot *growler, grumbler*
knorrig *grumbling, peevish*
knot ‹haar› *bun,* ‹wol› *skein*
knots *club, bludgeon*
knotwilg *pollard-willow*
knuffelen *cuddle, hug*
knuist *fist*
knul *chap, fellow, guy*
knuppel *cudgel,* ‹stuurknuppel›
joy-stick
knutselaar *handyman*
knutselen I [ov ww] ★ in elkaar ~ *put*
together II [on ww] *potter*
koddig *droll*
koe *cow*
koehandel *horse trading*

koeioneren *bully, dragoon*
koek • (zoet gebak) *gingerbread,* ≈ *cake*
• (koekje) ‹BE› *biscuit,* ‹AE› *cookie*
koekeloeren *stare, gaze*
koekenpan *frying-pan*
koekoek *cuckoo*
koel • (koud) *cool, cold, chilly* • (kalm)
cool, calm
koelbloedig I [bnw] *cold-blooded,*
imperturbable II [bijw] *cold-bloodedly,*
in cold blood
koelen I [ov ww] • (koel maken) *cool,*
‹drank› *ice* • (afreageren) ★ zijn
woede ~ *vent one's rage (on)* II [on
ww] *cool (down)*
koelkast *refrigerator,* ‹inf.› *fridge*
koelte *coolness*
koelwater *cooling water*
koepel *dome*
koeren *coo*
koers • (richting) *course* • (geldkoers)
rate
koesteren I [ov ww] *cherish,* ‹een
mening› *entertain,* ‹verdenking›
harbour II [wkd ww] *bask*
koeterwaals *gibberish*
koets *coach, carriage*
koetsier *driver, coachman*
koevoet *crowbar*
koffer • (valies) (suit)case, brief case,
‹voor geld› *coffer* • (bed) ★ de ~
induiken *jump in the sack; get*
between the sheets
koffie *coffee*
koffieboon *coffee bean*
koffiedik *coffee grounds*
koffiepauze *coffee break*
koffiezetapparaat *coffee*
maker/percolator
kogel ‹v. geweer› *bullet,* ‹v. kanon› *ball*
kogellager *ball bearing*
kogelstoten I [het] *shot-put(ting)*
II [on ww] *put the shot*
kogelvrij *bulletproof*
kok *cook*

koken I [ov ww] • (voedsel bereiden) *cook* • (laten koken) *boil* II [on ww] • (kwaad zijn) *seethe, fume* • (op het kookpunt zijn) ⋆ 't water kookt *the kettle is boiling*
koker • (houder) *case* • (stortkoker) *shoot*
koket *coquettish*
kokhalzen *retch*
kolder • (onzin) *giddy nonsense* • (ziekte) *staggers*
kolenmijn *coalmine,* ‹BE› *colliery*
kolenschop *coal shovel*
kolf • (handvat van vuurwapen) *butt* • (fles) ‹chem.› *receiver* • (vrucht van maïs) *cob*
kolibrie *hummingbird*
koliek *colic,* ‹inf.› *gripes*
kolk • (draaikolk) *eddy, whirlpool* • (luchtzak) (air-)pocket
kolken *eddy, swirl*
kolom *column*
kolonel *colonel*
koloniaal I [de] *colonial soldier* II [bnw] *colonial*
kolonie *colony*
kolonisatie *colonization*
koloniseren *colonize*
kolonist *colonist*
kolos *colossus*
kolossaal *colossal, huge*
kom • (beker) *bowl, basin* • (deel van gemeente) ⋆ bebouwde kom *built up area*
komaf *descent*
komediant • (aansteller) *play actor* • (acteur in komedie) *comedian*
komedie *comedy*
komeet *comet*
komen • (aankomen, bezoeken) ⋆ hoe kom ik daar? *how do I get there?* • (oorzaak vinden in) ⋆ hoe komt het dat... *how is it that...* ⋆ dat komt zo *well, it's like this* ⋆ zo komt het dat... *that is why...* • (gebeuren, zullen zijn)

⋆ daar komt niets van in *that's out of the question* ⋆ er komt nooit iets van it *never gets done* ⋆ iets te weten ~ *find out s.th.* • (geraken aan) ⋆ aan een baan ~ *get a job* ⋆ hoe ben je hieraan gekomen? *how did you come by this?* • (zich begeven) *come*
komiek I [de] *comedian* II [bnw] *comical*
komisch *comic(al)*
komkommer *cucumber*
komkommertijd *quiet/dull/slack/silly season*
komma *comma*
kommer *distress, trouble, sorrow*
kompas *compass*
kompres *compress*
komst *coming, arrival*
konfijten *preserve*
konijn *rabbit,* ‹inf.› *bunny*
koning *king*
koningin *queen*
koningschap *kingship*
koningsgezind *royalist*
koninklijk • (van het koningshuis) *royal* • (majestueus) *kingly*
koninkrijk *kingdom*
konkelen *intrigue*
konvooi *convoy*
kooi • (traliehok) *cage* • (hok) *pen* • (slaapplaats) *berth*
kooien *cage*
kook ⋆ aan de kook brengen/komen *bring/come to the boil*
kookplaat ‹elektra› *hot plate,* ‹gas› *gas ring*
kookpunt *boiling-point*
kool • (groente) *cabbage* • (steenkool) *coal*
koolhydraat *carbo-hydrate*
koolraap *Swedish turnip, swede*
koolwaterstof *hydrocarbon*
koolzaad *cole-seed, rape-seed*
koolzuur *carbonic acid*
koop *purchase*

koopakte *title deed*
koopavond *(late) shopping night*
koophandel *commerce, trade*
koopkracht *purchasing power*
kooplust *inclination to buy*
koopman *merchant,* <op straat> *seller, hawker*
koopvaardij *merchant navy, mercantile marine*
koopwaar *merchandise*
koor • *(zangkoor) choir* • *(koorzang) chorus*
koord *cord, string*
koorddanser *rope walker*
koorknaap *chorister*
koorts *fever*
koortsachtig *feverish*
koosjer *kosher*
kop • *(hoofd) head,* <inf.> *loaf, nut, pate* • *(bovenschrift) headline* • *(bovenste deel) top,* <v. golf> *crest* • *(voorste deel) head,* <v. vliegtuig> *nose* • *(drinkgerei) cup*
kopbal *header*
kopen *buy, purchase*
koper I [de] *buyer, purchaser* II [het] *copper*
koperen I [bnw] *copper, brass* II [ov ww] *copper*
kopergravure *copper-plate*
koperwerk *copperware, brassware*
kopie *copy, duplicate*
kopiëren *copy*
kopij *copy*
koplamp *headlight*
koppel *couple*
koppelbaas *recruiter, labour broker*
koppelen *couple, join*
koppeling • *(het koppelen) coupling, joining* • *(verbindingsdelen, overbrenging) clutch*
koppelteken *hyphen*
koppelwerkwoord *copula*
koppen <een bal> *head*
koppig • *(halsstarrig) obstinate*

• *(sterk) heady*
kopschuw *shy*
kopstuk • *(bovenstuk) headpiece* • *(belangrijk persoon) big man/shot, boss*
koptelefoon *headphone(s), earphone(s)*
kopzorg *worry*
koraal • *(bio.) coral* • *(muz.) choral*
koralen *coral(line)*
koran *Koran*
kordaat *resolute, firm*
kordon *cordon*
koren *corn*
korenbloem *cornflower*
korenschuur *granary*
korf *basket,* <bijenkorf> *hive*
kornuit *comrade, crony*
korporaal *corporal*
korps *corps*
korrel • *(bolletje) grain, pellet* • *(vizierkorrel) bead*
korrelig *granular*
korset *corset*
korst *crust,* <kaas> *rind,* <op wond> *scab*
kort *short,* <v. tijd> *brief* ★ *sinds kort recently*
kortaangebonden *short-tempered, curt*
kortademig *short-winded,* <tijdelijk> *short of breath*
kortaf *short, curt*
korten I [ov ww] • *(korter maken) shorten* • *(inhouden) cut (down)* II [on ww] *shorten*
kortharig *short-haired*
korting • *(inhouding) reduction (of)* • *(prijsverlaging) discount*
kortlopend *short-term*
kortom *in short, in brief*
kortsluiting *short-circuit*
kortstondig *brief, ephemeral, short-lived*
kortweg • *(in het kort) shortly, promptly* • *(kortaf) summarily*
kortwieken *clip the wings*

kortzichtig *short-sighted*
korzelig *crusty*
kosmisch *cosmic*
kosmonaut *cosmonaut*
kosmopolitisch *cosmopolitan*
kost ★ *kost en inwoning board and lodging* ★ *aan de kost komen make a living*
kostbaar *expensive, valuable, precious*
kostelijk *exquisite, splendid, glorious*
kosteloos I [bnw] *gratis, free* II [bijw] *gratis, free of charge*
kosten I [de] *expense(s)* II [on ww] *cost*
koster *sexton, verger*
kostganger *boarder*
kostgeld *board*
kosthuis *boardinghouse*
kostprijs *cost price*
kostschool *boarding school*
kostuum *suit*
kostwinner *bread-winner, wage earner*
kostwinning *livelihood*
kot ● (hok) <schapenkot> *pen,* <varkenskot> *sty* ● (gevangenis) *clink, nick*
kotelet *cutlet, chop*
kotsen *retch, puke*
kotter *cutter*
koud *cold*
koukleum *(house)tomato, a p. who feels the cold easily*
kous *stocking*
kouwelijk *chilly*
kozak *Cossack*
kozijn *window frame*
kraag *collar*
kraai ● (vogel) *crow* ● (doodbidder) *undertaker's man*
kraaien *crow*
kraakactie *squat*
kraakbeen *cartilage, gristle*
kraal ● (bolletje) *bead* ● (ompaald stuk land) *kraal, corral*
kraam *booth, stall*
kraambezoek *lying-in visit, visit to*

mother who has given birth
kraamverpleegster *maternity nurse, midwife*
kraamvrouw <bij bevalling> *woman in childbed,* <na bevalling> *new mother*
kraan ● (hijskraan) *crane, derrick* ● (uitblinker, kei) *dab, crack* ● (tap) *cock, tap,* <AE> *faucet*
kraanvogel *crane*
krab ● (kras) *scratch* ● (schaaldier) *crab*
krabbel *scrawl*
krabben *scratch*
kracht <die men bezit> *strength,* <die men gebruikt> *force,* <v. motor> *power*
krachtdadig *energetic*
krachteloos *powerless*
krachtens *by virtue of, on the strength of*
krachtig ● (sterk) *strong, powerful* ● (de maag vullend) *nourishing*
krachtsinspanning *effort, exertion*
krachtsport *power sport*
kraken I [ov ww] ● (openbreken) *crack* ● (vernielen) *wreck* II [on ww] *crack, (s)crunch,* <v. deur, schoenen> *creak,* <v. grind> *crunch,* <v. sneeuw> *crackle*
kraker *squatter*
kram *staple, cramp*
kramp *cramp*
krampachtig *spasmodic, convulsive*
kranig *plucky*
krankzinnig *insane, mad*
krankzinnigengesticht *mental home, lunatic asylum*
krans *wreath, garland*
krant *(news)paper*
krantenknipsel *press cutting*
krap ● (te klein) *tight* ● (met weinig geld)* ★ *zij hebben 't krap they are hard up* ● (met weinig marge) ★ *iets krap berekenen cut s.th. very fine* ★ *krap meten measure on the short side*
kras I [de] *scratch* II [bnw] *robust, strong*
krassen ● (een kras maken) *scrape, scratch* ● (rauw keelgeluid maken)*

screech, <v. kraai> *caw,* <v. raaf> *croak,*
<v. uil> *hoot*
krat *crate*
krater *crater*
krediet *credit,* <inf.> *tick*
kredietwaardig *credit worthy, solvent*
kreeft • (schaaldier) <rivierkreeft>
crayfish, <zeekreeft> *lobster*
• (sterrenbeeld) *Cancer, the Crab*
kreek *creek*
kreet *cry, shout*
krekel *cricket*
kreng <ding> *blighter,* <vrouw> *bitch*
krenken *offend, hurt*
krent *currant*
krenterig *niggling, mean, stingy*
kreukelig *creased*
kreunen *groan*
kreupel *lame (of one leg)*
kreupelhout *thicket*
kribbig *peevish*
kriebel *itch*
kriebelen I [ov ww] *tickle* II [on ww]
itch
kriebelig • (kriebelend) *ticklish*
• (kregel) *nettled* • (krabbelig)
squiggly
krijgen • (in een toestand
terechtkomen) ★ *ik krijg het koud I
am getting cold* • (getroffen worden
door) <schade> *sustain,* <verkoudheid>
catch • (ontvangen) *get, receive*
• (terechtkomen in) *get,* <regen> *have*
• (verkrijgen) <baby> *have,* <recht>
secure, <reputatie, wetenschap>
acquire • (in een toestand brengen)
★ *een vlek eruit* ~ *get out a stain*
krijger *warrior*
krijgertje ★ ~ *spelen play tag/tig*
krijgsdienst *military service*
krijgsgevangenschap *captivity,
imprisonment*
krijgshaftig *warlike*
krijgsmacht *(military) force*
krijgsraad *council of war,* <mil.

rechtbank> court-martial
krijt • (delfstof) *chalk* • (geologisch
tijdperk) *Cretaceous period*
• (strijdperk) *lists* [mv]
krijtwit I [het] *chalk dust* II [bnw]
chalk-white
krik *jack*
krimpen *shrink,* <v. pijn> *writhe*
kring • (cirkel) *circle, ring,* <v. ster>
orbit • (gezelschap) ★ *in alle* ~*en in all
walks of life*
kringloop • (cyclus) *cycle* • (omloop)
circular course, circle
krioelen *teem, swarm*
kristal *crystal*
kristalhelder *crystal-clear*
kristallen *crystal(line)*
kristalliseren *crystallize*
kritiek I [de] *criticism (of)* II [bnw]
critical
kritisch *critical*
kritiseren *criticize*
kroeg *public-house, pub*
kroes I [de] • (mok) *mug* • (smeltkroes)
crucible II [bnw] *crisp, frizzy*
kroezen *frizz*
krokodil *crocodile*
krokus *crocus*
krols *in heat*
krom • (gebogen) *crooked,* <lijn>
curved, <neus> *hooked,* <plank>
warped, <rug> *bent* • (gebrekkig)
★ *krom Engels bad English*
kromliggen *pinch and scrape*
krommen *curve, bend*
kromming *bend, curve*
kromtrekken *warp*
kronen *crown*
kroniek *chronicle*
kroning *coronation*
kronkel *twist, coil,* <in touw> *kink*
kronkelen *wind, wriggle,* <v. rivier>
meander
kroon *crown,* <v. boom> *top*
kroongetuige *chief witness for the*

Crown
kroonkurk *crown cap*
kroos *duckweed*
kroost *issue, offspring*
krot *hovel*
kruid *herb*
kruiden *spice, season*
kruidenier *grocer*
kruidig *spicy*
kruidnagel *clove*
kruien *wheel, trundle*
kruier *porter*
kruik • (kan) *jar, stone bottle*
   • (bedfles) * warme ~ *hot-water bottle*
kruimel *crumb*
kruimelen *crumble*
kruin *top,* ‹op hoofd› *crown,* ‹top v.
   golf› *crest*
kruipen *creep,* ‹v. dier› *crawl,*
   ‹vleierig› *grovel*
kruiperig *cringing, servile*
kruis • (kruisfiguur) *cross*
   • (lichaamsdeel) *crotch,* ‹v. broek› *fork*
   • (stuit v. dier) *croup,* ‹v. paard›
   crupper • (zwaar lot) *nuisance,*
   affliction • (zijde van munt) *tails*
   • (toonverhoging) *sharps*
kruisbeeld *crucifix*
kruisbes *gooseberry*
kruisen I [ov ww] • (over elkaar slaan)
   cross • (bevruchten) *interbreed* II [on
   ww] *cruise*
kruiser *cruiser*
kruisigen *crucify*
kruising • (bevruchting) *crossbreeding*
   • (kruispunt) *crossing*
kruispunt *intersection, crossing*
kruissnelheid *cruising speed*
kruistocht *crusade*
kruisvaarder *crusader*
kruisverhoor *cross-examination*
kruit *powder, gunpowder*
kruitdamp (gun)*powder-smoke*
kruiwagen (wheel)*barrow*
kruk • (zitmeubel) *stool* • (zitplaats v.

vogel) *perch* • (klink) *handle* • (as v.
machine) *crank* • (sukkel) *bungler*
   • (steunstok) *crutch*
krul • (haarlok) *curl* • (houtsnipper)
   shaving • (versiersel) *scroll* • (sierlijke
   pennenstreek) *flourish*
krulhaar *curly hair*
krullen I [ov ww] *curl* II [on ww] *curl*
kubiek *cubic*
kubus *cube*
kuch (dry) *cough*
kuchen *cough*
kudde *herd,* ‹schapen› *flock*
kuddedier *herd animal*
kuif *quiff,* ‹v. vogel› *tuft*
kuiken • (jong van kip) *chicken* • (dom
   persoon) *ninny, simpleton*
kuil • (gat) *pit, hole* • (scheepv.) *waist*
kuip *tub*
kuis *chaste*
kuisen • (schoonmaken) ‹Vl.› *chasten*
   • (censureren) *bowdlerize*
kuisheid *chastity*
kuit • (klomp viseitjes) *spawn*
   • (achterkant v. onderbeen) *calf*
kunde *knowledge*
kundig *able*
kundigheid *ability*
kunne *sex*
kunnen I [on ww] • (vermogen
   hebben) *can, be able to* • (mogelijk
   zijn) *may* II [hww]
   • (mogelijk/wenselijk zijn) * 't kan
   waar zijn *it may be true*
kunst • (creatieve activiteit) *art*
   • (kneep, foefje) *trick* • (toer) *feat*
kunstacademie *school/academy of
   art(s)*
kunstenaar *artist*
kunstgebit (a set of) *false teeth, denture*
kunstgeschiedenis *history of art*
kunstgreep *artifice*
kunstig *ingenious*
kunstmaan *satellite*
kunstmatig *artificial*

kunstmest *fertilizer*
kunstnijverheid *applied art*
kunstrijden *circus-riding,* <op
schaatsen> *figure-skating*
kunstschilder *painter, artist*
kunststuk *masterpiece,* <gevaarlijk
werk> *stunt*
kunstwerk *work of art*
kurk *cork*
kurkdroog *bone-dry, quite dry*
kurken I [bnw] *cork* II [ov ww] *cork*
kurkentrekker *corkscrew*
kus *kiss*
kussen I [het] *cushion,* <hoofdkussen>
pillow II [ov ww] *kiss*
kussensloop *pillowcase*
kust *coast, shore*
kustvaart *coasting trade*
kut <vulg.> *cunt*
kuur • (gril) *caprice, whim*
• (gezondheidskuur) <med.> *cure*
kwaad I [het] *evil, wrong* II [bnw]
• (slecht) *evil,* <geweten> *bad* • (boos)
angry III [bijw] *badly*
kwaadaardig *vicious, malicious,*
<gezwel> *malignant*
kwaadspreken *talk scandal*
kwaadwillig *malevolent*
kwaal *ailment, complaint, disease*
kwadraat *square*
kwajongen *urchin*
kwajongensstreek *monkey trick,*
practical joke, prank
kwaken <v. eend> *quack,* <v. kikker>
croak
kwakkelen *be ailing*
kwakken *dump, hurl*
kwakzalver *quack*
kwal *jelly-fish*
kwalificatie *qualification*
kwalificeren *qualify*
kwalijk • (bezwaarlijk) *ill*
• (nauwelijks) *hardly*
kwaliteit • (hoedanigheid) *quality*
• (waarde van schaakstuk) *value*

kwark *quark*
kwart • (vierde deel) *quarter, fourth*
part • (kwartier) * ~ *over/voor vijf a*
quarter past/to five
kwartaal *quarter*
kwartel *quail*
kwartet *quartet(te)*
kwartier • (deel v. uur) *quarter of an*
hour • (huisvesting v. militairen)
<mil.> *quarters* • (wijk) *quarter*
kwartje *25 cents*
kwarts *quartz*
kwartshorloge *quartz watch*
kwast • (raar persoon) *weirdo*
• (citroendrank) *lemon-squash*
• (verfkwast) *brush* • (noest) *knot*
kwebbelen *chatter*
kweekreactor *breeder (reactor)*
kweekschool *teacher training (college)*
kweken *grow, cultivate, breed, foster*
kweker *grower,* <bloemen, planten>
nurseryman, <groenten> *horticulturist*
kwekerij *nursery*
kwellen • (pijn/leed aandoen)
torment, vex • (obsederen) *haunt,*
torment, vex
kwelling *vexation, torment*
kwestie *question,* <zaak> *issue, matter*
kwetsbaar *vulnerable*
kwetsen • (verwonden) *injure, wound*
• (beledigen) *grieve, wound, offend*
kwetteren *twitter*
kwiek *spry, sprightly*
kwijlen *slaver*
kwijnen *languish,* <v. bloem> *wilt*
kwijt * ik ben het ~ *I have lost it*
kwijten • (voldoen) * een schuld ~
pay a debt
kwijtschelden *remit*
kwik *mercury*
kwinkslag *witticism*
kwintessens *quintessence*
kwintet *quintet(te)*
kwistig *lavish, liberal*
kwitantie *receipt*

L

la • (schuifbak) → lade
• (muzieknoot) la
laadruim *cargo hold, freight/cargo compartment*
laag I [de] *layer,* <geo.> *stratum,* <dun film,* <v. verf> *coat* II [bnw] • (niet hoog) *low* • (gemeen, minderwaardig) *base, mean*
laaghartig *vile, mean*
laagland *lowland*
laagte • (het laag zijn) *lowness* • (laag terrein) *depression, dip*
laagvlakte *lowlands*
laakbaar *reprehensible*
laan *avenue*
laars *boot* ★ rubberlaarzen *wellies*
laat *late*
laatdunkend *conceited, disdainful, arrogant*
laatst I [bnw] *last,* <meest recente> *latest* II [bijw] *lately, the other day, recently*
labiel *unstable, unbalanced*
laboratorium *laboratory,* <inf.> *lab*
labyrint *labyrinth*
lach *laugh, laughter,* <brede glimlach> *grin,* <glimlach> *smile,* <inwendig> *chuckle*
lachbui *fit of laughter*
lachen *laugh*
lachwekkend *laughable, ridiculous, absurd*
laconiek *laconic*
lacune *gap, break*
ladder *ladder*
lade *drawer,* <v. kassa> *till*
laden *load*
lading • (elektrische lading) *charge*
• (last) *cargo, load*
• (vuurwapens/explosieven) *charge,*

loading
laf • (niet moedig) *cowardly* • (flauw) *insipid*
lager <techn.> *bearing(s)*
lak *lacquer*
lakei *footman, lackey*
laken • (stof) *cloth* • (bedekking) <v. bed> *sheet,* <v. tafel> *cloth*
lakken *lacquer*
laks *remiss, lax, slack*
laksheid *slackness, laxity*
lam I [het] *lamb* II [bnw] • (verlamd) *paralysed* • (v. schroef) *stripped*
• (vervelend) *awkward, annoying*
lama *lama*
lambrisering *wainscot(ting)*
lamheid *paralysis*
lamlendig • (lui) *lazy* • (beroerd) *wretched*
lamp *lamp,* <peertje> *bulb*
lampenkap *lamp shade*
lampion *Chinese lantern*
lamsvlees *lamb*
lanceren *launch*
lancet *lancet*
land • (grond) *land* • (droge, vaste grond) *land* • (staat) *country*
• (platteland) *country* • (akker) *field*
landaard *national character*
landbouw *agriculture*
landbouwbedrijf *farm, agriculture*
landbouwhogeschool *agricultural college*
landbouwkunde *agriculture*
landelijk • (van het platteland) *rural*
• (nationaal) *national*
landen *land*
landengte *isthmus*
landerig *listless,* <inf.> *blue*
landgenoot *countryman, compatriot*
landgoed *(country) estate*
landhuis *country house*
landing *landing*
landingsgestel *landing gear, undercarriage*

landkaart *map*
landloper *tramp, vagabond, vagrant,*
  <AE> *bum*
landmacht *land forces*
landmeter *surveyor*
landschap *landscape*
landstreek *region, district*
landtong *spit (of land)*
landverraad *high treason, treason*
  against the state
landweg • (landelijke weg) *country*
  road • (route over land) *overland route*
lang I [bnw] • (v. gestalte, boom) *tall*
  • (een tijd durend) *long* II [bijw] *long*
langdradig *long-winded*
langdurig <afwezigheid, verblijf>
  prolonged, <vriendschap> *lasting*
langharig *long haired*
langs I [bijw] • (in de lengte
  naast/over) ★ de kerk ~ *en dan rechts*
  past the church and then right ★ bij
  iem. ~ gaan *drop in on s.o.* II [vz]
  • (via) *through, via* • (in de lengte
  naast/over) *along*
langspeelplaat *long-playing record,*
  L.P., album
languit (at) *full length*
langwerpig *oblong*
langzaam *slow*
langzamerhand *little by little,*
  gradually
lantaarn *lantern*
lantaarnpaal *lamp-post*
lanterfanten *idle, loaf (about)*
lap *rag, patch* <op kledingstuk>
  <grond>, <vlees> *slice*, <wrijfdoek> *cloth*
lapmiddel *expedient, makeshift*
lappen • (repareren) *mend, repair,*
  <kleren> *patch* • (ramen zemen) *clean*
  • (klaarspelen) ★ hij heeft het hem
  gelapt *he has pulled it off; he has done*
  it
lappendeken *patchwork quilt*
larderen *lard*
larie *bullshit, nonsense, rubbish,* <AE>
  boloney
larve *larva, grub*
las *joint, weld*
lassen *weld*
lasso *lasso,* <AE> *lariat*
last • (overlast) *trouble, nuisance*
  • (bevel) *order* • (vracht) <scheepv.>
  cargo, load, <fig.> *burden* • (geldelijke
  verplichting) ★ ten laste komen van
  be chargeable to • (beschuldiging)
  ★ iem. iets ten laste leggen *charge s.o.*
  with s.th.
lastdier *beast of burden*
laster *calumny, slander, defamation (of*
  character), smear
lasteren *slander, defame, insult*
lastig • (veeleisend) *exacting,*
  troublesome • (moeilijk) *difficult*
lat • (stuk hout) *slat* • (sport) *crossbar*
laten I [ov ww] • (toestaan) *let, permit*
  • (in een toestand laten) *leave*
  • (nalaten) *leave off, refrain from*
  • (zorgen dat iets gebeurt) *make,*
  cause, have, get • (bevelen) *tell, order*
  II [hww] *let*
latent *dormant, latent*
Latijn *Latin*
Latijns *Latin*
latwerk • (raamwerk) *lath-work,*
  lathing • (hekwerk) *lattice,* <v.
  bomen, planten> *trellis*
laurier *laurel, bay*
lauw • (niet erg warm) *tepid* • (mat,
  slap) *lukewarm, halfhearted*
lauweren I [de] *laurels* II [ov ww]
  crown with laurels
lauwerkrans *laurel wreath*
lava *lava*
laven *quench one's thirst*
lavendel *lavender*
laveren • (wankelend lopen) *reel,*
  stagger (about) • (schipperen)
  manoeuvre, steer a middle course
  • (scheepv.) *tack*
lawaai *noise, din, racket*

lawine *avalanche*
laxeren *purge*
lazaret *military hospital*
lectuur *reading (matter)*
ledematen *limbs*
ledigheid *idleness*
ledikant *bedstead*
leed • (verdriet) *grief, sorrow* • (letsel)
   injury, harm
leedvermaak *gloating, malicious*
   enjoyment
leedwezen *regret*
leefbaar *livable, habitable, fit to live in*
leefregel *regimen*
leeftijd *age*
leeftijdsgrens *age limit*
leeg • (zonder inhoud) *empty, vacant,*
   ‹fietsband, accu› *flat,* ‹huis›
   unoccupied
leeghoofd *rattlebrain, featherbrain,*
   ‹AE› *airhead*
leeglopen • (leegstromen) ‹v.
   fietsband, accu› *go flat* • (nietsdoen)
   idle, loaf (about/around)
leegte *emptiness*
leek *layman*
leem *clay,* ‹grond› *loam*
leemte *gap*
leen ‹gesch.› *fief*
leenheer *feudal lord, liege lord*
leep *cunning*
leer I [de] • (ladder) *ladder* • (doctrine)
   doctrine, theory • (het leren) *lesson,*
   apprenticeship II [het] *leather*
leerboek *textbook*
leergang • (cursus) *course (of*
   instruction) • (methode)
   (teaching/educational) method
leergeld *tuition fees*
leergierig *studious, eager to learn*
leerjaar *schoolyear, year's course,* ‹AE›
   ≈ *class*
leermeester • (docent) *teacher* • (iem.
   die wordt nagevolgd) *master*
leerplan *curriculum*

leerplichtig *of school age*
leerschool *school*
leerstelling *doctrine*
leerstoel *chair, professorship*
leerstof *subject matter*
leerzaam *instructive*
leesbaar • (wat te lezen is) *legible*
   • (aangenaam om te lezen) *readable*
leesboek • (boek om te leren lezen)
   reader • (boek om te lezen)
   recreational/light reading
leeslamp *reading lamp*
leest • (taille) *waist* • (gereedschap v.
   schoenmaker) *last*
leesteken *punctuation mark*
leeszaal *reading room*
leeuw *lion, the Lion,* ‹astrol.› Leo
leeuwerik *(sky)lark*
lef *pluck, guts*
leg *laying*
legaliseren *legalize*
legendarisch *legendary*
legende *legend*
leger • (rustplaats v. dier) *lair* • (mil.)
   army
leges *legal dues/charges*
leggen *lay*
legio *countless, legion*
legioen *legion*
legitimatie *identification*
legitimeren I [ov ww] *legitimize*
   II [wkd ww] *identify o.s., prove one's*
   identity
lei *slate*
leiband *leading strings* [mv]
leiden *lead*
leider *leader*
leiding • (het leiden) *guidance,*
   leadership, conduct • (het bestuur)
   management • (buis) *pipe* • (draad)
   wire
leidraad *guide(line)*
leien *slate*
leisteen *slate*
lek I [het] *leak(age),* ‹v. band› *puncture*

II [bnw] leaky, <v. band> punctured
* een lekke band hebben have a flat
tire
lekkage leak(age)
lekken leak, <v. schip> make water
lekker I [bnw] • (smakelijk) good,
delicious, tasty • (aangenaam) nice
II [bijw] * ~ rustig hier nice and quiet
here * ~ puh! serve you right!; pooh
(with knobs on)!
lekkerbek gourmet
lekkernij delicacy, tasty morsel
lelie lily
lelijk plain, <afstotend> ugly
lelijkerd • (lelijk persoon) ugly
fellow/bloke • (gemeen persoon)
brute, <inf.> ugly bastard
lenen • (uitlenen) lend (to) • (te leen
krijgen) borrow (from)
lengen lengthen
lengte length, <v. personen> height
lengtemaat linear measure
lenig lithe, supple
lenigen relieve, ease
lening loan
lens I [de] lens II [bnw] empty, dry
lente spring
lepel spoon
lepra leprosy
leraar teacher
leren I [bnw] leather II [on ww]
• (onderrichten) teach • (studeren)
study • (kennis, kundigheid
verwerven) learn
lering instruction
les lesson, lecture
lesbisch lesbian
lesrooster timetable
lessen quench
lessenaar desk, <in kerk> lectern
letsel injury
letter • (lettertype) font • (letterteken)
character
lettergreep syllable
letterkunde literature

letterkundig literary
letterlijk literal
letterteken character
leugen lie, <form.> falsehood
leugenaar liar
leugenachtig lying, false, <form.>
mendacious
leuk • (aardig, prettig) nice
• (amusant) amusing, funny
leunen lean (on/against)
leuning • (trapleuning) banisters, rail
• (leuning van stoel) <arm> arm rest,
<rug> back
leuren hawk, peddle
leus slogan, catchword
leuteren drivel
leven I [het] life [mv: lives] * een druk
~ leiden lead a busy life II [on ww] live
levend living, <predikatief> alive
levendig • (vol leven) lively, <persoon>
vivacious • (duidelijk) <beschrijving>
vivid
levenloos lifeless
levensbehoefte vital necessity
levensduur life (span)
levensgroot life-size, as large as life
levenslang lifelong
levenslicht light (of day)
levensloop • (leven) course of life
• (curriculum vitae) career,
curriculum vitae
levensmiddelen food(s), foodstuffs
levensonderhoud • (het voorzien in
levensbehoefte) support, sustenance
• (kost) livelihood
levensvatbaar viable
levensverzekering life insurance
levensvreugde joy of living
lever liver
leverancier purveyor, <algemeen>
supplier, <winkelier> tradesman
leverantie • (koopwaar) supply
• (levering) delivery, supply
leverbaar ready for delivery, available
leveren • (verschaffen, bezorgen)

supply, ‹afleveren› *deliver*
• (klaarspelen) *fix* • (aandoen) *try on*
levering *supply, delivery*
leverpastei *liver pie*
leverworst *liver sausage*
lexicon *lexicon*
lezen *read,* ‹vluchtig› *skim through*
lezer *reader*
lezing • (het lezen) *reading*
• (verhandeling) *lecture*
• (voorstelling v. zaken) *version*
libel *dragonfly*
liberaal *liberal*
licentie *licence*
lichaam *body*
lichaamsbeweging *(physical) exercise*
lichaamsbouw *physique, build*
lichamelijk *bodily*
licht I [het] • (schijnsel) *light*
• (opheldering) ⋆ *er gaat mij een ~ op
the penny has dropped; I'm beginning
to see the light* ⋆ *~ werpen op
throw/shed light on* • (openbaarheid)
⋆ *aan het ~ komen come to light*
II [bnw] • (niet donker) *bright, light*
• (niet zwaar) ‹maal› *light,* ‹muz.›
light, ‹sigaar› *mild* • (onbeduidend)
slight III [bijw] • (enigszins) *slightly*
• (gemakkelijk) *easily* • (soepel,
helder) *lightly*
lichtbron *source of light*
lichtbundel *pencil/shaft/beam of light*
lichtelijk *slightly*
lichten I [ov ww] • (weghalen) ⋆ *iem.
van het bed ~ drag s.o. from his bed;
arrest s.o. in his bed* • (legen) ⋆ *de bus
~ collect the letters/post; empty the
letter box* II [on ww] • (licht geven)
light (up), glow III [onp ww]
• (weerlichten) *lighten*
lichtgelovig *credulous, gullible*
lichtgeraakt *touchy*
lichtgevend *luminous*
lichtgewicht *lightweight*
lichting • (rekrutering) *conscription*

• (opgeroepen soldaten) *class*
• (postlichting) *collection*
lichtjaar *light-year*
lichtmatroos *ordinary seaman*
lichtnet *(electric) mains*
lichtpunt *power point, socket,* ‹fig.›
bright spot
lichtreclame • (reclame) *illuminated
advertisement* • (reclamebord)
sky-sign
lichtsterkte *brightness, intensity of
light*
lichtstraal *ray/beam of light*
lichtvaardig *rash*
lichtzinnig • (ondoordacht) *frivolous,
light-hearted* • (los van zeden) *loose*
lid • (beweegbaar lichaamsdeel)
‹lidmaat› *limb,* ‹v. oog› *lid* • (clublid)
member
lidmaatschap *membership*
lidwoord *article*
lied *song*
lieden *people, folk*
liederlijk ‹persoon› *debauched,* ‹v.
taal› *obscene*
lief I [bnw] • (geliefd) *dear*
• (beminnelijk) *sweet, nice*
• (dierbaar) *fond* II [bijw] *dear, sweet*
liefdadig *charitable*
liefde *love*
liefdeloos *loveless*
liefderijk *loving*
liefdevol *loving*
liefhebben *love*
liefhebber *lover*
liefhebberij *hobby*
liefkozen *caress, fondle*
lieftallig *sweet, pretty*
liegen *lie, tell a lie*
lier • (hijstoestel) *winch* • (muz.) *lyre*
lies *groin*
liesbreuk *(groin)rupture, hernia*
lieveheersbeestje *lady bird*
lieveling *darling, pet*
liever *rather, sooner*

lieverd *darling*
lift • (cabine van hijsinstallatie) *lift,*
elevator • (het meerijden) *lift*
liften *hitchhike*
lifter *hitchhiker*
liga *league*
liggeld *harbour-dues*
liggen • (uitgestrekt zijn) ∗ blijven ~
stay in bed; sleep in ∗ gaan ~ *lie down;*
drop ∗ op sterven ~ *be dying*
• (rusten) ∗ het werk is blijven ~ *the*
work has been left over ∗ iets laten ~
leave s.th. • (zich bevinden) *lie, be*
situated • (~ **aan**) *depend (on)*
ligging *situation, position*
ligplaats *berth*
ligstoel *reclining chair*
lij *lee*
lijdelijk *passive, resigned*
lijden I [het] *suffering(s)* II [ov ww]
suffer ∗ pijn ~ *be in pain* III [on ww]
• (~ **aan**) *suffer (from)*
lijdensweg *agony,* <v. Christus> *Way*
of the Cross
lijder • (iem. die lijdt) *sufferer*
• (patiënt) *patient*
lijdzaam *patient, resigned*
lijdzaamheid *patience*
lijf • (deel v. kledingstuk) *bodice*
• (lichaam) *body*
lijfarts *personal physician*
lijfelijk *bodily, physically*
lijfrente *annuity*
lijfspreuk *motto*
lijk *corpse, dead body*
lijken • (schijnen) *seem, appear*
• (aanstaan) *suit* • (~ **op**) *resemble,*
look like
lijkkist *coffin*
lijkrede *funeral oration*
lijkschouwing *autopsy, post-mortem*
examination, <jur.> *inquest*
lijm *glue*
lijmen • (plakken) *glue* • (bepraten)
talk round

lijn • (omtrek) ∗ in grote lijnen
broadly speaking • (route) *line*
• (touw, koord) *line,* <v. hond> *lead,*
leash • (streep) *line*
lijnen I [ov ww] *line* II [on ww] *go on a*
diet
lijnolie *linseed oil*
lijnrecht I [bnw] (dead) *straight*
II [bijw] ∗ ~ staan tegenover *be*
diametrically opposed to
lijnzaad *linseed*
lijst • (register) *list, register*
• (omlijsting) *frame*
lijster *thrush*
lijvig • (omvangrijk) *bulky* • (dik)
corpulent
lijzig *drawling*
lik • (het likken) *lick* • (slag) *lick, slap*
likdoorn *corn*
likeur *liqueur*
likken *lick*
lila *lilac*
limiet *limit*
limonade *lemonade,* <met prik> *fizzy*
lemonade
linde *lime (tree)*
lingerie *lingerie, women's underwear*
linguïstiek *linguistics*
linie *line*
linker *left, left-hand*
links I [bnw] • (aan de linkerkant) *on*
the left hand side • (onhandig)
awkward • (pol.) *left-wing, leftist*
II [bijw] • (aan linkerkant) *to/on/at*
the left
linksaf *to the left*
linnen *linen*
linnenkast *linen cupboard*
linoleum *linoleum*
lint *ribbon*
lintworm *tapeworm*
linze *lentil*
lip *lip*
liplezen I [het] *lipreading* II [ww]
lip-read, read s.o.'s lips

lippenstift lipstick
liquidatie liquidation, winding-up,
  <effectenbeurs> settlement
liquideren • (afwikkelen) settle
  • (opheffen) liquidate, wind up, go
  into liquidation • (uit de weg ruimen)
  eliminate
list trick
listig cunning, crafty
litanie litany
liter litre
litteken scar
liturgie liturgy
livrei livery
locomotief engine, locomotive
loden lead(en)
loeder bitch
loef luff
loeien • (bulken) <v. koe> low, <v. stier>
  bellow • (huilen) <v. sirene> shriek
loensen squint
loep magnifying glass, loupe
loeren leer (at), spy
lof I [de] praise II [het] chicory
loffelijk laudable
loflied hymn/song of praise
lofrede eulogy
lofzang ode
log <ding> unwieldy, <tred> heavy
logaritme logarithm
logboek log (book)
loge • (zitplaats in theater) box
  • (vereniging v. vrijmetselaars) lodge
  • (verenigingsgebouw v.
  vrijmetselaars) (freemasons') lodge
logeerkamer visitor's room, spare room
logement lodging-house
logen steep in lye
logenstraffen <hoop> belie
logeren stay, <inf.> stop
logica logic
logies accommodation, lodging(s),
  <scheepv.> living quarters
logisch logical, rational
logopedie speech therapy

lok lock
lokaal I [het] room II [bnw] local
lokaas bait
lokaliseren • (tot plaats beperken)
  localize • (plaats bepalen) locate
lokaliteit room, hall, premises [mv]
loket • (opbergvakje) pigeon hole, box
  • (raamvormige opening) ticket
  window, <v. kantoor> counter, <v.
  theater, bioscoop> booking/box office
lokken • (verleiden te komen) lure,
  entice • (aantrekken) tempt
lol fun, laugh
lollig funny
lommerd pawnshop
lomp • (onhandig) clumsy
  • (onbeleefd) rude
lonen be worth, pay
long lung
longontsteking pneumonia
lonken ogle
lont fuse
loochenen deny
lood • (metaal) lead • (schietlood)
  plummet, plumb line
loodgieter plumber
loodlijn ∗ een ~ oprichten/neerlaten
  erect/drop a perpendicular
loodrecht perpendicular
loods • (keet) shed, <v. vliegtuig>
  hangar • (gids voor schepen) pilot
loodsen pilot
loodzwaar leaden, heavy (as lead)
loof foliage
loofboom deciduous tree
looien tan
looier tanner
loom • (futloos) languid, listless
  • (traag) heavy
loon • (geldelijke betaling) wages, pay
  • (beloning) reward
loonbelasting P.A.Y.E., pay as you
  earn, income-tax
loondienst paid/salaried employment
loonlijst payroll

loonstop *wage freeze*
loonsverhoging *wage/pay rise*
loop • (vlucht) *run* • (het lopen) *walk,
gait* • (verloop) *course, development*
• (deel v. geweer) *barrel*
loopbaan *career*
loopbrug *footbridge,* <v. schip>
gangway
loopgraaf *trench*
loopje • (korte loop) (short) *run*
• (muz.) *run*
loopjongen *errand boy*
looppas *run, jog*
loopplank <v. schip> *gangway*
loops *in heat*
looptijd *term*
loos • (vals) *false* • (leeg) *empty*
loot • (uitloper) *shoot* • (nakomeling)
(off)shoot, <form.> *scion*
lopen • ((te voet) gaan) *walk, go, run*
• (z. ontwikkelen) ⋆ het boek loopt
goed *the book sells well* ⋆ het liep heel
anders *it turned out quite differently*
• (z. uitstrekken) ⋆ deze weg loopt
naar A *this road leads/goes to A* ⋆ de
weg liep langs de rivier *the road
followed the river* • (in werking zijn)
⋆ 1 op 7 ~ *do 7 kilometres to the litre*
lopend • (voortbewegend) *running*
• (voortgang hebbend) ⋆ ~e orders
standing orders ⋆ ~e schulden
running debts ⋆ ~e zaken *current
affairs*
loper • (sleutel) *master key*
• (schaakstuk) *bishop* • (tapijt) *carpet*
lor • (vod) *rag* • (prul) (a piece of) *junk*
los • (losbandig) <zeden> *loose, lax*
• (apart, vrij, afzonderlijk) *detachable*
• (niet vast, niet stevig) *loose* • (niet
strak) *loose, slack* • (niet stijf) *relaxed,
easy*
losbandig *lawless, loose, licentious*
losbarsten *break out, burst (out)*
losbladig *loose-leaf*
losbreken *break loose,* <v. onweer,
applaus> *burst out*
losgaan *come loose, come undone*
losgeld *ransom*
losjes *loosely,* <fig.> *lightly*
loskomen • (z. uiten) *let o.s. go,
express o.s.* • (losraken) *come loose/off,*
<vliegtuig, enz.> *get off the ground*
• (vrijkomen) *be set free*
loskoppelen *detach, uncouple,
disconnect*
loskrijgen • (in bezit krijgen) *secure*
• (losmaken) *get loose/undone*
loslaten • (vrijlaten) *let loose, set free*
• (laten blijken) *reveal* • (met rust
laten) *let go (of)*
loslippig *indiscreet*
loslopen • (vrij rondlopen) *walk
about freely,* <v. honden> *run free*
• (meevallen) ⋆ dat zal wel ~ *that is
sure to come right*
losmaken *unfasten, undo,* <schoenen>
unlace
losprijs *ransom*
losrukken *tear loose*
losscheuren *tear loose*
losschroeven *unscrew, screw off*
lossen • (uitladen) *unload*
• (afschieten) *discharge, fire* • (sport)
fall behind
losweken *soak off,* <door stoom> *steam
open*
lot • (loterijbriefje) (lottery) *ticket*
• (levenslot) *fate, lot*
loten I [ov ww] *draw lots (for)* II [on
ww] *draw by lot*
loterij *lottery*
lotgenoot *partner in distress,
fellow-sufferer*
loting *drawing lots, draw*
louter I [bnw] *sheer* II [bijw] *only,
purely*
louteren *purify, chasten*
loutering *purification, chastening*
loven *praise, commend*
lover *foliage*

loyaal *loyal*
loyaliteit *loyalty*
lozen • (spuien) *drain off* • (urineren) *pass (water)* • (z. ontdoen van) ★ iem. ~ *get rid of/ditch s.o.*
lucht • (dampkring) *air* • (adem) *air* • (hemel) *sky* • (reuk) *smell*
luchtballon *(hot-air) balloon*
luchtbed *air mattress, Lilo*
luchtbel *air bubble*
luchtdicht *airtight*
luchten • (uiten) *vent* • (ventileren) *air, ventilate*
luchter • (kroonluchter) *chandelier* • (kandelaar) *candelabrum*
luchthartig *light-hearted*
luchthaven *airport*
luchtig I [bnw] • (lucht doorlatend) *light* • (niet compact) *light, airy* II [bijw] *airy, light-hearted*
luchtkasteel *castle in the air, illusion*
luchtkoker *air shaft*
luchtledig *void of air, vacuous*
luchtmacht *air force*
luchtpijp *windpipe*, <med.> *trachea*
luchtruim • (territoriaal gebied) *airspace* • (dampkring) *atmosphere*
luchtschip *airship*
luchtvaart *aviation*
luchtvaartmaatschappij *air line (company)*
lucifer *match*
lucratief *lucrative*
lui I [de] *people, folk* II [bnw] *lazy, idle*
luiaard • (persoon) *lazy-bones* • (dier) *sloth*
luid *loud*
luiden I [ov ww] *ring* II [on ww] • (inhouden) *read, run* • (klinken) *ring, peal*
luidkeels *at the top of one's voice, loudly*
luidruchtig *clamorous, noisy*
luidspreker *loudspeaker*
luilak *lazybones*

luilekkerland *(land of) Cockaigne, land of plenty*
luipaard *leopard*
luis *louse* [mv: *lice*]
luister *lustre*
luisteraar *listener*
luisteren *listen* ★ ~ naar *listen to*
luisterrijk *glorious, magnificent*
luit *lute*
luitenant *lieutenant*
luitenant-kolonel <luchtmacht> *wing commander*
luiwagen *scrubbing-brush*
lukken *succeed*
lukraak I [bnw] *random, haphazard* II [bijw] *haphazardly*
lul • (klootzak) *sod, prick* • (penis) *cock, prick*
lullen *(talk) bullshit*
lummel *lout, oaf*
lummelen *hang about*
lunch *lunch(eon)*
lunchroom *tearoom*
lurken *suck noisely*
lus *loop*, <in tram> *strap*, <v. touw> *noose*
lust • (verlangen) *desire* • (plezier) *delight* • (zinnelijke lust) *lust*
lusteloos *listless*
lusten *like, enjoy*
lusthof • (paradijs) *(garden of) Eden* • (tuin) *pleasure garden*
lustig • (krachtig) *lusty* • (vrolijk) *cheerful*
lustrum • (vijfjarig bestaan) *lustrum* • (viering) *fifth, etc., anniversary*
luwen <v. ijver> *flag*, <v. vriendschap> *cool down*, <v. wind, boosheid> *die down*
luwte *lee, shelter*
luxe *luxury*
luxueus *sumptuous, luxurious*
lyceum <BE> ≈ *grammar school*, <AE> *high school*
lynchen *lynch*

lyriek *lyric poetry*
lyrisch *lyric(al)*

M

ma *mama, mum, mummy*
maag *stomach,* <inf.> *tummy*
maagbloeding *gastric h(a)emorrhage*
maagd • (meisje) *maid(en), virgin*
   • (Maria) *the Virgin* • (astrol.) *Virgo*
maagdelijk *virginal*
maagzuur *gastric acid, stomach acid*
maagzweer *gastric ulcer*
maaien *mow,* <v. gras> *cut*
maaier *mower, reaper*
maaimachine *mowing-machine,*
   <voor gras> *lawnmower*
maak *be under repair/construction*
maakloon *cost of making*
maaksel *make*
maakwerk *work made to order*
maal I [de] *time* II [het] *meal*
maalstroom *whirlpool, maelstrom*
maalteken *multiplication sign*
maaltijd *meal*
maan *moon*
maand *month*
maandag *Monday*
maandblad *monthly*
   (review/magazine)
maandelijks *monthly*
maandverband *sanitary towel*
maansverduistering *eclipse of the*
   moon
maar I [de] *but* II [bijw] *but, only*
   III [vw] *but*
maarschalk *marshal*
maart *March*
maarts (of) *March*
maas *mesh,* <in wet> *loophole*
maat • (muzikaal ritme) *measure,*
   time, <op muziekbalk> *bar* • (iets
   waarmee men meet) *measure*
   • (kameraad) *mate, comrade,* <inf.>
   chum • (afmeting) *measure,* <v.

kleding> size • (gematigdheid) ★ maat houden keep within bounds ★ met mate in moderation
maatgevoel sense of rhythm
maatglas measuring-glass, <AE> graduate
maatje • (0,1 liter) decilitre • (kameraad) mate, chum
maatregel measure
maatschappelijk social
maatschappij society, <handel> company
maatschappijleer social science
maatstaf standard, norm
maatwerk goods made to measure
machinaal mechanical, automatic
machine machine
machinebankwerker engineering fitter
machinegeweer machinegun
machinekamer engine-room
machinist (engine) driver
macht • (grote hoeveelheid) a great deal • (vermogen) power, might • (heerschappij) power, authority • (gezag) dominion, power • (wisk.) power
machteloos powerless, helpless
machthebber ruler, man in power
machtig I [bnw] • (het vermogen hebbend) powerful, mighty, tremendous • (zwaar op de maag liggend) rich II [bijw] powerfully
machtigen authorize
machtiging authorization
machtsmiddel weapon, means of power
machtsvertoon display of power
made maggot, grub
madonna Madonna
maffen kip ★ gaan ~ hit the sack/hay; turn in
magazijn • (ruimte voor patronen) magazine • (opslagruimte) warehouse, storehouse

mager <fig.> meagre, <v. personen> thin, <v. vlees> lean
magiër magician
magisch magic(al)
magistraal masterly
magistraat magistrate
magnaat magnate, <inf.> tycoon
magneet magnet
magneetnaald magnetic needle
magnesium magnesium
magnetisch magnetic
magnetiseren • (magnetisch maken) magnetize • (hypnotiseren) mesmerize
magnetisme magnetism
magnifiek magnificent
maïs maize, <AE> (sweet) corn
majesteit majesty
majesteitsschennis lèse-majesté, lese-majesty
majestueus majestic
majeur major
majoor major
mak tame, gentle
makelaar broker
makelaardij brokerage
makelij make
maken • (vervaardigen) make • (in een toestand brengen) render • (repareren) repair, mend • (verdienen) make • (doen) ★ het maakt niets uit it makes no difference; it does not matter
maker maker, author
makker comrade, mate
makreel mackerel
mal I [de] mould II [bnw] silly, foolish
malaise slump, depression
malaria malaria
malen I [ov ww] • (fijnmaken) grind II [on ww] • (~ om) worry, care
maling ★ iem. in de ~ nemen pull s.o.'s leg
mals tender
mammoet mammoth
man • (mannelijk persoon) man

• (echtgenoot) *husband* • (persoon) *person*

management *management*

manche <sport> *heat*, <whist> *game*

manchet *cuff*

manco • (tekort) *shortage* • (gebrek) *flaw*

mand *basket, pannier*

mandaat • (opdracht) *mandate* • (volmacht) *power of attorney*, <tot betaling> *pay-warrant*

mandarijn *mandarin*

mandoline *mandolin*

manege *manège, riding-school*

manen I [de] *mane* II [ov ww] • (aanmanen) *dun* • (~ tot) *urge*

maneschijn *moonlight*

mangel *mangle, wringer*

mangelen *mangle*

manhaftig *manly*

maniak *maniac, fiend*

manicure • (verzorger v. handen) *manicurist* • (verzorging v. handen) *manicure*

manie *mania, rage, craze, fad*

manier *manner, fashion, way*

manifest I [het] *manifesto* II [bnw] *manifest*

manifestatie *demonstration*

manifesteren I [ov ww] *manifest* II [on ww] *demonstrate* III [wkd ww] *manifest o.s.*

manipulatie *manipulation*

manipuleren *manipulate*

mank *lame, crippled*

mankement *defect, fault*

mankeren *fail, be absent*

manmoedig *manly, manfully*

mannelijk • (m.b.t. geslacht) *male* • (als v.e. man) *masculine* • (dapper) *manly* • (taalk.) *masculine*

mannequin *mannequin*

mannetje • (kleine man) *little fellow/man* • (mannelijk dier) *male*

manoeuvre *manoeuvre*

manometer *pressure gauge, manometer*

mans ∗ ik ben mans genoeg om... *I am man enough to...*

manspersoon *male, man*

mantel • (jas) <damesmantel> *coat*, <zonder mouwen> *cloak*

mantelpak *coat and skirt, lady's suit*

manufacturen *drapery, dry goods*

manuscript *manuscript*

manwijf <form.> *virago*

map <voor documenten> *folder*, <voor tekeningen> *portfolio*

marcheren *march*

marconist *wireless operator*

mare *news, report*

marechaussee *military police*

maretak *mistletoe*

margarine *margarine*, <inf.> *marge*

marge *margin*

marihuana *marihuana*, <inf.> *pot, grass*

marine *navy*

marinebasis *naval base*

marineblauw *navy blue*

marinier *marine*

marionet *marionette, puppet*

marjolein *marjoram*

markant *striking, outstanding*

markeren *mark*

markies • (markgraaf) *marquis, marquess* • (zonneluifel) *awning*

markt *market*

marmelade *marmalade*

marmer *marble*

marmeren I [het] *marbling, graining* II [bnw] *marble* III [ov ww] *marble, grain*

marmot *marmot, woodchuck*, <cavia> *guinea-pig*

mars *march*

marskramer *pedlar, hawker*

martelaar *martyr*

martelaarschap *martyrdom*

marteldood *martyrdom*

martelen *torture*
marter *marten*
marxisme *Marxism*
mascotte *mascot*
masker *mask*
massa • (hoeveelheid) *mass* • (groot aantal) *mass, loads* • (volk) *mass, crowd* • (nat.) *mass*
massaal *massive*
massage *massage*
massagraf *mass grave*
massamoord *mass murder*
massaproductie *mass production*
masseren *massage*
masseur *masseur*
massief • (niet hol) *solid* • (stevig) *massive*
mast *mast,* <hoogspanningsmast> *pylon*
mat I [de] *mat* II [bnw] • (vermoeid) *weary, languid* • (gematteerd) <foto> *mat(t)*
matador • (stierendoder) *matador* • (uitblinker) *crack (at, in), past master (in)*
mate *measure*
mateloos *unlimited*
materiaal *material(s)*
materialisme *materialism*
materie *matter*
materieel I [het] *materials* II [bnw] *material*
matglas *frosted glass*
mathematisch *mathematical*
matig *moderate*
matigen • (intomen) *moderate* • (verzachten) *mitigate*
matiging *moderation, mitigation*
matras *mattress*
matrijs *matrix*
matroos *sailor*
matrozenpak *sailor suit*
mattenklopper *carpet-beater*
mausoleum *mausoleum*
maximaal I [bnw] *maximum, top*

II [bijw] *at most*
maximum *maximum*
maximumsnelheid • (toegestane snelheid) *speed limit* • (topsnelheid) *top speed*
mayonaise *mayonnaise*
mazelen *measles*
mazen *darn*
mazzel *stroke/piece of luck*
mecanicien *mechanic*
mechanica *mechanics*
mechaniek *mechanism*
mechanisch *mechanical*
mechanisme *mechanism*
medaille *medal, medallion*
mededeelzaam *communicative*
mededeling (piece of) *information, announcement*
mededinging *competition*
mededogen *compassion*
medelijden *pity, compassion*
medelijdend *compassionate*
medemens *fellow-man*
medestander *supporter*
medewerker *colleague, fellow-worker,* <aan tijdschrift> *contributor*
medewerking *co-operation, collaboration*
medeweten ★ met ~ van *with the knowledge of*
medezeggenschap *workers' participation*
medicijn *medicine,* <iron.> *physic*
medicus *medical man, doctor, physician*
medisch *medical*
meditatie *meditation*
mediteren *meditate*
medium *medium*
mee ★ de wind mee hebben *have a tail wind* ★ ga je mee? *are you coming?*
meedoen *join (in),* <aan examen> *go in for,* <aan race> *compete*
meedogenloos *pitiless, ruthless*
meegaand *accommodating, compliant*

meekomen • (bijblijven) *keep up*
• (komen) *come (along, with)*
meel *meal,* <bloem> *flour*
meelokken *entice, lure*
meelopen ∗ met iem. ~ *accompany s.o.*
meemaken ∗ zij heeft veel
meegemaakt *she's been/gone through
a lot*
meenemen *take along/with*
meepraten • (meedoen in het
gesprek) *join in the conversation, put
in a word* • (naar de mond praten)
∗ met iem. ~ *play up to a person*
meer I [het] *lake* II [bijw] *more*
III [telw] ∗ onder meer *amongst others*
∗ zonder meer *simply; merely*
meerderheid *majority*
meerderjarig *of age*
meervoud *plural*
meervoudig *plural*
meerwaarde *surplus value*
mees *titmouse*
meesmuilen *smile ironically*
meespelen • (een rol spelen) *play a
part* • (meedoen) *join in the game*
meespreken • (meebeslissen) ∗ mag
ik ook een woordje ~? *may I put in a
word?; may I have a say in the matter?*
• (deelnemen aan gesprek) *take part
in a conversation*
meest I [bnw] *most* II [bijw]
• (meestal) *mostly* • (in hoogste mate)
most
meestal *mostly*
meestbiedende *highest bidder*
meester *master*
meesteres *mistress*
meesterlijk *masterly*
meesterschap *mastership, mastery*
meetellen I [ov ww] • (meerekenen)
include, count in II [on ww] • (van
belang zijn) *count (for anything)*
meetkunde *geometry*
meeuw *gull, sea-gull*
meevallen *exceed one's expectations*

mei *May*
meid • (jonge vrouw) *girl*
• (dienstbode) *servant, maid-servant,
maid*
meidoorn *hawthorn*
meineed *perjury*
meisje • (jonge vrouw) *girl*
• (verloofde) *fiancée, girl-friend,* <inf.>
sweetheart
meisjesachtig *girlish*
melaats *leprous*
melaatsheid *leprosy*
melden I [ov ww] • (aankondigen)
mention, state • (berichten) *report*
II [wkd ww] *report (to)*
melding *mention*
melig • (van meel) *mealy* • (grappig)
dull, slow
melk *milk*
melkachtig *milky*
melken *milk*
melkkoe *dairy-cow, milch cow*
melkpoeder *powdered milk, dried milk*
melktand *milk tooth*
melodie *melody*
melodieus *melodious, tuneful*
melodrama *melodrama*
meloen *melon*
memorandum *memorandum*
memoreren *recall to memory, mention*
memorie *memory*
memoriseren *commit to memory,
learn by heart*
men *a man, people, they, we, you, one*
meneer *mister*
menen • (bedoelen) *mean* • (denken)
think, fancy
mengeling *mixture*
mengelmoes *medley, jumble, farrago*
mengen I [ov ww] *mix, mingle, blend*
II [wkd ww] • (~ in) *interfere in*
mengsel *blend, mixture*
menie *red-lead, minium*
menig *many (a)*
menigeen *many a man*

menigmaal *many a time*
menigte *crowd, multitude*
mening *opinion*
meningsverschil *disagreement, difference of opinion*
mennen *drive*
menopauze *menopause*
mens I [de] *human being, man* II [het] • (vrouwelijk persoon) * 't arme mens *the poor soul*
mensaap *man-ape*, <bio.> *primate, anthropoid (ape)*
mensdom *mankind*
menselijk *human*
menselijkheid *humanity*
menseneter *man-eater*
mensengedaante *human shape*
mensenhater *misanthrope*
mensenheugenis * sinds ~ *within living memory*
mensenkennis *knowledge of human character*
mensenschuw *unsociable*
mensheid *humanity, mankind*
menslievend *humane, philantropic, charitable*
menstruatie *menstruation*
menswaardig *worthy of a human being, decent*
mentaliteit *mentality*
menthol *menthol*
menu *menu*
menuet *minuet*
mep *blow, crack, slap*
meppen *slap*
merel *blackbird*
meren *moor*
merendeel * 't ~ *the greater part/number*
merg *marrow*
mergel *marl*
meridiaan *meridian*
merk • (keur) *hall-mark* • (soort) *brand* • (handelsmerk) *trade-mark* • (teken) *mark* • (fabrikaat) *make*

merkbaar *noticeable*
merken • (van een merk voorzien) *stamp, brand* • (bemerken) *perceive, notice*
merkteken *mark, sign*
merkwaardig *remarkable*
merrie *mare*
mes *knife*
messing *brass*
messteek *knife-thrust*
mest *dung, manure*
mesten • (grond vruchtbaar maken) *dress, manure* • (dier vet maken) *fatten*
met • (op zekere wijze) *with* • (in gezelschap van) *with* * we zijn met z'n zevenen *we're seven* • (op zeker tijdstip) *at, in* • (voorzien van) *with* • (door middel van) *by, with*
metaal *metal*
metafysica *metaphysics*
metalen *metal*
metamorfose *metamorphosis*
meteen • (zo dadelijk) *at once* • (tegelijk) *at the same time*
meten *measure*, <land> *survey*
meteoor *meteor*
meteorologisch *meteorological*
meter • (lengtemaat) *metre* • (toestel om te meten) *meter* • (peetmoeder) *godmother* • (iem. die meet) *measurer, gauger*
methode *method*
methodiek *methodology*
methodisch *methodical*
meting *measurement, measuring*
metrum *metre*
metselaar *bricklayer, mason*
metselen *lay bricks*
metselwerk *masonry*, <v. bakstenen> *brickwork*
metten *matins*
metterdaad *actually*
mettertijd *in course of time*
meubel *piece/article of furniture* [mv: *furniture*]

meubelmaker *cabinet-maker*
meubilair *furniture*
meubileren *furnish*
meubilering • (de meubels) *furniture* • (het meubileren) *furnishing*
meug ⋆ ieder zijn meug *every man to his taste*
meute • (troep honden) *pack (of hounds)* • (groep mensen) *crowd*
mevrouw *Mrs., lady, Madam*
miauwen *miaow, mew*
mica *mica*
microbe *microbe*
microfilm *microfilm*
microfoon *microphone*
microscoop *microscope*
microscopisch *microscopic*
middag • (midden van de dag) *midday, noon* • (namiddag) *afternoon*
middageten *midday meal, lunch*
middel • (taille) *waist* • (iets om een doel te bereiken) *means, device* • (remedie) *remedy* • (bezittingen) *means* ⋆ mijn ~en laten dit niet toe I *can't afford this*
middelbaar *medium, average*
Middeleeuwen *middle ages*
middeleeuws *medi(a)eval*
middellijn *diameter*
middelmaat *medium size*
middelmatig • (gemiddeld) <v. lengte> *medium*, <v. prijs> *moderate* • (niet bijzonder) *mediocre*
middelpunt *centre*
middelpuntvliedend *centrifugal*
middelvinger *middle finger*
midden I [het] *middle, midst*, <v. stad e.d.> *centre* II [bijw] • (~ **in**) *in the middle of*
middenberm *central reservation*, <AE> *median*
middendoor *in two*
middengolf *medium wave*
middenstand *middle classes*
middenweg *middle course*

middernacht *midnight*
mier *ant*
mierenhoop *ant-hill*
miezerig • (nietig) *measly* • (regenachtig) *drizzly, dull, dreary*
migraine *migraine*
mijden *avoid, shun*
mijlpaal *mile-stone*
mijmeren *muse*
mijn I [de] • (kolenmijn, enz.) *mine, pit* • (mil.) *mine* II [bez vnw] *my*
mijnenlegger *minelayer*
mijnerzijds *on my part*
mijnheer *Mr., mister, Sir, gentleman*
mijnschacht *mineshaft*
mijt • (insect) *mite* • (stapel) *stack, pile*
mijter *mitre*
mijzelf *myself*
mikken (take) *aim (at)*
mikpunt *aim, target*, <v. spot, enz.> *butt*
mild • (zacht) *gentle* • (zachtaardig) *mild* • (royaal) *liberal, generous*
milieu I [het] • (leefklimaat) *environment* • (sociale kring) *milieu* II [voorv] *environmental*
militair I [de] *military man, soldier* [mv: the military] II [bnw] *military*
militant *militant*
militarisme *militarism*
militie *militia*
miljard *a thousand millions*, <AE> *billion*
miljardair *multi-millionaire*, <AE> *billionaire*
miljoen (a/one) *million*
miljoenennota *budget*
miljonair *millionaire*
millimeter *millimetre*
milt *spleen, milt*
mimiek *mimic art, mimicry*
min I [bnw] • (gering) *poor* • (gemeen) *mean* II [bijw] ⋆ min of meer *more or less* ⋆ zes min drie *six minus three*

minachten *disdain, slight*
minachting *contempt for/of*
minaret *minaret*
minder I [bnw] • (kleiner) *less*
• (geringer in waarde) *inferior*
• (zwakker) *worse* II [bijw] *less*
III [telw] • (niet telbaar) *less*
• (telbaar) *fewer*
mindere *inferior*
minderen I [ov ww] *decrease* II [on
ww] *diminish, decrease*
minderheid *minority*
mindering ∗ in ~ brengen *deduct*
minderwaardig *inferior*
mineraal *mineral*
mineraalwater *mineral water*
mineur *minor*
miniatuur *miniature*
miniem *slight, insignificant*
minimaal *minimum, minimal*
minimaliseren *minimalize*
minimum *minimum,*
minima [meervoud]
minimumloon *minimum-wage*
minister *minister,* ‹USA› *secretary*
ministerie • (gezamenlijke ministers)
the Cabinet • (departement) *ministry,*
department, Office
ministerieel *ministerial*
ministerraad *cabinet council*
minnaar *lover*
minst I [bnw] *least, fewest,* ‹slechtst›
worst II [bijw] *least* III [telw] ‹niet
telbaar› *least,* ‹telbaar› *fewest*
minstens *at (the) least*
minteken *minus sign*
minus I [het] *deficit* II [bijw] *minus, less*
minuut *minute*
minzaam *affable, bland*
miraculeus *miraculous*
mirakel *miracle*
mis I [de] *mass* II [bijw] • (onjuist)
wrong, amiss • (niet raak) *out* • (niet
gering van betekenis) ∗ dat is lang
niet mis *that is not half bad*

misbaar I [het] *clamour, uproar*
II [bnw] *dispensable*
misbaksel ‹fig.› *freak,* ‹v. aardewerk›
misfire
misbruik *abuse*
misbruiken *abuse, misuse*
misdaad *crime*
misdadig *criminal, wicked*
misdadiger *criminal*
misdeeld *poor, destitute*
misdienaar *server, acolyte*
misdrijf *criminal offence,*
misdemeanour
miserabel *miserable, wretched*
misgreep *mistake*
misgunnen *(be)grudge*
mishandelen *ill-treat, manhandle*
mishandeling *ill-treatment*
miskennen *misjudge, neglect*
miskleunen *slip up, blunder*
miskraam *miscarriage*
misleiden *deceive, mislead*
mislopen I [ov ww] *miss* II [on ww] *go*
wrong
mislukkeling *misfit, failure*
mislukken *fail*
mislukking *failure, flop, break-down*
mismaakt *deformed*
mismoedig *dejected, disheartened*
misnoegd *displeased (at/with)*
misnoegen *displeasure*
misoogst *bad harvest*
misplaatst *mistaken*
misschien *perhaps, maybe*
misselijk • (misselijk voelend) *sick*
• (misselijk makend) *sickening,*
disgusting
missen *miss* ∗ zij mist enthousiasme
she lacks spirit ∗ kun je een vijfje ~?
can you spare a fiver?
misser • (het missen) *miss* • (mislukte
poging) *fiasco*
missie *mission*
missionaris *missionary*
misslag • (slag die niet raak is) *miss*

• (vergissing) *error*
misstaan *be unbecoming,* <v. kleding>
not suit
misstand *abuse*
misstap • (verkeerde stap) *misstep*
• (vergissing) *false step, lapse*
mist *fog,* <nevel> *mist*
mistig *foggy*
mistlamp *fog lamp*
misvatting *misconception*
misverstand *misunderstanding*
mitrailleur *machine-gun*
mits *provided* (that)
mixen *mix*
mixer *mixer*
mobiel *mobile*
mobilisatie *mobilization*
mobiliseren *mobilize*
mobilofoon *radiotelephone*
modder *mud,* <met sneeuw> *slush*
modderen • (baggeren) *dredge*
• (knoeien) *mess about, bungle*
mode *fashion, style*
modeblad *fashion-paper,*
fashion-magazine
model *model*
modepop <man> *fop, dandy,* <vrouw>
doll
modern *modern, modernist*
moderniseren *modernize*
modeshow *fashion show/parade*
modieus *fashionable, stylish*
moduleren *modulate*
moe I [de] *mother* II [bnw] *tired, weary*
moed • (dapperheid) *courage* • (goede
hoop) *courage*
moedeloos *despondent*
moeder *mother*
moederlijk *maternal, motherly*
moederschap *motherhood*
moedertaal *mother tongue, native
language*
moedervlek *birthmark*
moedig *plucky, brave, courageous*
moedwil *wantonness, wilfulness*

moedwillig *wanton, wilful*
moeheid *weariness, fatigue*
moeilijk I [bnw] *arduous, difficult,
hard* II [bijw] • (met moeite) *with
difficulty* • (bezwaarlijk) *hardly*
moeilijkheid *trouble, difficulty*
moeite • (last) *difficulty, trouble*
• (inspanning) *trouble, pains*
moeizaam *laborious*
moer *nut*
moeras *marsh, bog, swamp*
moes I [de] *mums* II [het] *pulp*
moesson *monsoon*
moestuin *kitchen garden*
moeten • (verplicht zijn) *must, have
to, be obliged to* • (behoren) *should,
ought to* • (willen) *want*
• (noodzakelijk zijn) *must*
• (aannemelijk zijn) *must*
mof • (losse mouw) *muff* • (Duitser)
Hun, Jerry, Kraut
mogelijk *possible*
mogelijkheid *possibility*
mogen I [ov ww] *like* II [hww]
• (toestemming hebben) *be allowed*
• (wenselijk zijn) *should* • (kunnen)
may, be allowed
mogendheid *power*
moker *sledge*
mokken *sulk*
mol • (dier) *mole* • (muz.) *flat*
molecule *molecule*
molen *mill*
molenaar *miller*
molenwiek *wing/sail of a mill*
molesteren *importune, molest*
mollig *plump, chubby*
molm • (vergaan) *mould* • (vezels v.
turf) *peat-dust*
molshoop *mole-hill*
mom *mask*
moment *moment*
momenteel I [bnw] *momentary*
II [bijw] *at the moment*
momentopname *snapshot*

mompelen *mutter*
monarch *monarch*
monarchie *monarchy*
mond *mouth*
mondeling I [het] *viva*, <inf.> *oral*
  II [bnw] <afspraak> *verbal*,
  <overlevering> *oral* III [bijw] *orally, by
  word of mouth*
mondharmonica *mouth-organ*
monding *mouth*
mondjesmaat I [de] *scanty measure*
  II [bijw] *parsimoniously, in dribblets*
mondstuk *mouth-piece*
mondvol *mouthful*
monetair *monetary*
monitor *monitor*
monnik *monk*
monnikenwerk *drudgery*
monoloog *monologue*
monopolie *monopoly*
monotoon *monotonous*
monster • (eng wezen) *monster, freak*
  • (staal) *sample*
monsterachtig *monstrous*
monsteren • (scheepv.) *sign on*
  • (inspecteren) *inspect*
montage *assembling*, <v. film>
  montage
monter *brisk, lively, sprightly*
monteren *assemble*, <film> *edit, cut*
monteur *mechanic*
montuur *frame*
monument *monument*
monumentaal *monumental*
monumentenzorg ≈ *Department of
  the Environment Historic Buildings
  Bureau*
mooi *beautiful, handsome, fine, pretty,
  nice*
moord *murder*
moordaanslag *attempted murder*
moorddadig *murderous*
moorden (commit) *murder, kill*
moordenaar *murderer, killer*
moordpartij *massacre*

moot *slice*, <v. vis> *chunk*
mop • (grap) *joke, hoax* • (zwabber)
  mop
mopperaar *grumbler*
mopperen *grumble about/at*
moraal *moral*
moralist *moralist*
moreel I [het] *morale* II [bnw] *moral*
morfine *morphia, morphine*
morgen I [de] *morning* II [bijw]
  tomorrow
morgenavond *tomorrow evening*
morgenmiddag *tomorrow afternoon*
morgenochtend *tomorrow morning*
morgenrood *red morning-sky*
morgenstond *early morning*
morrelen *fumble*
morren *grumble* (at)
morsdood *stone-dead*
morsen I [ov ww] *mess* II [on ww] *spill*
morsig *dirty, grubby*
mortel *mortar*
mortier *mortar*
mos *moss*
mosgroen *moss-green*
moskee *mosque*
mossel *mussel*
most *must*
mosterd *mustard*
mot *moth*
motel *motel*
motie *motion, vote*
motief • (beweegreden) *motive*
  • (muz.) *motif*
motiveren *motivate*
motor • (aandrijfmachine) *motor*, <v.
  vliegtuig, auto> *engine* • (motorfiets)
  motorcycle
motoragent *motorcycle policeman*,
  <inf.> *speed cop*, <AE> *motor cop*
motorboot *motorboat, motor launch*
motorfiets *motor bicycle, motorbike*
motorisch *motorial*
motoriseren *motorize*
motorkap *bonnet*, <AE> *hood*

motorrijder *motorcyclist*
motregen *drizzle*
motregenen *drizzle*
motto *motto, device*
mout *malt*
mouw *sleeve*
mozaïek *mosaic*
mud *hectolitre*
muf <geur> *musty,* <v. kamer> *stuffy*
mug *gnat, mosquito*
muggenbeet *mosquito-bite*
muggenziften *split hairs*
muil • (bek) *muzzle* • (pantoffel) *slipper*
muilezel *hinny*
muis • (dier) *mouse* [mv: *mice*] • (deel
    v.d. hand) *ball of the thumb*
muiten *rebel, mutiny*
muiter *mutineer*
muiterij *mutiny*
muizenval *mouse-trap*
mul I [het] *mould* II [bnw] *loose*
mummelen *mumble*
mummie *mummy*
munitie *ammunition, munition*
munt *coin*
munten *mint, coin*
muntstuk *coin*
murmelen *murmur,* <v. stroompje>
    babble
murw *tender, soft*
mus *sparrow*
museum *museum, gallery*
musiceren *make music*
musicus *musician*
muskiet *mosquito*
muskus *musk*
muts *cap, bonnet*
muur *wall*
muurvast <fig.> *deep-rooted,*
    <letterlijk> *as firm as a rock*
muze *muse*
muziek *music*
muziekinstrument *musical
    instrument*
muzikaal *musical*

muzikant *musician*
mysterie *mystery*
mysterieus *mysterious*
mystiek I [de] *mysticism* II [bnw]
    mystic(al)
mythe *myth*
mythologie *mythology*

N

na I [bijw] • (behalve) ⋆ op een gulden na *less one guilder* ⋆ op twee na de grootste *the third biggest* • (later/toe) *after* • (na-/dichtbij) ⋆ zij stond hem zeer na *she was very dear to him* II [vz] • (later dan, achter) *after* • (over) *after*
naad *seam*
naaf *hub*
naaidoos *sewing box*
naaien *sew*
naaimachine *sewing machine*
naaister *seamstress*
naakt I [het] *nude* II [bnw] *bare, naked,* ‹persoon› *nude*
naald *needle*
naaldhak *stiletto heel*
naam • (benaming) *name* • (reputatie) *name, reputation*
naamgenoot *namesake*
naamloos • (anoniem) *nameless, anonymous* • (onnoemelijk) ⋆ ~ verdriet *untold misery*
naamval *case*
naamwoord *noun*
na-apen *mimic, ape*
naar I [bnw] *nasty, unpleasant* II [vz] ⋆ naar Londen gaan *go to London* ⋆ naar de dokter gaan *see the doctor* ⋆ naar huis lopen *walk home* ⋆ naar Frankrijk vertrekken *leave for France*
naargeestig *gloomy*
naarmate *as*
naarstig *industrious*
naast • (behalve) *as well as* • (terzijde van) ⋆ ~ elkaar *side by side* ⋆ de vrouw ~ haar *the woman next to her*
naaste *fellow man*
naastenliefde *neighbourly love,* ‹bijbels› *charity*
nabeschouwing *commentary, review,* ‹militair, diplomatiek› *debriefing*
nabestaande *relation, (surviving) relative*
nabij *near, close*
nabijgelegen *neighbouring, adjacent*
nabijheid • (het nabij zijn) *nearness* • (omgeving) *neighbourhood*
nablijven *stay behind*
nabootsen *imitate, copy*
naburig *neighbouring, nearby*
nacht *night*
nachtbraken ‹laat werken› *burn the midnight oil,* ‹uitgaan› *make a night of it*
nachtclub *nightclub*
nachtdienst *night shift*
nachtegaal *nightingale*
nachtelijk *nightly,* ‹form.› *nocturnal*
nachtkastje *night/bedside table,* ‹AE› *nightstand*
nachtrust *night's rest*
nachtvorst *night frost*
nadat *after*
nadeel *disadvantage, drawback*
nadelig *disadvantageous*
nadenken I [het] *thought, reflection* II [on ww] *think (about), reflect (upon), consider*
nader • (dichterbij) *nearer, closer* • (uitvoeriger) *closer,* ‹bijzonderheden› *further*
naderbij *closer, nearer*
naderen *approach, draw near*
naderhand *afterwards, later on*
nadien *since*
nadoen *imitate*
nadruk • (kracht, klemtoon) *emphasis, stress* • (herdruk) *reprint*
nadrukkelijk *emphatic*
nagaan • (volgen) *follow* • (controleren) *check (up on)* • (concluderen) *work out*
nagedachtenis *memory*
nagel *nail,* ‹v. dier› *claw*
nagellak *nail polish*

nagenoeg *almost, nearly*
nagerecht *dessert*
nageslacht • (nakomelingen)
offspring • (latere geslachten) *posterity*
nageven ⋆ dat moet ik hem ~ *I'll say that (much) for him*
naïef *naive*
naijver *jealousy, envy*
naïviteit *naivety*
najaar *autumn,* <AE> *fall*
najagen I [het] *pursuit* II [ov ww] *pursue*
nakijken *correct*
nakomeling *descendant*
nakomen <v. belofte> *keep,* <v. contract, regel> *observe*
nalaten *refrain from,* <verzuimen> *omit*
nalatenschap *inheritance,* <boedel> *estate*
nalatig *negligent*
nalatigheid *negligence*
naleven *observe, live up to*
nalopen • (controleren) *check* • (achternalopen) *run after, follow*
namaken *copy, counterfeit, imitate*
namelijk • (te weten) *namely* • (immers) ⋆ ik heb ~ geen geld *as it happens I have no money*
nameloos *indescribable, untold*
namens *on behalf of*
namiddag *afternoon*
napraten I [ov ww] *repeat, echo* II [on ww] *stay and talk (over)*
nar *jester, fool*
narcis *daffodil*
narcose *narcosis, anaesthesia*
narekenen *check*
narigheid *trouble*
naschrift *postscript*
naslaan <in naslagwerk> *consult,* <v. woord> *look up*
naslagwerk *reference book*
nasleep *aftermath*
nasmaak *aftertaste*
nastreven • (streven naar) *strive for,*

pursue • (proberen te evenaren) *emulate*
nat *wet*
natekenen *copy*
natellen *check, count over*
natie *nation*
nationaal *national*
nationalisatie *nationalization*
nationaliseren *nationalize*
nationalisme *nationalism*
nationalistisch *nationalist(ic)*
nationaliteit *nationality*
natrium *sodium*
nattigheid • (vochtigheid) *dampness* • (vocht) *damp, moisture*
natura ⋆ in ~ *in kind*
naturalisatie *naturalization*
naturaliseren *naturalize*
naturalisme *naturalism*
natuur *nature*
natuurgetrouw *true to nature*
natuurkunde *physics*
natuurlijk I [bnw] *natural* II [bijw] *of course, naturally*
natuurschoon *scenery, natural/scenic beauty*
nauw I [het] • (zeestraat) *narrows, strait(s)* • (moeilijkheid) *tight spot* II [bnw] *narrow, tight* ⋆ 't nauw nemen *be very particular*
nauwelijks *scarcely, hardly*
nauwgezet *scrupulous, painstaking*
nauwkeurig *accurate, precise*
navel *navel,* <kind.> *belly button*
navelstreng *umbilical cord*
navertellen *retell, repeat*
navolgen *imitate,* <v. voorbeeld> *follow*
navolging *imitation*
navraag *inquiry*
nawerken • (overwerken) *work overtime* • (zijn werking doen gelden) *have a lasting effect*
nazaat *descendant*
nazeggen *repeat, say after*
nazien • (volgen met blik) *follow with*

one's eyes • (controleren) *check*
nazomer *late summer*, ‹mooie
nazomer› *Indian summer*
nederig *humble*
nederlaag *defeat*
Nederland *the Netherlands*
nederzetting *settlement*
neef *cousin*, ‹oom-/tantezegger›
nephew
neer *down*
neerbuigend *condescending*
neerdalen *descend*
neergooien *throw down*
neerhalen • (naar beneden halen)
take/pull down • (slopen) *pull down*
• (afkammen) *run down*
neerkomen • (vallen) *come down*
• (betekenen) ⋆ erop ~ *come/boil
down to*
neerlaten *let down, lower*
neerleggen I [ov ww] • (op iets
leggen) *lay/put down* • (afstand doen
van) *lay down* II [wkd ww] • (~ **bij**)
put up with, resign o.s. to
neerschieten *shoot (down)*
neerslaan • (naar beneden slaan) ‹v.
ogen› *lower* • (tegen de grond slaan)
knock down
neerslachtig *dejected, depressed*
neerslag • (weerkundig verschijnsel)
precipitation, ‹regen› *rain(fall)*
• (bezinksel) *sediment, deposit*
neerstorten *plunge down*, ‹v.
vliegtuig› *crash*
neerstrijken • (neerdalen) *alight*
• (zich vestigen) *settle (on)* • (gaan
zitten) *descend (on)*
neervallen *fall down, drop*
neerzien • (naar beneden kijken) *look
down* • (~ **op**) *look down (up)on*
negatief *negative*
negen I [de] *nine* II [telw] *nine*
negentien *nineteen*
negentig *ninety*
neger *black*, ‹gesch.› *negro* [v: *negress*],

‹bel.› *nigger*
neigen I [ov ww] *bow, bend* II [on ww]
• (overhellen tot een mening)
incline/tend (to/towards)
• (omlaaggaan) *incline*
neiging *inclination, leaning, tendency*
nek *neck*
nekken • (doden) *kill (s.o.)*
• (kapotmaken) *wreck, ruin*
nekkramp *spotted fever*, ‹med.›
cerebro-spinal meningitis
nekslag *deathblow*
nemen • (aanpakken) *take* • (zich
verschaffen) *get* • (nuttigen) *have*
neon *neon*
nerf *vein*
nergens • (op geen enkele plaats)
nowhere • (niets) ⋆ hij geeft ~ om *he
cares for nothing* ⋆ ~ goed voor *good
for nothing* ⋆ dat slaat ~ op *that
makes no sense at all*
nering • (handel) (retail) *trade*
• (klandizie) *custom*
nerveus *nervous*
nest • (moeilijkheden) *spot, fix* • (bed)
⋆ naar zijn nest gaan *turn in; hit the
sack* • (broedplaats) *nest* • (nuffig
meisje) *chit (of a girl)* • (een worp)
litter
nestelen I [on ww] *nest* II [wkd ww]
lodge o.s., ensconce o.s.
net I [het] • (netwerk) *network, system*,
‹elektrisch› *mains* • (televisiezender)
channel • (weefsel met mazen) *net*
II [bnw] • (schoon) *tidy, clean*
• (keurig) *smart, neat* • (fatsoenlijk)
decent, nice III [bijw] • (keurig) *neatly*
• (precies) *just* • (zojuist) *just*
netel *nettle*
netelig *thorny*
netheid • (fatsoenlijkheid)
respectability • (ordelijkheid)
neatness, cleanliness
netjes • (net, orderlijk) *neat, clean, tidy*
• (fatsoenlijk) *proper*

netnummer *dialling code*, ‹AE› *area code*
netto *net(t), after tax*
netvlies *retina*
netwerk *network*
neuriën *hum, croon*
neurose *neurosis*
neurotisch *neurotic*
neus *nose*
neusgat *nostril*
neusholte *nasal cavity*
neushoorn *rhinoceros*
neusverkoudheid *cold*
neutraal *neutral*
neutraliseren *neutralize*
neutraliteit *neutrality*
neuzen *browse, nose (around)*
nevel • (mist) *haze*, ‹dichte nevel› *mist*
• (sterrennevel) *nebula*
nicht • (homoseksueel) *queer*
• (familierelatie) *cousin*,
‹oom-/tantezegster› *niece*
niemand *nobody, no one, none*
nier *kidney*
niet I [de] • (lot waar niets op valt)
blank • (nietje) *staple* II [het]
nothingness III [onb vnw] *nothing*
IV [bijw] *not*
nietig • (ongeldig) *void*
• (onbeduidend, gering) *insignificant,
paltry*, ‹v. reden› *futile*, ‹v. zaak›
trivial • (klein, schriel) *diminutive*, ‹v.
persoon› *puny*
nietigverklaring *nullification*
niets I [onb vnw] *nothing* II [bijw] *not
at all*
nietsnut *good-for-nothing*
nietszeggend *meaningless*
niettemin *nevertheless, nonetheless*
nieuw • (volgend op iets anders) *new,
modern* • (pas ontstaan) *new*
nieuwbakken • (vers) *freshly baked*,
‹fig.› *newfangled*
nieuweling *newcomer*
nieuwigheid *novelty, innovation*

nieuwjaar *New Year*
nieuwlichter *modernist*
nieuws • (actualiteiten) *news*
• (nieuwsuitzending) *news*
nieuwsbericht *news item/bulletin*
nieuwsblad *newspaper*
nieuwsgierig *inquisitive, curious*,
‹inf.› *nosey*
nieuwsgierigheid *inquisitiveness,
curiosity*
nieuwtje • (bericht) *news (item)*
• (nieuwigheid) *novelty*
niezen *sneeze*
nihil *nil*
nijd • (jaloezie) *envy, jealousy*
• (woede) *malice, spite*
nijdig *angry, cross*, ‹inf.› *huffy*
nijgen • (buigen) *bow, curts(e)y*
• (overhellen) *incline, lean (over)*
nijging *curts(e)y, bow*
nijptang *(pair of) pincers*
nijver *industrious*
nijverheid *industry*
nikkel *nickel*
niks *nothing*
nimf *nymph*
nimmer *never*
nippen *sip/nip (at)*
nis *niche*
niveau *level*
nivelleren *level (out/off)*
nobel *high-minded, noble*
noch *nor, neither*
node ★ node vertrekken *go reluctantly*
nodeloos *unnecessary, needless*
nodig I [het] *what is necessary* II [bijw]
• (noodzakelijk) *necessary, needful*
• (dringend) *necessarily*
noemen • (een naam geven) *name,
call* • (vermelden) *mention*
noemer *denominator*
nog • (tot nu toe) ★ nog altijd *still* ★ tot
nog toe *so far; as yet* • (geteld vanaf
nu) ★ nog twee dagen *two more days*
• (opnieuw) ★ nog een ei *another egg*

* (wil je) nog thee? *more tea?* * nog
vele jaren *many happy returns* * is er
nog melk? *is there any milk left?* * nog
eens *once more*
noga *nougat*
nogal *rather,* ‹inf.› *pretty*
nogmaals *once more/again*
nok • (daknok) *ridge* • (scheepv.)
yardarm
nominaal *nominal*
nominatie *nomination*
non *nun*
nonchalant *nonchalant, careless,*
off-hand
nonsens *nonsense, rot*
nood • (gevaar) *distress* • (gebrek) *need*
• (dringende omstandigheid)
necessity
noodgedwongen *out of/from*
necessity, ‹form.› *perforce*
noodklok *alarm (bell)*
noodkreet *cry of distress*
noodlanding *forced/emergency*
landing
noodlijdend • (behoeftig) *distressed,*
destitute • (niet renderend) * ~e
fondsen defaulted securities * ~e
wissel dishonoured bill
noodlot *fate, destiny*
noodlottig *fatal*
noodrantsoen *emergency ration*
noodrem *emergency brake*
noodtoestand *state of emergency*
nooduitgang *emergency exit*
noodweer I [de] *self-defence* II [het]
heavy weather
noodzaak *necessity*
noodzakelijk • (beslist nodig)
necessary • (onontkoombaar)
unavoidable
noodzaken *compel, force*
nooit *never*
Noor *Norwegian*
noord *north*
noordelijk *northern,* ‹v. wind›

northerly
noorden • (windstreek) *north*
• (noordelijke gebieden) *North*
noordenwind *north wind*
noorderbreedte *north latitude*
noorderkeerkring *tropic of Cancer*
noords *northerly,* ‹v. volkeren› *Nordic*
Noorwegen *Norway*
noot • (vrucht) *nut* • (aantekening)
note • (muz.) *note*
nootmuskaat *nutmeg*
nopen *compel, induce*
norm *norm, standard*
normaal I [de] *normal* II [bnw] *normal*
normalisatie *regulation,*
normalization
normaliseren • (regelmatig maken)
normalize • (standaardiseren)
standardize
normaliter *normally*
nors *gruff, surly*
nota • (geschrift) *note, memorandum*
• (rekening) *bill, invoice*
notariaat • (notarispraktijk) *notary's*
practice • (notarisambt) *profession of*
notary
notarieel *notarial*
notaris *notary*
notenbalk *staff* [mv: *staves*]
notendop *nutshell*
notenkraker *nutcracker, a pair of*
nutcrackers
noteren • (aantekenen/boeken) *note*
(down) • (opgeven/vaststellen) *quote,*
list
notering ‹v. effecten› *price,* ‹v. prijs›
quotation
notie *notion*
notitie • (aantekening) *note*
• (aandacht) *notice*
notulen *minutes*
notuleren I [ov ww] *enter in the*
minutes II [on ww] *minute*
novelle *short story*
november *November*

nu I [bijw] *now, at present* II [vw] *now
that* III [tw] *now, well*
nuance • (onderscheid) *nuance, shade
of meaning* • (kleurschakering) *shade*
nuanceren *modify, nuance, shade*
nuchter *sober* ∗ op de ~e maag *on an
empty stomach*
nucleair *nuclear*
nuf *prim/conceited girl*
nuffig *affected, haughty, conceited*
nuk *whim, caprice*
nukkig *whimsical, capricious*
nul I [de] • (cijfer) *nought, zero*
• (onbeduidend persoon) *nobody*
II [telw] *nought, zero, nil*
nulpunt *zero*
numeriek *numerical*
numero *number*
nummer • (cijfer) *number*, <v.
tijdschrift> *issue*
• (programmaonderdeel) *number,
item*, <v. circus, variété> *act* • (liedje)
number, <op cd, enz.> *track*
nummeren *number*
nurks I [de] *grumbler* II [bnw] *surly*
nut *use, benefit, profit*
nutteloos • (vergeefs) *fruitless, futile*
• (onbruikbaar) *useless, pointless*
nuttig *useful*
nuttigen *take, consume*, <form.>
partake of

oase *oasis*
o-benen *bandy-legs*
object *object*, <mil.> *objective*
objectief *objective*
objectiviteit *objectivity*
obligatie *bond, debenture*
obsceen *obscene*
observatie *observation*
observatorium *observatory*
obsessie *obsession*
obstinaat *obstinate*
obstructie *obstruction*
oceaan *ocean*
och *oh!*
ochtend *morning*
octaaf *octave*
octrooi <machtiging> *charter*, <op
uitvinding> *patent*
oecumenisch *ecumenic(al)*
oedeem *oedema*
oefenen I [ov ww] • (ergens in
bekwamen) *practise* • (betrachten)
exercise II [on ww] *practise*
oefening • (het oefenen) *practice,
exercise* • (opgave) *exercise*
oeroud *ancient*
oertijd *prehistoric times*
oerwoud *primaeval forest*
oester *oyster*
oever <v. meer> *shore*, <v. rivier> *bank*
of • (bij tegenstelling) *or*
• (gelijkstellend) *or* • (toegevend)
whether • (bij twijfel) *if, whether* • (na
ontkenning) *but* • (alsof) *as if*
• (bevestigend) ∗ nou en of! *rather!;
you bet!*
offensief I [het] *offensive* II [bnw]
offensive
offer • (offerande) *sacrifice*
• (slachtoffer) *victim* • (opoffering)

sacrifice
offerande • (offer) *offering, sacrifice*
• (deel v.d. mis) *offertory*
offeren • (ten offer brengen) *sacrifice*
• (bijdragen) *make an offering*
• (wijden aan) *sacrifice (to)*
offerte *quotation*
officier *officer*
officieus *unofficial*
ofschoon (al)though
ogenblik • (even) *moment, instant*
• (tijdstip) *moment*
ogenblikkelijk I [bnw] *immediate*
II [bijw] *immediately, at once*
ogenschouw ★ in ~ nemen *inspect;*
review
oker *ochre*
oksel • (lichaamsdeel) *armpit*
• (plantk.) *axil*
oktober *October*
olie *oil*
oliedom *as thick as a brick, as dumb as*
an ox
oliën *oil,* ‹form.› *lubricate*
olieraffinaderij *oil refinery*
oliesel *unction*
olieverf *oil paint*
olifant *elephant*
olijf *olive*
olijfolie *olive oil*
olijk *shy, roguish*
olm *elm*
om I [bnw] • (voorbij/langs) ★ de tijd is
om *time is up* ★ nog voor de week om
is *before the week is out* II [vz]
• (afwisselend) ★ om de beurt *turn*
and turn about ★ om de dag *every*
other day • (rond, rondom) *round,*
about • (doel) *to, in order to, so as to*
• (op zeker tijdstip) *at* • (vanwege) *on*
account of, for, because of
oma *grandma, granny*
omarmen *embrace*
ombrengen • (doden) *kill, murder*
ombudsman *ombudsman*

ombuigen I [ov ww] • (verbuigen)
bend • (veranderen) *adjust* II [on ww]
bend (over)
omdat *because*
omdoen *put on*
omdopen *rename*
omdraaien I [ov ww] ★ zich ~ *turn*
round II [on ww] • (draai maken) *turn*
• (omkeren) *turn back* • (van mening
veranderen) *change (one's mind)*
omelet *omelette*
omgaan • (rondgaan) *go round*
• (gebeuren) *happen* • (verstrijken)
pass • (~ **met**) *mix with,* ‹mensen›
associate with
omgang • (sociaal verkeer) *(social)*
intercourse, contact • (rondgang)
procession
omgangstaal *everyday speech,* ‹form.›
colloquial language
omgangsvormen *manners*
omgekeerd • (ondersteboven) *upside*
down • (tegenovergesteld) *reverse(d)*
★ 't ~e *the reverse*
omgeven *surround, envelop*
omgeving • (kennissenkring)
environment, acquaintances • (buurt)
neighbourhood, environs, vicinity
omgooien • (omvergooien) *overturn,*
upset • (omdraaien) *shift* • (omdoen)
throw... round • (veranderen) *change*
omhaal • (wijdlopigheid) *wordiness*
• (krul aan letter) *flourish* • (drukte,
omslag) *fuss, ado, ceremony* • (sport)
overhead kick
omhakken *fell, cut down*
omhelzen *embrace*
omhoog • (boven) *up* • (naar boven)
up/upwards
omhullen *wrap up,* ‹form.› *envelop*
omhulsel *covering, wrapping, casing*
omkeren I [ov ww] *turn (over)* II [on
ww] *turn back/round*
omkijken • (zorg, aandacht besteden)
look after, worry about • (omzien) *look*

back/round • (uitkijken) *look round/out*
omklemmen *hug, clasp*
omkomen • (ergens omheen komen) *come round* • (sterven) *die, perish*
omkoopbaar *corruptible*
omkopen *bribe, corrupt*
omlaag • (beneden) *below, down* • (naar beneden) *down(wards)*
omliggend *neighbouring, surrounding*
omlijnen • (omcirkelen) *(en)circle* • (afbakenen) *outline*
omloop *orbit* • (galerij) *gallery* • (verspreiding) *circulation*
omlopen I [ov ww] • (omverlopen) *knock over* II [on ww] • (rondlopen) *go round* • (langere weg volgen) *walk/go round* • (van richting veranderen) *shift/move round*
ommezien *moment*
ommezijde *back*
omploegen • (onderploegen) *plough (under)* • (ploegen) *plough (up)*
ompraten *talk/bring round*
omrekenen *convert*
omrijden I [ov ww] • (omverrijden) *run/knock down* II [on ww] • (een omweg maken) *go a long way round* • (ergens omheen rijden) *go round,* <met auto> *drive round*
omringen *surround*
omroep • (het uitzenden) (radio) *broadcast(ing)* • (omroepvereniging) *broadcasting corporation*
omroepen *page*
omroeper • (radio-omroeper) *announcer* • (gesch.) *town-crier*
omschakelen • (overschakelen) *change/switch over* • (aanpassen) *change (to), switch over (to)*
omschrijven • (beschrijven) *describe* • (definiëren) *define*
omschrijving • (beschrijving) *description* • (definitie) *definition*
omsingelen *surround, besiege*

omslaan I [ov ww] • (omverslaan) *knock down* • (omdoen) *put on* • (omkeren) <v. bladzij> *turn over,* <v. broekspijp> *turn up,* <v. mouwen> *tuck up* II [on ww] • (veranderen) <v. stemming> *turn,* <v. weer> *break* • (kantelen) *overturn,* <v. boot> *capsize*
omslachtig *roundabout*
omslag <losse omslag> *jacket,* <v. boek> *cover* • (verandering) *turn,* <v. weer> *break*
omsluiten *enclose*
omspannen • (omvatten) *span, enclose* • (spannend omsluiten) *fit tightly around/over*
omspitten *dig up*
omspringen ★ met iem./iets weten om te springen *know how to manage s.o./s.th.*
omstander *bystander*
omstandig I [bnw] *detailed, circumstantial* II [bijw] *in detail*
omstandigheid • (situatie) *circumstance* • (breedvoerigheid) *elaborateness*
omstreeks *about, round (about)*
omtrek • (afmeting) <v. cirkel> *circumference,* <v. veelhoek> *perimeter* • (buurt) *vicinity, neighbourhood*
omtrent I [bijw] *near* II [vz] • (omstreeks) *round (about)* • (betreffende) *about, concerning,*
omvallen *fall over/down*
omvang *size,* <v. schade> *extent*
omvangrijk *sizeable, extensive*
omvatten • (omsluiten) *enclose* • (bevatten) *include, comprise*
omver *down, over*
omvormen *convert, transform*
omweg *detour*
omwenteling • (draaiing om as) *revolution, rotation* • (ommekeer) *revolution*
omwerken • (herzien) <boek, artikel> *rewrite, redraft* • (grond omspitten)

dig up
omwisselen change
omwonend neighbouring
omzet • (koop en verkoop) turnover
• (geldsom) sales
omzetten • (veranderen) turn/convert
(into) • (verhandelen) turn over
• (anders neerzetten) change • (in
andere stand zetten) turn over
omzichtig cautious, wary
omzien • (een oogje houden op) look
after, take care of • (omkijken) look
back • (uitkijken) look out
omzwerving wandering, ramble
onaangedaan unmoved
onaantastbaar unassailable
onaanzienlijk • (zonder aanzien)
modest, ‹komaf› humble • (nietig)
insignificant, ‹som geld›
inconsiderable
onachtzaam inattentive, careless
onafgebroken continuous, unbroken
onafhankelijk independent (of)
onafhankelijkheid independence
onafscheidelijk inseparable
onafzienbaar vast, immense
onbaatzuchtig disinterested, unselfish
onbedaarlijk uncontrollable
onbeduidend insignificant, ‹reden,
enz.› trivial
onbegonnen ★ een ~ werk a hopeless
task
onbegrensd unlimited
onbegrijpelijk • (niet te begrijpen)
incomprehensible • (onvoorstelbaar)
incredible
onbehaaglijk • (niet op zijn gemak)
ill at ease • (onaangenaam) unpleasant
onbeholpen awkward
onbehouwen boorish
onbekend • (niet bekend) unknown
• (onwetend) ignorant (of),
unacqainted (with)
onbekommerd carefree, unconcerned
onbekwaam • (incompetent)

incompetent, incapable • (dronken)
incapacitated
onbeleefdheid • (onbeleefd zijn)
rudeness, impoliteness • (onbeleefde
uiting) incivility
onbemiddeld without means, ‹form.›
impecunious
onbenullig • (nietszeggend) trivial
• (dom) vapid, inane
onbepaald • (onbestemd) vague,
uncertain • (onbegrensd) indefinite
onbeproefd untried
onberaden ill-advised
onberekenbaar • (niet te berekenen)
incalculable • (onvoorspelbaar)
unpredictable
onberispelijk irreproachable, faultless
onbeschaamd insolent, impudent
onbeschoft impudent
onbesproken • (niet behandeld)
undiscussed • (niet gereserveerd) not
reserved, not booked • (onberispelijk)
irreproachable, blameless
onbesuisd rash, reckless
onbetaalbaar • (onschatbaar)
invaluable • (kostelijk) priceless • (niet
te betalen) prohibitive
onbetuigd ★ zich niet ~ laten keep
one's end up; be quick to respond; do
justice to a meal
onbetwist undisputed
onbetwistbaar indisputable
onbevangen • (onbevooroordeeld)
unprejudiced, open-minded
• (vrijmoedig) frank, candid
onbewaakt unguarded
onbeweeglijk • (roerloos) motionless
• (onwrikbaar) immovable
onbewogen • (onbeweeglijk)
motionless • (onaangedaan) unmoved
onbewoonbaar uninhabitable
onbewust • (niet bewust) unconscious
• (onwillekeurig) unwitting,
unintentional
onbezonnen rash

onbezorgd *carefree*
onbreekbaar *unbreakable*
onbruik *disuse*
ondank *ingratitude*
ondankbaar *ungrateful*
ondanks *despite, in spite of*
ondeelbaar • (niet deelbaar) *indivisible* • (zeer klein) *infinitesimal*
onder I [bijw] *underneath, below* II [vz] • (minder/lager dan) *under* • (dichtbij) *nearby* • (tijdens) *during* • (te midden van) *among(st)* • (tussen dingen/personen) ‹meer dan twee› *among*, ‹twee› *between* • (beneden) *under*
onderaan *at the foot of*
onderaards *underground, subterranean*
onderarm *forearm*
onderbouw • (fundament) *substructure* • (v. school) *lower school*
onderbreken *interrupt*
onderbreking • (het onderbreken) *interruption* • (pauze) *break*, ‹film› *intermission*
onderbrengen *lodge, house*
onderbroek *underpants*
onderbuik *abdomen*
onderdaan *subject*
onderdak *shelter, accommodation*
onderdanig *submissive*
onderdeel *part*, ‹v. seconde› *fraction*
onderdirecteur *assistant director/manager*, ‹v.e. school› *assistant/deputy head*
onderdoen ★ niet ~ voor *hold one's own with* ★ voor niemand ~ *be second to none*
onderdompelen *immerse*
onderdoor *under, underneath*
onderdrukken • (ondergeschikt houden) *oppress* • (bedwingen) ‹gevoel› *suppress*, ‹lachen, geeuw› *stifle*, ‹snik, tranen› *choke back*
onderdrukking *oppression*

onderduiken • (duiken) *dive, take a nosedive* • (verschuilen) *go underground, go into hiding*
ondergang • (het ten onder gaan) *(down)fall* • (het ondergaan) *setting*
ondergeschikt • (van lagere rang) *subordinate* • (van minder belang) ★ van ~ belang *of minor importance*
ondergetekende ★ (de) ~ *the undersigned; yours truly*
ondergoed *underwear*
ondergraven *undermine*
ondergronds • (onder de grond) ★ de ~e *the underground (railway)*; ‹AE› *subway* • (clandestien) ★ de ~e beweging *the resistance movement*
onderhandelaar *negotiator*
onderhandelen *negotiate*
onderhandeling *negotiation*
onderhavig ★ 't ~e geval *the present case*
onderhevig *liable/subject (to)*
onderhoud • (gesprek) *interview* • (verzorging) *maintenance, upkeep, keep*
onderhoudend *entertaining*
onderhuids *subcutaneous*
onderin *at the bottom*
onderkaak *lower jaw*
onderkant *bottom*
onderkennen • (onderscheiden) *distinguish* • (herkennen) *recognize*
onderkin *double chin*
onderlaag • (onderste laag) *bottom layer*, ‹verf› *undercoat* • (basis) *foundation*
onderlegd ★ goed ~ zijn in *have a good grounding in*
onderlegger ‹onder matras› *underlay*, ‹op tafel› *table/place mat*, ‹vloeipapier› *blotting-paper*
onderlijf *lower part of the body*
onderling ★ ~ beraadslagen *consult one another*

onderlopen *be flooded/swamped*
ondermijnen *undermine*
ondernemen *undertake*
ondernemer *entrepreneur*
onderneming • (karwei) *undertaking*
• (bedrijf) *business, concern*
ondernemingsraad *works/company council*
onderofficier *non-commissioned officer*
onderonsje *tête-à-tête, informal chat*
onderpand *pledge, security*
onderricht *instruction*
onderrichten *instruct*
onderschatten *underrate*
onderscheid • (verschil) *difference* • (inzicht, begrip) *distinction*
onderscheiden I [ov ww] • (verschil maken) *distinguish* • (een onderscheiding verlenen) *decorate* II [wkd ww] *distinguish o.s.*
onderscheiding • (het onderscheiden) *distinction* • (respect) *distinction* • (eerbewijs) *decoration*
onderscheppen *intercept*
onderschrift *caption, legend*
onderschrijven *subscribe to, endorse*
onderspit ★ 't ~ delven *get the worst of it*
onderstaand *below, hereunder*
onderstel *undercarriage*
ondersteunen *support,* <voorstel> *back up*
onderstrepen • (ergens een streep onder zetten) *underline* • (met nadruk zeggen) *stress*
ondertekenaar *signer,* <v. verdrag> *signatory*
ondertekenen *sign*
ondertrouw ★ in ~ gaan *have the banns published; take out a marriage license*
ondertussen • (toch) *yet* • (in de tussentijd) *meanwhile*
onderuit *from below*

ondervangen <bezwaren> *meet,* <gevaar, moeilijkheid> *remove*
onderverhuren *sublet*
ondervinden *experience, meet with*
ondervinding *experience*
ondervoeding *malnutrition*
ondervragen *question, examine*
ondervraging *interrogation, examination*
onderweg *on the way*
onderwereld *underworld*
onderwerp • (waarover gesproken wordt) *subject, topic* • (taalk.) *subject*
onderwerpen • (doen gehoorzamen) *subject to* • (voorleggen) *submit (to)* • (blootstellen aan) *subject to*
onderwijs • (onderricht) *education, instruction* • (onderwijsinstelling) *education*
onderwijzen *teach*
onderwijzer (school)*teacher*
onderzeeboot *submarine*
onderzoek • (bestudering) *inquiry, examination, investigation,* <wetenschappelijk> *research* • (med.) *check-up,* <v. lichaamsfuncties> *test*
onderzoeken *examine, investigate,* <wetenschappelijk> *research, study*
onderzoeker *investigator,* <wetenschap> *researcher, research worker*
ondeugd • (slechte daad) *vice* • (persoon) *scamp* • (ondeugendheid) *mischief*
ondeugdelijk *unsound*
ondeugend *naughty*
onding • (iets onmogelijks) *absurdity* • (prul) *trash*
ondoorgrondelijk *inscrutable*
ondraaglijk *unbearable*
ondubbelzinnig *unequivocal*
onecht • (niet echt) *not genuine, spurious, false, counterfeit* • (buitenechtelijk) *illegitimate (child)*
oneens ★ 't ~ zijn met *disagree with*

oneerbaar *indecent*
oneerlijk *dishonest, unfair*
oneffenheid *roughness*
oneigenlijk * ~ gebruik van iets *improper use of s.th.*
oneindig • (zonder einde) *infinite* • (buitengewoon) *infinite*
onenigheid *discord*
oneven *odd*
onevenredig *disproportionate*
onfeilbaar *infallible, foolproof*
onfris • (niet fris) <bedompt> *stuffy*, <oud> *stale* • (dubieus) *unsavoury, fishy*
ongaarne *unwillingly, reluctantly*
ongeacht I [bnw] *unesteemed* II [vz] *in spite of*
ongebreideld *unbridled*
ongedaan *undone*
ongedeerd *unhurt*
ongedierte *vermin*
ongeduld *impatience*
ongeduldig *impatient*
ongedurig *fidgety, restless*
ongedwongen • (ongekunsteld) *natural, easy* • (vrijwillig) *unconstrained*
ongeëvenaard *unequalled, unrivalled*
ongegrond *unfounded*
ongehoord • (onvoorstelbaar) *unprecedented, unheard-of* • (buitengewoon) *strange* • (niet gehoord) *unheard*
ongehoorzaamheid *disobedience*
ongekend *unprecedented*
ongekunsteld *unaffected, artless*
ongelegen *inconvenient*
ongeletterd • (analfabeet) *illiterate* • (zonder onderricht) *uneducated*, <lit.> *unlettered*
ongelijk *wrong* * ~ hebben *be (in the) wrong* * ik geef je geen ~ *I can't blame you*
ongelofelijk *incredible*
ongeloof *disbelief*, <rel.> *unbelief*

ongeloofwaardig *incredible, implausible*
ongelovig • (iets niet gelovend) *incredulous* • (niet gelovig) <rel.> *unbelieving*
ongeluk • (gemoedstoestand) *unhappiness* • (tegenspoed) *misfortune* • (ongeval) *accident*
ongelukkig • (niet gelukkig) *unhappy* • (rampspoedig) *unfortunate*, <door pech> *unlucky* • (gehandicapt) *handicapped*
ongemak • (hinder) *discomfort, inconvenience* • (euvel) *trouble*
ongemakkelijk • (ongerieflijk) *uneasy, uncomfortable* • (ongelegen) *awkward, inconvenient* • (moeilijk in de omgang) *difficult*
ongemanierd *ill-mannered*
ongemeen • (ongewoon) *uncommon* • (buitengewoon) *extraordinary*
ongemerkt I [bnw] • (zonder merkteken) *unmarked* • (niet bemerkt) *unnoticed* II [bijw] *imperceptibly*
ongemoeid *undisturbed*
ongenaakbaar *unapproachable*
ongenade *disgrace*
ongenadig *merciless*
ongeneeslijk *incurable*
ongenietbaar <v. eten, drinken> *indigestible*, <v. persoon> *disagreeable*
ongenoegen *displeasure*
ongeoorloofd *unlawful, illicit*
ongepast • (onfatsoenlijk) *improper, unbecoming* • (misplaatst) *inappropriate*
ongerechtigheid • (onrechtvaardigheid) *iniquity* • (fout) *flaw*
ongeregeld <leven> *disorderly*, <studie> *haphazard*, <v. tijd> *irregular*
ongerept *intact*, <natuur, schoonheid> *unspoilt*
ongerief *inconvenience*

ongerijmd *absurd*
ongerust *uneasy, anxious*
ongeschonden *undamaged*
ongeschoold *untrained, unskilled*
ongesteld ⋆ zij is ~ *she is having her period*
ongesteldheid • (menstrueren) *menstrual period* • (onwel zijn) *indisposition*
ongestraft *unpunished*
ongeval *accident*
ongeveer *about, roughly*
ongewild *unintentional, not intended*
ongezond *unhealthy, unwholesome*
ongezouten • (zonder zout) *unsalted* • (openhartig) *straight*
onguur *unsavoury, sinister*
onhandelbaar *unmanageable*
onhandig *clumsy, awkward*
onhebbelijk *rude, offensive*
onheil *disaster, calamity*
onheilspellend *ominous*
onherbergzaam *inhospitable*
onherroepelijk *irrevocable*
onherstelbaar *irreparable, irretrievable*
onheus *discourteous, unkind, ungracious*
onkies *indelicate*
onklaar *out of order*
onkosten *charges, expenses*
onkreukbaar • (van stof) *uncrushable* • (integer) *unimpeachable*
onkruid *weeds*
onkunde *ignorance*
onkundig *ignorant*
onlangs *recently, the other day*
onleesbaar *illegible*
onmacht *impotence*
onmatig *immoderate*
onmens *brute*
onmenselijk *inhuman*
onmiddellijk I [bnw] • (meteen) *immediate* II [bijw] *immediately, at once, straight away*

onmin *discord*
onmisbaar *indispensable*
onmiskenbaar *unmistakable*
onmogelijk I [bnw] • (niet uitvoerbaar) *impossible* • (onverdraaglijk) *impossible* • (potsierlijk) *impossible, preposterous* II [bijw] *impossibly, not possibly*
onmogelijkheid *impossibility*
onmondig • (minderjarig) *under age* • (niet mondig) ⋆ ~ houden *keep in a state of tutelage*
onnadenkend *thoughtless*
onnatuurlijk • (niet natuurlijk) *unnatural* • (gekunsteld) *affected*
onnozel • (dom) *stupid, silly* • (argeloos) *innocent* • (lichtgelovig) *gullible* • (onervaren) *green*
onomstotelijk *incontrovertible*
onomwonden *plain*
onontbeerlijk *indispensable*
onontkoombaar *inevitable*
onooglijk *unsightly*
onophoudelijk *unceasing*
onoverkomelijk *insuperable*
onpartijdig *impartial*
onpasselijk *sick*
onraad *danger*
onrecht *wrong, injustice*
onrechtmatig *unlawful, illegal, wrongful*
onrechtvaardig *unjust*
onregelmatig *irregular*
onregelmatigheid *irregularity*
onroerend ⋆ ~e goederen *real estate; immovables*
onrust • (beroering) *unrest, agitation* • (rusteloosheid) *restlessness*
onrustbarend *alarming*
onrustig *restless,* <v. slaap> *fitful, uneasy*
onruststoker *trouble-stirrer*
ons I [het] *100 grammes, hectogram,* <Engels ons> *ounce* II [pers vnw] *us* III [bez vnw] *our*

onsamenhangend *incoherent*
onschatbaar *invaluable*
onschendbaar • (niet te schenden) *inviolable* • (geen verantwoording hoeven af te leggen) *immune*
onsmakelijk *unsavoury, distasteful*
onsterfelijk *immortal*
onstuimig ‹v. persoon› *impetuous,* ‹v. zee› *turbulent*
ontbieden *summon*
ontbijt *breakfast*
ontbijten *have breakfast*
ontbinden *dissolve*
ontbinding • (het opheffen) *dissolution* • (rotting) *decomposition*
ontboezeming *outpouring, unburdening*
ontbranden *take fire, ignite*
ontbreken *be absent, be missing*
ontcijferen *decipher*
ontdaan *dismayed, upset*
ontdekken *discover,* ‹v. fout› *detect*
ontdoen • (vrijmaken) *strip* • (uit de weg ruimen) *dispose of, get rid of*
ontdooien ‹ingevroren voedsel› *defrost,* ‹ook fig.› *thaw*
ontegenzeglijk *unquestionable*
onteigenen *expropriate*
ontelbaar *innumerable, countless*
ontembaar *indomitable*
onteren • (van eer beroven) *dishonour* • (verkrachten) *rape, violate* • (schenden) *violate*
onterven *disinherit*
ontfermen *take care of*
ontfutselen ∗ iem. iets ~ *filch/pilfer s.th. from s.o.*
ontgaan *escape*
ontgelden ∗ hij moest het ~ *he had to pay for it*
ontginnen ‹fig.› *explore,* ‹v. bos› *clear,* ‹v. land› *reclaim,* ‹v. mijn› *exploit*
ontglippen *slip from one's hands*
ontgoochelen *disillusion*
onthaal *reception*

onthalen • (ontvangen) *welcome* • (vergasten op) *treat (to), regale (with),* ‹inf.› *do s.o. proud*
ontharen *remove hair, depilate*
ontheffen • (vrijstellen) *release* • (ontslaan) *discharge, dismiss*
onthoofden *behead*
onthouden I [ov ww] • (niet vergeten) *remember* • (achterhouden) *deny* II [wkd ww] *abstain (from)*
onthouding *abstinence,* ‹v. stemming› *abstention,* ‹vnl. v. geslachtsverkeer› *continence*
onthullen • (tonen) *unveil* • (bekendmaken) *reveal*
onthulling • (wat bekendgemaakt wordt) *revelation* • (het tonen) *unveiling* • (bekendmaking) *revelation*
ontijdig *untimely, premature*
ontkennen *deny*
ontkenning • (het ontkennen) *denial,* ‹form.› *negation* • (taalk.) *negation*
ontketenen ‹v. aanval› *launch,* ‹v. oorlog, reactie› *spark off*
ontkiemen *germinate, sprout*
ontknoping *dénouement, outcome*
ontkomen *escape, elude*
ontkoppelen *uncouple,* ‹motor› *declutch*
ontkurken *uncork*
ontladen I [ov ww] *unload* II [wkd ww] ‹emoties› *release*
ontlasten I [ov ww] • (van een last ontdoen) *unburden, relieve* II [wkd ww] *defecate, empty one's bowels*
ontlasting • (het ontlasten) *relief, discharge* • (stoelgang) *motion* • (uitwerpselen) *stools, faeces*
ontleden *analyse,* ‹dier, lijk, plant› *dissect*
ontlenen • (overnemen uit) *borrow/take from* • (te danken hebben aan) *derive from*

ontlokken *elicit/draw (from)*
ontlopen *avoid*
ontluiken • (uit de knop komen) *open*
• (zich ontwikkelen) *bud*
ontmantelen *dismantle*
ontmaskeren ‹fig.› *expose,* ‹ook fig.›
unmask
ontmoedigen *discourage*
ontmoeten • (tegenkomen) *meet,*
‹per toeval› *come across, run into*
ontmoeting *meeting, encounter*
ontnemen *take (away) from, deprive of*
ontnuchteren *sober up,* ‹fig.›
disenchant
ontoereikend *inadequate*
ontploffen *explode*
ontploffing *explosion, detonation*
ontplooien *unfold,* ‹v. zaak› *expand*
• (tentoonspreiden) *display*
ontreddering ‹v. persoon›
desperation, ‹v. situatie› *upheaval,*
disorder
ontroeren *move, touch*
ontroering *emotion*
ontroostbaar *inconsolable*
ontrouw • (niet loyaal) *disloyal*
• (overspelig) *unfaithful*
ontruimen *evacuate, clear*
ontrukken *snatch/wrest from*
ontschepen ‹goederen› *discharge,*
‹passagiers› *disembark*
ontschieten • (per ongeluk zeggen)
escape, slip out • (vergeten) ⋆ *het is*
mij ontschoten it slipped my memory
ontsieren *mar, disfigure*
ontslaan • (ontslag geven) *dismiss,*
‹inf.› *fire* • (laten vertrekken) ‹uit
gevangenis› *release,* ‹uit ziekenhuis›
discharge
ontslag *discharge*
ontsluieren *unveil, reveal*
ontsluiten • (openen) *open, unlock*
• (blootleggen) *open up*
• (toegankelijk maken) *open*
ontsmetten *disinfect*

ontsnappen *escape, get away*
ontspannen *relax*
ontspanning *relaxation*
ontsporen *be derailed,* ‹fig.› *go off the*
rails
ontspruiten • (uitspruiten) *sprout*
• (afkomstig zijn) ⋆ ~ *uit arise from*
ontstaan I [het] *origin* II [on ww] *arise*
ontsteken I [ov ww] • (aansteken)
light, ‹techn.› *ignite* II [on ww]
• (med.) *become inflamed*
ontsteking • (het ontsteken) ‹techn.›
ignition • (med.) *inflammation*
ontsteltenis *alarm, dismay*
ontucht *vice,* ‹bijbel› *fornication*
ontvallen • (verliezen) ⋆ *zijn moeder*
is hem ~ *he has lost his mother* • (per
ongeluk zeggen) ⋆ *het ontviel me it*
just slipped out
ontvangen *receive*
ontvanger • (iem. die iets ontvangt)
receiver • (inner van belasting) *tax*
collector • (ontvangtoestel) *receiver*
ontvangst • (het ontvangen) *receipt*
• (radio-/tv-ontvangst) *reception*
• (onthaal) *reception, welcome*
ontvankelijk ⋆ ~ *voor susceptible to;*
open to
ontvlambaar *inflammable*
ontvlammen *inflame*
ontvluchten *escape*
ontvoerder *kidnapper*
ontvoeren *carry off, kidnap*
ontvouwen *unfold*
ontvreemden *steal*
ontwaken • (wakker worden) *awake,*
wake up • (tot leven komen) *arouse*
ontwapenen *disarm*
ontwarren *disentangle, straighten out*
ontwenningskuur *cure for addiction*
ontwerp *design*
ontwerpen *design*
ontwijken *evade, avoid*
ontwikkelen *develop*
ontwikkeling • (groei) *development*

• (het doen ontstaan) *generation*
• (het ontwikkeld zijn) *education*
• (gang van zaken) *development*
ontwikkelingshulp *development aid*
ontworstelen *wrest from*
ontwrichten • (v. ledematen)
dislocate • (ontregelen) *unsettle*
ontzag *respect, awe*
ontzaglijk • (ontzagwekkend)
awesome • (zeer groot) *enormous*
ontzagwekkend *awe-inspiring*
ontzeggen I [ov ww] • (weigeren)
deny • (iets niet toekennen) ∗ *gevoel
voor humor kan men hem niet ~ it
can't be denied that he has a sense of
humour* II [wkd ww] ∗ *zich elk
genoegen ~ deny o.s. all pleasure*
ontzenuwen *refute*
ontzet I [het] *relief* II [bnw]
• (ontsteld) *appalled, aghast*
• (ontwricht) *twisted, buckled*
ontzetten • (bevrijden) <persoon>
rescue, <stad> *relieve* • (verbijsteren)
appal, horrify • (ontwrichten) *twist,
buckle*
ontzettend *dreadful, awful*
ontzetting • (bevrijding) <persoon>
rescue, <stad> *relief* • (ontslag uit
ambt) *removal* • (verbijstering)
dismay
ontzien *spare*
onuitputtelijk *inexhaustible*
onuitsprekelijk *unspeakable,
inexpressible*
onuitstaanbaar *insufferable*
onvast • (niet stevig) *unsteady*
• (onbestendig) *unsettled*
onveranderlijk I [bnw] *unchanging*
II [bijw] *invariably*
onverantwoord • (niet te
verantwoorden) *unwarranted,
irresponsible* • (niet gespecificeerd)
unaccounted for
onverbeterlijk *incorrigible*
onverbiddelijk • (onvermurwbaar)

inexorable • (onvermijdelijk)
unrelenting
onverbloemd *plain*
onverdeeld *undivided*
onverdraaglijk *unbearable,
intolerable*
onverdraagzaam *intolerant*
onverenigbaar *incompatible*
onvergankelijk • (niet vergaand)
imperishable • (blijvend) *everlasting*
onvergeeflijk *unforgivable,
unpardonable*
onverhoeds *unexpected*
onverholen I [bnw] *unconcealed*
II [bijw] *candidly, openly*
onverhoopt I [bnw] *unexpected*
II [bijw] *in the unlikely event that*
onverkort • (niet ingekort)
unabridged • (ongewijzigd)
uncurtailed
onverkwikkelijk *distasteful,
unpalatable,* <onderwerp> *unsavoury*
onvermijdelijk *inevitable*
onverminderd *undimished*
onvermoeibaar *indefatigable*
onvermogen • (onmacht) *impotence,
incapacity, inability* • (v. schuldenaar)
insolvency
onvermurwbaar *inexorable*
onversaagd *undaunted*
onverschillig *careless* • (~ **voor**)
indifferent to
onversneden <v. vaste stoffen>
unadulterated, <v. vloeistof> *undiluted*
onverstandig *unwise*
onverstoorbaar *imperturbable*
onvertogen *improper*
onvervaard *undaunted, fearless*
onvervalst • (door en door)
unmitigated • (niet vervalst)
unadulterated, unalloyed
onverwacht *unexpected*
onverzadigd • (niet tevreden) *not
satiated, unsatisfied* • (chem.)
unsaturated

onverzettelijk *inflexible, immovable*
onvindbaar *untraceable, not to be found*
onvoldaan • (niet betaald) *unpaid,* ‹schulden› *outstanding* • (niet tevreden) *unsatisfied*
onvolkomen *imperfect*
onvolprezen *one and only, unsurpassed, unparalleled*
onvoltooid *unfinished*
onvoorwaardelijk *unconditional*
onvoorzien *unforeseen*
onvruchtbaar *infertile, barren*
onwaar *untrue, false*
onwaardig • (iets niet waard zijnd) *unworthy* • (verachtelijk) *undignified*
onwaarheid • (het onwaar zijn) *untruthfulness* • (leugen) *lie, untruth*
onweer *thunderstorm*
onweerlegbaar *irrefutable, unanswerable*
onweersbui *thundery rain*
onweerstaanbaar *irresistible*
onwel *unwell*
onwennig *unaccustomed*
onweren *thunder*
onwetend • (onbewust) *unknowing* • (iets niet wetend) *ignorant*
onwetendheid *ignorance*
onwettig • (v. kind) *illegitimate* • (tegen de wet) *illegal, unlawful*
onwijs I [bnw] *unwise, foolish* II [bijw] *extremely*
onwil *unwillingness*
onwillekeurig *involuntary*
onwillig *unwilling*
onwrikbaar • (onomstotelijk) *irrefutable* • (rotsvast) *immovable, unshakable*
onzacht *rough, rude*
onzedelijk • (onkuis) *indecent, obscene* • (immoreel) *immoral*
onzeker • (niet vaststaand) *uncertain* • (niet zelfverzekerd) *insecure*
onzekerheid • (twijfel) *uncertainty*

• (onvastheid) *unsteadiness*
• (onzekere zaak) *uncertainty, insecurity*
onzent ⋆ te ~ *at our house* ⋆ om ~ wil *for our sake*
onzerzijds *on our part*
onzichtbaar *invisible*
onzijdig *neutral,* ‹taalk.› *neuter*
onzin *nonsense*
onzinnig *absurd*
onzuiver *impure,* ‹v. toon› *false, out of tune*
oog *eye*
oogappel *apple of one's eye*
oogarts *eye-specialist, ophthalmic surgeon*
ooghoek *corner of the eye*
oogklep *blinker*
ooglid *eyelid*
oogluikend ⋆ ~ toelaten *ignore*
oogopslag *look, glance*
oogpunt *angle, point of view*
oogst • (het oogsten) *harvesting* • (het geoogste) *harvest, crop(s)*
oogsten *reap, harvest*
oogverblindend *dazzling*
ooievaar *stork*
ooit *ever, at any time*
ook • (evenzo) *also, as well, too* • (zelfs) *even* • (immers) *thus, therefore* • (misschien) *perhaps, by any chance* • (als versterking) *again, whatever*
oom *uncle*
oor • (gehoororgaan) *ear* • (oorschelp) *ear* • (handvat) *handle*
oorbel *earring*
oord • (plaats) *region, place* • (verblijf) *residence*
oordeel • (vonnis) *judgment, sentence* • (mening) *judgment, opinion*
oordelen I [ov ww] • (menen) *deem, judge* II [on ww] • (concluderen) *judge* • (rechtspreken) *judge, pass judgement*
oorkonde *document, charter*

oorlog *war*
oorlogsinvalide *war invalid*
oorlogsverklaring *declaration of war*
oorsprong *origin, source*
oorspronkelijk • (origineel)
innovative • (v.d. oorsprong) *original*
oorverdovend *deafening*
oorzaak *cause, origin*
oorzakelijk *causal*
oost *east* ★ de Oost *the East*
Oost-Duits *East German*
Oost-Duitsland *East Germany,*
German Democratic Republic
oosten • (windstreek) *east* ★ ten ~ van
(to the) east of • (gebied) ★ 't ~ *the*
East; the Orient ★ 't Midden-Oosten
the Middle East
Oostenrijk *Austria*
oostenwind *east wind*
oosterling *Oriental*
oosters *eastern, oriental*
ootmoedig *humble*
op I [bijw] • (uit bed) *up (and about)*
• (uitgeput) *exhausted* • (verbruikt)
★ het water is op *we've run out of*
water • (omhoog) ★ op en neer *up and*
down ★ trap op, trap af *up and down*
the stairs II [vz] • (bovenop) *on* • (in)
in • (tijdens) *on* • (verwijderd van)
★ op drie km afstand *at three*
kilometers' distance • (uitgezonderd)
★ op twee na *all but two* • (met) ★ op
gas koken *cook with gas* ★ op
waterstof lopen *run on hydrogen*
opa *grandpa, grandad*
opaal *opal*
opbellen *call/phone/ring up, give (s.o.)*
a ring
opbergen *put away,* <documenten>
file, <in pakhuis> *store (away)*
opbeuren *lift up,* <fig.> *cheer (up)*
opbiechten *confess, own up*
opbieden ★ ~ tegen *outbid; bid*
against
opblaasbaar *inflatable*

opblijven *stay up*
opbloei *flourishing, revival*
opbloeien • (gaan bloeien) *bloom*
• (beter gaan bloeien) *flourish, revive*
opbod • (hoger bod) *higher bid* • (het
opbieden) ★ bij ~ verkopen *sell by*
auction
opborrelen *bubble up*
opbouw • (het gebouwde)
superstructure • (structuur) *structure*
• (totstandkoming) *building,*
construction
opbouwen • (bouwen) *build up,*
construct • (opzetten) *set/build up*
opbreken *strike camp, break up*
opbrengen • (opleveren) *bring in,*
yield • (betalen) *pay*
opbrengst <v. oogst, belasting> *yield,*
<v. productie> *output,* <v. winst>
proceeds, revenue
opdagen *turn up*
opdat *so that, in order that*
opdienen *serve (up)*
opdirken *dress up*
opdissen *serve/dish up*
opdoeken I [ov ww] *do away with,*
<zaak> *shut up shop* II [on ww]
• (weggaan) *clear out*
opdoemen *loom (up)*
opdoen • (opzetten) *put on*
• (aanbrengen) *put on* • (verkrijgen)
acquire, <v. ervaring> *gain* • (oplopen)
catch
opdonderen ★ donder op! *get lost!*
opdraaien I [ov ww] • (opwinden)
wind up II [on ww] • (~ voor)
★ ergens voor ~ *suffer for it*
opdracht • (levenstaak) *mission*
• (opdracht in boek) *dedication*
• (bevel) *charge, instruction*
opdrachtgever <jur.> *principal,* <v.
aannemer> *client, customer*
opdragen • (opdracht geven) *charge,*
instruct • (verslijten) *wear out*
• (~ aan) *dedicate to*

opdreunen *rattle off*
opdrijven • (opdrijven) *drive* • (laten stijgen) *force up*
opdringen I [ov ww] * iem. iets ~ *force s.th. on s.o.* II [on ww] *press forward* III [wkd ww] • (~ **aan**) *inflict o.s. on*
opdringerig *obtrusive, intrusive*
opdrinken *empty, drink (up), finish*
opdrogen *dry up*
opdruk *print*
opdrukken • (van opdruk voorzien) *impress on* • (omhoogdrukken) *press up* • (sport) *do press/push-ups*
opduiken • (boven water komen) *surface, emerge* • (verschijnen) *turn up*
opeen *together*, ‹boven op elkaar› *one on top of another*
opeenhoping • (het opeenhopen) ‹v. verkeer› *congestion*, ‹v. werk› *accumulation* • (hoeveelheid) ‹v. mensen› *crowd, mass*, ‹v. sneeuw› *snowdrift*
opeenvolging *succession*
opeisen *claim, demand*
open • (niet dicht) *open*, ‹v. kraan› *on* • (nog niet bezet) *vacant* • (onbedekt) *open*
openbaar *public*
openbaarheid *publicity*
openbaren *reveal, disclose*
openbaring • ('t openbaar maken) *disclosure* • (rel.) *revelation*
openbreken *break/force open*
openen *open (up)*, ‹kraan› *turn on*
opener *opener*
opengaan *open*
openhartig *outspoken, frank*
openheid *openness, frankness*
opening • (het openen) *opening* • (begin) *beginning* • (gat) *opening*
openleggen *lay open, disclose*
openlijk *open, public*
openmaken ‹v. deur› *open, unlock*, ‹v. pakje› *undo*

openspringen *burst (open)*, ‹v. huid/lippen› *chap*
openstaan *be open* • (~ **voor**) *be open to*
openstellen *open*
openvallen • (opengaan) *fall open* • (vacant komen) *fall vacant*
opera *opera*
operatie *operation*
operatief *operative*
operatiekamer (operating) *theatre*
operationeel *operational*
opereren I [ov ww] *operate* II [on ww] *work*
operette *operetta, musical comedy*
opeten *eat (up), finish*
opfleuren *brighten (up), cheer up*
opfokken • (grootbrengen) *breed, rear* • (op stang jagen) *work up*
opfrissen I [ov ww] *refresh*, ‹fig.› *brush up* II [on ww] *freshen (up)*
opgaan • (omhooggaan) *go up*, ‹v. zon› *rise* • (juist zijn) *hold good* • (in elkaar overgaan) *merge into* • (verdiept zijn in) *be absorbed in* • (opgaan voor examen) *sit for* • (verbruikt worden) *be finished* • (wisk.) *terminate*
opgang • (opkomst) *success*, ‹fig.› *rise* • (trap) *staircase*
opgave *task*, ‹bij examen› *paper*
opgeblazen • (opgezwollen) *puffy, swollen* • (verwaand) *puffed up, conceited*
opgeruimd *cheerful*
opgeschoten *lanky, gangling*
opgetogen *elated, delighted*
opgeven • (zich, iets gewonnen geven) *abandon* • (overgeven) *spit, bring up* • (mededelen) *give, state*, ‹v. inkomen› *declare* • (opdragen) ‹v. raadsel› *ask*, ‹v. taak› *set* • (aanmelden) *enter*
opgewassen * hij is er niet tegen ~ *het can't cope with it*

opgewonden *excited*
opgooien *toss (up)*
opgraven *dig up*
opgraving *excavation*
opgroeien *grow up*
ophaalbrug *drawbridge*
ophalen • (omhooghalen) *draw up, pull up,* ‹v. anker› *weigh,* ‹v. gordijn› *raise,* ‹v. neus› *sniff* • (komen halen) *collect* • (in herinnering roepen) ★ oude herinneringen ~ *revive old memories*
ophanden *at hand*
ophangen I [ov ww] • (bevestigen) *hang (up)* • (ter dood brengen) *hang* II [on ww] • (telefoongesprek beëindigen) *hang up, ring off*
ophebben • (dragen) *wear, have on* • (genuttigd hebben) ‹v. drank› *have drunk,* ‹v. eten› *have eaten* • (~ met) ★ veel ~ met iem. *be fond of s.o.* ★ met zichzelf ~ *be complacent*
ophef *fuss, song and dance*
opheffen • (optillen) *lift (up), raise* • (beëindigen) *discontinue,* ‹v. partij, zaak› *liquidate*
opheffing *cancellation, lifting, raising,* ‹dienst, zaak› *removal,* ‹praktijken, verbod› *abolition*
ophelderen I [ov ww] *clear up, explain, clarify* II [on ww] *clear (up),* ‹v. gelaat, weer› *brighten*
opheldering • (uitleg) *explanation* • (opklaring) *brightening*
ophemelen *extol*
ophitsen • (opruien) *incite, stir up* • (aanmoedigen) *set on*
ophoepelen *get lost*
ophogen *raise*
ophouden I [ov ww] • (tegenhouden) *hold up* • (niet afzetten) *keep on* • (omhooghouden) *hold up* • (vasthouden aan) *uphold* II [on ww] • (stoppen) *stop, come to an end* III [wkd ww] • (ergens zijn) *stay,*

‹rondhangen› *hang around* • (~ met) *deal in lies*
opinie *opinion*
opium *opium*
opjagen • (opdrijven) ‹v. persoon› *hunt,* ‹v. wild› *put up* • (opjutten) *rush* • (omhoog doen gaan) *blow up,* ‹stof, enz.› *raise*
opkijken • (omhoogkijken) *look up (at)* • (verrast worden) *surprise*
opkikkeren *buck/cheer up*
opklapbed *foldaway bed*
opklaren *clear/brighten up*
opklaring *bright interval/period*
opklimmen • (omhoogklimmen) *climb (up), mount* • (in rang stijgen) *rise*
opknappen I [ov ww] • (netjes maken) *tidy up, smarten up* • (verrichten) *fix* II [on ww] *improve*
opkomen • (ontstaan) ‹v. onweer› *come on,* ‹v. wind› *rise* • (omhoogkomen) *rise, come up* • (op toneel komen) *come on (stage)* • (in gedachten komen) *occur,* ‹vraag› *arise, crop up* • (~ voor) *stand up for*
opkomst • (het opkomen) *rise* • (komst na oproep) *attendance*
opkopen *buy up*
opkoper *wholesale buyer,* ‹v. oude rommel› *junk dealer*
opkrabbelen *scramble to one's feet,* ‹fig.› *recover, pick up*
opkroppen *bottle up*
oplaaien *flare/blaze up*
opladen *charge*
oplappen *patch up*
oplaten *fly*
opleggen *impose*
oplegger *trailer*
opleiden *train, educate, school*
opleiding *education, training*
opletten *pay attention, attend (to)*
oplettend *attentive*
opleven *revive*

opleveren • (voortbrengen) *furnish, produce* • (opbrengen) *yield, bring in* • (werk afleveren) *deliver*

opleving *revival,* <econ.> *recovery*

oplichten I [ov ww] • (optillen) *lift (up), raise* • (afhandig maken) *swindle* II [on ww] *lighten*

oplichter *fraud, swindler, con (wo)man/artist*

oplopen I [ov ww] <v. schade> *sustain,* <v. straf> *incur,* <v. verkoudheid> *catch,* <v. ziekte> *contract* II [on ww] • (naar boven lopen) *go/walk up,* <trap> *mount* • (naar boven gaan) *rise,* <schuin> *slope up* • (toenemen) *rise,* <prijzen> *increase,* <v. spanning> *mount*

oplosbaar *soluble,* <fig.> *solvable*

oplosmiddel *solvent*

oplossen I [ov ww] • (de uitkomst vinden) *solve* • (chem.) *dissolve* II [on ww] *dissolve*

oplossing *solution*

opluchten *relieve*

opluchting *relief*

opluisteren *grace, add lustre to*

opmaak • (druk) *layout* • (make-up) *make-up*

opmaken • (verbruiken) *consume,* <v. geld> *spend,* <v. voedsel> *eat,* <v. voorraad> *use up* • (in orde maken) <v. bed> *make,* <v. haar> *dress,* <v. schotel> *garnish* • (opstellen) <v. rekening> *make out* • (concluderen) *gather*

opmerkelijk *striking*

opmerken • (bemerken) *notice* • (opmerking maken) *observe, remark*

opmerking *observation, remark, comment*

opname • (registratie) *recording* • (het opnemen in ziekenhuis) *admission*

opnemen I [ov ww] • (laten doordringen) *take in* • (meten) *take* • (oppakken) *lift (up),* <fig.> *take up* • (vastleggen) <v. film> *shoot,* <v.

geluid> *record* • (van tegoed halen) *take up, withdraw* • (opbreken) *take up* • (beantwoorden) *answer* • (een plaats geven) <v. artikel> *insert,* <v. patiënt> *admit* • (absorberen) *absorb* • (in ogenschouw nemen) *size up, survey* • (noteren) *take down* • (opvatten) *take* II [on ww] *catch on*

opnieuw *again, once more*

opnoemen *name, mention*

opofferen *sacrifice*

opoffering *sacrifice*

oponthoud • (verblijf) *stay*

oppakken • (bijeenpakken) *pack up* • (arresteren) *run in*

oppas *baby-sitter*

oppassen I [ov ww] • (iets passen) *try on* • (verzorgen) *take care of, nurse* II [on ww] • (voorzichtig zijn) *be careful, look out* • (zich goed gedragen) *behave well* • (babysitten) *babysit*

oppasser *keeper, caretaker*

opperbevel *supreme command*

opperbevelhebber *commander-in-chief*

opperen *propose, suggest*

opperhoofd *chief(tain)*

oppermachtig *supreme*

oppervlak *surface*

oppervlakkig *superficial*

oppervlakte • (gebied) *area* • (maat) *surface area* • (bovenkant) *surface*

oppoetsen *polish*

opponent *opponent*

opportunisme *opportunism*

oppositie *opposition*

oprapen *pick up*

oprecht *sincere*

oprichten • (stichten) *establish* • (overeind zetten) *erect, set up (right), raise (up)*

oprichter *founder*

oprichting *foundation,* <v. zaak> *establishment*

oprijden ‹met auto› *drive up*, ‹met fiets, paard› *ride up*

oprijlaan *drive, sweep*

oprijzen *rise*

oprisping *belch*

oprit • (oprijlaan) *drive* • (invoegstrook) *access*

oproep ‹om hulp› *call, appeal*, ‹voor betrekking› *notice*

oproepen ‹v. geesten› *conjure up*, ‹v. herinnering› *evoke, recall*

oproer *rebellion, revolt*

oprollen • (in elkaar rollen) *roll up* • (arresteren) *round up*

opruien *incite, stir up*

opruimen *clear (away)*

opruiming • (schoonmaak) *clearing away/up* • (uitverkoop) *clearance (sale)*

oprukken *advance (on)*

opscharrelen *pick up, hunt out*

opschepen ⋆ iem. met iets ~ *saddle s.o. with s.th.*

opscheppen I [ov ww] • (eten opscheppen) *ladle out, dish out* II [on ww] • (pochen) *show off, brag*

opschepper *show off*

opschepperij *boasting*

opschieten • (zich haasten) *hurry up* • (~ met) *get on/along*

opschorten ‹v. beslissing› *postpone*, ‹v. vergadering› *adjourn*

opschrift *inscription*

opschrijven *note/write down*

opschrikken I [ov ww] *startle* II [on ww] *start*

opschroeven • (iets ergens op schroeven) *screw up* • (opdrijven) *drive up* • (overdrijven) *force up, inflate*

opschudding *commotion, stir*

opschuiven I [ov ww] • (opzij schuiven) *push up, shift* • (uitstellen) *put off* II [on ww] *move up/over*

opslaan • (bergen) ‹in pakhuis› *store*, ‹v. voedsel› *lay in* • (opzetten) ‹kamp›

pitch, ‹tent› *put up* • (omhoogdoen) *raise*

opslag • (verhoging) *rise* • (berging) *storage*

opsluiten *lock/shut up*

opsluiting *confinement*

opsnuiven *inhale, sniff*

opsommen *sum up, enumerate*

opsomming *enumeration, summing up*

opsparen *save up*

opsporen *trace, track (down)*, ‹v. vermisten› *locate*

opsporing *tracing*

opspraak *scandal*

opstaan *get up, rise*

opstand • (verzet) *rising, rebellion, revolt* • (geboomte) *stand*

opstandeling *rebel, insurgent*

opstandig *rebellious*

opstanding *resurrection*

opstapelen I [ov ww] *pile up, stack* II [wkd ww] *accumulate*

opstappen • (op iets stappen) ‹op fiets› *get on* • (weggaan) *go away, push off* • (ontslag nemen) *resign*

opsteken • (omhoogdoen) ‹haar› *pin up*, ‹v. hand› *put up* • (aansteken) *light (up)* • (te weten komen) *learn, pick up*

opstel *essay, paper*

opstellen I [ov ww] • (ontwerpen) *draw up, draft* II [wkd ww] *line up*, ‹fig.› *adopt an attitude*

opstelling • (plaatsing) *placing* • (houding) *attitude* • (het ontwerpen) *drafting* • (sport) *line-up* • (mil.) *deployment, formation*

opstijgen • (omhooggaan) *rise*, ‹v. vliegtuig› *take off* • (paard bestijgen) *mount*

opstoken • (harder stoken) *stir/poke (up)* • (geheel verbranden) *burn (up)* • (ophitsen) *incite*

opstootje *disturbance*

opstopping *traffic jam, congestion*
opstrijken • (gladstrijken) *iron*
 • (ontvangen) *rake in*
opstropen *tuck up*
opsturen *send, post*
optekenen *record, note down*
optellen *add (up)*
optelling *addition*
optie *option*
optillen *lift up*
optimisme *optimism*
optimist *optimist*
optimistisch *optimistic*
optisch *optical*
optocht *procession,* <gesch.> *pageant*
optornen * ~ tegen *cope/battle with*
optreden I [het] • (uitvoering)
 appearance • (handelwijze)
 <houding> *attitude,* <v. politie> *action*
 II [on ww] • (op toneel verschijnen)
 enter, go on • (zich voordoen) *appear*
 • (handelen) *act*
optrekken I [ov ww]
 • (omhoogtrekken) *pull up, raise,* <v.
 schouders> *shrug* • (verhogen) *raise*
 II [on ww] • (wegtrekken) *lift*
 • (accelereren) *accelerate, pick up speed*
 • (~ met) *hang around with*
optuigen • (van tuig voorzien) <v.
 paard> *harness,* <v. schip> *rig*
 • (versieren) *decorate*
opvallen *attract attention, strike*
opvallend *striking, marked*
opvangen • (vangen) *catch, receive*
 • (horen) *pick up,* <v. gesprek> *overhear*
opvatten • (opnemen) *take up* • (gaan
 koesteren) *conceive* • (beschouwen)
 understand, conceive
opvatting • (idee) *conception*
 • (mening) *opinion, notion, idea*
opvissen *fish up*
opvliegen • (driftig uitvallen) *flare up*
 • (omhoogvliegen) *fly up*
opvoeden *educate, bring up, raise*
opvoeding • (het opvoeden)

upbringing • (vorming) *education*
opvoedkundig *pedagogic(al)*
opvoeren • (verhogen) <v. productie>
 increase, step up • (motorvermogen
 vergroten) *tune up* • (ten tonele
 voeren) *perform*
opvoering *performance*
opvolgen I [ov ww] <v. advies> *follow,*
 <v. bevel> *obey* II [on ww] *succeed*
opvolger *successor*
opvouwbaar *folding,* <v. bed>
 collapsible
opvouwen *fold up*
opvragen *claim, ask for, reclaim,*
 <gegevens> *retrieve,* <v. geld v.
 rekening> *withdraw,* <v. hypotheek>
 recall
opvreten I [ov ww] *devour* II [wkd ww]
 • (~ van) *be consumed with*
opvrolijken *cheer (up), enliven*
opvullen *fill up*
opwaarts *upward(s)*
opwachten *wait for,* <met vijandige
 bedoeling> *waylay*
opwachting * zijn ~ maken bij *pay
 one's respect to*
opwarmen I [ov ww] • (opnieuw
 verwarmen) *heat/warm up*
 • (enthousiast maken) *inspire* II [on
 ww] *warm up*
opwegen *be equal to*
opwekken *arouse,* <gevoelens> *evoke,*
 <v. eetlust> *stimulate*
opwellen *well up*
opwelling *impulse,* <v. woede> *surge,
 fit*
opwerken • (naar boven brengen)
 work up • (bewerken) *touch up*
opwerpen I [ov ww] • (bouwen) *erect*
 • (opgooien) *throw up* • (opperen)
 raise II [wkd ww] * zich ~ als *set o.s.
 up as*
opwinden • (oprollen) *wind*
 • (spannen) *wind (up)* • (geestdriftig
 maken) *excite*

opwinding *excitement*

opzeggen • (voordragen) <v. gedicht> *recite*, <v. les> *read* • (doen ophouden) *terminate*, <v. betrekking> *resign*

opzet • (plan) *design* • (doelbewust) ⋆ met ~ *on purpose*

opzettelijk *intentional, deliberate*

opzetten • (op het vuur zetten) *put on* • (overeind zetten) *set up, put up*, <v. kraag> *turn up* • (iets beginnen) *set up, start* • (opdoen) *put on* • (prepareren) *stuff* • (~ **tegen**) *set on*

opzicht • (oogpunt) ⋆ in dit ~ *in this respect* ⋆ in zeker ~ *in a way* ⋆ ten ~e van *with regard to*

opzichter *overseer, supervisor*, <v. park> *keeper*

opzichtig <v. kleren> *flamboyant, showy*, <v. kleuren> *loud*

opzien I [het] ⋆ ~ baren *cause a sensation; make a splash* II [on ww] • (opkijken) *look up* • (~ **tegen**) ⋆ ik zie er tegen op *I'm not looking forward to it*

opzienbarend *sensational*

opzitten *sit up*, <v. hond> *beg*

opzoeken *look up*

opzuigen • (naar boven zuigen) *suck in/up*, <met stofzuiger> *hoover* • (absorberen) *absorb*

opzwellen *swell (up)*

opzwepen *whip up*

orakel *oracle*

oranje *orange*, <v. stoplicht> *amber*

orchidee *orchid*

orde *order* ⋆ er is iets niet in orde *there is s.th. wrong* ⋆ orde houden *keep order* ⋆ in orde! *all right!; righto!*

ordeloos *disorderly*

ordenen • (rangschikken) *put s.th. in order* • (regelen) *order, arrange* • (iem. in een orde opnemen) *ordain*

ordening • (regulering) *planning* • (rangschikking) *arrangement*

ordentelijk • (fatsoenlijk) *decent*

• (billijk) *fair, reasonable*

order • (bevel) *order, command* • (bestelling) *order*

ordinair *common, vulgar*

orgaan *organ*

organisatie *organization*

organisator *organizer*

organisch *organic*

organiseren *organize*

organisme *organism*

organist *organist, organ-player*

orgasme *orgasm*

orgel *organ*

orgie *orgy*

originaliteit *originality*

origineel I [het] *original* II [bnw] • (oorspronkelijk) *original* • (apart) *strange, original*

orkaan *hurricane*

orkest *orchestra*

ornaat ⋆ in vol ~ *in state; in full vestments*

ornament *ornament*

orthodox *orthodox*

os • (persoon) *ass* • (dier) *ox* [mv: oxen]

otter *otter*

oud *old*, <v. brood> *stale*

oudbakken *stale*

ouder I [de] *parent* II [bnw] *older, elder*

ouderdom • (leeftijd) *age* • (hoge leeftijd) *old age*

ouderlijk *parental*

ouderling *elder*

ouderwets I [bnw] • (uit de mode) *old-fashioned, out of date* • (degelijk) *proper* II [bijw] *in an old-fashioned way*

oudgediende • (ex-militair) *veteran, ex-serviceman* • (ervaren persoon) *old hand*, <inf.> *old-timer*

oudheid *antiquity*

oudheidkunde *archaeology*

oudoom *great uncle*

outillage *equipment*

ouwelijk *oldish, elderly*

ovaal *oval*
ovatie *ovation*
oven *oven*
over I [bijw] • (van/naar een andere plaats) *across, over* • (resterend) *left* • (opnieuw) *again* • (afgelopen) *over, finished* II [vz] • (bovenop/-langs) *across, over* • (via) *by way of, via* • (meer/langer dan) *over, past* • (na) ★ vandaag over een week *a week today* ★ over enige tijd *after some time* • (betreffende) *about, concerning* • (van/naar een andere plaats) *across, over*
overal *everywhere,* <inf.> *all over the place*
overbevolking *overpopulation*
overbevolkt *overpopulated*
overblijfsel <afval, restanten> *remains,* <vnl. etensresten> *left-overs* [mv]
overboord *overboard*
overbrengen • (transporteren) *bring, take, move* • (doorgeven) <boodschap> *take,* <groeten> *give* • (overdragen) *carry* • (overboeken) *transfer* • (techn.) *transmit*
overbrenging • (middel van overbrenging) *transmission* • (het overbrengen) *transport, transfer, removal*
overbruggen *bridge,* <fig.> *tide over*
overbrugging *bridging*
overcompleet *surplus*
overdaad *excess*
overdadig *excessive*
overdag *during the day, in the daytime*
overdekken *cover (over)*
overdenken *reflect on, consider*
overdenking *reflection, consideration*
overdoen • ((iets) opnieuw doen) *do (s.th.) over again* • (overdragen) *transfer, take over* • (verkopen) *sell (off)*
overdonderen *browbeat*
overdracht *transfer*

overdrachtelijk *metaphorical*
overdragen • (vervoeren) *carry/take (over/across)* • (overgeven) *hand over,* <taak> *delegate* • (overbrengen) *pass on, transmit*
overdreven *exaggerated, gushing*
overdruk • (hogere druk) *overpressure* • (wat over iets gedrukt is) *overprint* • (postzegel) *overprint*
overduidelijk *manifest, obvious*
overdwars *across, crosswise*
overeenkomen I [ov ww] • (afspreken) *agree (on)* II [on ww] • (overeenstemmen) *correspond (to)* • (samengaan) *go together*
overeenkomst • (gelijkenis) *correspondence, resemblance* • (afspraak) *agreement*
overeenkomstig I [bnw] • (volgens) *consistent with* • (gelijk) *similar, corresponding* II [vz] *in accordance with*
overeenstemmen • (het eens zijn) *agree* • (gelijk zijn aan) *correspond to*
overeenstemming • (het overeenstemmen) *agreement* • (gelijkenis) *correspondence, resemblance* • (afspraak) *agreement*
overeind • (rechtop) *upright, on end* • (staand) *standing*
overgaan • (oversteken) *cross* • (bevorderd worden) *move up* • (voorbijgaan) <v. bui> *blow over,* <v. pijn> *pass off* • (~ in) *pass into* • (~ tot) *proceed to*
overgang • (oversteekplaats) <spoorlijn> *(level)crossing,* <v. rivier> *crossing* • (menopauze) *change of life, menopause* • (tussenvorm) *link*
overgankelijk *transitive*
overgave • (overdracht) *transfer, delivery* • (capitulatie) *surrender* • (toewijding) *devotion, dedication*
overgeven I [ov ww] • (overdragen) *hand (over), pass* II [on ww] *vomit* III [wkd ww] *surrender*

overgevoelig *hypersensitive,
over-sensitive*
overgordijn *curtain*
overhalen • (trekken aan) *pull*
• (overreden) *persuade, talk (s.o.) into*
overhand ⋆ de ~ hebben *have the
upper hand*
overhandigen *hand (over), deliver*
overhebben ⋆ dat heb ik er wel voor
over *it's worth it*
overheen *over, across*
overheersen I [ov ww] *dominate* II [on
ww] *predominate*
overheersing *domination*
overheid *government*
overheidswege ⋆ van ~ *by the
authorities* ⋆ van ~ wordt verklaard
the authorities announce
overhellen • (hellen) *lean over, incline*
• (neigen) *tend*
overhemd *shirt*
overhoop *in disorder,* ‹fig.› *at odds*
overhoren *test*
overhouden *have s.th. left,* ‹v. geld›
save
overig *remaining*
overigens • (trouwens) *for that
matter, indeed* • (voor het overige) *for
the rest*
overjas *overcoat*
overkant *opposite/far side*
overkoken *boil over*
overladen • (te zwaar beladen)
overload • (overstelpen) *shower, heap
on*
overlangs *lengthwise*
overlappen *overlap*
overlast *annoyance, nuisance*
overlaten • (doen overblijven) *leave*
• (toevertrouwen) *leave*
overleden *dead, deceased*
overleg • (bedachtzaamheid)
discretion, judgement
• (beraadslaging) *deliberation,*
‹bespreking› *consultation*

overleven • (blijven leven) *survive*
• (langer leven dan iets/iem.) *outlive*
overlevende *survivor*
overleveren • (overdragen) *hand over*
• (doorgeven) *hand down*
overlevering *tradition*
overlijden I [het] *death,* ‹form.›
decease II [on ww] *die, pass away*
overloop • (bovenportaal) *landing*
• (het overstromen) *flooding*
• (overloopbuis) *overflow*
overlopen • (naar andere partij gaan)
defect, desert • (overstromen) *run over,*
‹fig.› *brim over*
overloper *deserter, defector, turncoat*
overmaat *excess*
overmacht • (grotere macht) *superior
forces/numbers* • (force majeure)
*circumstances beyond one's control, an
Act of God*
overmaken • (opnieuw maken) *redo,
do over again* • (overschrijven) ‹v.
geld› *transfer*
overmannen *overpower*
overmatig *excessive*
overmeesteren *overcome, overpower*
overmoed *recklessness*
overmoedig *reckless*
overmorgen *the day after tomorrow*
overnachten *stay the night*
overname • (koop) *taking over,
purchase* • (ontlening) *borrowing*
overnemen • (uit handen nemen)
take over • (kopen) *buy* • (opschrijven)
copy
overpeinzing • (het overpeinzen)
meditation • (wat overdacht wordt)
reflection
overplaatsen *transfer*
overproductie *over-production*
overreden *persuade*
overredingskracht *power of
persuasion*
overrompelen (take by) *surprise*
overschaduwen • (schaduw op iets

werpen) *overshadow* • (overtreffen)
eclipse
overschakelen • (andere verbinding
maken) *switch over* • (overstappen op)
switch over • (in andere versnelling
gaan) *change gear*
overschatten *overrate*
overschot • (restant) *remainder*, <aan
geld> *balance* • (teveel) *surplus*
overschreeuwen * iem. ~ *shout s.o.
down*
overschrijden • (over iets heen
stappen) *cross* • (te buiten gaan)
exceed
overschrijven • (overmaken) <v. geld>
transfer • (opschrijven) *copy (out)*
overslaan I [ov ww] • (voorbij (laten)
gaan) *omit, miss (out)*, <bij uitdeling>
pass over II [on ww] • (op iets anders
overgaan) *jump over, spread to* • (van
toon veranderen) <v. stem> *break,
catch*
overspannen I [bnw] • (te gespannen)
overstrained • (doorgedraaid)
overwrought II [ov ww] • (overdekken)
span • (te sterk spannen) *overstrain*
overspel *adultery*
overspringen *jump/leap over*
overstaan * ten ~ van *before; in the
presence of*
overstappen • (van trein wisselen)
change • (op iets anders overgaan)
change over
overste • (mil.) *lieutenant-colonel*
• (rel.) *prior* [v: *prioress*]
oversteekplaats *crossing*
oversteken • (naar overkant gaan)
cross • (ruilen) *exchange*
overstelpen • (bedelven) *shower, heap*
• (overmannen) *overwhelm*
overstemmen • (meer lawaai maken)
drown out • (meerderheid van
stemmen behalen) *outvote*
overstroming *flood*
overstuur *upset*

overtocht *passage, crossing*
overtollig *superfluous*
overtreden *break, infringe*, <form.>
offend against
overtreffen *exceed, surpass, outstrip*
overtrek *cover*
overtroeven • (aftroeven) *overtrump*
• (overtreffen) *outdo, outwit*
overtuigen *convince, satisfy*
overtuiging *conviction*
overval <v. politie> *raid* * gewapende ~
armed robbery
overvallen • (onverhoeds aanvallen)
<v. bank, winkel, enz.> *hold up*, <v.
personen> *assault* • (verrassen)
surprise
overvleugelen *outstrip*
overvloed *abundance, plenty, profusion*
overvloedig *abundant, plentiful,
copious*
overvloeien • (overstromen) *overflow*
• (in elkaar opgaan) *flow over*
• (~ van) *brim (with)*
overvoeren • (te veel voeren) *overfeed*
• (v. markt) *glut, oversupply*
overvol *crowded, overcrowded,
crammed (with)*
overwegen I [ov ww] • (overdenken)
consider, weigh II [on ww] • (de
doorslag geven) *prevail*
overwegend I [bnw] *paramount*
II [bijw] *predominantly, mainly*
overweging • (overdenking)
consideration • (beweegreden)
ground, reason
overweldigen • (overmeesteren)
overpower • (overstelpen) *overwhelm*
overwicht • (hoger gewicht)
overweight • (invloed) *preponderance*
overwinnaar *victor, conqueror*
overwinnen • (verslaan) *gain the
victory, conquer* • (te boven komen)
overcome
overwinning *victory*, <sport> *win*
overwinteren *hibernate, winter*

overzees *overseas*
overzetten *take across,* <met pont>
ferry (across)
overzicht • (het overzien) *survey*
• (samenvatting) *summary*
overzichtelijk *well-organized, clear*
overzien *look over, survey*
oxidatie *oxidation*
oxideren *oxidize*
ozon *ozone*

P

paaien I [ov ww] *placate, appease* II [on
ww] *spawn*
paal *pole, post*
paalwoning *pile dwelling*
paar • (klein aantal) *couple* • (koppel)
couple, pair
paard • (dier) *horse* • (schaakstuk)
knight • (sport) (vaulting) *horse*
paardensport *equestrian/hippic sport*
paardrijden *ride (horseback)*
paars *purple*
paarsgewijs *in pairs*
paartijd *mating season*
paasdag *Easter Day*
pacht • (huurovereenkomst) *lease*
• (pachttermijn) *tenancy*
• (pachtgeld) *rent*
pachten • (huren) *rent* • (een recht
kopen) *farm*
pachter *leaseholder, lessee,* <v.
boerderij> *tenant*
pacifisme *pacifism*
pad I [de] *toad* II [het] *path*
paddestoel • (zwam) *mushroom,*
<altijd giftig> *toadstool* • (wegwijzer)
road marker
padvinder <jongen> (boy) *scout,*
<meisje> *girl guide,* <AE> *girl scout*
padvinderij (boy) *scout movement*
paf I [de] *bang* II [bnw] ∗ daar sta ik paf
van *I'm staggered* III [tw] *bang!*
paffen *puff*
pagina *page*
pak • (verpakking) *package,* <klein>
packet • (kostuum) *suit*
pakezel • (lastdier) *pack donkey*
• (persoon) *dogsbody*
pakhuis *warehouse*
pakken I [ov ww] • (aanhouden) *catch,
seize* • (boeien) *grip* • (beetpakken)

catch, <omhelzen> *hug* • (inpakken)
pack, do up • (te voorschijn halen) *get,*
fetch, take II [on ww] <v. sleutel> *bite,*
<v. sneeuw> *ball,* <v. verf> *take*
pakket *parcel, packet*
pakking *packing, gasket*
pakpapier *wrapping paper*
pal I [de] *catch* II [bijw] • (onwrikbaar)
firmly • (precies, vlak) *directly*
paleis *palace*
palet *palette*
paling *eel*
paljas *buffoon, clown*
palm • (boom) *palm* • (handpalm)
palm
palmboom *palm (tree)*
pamflet *pamphlet*
pan • (kookpan) *pan* • (duinpan)
hollow, dip • (dakpan) *tile* • (janboel)
mess
pand • (onderpand) *security*
• (gebouw) *property, building,* <huis
en erf> *premises* • (slip v. jas) *tail*
pandverbeuren *game of forfeits*
paneel *panel*
paneren *coat with breadcrumbs*
paniek *panic, scare*
panisch *frantic, panic*
panklaar *oven-ready, ready for cooking*
pannenkoek *pancake*
panorama *panorama*
pantalon *trousers,* <AE> *pants*
panter *panther*
pantoffel *slipper*
pantoffelheld • (man onder de plak)
henpecked husband • (lafaard) *coward*
pantomime *dumb show, mime*
pantser • (stalen bekleding)
armour-plate, armour-plating • (huid
v. dier) *armour*
pantseren *armour, steel*
panty *tights, panty hose*
pap • (voedsel) *porridge* • (papachtig
mengsel) *pulp*
papa *dad(dy)*

papaver *poppy*
papegaai *parrot*
paperassen *papers*
papier *paper*
papieren • (van papier) *paper* • (niet
werkelijk) *paper*
pappen I [ov ww] <v. ontsteking>
poultice, <v. stoffen> *dress* II [on ww]
become pulpy
paprika • (vrucht) *pepper, paprika*
• (plant) *paprika*
papzak *fatty*
paraaf *initials*
paraat *ready, prepared*
parabel *parable*
parabool *parabola*
parachute *parachute*
parachutist *parachutist*
parade *review, parade*
paraderen • (parade houden) *parade*
• (pronken) *show off, make a show of*
paradijs *paradise*
paradox *paradox*
paraferen *initial*
paraffine *paraffin*
paragraaf • (onderdeel v. tekst) *section*
• (paragraafteken) *paragraph*
parallel I [de] *parallel* II [bnw] *parallel*
paraplu *umbrella*
parasiet • (soort plant, dier) *parasite*
• (klaploper) *sponger*
parasiteren *parasitize*
parasol *parasol, sunshade*
pardoes *bang, slap, smack*
pardon I [het] *pardon* II [tw] ★ ~! *(I beg
your) pardon; pardon me*
parel • (sieraad) *pearl* • (kostbaar
iets/iem.) *jewel* • (parelvormig
voorwerp) *bead*
parelen I [ov ww] *pearl* II [on ww]
• (bellen, druppels vormen) *pearl,
bead,* <v. vloeistof> *sparkle* • (zuiver
klinken) *ripple*
parelhoen *guinea fowl* [v: *guinea hen*]
paren I [ov ww] • (tot paar maken)

pair off • (doen samengaan) *combine
(with), couple (with)* II [on ww] *mate
with, copulate*
pareren *parry, ward off*
parfumeren *scent, perfume*
paria *pariah*
paring • (het koppels vormen) *pairing*
• (de copulatie) *mating, copulation*
pariteit *parity*
park *park*
parkeermeter *parking meter*
parkeerplaats • (parkeervak) *parking
place*, ‹langs weg› *lay-by*
• (parkeerterrein) *car park*
parkeerterrein *parking place/space*,
‹AE› *parking lot*
parkeren *park*
parket • (rang in theater) *parquet*
• (bureau v.h. Openbaar Ministerie)
office of the Public Prosecutor
parkiet *parakeet*
parlement *parliament*
parlementair • (beleefd)
parliamentary, civil • (m.b.t. het
parlement) *parliamentary* • (m.b.t.
onderhandelaar) *parliamentary*
parlementslid *Member of Parliament,
MP*
parochiaan *parishioner*
parochie *parish*
parodie *parody*
parodiëren *parody*
parool • (wachtwoord) *password*
• (leus) *slogan* • (erewoord) *parole*
part I [de] * je geheugen speelt je
parten *your memory is playing tricks
on you* II [het] *part, share*
parterre • (benedenverdieping)
ground floor, ‹AE› *first floor* • (rang in
theater) *pit*
participatie *participation*
particulier I [de] *private person*
II [bnw] *personal*, ‹v. secretaresse,
school, enz.› *private*
partij • (onbepaalde hoeveelheid) *set,*

bunch, ‹v. goederen› *lot*
• (gezamenlijk spel) *game* • (feest)
party • (belangengroep) *party*
• (deelhebber) *party* • (muz.) *part*
partijdig *partial, bias(s)ed*
partijgenoot *party-member*
partituur *score*
partizaan *partisan*
partner *partner*
parvenu *upstart, parvenu*
pas I [de] • (stap) *step, pace* • (bergpas)
pass • (legitimatiebewijs) *pass, permit*
II [bnw] • (passend) *fit* • (waterpas)
level III [bijw] • (niet
meer/eerder/verder dan) *just* • (in
hogere mate) ★ dat is pas lekker *that's
really delicious!*
Pasen *Easter*, ‹joods› *Passover*
pasfoto *passport photo*
paskamer *fitting room*
pasklaar • (zo gemaakt dat het past)
made to measure • (gereed om gepast
te worden) *ready for trying on*
paspoort *passport*
passage *passage*, ‹in de bergen› *pass*,
‹winkelgalerij› *arcade*
passagier *passenger*
passen I [ov ww] • (juiste maat
proberen) *try on, fit* • (juist plaatsen)
★ aan/in elkaar ~ *fit together/in* II [on
ww] • (de juiste maat hebben) *fit*
• (betamen) *become* • (schikken) *suit*
• (~ bij) *fit, match, suit, become*
passend • (v.d. goede maat) *fitting*
• (geschikt) *fit, suitable* • (gepast)
proper, appropiate
passer *compass, (pair of) compasses*
passeren • (door-/overtrekken) *pass
through, cross* • (gaan langs) *pass (by)*
• (inhalen) *overtake*
passie • (het lijden v. Christus)
Passion • (hartstocht) *passion*
passief *passive*
pasta • (dik smeersel) *paste*
• (deegwaar) *pasta*

pastei *pie*
pastel *pastel*
pasteuriseren *pasteurize*
pastille *pastille*
pastoor *priest*
pastoraal • (m.b.t. pastor/pastoraat)
pastoral • (m.b.t. het landleven)
pastoral, rustic
pastorie <protestants> *parsonage,*
vicarage, <rooms-katholiek>
presbytery
pat *stalemate*
patent I [het] <voor bedrijf> *licence,*
<voor uitvinding> (letters) *patent*
II [bnw] *first-rate, excellent*
pater *father*
paternoster I [de] *rosary, paternoster*
II [het] *paternoster, Lord's Prayer*
pathetisch *pathetic*
pathologisch *pathological*
pathos *pathos*
patiënt *patient*
patriarch *patriarch*
patriarchaal *patriarchal*
patriarchaat <rechtstoestand>
patriarchy, <waardigheid, gebied>
patriarchate
patriciër *patrician*
patrijs *partridge*
patrijspoort *porthole*
patronaat • (beschermheerschap)
patronage • (kath. jeugdvereniging)
confraternity
patroon I [de] • (huls met
springlading, inkt, enz.) *cartridge*
• (beschermheer) *patron*
• (beschermheilige) *patron saint*
• (baas) *employer, master* II [het]
• (model, voorbeeld) *pattern* • (dessin)
pattern, design
patrouille *patrol*
patrouilleren *patrol*
pats I [de] *slap* II [tw] *wham*
pauk *kettledrum*
paus • (geestelijk leider) *pope* • (bazig

persoon) *autocrat*
pauselijk *papal, pontifical*
pauw *peacock* [v: *peahen*]
pauze *pause,* <in schouwburg, enz.>
interval, <AE> *intermission,* <in
wedstrijd> *half-time,* <op school>
break
pauzeren *pause, stop, have a break*
paviljoen • (buitenverblijf) *pavilion*
• (bijgebouw) *outbuilding*
pech • (panne, mankement) *trouble,*
breakdown • (tegenspoed) *bad luck*
pechvogel *unlucky person*
pedaal *pedal*
pedaalemmer *pedal bin*
pedagogisch *pedagogic(al),*
<opvoedend> *educational*
pedagoog • (leermeester) *pedagogue*
• (opvoedkundige) *educationalist*
pedant *pedantic, conceited*
pedanterie *pedantry*
pedicure • (voetverzorging) *pedicure*
• (voetverzorger,-ster) *chiropodist*
pee ✶ de pee hebben aan *hate*
peen *carrot*
peer • (vent) *guy, bloke* • (vrucht) *pear*
• (lamp) *bulb*
pees • (bindweefsel) *tendon, sinew*
• (boogpees) *string*
peil *level*
peilen • (bepalen) <v. diepte> *sound,*
fathom, <v. gehalte, inhoud> *gauge,*
<v. positie> *take (one's) bearings*
• (onderzoeken) <v. gedachten>
fathom, probe, sound out, <v. kennis>
test, gauge
peiling <ter oriëntatie> *bearing,* <v.
gehalte> *gauging,* <v. hoogte, diepte>
sounding
peillood *plumb line*
peilloos *unfathomable*
peinzen *ponder, brood*
pek *pitch*
pekel • (strooizout) *salt*
• (zoutoplossing) *brine, pickle*

pekelen • (zouten) *pickle*
• (bestrooien) *salt*
pekelvlees *salt(ed) meat*
pelgrim *pilgrim*
pelikaan *pelican*
pellen *peel,* <v. noten> *shell*
peloton • (sectie) *platoon* • (sport) *pack*
pels • (vacht) *pelt* • (bewerkt bont) *fur*
pelsjager *trapper*
pen • (klem, knijper) *peg* • (schrijfpen)
pen
pendant *pendant, counterpart,*
opposite number
pendelaar *commuter*
pendeldienst *shuttle service*
pendelen *commute*
penibel *awkward*
penicilline *penicillin*
penis *penis*
pennen • (vastzetten bij schaken) *pin*
• (schrijven) *pen, scribble, jot down*
pennenlikker *penpusher, inkslinger*
pennenstrijd *controversy*
pennenvrucht *product of one's pen*
penning *medal,* <v. koffieautomaat,
enz.> *token,* <v. politieagent> *badge*
penningmeester *treasurer*
pens • (etenswaar) *tripe* • (buik)
paunch
penseel *brush*
pensioen *pension,* <v. militairen>
retirement pay
pensioenfonds *pension fund*
pensioengerechtigd *pensionable*
pension • (kosthuis) *boarding house*
• (kostgeld) *board* • (kost en
inwoning) *bed and board*
• (dierenverblijf) *kennel*
pensioneren *pension off*
peper *pepper*
peperduur *very expensive*
peperen *pepper*
pepermunt *peppermint*
pepernoot ≈ *gingernut*
per • (vanaf) *from* • (door middel van,

met) *by* • (in/voor) *per, by*
perceel *property,* <kaveling> *lot,* <land>
plot
percent *per cent*
percentage *percentage*
perenboom *pear tree*
perfect *perfect*
perfectie *perfection*
perforeren *perforate*
pergola *pergola*
periode *period*
periodiek I [de] • (tijdschrift)
periodical • (salarisverhoging)
increment II [bnw] *periodical*
periscoop *periscope*
perk • (stuk tuin) *bed, flowerbed*
• (grens) *bound, limit*
perkament *parchment*
permanent I [de] *permanent (wave)*
II [bnw] *permanent*
permissie *permission, leave*
permitteren *allow, permit*
perplex *perplexed, baffled*
perron *platform*
pers • (toestel om te persen) *press*
• (drukpers) (printing) *press*
• (kranten, tijdschriften,
journalisten) *press* • (tapijt) *Persian
carpet/rug*
persbureau *news agency*
persen *press*
personage • (persoon) *person* • (rol,
figuur, karakter) *personage, character*
personeel I [het] *personnel, staff,
employees* II [bnw] *personal*
personenauto *passenger car*
personificatie *personification*
personifiëren *personify*
persoon • (individu) *person*
• (personage) *figure, character, role*
persoonlijk I [bnw] • (van/voor een
persoon) *personal, private* • (in eigen
persoon) *personal* • (met persoonlijk
karakter) *individual, private* II [bijw]
personally

persoonlijkheid *personality*
persoonsbewijs *identity card, ID*
perspectief I [de] • (uitbeelding in plat vlak) *perspective* II [het] • (gezichtspunt) *perspective, point of view* • (vooruitzicht) *perspective, prospect* • (context) *perspective, context*
persvrijheid *freedom of the press*
pertinent *positive*
perzik *peach*
pessimisme *pessimism*
pest • (ziekte) *plague* • (plaag) *pest, blight* • (vervelend) *rotten*
pesten *plague, badger, pester*
pestkop *bully, tormentor*
pet I [de] *(peaked) cap* II [bnw] *lousy*
petekind *godchild*
peterselie *parsley*
petitie *petition*
petrochemie *petrochemistry*
petroleum ‹gezuiverd› *paraffin*, ‹AE› *kerosene*, ‹ruw› *petroleum*
petto ∗ iets in ~ houden *have/keep s.th. in reserve*
peul • (doosvrucht) *pod* • (soort erwt) *mange-tout*
peuter *toddler*
peuteren • (pulken) *pick* • (friemelen) *fumble, fiddle* • (~ aan) *tamper (with)*
peuterig • (klein) *finicky* • (prutserig) *slapdash*
peuzelen *munch, nibble*
piano *piano*
piccolo • (hotelbediende) *bellboy, buttons*, ‹AE› *bellhop* • (kleine dwarsfluit) *piccolo*
piek *peak, summit*
piekeren *puzzle over, brood, worry, fret*
piekfijn ‹v. uiterlijk› *spruce, natty*
pienter *bright, clever, smart*
piepen ‹v. adem› *wheeze*, ‹v. muizen› *squeak*, ‹v. scharnier› *creak*
pieper • (oproepapparaat) *bleeper* • (aardappel) *spud*
piepjong *extremely young*

pier • (worm) *earthworm* • (landhoofd) *pier*, ‹golfbreker› *jetty* • (loopbrug) *pier*
pietlut *niggler*
pietluttig *niggling, petty*
pigment *pigment*
pij (monk's) *habit*
pijl *arrow*, ‹klein› *dart*
pijler *pillar, column*, ‹v. brug› *pier*
pijlsnel (*as*) *swift as an arrow*
pijn • (lichamelijk lijden) *pain*, ‹aanhoudend› *ache*, ‹plotseling› *pang*
pijnbank *rack*
pijnboom *pine (tree)*
pijnigen *torment*
pijnlijk • (pijn doend) *painful* • (onaangenaam) *awkward* • (zeer nauwgezet) *painstaking*
pijnloos *painless*
pijnstillend *soothing*
pijp • (deel v.e. broek) *leg* • (rookgerei) *pipe* • (buis) *tube*
pijpleiding *pipeline*
pik • (wrok) *spite, grudge* • (penis) *cock*
pikant • (scherp) *piquant, savoury* • (prikkelend) *salty, racy*
pikdonker I [het] *pitch darkness* II [bijw] *pitch-dark*
pikhouweel *pickaxe*
pikken *pick*
pikzwart *pitch-black*
pil *pill*
pilaar *pillar, column*
piloot *pilot*
pimpelen *booze, tipple*
pin • (staafje, pen) *peg, pin* • (pinnig mens) *shrew*
pincet (*pair of*) *tweezers*
pinda *peanut*
pindakaas *peanut butter*
pingelen • (tikken v. automotor) *pink* • (afdingen) *haggle, chaffer, dicker* • (dribbelen) *dribble*
pink • (vinger) *little finger* • (kalf) *yearling* • (vissersboot) *smack*

pinken blink
Pinksteren Whitsun(tide),
<pinksterzondag> Pentecost
pinnig • (bits) tart, sharp • (zuinig)
mingy, stingy
pion counter, <bij schaken> pawn
pionier pioneer
pipet pipette
pips off colour
piraat • (zeerover) pirate • (illegale
zender) pirate (station)
piramide pyramid
pis piss, ↑ urine
pistache • (noot) pistachio • (bonbon)
cracker
piste • (circusarena) ring • (skipiste)
(ski) run
pistool pistol
pit • (energie) spirit • (kern v. vrucht)
stone, <v. appel> pip • (gaspit) jet,
burner • (lont) wick
pitten I [ov ww] stone II [on ww] sleep,
<inf.> snooze
pittig spicy
plaag nuisance, pest, plague
plaagziek teasing
plaat • (grammofoonplaat) record
• (prent) picture, plate
plaats • (waar iem./iets zich bevindt)
place, position • (ruimte) room, space,
<zitplaats> seat • (functie, post) post,
place • (woonplaats) town, <dorp>
village
plaatsbepaling • (lokalisatie)
position-finding, <luchtvaart> fix
• (taalk.) adjunct of place
plaatsbespreking booking
plaatsbewijs ticket
plaatselijk local
plaatsen place
plaatsgebrek lack of space
plaatsruimte room, accommodation
plaatsvervangend substitute
plaatsvervanger replacement,
substitute, <v. dokter> locum (tenens)

plagiaat plagiarism, plagiary
plaid plaid
plak slice, <chocolade> slab, <v. spek>
rasher
plakband adhesive, sticky tape
plakboek scrapbook
plakkaat • (aanplakbiljet) placard,
poster • (vlek, klodder) blotch, blob
plakken I [ov ww] paste, stick, glue
II [on ww] stick
plakker • (plakstrookje) sticker • (iem.
die lang blijft hangen) sticker • (iem
die plakt) paster, sticker
plamuren fill
plan plan
planeet planet
planetarium planetarium
plank plank, <dun> board
plankenkoorts stage fright
plankgas ★ ~ geven step on the gas
planmatig systematic
planning plan(ning)
plant plant
plantaardig vegetable
plantage plantation, estate
planten plant
plantengroei vegetation
planter planter
plantkunde botany
plantsoen public garden(s)
plas • (urine) ★ een plas doen go to the
toilet • (stilstaand water) pool, puddle,
<meer> lake • (natte plek) puddle
• (hoeveelheid) puddle
plassen I [ov ww] • (in plassen doen
stromen) splash, spatter II [on ww]
• (in een vloeistof bewegen) splash,
paddle • (urineren) pass water, go to
the loo
plastic I [het] plastic II [bnw] plastic
plastiek
• (boetseer-/beeldhouwkunst) plastic
art(s), <beeldhouwen> sculpture
• (voorwerp) <gebeeldhouwd>
sculpture, <geboetseerd> model

plat I [het] • (plat vlak) *plateau, shelf*
• (platte kant) *flat* • (dakterras) *sun
roof, terrace(roof)* II [bnw] • (vlak en
ondiep) *flat, low, shallow* • (niet in
bedrijf) *closed, shut down*
• (platvloers) *coarse, vulgar*
• (dialectisch) *broad*
platenspeler *record player*
platform *platform,* <v. vliegveld>
tarmac, apron
platina *platinum*
plattegrond • (kaart) *street plan/map*
• (tekening van huisindeling)
floor/ground plan
platteland *country(side)*
platvoet *flat foot*
platweg *bluntly, straight out*
platzak *broke*
plaveien *pave*
plaveisel *pavement*
plavuis *tile,* <v. steen> *flag(stone)*
plechtig *solemn, stately, ceremonious*
plechtigheid • (ceremonie) *solemnity,
ceremony* • (het stemmige) *solemnity*
plechtstatig *solemn, stately*
plegen *do, perform,* <v. misdaad>
perpetrate, commit
pleidooi *plea(ding)*
plein *square*
pleister I [de] (sticking) *plaster,* <AE>
band-aid II [het] • (kalkmengsel)
plaster
pleisteren I [ov ww] • (een pleister
plakken op) *put a plaster/band-aid on*
• (met gipskalk bestrijken) *plaster*
II [on ww] • (onderweg ergens
rusten) *stop (for refreshment)*
pleisterplaats • (plaats waar men
even blijft) *port of call* • (plaats waar
men reis onderbreekt) *stopping place*
pleisterwerk *plaster work, stucco*
pleitbezorger *advocate*
pleiten *plead*
pleiter • (pleitbezorger) *advocate*
• (iem. die een rechtsgeding voert)

litigant • (advocaat) *counsel*
plek • (vlek) *stain* • (plaats) *spot, place*
pletten *flatten*
pletter ★ te ~ slaan *smash* ★ te ~
vallen *plunge to (one's) death* ★ zich te
~ vervelen *be bored to tears*
pleuris *pleurisy*
plezier *pleasure, fun*
plezierig *pleasant*
plicht *duty, obligation*
plichtpleging *ceremony, compliment*
plint *skirting board*
ploeg • (landbouwwerktuig) *plough*
• (team) *team* • (arbeiders in
ploegendienst) *shift*
ploegen I [ov ww] • (met de ploeg
omwerken) *plough* II [on ww]
• (moeizaam vooruitkomen) *plough,
plod*
ploert *cad, bastard*
ploeteren • (spetteren) *splash*
• (zwoegen) *toil, plod*
plof *thud, flop*
ploffen I [ov ww] • (neergooien)
dump, chuck II [on ww] • (met een
plof vallen) *thud, flop* • (geluid van
ontsnappend gas geven) *pop, bang*
plomberen • (kiezen vullen) *fill*
• (met lood verzegelen) *seal with lead*
plomp *plump,* <mens> *squat*
plonzen *splash*
plooi • (rimpel in huid) *wrinkle, line*
• (kreukel) *crease* • (rimpel in stof)
fold, pleat
plooibaar *pliable*
plooien *fold, pleat*
plooirok *pleated skirt*
plug *plug,* <in vat, enz.> *bung*
pluim *feather, plume*
pluimage *plumage*
pluimvee *poultry*
pluis *fluff*
pluizen I [ov ww] • (iets uitrafelen)
fluff II [on ww] • (gaan rafelen)
become fluffy, fluff up

pluk • (bosje) *tuft* • (oogst) *pickings, crop* • (het plukken) *picking*
plukken I [ov ww] • (grijpen) *pluck* • (van veren ontdoen) *pluck* • (oogsten) *gather, pick* • (beroven) *fleece, pluck* II [on ww] • (peuteren aan) *pull (at), pick/pluck (at)*
plunderen *plunder, loot*
plunje • (kleding) *duds, togs* • (bagage) *kit, gear*
plunjezak *kit bag*
plus I [het] • (het teken +) *plus* II [bijw] • (boven nul) *plus, over*
pluspunt *advantage*
pneumatisch *pneumatic*
pochen *boast, brag*
podium *platform, dais,* <v. toneel> *stage*
poedel • (misgooi, -stoot) *missthrow,* <biljart> *miscue* • (hond) *poodle*
poedelnaakt *stark naked*
poeder I [de] • (geneesmiddel) *powder* II [het] • (fijn verdeelde vaste stof) *powder*
poederdoos *(powder) compact*
poederen *powder*
poeha *fuss*
poel • (ondiepe plas) <op straat> *pool, puddle* • (broeiplaats) *cesspool*
poelier *poulterer*
poen • (patser) *show-off,* <vero.> *bounder* • (geld) *dough, bread*
poenig *flashy*
poep *crap,* <v. hond, enz.> *mess,* <v. koe, enz.> *dung*
poepen *(have a) crap,* <kind> *do a jobby*
poes • (kat) *(pussy)cat* • (mooie meid) ↓ *pussycat*
poeslief *smooth,* <glimlach, woorden> *sugary,* <woorden> *honeyed*
poesta *puszta*
poëtisch *poetic(al)*
poets *trick, prank*
poetsen *clean,* <v. schoenen> *polish,* <v. tanden> *brush*

poetskatoen *waste cotton*
poëzie *poetry*
pofbroek *knickerbockers* [mv]
poffen I [ov ww] • (in de schil stoven) *roast,* <maïs> *pop* II [on ww] • (op krediet kopen) *buy on credit/tick* • (op krediet verkopen) *sell on tick*
poffertje ≈ *tiny puff-pancakes*
pogen *endeavour, try, attempt*
pogrom *pogrom*
polair • (van de polen) *polar* • (chem.) *dipolar*
polarisatie *polarization*
polariseren *polarize*
polder *polder*
polemiek *polemic(s), controversy*
polemisch *polemic(al), controversial*
Polen *Poland*
poliep • (dier) *polyp, polipite* • (med.) *polyp, polypus*
polijsten *polish*
polikliniek *polyclinic, out-patients' clinic*
polis *policy*
politicus *politician*
politie *police*
politiek I [de] • (overheidsbeleid) *politics* • (tactisch beleid) *policy* II [bnw] • (m.b.t. tactisch beleid) *politic, diplomatic* • (m.b.t. overheidsbeleid) *political* III [bijw] *political*
politiseren *politicize*
pollepel *ladle*
pols • (gewricht) *wrist* • (polsslag) *pulse*
polshorloge *wristwatch*
polsslag *pulse*
polsstok *jumping/vaulting pole*
polyester *polyester*
polygaam *polygamous*
pomp • (tankstation) *petrol station,* <langs autoweg> *service station* • (werktuig) *pump*
pompbediende *petrol/service station attendant*

pompen *pump*
pompoen *pumpkin*
pompstation • (gebouw voor het oppompen v. water) *pumping-station* • (tankstation) *filling/service station*
pond • (gewichtseenheid) *pound* • (Eng. munteenheid) *pound*
poneren *postulate, put forward*
ponsen *punch*
ponskaart *punch(ed) card*
pont *ferryboat*
pontificaal *pontifical*
pony • (paardenras) *pony* • (haardracht) *fringe, bang*
pook • (vuurpook) *poker* • (versnellingshendel) *(gear)stick*
pool • (uiteinde van magneet) *pole* • (poolstreek) *pole* • (opstaande haren van stoffen) *pile*
poolshoogte *latitude*
poolster *polar star*
poolzee *polar sea*
poort • (hoofdingang) *gate* • (nauwe doorgang) *alley(way)* • (boogvormige doorgang) *gate(way)*
poos *while, time*
poot • (lidmaat) *leg* • (voet) <v. dier> *paw, foot* • (steun van een voorwerp) *leg*
pootjebaden *paddle*
pop *doll,* <paspop> *dummy* • (marionet) *puppet* • (ingesponnen larve) *pupa*
poppenkast • (de kast) *puppet theatre, tomfoolery* • (poppenspel) *Punch and Judy show, puppet show*
popperig *doll-like*
populair • (algemeen bekend) *familiar* • (algemeen geliefd) *popular* • (algemeen begrijpelijk) *popular*
populariteit *popularity*
populier *poplar*
por *prod*
poreus *porous*

porie *pore*
porren *prod*
porselein *porcelain, china*
porseleinen *china, porcelain*
portaal *porch, hall*
portefeuille *portfolio,* <voor geld> *wallet*
portemonnee *purse*
portie • (aandeel) *share, portion, part* • (hoeveelheid eten) <aan tafel> *helping*
portiek *porch*
portier I [de] • (conciërge, enz.) *door-/gatekeeper,* <bank, hotel> *porter* II [het] *door*
porto *postage*
portret • (afbeelding van iem.) *portrait, photo(graph)* • (persoonsbeschrijving) *portrait*
portretteren *portray*
Portugal *Portugal*
poseren • (gemaakt doen) *pose (as), masquerade (as))* • (model zijn) *sit (for one's portrait), pose*
positie • (maatschappelijke stand) *position* • (lichaamshouding) *position, posture* • (innerlijke houding) *position, attitude* • (plaats) *position* • (toestand) *situation* • (betrekking) *position, post*
positief • (bevestigend) *positive,* <antwoord> *affirmative* • (stellig) *definite* • (gunstig) *positive, favourable* • (niet negatief) *positive*
post *post,* <poststukken> *mail*
postbode *postman*
postduif *carrier/homing pigeon*
postelein *purslane*
posten I [ov ww] • (op de post doen) *post* II [on ww] • (op wacht staan) *stand guard,* <v. stakers> *picket*
posteren *post, station*
posterijen *postal services, the Post Office*
postgiro *post office giro, national giro*

postkantoor *post office*
postmerk *post mark*
postpakket *postal parcel*
poststuk *postal packet/parcel*
postuur • (gestalte) *figure, build*
• (houding) *posture*
postwissel *postal/money order*
postzegel *(postage) stamp*
postzegelverzamelaar *stamp collector, philatelist*
pot • (pot om iets in te bewaren) ‹v. aardewerk› *pot,* ‹v. glas› *jar* • (po) (chamber) *pot* • (kookpot) *cooking pot, saucepan* • (inzet) *pool, stakes* • (marihuana) *pot*
potdicht *locked, sealed, hermetically closed,* ‹eigenschap v. iem.› *as closed as an oyster*
potentaat *potentate*
potentie *power,* ‹ook seksueel› *potency,* ‹seksueel› *virility*
potentieel I [het] *potential, capacity* II [bnw] *potential*
potig *burly, robust, husky*
potlood • (grafiet) *black lead* • (schrijfgerei) *pencil*
potpourri *potpourri,* ‹muz.› *medley*
potsierlijk *clownish, grotesque*
potten • (sparen) *hoard* • (in potten doen) *pot*
pottenbakker *potter*
pottenbakkerij *pottery*
pottenkijker *nosy parker, snooper*
potverteren *squander money*
potvis *sperm whale*
pover *poor*
praal *pomp, splendour*
praat • (het spreken) *talk* • (wat gezegd wordt) *talk*
praatje • (gerucht) *rumour, story* • (gesprekje) *talk, chat* • (kleine voordracht) *talk*
praatjesmaker *gasbag, boaster*
praatpaal *emergency telephone,* ‹fig.› *confidant*

praatziek *talkative, chatty*
pracht • (grote schoonheid) *splendour, magnificence* • (prachtig exemplaar) *beauty*
prachtig • (heel mooi) *splendid, magnificent* • (heel goed) *fine, wonderful*
praktijk • (gewoonte) *practice* • (beroepsuitoefening) *practice* • (toepassing) *practice*
pralen *parade, flaunt*
prat *proud*
praten *talk*
precair *precarious*
precedent *precedent*
precies • (geheel en al) *precise, exact* • (nauwkeurig) ★ ~ op tijd *right on time* ★ ~ in het midden *right smack in the middle* ★ om tien uur ~ *at ten precisely/sharp*
preciseren *define, state precisely, specify*
predestinatie *predestination*
predikant ‹anglicaans› *vicar,* ‹protestant› *clergyman,* ‹rooms-katholiek› *preacher*
preek • (leerrede) *sermon* • (vermaning) *sermon, lecture*
preekstoel *pulpit*
prei *leek*
preken *preach*
prelaat *prelate*
prematuur *premature*
premie *premium*
premier *premier, prime minister*
premisse *premise*
prent • (afdruksel v. plaat) *print, picture* • (bekeuring) *ticket*
prentbriefkaart *picture postcard*
prenten *impress, fix*
preparaat *preparation*
prepareren *prepare*
present I [het] • (cadeau) *present* II [bnw] *present*
presentator *presenter*

presenteerblad *salver, tray*
presenteren • (iem. voorstellen)
present, introduce • (iets aanbieden)
present, offer • (introduceren op tv)
host
presentexemplaar <als geschenk>
presentation copy, <extra> *free copy*
presentielijst *roll, attendance*
list/register
pressie *pressure*
pressiegroep *pressure group*
prestatie *performance, achievement*
presteren • (iets verrichten) *achieve,*
perform
prestige *prestige*
pret *fun, pleasure*
pretentie • (aanspraak) *claim,*
pretension • (aanmatiging) *pretension*
pretentieus *pretentious*
prettig *pleasant, nice*
preuts *prudish, prim*
prevelen *mutter*
preventief *preven(ta)tive,*
precautionary
prieel *summerhouse, gazebo*
priem *awl, bodkin*
priemen *pierce*
priemgetal *prime number*
priester *priest* [v: *priestess*]
prijken *figure*
prijs • (kostprijs) *price* • (prijskaartje)
price (tag) • (gewonnen beloning)
prize, award • (uitgeloofde beloning)
reward • (buit) *prize* • (lof) *praise*
prijsbewust *cost-conscious*
prijsgeven *abandon, give up,*
<geheimen> *divulge*
prijsvraag *prize contest, competition*
prijzen • (de prijs aangeven) *price,*
ticket • (loven) *praise, commend*
• (achten) *prize*
prijzig *expensive,* <inf.> *pricey*
prik • (limonade) *pop, fizz* • (steek)
prick, stab • (injectie) *injection*
prikkel • (doorn) *prickle*

• (aansporing) *incentive, stimulus,*
spur • (prikkeling) *tingle,* <bio.>
stimulus
prikkelbaar • (lichtgeraakt) *irritable,*
touchy • (bio.) *sensitive*
prikkeldraad *barbed wire*
prikkelen I [ov ww] • (aanzetten)
stimulate, excite • (ergeren) *irritate,*
nettle • (prikken) *prickle* II [on ww]
• (prikkelend gevoel geven) *tingle*
prikkeling *stimulation*
prikken I [ov ww] • (steken) *prick*
• (injectie geven) *inject*
• (vastprikken) *stick to/on* II [on ww]
• (tintelen) *tingle*
pril *early, tender*
prima • (eerste) *prime* • (uitstekend)
excellent, great, first-rate
primaat I [de] • (titel van geestelijke)
primate • (aapachtig zoogdier)
primate II [het] *primacy*
primair *primary*
primeur <v. journalist> *scoop*
primitief *primitive*
primula *primrose, primula*
primus *primus (stove)*
principieel *essential, fundamental*
prins *prince*
prinselijk *princely*
prioriteit *priority*
prisma *prism*
privaatrecht *private law*
privé *private, personal*
pro *pro*
probaat *approved, effective*
probeersel *experiment*
proberen *try, attempt*
probleem *problem*
problematiek *problem(s), question at*
hand
procédé *process*
procederen • (een proces voeren)
litigate • (te werk gaan) *proceed*
procent *per cent*
proces • (rechtszaak) *trial* • (wijze

waarop iets verloopt) *process*
processie *procession*
proclamatie *proclamation*
proclameren *proclaim*
procuratiehouder *confidential clerk,
deputy manager*
procureur *solicitor, attorney*
producent *producer*
produceren *produce*
productie • (de opbrengst) *output*
• (het produceren) *production*
productief *productive*
productiviteit *productivity*
proef • (onderzoek) *test* • (experiment)
test, experiment • (bewijs) *test, proof*
• (voorlopig product) *proof* • (staal)
try, sample • (keur) *sample (test)*
proefdier *laboratory animal,* ‹fig.›
guinea pig
proefdraaien *(give a) trial/test run*
proefkonijn *laboratory rabbit,* ‹fig.›
guinea pig
proefneming *experiment*
proefondervindelijk • (door middel
van experiment) *experimental* • (op
grond van experiment) *empirical*
proefrit *trial run, test drive*
proefschrift *thesis*
proeftijd *probation*
proefwerk *test paper*
proeven *taste,* ‹een beetje v. iets›
sample
profaan *profane*
profeet *prophet* [v: *prophetess*]
professor *professor*
profetie *prophecy*
profetisch *prophetic*
profiel • (loopvlak op band) *tread*
• (profielschets) *profile* • (zijaanzicht)
profile
profijt *profit, gain*
profiteren *profit (by/from), benefit
(by/from), avail o.s. of, take advantage
(of)*
prognose *prognosis*

programma *programme*
programmeren *program*
progressie • (trapsgewijze
toeneming) *progression*
• (vooruitgang) *progress*
progressief *progressive*
project *project*
projecteren *project*
projectie *projection*
projectiel *missile, projectile*
projector *projector,* ‹v. dia's› *slide
projector*
proletariaat *proletariat*
proletariër *proletarian*
proletarisch *proletarian*
proloog *prologue*
prominent *prominent*
promotie • (bevordering naar hogere
rang) *promotion, rise*
• (verkoopbevordering) *promotion*
• (doctor worden) *taking one's
Ph.D./doctor's degree,* • (ceremonie)
degree (of doctorate) ceremony
promotor • (zakelijk) *promoter*
• (hoogleraar) ≈ *supervisor of a Ph.D.
student*
promoveren I [ov ww] • (iem. de
doctorstitel verlenen) *doctor, confer a
degree of doctor on* II [on ww] • (de
doctorstitel verwerven) *take a
doctor's degree* • (sport) *be promoted*
prompt I [bnw] • (punctueel)
punctual, prompt • (vlot) *prompt,
quick* II [bijw] *promptly, at once*
pronken *show (o.s./s.th.) off, flaunt
(o.s./s.th.)*
pronkstuk *showpiece*
prooi • (buit van een roofdier) *prey*
• (slachtoffer) *prey, victim*
proost *bottoms up!, cheers!,* ‹bij
niezen› *bless you!*
prop *wad,* ‹in de mond› *gag,* ‹papier›
ball
propaganda *propaganda*
propagandistisch *propagandist(ic)*

propedeuse *foundation course*
propeller *propeller*
proper • (netjes) *neat* • (schoon) *clean*
proportie • (onderlinge verhouding) *proportion* • (afmeting) *proportion, dimension*
proportioneel *proportional*
proppen *stuff, cram*
propvol *chock-full, packed, chock-a-block*
prostituee *prostitute*
prostitutie *prostitution*
protectie • (bescherming) *protection* • (steun) *influence*
protectionisme *protectionism*
protest *protest*
protesteren *protest*
prothese *prosthesis,* <v. ledemaat> *artificial limb,* <v. tanden> *dentures, false teeth*
protocol • (verslag/proces-verbaal) *protocol, record* • (diplomatieke etiquette) *protocol*
proviand *provisions*
provinciaal *provincial*
provincie *province*
provisie • (mondvoorraad) *provisions, stock of food* • (procentueel commissieloon) *commission,* <makelaar> *brokerage*
provocatie *provocation*
provoceren *provoke*
proza *prose*
prozaïsch *prosaic*
pruik • (vals haar) *wig* • (haardos) *mop of hair*
pruilen *pout, sulk*
pruim • (vrucht) *plum* • (plukje kauwtabak) *quid*
pruimen • (pruimtabak kauwen) *chew* • (accepteren) ★ *ik kan die man niet ~ I can't stand that man*
pruimtabak *chewing tobacco*
prul *trash, gimcrack*
prutsen • (knutselen) *tinker*

(about/with), *mess about with*
• (klungelen) *bungle*
prutswerk • (knutselwerk) *fiddling work* • (knoeiwerk) *bungle, shoddy work, botch(-up)*
psalm *psalm*
pseudoniem *pseudonym*
psyche *psyche*
psychiater *psychiatrist*
psychiatrisch *psychiatric*
psychisch *psychic(al)*
psychoanalyse *psychoanalysis*
psychologisch *psychological*
psycholoog *psychologist*
psychopaat *psychopath*
psychose *psychosis*
puber *adolescent*
puberteit *puberty*
publiceren *publish*
publiciteit *publicity*
publiek I [het] • (toeschouwers) *public,* <v. culturele gebeurtenis> *audience,* <v. sport> *crowd* • (het volk) *public* **II** [bnw] • (algemeen bekend) *public* • (voor iedereen) *public*
publicatie *publication*
pudding *pudding*
puf *energy*
puffen • (zuchten) *puff, pant* • (tuffen van motor) *chug*
pui *front,* <winkel> *shopfront*
puik • (van goede kwaliteit) *choice* • (voortreffelijk) *great*
puilen *bulge*
puin *debris, rubbish, rubble*
puinhoop *mess*
puist • (zweer) *pustule* • (pukkel) *pimple*
pul • (vaas) *vase, jug* • (bierpul) *tankard*
pulken *pick*
pulp *pulp*
punaise *drawing pin,* <AE> *thumbtack*
punctueel *punctual*
punt I [de] • (leesteken) *full stop, period,* <decimaalpunt> *decimal*

(point) • (waarderingseenheid) point,
mark • (stuk taart, pizza) slice, <groot>
wedge • (spits uiteinde) tip, point, <v.
zakdoek, tafel> corner II [het] point

punten • (een punt maken aan) point,
sharpen • (de punten verwijderen)
trim

puntenslijper pencil sharpener

puntig • (spits) pointed, sharp
• (snedig) pointed, sharp, witty

puntje • (kleine punt) tip, dot
• (broodje) roll

puntsgewijs point by point

pupil • (onderdeel v.h. oog) pupil
• (kind onder voogdij) pupil, ward
• (leerling) pupil, student • (sport)
junior

puree puree

put • (waterput) well • (kuil) <ook fig.>
pit

putten • (water halen) draw • (iets
ontlenen aan) draw (from/on)

puur pure, straight, <alcoholische
dranken> neat, <chocola> plain

puzzel puzzle

pygmee pygmy

pyjama (pair of) pyjamas

Q

quarantaine quarantine

quasi quasi, pseudo, mock

quatre-mains ★ à ~ for four hands
★ een ~ a (piano) duet ★ ~ spelen play
(piano) duets

querulant querulous person, <inf.>
grouser

quitte quits

quota quota, contingent, share

quotiënt quotient

R

ra *yard*
raad • (advies) *advice, counsel*
• (adviserend orgaan) *council*
raadgeving *advice*
raadhuis *town hall,* <v. stad> *city hall*
raadplegen • (inlichtingen
inwinnen) *consult* • (advies vragen)
consult, to seek advice
raadsel • (opgave, vraag) *riddle* • (iets
onbegrijpelijks) *mystery, puzzle,*
enigma
raadselachtig *enigmatic, mysterious*
raadsheer • (raadsman) *councillor*
• (schaakstuk) *bishop*
raadslid *councillor*
raadsman • (raadgever) *adviser,* <jur.>
counsel • (advocaat) *counsel*
raadzaam *advisable, wise*
raaf *raven*
raak • (treffend juist) *to the point* • (het
doel treffend) ★ raak schieten *hit the*
mark
raakvlak • (gemeenschappelijk
gebied) *interface* • (wisk.) *tangent*
plane
raam • (venster) *window* • (lijst) *frame*
• (kader) *context, frame*
raap • (gewas) *turnip* • (afgevallen
fruit) *windfall*
raar *strange, odd, weird*
raaskallen *rave, talk gibberish*
raat *honeycomb*
rabarber *rhubarb*
race *race*
racen • (aan een race deelnemen) *race*
• (zeer snel gaan) *speed*
radeloos *desperate*
raden • (gissen) *guess* • (raad geven)
advise, counsel
raderwerk *wheels,* <v. klok> *clockwork*

radiator • (koelelement) *radiator*
• (verwarmingselement) *radiator*
radicaal I [de] *radical* II [het] • (bewijs
van aanspraak) *entitlement* • (chem.)
radical III [bnw] • (extremistisch)
radical • (drastisch) *drastic*
radijs *radish*
radio • (radiotoestel) *radio*
• (radio-uitzending) *radio*
• (radio-omroep) *radio*
radioactief *radioactive*
radioactiviteit *radioactivity*
radiografisch *radiographic*
radiostation *radio station*
radiozender *radio transmitter*
radium *radium*
rafel *frayed end, loose end*
rafelig *frayed, unravelled*
raffinaderij *refinery*
raffineren *refine*
rag *cobweb*
rage *craze, rage, trend*
rail *rail*
rakelings ★ iem./iets ~ voorbijgaan
brush past s.o./a thing
raken I [ov ww] • (treffen) *hit*
• (aanraken) *touch* • (ontroeren)
touch, move II [on ww] ★ in
moeilijkheden ~ *get into difficulties*
raket • (projectiel) *rocket* • (vuurpijl)
rocket
rakker *rascal, scamp*
ram • (mannetjesschaap) *ram*
• (sterrenbeeld) *Aries, the Ram*
• (klap) *whack, thump* • (gesch.)
battering ram
ramen *estimate*
raming *estimate*
rammelaar • (speelgoed) *rattle*
• (mannetjeskonijn) *buck rabbit*
rammelen *rattle,* <v. geld> *jingle*
rammen *ram*
ramp *catastrophe, disaster*
rampspoed *adversity, misfortune*
rampzalig *disastrous*

rand *edge*, ‹richel› *ledge*, ‹v. cilindervormig voorwerp› *brim*, ‹v. kopje› *rim*
rang *rank*
rangeren *shunt*
ranglijst *list*
rangorde *order of rank, hierarchy*
rangschikken *arrange*
rangtelwoord *ordinal*
rank I [de] *tendril* II [bnw] *slender*
ransel • (knapzak) *knapsack* • (slaag) *hiding*
ranselen *thrash, flog, beat*
rantsoen *ration*
rap *quick*
rapen • (oppakken) *pick up* • (verzamelen) *gather*
rapport • (verslag) *report* • (cijferlijst) *report*
rapporteren • (verslag uitbrengen) *report* • (melden) *report*
rariteit *curiosity*
ras ‹v. dieren› *breed*, ‹v. mensen› *race*, ‹v. planten› *variety*
rasecht • (echt) *born* • (raszuiver) *thoroughbred*
rasp • (keukengereedschap) *grater* • (vijl) *rasp*
raspen I [ov ww] *grate* II [on ww] *rasp*
raster • (puntenpatroon) *screen* • (hekwerk) *fence*, ‹v. hout› *picket fence*
rat *rat*
ratel *rattle*
ratelen *rattle*
ratelslang *rattlesnake*
ratificatie *ratification*
rationeel *rational*
rauw *raw*
rauwkost *raw/uncooked food, raw vegetables*, ‹als gerecht› *vegetable salad*
ravijn • (afgrond) *ravine, gorge* • (holle weg) *sunken road*
ravotten *romp*
rayon • (werkgebied) *area*

• (kunstzijde) *rayon*
razen • (tekeergaan) *rage, rave* • (zoeven) *race*
razend • (woedend) *furious* • (hevig) ★ ~e honger *ravenous appetite*
razernij • (woede) *frenzy, rage* • (krankzinnigheid) *madness*
razzia *raid, round-up*, ‹gesch.› *razzia*
reactie • (antwoord) *reaction* • (tegenkracht) *reaction* • (chemisch proces) *reaction*
reactionair I [de] *reactionary* II [bnw] *reactionary*
reactor *reactor*
reageren • (reactie vertonen) *react* • (chem.) *react*
realisme *realism*
realistisch *realistic*
realiteit *reality*
rebel *rebel*
rebelleren *rebel*
rebellie • (opstand) *rebellion* • (opstandigheid) *rebelliousness*
rebels *rebellious*
recensent *reviewer, critic*
recensie *review, criticism*
recept • (doktersrecept) *prescription* • (keukenrecept) *recipe*
receptie *reception*
receptionist *receptionist*
reces *recess*
recessie *recession*
recherche • (afdeling) *criminal investigation department* • (team) *team of detectives*
rechercheur *detective*
recht I [het] • (bevoegdheid) *right* • (aanspraak) *right, claim* • (rechtsgeleerdheid) ‹inf.› *law*, ‹form.› *jurisprudence* • (rechtsregels) *law* • (gerechtigheid) *right, justice* II [bnw] • (niet krom of scheef) *straight* • (rechtstreeks) *direct, straight* III [bijw] *straight, right*
rechtbank • (college van rechters) *law*

court, court of justice
• (gerechtsgebouw) court
rechtens by right(s)
rechter I [de] judge, justice II [bnw]
★ de ~ voet the right foot
rechterlijk judicial
rechtgeaard right-minded
rechthebbende (rightful) claimant
rechthoek rectangle
rechthoekig • (m.b.t. hoek) right
angled • (m.b.t. vorm) rectangular
rechtlijnig • (strikt logisch) ★ ~
denken linear thought
rechtmatig rightful, legitimate
rechtop upright, erect
rechts • (conservatief) right-wing
• (aan/naar rechterkant) on/to/at the
right • (rechtshandig) right-handed
rechtsaf to the right
rechtsbijstand legal aid
rechtschapen righteous, honest
rechtsgeldig legal, valid
rechtsgevoel sense of justice
rechtsgrond legal ground
rechtshandig right-handed
rechtskundig legal
rechtsorde legal system
rechtspersoon legal body, statutory
body, <vereniging> corporation
rechtspraak • (jurisdictie) jurisdiction
• (jurisprudentie) jurisprudence
rechtspreken administer justice
rechtsstaat constitutional state
rechtstandig perpendicular
rechtstreeks • (zonder tussenkomst)
direct • (zonder omwegen) direct
rechtsvervolging prosecution
rechtsvordering • (procesrecht) <het
proces v.h. recht> legal procedure,
<onderdeel v. rechtswetenschappen>
procedural law • (vordering) legal
action, legal claim
rechtswege ★ van ~ by law; legally
rechtswetenschap jurisprudence
rechtszaak lawsuit

rechtszitting session in court, court
case
rechtuit • (rechtdoor) straight on
• (ronduit) outright
rechtvaardig just
rechtvaardigen justify, warrant
rechtvaardigheid justice
rechtzetten • (recht/overeind zetten)
adjust • (rectificeren) rectify
rechtzinnig orthodox
recidivist recidivist, backslider, <m.b.t.
misdrijf> hardened offender
reciteren recite, <met passie> declaim
reclame • (aanprijzing) advertising,
publicity • (middel, voorwerp) neon
sign, <advertentie> advertisement,
<radio, tv> spot • (vordering) claim
• (bezwaar) protest
reclameren ★ betaling ~ request a
refund ★ ~ bij afzender demand
remittance
reclasseren rehabilitate
reclassering • (heraanpassing)
rehabilitation of discharged prisoners
• (reclasseringsdienst) probation
officer and social services
record record
recordhouder record-holder
recreatie recreation
rector • (hoofd v. school) headmaster
• (hoofd v. academisch bestuur) rector
• (hoofd v. de senaat) rector • (hoofd v.
klooster) rector
redacteur editor
redactie • (het redigeren) editorship
• (de redacteur(en)) editors
• (afdeling) editorial office
redactioneel editorial
reddeloos irretrievable, beyond repair
redden I [ov ww] • (in veiligheid
brengen) save, rescue II [wkd ww]
★ hij redt zich wel he'll manage
redder • (iem. die redt) rescuer
• (verlosser) saviour
redding • (het redden) rescue

• (verlossing) *deliverance* • (uitkomst) *salvation, redemption*

rede ★ iem. in de rede vallen *interrupt s.o.*

redelijk I [bnw] • (met verstand) *rational* • (verstandig) *sensible* • (billijk) *reasonable, fair* • (vrij goed) *passable, tolerable* II [bijw] *rather*

redelijkheid • (billijkheid) *fairness* • (verstandigheid) *reasonableness*

redeloos *irrational, senseless*

reden • (beweegreden) *reason, motive* • (motief, argument) *ground, cause* • (wisk.) *ratio*

redenaar *orator*

redeneren *reason, argue*

redenering • (gedachtegang) *reasoning, argument* • (betoog) *argument, <form.> discourse*

reder *ship owner*

rederij • (onderneming) <v. goederenvervoer> *shipping company,* <v. passagiersvervoer> *shipping line*

redetwisten *dispute*

redevoering *speech*

redmiddel *remedy*

reduceren *reduce*

reductie *reduction*

ree *roe(-deer),* <vrouwelijk> *doe*

reeds *already*

reëel • (werkelijk) *real* • (zakelijk) *realistic*

reeks *row, series,* <woorden, cijfers> *string*

reep • (strook) *strip* • (tablet chocola) *bar*

reet • (spleet) *crack, chink, fissure* • (achterwerk) *arse*

referaat • (verslag) *report* • (voordracht) *lecture*

referendum *referendum*

reflecteren • (weerspiegelen) *reflect* • (~ op) <advertentie, aanbod> *answer* • (~ over) *reflect upon,* <voorstel> *entertain*

reflector *reflector*

reflex *reflex*

reformatie *reformation*

reformeren *reform*

refrein *refrain, chorus*

regel • (tekstregel) *line* • (voorschrift) *rule*

regelbaar *adjustable*

regelen *arrange*

regeling *arrangement*

regelmaat *regularity*

regelmatig *regular*

regelrecht *straight*

regen *rain*

regenachtig *rainy*

regenboog *rainbow*

regenbui *shower*

regenen • (het vallen v. regen) *rain* • (veel voorkomen) ★ 't regende klachten *complaints poured in*

regenjas *raincoat, mackintosh*

regent • (autoritaire bestuurder) *dictator* • (gesch.) *governor*

regentschap *rule,* <v. vorst> *reign*

regenval *rainfall*

regenvlaag *squall*

regeren *rule*

regering *government*

regeringswege ★ van ~ *officially; by the government*

regie *direction, production*

regime • (staatsbestel) *regime* • (leefregels) *regimen*

regiment *regiment*

regisseren *direct*

regisseur *director*

register • (lijst) *register* • (index) *index* • (toonomvang) *register* • (orgelregister) *stop, organ stop*

registratie *registration*

registreren • (inschrijven) *register* • (vastleggen) *register* • (waarnemen) *register, notice*

reglement *rules,* <geschreven> *regulations*

reglementair I [bnw] *prescribed* II [bijw] *as prescribed/laid down, according to the regulations/rules*
reglementeren *regulate*
reguleren *regulate*
regulier *regular*
rehabilitatie *rehabilitation*
rei • (reidans) *round/choral dance* • (koor) *chorus*
reiger *heron*
reiken *reach*
rein • (schoon) *clean* • (zuiver) ⋆ de reinste dwaasheid *sheer/utter folly*
reinigen *clean,* ‹wond› *cleanse*
reis *journey,* ‹op zee› *voyage,* ‹rondreis› *trip, tour*
reisbureau *travel bureau/agency, tourist office*
reischeque *traveller's cheque*
reisgenoot *travelling companion*
reisgezelschap *party (of travellers)*
reisgids *guide*
reizen *travel, journey*
reiziger • (iem. die reist) *traveller* • (handelsreiziger) *commercial traveller*
rek • (klimrek) *climbing frame* • (opbergrek) ‹v. bagage, enz.› *rack*
rekbaar *elastic*
rekenen I [ov ww] • (tellen) *count* • (schatten) *reckon, estimate* • (als betaling vragen) *charge* II [on ww] • (met getallen werken) *calculate, work out, cipher,* ‹sommen maken› *do sums* • (~ op) *depend/count (on)*
rekening • (nota) *bill* • (bankrekening) *account*
rekenkunde *arithmetic*
rekenkundig *arithmetical*
rekenmachine *calculator*
rekenschap *account*
rekken • (uitrekken) *stretch* • (lang aanhouden) *prolong*
rekruteren *recruit*
rekruut *recruit,* ‹AE› *draftee*

rekstok *horizontal bar*
rel *riot*
relaas • (verhaal) *story* • (verslag) *account*
relatie • (zakenrelatie) *business aquaintance/contact* • (onderlinge betrekking) *relationship, connection* • (liefdesrelatie) *relationship, (love) affair*
relatief *relative*
reliëf *relief*
religie *religion*
religieus *religious*
relikwie *relic*
reling *rail(ing)*
rem *brake*
remblok *brake block, shoe*
rembours ⋆ onder ~ *C.O.D.; cash on delivery*
remedie *remedy*
remise • (loods) *depot* • (overmaking v. geld) *remittance* • (onbesliste dam-/schaakpartij) *draw*
remmen I [ov ww] • (afremmen) *stop, brake* • (belemmeren) *inhibit, brake, hinder* II [on ww] *put on the brake(s), brake*
remming *restraint, inhibition*
renaissance *renaissance*
renbaan ‹atletiek› *race track,* ‹autosport› *speedway,* ‹motorsport› *race circuit,* ‹paardensport› *racecourse*
rendabel *paying, profitable*
renderen *pay (its way)*
rendez-vous *rendez-vous*
rendier *reindeer*
rennen *run,* ‹hard› *race*
renner ‹coureur› *racing driver,* ‹te voet› *runner*
renovatie *renovation*
renoveren *renovate*
rentabiliteit *earning capacity,* ‹econ.› *return*
rente • (vergoeding voor lenen) *interest* • (inkomsten uit kapitaal)

interest
renteloos • (rentevrij) *without interest*
• (geen rente gevend) ★ ~ kapitaal
idle capital
rentenieren *live of one's investments*
rentmeester *manager, steward, estate*
agent
reorganisatie *reorganization*
reorganiseren *reorganize*
reparateur *repairman*
reparatie *repair(s)*
repareren *fix, mend, repair*
repeteren I [ov ww] *rehearse* II [on
ww] *repeat*
repetitie • (proefwerk) *test* • (het
repeteren van toneel/muz.) *rehearsal*
• (herhaling) *repetition*
repliek • (weerwoord) *reply*
• (antwoord op het eerste verweer)
reply, ‹jur.› *replication*
reportage *report, commentary*
reppen I [on ww] • (gewag maken van
iets) *mention* II [wkd ww] • (zich
haasten) *hurry*
representatie *representation*
representatief *representative (of)*
repressief *repressive*
reproduceren *reproduce*
reptiel *reptile*
republiek *republic*
reputatie *reputation*
requiem *Requiem (mass)*
reservaat *reserve*
reserve • (voorbehoud) *reservation*
• (noodvoorraad) *reserve*
reserveren • (in reserve houden)
reserve, set aside • (voorbehouden)
reserve • (bespreken) *book*
resideren *reside*
resolutie *resolution*
resoluut *resolute*
respect *respect, regard*
respectabel • (aanmerkelijk)
considerable • (eerbiedwaardig)
respectable

respecteren • (achten) *respect*
• (naleven) *observe*
respectievelijk *respectively*
ressorteren ★ ~ onder *come under*
★ dat ressorteert niet onder ons *that's
outside our province*
rest *rest, remainder*
restant *remainder, remnant*
restaurant *restaurant*
restaurateur • (hersteller) *restorer*
• (restauranthouder) *restaurateur*
restauratie • (eetgelegenheid)
restaurant, ‹in trein, e.d.› *buffet*
• (herstel) *restoration*
restaureren *restore*
resten *remain, be left*
restitutie *restitution*
restrictie *restriction*
resultaat • (gevolg) *result* • (gunstige
uitkomst) *result, outcome*
resumé *résumé, summary,* ‹v. rechter›
summing-up
retoriek *rhetoric*
retorisch *rhetorical*
retort *retort*
retoucheren *retouch, touch up*
retraite *retreat*
reuk *smell*
reukwater *scent, perfume*
reünie *reunion*
reus *giant*
reusachtig I [bnw] • (zeer groot)
gigantic, huge • (zeer goed) *grand,
great* II [bijw] *immensely, enormously*
reutelen *rattle*
reuzel *lard*
revalidatie *rehabilitation*
reveil *revival*
reviseren *overhaul*
revisie • (controlebeurt v. motor)
overhaul • (herziening) ‹tekst›
revision, ‹v. vonnis› *review*
revolutie *revolution*
revolutionair *revolutionary*
revolver *revolver*

revue *revue*
ribbenkast *ribcage*
richel *ledge,* <opstekende rand> *ridge*
richten I [ov ww] • (in een richting
laten gaan) *direct* • (instellen op een
doel) <v. camera> *point (at),* <v. kijker>
train (on), <v. wapen> *aim* II [wkd ww]
• (~ **naar**) *conform to* • (~ **op**)
concentrate on • (~ **tot**) *address*
richting *direction*
richtlijn *guideline*
richtsnoer *guide*
ridder *knight*
ridderlijk *chivalrous*
ridderorde • (ridderstand)
knighthood • (onderscheiding)
decoration
riem • (band) *strap,* <v. hond> *lead,*
leash • (ceintuur) *belt* • (roeiriem) *oar*
riet *reed,* <dik> *cane*
rieten *reed*
rietje • (stokje) *cane* • (limonaderietje)
straw
rietsuiker *cane sugar*
rif *reef*
rij • (reeks in rechte lijn) *row, line,* <v.
mensen> *file, queue* • (reeks) *row*
rijbaan *roadway,* <rijstrook> *lane*
rijbewijs *(driving) licence,* <AE> *driver's
license*
rijden I [ov ww] • (besturen en rijden)
<auto, bus, enz.> *drive,* <v. fiets, paard>
ride II [on ww] • (zich voortbewegen)
ride • (op en neer bewegen) *fidget
(about)*
rijdier *mount*
rijexamen *driving test*
rijgen • (met grote steken naaien)
baste, tack • (met snoer
vast-/dichtmaken) *lace* • (aan een
snoer rijgen) *string, thread*
rijglaars *lace-up boot*
rij-instructeur *driving instructor*
rijk I [het] • (soevereine staat) *state,*
<internationaal> *empire,* <koninkrijk>

kingdom II [bnw] • (vermogend) *rich,
wealthy, well-to-do, well off*
• (overvloedig) *abundant, rich,* <v.
maaltijd> *sumptuous, lavish*
rijkaard *rich/wealthy person*
rijkdom • (kostbaar bezit) *riches* • (het
in overvloed aanwezig zijn)
abundance, richness, wealth • (het rijk
zijn) *affluence, wealth*
rijkelijk • (overvloedig) *rich(ly)* • (in te
ruime mate) *excessive, ample*
rijksambtenaar *public servant,
government official*
rijksdaalder *two-and-a-half guilder
coin*
rijkswege ★ van ~ *by authority of the
government; by/from the state*
rijles <auto> *driving lesson,* <te paard>
riding lesson
rijm • (overeenkomst in klank) *rhyme*
• (gedicht) *poem, verse*
rijmen I [ov ww] • (~ **met**) *reconcile*
II [on ww] • (rijm hebben) *rhyme*
• (rijmen maken) *rhyme* • (in
overeenstemming zijn) *be in
accordance with, tally with*
rijp I [de] (white) *frost, hoarfrost*
II [bnw] • (geheel ontwikkeld)
<bomen, personen, wijn, zaken>
mature, <gewassen, vruchten> *ripe*
• (~ **voor**) *fit/ready/ripe for*
rijpaard *mount, (riding) horse*
rijpen • (rijp doen worden) <personen,
zaken> *mature,* <vruchten> *ripen*
rijpheid *maturity, ripeness*
rijs • (rijshout) *brushwood* • (twijg)
sprig, twig
rijschool <v. autorijden> *driving
school,* <v. paardrijden> *riding school*
rijst *rice*
rijstebrij *rice pudding*
rijstrook *lane*
rijsttafel *(Indonesian) rice table*
rijtuig • (koets) *carriage* • (treinstel)
carriage

rijweg *carriageway, road(way)*
rijwiel *bicycle, ‹inf.› bike*
rijzen • (omhoogkomen) *rise* • (zich voordoen) *occur, arise*
rijzig *tall*
rijzweep *(riding) crop, riding whip*
rillen ‹v. angst› *shudder,* ‹v. kou› *shiver*
rilling *shiver, shudder*
rimboe • (wildernis) *jungle* • (afgelegen gebied) *wilds, back of beyond*
rimpel • (plooi) *wrinkle,* ‹diep› *furrow* • (rimpeling op water) *ripple*
rimpelen ‹v. gezicht› *wrinkle,* ‹v. water› *ruffle, ripple*
rimpelig *wrinkled,* ‹v. gezicht› *lined*
rimpeling ‹golfje› *ripple*
ring *ring, circle*
ringbaard *fringe of beard*
ringeloren *bully*
ringslang *grass snake*
ringvinger *ring finger*
rinkelen *jingle, tinkle,* ‹glas, metaal› *rattle,* ‹v. bel, telefoon› *ring*
riolering *sewerage*
riool *sewer,* ‹vanaf huis› *drain*
risico *risk*
riskant *risky*
riskeren • (op het spel zetten) *risk* • (gevaar lopen) *run the risk of*
rit ‹in auto› *drive,* ‹in trein, bus› *ride,* ‹v. trein› *run*
ritme *rhythm*
ritmisch *rhythmic(al)*
ritselen I [ov ww] • (regelen) *fix, wangle* II [on ww] • (geluid maken) *rustle*
ritueel *ritual*
ritus *rite*
rivier *river*
rivierpolitie *river police*
rob *seal*
robbedoes ‹jongetje› *wild boy,* ‹meisje› *hoyden, tomboy*
robijn *ruby*

robot *robot*
robuust *robust,* ‹v. gestalte› *sturdy*
rochelen • (ophoesten) *cough, hawk up, spit* • (reutelen) *rasp,* ‹v. stervende› *rattle*
roddelaar *backbiter, gossip*
roddelen *backbite, gossip*
rododendron *rhododendron*
roebel *rouble*
roeiboot *rowing boat*
roeien *row,* ‹sport› *scull*
roeier *oarsman* [v: *oarswoman*], *rower*
roekeloos *reckless, rash*
roem *fame, glory*
roemen I [ov ww] *praise, speak highly of* II [on ww] ⋆ ~ *op boast of*
Roemenië *Romania*
roemrijk *glorious*
roep *call,* ‹vogel› *cry*
roepen I [ov ww] *call* II [on ww] *call (out), cry (out), shout*
roeping • (het geroepen zijn) *call(ing), vocation* • (levenstaak) *mission*
roer • (roerblad) *rudder* • (stuurinrichting) *helm*
roeren I [ov ww] • (ontroeren) *move, touch* • (mengen) *stir, mix* II [on ww] ⋆ *goed* ~ *stir well*
roerend *moving, touching*
roerganger *helmsman*
roerig • (beweeglijk) *lively, restless* • (oproerig) *turbulent,* ‹massa› *riotous*
roerloos *motionless*
roes • (bedwelming) *intoxication,* ‹v. drank, drugs› *high* • (euforie) *flush*
roest *rust*
roesten *rust*
roestvrij *rustproof*
roet *soot*
roffel *roll*
roffelen • (een roffel slaan) *roll* • (knoeiwerk leveren) *scamp, do (things) by halves*
rog *ray*
rok • (kledingstuk v. vrouwen) *skirt*

- (rokkostuum) *dress coat*, ‹inf.› *tails*
roken I [ov ww] *smoke* II [on ww]
- (rook afgeven) *smoke*
roker *smoker*
rol • (voorwerp) *roll, cylinder*
- (register) *list, roll* • (hoeveelheid) *coil* • (toneelrol) *part, role* • (functie) *role*
rolgordijn (roller) *blind*, ‹AE› (window) *shade*
rollade *meat roll*
rollen *roll*
rollenspel *role-playing, role play*
rolluik *roll-down shutter*
rolstoel *wheelchair*
roltrap *escalator*
Romaans ‹taalk.› *Romance*, ‹kunst› *Romanesque*
roman *novel*
romanist *student of Romance languages, Romanist*
romanschrijver *novelist*
romantiek I [de] • (stroming in de kunst) *Romanticism* • (romantisch gevoel) *romance* II [bnw] *romantic*
romantisch *romantic*
Rome *Rome*
rommel • (waardeloze prullen) *rubbish* • (vuile boel) *mess*, ‹achtergelaten rommel› *litter*
rommelen • (zoekend overhoop halen) *rummage* • (dof rollend geluid maken) *rumble, roll* • (prutsen) *mess/fart about/around*
rommelig *messy, untidy*
rommelkamer *lumber/junk room*
romp • (torso) *trunk* • (casco) *body*
rompslomp • (gedoe) *bother, fuss*
rond I [het] *round* II [bnw]
- (bol-/cirkelvormig) *round*
- (afgerond) *round* • (gevuld) ⋆ ronde vormen *rounded shapes* III [bijw]
- (met een cirkelbeweging) ⋆ de wereld rond *around the world* ⋆ het gerucht ging rond *rumour had it*

- (afgerond, voltooid) *completed*
IV [vz] • (om(heen)) (a)*round*
- (ongeveer, in de buurt van) *around*
rondbazuinen *trumpet, noise abroad, broadcast*
rondborstig *candid, frank*
rondbrengen *deliver*
ronddraaien *turn* (round), *rotate*
ronddwalen *wander about*
ronde *round*
rondedans *round dance*
rondgaan • (de ronde doen) *go round*
rondhangen *hang around, stand about*
ronding *curve, rounding*
rondje ⋆ een ~ geven *buy a round of drinks*
rondkijken *look about*
rondkomen *make ends meet, manage*
rondleiden *lead round*
rondlopen *walk about*
rondom I [bijw] • (overal) *all around*
- (eromheen) *on all sides* II [vz] • (in de buurt van) ⋆ ~ het centrum van de stad *around the town centre* • (om ... heen) ⋆ ~ het vuur *around the fire*
rondreis *tour, round trip*
rondrit *tour*
rondschrijven *circular* (letter)
rondte ⋆ in de ~ *in a circle*
ronduit I [bnw] *straightforward* II [bijw] *frankly, plainly*
rondvliegen • (in een kring vliegen) *fly round, circle* • (alle kanten opvliegen) *fly about/around*
rondvraag *matters arising*, ‹als punt op agenda› *any other business*
rondweg *bypass, orbital motorway*
rondzwerven *wander about*
ronken • (snurken) *snore* • (ronkend geluid maken) ‹v. motor› *throb*, ‹v. vliegtuig› *roar*
ronselen *press-gang, recruit*
röntgenfoto *X-ray*
rood *red*

roodborstje *robin (redbreast)*
roodgloeiend *red-hot*
roodharig *ginger, red-haired*
roodhuid *redskin*
roodvonk *scarlet fever*
roof *robbery*
roofbouw • (overdadige landbouw) *overcropping* • (exploitatie) <fig.> *exhaustion, overuse,* <v. landbouw> *depletion of the soil*
roofdier *beast of prey, predator*
roofoverval *hold-up, armed robbery*
roofvogel *bird of prey*
rooien • (uit de grond halen) *dig (up),* <v. aardappels> *lift* • (bolwerken) *manage*
rook *smoke*
rookcoupé *smoker, smoking compartment*
rookgordijn *smoke screen*
rookvlees *smoked beef*
room *cream*
roomboter *(full-cream) butter*
roomijs *ice cream*
roos • (bloem) *rose* • (huidschilfers op hoofd) *dandruff* • (afleesschijf v. kompas) *rose, card* • (middelpunt van schietschijf) *bull's eye*
rooskleurig *rosy,* <form.> *roseate*
rooster • (raamwerk) *grid,* <braadrooster> *grill* • (schema) <lesrooster> *timetable,* <werkrooster> *roster*
roosteren *roast,* <v. brood> *toast,* <v. vlees> *grill*
ros I [het] *steed* II [bnw] ∗ de rosse buurt *the red-light district*
rosbief *roast beef*
rossen *career, ride recklessly*
rossig *ginger, reddish, sandy-haired*
rot I [het] *rot, decay* II [bnw] *rotten,* <rottend> *putrid*
roteren *rotate*
rotonde • (rond gebouw) *rotunda* • (verkeersrotonde) *roundabout*

rots *rock,* <aan zee> *cliff,* <steil> *crag*
rotsachtig *rocky*
rotstuin *rock garden, rockery*
rotsvast *solid as a rock*
rotten *decay, rot*
rotting • (het bederf) *rot, decay* • (stok) *cane*
rotzooi • (slechte waar) *rubbish, junk* • (rommel) *mess*
roulatie *circulation*
rouleren • (in omloop zijn) *circulate* • (bij toerbeurt gedaan worden) *take turns,* <m.b.t. ploegendienst> *work in shifts*
roulette *roulette*
route *route, way*
routine • (sleur) *routine* • (geoefendheid) *practice*
rouw *mourning*
rouwen • (treuren) *grieve, mourn* • (in de rouw zijn) *be in mourning*
rouwig ∗ ik ben er niet ∼ om *I'm not sorry about it; I don't regret it*
roven *rob*
rover *robber*
royaal *generous* ∗ een ∼ inkomen *an ample income*
roze *pink*
rozengeur *scent of roses*
rozenkrans • (krans van rozen) *garland of roses* • (bidsnoer) *rosary*
rozet *rosette*
rozig *rosy*
rozijn *raisin*
rubber *rubber*
rubriceren • (indelen) *classify* • (in rubrieken onderbrengen) *class (under)*
rubriek • (vast stuk in krant) *column* • (opschrift) *heading* • (categorie) *category, class, division*
ruchtbaar *known, public*
ruchtbaarheid *public knowledge, publicity*
rug • (deel van lichaam) *back* • (bovenvlak) <bergrug> *ridge,* <v.

neus> bridge
rugby rugby (football), <inf.> rugger
ruggelings I [bnw] backward II [bijw]
• (achterwaarts) backwards • (op de
rug) on one's back
ruggengraat • (wervelkolom)
backbone, spine, spinal/vertebral
column • (wilskracht) backbone,
determinaton
ruggenmerg spinal cord
ruggensteun • (steun in de rug) back
support • (hulp) support, backing
ruggenwervel dorsal vertebra
ruggespraak consultation
rugleuning back rest
rugzak backpack, <klein> rucksack
rugzijde back
rui moulting
ruig rugged, rough
ruiken I [ov ww] smell II [on ww]
• (geur dragen) smell • (~ naar)
smack of
ruiker bouquet, <klein> nosegay
ruil exchange, <inf.> swop
ruilen exchange, <inf.> swop
ruilhandel barter
ruilverkaveling legal re-division and
re-allotment of land
ruim I [het] hold II [bnw] • (veel
ruimte biedend) large, spacious
• (uitgebreid) extensive • (meer dan
voldoende) ★ ruim inkomen
comfortable/liberal income ★ zij had
het niet ruim she was not well off
★ ruime keus wide/large choice
III [bijw] • (meer dan) ★ ruim zestig
(well) over sixty
ruimen I [ov ww] • (leegmaken) empty
• (schoonmaken) clear out II [on ww]
veer
ruimschoots abundantly, amply
ruimte • (heelal) space • (plaats) room,
space • (vertrek) room
ruimtelijk • (driedimensionaal)
three-dimensional • (de ruimte

betreffend) spatial
ruimtevaart space travel
ruïne • (vervallen bouwwerk) ruin
• (resten) ruins
ruïneren ruin
ruisen <v. water> murmur, <v. wind,
bladeren, kleren> rustle
ruit • (geometrische figuur) diamond
• (motief) check • (glasplaat) pane
ruitensproeier windscreen washer,
<AE> windshield washer
ruitenwisser windscreen wiper, <AE>
windshield wiper
ruiter horseman, rider
ruiterij cavalry
ruiterlijk frank
ruiterpad bridle path
ruk • (trekkende beweging) jerk, pull,
tug • (tijdsduur) period • (afstand)
distance
rukken I [ov ww] • (met een ruk
trekken) snatch II [on ww] • (hard
trekken) jerk, pull, tug
rukwind squall
rum rum
rumoer • (lawaai) noise • (ophef)
uproar, commotion
rumoerig • (onstuimig) boisterous
• (lawaaiig) noisy
run run
rund • (dier) <koe> cow [mv: cattle], <os>
ox [mv: cattle], <stier> bull
• (stommeling) idiot
rundvlees beef
rups caterpillar
Rusland Russia
Russisch I [het] Russian II [bnw]
Russian
rust • (pauze in muziekstuk) rest
• (pauze tijdens wedstrijd) half-time,
interval • (ontspanning) rest
• (kalmte) calm, quiet • (nachtrust,
slaap) repose
rusten • (uitrusten) repose, rest
• (steunen op) rest (upon) • (begraven

liggen) * hier rust... here lies...
rustig • (in rust) peaceful, quiet
• (ongestoord) quiet, untroubled
• (bedaard) calm • (vredig) peaceful,
tranquil
rustplaats resting place
rustpunt pause, rest
rustverstoorder <herrieschopper>
hooligan, <ordeverstoorder> rioter
ruw • (niet glad) rough, <huid> coarse
• (onbeschaafd) coarse • (onbewerkt)
crude, raw • (onbehouwen) rough
• (globaal) rough
ruzie quarrel, row
ruzieachtig • (twistziek) quarrelsome
• (als bij ruzie) argumentative

S

saai I [het] serge II [bnw] tedious,
boring, dull, slow
sabbat sabbath
sabbelen suck
sabel I [de] sword II [het] • (bont) sable
• (kleur) sable
sabotage sabotage
saboteren sabotage
sacrament sacrament
sadisme sadism
saffraan saffron
sage saga
salade salad
salamander salamander
salaris salary, pay
saldo balance
salon • (kapper) hair salon, hairdressers
• (zitkamer) drawing room
salpeter saltpetre, potassium nitrate
salueren salute
salvo • (van schoten) salvo, volley
• (stortvloed) volley
samen together
samenhang connection, connexion
samenhangen be connected
samenleving society
samenloop • (samenkomst van
invloeden e.d.) concurrence
• (samenvloeiing) convergence, <v.
rivieren> confluence
samenpakken I [ov ww] pack up
II [wkd ww] gather
samenraapsel jumble, hotchpotch
samenscholing • (het samenscholen)
gathering • (menigte) assembly
samensmelten I [ov ww] melt
together, fuse II [on ww] • (door
smelten een geheel worden) fuse
• (samengaan) amalgamate
samenspannen plot, conspire

samenspel <muz.> *ensemble*, <sport> *teamwork*

samenstellen • (onderdelen tot geheel vormen) *arrange* • (opstellen) *compose*

samensteller *compiler, assembler, composer*

samenstelling • (het samenstellen) *compilation* • (manier van samenstellen) *composition*, <v. programma> *arrangement*

samentrekken *contract*

samenvallen • (tegelijk gebeuren) *coincide* • (samenkomen) *converge*

samenvatten • (bij elkaar pakken) *take together* • (kort weergeven) *summarize, sum up*

samenvatting *summary*

samenvoegen *join, combine, unite*

samenwerken • (samenlopen) *combine* • (met elkaar werken) *work/act/pull together, co-operate, collaborate*

samenwerking *cooperation*

samenwonen *live together*

samenzijn *gathering, meeting*

samenzweerder *conspirator*

samenzweren *plot, conspire*

samenzwering *plot*

sanatorium *sanatorium*

sanctie *sanction*

sandaal *sandal*

saneren • (onderhouden) *put in order* • (op orde brengen) *clean up*, <bedrijf> *reorganize*, <buurt> *redevelop*

sanitair • (badkamer-/toiletartikelen) *sanitary* • (hygiënisch) *sanitary*

sap • (vocht v. plant) *sap* • (vruchtensap) *juice*

sappig • (vol sap) *tender*, <fruit> *juicy*, <plant> *sappy*, <vlees> *succulent* • (levendig) *juicy*

sarcasme *sarcasm*

sarcastisch *sarcastic*

sarren *nag, bait, tease*

sas ★ in zijn sas zijn *be in high spirits*

Satan *Satan*

satanisch *satanic*

satelliet • (hemellichaam) *satellite* • (kunstmaan) *satellite* • (persoon) *henchman*

satire *satire*

satirisch *satiric(al)*

saucijzenbroodje *sausage roll*

sauna *sauna*

saus *sauce*

sausen • (van smaak voorzien) *sauce* • (verven) *whitewash*

saxofoon *saxophone*

scalperen *scalp*

scenario • (draaiboek) *scenario, film script, script* • (plan) *scenario*

scenarioschrijver *scriptwriter, scenarist*

scepter *sceptre*

scepticisme *scepticism*

sceptisch *sceptical*

schaaf • (schuurgereedschap) *plane* • (plakjessnijder) *slicer*

schaak I [het] *chess* II [tw] ★ ~! *check!*

schaakbord *chessboard*

schaakmat *checkmate*

schaal • (schotel) *dish, bowl* • (schaalverdeling) *scale*

schaalverdeling *scale division*

schaambeen *pubic bone*

schaamrood *blush*

schaamte *shame*

schaamteloos • (zonder schaamtegevoel) *shameless* • (onbeschaamd) *unashamed*

schaap *sheep* [mv: *sheep*]

schaapachtig *sheepish*

schaapherder *shepherd*

schaapskooi *sheepfold*

schaar (pair of) *scissors*

schaars I [bnw] *scarce, rare* II [bijw] ★ ~ gekleed *scantily dressed*

schaats *skate*

schacht *shaft*

schade • (verlies, nadeel) *loss*
• (beschadiging) *damage, injury, harm*
schadelijk *harmful*
schaden *damage, harm, hurt*
schadepost *loss*
schadevergoeding *compensation,
indemnification*
schaduw *shadow* ∗ in de ~ *in the shade*
schaduwen • (schaduw aanbrengen)
shade • (volgen) *shadow*
schaduwrijk *shadowy, shady*
schaften *take time off (for a meal)*
schakel *link*
schakelaar *switch*
schakelbord *switchboard*
schakelen *change gear*
schakeling <elektriciteit> *circuit*
schaken I [ov ww] *abduct (a girl)* II [on
ww] *play chess*
schaker • (iem. die schaakt speelt)
chess player • (ontvoerder) *abductor*
schakeren • (kleuren schikken)
variegate • (afwisselen) *pattern*
schakering • (afwisseling) *variegation*
• (nuance) *shade*
schalks *roguish*
schallen *sound, resound*
schamel *poor*
schamper *scornful*
schampschot *graze*
schandaal *scandal*
schandalig *scandalous, shameful,
outrageous*
schande • (oneer) *disgrace, shame,
ignominy* • (oneervolle toestand)
shame, disgrace
schandelijk *disgraceful, shameful,
ignominious*
schandvlek *stain, blemish, stigma,
<persoon> disgrace, dishonour*
schans • (bolwerk) *entrenchment*
• (springschans) *ski jump*
schapenvacht *sheepskin*
schapenvlees *mutton*
schappelijk *fair, reasonable*

scharen *range, draw up*
scharnier *hinge*
scharrelen I [ov ww] *scrape together*
II [on ww] • (rommelen) *grub (about)*
• (flirten) *flirt* • (moeizaam bewegen)
stumble along
schat • (overvloed) *wealth, treasure*
• (geliefd persoon) *dear, darling, love,
honey* • (verzameling
kostbaarheden/geld) *treasure*
• (waardevol bezit) *treasure*
schateren *roar with laughter*
schatkamer *treasury*
schatkist • (geldkist) *treasure chest*
• (staatskas) *exchequer, The Treasury*
schatrijk *wealthy*
schatten • (waarderen) *value*
• (waarde bepalen) *estimate*
schattig *sweet*
schatting • (raming) *estimation* • ('t
geraamde) *estimate* • (heffing) *tribute*
schaven *plane*
schavot *scaffold*
schede • (omhulsel) *sheath* • (vagina)
vagina
schedel *skull*
scheef • (niet recht) *crooked,* <het
hoofd> *cocked,* <ogen> *slanting*
• (asymmetrisch) *lopsided*
scheel *squinting, cross-eyed*
scheen *shin*
scheepslading *shipload*
scheepsrecht *maritime law*
scheepvaart • (bedrijf) *shipping* • (het
varen) *navigation*
scheerapparaat *electric shaver*
scheerkwast *shaving brush*
scheermes *razor*
scheiden I [ov ww] • (uit elkaar halen)
part II [on ww] *separate, part,* <v.
gehuwd paar> *divorce*
scheiding *separation*
• (haarscheiding) *parting*
• (verbreking v. relatie) *separation,*
<echtscheiding> *divorce*

scheidsrechter <tennis> umpire, <voetbal> referee
scheikunde chemistry
scheikundig chemical
schel <geluid> shrill, <licht> glaring
schelden I [ov ww] call names, scold, rail at II [on ww] curse, swear, use abusive language
scheldnaam term of abuse, nickname
scheldwoord term of abuse
schelen make a difference, differ
schelm rascal
schelp shell
schelvis haddock
schema • (tijdsplanning) schedule • (tekening) diagram • (weergave van hoofdpunten) outline
schematisch schematic
schemer twilight, dusk
schemeren <'s avonds> turn to dusk, <'s morgens> dawn
schemering twilight, dusk
schemerlamp floor/table lamp
schenden • (ontheiligen) desecrate • (verminken) mutilate • (verbreken) <v. rechten> violate, <wet> infringe
schending • (ontering) violation • (ontheiliging) desecration • (overtreding) transgression • (verminking) mutilation
schenken • (gieten) pour • (serveren) serve • (geven) give, grant, make a present of
schenking gift, donation
schep scoop, shovel
schepnet landing net, scoop net
scheppen • (opscheppen) scoop, <eten> ladle, <papier> dip • (maken) create • (ontlenen) take
schepper creator
schepping creation
schepsel creature
scheren shave
scherf splinter, <aardewerk> potsherd
schering warp

scherm screen, <zonnescherm> awning
schermen • (sport) fence • (~ met) talk big
schermutseling skirmish
scherp sharp ★ ~ stellen focus
scherpen sharpen
scherpschutter sharpshooter
scherpte sharpness
scherpzinnig • (intelligent) acute • (vernuftig) shrewd
scherts joke, fun
schertsen • (grappen maken) jest, joke • (spotten) make fun of
schets • (kort verhaal) sketch • (tekening) sketch • (beschrijving in hoofdlijnen) outline
schetsboek sketchbook
schetsen • (tekenen) sketch • (in hoofdlijnen beschrijven) outline
scheur • (spleet) crack, <in kleding> tear • (mond) big mouth
scheurbuik scurvy
scheuren I [ov ww] tear II [on ww] • (een scheur krijgen) tear, <v. ijs, enz.> crack • (hard rijden) speed
scheuring • (het scheuren) tearing, rupture • (splitsing) rupture, split, <kerkelijk> schism
scheurkalender block-calendar
scheut • (steek v. pijn) twinge • (hoeveelheid vloeistof) dash • (loot) shoot, sprig
scheutig • (vrijgevig) liberal • (bereidwillig) willing
schicht flash (of lightning)
schichtig shy, skittish
schielijk • (snel) quick • (plotseling) sudden
schiereiland peninsula
schietbaan rifle range
schieten shoot
schietlood plummet
schietschijf target
schietstoel ejector seat
schiettent shooting gallery

schiften I [ov ww] *sift, sort (out), separate, sort through* II [on ww] *curdle*
schijf *disk*
schijn *appearance*
schijnbaar I [bnw] *seeming, apparent* II [bijw] *evidently*
schijnbeweging *feint*
schijndood I [de] *apparent death, suspended animation* II [bnw] *apparently dead, seemingly in a state of suspended animation*
schijnen • (stralen) *shine* • (lijken) *seem*
schijnheilig *hypocritical*
schijnsel *shine, radiance, glimmer*
schijnwerper *floodlight,* <toneel> *spotlight*
schijt *shit*
schijten *shit*
schik • (plezier) *fun* • (tevredenheid) ★ hij was er erg mee in zijn ~ *he was very pleased with it*
schikken I [ov ww] *arrange* II [on ww] *suit* III [wkd ww] ★ zich ~ in zijn lot *resign o.s. to one's fate*
schikking • (ordening) *arrangement* • (vergelijk) *agreement, arrangement, settlement*
schil <banaan, sinaasappel> *peel,* <meloen, sinaasappel> *rind,* <v. bessen, druiven, bananen> *skin,* <v. ei> *shell*
schild *shield*
schilder *painter*
schilderachtig *picturesque*
schilderen I [ov ww] • (verven) *paint* • (beschrijven) *paint, picture* II [on ww] *stand guard*
schilderij • (iets schilderachtigs) *picture* • (geschilderde afbeelding) *picture, painting*
schildklier *thyroid gland*
schildpad I [de] *tortoise,* <zeeschildpad> *turtle* II [het] *tortoiseshell*

schildwacht *sentry, sentinel*
schilfer *flake, scale*
schilferen *peel off, flake*
schillen *peel*
schim • (vage gedaante) *shadow, shade* • (geest) *shade, ghost* • (schaduwbeeld) *silhouette*
schimmel • (uitslag) *mould, mildew* • (zwam) *fungus* • (paard) *grey*
schimmelen *become/get mouldy*
schimmelig • (beschimmeld) *mouldy* • (schimmelachtig) *fungoid*
schimpscheut *gibe*
schip • (boot) *ship, vessel* • (middenbeuk v. kerk) *nave*
schipbreuk *shipwreck*
schipbreukeling *shipwrecked person*
schipper *master, skipper,* <v. binnenvaartuig> *bargeman,* <v. kleine boot> *boatman*
schipperen I [ov ww] *manage* II [on ww] *give and take*
schitteren *shine,* <v. ogen, diamanten, enz.> *glitter, sparkle*
schitterend • (glinsterend) *glittering, sparkling* • (fantastisch) *brilliant, splendid*
schittering • (het schitteren) *brilliance* • (pracht) *lustre, splendour*
schizofreen *schizophrenic*
schmink *paint, make up*
schminken *make up*
schoeisel *footwear*
schoen *shoe*
schoener *schooner*
schoenmaker *shoemaker*
schoenpoetser *shoeblack, shoeshine boy, shoeshine machine*
schoffel *hoe, shovel*
schoffelen • (tackelen) *chop* • (onkruid) *hoe, weed*
schoft • (klootzak) *cad, scoundrel, bastard* • (schouder v. dier) *withers*
schok *shock*
schokbeton *vibrated concrete*

schokbreker *shock absorber*
schokgolf *shock wave*
schokken I [ov ww] • (choqueren)
shock • (doen wankelen) *shake* II [on
ww] *shake, jerk*
schol *plaice*
scholen • (onderwijzen) *school, teach*
• (samenscholen) *flock together*
scholengemeenschap *comprehensive
school, community school*
scholier *pupil,* <AE> *student*
scholing *schooling*
schommel • (speeltuig) *swing*
• (dikkerd) *fat person, fatty*
schommelen *rock,* <v. boot> *roll*
schommeling *swing, fluctuation*
schommelstoel *rocking chair*
schoof *sheaf*
schooien *beg*
schooier • (zwerver) *beggar, bum,
tramp* • (schoft) *bastard*
school *school*
schoolblijven I [het] *detention* II [on
ww] *be kept in*
schoolboek *schoolbook, textbook*
schoolgeld *tuition*
schoolhoofd *principal, headmaster,
headmistress*
schooljaar • (leerjaar) *school year*
• (jaar op school) *scholastic year*
schoollokaal *classroom*
schoolmeester • (leerkracht)
schoolmaster • (schoolmeesterachtig
type) *pedant*
schools *scholastic*
schoolslag *breaststroke*
schooltas *schoolbag,* <over schouder>
satchel
schooltijd • (schooltijdjaren)
schooldays • (lestijd) *school hours,
school time*
schoon I [bnw] *clean* II [bijw] ⋆ er ~
*genoeg van hebben be sick and tired
of it*
schoondochter *daughter-in-law*

schoonheid *beauty*
schoonhouden *keep clean*
schoonmaak *cleaning,* <voorjaar>
spring-cleaning
schoonmaakbedrijf *cleaning firm*
schoonmaken *clean*
schoonmoeder *mother-in-law*
schoonouders *parents-in-law, in-laws*
schoonvader *father-in-law*
schoonzoon *son-in-law*
schoorsteen *chimney,* <v. stoomboot>
funnel
schoorsteenmantel *mantelpiece*
schoorsteenveger *chimney sweep*
schoorvoetend *reluctant*
schoot • (baarmoeder) *womb*
• (binnenste) *insides* • (rok v.
kledingstuk) *skirt* • (uitloper)
<plantk.> *shoot* • (voorkant v.
bovenbenen) *lap* • (touw) <scheepv.>
sheet
schop • (spade) *shovel, spade* • (trap)
kick
schoppen I [de] *spades* II [ov ww] *kick
(at)*
schor I [de] *salt marsh* II [bnw] *hoarse*
schorem I [het] *scum, riffraff* II [bnw]
shabby
schorpioen • (dier) *scorpion*
• (sterrenbeeld) *Scorpio, the Scorpion*
schors *bark, rind*
schorsen • (buiten dienst stellen)
suspend • (tijdelijk opheffen) *adjourn*
schorsing • (tijdelijke uitsluiting)
suspension • (uitstel v. vergadering)
adjournment
schort *apron,* <overgooier> *pinafore*
schorten ⋆ wat schort er aan? *what is
wrong?*
schot • (ontlading v. vuurwapen) *shot,
crack,* <knal> *report* • (trap tegen bal)
shot • (tussenschot) *partition* • (vaart)
⋆ er zit geen ~ in things *are at a
standstill*
schotel • (serviesstuk) *saucer*

• (gerecht) *dish*
Schotland *Scotland*
schots *(ice-)floe*
schouder *shoulder*
schouderband *shoulder strap*
schouderblad *shoulder blade*
schouderophalen *shrug*
schouw • (stookplaats) *fireplace*
• (binnenvaartuig) *scow* • (inspectie
v. wegen) *survey*
schouwburg *theatre*
schouwspel *spectacle, scene*
schraag *trestle*
schraal • (guur) *bleak* • (mager) *lean,
thin* • (karig) *scant(y)* • (uitgedroogd)
<v. huid> *irritated, rough*
schraapzucht *stinginess*
schrammen *scratch*
schrander *clever, smart, bright*
schranderheid *cleverness, smartness,
brightness*
schransen *stuff, gorge*
schrap ★ zich ~ zetten *brace o.s.*
schrapen *scrape*
schrappen *delete,* <naam> *strike out*
schrede *step, pace*
schreef • (lijn) *scratch, line*
• (dwarsstreepje v. drukletter) *serif*
schreeuw *shout, cry*
schreeuwen • (hard roepen) *shout*
• (~ om) *cry out for*
schreeuwend • (roepend) *crying*
• (opzichtig) *loud*
schreeuwerig *noisy, clamorous*
schreien *weep, cry*
schriel ★ een ~ mannetje *a skinny
little man*
schrift I [de] ★ de Heilige Schrift *Holy
Scripture* II [het] • (handschrift)
handwriting, script • (het
geschrevene) *writing* • (cahier)
notebook
schriftelijk I [bnw] *written* II [bijw] *in
writing*
schrijden *stride, stalk*

schrijfmachine *typewriter*
schrijftaal *written language*
schrijfwijze • (spelling) *spelling,* <v.
getallen> *notation* • (handschrift)
handwriting
schrijlings *astride*
schrijnen *smart*
schrijven I [het] *letter* II [ov ww]
• (opschrijven) *write down* ★ iem. ~
write to s.o. III [on ww] *write*
schrijver • (briefschrijver) *writer*
• (klerk) *clerk, secretary* • (auteur v.
een boek) *author, writer*
schrik • (vrees) *terror, dread*
• (plotseling angstgevoel) *fright,
alarm*
schrikaanjagend *terrifying*
schrikbarend • (angstaanjagend)
terrifying • (ontzettend) *appalling*
schrikbeeld *spectre, bogey*
schrikbewind *reign of terror*
schrikdraad *electric wire, electric fence*
schrikkeljaar *leap year*
schrikken *be frightened,*
<opschrikken> *start*
schril *shrill*
schrobben *scrub*
schrobber *scrubbing brush*
schrobbering *scolding, dressing down*
schroef • (draaiende beweging) *screw*
• (pin met schroefdraad) *tuning peg,
screw* • (aandrijfwerktuig) *propeller*
• (bankschroef) *vice*
schroefdop *screw-top*
schroefdraad *thread*
schroeien I [ov ww] *singe,* <haar>
scorch II [on ww] *singe, burn*
schroeven *screw*
schroevendraaier *screwdriver*
schrokken *gorge, gobble*
schromelijk *gross*
schromen • (vrezen) *fear* • (aarzelen)
hesitate
schroot I [de] *lath* II [het]
• (metaalafval) *scrap iron* • (als

schietlading) *grapeshot, shrapnel, pellet*
schuchter *shy*
schudden *shake*
schuif • (grendel) *bolt* • (luik) *slide,* ‹v. kachel› *damper,* ‹v. machine› *valve*
schuifdak *sliding roof,* ‹v. auto› *sunroof*
schuifdeur *sliding door*
schuifelen • (schuivend voortbewegen) *shuffle* • (dansen) *smooch*
schuilen • (beschutting zoeken) *take shelter* • (zich verbergen) *hide*
schuilgaan • (zich verbergen) *hide* • (~ achter) *be hidden behind*
schuilkelder *air-raid shelter*
schuilnaam *pen name, pseudonym*
schuim *foam,* ‹op bier, enz.› *froth,* ‹op soep, enz.› *scum,* ‹v. zeep› *lather*
schuimen I [ov ww] *skim* II [on ww] *foam,* ‹v. bier› *froth,* ‹v. zeep› *lather*
schuimrubber *foam rubber*
schuin I [bnw] • (scheef) *slanting, sloping, oblique* • (schunnig) *broad* II [bijw] *obliquely, slantwise, aslant, awry*
schuinte • (helling) *slope* • (schuine richting) *bias*
schuit *boat, barge*
schuiven I [ov ww] *push, shove* II [on ww] • (voortschuiven) *slide* • (betalen) *shell out*
schuld • (geldelijke verplichting) *debt* • (fout, tekortkoming) *guilt, fault, blame*
schuldbekentenis • (promesse) *IOU, bond* • (bekennen van schuld) *confession of guilt*
schuldbesef *sense of guilt*
schuldeiser *creditor*
schuldenaar *debtor*
schuldig • (verschuldigd) *owing* • (schuld hebbend) *guilty, culpable*
schulp *shell*

schunnig ‹taalgebruik› *filthy*
schuren I [ov ww] • (schrapend schuiven) *scour, grate* • (met schuurpapier bewerken) *sand(paper)* II [on ww] *chafe*
schurft *scabies,* ‹v. dieren› *mange*
schurftig *scabby,* ‹dieren› *mangy*
schurk *scoundrel, villain*
schut *lock*
schutter *marksman, shot*
schutterig *awkward, clumsy*
schutting *fence*
schuur *barn,* ‹klein› *shed*
schuurpapier *sandpaper*
schuw *shy, timid*
schuwen *shun, shrink (from),* ‹form.› *eschew*
schuwheid *shyness*
scooter *scooter*
scoren *score*
scrupule *scruple*
scrupuleus *scrupulous*
seconde *second*
secondewijzer *second hand*
secretariaat *secretary's office, secretariat*
secretaris • (ambtenaar v. gemeentebestuur) ≈ *town clerk* • (adm.) *secretary*
sectie • (deel/afdeling) *section,* ‹v. school, enz.› *department* • (med.) ‹op kadaver› *dissection,* ‹op lijk› *autopsy*
sector *sector*
secundair *secondary*
secuur • (veilig) *safe, secure* • (precies) *accurate, precise*
segment *segment*
sein • (waarschuwing, hint) *tip, hint* • (teken) *sign, signal* • (voorwerp waarmee men seint) *signal*
seinen I [ov ww] *radio, flash* II [on ww] *signal*
seinpaal *semaphore*
seizoen *season*
sekse *sex*

seksueel *sex, sexual*
sekte *sect*
selectie *selection*
selectief *selective*
semantiek *semantics*
semester *term of six months,* <AE>
semester
seminarie *seminary*
senaat *senate*
senator *senator*
senior *senior*
sensatie • (gewaarwording) *sensation*
• (opschudding) *thrill, sensation*
sensueel *sensual*
sentimenteel *sentimental,* <inf.>
sloppy
separaat *separate*
seponeren *dismiss*
september *September*
sergeant *sergeant*
sergeant-majoor *sergeant-major*
serie *series*
serpent • (slang) *serpent* • (persoon)
shrew, bitch
serpentine (paper) *streamer*
serre • (vertrek) *sun lounge/room*
• (broeikas) *conservatory*
serum *serum*
serveren • (opdienen) *serve* • (sport)
serve
servet (table) *napkin, serviette*
servies *dinner-service,* <theeservies>
tea-set
sextant *sextant*
sextet *sextet*
sfeer *atmosphere*
sfinx *sphinx*
sherry *sherry*
Siberisch *Siberian*
sidderen *tremble, shake*
siddering *shudder*
sier *show*
sieraad • (juweel) *jewel, (piece of)*
jewellery • (opschik) *ornament*
sieren • (tot sieraad zijn) *adorn*

• (versieren) *decorate*
sierlijk *graceful*
sigaar *cigar*
sigaret *cigarette*
sigarettenpijpje *cigarette holder*
signaal *signal*
signalement *description*
signaleren • (attenderen op) *point
out, draw attention to* • (opmerken)
observe
signatuur • (handtekening) *signature*
• (kenmerk, aard) *nature, character*
sijpelen *seep, ooze, trickle, filter*
sik • (puntig baardje) *goatee* • (geit)
goat
sikkel • (sikkelvormig mes) *reaping
hook, sickle* • (v. maan) *crescent, sickle*
silhouet *silhouette*
silo *silo*
simpel • (eenvoudig) *simple*
• (onnozel) *silly, simple*
simultaan *simultaneous*
sinaasappel *orange*
sinds I [vz] • (vanaf tijdstip) *since*
• (gedurende) *for* II [vw] *since*
singel • (gracht) *moat* • (weg)
boulevard • (gordel) *girdle*
sint • (Sinterklaas) *Saint Nicholas*
• (heilige) *saint*
sintel *cinder*
sintelbaan *cinder-track,* <vnl. v.
motoren> *dirt-track*
sinterklaas *feast of St Nicholas*
Sinterklaas *St Nicholas*
sip *glum, crestfallen*
sirene *siren*
siroop *treacle, syrup*
sissen • (iets sissend zeggen) *hiss*
• (sissend geluid maken) *sizzle*
sisser *squib*
situatie *situation*
sjaal *shawl, scarf*
sjacheren *haggle, barter*
sjalot *shallot*
sjeik *sheik(h)*

sjerp *sash*
sjezen • (studie of loopbaan staken)
drop out • (hard lopen/rijden) *tear*
• (zakken) *be ploughed*
sjilpen *chirp, cheep*
sjirpen *cheep, chirp*
sjofel *shabby, shoddy*
sjokken *trudge*
sjorren • (vastbinden) *lash (down)*
• (trekken) *lug*
sjouwen *lug*
skelet *skeleton*
ski *ski*
skiën I [het] *skiing* II [on ww] *ski*
skiër *skier*
sla • (salade) *salad* • (groente) *lettuce*
slaaf *slave*
slaag ★ een stevig pak ~ geven *give a
good hiding/beating*
slaags ★ ~ raken met iem. *come to
blows with s.o.*
slaan I [ov ww] • (slagen geven) *strike,
hit*, ‹herhaaldelijk› *beat*, ‹met platte
hand› *spank* • (bij bordspel) *take,
capture* • (in toestand brengen) *strike,
beat* II [on ww] • (slaande beweging
maken) *hit out, strike out* • (door
slagen geluid maken) *strike* • (~op)
refer (to)
slaap • (rust) *sleep* • (neiging tot
slapen) *sleepiness* • (afscheiding in
ooghoeken) *sleep* • (zijkant van het
hoofd) *temple*
slaapdronken *half asleep, drowsy*
slaapkamer *bedroom*
slaapkop • (slaperig persoon)
sleepyhead • (sukkel) *dope*
slaapmiddel *sedative, sleeping pill,
‹med.› opiate*
slaapwandelaar *sleepwalker*
slaapwandelen I [het] *sleepwalking*
II [on ww] *sleepwalk*
slaapzaal *dormitory*
slaapzak *sleeping bag*
slachten • (doden v. slachtvee) *kill,*

slaughter • (afslachten v. mensen)
butcher, massacre
slachter *slaughterer*
slachthuis *slaughterhouse*
slachting • (het slachten)
slaughtering • (moordpartij) *slaughter*
slachtoffer • (persoon) *victim*
• (offerdier) *sacrifice, sacrificial animal*
slag • (het slaan) ‹v. hart, pols› *beat*, ‹v.
klok› *stroke* • (klap, knal) *blow* • (mil.)
battle
slagader *artery*
slagboom *barrier*
slagen • (succes hebben) *succeed*
• (examen halen) *pass, qualify*
slager *butcher*
slagerij *butcher's shop*
slagorde *battle array*
slagregen *downpour*
slagroom ‹na het kloppen› *whipped
cream*, ‹voor het kloppen› *whipping
cream*
slagschip *battleship*
slagtand ‹v. hond, wolf› *fang*, ‹v.
olifant› *tusk*
slagvaardig • (voortvarend) *decisive*
• (strijdvaardig) *ready for battle*
• (gevat) *quick-witted, on the ball,
adroit*
slagveld *battlefield*
slagwerk • (slaand werk in uurwerk)
striking-mechanism • (muz.)
percussion instruments
slagzin *slogan*
slak *snail*, ‹naaktslak› *slug*
slaken • (uiten) *give, utter*
• (losmaken) *loosen*
slang • (dier) *snake* • (buis) *tube, hose*
slank *slender, slim*
slaolie *salad oil*
slap *weak*, ‹slap hangend› *limp*, ‹v.
bier› *thin*, ‹v. touw› *slack*
slapeloos *sleepless, wakeful*
slapeloosheid *sleeplessness, insomnia*
slapen *sleep, be asleep*

slaper • (logé) *guest (for the night)* • (dijk) *inner-dike* • (iem. die slaapt) *sleeper*

slaperig *sleepy, drowsy*

slappeling *weakling, softie, wimp*

slapte *slackness*

slavenarbeid • (werk als voor een slaaf) ‹op het werk› *slave labour,* ‹thuis› *drudgery* • (slavenwerk) *slavery, slave labour*

slavernij • (onderworpenheid) *bondage, slavery* • (het stelsel) *slavery*

slecht I [bnw] • (moreel slecht) *evil, wicked* • (ongunstig) *bad* • (niet deugdelijk) *bad* II [bijw] • (nauwelijks) *badly, ill, hardly* • (ongunstig) *badly*

slechten • (effen maken) *level* • (slopen) *demolish, level/raze (to the ground)*

slechthorend *hard of hearing*

slechts *only, merely, just*

slee • (slede) *sledge* • (grote auto) *big car, limousine* • (vrucht) *sloe*

sleeën *sleigh, sledge*

sleep *train*

sleepboot *tug, tug boat*

sleepkabel ‹auto› *towrope*

sleeptouw *towrope*

slenteren *saunter*

slepen I [ov ww] • (voortslepen) *haul, drag* • (op sleeptouw nemen) *tow* II [on ww] • (over de grond gaan) *drag* • (traag voortgaan) *drag on*

slet *slut, trollop*

sleuf • (gleuf) *groove* • (opening) *slot,* ‹lang› *slit*

sleur *routine, rut*

sleuren *drag*

sleutel • (werktuig dat slot opent) *key* • (gereedschap) *spanner, wrench* • (middel tot oplossing) *key, clue, secret* • (muz.) *clef*

sleutelbeen *collarbone*

sleutelbos *bunch of keys*

sleutelgat *keyhole*

slib *silt, slime*

slijk *dirt, mud, mire*

slijm • (fluim) *phlegm* • (huidbedekking) *slime*

slijmerig • (slijmachtig) *slimy* • (vleierig) *grovelling, slimy*

slijmvlies *mucous membrane*

slijpen I [ov ww] • (scherp maken) *grind, sharpen* • (polijsten) *polish,* ‹edelstenen› *cut* • (graveren) *cut* II [on ww] *grind, polish,* ‹v. edelstenen› *cut*

slijpsteen *grindstone*

slijtage *wear and tear*

slijten I [ov ww] • (verslijten) *wear out* • (doorbrengen) *pass, spend* • (verkopen) *sell* II [on ww] *wear out,* ‹fig.› *wear off/away*

slikken • (doorslikken) *swallow* • (accepteren) *put up with, stomach, swallow*

slim *cunning, clever,* ‹pej.› *sly*

slimheid *astuteness*

slimmerd *smart cookie, a sly one*

slinger • (feestdecoratie) *paper chain,* ‹v. bloemen› *garland* • (zwaai) *swing* • (voorwerp v. klok) *pendulum* • (hefboom) *handle*

slingeren I [ov ww] • (zwaaiende beweging maken) *swing* • (werpen) *fling, hurl* II [on ww] • (bewegen v. schip) *roll* • (zwaaien) *swing, oscillate* • (kronkelen v. pad, rivier) *wind* • (overal liggen) *lie about* III [wkd ww] *meander, wind*

slinken *shrink, run low,* ‹door koken› *boil down,* ‹v. voorraad› *dwindle*

slip • (ondergoed) *briefs,* ‹dames› *panties,* ‹heren› *men's (short) pants* • (afhangend stuk v. kledingstuk) *lappet, tail, coat-tail, flap*

slippen • (wegglijden) *slip* • (uitglijden v. voertuig) *skid*

slippertje ★ een ~ maken *go off on the sly*

slobberen I [ov ww] *eat/drink noisily, slobber, slurp* II [on ww] *bag, sag*
sloddervos *slob, grub*
sloep • (kleine boot) *boat, smack* • (reddingsboot) *sloop*
slof • (pantoffel) *slipper* • (het sloffen) *shuffle* • (pak met pakjes sigaretten) *carton* • (spanblokje aan strijkstok) *nut* • (mandje) *punnet* • (briket) *briquette*
sloffen • (manier van lopen) *shuffle, shamble* • (nalatig zijn) *slack*
slok • (een keer slikken) *gulp* • (teug) *draught,* ‹inf.› *swig,* ‹groot› *pull* • (borreltje) *drop, dram*
slokdarm *gullet,* ‹med.› *oesophagus*
slons *frump*
slonzig *dowdy, slovenly*
sloof *drudge*
sloom *slow, listless*
sloop • (kussensloop) *pillowcase* • (het slopen) *demolition*
sloot • (waterloop) *ditch* • (grote hoeveelheid) *gallons*
slop *alley,* ‹doodlopend› *blind alley*
slopen *demolish,* ‹huis› *pull down*
slordig *untidy, careless, sloppy*
slot • (kasteel) *castle, manor-house* • (einde) *end, conclusion* • (sluitmechanisme) *lock*
slotsom *result, upshot*
sloven *drudge, toil*
sluier *veil*
sluik *lank*
sluikhandel ‹illegaal› *illicit trade,* ‹smokkel› *smuggling*
sluimeren *slumber*
sluipen • (voorzichtig lopen) *sneak, steal* • (ongemerkt opkomen) *creep*
sluis ‹schutsluis› *lock,* ‹uitwateringssluis› *sluice*
sluiten I [ov ww] • (verbieden) *close* • (dichtmaken) *shut, close,* ‹op slot doen› *lock* • (buitensluiten) *lock out* • (aansluiten) *close* • (aangaan)

conclude • (afsluiten) *close* • (opmaken) *close, balance* II [on ww] • (dichtgaan) *shut, close* • (aansluiten) *close,* ‹v. kleding› *fit* III [wkd ww] *close*
sluiting • (het sluiten) *closing* • (sluitingsmechanisme) *fastening, clasp, lock*
slungel *beanpole*
slungelig *lanky, gangling*
slurf • (flexibele buis) *hose,* ‹m.b.t. vliegtuig› *pneumatic gateway* • (snuit v. olifant) *trunk*
sluw *sly, cunning, sneaky*
smaad *defamation*
smaak *taste,* ‹wat men proeft› *flavour*
smaakvol *tasteful, in good taste*
smachten • (kwijnen) *languish* • (~ naar) *yearn/long (for)*
smadelijk • (vernederend) *humiliating* • (beledigend) *insulting, opprobrious*
smak • (val) *fall* • (bons) *thud, crash* • (smakkend geluid) *smack(ing)* • (grote hoeveelheid) *heap*
smakelijk • (lekker) *savoury, tasty* • (met graagte) *vivid, merry*
smakeloos *tasteless,* ‹fig.› *in bad taste*
smaken • (smaak hebben) *taste* • (naar de zin zijn) ★ smaakt het? *do you like it?* • (~ naar) *taste of*
smakken I [ov ww] *dash* II [on ww] • (geluid maken met de lippen) *smack* • (vallen) *crash*
smal *narrow*
smaldeel *squadron*
smalfilm 8/16mm. *film, cine film*
smaragd *emerald*
smart • (leed) *sorrow, grief, affliction* • (verlangen) *yearning*
smartegeld *smart money, compensation*
smartelijk *painful, smarting*
smeden *forge,* ‹aan elkaar› *weld*
smeekbede *appeal, plea*
smeer • (smeersel) *grease, fat,*

<schoensmeer> polish • (vlek) smear

smeerboel mess

smeerkaas cheese spread

smeerlap • (gemeen persoon) swine, bastard • (smeerpoets) slob • (vunzige vent) dirty fellow, pervert

smeerlapperij • (viezigheid) filth • (gemeenheid) dirty tricks

smeerolie lubricating oil

smeersel • (zalf) ointment, <vloeibaar> liniment • (beleg voor boterham) (sandwich) spread

smeken beg, entreat, implore

smelten melt

smeltkroes melting pot

smeren • (insmeren) <met olie> lubricate, oil, <met vet> grease, <v. lichaam> rub in • (uitsmeren) smear • (met boter bestrijken) butter

smerig dirty

smeris cop(per)

smet • (vlek) spot, stain • (schandvlek) blot, blemish

smetteloos spotless, immaculate

smeuïg • (zacht) smooth, <soep> thick • (pikant) savoury, <roddels, anekdotes> racy

smeulen smoulder

smid blacksmith

smijten fling, throw, dash

smikkelen ⋆ iets ~ tuck into s.th.

smoezelig dingy, grubby

smoezen whisper

smoking dinner jacket

smokkelen I [ov ww] smuggle II [on ww] cheat, dodge

smokkelwaar contraband

smoor ⋆ Mathilde was ~ op hem Mathilde had a crush on him ⋆ hij had er de ~ in he was fed up

smoorheet sweltering, broiling hot

smoren I [ov ww] • (gaar laten worden) braise • (onderdrukken) smother, strangle II [on ww] • (sudderen) braise • (stikken) stifle,

choke

smullen feast (upon), <fig.> lap up, revel in

smulpaap gourmet

snaak joker

snaar string, <v. harp> chord, <v. trommel> snare

snackbar snack bar

snakken • (smachten) yearn for • (naar adem happen) gasp

snappen I [ov ww] • (begrijpen) get, <inf.> twig • (betrappen) nick, catch out II [on ww] snap (at)

snars ⋆ 't kan me geen ~ schelen I couldn't care less; I don't give a toss ⋆ hij weet er geen ~ van he hasn't got a clue

snateren chatter, <v. ganzen> gaggle

snauw snarl

snauwen snarl (at), snap (at)

snavel bill, <krom> beak

snedig witty, smart

sneeuw snow

sneeuwen snow

sneeuwketting snow chain

sneeuwklokje snowdrop

sneeuwwit snow-white

snel • (vlug) quick, fast, swift, rapid • (modern) trendy

snelbuffet quick-service buffet

snelheid speed, <v. licht, geluid> velocity

snellen rush, hurry

sneltrein fast train

snelweg motorway, <AE> freeway

snerpen • (striemen) cut, bite • (schril klinken) shriek, shrill

snert • (erwtensoep) pea soup • (troep) trash, tripe

sneu hard, disappointing

sneuvelen • (omkomen) fall in battle, be killed • (kapotgaan) break

snibbig snappish

snijboon French bean

snijden • (in-/uit-/afsnijden) cut, <aan

stukken> *cut up*, <hout, vlees> *carve*,
<in plakken> *slice*
snijpunt *intersection*
snijtand *incisor*
snik • (ademtocht) *gasp* • (schokkende
ademhaling) *sob*
snikheet *stifling hot, sweltering*
snikken *sob*
snip • (vogel) *snipe* • (briefje van
honderd) *one-hundred guilder note*
snipper *shred*
snit *cut*
snoeien <bomen> *prune*, <struik> *trim,
clip*
snoek • (vis) *pike* • (misslag bij 't
roeien) *crab*
snoep *sweets* [mv], <AE> *candy*
snoepen I [ov ww] *eat sweets/candy*
II [on ww] *(have a) nibble*
snoepreisje *jaunt*, <afkeurend> *junket*
snoer • (draad) *rope, cord*
• (elektriciteitsdraad) *flex*, <netsnoer>
mains lead • (geregen draad) *string*
snoeren <kralen, enz.> *string*, <vast
rijgen> *lace*
snoeshaan ★ *rare* ~ *queer fish/customer*
snoet • (snuit) *snout* • (gezicht) *face*,
<inf.> *mug*
snoezig *sweet, lovely*
snood *malicious, wicked*
snor *moustache*, <v. dieren> *whiskers*
snorren • (snel voortbewegen) *whiz*
• (brommend geluid maken) *buzz,
hum*, <v. kat> *purr*, <v. machine, enz.>
whirr
snot (nasal) *mucus/discharge*, <inf.> *snot*
snotneus • (snotaap) *brat, (arrogant)
youngster* • (loopneus) *runny nose*,
<vulg.> *snotty nose*
snotteren • (huilen) *snivel, blubber*
• (neus snuiten) *blow one's nose,
snivel* • (neus ophalen) *sniffle*
snuffelen • (ruiken) *sniff* • (speuren)
nose, <in boek> *browse*
snufje • (nieuwigheidje) *novelty*

• (klein beetje) *touch*
snugger *smart, bright*, <inf.> *brainy*
snuisterij *trinket, knick-knack, bauble*
snuit *snout, muzzle*
snuiten • (uitsnuiten) *blow one's nose*
• (pit van kaars knippen) *snuff*
snuiter *chap, guy*
snuiven *sniff, snort*
snurken *snore*
sober *sober, frugal*
sociaal • (maatschappelijk) *social* • (in
groepsverband levend) *social*
• (maatschappelijk verantwoord)
socially minded
sociaal-democraat *social democrat*
socialisme *socialism*
sociëteit • (gezelligheidsvereniging)
association, club
• (verenigingsgebouw) *club-house*
• (genootschap) *society*
sociologie *sociology*
socioloog *sociologist*
soda • (natrium(bi)carbonaaat) *soda*
• (sodawater) *soda (water)*
soep • (gerecht) *soup* • (rommeltje)
mess
soepballetje *forcemeat ball*
soepel • (buigzaam) *pliable* • (lenig)
supple • (niet streng) *flexible*
• (gemakkelijk) *smooth*
soeplepel • (pollepel) *soup ladle*
• (eetlepel voor soep) *soup spoon*
soeverein I [de] *ruler, sovereign*
II [bnw] *sovereign*
soevereiniteit *sovereignty*
soezen • (dommelen) *doze*
• (mijmeren) *daydream*
soezerig *drowsy*
soja *soy sauce*
sok • (korte kous) *sock* • (techn.) *socket*
• (bio.) *sock*
sokkel *pedestal*
solarium *solarium*
soldaat *soldier, private (soldier)*
soldeer *solder*

soldeerbout *soldering bolt*
solderen *solder*
soldij *pay*
solidair *sympathetic*
solidariteit *solidarity*
solide *solid*
solist • (iem. die alleen optreedt) *solo performer* • (muz.) *soloist*
sollen *trifle (with)*
sollicitant *candidate, applicant*
sollicitatie *application*
solliciteren *apply*
solo *solo*
som *sum*
somber *gloomy*, ‹v. kleur› *sombre*
sommeren • (aanmanen) *summon* • (wisk.) *find the sum of, sum*
soms • (af en toe) *sometimes, now and then* • (misschien) *perhaps*
sonate *sonata*
sonnet *sonnet*
soort I [de] • (bio.) *species* II [het] *sort, kind*
soortelijk *specific*
soortgelijk *similar*
soortgenoot *one of the same kind*
sop • (zeepsop) *suds, soapsuds* • (zee) *blue, deep*
soppen • (boenen) *wash* • (in vloeistof dopen) *dunk*
sopraan *soprano*
sorbet *ice-cream soda*, ‹met vruchten› *knickerbocker glory*
sorteren *sort*
sortering • (kwaliteit) *grade* • (het sorteren) *sorting* • (collectie) *assortment, selection*
souffleur *prompter*
souteneur *pimp*
souterrain *basement*
souvenir • (aandenken) *keepsake* • (geschenk) *souvenir*
spaarbank *savings bank*
spaarbankboekje *savings account book, savings account*

spaarpot • (busje) *money-box* • (gespaard geld) ★ een ~je maken *put a little money by*
spaarzaam • (zuinig) *thrifty, sparing, economical* • (schaars) *sparse*
spaarzegel ‹v. bank› *savings stamp*, ‹v. winkel› *trading stamp*
spade *spade*
spalk *splint*
spalken *splint*
span *team (of horses)*
spandoek *banner*
Spanje *Spain*
spankracht • (veerkracht) *elasticity* • (door spanning opgewerkte kracht) *tension*
spannen I [ov ww] • (strak trekken, strekken) *tighten, stretch*, ‹fig.› *strain*, ‹v. spieren› *strain* • (uitrekken) *stretch* II [on ww] • (nauw zijn) *be tight* • (spannend zijn) ★ het zal erom ~ *it will be a tense struggle*
spannend *exciting, thrilling*, ‹v. moment› *tense*
spanning • (gespannen sfeer) *tension*, ‹onzekerheid› *suspense* • (elektrische spanning) *voltage*
spar *spruce*
sparen • (niet uitgeven) *save (up)* • (ontzien) *spare, save* • (verzamelen) *collect* • (uitsparen) *save*
spartelen *thrash, struggle, flounder*
spat • (vlek) *speck, spot* • (spetter) *drop, splash*
spatbord *mudguard*, ‹v. auto› *wing*
spatie *space*
spatten I [ov ww] • (bespatten) *splatter, splash* • (spetteren) *splash*, spatter II [on ww] *splash, splutter*
specerij *spice*
specht *woodpecker*
speciaal I [bnw] *special, particular* II [bijw] *in particular*
specialiseren *specialize*
specialist *specialist, expert*

specialiteit *speciality, specialty*
specie *mortar*
specificatie *specification*
specificeren *specify, itemize*
specifiek I [bnw] *specific* II [bijw] *specifically, particularly*
spectrum *spectrum* [mv: *spectrums/spectra*]
speculatie *speculation*
speculeren *speculate*
speech *speech*
speeksel *saliva, spit(tle)*
speelbal • (speelgoed) *player's/playing ball* • (weerloos slachtoffer) *toy, plaything* • (biljartbal) *cue ball*
speelgoed *toy(s)*
speelkameraad *playmate*
speelruimte • (speling) *elbow-room, latitude,* ‹tussen onderdelen› *play* • (ruimte om te spelen) *play area*
speels *playful*
speeltuin *playground, recreation area*
speen • (tepel) *teat* • (dop op fles) *dummy*
speenvarken *sucking pig*
speer *spear,* ‹sport› *javelin*
speerpunt *spearhead*
speerwerpen I [het] *the javelin (event)* II [onv ww] *javelin throwing*
spek *bacon,* ‹vers› *pork*
spektakel • (drukte) *uproar, hubbub* • (schouwspel) *spectacle, show* • (lawaai) *racket*
spel *game,* ‹v. muz., toneel› *performance*
speld *pin*
spelden *pin*
speldenprik *pinprick*
spelen I [ov ww] • (zich vermaken) *play, have a game (of)* • (aanpakken) *play* • (bespelen) *play* II [on ww] • (speculeren) *gamble, speculate (on)* • (lichtzinnig omgaan met) *trifle with* • (zich afspelen) ★ *het stuk speelt in... the scene is set in...*

spelenderwijs *without effort*
speler *player,* ‹gokker› *gambler,* ‹toneel› *actor* [v: *actress*]
spelfout *spelling mistake*
speling • (speelruimte) *play* • (marge) *margin, leeway* • (toevalligheid) ★ ~ *der natuur freak of nature*
spellen *spell*
spelling *spelling*
spelonk *cave, cavern*
spelregel • (regel voor spel) *rule of the game* • (taalk.) *spelling rule*
sperma *sperm*
spervuur *barrage*
sperwer *sparrowhawk*
speuren I [ov ww] *detect, sense* II [on ww] *investigate, track*
spichtig *lanky, weedy*
spieden *spy*
spiegel • (weerkaatsend glas) *mirror, looking-glass* • (med.) *level*
spiegelbeeld • (omgekeerd beeld) (mirror) *image* • (teruggekaatst beeld) *reflection*
spiegelei • (gebakken ei) *egg sunny side up* • (seinstok) *signalling disc*
spiegelen I [on ww] *mirror, reflect* II [wkd ww] • (~ **aan**) *take warning by, take an example from*
spiegelglad ‹weg› *slippery, icy*
spieken *crib, copy*
spier *muscle*
spiering *smelt*
spiernaakt *stark naked*
spierpijn *muscular pain, aching muscles*
spierwit *as white as a sheet*
spijbelen I [het] *truancy* II [on ww] *dog/skip school, play truant,* ‹AE› *play hooky*
spijker *nail*
spijkerbroek *jeans*
spijkeren *nail*
spijkerschrift *cuneiform writing*
spijl *bar*

spijs • (voedsel) *food, fare* • (mengsel voor vulling) *paste*
spijskaart *menu*
spijsvertering *digestion*
spijt *regret, remorse*
spijten *regret, be sorry*
spijtig *regrettable, unfortunate*
spiksplinternieuw *brand new*
spil *pivot, axis*
spin • (dier) *spider* • (snelbinder) *spinbinder*
spinazie *spinach*
spinnen I [ov ww] *spin* II [on ww] *purr*
spinnenweb *cobweb*
spinnewiel *spinning wheel*
spinnijdig *furious*
spinrag *cobweb*
spiraal • (schroeflijn) *spiral* • (spiraalvormig voorwerp) *coil* • (ontwikkeling) *spiral*
spiritisme *spiritualism*
spiritus *(methylated) spirit(s)*
spit • (pen) *spit* • (med.) *lumbago*
spits I [de] • (top) *point*, <v. berg> *peak*, <v. toren> *spire* • (spitsuur) *rush hour*, <m.b.t. tarieven> *peak hour* • (sport) *forward, striker* II [bnw] • (puntig) *pointed, sharp* • (spits toelopend) *tapering*
spitsuur <m.b.t. tarieven> *peak hour*, <v. verkeer> *rush hour*
spitsvondig *smart, clever, ingenious*
spitten *dig*
spleet *chink, crack, crevice*
splijten I [ov ww] *split, cleave* II [on ww] *split, crack*
splijtstof *fissionable material*, <AE> *fissile material*
splinter *splinter*, <v. glas> *sliver*
splitsen I [ov ww] *split, divide* II [wkd ww] *split (up)*, <v. weg> *branch off*
splitsing *bifurcation*
spoed *haste, speed*
spoedgeval *emergency (case)*
spoedig I [bnw] *speedy* II [bijw] *soon, speedily*

spoel *spool*, <v. film, tape> *reel*
spoelen I [ov ww] • (wassen) *wash, rinse* • (opwinden) *reel* II [on ww] *wash*
spoeling *rinse*, <v. toilet> *flush*
spoken I [on ww] *haunt, prowl* II [onp ww] ∗ het spookt in dat huis *the house is haunted*
sponning <v. raam> *runway*
spons *sponge*
sponsoren *(be) sponsor (for)*
spontaan *spontaneous*
spook • (geest) *ghost* • (schrikbeeld) *spectre* • (hersenschim) *phantom*
spookachtig *ghostly*
spookhuis • (huis waar het spookt) *haunted house* • (kermisattractie) *ghost train*
spoor I [de] *spur* II [het] • (afdruk) *track*, <geurspoor> *scent*, <v. voet> *footprint* • (overblijfsel) *sign, vestige, trace* • (v. taperecorder, film, enz.) *track* • (rails) *rail(s), track*
spoorbaan *railway*
spoorboekje *rail(way) guide, timetable*
spoorloos *without a trace, trackless*
spoorslags *at full speed*
spoorweg *railway*
spoorwegovergang *level crossing*
sporadisch *sporadic*
sporen • (in hetzelfde spoor lopen) *track* • (met het spoor reizen) *go by rail*
sport • (tree) *rung* • (lichaamsoefening) *sport*
sportief • (de sport betreffend) *sporty* • (van sport houdend) *fond of sports* • (eerlijk) *sportsmanlike*
spot • (hoon) *mockery, ridicule* • (lamp) *spotlight*
spotgoedkoop *dirt cheap*
spotprijs *bargain/basement price*
spotten • (schertsen) *joke* • (belachelijk maken) *mock, scoff, sneer*

spotter *mocker*
spraak • (het vermogen te spreken)
speech • (manier van spreken)
language
spraakgebrek *speech impediment*
spraakkunst *grammar*
spraakvermogen *power of speech*
spraakzaam *talkative,* ‹inf.› *chatty*
sprake * er is ~ van *there is (some) talk
of* * geen ~ van! *out of the question!*
* iets ter ~ brengen *raise a subject*
sprakeloos *speechless, dumb*
sprankelen *sparkle*
spreekbeurt *talk*
spreekbuis • (vertolker v. mening)
mouthpiece • (spreekhoorn)
megaphone
spreekkamer *consulting room*
spreektaal *spoken language,*
vernacular
spreekuur *office hours,* ‹v. huisarts›
surgery, ‹v. welzijnswerker›
consulting hour(s)
spreekwoord *proverb*
spreekwoordelijk *proverbial*
spreeuw *starling*
sprei *bedspread, counterpane*
spreiden *spread*
spreiding *spreading*
spreken *speak*
sprekend * ~ lijken op *be the spitting
image of*
spreker *speaker, lecturer*
sprenkelen *sprinkle*
spreuk *motto, aphorism*
spriet • (grasspriet, enz.) *blade (of
grass)* • (haarpiek) *wisp* • (voelhoorn)
antenna [mv: *antennae*], *feeler*
springconcours *show jumping contest*
springen *spring, jump, leap,* ‹met
handen/polsstok› *vault*
springlading *explosive charge*
springlevend *alive and kicking, very
much alive*
springplank *springboard*

springstof *explosive*
springvloed *spring tide*
sprinkhaan *locust, grasshopper*
sproeien *water, sprinkle,* ‹tegen
ongedierte› *spray*
sproeier • (sproeitoestel) *sprinkler,
sprayer* • (v. carburateur) *nozzle*
• (verstuiver op een fles) *spray nozzle*
sproet *freckle*
sprokkelen *gather wood*
sprong *jump, leap*
sprookje *fairy tale*
sprookjesachtig *fairy-tale like*
spruit • (groente) *Brussels sprout*
• (kind) *sprig, sprout* • (uitloper)
sprout, shoot
spruiten • (uitlopen) *sprout, shoot*
• (voortkomen uit) *spring/descend
from*
spugen • (speeksel uitspugen) *spit*
• (braken) *throw up, be sick,* ‹inf.› *spew*
spuien I [ov ww] • (uiten) *unload,
spout, get (s.th.) off one's chest* • (lozen)
sluice, drain (off) II [on ww] *let in fresh
air, ventilate*
spuigat *scupper(hole)*
spuit • (injectienaald) *needle, syringe*
• (injectie) *injection* • (werktuig om
mee te spuiten) *squirt,* ‹tegen
insecten› *sprayer*
spuiten I [ov ww] • (naar buiten
persen) *spout, spurt, squirt*
• (bespuiten) *spray* II [on ww]
• (med.) *inject*
spuitwater *soda(-water)*
spul *stuff*
spurten *spurt, sprint*
sputteren • (pruttelen, spetteren)
sp(l)utter • (mopperen) *mutter*
spuug *spittle, saliva*
spuwen • (braken) *vomit, spew*
• (spugen) *spit, spew*
staaf *rod*
staak *stake, pole, beanpole*
staal • (monster) *sample* • (metaal) *steel*

staan • (rechtop staan) *stand* • (passen)
suit • (opgeschreven staan) ⋆ *het
staat in de brief/krant dat... it says in
the letter/paper that...* • (~ **op**) *insist
on*

staand ⋆ ~e *lamp standard lamp* ⋆ ~e
klok long-case clock

staanplaats • (plaats om te staan)
standing room • (standplaats) ‹op
markt› *stand*, ‹v. taxi› *taxi rank*

staar *cataract*

staart • (eindstuk v. ruggengraat) *tail*
• (neerhangend haar) *pigtail*
• (uiteinde) *tail(end)* • (nasleep)
aftermath

staat • (toestand) *condition, state*
• (rijk) *state* • (lijst) *list* • (rang) *rank*
• (gelegenheid) ⋆ *in* ~ *stellen enable*
⋆ *in* ~ *zijn be able; be capable*

staathuishoudkunde *political
economy*

staatkundig *political*

staatsblad ≈ *Government Gazette*

staatsgreep *coup d'état*

staatsie *state, pomp, ceremony*

staatsrechtelijk *constitutional*

staatssecretaris *State Secretary*

stabiel *stable*

stabiliseren *stabilize*

stabiliteit *stability*

stad • (plaats) *town*, ‹grote stad› *city*
• (stedelijke gemeente) *borough*

stadhouder *stadtholder*

stadhuis *town hall*

stadion *stadium* [mv: *stadiums*]

stadium *stage, phase*

staf • (leiding) *staff* • (stok) *staff*
• (toverstaf) *wand* • (bisschopsstaf)
crosier

stafkaart *ordnance (survey) map*

stagnatie *stagnation*

stagneren *stagnate*

staken I [ov ww] • (stoppen) *stop,
cease*, ‹voor korte tijd› *suspend* II [on
ww] *go on strike*

staker *striker*

staking • (het ophouden met iets)
suspension • (het gelijk staan) *tie*
• (werkstaking) *stoppage (of work),
strike*

stal *stable*, ‹v. koeien› *cowshed*, ‹v.
varkens› *pigsty*

stalen *steel*

stallen *stable, stall*, ‹v. auto› *garage*

stalles *stalls*

stalling ‹overdekte fietsenstalling›
shelter, ‹v. auto's› *garage*

stam • (volksstam) *tribe* • (plantk.)
‹plant› *stem*, ‹v. boom› *trunk*

stamboom *genealogical/family tree,
pedigree*

stamelen I [ov ww] *stammer* II [on
ww] *falter, stammer*

stamgast *regular (customer)*

stammen • (afstammen van) *stem
(from)* • (taalk.) *derive*

stampen *pound*, ‹met voet› *stamp*, ‹v.
aardappels› *mash*, ‹v. machine›
thump

stamper • (bio.) *pistil*

stamppot *hotchpotch*

stampvoeten *stamp one's foot/feet*

stampvol *crowded, packed (full)*

stamvader *ancestor*

stand • (toestand) *state* • (wijze van
staan) ‹v. maan› *phase*, ‹v. water,
barometer› *height* • (houding)
posture, bearing, ‹gymnastiek›
position • (maatschappelijke stand)
rank, station, standing • (ruimte op
tentoonstelling) *stand* • (bestaan)
⋆ *in* ~ *blijven survive; endure* ⋆ *in* ~
houden maintain ⋆ *tot* ~ *brengen
bring about; achieve* • (sport) *score*

standaard *standard*

standbeeld *statue*

standje • (berisping) *scolding, talking
to* • (houding) *position*

standplaats • (vaste plaats) *stand*,
‹taxi› *taxi rank*, ‹v. venter› *pitch*

standpunt *standpoint, point of view*
standvastig • (volhardend) *firm, steadfast* • (onveranderlijk) *constant*
stang *rod, bar,* <v. fiets> *crossbar*
stank *stench, bad/foul smell*
stap • (pas) *step, footstep* • (maatregel) *step, measure*
stapel I [de] *stack, heap, pile* II [bnw] • (~ **op**) *crazy about*
stapelen *pile (up), stack, heap*
stapelgek *stark raving mad, bonkers*
stappen • (lopen) *step, walk* • (uitgaan) *go out for a drink*
stapvoets *at walking pace*
star *stiff, rigid*
staren *stare, gaze*
start *start, starting point*
startbaan *runway*
starten I [ov ww] *start* II [on ww] • (vertrekken) *start,* <v. vliegtuig> *take off*
starter *starter*
statiegeld *deposit*
statig • (waardig) *stately* • (plechtig) *solemn*
station *station*
stationair * ~ *lopen tick over; idle*
stationeren *station*
statistiek • (methode) *statistics* • (tabel) *statistics,* <officieel> *returns*
status • (positie) *status* • (med.) *case history*
statuut • (voorschrift) *statute, charter* • (grondregels) * *statuten articles of association; regulations*
staven • (bewijzen) *substantiate* • (bekrachtigen) *support, corroborate, confirm*
stedelijk • (van de stad) *municipal* • (stads) *urban*
steeds I [bnw] *townish* II [bijw] • (telkens) *always, ever* • (voortdurend) *continuously, all the time*
steeg *alley(way), lane*

steek • (stoot v. iets scherps) <v. insect> *sting,* <v. mes, dolk> *stab,* <v. zwaard> *thrust* • (pijnscheut) *pang,* <in de zij> *stitch*
steekhoudend *sound, valid*
steekproef *spot check*
steekspel • (discussie) *sparring match* • (gesch.) *joust*
steekvlam *tongue/jet of flame*
steekwapen *pointed weapon*
steel • (handvat) *handle* • (stengel) *stem*
steels *stealthy*
steen • (natuurlijke steen) *stone* • (bouwsteen) <baksteen> *brick,* <natuursteen> *stone*
steenbok • (dier) *ibex* • (teken van de dierenriem) *Capricorn*
steengroeve *quarry*
steenkool *coal*
steenkoud • (ijskoud) *stone-cold, freezing* • (gevoelloos) *stony, ice-cold*
steenpuist *boil*
steenslag • (vallend gesteente) *broken stones, rubble* • (voor wegverharding) *roadmetal*
steenworp *stone's throw*
steevast *regular*
steiger • (bouwsteiger) *scaffolding* • (landingssteiger) *landing stage*
steigeren • (op de achterste benen gaan staan) *rear* • (protesteren) *get up on one's hind legs*
steil *steep*
stek • (plekje) *niche* • (takje) *cutting*
stekeblind *stone-blind*
stekel *prickle,* <v. egel> *quill*
stekelbaars *stickleback*
stekelig • (hatelijk) *caustic, sharp* • (met stekels) *prickly*
stekelvarken *porcupine*
steken I [ov ww] • (uitspitten) *dig* • (met iets scherps raken) <met mes> *stab,* <v. insect> *sting* • (grievend zijn) *sting* • (in genoemde plaats/toestand*

brengen) *put into, plug in* II [on ww]
• (gevoel als van prikken
veroorzaken) <v. zon> *burn,* <wond>
sting • (vastzitten) ⋆ *blijven* ~ *get
stuck* ⋆ daar steekt wat achter *there is
s.th. behind it*
stekker *plug*
stel ⋆ 'n aardig stel *a nice couple*
stelen *steal*
stellage *stand, stage, scaffolding*
stellen • (formuleren) *put, pose*
• (beweren) *posit, declare, postulate*
• (plaatsen) *place, put,* <v. machine>
erect • (afstellen) *set*
• (veronderstellen) *suppose*
• (vaststellen) *fix, make*
stellig *positive*
stelling • (steiger) *scaffolding*
• (stellage) *rack*
stelpen *staunch, stem, stop*
stelregel *principle, maxim*
stelsel *system*
stelselmatig *systematic(al)*
stelt • (om op te lopen) *stilt* • (lang,
dun been) *pin*
stem • (spraakvermogen) *voice*
• (voorkeur bij stemming) *vote*
stembiljet *ballot(paper)*
stembureau *polling station*
stembus • (de stemming) *poll* • (bus)
ballot box
stemgerechtigd <v. burgers>
enfranchised, <v. lid> *entitled to vote*
stemhokje *voting/polling booth*
stemmen I [ov ww] • (in zekere
stemming brengen) ⋆ *gunstig* ~
placate ⋆ optimistisch gestemd zijn
be in an optimistic mood • (muz.) *tune*
II [on ww] • (stem uitbrengen) *vote,
(go to the) poll*
stemmig *quiet*
stemming • (het stemmen) *vote*
• (gemoedsstemming) *mood* • (muz.)
tuning
stempel *stamp,* <v. post> *postmark*

stempelen I [ov ww] *stamp,* <v. post>
postmark II [on ww] *sign the register,
be on the dole, sign(ing) on*
stemrecht *franchise, suffrage*
stemvork *tuning fork*
stencil *stencil, handout*
stenen • (gemaakt van steen)
<baksteen> *brick,* <natuursteen> *stone*
• (als van steen) *stone*
stengel *stalk, stem*
stenigen *stone*
stenografisch *shorthand, stenographic*
step • (autoped) *scooter* • (voetsteun)
footrest • (danspas) *step*
steppe *steppe*
ster • (hemellichaam) *star*
• (beroemdheid) *star, celebrity*
sterfbed *deathbed*
sterfdag *day of s.o.'s death*
sterfgeval *death*
sterftecijfer *death/mortality rate*
steriel • (onvruchtbaar) *barren* • (vrij
van ziektekiemen) *sterile* • (doods)
sterile, unimaginative
steriliseren *sterilize*
sterk • (krachtig) *strong, powerful*
• (kras) ⋆ ~ *verhaal tall story*
• (alcoholisch) ⋆ ~e *drank spirits;
liquor*
sterken *strengthen, fortify*
sterkte *strength, power*
sterrenbeeld • (groep sterren)
constellation • (teken van de
dierenriem) *sign of the zodiac*
sterrenkunde *astronomy*
sterveling *mortal*
sterven I [on ww] • (doodgaan) *die,
expire* • (afsterven) *die, fade* II [onp
ww] *be swarming with*
steun • (stut) *support, prop* • (hulp)
help, support • (bijstandsuitkering)
unemployment benefit
steunen I [ov ww] *support, back (up)*
II [on ww] • (kreunen) *moan, groan*
• (~ **op**) *lean on,* <fig.> *relie on*

steunpilaar • (pilaar) *pillar*
• (persoon) *pillar, mainstay*
steunpunt • (punt waarop iets
steunt) *point of support,* ‹v. hefboom›
fulcrum • (mil.) *base*
stevig • (solide) *solid, strong,* ‹v.
persoon› *sturdy,* ‹v. vlees, weefsel›
firm • (krachtig) ‹v. maal› *hearty,
substantial,* ‹v. wind› *stiff*
stichtelijk • (verheffend) *edifying*
• (vroom) *pious*
stichten *found*
stichter • (oprichter) *founder*
• (aanstichter) *instigator*
stichting • (rechtsvorm) *corporation,
foundation* • (het oprichten)
establishment • (geestelijke
verheffing) *edification*
stiefmoeder *stepmother*
stiekem I [bnw] • (achterbaks)
underhand, devious, ‹inf.› *dodgy* • (in
het geheim) *furtive, underhand, sly*
II [bijw] *on the sly*
stiekemerd *sneak*
stier • (teken van de dierenriem)
Taurus, the Bull • (dier) *bull*
stierlijk ★ zich ~ vervelen *be bored to
tears*
stift • (staafje) *peg, pin* • (viltstift)
felt-tip
stijf • (niet buigzaam) *stiff, rigid*
• (houterig) *awkward, wooden*
• (vormelijk) *formal, starchy*
• (koppig) *stubborn*
stijfsel *starch,* ‹behanglijm› *paste*
stijgbeugel *stirrup*
stijgen • (naar hogere plaats gaan)
rise, ‹v. vliegtuig› *climb* • (stijgen in
rangorde) *rise, go up* • (toenemen) *rise*
stijl • (schrijfstijl) *style* • (vormgeving)
style, tradition • (handelwijze) *style*
• (raam-/deurpost) *post, jamb* • (spijl)
baluster
stijlvol *stylish*
stijven • (stijf maken) *stiffen*

• (sterken) *stiffen, strengthen* • (met
stijfsel behandelen) *starch*
stikdonker I [het] *pitch darkness*
II [bnw] *pitch-dark*
stikken *choke*
stikstof *nitrogen*
stil • (geluidloos) *silent* • (rustig) *quiet*
• (niet geuit) *silent* • (roerloos) *still*
• (verborgen) *secret*
stilhouden I [on ww] *stop* II [wkd
ww] *keep quiet*
stillen *allay*
stilletjes • (zachtjes) *quietly*
• (heimelijk) *secretly* • (ongestoord) *in
peace*
stilleven *still life*
stilstaan • (niet bewegen) *stand still*
• (niet vooruitkomen) *stagnate, stand
still* • (buiten bedrijf zijn) *be/lie idle*
• (~ bij) ★ ~ bij 'n feit *dwell on a fact*
★ zij heeft er nooit bij stilgestaan dat
... *it has never occurred to her that ...*
stilstand • (bewegingloosheid)
standstill, stoppage • (stagnatie)
stagnation
stilte • (zonder ruchtbaarheid) *quiet,
secrecy* • (geluidloosheid) *silence,
quiet, stillness* • (rust) *calm,
tranquillity*
stilzwijgen I [het] *silence* II [on ww]
keep silent
stimulans • (aanmoediging) *stimulus*
• (opwekkend middel) *stimulant*
stimuleren *stimulate, encourage*
stinken *stink, smell*
stip *dot,* ‹op kleding› *polka dot*
stippelen *dot, speckle*
stipt *punctual*
stiptheidsactie *work-to-rule action*
stoeien • (ravotten) *romp* • (speels
omgaan met) *play with*
stoel *chair, seat*
stoelgang *bowel movement, defecation*
stoeltjeslift *chairlift*
stoep • (stenen opstapje) *doorstep*

• (trottoir) pavement
stoer ⋆ ~ doen show off; act tough
stoet procession
stof I [de] • (substantie) matter
• (weefsel) material, stuff
• (onderwerp) subject matter II [het] dust
stoffelijk • (de materie betreffend) material • (materieel) material, tangible
stoffen I [bnw] cloth II [ov ww] dust
stoffer brush, duster
stofferen • (bekleden) upholster
• (aankleden van een huis, enz.) decorate, furnish with carpets, etc.
stoffering upholstery
stofwisseling metabolism
stofzuiger vacuum cleaner, hoover
stok stick
stokdoof stone deaf
stoken I [ov ww] • (laten branden) stoke • (als brandstof gebruiken) burn
• (distilleren) distil II [on ww]
• (verwarmen) heat, have a fire
• (opruien) make trouble, stir things up
stoker • (machinestoker) stoker, fireman • (distilleerder) distiller
• (opruier) firebrand, agitator
stokken <v. motor> stall, <v. spreker> break down
stokstijf • (roerloos) stock-still
• (halsstarrig) stubborn • (geheel stijf) stiff as a rod
stokvis stockfish
stola stole
stollen coagulate, congeal, <v. bloed> clot, <v. jus, gelei> set
stolp glass cover, bell glass
stom • (zonder spraakvermogen) mute
• (dom) stupid • (vervelend) stupid, tedious • (zonder geluid) ⋆ stomme film silent film • (toevallig) ⋆ stom toeval pure chance
stomdronken dead/blind drunk
stomen I [ov ww] • (gaar maken)

steam • (reinigen) dry-clean • (met stoom losweken) steam off II [on ww] steam
stomheid • (het niet kunnen spreken) dumbness • (stommiteit) stupidity
stommelen clatter (about)
stommeling idiot, blockhead
stomp I [de] • (overblijfsel) stump
• (stoot) punch II [bnw] • (bot) blunt, dull
stompen thump, punch
stomvervelend deadly dull
stookolie fuel oil
stoom steam
stoomboot steamer, steamship
stoomcursus crash/intensive course
stoornis disturbance, disorder
stoot push, <bij biljart> shot
stop • (afsluiter) <v. bad> plug, <v. fles> stopper, <v. vat> bung • (zekering) plug
• (pauze) stop, break
stopbord stop sign
stopcontact (plug-)socket, power-point
stoplicht • (verkeerslicht) traffic light
• (remlicht) brake light/lamp
stopnaald darning-needle
stoppen I [ov ww] • (opvullen) plug up
• (gat in sok repareren) darn
• (tegenhouden) stop II [on ww] stop
stoptrein stop(ping) train, slow/local train
stopverbod <op bord> no stopping
stopverf putty
stopzetten stop, <voor korte tijd> suspend
storen I [ov ww] disturb, interfere with, interrupt, <v. radio> jam II [wkd ww]
⋆ stoor je niet aan hem don't mind him; don't bother about him
storing • (onderbreking) disturbance
• (zenderstoring) <atmosferisch> atmospherics, <v. radio> interference, jamming
storm storm, gale

stormachtig • (met storm) *stormy*
• (heftig) *tempestuous, tumultuous*
stormen ★ 't stormt *there is a gale*
★ het gaat ~ *it is blowing up a gale*
stormloop • (run) <op kaartjes> *rush,*
<op winkels> *run* • (aanval) *assault*
stortbad *shower*
stortbui *downpour*
storten I [ov ww] • (laten vallen)
dump, shoot • (geld overmaken) *pay*
II [on ww] *fall, plunge* III [onp ww]
★ het stort *it is pouring*
storting • (het storten) <v. afval>
dumping • (overmaken) *payment*
stortplaats *dump, dumping ground*
stortvloed *torrent*
stoten I [ov ww] • (duwen) *push*
• (bezeren) *bump* II [on ww]
• (schokken) *jolt* • (botsen met) *bump*
III [wkd ww] *bump*
stotteren *stutter, stammer*
stout • (ondeugend) *naughty*
• (moedig) *bold*
stouterd *naughty child*
stoven *stew, simmer*
straal *stream*
straaljager *fighter jet*
straalvliegtuig *jet*
straat • (weg) *street, waterweg* ★ ~ van
Malakka *strait of Malacca*
straatarm *penniless*
straathond *stray dog*
straatweg *highroad*
straf *punishment*
strafbaar *punishable*
strafbepaling • (clausule) *penalty
clause* • (het bepalen) *determining the
punishment*
straffeloos *with impunity*
straffen *punish*
strafrecht *criminal law*
strafschop *penalty (kick)*
strak *tight,* <touw> *taut*
stralen • (licht, enz. uitzenden) *beam,
radiate* • (uitdrukking van geluk

tonen) *shine, beam* • (zakken) *flunk,
fail*
straling *radiation*
stram • (stijf) *stiff, rigid* • (fier) *ramrod*
strand *beach, seaside*
stranden • (mislukken) *strand, fail*
• (op reis blijven steken) *be stranded*
• (aanspoelen) *be washed ashore*
• (scheepv.) *run ashore*
strandstoel *beach-chair, beehive chair*
streek • (strijkende beweging) <op
viool> *bow,* <v. pen> *stroke*
• (windstreek) *point* • (landstreek)
region, district • (omgeving v. orgaan)
region • (poets) *trick*
streekroman *regional novel*
streep *line*
strekken *stretch, extend*
strekking <v. betoog> *tenor,* <v.
verhaal> *drift*
strelen • (aaien) *caress, stroke, fondle*
• (aangenaam aandoen) *gratify, flatter*
streling • (aai) *caress* • (aangename
gewaarwording) *gratification*
stremmen • (schiften) *coagulate,* <v.
melk> *curdle* • (belemmeren) *obstruct*
stremming • (stagnatie) *obstruction*
• (het stremmen) *curdling*
streng I [de] • (bundel draden) *twine,*
<v. garen, wol> *skein* • (iets wat
geregen is) *string* II [bnw] • (strikt)
strict • (hard) *severe,* <v. uitdrukking>
stern
streven I [het] *endeavour* II [on ww]
• (~ naar) *strive after/for, aim at*
striem *weal, welt*
striemen • (striemen toebrengen)
welt, slash • (pijn doen) *lash*
strijd *struggle, fight*
strijdbaar *warlike, militant*
strijdbijl *battle-axe, hatchet*
strijden • (vechten) *fight, struggle*
• (wedijveren) *compete, contend*
strijder *warrior*
strijdig • (in strijd) *contrary (to)*

• (tegenstrijdig) *conflicting*
strijdkrachten *armed (military) forces*
strijdperk • (slagveld) *battleground*
• (arena) *arena*
strijken • (strijkend over iets gaan) *stroke, brush,* <op 'n snaar> *bow*
• (gladmaken met strijkijzer) *iron*
• (laten zakken) <v. vlag> *lower,* <v. zeil> *strike*
strijkinstrument *stringed instrument*
strijkplank *ironing board*
strijkstok *bow*
strik • (valstrik) *snare* • (soort knoop) *knot,* <met schuifknoop> *noose*
• (gestrikt lint) *bow*
strikken • (knopen) *tie* • (vangen) *snare* • (overhalen) *ensnare*
strikt *strict*
strikvraag *trick/catch question*
stripverhaal *strip (cartoon)*
stro *straw*
stroef *stiff*
strofe *strophe*
stroken *agree (with)*
stroman *straw man*
stromen • (vloeien) *pour, flow, stream*
• (in groten getale komen) *stream, pour*
stroming • (stroom) *current*
• (denkwijze) *tendency, trend* • (het stromen) *flowing*
strompelen *stumble, stagger, hobble*
stronk • (boomstomp) *stump*
• (koolplant) *stalk*
stront • (poep) *dung, shit, muck, filth*
• (ruzie) *row, kick up*
strooien *strew, scatter,* <poeder> *sprinkle*
strook *strip*
stroom • (stromende vloeistof) *stream*
• (elektrische spanning) *current*
• (rivier) *stream*
stroomlijnen *streamline*
stroomversnelling • (versnelling v. stroom) *rapid(s)* • (versnelling v.

ontwikkeling) *acceleration*
stroop *treacle*
strooplikker *toady, lickspittle*
strooptocht *raid*
strop • (lus) *noose* • (pech) *bad/tough luck,* <verlies> *loss*
stropdas *(neck)tie*
stropen • (illegaal jagen) *poach*
• (villen) *skin* • (oprollen) <mouwen> *roll up*
stroper *poacher*
stroperij *poaching*
strot • (keel) *throat* • (strottenhoofd) *larynx*
strottenhoofd *larynx*
strubbeling • (moeilijkheid) *difficulty, trouble* • (onenigheid) *squabble, bickering*
structureel *structural*
structuur *structure*
struik *bush, shrub*
struikelblok *stumbling block*
struikelen • (ergens over vallen) *trip (over), stumble* • (zijn positie verliezen) *falter, founder* • (een misstap doen) *trip up*
struikgewas *brushwood, shrubs*
struikrover *highwayman*
struis *sturdy, robust*
struisvogelpolitiek *head-in-the-sand politics*
studeerkamer *study*
studeren I [ov ww] • (studie volgen) *study,* <op universiteit> *go to college/university* • (muz.) *practise*
II [on ww] *study*
studie • (opleiding) *study* • (het bestuderen van iets) *study*
• (onderzoeksverslag) *study, paper, essay* • (schets) *study, sketch*
studiebeurs <als beloning> *scholarship,* <v. regering> *student grant*
studieboek *textbook*
studiejaar • (cursusjaar) *academic/school year* • (jaar van

iemands studie) * hij is van mijn ~
he's in my year
studietoelage scholarship, student
grant
studio studio
stug • (niet soepel) stiff, tough • (niet
aardig) surly
stuifmeel pollen
stuip • (stuiptrekking) convulsion
• (krampaanval) fit
stuiptrekken twitch, be convulsed
stuiptrekking convulsion, spasm
stuiten I [ov ww] arrest, stop, stem
II [on ww] • (kaatsen) bounce • (~ op)
encounter, chance, happen upon, meet
(up) with
stuitend shocking
stuiven • (opwaaien) blow, fly about
• (met grote snelheid gaan) rush, dash
stuiver five cent piece
stuk I [het] • (gedeelte) piece, part,
fragment, <op broek, mouw> patch
• (exemplaar) piece • (geschrift)
document • (schaakstuk, damsteen)
piece • (aantrekkelijk persoon) <v.
man> hunk, <v. vrouw> beauty,
darling • (hoeveelheid) * op geen
stukken na not nearly; not by a long
shot * 'n heel stuk beter quite a lot
better • (kunst) <muz.> piece of music,
<toneel> play, piece II [bnw] broken,
<defect> out of order
stukadoor plasterer
stukloon piece-rate
stuntelig clumsy, bungling
sturen I [ov ww] • (besturen) steer,
<auto> drive • (bedienen) operate
• (zenden) <v. brief> send, post II [on
ww] steer
stut prop, support
stutten prop, buttress, support
stuur <v. auto> wheel, <v. fiets>
handlebar
stuurboord starboard
stuurknuppel control column, <inf.>

joystick
stuurloos out of control
stuurman • (scheepsofficier)
chief/first mate • (roerganger)
helmsman, <sport> cox
stuurs surly
stuwdam dam, weir
stuwen • (voortbewegen) drive, propel
• (water keren) dam (up) • (scheepv.)
stow
stuwkracht propulsion
subiet • (dadelijk) right away, at once
• (zeker) certainly
subject subject
subjectief subjective
subliem • (groots) sublime
• (fantastisch) fantastic
subsidie subsidy, grant
subsidiëren subsidize
substantie substance, matter
substantieel substantial
substituut substitute
subtiel subtle, delicate
subtropisch subtropical
subversief subversive
succes • (gunstig resultaat) success,
luck • (iets dat geslaagd is) success
succesvol successful
sudderen simmer
suf drowsy
suffen • (suf zijn) doze • (soezen)
day-dream, drowse
suggereren suggest
suggestie suggestion
suiker • (zoetstof) sugar
• (suikerziekte) diabetes
suikerbiet sugar beet
suikergoed confectionery, sweetmeats
suikeroom rich uncle
suikerriet sugar cane
suikerziekte diabetes
suite • (kamers) suite • (muz.) suite
suizen <v. regen> rustle, <v. wind> sigh
sujet fellow
sukade candied peel

sukkelen • (sjokken) *jog, trudge*
• (ziekelijk zijn) *be ailing*
sukkelgangetje *jogtrot*
sul • (goedzak) *softy* • (sufferd) *mug,*
dope
sullig • (goeiig) *soft, goody-goody*
• (dom) *goofy*
summier • (bondig) *brief, concise,*
summary • (gering) *summary, scanty*
superieur *superior*
superioriteit *superiority*
supermarkt *supermarket*
supersonisch *supersonic*
supplement *supplement*
suppoost ‹in museum› *attendant*
surfen • (windsurfen) *surf,* ‹in
branding› *go surfing* • (plankzeilen)
go windsurfing
Suriname *Surinam*
surplus *surplus*
surprise *surprise*
surrogaat *surrogate, substitute*
surveillance *surveillance*
surveilleren I [ov ww] *supervise,* ‹bij
examen› *invigilate* II [on ww] ‹leraar,
politieman› *be on duty,*
‹politiewagen› *patrol*
sussen ‹kind› *soothe,*
‹ontevredenheid› *appease,* ‹ruzie›
hush up
symboliek • (het symbolische)
symbolism • (leer van de symbolen)
symbolics
symbolisch • (zinnebeeldig)
symbolic(al) • (een teken vormend)
token
symboliseren *symbolize*
symbool *symbol*
symfonie *symphony*
symmetrie *symmetry*
sympathie • (genegenheid) *sympathy*
• (medegevoel) *sympathy, affinity*
sympathiek *sympathetic, likeable*
sympathiseren *sympathize*
symptoom *symptom*

synagoge *synagogue*
syndicaat *syndicate*
syndroom *syndrome*
synode *synod*
synoniem I [het] *synonym* II [bnw]
synonymous
syntaxis *syntax*
synthese *synthesis*
synthetisch *synthetic*
systeem *system*
systematiek • (systeemleer)
systematics, taxonomy
• (ordeningsprincipe) *system*
systematisch *systematic*

T

taai *tough*
taaiheid *toughness*
taak *task*, ‹inf.› *job*, ‹officieel
toegekend› *assignment*
taal *language, speech*
taaleigen *idiom*
taalfout *grammatical error/mistake*
taalgebruik *usage*
taalkunde *linguistics*
taalkundig *linguistic, grammatical*
taalonderwijs *language teaching*
taart • (gebak) *cake, tart*, ‹AE› *pie*
• (vrouw) *frump*
tabak *tobacco*
tabaksdoos *tobacco tin*
tabel *chart, table*
tabernakel *tabernacle*
tableau *tableau, picture*
tablet *tablet*
taboe *taboo*
tachtig *eighty*
tact *tact*
tacticus *tactician*
tactiek *tactics*
tactisch *tactical*
tactloos *tactless*
tactvol *tactful*
tafel *table*
tafelblad *table-top*
tafelkleed *tablecloth*
tafeltennis *table tennis*
tafereel *scene, picture*
taille *waist*
tailleren *cut in*
tak *branch*
takel *tackle, pulley block*
takelen • (optuigen) *rig* • (ophijsen)
hoist (up)
taks • (hoeveelheid) *portion, share*
• (dashond) *dachshund, basset*

tal *number*
talent *talent*
talentvol *talented*, ‹form.›
accomplished
talisman *talisman, amulet*
talk *tallow*
talkpoeder *talcum/powder, talc*
talloos *countless, innumerable*
talmen *linger, delay*
talrijk *numerous*
tam *tame*, ‹dieren› *domesticated*
tamboerijn *tambourine*
tamelijk I [bnw] *fair* II [bijw] *fairly,
rather, pretty*
tampon *tampon*
tamtam • (trommels) *tomtom*
• (ophef, poeha) *fuss, to-do*
tand *tooth* [mv: *teeth*]
tandarts *dentist*
tandem *tandem*
tandenborstel *tooth brush*
tanen I [ov ww] *tan* II [on ww] *be on
the wane, fade*
tang • (gereedschap) (pair of) *tongs*, ‹v.
chirurg› *forceps* • (kwaadaardige
vrouw) *hag*
tango *tango*
tanig *tawny*
tank *tank*
tanken *(re)fuel*
tankstation *petrol station*
tante *aunt*
tap • (kraan) *tap* • (spon) *bung*
tapijt *carpet*
tapkast *bar*
tappen • (bier tappen) *tap/draw/pull
beer* • (vertellen) ∗ moppen ~ *crack
jokes*
taps *tapering*
taptoe • (parade) *tattoo* • (signaal) *last
post*
tarbot *turbot*
tarief *tariff, rate*, ‹prijs› *charge*
tarten • (trotseren) *defy, brave*
• (uitdagen) *challenge, dare*

• (overtreffen) *defy, baffle*
tarwe *wheat*
tarwebloem *wheat flour*
tarwebrood *wheat bread*
tas *bag,* <aktetas> *brief-case*
tastbaar *tangible, palpable*
tasten I [ov ww] *touch, feel* II [on ww]
grope, fumble for
tastzin *sense of touch*
tatoeëren *tattoo*
taxateur *assessor, valuer,* <v. huis>
surveyor
taxatie *valuation, appraisal, assessment*
taxeren *value, appraise, estimate,
assess,* <v. huis> *survey*
taxi *taxi(cab)*
taxichauffeur *taxi driver*
taxistandplaats *taxi/cab rank*
te I [bijw] • (meer dan gewenst) *too*
II [vz] • (in/op) *at, in* • (voor
infinitieven) *to*
technicus *technician*
techniek • (werktuigkundige
bewerking) *technology, engineering*
• (vakkunde) *technique*
technisch *technical*
tederheid *tenderness*
teef *bitch*
teelaarde *earth, soil*
teelbal *testicle*
teelt *culture, cultivation,* <v. vee>
breeding
teen • (wilgentwijg) *willow shoot*
• (deel van voet) *toe*
teer I [de] *tar* II [bnw] • (broos) *delicate,
fragile* • (gevoelig) *tender, delicate*
tegel *tile*
tegemoetkoming • (toelage)
allowance • (vergoeding)
compensation • (concessie)
accommodation, concession
tegen I [het] *contra, disadvantage*
II [bijw] • (anti) *against* • (niet mee)
against III [vz] • (in tegengestelde
richting) *against* • (in aanraking

met) ⋆ *het staat* ~ *de muur it's
against the wall* • (bijna) *towards, by*
• (ter bestrijding van) *against* • (in
strijd met) *against, contrary to* • (in
ruil voor) *against, for* • (jegens)
to(wards), with • (aan) *to*
tegenaan *against*
tegenaanval *counter-attack*
tegendeel *contrary, opposite, reverse*
tegengaan *prevent, fight, discourage*
tegengesteld *opposite, contrary*
tegenhanger *counterpart*
tegenhouden • (stoppen) *check,
arrest, stop* • (vertragen) *hold up*
tegenkomen *meet, come across*
tegenligger *oncoming car/ship*
tegenlopen *go wrong*
tegennatuurlijk *unnatural*
tegenover I [bijw] *across (from),
opposite* II [vz] • (aan de overkant) ⋆ ~
het station opposite the station
tegenovergesteld *opposite*
tegenpartij *opposite side,*
<tegenstander> *opponent*
tegenpool *opposite*
tegenprestatie *quid pro quo,
compensation*
tegenslag *reverse, set back, hitch*
tegenspartelen *raise objections, resist*
tegenspoed *adversity*
tegenspraak *contradiction*
tegenspreken *contradict, deny*
tegenstaan ⋆ *het eten/idee staat mij
tegen the food/idea puts me off* ⋆ *alles
stond hem tegen he was sick of
everything* ⋆ *zoiets gaat* ~ *that sort of
thing palls on one*
tegenstand *resistance*
tegenstander *opponent, adversary*
tegenstelling *antithesis, contrast*
tegenstribbelen *resist*
tegenstrijdig *contradictory, conflicting*
tegenstrijdigheid *inconsistency,
contradiction*
tegenvallen *be disappointing*

tegenvaller *disappointment, bit of bad luck*

tegenvoeter • *(iem. aan andere kant van de wereld) antipodean* • *(tegenpool) opposite, antipode*

tegenvoorstel *counter-proposal, counter-suggestion*

tegenwerken *cross, ‹iem.› work against, ‹v. plannen› thwart*

tegenwerking *opposition*

tegenwerpen *object*

tegenwerping *objection*

tegenwicht *counterpoise*

tegenwoordig I [bnw] • *(aanwezig) present* • *(huidig) present-day, current* II [bijw] *at present, nowadays*

tegenwoordigheid *presence*

tegenzin *dislike (of), aversion (to)*

tegoed *balance*

tehuis *home, shelter, refuge*

teil • *(teiltje) bowl* • *(wasteil) washtub*

teisteren *afflict, ravage, harass, sweep*

teken • *(aanduiding) sign, token, indication, ‹signaal› signal* • *(kenmerk) symptom*

tekenaar *draughtsman*

tekenen • *(een afbeelding maken) draw, sketch* • *(ondertekenen) sign* • *(kenmerken) stamp, characterize*

tekenfilm *cartoon*

tekening *drawing*

tekort *shortage, deficiency*

tekortkoming *shortcoming*

tekst *text*

tel • *(het tellen) count* • *(aanzien)* ⋆ *niet in tel zijn be of no account*

telefoneren *telephone, phone*

telefonisch *by telephone*

telefoon • *(toestel) (tele)phone* • *(gesprek)* ⋆ *er is ~ voor je there's a phone-call for you* ⋆ *ik geef je wel een ~tje I'll give you a ring*

telefoongesprek *telephone conversation/call*

telefoonnummer *telephone number*

telegraaf *telegraph*

telegraferen *wire, telegraph*

telegrafisch *telegraphic*

telegram *telegram, wire*

telegramstijl *telegram style*

telelens *tele-lens*

telen *‹dieren› breed, ‹gewassen› grow*

telescoop *telescope*

teleurstellen *disappoint*

teleurstelling *disappointment*

televisie *television, TV, ‹inf.› telly*

televisietoestel *television (set)*

telex • *(dienst) telex (teleprinter exchange)* • *(bericht) telex* • *(apparaat) teleprinter*

tellen *count*

teller • *(persoon) counter* • *(wisk.) numerator*

telling *count(ing)*

temmen *tame*

tempel *temple*

temperament *temperament, temper*

temperatuur *temperature*

temperen *‹m.b.t. geestdrift› damp, ‹v. geluid› subdue, soften, ‹v. licht› dim, ‹v. pijn› ease, ‹v. staal, hitte› temper*

tempo • *(snelheid) pace, speed, tempo* • *(muz.) tempo, time*

tendens *tendency*

tendentieus *tendentious, bias(s)ed*

tenger *slight, slender*

tenminste *at least*

tennis *tennis, lawn-tennis*

tennissen *play tennis*

tent *ridge tent*

tentamen *exam*

tentoonstellen *exhibit, display*

tentoonstelling *exhibition, show*

tenue *dress, uniform*

tenzij *unless*

tepel *nipple, teat*

teraardebestelling *funeral, burial, ‹form.› interment*

terdege *thoroughly*

terecht I [bnw] ∗ zeer ~ *quite rightly*
II [bijw] • (met recht) *justly, rightly*
• (teruggevonden) ∗ *mijn fiets is ~
my bicycle has been found* • (op de
juiste plaats) ∗ *ben ik hier ~ bij A.?
does A. live here?* ∗ *je kunt daar nu
niet ~ it's closed now* ∗ *met Engels
kun je overal ~ you can get by
everywhere in English*
terechtkomen • (teruggevonden
worden) *turn up* • (in orde komen)
turn out all right • (belanden) *fall,
land, end up/in/at*
terechtstellen *execute*
terechtstelling *execution*
terechtwijzing *reprimand*
teren I [ov ww] • (met teer insmeren)
tar II [on ww] • (leven van) *live on/off*
tergen *provoke*
terloops *casual, incidental*
term • (benaming) *term* • (reden)
ground
termijn • (periode) *term, period*
• (tijdslimiet) *deadline* • (deel van
schuld) ∗ *in ~en betalen pay by/in
instalments*
terpentijn *turpentine*
terras *terrace*
terrein • (grond) *ground*,
<bouwterrein> *(building-)site*,
<landschap> *terrain*, <om gebouw>
grounds
territoriaal *territorial*
territorium *territory*
terroriseren *terrorize*
terrorisme *terrorism*
terstond *at once, forthwith*
terts *third*
terug • (weerom) *back* • (geleden) *back*
• (achteruit) *back*
terugbetalen *pay back, refund*
terugblik *retrospect*
terugbrengen • (weer op de plaats, in
de toestand brengen) *bring/take
back, return* • (~ tot) *reduce to*

terugdeinzen *shrink back*
teruggaan • (terugkeren) *go back,
return* • (ontstaan zijn uit) *date back
to*
teruggetrokken *retiring*
teruggeven *give back, restore, return*
terughoudend *reserved, reticent, aloof*
terugkeer *return*
terugkeren *return, come back*
terugkomen *come back, return*
• (~ op) *get back to*, <een belofte,
oordeel> *go back on*
terugkomst *return*
terugkrabbelen *back out*
terugkrijgen *recover, get back*
teruglopen *walk back*
terugnemen *take back, withdraw*
terugreis *return-journey*
terugroepen *recall, call back*
terugschrikken *recoil*
terugslag • (terugstoot) *backlash*, <v.
wapen> *recoil* • (nadelig gevolg) <fig.>
repercussion
terugtocht *retreat, return journey*
terugtrekken I [ov ww] *withdraw*
II [on ww] *retreat, fall back* III [wkd
ww] *withdraw*, <uit zaken, naar zijn
kamer> *retire*, <v. leger> *retreat*
terugverlangen *want back*
terugvinden *find again*
terugweg *way back*
terugwinnen *win back, regain*
terwijl *as, while*
terzijde *aside*
test *test*
testament • (laatste wil) *(last) will*
• (bijbeldeel) *Testament*
testen *test*
teug *draught*
teugel *rein*, <met hoofdstel> *bridle*
teuten *dawdle*
tevens • (ook) *also, besides*
• (tegelijkertijd) *at the same time*
tevergeefs *in vain, vainly*
tevoren • (van tevoren) *beforehand*

• (vroeger) *before, previously*
tevreden ‹over iets› *satisfied,* ‹v. aard›
contented
tevredenheid *satisfaction*
tewaterlating *launching*
teweegbrengen *bring about, cause*
textiel • (stof) *textile* • (industrie)
textiles [mv]
thans *at present, now*
theater *theatre*
theatraal • (melodramatisch) ★ ~
gedrag histrionics • (het toneel
betreffend) *theatrical*
thee *tea*
theelichtje *tea warmer*
theepot *teapot*
thema • (onderwerp) *theme, subject*
(matter) • (oefening) *translation*
exercise
theologie *theology*
theoloog *student training for the*
ministry, ‹geleerde› *theologian,*
‹student› *theological student*
theoreticus *theorist*
theoretisch *theoretical*
theorie *theory*
therapeut *therapist*
therapie *therapy*
thermometer *thermometer*
thermosfles *thermos (flask)*
thuis I [het] *home* II [bijw] *at home*
thuisfront *home front*
thuishaven *home port,* ‹fig.› *home base*
thuiskomst *homecoming*
thuisreis *homeward journey/voyage*
thuiswedstrijd *home match*
tien *ten*
tiener *teenager (boy/girl)*
tiental *decade, ten*
tientje • *ten-guilder note, ten guilders*
tieren • (razen) *rage* • (gedijen) *thrive*
tiet *tit*
tij *tide*
tijd • (tijdsduur) *time* • (tijdvak) *time,*
period, season • (tijdstip) *time*

• (grammaticale tijd) *tense*
tijdbom *time bomb*
tijdelijk • (voorlopig) *temporary*
• (vergankelijk) ‹form.› *temporal*
tijdens *during*
tijdgeest *spirit of the age*
tijdperk *period,* ‹gesch.› *age*
tijdrekening *chronology, era*
tijdrovend *time-consuming*
tijdschrift *periodical, magazine*
tijdsein *time signal*
tijdstip (point in) *time*
tijdvak *period,* ‹gesch.› *age, era*
tijdverdrijf *pastime*
tijger *tiger*
tijm *thyme*
tik *tap,* ‹harde tik› *rap*
tikje • (klopje) (light) *tap* • (een beetje)
a touch
tikken • (geluid geven) *tick*
• (kloppen) ‹bij tikkertje› *touch,*
‹tegen ruit, deur› *tap/rap* • (typen)
type
til • (duiventil) *dovecot(e)* • (het tillen)
lifting
tillen *lift*
timmeren I [ov ww] *build, knock*
together II [on ww] *hammer*
timmerman *carpenter*
tin *tin,* ‹legering› *pewter*
tinctuur *tincture*
tint • (kleur) *tint, hue* • (gelaatskleur)
complexion
tintelen • (flonkeren) ‹v. geest, wijn›
sparkle, ‹v. sterren, ogen› *twinkle*
• (prikkelen) *tingle*
tinten *tint, tinge*
tip *tip*
tippelen • (lopen) *tramp, walk*
• (prostitutie bedrijven) *walk the*
streets, solicit
tiptop *tip-top, A 1*
tiran *tyrant*
tirannie *tyranny*
tiranniek *tyrannical*

tiranniseren tyrannize (over), bully
titel • (benaming) title • (waardigheid) title
titelblad title page
titelhouder title holder
tjilpen chirp, twitter
tjokvol ‹inf.› chock-full
tl-buis fluorescent light
toast toast
tobbe tub
tobben • (sloven) slave • (piekeren) worry
toch • (desondanks) yet, still, for all that, all the same • (bij nader inzien) ★ hij heeft het toch maar gedaan he did it after all
tocht • (reis) journey, trip, expedition • (wind) draught
tochten ★ het tocht there is a draught
tochtig • (met veel tocht) draughty • (bio.) on heat
tochtstrip ‹binnen en buiten› draught-excluder, ‹buitenkant› weather-strip
toe I [bijw] • (dicht) shut, closed • (richting) ★ waar ga je naar toe? where are you going? ★ naar het oosten toe towards the east II [tw] ★ toe maar go ahead
toebehoren I [het] accessories II [on ww] • (~ aan) belong to
toebrengen ‹letsel, nederlaag› inflict, ‹schade› do, ‹slag› deal
toedekken cover up
toedienen administer
toedoen close, shut
toedracht facts
toe-eigenen appropriate, annex
toegang • (ingang) entrance, entry, access • (mogelijkheid tot toegang) admittance, admission, access
toegangsbewijs entry ticket
toegangsweg access (road), approach
toegankelijk open, accessible
toegedaan ★ 'n mening ~ zijn hold an opinion/view ★ iem. ~ zijn be devoted to a person
toegeeflijk indulgent
toegeven I [ov ww] • (erkennen) admit, grant, ‹form.› concede • (extra geven) throw in, add • (inschikkelijk zijn) indulge, humour II [on ww] give in, yield
toegift encore
toehoorder auditor, hearer
toejuichen applaud, cheer
toekennen allow
toekijken look on
toeknikken nod to
toekomen • (rondkomen) get by • (toebehoren) belong to • (toezenden) ★ doen ~ send • (aan toekomen) ★ ergens aan ~ get round to s.th. • (naderen) ★ ~ op come up to; make for
toekomst future
toelaatbaar acceptable, ‹te dulden› tolerable, ‹v. bewijs(stuk)› admissible
toelachen • (zich gunstig voordoen) ‹v. fortuin› smile on, ‹v. idee› appeal to • (naar iem. lachen) smile at
toelage allowance, ‹beurs› grant
toelaten • (toestaan) allow, permit • (binnenlaten) admit • (laten slagen) pass
toelating • (toestaan) permission, leave • (binnenlaten) admission, admittance
toelatingsexamen entrance examination
toeleggen I [ov ww] • (meer betalen) add (to) • (moeite doen) be bent (on) II [wkd ww] • (~ op) apply o.s. to
toelichten explain, ‹met voorbeelden› illustrate
toelichting comment, explanation, illustration
toeloop rush
toelopen • (komen aanlopen) walk up to, come up to • (uitlopen) ★ spits ~

taper
toen I [bijw] *then* II [vw] *when*
toenadering *approach*
toename *increase*
toenemen *increase, grow*
toenmalig *of the day, of that time*
toepasselijk *appropriate, suitable*
toepassen *apply*
toepassing *application*
toer • (reis) *tour* • (omwenteling) *turn, revolution*
toerbeurt *turn*
toeren *take a trip/ride*
toerental *number of revolutions*
toerisme *tourism*
toerist *tourist*
toernooi *tournament*
toeschietelijk *accommodating, forthcoming*
toeschouwer *onlooker, spectator*
toeschrijven ∗ ~ aan *attribute to*
toeslaan I [ov ww] • (dichtslaan) <deur> *slam* II [on ww] • (aanvallen) *strike*
toeslag <op rekening> *additional charge*, <trein> *excess fare*
toespeling *allusion*
toespitsen I [ov ww] • (aanscherpen) *aggravate* II [wkd ww] *become acute*
toespraak *speech*, <form.> *address*
toespreken *speak to, address*
toestaan • (goedkeuren) *allow, permit* • (verlenen) *grant*, <form.> *concede*
toestand • (situatie) <leef-/werksituatie> *condition*, <v. zaken> *state of things/affairs*, <v.h. ogenblik> *situation, position* • (nare situatie) *muddle*
toestel • (apparaat) *apparatus* • (vliegtuig) *machine*
toestemmen *agree/consent (to)*
toestemming *consent*
toestoppen • (instoppen) *tuck in* • (geven) *slip* • (dichtmaken) *plug*,
toestromen *pour/flood in*

toet *face*
toetakelen • (afranselen) *beat up* • (verfomfaaien) *crumple (up)/rumple*
toetasten • (aanpakken) *take action* • (eten) *fall to*
toeten *toot*
toeter *hooter*, <claxon> *horn*
toetreden ∗ ~ tot *join*
toets • (examen) *test* • (figuurlijk) *test* • (muz.) *key*
toetsen *test*
toetssteen *touchstone*
toeval • (ziekte) *an epileptic fit* • (samenloop van omstandigheden) *accident, chance*
toevallen • (dichtvallen) *fall to* • (v. bezit) *devolve to/on*
toevallig I [bnw] *accidental, fortuitous* II [bijw] *by chance/accident*
toevertrouwen ∗ iem. iets ~ *(en)trust s.o. with s.th.*
toevloed *influx*
toevlucht *refuge, resort*
toevoegen *add*
toevoeging *addition*
toevoer *supply*
toewijding *devotion*
toewijzen <v. deel> *allot*, <v. taak> *assign*
toezeggen *promise*
toezegging *promise*
toezicht *supervision*
toezien • (toekijken) *look on* • (oppassen) *take care, see to it*
tof *great*
toga *gown*, <v. Romein> *toga*
toilet • (het zich kleden en opmaken) *toilet* • (wc) *lavatory, toilet*
toilettafel *dressing table*
tol • (speelgoed) *top* • (tolhuis) *toll house* • (tolgeld) *toll* • (tolboom) <AE> *turnpike*
tolerantie *toleration, tolerance*
tolk *interpreter*
tollen • (met een tol spelen) *spin a top*

• (snel ronddraaien) *spin round*
tolvrij *toll-free*
tomaat *tomato*
ton • (gewicht, maat) *ton* • (vat) *cask, barrel* • (geld) *a hundred thousand guilders*
toneel • (podium) *stage* • (genre) *drama* • (tafereel) *scene*
toneelgezelschap *theatre/theatrical company*
toneelschool *drama school/college*
toneelschrijver *playwright, dramatist*
toneelspel • (stuk) *play* • (het spelen) *acting*
toneelspeler *actor*
toneelstuk *play*
tonen I [ov ww] • (laten zien) *show*, <uitstallen> *display* • (aantonen) *prove, demonstrate, manifest* II [on ww] *look*
tong • (smaakorgaan) *tongue* • (vis) *sole*
tongval *accent, dialect*
tonijn *tunny*, <AE> *tuna*
tonnage *tonnage*
tonsuur *tonsure*
tooien *decorate*
toom • (teugel) *bridle* • (kippen) *brood*
toon *tone, sound*
toonaangevend *leading*
toonaard *key*
toonbaar *presentable, fit to be seen*
toonbeeld *model, paragon*
toonder *bearer*
toonladder *scale*
toonzaal *showroom*
toorn *wrath, rage*
toorts *torch*
top *top*, <v. berg> *summit*
topaas *topaz*
topconferentie *summit meeting/conference*
topografie *topography*
topprestatie *a record/top-notch performance/achievement*

toppunt • (uiterste) *top, peak, summit* • (hoogtepunt) *climax*
topsnelheid *top speed*
topvorm *top form*
topzwaar *top-heavy*
tor *beetle*
toren *tower*, <met spits> *steeple*
torenklok *church bell/clock*
tornado *tornado*
tornen I [ov ww] *unsew, unstitch, rip* II [on ww] *meddle with*
torpederen *torpedo*
torpedo *torpedo*
torsen *bear, carry*
tot I [vz] • (als/voor) *to, for* • (tegen) ⋆ *tot elke prijs at any price* • (zo ver als) *to, until* II [vw] ⋆ *hij sliep tot het donker werd he slept until dusk*
totaal I [het] *sum total* II [bnw] *total*
totalisator *totalizator*, <inf.> *tote*
totdat *till, until*
touringcar *coach*
tournee *tour*
touw *rope*
touwladder *rope ladder*
touwtrekken *tug of war*
tovenaar *magician*
toveren *practise witchcraft*, <goochelen> *conjure*
toverij *magic*
traag *slow*
traagheid *slowness, slow-wittedness, obtusity*
traan *tear*
traangas *tear gas*
traanklier *tear gland*
trachten *attempt, try*, <form.> *endeavour*
traditie *tradition*
traditioneel *traditional*
tragedie *tragedy*
tragisch *tragic*
trainen *train*
trainingspak *tracksuit*
traject <v. weg, spoorlijn> *section*

traktaat • (verdrag) treaty • (verhandeling) tract
traktatie treat
trakteren I [ov ww] treat (s.o. to) II [on ww] ∗ ik trakteer this one's on me
tralie bar
tram tram (car)
tramhalte tram stop
tranen water
transactie transaction
transatlantisch transatlantic
transformatie transformation
transformator transformer
transparant I [het] transparency II [bnw] transparent
transpireren perspire
transplantatie transplant(ation)
transplanteren transplant
transport transport
transporteren transport
trant style, manner
trap • (alle treden) stairs, staircase • (schop) kick
trapeze trapeze
trapezium trapezium
trapgevel step gable
trapleuning banisters
trappelen trample
trappen I [ov ww] • (schoppen) kick II [on ww] • (op of in iets stappen) tread/step on • (fietsen) pedal
trapper pedal
trapportaal landing
trauma trauma
traumatisch traumatic
travestie travesty
trechter funnel
tred step, pace
trede ‹v. ladder› rung, ‹v. trap› step
treden step, tread
tredmolen treadmill
treffen I [het] engagement, encounter II [ov ww] • (raken) hit, ‹bliksem› strike, ‹maatregel› affect • (aantreffen) meet (up with), come

across • (ontroeren) move • (opvallen) strike
treffend striking
treffer • (raak schot, enz.) hit • (toeval) stroke/bit of luck
trefwoord catchword, ‹inf.› buzz word
trein train
treinstel train
treiteren nag
trek • (het trekken) ‹v. vogels› migration • (gelaatstrek) feature • (kenmerk) trait, feature • (tocht) draught • (zin, eetlust) appetite
trekken I [ov ww] • (slepen) pull, draw, tow • (in genoemde toestand brengen) draw, pull • (aantrekken) attract, ‹v. publiek, klanten› draw • (eruit halen) pull out II [on ww] • (reizen, gaan) travel, ‹te voet› hike • (vervormd worden) warp • (spierbeweging maken) twitch
trekker • (onderdeel v. vuurwapen) trigger • (wandelaar) hiker • (auto) truck, lorry
trekking draw
trekkracht traction, pull
trekpleister • (attractie) attraction, ‹inf.› draw • (pleister) ≈ (blistering) plaster
trekvogel migratory bird, bird of passage
treuren mourn, grieve
treurig sad, mournful
treurspel tragedy
treurwilg weeping willow
treuzelen dawdle (over)
triangel triangle
tribunaal tribunal
tribune stand
tricot • (materiaal) tricot • (ballet-/gympakje) leotard
trillen • (heen en weer gaan) tremble, quiver, vibrate • (beven) tremble
triller ‹muz.› trill
trilling trembling, quiver(ing),

vibration
trio trio
triomf triumph
triomfboog triumphal arch
triomftocht triumphal procession
trip • (uitstapje) outing, trip • (effect van drugs) trip
trippelen patter, scurry
troebel muddy, murky, cloudy
troef • (kleur die troef is) trumps • (troefkaart) trump (card)
troep • (groep) troop, <honden> pack, <mensen> crowd • (rommel) mess
troepenmacht military forces
troetelnaam pet name
troeven (play) trump
trofee trophy
troffel trowel
trog trough
trolleybus trolley bus
trom drum
trombone trombone
trombose thrombosis
tromgeroffel drum roll
trommel • (slaginstrument) drum • (doos) box, tin • (cilinder) drum, barrel
trommelen (beat the) drum
trommelrem drum brake
trommelvlies eardrum
trompet trumpet
trompetten trumpet
tronen throne, sit enthroned
tronie mug
troon throne
troonopvolger heir to the throne
troonrede speech from the throne, king's/queen's speech
troonsafstand abdication
troost comfort, consolation
troosteloos • (mistroostig) disconsolate, drab, dreary • (ontroostbaar) disconsolate
troosten I [ov ww] comfort, console II [wkd ww] comfort o.s. (with)

tropen tropics
tropisch tropical
tros bunch
trots I [de] pride II [bnw] proud
trotseren • (het hoofd bieden) defy, brave • (bestand zijn tegen) stand up (to)
trottoir pavement
trouw I [de] fidelity, loyalty II [bnw] faithful, loyal, true
trouwdag wedding day
trouwen I [ov ww] marry II [on ww] get married
trouwens for that matter, by the way, mind you
trouwpartij wedding party
trouwring wedding ring
truc trick
truffel truffle
trui sweater, jumper, jersey
trust trust
T-shirt T-shirt, tee shirt
tube tube
tuberculose tuberculosis
tucht discipline
tuchtschool borstal, institution/prison for young offenders
tuig • (hoofdstel van paard) harness • (vistuig) gear, tackle • (scheepstuig) rigging • (plebs) scum
tuimelen tumble
tuimelraam pivot window, flap-window
tuin garden
tuinbouw horticulture
tuinder market gardener
tuinieren garden
tuinman gardener
tuinslang (garden) hose
tuit • (schenktuit) spout • (spits einde) nozzle
tuiten I [ov ww] ★ de lippen ~ purse one's lips II [on ww] ★ mijn oren ~ my ears are ringing
tuk ★ tuk zijn op be keen on ★ iem. tuk

hebben *pull s.o.'s leg*
tulband • (hoofddeksel) *turban*
• (gebak) *fruitcake*
tulp *tulip*
tulpenbol *tulip bulb*
tumor *tumour*
tumult *tumult*
tunnel *tunnel*
tureluurs *mad*
turen *peer* (at)
turf *peat*
turfmolm *peat dust*
Turkije *Turkey*
turkoois *turquoise*
Turks I [het] *Turkish* II [bnw] *Turkish*
turnen *practise/do gymnastics*
turven *score, keep a tally*
tussen ‹tussen meer› *among*, ‹tussen twee› *between*
tussendeur *communicating door*
tussendoor • (tussen twee door) *through it/them* • (tussentijds) *in between*
tussenhandel *intermediate trade*
tussenin *in between*
tussenkomst *intervention*
tussenlanding *stop(over)*
tussenpersoon *intermediary,* ‹bij geschil› *mediator,* ‹handel› *middleman*
tussenpoos *interval*
tussenruimte *space,* ‹v. tijd› *interval*
tussentijd ‹form.› *interim*
tussentijds I [bnw] ★ ~e vacature *casual vacancy* ★ ~e verkiezing *by-election* ★ ~e vakantie *half-term holiday* II [bijw] *between times*
tussenuit ★ er ~ knijpen *do a bunk*
tussenvoegen *insert, put in*
tutoyeren *be on first-name terms*
twaalf *twelve*
twaalfuurtje *midday meal/snack, lunch*
twee *two*
tweede *second*

tweedehands *secondhand*
tweederangs *second-rate*
tweedracht *discord*
tweegevecht *duel*
tweeling(en) (pair of) *twins,* ‹sterrenbeeld› *Gemini*
tweeslachtig • (ambivalent) *ambiguous, ambivalent* • (hermafrodiet) *hermaphrodite,* ‹v. planten› *androgynous* • (amfibisch) *amphibious*
tweespalt *discord*
tweesprong *cross-roads* [mv]
tweestrijd *internal conflict*
tweetal *two, pair*
tweetalig *bilingual*
twijfel *doubt*
twijfelachtig *doubtful, dubious*
twijfelen *doubt*
twijg *twig*
twintig *twenty*
twist *quarrel, dispute*
twisten • (redetwisten) *dispute* • (ruzieën) *quarrel*
twistgesprek *argument, dispute*
twistpunt *point of contention,* (point at) *issue*
type *type*
typen *type(write)*
typeren *typify*
typisch • (typerend) *typical (of)* • (eigenaardig) *curious*

U

ui • (bolgewas) *onion* • (grap) *joke*
uier *udder*
uil • (nachtvogel) *owl* • (sukkel) *fool*
uilskuiken *nincompoop, silly fool,*
‹inf.› *idiot*
uit I [bnw] • (niet thuis) *out* • (op de
markt) *out* II [bijw] • (beëindigd) *out,
finished* • ((naar) buiten) *out* • (niet
populair (meer)) *out* • (niet
brandend) *out* III [vz] • (vanwege) *out
of* • ((naar) buiten) *out (of)*
• (van(daan)) *from*
uitademen • (adem uitblazen)
breathe out • (uitwasemen) *exhale*
uitbannen • (verbannen) *banish*
• (verdrijven) *drive away,* ‹geesten›
exorcize
uitbarsten *burst out,* ‹v. vulkaan›
erupt
uitbarsting *outburst,* ‹v. vulkaan›
eruption
uitbeelden *portray, depict*
uitbesteden • (in de kost doen) *board
out* • (aan anderen overdragen)
contract out
uitbetalen *pay,* ‹v. cheque› *cash*
uitblazen I [ov ww] *blow out* II [on
ww] ⋆ *even* ∼ *take a breather*
uitblijven • (wegblijven) ‹v. regen,
enz.› *hold off* • (achterwege blijven)
fail to occur
uitblinken *shine, excel*
uitblinker *star, brilliant person,*
‹kind› *prodigy*
uitbloeien ⋆ uitgebloeid zijn *be out of
flower* ⋆ uitgebloeide rozen *overblown
roses*
uitbouw • (aanbouwsel) *annex(e)*
• (het uitbouwen) *extension*
uitbouwen *extend*

uitbraak *escape (from prison)*
uitbrander *reprimand*
uitbreiden I [ov ww] *expand, extend*
II [wkd ww] *spread, expand*
uitbreken *break out*
uitbrengen • (zeggen, uiten) *say,
utter* • (kenbaar maken) ‹geheim›
reveal, ‹rapport› *deliver* • (op de
markt brengen) *launch, bring out,*
‹film, muz.› *release*
uitbroeden *hatch*
uitbuiten *exploit*
uitbundig *exuberant,* ‹gejubel›
enthusiastic
uitdagen *challenge,* ‹tarten› *defy*
uitdager *challenger*
uitdaging *challenge*
uitdelen *distribute, deal (out), hand out*
uitdenken *devise, contrive, invent*
uitdeuken ‹auto› *panel-beat*
uitdiepen *deepen*
uitdijen *expand*
uitdoen • (uittrekken) *take off*
• (uitschakelen) *switch/turn off*
uitdossen *dress up*
uitdraaien • (uitdoen) *turn off, switch
off, turn/put out* • (uitschroeven)
unscrew • (printen) *run off,*
‹computer› *print (out)*
uitdragen • (verbreiden) ‹ambtelijk›
proclaim, ‹informatie, kennis›
disseminate, ‹nieuws, boodschap›
spread, ‹standpunt› *propagate* • (naar
buiten dragen) *carry out*
uitdrijven *drive/cast out, exorcise*
uitdrogen *dry out,* ‹bron, rivier› *dry
up,* ‹med.› *dehydrate*
uitdrukkelijk *express, explicit*
uitdrukken *express*
uitdrukking *expression*
uitdunnen *thin (out)*
uiteengaan *separate, part,* ‹in alle
richtingen› *disperse*
uiteenlopen • (niet dezelfde kant
uitlopen) *diverge* • (verschillen) *differ,*

vary, diverge
uiteenzetten *explain*
uiteenzetting • (uitleg) *explanation, statement* • (het uiteenzetten) *exposition, description*
uiteinde *extremity, (far) end*
uiteindelijk I [bnw] *ultimate, final,* ‹doel› *eventual* II [bijw] *eventually*
uiten I [ov ww] *express, voice,* ‹klanken, woorden› *utter* II [wkd ww] *express o.s.*
uiteraard *naturally, of course*
uiterlijk I [het] • (voorkomen) *(outward) appearance, looks, exterior* II [bnw] *external, outward* III [bijw] • (op zijn laatst) *at the latest* • (van buiten) *outwardly*
uitermate *exceedingly, extremely*
uiterst I [bnw] • (het meest verwijderd) *out(er)most, extreme, farthest* • (grootst) *utmost, utter* • (laatste) *final, last* II [bijw] *extremely, exceedingly*
uitgaan • (naar buiten gaan) *go out, leave* • (zich ergens gaan vermaken) *go out* • (als uitgangspunt nemen) *depart (from)*
uitgang • (doorgang naar buiten) *exit, way out* • (einde v. woord) *ending* • (techniek) *output*
uitgave • (kosten) *expense* • (druk) *edition*
uitgebreid • (van grote omvang) *extensive* • (veelomvattend) *comprehensive, elaborate* • (uitvoerig) *detailed*
uitgebreidheid • (grootte) *extent* • (grote omvang) *extensiveness*
uitgelaten *elated, exuberant*
uitgeleide ★ iem. ~ doen *show s.o. out; see s.o. off*
uitgelezen *choice, select*
uitgemaakt ★ dat is een ~e zaak *that is a foregone conclusion*
uitgerekend ★ ~ vandaag *today of all*

days
uitgeslapen • (uitgerust) *refreshed, wide awake* • (pienter) *shrewd, smart*
uitgestrekt *extensive, vast*
uitgestrektheid • (oppervlak) *expanse* • (uitgebreidheid) *extensiveness*
uitgeven I [ov ww] • (publiceren) *publish* • (besteden) *spend* • (in omloop brengen) *emit,* ‹aandelen, geld› *issue* • (uitdelen) *distribute* II [wkd ww] *pass o.s. off as*
uitgever *publisher*
uitgeverij *firm of publishers, publishing house*
uitgezonderd *barring, except,* ‹form.› *save*
uitgifte *issue*
uitglijden *slip, lose one's footing*
uitgraven *dig out, excavate*
uitgroeien *outgrow*
uithalen • (ergens iets uitnemen) *extract, draw/pull out* • (los-/leeghalen) *clean/clear out,* ‹breiwerk› *unpick* • (uitvoeren) *play* • (baten, helpen) *help*
uithangbord *signboard*
uithangen • (naar buiten hangen) *hang out* • (zich voordoen als) *play*
uitheems *foreign, exotic*
uithoek *remote/out-of-the-way place*
uithollen *hollow out*
uithoren *question, interrogate*
uithouden • (verduren) *bear, endure* • (volhouden) ★ het ~ *hold out; stand it; stick it out*
uithoudingsvermogen ‹lichamelijk› *stamina,* ‹mentaal› *endurance*
uithuilen *cry one's heart out, have a good cry*
uithuizig *gadding about, always out*
uiting *utterance* ★ ~ van *expression of*
uitje • (uitstapje) *outing* • (zilveruitje) *cocktail onion*

uitjouwen *hoot (at), boo, jeer (at)*
uitkeren *pay*
uitkering *benefit*
uitkienen *puzzle out,* ‹een plan› *think out*
uitkiezen *choose, select*
uitkijk *lookout*
uitkijken • (verlangen naar) *look forward to* • (steeds kijken) *be on the lookout (for)* • (oppassen) *watch, look out* • (uitkijken op) *look out over, overlook*
uitkijktoren *watchtower*
uitklaren *clear*
uitkleden *undress*
uitknijpen *squeeze (out)*
uitkomen • (terechtkomen) *arrive at* • (toegang geven tot) ‹deur› *open onto,* ‹v. kamer› *give on* • (uit ei komen) *hatch (out)* • (opgaan/kloppen) *prove to be correct,* ‹som› *come/work out,* ‹v. droom› *come true* • (verschijnen) *appear,* ‹boek› *come out* • (rondkomen) *make (both) ends meet* • (bekend worden) *transpire, emerge, come out* • (gelegen komen) *suit* • (niet verbergen) ∗ *voor zijn mening* ~ *be candid; speak one's mind* • (plantk.) *come out, sprout* • (sport) *play,* ‹bij kaartspel› *lead*
uitkomst • (resultaat) *result* • (redding) *relief, solution*
uitkopen • (vrijkopen) *buy out* • (afkopen) *buy off*
uitkramen *talk,* ‹geleerdheid› *parade*
uitlaat *exhaust*
uitlaatklep *exhaust valve,* ‹fig.› *outlet*
uitlachen *laugh at*
uitladen *unload*
uitlaten I [ov ww] • (naar buiten laten) ‹bezoeker› *show out,* ‹persoon, dier› *let out* • (niet aantrekken) *leave off* II [wkd ww] *express o.s. on, give one's opnion on*
uitlating *utterance*

uitleg *explanation, interpretation*
uitleggen • (verklaren) *explain, interpret, expound* • (uitspreiden) *spread out*
uitlekken • (wegsijpelen) *leak (out)* • (bekend worden) *leak out,* ‹form.› *transpire*
uitlenen *lend (out), loan*
uitleven *let o.s. go*
uitleveren *hand over,* ‹aan ander land› *extradite*
uitlevering ‹personen› *extradition,* ‹zaken› *surrender*
uitlezen • (tot aan het eind lezen) *read from cover to cover, finish (reading), read to the end* • (comp.) *read out*
uitlokken *provoke, elicit*
uitlopen • (uitkomen op) *end in, lead to* • (leiden tot) *result/end in* • (meer tijd kosten) *overrun*
uitloper • (uitgroeisel) *offshoot, runner* • (deel van gebergte) *foothill(s)*
uitloten • (bij loting aanwijzen) *draw (out)* • (door loting uitsluiten) *eliminate by lottery*
uitloven *offer*
uitmaken • (afbreken) *end,* ‹relatie› *break off* • (doven) *put out* • (vormen) *form, constitute* • (invloed hebben) *matter, be of importance*
uitmeten • (afmeten) *measure (out)* • (uitvoerig bespreken) ∗ *breed* ~ *enlarge on*
uitmonden *discharge into, flow into*
uitmonsteren • (versieren) *trim* • (uitdossen) *dress up,* ‹inf.› *doll up* • (uitrusten) *equip*
uitmoorden *massacre, slaughter*
uitmunten *excel, stand out*
uitmuntend *excellent, outstanding*
uitnodiging *invitation*
uitoefenen *practise, exercise*
uitpakken ‹bagage› *unpack,* ‹uit verpakking› *unwrap*

uitpersen *press out, squeeze*
uitpluizen <gegevens> *sift (out),*
<raadsel> *unravel*
uitpraten *have one's say*
uitpuilen *bulge,* <v. ogen> *goggle*
uitputten *exhaust*
uitputting *exhaustion*
uitreiken *distribute,* <paspoort> *issue,*
<prijs> *present*
uitrekenen *figure out, calculate*
uitrekken *stretch (out)*
uitrukken I [ov ww] *pull/pluck out*
II [on ww] *march (out),* <brandweer>
turn out
uitrusten I [ov ww] *equip, fit out* II [on
ww] *(have a) rest*
uitrusting *equipment,* <v. reiziger>
outfit
uitschakelen • (afzetten) *switch off,*
disconnect • (elimineren) *eliminate,*
rule out
uitscheiden I [ov ww] *secrete* II [on
ww] *stop, leave off*
uitschelden *call (s.o.) names, swear at*
s.o., abuse
uitschieten I [ov ww] • (haastig
uittrekken) *slip/throw off* II [on ww]
• (een plotselinge beweging maken)
shoot/dart out
uitschieter *highlight,* <naar beneden>
dip, <naar boven> *peak*
uitschot *scum, riff-raff*
uitschrijven <cheque, recept> *write out*
uitschuiven *pull out, extend,* <tafel,
enz.> *draw out*
uitslaan I [ov ww] • (uitkloppen)
beat/shake out • (naar buiten slaan)
knock/beat/strike out, <vleugels>
spread • (uitvouwen) *unfold* II [on
ww] • (met aanslag bedekt worden)
<brood, enz.> *become/grow mouldy,*
<muur> *sweat* • (naar buiten komen)
break/burst out
uitslag • (puistjes) *rash* • (afloop) *result*
uitslapen *sleep in*

uitsluiten *exclude,* <mogelijkheid>
rule out
uitsluitend *only, exclusively*
uitsluiting *exclusion*
uitsluitsel *definite/decisive answer*
uitsmeren *spread*
uitsmijter • (portier) *bouncer*
• (gebakken eieren met brood, kaas
of ham) *fried bacon, cheese and eggs on*
slice of bread
uitspannen *unharness*
uitspansel *firmament*
uitsparen • (besparen) *save* • (open
laten) *leave open*
uitspatting *excess,* <drank, seks>
debauchery
uitspelen • (tot het eind spelen) *play*
out, <spel> *finish* • (in het spel
brengen) *lead*
uitspraak • (wijze van uitspreken)
pronunciation, <v. persoon> *accent*
• (verklaring) *pronouncement,*
utterance • (jur.) *judg(e)ment, verdict,*
sentence
uitspreiden *spread (out)*
uitspreken I [ov ww] • (in
spraakklanken weergeven)
pronounce, <duidelijk> *articulate*
• (uiten) *express, utter*
• (bekendmaken) *declare,* <vonnis>
pronounce II [on ww] ★ laat mij ~ *let*
me finish
uitstaan *stand, bear*
uitstallen *show, display*
uitstalling *display, shop window*
display
uitstappen • (eruit stappen) *get*
off/out • (ermee ophouden) *quit*
uitsteeksel *projection, protuberance*
uitstek ★ bij ~ *geschikt om*
exceptionally suited for ★ bij ~
pre-eminently
uitsteken I [ov ww] • (naar
buiten/voren steken) *stick out,*
<hand> *hold out,* <vlag> *put out*

• (uitstrekken) *extend*, ‹hand, voet›
stretch out II [on ww] • (omhoog/naar
buiten steken) *stick out, project,
protrude* • (zichtbaar zijn) *rise/tower
above, excel,* ‹fig.› *tower above*
uitstel *postponement, delay*
uitstellen *postpone, put off*
uitsterven *die out, become extinct*
uitstorten *pour out*
uitstoten ‹gassen, rook› *emit*
uitstralen *radiate*
uitstrekken I [ov ww] *stretch (out)*
II [wkd ww] • (lengte/oppervlakte
beslaan) *stretch (out), lie down*
• (gelden) *extend*
uitsturen *send out*
uittekenen *draw*
uittocht *exodus*
uittreden *resign (from), retire (from)*
uittrekken • (door trekken
verwijderen) *pull out,* ‹vooral v. kies›
extract • (uitdoen) *take off*
uittreksel • (verkorte versie) *extract,*
‹v. boek› *summary* • (akte) *certificate*
uitvaardigen *issue,* ‹jur.› *enact*
uitval *outburst*
uitvallen • (wegvallen) *fall out,*
‹sport› *drop out,* ‹v. trein› *be
cancelled,* ‹verbinding› *break down*
• (tot resultaat hebben) *turn/work out*
• (agressief spreken) *fly (at)* • (sport)
lunge (at)
uitvaren • (de zee kiezen) *sail (out),
put to sea* • (uitvallen) *fly at*
uitvechten *fight out*
uitverkoop *sale, clearance sale*
uitverkoren *chosen, elect*
uitvinden • (iets nieuws uitdenken)
invent • (te weten komen) *find out,
discover*
uitvinder *inventor*
uitvinding *invention*
uitvissen *fish out, dig/ferret out*
uitvloeisel *result, consequence*
uitvlucht *pretext, evasion, subterfuge*

uitvoer • (export) *export*
• (exportgoederen) *exports*
• (uitvoering) * ten ~ brengen *carry
out; execute*
uitvoerbaar *practicable, feasible*
uitvoeren • (exporteren) *export*
• (volbrengen) *implement,* ‹jur.›
execute, ‹belofte› *fulfil,* ‹besluit,
instructies, plan› *carry out,* ‹functie,
plicht, taak› *perform* • (vertonen,
spelen) ‹kunst› *perform,* ‹muz.›
execute • (verrichten) * niets ~ *do
nothing*
uitvoerig I [bnw] *detailed,
comprehensive, full* II [bijw] *in detail,
comprehensively, fully*
uitvoering *execution,* ‹toneel, muz.›
performance
uitvragen • (uithoren) *question,* ‹inf.›
pump • (uitnodigen) *ask out*
uitvreten *be up to s.th.*
uitwaaien • (uitgeblazen worden) *be
blown out* • (frisse lucht happen) *get a
breath of fresh air*
uitwas • (ongewenste ontwikkeling)
excess • (uitgroeisel) *outgrowth*
uitwedstrijd *away game*
uitweg *way out*
uitweiden • (lang spreken) *dwell*
• (afdwalen) *digress (on)*
uitwendig *outward, external*
uitwerken ‹plan› *work out, devise,*
‹theorie› *develop*
uitwerking • (resultaat) *effect, result*
• (het uitwerken) *working out (of a
plan)*
uitwijken • (uit de weg gaan)
turn/step aside, ‹voertuig› *swerve*
• (emigreren) *emigrate (to)*
uitwijzen • (aantonen) *show, prove*
• (verdrijven) *expel,* ‹form.› *extradite*
uitwisselen *exchange*
uitwissen *wipe out*
uitwringen *wring out*
uitzaaien • (zaaiend verspreiden) *sow,*

<fig.> sow, disseminate • (med.)
metastasize, <inf.> spread
uitzendbureau = (temporary)
employment agency
uitzenden broadcast, transmit
uitzending broadcast, transmission
uitzet <v. baby> layette, <v. bruid>
trousseau
uitzetten I [ov ww] • (buiten iets
zetten) expel, <uit land> deport
• (verspreid zetten) set, <vis> plant
• (op interest plaatsen) put out II [on
ww] • (groter worden) swell
uitzicht • (gelegenheid naar buiten te
kijken) view • (vooruitzicht) outlook,
prospect
uitzien • (uitkijken naar) look out
• (verlangen naar) look forward to
• (zicht geven op) look out (over)
uitzingen • (volhouden) * ik kan het
nog wel even ~ I can hold out for a
while; I can swing it; I can carry on for
some time
uitzinnig mad, crazy, delirious, out of
one's wits
uitzitten sit out
uitzoeken • (kiezen) select, pick out
• (sorteren) sort (out) • (te weten
komen) find out
uitzonderen exclude
uitzondering exception
uitzonderlijk exceptional
uitzuigen • (uitbuiten) bleed
white/dry, <werkgever> sweat
• (zuigend verwijderen) suck (out)
uitzwermen swarm
ultimatum ultimatum
unie union
uniform I [het] uniform II [bnw]
uniform
universeel universal
universiteit university
uranium uranium
urgent urgent, pressing
urgentie urgency

urine urine
urineren urinate
urinoir urinal
utopie utopia
utopisch utopian
uur • (tijdsaanduiding) * om één uur
at one o'clock • (tijdmaat) hour
uurloon hourly wage(s)
uurwerk • (klok) timepiece • (het
binnenwerk van een klok) movement,
clockwork
uw your
uwerzijds on your part

V

vaag • (niet goed zichtbaar) *vague, hazy, dim* • (onduidelijk) *vague*
vaak I [de] *sleepiness* II [bijw] *often, frequently*
vaal *faded*
vaalbleek *sallow, pallid*
vaandel *colours, standard, banner*
vaandrig *ensign,* <v. cavalerie> *cornet*
vaardig • (bedreven) *skilled, skilful, adroit, proficient* • (gereed) *ready*
vaargeul *channel, fairway,* <in mijnenveld> *(sea-)lane*
vaars *heifer*
vaart • (snelheid) *speed* • (kanaal) *canal* • (scheepv.) *navigation*
vaartuig *vessel, craft*
vaarwater • (vaargeul) *channel, fairway* • (waterweg) *waterway*
vaarwel I [het] *farewell* II [tw] *farewell*
vaas *vase*
vaatdoek *dishcloth*
vaatwerk • (keukenvaatwerk) *plates and dishes* • (vaten) *casks*
vacant *vacant*
vacature *vacancy*
vacht *fur, coat,* <v. schaap> *fleece*
vacuüm *vacuum*
vader *father*
vaderland *(native) country, homeland*
vaderlands • (v. het vaderland) ★ ~e liederen/geschiedenis *national songs/history* ★ ~e bodem *native soil* • (nationalistisch) ★ ~ gevoel *patriotic feeling*
vaderlijk *fatherly*
vaderschap *paternity, fatherhood*
vadsig *indolent, lazy*
vagebond *vagabond, tramp*
vagevuur *purgatory*
vagina *vagina* [mv: *vaginae, vaginas*]

vak • (door rechte lijnen begrensd vlak) *section,* <v. kast, enz.> *compartment* • (beroep) *profession, trade* • (tak v. wetenschap) *subject*
vakantie *holiday(s), vacation*
vakantiedag *holiday*
vakantieganger *holidaymaker, tourist*
vakbeweging • (de vakorganisaties) *trade unions,* <AE> *labor unions* • (streven zich te organiseren) *trade unionism*
vakbond *trade(s) union*
vakcentrale *federation of trade unions*
vakgroep • (deel v.e. vakvereniging) *union branch* • (deel v.e. faculteit) *department*
vakkennis *professional knowledge*
vakkundig *skilled, professional*
vakman *expert,* <in ambacht> *craftsman*
vakopleiding *vocational training,* <hogere beroepen> *professional training*
vakterm *specialist term, technical term*
vakvereniging *trade(s) union,* <v. werkgevers> *employer's association*
vakwerk • (werk v.e. vakman) *professional job* • (wandconstructie) ★ ~ huizen *half-timbered houses*
val • (het vallen) *fall,* <v. vliegtuig> *crash* • (daling) *fall* • (vangtoestel) *trap* • (hinderlaag) *trap* • (ondergang) ★ ten val brengen *overthrow; bring down*
valeriaan *valerian*
valhelm *crash helmet*
valk *falcon*
valkuil *pitfall*
vallei *valley*
vallen I [het] *fall,* <v. avond> *nightfall* II [on ww] • (ten onder gaan) *fall* • (sneuvelen) *fall* • (neervallen) *fall, drop* • (neerhangen) *hang* • (terechtkomen) *fall* ★ ~ onder *fall/come under* • (op bepaalde wijze

zijn) ∗ dat valt nog niet te zeggen *that can't be said yet* ∗ er viel een stilte *there was a hush* ● (~ **op**) *fancy, take* (to)

valluik *trapdoor*

valreep *gangway, gangplank*

vals I [bnw] ● (gemeen) *vicious, nasty, savage* ● (namaak) *false, <scherts> bogus* (antique) ● (oneerlijk) *false* ● (onzuiver) *false* ● (verkeerd) *false* II [bijw] ● (onzuiver) *out of key* ● (bedrieglijk) *falsely*

valscherm *parachute*

valselijk *falsely*

valsheid *falseness* ● (het vervalsen) ∗ ~ in geschrifte *forgery*

valstrik ● (strik om te vangen) *snare* ● (hinderlaag) *trap, snare*

valuta ● (munt) *currency* ● (koers) (rate of) *exchange*

vampier *vampire*

van I [bijw] ● (over) *of, about* ● (weg) *from, of* ● (door) *by, from* II [vz] ● (door) *by, of, with* ● (in bezit van, toebehorend aan) *of* ● (bestaande uit) *of* ● (gebeurend met/aan) *of* ● (afkomstig van) *from, of* ● (wat ... betreft) *of* ● (vanaf) *from*

vanaf ● (met ingang van) *from, as from, since* ● (daar vandaan) *from*

vanavond *tonight, this evening*

vandaag *today*

vandaan ● (weg van) ∗ blijf er ~ *keep away from it* ● (aanduiding v. herkomst) ∗ ik kom er juist ~ *I just came from there* ∗ waar ~? *from where?*

vandaar ● (daarom) *that's why, <form.> hence* ● (daar vandaan) *from there*

vandalisme *vandalism*

vangen ● (opvangen) *catch* ● (gevangen nemen) *capture* ● (vervatten) *capture*

vangrail *crash barrier, guard-rail, safety-fence*

vangst ● (buit) *haul* ● (het vangen) *catch*

vanille *vanilla*

vannacht ● (afgelopen nacht) *last night* ● (komende nacht) *tonight*

vanouds *of old*

vanwaar ● (waarvandaan) *from where, <form.> whence* ● (waarom) *why*

vanwege ● (van de zijde van, namens) *on the part of, on behalf of* ● (wegens) *because of, on account of, owing to, due to*

vanzelf ● (uit eigen beweging) *of itself* [mv: *of themselves*], *automatically* ● (vanzelfsprekend) *naturally*

vanzelfsprekend I [bnw] *self-evident* II [bijw] *as a matter of course*

varen I [de] *fern, <heidevaren> bracken* II [on ww] ● (per vaartuig gaan) *sail, navigate* ● (~ **op**) *trade to* ∗ laten ~ *abandon*

variatie ● (afwisseling) *variation* ● (verscheidenheid) *variety*

variëren I [ov ww] *diversify* II [on ww] *vary*

variëteit ● (verscheidenheid) *variety* ● (afwijkende vorm) *variety*

varken *pig*

vaseline *vaseline*

vast I [bnw] ● (onveranderlijk) *permanent* ● (scherp afgetekend) *definite* ● (niet los) *fast, fixed* ● (stevig) *firm, <niet vloeibaar> solid* ● (bestendig) *steady* ● (onwankelbaar) *firm* II [bijw] ● (stevig) *fast, firmly* ● (onveranderlijk) *regularly, steadily* ● (stellig) ∗ vast (en zeker) *certainly*

vastberaden *resolute*

vastbinden *fasten, tie up*

vasteland ● (landmassa) *continent* ● (de vaste wal) *mainland*

vasten *fast*

Vastenavond Shrove Tuesday

vastgrijpen *grip, catch hold of, clutch*

vasthechten *attach, fasten*

vastheid *firmness, solidity, stability*
vasthouden I [ov ww] • (in handen houden) *hold (fast)*, ‹in arrest› *detain* • (in bezit houden) *retain*, ‹v. goederen› *hold up* II [on ww] *stick to*
vasthoudend *tenacious*
vastigheid *certainty*
vastleggen • (registreren) *record* • (vastmaken) *fix, fasten*, ‹v. boot› *moor*
vastliggen • (vastgesteld zijn) *be laid down* • (vastgebonden zijn) *be (firmly) fixed, be fastened*, ‹v. schip› *be moored*
vastlopen • (blokkeren) *jam* • (vast komen te zitten) *get stuck*
vastmaken *fasten*
vastroesten *rust*
vastschroeven *screw down*
vaststaan ⋆ ~d feit *established fact*
vaststellen • (bepalen) *determine* • (constateren) *conclude*
vastzetten *fix, fasten*, ‹v. wiel› *chock*
vastzitten • (bevestigd zijn) *stick* • (gevangen zitten) *be in prison* • (klem zitten) ‹fig.› *be stuck*, ‹v. deur, stuur› *be jammed*, ‹v. schip› *be aground* • (~ aan) ⋆ dan zit je eraan vast *then you are committed to it*
vat I [de] *hold, grip* II [het] • (ton) *barrel, cask* • (bio.) *vessel*
vatbaar *susceptible*
Vaticaan *the Vatican*
vatten • (in iets vastzetten) *mount, embed*, ‹v. juweel› *set* • (beetpakken) *catch, seize* • (begrijpen) *understand, see* • (opdoen) ⋆ kou ~ *catch cold*
vazal *vassal*
vechten *fight*
vechtlust *fighting spirit, combativeness, eagerness to fight*, ‹form.› *pugnacity*
vechtpartij *scuffle, scrap*
vedergewicht *featherweight*
vee *cattle*

veearts *veterinary surgeon*, ‹inf.› *vet*
veeg *wipe*
veel I [onb vnw] ‹voor enkelvoud› *much*, ‹voor meervoud› *many* II [bijw] • (in ruime mate) *much* • (vaak) ⋆ hij komt hier veel *he often comes here* III [telw] ⋆ veel boeken lezen *read a lot of books; read many books*
veelal *mostly*
veelbelovend *promising*
veelbetekenend *significant*
veelbewogen *stirring*
veeleer *rather, sooner*
veeleisend *exacting, demanding*
veelheid *multitude*
veelhoek *polygon*
veelkleurig *multi-coloured*
veelomvattend *comprehensive*
veelsoortig *varied*, ‹form.› *manifold*
veelstemmig ‹muz.› *polyphonic*
veelvoud *multiple*
veelvoudig • (in veelvoud) *multiple* • (veelvuldig) *frequent*
veelvraat *glutton*
veelvuldig *frequent*
veelzeggend *significant*
veemarkt *cattle market*
veen *peat*
veer I [de] • (slag-/staart-/vleugelpen) *feather* • (spiraalvormig draad) *spring* II [het] *ferry*
veerboot *ferry*
veerkracht *elasticity*, ‹fig.› *resilience*
veerkrachtig *elastic*, ‹fig.› *resilient*
veerman *ferryman*
veertien *fourteen*
veertig *forty*
veestapel *livestock*
veeteelt *cattle-breeding*
vegen I [ov ww] • (met borstel/bezem reinigen) ‹v. kleed› *brush*, ‹v. vloer› *sweep* • (af-/wegvegen) *wipe* II [on ww] *brush*
veger • (bezem, stoffer) *brush*

• (persoon) *sweeper*
vegetariër *vegetarian*
vegetarisch *vegetarian*
vegeteren • (leven als een plant) *vegetate,* ‹fig.› *lead a vegetative live* • (parasiteren) *sponge on s.o.*
vehikel *vehicle*
veilen *put up for auction*
veilig *safe*
veiligheid *safety* • (beveiliging) *security*
veiligheidsdienst *security services*
veiligheidshalve *for safety('s sake)*
veiligheidsspeld *safety pin*
veiling *auction, public sale*
veinzen I [ov ww] *simulate, feign* II [on ww] *feign, dissemble*
vel • (huid) *skin* • (afgestroopte huid) *hide* • (vlies) *skin* • (blad papier) *sheet*
veld • (vakgebied) *field* • (vlakte) *field* • (vlak) *field,* ‹sportveld› *ground,* ‹v. schaakbord› *square*
veldbed *camp-bed,* ‹AE› *cot*
veldfles *flask,* ‹mil.› *canteen*
veldheer *general*
veldmaarschalk *field marshal*
veldsla *corn salad*
veldslag *battle*
veldtocht *campaign*
velen *stand, endure*
velg *rim*
vellen *fell*
venijn *venom*
venijnig *venomous, vicious*
vennoot *partner*
vennootschap *partnership*
venster *window*
vent *fellow, chap,* ‹AE› *guy*
venten *hawk, peddle*
venter *hawker, huckster,* ‹v. groente, fruit› *coster(monger)*
ventiel *valve*
ventilatie *ventilation*
ventilator *ventilator, fan*
ventileren *ventilate*

ver I [bnw] *far* II [bijw] • (punt v. voortgang) ∗ *hoe ver ben je? how far have you got?*
verachtelijk • (laag) ∗ ~ *gedrag contemptible conduct* • (minachtend) ∗ ~e *blik contemptuous look*
verachten • (minachten) *despise, scorn* • (trotseren) *scorn*
verachting *contempt, scorn*
verademing *relief*
veraf *far (away)*
verafgoden *idolize*
verafschuwen *detest,* ‹form.› *abhor*
veralgemenen *generalize*
veranda *verandah*
veranderen *change*
verandering *change*
veranderlijk • (kunnende veranderen) *variable* • (geneigd tot veranderen) *changeable*
verankeren ‹v. schip› *moor*
verantwoordelijk *responsible*
verantwoordelijkheid *responsibility*
verantwoorden *answer/account for*
verantwoording • (rekenschap) *account* • (verantwoordelijkheid) *responsibility*
verarmen I [ov ww] *impoverish* II [on ww] *become impoverished*
verbaasd *astonished, surprised*
verbaliseren • (verwoorden) *put into words* • (proces-verbaal opmaken) ∗ *iem.* ~ *take s.o.'s name and address*
verband • (zwachtel) *bandage, dressing* • (samenhang) *connection, context*
verbannen • (uitwijzen) *exile* • (verjagen) *banish*
verbasteren I [ov ww] *corrupt* II [on ww] • (vervormd worden) *be corrupted* • (ontaarden) *degenerate*
verbazen *astonish, surprise*
verbazend *surprising, astonishing*
verbeelden I [ov ww] *represent* II [wkd ww] • (zich voorstellen) *imagine,*

fancy • (inbeelden) ✶ *hij verbeeldt zich heel wat* he fancies himself a great deal ✶ *wat verbeeld jij je wel?* who do you think you are?

verbeelding
• (voorstellingsvermogen) *imagination, fancy* • (verwaandheid) *conceit, self-conceit* • (inbeelding) *imagination*
verbeeldingskracht *imagination*
verbergen *hide, conceal*
verbeten *grim*
verbeteren I [ov ww] • (beter maken) *(make) better, improve,* ‹zedelijk› *reform* • (herstellen) *correct* • (corrigeren) *revise, correct* • (overtreffen) ✶ *een record* ~ *break a record* II [on ww] *improve*
verbetering • (het beter worden) *improvement* • (correctie) *correction*
verbeuren ✶ *een recht* ~ *forfeit a right*
verbieden *forbid,* ‹v. rechtswege› *prohibit*
verbijstering *bewilderment, perplexity*
verbijten I [ov ww] *stifle, suppress* II [wkd ww] ✶ *zich* ~ *van woede rage/burn inwardly; steam with anger*
verbinden • (verband aanleggen) *dress* • (aansluiten) *join, connect, link up* • (telefonisch aansluiten) • (~ **met**) *connect with, put through to* ✶ *verkeerd verbonden wrong number*
verbinding • (relatie, contact) *connection, contact* • (aansluiting) *communication,* ‹elektriciteit› *connection* • (samenvoeging) *combination, connection* • (chem.) *compound*
verbintenis • (verplichting) *engagement* • (overeenkomst) *agreement*
verbleken • (bleek worden) ‹v. gezicht› *(grow) pale,* ‹v. kleuren› *fade*
verblijden *gladden, cheer*
verblijf • (het verblijven) *stay* • (het

wonen) *residence* • (verblijfplaats) *residence, abode, home*
verblijfplaats *residence,* ‹form.› *abode*
verblijven *stay, remain*
verblinden • (obsederen) *infatuate, dazzle* • (als blind maken) *blind, dazzle*
verbloemen *disguise, camouflage, veil*
verbolgen *incensed*
verbond • (vereniging) *league,* ‹v. politieke machten› *alliance* • (verdrag) *pact, treaty,* ‹bijbels› *covenant*
verbouwen *grow, cultivate*
verbouwereerd *perplexed, bewildered*
verbouwing • (het anders bouwen) *rebuilding* • (het telen) *cultivation, growth*
verbranden I [ov ww] *burn* II [on ww] • (door vuur verteerd worden) *be burnt* • (rood worden door de zon) *get sunburnt*
verbrandingsmotor *internal combustion engine*
verbrassen *dissipate, squander*
verbreden *widen*
verbreiden *spread*
verbreken *break*
verbrijzelen *smash, shatter*
verbroederen *fraternize*
verbrokkelen *crumble*
verbruik ‹v. energie› *expenditure,* ‹v. voedsel› *consumption*
verbruiken *use,* ‹v. voedsel› *consume*
verbuigen • (ombuigen) *bend, twist, buckle* • (vervoegen) *decline*
verdacht • (onder verdenking) *suspected* • (aanleiding gevend tot verdenking) *suspicious, open to suspicion, suspect* • (~ **op**) *prepared for*
verdachtmaking *insinuation*
verdagen *adjourn*
verdampen *evaporate, vaporize*
verdedigen *defend*
verdediger • (voorvechter) *defender*

• (sport) *defender, back* • (jur.) *counsel (for the defence)*
verdediging *defence* • (het verdedigen) *defence*
verdekt <mil.> *under cover*
verdelen • (in delen scheiden) *divide* • (uitdelen) *divide/distribute (among)*
verdelgen *exterminate*
verdenken *suspect*
verdenking *suspicion*
verder • (meer verwijderd) *farther, further* • (voorts) *further* • (overigens) ⋆ ~ nog iets? *anything else?* • (met iets voortgaand) ⋆ ~ eten/lezen/rijden *eat/read/drive on* ⋆ ga ~! *go on!; proceed!*
verderf *ruin, destruction*
verderfelijk *pernicious, noxious*
verdienen • (als loon krijgen) *earn, make* • (waard zijn) *deserve*
verdienste *merit*
verdienstelijk *deserving, meritorious*
verdiepen I [ov ww] *deepen* II [wkd ww] • (~ in) ⋆ verdiept zijn in *be absorbed in*
verdieping • (etage) *floor, storey,* <AE> *story* • (het verdiepen) *deepening*
verdisconteren • (incalculeren) *discount, allow for* • (verkopen v. wissels) *negotiate*
verdoemen *damn*
verdoemenis *damnation*
verdoen <v. tijd> *waste*
verdoezelen *obscure*
verdommen • (vertikken) ⋆ ik verdom het (I'm) *damned if I do/will* • (schelen) ⋆ het kan me niks ~ I *couldn't care less*
verdonkeremanen <v. geld> *embezzle*
verdorren I [ov ww] *scorch* II [on ww] *wither*
verdorven *depraved, wicked*
verdoven <door een slag> *stun,* <v. pijn> *deaden,* <voor operatie> *anaesthetize*

verdoving • (het verdoven) *anaesthesia* • (gevoelloosheid) *stupor*
verdraagzaam *tolerant*
verdraaid I [bnw] ⋆ ~ hard *damned hard* II [tw] ⋆ wel ~! *damn it!*
verdraaien *twist*
verdraaiing *distortion, perversion*
verdrag *treaty, pact*
verdragen *endure, stand, suffer, bear*
verdriet *sorrow, distress, grief*
verdrietig *sorrowful, sad, mournful*
verdrijven *drive away*
verdringen I [ov ww] • (naar de achtergrond dringen) <v. gedachte, gevoel> *cut out,* <v. persoon> *repress* • (wegdringen) *push aside, crowd out* • (v. plaats dringen) *supersede, drive out, oust* II [wkd ww] *crowd (round)*
verdrinken I [ov ww] • (doen omkomen in water) *drown* II [on ww] • (de verdrinkingsdood sterven) *be drowned, drown*
verdrogen *dry up*
verdrukking *oppression*
verdubbelen I [ov ww] (re)double II [on ww] *double*
verduidelijken *explain, illustrate*
verduisteren • (donker maken) *darken,* <bij luchtaanval> *black out* • (stelen) *embezzle*
verduistering • (het donker maken) *darkening,* <in de oorlog> *black-out* • (eclips) *eclipse* • (het stelen) *embezzlement*
verdunnen *dilute*
verdunning • (graad v. verdunning) *dilution* • (het verdunnen) *thinning,* <v. gas> *rarefaction,* <v. vloeistof> *dilution*
verduren *endure, bear*
verdwalen *lose one's way, get lost*
verdwijnen *disappear,* <langzaam> *fade away,* <snel, geheel> *vanish*
veredelen *ennoble,* <v. vee, fruit> *improve*

vereenvoudigen *simplify*
vereenzamen *become lonely*
vereenzelvigen *identify*
vereeuwigen *immortalize*
vereffenen • (voldoen) *settle*
• (bijleggen) *settle*
vereisen *require, demand*
vereiste *requirement, requisite*
veren I [bnw] *feather* II [on ww] • (zich verend bewegen) *be springy*
• (veerkrachtig zijn) *be elastic/springy*
verenigbaar *consistent, compatible*
verenigen *combine, join, unite*
vereniging • (het verenigen) *union*
• (club) *society, club, association*
vereren • (aanbidden) *honour, revere, worship* • (eer bewijzen) *honour (with)*
verergeren I [ov ww] *aggravate, worsen* II [on ww] *grow worse, worsen*
verering *worship*
verf ‹in lagen aan te brengen› *paint,* ‹voor verfbad› *dye*
verfijnen *refine*
verfilmen *film*
verflauwen *fade*
verfoeien *abominate, detest*
verfoeilijk *detestable, abominable*
verfomfaaien *crumple, dishevel*
verfraaien *embellish, beautify*
verfrissen *refresh*
verfrissing *refreshment*
vergaan I [het] ‹v. materiaal› *decay,* ‹v. schip› *wreck* II [on ww] • (ten onder gaan) *perish,* ‹v. schip› *be wrecked*
• (verteren) *decay*
vergaarbak • (reservoir) *receptacle,* ‹voor vloeistof› *reservoir*
• (verzamelplaats) *repository*
vergaderen I [ov ww] *gather, collect* II [on ww] *meet, assemble*
vergadering *meeting*
vergallen ‹v. pret› *spoil*
vergankelijk *transitory*
vergapen I [ov ww] *waste/fritter away* II [wkd ww] *gape/goggle at*

vergaren *gather, collect*
vergassen I [ov ww] • (met gas doden) *gas* • (in gas omzetten) *gasify* II [on ww] *gasify*
vergasten *treat (to), regale (with)*
vergeeflijk *pardonable*
vergeefs I [bnw] *idle, vain, futile* II [bijw] *in vain, vainly*
vergeetachtig *forgetful*
vergelden *repay*
vergeldingsmaatregel *retaliatory measure, reprisal*
vergelijk *compromise, agreement*
vergelijkbaar *comparable, similar*
vergelijken *compare (with/to), liken (to)*
vergelijking • (het vergelijken) *comparison* • (taalk.) *simile* • (wisk.) *equation*
vergemakkelijken *make easier,* ‹form.› *facilitate*
vergen *ask, require, demand*
vergetelheid • (het vergeten zijn) *oblivion* • (het vergeten) *forgetfulness*
vergeten I [ov ww] *forget* II [wkd ww] *forget*
vergeven • (vergiffenis schenken) *forgive,* ‹form.› *pardon* • (weggeven) *give away* • (vergiftigen) *poison*
vergevensgezind *forgiving*
vergeving • (vergiffenis) *forgiveness,* ‹form.› *pardon* • (het weggeven) *giving away*
vergezellen ‹v. gelijken› *accompany,* ‹v. meerderen› *attend*
vergezicht *prospect,* ‹doorkijk› *vista*
vergezocht *far-fetched*
vergiffenis *forgiveness,* ‹form.› *pardon*
vergiftig *poisonous,* ‹v. dieren› *venomous*
vergiftigen *poison*
vergissing *mistake, error, slip*
vergoeden *compensate for, refund,* ‹v. verlies, kosten› *make good*
vergoeding • (het vergoeden)

compensation • (beloning)
recompense, reward
• (schadeloosstelling) *damages*
vergoelijken <v. fouten> *smooth/gloss over*, <v. gedrag> *excuse*
vergooien *throw away*
vergrijp *offence, delinquency*
vergrijzen *grow grey*
vergroeien *grow together*
vergrootglas *magnifying glass*
vergroten • (vermeerderen) *increase* • (groter maken) *enlarge*, <door kijkglas> *magnify*
vergroting • (het vergroten) *enlargement* • (foto) *blow-up*
verguizen *abuse*, <form.> *vilify*
vergulden • (met goud bedekken) *gild* • (verblijden) *please*
vergunnen *permit, allow, grant*
vergunning *permit*, <v. café> *licence*
verhaal *story, tale*
verhalen *tell, relate, narrate*
verhandelen • (handelen in) *deal in, sell*, <v. wissel> *negotiate* • (behandelen) *discuss*
verhandeling *treatise, essay*, <mondeling> *lecture*
verharden I [ov ww] *harden* II [on ww] *harden*
verharen <v. dier> *moult*, <v. vacht> *shed hair*
verheerlijken *glorify*
verheffen I [ov ww] • (naar boven brengen) *lift, raise* II [wkd ww] • (verrijzen) *rise*
verhelderen I [ov ww] *clarify* II [on ww] *brighten, clear up*
verhelen *conceal, hide*
verhelpen *set to rights, remedy*
verhemelte • (gehemelte) *palate* • (baldakijn) *canopy*
verheugd *glad, pleased, happy*
verheugen ★ zich ~ op *look forward to*
verheven • (hoogstaand) *elevated, exalted, lofty* • (hoger liggend) *raised*

verhinderen *prevent*
verhindering • (het verhinderen) *prevention* • (beletsel) *hindrance, obstacle* • (het verhinderd zijn) ★ bericht van ~ *apology* ★ ~ wegens ziekte *absence through illness*
verhitten *heat*
verhoeden *prevent*
verhogen *raise*
verhoging • (het vermeerderen) *increase, rise* • (verhoogde plaats) <in terrein> *rise*, <podium> *dais, platform* • (het hoger maken) *heightening, raising* • (lichte koorts) *temperature*
verhongeren *starve (to death)*
verhoor *questioning, interrogation, trial*
verhoren • (vervullen) <v. wens> *grant* • (ondervragen) *question*
verhouding • (betrekking) *relation(s)* • (liefdesrelatie) (love) *affair* • (evenredigheid) *proportion, ratio*
verhuizen I [ov ww] *move* II [on ww] *move*
verhuizer *remover*
verhuren *let out (for hire), hire out*
verhuurder <op huurcontract> *lessor*, <v. huis> *landlord*
verijdelen *frustrate, defeat, foil*
vering *springs*, <v. auto> *suspension*
verjaardag *birthday*, <v. gebeurtenis> *anniversary*
verjagen *drive/chase away, expel*
verjaren <v. misdrijf> *go out of date*
verjongen I [ov ww] *rejuvenate* II [on ww] *become young again*
verkavelen *parcel out*
verkeer • (gebruik v. wegen) *traffic* • (voertuigen, personen) *traffic* • (omgang) *intercourse*
verkeerd • (niet juist) *wrong* • (slecht) *bad*
verkeersbord *road sign*
verkeersdrempel *sleeping policeman, judder bar, speed hump*

verkeersleider *air-traffic controller*
verkeerslicht *traffic light*
verkeersopstopping *traffic jam*
verkeerstoren *control tower*
verkennen *survey, explore, ‹mil.›*
reconnoitre
verkenner • (verspieder) *scout*
• (padvinder) (*Boy*) *Scout* [v: *Girl
Scout*]
verkenning *reconnoitring*
verkeren ★ in gevaar ~ *be in danger*
★ aan 't hof ~ *move in court circles*
verkering *courtship*
verkiesbaar *eligible*
verkiezen • (prefereren) *prefer (to)*
• (door keuze aanwijzen) *elect, choose*
• (liever willen) *choose*
verkiezing • (het stemmen) *election*
• (keuze, voorkeur) *choice, preference*
verkijken • (verkeerd beoordelen)
misjudge • (~ **op**) *be mistaken in*
verkikkerd ★ ~ op iets *keen on s.th.*
★ ~ op een meisje *crazy about a girl;
sweet on a girl*
verklaarbaar *explicable*
verklaren • (formeel mededelen)
state, declare • (uitleggen) *explain*
verklaring • (uitleg) *explanation*
• (getuigenis) *statement*
verkleden • (omkleden) *change, get
dressed* • ((zich) vermommen)
disguise, dress up
verkleinen *reduce*
verkleinwoord *diminutive*
verkleumen *get numb with cold*
verkleuren *fade, lose colour*
verklikken *squeal on a person*
verklikker • (verrader) *snitch, ‹inf.›
telltale, ‹politiespion› informer*
• (alarmtoestel) *alarm*
verkneukelen ★ zich ~ *in revel in;
‹ongunstig› gloat over*
verknippen • (in stukken knippen)
cut up • (met knippen bederven) *cut
to waste*

verknocht *devoted, attached*
verknoeien *spoil, ruin, ‹v. werk›
bungle*
verkondigen *proclaim, preach*
verkoop *sale*
verkoopbaar *saleable*
verkopen *sell*
verkoper *salesman*
verkorten *shorten*
verkouden ★ ~ zijn *have a cold*
verkoudheid *cold*
verkrachten • (tot geslachtsgemeenschap dwingen) *rape,
(sexually) assault* • (schenden)
violate
verkrijgbaar *obtainable*
verkrijgen *get, acquire, obtain*
verkroppen *stomach, swallow*
verkruimelen *crumble*
verkwanselen *barter away*
verkwikken *refresh*
verkwisten *squander, waste*
verlagen I [ov ww] • (minder maken)
reduce • (lager maken) *lower* II [wkd
ww] *debase o.s.*
verlammen *paralyse*
verlamming • (lamheid) *paralysis*
• (het verlammen) *crippling*
verlangen I [het] *desire, longing* II [ov
ww] • (wensen) *desire, want* • (eisen)
demand III [on ww] • (~ **naar**) *long for*
verlaten I [bnw] • (afgelegen,
onbewoond) *lonely, deserted* • (in de
steek gelaten) *lonely* II [ov ww]
• (weggaan) *leave* • (in de steek laten)
abandon, desert • (later komen) *delay,
postpone* III [wkd ww] • (later komen)
be late • (~ **op**) *rely on, put one's trust
in*
verlatenheid *loneliness, desolation*
verleden I [het] *past* II [bnw] ★ ~ week
last week ★ ~ tijd *past tense*
verlegen • (schuchter) *shy, bashful*
• (geen raad wetend) *embarrassed
(with)* • (~ **om**) *in want of, in need of*

verlegenheid • (het verlegen zijn)
shyness, bashfulness • (moeilijke
omstandigheid) *embarrassment*
verleggen *shift, move*
verleidelijk *tempting, alluring,
seductive*
verleiden • (tot zonde verleiden) *lead
astray* • (tot geslachtsgemeenschap
brengen) *seduce* • (verlokken) *tempt*
verleiding *seduction, temptation*
verlenen *grant*
verlengen • (langer maken) *lengthen*
• (prolongeren) *extend, prolong,* ‹v.
officieel document› *renew*
verlenging • (waarmee verlengd
wordt) *extension,* ‹sport› *extra time*
• (het verlengen) *lengthening,
prolongation, renewal*
verleren *forget (how to)*
verlevendigen *revive, enliven*
verlichten • (v. licht voorzien) *light
(up)* • (verzachten) ⋆ pijn ~
relieve/ease pain
verlichting • (licht) *lighting* • (het
minder zwaar maken) *lightening*
• (opbeuring, opluchting) *relief, ease*
• (gesch.) *enlightenment*
verliefd • (liefde voelend) *in love
(with), enamoured* • (liefde tonend)
amorous
verliefdheid *being in love*
verlies *loss*
verliezen *lose*
verlof *leave*
verlokken *tempt, allure*
verloochenen *renounce, repudiate*
verloop • (het verstrijken) *course,
lapse* • (ontwikkeling) *progress,* ‹v.
ziekte, enz.› *course* • (teruggang)
falling off • (wisseling van personeel)
wastage
verlopen I [bnw] • (verliederlijkt) ‹v.
persoon› *seedy,* ‹v. zaak› *run-down*
• (ongeldig) *expired* II [on ww]
• (verstrijken) *pass (away), elapse*

• (geldigheidsduur overschrijden)
expire • (achteruitgaan) *decline, decay,*
‹v. staking› *peter out* • (zich
ontwikkelen) *pass off*
verloren *lost*
verloskunde *obstetrics,* ‹v.
vroedvrouw› *midwifery*
verloskundige ‹arts› *obstetrician,*
‹vroedvrouw› *midwife*
verlossen • (bevrijden) *deliver,* ‹rel.›
redeem • (bij bevalling helpen) *deliver*
verlosser *deliverer, liberator*
verlossing • (bevrijding) *deliverance,*
‹rel.› *redemption* • (bevalling) *delivery*
verloten *raffle*
verloven ⋆ zich ~ met get engaged to
verloving *engagement,* ‹form.›
betrothal
verluiden ⋆ naar verluidt *reputedly; it
is rumoured that*
vermaak *entertainment, pleasure,
amusement*
vermaard *famous,* ‹form.› *renowned*
vermageren I [ov ww] *emaciate* II [on
ww] *become thin, lose weight*
vermaken • (amuseren) *amuse,
entertain* • (veranderen) *alter*
• (~ aan) *bequeath*
vermanen *admonish, warn*
vermaning *admonition, warning*
vermannen *pull (o.s.) together*
vermeend *supposed, alleged*
vermeerderen *increase,* ‹form.›
augment
vermelden *mention, report*
vermelding *mention*
vermengen *mix,* ‹v. aroma's› *blend*
vermenigvuldigen I [ov ww]
• (verveelvoudigen) *duplicate*
• (wisk.) *multiply* II [wkd ww]
multiply, reproduce
vermenigvuldiging • (het
vermenigvuldigen) *multiplication*
• (voortplanting) *reproduction*
vermetel *audacious*

vermicelli *vermicelli*
vermijden *avoid*
verminderen *reduce*
vermissen *miss*
vermoedelijk *presumable, probable*
vermoeden I [het] *suspicion* II [ov ww]
• (veronderstellen) *suspect, suppose*
vermoeid *tired, weary, ‹form.› fatigued*
vermoeidheid *tiredness, weariness,*
‹form.› fatigue
vermoeien *tire, weary, ‹form.› fatigue*
vermogen • (bezit) *property, ‹v. geld›*
fortune • (macht) *power* • (capaciteit)
power, capacity
vermogend • (rijk) *wealthy*
• (invloedrijk) *influential*
vermommen *disguise*
vermomming *disguise*
vermoorden *murder*
vermorzelen *crush, pulverize*
vermurwen *soften, mollify*
vernauwen *narrow*
vernederen *humiliate, humble*
vernedering *humiliation*
vernemen *hear, learn, understand*
vernielen *destroy, smash (up)*
vernieling *destruction*
vernielzucht *destructiveness*
vernietigen • (verwoesten) *destroy,*
annihilate • (nietig verklaren) *annul,*
quash
vernieuwen • (moderniseren)
renovate • (vervangen) *renew*
vernissen *varnish*
vernuft *genius, ingenuity*
vernuftig *ingenious*
veronachtzamen • (verwaarlozen)
neglect • (negeren) *disregard, ignore*
veronderstellen • (vermoeden)
suppose, assume • (uitgaan v.)
(pre)suppose, assume
veronderstelling *supposition,*
assumption
verongelukken *die in an accident, be*
in a fatal accident

verontreinigen *pollute*
verontrusten *disquiet, disturb, alarm*
verontschuldigen I [ov ww] *excuse*
II [wkd ww] *apologize*
verontschuldiging *apology, excuse*
verontwaardiging *indignation*
veroordelen • (een vonnis vellen)
sentence • (afkeuren) *condemn*
• (~ tot) *condemn to, ‹in vonnis›*
sentence to
veroorloven *allow, permit*
veroorzaken *cause, bring about,*
‹form.› occasion
verorberen *dispatch, dispose of*
verordenen • (bevelen) *order*
• (wettelijk voorschrijven) *ordain, ‹in*
wet› provide
verordening *regulation*
verouderen I [ov ww] *age* II [on ww]
• (in onbruik raken) *become obsolete*
• (oud worden) *grow old, age*
veroveraar *conqueror*
veroveren *conquer*
verovering *conquest*
verpachten *lease (out)*
verpakken *pack/wrap (up)*
verpakking • (verpakkingsmateriaal)
packing • (het verpakken) *packing*
verpanden • (belenen) *pawn,*
‹onroerend goed› mortgage • (op het
spel zetten) pledge
verpatsen *flog*
verpesten *spoil*
verplaatsen I [ov ww] *move, shift*
II [wkd ww] *move*
verplanten *transplant, plant out*
verplegen *tend, nurse*
verpleging *nursing*
verpletteren • (vermorzelen) *crush,*
smash • (overweldigen) *shatter*
verplicht • (voorgeschreven)
compulsory • ((dank) verschuldigd)
obliged
verplichten *oblige*
verplichting *obligation, commitment*

verpotten *repot*
verprutsen *spoil*
verraad *treason, treachery, betrayal*
verraden I [ov ww] • (verraad plegen)
betray • (verklappen) *give away*
II [wkd ww] *give o.s. away*
verrader *traitor, betrayer*
verraderlijk • (als een verrader)
treacherous • (gevaarlijk) *tricky,*
treacherous • (iets verradend) *telltale*
verrassen *surprise, take by surprise*
verrassing *surprise*
verregaand *far-reaching, extreme*
verrekenen I [ov ww] *settle* II [wkd
ww] *miscalculate*
verrekijker • (telescoop) *telescope*
• (kijker met twee lenzen) *binoculars*
verrekken I [ov ww] *sprain* II [on ww]
★ *verrek! damn!*
verreweg *by far, far and away*
verrichten *perform, do*
verrichting • (uitvoering)
performance • (handeling) *action,*
activity, <zakelijk> *transaction*
verrijken *enrich*
verrijzen • (oprijzen) *arise,* <v.
industrie, stad> *spring up* • (opstaan)
rise
verrijzenis *resurrection*
verroeren *stir, move, budge*
verroesten *rust, get rusty*
verruilen *exchange/swap (for)*
vers I [het] *poem* II [bnw] *fresh*
verschaffen *provide/supply (with)*
verschalen *go flat/stale*
verschalken • (te slim af zijn) *outwit,*
outmanoeuvre, get round
• (verorberen) *polish off, dispose of*
verschansen *entrench*
verscheiden I [het] *decease* II [bnw]
diverse, various III [on ww] *depart*
IV [telw] *several*
verscheidenheid • (verschil) *variety,*
diversity • (gevarieerde veelheid)
range

verschepen • (per schip verzenden)
ship • (overladen in ander schip)
transship
verscherpen *sharpen*
verscheuren • (in stukken scheuren)
tear (apart/up), tear to pieces
• (verslinden) *maul* • (pijnlijk
aandoen) *rend, lacerate* • (verdelen)
tear (apart)
verschiet • (toekomst) *offing, prospect*
• (verte) *distance*
verschieten I [ov ww] *use up, shoot*
II [on ww] • (verbleken) <v. gezicht>
change colour, <v. kleur> *fade*
• (wegschieten) *shoot*
verschijnen • (zich vertonen) *make
one's appearance, appear* • (komen
opdagen) *appear, turn up*
• (uitkomen) *come out, be published*
• (vervallen) *fall due, expire*
verschijning • (het verschijnen)
appearance • (persoon) *figure, person*
verschijnsel *phenomenon*
verschil • (onderscheid) *difference,
distinction* • (uitkomst v. aftreksom)
difference
verschillen *differ (from)*
verschillend I [bnw] *different (from)*
II [telw] • (verscheiden) *several*
• (allerlei) *various*
verschonen *change*
verschoning • (schoon goed) *change
(of linen)* • (verontschuldiging) *excuse*
verschoppeling *outcast, pariah*
verschrikkelijk *terrible, dreadful*
verschrikking *terror, horror*
verschroeien *scorch,* <door zon> *parch*
verschrompelen I [ov ww] *shrivel*
II [on ww] • (rimpelig worden) *shrivel
(up)* • (ineen schrompelen) *shrink*
verschuiven I [ov ww] • (uitstellen)
postpone • (verplaatsen) *shove (away),
shift, move* II [on ww] *shift*
verschuldigd ★ ik ben haar dat ~ *I
owe it to her*

versie *version*
versieren • (verfraaien) *decorate*
• (voor elkaar krijgen) *fix*
• (verleiden) *pick up*
versiering • (het versieren)
adornment, decoration • (decoratie)
decoration
versjacheren *flog*
versjouwen *drag away*
verslaafd *addicted* (to), ‹inf.› *hooked*
(on)
verslag *report, account*
verslagen • (overwonnen) *defeated*
• (terneergeslagen) *dismayed*
verslaggever *reporter*
verslapen • (te lang slapen) *oversleep*
• (slapend doorbrengen) *sleep away*
verslappen I [ov ww] *relax, slacken*
II [on ww] *weaken, slacken*
versleten *worn* (out), ‹v. textiel,
kleding› *threadbare*
verslijten *wear out*
verslinden *devour*
verslonzen *allow to go to pot, neglect*
versmaden *despise, disdain, scorn*
versmallen *narrow*
versmelten *blend*
versnapering *snack*
versnellen I [ov ww] *accelerate, speed
up* II [on ww] *quicken*
versnelling • (schakelinrichting) *gear*
• (het versnellen) *acceleration*
versnellingsbak *gearbox*
versnijden • (in stukken snijden) *cut
up* • (aanlengen) *dilute, adulterate*
versnipperen *shred*
verspelen • (verbeuren) *lose, forfeit*
• (vergokken) *gamble away*
versperren *block, bar*
verspillen *squander, waste*
versplinteren I [ov ww] *splinter,
sliver, smash* (up) *into matchwood*
II [on ww] *splinter, shatter*
verspreiden *spread*, ‹v. geur› *give out*
verstaan • ((kunnen) horen) *hear*

• (begrijpen) *understand*
verstand • (vermogen te denken)
mind, intellect, intelligence
• (vermogen te oordelen) *judgement,
understanding*, ‹kennis› *knowledge*
verstandelijk *intellectual*
verstandhouding *understanding,
relations*
verstandig • (verstand hebbend)
reasonable, intelligent • (v. inzicht
getuigend) *sensible*
verstandskies *wisdom tooth*
verstandsverbijstering *mental
derangement, insanity*
verstarren I [ov ww] *make rigid, stiffen*
II [on ww] *become rigid*
verstek • (verzuim) *default* • (techn.)
mitre
verstekeling *stowaway*
versteld ★ ~ *staan be dumbfounded* ★ ~
doen staan stupefy s.o.
verstellen • (repareren) *mend, patch*
• (stand veranderen) *adjust*
verstenen *petrify*
versterken *strengthen*, ‹m.b.v. een
versterker› *amplify*
versterker • (radio) *amplifier* • (foto.)
intensifier
versterking • (het versterken)
*fortification, reinforcement,
intensification, strengthening*, ‹v.
geluid› *amplification*
verstijven *stiffen*
verstikken I [ov ww] *stifle, suffocate,
choke* II [on ww] *choke, suffocate*
verstoken I [bnw] *devoid* (of) II [ov
ww] *burn up*
verstommen *fall silent, die down*
verstoord *annoyed*
verstoppen • (blokkeren) ‹v. buis›
clog, ‹v. doorgang› *obstruct/block*
• (verbergen) *hide*
verstoppertje ★ ~ *spelen play
hide-and-seek*
verstopping • (het verstopt zijn)

blockage • (obstipatie) *constipation*
verstoren ∗ de openbare orde/rust ~
disturb the peace
verstoten *cast off*
verstrakken *set, tighten*
verstrekken *provide/supply with,*
<mil.> *issue*
verstrijken *pass (by), go by*
verstrikken • (in strik vangen)
ensnare • (doen vastlopen) *entangle*
verstrooid • (verspreid) *scattered*
• (afwezig) *absent-minded*
verstrooien • (iem./zich afleiding
bezorgen) *entertain* • (verspreiden)
scatter, disperse
verstrooiing • (verspreiding)
dispersion • (ontspanning) *diversion*
verstuiken *sprain*
verstuiven I [ov ww] *vaporize, spray*
II [on ww] *be blown away*
verstuiving • (het verstuiven)
dispersion, scattering, spraying
• (zandverstuiving) *sand-drift*
vertalen *translate*
vertaler *translator*
vertaling *translation*
verte *distance*
vertederen *soften, mollify*
verteerbaar *digestible*
vertegenwoordigen • (handelen
namens) *represent* • (uitdrukken)
stand for • (equivalent zijn met)
represent
vertegenwoordiging • (het
vertegenwoordigen) *representation*
• (delegatie) *representative(s)*
vertellen *tell*
verteller *story-teller, narrator*
vertelling *story, tale*
verteren I [ov ww] • (voedsel
afbreken) *digest* • (doen vergaan)
corrode, eat away II [on ww] <v.
voedsel> *digest,* <wegteren> *waste
(away)*
verticaal *vertical*

vertier *entertainment, amusement*
vertikken *refuse flatly*
vertillen *strain o.s. (in) lifting*
vertoeven *stay,* <tijdelijk> *sojourn*
vertolken • (vertalen) *interpret*
• (weergeven) *voice, express*
• (uitbeelden) *render, play,
impersonate*
vertonen I [ov ww] • (laten
zien/blijken) *exhibit, display*
• (opvoeren) *show, present* II [wkd
ww] *show (o.s.), appear, show up*
vertoning *show, display*
vertoon • (het vertonen) *showing,
producing* • (tentoonspreiding)
demonstration, manifestation
vertragen *slow down*
vertrappen *tread/trample on/down*
vertrek • (kamer) *room* • (het
weggaan) *departure*
vertrekken *leave,* <v. boot> *sail,* <v.
vliegtuig> *take off*
vertroebelen I [ov ww] *make
turbid/muddy,* <fig.> *confuse, obscure*
II [on ww] *become/get muddy/turbid*
vertroetelen *baby, pamper,* <pej.>
(molly)coddle
vertrouwd • (vertrouwen genietend)
reliable • (wat gewoon is) *familiar*
• (wat veilig is) *safe*
vertrouwelijk • (blijkgevend van
vertrouwen) *intimate, familiar*
• (geheim) *confidential*
vertrouweling *confidant* [v:
confidante]
vertrouwen I [het] *confidence, faith*
II [ov ww] *trust* III [on ww] *trust (in),
rely on*
vertwijfeling *despair, desperation*
vervaardigen *manufacture,* ↓ *make*
vervaarlijk *awful, tremendous*
vervagen I [ov ww] *blur, dim* II [on
ww] *fade (out/away), become blurred*
verval • (het vervallen) *decline,
deterioration, decay* • (hoogteverschil)

drop, fall • (het niet meer geldig zijn) *maturity*

vervallen I [bnw] • (niet onderhouden) *dilapidated, ramshackle* • (verlopen) *ravaged, wasted* • (verstreken) *due* • (afgeschaft) *lapsed* II [on ww] • (eigendom worden van) *fall to* • (bouwvallig worden) *fall into disrepair* • (afnemen) *decay, decline* • (verstreken zijn) *expire,* <polis> *lapse,* <v. wedstrijd> *be cancelled* • (invorderbaar worden) *mature, become/be payable, fall due*

vervalsen • (namaken) *forge, counterfeit* • (met kwade opzet veranderen) *doctor, tamper with*

vervalsing • (het vervalsen) *forging, counterfeiting* • (het vervalste) *forgery, counterfeit,* <inf.> *fake*

vervangen *replace*

vervanging *replacement, substitution*

vervelen I [ov ww] • (ergeren) *annoy* • (verveling veroorzaken) *bore* II [wkd ww] *be bored*

vervelend • (saai) *boring, tedious, tiresome* • (onplezierig) *tedious, annoying* • (onhebbelijk) *annoying*

verveling *boredom,* ↑ *tedium*

vervellen *peel*

verven • (schilderen) *paint* • (kleuren) *dye*

verversen • (weer vers maken) *refresh* • (vervangen) *change*

vervlakken • (afstompen) *become numb* • (verflauwen) *wane,* <v. kleuren> *fade (away)* • (vlakmaken) *make smooth/even*

vervliegen • (verdampen) *evaporate* • (verdwijnen) *vanish*

vervloeken *curse, damn,* <rel.> ↑ *anathematize*

vervoegen I [ov ww] *conjugate* II [wkd ww] <bij een persoon> *report to,* <m.b.t. plaats> *apply (at)*

vervoer *transport*

vervoeren *carry, transport*

vervoering *ecstasy, rapture*

vervolg • (de volgend tijd) *future* • (voortzetting) *continuation* • (het vervolgen) *continuation*

vervolgen • (doorgaan) *continue* • (achtervolgen) *pursue,* <vanwege een overtuiging> *persecute* • (jur.) *prosecute*

vervolgens *further, next*

vervolging • (het voortzetten) *pursuit, continuation* • (het vervolgd worden) *persecution* • (rechtsvervolging) *prosecution*

vervolmaken *perfect*

vervormen *distort*

vervreemden ★ ~ van *alienate from;* <persoon> *estrange from*

vervroegen *bring/move/put forward, advance,* <betalingen, enz.> *accelerate*

vervuilen *pollute,* <v. voedsel/water> *contaminate*

vervullen *fulfil*

vervulling *fulfilment, accomplishment,* <v. droom, wens> *realization*

verwaand *conceited, cocky*

verwaarlozen *neglect*

verwachten *expect,* <v. gebeurtenis> *anticipate*

verwachting *expectation, anticipation*

verwant ★ ~ aan *related to*

verwantschap • (het verwant zijn) *relation(ship), kinship* • (overeenkomst) *relationship, affinity*

verward • (onordelijk) <haar> *tousled,* <v. draden> *tangled (up)* • (in de war) *confused*

verwarmen *heat, warm*

verwarming • (het verwarmen) *heating, warming* • (installatie) *heating (system), heater*

verwarren • (in de war maken) *confuse,* <v. draden> *tangle (up)*

• (verwisselen met elkaar) *confuse, mix up*

verwarring • (het verwarren) *confusion, entanglement* • (het verward zijn) *muddle, confusion*

verwateren I [ov ww] *dilute* II [on ww] • (waterig worden) *become diluted* • (verslappen) *lose vigour*

verwedden • (inzetten bij wedden) *bet, wager, gamble* • (vergokken) *gamble (away)*

verweer *defence,* ‹jur.› *plea*

verwekken *father*

verwelken *wither, wilt*

verwelkomen *welcome*

verwennen *spoil, pamper, coddle*

verwensen *curse*

verwensing *curse*

verweren I [on ww] ‹ook v. steen› *weather,* ‹steen› *erode* II [wkd ww] *defend o.s.*

verwerkelijken *realize*

verwerken • (opnemen) ‹informatie› *digest* • (emotioneel te boven komen) *cope with* • (maken tot) *process*

verwerpelijk *reprehensible, objectionable*

verwerpen *reject*

verwerven *acquire*

verwezenlijken *realize,* ‹v. hoop, wens› *fulfil*

verwijden *widen*

verwijderd *remote, distant, far off*

verwijderen I [ov ww] *remove* II [wkd ww] *leave*

verwijdering • (de toestand) ‹ook fig.› *estrangement* • (het verwijderen) *removal,* ‹fig.› *alienation,* ‹v. school/universiteit› *expulsion*

verwijfd *effeminate, womanish, sissy*

verwijt *reproach, blame,* ‹form.› *reproof*

verwijten *blame, reproach*

verwijzen *refer (to),* ‹pej.› *relegate*

verwijzing • (het verwijzen) *reference* • (verwijzingsbriefje van arts) *referral*

verwikkelen *involve, mix up,* ‹vnl. in lijdende vorm› *entangle*

verwikkeling • (de moeilijkheid) *entanglement* [alleen ev], ‹jur.› *complication* • (plot van boek) *plot* [alleen ev], *complication* • (het verwikkelen) *involvement,* ‹scandaleus› *entanglement*

verwilderen *go wild*

verwisselbaar *exchangeable,* ‹onderling› *interchangeable*

verwisselen • (omruilen) *exchange* • (verwarren) *confuse, mistake*

verwittigen *notify, advise, inform*

verwoed *ardent, passionate, avid*

verwoesten *destroy, devastate, ruin*

verwoesting *destruction, devastation*

verwonden I [ov ww] *injure, hurt,* ‹met opzet› *wound* II [wkd ww] *hurt/injure o.s.*

verwonderen I [ov ww] • (verrassen) *surprise* • (verbazen) ‹in grote mate› *astonish, amaze* II [wkd ww] ∗ zich ~ over *marvel at*

verwondering • (verrassing) *surprise* • (verbazing) *wonder, astonishment*

verwonderlijk *surprising, astonishing,* ‹zonderling› *strange*

verwonding *injury*

verworden *decay, degenerate*

verwringen *distort, twist*

verzachten *ease*

verzadigen *satisfy,* ‹chem.› *saturate*

verzaken I [ov ww] • (niet nakomen) *neglect* • (afvallen) ‹v. geloof› *renounce,* ‹v. vriend› *desert, forsake* II [on ww] ‹in kaartspel› *revoke*

verzakken *sag,* ‹v. bodem› *subside*

verzamelaar *collector*

verzamelen I [ov ww] *gather, collect* II [wkd ww] *gather, assemble*

verzameling • (het verzamelen) *collection, gathering* • (collectie) *collection*

verzamelnaam *collective noun*

verzamelplaats *meeting place,*
rallying point
verzanden *silt up*
verzegelen *seal* (up)
verzekeraar *insurer*
verzekeren I [ov ww] • (stellig
verklaren) *guarantee, ensure*
• (assureren) *insure* II [wkd ww] *ensure*
verzekering • (stellige verklaring)
guarantee, assurance • (assurantie)
insurance
verzenden *send, dispatch,* <per post>
mail
verzengen *scorch*
verzet *resistance*
verzetsbeweging *resistance*
(movement)
verzetten I [ov ww] • (elders zetten)
move • (wegwerken) <werk> *get*
through II [wkd ww] *resist*
verzilveren • (met zilver bedekken)
(coat/plate with) silver • (innen) *cash*
verzinken I [ov ww] • (met zink
overtrekken) *galvanize* • (diep
leggen) *sink* II [on ww] *sink*
verzinnen • (uitvinden) *invent*
• (fantaseren) *make up*
verzinsel *invention*
verzoek *request,* <form.> *petition*
verzoeken • (vragen) *request, beg, ask*
• (tarten) *tempt*
verzoeking *temptation*
verzoekschrift *petition, appeal*
verzoenen *reconcile, conciliate*
verzoening *reconciliation*
verzolen *resole*
verzorgd <v. kleding> *well-groomed,*
<v. maaltijd> *excellent,* <v.
taalgebruik> *polished,* <v. tuin>
well-kept
verzorgen *look after, take care of,* <v.
dier, zieke> *tend*
verzorger *attendant*
verzot ★ ~ op *crazy/mad/wild about*
verzuchten *sigh*

verzuchting *sigh,* <klacht>
lamentation
verzuim • (nalatigheid) *neglect,*
omission • (het wegblijven) <op 't
werk> *absenteeism,* <op school>
non-attendance, truancy
verzuimen I [ov ww] • (nalaten,
veronachtzamen) *neglect, omit* II [on
ww] • (niet opdagen) <v. school> *be*
absent
verzuipen I [ov ww] • (doen
verdrinken) *drown* • (uitgeven aan
drank) ↑ *squander one's money on*
drink II [on ww] *drown, be drowned*
verzwakken I [ov ww] *weaken,*
enfeeble II [on ww] *weaken, grow weak*
verzwaren • (versterken) <v. dijken>
strengthen • (zwaarder maken) *make*
heavier
verzwelgen <drank> *guzzle,* <eten>
gobble
verzwijgen • (verbergen) *conceal*
• (achterhouden) *suppress*
verzwikken *sprain, twist*
vesper • (gebed) *vespers*
• (avonddienst) *vespers, evensong*
vest • (onderdeel v. pak) *waistcoat,*
<AE> *vest* • (gebreid jasje) *cardigan*
vestibule *(entrance-)hall, lobby*
vestigen • (nederzetten) *establish*
• (~ op) *focus*
vestiging • (het vestigen)
establishment • (filiaal) *establishment,*
branch
vesting *fortress, stronghold*
vet I [het] • (smeer) *grease* • (weefsel
tussen vlees) *fat* II [bnw] • (rijk aan
vet) *fat* • (dik gedrukt) *bold*
vete *feud*
veter *lace*
veteraan *veteran*
vetgehalte *fat content*
vetmesten *fatten* (up)
veto *veto*
vettig • (vet bevattend) *fatty* • (met

vet bedekt) *greasy*
veulen *foal*, ‹hengst› *colt*, ‹merrie› *filly*
vezel *fibre, thread, filament*
via • (over, langs) *via* • (door bemiddeling van) *via, by way of*
viaduct ‹bij elkaar kruisende wegen› *flyover*, ‹voor weg of spoor› *viaduct*
vibreren *vibrate*
videocassette *video cassette*
vier I [de] *four* II [telw] *four*
vierde I [bnw] *fourth* II [telw] *fourth*
vieren *celebrate*
viering *celebration*
vierkant *square*
vierling *quadruplets, quads*
viersprong *crossroads*
vies • (vuil) *dirty* • (schunnig) *obscene, filthy* • (onsmakelijk) *nasty*
viezerik *slob*, ‹seksueel› *pervert*
vignet • (boekversiering) *vignette* • (handelsmerk) *device, logo*
vijandelijk *hostile, enemy*
vijandig • (vijandelijk) *enemy* • (agressie vertonend) *hostile*
vijandschap *hostility, enmity*
vijf I [de] *five* II [telw] *five*
vijfkamp *pentathlon*
vijftien *fifteen*
vijftig *fifty*
vijg • (vrucht) *fig* • (paardenvijg) *horsedung*
vijgenblad *fig leaf*
vijl *file*
vijlen *file*
vijver *pond*
vijzel • (krik) *jack(screw)* • (stampvat) *mortar*
villa *villa*
villen • (huid afstropen) *skin, flay* • (afpersen) *fleece*
vilt *felt*
vilten *felt*
viltstift *felt-tip (pen)*
vin *fin*
vinden • (menen) *find, think*

• (aantreffen) *find, discover*
vinding • (het vinden) *finding* • (uitvindig) *invention, discovery*
vindingrijk *inventive, resourceful*
vindplaats • (plaats van een vondst) *place where s.th. is found* • (plaats van opgraving) *site of find/discovery*
vinger *finger*
vingerafdruk *fingerprint*
vingerhoed *thimble*
vingertop *fingertip*
vingerwijzing *hint, clue*
vink • (vogel) *finch* • (vleeswaar) ★ blinde vinken *veal/beef olives*
vinnig *sharp, snappy*
violet *violet*
violist *violinist*
viool *violin*
virtuoos *virtuoso*
virtuositeit *virtuosity*
vis *fish*
visafslag *fish auction, fish market*
visboer *fish dealer, fishmonger*
visie • (mening) (point of) *view* • (zienswijze) *vision*
visioen *vision*
visionair *visionary*
visite • (het bezoeken) *visit*, ‹kort› *call* • (personen op bezoek) ★ ~ hebben/verwachten *have/expect visitors/guests*
visitekaartje *business/calling card*
vissen I [de] • (astrol.) *Pisces* II [on ww] *fish*, ‹sport› *fish, angle*
visser • (beroepsvisser) *fisherman* • (sportvisser) *angler*
visserij *fishery*
visueel *visual*
visum *visa*
vitaal *vital*
vitamine *vitamin*
vitrage • (stof) *net* • (gordijn) *net (curtain)*
vitten *find fault (with), carp/cavil (at)*
vivisectie *vivisection*

vizier I [de] vizier II [het] • (klep op helm) visor • (deel van vuurwapen) sight
vla • (toetje) ≈ custard • (vlaai) flan
vlaag • (windstoot) gust • (opwelling) fit
Vlaams I [het] Flemish II [bnw] Flemish
Vlaanderen Flanders
vlag flag, colours
vlaggen • (de vlag uithangen) hang/put out the flag(s) • (sport) raise the flag
vlaggenschip flagship
vlaggenstok flagstaff/-pole
vlak I [het] • (platte kant) surface, <v. hand, zwaard> flat • (gebied) field, <niveau> level • (wisk.) plane II [bnw] • (glad) flat, level • (niet contrasterend) flat III [bijw] right
vlakte plain
vlaktemaat square measure, surface measurement
vlam • (vuur) flame • (tekening in hout) grain
Vlaming Fleming
vlammenwerper flame-thrower
vlas flax
vlasblond flaxen(-haired), tow-coloured
vlassen I [bnw] flaxen II [on ww] * ~ op iets look forward to s.th.; be eager for s.th.
vlecht plait, braid
vlechten plait, <AE> braid, <v. krans> wreathe, <v. manden> make, <v. matten> weave
vlechtwerk <v. mand> wicker-work
vleermuis bat
vlees • (voedsel) meat • (weefsel) flesh
vleesboom fleshy growth, <med.> fibroid, myoma
vleeskleurig flesh-coloured
vleesmolen mincer
vleeswaren meat-products, meats
vleet herring net

vlegel • (vlerk) lout, yob • (kwajongen) brat • (dorsvlegel) flail
vleien flatter
vleierij flattery
vlek stain, <veeg> smear, smudge
vlekkeloos • (smetteloos) spotless • (feilloos) perfect, immaculate
vlekken stain, soil
vleselijk • (lichamelijk) physical • (zinnelijk) carnal
vleugel • (vlerk, deel gebouw) wing • (piano) grand piano
vleugellam broken-winged
vleugelmoer wing/butterfly nut
vlezig fleshy, meaty, plump
vlieg fly
vliegbasis air base
vliegbrevet pilot's licence
vliegdekschip aircraft carrier
vliegen fly
vliegengaas (window/door) screen(ing)
vlieger • (speelgoed) kite • (vliegenier) pilot, flyer
vliegtuig airplane, aircraft
vliegtuigkaping hijacking
vliegveld <groot> airport, <klein> airstrip
vliering attic, loft
vlies skin, membrane, <op vloeistof> film
vlijmscherp razor sharp
vlijt diligence, industry
vlijtig diligent, industrious
vlinder butterfly
vlinderslag butterfly stroke
vlo flea
vloed • (grote hoeveelheid) flood • (getijde) (high) tide
vloedgolf tidal wave
vloeibaar liquid, fluid
vloeien flow
vloeiend flowing, <v. taal> fluent
vloeipapier • (dun papier) tissue paper • (absorberend papier) blotting-paper
vloeistof liquid

vloek • (verwensing) *curse*
• (vloekwoord) *oath, curse*
vloeken • (krachttermen uiten) *swear,*
curse • (~ met) ⋆ deze kleuren ~ met
elkaar *these colours clash*
vloer *floor*
vloerbedekking *floor-covering*
vloeren *floor, knock down*
vloerkleed *carpet,* ‹klein› *rug*
vlok *flake*
vlonder • (slootplank) *plank bridge*
• (losse vloer) *planking*
vlooien *flea*
vloot • (groep vaar-/vlieg-
/voertuigen) *fleet* • (oorlogsvloot)
fleet, navy
vlot I [het] *raft* II [bnw]
• (gemakkelijk) *smooth*
• (ongedwongen) *easy-going*
vlotten *go smoothly*
vlotter *float*
vlucht • (het vluchten) *flight*
• (vliegtuigreis) *flight* • (spanwijdte)
wing-span • (troep vogels) *flock, flight*
vluchteling • (voortvluchtige)
fugitive • (dissident) *refugee*
vluchten • (toevlucht zoeken) *flee,*
take refuge • (ontvluchten) *escape, flee*
vluchtheuvel *traffic island*
vluchtig • (haastig, oppervlakkig)
cursory • (snel vervliegend) *volatile*
vluchtstrook *hard shoulder*
vlug • (in snel tempo) *quick, fast*
• (snel en handig) ‹m.b.t.
lichaamsbeweging› *agile,* ‹v. geest›
bright • (spoedig) *quick*
vlugschrift *pamphlet*
vlugzout *sal volatile, smelling salts*
vocht • (vloeistof) *liquid,* ‹med.› *fluid*
• (vochtigheid) *moisture, dampness*
vochtig • (ietwat nat) *moist,* ‹klimaat›
humid • (onprettig vochtig) *damp*
vod *rag, tatter*
voeden I [ov ww] *feed* II [on ww] *be*
nourishing

voeding *food, nutrition,* ‹voor baby,
dieren› *feed*
voedingsbodem ‹fig.› *breeding*
ground, ‹v. bacteriën› *medium*
voedingsleer *dietetics*
voedingsmiddel *(article of) food,*
foodstuff
voedingswaarde *food/nutritional*
value
voedsel *food*
voedselpakket • (ingepakt eten) *food*
parcel • (keuze in voedingsmiddelen)
food range
voedzaam *nutritious, nourishing*
voeg *joint*
voegen I [ov ww] • (verenigen met)
join • (opvullen met specie) *point*
• (voegen bij) *add (to)* • (verbinden)
join II [on ww] • (betamen) *become*
• (gelegen komen) *suit* III [wkd ww]
⋆ zich ~ naar *adjust/conform (to)*
voegwoord *conjunction*
voelbaar *tangible, perceptible, palpable*
voelen I [on ww] *feel* II [wkd ww]
⋆ zich goed/ziek ~ *feel well/ill*
voelhoorn *tentacle*
voeling *feeling, touch*
voer *feed, food*
voeren • (verrichten) *carry on,*
‹onderhandelingen› *conduct*
• (voeden) *feed* • (v. voering voorzien)
line • (op stang jagen) *bait, badger*
• (leiden) *lead, bring (s.o.)*
voering *lining*
voertaal *official language, medium of*
communication
voertuig *vehicle*
voet *foot*
voetbal I [de] *football* II [het] *football,*
soccer, ↑ *Association football*
voetballen *play football*
voetballer *football player, footballer*
voetganger *pedestrian*
voetlicht *footlights*
voetpad *footpath*

voetreis *walking-trip*
voetspoor *footprint, track*
voetstap *footstep*
voetstoots *out of hand, without further ado*
voetstuk *pedestal*
voetzoeker *firecracker, jumping jack*
voetzool *foot sole, sole (of one's foot)*
vogel • (dier) *bird* • (persoon) *customer, character*
vogelkooi *birdcage*
vogelverschrikker *scarecrow*
vogelvlucht *bird flight*
vogelvrij *outlawed*
voile • (sluier) *veil* • (materiaal) *voile*
vol *full* ∗ vol met *filled with*
volbloed I [de] *thoroughbred* II [bnw] *full-blooded, pedigree*
volbrengen *fulfil*
voldaan *satisfied, content*
voldoen I [ov ww] • (betalen) *pay, settle* II [on ww] • (aan verwachting beantwoorden) *be satisfactory* • (~ aan) *satisfy*
voldoening • (tevredenheid) *satisfaction* • (betaling) *payment, settlement*
voldragen *full-born, full-term,* <fig.> *mature*
volgeling *follower,* <rel.> *disciple*
volgen *follow*
volgens • (naar mening van) *according to* • (overeenkomstig) *in accordance with*
volgooien *fill (up)*
volgorde *order, sequence*
volgroeid *full(y)-grown, mature*
volgzaam *docile*
volharden *persevere, persist (in)*
volheid *fullness*
volhouden I [ov ww] • (doorgaan met) *carry on, keep up* • (blijven beweren) *maintain, insist* II [on ww] *hold on*
volk *people*

volkenkunde *cultural anthropology,* <beschrijvend> *ethnography,* <vergelijkend> *ethnology*
volkenrecht *international law*
volkomen I [bnw] • (volmaakt) *perfect* • (totaal) *complete* II [bijw] *absolutely, completely*
volkorenbrood *wholemeal bread*
volksgezondheid *public health*
volkslied • (nationaal lied) *national anthem* • (traditioneel, overgeleverd lied) *folk-song*
volksmond ∗ in de ~ in *everyday/popular language* ∗ in de ~ noemt men dit *it is popularly called*
volksstam • (volk) *tribe* • (menigte) *crowd, horde*
volkstelling *census*
volksuniversiteit ≈ *adult education centre*
volksverhuizing • (het trekken van een volk) *migration of a nation* • (gesch.) *the migration of the nations*
volksvertegenwoordiger *representative (of the people), member of parliament,* <AE> *Congressman,* <BE> *M.P.*
volksvertegenwoordiging • (parlement) *house of representatives, parliament* • (het vertegenwoordigen) *representation of the people*
volledig *complete, full*
volleerd • (volledig geschoold) *fully qualified* • (doorkneed) *accomplished, consummate, perfect*
vollopen *get filled, fill (up)*
volmaakt *perfect*
volmacht *power, authority, mandate,* <jur.> *power (of attorney)*
volmondig *full, whole-hearted, unconditional, frank*
volop *plenty of, in abundance*
volslagen *complete, utter*
volstaan • (voldoende zijn) *do, be sufficient, suffice* • (~ met) *limit o.s.*

volstrekt *complete, absolute*
volt *volt*
voltallig *complete*
voltooien *finish, complete*
voltooiing *completion*
voltreffer *direct hit*
voltrekken I [ov ww] <v. huwelijk> *perform,* <v. vonnis> *execute* II [wkd ww] *occur, happen*
voluit *in full*
volume *volume*
volvet *full-cream*
volwaardig <v. lid> *full,* <v. munt> *sound*
volwassen *adult*
volzin *(complete) sentence,* <taalk.> *period*
vondeling *abandoned child*
vondst • (ontdekking) *discovery* • (het gevondene) *find* • (het vinden) *discovery, finding*
vonk *spark*
vonnis • (uitspraak v. rechter) *judg(e)ment* • (strafmaat) *sentence* • (oordeel) *verdict*
vonnissen I [ov ww] *pass sentence on* II [on ww] *pass sentence, condemn*
voogdij *custody, guardianship*
voor I [bijw] • (ten gunste van) *for* • (aan voorzijde) *in front* • (voorafgaand in tijd) *before* II [vz] • (plaatsbepaling) *in front of* • (tijdsbepaling) *before* • (gedurende) *for* • (ten voordele van) *for* III [vw] *before*
vooraan *in front*
vooraanstaand *leading, prominent*
vooraf *beforehand, previously*
voorafgaan *precede, go before*
vooral *especially, particularly*
vooralsnog *as yet, for the time being*
voorarrest *detention on remand*
vooravond • (avond voor belangrijke dag) *eve* • (eerste deel van de avond) *early evening*

voorbaat ★ bij ~ *in anticipation; in advance*
voorbarig • (te vroeg) *premature* • (onbezonnen) *hasty, rash*
voorbeeld • (illustratie) *instance, specimen, example* • (iets dat nagevolgd kan worden) *example, model, pattern*
voorbeeldig *exemplary*
voorbehoedmiddel *contraceptive*
voorbehoud • (beperking) *reserve, reservation* • (voorwaarde) *reservation*
voorbehouden *reserve*
voorbereiden *prepare, be ready*
voorbereiding *preparation*
voorbeschikken *predestine*
voorbestemmen *predetermine, predestine*
voorbij I [bijw] • (voor iets/iem. langs) *past, by* • (verleden tijd) *over* • (verder dan) *beyond* II [vz] • (verder dan) *past, beyond* • (langs) *past*
voorbijgaan *pass (by), go by*
voorbijgaand *passing, transitory*
voorbijganger *passer-by*
voorbijstreven *outstrip, outpace, surpass*
voorbode *forerunner, herald,* <voorteken> *omen*
voordeel *benefit, advantage*
voordeur *front door*
voordoen I [ov ww] *show, demonstrate* II [wkd ww] • (plaatsvinden) *occur, turn up,* <v. vraag, omstandigheid> *arise* • (zich gedragen/uitgeven als) *present o.s., pose as, make o.s. out*
voordracht • (aanbevelingslijst) *short list, list of candidates* • (aanbeveling) *nomination* • (lezing) *lecture, speech* • (poëzie-/muziekvoordracht) <muz.> *recital,* <v. gedicht> *recitation* • (wijze v. voordragen) *execution,* <v. toespraak> *delivery*
voordragen <v. gedicht> *recite*
voorgaan • (eerst komen/gaan)

precede • (de weg wijzen) lead the way • (de voorrang hebben) take precedence
voorgaand preceding, former, last
voorganger • (iem. die men opvolgt) predecessor • (rel.) pastor, minister
voorgerecht first course, ‹form.› entrée
voorgeschiedenis ‹v. pers.› past history, ‹v. zaak› (previous) history
voorgevel • (voorzijde) face, façade • (boezem) ‹inf.› boobs
voorgeven • (voorwenden) pretend, make out, claim • (als voorsprong geven) give odds/points, grant a handicap
voorgevoel presentiment, ‹inf.› hunch
voorgoed for good, once and for all
voorgrond foreground
voorhanden available
voorhebben • (dragen) have on • (bedoelen) mean, intend • (tegenover z. hebben) ★ wie denk je dat je voor je hebt? who(m) do you think you are talking to? • (als voordeel hebben) ★ dat heeft hij op je voor there he has the advantage of you
voorheen formerly
voorhistorisch prehistoric
voorhoede • (voorste legertroepen) advance guard • (voorvechters) vanguard • (sport) forward-line
voorhoofd forehead
voorhouden • (wijzen op) impress (upon), confront • (omhooghouden) hold (s.th.) before (s.o.) • (aanhouden) keep on
voorhuid foreskin
voorin ‹in bus, enz.› in front
vooringenomen prejudiced, biased
voorjaar spring
voorkamer front room
voorkant front
voorkennis foreknowledge
voorkeur preference
voorlaatst last but one, penultimate

voorleggen submit (to), lay/put before (s.o.)
voorletter initial (letter)
voorlezen ‹aan kinderen› read (to), ‹aankondiging› read (out)
voorlichten • (onderrichten) inform, enlighten (on) • (seksuele voorlichting geven) tell s.o. the facts of life
voorlichting information, guidance, advice
voorliefde preference, predilection
voorliegen lie (to)
voorlopen • (voorop lopen) walk in front • (te snel gaan) be fast, gain
voorloper precursor, forerunner
voorlopig I [bnw] provisional, temporary II [bijw] for the time being, for now
voormalig former
voorman • (leider) leader • (ploegbaas) foreman
voormiddag • (ochtend) morning • (vroeg in de middag) early afternoon
voornaamwoord pronoun
voornamelijk mainly, principally, chiefly
voornemen I [het] resolve, resolution, intention II [wkd ww] resolve, determine, make up one's mind (to)
voornoemd above-/afore-mentioned
vooronderzoek preliminary investigation
vooroordeel prejudice, bias
voorop • (aan het hoofd) in front, in the lead • (aan de voorkant) in front
voorover forward, prostrate, head first, headlong
voorpagina front page
voorpoot foreleg, forepaw
voorportaal vestibule, porch
voorpost outpost
voorraad stock, supply, store
voorradig in stock, in store
voorrang • (prioriteit) precedence,

priority • (recht vóór te gaan in verkeer) *right of way*
voorrangsweg *major road, main road*
voorrecht *privilege,* <form.> *prerogative*
voorruit *windscreen*
voorschieten *advance*
voorschijn * te ~ komen *appear*
voorschot *advance, loan*
voorschrift *prescription*
voorsorteren • (voorlopig sorteren) *presort* • (rijbaan kiezen) *get in lane*
voorspel *foreplay*
voorspelen I [ov ww] *play* II [on ww] *lead*
voorspiegelen * iem. iets ~ *hold out false hopes to s.o.*
voorspoed *prosperity*
voorspoedig *prosperous, successful, flourishing*
voorspraak • (bemiddeling) *intercession (with), mediation* • (persoon) *advocate, intercessor, mediator*
voorsprong (head)*start, lead,* <fig.> *advantage*
voorstaan • (voorstander zijn van) <v. doel> *champion,* <v. idee> *advocate* • (voor iets staan) *be in front*
voorstad *suburb*
voorstander *advocate, champion*
voorstel *suggestion, proposal*
voorstellen I [ov ww] • ('n voorstel doen) *propose, suggest, make a suggestion* • (de rol spelen) *represent* • (verbeelden) *depict, represent* • (introduceren) *introduce* II [wkd ww] • (zich een denkbeeld vormen van iets) *imagine* • (v. plan zijn) *intend, mean*
voorstelling • (beeld) *representation* • (vertoning) *show, performance*
voorstellingsvermogen *imagination*
voorsteven *stem*
voort *on, onwards, forward*
voortaan *from now on, in future,*

<form.> *henceforth*
voortand *front tooth*
voortbestaan I [het] *survival, (continued) existence* II [on ww] *survive*
voortbewegen I [ov ww] *drive, propel* II [wkd ww] *move (on)*
voortbrengen • (doen ontstaan) *produce, create* • (opleveren) *bring forth* • (veroorzaken) *generate*
voortbrengsel *product*
voortduren *continue, last, wear/drag on*
voortdurend • (aanhoudend) *constant, continual* • (doorlopend) *continuous*
voorteken *sign, omen*
voortgaan *go on, continue*
voortgang • (vordering) *progress* • (voortzetting) *advancement, continuation* • (het voortgaan) *continuation*
voortijdig *premature*
voortkomen *stem from,* <form.> *proceed/spring/arise from*
voortleven *live on*
voortmaken *hurry (up), make haste*
voortplanten • (zich vermenig-vuldigen) *reproduce, multiply, propagate* • (zich verbreiden) *be transmitted, travel*
voortreffelijk *excellent*
voortrekken *favour, give preference to*
voorts *furthermore, besides, moreover*
voortslepen I [ov ww] *drag along* II [wkd ww] *linger,* <fig.> *drag on*
voortspruiten *spring/stem/result from*
voortstuwen *drive on, propel*
voortvarend *dynamic*
voortvloeien *result (from), arise (out of/from)*
voortvluchtig *fugitive*
voortzetten *continue, go on with, carry on, proceed with*
voortzetting *continuation,* <na pauze> *resumption*

vooruit I [bijw] • (verder) *forward*
• (van te voren) *in advance,*
beforehand II [tw] *come on!, go ahead!*
vooruitgaan • (vóórgaan) *lead the*
way • (beter worden) *improve* • (v.
tevoren gaan) *go on ahead*
vooruitgang • (verbetering) *progress,*
improvement • (het voorwaarts gaan)
advance, progress
vooruitkomen *make headway, get*
on/ahead
vooruitlopen • (voor anderen uit
lopen) *go on ahead* • (~ op) *anticipate*
vooruitstrevend *progressive,*
go-ahead
vooruitzicht *prospect, outlook*
vooruitzien I [ov ww] *foresee* II [on
ww] *look ahead/forward, anticipate*
voorvader *ancestor, forefather*
voorval *incident*
voorvallen *happen, occur*
voorvechter *champion, advocate*
voorwaarde *condition, terms* [mv]
voorwaardelijk *conditional*
voorwaarts *forward*
voorwenden *feign, pretend*
voorwendsel *pretext, pretence,* <inf.>
blind
voorwerp *object*
voorwiel *front wheel*
voorwoord *preface, foreword*
voorzetsel *preposition*
voorzetten • (voor iets/iem. zetten)
put (s.th.) before (s.o.) • (voor laten
lopen) *put/set forward* • (sport) *centre,*
feed
voorzichtig *cautious, careful,* <form.>
prudent
voorzichtigheid *prudence, care,*
caution
voorzichtigheidshalve *by way of*
precaution
voorzien • (verwachten) *anticipate*
• (~ van) *provide/supply with* • (~ in)
<behoefte> *meet, supply*

voorzienigheid *providence*
voorziening • (maatregel) *provision,*
supply • (faciliteit) *facilities* • (het
voorzien) *provision*
voorzijde *front*
voorzitten *chair, preside*
voorzorg *precaution*
voos • (saploos, taai) *withered,*
dried-out • (niet deugend) *rotten*
vorderen I [ov ww] • (eisen) *demand,*
claim • (opeisen door overheid)
requisition II [on ww] *make progress*
vordering *progress*
voren ∗ *nooit te ~ never before*
vorig *previous, last*
vork *fork*
vorkheftruck *forklift (truck)*
vorm *form, shape*
vormelijk *formal*
vormen • (doen ontstaan) *form*
• (uitmaken) *make up, constitute*
• (een vorm geven) *shape, mould*
vormgeving *design*
vorming • (het vormen) *moulding*
• (geestelijke ontwikkeling)
education, training
vorsen *investigate, research*
vorst • (heerser) *sovereign, monarch*
• (het vriezen) *frost*
vorstelijk *royal*
vorstendom *principality*
vorstenhuis *dynasty, royal house*
vos • (roofdier) *fox* [v: *vixen*] • (paard)
sorrel, bay • (bont) *fox stole* • (sluw
mens) *fox*
vouw *fold,* <in broek, papier> *crease*
vouwblad *folder*
vouwen *fold*
vraag • (handeling v. vragen) *question,*
query • (verzoek) *request* • (kooplust)
demand • (vraagstuk) *question, issue*
vraagbaak • (bron van informatie)
source of information, <persoon> *oracle*
• (informatief boek) *encyclopedia*
vraaggesprek *interview*

vraagstuk *problem,* <ter discussie> *issue*

vraagteken • *(leesteken) question mark, interrogation mark* • *(niet opgeloste vraag) question mark*

vraatzucht *gluttony,* <med.> *bulimia (nervosa)*

vraatzuchtig <lit.> *voracious,* <v. mensen> *gluttonous*

vracht *load,* <v. voertuig> *cargo, freight*

vrachtbrief *waybill,* <v. schip> BL, *bill of lading,* <v. schip, trein, vliegtuig> *consignment-note*

vrachtschip *freighter, cargo ship*

vrachtwagen *lorry, truck*

vragen I [ov ww] • *(een vraag stellen) ask, inquire (after)* • *(verlangen, verzoeken) want* • *(uitnodigen) ask* II [on ww] • *(~ naar) ask, inquire (after)* • *(~ om) ask (for)*

vragenlijst *questionnaire*

vrede *peace*

vredelievend *peace loving, peaceful*

vredestijd *peacetime*

vredig *peaceful, quiet*

vreedzaam *peaceable, peaceful*

vreemd • *(uitheems) foreign, exotic, alien* • *(onbekend) strange, alien* • *(raar) strange, odd,*

vreemdsoortig *odd, peculiar, singular*

vrees *fear*

vrek *miser, skinflint*

vreselijk *dreadful, terrible, frightful*

vreten *feed*

vrezen I [ov ww] *fear, dread* II [on ww] ∗ *~ voor fear for*

vriend *friend, chum, pal*

vriendelijk I [bnw] • *(aardig) kind, friendly* • *(aangenaam) pleasant, cheerful* II [bijw] *kind*

vriendendienst *friendly turn*

vriendenkring *circle of friends*

vriendschap *friendship*

vriendschappelijk I [bnw] *friendly, amicable* II [bijw] *in a friendly way*

vriespunt *freezing (point)*

vriesweer *frosty weather*

vriezen *freeze*

vrij I [bnw] *free* II [bijw] • *(tamelijk) rather, pretty* • *(~ van) free from,* <v. plichten> *exempt from*

vrijaf *off*

vrijage *courtship,* <inf.> *necking, snogging,* <seksueel> *love-making*

vrijblijvend *non-committal, free of obligations*

vrijbrief *licence, permit*

vrijbuiter • *(zeerover) freebooter* • *(ongebonden persoon)* <negatief> *libertine,* <positief> *free spirit*

vrijdag *Friday*

vrijdenker *freethinker*

vrijelijk *freely*

vrijen • *(de liefde bedrijven) make love* • *(kussen en knuffelen) neck, pet*

vrijer *lover, sweetheart*

vrijetijdsbesteding *leisure activities, recreation*

vrijgeleide *safe-conduct*

vrijgeven I [ov ww] *release,* <hand.> *decontrol* II [on ww] *give a holiday, give a day off*

vrijgevig *liberal, generous*

vrijgevochten • *(tuchteloos) undisciplined, lawless* • *(ongebonden) easy-going, unconventional*

vrijgezel I [de] *bachelor* II [bijw] *single*

vrijhandel *free trade*

vrijhaven *free port*

vrijheid *liberty, freedom*

vrijheidsberoving *deprivation of freedom*

vrijhouden *reserve,* <v. tijd> *set aside*

vrijkaart *free ticket, free pass*

vrijkomen • *(vrijgelaten worden) be released* • *(beschikbaar komen) become available*

vrijlaten *release*

vrijmaken I [ov ww] • *(beschikbaar maken) liberate, (set) free* • *(apart*

zetten) *reserve* II [wkd ww] *free (o.s.)*
vrijmetselarij *Freemasonry*
vrijmoedig *frank, free, bold, candid*
vrijpleiten *clear (of)*, ‹form.› *exculpate*
vrijpostig *impertinent, bold,* ‹inf.›
saucy
vrijspraak *acquittal*
vrijspreken *acquit (from), clear*
vrijstellen ‹v. lessen› *excuse from,* ‹v.
plichten› *exempt from*
vrijstelling *exemption*
vrijuit *freely, frankly*
vrijwaren * ~ tegen *protect against*
vrijwel *practically, nearly, almost*
vrijwillig *voluntary*
vrijwilliger *volunteer*
vrijzinnig *liberal*
vroedvrouw *midwife*
vroeg • (eerder dan verwacht) *early,
soon, premature* • (aan het begin) *early*
vroeger I [bnw] • (voorheen) *earlier,
former, previous* • (vorig) *former,
previous* II [bijw] *formerly, earlier*
vroegrijp *precocious*
vroegte * in de ~ *early in the morning*
* in alle ~ *at the crack of dawn*
vroegtijdig • (bijtijds) *early, timely*
• (eerder dan verwacht) *premature,* ‹v.
dood› *untimely*
vrolijk • (blij) *merry, cheerful, gay*
• (aangenaam) *cheerful*
vrolijkheid • (het vrolijk zijn) *gaiety,
cheerfulness* • (vermaak) *mirth,
merriment*
vroom *pious*
vrouw • (vrouwelijk persoon) *woman*
• (echtgenote) *wife,* ‹jur.› *spouse*
• (speelkaart) *queen* • (bazin) *mistress*
vrouwenarts *gynaecologist*
vrucht • (fruit) *fruit* • (resultaat) *fruit,
result* • (ongeboren kind) *foetus*
vruchtafdrijving *abortion*
vruchtbaar • (in staat tot
voortplanten) *fertile* • (productief)
fruitful

vruchtbeginsel *ovary*
vruchteloos *fruitless, vain, ineffectual*
vruchtensap *fruit juice*
vruchtgebruik *usufruct*
vruchtvlees *pulp*
vuil I [het] *dirt, grime, filth* II [bnw]
• (vies) *dirty, grimy, grubby*
• (bedorven) *rotten* • (onaangenaam)
foul • (vulgair) ‹taal› *foul, scurrilous,*
‹v. grap, verhaal› *dirty, smutty*
• (laaghartig) *dirty* • ((nog)
ongezuiverd) *gross* • (nijdig) *dirty*
vuilnis *dirt, rubbish,* ‹AE› *garbage*
vuilnisbak *dust-bin,* ‹AE› *trashcan,
garbage can*
vuilnisman *refuse-collector,* ‹AE›
garbage collector
vuiltje *speck of dust, grit*
vuilverbranding *incineration of refuse*
vuist *fist*
vuistslag *punch, thump, blow with the
fist*
vulgair *vulgar*
vulkaan *volcano*
vulkanisch *volcanic*
vullen *fill*
vulling • (vulling in gebit) *filling,
inlay* • (het vullen) *filling* • (vulsel)
filling, stuffing
vulpotlood *propelling pencil*
vuren I [bnw] *deal, pine, fir* II [on ww]
fire (at)
vurig *passionate*
vuur • (brand) *fire* • (het schieten) *fire*
• (enthousiasme) *ardour, warmth*
• (bederf in hout) *dry rot* • (brand in
koren) *blight*
vuurdoop *baptism of fire*
vuurmond • (kanon) *gun* • (uiteinde
van de loop) *muzzle*
vuurpeloton *firing squad*
vuurpijl *rocket*
vuurproef *trial by fire,* ‹fig.› *crucial
test, ordeal*
vuurrood *(as) red as a beetroot*

vuurtoren *lighthouse*
vuurvast *fireproof, heat resistant*
vuurwapen *firearm*
vuurwerk • (materiaal) *firework*
• (voorstelling v. vuurwerk) *fireworks*
vuurzee *sea of fire*

W

waag • (weegschaal) *balance*
• (gebouw) *weigh-house*
waaghals *dare-devil*
waagstuk *bold venture, risky
undertaking*
waaien *blow*
waaier *fan*
waakhond *watchdog*
waaks *watchful*
waakvlam *pilot light*
waakzaam *watchful, wakeful, vigilant*
Waal *Walloon*
Waals *Walloon*
waan *delusion*
waanzin • (krankzinnigheid)
madness, insanity • (absurditeit)
nonsense
waanzinnig *insane, mad, demented,
deranged*
waar I [de] *merchandise, goods, wares*
II [bnw] • (waarheidsgetrouw) *true,
real* III [bijw] *where*
waarachtig I [bnw] *true, real* II [bijw]
truly, really, indeed
waarborg *guarantee, warrant,
safeguard*
waarborgen *warrant, safeguard,
guarantee*
waard I [de] • (kastelein) *landlord*
II [bnw] *worth*
waarde *value*
waardebon *gift coupon*
waardeloos *worthless, valueless*
waardeoordeel *value judgement*
waarderen *value,* ‹op prijs stellen›
appreciate
waardering *appreciation*
waardevast *stable price, index-linked*
waardevermindering *depreciation,*
‹v. geld› *devaluation*

waardevol *valuable*
waardig • (eerbiedwaardig) *dignified* • (waard) *worthy*
waardigheid *dignity*
waarheen *where, where to*
waarheid *truth*
waarin *in which/what*
waarlangs *past/along which*
waarlijk *truly, actually, really*
waarmaken • (bewijzen) *prove* • (verwezenlijken) *fulfil*
waarna *after which*
waarnaar *to which*
waarneembaar *perceptible, discernible*
waarnemen • (gewaarworden) *discern, perceive, observe,* <gadeslaan> *watch* • (benutten) ⋆ *zijn kans ~ take one's chance* • (tijdelijk vervullen) *perform*
waarneming • (observatie) *observation, perception* • (vervanging) *deputizing*
waarom *why*
waaronder *including*
waarop *on which*
waarover • (over welke) *about/over which* • (over iets heen) *across which*
waarschijnlijk *probable, likely*
waarschijnlijkheid *probability, likelihood*
waarschuwen • (verwittigen) *warn* • (vermanen) *warn, caution (against)*
waarschuwing *warning, admonition, demand*
waas *haze,* <voor de ogen> *mist*
wacht • (wachter(s)) *watchman, guard,* <militair> *sentry* • (wachthuis) *guard-house* • (wachtdienst) *guard*
wachten I [ov ww] *expect* II [on ww] *wait*
wachter *watchman,* <in park> *keeper*
wachtgeld *reduced pay, redundancy pay*
wachtkamer *waiting room*
wachtmeester *sergeant*

wachtpost • (plaats waar men wacht houdt) *watch post, guard post* • (wacht) *sentry*
wachtwoord • (herkenningswoord) *password* • (leus) *catchword, motto, slogan*
wad *mud-flat*
waden *ford, wade*
wafel *wafer, waffle*
wagen I [de] *carriage, coach,* <auto> *car* II [ov ww] • (riskeren) *risk, venture, hazard* • (durven) *venture, hazard* III [wkd ww] *venture (upon)*
wagenwijd *wide(open)*
waggelen • (wankelend voortbewegen) *totter, stagger, reel,* <v. klein kind> *toddle* • (wiebelen) *wobble*
wagon *carriage*
waken • (wakker zijn) *wake, stay awake* • (opletten) *watch, keep vigil/watch* • (~ over) *watch over*
wakker • (niet slapend) *awake* • (flink) *smart* • (waakzaam) *alert, watchful*
wal • (dijkje) *embankment, bank* • (verdikking onder de ogen) *bag* • (het vasteland) *shore*
walgen ⋆ *ik walg ervan I loathe it; it makes me sick* ⋆ *tot ~s toe ad nauseam*
walging *loathing, disgust*
walm (dense) *smoke, smother*
walmen *smoke*
walnoot *walnut*
walrus *walrus*
wals • (dans) *waltz* • (pletter) *roadroller*
walsen I [ov ww] *roll* II [on ww] *waltz*
walvis *whale*
wanbeheer *mismanagement*
wanbetaler *defaulter*
wand *wall,* <v. rots, berg> *face*
wandelen *walk*
wandeling *walk, stroll*
wandelpad *footpath*
wandelstok *walking stick, cane*
wanen *imagine, fancy*
wang *cheek*

wangedrag *misbehaviour, misconduct*
wanhoop *despair*
wanhopen *despair*
wanhopig *desperate, despairing*
wankel • (onzeker) *shaky, insecure*
• (onvast) *unsteady, unstable, tottering*
wankelen • (onzeker lopen, staan)
totter, stagger, sway • (weifelen) *waver*
wanklank *discordant sound,*
dissonance, ‹fig.› *jarring/discordant*
note
wanneer I [bijw] *when* II [vw]
• (indien) *if* • (als) *when*
wanorde *disorder*
wanordelijk *disorderly*
wansmaak *bad taste*
want I [de] *mitten* II [het] *rigging*
III [vw] *for, because*
wantoestand *abuse*
wantrouwen I [het] *distrust, mistrust*
II [ov ww] *distrust, mistrust*
wanverhouding *discrepancy,*
disproportion, ‹misstand› *abuse*
wapen *weapon, arms* [mv]
wapenen *arm,* ‹v. beton› *reinforce*
wapenfeit *feat of arms*
wapenstilstand *armistice, cease-fire*
wapperen ‹v. vlag› *fly*
war *muddle, confusion, mix-up, mess*
warboel *muddle, mess, confusion*
warempel *actually, really, indeed*
warenhuis *department store*
warhoofd *scatterbrain*
warm *hot, warm*
warmbloedig • (temperamentvol)
hot-blooded, passionate • (bio.)
warmblooded
warmen *warm, heat*
warmte • (het warm zijn) *warmth,*
‹nat.› *heat* • (hartelijkheid) *warmth*
warrelen *whirl*
wars *averse*
wartaal *gibberish, ravings*
warwinkel *chaos, muddle, mess*
was I [de] • (het wassen) *wash(ing)*

• (wasgoed) *laundry* II [het] *wax*
wasdom *growth*
wasem *steam, vapour*
wasemen *steam*
wasgoed *washing, laundry*
washandje *face cloth/flannel,* ‹AE›
wash cloth
waslijst *laundry list*
wasmand *laundry basket*
wasmiddel *detergent*
wassen I [bnw] *wax(en)* II [ov ww]
• (reinigen) *wash* III [on ww]
• (groeien) *grow* • (toenemen) ‹v.
maan› *wax,* ‹v. waterpeil› *rise*
wasserette *launderette*
wasserij *laundry*
wastafel *washbasin*
wat I [vr vnw] • (in vragen en
uitroepen) *what* II [betr vnw] *what,*
which, that III [onb vnw] ‹bijvoeglijk
gebruikt› *some, any,* ‹zelfstandig
gebruikt› *anything, something*
IV [bijw] • (iets, enigszins) *a little*
• (erg) *very, jolly* V [tw] *what*
water *water*
waterafstotend *water-repellent*
waterbouwkunde *hydraulic*
engineering, hydraulics
waterdicht *waterproof*
wateren *make/pass water, urinate*
watergolf *artificial curl, wave*
waterig *watery*
waterkant *waterside,* ‹in stad, enz.›
waterfront
waterkering *embankment, dam, dike*
waterkraan *water tap*
waterleiding *waterworks*
waterlelie *water lily*
waterpas I [het] *spirit level* II [bnw]
level
waterpokken *chickenpox*
waterpolo *water polo*
waterput *well*
waterskiën *water-skiing*
watersnood *flood(s)*

watertanden ⋆ 't doet mij ~ it makes my mouth water
waterval waterfall
waterverf watercolour(s), water-based paint
watervliegtuig hydroplane, seaplane
watervrees hydrophobia
waterweg waterway
watje • (propje watten) wad of cotton wool • (halfzacht persoon) softy
watt watt
watten I [de] wadding, cotton wool II [bnw] cotton wool
watteren wad, quilt, pad
wauwelen waffle, blather (on)
wazig hazy, foggy
we we
wedde salary, pay
wedden bet, lay a wager
weddenschap bet, wager
wederdienst service in return
wedergeboorte rebirth
wederhelft ‹inf.› better half
wederkerend reflexive
wederkerig mutual, reciprocal
wederom again, once more
wederopbouw reconstruction, rebuilding, redevelopment
wederopstanding resurrection
wederrechtelijk unlawful, illegal, wrongful
wedervaren I [het] adventures II [on ww] befall
wedervraag ≈ counter-question
wederzijds mutual, reciprocal
wedijveren compete
wedloop race
wedstrijd competition, match, contest
weduwe widow
wee I [de] ⋆ weeën labour pains; contractions II [bnw] faint, ‹geur/smaak› sickly, ‹onwel› shaky
weefgetouw loom
weefsel • (stof) texture, fabric • (celweefsel) tissue

weegschaal • (weeginstrument) (pair of) scales, balance • (sterrenbeeld) Libra
week I [de] • (periode) week • (het weken) ⋆ de was in de week zetten put the clothes in to soak II [bnw] soft, ‹weekhartig› weak
weekblad weekly magazine/journal
weeklagen wail, lament
weekloon weekly wages
weelde • (overvloed) profusion, wealth, abundance • (luxe) luxury
weelderig ⋆ ~(e) haar/groei luxuriant hair/growth ⋆ ~e vegetatie lush vegetation ⋆ ~ leventje luxurious life
weemoed melancholy, sadness
weemoedig melancholy, sad
weer I [het] weather II [bijw] • (opnieuw) again • (terug) back
weerbaar able-bodied
weerbarstig unruly, obstinate, recalcitrant, intractable
weerga equal, peer, match
weergalmen reverberate, echo, resound
weergaloos matchless, unequalled, unparalleled
weergave reproduction
weergeven • (vertolken) perform • (reproduceren) reproduce
weerhaak barb
weerhaan weathercock
weerklank echo
weerklinken resound, ring out
weerleggen refute, counter
weerlicht blazes, summer lightning, like hell
weerloos defenceless
weerschijn lustre, reflection
weersgesteldheid weather conditions
weerskanten ⋆ aan ~ on both sides
weerslag repercussion
weerspannig recalcitrant, refractory
weerspiegelen reflect
weerstaan resist
weerstand resistance

weersverwachting *weather forecast*
weerwil ⋆ in ~ van *in spite of*
weerzien I [het] *meeting again,*
  reunion II [ov ww] *see again*
weerzin *reluctance, repugnance (to)*
weerzinwekkend *repulsive, revolting,*
  repugnant
wees *orphan*
weeshuis *orphanage*
weet ⋆ het is maar een weet *it's only a*
  knack ⋆ aan de weet komen *find out*
weetgierig *inquisitive, eager to learn*
weg I [de] • (pad, straat) *path, road*
  • (traject, juiste route) *way, course*
  • (doortocht) *way* II [bijw] • (afwezig)
  away • (vertrokken) *gone* • (verloren)
  gone, lost
wegbereider *pioneer*
wegblijven *stay away*
wegbrengen • (naar een andere
  plaats brengen) *take away (s.th.)*
  • (iem. begeleiden) *see (s.o.) off*
wegcijferen *ignore*
wegdek *road-surface*
wegdenken *think away*
wegdoen • (afdanken) *dispose of, scrap*
  • (opbergen) *put away*
wegdragen *carry away/off*
wegduiken *dive/duck away*
wegen *weigh*
wegenaanleg *road building*
wegens *because of, on account of, owing*
  to, due to
wegenwacht • (dienst) *A.A. (rescue)*
  service, R.A.C. • (monteur) *A.A.-man,*
  R.A.C.-man, road-scout
weggaan *go away, leave*
weggeven • (ten beste geven)
  give/offer s.th. • (cadeau geven) *give*
  away
weggooien • (wegdoen) *throw/fling*
  away • (afwijzen) *discard*
wegjagen *drive off, chase away*
wegkomen *get/come away*
wegkruipen *creep away*

wegkwijnen *pine away, languish*
weglaten *leave/miss out, omit*
wegleggen *lay/put aside*
wegligging <v. auto> *roadholding*
weglopen • (naar elders lopen) *walk*
  away • (ervandoor gaan) *run away*
wegmaken • (verdoven) *anaesthetize*
  • (zoekmaken) *lose, mislay*
  • (verduisteren) *embezzle*
  • (verwijderen) *remove*
wegnemen *take away, remove*
wegpesten *freeze s.o. out*
wegraken *be mislaid, get lost*
wegrestaurant *roadhouse*
wegscheren I [ov ww] *shave off*
  II [wkd ww] *make off*
wegsmelten *melt away*
wegsterven • (wegkwijnen) *die away*
  • (verdwijnen v. geluid) *fade away,*
  trail off
wegstoppen • (opbergen) *put away*
  • (verstoppen) *hide, conceal*
wegsturen *send away, dismiss*
wegtrekken I [ov ww] *draw/pull away*
  II [on ww] *withdraw*, <v. bui> *blow*
  over, <v. mist> *lift*, <v. pijn> *ease*, <v.
  toeristen> *leave*
wegvagen *sweep away, wipe out*
wegvallen • (uitvallen) *fall/drop off*
  • (weggelaten worden) *be left out, be*
  omitted
wegverkeer *road traffic*
wegvoeren *carry off*
wegwijs *familiar*
wegwijzer • (richtingbord) *sign(post)*
  • (gids) *guide*
weiden *graze*
weids *magnificent, stately, grand*
weifelaar *waverer, wobbler*
weifelen *waver, hesitate*
weigeren I [ov ww] • (niet willen
  doen) *refuse* • (afslaan) *decline* II [on
  ww] *refuse*, <v. rem, enz.> *fail*
weigering *refusal*
weinig I [onb vnw] *little, not much*

II [bijw] • (nauwelijks) little • (zelden) rarely, seldom III [telw] few, not many

wekelijks weekly

weken soften, soak

wekken • (wakker maken) wake • (opwekken) ‹belangstelling› excite, ‹hoop, argwaan› raise

wekker • (klok) alarm (clock)

wel I [bnw] well II [bijw] ⋆ ik denk het wel I think so ⋆ ik houd er wel van I rather like it; I do like it ⋆ wel wat duur rather expensive • (waarschijnlijk) ⋆ het kan wel (waar) zijn it may be (true) • (minstens) ⋆ wel 1000 mensen as many as 1000 people • (tamelijk) ⋆ het was wel aardig it was quite nice • (vragend) ⋆ komt hij wel? is he coming?

welbehagen pleasure, well-being

welbekend well-known

welbespraakt eloquent, fluent, voluble

weldaad • (goede daad) benefaction, boon • (genoegen) blessing

weldadig • (liefdadig) ‹v. instelling› charitable, ‹v. persoon› benevolent • (aangenaam) pleasant, soothing

weldenkend right-thinking

weldoen do good

weldoener benefactor

weldra soon, presently

welgemanierd well-mannered, well-bred

welgemeend • (gemeend) sincere • (goed bedoeld) well-meant, well-meaning

welgemoed cheerful

welgeschapen well-made, shapely

welgesteld well-to-do, comfortably off

welgevallen I [het] pleasure II [onv ww] ⋆ zich iets laten ~ put up with s.th.; submit to s.th.

welgezind well-disposed (towards)

welig luxuriant

welingelicht well-informed

weliswaar it is true, indeed

welk I [vr vnw] which, what II [betr vnw] which, that III [onb vnw] whatever, whichever

welkom I [het] welcome II [bnw] welcome

welletjes ⋆ zo is 't ~ we'll call it a day; that will do

wellicht perhaps, maybe

welluidend harmonious, melodious

wellust sensuality, lasciviousness, lust

wellustig lustful, sensual, lascivious

welnemen ⋆ met uw ~ by your leave

welp cub

welslagen success

welstand • (welvaren) well-being • (welvaart) prosperity

welvaart prosperity, affluence

welvarend • (voorspoedig) prosperous, thriving, flourishing • (gezond) healthy

welven arch, vault

welving ‹v. lichaam› curve

welwillend kind, sympathetic, obliging, benevolent

welzijn welfare, well-being

wemelen swarm/teem (with)

wenden I [ov ww] turn II [wkd ww] ⋆ zich ~ tot turn to

wending turn

wenen weep, cry

wenk • (gebaar, blik) sign • (aanwijzing) hint

wenkbrauw eyebrow

wenken beckon

wennen I [ov ww] accustom to II [on ww] get used/accustomed to

wens • (verlangen) wish, desire • (gelukwens) wish

wenselijk • (gewenst) desirable • (raadzaam) advisable

wensen • (verlangen) wish, want, desire • (toewensen) wish

wentelen I [ov ww] roll (over), turn about, revolve II [on ww] turn, rotate,

revolve
wenteltrap *winding/spiral staircase*
wereld *world*
wereldberoemd *world-famous*
wereldbeschouwing *world view,*
outlook (on life)
wereldbol *globe*
wereldburger *world citizen*
werelddeel *continent, part of the world*
wereldkundig *known all over the*
world, public
wereldlijk *worldly, secular*
wereldoorlog *world war*
wereldrecord *world record*
werelds ⋆ ~e genoegens *worldly*
pleasures
wereldschokkend *world-shaking*
wereldvrede *world peace*
weren I [ov ww] *avert, prevent* II [wkd
ww] • (zich inspannen) *exert o.s.*
• (zich verdedigen) *defend o.s.*
werf • (scheepswerf) *shipyard* • (kaai)
quay, wharf
werk • (arbeid) *work* • (betrekking)
employment, job • (taak) *duty*
• (product) *work* • (daad) *work*
• (mechanisme) *works, mechanism*
werkbank *workbench, bench*
werkdag *working day*
werkelijk *real*
werken • (arbeid verrichten) *work,*
<techn.> *operate* • (beroep/bedrijf
uitoefenen) *work* • (in werking zijn)
function, <v. fontein> *play,* <v.
machine> *work* • (effect hebben)
work, act, be effective • (vervormen)
warp
werker *worker*
werkgelegenheid *employment*
werkgever *employer*
werking • (het in werking zijn)
action, working, operation, <v.
vulkaan> *activity* • (effect) *effect*
• (vervorming van hout) *warping*
• (het van kracht zijn) ⋆ buiten ~

stellen render inoperative ⋆ in ~
treden come into force; come into
operation
werkkamer *study*
werkkamp *labour camp*
werkkracht • (werknemer) *employee,*
worker • (arbeidsvermogen) *energy*
werkkring • (werkomgeving) *working*
environment • (ambt) *job, position,*
post
werklust *willingness to work, zest for*
work
werknemer *employee*
werkplaats *workshop*
werkster • (schoonmaakster)
charwoman, cleaning lady
werkstudent *student working his/her*
way through college
werkstuk *piece of work,* <school> *paper*
werktafel *worktable,* <werkbank>
bench
werktijd *working hours,* <v. ploeg
werklieden> *shift*
werktuig *instrument, tool, implement*
werktuiglijk *mechanical*
werkvergunning *work permit*
werkverschaffing (unemployment)
relief work
werkwijze *working-method, procedure,*
method
werkwoord *verb*
werkzaam • (werkend) *working,*
employed • (arbeidszaam) *active,*
industrious • (uitwerking hebbend)
effective
werpen *throw,* <met een zwaai> *fling,*
hurl
wervel *vertebra* [mv: *vertebrae*]
wervelstorm *cyclone, hurricane*
werven • (in dienst nemen) *recruit,*
<soldaten> *enlist* • (trachten te
winnen) <v. klanten> *attract,* <v.
leden> *bring in,* <v. stemmen> *canvass*
wesp *wasp*
wespennest *wasps' nest*

west I [de] West II [bnw] west
westelijk westerly, western
westen west
westerling Westerner
westers western, occidental
wet law
wetboek code (of law)
weten know
wetenschap • (kennis, regels)
learning, <exact> science • ('t weten)
knowledge
wetenschappelijk scientific
wetenswaardig interesting,
informative, <inf.> worth knowing
wetenswaardigheid information
wetgevend legislative
wetgever legislator
wetgeving legislation
wethouder alderman
wetsbepaling statutory/legal
provision
wetsontwerp bill
wettelijk legal, statutory
wetten whet, sharpen
wettig legal, lawful, legitimate
weven weave
wezel weasel
wezen • (schepsel) being, creature • ('t
wezenlijke) essence
wezenlijk • (essentieel) essential
• (werkelijk) real
wezenloos vacant, blank,
expressionless
wichelroede divining rod
wicht • (kind) baby, child • (meisje)
chit
wie I [vr vnw] <keuze uit twee of meer>
which, <onderwerp> who, <voorwerp>
whom, <wiens> whose II [betr vnw]
<met antecedent> who, whose, <na vz>
whom III [onb vnw] whoever
wiebelen wobble
wieden weed
wieg • (babyledikant) cradle
• (bakermat) birthplace

wiegen rock
wiek • (vleugel) wing • (molenwiek)
sail
wiel wheel
wieldop wheel cover, hub cap
wielerbaan cycling track
wielersport cycling
wielrenner racing cyclist
wier seaweed
wierook incense
wij we
wijd I [bnw] wide, spacious, large,
broad II [bijw] wide(ly)
wijdbeens with legs wide apart
wijden ★ ~ aan dedicate/devote to
wijdte breadth, width
wijf bitch
wijfje <v. dier> female
wijk • (stadsdeel) neighbourhood,
district • (rayon) <kiesdistrict> ward,
<v. melkboer, enz.> round, <v.
politieagent> beat
wijken give way (to)
wijkplaats refuge, asylum, sanctuary
wijlen I [bnw] late, deceased II [on ww]
sojourn
wijn wine
wijnbouw wine growing, viniculture
wijnbouwer viniculturalist, wine
grower
wijngaard vineyard
wijnoogst vintage
wijnstok vine
wijs I [de] • (melodie) melody, air, tune
II [bnw] • (wetend) wise • (van inzicht
getuigend) wise, sensible
wijsbegeerte philosophy
wijselijk wisely
wijsgeer philosopher
wijsgerig philosophic(al)
wijsheid wisdom
wijsneus wiseacre, know-all
wijsvinger forefinger, index finger
wijten attribute/impute (to)
wijwater holy water

wijze <taalk.> mood • (wijs persoon) *wise person, sage* • (manier) *way, manner, fashion*
wijzen • (aanduiden) *indicate* • (~ **naar**) *point at/to*
wijzer *pointer,* <v. klok> *hand*
wijzerplaat *dial,* <v. klok> *face*
wijzigen *modify, alter, change*
wikkelen *wrap (up),* <v. draad> *wind*
wikken *weigh*
wil *will, wish, desire*
wild I [het] *game* II [bnw] *wild*
wilde *savage*
wildernis *wilderness*
wildvreemd ★ een ~e *a perfect stranger*
wilg *willow*
willekeur *arbitrariness*
willekeurig *arbitrary, random*
willen I [het] *volition* II [ov ww] • (verlangen) *want, wish, choose,* <graag willen> *like,* <v. plan zijn> *intend* • (genegen zijn) *be willing, will* III [hww] • (uitdrukking van gebod/vraag) *will, would* • (zullen) *will*
willens *deliberately, on purpose*
willig *willing, obedient*
willoos *apathetic*
wilsbeschikking *last will, testament*
wilskracht *willpower, energy*
wimpel *pennant*
wimper *(eye)lash*
wind • (luchtstroom) *wind* • (scheet) *fart* • (opgewekte luchtstroom) *wind, draught*
windbuks *air gun*
winden *wind, twist*
winderig • (met veel wind) *windy, blowy* • (opgeblazen) *flatulent*
windhond *greyhound*
windhoos *whirlwind,* <zwaar> *tornado*
windkracht *wind force*
windmolen *windmill*
windscherm *windshield*
windstil *calm*

windstreek *quarter, point of the compass*
windtunnel *wind tunnel*
wingerd <wijnstok> *vine*
winkel *shop, store*
winkelcentrum *shopping centre,* <verkeersvrij> *shopping precinct*
winkelen *shop, go/be out shopping*
winkelhaak • (scheur) *tear* • (gereedschap) *try-square*
winkelstraat *shopping street*
winnaar *winner,* <form.> *victor*
winnen • (verwerven) *harvest, mine, extract,* <land> *reclaim,* <tijd> *gain* • (zegevieren) *win* • (behalen) *win*
winning *winning, production,* <v. kolen> *extraction*
winst *profit, gain, benefit,* <bij spel> *winnings*
winstbejag *pursuit of gain, profit seeking*
winstdeling *profit-sharing*
winstgevend *profitable, lucrative*
winter *winter*
winters *wintry*
wintersport *winter sports*
wip • (sprongetje) *skip, hop* • (nummertje) *lay* • (speelgoed) *seesaw*
wipneus *turned-up nose*
wippen • (op een wip spelen) *seesaw* • (vrijen) *bonk*
wiskunde *mathematics,* <inf.> *maths*
wiskundig *mathematical*
wispelturig *fickle, inconstant*
wissel *points,* <toestel> *switch*
wisselbeker *challenge cup*
wisselen I [ov ww] *exchange,* <v. geld> *change,* <v. tanden> *shed* II [on ww] *change, vary*
wisselgeld *(small) change*
wisselkantoor *exchange office*
wisselstroom *alternating current*
wisselvallig *unstable*
wisselwerking *interaction*

wissen *wipe*
wissewasje *trifle*
wit I [het] *white* II [bnw] *white*
wittebrood *white bread*
wittebroodsweken *honeymoon*
witten *whitewash*
woede *rage, fury, anger*
woeden *rage*
woekeren • (woeker drijven) *profiteer*
• (groeien) <v. kwaad> *be rampant/rife,* <v. onkruid> *be/grow rank*
woekering *uncontrolled/rampant growth*
woelen *toss about*
woelig *turbulent*
woensdag *Wednesday*
woensdags *on Wednesdays, Wednesday*
woerd *drake*
woest • (ongecultiveerd) <onbebouwd> *waste,* <onbewoond> *deserted, desolate* • (wild) *savage,* <strijd> *fierce,* <zee> *wild, turbulent* • (woedend) ★ ~ worden *see* red
woestenij *wasteland, wilderness*
woestijn *desert*
wol *wool*
wolf *wolf*
wolk *cloud*
wolkbreuk *cloudburst, downpour*
wolkeloos *cloudless*
wolkenkrabber *skyscraper*
wond *wound, injury*
wonder I [het] • (iets buitengewoons) *marvel, prodigy, wonder* • (bovennatuurlijke zaak) *miracle* II [bnw] *strange*
wonderdokter *quack*
wonderkind *infant prodigy*
wonderlijk *strange, odd*
wonderolie *castor oil*
wonen *live, reside,* <form.> *dwell*
woning *dwelling, house*
woninginrichting
• (benodigdheden) *home-furnishings*

• (het inrichten) *furnishing*
woningnood *housing shortage*
woonachtig *resident*
woonkamer *living room, sitting room, lounge*
woonplaats *dwelling-place, place of residence*
woord • (spraakklank, uiting) *word, term* • (erewoord) *word, honour* • (het spreken) *word*
woordelijk *literally, word for word*
woordenboek *dictionary*
woordenlijst *vocabulary*
woordenschat *vocabulary*
woordenwisseling *altercation, disagreement*
woordspeling *pun*
woordvoerder *spokesman*
worden I [hww] *be* II [kww] <met bnw> *grow, get, go, turn,* <met bnw & znw> *become*
wording *origin, genesis*
worm • (pier) *worm* • (made) *grub, maggot*
wormstekig *wormy, worm-eaten*
worp • (gooi) *throw* • (nest jongen) *litter*
worst *sausage*
worstelaar *wrestler*
worstelen • (sport) *wrestle* • (~ met) *struggle with*
wortel • (plantorgaan) *root* • (peen) *carrot* • (wisk.) *root*
wortelen ★ ~ in *be rooted in*
woud *forest*
wraak *revenge, vengeance*
wraakzuchtig *(re)vengeful*
wrak I [het] *wreck* II [bnw] *rickety, shaky*
wrang • (zuur) *sour, tart* • (bitter) *unpleasant, wry*
wrat *wart*
wreed *cruel*
wreef *instep*
wreken *revenge, avenge*

wreker *avenger, revenger*
wrevel • (wrok) *resentment*
• (knorrigheid) *peevishness*
wrevelig • (misnoegd) *resentful*
• (prikkelbaar) *peevish*
wriemelen *wriggle, squirm*
wrijven • (strijken) *rub* • (boenen)
polish • (fijnmaken) *grind*
wrijving *friction*
wrikken • (heen en weer bewegen)
pry, wrench • (een boot
voortbewegen) *scull*
wringen I [ov ww] *wrench, wring,*
wrest, twist II [on ww] • (knellen)
pinch • (kronkelen) ⋆ zich in allerlei
bochten ~ *wriggle; squirm*
wroeging *remorse, compunction*
wroeten *grub, root*
wrok *grudge, resentment*
wrong *bun, knot*
wuft *frivolous, flighty*
wuiven *wave*
wulps *voluptuous, salacious*
wurm • (pier) *worm* • (kind) *mite*

X/Y/Z

x-as *x-axis*
xylofoon *xylophone*

y-as *y-axis*
yoghurt *yogurt*

zaad • (kiem) *seed* • (sperma) *semen,*
sperm
zaag *saw*
zaagsel *sawdust*
zaak • (kwestie) *affair, business, matter*
• (bedrijf, handel) *business* • (winkel)
shop • (transactie) *deal, transaction*
• (onderwerp) ⋆ ter zake komen
come/get to the point ⋆ niet ter zake
doend *irrelevant*
zaakgelastigde *agent, proxy,*
representative, <diplomatieke
zaakgelastigde> *chargé d'affaires*
zaakregister *index of subjects*
zaakwaarnemer *solicitor*
zaal • (vertrek) *room* • (aula) *hall,*
auditorium • (ziekenhuisafdeling)
ward
zacht • (niet snel) *slow* • (niet streng)
mild • (niet hard) *soft* • (zachtaardig)
gentle • (niet luid) *soft, low*
zachtaardig *gentle, sweet, mild*
tempered
zachtjes *softly, gently, slowly*
zachtmoedig *meek*
zadel *saddle*
zadelen *saddle*
zagen I [ov ww] *saw* II [on ww] • (vals
viool spelen) *scrape (on the violin)*
zak • (verpakking) *bag,* <groot> *sack*
• (bergplaats op kleding) *pocket*
zakboekje *notebook*
zakdoek *handkerchief*
zakelijk • (nuchter, bondig) *concise*

• (m.b.t. zaken) *commercial*, ‹houding› *business-like*
zakelijkheid • (het zakelijk zijn) *objectivity, pragmatism* • (bondigheid) *soberness, conciseness*
zakenman *businessman*
zakgeld *pocket money*
zakken • (niet slagen) *fail* • (dalen) *sink* • (in niveau dalen) *fall, drop*
zakkenroller *pickpocket*
zaklopen I [het] *sack race* II [ww] *run a sack race*
zakmes *pocketknife*
zalf *ointment, salve*
zalig *glorious, divine*, ‹m.b.t. voedsel, drinken› *delicious*
zaliger *late, deceased*
zaligheid • (iets verrukkelijks) *delight, bliss* • (staat van geluk) *bliss(fulness), happiness* • (rel.) *beatitude*, ‹verlossing› *salvation*
zaligmakend *soul-saving, beatific*
zalm *salmon*
zalmkleurig *salmon, salmon-coloured*
zalven • (wijden) *anoint* • (wond, enz.) *rub with ointment*
zalvend *unctuous*
zand *sand*
zandbak *sand pit/box*
zandbank *sandbank, shallow*
zandloper *hour-glass*
zandsteen *sandstone*
zang • (het zingen) *singing*, ‹vogels› *warbling* • (gezang) *song*
zanger *singer*
zangerig *melodious, tuneful*
zangkoor *choir*
zangstem *singing voice*
zangvereniging *choir, choral society*
zangvogel *song bird*
zaniken *bother, nag*
zat I [bnw] • (verzadigd) *satiated* • (dronken) *pissed, tight* • (beu) ★ ik ben 't zat *I'm fed up with it* II [bijw] *plenty*

zaterdag *Saturday*
zaterdags *on Saturdays*
ze • (enkelvoud) *she* • (meervoud) *they* ‹lijd. vw.› *them*
zebra • (dier) *zebra* • (oversteekplaats) *zebra crossing*
zebrapad *zebra crossing*
zede *custom*
zedelijk *moral*
zedelijkheid *morality*
zedeloos *immoral*
zedenbederf *corruption (of morals)*
zedenleer *ethics, morality*
zedenmeester *moralist*
zedenpolitie *vice squad*
zedig ‹ingetogen› *demure*, ‹kleding› *modest*
zee *sea, ocean*
zeebeving *seaquake*
zeebodem *seabed, oceanfloor*
zee-engte *straits* [mv]
zeef *sieve*
zeegat (tidal) *inlet/outlet*, ‹Schots› *lochan*
zeehaven *seaport*
zeeklimaat *maritime/oceanic climate*
zeelucht *sea air*
zeem *shammy, chamois (leather)*
zeemacht *naval forces, navy*
zeeman *seaman, sailor*
zeemeermin *mermaid*
zeemeeuw (sea) *gull*
zeemijl *nautical mile*
zeemogendheid *naval/maritime power*
zeep *soap*
zeepbel *soap bubble*
zeeppoeder *washing powder*
zeepsop *soap suds*
zeer I [het] *sore, ache* II [bnw] *painful, aching, sore* III [bijw] *very, (very) much, extremely*
zeereis *sea voyage*
zeerob • (dier) *seal* • (persoon) *sea dog*
zeerover *pirate*

zeeschip *sea/ocean-going vessel*
zeeschuimer *pirate*
zeester *starfish*
zeestraat *straits* [mv]
zeevaarder *navigator, seafarer*
zeevaart *navigation*
zeevaartschool <marine> *naval college,* <zeevaart> *nautical college*
zeevarend *seafaring*
zeevis *salt-water fish,* <bio.> *marine fish*
zeewaardig *seaworthy*
zeewaarts *seaward*
zeewater *seawater*
zeeweg *sea route*
zeeziek *seasick*
zege *triumph, victory*
zegel I [de] *stamp* II [het] • *(zegelafdruk) seal* • *(stempel) seal, stamp* • *(papier) paper seal*
zegelen *seal (up)*
zegelring *signet ring*
zegen *blessing*
zegenen *bless*
zegening *blessing*
zegenrijk *salutary, beneficial*
zegeteken *trophy*
zegetocht *triumphal march*
zegevieren *triumph*
zeggen • *(beduiden, betekenen)* ★ *dat wil* ~ *(d.w.z.) that is (i.e.)* • *(vertellen) say*
zeggenschap *(right of) say, control*
zeggingskracht *eloquence, expressiveness*
zegsman *informant*
zegswijze *saying, phrase, expression*
zeil • *(vloerbedekking) lino(leum)* • *(dekkleed) tarpaulin* • *(scheepv.) sail*
zeilboot *sailing boat*
zeildoek *canvas*
zeilen *sail*
zeilschip *sailer, sailing ship*
zeilsport *yachting*
zeilwedstrijd *sailing match/race*
zeis *scythe*

zeker *certain, sure*
zekering *fuse*
zelden *seldom, rarely*
zelf *self*
zelfbedrog *self-deceit*
zelfbeheersing *self-control, self-restraint*
zelfbehoud *self-preservation*
zelfbestuur *self-government*
zelfbewust *self-assured, confident*
zelfde *same*
zelfgenoegzaam *self-satisfied*
zelfkant • *(buitenkant van stof) selvage, list* • *(dubieus grensgebied) seamy side (of life)*
zelfkennis *self-knowledge*
zelfmoord *suicide*
zelfrespect *self-respect*
zelfs *even*
zelfstandig *independent, self-employed*
zelfstandigheid • *(onafhankelijkheid) independence, autonomy* • *(entiteit) entity, being*
zelfstudie *self-directed learning*
zelfverdediging *self-defence*
zelfvertrouwen *self-confidence*
zelfverzekerd *self-confident*
zelfvoldaan *complacent, smug*
zelfwerkzaamheid *self-motivation*
zelfzuchtig *egotistic, self-centred, selfish*
zemelen I [de] *bran* [ev] II [on ww] *bother*
zemen I [bnw] *(chamois) leather* II [ov ww] *shammy*
zendeling *missionary*
zenden • *(overseinen) transmit, broadcast* • *(sturen) send*
zender • *(zendapparaat) transmitter* • *(iem. die zendt) sender* • *(zendstation) broadcasting station*
zending • *(het zenden) sending* • *('t gezondene) shipment, consignment* • *(missie) mission*
zendingswerk *mission work*

zendstation broadcasting/radio station
zenuw • (zenuwvezel) nerve • (psychische gesteldheid) nerves
zenuwachtig nervous
zenuwarts neurologist
zenuwinrichting mental institute
zenuwontsteking neuritis
zenuwpees fusspot, bundle of nerves
zerk tombstone
zes I [de] six II [telw] six
zestien sixteen
zestig sixty
zet • (het zetten, handeling) move • (duw) push, shove
zetel seat
zetelen • (gevestigd zijn) be registered/established • (gezeten zijn) reside
zetfout printer's error, misprint
zetmeel starch, farina
zetpil suppository
zetten • (plaatsen) put, place • (bereiden) * thee/koffie ~ make tea/coffee
zetter typesetter, compositor
zeug sow
zeulen drag, lug
zeuren • (talmen) dawdle • (kletsen) waffle, rabbit on
zeurkous bore, waffler, whinger
zeven I [ov ww] sift, sieve II [telw] seven
zeventien seventeen
zeventig seventy
zich himself, herself, itself, oneself [mv: themselves]
zicht • (gezichtsveld, uitzicht) sight, view • (beoordeling) sight
zichtbaar • (waarneembaar) visible • (merkbaar) perceptible
ziek sick, <predikatief> ill
ziekbed sickbed
ziekelijk • (sukkelend) sickly, ailing • (abnormaal) morbid, sickly
ziekenauto ambulance

ziekenbezoek <door arts> house call, <door familie, enz.> visit to a patient
ziekenboeg sickbay
ziekenfonds National Health Service
ziekenhuis hospital, <AE> infirmary
ziekenverpleger (male) nurse
ziekte • (het ziek zijn) sickness, illness • (vorm van het ziek zijn) disease • (kwaal) complaint • (v. planten) disease, blight • (v. dieren, vooral hond en konijn) distemper
ziektekiem germ, pathogen
ziekteverlof sick leave
ziekteverzuim sick leave, <verschijnsel> sickness absenteeism
ziel soul
zielenheil salvation
zielenrust peace of mind
zielig pitiful, pathetic
zieltogen be dying
zien I [het] sight, vision II [ov ww] • (waarnemen, opmerken) see • (inzien) interpret • (als uitkomst verwachten) see • (proberen) see III [on ww] • (niet blind zijn) see • (uitzicht geven op) look (out) on
zienderogen visibly
zier whit, iota, least bit
ziezo all right, that's it
zigzag zigzag
zij I [de] • (zijde) * zij aan zij side by side II [pers vnw] • (enkelvoud) she • (meervoud) they
zijdelings I [bnw] sidelong, sideways II [bijw] sideways
zijden silk
zijderups silkworm
zijdeur side door
zijkamer side room
zijlijn • (zijspoor) branch line • (sport) sideline, <rugby> touch-line
zijn I [het] being II [on ww] be III [hww] • (van tijd) have • (van de lijd. vorm) be IV [bez vnw] his, <m.b.t.

dingen, dieren> its, <m.b.t. niet nader aangeduide persoon> one's
zijpad side-path
zijrivier tributary
zijspoor siding
zijstraat side street, turning
zijwaarts sideways
zijweg crossroad
zijwind crosswind
zilver silver
zilveren silver
zilvergeld silver coins
zilverwerk silver ware, silver plate
zin • (zintuig) sense • (betekenis) meaning, sense • (lust) mind ★ ik heb er geen zin in I don't feel like it • (mening, wil, streven) mind • (doel, nut) sense, meaning • (verstand) senses • (gevoel) sense • (volzin) sentence
zindelijk <v. hond, enz.> house-trained, <v. kind> toilet-trained
zingen sing, chant
zink zinc
zinken I [bnw] zinc II [on ww] • (ondergaan) sink
zinnebeeld symbol
zinnelijk sensual, sensuous
zinnen muse, ponder
zinnig sane, sensible
zinsbouw sentence structure
zinsnede passage, phrase, <vnl. taalkunde> clause
zinspelen allude (to), hint (at)
zinsverband context
zinswending turn of phrase
zintuig sense (organ/faculty), (organ of) sense
zintuiglijk sensory
zionisme Zionism
zit ★ een hele zit a long time to sit; a long haul
zitkamer sitting room, living room
zitplaats seat
zitten sit • (verblijven) ★ waar zit die jongen? where is that boy? • (~ aan)

touch
zittenblijver repeater
zittend sitting, seated
zitting seat
zitvlak bottom, seat
zo I [bijw] • (aldus, op die wijze) so, in this way, like this • (aanstonds) presently, in a minute • (in overeenstemming met maat, graad) as, so • (op bepaalde wijze) so, thus • (zeer) so II [vw] • (zoals) as • (indien) if III [tw] well
zoals I [bijw] how much, the way/manner II [vw] as, such as, like
zodanig I [aanw vnw] such II [bijw] so, in such a way
zodat so that
zode sod, turf
zodoende • (op die manier) thus, in this/that way • (derhalve) consequently, accordingly
zodra as soon as
zoek missing, gone
zoeken look/search for
zoeklicht searchlight, spotlight
zoemen buzz, hum
zoemer buzzer
zoen kiss
zoenen kiss
zoet sweet, <m.b.t. water> fresh
zoethout liquorice
zoetig sweetish
zoetigheid • (wat zoet is) sweetness • (snoep) sweets
zoetsappig sugary
zoetzuur I [het] (sour and) sweet pickles II [bnw] sweet and sour
***zoëven** (Wdl: zo-even) just now, a moment ago
zog • (moedermelk) (mother's) milk • (kielzog) wake
zogen suckle, nurse
zogenaamd I [bnw] self-styled, would-be, so-called II [bijw] ostensibly
zogezegd • (bij wijze v. spreken) so to

say, so to speak • (vrijwel) all but, as good as

zolang so long as, as long as

zolder garret, loft, attic

zoldertrap attic/loft-stairs

zomen hem

zomer summer

zomers summery

zomin as little as

zon sun

zondaar sinner

zondag Sunday

zonde I [de] sin II [tw] • ~! pity!

zondebok scapegoat

zonder without • (~ te) • ~ te klagen without complaining

zonderling I [de] eccentric, freak II [bnw] odd, singular, peculiar

zondeval • de ~ the Fall

zondig sinful

zondigen sin, offend

zondvloed <fig.> deluge

zone zone

zonnebaden sunbathe

zonnebril sunglasses

zonneklaar obvious, crystal clear

zonnen sunbathe, sun o.s.

zonnescherm sunshade, parasol

zonneschijn sunshine

zonnesteek sunstroke, touch of the sun

zonnetje • Janneke is een ~ in huis Janneke is a ray of sunshine; Janneke is our little ray of sunshine • iem. in 't ~ zetten make s.o. the centre of attention; poke fun at s.o.

zonnig sunny

zonsondergang sunset

zonsverduistering solar eclipse

zoogdier mammal

zooi • (troep) lot, heap • (rommel) mess

zool sole

zoölogie zoology

zoom • (omgenaaide rand) hem • (buitenrand) edge

zoon son

zootje • (hoeveelheid) lot, heap, load • (vuile boel) mess

zorg • (verzorging) care • (bezorgdheid) concern, anxiety, solicitude • (last) trouble

zorgen • (verzorging geven) care for, look after, take care of • (oppassen) see (to), take care (to) • (regelen) take care of, see to

zorgvuldig • (met zorg) careful • (nauwkeurig) meticulous, painstaking

zorgwekkend alarming, critical

zot I [de] fool II [bnw] foolish, silly

zout I [het] salt II [bnw] • (zoutig) salt • (gezouten) salted

zouteloos insipid

zouten salt

zoutzuur hydrochloric acid

zoveel • (een zeker getal of bedrag) as much/many • (onbepaald getal of bedrag) so much/many, as much/many

zowat about

zowel • ~ als as well as; both... and...

zozeer so much

zucht • (diepe uitademing) sigh • (begeerte) desire (for), craving (for), longing (for)

zuchten • (diep uitademen) sigh • (begeren) sigh, yearn

zuchtje • er is geen ~ wind there is not a breath of wind

zuid south

zuidelijk I [bnw] • (in het zuiden) southern • (uit het zuiden) south(ern), <wind> southerly II [bijw] southward(s)

zuiden south • op het ~ liggen face south • ten ~ van (to the) south of

zuiderbreedte south(ern) latitude

zuidpool south pole, antarctic

zuidwaarts southward

zuigeling baby, infant, suckling

zuigen • (opzuigen) suck • (stofzuigen) vacuum, <inf.> hoover

zuiger • (v. motor, enz.) piston • (etter)

badger
zuigfles *feeding bottle*
zuil *pillar, column*
zuinig *economical,* <persoon> *thrifty*
zuinigheid *economy, thrift*
zuipen I [ov ww] *swill* II [on ww]
booze, tipple
zuivel *dairy produce*
zuivelfabriek *dairy factory*
zuiver *pure*
zuiveren *clean*
zuivering *cleaning, cleansing,*
purification, <politieke> *purge*
zuiveringsinstallatie *purifying plant*
zuiveringszout *bicarbonate of soda*
zulk • (zodanig) *such* • (groot) *this, that*
zullen <I, we> *shall,* <you, he, they> *will*
zurig *sourish*
zus I [de] • (zuster) *sister,* <inf.> *sis*
• (meisje) *girl* II [bijw] *thus*
zuster • (zus) *sister* • (verpleegster)
nurse
zuur I [de] • (iets in zuur) *pickle*
• (maagzuur) *heartburn, indigestion*
• (chem.) *acid* II [bnw] • (smaak) *sour*
• (onprettig) *hard* • (chem.) *acid*
zuurkool *sauerkraut*
zuurpruim *sourpuss, grouch*
zuurstof *oxygen*
zuurstofapparaat *oxygen-apparatus,*
resusitator
zuurtje *acid drop*
zwaai *swing, sweep,* <met armen> *wave*
zwaaien I [ov ww] • (heen en weer
bewegen) *wave* II [on ww] • (heen en
weer bewogen worden) *sway, swing*
• (zwalken) *sway*
zwaailicht *flashing light*
zwaan *swan*
zwaar I [bnw] *heavy* II [bijw] *heavily*
zwaargebouwd *heavily built, massive*
zwaarlijvig *corpulent, stout*
zwaarmoedig *melancholy*
zwaarte *heaviness, weight*
zwaartekracht *gravity, gravitation*

zwaartepunt • (hoofdzaak) *main
point* • (nat.) *centre of gravity*
zwaarwichtig *weighty*
zwabber *swab, mop*
zwabberen I [ov ww]
• (schoonmaken) *mop, swab* II [on
ww] *lead a loose life*
zwachtel *bandage*
zwachtelen *bandage, swathe*
zwager *brother-in-law*
zwak • (weinig kracht hebbend) *weak,
feeble* • (weinig presterend) *weak,
poor,* <poging> *feeble*
zwakheid *weakness, feebleness, frailty*
zwakjes *weakly*
zwakkeling *weakling*
zwakstroom *weak current*
zwakte *weakness*
zwakzinnig *mentally handicapped,
feeble-minded*
zwalken *drift/wander about*
zwaluw *swallow*
zwam *fungus*
zwammen *drivel*
zwanger *pregnant*
zwangerschap *pregnancy*
zwangerschapsverlof *maternity leave*
zwart • (m.b.t. de kleur) *black*
• (onwettig) *black* • (somber) *black*
zwartgallig *melancholic, pessimistic*
zwavel *sulphur*
zwavelzuur *sulphuric acid*
Zweden *Sweden*
zweefmolen *giant('s) stride*
zweefvliegen I [het] *gliding, soaring*
II [on ww] *glide, soar*
zweefvliegtuig *glider*
zweem *hint*
zweep *whip*
zweepslag • (slag met zweep) *lash*
• (spierblessure) *whiplash*
zweer *ulcer, sore*
zweet • (transpiratie) *sweat,
perspiration* • (vochtuitslag) *moisture*
zwelgen I [ov ww] • (gulzig eten en

drinken) *guzzle*, <drank> *swill* II [on ww] • (volop hebben) *wallow*
zwellen *swell, expand*
zwelling *swelling*
zwembad *swimming pool*
zwemmen *swim*
zwemmer *swimmer*
zwempak *swimsuit*
zwemvest *life-jacket*
zwemvlies • (vlies tussen tenen) *web* • (duikschoeisel) *flipper*
zwendel *swindle, fraud*
zwendelaar *swindler, fraud*
zwendelen *swindle*
zwengel • (arm van hefboom) *handle* • (draaikruk) *crank*
zwenken *turn/face about, swing round*
zweren I [ov ww] • (onder ede verklaren) *swear* II [on ww] • (geïnfecteerd zijn) *fester* • (eed afleggen) *swear*
zwerftocht *ramble*
zwerm *swarm*
zwerven • (ronddwalen) *wander, ramble, roam, rove* • (rondslingeren) *lie about/around*
zwerver • (iem. zonder vaste verblijfplaats) *wanderer, traveller* • (landloper) *vagabond, tramp* • (dier) *stray*
zweten • (transpireren) *sweat, perspire* • (vochtig uitslaan) *sweat*
zweterig *sweaty*
zwetsen • (dom kletsen) *blether* • (pochen) *brag, boast*
zweven *float, hover*
zwichten *submit to, yield, give in* (to)
zwiepen • (krachtig slaan) *swish, lash* • (doorbuigen) *sway*
zwier • (zwaai) *flourish* • (gratie) *grace* • (allure) *jauntiness, dash*
zwieren • (slingerend lopen, rijden, enz.) <over ijs> *glide*, <v. dansers> *whirl about* • (heen en weer zwaaien) *sway*
zwierig *dashing*

zwijgen I [het] *silence* II [on ww] • (niet spreken) *be silent, keep silence* • (zich niet meer doen horen) *keep silent*
zwijgzaam • (niet spraakzaam) *taciturn* • (terughoudend) *reticent*
zwijm *faint*
zwijmelen *feel giddy, swoon*
zwijn • (varken) *swine* • (vuilak) *swine* • (gelukje) *fluke*
zwijnerij • (vuiligheid) *filth* • (smerige taal) *smut*
zwikken *sprain*
Zwitserland *Switzerland*
zwoegen *toil, slave, labour*
zwoel *sultry*
zwoerd (pork-/bacon-)*rind*